Scottish Football Alamanac
2014 / 15

Edited by Andy McGregor

Rel8Media

SCOTTISH FOOTBALL ALMANAC
2014/15

Published by Rel8 Media
Unit 7, Woodend Business Centre, Cowdenbeath, Fife, KY4 8HG.

© Rel8 Media , Andy McGregor, 2014

A great deal of effort has been made to ensure that the information in this book is as accurate as possible. However, in a work of this nature there will inevitably be some inaccuracies. Neither the publishers nor the author can accept responsibility for any consequences arising from using this book.

The right of Andy McGregor to be identified as the Author of this work has been asserted in accordance with the Copyrights, Designs and Patents Act, 1988.

Sources used have been acknowledged where appropriate. The author has tried to clear all copyright permissions but where this has not been possible and where amendments are required, then the publisher will be pleased to make any necessary arrangements at the earliest opportunity.

British Library in Publication Data.
A catalogue record for this volume is available from the British Library.

ISBN 978-0-9574645-3-7

CONTENTS

SOURCES / ACKNOWLEDGEMENTS

Most of the information for this book has been culled from media sources. The websites of the SFA and SPFL have been most informative, as have official club websites. "Unofficial" web sources, including the mine of information that is Pie and Bovril, have also been useful in clarifying certain points.

Club match programmes have also been useful. Those that provide a "record" of club news and events are particularly helpful when putting together a project of this nature.

Historical records have come mainly from Rothmans and Sky Sports Year Books. For football outwith the Scottish Professional Football League extensive use was made of back issues of the invaluable Scottish Non League Review, published annually by Stewart Davidson since the late 1980s.

My thanks go to everyone who takes the time to update and disseminate information about football, via websites, Twitter, Facebook and printed media.

INTRODUCTION

It may seem strange to publish a new statistical book on Scottish football in this digital age. However, it was the very nature of that digital age which prompted this publication. The volume of information available to football fans through the internet is greater than ever before but it is ephemeral. Fantastic websites can come and go at the whim of their owners ad some already have disappeared into the ether.

For several years now there has been no adequate printed record of the entire game in Scotland. The *Scottish Non League Review*, published annually by Stewart Davidson, gives an overview of football beyond the SPFL. The *Sky Sports Yearbook* (I still call it the Rothmans) provides coverage of the game at SPFL level. Both are highly recommended but neither gives a truly comprehensive picture of Scotland's national sport.

In aiming to provide such a comprehensive record I am acutely aware of the shortcomings of this publication. The most serious omission is Women's Football. If there is a second edition of this book next year then that will be rectified.

Whether or not there is a second edition will depend on the sales of this version. It is extremely difficult to sell books in the current market and even more difficult to make them profitable. If you have purchased the book you are reading just now then you have my heartfelt thanks. If you like it, then you might consider buying one as a Christmas / Birthday present for someone! If you are looking at a borrowed copy then shame on you.

The researching of football history is a popular hobby these days. However, it would be wrong not to keep a complete record of contemporary football to augment the burgeoning archives of historical material.

All being well Rel8 Media intend to publish a range of books on aspects of Scottish football history over the next few years. Details of these will be available through our website.

2013/14 was one of the best Scottish seasons for many years. The national team looked to be getting back on track. There was international success at Under 19 and Under 17 youth level. The introduction of Play Offs made the end of the Premiership and Championship seasons more exciting than ever before. Dare it be said that the absence of a certain direct rivalry at the of the game has been a breath of fresh air. The national silverware was spread around different clubs. At Junior level the Super Leagues are thriving and providing a high quality competition. Hopefully 2014/15 will be as good, if not better.

Personally I watched over 170 matches during 2013/14 at all levels from the Scottish Cup Final down to Amateurs. In many cases the entertainment provided has been superb. Scotland was lauded for introducing the "passing game" in late Victorian times and it is great to see that tradition being continued. "Long ball" football is rare in this country and long may that continue to be the case.

Andy McGregor
June 2014

SCOTTISH FOOTBALL ASSOCIATION

SFA STRUCTURE (Source: SFA website)

It is remarkably difficult to obtain accurate information about the make-up of the SFA Boards. The information provided on the SFA's own website is several years out of date. No minutes of meetings are available for public scrutiny.

The SFA's Board, the main power-broking body, appears to comprise::
Stewart Regan (SFA Chief Executive), Campbell Ogilvie (SFA President), Alan McRae (SFA Vice President), Rod Petrie (SFA Second Vice President), Peter Lawell (SPFL Representative), Barrie Jackson (Independent Non Executive Director) and Tom Johnston (Scottish Junior FA).

There are also two subsidiary boards, the Professional Game Board and the Non Professional Game Board. When these were established membership was as follows:

Professional Game Board:
Chairman: Rod Petrie (Scottish FA)
Members: Jim Ballantyne (SFL), Neil Doncaster (SPL), Peter Lawwell (SPL), David Longmuir (SFL), Alan McRae (Scottish FA), Campbell Ogilvie (Scottish FA), Stewart Regan (Scottish FA), Sandy Stables (SHFL) and Ralph Topping (SPL).

Non-Professional Game Board:
Chairman: Alan McRae (Scottish FA)
Members: Donald Beaton (Welfare FA), John Gold (Schools FA), Colin Holden (South of Scotland), Tom Johnston (Junior FA), David Little (Youth FA), Maureen McGonigle (Scottish Women's Football), Campbell Ogilvie (Scottish FA), Rod Petrie (Scottish FA), Stewart Regan (Scottish FA), Andrew Renwick (East of Scotland), Graham Harkness (Scottish Amateur FA).

This remains the information carried on the SFA website although clearly it is out of date, at least one member being deceased.

In addition the SFA website lists the various affiliated bodies, registered competitions etc. which fall under their auspices. These are listed below:

ASSOCIATIONS AND LEAGUES

AFFILIATED ASSOCIATIONS

ABERDEENSHIRE AND DISTRICT F.A.
Secretary: Brian Christie

EAST OF SCOTLAND F.A.
Secretary: John Greenhorn

FIFE F.A.
Secretary: James Stevenson

FORFARSHIRE F.A.
Secretary: Ken Ferguson

GLASGOW F.A.
Secretary: John Taylor

NORTH OF SCOTLAND F.A.
Secretary : Roderick Houston

SOUTHERN COUNTIES F.A.
Secretary: Richard Osborne

STIRLINGSHIRE F.A.
Secretary: Terry Bulloch

WEST OF SCOTLAND F.A.
Secretary: Scott Struthers

AFFILIATED NATIONAL ASSOCIATIONS

SCOTTISH AMATEUR F.A.
Secretary: Hugh Knapp, Hampden Park Glasgow G42 9DB

SCOTTISH JUNIOR F.A.
Secretary: Tom Johnston Hampden Park Glasgow G42 9DD

SCOTTISH SCHOOLS F.A.
Secretary: John Watson Hampden Park Glasgow G42 9AZ

SCOTTISH WELFARE F.A.
Secretary: John Campbell, 61 High Street, Rothes
AB38 7AY

SCOTTISH WOMEN'S FOOTBALL
Exec. Admin: Maureen McGonigle Hampden Park
Glasgow G42 9DF

SCOTTISH YOUTH FOOTBALL ASSOCIATION
Secretary: David Little Hampden Park Glasgow G42
9BF

RECOGNISED LEAGUES

THE SCOTTISH PROFESSIONAL FOOTBALL
LEAGUE
Secretary: Iain Blair Hampden Park Glasgow G42 9DE

THE SCOTTISH HIGHLAND FOOTBALL LEAGUE
Secretary: John Grant 35 Hamilton Drive Elgin Moray
IV30 4NN

THE SCOTTISH LOWLAND FOOTBALL LEAGUE
Secretary: David Baxter, 23/5 South Elixa Place,
Edinburgh, EH8 7PG

THE EAST OF SCOTLAND FOOTBALL LEAGUE
Secretary: David Baxter, 23/5 South Elixa Place,
Edinburgh, EH8 7PG

THE SOUTH OF SCOTLAND FOOTBALL LEAGUE
Secretary: Richard Osborne, 29 Castle Street,
Dumfries,DG1 1DL

REGISTER OF COMPETITIONS 2013/2014
The following is a list of competitions approved by the
Scottish Football
Association.

AFFILIATED ASSOCIATIONS

Aberdeenshire & District F.A.
Aberdeenshire & District F.A. Challenge Cup
Aberdeenshire & District F.A. Shield

East of Scotland F.A.
East of Scotland Cup
East of Scotland Shield
King Cup
East of Scotland Qualifying Cup
Alex Jack Cup

Fife F.A.
Fife Cup

Forfarshire F.A.
Forfarshire F.A. Challenge Cup

Glasgow F.A.
The Glasgow Cup

North of Scotland F.A.
North of Scotland Cup

Southern Counties F.A.
Challenge Cup
J Haig Gordon Memorial Trophy
Potts Cup

Stirlingshire F.A.
Stirlingshire Cup

West of Scotland F.A.
Renfrewshire Cup
Renfrewshire Victoria Cup

LEAGUES

Aberdeenshire & District League
League

East of Scotland League
EOS League Championship
EOS League Cup
Qualifying League
South Challenge Cup
League Cup
Under 19 League Championship
South Challenge Cup
Under 19 League Cup
Jimmy Lynch Memorial Cup (U19s)
Central Taxis League Championship

Scottish Highland Football
LeagueSHFL Championship
SHFL Morganti Cup
Under 17 League Championship

North Caledonian League
League Championship

Scottish Professional Football League
Scottish Premiership
Scottish Championship
Scottish League 1
Scottish League 2
SPFL U20 League
SPFL U19 League
SPFL Reserve League

South of Scotland Football League
League
League Cup
Scottish Lowland League
League
League Cup

RECOGNISED BODIES & COMPETITIONS

North Caledonian F.A.
North Caledonian Cup
Football Times Cup
Jock Mackay Memorial Cup
Ness Cup
SWL Cup

Wigtownshire & District F.A.
Cree Lodge Cup
Tweedie Cup

INTERNATIONAL FITBA

FULL INTERNATIONALS 2013/14

				Aug 14	Sep 6	Sep 10	Oct 15	Nov 15	Nov 19	Mar 5	May 28
				A	H	A	H	H	A	A	N
				England	Belgium	Macedonia	Croatia	USA	Norway	Poland	Nigeria
				Fr	WC	WC	WC	Fr	Fr	Fr	Fr
			Total	2-3	0-2	2-1	2-0	0-0	1-0	1-0	2-2
			Caps	80485	36000	16000	30172	21079	9750	41652	20156
McGregor	Allan	Hull City	32	1			1				1
Hutton	Alan	Aston Villa	40	2	2	2	2	2	2	^2	2
Martin	Russell	Norwich City	11	3	4	4	4		4	4	
Hanley	Grant	Blackburn Rovers	13	4	5	5	5	4			5
Whittaker	Steven	Norwich City	24	5	3	$3			3	3	*12
Forrest	James	Celtic	9	>6	$11						
Brown	Scott	Celtic	38	7	8	8	7	8	8G	8G	8
Snodgrass	Robert	Norwich City	15	$8	*10			+10G	10	10	
Maloney	Shaun	Wigan Athletic	32	*9	6	6G					10
Miller	Kenny	Vancouver Whitecaps	69	^10G							
Morrison	James	West Bromwich Albion	31	+11G				8		+7	$6
Naismith	Steven	Everton	29	*12		9	9G	*12	+9	*12	+9
Rhodes	Jordan	Blackburn Rovers	11	+13	+13						
Conway	Craig	Cardiff City	7	$14					$11	^15	
Griffiths	Leigh	Wolves / Celtic	4	^15	+9						
Mulgrew	Charlie	Celtic	13	>16	7	7	3	^7		3	7G
Marshall	David	Cardiff City	11		1	1		1	1	1	
Anya	Ikechi	Watford	6		*12	11G	*11		^7	<11	*11
McCormack	Ross	Leeds United	11		$14			^15		>10	
Bannan	Barry	Crystal Palace	17			+10	$6	*6	$14	$6	
Gilks	Matt	Blackpool	3			*12					
Wallace	Lee	Rangers	8			$14		+13			
Dorrans	Graham	West Bromwich Albion	10				*12				
Burke	Chris	Birmingham City	7				$14			<17	
Greer	Gordon	Brighton	4					5	5	5	4
Fletcher	Steven	Sunderland	14					+9		*9	
Mackay-Steven	Gary	Dundee United	1					$14			
Adam	Charlie	Stoke City	25						*6	>16	
Bryson	Craig	Derby County	2						$11		
Berra	Christophe	Ipswich Town	28						+13		
Fletcher	Darren	Manchester United	62							+13	
Robertson	Andrew	Dundee United	2							$14	^3
Bardsley	Phil	Sunderland	13							^15	
Martin	Chris	Derby County	1								13+
Boyd	George	Hull City	2								$14
Forsyth	Craig	Derby County	1								^15
Own Goal											G

Gordon Strachan, assisted by Stuart McCall and Mark McGhee, put together a consistent run of results. More importantly, the performances looked solid with a team playing to its strengths and prepared to attack. This was the perfect antidote to the Levein period when Scotland seemed to be set up primarily to defend.

Kenny Miller announced his retirement from International football after a decent performance against England at Wembley in a match to celebrate the 150th Anniversary of the F.A.

Of the new players introduced one of the most promising talents was young Andrew Robertson of Dundee United who looked comfortable in the left back position. Former skipper Darren Fletcher made a brief return following his long-term illness absence for the Friendly in Poland.

UNDER 21 INTERNATIONALS 2013/14

			Aug 13	Sep 5	Oct 10	Oct 14	Nov 14	Mar 5	May 28
			A	A	H	A	H	H	H
			England	Netherlands	Slovakia	Georgia	Georgia	Hungary	Netherlands
			Fr	UEFA	UEFA	UEFA	UEFA	Fr	UEFA
			0-6	0-4	2-1	1-2	1-1	2-2	1-6
			26942	5700	2014	n/a	1737	4537	3002
			Sheffield	Nijmegen	Paisley	Tbilisi	Paisley	Tannadice	Paisley
Archer	Jordan	Tottenham Hotspur	1	1	1	1	1	*1	1
Jack	Ryan	Aberdeen	*2	2	2	2	2		
McKay	Brad	Hearts	3						
Robertson	Clark	Aberdeen	4	5	5	5			
McHattie	Kevin	Hearts	5						5
Fyvie	Fraser	Wigan Athletic	6	*6	+6	+6			
McGeouch	Dylan	Celtic	7	7	7	*7	*5		
Bannigan	Stuart	Partick Thistle	+8						
Feruz	Islam	Chelsea	^9						
Armstrong	Stuart	Dundee United	$10	10	9G	10	8	^7	10
Watt	Tony	Celtic / Lierse	>11	+9					
Duffie	Kieran	Falkirk	*12						
McLeod	Lewis	Rangers	+13	*12	*10	+13G	10		
May	Stevie	St Johnstone	$14	+13	11G	11	11		9G
Smith	David	Hearts	^15						
Holt	Jason	Hearts	>16	8	*12	$8			
McGhee	Jordan	Hearts		3	3	3	3	3	3
Findlay	Stuart	Celtic		4	4	4	4	4	4
Fraser	Ryan	AFC Bournemouth		$11				11G	*7
Paterson	Calum	Hearts		$14	$14	$14	+13G	<9	2
McGregor	Callum	Celtic / Notts County			$8	9	+7	10G	$11
Gauld	Ryan	Dundee United					6		
Mclean	Kenny	St Mirren					*12	>8	8
Fraser	Marcus`	Celtic						%2	
Kelly	Liam	St Mirren						$5	
Slater	Craig	Kilmarnock						+6	13+
Kettings	Chris	Blackpool						*12	
Grimmer	Jack	Fulham / Port Vale						+13	
Chalmers	Joe	Celtic / Falkirk						$14	
Stanton	Sam	Hibernian						^15	
McGinn	John	St Mirren						>16	+6
Herron	John	Celtic						<17	
Handling	Ryan	Hibernian						%18	
Scougall	Stefan	Sheffield United							12*
McKenzie	Rory	Kilmarnock							14$

Whilst Scotland enjoyed comparative success at Full, Under 19 and Under 17 levels, the results of Billy Stark's Under 21 team were very disappointing.

The season began with a humiliating 6-0 defeat away to England in a Friendly; It ended with an equally humiliating 6-1 home defeat from the Netherlands. The Scots have no chance now of qualifying for the Under 21 Championships.

UEFA EURO 2016 QUALIFYING DATES

14/9/14	Sat	A	v Germany (Dortmund)	19.45
11/10/14	Sat	H	v Georgia	17.00
14/10/14	Tue	A	v Poland	19.45
14/11/14	Fri	H	v Republic of Ireland	19.45
29/3/15	Sun	H	v Gibraltar	17.00
13/6/15	Sat	A	v Republic of Ireland	17.00
4/9/15	Fri	A	v Georgia	17.00
7/9/15	Mon	H	v Germany	19.45
8/10/15	Thu	H	v Poland	19.45
11/10/15	Sun	A	v Gibraltar	19.45

UNDER 21

4/9/14	A	v Slovakia
8/9/14	A	v Luxembourg

At the time of going to press no venues had been confirmed for the home matches against Georgia or the Republic of Ireland. Hampden would still be unavailable for these games due to the re-instatement works following the Commonwealth Games.

UNDER 19 INTERNATIONALS 2013/14

			Sep 3	Oct 10	Oct 12	Oct 15	Mar 5	May 24	May 26	May 29
			H	N	A	A	H	N	A	N
			Iceland	Latvia	Belarus	Germany	Switzerland	Ukraine	England	Montenegro
			Fr	UEFAQ	UEFAQ	UEFAQ	Fr	UEFAER	UEFAER	UEFAER
			1-1	1-1	1-0	1-1	4-2	0-0	1-2	0-1
			617							
			Stirling	Minsk	Borisov	Minsk	Livingston	Burton	Burton	Walsall
Kelly	Liam	Rangers	1	1	1	1				1
O'Hara	Mark	Kilmarnock	2	2		*12				
Soutar	John	Dundee United	3	3	2	2		3	2G	2
Burgess	Cammy	Fulham	4	4			+4			
Targett	Matthew	Southampton	5							
Lindsay	James	Celtic	*6	7	5	*5	<17	5	6	12*
Aird	Fraser	Rangers	+7				7G			
Petrie	Darren	Dundee United	$8	6	$4	$4	<6			*6
Johnstone	Denny	Celtic	^9	*12	*7G	6G		*9	+11	13+
Smith	Cammy	Aberdeen	>10				&19G	+10		+10
Gauld	Ryan	Dundee United	<11G	8G	6			7	8	8
King	Adam	Hearts / Swansea City	*12				8G	8	9	9
Kidd	Lewis	Celtic	+13				^2			
Nicholson	Sam	Hearts	$14	10	+13	$14	>11	12*	*10	
Preston	Jordan	Blackburn Rovers	^15							
Gallagher	Sam	Southampton	>16							
Connolly	Aiden	Dundee United	<17	+13						
Hendrie	Stephen	Hamilton Accies		5	3	3	$5		$3	
Walsh	Tom	Rangers		+9	11	11				
Oliver	Scott	Hearts		*11	*12	+13	%9G			
McKenna	Scott	Aberdeen			8	7	3	4		3
Henderson	Liam	Celtic			+10	9	>16	6	7	7
Telfer	Charlie	Rangers			$15	+10	%18		13+	14$
Stewart	Ross	Motherwell					*1			
Cummings	Jason	Hibernian					&10			
Hurst	Mark	St Johnstone					*12			
Halkett	Craig	Rangers					+13			
McLennan	David	Reading					$14		4	4
Fulton	Ryan	Liverpool						1	1	
Sinnamon	Ryan	Rangers						2	12*	
Hyam	Dominic	Reading						11	5	5
Cardwell	Harry	Reading						14+	15$	$11

Scotland made excellent progress at Under 19 level under the management of Ricky Sbragia. They qualified for the UEFA Elite Round, playing in England against the hosts, Ukraine and Montenegro. A missed penalty in the opening match against Ukraine could have made all the difference had it been scored.

Several players established themselves in their respective first teams. John Soutar and Ryan Gauld excelled for Dundee United while Liam Henderson was given a run in the had clearly gained in confidence as the season progressed.

Many of these players will progress to the Under 21 set up next season and hopefully they can bring about an improvement in results at that level.

The Under 17 squad, managed by Scott Gemmill, did even better. They worked their way through the Qualifying and Elite rounds to reach the UEFA Championship Finals, held in Malta. In that event they reached the Semi Finals before losing to the Netherlands. On the way they defeated Germany - a quite outstanding result at any level.

Craig Wighton of Dundee played a significant number of Championship games for his club side during the season and is regarded as an outstanding prospect.

UNDER 17 INTERNATIONALS 2013/14			Aug 26	Aug 28	Aug 30	Sep 23	Sep 25	Sep 28	Feb 11	Mar 24	Mar 26	Mar 29	May 9	May 12	May 15	May 18
			N	N	A	A	N	N	H	H	H	H	N	N	N	N
			Bulgaria	Czech Rep	Romania	Slovenia	Wales	Hungary	Serbia	Bosnia	Belgium	Romania	Portugal	Germany	Switzerland	Netherlands
			Tnt	Tnt	Tnt	UEFAQ1	UEFAQ1	UEFAQ1	Fr	UEFAQE	UEFAQE	UEFAQE	UEFA	UEFA	UEFA	UEFASF
			0-1	2-0	2-2	3-1	0-0	2-1	2-0	2-0	3-1	1-0	0-2	1-0	3-1	0-5
			Buftea	Buftea	Buftea	Slovenska B.	Slovenska B.	Bakovci	Kilmarnock	Kilmarnock	Greenock	Kilmarnock	Gozo	Paola	Paola	Ta Qali
McCrorie	Robbie	Rangers	1	1	1	1	1	1	>1	1	1	1	1	1	1	1
Breslin	Jack	Celtic	2	4	4	4	4	4	4G	4	3	3	4	3	3	2
Lang	Tom	Birmingham City	3		3	3	3	3		3G	2	2	$3	+13		+13
Lacovitti	Alex	Nottingham Forest	4	+6												
McIlduff	Aidan	Celtic	5	*5	5G	5	5	$5	^15				+10	$14	$14	
Scott	Aaron	Hearts	*6	+14	+7	7	$14	6	^6	7	5					
Kelly	Michael	Aberdeen	7	*12	6	*6	6	+8	+13	+9		7	*12			*12
Boyd	Steven	Celtic	$8		$14	$14	+10		$14	*12	+11		$14		+13G	8
Hardie	Ryan	Rangers	^9	$15	>16G	+10	*12	10GG	*11G	*10	*10	$14	$14		+13G	8
Kiltie	Greg	Kilmarnock	>10	^16	^10	8	+13	+13	+10	$6	8G	+13	7	6	6	5
Nesbitt	Aidan	Celtic	+11	9	$9	8		$14	+10	11	7		6	5	5	4
Thomson	Joseph	Celtic	*12	^8	*12	*12			7							
Armstrong	Daniel	Hamilton Accies	+13													
Wighton	Craig	Dundee	$14	>11G	>11	$11GGG	9	11	9	8G	$9	$6	8	*12	*12G	$6
Pooler	Dylan	Kilmarnock	^15	10G	8	9	8	*9	$8							
Petrie	Richie	Aberdeen	>16	>17	^15											
Wardrope	Sam	Celtic		2	*12	2	2	2	2	2	2	*12	2	2	2	$14
Ballantyne	Cammy	Dundee United		3	*2			*12	3	$15	6G	10	11	10	+10	10
Finnie	Ross	Wolves		$7	+13		$7	7				5				
Miller	Calvin	Celtic				+13	*11		5	5	$14	+8	+13	+8	*8	3
Cameron	Kyle	Newcastle United								5	4	4	5	$14	4	+7
Wright	Scott	Aberdeen							*12	+13	*12	*9G	*9	*7G	$7	+7
McKay	Devlin	Kilmarnock							>16		*12	+13G	1			
Shepherd	Jake	Reading		$7	+13	+13					+13G	11	+13	11	11G	*11
Jules	Zak	Reading										11	9	9	9	9

UNDER 16 INTERNATIONALS 2013/14

			Aug 13	Aug 14	Aug 16	Aug 17	Sep 4	Oct 17	Oct 31	Nov 12	Jan 20	Jan 21	Jan 23	Jun 10	Jun 11
			N	N	N	A	H	A	A	H	N	N	N	A	N
			Ukraine	Hungary	Cyprus	Russia	Italy	N Ireland	Wales	England	Norway	France	USA	Bosnia	Azerbaijan
			Tnt	Tnt	Tnt	Tnt	Fr	VS	VS	VS	Tnt	Tnt	Tnt	Tnt	Tnt
			2-2	0-1	3-2	1-0	3-1	3-0	2-2	1-0	0-3	1-1	1-1	3-3	3-1
							910			2294					
			Krilya	Krilya	Krilya	Krilya	Kirkcaldy	Ballymena	Aberystwyth	Kirkcaldy	Turkey	Turkey	Turkey	Bosnia	Bosnia
Doohan	Ross	Celtic	1				1	1	1		1		1	1	
Lyon	Ross	Rangers	2	2	1	12*	2	2	2		11	6	9	1	12
Jones	Leon	Hearts	>3	3	2	3	3	3	3	3	5	3	3	4	3
Higgins	Daniel	Celtic	4	17<	3					4					
Waugh	Kevin	Hibernian	5		4	4	4	4	4					5	
McKirdy	Sean	Hearts	6G	14$	*5	14$	$8G	7	6	6	6	^8	5		15
Ross	Frank	Aberdeen	+7	16>	6	+7	7	*6		12*					6G
Hamilton	Ethan	Hutchison Vale	$8		+7	>11									
Jeffries	Josh	Rangers	9	13+	$8	9									
Miller	Calvin	Celtic	*10	15^	^10G	13+	+9	^9	7	+9G					
Coote	Alistair	Dundee United	^11	^11	9G	15^			*11	11	10	12*	16>	8G	18
Laws	Joshua	Fortuna Dusseldorf	12*	>7	13+	6	13+G	$11GG	14$		12*	7			5
Gilmour	Charlie	Arsenal	13+	8	14$	$8	^10	12*							
Page	Greg	Hearts	14$G	<5		*5									
Quinn	Aidan	Celtic	15^	^10	15^	^10	*5	5							
McCrorie	Ross	Rangers	16>	4	12*	2				2	4	17<	2	3	7
Booth	Ryan	Dundee United		1		1						1			2
Stirling	Ben	Hibernian		$6			6	8							
Hendrie	Regan	Celtic		+9	16>G	16>G	>11				7	13+			
Archibald	Theo	Celtic		12*	>11		15^		12*G	7		>5	15^	6	16
White	Lewis	Rangers					12*								
Clark	David	Rangers					14$								
Watters	Ryan	Motherwell					16>G	14$	1	1			14$		
McCrorie	Robbie	Rangers						1							
O'Hara	Kevin	Forth Valley						+10	+9G				+6		
Runciman	Liam	Motherwell						13+					13+		
Hill	Mark	Celtic						15^G	$8	*8	3	14$	17<	11GG	21
Harvie	Daniel	Aberdeen							5	5	8	*11	*4		
Heaney	McKenzi	Newcastle United													
Norris	Aaron	Aberdeen							10	10	2	<4	$7	7	17
McMahon	Jack	St Mirren							13+	13+		16>	12*		
Holmes	Jamie	Newcastle United									14+	15^	<11		
McAdams	Aidan	Celtic										+10			1
McIntyre	Tom	Reading										2			4G
Woodcock	Ross	Crewe Alexandra										$9G		2	14
Kidd	Blair	Celtic												9	19
Furlong	Connor	MK Dons													20
Murray	Innes	Celtic												10	9
Yuill	Louis	West Ham United													10G
Frizell	Adam	Kilmarnock													8
Smith	Ian	Hearts													11
Finlayson	Mark	Falkirk													

UNDER 15 INTERNATIONALS 2013/14			Sep 10	Apr 7	June 17
			A	H	H
			Switzerland	Rep of Ireland	Poland
			Fr	Fr	Fr
			3-4	2-3	2-1
			Kerzers	Dunfermline	Hamilton
McAdams	Aidan	Celtic	1	1	12*
Bowers	Shaun	Celtic	2	2	+3
Strachan	Conor	Aberdeen	3		
Baur	Daniel	Hearts	4	S	2
Thorburn	Grant	Celtic	5		
Docherty	Lewis	Celtic	6	6	
Nelson	Grant	Rangers	7	7	
McLaughlin	Ross	Celtic	8		
Sutherland	Scott	Dunfermline Ath	9*GG	9	
Johnston	Michael	Celtic	10$		
Jamieson	Samuel	Rangers	11G	11	
Manderson	Joseph	Queen's Park	12*		
Burt	Liam	Rangers	14$		6>
Henry	Chris	St Mirren	S		
Wilson	Aidan	St Mirren	S		
McKendry	Dylan	Celtic	S		
Boyd	Jamie	Hamilton Accies	S		
Breen	Jack	Hibernian	S		
Henderson	John James	Dunfermline Ath	S		
Watson	Broque	Celtic	S		
Murray	Blair	Queen's Park		3G	S
Smith	Robbie	Rangers		4	
Bell	Lewis	Celtic		5G	4
Heaney	Mackenzie	Newcastle United		8	
Connelly	Lee	Queen's Park		10	15^
Yates	Cameron	Leicester City		S	*1
Quitongo	Rico	Hamilton Accies		S	
Young	Jordan	Swindon Town		S	
Gunnar	Callum	Swindon Town		S	
McAllister	Daniel	Celtic		S	S
Adamson	Jack	Hibernian		S	9
Bradley	Kyle	Rangers		S	
Falconer	Dylan	Motherwell		S	
Christopher	Will	Swindon Town		S	
Krones	Jason	Rangers			5
Barjonas	Jamie	Rangers			7^
Gilmour	Charlie	Arsenal			8
Morrison	Lewis	Kilmarnock			$10
Gallagher	Owen	Newcastle United			11<
Freeman	Kieran	Dundee United			13+
Antoniazzi	Christian	Aberdeen			14$
Marku	Kristi	Celtic			16>
Aitchison	Jack	Celtic			17<
Church	Daniel	Celtic			S

Scottish Junior FA

The Bi-Annual Quadrangular Tournament took place in Ireland in October 2013.

4/10/13	Republic of Ireland	Scotland	3 0	Pike Rovers Complex, Limerick
4/10/13	Northern Ireland	Isle of Man	2 1	
5/10/13	Scotland	Northern Ireland	4 1	Fairgreen, Limerick
5/10/13	Republic of Ireland	Isle of Man	5 0	
6/10/13	Scotland	Isle of Man	6 0	Pike Rovers Complex, Limerick
6/10/13	Republic of Ireland	Northern Ireland	1 0	

Team	Pld	W	D	L	GF	GA	GD	Pts
Republic of Ireland	3	3	0	0	9	0	+9	9
Scotland	3	2	0	1	10	4	+6	6
Northern Ireland	3	1	0	2	3	6	-3	3
Isle of Man	3	0	0	3	1	13	-12	0

			v ROI	v NI	V IOM
Fleming	Greg	Kelty Hearts	1	S	S
Snowdon	Will	Bo'ness United	2	S	2
Courts	Tom	Kelty Hearts	3	S	S
Campbell	Ross	Clydebank	4	S	S
Malone	Chris	Kilbirnie Ladeside	5	2	S
Mckenna	Michael	Musselburgh Athletic	6	S	S
Batchelor	Blair	Camelon	7	S	4
Masterton	Stevie	Hurlford United	8	S	6
Tansey	Paul	Newtongrange Star	9	S	S
Barr	Richie	Pollok	10	SG	7GG
Renton	Kris	Bonnyrigg Rose	11	S	S
Barnard	Richie	Camelon	S	1	S
Diack	Ian	Pollok	S	9	11
McElroy	Ciaran	Clydebank	S	S	S
Jamieson	Sean	Newtongrange Star	S	7	S
Donnelly	Chris	Bo'ness United	S	8G	8
Pittman	Scott	Broxburn Athletic	S	4	S
Leiper	Colin	Camelon	S	10G	10G
Wilson	Chris	Clydebank	S	11	3
Hislop	Steve	Bo'ness United	S	6	9GGG
Campbell	Mark	Iirvine Meadow		3G	S

The UEFA Regions Cup

In previous years the Scottish Amateur FA have entered one of their Amateur Associations into this tournament, often represented by a single club. Results have been poor.

This season a proper SAFA Select team has been entered and won through the Preliminary Round stage, held in Slovenia.

June 15 2014
San Marino v Scotland, 0-0
Sportni Park, Radenci

Scotland
Jordan Longmuir	Colville Park
Scott Wightman	Strathclyde Uni
Colin Mcleod	Bannockburn
Gary Gaitens	Wellhouse
Gary Currie	Bannockburn
Steven McDevitt	Wellhouse
Kevin Fotheringham	Bannockburn
Michael Brown	Colville Park
Andrew McLay	Glasgow Harp
Martyn Shields	Eastfield
Allan McPherson	Haldane Ams

Sub
John Nisbet	Tollcross Thistle
Robert Peebles	Wellhouse
James Bradley (for McDevitt)	Greenock HSFP
Alan Inglis (for McPherson)	Doune Castle
Ross Fletcher (for Fotheringham)	Blantyre Celtic
Mark McCormack	Bowhill Rovers
Brian Hughes	Wellhouse

June 17
Scotland v Greece (Evia Region), 1-2
Sportni Park, Radenci

Jordan Longmuir
Robert Peebles
Scott Wightman
Colin Mcleod
Gary Gaitens
James Bradley
Gary Currie

Steven McDevitt
Ross Fletcher (1 goal)
Andrew McLay
Allan McPherson

Subs
John Nisbet
Alan Inglis (for McLay)
Kevin Fotheringham
Michael Brown
Mark McCormack
Brian Hughes (for McPherson)
Martyn Shields (for McDevitt)

June 19
Scotland v Slovenia (Murska Sobota), 3-1
Sc Bakovci Stadium

John Nisbet
Robert Peebles
Colin McLeod
James Bradley (1 goal)
Gary Currie
Alan Inglis (1 goal)
Kevin Fotheringham (1 goal)
Michael Brown
Mark McCormack
Andrew McLay
Martyn Shields

Subs
Jordan Longmuir
Scott Wightman (for Peebles)
Gary Gaitens
Stephen McDevitt (for Bradley)
Ross Fletcher
Brian Hughes (for Inglis)

The next group stage takes place in Slovakia, with Scotland playing the hosts, England and Germany.

Final Standings

	P	W	D	L	F	A	PTS
Scotland	3	1	1	1	4	3	4
Greece	3	1	1	1	4	4	4
Slovakia	3	1	1	1	4	5	4
San Marino	3	0	3	0	2	2	3

SPFL FITBA

SCOTTISH PROFESSIONAL FOOTBALL LEAGUE

The Scottish Professional Football League was formed on June 27, 2013 when The Scottish Football League and The Scottish Premier League merged to create a single body to govern the 42 league clubs in Scotland. Most observers felt this was a long overdue development.

According to the SPFL's own website, the current SPFL Board is made up of Neil Doncaster (CEO), Ralph Topping (Chairman), Eric Riley (Celtic), Stephen Thompson (Dundee United), Duncan Fraser (Aberdeen), Les Gray (Hamilton Academical), Mike Mulraney (Alloa Athletic) and Bill Darroch (Stenhousemuir).

The League structure is as follows:

Premiership
12 clubs. Play each other three times before split into top six and bottom six. Each group then plays each other once more - where possible maintaining an even split of home and away games. Bottom club relegated, 11 th club goes into Play Off.

Championship
10 clubs. Play each other four times. Top team promoted. 4th plays 3rd in Round 1 of Play Off. Winners Plays 2nd in Play Off Semi Final. Winner of that then plays Premiership 11th in the Play Off Final. Bottom team relegated. 9th goes into relegation Play Off.

League One
10 clubs. Play each other four times. Top team promoted. Teams 2, 3 and 4 go into Play Off with 9th in Championship. One team relegated, 9th goes into relegation Play Off.

League Two
10 clubs. Play each other four times. Top team promoted. Teams 2, 3 and 4 go into Play Off with 9th in League One. Bottom team goes into Play off against winners of Highland League / Lowland League Play Off.

LEAGUE STRUCTURE 2014/15

PREMIERSHIP
Aberdeen
Celtic
Dundee
Dundee United
Hamilton Accies
Inverness Caledonian Thistle
Kilmarnock
Motherwell
Partick Thistle
Ross County
St Johnstone
St Mirren

CHAMPIONSHIP
Alloa
Cowdenbeath
Dumbarton
Falkirk
Heart of Midlothian
Hibernian
Livingston
Queen of the South
Raith Rovers
Rangers

LEAGUE ONE
Airdrieonians
Ayr United
Brechin City
Dunfermline Athletic
Forfar Athletic
Morton
Peterhead
Stenhousemuir
Stirling Albion
Stranraer

LEAGUE TWO
Albion Rovers
Annan Athletic
Arbroath
Berwick Rangers
Clyde
East Fife
East Stirlingshire
Elgin City
Montrose
Queen's Park

NOTES ON THE CLUB INFORMATION SECTION

DATES OF BIRTH
Where possible these have been taken from club websites. However, there appears to be considerable inaccuracy, with even some club sites taking information from unreliable sources. Consequently, the dates of birth given must be regarded with some degree of caution.

APPEARANCES
Information refers to Appearances (A), Used Substitute Appearances (S) and Goals (G) in League (L), Scottish Cup (SC), League Cup (LC), Ramsdens Cup (RC) and European Ties (UC), The UNS column refers to Unused substitute appearances in all competitions.

Most media sources use information from a single reporter at matches via an Agency. Sometimes it is clear that mistakes have been made and I have corrected these. Where possible I have cross-referenced media reports with club sources such as websites and programmes and clarified any discrepancies.

CONTRACT
The information given is for guidance only. It has been gleaned primarily from club websites.

SCORERS
Where possible these have been double checked but there may still be disputed goals. The information on the SPFL website is sometimes updated and changed following such instances.

ATTENDANCES
Most clubs publish accurate attendances for games. In some cases, notably Celtic and Rangers, these include all tickets sold, including season tickets. Matchday attendances are, in some cases, little more than 50% of the published figure. Two matches from 2013/14 have caused particular problems. At an Ayr v Dunfermline match and at the Cup tie between Inverness CT and Morton, power failures caused the computerised turnstile systems to fail. As I understand it the figure for Ayr v Dunfermline is the number admitted before the system failed, but no official figure has been given for the Inverness CT game.

PLAYER NUMBERING
Numbers 1-11 refer to players who started the match but bear no relation to actual numbers worn. Used substitutes are listed as 12,14 and 15, again regardless of actual numbers worn. Press Agencies ask for teams to provided in "formation" rather than numerical order which causes problems for reporters unfamiliar with the teams. Squad numbering is mandatory in the Premiership and was optional in the other divisions for 2013/14. Most Championship sides chose to adopt squad numbering systems.

TRIALISTS
In almost all cases trialists have been identified are entered under their correct names.

FRIENDLY MATCHES
The lists of Friendly games may not be 100% comprehensive. Some clubs are very good at detailing games. Others publish details of matches which are really closed-door "joint training sessions" rather than proper matches.

Aberdeen FC   2013/14

Founded	1903
Ground	Pittodrie Stadium
Postcode	AB24 5QH
Tel	01224 650400
Closest Railway Station	Aberdeen
Record Attendance	45061 v Hearts, SC, 1953/4
Record Win	13-0 v Peterhead, SC, 10/2/1923
Record Defeat	0-9, v Celtic, Lge, 6/11/2010
Most League Goals in a Season	38, Benny Yorston, 1929/30
Most Goals in Career	199, Joe Harper
Chairman	Stewart Milne
Chief Executive	Duncan Fraser
Secretary	Steven Gunn
Manager	Derek McInnes
Assistant Manager	Tony Docherty
Colours 2013/14 Top	Red
Shorts	Red
Sponsor	Team Recruitment
Manufacturer	Adidas
Change Colours 2013/14 Top	White with Black Flash
Shorts	Black
Nicknames	Dons, Dandies, Sheep
Web	www.afc.co.uk

PREDICTION FOR 2014/15
Top three finish, either second or third.

After years of under-achieving, 2013/14 finally brought signs that Aberdeen might be awakening. The appointment of Derek McInnes as Manager seemed like a breath of fresh air and blew away the staleness that had settled over Pittodrie.

There were several highlights to the season. The Dons were the first team to beat Celtic. They finally managed to win a penalty shoot out in the League Cup. And, of course, they lifted the League Cup in March at Celtic Park. The Final, against ICT, is best forgotten but the final outcome and the outpouring of support for Aberdeen demonstrated the potential that this club has.

For 2014/14 the Dons will be looking for a little more consistency. They need to turn Pittodrie into a fortress that other teams fear to visit.

The team have tremendous attacking ability. Rooney, Hayes and McGinn are proven goalscorers and at the time of going to press the Dons were chasing the signature of Kris Boyd. The capture of Shaleum Logan looks like a good bit of business - he has the talent to be a big personality in the SPFL.

Surname	First Name	DOB	SQ	Pos	L (A S G)	SC (A S G)	LC (A S G)	UNS	Signed Previous Club	Notes	Contract
Anderson	Russell	25/10/78	4	D	27 3 1	4	1 4	4	2012 Derby County		C (2015)
Considine	Andrew	01/04/87	5	D	21	4	1 2 1 1	3	2004 Aberdeen Youth		C (2015)
Flood	Willo	10/04/85	8	M	31 2 3	3	4		2013 Dundee United		C (2015)
Hayes	Johnny	09/07/87	11	F	28 3 2	2	5 3		2012 Inverness CT		C (2016)
Hector	Michael	19/07/92	27	D	18 2 1	1	1	1	2013 Reading (loan)		▮
Jack	Ryan	27/02/92	22	M	34	2 3	4		2010 Aberdeen Youth		C (2016)
Langfield	Jamie	22/12/79	1	GK	37	4	5		2005 Dunfermline Athletic		C (2016)
Logan	Shaleum	29/01/88	29	D	13	1 3	2		2014 Brentford (loan)	Signed pre-contract May 2014	C (2016)
Low	Nicky	06/01/92	18	M	3 9 1	1	1 3	20	2011 Aberdeen Youth		C (2015)
Magennis	Josh	15/08/90	21	F	1 17 1	1	1	2	2010 Cardiff City	On loan to St Mirren (Mar-May)	F
McGinn	Niall	20/07/87	10	F	35 1 13	3 1 1	4		2012 Celtic		C (2016)
McManus	Declan	03/08/94	24	F	3			9	2013 Aberdeen Youth	On loan to Alloa, Aug-Dec 2013	C (2015)
Murray	Craig	01/01/94	35	M	2		1	13	2012 Aberdeen Youth		C (2015)
Pawlett	Peter	03/02/91	16	F	33 2 5	3	1 4 1		2007 Aberdeen Youth		C (2017)
Reynolds	Mark	07/05/87	6	D	37	2 4	5		2012 Sheffield Wednesday		C (2018)
Robertson	Clark	05/09/93	3	D	5 3		4	9	2009 Aberdeen Youth		C (2016)
Robson	Barry	07/11/78	15	M	20 8 4	4	1 1		2013 Sheffield United		C (2015)
Rogers	Danny	23/03/94	30	GK				2	2013 Aberdeen Youth	On loan to Airdrie (Dec 2013)	C (2015)
Rooney	Adam	21/04/88	17	F	13	7 3	1 2 1		2014 Oldham Athletic		C (2016)
Rose	Michael	11/10/95	36	D				2	2010 Lewis United		C (2015)
Shankland	Lawrence	10/08/95	25	F				3	2013 Queen's Park	On loan to Dunfermline Jan 2014	C (2015)
Shaughnessy	Joe	06/07/92	2	D	20 6	1	2 1	11	2011 Aberdeen Youth		C (2015)
Smith	Cammy	24/08/95	14	F	8 10	1 1	1 1 1	14	2012 Aberdeen Youth		C (2017)
Storrie	Craig	13/01/96	26	M	1			3	2013 Aberdeen Youth	On loan to Forfar Ath	C (2015)
Tate	Alan	02/09/82	28	D	5 2		1	1	2114 Swansea City (Loan)		
Vernon	Scott	13/12/83	9	F	14 11 6	4	5 3	13	2010 Colchester United	Joined Shrewsbury Town, June 2014	F
Weaver	Nicky	02/03/79	20	GK	1 1			44	2013 Sheffield Wednesday		F
Wylde	Gregg	23/02/91	17	M	3 5 1 1		1	11	2013 Bolton Wanderers	Freed Jan, joined St Mirren	
Zola	Calvin	31/12/84	7	F	11 9 3 1		3	15	2013 Burton Albion	Contract Cancelled, June 2014	▮

New Signings 2014/15

Surname	First Name	DOB		Pos					Signed Previous Club		
Brown	Scott	26/04/85		GK					2014 Cheltenham Town		
Taylor	Ash	02/09/90		D					2014 Tranmere Rovers		

Date	Comp	H/A	Opponents	F	A		Crowd	Scorers
03/08/2013	Prem	H	Kilmarnock	2	1		13149	Hayes, Flood
11/08/2013	Prem	A	Motherwell	3	1		6242	McGinn 2, Reynolds
17/08/2013	Prem	H	Celtic	0	2		20017	
24/08/2013	Prem	A	Hearts	1	2		15218	McGinn
27/08/2013	LC2	H	Alloa	0	0	*6-5 p	4897	
31/08/2013	Prem	H	St Johnstone	0	0		9478	
14/09/2013	Prem	A	Partick Thistle	3	0		6193	Zola, Pawlett, Magennis
21/09/2013	Prem	H	Inverness CT	1	0		11251	Vernon
25/09/2013	LC3	A	Falkirk	5	0		2838	Shaughnessy, Smith, Vernon 3
30/09/2013	Prem	A	St Mirren	1	1		4051	Pawlett
05/10/2013	Prem	A	Ross County	0	1		5290	
19/10/2013	Prem	H	Dundee United	1	0		12654	Zola
26/10/2013	Prem	A	Hibernian	2	0		12810	Vernon, Wylde
30/10/2013	LC4	A	Motherwell	2	0		6995	Considine, Hayes
04/11/2013	Prem	H	Partick Thistle	4	0		10057	McGinn 2, Zola, Hector
09/11/2013	Prem	H	Hearts	1	3		13940	McGinn
23/11/2013	Prem	A	Celtic	1	3		49683	McGinn
01/12/2013	SC4	A	Partick Thistle	1	0		3642	Considine
07/12/2013	Prem	A	St Johnstone	2	0		4741	Pawlett, McGinn
14/12/2013	Prem	H	St Mirren	2	0		9332	Vernon, Robson
21/12/2013	Prem	A	Inverness CT	4	3		4810	Robson 2, Pawlett, McGinn
26/12/2013	Prem	H	Motherwell	0	1		12494	
29/12/2013	Prem	H	Ross County	1	0		11602	Low
01/01/2014	Prem	A	Dundee United	2	1		12601	Robson, Pawlett
05/01/2014	Prem	A	Kilmarnock	1	0		4073	Reynolds
10/01/2014	Prem	H	Hibernian	1	0		12734	Flood
18/01/2014	Prem	H	Inverness CT	0	1		12021	
25/01/2014	Prem	A	Motherwell	2	2		5756	Rooney, Anderson
01/02/2014	LCSF	N	St Johnstone	4	0		16761	Hayes 2, Pawlett, Rooney
08/02/2014	SC5	A	Celtic	2	1		30413	Anderson, Pawlett
15/02/2014	Prem	A	St Mirren	1	0		4073	Rooney
22/02/2014	Prem	A	Partick Thistle	1	3		4554	Rooney
25/02/2014	Prem	H	Celtic	2	1		16634	Hayes, Rooney
01/03/2014	Prem	H	St Johnstone	1	0		11487	jack
08/03/2014	SC6	H	Dumbarton	1	0		10600	Rooney
16/03/2014	LCF	N	Inverness CT	0	0	*4-2 p	51143	
22/03/2014	Prem	H	Kilmarnock	2	1		14029	Rooney, Jack
25/03/2014	Prem	A	Ross County	1	1		3775	Rooney
29/03/2014	Prem	H	Dundee United	1	1		14627	McGinn
02/04/2014	Prem	A	Hearts	1	1		13193	Flood
07/04/2014	Prem	A	Hibernian	2	0		9321	McGinn 2
13/04/2014	SCSF	N	St Johnstone	1	2		19057	McGinn
19/04/2014	Prem	A	Inverness CT	0	0		4224	
26/04/2014	Prem	H	St Johnstone	1	1		10003	Rooney
03/05/2014	Prem	A	Celtic	2	5		47468	McGinn, Logan
06/05/2014	Prem	A	Dundee United	3	1		8677	Vernon 3
11/05/2014	Prem	H	Motherwell	0	1		17016	

* AET

Friendly Matches

Date	Comp	H/A	Opponents	F	A			
9/7/13	Fr	A	Buckie Thistle	3	0			
9/7/13	Fr	A	Turriff United	6	3		300	U20
13/7/13	Fr	A	Clachnacuddin	2	0			U20
13/7/13	Test	A	Huntly	4	1			
16/7/13	Fr	A	Arbroath	3	3			U20
16/7/13	Fr`	A	University College Dublin	4	0			
18/7/13	Fr	A	Malahide United	4	1			
20/7/13	Fr	A	Shelbourne	2	1			
23/7/13	Fr	A	Elgin City	1	2			U20
23/7/13	Fr	A	Peterhead	2	3			
26/7/13	Fr	H	Twente Enschede	2	0		7336	
27/7/13	Fr	A	Inverurie Loco Works	0	1			U20
30/7/13	Fr	H	Dundee U20					U20
26/8/13	Fr	A	Fraserburgh	9	1			U20
4/9/13	Fr	H	Viking Stavanger	3	2			
29/4/13	Test	A	Cove Rangers	5	5			Martin Johnston Test

Date	Comp	H/A	Opponents	F	A	1	2	3	4	5	6	7	8	9	10	11	12	13	14	15	16	17	18
03/08/2013	Prem	H	Kilmarnock	2	1	Langfield	Anderson	Reynolds	Robertson+	Shaughnessy	Robson"	Flood	Hayes	jack	Zola*	McGinn	Magennis*	Hector+	Pawlett"	Vernon	Wylde"	Murray	Weaver
11/08/2013	Prem	A	Motherwell	3	1	Langfield	Anderson*	Reynolds	Hector	Shaughnessy	Pawlett"	Flood	Hayes	jack	Zola+	McGinn	Robertson"	Magennis+	Wylde"	Vernon	Murray	Storie	Weaver
17/08/2013	Prem	H	Celtic	0	2	Langfield	Anderson"	Reynolds	Hector	Shaughnessy	Pawlett+	Flood	Hayes	jack	Zola*	McGinn	Weaver*	Magennis+	Wylde"	Vernon	Considine	Lowe	Robertson
24/08/2013	Prem	A	Hearts	1	2	Weaver	Robertson+	Reynolds	Hector	Shaughnessy	Pawlett"	Flood*	Hayes+	jack	Zola	McGinn	Zola*	Wylde+	Magennis"	Anderson	Considine	Lowe	Rogers
27/08/2013	LC2	H	Alloa	0	0 *6-5 p	Langfield	Anderson	Reynolds	Robertson"	Murray	Pawlett"	Flood*	Hayes+	jack	Zola	McGinn	Vernon"	Wylde+	Vernon"	Shaughnessy"	Weaver	Lowe	Considine
31/08/2013	Prem	H	St Johnstone	0	0	Langfield	Anderson	Reynolds	Hector	Shaughnessy"	Pawlett"	Hector+	Wylde*	jack	Magennis	McGinn	Zola*	Smith+	Vernon"	Vernon	Weaver	Lowe	Murray
14/09/2013	Prem	A	Partick Thistle	3	0	Langfield	Considine"	Reynolds	Hayes	Shaughnessy	Pawlett"	Hector	Wylde"	jack	Zola*	McGinn	Low*	Smith+	Murray"	Vernon	Weaver	Lowe	Murray
21/09/2013	Prem	H	Inverness CT	1	0	Langfield	Considine	Reynolds	Hayes	Shaughnessy	Pawlett	Hector	Shaughnessy	jack	Zola*	Smith+	Magennis*	Magennis+	Robertson"	Robertson"	Weaver	Storie	Murray
25/09/2013	LC3	H	Falkirk	5	0	Langfield	Robertson	Reynolds	Hayes+	Shaughnessy	Pawlett	Hector	Low	jack	Zola+	Smith"	Low*	Murray+	Vernon"	Wylde	Weaver	Storie	Murray
30/09/2013	Prem	H	St Mirren	1	1	Langfield	Considine	Reynolds	Hayes	Shaughnessy	Pawlett	Hector	Vernon"	jack	Zola+	Smith"	Vernon"	Murray+	Magennis"	Robertson"	Wylde	Anderson	Weaver
05/10/2013	Prem	A	Ross County	0	1	Langfield	Considine"	Reynolds	Hayes	Shaughnessy	Pawlett"	Anderson	Flood	jack"	Zola*	Smith+	Robertson"	Flood+	McGinn"	Wylde	Weaver	Lowe	Smith
19/10/2013	Prem	A	Dundee United	1	0	Langfield	Considine*	Reynolds	Hayes+	Shaughnessy"	Pawlett"	Anderson	Flood	jack	Zola*	McGinn	Vernon"	Vernon+	Hector"	Wylde	Weaver	Lowe	Smith
26/10/2013	Prem	H	Hibernian	2	0	Langfield	Robertson+	Reynolds	Hayes	Shaughnessy	Pawlett"	Anderson	Flood	jack	Zola+	McGinn	Vernon"	Robson+	Wylde"	Considine	Weaver	Smith	Hector
30/10/2013	LC4	A	Motherwell	2	0	Langfield	Considine	Reynolds	Hayes+	Smith*	Hector	Anderson	Flood	jack	Zola+	McGinn	Considine"	Vernon+	Robson"	Wylde	Weaver	Lowe	Shankland
04/11/2013	Prem	H	Partick Thistle	4	0	Langfield	Considine	Reynolds	Hector	Anderson	Hayes+	Flood	Flood	jack	Zola*	McGinn	Robson"	Vernon+	Anderson"	Wylde	Weaver	Lowe	Wylde
09/11/2013	Prem	H	Hearts	1	3	Langfield	Considine	Reynolds	Hector"	Anderson	Hayes+	Hayes"	Flood*	jack	Zola+	McGinn	Robson"	Vernon+	Smith"	Shaughnessy	Weaver	Lowe	Murray
23/11/2013	Prem	A	Celtic	1	3	Langfield	Anderson	Reynolds	Hector	Anderson	Hector	Hayes+	Shaughnessy"	jack	Zola*	McGinn	Vernon"	Magennis+	Vernon"	Shaughnessy	Weaver	Lowe	Murray
01/12/2013	SC4	A	Partick Thistle	1	0	Langfield	Anderson*	Reynolds	Hector	Anderson	Hector	Hayes+	Wylde+	jack	Zola*	McGinn	Smith*	Magennis+	Anderson"	Smith	Weaver	Lowe	Magennis
07/12/2013	Prem	H	St Johnstone	2	0	Langfield	Shaughnessy"	Reynolds	Hector	Anderson	Hector	Hayes	Vernon	jack*	Flood*	McGinn	Wylde*	Magennis+	Smith"	Shaughnessy"	Weaver	Wylde	Lowe
14/12/2013	Prem	A	Inverness CT	4	3	Langfield	Shaughnessy	Hayes	Hector	Anderson	Hector	Robson"	Vernon"	jack	Flood*	McGinn	Smith*	Murray+	Zola+	Zola	Weaver	Wylde	Lowe
21/12/2013	Prem	A	Inverness CT	1	0	Langfield	Anderson	Hayes	Hector	Anderson	Hector"	Robson"	Vernon"	jack	Flood	McGinn	Hayes*	Smith+	Magennis*	Zola	Weaver	Wylde	Anderson
26/12/2013	LC4	H	Hearts	0	1	Langfield	Anderson	Hayes+	Hector	Reynolds	Hector"	Robson"	Vernon"	jack	Flood	McGinn	Magennis*	Shaughnessy+	Smith"	Shankland	Weaver	Wylde	Shankland
29/12/2013	Prem	H	Ross County	1	0	Langfield	Shaughnessy	Reynolds	Hector	Reynolds	Hector	Robson"	Vernon"	jack"	Flood	McGinn	Robson*	Low+	Zola+	Wylde	Weaver	Lowe	Murray
01/01/2014	Prem	A	Dundee United	2	1	Langfield	Shaughnessy	Reynolds	Hector	Reynolds	Hector	Robson"	Vernon"	jack	Flood	McGinn	Magennis*	Shaughnessy+	Magennis"	Wylde	Weaver	Lowe	Zola
05/01/2014	Prem	A	Kilmarnock	2	1	Langfield	Anderson	Reynolds	Hector	Reynolds	Pawlett+	Robson+	Vernon"	jack	Flood	McGinn	Zola*	Anderson+	Smith"	Smith	Weaver	Smith	Murray
10/01/2014	Prem	H	Hibernian	1	0	Langfield	Anderson*	Reynolds	Hector	Reynolds	Pawlett+	Low	Vernon"	jack	Flood	McGinn	Shaughnessy*	Hayes+	Smith"	Smith	Weaver	Storie	Rogers
18/01/2014	Prem	A	Inverness CT	0	1	Langfield	Anderson	Reynolds	Tate*	Reynolds	Pawlett	Robson+	Vernon"	jack	Flood	McGinn+	Pawlett*	Vernon+	Low"	Vernon	Weaver	Magennis	Tate
25/01/2014	LC5F	N	Motherwell	2	2	Langfield	Tate	Considine	Shaughnessy	Considine	Hayes	Robson+	Rooney	jack	Flood	McGinn+	Tate*	Low+	Low"	Zola	Smith	Smith	Tate
01/02/2014	Prem	H	Motherwell	4	0	Langfield	Anderson	Considine	Logan	Considine	Hayes	Robson"	Rooney	jack	Flood	McGinn	Zola*	Vernon+	Low"	Zola	Weaver	McManus	Murray
02/02/2014	SC5	A	Celtic	2	1	Langfield	Anderson+	Considine+	Logan	Considine	Hayes	Robson"	Rooney	jack	Flood	McGinn	Tate*	McManus+	Low"	Zola	Weaver	McManus	Murray
15/02/2014	Prem	A	St Mirren	1	0	Langfield	Tate*	Considine	Logan	Considine	Hayes	Low*	Rooney	jack	Flood	McGinn	Low*	Vernon+	Vernon	Smith	Weaver	McManus	Tate
22/02/2014	Prem	A	Partick Thistle	1	3	Langfield	Anderson	Considine	Considine+	Considine	Hayes	Low+	Rooney	jack	Flood	Robson	Tate*	Vernon+	Vernon	Zola	Weaver	Zola	Low
25/02/2014	Prem	A	Celtic	1	2	Langfield	Anderson*	Considine	Robson*	Considine	Hayes	Pawlett"	Rooney	jack	Flood*	Robson"	Shaughnessy"	Anderson+	Vernon"	Shaughnessy	Weaver	Vernon	Anderson
01/03/2014	Prem	H	St Johnstone	1	0	Langfield	Anderson	Considine*	jack+	Considine	Hayes	Pawlett	Rooney	jack"	Flood	Robson"	Smith"	Robson+	Low"	Shaughnessy	Weaver	Vernon	Zola
08/03/2014	SC6	H	Dumbarton	1	0	Langfield	Anderson	Considine	jack	Considine	Hayes	Hayes	Rooney	Smith*	Flood	Hayes	McGinn*	Anderson+	Low"	Shaughnessy"	Weaver	Tate	Zola
16/03/2014	LCF	N	Inverness CT	0	0 *4-2 p	Langfield	Anderson	Considine+	jack	Considine	Hayes	Robson"	Rooney+	Smith*	Flood	Hayes*	Robson"	Robson+	Vernon"	Tate	Weaver	Zola	Shaughnessy
22/03/2014	Prem	A	Kilmarnock	2	1	Langfield	Tate*	Considine	jack	Considine	Hayes	Smith	Rooney	McGinn+	Flood	Hayes"	McGinn*	Vernon+	Vernon	Tate	Weaver	Zola	McManus
29/03/2014	Prem	A	Ross County	1	1	Langfield	Anderson	Considine	jack	Considine	Hayes	Smith+	Rooney	McGinn	Flood	Robson	Robson*	Low+	Zola"	Robertson	Weaver	Low	Robertson
03/04/2014	Prem	H	Dundee United	1	1	Langfield	Anderson	Shaughnessy	jack	Reynolds	Logan	Pawlett+	Rooney	McGinn	Flood	Robson+	Smith*	Low+	Low"	Vernon	Weaver	Zola	Low
02/04/2014	Prem	A	Hearts	1	1	Langfield	Shaughnessy	Considine	jack	Considine	Logan	Pawlett"	Rooney	McGinn	Flood	Robson	Vernon"	Low+	Low"	Shaughnessy	Weaver	Robertson	McManus
07/04/2014	Prem	H	Hibernian	2	0	Langfield	Anderson	Considine	Hayes*	Reynolds	Logan	Pawlett	Rooney	McGinn"	Flood*	Robson"	Smith*	Shaughnessy	Robertson	Tate	Weaver	Low	McManus
13/04/2014	SCSF	N	St Johnstone	1	1	Langfield	Anderson	Considine	Hayes	Reynolds	Logan	Pawlett+	Rooney*	McGinn"	Flood	Robson+	Vernon"	Zola+	Low"	Shaughnessy	Weaver	Robertson	McManus
19/04/2014	Prem	A	Inverness CT	1	2	Langfield	Anderson	Considine*	Hayes	Reynolds	Logan	Pawlett+	Rooney*	McGinn"	Flood	Robson	Vernon"	Smith+	Zola"	Smith	Weaver	Low	Vernon
26/04/2014	Prem	H	St Johnstone	1	1	Langfield	Robertson"	Considine	Hayes	Reynolds	Logan	Pawlett+	Rooney*	Vernon"	Flood*	jack	Zola*	Smith+	Smith"	Robertson	Weaver	McManus	Murray
03/05/2014	Prem	A	Celtic	2	5	Langfield	Anderson	jack	Hayes	Reynolds	Logan	Pawlett	Rooney	Vernon"	Flood	Robson+	Vernon*	Tate+	Zola"	Murray	Weaver	Zola	Tate
06/05/2014	Prem	H	Dundee United	0	1	Langfield	Anderson	jack	Hayes	Reynolds	Logan	Pawlett	Rooney	McGinn	Flood	McGinn	Smith*	Smith+	McManus"	Tate	Weaver	Rose	McManus
11/05/2014	Prem	H	Motherwell	0	1	Langfield	Anderson	jack	Hayes	Reynolds	Logan	Pawlett	Robson	Vernon	Flood	McGinn	Zola	Smith	McManus	Tate	Weaver	Rose	Murray

Airdrieonians FC — 2013/14

AIRDRIEONIANS

Founded	2002 (as Airdrie United)
Ground	Excelsior Stadium
Postcode	ML6 8QZ
Tel	07710 230775 (Club Office) / 01236 622000 (Ground)
Closest Railway Station	Drumgelloch
Record Attendance	9044, 23/8/2013
Ground Record	
Record Win	11-0, v Gala Fairydean, 19/11/2011
Record Defeat	0-6, v Rangers, Lge, 23/8/2013
Most Goals in a Season	19, Alan Russell, 2007/8
Most Goals in Career	33, Stephen McKeown
Chairman	James Ballantyne
Secretary	Anne Marie Ballantyne
Manager	Jimmy Boyle (until Oct) / Gary Bollan
Assistant Manager	Paul Lovering (until Oct) / Stuart Balmer
Colours 2013/14 Top	White with red diamond
Shorts	White or Red
Sponsor	Advance Construction Scotland
Manufacturer	Puma
Change Colours 2013/14 Top	Black with red shoulder flash
Shorts	Black
Nicknames	Diamonds, Waysiders
Web	www.airdriefc.com

Airdrie started 2013/14 by adopting the old name of Airdrieonians in preference to Airdrie United. The change didn't prevent some dreadful form and by the turn of the year they looked odds-on for relegation. They were giving away soft goals and crowds were down to an all-time low.

Jimmy Boyle departed the Manager's office and was replaced by former Livingston boss Gary Bollan. The turnaround in Airdrie's fortunes was remarkable. They made a steady climb up the table, crowds at home and away began to rise, and a mood of confidence and optimism surrounded the club. Bollan used his contacts to recruit some decent players.

Several of Airdrie's best players moved on in the Summer of 2014. However, Bollan has been quick to bring in a decent quality of replacement.

PREDICTION FOR 2014/15
Promotion play offs, or better.

Surname	First Name	DOB	Pos	L A	L S	L G	SC A	SC S	SC G	LC A	LC S	LC G	RC A	RC S	RC G	US	Signed Previous Club	Notes	Contract
Adam	Grant	16/04/91	GK	16													2014 Cowdenbeath		
Bain	Jamie	08/08/91	M	26	6	1	1						2	2		3	2008 Airdrie United Youth		C (2015)
Barclay	Jamie	01/03/95	M							1						2	2012 Falkirk	Freed Jan 2014, Joined Pollok	
Barr	Craig	29/03/87	M	11	2												2014 Ostersunds FK (Sweden)	Signed for Raith Rovers May 2014	
Bjekovic	Stefan Milojevic	20/02/91	D	17													2014 FK Bezanija (Serbia)	Signed for Morton, June 2014	
Blockley	Nathan	15/06/92	M	21	4	2	1			2			1	1	1	3	2014 Queen's Park		C (2015)
Boyle	Patrick	20/03/87	D	30			1	1					1			7	2013 Dunfermline Athletic		C (2015)
Boyle	John`	22/10/86	F														2011 Auchinleck Talbot		C (2015)
Buchanan	Gregor	31/03/90	D	28	4	4	1						1			1	2012 Bathgate Thistle	Signed for Dunfermline Ath May 2014	
Bullock	Tony	18/02/72	GK				1											Goalkeeper Coach	
Cadden	Nicky	19/09/96	M	8	4											10	2013 Motherwell		c (2015)
Coogans	Liam	31/10/96	F	9	14	3	1			2			1	1		12	2012 Airdrie United Youths		
Coult	Lewis	07/06/88	F	14	7	7	1			2			1	1		9	2013 Cowdenbeath		F
Drummond	Grant	16/01/95	D	3	1		1						1			2	2014 Airdrie Youths		
Duncan	Andrew		GK	3												19	2011 Dumbarton	Freed Jan 2014, joined Pollok	
Evans	Grant	03/01/90	D	10	3					2			2			6	2012 Morton		F
Gallagher	Scott	15/07/89	GK	8													2013 Rangers (Loan Sep-Nov)		
Gilmour	Ross	05/07/94	D	11	1											2	2013 Dundee United (Loan Dec-Feb)	Returned to Dundee United	
Glackin	Reece	23/06/96	M	9													2013 Airdrie Youths		Youth
Grier	Jonathan	13/04/95	GK	6													2013 Airdrieonians Youth		
Hardie	Martin	22/04/76	F	11	1	2	1			2						1	2013 Morton	Freed Jan 2014	
Hay	Gary	07/09/77	D	2	2								1	1		1	2013 Kilmarnock	Freed Sep 2013	
Higgins	John									1						2			Youth
Lamie	Ricky	20/06/93	D													5	2012 Airdrie United Youth	Loaned to East Stirlingshire	F
Lister	Jim	26/02/81	F	28	5	10	1			2						1	2013 Dumbarton		C (2015)
McAleer	Caolen	19/08/93	M	19	1	3											2013 Partick Thistle (Loan)	Returned to Partick Thistle	
McCluskey	Chris	30/01/87	GK													14	2013 North Star (Brisbane)		
McCormack	Darren	29/09/88	D	34	1											2	2013 East Fife		
McLaren	Willie	06/11/84	F	7	6	2	1	1		2	1					5	2012 Hamilton Accies	Freed Jan 2014, joined Irvine Meadow	
McMillan	Marcus		D													1	2013 Airdrie Youths		Youth
O'Byrne	Michael	07/09/88	D	6	2		1	1		1	1					12	2012 Albion Rovers	Freed, Joined Stirling Albion Jan 2014	
O'Neill	Chris	24/08/95	D	6						1	1					5	2012 Airdrie Youths		
Parker	Keigan	08/06/82	F	20	1	4											2013 Shettleston		C (2015)
Pollock	Jamie	20/02/92	M	1												1		Trialist, Ex Motherwell, E Fife	
Richford	Kyle	21/03/96	F													1	2013 Campsie Black Watch		
Rogers	Daniel	23/03/94	GK	6													2013 Aberdeen (Loan Dec-Jan)		
Sinclair	David	23/07/90	M	12	2	1	1			2			1	1		3	2013 Ayr United	Freed Jan 2014, joined BI (Faroes)	
Stewart	Colin	10/01/80	GK	3	1					2			2				2013 Cowdenbeath	Freed Aug 2013, Joined Raith Rovers	
Stewart	Scott	29/04/96	D	2	6											10	2013 Airdrie Youths		C (2015)
Ward	Aiden	25/07/96	M													5	2013 Airdrieonians Youth		
Watt	Liam	21/01/94	M	24	1	2	1						1	1		7	2012 Airdrieonians Youth		C (2015)
Own Goal						1													

NEW SIGNINGS 2014/15

Surname	First Name	Pos	Signed Previous Club
McNeill	Andy	GK	2014 New Zealand Football
Gray	Scott	M	2014 St Johnstone
Hamill	Joe	F	2014 Formartine United (ex Hearts)
Fitzpatrick	Marc	D	2014 Morton

Date	Comp	H/A	Opponents	F	A	Crowd	Scorers
27/07/2013	RC1	H	Hamilton Accies	2	1	880	McLaren, Blockley
03/08/2013	LC1	H	Stenhousemuir	4	3	647	O'Byrne, Sinclair, Blockley, Coult
10/08/2013	L	A	Forfar Athletic	3	3	704	Lister, McLaren, Coult
17/08/2013	L	H	Stenhousemuir	0	1	722	
20/08/2013	RC2	H	Queen of the South	0	2	637	
23/08/2013	L	H	Rangers	0	6	9044	
27/08/2013	LC2	H	Livingston	0	2	483	
31/08/2013	L	A	Ayr United	2	2	1339	Boyle, Blockley
14/09/2013	L	H	Stranraer	3	2	679	Sinclair, Coult, Buchanan
21/09/2013	L	A	Dunfermline Athletic	1	2	2607	Coogans
28/09/2013	L	A	East Fife	0	1	665	
05/10/2013	L	H	Brechin City	3	1	606	Hardie, Coogans, Coult
12/10/2013	L	A	Arbroath	2	3	747	McLaren, Coult
19/10/2013	L	H	Forfar Athletic	0	2	579	
26/10/2013	L	H	Ayr United	0	1	1012	
01/11/2013	SC3	A	Rangers	0	3	22533	
09/11/2013	L	A	Rangers	0	2	43158	
16/11/2013	L	H	Dunfermline Athletic	0	3	1219	
23/11/2013	L	A	Stranraer	1	3	461	Hardie, Coogans, Coult
14/12/2013	L	H	East Fife	1	3	624	Coult
17/12/2013	L	A	Brechin City	3	4	445	Lister, Coult, Blockley
21/12/2013	L	A	Stenhousemuir	1	1	419	Buchanan
28/12/2013	L	H	Arbroath	2	1	641	Buchanan, Parker
02/01/2014	L	H	Rangers	0	1	6522	
11/01/2014	L	A	Ayr United	0	3	1037	
18/01/2014	L	A	Dunfermline Athletic	1	0	2711	McAleer
25/01/2014	L	H	Stranraer	1	1	726	Lister
01/02/2014	L	A	Forfar Athletic	1	1	542	Lister
15/02/2014	L	H	Brechin City	2	1	690	Gilmour, Coult
22/02/2014	L	A	East Fife	0	0	815	
25/02/2014	L	H	Stenhousemuir	1	1	586	Lister
01/03/2014	L	H	Ayr United	3	0	880	Barr, Watt, Parker
12/03/2014	L	A	Rangers	0	3	41343	
15/03/2014	L	A	Arbroath	1	0	823	Lister
22/03/2014	L	H	Forfar Athletic	5	1	712	Buchanan, Lister, Watt, Parker, Bain
29/03/2014	L	A	Stranraer	1	1	404	Rumsby og
05/04/2014	L	H	Dunfermline Athletic	2	0	1142	Parker, Lister
12/04/2014	L	A	Brechin City	1	1	646	Lister
19/04/2014	L	H	East Fife	2	1	1033	McAleer, Lister
26/04/2014	L	A	Stenhousemuir	2	1	812	Stewart, Barr
03/05/2014	L	H	Arbroath	2	0	1243	McAleer, Coogans

Friendly Matches			Versus	F	A	Att	Notes
8/7/13	Fr	A	Alloa	2	3	229	
13/7/13	Fr	A	Deveronvale	3	2		
15/7/13	Fr*	N	Motherwell U17	2	0		at Carluke
20/7/13	Fr*	A	Carlisle United U18	1	2		
25/7/13	Fr*	A	St Anthonys	0	0		
28/7/13	Fr*	A	Spartans	2	2		
29/7/13	Fr	H	Linlithgow Rose	2	3		
31/7/13	Fr*	A	Rossvale U21	5	1		
1/8/13	Fr*	A	Amiston Rangers	0	3	ABD	
4/8/13	Fr*	H	Chester U18	1	2		
10/8/13	Fr*	A	Hearts U17	1	1		
20/9/13	Fr*	H	EDUSPORT Academy	2	5		

* Mainly youth players

Date	Comp	H/A	Opponents	F	A	1	2	3	4	5	6	7	8	9	10	11	12	13	14	15	16	17	18
27/07/2013	RC1	H	Hamilton Accies	2	1	Stewart	McNeil	McCormack	O'Byrne	Evans	Bain*	Sinclair	Blockley	McLaren"	Coult+	Lister	Hardie*	Coogans+	Watt*	Drummond	Duncan		
03/08/2013	LC1	A	Stenhousemuir	4	3	Stewart	O'Neill	McCormack	O'Byrne	Evans	Hardie	Sinclair	Blockley	McLaren	Coult+	Lister	Bain*	Coogans+	Watt	Lamie	Duncan		
10/08/2013	L	A	Forfar Athletic	3	3	Stewart	Hay	McCormack	O'Byrne	Evans	Hardie*	Sinclair	Blockley	McLaren	Coult+	Lister	Bain*	Coogans+	Watt	Boyle	Duncan		
17/08/2013	L	H	Stenhousemuir	0	1	Stewart	Hay+	McCormack	O'Byrne	Boyle	Hardie	Sinclair	Blockley*	O'Neill"	Coult	Lister	Bain*	McLaren+	Coogans"	Evans	Duncan		
20/08/2013	RC2	H	Queen of the South	0	2	Stewart	Hay	Drummond	Buchanan+	Evans	McLaren	Bain	Watt	Barclay*	Coogans	Richford"	Higgins*	O'Byrne+	McMillan"	S Stewart	Duncan		
23/08/2013	L	H	Rangers	0	6	Stewart	O'Neill	McCormack	Buchanan	Boyle	Bain+	Sinclair	Blockley	McLaren*	Coult	Lister	Hardie*	Hay+	Coogans"	Evans	Duncan	O'Byrne	
27/08/2013	LC2	L	Livingston	0	2	Stewart	Hay+	McCormack*	Buchanan	Boyle	Evans	Sinclair	Blockley	Hardie*	Coult*	Lister	Bain*	McLaren-	Coogans"	O'Byrne	Duncan		
31/08/2013	L	A	Ayr United	2	2	Duncan	O'Neill	McCormack*	O'Byrne	Boyle	McLaren	Sinclair	Blockley	Watt	Coult*	Lister+	Bain*	Buchanan"'	Coogans"	S Stewart	Watt	Stewart	
14/09/2013	L	H	Stranraer	3	2	Gallagher	Evans	McCormack	Buchanan	Boyle	Hardie	Sinclair	Blockley	Bain	Coult*	Coogans	Coogans*	Drummond+	Duncan	S Stewart	Watt		
21/09/2013	L	A	Dunfermline Athletic	1	2	Gallagher	Evans	McCormack	Buchanan"	Boyle	Hardie+	Sinclair	Blockley	Bain	Watt	Coogans	McLaren*	Drummond	Duncan	O'Byrne	Cadden		
28/09/2013	L	A	East Fife	0	1	Gallagher	Evans	McCormack	O'Neill*	Boyle	Hardie+	Sinclair	Blockley	Bain	Watt	Coogans"	McLaren"	Coult+	Duncan	Cadden	Duncan		
05/10/2013	L	H	Brechin City	3	1	Gallagher	Evans	McCormack	O'Neill*	Boyle	Hardie+	Sinclair	Blockley	Lister"	Watt+	Coogans	O'Byrne*	Bain+	Coult*	Cadden	Duncan		
12/10/2013	L	A	Arbroath	2	3	Gallagher	Evans	McCormack	O'Neill*	Boyle	Hardie*	Sinclair"	Blockley*	Coult	Watt+	Coogans	Bain*	McLaren+	Buchanan*	O'Byrne	Duncan		
19/10/2013	L	H	Forfar Athletic	0	2	Gallagher	Evans	McCormack	Buchanan	Boyle	Hardie	Sinclair+	Bain*	Coult	Coogans	Lister	McLaren*	Stewart+	Duncan	O'Byrne	Higgins		
26/10/2013	L	H	Ayr United	0	1	Gallagher	Evans*	McCormack	Buchanan	Boyle	Hardie	Sinclair	Blockley	McLaren+	Coogans	Lister	Coult*	Bain+	Duncan	O'Byrne	Higgins	Stewart	
01/11/2013	SC3	A	Rangers	0	3	Bullock	Drummond	McCormack	Buchanan	Boyle	Hardie	Sinclair	Blockley	Coult*	Bain+	Lister	Watt*	Coogans+	Duncan	O'Byrne	Barclay	McLaren	
09/11/2013	L	A	Rangers	0	2	Duncan	Drummond	McCormack	Buchanan	Boyle	Hardie	Sinclair*	Blockley	McLaren+	Bain	Lister	Watt*	Barclay	Grier	Coult	O'Byrne	McLaren	
16/11/2013	L	H	Dunfermline Athletic	0	3	Duncan	Drummond*	McCormack*	Buchanan	Boyle	Hardie	Pollock+	Cadden	Coogans	Bain	Lister"	O'Byrne*	Grier+	Blockley*	Coult	Sinclair		
23/11/2013	L	A	Stranraer	1	3	Gallagher	O'Byrne*	Drummond*	Buchanan	Boyle	Sinclair	McAleer	Cadden+	Blockley	Coult*	Lister"	Bain*	Coogans+	Sinclair"	O'Byrne	Bain	McLaren	Duncan
14/12/2013	L	H	East Fife	1	3	Rogers	Gilmour	McCormack	Buchanan	Boyle"	Watt	McAleer	Cadden+	Blockley	Coult*	Parker	Lister*	Coogans+	Sindair"	O'Byrne	Bain	McLaren	Duncan
17/12/2013	L	A	Brechin City	3	4	Rogers	Gilmour	McCormack	Buchanan	Boyle"	Watt	McAleer	Coogans+	Blockley	Coult*	Parker	Lister*	McAleer+	Cadden"	O'Byrne	Bain	Duncan	
21/12/2013	L	A	Stenhousemuir	1	1	Rogers	Gilmour	McCormack	Buchanan	Lister	Watt	Sinclair*	Caden	Blockley	Coult	Bain	O'Byrne	McLaren	Coogans	Stewart	Duncan		
28/12/2013	L	A	Arbroath	2	1	Rogers	Gilmour	McCormack	Buchanan	O'Byrne	Watt	McAleer	Caden+	Blockley	Coult+	Bain	Lister*	McLaren+	Stewart*	Coogans	Grier	Ward	McCluskey
02/01/2014	L	H	Rangers	0	1	Rogers	Gilmour	McCormack	Buchanan	O'Byrne	Watt	McLaren	McLaren	Parker"	Lister	Bain	Parker"	Boyle	O'Burne	Cadden	Grier		
11/01/2014	L	A	Ayr United	0	3	Adam	Gilmour	McCormack	Buchanan	Bjekovic	Watt	Boyle	Blockley	Blockley*	Coult*	Bain	Lister*	Boyle	Lamie	Watt	Grier		
18/01/2014	L	H	Dunfermline Athletic	1	0	Adam	Gilmour	McCormack	Buchanan	Bjekovic	Lister	Boyle	Blockley	McAleer	McAleer	Bain	Cadden	Coogans	Lamie	Watt	Cadden		
25/01/2014	L	A	Stranraer	1	1	Adam	Gilmour	McCormack	Buchanan	Bjekovic	Lister	Boyle	Blockley	McAleer	McAleer	Bain	Coult*	Coogans	Lamie	Watt	Cadden		
01/02/2014	L	H	Forfar Athletic	1	1	Adam	Gilmour	Watt	Evans	Bjekovic	Lister	Boyle	Blockley	Cadden*	McAleer	McCormack	Coogans*	Cadden	McCluskey	Glackin	Glackin	Coult	Stewart
15/02/2014	L	H	Brechin City	2	1	Adam	Gilmour	Watt	Evans+	Bjekovic	Lister	Boyle	Parker*	McCormack	McAleer	McCormack	Coult*	Buchanan+	Coult*	Lamie	Glacken	Evans	McCluskey
22/02/2014	L	A	East Fife	0	0	Adam	Gilmour	Watt	Buchanan	Bjekovic	Lister	Boyle	Parker*	McCormack	McAleer	Bain	Richford	Cadden	Coogans*	Stewart	Glacken	Blockley	McCluskey
25/02/2014	L	H	Stenhousemuir	1	1	Adam	Barr	Watt	Buchanan	Bjekovic	Lister"	Boyle	Parker	McCormack	McAleer+	Bain	Blockley*	Cadden	Coogans*	Stewart	Gilmour	Blockley	McCluskey
01/03/2014	L	A	Ayr United	3	0	Adam	Barr*	Watt	Buchanan	Bjekovic	Lister*	Boyle	Parker*	McCormack	McAleer	Bain	Blockley"	Cadden+	Coogans"	Stewart	Gilmour	Richford	McCluskey
12/03/2014	L	A	Rangers	0	3	Adam	Barr*	Watt	Buchanan	Bjekovic	Lister	Boyle	Parker+	McCormack	McAleer	Bain	Stewart*	Cadden+	Coogans*	Coult	McCluskey	Evans	Ward
15/03/2014	L	A	Arbroath	1	0	Adam	Barr	Watt+	Buchanan	Bjekovic	Lister	Boyle	Parker"	McCormack	McAleer	Bain	Evans*	Stewart+	Coogans"	Ward	Cadden	Ward	McCluskey
22/03/2014	L	H	Forfar Athletic	5	1	Adam	Barr	Watt	Buchanan	Bjekovic	Lister	Boyle	Parker+	McCormack*	Stewart	Bain	Coult*	Coogans+	Coult	Ward	McCluskey	Glacken	Stewart
29/03/2014	L	A	Stranraer	1	1	Adam	Barr	Watt	Buchanan	Bjekovic	Lister	Boyle	Parker+	McCormack*	McAleer*	Bain	Stewart*	Evans+	Coogans+	Cadden	McCluskey	Glacken	Evans
05/04/2014	L	H	Dunfermline Athletic	2	0	Adam	Barr	Watt	Buchanan	Bjekovic	Lister	O'Neill	McCormack	McCormack	Stewart	Bain	Stewart*	Coogans+	Glackin	Cadden	McCluskey	Evans	O'Neill
12/04/2014	L	A	Brechin City	1	1	Adam	Barr	Watt	Buchanan	Bjekovic	Lister	O'Neill	McCormack	McCormack	McAleer*	Bain	Stewart*	Coogans	Glackin	Cadden	McCluskey	Coogans	Coult
19/04/2014	L	H	East Fife	2	1	Adam	Barr	Watt	Stewart	Bjekovic	Lister	O'Neill	Parker+	McCormack	McAleer	Bain	Stewart*	Evans+	O'Neill	Cadden	McCluskey	Evans	Ward
26/04/2014	L	A	Stenhousemuir	2	1	Adam	Barr	Watt	Buchanan	Bjekovic	Lister	Cadden+	Parker*	Boyle	McAleer*	Bain	Buchanan"	Lister+	Stewart*	Coogans	McCluskey	Coult	O'Neill
03/05/2014	L	H	Arbroath	2	0	Adam	Barr	Watt	Buchanan	Bjekovic	Lister	McCormack+	Parker*	Boyle	McAleer"	Bain	Coogans*	Blockley+	Stewart*	Glackin	Cadden	O'Neill	Cadden

Albion Rovers FC   2013/14

ALBION ROVERS

Founded	1882
Ground	Cliftonhill Stadium
Postcode	ML5 3RB
Tel	01236 606334
Capacity	1238
Closest Railway Station	Coatdyke
Record Attendance	27381, SC, v Rangers 8/2/36
Record Win	12-0, v Airdriehill, 3/9/1887
Record Defeat	1-11, v Partick Thistle, LC, 11/8/1993
Most League Goals in a Season	John Renwick, 41, 1932/3
Most Goals in Career	105, Bunty Weir
Chairman	John Devlin
Secretary	Paul Reilly
General Manager	Stevie Kirk
Manager	James Ward (until June) / Darren Young
Assistant Manager	Mark Cameron (until June) / Sandy Clark
Colours 2013/14 Top	Yellow
Shorts	Red
Sponsor	Reigart Demolition
Manufacturer	Macron
Change Colours 2013/14 Top	Red with yellow flashes
Shorts	Blue
Nicknames	Wee Rovers
Web	www.albionroversfc.com

Albion Rovers gained substantial publicity, and income, from their Scottish Cup run, which culminated in taking Rangers to a replay in the Quarter Final. That success disguised a somewhat disappointing League season with the Coatbridge side well off the pace in League Two.

During the Summer Rovers decided to change their management team bringing in Darren Young as player-manager with Sandy Clark as his Assistant. Off the field Rovers have been re-energised with an injection of new ideas and enthusiasm in the Boardroom. The idea of "Pay What You Can" season tickets has led to a large increase in sales with no loss of revenue.

Work is to start soon on improving facilities at Cliftonhill with the club accepting that the old ground will remain their home - they have no plans now to move.

PREDICTION FOR 2014/15
Play Offs or better.

Surname	First Name	DOB	Pos	L			SC			LC			RC			UNS	Signed Previous Club	Notes	Contract
				A	S	G	A	S	G	A	S	G	A	S	G				
Allan	Jordan	07/02/95	F	5												1	2013 Dundee United (Loan)		
Bosley	Lee		D	1													Trialist Arthurlie U21		
Chaplain	Scott	09/10/83	M	26	4	9	5			1			1			3	2013 Annan Athletic		C(2015)
Crawford	David	16/02/92	M	13	8	2	2	2		1			1			7	2012 Hibernian		
Cusack	Liam	27/07/93	F	30	2	3	5						1			1	2013 Cowdenbeath		C(2015)
Dallas	Chris	10/04/87	M	18	5	5	4	1		1						6	2013 Arthurlie		C(2015)
Donnelly	Ciaran	30/04/86	M	29	2	1	6			1	1		1			3	2005 Hamilton Accies		C(2015)
Donnelly	Ryan	23/10/91	M	12	2	3										3	2014 Brechin City		
Dunlop	Mick	05/11/82	D	32			2		5				1			5	2013 Stranraer	Brother of Ross	C(2015)
Dunlop	Ross	20/06/88	D	34			6						1			1	2013 Pollok	Brother of Mick	C(2015)
Flood	Joshua	02/02/92	M	11	12		1	4					1			14	2013 Stirling Albion		F
Innes	Peter	26/04/91	D	5	2					1			1			13	2012 East Kilbride Thistle		F
Kennedy	Dominic	14/05/92	D	9			1									5	2014 Workington		
Lamont	Mark	04/02/93	M	1													Trialist, ex St Mirren, Dumbarton		
Maguire	Martin	17/02/94	D	2	2											26	2013 Morton		C(2015)
McGinley	Matt	15/08/88	GK	4	2											37	2012 Morton		F
McGuigan	Mark	07/11/88	F	30	1	3	6			2	1		1			3	2013 Partick Thistle (Loan)		C(2015)
Mercer	Scott	18/06/95	M	1												4	2013 Dunfermline Athletic (Loan)		
Miller	Darren	04/08/92	D	3	2	1	1						1			4	2013 Knightswood Juveniles	Freed November 2013	
Nicoll	Kevin	16/06/86	M	2	2		1			1			1			4	2013 Clyde	Transferred to Arbroath Jan 2014	
Parry	Neil	08/11/85	GK	32			6			1						1	2013 Queen's Park		C(2015)
Phillips	Gary	01/05/88	M	31	4	5	6	2		1			1			1	2012 Largs Thistle		F
Reid	Alan	12/07/88	M	34	1	6				1			1				2007 Hamilton Accies		
Russell	Barry	01/06/89	M	21	2	1	4	1								4	2011 East Kilbride Thistle		F
Sally	Scott	17/07/93	F													4	2013 Airdrie United	Freed October 2013	
Shankland	Mark	11/07/95	M	3	1											1	2013 Ayr United (Loan)		
Shepherd	Graeme	13/03/92	GK													1	2011 Partick Thistle		F
Tiffney	Ryan	11/05/90	M	3	18		2	3					1			16	2012 Drumchapel Amateurs		F
Walker	Pat	14/09/84	F	9	7	2	1									11	2013 Dumbarton		F
Trialist			GK													1			
Own Goals						3			1										

New Signings 2014/14

Surname	First Name	DOB	Pos	Signed Previous Club	Contract
McNeill	Ross	01/11/91	F	2014 Stenhousemuir	
Love	Ally	22/08/91	M	2014 Annan Athletic	
Gemmell	John	06/09/84	F	2014 Stenhousemuir	C(2016)
McKenzie	Marc	11/07/85	M	2014 Cowdenbeath	

Date	Comp	H/A	Opponents	F	A		Crowd	Scorers
28/07/2013	RC1	H	Rangers	0	4	at Livingston	5345	
03/08/2013	LC1	A	Dumbarton	0	1		505	
10/08/2013	L	A	Elgin City	2	1		541	Walker, Crawford
17/08/2013	L	H	Clyde	3	0		528	Philips 2, Walker
24/08/2013	L	A	Annan Athletic	1	1		492	Crawford
31/08/2013	L	H	Montrose	0	2		311	
14/09/2013	L	H	Berwick Rangers	0	2		322	
21/09/2013	L	A	East Stirlingshire	4	1		336	Dunlop, Dallas 2, McGuigan
28/09/2013	L	H	Peterhead	1	2		354	Miller
05/10/2013	SC2	H	Spartans	1	0		437	McGuigan
19/10/2013	L	H	Elgin City	0	0		337	
26/10/2013	L	A	Queen's Park	1	1		541	Quinn
29/10/2013	L	A	Stirling Albion	1	2		423	Dallas
02/11/2013	SC3	H	Deveronvale	1	0		484	McGuigan
09/11/2013	L	H	Annan Athletic	2	0		319	Watson og, Shankland
16/11/2013	L	A	Montrose	1	2		343	McGuigan
23/11/2013	L	A	Berwick Rangers	1	2		388	Dunlop og
30/11/2013	SC4	H	Motherwell	1	0	at Hamilton	2950	Phillips
03/12/2013	L	H	East Stirlingshire	3	2		323	Phillips, Dallas, Chaplain
07/12/2013	L	H	Stirling Albion	2	1		396	Russell, Dallas
14/12/2013	L	A	Peterhead	1	1		423	McGuigan
21/12/2013	L	A	Clyde	2	2		508	M Dunlop, Cusack
28/12/2013	L	H	Queen's Park	2	1		538	Cusack, Chaplain
04/01/2014	L	A	Annan Athletic	0	2		403	
11/01/2014	L	H	Montrose	1	0		718	Chaplain
18/01/2014	L	A	East Stirlingshire	1	1		319	Chaplain
25/01/2014	L	H	Berwick Rangers	0	3		366	
01/02/2014	L	A	Elgin City	1	1		519	Chaplain
08/02/2014	SC5	H	Stenhousemuir	2	0		748	McMillan og, Phillips
15/02/2014	L	A	Stirling Albion	0	2		541	
22/02/2014	L	H	Peterhead	0	0		442	
25/02/2014	L	H	Clyde	1	0		423	Chaplain
01/03/2014	L	A	Montrose	1	2		334	Phillips
09/03/2014	SC6	A	Rangers	1	1		23976	C Donnelly
15/03/2014	L	A	Queen's Park	0	4		361	
17/03/2014	SC6R	H	Rangers	0	2		5354	
22/03/2014	L	H	Elgin City	5	2		286	C Donnelly, Cusack, Phillips, Chaplain 2
25/03/2014	L	H	Annan Athletic	0	2		323	
29/03/2014	L	A	Berwick Rangers	1	3		471	R Donnelly
05/04/2014	L	H	East Stirlingshire	2	1		287	R Donnelly 2
12/04/2014	L	H	Stirling Albion	0	2		480	
19/04/2014	L	A	Peterhead	0	2		775	
26/04/2014	L	A	Clyde	0	4		620	
03/05/2014	L	H	Queen's Park	1	0		503	Chaplain

Friendly Matches			Versus	F	A	Att	Notes
6/7/13		Fr	A Stenhousemuir	1	0		
16/7/13		Fr	H Stranraer	3	1		at St Ambrose HS
20/7/13		Fr	A Kirkintilloch Rob Roy	1	2		at Arthurlie
23/7/13		Fr	A St Anthonys	8	0		
9/9/13		Fr	A Rutherglen Glencairn	3	1		
13/1/14		Fr	N Shotts Bon Accord	1	2		at St Ambrose HS

Date	Comp	H/A	Opponents	F	A	1	2	3	4	5	6	7	8	9	10	11	12	13	14	15	16	17	18
28/07/2013	RC1	H	Rangers	0	4	Parry	Reid	Donnelly	M Dunlop	R Dunlop	Phillips	Nicol	Innes+	Flood*	Crawford	McGuigan	Chaplain	Tiffney	Dallas	Miller"	McGinley		
03/08/2013	LC1	A	Dumbarton	0	1	Parry	Reid	Donnelly	M Dunlop	R Dunlop	Cusack*	Nicol	Innes	Chaplain+	Crawford	McGuigan	Dallas*	Phillips+	Miller	Tiffney	McGinley		
10/08/2013	L	A	Elgin City	2	1	Parry	Reid	Donnelly	M Dunlop	R Dunlop	Cusack*	Phillips"	Innes	Walker+	Crawford	McGuigan	Tiffney*	McGinley"	Flood"	Miller	Sally	Maguire	
17/08/2013	L	H	Clyde	3	0	McGinley	Reid	Donnelly	M Dunlop	R Dunlop	Cusack+	Phillips	Innes	Walker*	Crawford"	McGuigan	Chaplain*	Tiffney+	Flood"	Dallas	Miller	Shepherd	Maguire
24/08/2013	L	A	Annan Athletic	1	1	Parry	Reid	Donnelly	M Dunlop	R Dunlop	Cusack	Phillips	Innes*	Walker+	Crawford	McGuigan	Chaplain*	Dallas	Miller"	Flood	McGinley	Maguire	Tiffney
31/08/2013	L	A	Montrose	0	2	Parry	Reid	Donnelly	M Dunlop	R Dunlop	Cusack"	Phillips	Miller	Chaplain*	Crawford	McGuigan	Nicol*	Dallas+	Miller"	Flood	McGinley	Chaplain	Tiffney
14/09/2013	L	H	Berwick Rangers	0	2	Parry	Reid	Donnelly	M Dunlop	R Dunlop	Cusack"	Phillips	Miller	Chaplain+	Dallas+	McGuigan+	Flood*	Dallas+	Tiffney"	McGuire	McGinley	Walker	Sally
21/09/2013	L	A	East Stirlingshire	4	1	Parry	Reid	Donnelly	M Dunlop	R Dunlop	Cusack	Phillips	Miller	Flood*	Dallas-	McGuigan+	Crawford*	Walker+	Maguire	Tiffney	McGinley	Chaplain	Sally
28/09/2013	L	H	Peterhead	1	2	Parry	Reid	Donnelly	Chaplain	R Dunlop	Cusack	Phillips	Miller	Flood*	Dallas"	McGuigan*	Walker+	Tiffney+	McGuire"	Nicol	McGinley	M Dunlop	Sally
05/10/2013	SC2	H	Spartans	1	0	Parry	Reid	Donnelly	Chaplain	R Dunlop	Nicol	Phillips	Miller	Flood*	Tiffney"	McGuigan"	Dallas"	Russell+	McGuire"	M Dunlop	McGinley		
19/10/2013	L	H	Elgin City	0	0	Parry	Reid	Donnelly	M Dunlop	R Dunlop	Nicol	Phillips	Cusick*	Chaplain	Dallas*	McGuigan	Russell!**	Crawford+	Miller"	Flood	McGinley	Maguire	Tiffney
26/10/2013	L	A	Queen's Park	1	1	Parry	Reid	Donnelly	M Dunlop	R Dunlop	Nicol+	Phillips	Flood"	Chaplain	Crawford*	McGuigan	Russell!**	Cusack*	Tiffney"	McGuire	McGinley	Walker	Innes
29/10/2013	L	A	Stirling Albion	1	2	Parry	Reid	Donnelly	M Dunlop	R Dunlop	Russell!*	Phillips	Flood"	Chaplain	Dallas-	McGuigan	Cusack*	Flood+	Crawford"	McGuire	McGinley	Innes	
02/11/2013	SC3	A	Deveronvale	1	0	Parry	Reid	Donnelly	M Dunlop	R Dunlop	Cusack	Phillips	Tiffeny*	Crawford+	Dallas	McGuigan	Flood*	McGuire+	Russell	Walker	McGinley	Innes	
09/11/2013	L	H	Annan Athletic	2	0	Parry	Reid*	Donnelly	M Dunlop	R Dunlop	Cusack	Phillips	Tiffeny"	Crawford"	Dallas	McGuigan	Tiffeny+	McGuire+	Flood"	Walker	Russell	Russell	
16/11/2013	L	A	Montrose	1	2	Parry	Reid	Donnelly	M Dunlop	R Dunlop	Cusack	Phillips	Shankland	Crawford	Dallas*	McGuigan	Flood*	McGuire	Flood	Mercer	McGinley	Russell	Chaplain
23/11/2013	L	A	Berwick Rangers	1	2	Parry	Reid*	Donnelly"	M Dunlop	R Dunlop	Cusack	Phillips	Shankland*	Mercer+	Dallas	McGuigan	Chaplain+	McGuire	Tiffeny"	Russell	McGinley	McGuire	
30/11/2013	SC4	H	Motherwell	1	0	Parry	Reid	Donnelly	M Dunlop	R Dunlop	Phillips	Phillips	Russell	Chaplain	Dallas*	McGuigan	Flood+	Flood+	McGuire"	Mercer	McGinley	Innes	Walker
03/12/2013	SC4	A	East Stirlingshire	3	2	Parry	Reid	Donnelly	M Dunlop	R Dunlop	Cusack+	Phillips	Russell!*	Chaplain	Dallas-	McGuigan	Russell!**	Cusack*	Mercer	McGuire	McGinley	Shankland	Crawford
07/12/2013	L	H	Stirling Albion	2	1	Parry	Reid	Donnelly	M Dunlop	R Dunlop	Cusack	Phillips	Russell	Chaplain	Dallas-	McGuigan	Crawford*	Tiffeny	Mercer	Flood	McGinley	Innes	Maguire
14/12/2013	L	A	Peterhead	1	1	Parry	Reid	Donnelly	M Dunlop	R Dunlop	Russell!*	Phillips	Russell	Chaplain	Dallas*	McGuigan	Tiffeny*	Crawford	Flood	McGuire	McGinley	Nicol	
21/12/2013	L	A	Clyde	2	2	Parry	Reid	Donnelly	M Dunlop	R Dunlop	Cusack	Phillips	Russell	Chaplain+	Dallas+	McGuigan	Allan*	Crawford+	Nicol"	McGuire	Nicoll		
28/12/2013	L	H	Queen's Park	2	1	Parry	Reid	Donnelly"	M Dunlop	R Dunlop	Cusack	Phillips"	Russell	Chaplain+	Dallas+	McGuigan	Allan*	Flood+	Tiffeny"	McGuire	McGinley	Crawford	Tiffney
04/01/2014	L	A	Annan Athletic	1	0	Parry	Reid	Donnelly"	M Dunlop	R Dunlop	Cusack	Phillips	Russell	Chaplain+	Dallas*	McGuigan	Crawford*	Allan+	Tiffeny"	McGuire	McGinley	Flood	Nicol
11/01/2014	L	A	Montrose	1	0	Parry	Reid	Donnelly	M Dunlop	R Dunlop	Cusack	Flood +	Russell	Chaplain	Dallas	McGuigan	Tiffeny*	Allan+	Crawford	McGuire	McGinley	Phillips	
18/01/2014	L	A	East Stirlingshire	1	1	Parry	Reid	Donnelly"	M Dunlop	R Dunlop	Cusack	Flood +	Russell	Chaplain	Dallas*	R Donnelly+	Tiffeny*	Phillips+	Allan"	McGuire	McGinley	Crawford	
25/01/2014	L	H	Berwick Rangers	0	3	Parry	Reid	Crawford"	M Dunlop	R Dunlop	Cusack+	R Donnelly+	Russell	Chaplain+	Dallas*	McGuigan	Phillips*	Crawford+	Flood	Allan	McGinley	McGuire	Tiffney
01/02/2014	L	H	Elgin City	1	1	Parry	Reid	Phillips	M Dunlop	R Dunlop	Cusack"	C Donnelly	Russell	Chaplain	Phillips	McGuigan+	C Donnelly*	C Donnelly*	Flood	Flood	McGinley	Walker	Tiffney
08/02/2014	SC5	A	Stenhousemuir	0	0	McGuire	McGuire	Phillips	M Dunlop	R Dunlop	Cusack"	C Donnelly	Russell	Chaplain+	Dallas*	McGuigan+	Crawford*	Crawford+	Innes"	Flood	McGinley	Walker	Innes
15/02/2014	L	A	Stirling Albion	0	2	Parry	Reid	Phillips	M Dunlop	R Dunlop	Cusack"	Kennedy+	Russell	Chaplain	Phillips	McGuigan	Tiffeny*	McGuire	R Donnelly+	Flood	McGinley	Tiffney	
22/02/2014	L	H	Peterhead	0	0	Parry	Reid	Phillips	M Dunlop	R Dunlop	C Donnelly*	Kennedy	Russell	Chaplain	Flood+	McGuigan	Flood	McGuire	McGuire	Innes	McGinley	Tiffney	Walker
25/02/2014	L	A	Montrose	1	0	Parry	Reid	Phillips	M Dunlop	R Dunlop	C Donnelly*	R Donnelly+	Russell	Kennedy*	Flood +	McGuigan	Walker*	Dallas+	Tiffeny"	Innes	McGinley	Tiffney	Kennedy
01/03/2014	L	H	Rangers	1	1	Parry	Reid	Phillips	McGuigan+	R Dunlop	C Donnelly	Cusack+	Russell"	Chaplain	Walker"	McGuigan	Dallas*	Chaplain+	Flood"	McGuigan	McGinley	Walker	Maguire
09/03/2014	SC6	A	Queen's Park	0	4	McGinley	Bosley	Lamont*	McGuire+	Kennedy	Innes	Crawford"	Tiffeney	Flood	R Donnelly	Walker	Reid*	C Donnelly+	Phillips"	M Dunlop	Parry	McGuigan	Cusack
15/03/2014	SC6R	L	Rangers	0	4	Parry	Reid	Phillips"	M Dunlop	R Dunlop	C Donnelly	Cusack+	Russell	Chaplain	Crawford*	McGuigan	Walker*	Flood+	Phillips"	M Dunlop	McGuigan	McGuire	Kennedy
17/03/2014	L	A	Rangers	0	2	McGinley	Reid	Phillips"	M Dunlop	R Dunlop	Kennedy	Cusack+	Russell	Chaplain+	Crawford+	McGuigan	Walker*	Flood+	Phillips"	M Dunlop	Parry	McGuigan	Cusack
22/03/2014	L	H	Elgin City	5	2	Parry	Reid	Phillips	M Dunlop	R Dunlop	C Donnelly	Cusack"	Russell	Chaplain+	Crawford*	McGuigan+	Walker*	R Donnelly+	Tiffeny"	Innes	McGinley	Kennedy	Flood
25/03/2014	L	A	Annan Athletic	0	2	Parry	Reid	Phillips	M Dunlop	R Dunlop	C Donnelly	Cusack	Flood	Chaplain	Crawford*	McGuigan	Walker+	R Donnelly+	Flood"	Kennedy	McGinley	McGuire	Kennedy
29/03/2014	L	H	East Stirlingshire	1	3	Parry	Reid	Phillips	M Dunlop	R Dunlop	C Donnelly*	Cusack	Russell	Chaplain	Crawford*	McGuigan	Walker+	Tiffeny+	Flood*	Flood	McGinley	Tiffney	
05/04/2014	L	H	Rangers	1	1	Parry	Reid	Phillips	McGuigan"	Kennedy+	Kennedy*	Cusack+	Russell	Chaplain	Walker+	R Donnelly*	Flood*	McGuigan	Innes"	McGuigan	McGinley	Tiffney	
12/04/2014	L	A	Stirling Albion	0	2	Parry	Reid	Phillips	M Dunlop	R Dunlop	Kennedy	Cusack+	Russell	Chaplain	Walker	R Donnelly	Flood+	Dallas+	C Donnelly"	Innes	McGinley	Tiffney	Crawford
19/04/2014	L	A	Peterhead	0	2	Parry	Reid	Phillips	McGuigan+	Tiffeny*	Kennedy	Cusack"	Russell	Chaplain	Walker*	R Donnelly	McGinley*	Flood+	Tiffeny"	McGuigan	McGinley	Tiffney	
26/04/2014	L	A	Clyde	0	4	McGinley	Reid	Phillips	C Donnelly	Tiffeny*	Kennedy+	Cusack"	Flood	Chaplain	Walker	R Donnelly	Flood+	R Dunlop	M Dunlop	Crawford	Dallas	Dallas	
03/05/2014	L	H	Queen's Park	1	0	McGinley	Reid	McGuigan	M Dunlop	R Dunlop	Kennedy+	Flood	Russell	Chaplain	Cusack"	R Donnelly"	Phillips*	Tiffeny+	Walker"	Dallas	C Donnelly	Trialist	

Alloa FC   2013/14

Founded	1878
Ground	Recreation Park
Postcode	FK10 1RY
Tel	01259 722695
Capacity	3100
Closest Railway Station	Alloa
Record Attendance	13000 v Dunfermline, SC, 26/2/1939
Record Win	9-0 v Selkirk, SC, 28/1/2005
Record Defeat	0-10 v Dundee, Lge, 82/47; v T Lanark, LC, 8/8/53
Most League Goals in a Season	49, Willie Crilley, 1921/2
Chairman	Mike Mulraney
Secretary	Ewan Cameron
Manager	Paul Hartley (until Jan) / Barry Smith
Assistant Manager	Paddy Connolly
Colours 2013/14 Top	Black and Gold Hoops
Shorts	Black and Gold Hoops
Sponsor	Marshall Construction
Manufacturer	Pendle
Change Colours 2013/14 Top	Maroon
Shorts	Maroon
Nicknames	Wasps
Web	www.alloaathletic.co.uk

During the early part of 2013/14 Alloa were the surprise package of the Championship. With a settled team and a particular style of play under Paul Hartley they were safely placed in the upper middle of the table.

Towards the turn of the year results started to slide and Hartley resigned, saying that he had taken the club as far as he could. A few weeks later he was back in the game with Dundee. Meantime Alloa turned to a former Dundee Manager, Barry Smith, to arrest their slide.

He found the going hard and going into the Final game of the season Alloa needed a point at Falkirk to be sure of avoiding the relegation play off. They failed to get it and only escaped the play off courtesy of a 96th minute Queen of the South equaliser against Cowdenbeath.

Off the field the club are successful and high-profile in their community thanks to a hard working Board of Directors led by Mike Mulraney.

PREDICTION FOR 2014/15
Tough season ahead for Alloa - will be happy to finish in the top eight and avoid relegation or the play offs.

				L			SC			LC			RC							
Surname	First Name	DOB	Pos	A	S	G	A	S	G	A	S	G	A	S	G	UNS	Signed	Previous Club	Notes	Contract
Bain	Scott	22/11/91	GK	35			3			2				1		1	2011	Aberdeen	Joined Dundee May 2014	ONC
Caddis	Liam	20/09/93	F	12	5	1										2	2013	St Johnstone (Loan Dec-May)	Returned to St Johnstone	
Caldwell	Ross	26/10/93	F	4	8	1										4	2014	Hibernian (Loan Jan-May)	Returned to Hibernian	
Cawley	Kevin	17/03/89	F	35		8	3			1	2			1			2011	East Stirlingshire		C (2015)
Creaney	James	19/10/88	D	7	1					2			1			13	2013	Dumbarton		OTF
Doyle	Michael	01/08/91	D	36			2			2			1			1	2011	Kilmarnock		ONC
Ferns	Edward	18/04/91	M	6	17	3	2			1						4	2012	Drumchapel United		C (2015)
Flannigan	Iain	15/01/88	M	1	11		1									13	2013	Falkirk		OTF
Forsyth	Graham	19/01/95	M													2	2013	Castlehill United		Youth
Gemmell	Ryan	26/04/96	M	1												8	2013	Rangers SABC		Youth
Gordon	Ben	07/10/85	D	36			3	3		1	2			1			2011	Dumbarton		C (2015)
Hardie	Michael	06/03/96	M													1	2013	Alloa Youths		Youth
Holmes	Graeme	26/03/84	M	33	1	2	3			1	2			1			2011	Morton		C (2015)
Hynd	Scott	10/08/97	F													4	2013	Alloa Youths		Youth
Kirk	Andy	29/05/79	F	27	5	5	3			2		1	1			4	2013	Dunfermline Athletic		F
Lindsey	Liam	12/10/95	D	10			1										2014	Partick Thistle (Loan Jan-May)	Returned to Partick Thistle	
Marr	Jason	23/02/89	D	12	1		1		1	1						6	2012	Clyde		OTF
McCord	Ryan	21/03/89	M	34	1	6	3		1	2		1	1				2011	Dundee United		C (2015)
McDowall	Craig	24/08/90	GK	1			1									40	2011	Livingston		C (2015)
McLelland	Lee	02/05/96	M													3	2013	Lenzie United		Youth
McManus	Declan	03/08/94	F	7	11	1				1						1	2013	Aberdeen (Loan Aug-Oct)	Returned to Aberdeen	
Meggatt	Darryll	20/10/90	D	34		1	3			1	2			1			2012	Queen's Park		C (2015)
Moore	Nathan	12/08/96	M													3	2013	Clyde		Youth
Riordan	Derek	16/01/83	F		2											6	2014	Bristol Rovers		F
Robertson	Willie	14/04/93	M	5	5		1									20	2013	Dundee United		OTF
Salmon	Alex	09/07/94	F	1				2	1							6	2014	Carlisle United (Loan Nov-Dec)	Returned to Carlisle United	
Simmons	Stephen	27/02/82	M	29	1	2	3			2			1				2012	Queen of the South		C (2015)
Tiffoney	Jonathan	07/05/91	D	17	6		2	1			1		1			13	2013	Ayr United		C (2015)
Ward	Andrew	30/10/97	D													2	2013	Cadzow BC		Youth
Wilson	Lewis	01/08/96	D				1									4	2013	Alloa Youths		Youth
Young	Darren	13/10/78	M	14	3		1	1		1						17	2011	Morton	Joined Albion Rovers June 2014	F

New Signings 2014/15																				
Weatherston	David	25/08/86	M														2014	Stirling Albion		
Gibson	John	31/01/89	GK														2014	Dundee		
Docherty	Mark	15/03/88	M														2014	Stranraer		

Date	Comp	H/A	Opponents	F	A		Crowd	Scorers
27/07/2013	RC1	H	Dundee	0	1		880	
03/08/2013	LC1	A	Peterhead	2	0		429	McCord, Kirk
10/08/2013	L	H	Livingston	1	0		714	Simmons
17/08/2013	L	A	Dundee	0	1		4167	
24/08/2013	L	H	Cowdenbeath	3	1		611	Gordon, Kirk, Ferns
27/08/2013	LC2	A	Aberdeen	0	0	AET, 5-6 pens	4897	
31/08/2013	L	A	Queen of the South	0	0		1607	
14/09/2013	L	H	Dumbarton	1	2		626	Simmons
21/09/2013	L	A	Raith Rovers	2	4		1397	Cawley, McCord
28/09/2013	L	H	Hamilton Accies	1	0		653	McCord
05/10/2013	L	A	Morton	2	0		1478	Holmes, Kirk
12/10/2013	L	H	Falkirk	0	0		1625	
19/10/2013	L	A	Livingston	2	3		869	Cawley, Gordon
26/10/2013	L	H	Queen of the South	0	3		724	
02/11/2013	SC3	H	Inverurie Locos	3	0		403	Cawley, Gordon, Salmon
09/11/2013	L	A	Cowdenbeath	2	0		346	Cawley, Kirk
16/11/2013	L	H	Raith Rovers	1	0		858	Kirk
30/11/2013	SC4	H	Stirling Albion	3	2		1278	McCord, Holmes, Marr
04/12/2013	L	A	Dumbarton	1	1		463	Cawley
07/12/2013	L	A	Hamilton Accies	1	0		860	Meggatt
14/12/2013	L	H	Morton	2	0		546	Kirk, McManus
21/12/2013	L	H	Dundee	0	1		1170	
28/12/2013	L	A	Falkirk	0	0		3417	
02/01/2014	L	H	Cowdenbeath	0	1		818	
11/01/2014	L	A	Queen of the South	1	3		1476	Caldwell
18/01/2014	L	H	Dumbarton	1	5		602	Cawley
01/02/2014	L	A	Dundee	1	1		4021	Gordon
08/02/2014	SC5	H	Dumbarton	0	1		749	
15/02/2014	L	H	Livingston	0	3		605	
22/02/2014	L	A	Morton	1	0		1628	McCord
25/02/2014	L	A	Raith Rovers	1	1		978	Ferns
01/03/2014	L	H	Hamilton Accies	0	3		656	
08/03/2014	L	A	Cowdenbeath	2	2		458	Holmes, McCord
15/03/2014	L	H	Queen of the South	0	1		644	
22/03/2014	L	H	Falkirk	3	0		1025	Ferns, Cawley, McCord
25/03/2014	L	A	Livingston	0	2		709	
29/03/2014	L	H	Raith Rovers	0	1		726	
05/04/2014	L	A	Dumbarton	1	4		677	Caddis
12/04/2014	L	H	Morton	2	0		615	Cawley, McCord
19/04/2014	L	A	Hamilton Accies	1	2		1087	Caldwell
26/04/2014	L	H	Dundee	0	3		2552	
03/05/2014	L	A	Falkirk	1	3		3998	Cawley

Friendly Matches			Versus	F	A		Att	Notes
6/7/13		Fr	H	East Fife	1	1		
8/7/13		Fr	H	Airdrieonians	3	2	229	
10/7/13		Fr	H	Oxford United	1	1	245	
13/7/13		Fr	A	Cove Rangers	2	0		
14/7/13		Fr	A	Peterhead	2	1		at Banks o' Dee
17/7/13		Fr	H	Burntisland Shipyard	5	1	U19	
20/7/13		Fr	A	Queen's Park	0	0		
31/7/13		Fr	A	Easthouses Lily	?	?	U19	
27/8/13		StC1	H	East Stirlingshire	2	2	2-4 pens	

Date	Comp	H/A	Opponents	F	A	1	2	3	4	5	6	7	8	9	10	11	12	13	14	15	16	17	18
27/07/2013	RC1	H	Dundee	0	1	Bain	Creaney	Gordon	Meggat	Simmons	McCord*	Holmes*	Doyle	Kirk	Cawley	Tiffoney	Ferns*	Ward	McDowell	Robertson	Moore		
03/08/2013	LC1	A	Peterhead	2	0	Bain	Creaney	Gordon	Meggat	Simmons	McCord	Holmes*	Doyle	Kirk	Cawley	McManus	Tiffoney*	Tiffoney*	Ferns	McDowell	Moore		
10/08/2013	L	H	Livingston	1	0	Bain	Creaney	Gordon	Meggat	Simmons	McCord	Holmes+	Doyle	Kirk	Cawley	McManus	Tiffoney*	Ward	McDowell	Forsyth	Gemmell	Gemmell	
17/08/2013	L	A	Dundee	0	1	Bain	Creaney	Gordon	Meggat	Simmons+	McCord	Holmes+	Doyle	Kirk*	Cawley	McManus*	Robertson*	Robertson*	McDowell	Forsyth	Marr	Gemmell	Hynd
24/08/2013	L	H	Dundee	3	1	Bain	Creaney	Gordon	Meggat	Simmons+	McCord	Holmes	Doyle	Kirk	Cawley	McManus*	McManus*	Tiffoney+	McDowell	Young	Marr	Tiffoney	Gemmell
27/08/2013	LC2	A	Aberdeen	0	0	Bain	Creaney	Gordon	Meggat	Simmons	McCord	Holmes	Doyle	Kirk*	Cawley	McManus	Salmon*	Robertson*	McDowell	Tiffoney	Robertson	Tiffoney	
31/08/2013	L	A	Dumbarton	0	0	Bain	Creaney*	Gordon	Meggat	Simmons	McCord	Holmes	Doyle	Kirk	Cawley	Salmon+	Ferns*	Young*	McDowell	Tiffoney	Robertson	McDowell	Salmon
14/09/2013	L	H	Queen of the South	1	2	Bain	Marr	Gordon	Meggat	Simmons	McCord	Holmes	Doyle	Kirk+	Cawley	Tiffoney*	Young*	Ferns*	Young*	Tiffoney	Young	Young	
21/09/2013	L	A	Raith Rovers	2	4	Bain	Marr	Gordon	Meggat	Simmons	McCord	Holmes*	Doyle	Kirk	Cawley	Salmon+	Salmon*	McManus*	McDowell	Tiffoney	Moore	Mclelland	
28/09/2013	L	H	Hamilton Accies	1	0	Bain	Marr	Gordon	Meggat	Simmons	McCord	Holmes*	Doyle	Kirk+	Cawley	Tiffoney"	McManus+	Salmon+	Salmon&	Young	Tiffoney	McDowell	
05/10/2013	L	A	Morton	2	0	Bain	Creaney	Gordon	Meggat	Simmons	McCord	Holmes	Doyle	Kirk+	Cawley	McManus*	McManus*	Robertson+	Young"	Young"	Robertson	McDowell	
12/10/2013	L	H	Falkirk	0	0	Bain	Tiffoney	Gordon	Meggat	Simmons	McCord	Holmes	Doyle	Kirk+	Cawley	Salmon*	McManus*	Salmon+	Young"	Tiffoney	Robertson	McDowell	
19/10/2013	L	A	Livingston	2	3	Bain	Tiffoney	Gordon	Meggat	Simmons	McCord+	Holmes-	Doyle	Kirk	Cawley	Robertson*	Flannigan*	Ferns+	Ferns"	Tiffoney	Young	McDowell	
26/10/2013	L	H	Queen of the South	0	3	Bain	Tiffoney*	Gordon	Meggat	Simmons	McCord+	Holmes	Doyle	Kirk+	Cawley	Flannigan*	McManus*	Salmon*	Salmon	McDowell	Young	Creaney	
02/11/2013	SC3	H	Inverurie Locos	3	0	Bain	Tiffoney*	Gordon	Meggat	Simmons*	McCord+	Holmes+	Doyle	Kirk+	Cawley	Flannigan*	McManus*	McManus+	Young"	McDowell	Doyle	Robertson	
09/11/2013	L	A	Cowdenbeath	2	0	Bain	Tiffoney	Gordon	Meggat	Simmons*	McCord*	Holmes-	Wilson	Kirk	Cawley	Flannigan*	McManus+	McManus*	Salmon	Fems	Robertson	Robertson	
16/11/2013	L	H	Raith Rovers	1	0	Bain	Tiffoney	Gordon	Meggat	Simmons	McCord	Holmes	Doyle	Kirk+	Cawley	Marr	Ferns*	McManus*	Salmon	McDowell	Robertson	McDowell	
30/11/2013	SC4	A	Stirling Albion	3	2	Bain	Tiffoney	Gordon	Meggat	Simmons	McCord+	Holmes	Doyle	Kirk*	Cawley	Salmon*	Salmon*	Young	McManus*	Fems	Robertson	Young	
04/12/2013	L	H	Dumbarton	1	1	Bain	Marr	Gordon	Meggat	Simmons	McCord	Holmes*	Doyle	Kirk*	Cawley	Marr	McManus*	Robertson+	McDowell	McDowell	Robertson	Creaney	
07/12/2013	L	A	Hamilton Accies	1	0	Bain	Marr	Gordon	Meggat	Simmons	McCord	Holmes	Doyle	Young	Cawley	Robertson*	Salmon*	Ferns+	Salmon	McDowell	Kirk	Creaney	
14/12/2013	L	H	Morton	2	0	Bain	Marr	Gordon	Meggat	Simmons	McCord*	Holmes	Doyle	Kirk+	Cawley	Gordon	Tiffoney*	McManus+	Gemmell"	Young	McDowell	Creaney	
21/12/2013	L	A	Dundee	0	1	Bain	Marr	Gordon	Meggat	Holmes	McCord"	Tiffoney	Doyle	Kirk+	Cawley	Robertson	Ferns*	McManus+	Young	McDowell	Robertson	Creaney	
28/12/2013	L	A	Falkirk	0	0	Bain	Marr"	Young	Young	Holmes	McCord	Tiffoney*	Doyle	Kirk	Cawley	Robertson*	Ferns*	Creaney	Ferns"	Young	Robertson	Creaney	
02/01/2014	L	H	Cowdenbeath	0	1	Bain	Marr"	Gordon	Meggat	Holmes	McCord*	Tiffoney	Doyle	Robertson*	Cawley	Caddis	McManus*	Simmons+	Ferns"	McDowell	Hynd	Robertson	
11/01/2014	L	A	Dumbarton	1	3	Bain	Creaney+	Gordon	Meggat	Caldwell+	Tiffoney	Young"	Doyle	Kirk+	Cawley	Caddis	McManus*	Ferns+	Creaney"	Young	Tiffoney	Gemmell	
18/01/2014	L	A	Dumbarton	1	5	Bain	McCord	Gordon	Meggat	Young	Tiffoney	Simmons	Doyle	Kirk	Cawley	Caddis	Caldwell	Ferns+	Kirk"	Creaney	Flannigan	Gemmell	
01/02/2014	L	A	Dundee	1	1	Bain*	McCord	Gordon	Meggat*	Tiffoney*	Lindsey	Simmons	Doyle	Caldwell	Kirk+	Caddis	McCord*	Fearns+	Tiffoney"	Creaney	McLelland	Gemmell	
08/02/2014	SC5	H	Dumbarton	0	1	McDowall	Ferns	Gordon	Meggat	Caddis*	Lindsey	Simmons	Doyle	Caldwell*	Kirk	Caddis	Flannigan*	Riordan+	Tiffoney	Creaney	Flannigan	Kirk	
15/02/2014	L	H	Livingston	0	3	Bain	Ferns*	Gordon	Meggat	Kirk*	Lindsey	Simmons	Doyle	Cawley	Holmes*	Young"	Flannigan*	Riordan+	Young	Caldwell	Young	Caddis	
22/02/2014	L	A	Morton	1	0	Bain	Ferns+	Gordon	Meggat	Tiffoney*	Lindsey	Simmons-	Doyle	Cawley	Holmes+	Robertson+	Caddis*	Kirk+	Tiffoney"	Creaney	Kirk	Riordan	
25/02/2014	L	A	Raith Rovers	1	1	Bain	Ferns+	Gordon	Meggat	Tiffoney*	Lindsey	Simmons	Doyle	Cawley	Holmes	Robertson*	Caddis*	Kirk+	Flannigan	Creaney"	Flannigan	Caldwell	
01/03/2014	L	H	Hamilton Accies	0	3	Bain*	Ferns+	Gordon	Meggat	Tiffoney*	Lindsey+	Simmons"	Doyle	Cawley	Holmes	Caddis	Flannigan+	Tiffony+	Caddis+	Creaney	Riordan	Caldwell	
08/03/2014	L	H	Cowdenbeath	2	2	Bain	Young	Gordon	Meggat	Tiffoney	Lindsey	Simmons	Doyle	Cawley	Holmes*	Caddis	Caldwell*	Tiffony+	Caddis"	Robertson"	Riordan	Robertson	
15/03/2014	L	H	Queen of the South	0	1	Bain	Young+	Gordon	Meggat	Caddis"	Lindsey	Simmons	Doyle	Cawley	Holmes*	McCord	Caldwell*	Flannigan+	Caldwell"	Robertson	Caddis	McDowall	McLelland
22/03/2014	L	H	Falkirk	3	0	Bain	Young*	Gordon	Holmes	Kirk*	Kirk"	Simmons"	Doyle	Cawley	Kirk*	McCord	Caldwell*	Caddis*	Kirk"	Robertson	Hynd	McDowall	Flannigan
25/03/2014	L	A	Livingston	0	2	Bain	Young*	Gordon	Holmes	Tiffoney*	Lindsey	Caddis"	Doyle	Cawley	Kirk	McCord	Ferns*	Flannigan+	Caldwell"	Marr	Caldwell	McDowall	McDowell
29/03/2014	L	H	Raith Rovers	0	1	Bain	Young+	Gordon	Holmes	Tiffoney	Lindsey	Ferns*	Doyle	Cawley	Ferns	McCord	Robertson*	Ferns+	Caldwell"	Tiffoney	Flannigan	Hynd	McDowell
05/04/2014	L	A	Dumbarton	1	4	Bain	Young+	Gordon	Meggat	Meggat	Lindsey	Caddis	Doyle	Cawley	Kirk	McCord	Caddis+	Caddis+	Flannigan	Riordan	Robertson	Marr	McDowell
12/04/2014	L	H	Hamilton Accies	2	0	Bain	Young	Gordon	Holmes	Meggat	Tiffoney	Caddis	Doyle	Cawley	Kirk*	McCord	Caldwell*	Flannigan+	Robertson	Riordan	Wilson	McDowall	McDowell
19/04/2014	L	A	Dundee	1	2	Bain	Young	Gordon	Holmes	Meggat	Tiffoney	Caddis	Doyle	Cawley	Kirk*	McCord	Caldwell*	Caddis+	Flannigan	Riordan	Wilson	McDowall	McDowell
26/04/2014	L	H	Dundee	0	3	Bain	Young"	Gordon	Holmes	Meggat	Tiffoney	Simmons	Doyle	Cawley	Kirk	McCord	Caldwell*	Robertson	Robertson"	Riordan	Wilson	McDowall	Gemmell
03/05/2014	L	A	Falkirk	1	3	Bain	Young*	Gordon	Holmes	Robertson	Caddis+	Simmons	Doyle	Cawley	Caldwell	NcCord	Ferns*	Kirk+	Flannigan	Riordan	Wilson	McDowall	Marr

Annan Athletic FC

Founded	1942
Ground	Galabank
Postcode	DG12 5DQ
Tel	01461 204108
Capacity	2514
Closest Railway Station	Annan
Record Attendance	2517 v Rangers, Sep 2013
Record Win	Annan Athletic 6 Elgin City 0, 07.03.2009
Record Defeat	Inverness CT 8 Annan Athletic 1, 24.01.1998
Most League Goals in a Season	15, Mike Jack, 2008/9
Chairman	Henry McClelland
Secretary	Alan Irving
Manager	Jim Chapman
Assistant Manager	John Joyce
Colours 2013/14 Top	Gold with Black Flashes
Shorts	Black
Sponsor	M and S Engineering
Manufacturer	Stanno
Change Colours 2013/14 Top	Mauve with White Sleeves
Shorts	White
Nicknames	Galabankies
Web	www.annanathleticfc.co.uk

In some respects season 2013/14 will be regarded as a success for Annan Athletic. They reached the Semi Final of the Ramsdens Cup and comfortably qualified for the promotion play offs. However, their performance in the play offs when they were heavily defeated by Stirling Albion was a major disappointment.

However, Annan can be well pleased with their achievements since joining the League in 2008. As well as establishing themselves in playing terms, they have made Galabank into an impressive small stadium.

2014/15 will be a vital season for the club. They need to kick on from last season's near-thing and establish the sort of consistency that wins titles.

PREDICTION FOR 2014/15
More play off disappointment for Annan.

Name		DOB	Pos	L A	S	G	SC A	S	G	LC A	S	G	RC A	S	G	UNS	Signed		Notes	Contract
Anderson	Gregor	02/12/94	D										1			18	2013	Queen of the South	Released and joined Dalbeattie Star	
Arthur	Kenny	07/12/78	GK	35			3						3			3	2013	Grimsby Town		OOC
Black	Steven	17/06/92	D	17	2	1	2						2			4	2013	Queen of the South		C (2015)
Black	Gary	08/05/97	GK													9	2013	Jimmy Johnstone Academy		Youth
Bradley	Peter	26/05/91	D	15		3					1		3	1		22	2013	Queen's Park		OOC
Brannan	Keiran	17/05/91	M	15	16	1	1	2	1				1	3	1	8	2013	Albion Rovers		C (2015)
Brown	Jordan		M													2				Youth
Caldwell	Zak															6		Annan Athletic Youth		Youth
Chisholm	Ian	29/08/85	D	22	1		2			1			4			2	2013	Arthurlie		C (2015)
Davidson	Scott	01/01/92	F	18	15	10	4			1			2	2		5	2013	Stirling Albion		C (2015)
Flynn	Matt	15/05/88	M	19	5	1	1	1	2	1			4			5	2013	Rutherglen Glencairn		C (2015)
Graham	Danny		M													4	2013	Annan Athletic Youth		Youth
Henderson	Blair	10/08/94	F	8	5	3										1	2014	Dunfermline Athletic		OOC
Hopkirk	David	17/01/93	F	17	4	8	4		1	1			4	2		1	2013	Queen of the South		C (2015)
Jardine	Chris	26/11/78	M	11	2		2			1						11	1998			R
Logan	Steven		M	1	1		1											2013	Newcastle United (loan)	Returned to Newcastle Utd	
Love	Ally	22/08/91	M	28	5	8	4		1	1			3	1		1	2012	St Mirren	Joined Albion Rovers May 2014	OOC
McAnespie	Michael		M	1																Youth
McCrudden	Keiran	27/10/96	M	1												5	2013			Youth
MacKay	Kenny	10/09/90	F	28	2	13	1	2	1				3	3		1	2013	Greenock Juniors		OOC
McNiff	Martin	16/03/90	D	33		4	4	1										2013	Dumbarton (loan)		OOC
Mitchell	Alex	21/03/91	GK	3			1			1			1			36	2011	Gretna		C (2015)
Mitchell	Andrew	06/04/92	M	28	1	5	4						1				2013	Rangers (loan)	Made permanent Jan 2014	OOC
Moffat	Jordan	21/03/94	F	9					1					2		20	2013	Partick Thistle		OOC
Murray	C		M													1				Youth
Orsi	Dan	31/03/92	M	1	7											5	2014	Queen of the South		OOC
Sloan	Steven	21/03/84	M	24	4		3			1			3			6				C (2015)
Swinglehurst	Steven	23/10/92	D	25	1	2	2			1			2	1		9	2012	Carlisle United		C (2015)
Todd	Josh	11/06/94	M	25	5	12	3	1	1				2			2	2013	Carlisle United (loan)		C (2015)
Watson	Peter	20/08/86	D	33		1	4	1					4					Albion Rovers		OOC
Weatherson	Peter	29/05/80	F	11		2	4	1					4	1			2013	Morton		OOC
Wood	Daniel		M				2									10		Annan Athletic Youth		Youth
Own Goals							2													

NEW SIGNINGS 2014/15

Carcary	Derek					2014 Brechin City

Date	Comp	H/A	Opponents	F	A		Crowd	Scorers
27/07/2013	RC1	H	Morton	1	0		732	Weatherston
03/08/2013	LC1	A	Queen of the South	0	3		1588	
10/08/2013	L	A	Peterhead	2	2		504	Hopkirk 2
17/08/2013	L	H	Montrose	2	1		286	McKay, Black
20/08/2013	RC2	A	Stranraer	3	2		290	McKay 2, Hopkirk
24/08/2013	L	H	Albion Rovers	1	1		492	Davidson
31/08/2013	L	A	Berwick Rangers	2	4		448	Hopkirk, Love
07/09/2013	RC3	H	Formartine United	4	0		506	Love, Brannan, McKay, Hopkirk
14/09/2013	L	A	Stirling Albion	2	0		608	Love, Hopkirk
21/09/2013	L	H	Clyde	1	2		483	Weatherston
28/09/2013	L	A	Queen's Park	5	2		413	MacKay 2, Todd 2, Love
05/10/2013	SC2	A	Buckie Thistle	0	0		320	
13/10/2013	RCSF	A	Raith Rovers	0	3		2119	
19/10/2013	SC2R	H	Buckie Thistle	4	0		338	Love, Flynn 2, Mackay
26/10/2013	L	A	Elgin City	3	2		648	Weatherston, Todd, McKay
29/10/2013	L	H	East Stirlingshire	1	2		301	Hopkirk
02/11/2013	SC3	A	Stenhousemuir	2	2		309	McNiff, Brannan
05/11/2013	L	H	Peterhead	2	0		277	Todd, McGeever og
09/11/2013	L	A	Albion Rovers	0	2		319	
12/11/2013	SC3R	H	Stenhousemuir	2	4	AET	421	Todd, Hopkirk
16/11/2013	L	H	Berwick Rangers	3	2		395	McNiff, Davidson, Brannan
23/11/2013	L	H	Stirling Albion	4	4		384	Davidson, Mitchell, McKay, Love
03/12/2013	L	A	Clyde	1	2		422	McKay
07/12/2013	L	A	East Stirlingshire	1	1		218	Mitchell
26/12/2013	L	A	Montrose	2	0		350	Todd, McKay
28/12/2013	L	H	Elgin City	2	1		401	Davidson, McKay
04/01/2014	L	H	Albion Rovers	2	0		403	Todd, McKay
11/01/2014	L	A	Berwick Rangers	4	1		429	Flynn, Swinglehurst, Todd 2
18/01/2014	L	H	Clyde	0	1		456	
25/01/2014	L	A	Stirling Albion	1	1		509	Davidson
08/02/2014	L	H	Montrose	1	0		354	Todd
15/02/2014	L	H	East Stirlingshire	2	3		401	Davidson, Mitchell
22/02/2014	L	A	Queen's Park	1	0		356	McKay
25/02/2014	L	H	Queen's Park	3	2		345	McNiff, Davidson 2
01/03/2014	L	H	Berwick Rangers	4	0		473	Love, McKay 2, Watson
04/03/2014	L	A	Peterhead	1	3		607	Ross og
15/03/2014	L	A	Elgin City	3	2		485	Love, Swinglehurst, Henderson
22/03/2014	L	H	Peterhead	2	1		452	Mitchell. Love
25/03/2014	L	A	Albion Rovers	2	0		323	Todd, McKay
29/03/2014	L	H	Stirling Albion	1	2		479	Henderson
05/04/2014	L	A	Clyde	3	0		516	Davidson. Todd 2
12/04/2014	L	A	East Stirlingshire	1	2		253	Henderson
19/04/2014	L	H	Queen's Park	1	1		560	Mitchell
26/04/2014	L	A	Montrose	1	2		264	Hopkirk
03/05/2014	L	H	Elgin City	2	0		428	Hopkirk, McNiff
07/05/2014	PO	A	Stirling Albion	1	3		972	Hopkirk
10/05/2014	PO	H	Stirling Albion	3	5		912	McNiff, Love, Davidson

Friendly Matches

Date		H/A	Opponents	F	A			
6/7/13	Fr	A	Workington	2	2			
9/7/13	Fr	H	Partick Thistle	1	5			
11/7/13	Fr	A	Dalbeattie Star	1	4			
13/7/13	Fr	H	Queen of the South	0	2	710		
16/7/13	Fr	H	East Kilbride	1	3		U19	
19/7/13	Fr	H	Carlisle United	2	1			
23/7/13	Fr	H	Carlisle United U20	2	2		U19	
31/7/13	Fr	A	Cumnock	2	2	5-6 pens		

Date	Comp	H/A	Opponents	F	A	1	2	3	4	5	6	7	8	9	10	11	12	13	14	15	16	17	18
27/07/2013	RC1	H	Morton	1	0	Mitchell	Chisholm	Bradley	Sloan	Weatherson	Swinglehurst	Hopkirk	Watson	McKay+	Flynn	Love*	Brannan*	Davidson+	Anderson*	Moffat	Arthur		
03/08/2013	LC1	A	Queen of the South	0	3	Mitchell	Chisholm	Bradley	Sloan	Weatherson	Swinglehurst	Hopkirk	Watson	McKay*	Flynn	Love*	Davidson*	Davidson+	Moffat*	Brannan	Arthur		
10/08/2013	L	A	Peterhead	2	2	Mitchell	Chisholm	Bradley	Sloan	Weatherson	Black	Hopkirk	Watson	Black	Flynn	Love	Jardine*	Moffat	Brannan	Davidson	McCrudden	Graham	Arthur
17/08/2013	L	H	Montrose	2	1	Arthur	Chisholm	Bradley	Sloan	Weatherson	Black	Hopkirk+	Watson	McKay*	Flynn+	Love*	McCudden*	Davidson+	Brannan*	Moffat	Mitchell		
20/08/2013	RC2	A	Stranraer	3	2	Arthur	Chisholm	Bradley"	Sloan	Weatherson	Black	Hopkirk	Watson	McKay	Flynn+	Love+	Brannan*	Swinglehurst+	Davidson*	Moffat	Mitchell	Swinglehurst	Swinglehurst
24/08/2013	L	A	Albion Rovers	1	1	Arthur	Chisholm	Bradley"	McNiff	Weatherson	Black*	Hopkirk	Watson	McKay	Flynn	Love+	Brannan*	Davidson+	Moffat*	Moffat	Anderson	Mitchell	Mitchell
31/08/2013	L	A	Berwick Rangers	2	4	Arthur	Chisholm	Bradley"	McNiff	Weatherson	Davidson*	Hopkirk	Watson	McKay+	Flynn	Love*	Brannan*	Todd+	Moffat*	McCudden	Anderson	Swinglehurst	Mitchell
07/09/2013	RC3	H	Formartine United	4	0	Arthur	Chisholm	Bradley	Bradley"	Davidson*	Mitchell	Davidson*	Watson	McKay	Flynn	Love*	Davidson*	Brannan+	Moffat*	McCudden	Anderson	Swinglehurst	Mitchell
14/09/2013	L	A	Stirling Albion	2	0	Arthur	Chisholm	Bradley	Sloan	Weatherson"	Mitchell	Hopkirk"	Watson	McKay+	Flynn*	Flynn*	McNiff	Todd+	Moffat*	Black G	Black G	Moffat	Todd
21/09/2013	L	H	Clyde	1	2	Arthur	Chisholm	Bradley+	Sloan"	Mitchell	Mitchell	Mitchell	McNiff	McKay	Flynn*	Love	Logan*	Davidson+	Brannan*	Davidson	Anderson	Swinglehurst	Mitchell
28/09/2013	L	H	Queen's Park	5	2	Arthur	Chisholm	McNiff	Todd"	Weatherson	Todd*	Hopkirk	McNiff	McKay+	Flynn	Love	Logan	Todd+	Brannan*	Davidson	Anderson	Moffat	Sloan
05/10/2013	SC2	A	Buckie Thistle	0	0	Arthur	Chisholm	McNiff	Todd*	Weatherson+	Mitchell	Hopkirk	Watson	McKay	Flynn	Love*	Brannan*	Swinglehurst+	Davidson*	Mitchell	Anderson	Swinglehurst	Mitchell
13/10/2013	RCSF	A	Raith Rovers	0	3	Arthur	Chisholm	Black	Swinglehurst+	Weatherson	A Mitchell	Andrew Mitchell	Watson	Brannan*	Flynn	Davidson*	Todd*	Bradley+	Moffat*	Mitchell	Alex Mitchell	Anderson	Jardine
19/10/2013	SCQR	H	Buckie Thistle	4	0	Arthur	Chisholm"	McNiff	McKay	Weatherson	A Mitchell	Mitchell	Watson	Brannan*	Flynn	Love	Mackay*	Davidson+	Black*	Swinglehurst	A Mitchell	Bradley	Jardine
26/10/2013	L	A	Elgin City	3	2	Arthur	Chisholm*	McNiff	Todd+	Weatherson	A Mitchell	Mitchell	Watson	McKay	Flynn+	Love	Sloan*	Todd+	Anderson	Mitchell	Mitchell	Moffat	Swinglehurst
29/10/2013	L	A	East Stirlingshire	1	2	Arthur	Bradley*	McNiff	Todd+	Weatherson	A Mitchell	A Mitchell	Watson	McKay	Flynn	Love	Brannan*	Davidson+	Davidson*	Mitchell	A Mitchell	Jardine	Flynn
02/11/2013	SC3	A	Stenhousemuir	2	2	Arthur	Sloan*	McNiff	Jardine-	Weatherson	A Mitchell	A Mitchell	Watson	McKay*	Swinglehurst	Love*	Todd*	Brannan+	Davidson*	Mitchell	Mitchell	Moffat	Bradley
05/11/2013	L	H	Peterhead	2	0	Arthur	Sloan	McNiff	Jardine	Bradley*	A Mitchell	A Mitchell	Watson	McKay"	Swinglehurst	Love+	Todd*	Brannan+	Henderson	Mitchell	Bradley	Bradley	Moffat
09/11/2013	L	A	Albion Rovers	0	2	Arthur	Sloan	McAnespie	Jardine	Weatherson	Weatherson	A Mitchell	Weatherson	Todd*	Swinglehurst	Love+	Davidson*	Brannan+	Davidson*	McCudden	Bradley	Flynn	Black
12/11/2013	SC3R	A	Stenhousemuir	2	4	Mitchell	Sloan	McNiff	Jardine-	Weatherson"	Bradley*	A Mitchell	Watson	Todd"	Swinglehurst	Davidson*	Black"	McKay*	Davidson"	Black G	Bradley	G Black	McKay
16/11/2013	L	H	Berwick Rangers	3	2	Mitchell	Sloan	McNiff	Jardine	Bradley*	Brannan	Hopkirk*	Watson	Todd+	Swinglehurst	Love+	Love*	Flynn+	Brannan*	Anderson	S Black	G Black	Bradley
23/11/2013	L	H	Stirling Albion	4	4	Arthur	Sloan	McNiff	Jardine-	Davidson	Brannan	Flynn	Watson	Todd"	Swinglehurst	Davidson*	Mackay*	Flynn+	Brannan*	Anderson	Anderson	G Black	Todd
03/12/2013	L	A	Clyde	1	2	Arthur	Sloan	McNiff	Todd	Black*	Brannan	Flynn	Watson	Todd+	Swinglehurst	Love	Bradley*	Flynn+	Wood"	Anderson	Moffat	G Black	Bradley
07/12/2013	L	A	East Stirlingshire	1	1	Arthur	Sloan	McNiff	Todd	Brannan	Brannan	Flynn	Watson	Todd"	Swinglehurst	Love	Anderson	G Black	Brannan	Bradley	Davidson	Graham	Todd
26/12/2013	L	H	Montrose	2	0	Arthur	Sloan	McNiff	Todd	Davidson+	Brannan	Flynn	Watson	McKay	Swinglehurst	Love	Moffat*	Bradley+	Brown	Bradley	Murray	Graham	Wood
28/12/2013	L	A	Queen's Park	2	1	Arthur	Sloan	McNiff	Todd	Davidson*	Brannan*	Flynn	Watson	McKay	Swinglehurst	Love	Moffat*	Bradley+	Brown	Mitchell	Graham	Anderson	Caldwell
04/01/2014	L	A	Albion Rovers	2	0	Arthur	Sloan	McNiff	Todd"	Davidson*	Brannan	Flynn	Watson	McKay	Swinglehurst	Bradley	Moffat*	Bradley	Anderson	Caldwell	Mitchell	McCrudden	Moffat
11/01/2014	L	A	Berwick Rangers	4	1	Arthur	Sloan	McNiff	Todd"	Davidson*	McKay*	Flynn	Watson	McKay	Swinglehurst	Bradley	Moffat*	Wood+	Anderson	Bradley	Mitchell	McCrudden	Moffat
18/01/2014	L	A	Clyde	0	1	Arthur	Sloan	McNiff	Todd	Davidson*	McKay*	Flynn"	Watson	McKay	Swinglehurst	Love+	Mitchell*	Moffat+	Black*	Bradley	Bradley	Jardine	Wood
25/01/2014	L	A	Montrose	1	0	Arthur	Sloan	McNiff	Todd	Davidson*	McKay	Flynn	Watson	Mitchell	Swinglehurst	Watson	Orsi*	Moffat*	Black	Chisholm	Mitchell	Jardine	Wood
08/02/2014	L	H	Montrose	1	0	Arthur	Sloan	McNiff	Todd	Davidson*	McKay	Flynn	Black	Mitchell	Swinglehurst	Watson	Moffat*	Moffat	Caldwell	Chisholm	Mitchell	Jardine	Wood
15/02/2014	L	A	East Stirlingshire	2	3	Arthur	Sloan	McNiff	Todd*	Davidson*	McKay	Flynn	Black	Mitchell"	Swinglehurst*	Watson	Orsi+	Orsi+	Love"	Caldwell	Mitchell	Jardine	Mitchell
22/02/2014	L	A	Queen's Park	1	0	Arthur	Henderson+	McNiff	Chisholm	Davidson-	McKay*	Henderson+	Love*	Mitchell*	Swinglehurst	Watson	Brannan*	Chisholm+	Orsi+	Black	Bradley	Jardine	Sloan
25/02/2014	L	H	Queen's Park	3	2	Arthur	Todd	McNiff	Chisholm	Black	McKay*	Henderson"	Love*	Mitchell	Swinglehurst	Watson	Black*	Davidson-	Brannan+	Mitchell	Bradley	Jardine	Bradley
01/03/2014	L	H	Berwick Rangers	4	0	Arthur	Todd	McNiff	Chisholm	Black	McKay	Henderson"	Love+	Mitchell	Swinglehurst	Watson	Flynn*	Bradley	Henderson*	Mitchell	Moffat	Hopkirk	Caldwell
04/03/2014	L	A	Albion Rovers	1	3	Arthur	Todd	McNiff	Chisholm	Black	McKay	Henderson-	Branman	Mitchell*	Swinglehurst	Watson	Davidson*	Brannan*	Orsi+	Mitchell	Moffat	Wood	Caldwell
15/03/2014	L	A	Elgin City	3	2	Arthur	Todd	McNiff	Chisholm	Jardine"	McKay*	Henderson"	Branman	Mitchell	Swinglehurst	Watson	Brannan*	Brannan+	Brannan*	Mitchell	Moffat	Wood	Sloan
22/03/2014	L	H	Peterhead	1	2	Arthur	Todd	McNiff	Chisholm	Jardine"	Davidson*	Henderson"	Branman	Mitchell	Swinglehurst	Watson	Davidson*	Hopkirk+	Sloan"	Mitchell	Moffat	Bradley	Wood
25/03/2014	L	H	Albion Rovers	2	0	Arthur	Todd	McNiff	Chisholm	Jardine"	Davidson*	Henderson"	Branman	Mitchell	Swinglehurst	Bradley	Hopkirk*	Love+	Sloan*	Mitchell	Moffat	Orsi	Wood
29/03/2014	L	H	Stirling Albion	1	2	Arthur	Todd	McNiff	Chisholm	Jardine	Love	Henderson"	Branman	Mitchell	Swinglehurst	Bradley	Hopkirk*	Love++	Love"	Mitchell	Sloan	Orsi	Black
05/04/2014	L	A	Clyde	3	0	Arthur	Todd	McNiff	Chisholm	Jardine"	Watson	Black	Branman	Swinglehurst	McKay+	Bradley	Davidson*	McKay+	Black	Flynn	Mitchell	Bradley	Wood
12/04/2014	L	H	East Stirlingshire	1	1	Arthur	Todd	McNiff	Chisholm	Jardine"	Watson	Watson	Branman	Todd+	McKay	Bradley	Davidson*	Henderson*	Love*	Moffat	Moffat	Orsi	Mitchell
19/04/2014	L	H	Queen's Park	1	1	Arthur	Todd	McNiff	Chisholm	Jardine"	Watson	Black	Branman	Mitchell	Swinglehurst	Bradley	Hopkirk*	Love++	Love*	Flynn	Moffat	Sloan	Wood
26/04/2014	L	A	Montrose	1	2	Arthur	Todd	McNiff	Chisholm	Branman*	Watson"	McKay	Hopkirk	Hopkirk	McKay*	Bradley	Davidson*	McKay+	Love+	Flynn	Sloan	Orsi	Mitchell
03/05/2014	L	H	Elgin City	2	0	Arthur	Todd*	McNiff+	Chisholm	Branman"	Watson"	Black	Mitchell	Hopkirk	McKay	Bradley	Davidson"	Henderson+	Davidson	Moffat	Love	Swinglehurst	Mitchell
07/05/2014	PO	A	Stirling Albion	1	3	Arthur	Todd*	McNiff	Chisholm	Sloan+	Sloan+	McKay	Mitchell	Hopkirk	Swinglehurst	Love	Jardine*	Davidson+	Henderson-	Mitchell	Mitchell	Mitchell	Brannan
10/05/2014	PO	H	Stirling Albion	3	5																		

Arbroath FC   2013/14

Founded	1878
Ground	Gayfield Park
Postcode	DD11 1QB
Tel	01241 872157
Capacity	6600
Closest Railway Station	Arbroath
Record Attendance	13510, v Rangers, SC, 23/2/1952
Record Win	36-0 v Bon Accord, SC, 12/9/1885
Record Defeat	1-9 v Celtic, LC, 25/8/1993
Most League Goals in a Season	45, Dave Easson, 1958/9
Most Goals in Career	120, Jimmy Jack
Chairman	John Christison
Secretary	Gary Callon
Manager	Paul Sheerin (until June) / Allan Moore
Assistant Manager	Stewart Petrie (until June) / Todd Lumsden
Colours 2013/14 Top	Maroon with White Sleeves
Shorts	White
Sponsor	Prosperity Offshore Investment
Manufacturer	Pendle
Change Colours 2013/14 Top	Yellow
Shorts	Blue
Nicknames	Red Lichties
Web	www.arbroathfc.co.uk

Arbroath's relegation at the end of 2013/14 was disappointing. They have the potential to be the biggest of the four Angus clubs, just as they were in the 1970s, but they have consistently underperformed in recent times. First round exits in all 3 Cup competitions summed up a poor season at Gayfield.

The loss of Manager Paul Sheerin in June 2014 is another blow. He was tempted by the offer of a full-time post in charge of Aberdeen's Under 20s. His replacement, Allan Moore, has done well in the past at this level and looks a decent appointment.

The new gaffer will inherit the nucleus of a decent squad but new blood will be essential. Bobby Linn is a key player for the Red Lichties and they need to get the best from him.

PREDICTION FOR 2014/15
Play Offs at best

Surname	First Name	DOB	Pos	L A	S	G	SC A	S	G	LC A	S	G	RC A	S	G	UNS	Signed	Previous Club	Notes	Contract
Adams	Scott		M	1													2013	Arbroath Youths		Youth
Banjo	David	19/01/91	M	23	8	2	1			1			1	1		4	2013	Ilford		OOC
Bayne	Graham	22/08/79	F	3	11		1			1						1	2013	Wick Academy	On loan to Elgin City, then permanent	
Bullock	Tony	18/02/72	GK													7	2012	Livingston	Joined Airdrieonians, October 2013	
Butter	Jim	14/12/66	GK							1						1		Goalkeeper Coach		Coach
Chisholm	Ross	14/01/88	M	28	3		1			1						2	2013	Shumen 2010 (Bulgaria)		F
Cook	Alan	24/04/92	M	30	5	12	1			1							2013	Airdrieonians	Joined East Fife May 2014	OOC
Deuchar	Kenny	08/07/80	F	4	5	2										2	2014	Unattached		OOC
Donaldson	Bradley	02/07/94	D	9	1	1										5	2013	Hibernian (Loan)	Returned to Hibs	
Doris	Steven	09/08/88	F	2	1												2013	Dundee (Loan)	Returned to Dundee	
Erwin	Lee	19/03/94	F	11	8												2013	Motherwell (Loan)	Returned to Motherwell	
Gray	Josh		GK													3	2013	Arbroath Youths		
Hamilton	Colin	07/05/92	D	35		1	1			1							2012	Hearts	Joined Brechin City May 2014	
Keddie	Alex	23/01/81	D	27	1		1			1						1	2012	Dunfermline Athletic		R
Lindsay	Johnny	16/10/92	D	7	2								1			19	2013	Stalybridge Celtic		F
Linn	Bobby	10/10/85	F	36		6	1			1			1	1			2013	Ballingry Rovers		C (2016)
Little	Ricky	20/05/89	D	8	2								1			3	2013	Queen's Park		OOC
Martin	Pat		F		2											2	2013	Arbroath Youths		Youth
McGeever	Ryan	30/04/94	D	5													2014	Falkirk (Loan Mar-May)	Returned to Falkirk	
McIntosh	Leighton	11/02/93	F	4	5	2											2014	Dundee (Loan)	Returned to Dundee	
McManus	Paul	26/12/82	F	12	6											1	2014	Forfar Athletic (Loan)	Returned to Forfar Ath	
McWalter	Kieran	06/10/95	M	1	2		1									14	2012	Arbroath Youths		C (2015)
Milne	Steven	05/05/80	F	6	5	1	1			1			1	1		2	2013	Dundee		R
Morrison	Scott	22/10/81	GK	28			1			1						4	2012	Brechin City		OOC
Nicoll	Kevin	16/06/86	M	16													2014	Albion Rovers		OOC
Robertson	Dayle	17/09/95	F	2	10	1										6		Arbroath Youths	Taking up Soccer Scholarship in USA, 2014	R
Rosscraig	John			1												1		Arbroath Youths		Youth
Scott	Christopher	12/03/96		8	4	1										16		Arbroath Youths		C (2015)
Sheerin	Paul	28/08/74	M	30	4	2		1								4	2010	St Johnstone		Manager
Sibanda	Lee	25/05/84	M	1	12	1	1						1			7	2011	Cowdenbeath	Freed Jan 2014, Joined St Andrews Utd	
Smith	Darren	04/06/80		16	2		1			1	1						2013	East Fife	Freed Jan 2014, joined Stirling Albion	
Smith	Patrick															1		Arbroath Youths		Youth
Thomson	Jamie															4		Arbroath Youths		Youth
Travis	Michael	06/05/93	D	34		5	1			1			1			1	2012	Livingston		OOC
Wilson	Leonard	29/12/96	GK													19		Arbroath Youths		Youth
Wood	Sandy	02/04/86	GK	8												5	2014	Montrose		OOC
Yao	Lari	14/12/92	M	1	9		1			1						26	2013	Croydon		OOC

NEW SIGNINGS 2014/15

Surname	First Name	DOB	Pos														Signed	Previous Club		
Whatley	Mark		M														2014	Spartans		

Date	Comp	H/A	Opponents	F	A		Crowd	Scorers
27/07/2013	RC1	A	Stenhousemuir	4	4	AET, 2-3 pens	280	Linn, Banjo, Milne 2
03/08/2013	LC1	H	Montrose	0	1		903	
10/08/2013	L	H	Ayr United	0	3		775	
17/08/2013	L	A	Dunfermline Athletic	2	3		3242	Milne, Cook 2
24/08/2013	L	A	East Fife	1	2		809	Cook
31/08/2013	L	H	Brechin City	2	1		801	Erwin 2
14/09/2013	L	A	Rangers	1	5		43562	Cook
21/09/2013	L	H	Stenhousemuir	3	4		596	Erwin, Hamilton, Cook
28/09/2013	L	H	Forfar Athletic	3	0		855	Cook, Sibanda, Erwin
05/10/2013	L	A	Stranraer	2	3		334	Erwin, Cook
12/10/2013	L	H	Airdrieonians	3	2		747	Linn, Banjo, Erwin
19/10/2013	L	A	Ayr United	0	2		990	
26/10/2013	L	A	Brechin City	1	3		765	Cook
02/11/2013	SC3	H	Brechin City	0	2		634	
09/11/2013	L	H	East Fife	2	2		603	Cook, Erwin
16/11/2013	L	A	Stenhousemuir	2	3		469	Travis, Erwin
25/11/2013	L	H	Rangers	0	3		3902	
07/12/2013	L	H	Stranraer	1	2		521	Doris
14/12/2013	L	A	Forfar Athletic	1	1		609	Travis
21/12/2013	L	H	Dunfermline Athletic	0	3		967	
28/12/2013	L	A	Airdrieonians	1	2		641	Donaldson
02/01/2014	L	A	East Fife	0	1		910	
11/01/2014	L	H	Brechin City	0	1		777	
18/01/2014	L	H	Stenhousemuir	2	1		498	Scott, Robertson
25/01/2014	L	A	Rangers	2	3		41207	Banjo, Linn
01/02/2014	L	H	Ayr United	2	3		605	Linn, McIntosh
15/02/2014	L	A	Stranraer	1	1		377	McManus
22/02/2014	L	H	Forfar Athletic	2	3		823	Cook, McIntosh
25/02/2014	L	A	Dunfermline Athletic	0	3		1983	
01/03/2014	L	A	Brechin City	4	2		668	Linn 2, Travis, McManus
08/03/2014	L	H	East Fife	2	1		679	Travis, McManus
15/03/2014	L	H	Airdrieonians	0	1		823	
22/03/2014	L	A	Ayr United	1	2		766	Deuchar
29/03/2014	L	H	Rangers	1	2		3400	McManus
05/04/2014	L	A	Stenhousemuir	2	2		518	McManus, Linn
12/04/2014	L	H	Stranraer	4	2		528	McManus, Cook 2, Sheerin
19/04/2014	L	A	Forfar Athletic	2	0		833	Sheerin, Deuchar
26/04/2004	L	H	Dunfermline Athletic	1	2		1079	Travis
03/05/2014	L	A	Airdrieonians	0	2		1243	

Friendly Matches			Versus	F	A	Att	Notes
6/7/13	Fr	A	Craigroyston	0	1		
13/7/13	Fr	H	Lossiemouth`	3	2	207	
16/7/13	Fr	H	Aberdeen U20	3	3		
20/7/13	Fr	H	Partick Thistle	1	0		
23/7/13	Fr	H	Inverness CT	1	7		
1/8/13	Fr	A	Forfar West End	3	3		U19
3/8/13	Fr	A	Brechin Vics	3	2		U19
5/8/13	Fr	A	Jeanfield Swifts	2	2		
6/8/13	Fr	A	Forfar Albion	?	?		U19

Date	Comp	H/A	Opponents	F	A	1	2	3	4	5	6	7	8	9	10	11	12	13	14	15	16	17	18
27/07/2013	RC1	A	Stenhousemuir	4	4	AET, 2-3 pens	Morrison	Banjo	Lindsay	Chisholm	Travis	Little*	Milne	Linn	Bayne	Cook*	Rowson	Sibanda*	Yao+	Sheerin"	McWalter	Bullock		
03/08/2013	LC1	H	Montrose	0	1	Morrison	Keddie	Hamilton	Chisholm"	Travis	Smith	Banjo+	Linn	Bayne	Cook*	Milne"	Yao*	Sheerin+	Lindsay	Lindsay	Bullock		Scott
10/08/2013		H	Ayr United	0	3	Morrison	Keddie	Hamilton	Chisholm*	Travis"	Smith	Lindsay	Linn	Bayne	Yao+	Milne"	Cook*	Sheerin+	Martin"	Sibanda	Bullock	Banjo	
17/08/2013		A	Dunfermline Athletic	2	3	Morrison	Keddie*	Hamilton	Sheerin	Travis	Smith	Banjo	Linn"	Scott*	Cook*	Milne	Lindsay*	Sibanda+	Chisholm"	McWalter	Bullock	Yao	
24/08/2013		A	East Fife	1	2	Morrison	Lindsay	Hamilton	Sheerin+	Travis	Smith	Banjo	Linn"	Scott*	Cook	Milne	Chisholm*	Bayne+	Yao"	McWalter	Bullock	Sibanda	
31/08/2013		H	Brechin City	2	1	Morrison	Lindsay	Donaldson	Sheerin*	Travis	Smith*	Banjo	Linn"	Chisholm"	Erwin"	Milne+	Cook*	Sibanda+	Bayne"	Scott	Gray	Yao	Walker
14/09/2013		H	Stenhousemuir	1	5	Morrison	Hamilton	Donaldson	Sheerin*	Travis	Smith+	Banjo	Linn"	Chisholm	Cook	Erwin"	Milne"	Bayne+	Sibanda"	McWalter	Bullock	Yao	Lindsay
21/09/2013		H	Rangers	3	4	Morrison	Hamilton	Donaldson	Sheerin*	Travis"	Smith*	Banjo	Linn	Chisholm	Erwin	Erwin"	Milne*	Bayne+	Lindsay	Sibanda	Bullock	Yao	McWalter
28/09/2013		H	Forfar Athletic	0	0	Morrison	Hamilton	Keddie	Sheerin	Travis"	Smith*	Banjo	Linn	Chisholm	Cook+	Erwin	Cook*	McWalter+	Bayne"	Donaldson	Gray	Yao	Milne
05/10/2013		A	Stranraer	2	3	Morrison	Hamilton*	Keddie	Sheerin"	Travis	Smith	Banjo	Linn+	Chisholm	Cook	Erwin	Sibanda*	Milne+	Sibanda"	Donaldson	Gray	Yao	McWalter
12/10/2013		H	Airdrieonians	3	2	Morrison	Hamilton	Keddie	Milne*	Travis	Smith	Banjo	Linn"	Chisholm	Cook+	Erwin	Lindsay*	Milne+	Sheerin"	Lindsay	McWalter	Yao	Wilson
19/10/2013		A	Ayr United	0	2	Morrison	Hamilton	Keddie	Sheerin*	Travis	Smith	Banjo"	Linn	Chisholm	Cook+	Erwin	Sheerin"	Bayne+	Donaldson"	Donaldson	McWalter	Lindsay	Wilson
26/10/2013		A	Brechin City	1	3	Morrison	Hamilton	Keddie	Sheerin*	Travis"	Smith	Banjo	Linn	Rosscraig"	Cook	Erwin	Yao*	Bayne"	Sibanda"	Donaldson	Chisholm	Lindsay	Wilson
02/11/2013	SC3	H	East Fife	0	2	Morrison	Hamilton	Keddie	Chisholm*	Donaldson	Smith+	Banjo+	Linn	Bayne	Sibanda"	Milne	Cook*	Yao+	McWalter"	Lindsay	Sheerin	Smith	Wilson
09/11/2013		A	East Fife	2	2	Morrison	Hamilton	Keddie	Chisholm"	Donaldson	Scott*	Banjo	Linn	Cook	Sibanda*	Erwin	Milne*	Sheerin+	Yao"	Wilson	Travis	Yao	Smith
16/11/2013		H	Stenhousemuir	2	3	Morrison	Hamilton	Banjo	Chisholm	Donaldson	Scott*	Travis	Linn	Cook	Sheerin+	Erwin	Sibanda*	Smith+	Bayne"	Wilson	Milne	Smith	Banjo
25/11/2013		H	Stranraer	0	3	Morrison	Hamilton	Banjo	Chisholm	Donaldson	Scott*	Travis	Linn	Cook	Sheerin+	Erwin"	Bayne*	Yao+	Yao"	Sibanda	Wilson	Yao	Keddie
07/12/2013		H	Stranraer	1	2	Morrison	Hamilton	Lindsay	Chisholm	Donaldson	Keddie	Travis	Linn	Cook*	Smith	Doris	Bayne*	Scott+	McWalter	Banjo	Banjo	Sheerin	Wilson
14/12/2013		H	Forfar Athletic	1	1	Morrison	Hamilton	Banjo	Chisholm	Sheerin"	Keddie	Travis	Linn	Cook	Smith+	Doris	Bayne+	Bayne+	McWalter	Scott	Wilson	Yao	Lindsay
21/12/2013		A	Dunfermline Athletic	0	3	Morrison	Hamilton	Banjo	Sheerin+	Chisholm	Keddie	Travis	Linn	Cook*	Cook*	Robertson*	Sibanda*	Scott+	Martin"	Scott	Wilson	Yao	Thomson
28/12/2013		H	Airdrieonians	1	2	Morrison	Hamilton	Banjo	Sheerin+	Donaldson*	Keddie	Travis	Linn	Cook	Robertson	Smith	Sibanda*	Yao+	McWalter	Scott	Wilson	Thompson	Martin
02/01/2014		A	East Fife	0	1	Morrison	Hamilton	Banjo"	Sheerin	Chisholm	Keddie	Travis	Linn	Cook*	Bayne	Smith+	Sibanda*	Robertson*	Sibanda"	Lindsay	Wilson	Thompson	McWalter
11/01/2014		H	Brechin City	0	1	Morrison	Hamilton	Banjo	Little	Chisholm"	Keddie	Travis	Linn	Cook	Bayne	Nicoll*	Robertson*	Scott	Yao	Lindsay	Wilson	Yao	Smith
18/01/2014		A	Stenhousemuir	2	1	Morrison	Hamilton	Banjo+	Little	Chisholm"	Keddie	Travis+	Linn	Cook*	Scott	Nicoll	Robertson*	McManus+	Bayne"	Lindsay	Wilson	Scott	Yao
25/01/2014		A	Rangers	2	3	Morrison	Hamilton	Banjo+	Little+	Chisholm	Keddie	Travis	Linn	Cook*	Scott+	Nicoll"	Sheerin*	Yao*	Robertson"	Lindsay	Yao	Martin	Smith
01/02/2014		H	Ayr United	2	3	Morrison	Hamilton	Banjo+	Little*	Chisholm	Keddie	Travis	Linn	Cook*	Scott+	Nicoll	McManus*	Cook+	Bayne"	Scott	Scott	Robertson"	Wood
15/02/2014		A	Stranraer	1	1	Wood	Hamilton	Sheerin*	Little	Chisholm	Keddie	Sheerin	Linn	McManus	McIntosh	Nicoll"	Scott*	Yao+	Robertson"	Scott	Yao	Thompson	Wilson
22/02/2014		H	Forfar Athletic	0	3	Wood	Hamilton*	Sheerin*	Little	Chisholm	Keddie	Travis	Linn	Cook+	McIntosh	Nicoll	Deuchar*	Robertson*	Deuchar"	Sheerin	McManus	Robertson	Wilson
25/02/2014		A	Dunfermline Athletic	0	3	Wood	Hamilton	Scott*	Little	Chisholm	Keddie	Travis	Linn	Cook*	McIntosh"	Nicoll	Banjo*	McWalter+	Banjo"	Lindsay	Yao	Yao	Wilson
01/03/2014		H	Brechin City	4	2	Wood	Hamilton	Sheerin	Little	Banjo	Chisholm	Travis	Linn*	Cook*	McManus+	Nicoll	McIntosh*	Scott+	Banjo"	Yao	Smith	Robertson	Wilson
08/03/2014		H	East Fife	0	1	Wood	Hamilton	Sheerin	Banjo	Banjo+	Keddie	Travis	Linn	Deuchar	McManus+	Nicoll	Deuchar*	Adams+	Lindsay	Yao	Scott	Scott	Deuchar
15/03/2014		A	Airdrieonians	0	1	Wood	Hamilton	Sheerin	Little	Cook+	Keddie	Travis	Linn	Lindsay*	McManus	Nicoll	Robertson*	Banjo+	Robertson+	Robertson"	McWalter	Morrison	Deuchar
22/03/2014		A	Ayr United	1	2	Wood	Hamilton	Sheerin	Chisholm"	Cook+	McGeever	Travis	Linn	Lindsay"	McManus	Nicoll	Deuchar*	Scott+	Scott	Robertson"	McWalter	McWalter	Morrison
29/03/2014		H	Rangers	1	2	Wood	Hamilton	Sheerin	Chisholm	Cook*	Keddie	Travis	Linn	Keddie	McManus	Nicoll	Robertson*	Robertson*	Keddie"	Keddie"	Robertson	Lindsay	Morrison
05/04/2014		A	Stenhousemuir	2	2	Morrison	Hamilton	Sheerin"	Chisholm	Cook*	McGeever	Travis	Linn	Keddie	McManus+	Nicoll	Deuchar*	Adams+	Robertson"	Scott	Little	Thompson	Butter
12/04/2014		H	Stranraer	4	2	Morrison	Hamilton	Sheerin"	Chisholm	Cook*	McGeever	Travis	Linn"	Keddie	McManus	Nicoll"	Banjo*	Banjo+	Little+	Yao	Robertson	Scott	Deuchar
19/04/2014		A	Forfar Athletic	2	0	Morrison	Hamilton	Sheerin+	Little"	Cook*	McGeever	Travis	Linn"	Keddie	McManus	Deuchar+	McIntosh*	McIntosh*	Banjo"	Yao	Little	Wood	Scott
26/04/2004		H	Dunfermline Athletic	1	2	Morrison	Hamilton	Sheerin+	Nicoll	Cook*	McGeever	Travis	Linn	Keddie	McManus	Deuchar+	McIntosh*	Chisholm*	Chisholm"	Yao	Little	Wood	Scott
03/05/2014		A	Airdrieonians	0	2	Morrison	Hamilton	Sheerin	Nicoll	Cook*	McGeever	Travis	Linn	Keddie	McManus	Deuchar+	McIntosh*	Banjo+	Chisholm	Yao	Little	Wilson	Scott

Ayr United FC

Founded	1910
Ground	Somerset Park
Postcode	KA8 9NB
Capacity	10185
Tel	01292 263435
Closest Railway Station	Ayr
Record Attendance	25225, v Rangers, Lge, 13/9/1969
Record Win	11-1 v Dumbarton, LC 13/8/1952
Record Defeat	0-9, v Rangers 1929, v Hearts 1931, v Third Lanark 1954
Most Goals in a Season	66 Jimmy Smith, 1927/8
Most Goals in Career	213 Peter Price
Chairman	Lachlan Cameron
Managing Director	Lewis Grant
Secretary	Tracy McTrusty
Manager	Mark Roberts
Assistant Manager	David White & Andy Millen
Colours 2013/14 Top	White with Black side stripe
Shorts	White or Black
Sponsor	Bodog
Manufacturer	Nike
Change Colours 2013/14 Top	Red with White side stripe
Shorts	White
Nicknames	Honest Men
Web	www.ayrunitedfc.co.uk

Ayr United's fans made their feelings known during he Play Off defeat at the hands of Cowdenbeath. They clearly feel that their club is underachieving and that another season in League One is totally unacceptable.

This prompted the Chairman to defend Manager Mark Roberts but he also set out the targets for 2014/15. He specifically stated that a sustained period in the lower half of the table would lead to termination of the Manager's contract.

It was a season of good spells and bad spells for Ayr. On their day they could match the best but they also produced some desperately poor performances.

Roberts' task will be made harder by the loss of striker Michael Moffat to rivals Dunfermline Athletic. Ayr have relied heavily on Moffat for goals in recent seasons and he has been a shining light for the Somerset Park club.

Craig Malcolm and Alan Lithgow have also opted to leave Somerset Park for other League One sides, suggesting that the wage budget at Ayr is restricted.

PREDICTION FOR 2014/15

Mid table, perhaps scraping into the Play off positions.

Surname	First Name	DOB	Pos	L A	L S	L G	SC A	SC S	SC G	LC A	LC S	LC G	RC A	RC S	RC G	UNS	Signed Previous Club	Notes	Contract
Campbell	Martyn	17/01/81	D	18	1	1				1			2			1	2005 Irvine Meadow		OOC
Crawford	Robbie	22/06/94	M	12	3	3				1			1			15	2010 Ayr United Youths		OOC
Donald	Michael	20/01/89	M	35	7	3				1	1					2	2013 Maybole Juniors		OOC
Forrest	Alan	09/09/96	M	12	17	8	2			1			1	1	1	4	2013 Ayr United Youths	Brother of J Forrest (Celtic)	OOC
Gilmour	Brian	08/05/87	M	23	1	3	2									1	2013 KA Akureyri		C (2015)
Holland	Jai	27/03/98	F													2	2013 Ayr United Youths		Youth
Hunter	Adam	25/01/86	M	30	1	1	3			1			1			6	2012 Rangers		F
Hutton	David	18/05/85	GK	38			3			1						2	2013 Morton		OOC
Kyle	Kevin	07/06/81	F	23	5	5	2			1						4	2013 Rangers		F
Lithgow	Alan	12/03/88	D	36		3				1	1					2	2013 Dumbarton	Joined Stenhousemuir June 2014	
Longridge	Jackson	12/04/95	M	2	2											26	2013 Ayr United Youths		OOC
Malcolm	Craig	30/12/86	M	30	5	8	1		1	1		1	2		1	3	2013 Stranraer	Signed for Stranraer May 2014	
Marenghi	Anthony	11/06/93	M	17	5	2	3			1	1		1			15	2012 Rangers		F
McArthur	Josh	22/04/96	D	1						1						9	2013 St Mirren		OOC
McAusland	Kyle	19/01/93	D	14	5											1	2013 Rangers (Loan)	Returned to Rangers	
McCracken	Craig	22/03/96	D													3	2013 Ayr United Youths		Youth
McGowan	Michael	22/02/85	M	17	8	2	1			1			1	1		14	2011 Alloa		OOC
McLaughlin	Scott	20/01/84	M	37	1	3	1									2	2013 Peterhead		C (2015)
Moffat	Michael	17/01/84	F	34		26	3			1			2	1			2011 Girvan Juniors	Signed for Dunfermline May 2014	
Muir	William	16/03/93	GK													29	2012 Motherwell	Freed February 2014	
Newman	Shaun	03/11/96	GK													15	2013 Ayr United Youths		Youth
Pope	Gordon	02/04/89	M	34	2	3	1									1	2013 Auchinleck Talbot	Rejoined Auchinleck Talbot May 2014	F
Roberts	Mark	29/09/75	F	5	2	1	1									14	2009 Partick Thistle		Manager
Shankland	Mark	11/07/95	M	13						1	1		2			17	2011 Ayr United Youths		OOC
Wardrope	Michael	17/12/96	M	1												19	2013 Ayr United Youths		OOC
Wylie	Aaron	12/08/93	M	1						1						7	2012 Ayr United Youths	Freed November 2013	

NEW SIGNINGS 2014/15

Surname	First Name	DOB	Pos	Signed Previous Club
McKinley	Kevin		D	2014 Stenhousemuir

Date	Comp	H/A	Opponents	F	A		Crowd	Scorers
27/07/2013	RC1	A	Queen's Park	2	1		887	Moffat, Forrest
06/08/2013	LC1	A	Partick Thistle	1	2		2145	Shankland
10/08/2013	L	A	Arbroath	3	0		775	Moffat 2, Forrest
17/08/2013	L	H	Forfar Athletic	2	0		1056	Malcolm, Moffat
20/08/2013	RC2	H	Falkirk	1	2	AET	921	Malcolm
24/08/2013	L	A	Stranraer	1	1		845	McGowan
31/08/2013	L	H	Airdrieonians	2	2		1339	Moffat 2
14/09/2013	L	A	Stenhousemuir	1	1		657	Roberts
21/09/2013	L	H	Brechin City	2	2		987	Moffat, McGowan
28/09/2013	L	A	Dunfermline Athletic	1	5		2743	Moffat
05/10/2013	L	H	Rangers	0	2		8968	
12/10/2013	L	A	East Fife	4	1		753	Donald 2, Moffat, McLaughlin
19/10/2013	L	H	Arbroath	2	0		990	Kyle, Hunter
26/10/2019	L	A	Airdrieonians	1	0		1012	Marenghi
02/11/2013	SC3	H	Queen's Park	3	2		879	Marenghi, Lithgow, Malcolm
12/11/2013	L	H	Stranraer	3	6		986	Moffat 3
16/11/2013	L	A	Brechin City	1	1		518	Marenghi
23/11/2013	L	H	Stenhousemuir	4	3		986	Moffat 2, Donald, Kyle
30/11/2013	SC4	H	Dunfermline Athletic	1	1		1391	Donald
04/12/2013	SC4R	A	Dunfermline Athletic	0`	1		1932	
07/12/2013	L	A	Rangers	0	3		45227	
14/12/2013	L	H	Dunfermline Athletic	2	4		643	Gilmout, Moffat
21/12/2013	L	A	Forfar Athletic	1	0		473	Kyle
28/12/2013	L	H	East Fife	2	0		1059	Moffat 2
04/01/2014	L	A	Stranraer	0	4		1097	
11/01/2014	L	H	Airdrieonians	3	0		1037	Kyle, Moffat, Forrest
18/01/2014	L	H	Brechin City	1	3		1018	Pope
25/01/2014	L	A	Stenhousemuir	1	1		467	Malcolm
01/02/2014	L	A	Arbroath	3	2		605	Moffat 2, Donald
15/02/2014	L	H	Rangers	0	2		8449	
22/02/2014	L	A	Dunfermline Athletic	0	3		2773	
01/03/2014	L	A	Airdrieonians	0	3		880	
04/03/2014	L	H	Forfar Athletic	2	3		656	Malcolm, Campbell
08/03/2014	L	H	Stranraer	5	0		1141	Moffat 2, Malcom, Donald, Forrest
15/03/2014	L	A	East Fife	5	0		647	Moffat 2, Kyle, Donald, Forrest
22/03/2014	L	H	Arbroath	2	1		766	Moffat, Malcolm
29/03/2014	L	H	Stenhousemuir	2	3		992	Moffat, Forrest
05/04/2014	L	A	Brechin City	1	2		507	Forrest
19/04/2014	L	H	Dunfermline Athletic	1	1		1272	Forrest
22/04/2014	L	A	Rangers	1	2		40651	Forrest
26/04/2014	L	A	Forfar Athletic	2	4		532	Moffat, Gilmour
03/05/2014	L	H	East Fife	4	1		1952	Malcolm 3, Gilmour
07/05/2014	PO	H	Cowdenbeath	1	2		1495	Pope
10/05/2014	PO	A	Cowdenbeath	1	3		933	Donald

Friendly Matches

7/7/13	Fr	N	Dinamo Bucharest	1	1			at Woodlesford, Leeds
9/7/13	Fr	A	Queen's Park	3	0			at Lesser Hampden
13/7/13	Fr	H	Rotherham United	1	4		633	
21/7/13	Fr	A	Cumnock	5	0			
24/7/13	Fr	A	Kilwinning Rangers	3	2			
27/7/13	Fr	A	Girvan	3	4			U19
29/7/13	Fr	H	AEL Limassol	0	2		461	
29/7/13	Fr	A	Troon	3	1			U19
31/7/13	Fr	A	Greenock	1	7			U19

39

Date	Comp	H/A	Opponents	F	A	1	2	3	4	5	6	7	8	9	10	11	12	13	14	15	16	17	18
27/07/2013	RC1	A	Queen's Park	2	1	Hutton	Hunter	Pope	McLaughlin	Campbell	Uthgow	McGowan+	Malcolm*	Moffat	Donald	Crawford	Shankland*	Forrest+	McArthur	Marenghi	Muir		
06/08/2013	LC1	A	Partick Thistle	1	2	Hutton	Hunter	Pope	McLaughlin	Campbell*	Uthgow	McGowan+	Malcolm*	Moffat	Donald	Marenghi	McArthur*	Forrest+	Shankland"	Roberts	W Muir	Wardrope	
10/08/2013	L	A	Arbroath	3	0	Hutton	Hunter	Pope	McLaughlin	McArthur*	Uthgow	McGowan*	Malcolm"	Moffat	Donald	Marenghi+	Forrest*	Shankland+	Wylie	Longridge	Roberts	Wardrope	Muir
17/08/2013	L	H	Forfar Athletic	2	0	Hutton	Hunter	Pope	McLaughlin	Campbell+	Uthgow	McGowan*	Malcolm"	Moffat	Donald	Marenghi+	Forrest*	Crawford+	Shankland"	Longridge	McArthur	Roberts	W Muir
20/08/2013	RC2	H	Falkirk	1	2	Hutton	Forrest*	Pope	McLaughlin	Campbell	Uthgow	Wylie"	Malcolm+	Moffat	Donald	Marenghi+	McGowan*	Crawford+	Roberts"	McArthur	Muir		
24/08/2013	L	A	Stranraer	1	1	Hutton	Hunter	Pope	McLaughlin	Campbell	Uthgow	McGowan+	Malcolm	Moffat	Donald	Marenghi"	Crawford*	Forrest+	Shankland"	McArthur	Muir	Shankland	Wylie
31/08/2013	L	H	Airdrieonians	2	2	Hutton	Hunter	Pope	McLaughlin	Campbell*	Uthgow	McGowan+	Malcolm	Moffat	Donald	Marenghi"	Forrest"	Crawford+	Shankland"	Roberts	Muir	Wylie	Longridge
14/09/2013	L	A	Stenhousemuir	1	1	Hutton	Hunter	Crawford	McLaughlin	Roberts*	Uthgow	McGowan*	Malcolm	Moffat	Donald	Marenghi	Trialist*	McArthur	Shankland	Wardrope	Muir	Wylie	Longridge
21/09/2013	L	H	Brechin City	1	5	Hutton	Hunter	Crawford	McLaughlin	Roberts+	Uthgow	McGowan*	Malcolm	Moffat	Donald	Marenghi	Kyle*	Wylie+	Shankland	Wardrope	Muir	Wardrope	Longridge
28/09/2013	L	A	Dunfermline Athletic	1	0	Hutton	Hunter	Pope	McLaughlin	Forrest+	Uthgow	McGowan++	Malcolm	Moffat	Donald	Crawford"	Roberts+	Roberts+	Kyle"	Marenghi	Muir	Wylie	Shankland
05/10/2013	L	H	Rangers	0	2	Hutton	Hunter	Pope	McLaughlin	Campbell	Uthgow	Roberts*	Kyle+	Moffat	Donald	Crawford"	Marenghi"	Malcolm+	Forrest"	Longridge	Muir	Shankland	McGowan
12/10/2013	L	A	East Fife	4	1	Hutton	Hunter	Pope	McLaughlin	Campbell	Uthgow	Roberts*	Kyle"	Moffat	Donald	Crawford	Malcolm*	Malcolm"	Forrest	Longridge	Muir	Shankland	Marenghi
19/10/2013	SC3	H	Arbroath	2	0	Hutton	Hunter	Pope	McLaughlin	McAusland	Uthgow	Marenghi	Malcolm	Moffat+	Donald	Crawford+	McGowan"	Marenghi+	Malcolm"	Wylie	Muir	Longridge	McGowan
26/10/2019	L	H	Airdrieonians	2	6	Hutton	Hunter	Pope	McLaughlin	McAusland	Uthgow	Marenghi	Kyle	Moffat	Donald	Crawford	Forrest*	Wylie	Longridge	Wardrope	Muir	Longridge	Malcolm
02/11/2013	SC3	H	Queen's Park	3	2	Hutton	Hunter	Pope	McLaughlin	Roberts*	Uthgow	Marenghi	Malcolm	Moffat+	Donald	Crawford	Gilmour*	Kyle+	McArthur	Wylie	Muir	Longridge	Roberts
12/11/2013	L	A	Stranraer	1	1	Hutton	Hunter	Pope	McLaughlin	McAusland	Gilmour	Marenghi	Kyle	Moffat	Donald	Crawford	Malcolm*	McGowan	McArthur	Roberts	Muir	Longridge	Wardrope
16/11/2013	L	A	Brechin City	4	1	Hutton	Hunter	Pope	McLaughlin	McAusland	Gilmour	Marenghi	Kyle	Moffat	Donald	Crawford	Malcolm"	McGowan	McArthur	Roberts	Muir	Holland	McGowan
23/11/2013	L	H	Stenhousemuir	1	3	Hutton	Hunter	Pope	McLaughlin	Gilmour*	Uthgow	Malcolm+	Kyle	Moffat	Donald	Campbell+	Forrest*	Marenghi+	Wardrope	McGowan	Muir	Holland	Wardrope
30/11/2013	SC4	H	Dunfermline Athletic	0	1	Hutton	Hunter*	Pope	McLaughlin	Gilmour*	Uthgow	Malcolm	Kyle+	Moffat*	Donald+	Marenghi+	Forrest*	Shankland+	Shankland	Crawford	Muir	Hunter	Wardrope
04/12/2013	SC4R	A	Dunfermline Athletic	0	1	Hutton	Hunter+	Pope	McLaughlin	Gilmour+	Uthgow	Malcolm	Kyle+	Moffat*	Donald+	Forrest*	Forrest*	Shankland+	Wardrope*	McCracken	Muir	Forrest	Crawford
07/12/2013	L	A	Rangers	3	0	Hutton	McAusland	Crawford	McLaughlin	Gilmour	Uthgow	Malcolm	Kyle+	McGowan	Donald	Forrest+	McGowan*	Marenghi+	Longridge	McCracken	Muir	Forrest	Wardrope
14/12/2013	L	H	Forfar Athletic	0	3	Hutton	McAusland	Pope	McLaughlin+	Gilmour	Uthgow	Malcolm	Kyle*	Moffat*	Donald	Campbell*	McAusland*	Marenghi+	Shankland	Crawford	Muir	Forrest	McGowan
21/12/2013	L	H	East Fife	0	1	Hutton	McAusland	Pope	McLaughlin	Gilmour+	Uthgow	Malcolm	Kyle*	Moffat*	Donald	Campbell+	Longridge"	Shankland	Wardrope	McGowan	Muir	Forrest	Crawford
28/12/2013	L	A	Airdrieonians	2	3	Hutton	McAusland	Pope	Gilmour	Campbell*	Uthgow	Malcolm	Kyle*	Moffat	Donald	Hunter	Shankland"	Forrest	Longridge	McGowan	Muir	Roberts	Newman
04/01/2014	L	H	Stranraer	0	0	Hutton	McAusland	Pope	Gilmour	Campbell*	Uthgow	Malcolm	Kyle	Moffat	Donald	Hunter	Forrest*	Shankland	Gilmour	Pope	Muir	Crawford	Newman
11/01/2014	L	H	Airdrieonians	3	0	Hutton	Forrest*	Pope	Gilmour+	Gilmour*	Uthgow	Malcolm	Moffat	McGowan	Donald	Hunter	Forrest*	Shankland	Marenghi"	Crawford	Roberts	Longridge	Newman
18/01/2014	L	H	Brechin City	2	1	Hutton	Forrest*	Pope	Gilmour+	Campbell	Uthgow	Malcolm	Moffat	McGowan	Donald	Hunter	Forrest*	McAusland+	Marenghi"	McGowan	Wardrope	Roberts	Newman
25/01/2014	L	A	Stenhousemuir	1	1	Hutton	Forrest	Pope	Gilmour	Campbell	Uthgow	Malcolm+	Kyle	McGowan	Donald	Hunter	Forrest*	Marenghi	Crawford	Longridge	Muir	Roberts	Newman
01/02/2014	L	A	Arbroath	3	2	Hutton	Marenghi	Pope	McLaughlin	Campbell	Uthgow	Malcolm	Kyle+	McGowan	Donald*	Hunter	McGowan*	Marenghi+	Campbell	Shankland	Muir	Marenhi	Wardrope
15/02/2014	L	H	Rangers	0	3	Hutton	Marenghi*	Pope	McLaughlin+	Gilmour+	Uthgow	Malcolm	Kyle*	Crawford*	Donald	Hunter	Shankland*	McGowan*	Marenghi+	Longridge	Newman	Marenhi	Wardrope
22/02/2014	L	A	Dunfermline Athletic	0	1	Hutton	McLaughlin	Pope	McLaughlin	Gilmour+	Uthgow	Malcolm	Kyle*	Crawford*	Donald	Hunter	Shankland"	Forrest	Wardrope	Wardrobe	Newman	Roberts	Wardrope
01/03/2014	L	A	Airdrieonians	2	2	Hutton	McLaughlin	Pope	Gilmour	Campbell	Uthgow	Malcolm	Moffat	McGowan	Donald	Forrest	Forrest*	Shankland	Gilmour	Crawford	Roberts	Crawford	Newman
04/03/2014	L	H	Forfar Athletic	0	0	Hutton	McLaughlin*	Pope	Gilmour+	Campbell*	Uthgow	Malcolm	Moffat	McGowan	Donald	Forrest	Forrest*	Shankland	Marenghi"	McGowan	Wardrope	Longridge	Newman
08/03/2014	L	A	Stranraer	1	0	Hutton	McLaughlin	Pope	Gilmour	Campbell	Uthgow	Malcolm+	Moffat	McGowan*	Donald	Forrest+	Forrest*	Marenghi"	Marenghi+	Shankland	Roberts	Shankland	Newman
15/03/2014	L	A	East Fife	2	0	Hutton	McLaughlin	Pope	Gilmour	Campbell*	Uthgow	Malcolm	Moffat	McGowan	Donald	Forrest+	Forrest*	Shankland	Marenghi	McAusland	Wardrope	Roberts	Newman
22/03/2014	L	H	Arbroath	2	1	Hutton	McLaughlin	Pope	Gilmour	Campbell	Uthgow	Malcolm+	Moffat	McGowan	Donald	Hunter	Forrest*	McAusland+	Shankland	McAusland	Wardrope	Longridge	Newman
29/03/2014	L	A	Stenhousemuir	2	3	Hutton	McLaughlin	Shankland	Gilmour	Campbell	Uthgow	Malcolm+	Moffat	McGowan	Marenghi"	Hunter	Forrest*	Kyle+	Kyle+	Marenghi	Wardrope	Longridge	Newman
05/04/2014	L	A	Brechin City	1	2	Hutton	McLaughlin	Pope	Gilmour	Campbell	Uthgow	Malcolm+	Moffat	McAusland	Donald	Forrest	Forrest*	Shankland	Crawford	Hunter	Marenghi	Longridge	Newman
19/04/2014	L	H	Dunfermline Athletic	1	1	Hutton	McLaughlin	Pope	Gilmour	Campbell	Uthgow	Malcolm+	Moffat	McGowan*	Donald	Forrest	Kyle	Shankland+	Crawford	Hunter	Marenghi	Longridge	Newman
22/04/2014	L	H	Forfar Athletic	2	4	Hutton	McLaughlin	Pope	Gilmour	Campbell	Uthgow	Malcolm+	Moffat	McGowan"	Donald	Forrest+	Kyle	Shankland+	Crawford	Kyle	Marenghi	Kyle	Newman
26/04/2014	L	A	Forfar Athletic	4	1	Hutton	McLaughlin	Pope	Gilmour	Campbell*	McAusland	Malcolm+	Moffat	McGowan*	Donald	Forrest+	McAusland*	Shankland+	Crawford	Shankland	Longridge	McGowan	Newman
03/05/2014	L	A	Cowdenbeath	1	2	Hutton	McLaughlin	Pope	Gilmour	Campbell*	Uthgow	Malcolm+	Moffat	Hunter	Donald	Forrest	Kyle*	Shankland+	Crawford	Kyle	Marenghi	Wardrope	Newman
07/05/2014	PO	H	Cowdenbeath	1	2	Hutton	McLaughlin	Pope+	Gilmour	McAusland*	Uthgow	Malcolm	Moffat	Hunter	Marenghi+	Forrest+	Kyle*	Shankland+	Crawford	Shankland	Longridge	Wardrope	Newman
10/05/2014	PO	A	Cowdenbeath	1	3	Hutton	McLaughlin	Pope	Gilmour	McAusland	Uthgow	Malcolm	Moffat	Hunter	Donald	Forrest	Forrest*	McGowan+	Crawford	Shankland	Marenghi	Longridge	Newman

Berwick Rangers FC

Founded	1884
Ground	Shielfield Park
Postcode	TD12 2EF
Tel	01289 307424
Capacity	4131
Closest Railway Station	Berwick-upon-Tweed
Record Attendance	13283, v Rangers, SC 28/1/1967
Record Win	8-1 v Forfar, Lge, 25/12/1965; v Vale of Leithen, SC, 1966/7
Record Defeat	1-9 v Hamilton Accies, Lge 9/8/1980
Most League Goals in a Season	33 Ken Bowron, 1963/4
Most Appearances Career	439 Eric Tait
Chairman	Brian Porteous
Secretary	Dennis McCleary
Manager	Ian Little (until Jan) / Colin Cameron
Assistant Manager	Robbie Horn
Colours 2013/14 Top	Black with Gold Centre Panel
Shorts	Black
Sponsor	JB Site Investigations
Manufacturer	Zoo Sport
Change Colours 2013/14 Top	Blue
Shorts	White
3rd Kit 2013/14 Top	White with Black and Gold Diagonal Band
Shorts	White
Nicknames	Borderers, Wee Rangers, Black & Gold
Web	www.berwickrangersfc.co.uk

For much of the season Berwick looked like potential play off qualifiers but in the end they failed to make it.

In reality it was a season of transition for the Shielfield side. Manager Ian Little left mid season and was replaced by former Cowdenbeath Manager Colin Cameron. Inconsistency was the main problem - there was no lack of ability at Shielfield but performance levels varied.

For 2014/15 Berwick have decided to withdraw their reserve side from the East of Scotland League and concentrate on the Reserve League. Their resources were often stretched in fielding two teams on a Saturday and they should see the benefit of midweek reserve football.

Most of their key players have re-signed or are under contract. Colin Cameron will doubtless have them well prepared for the new season.

PREDICTION 2014/15
Potential League winners, Play Offs at least

Surname	First Name	DOB	Pos	L-A	L-S	L-G	SC-A	SC-S	SC-G	LC-A	LC-S	LC-G	RC-A	RC-S	RC-G	UNS	Signed Previous Club	Notes	Contract
Andrews	Michael	25/03/90	GK	8												9	2014 East Fife		C (2015)
Bald	William	21/08/93	GK	13				3								16	2013 Penicuik Athletic		C (2015)
Beveridge	Kieran	15/07/94	GK													1	2012 Leith Athletic	Transferred to Tranent, Jan 2014	
Brady	Ross	22/05/94	F													1	2013 Livingston		
Brydon	Dougie	23/03/87	D	1												1	2012 Duns		
Cameron	Colin	23/10/72	M	10												2	2013 Burntisland Shipyard		C (2015)
Carse	Dean	28/04/94	F		8						1					9	2013 Aberdeen		C (2015)
Currie	Lee	12/02/90	M	36	16	3				1	1					2	2011 Hibernian		
Currie	Paul	30/01/85	M	12	3	4											2014 Bonnyrigg Rose		C (2015)
Dalziel	Scott	29/12/85	F	28	7	9	3	1	1	1			1	1			2013 Brechin City		C (2015)
Downie	Jack	23/03/94	D		2											5	2014 Livingston		
Drummond	Ross	20/03/94	D	11													2014 Dunfermline Athletic (Loan Feb-May)	Returned to Dunfermline	
Dunlop	Michael	11/01/93	D	26	2	4					1					4	2013 Forfar Athletic (Loan)	Returned to Forfar	
Fairbairn	Jonny	10/01/90	D	15	2	1										10	2012 Mississippi Storm		C (2015)
Gielty	Damien	22/02/84	M	15	11	1	3	1		1	1		1	1		4	2012 Avenir Beggen	Moved to Netherlands to work, May 2014	F
Grant	Paul	23/03/93	GK	15						1			2			4	2013 Hibernian (Loan)	Returned to Hibs	
Gray	Ross	21/09/92	M	26	7	1	2	1		2	1	1				1	2013 Livingston		C (2015)
Hoskins	Dean	27/03/86	D	26	5	2	4			1			2			4	2012 Spartans		C (2015)
Jacobs	Devon	14/06/91	D	32	2	4				1							2013 Stirling Albion		C (2015)
Janczyk	Neil	07/04/83	M	8	1	4				1						4	2012 East Fife	Released Jan 2014, Joined Clyde	
Lavery	Darren	13/12/91	F	31	2	15	4			2	1		2			2	2011 Leith Athletic		c (2015)
McMullen	Ross	02/10/91	GK													1	2014 Tranent		
Miller	Ben	08/11/94	M	5	7					1			1			13	2011 Seton Boys Club		C (2015)
Morris	Josh	03/09/91	F	6	18	2	4			1			2	1		6	2012 Tynecastle		C (2015)
Notman	Steven	29/08/86	M	25	2	4	1	1		2							2009 Vale of Leithen		C (2015)
O'Brien	Kenny	23/05/93	M	16	7	2	1	3	2	1	1		1			5	2012 Alloa	Joined Vale of Leithen May 2014	
O'Connor	Gary	07/04/74	GK				1									7	2012 Raith Rovers	Goalkeeping Coach	
Ronald	Owen	09/05/93	F	3	6				1	1			1			3	2013 Dumbarton (Loan)	Returned to Dumbarton	
Russell	Andy	30/03/93	F	8	3	3											2014 Cowdenbeath		C (2015)
Scott	Conor	16/06/93	M													1	2013 Preston Athletic		
Sloan	Lyle	29/10/94														1	2013 East Fife		
Tufail	Asher	18/08/93	GK													4	2013 Lothian Thistle HV		
Tulloch	Stephen	04/12/87	D	19		1	4			1			2			2	2013 Forfar Athletic		C (2015)
Turner	Lewis	24/10/92	F	1	2					1						3	2013 Newtongrange Star	On Loan to Musselburgh Ath (Nov	F
Own Goals						1													

NEW SIGNINGS 2014/15

Surname	First Name																Signed Previous Club		
Maxwell	Scott																2014 East Stirlingshire		

Date	Comp	H/A	Opponents	F	A		Crowd	Scorers
27/07/2013	RC1	H	Livingston	3	2	AET	460	Gray, Morris, Ronald
03/08/2013	LC1	H	Cowdenbeath	0	5		465	
10/08/2013	L	A	Clyde	0	1		469	
17/08/2013	L	H	Queen's Park	4	0		439	Keenan og, Dalziel, Lavery 2
24/08/2013	L	A	Montrose	1	1		285	Lavery
27/08/2013	RC2	A	Rangrs	0	2		16097	
31/08/2013	L	H	Annan Athletic	4	2		448	Dalziel 2, O'Brien, Lavery
14/09/2013	L	A	Albion Rovers	2	0		322	O'Brien, Dalziel
21/09/2013	L	H	Stirling Albion	1	1		491	Lavery
28/09/2013	L	A	East Stirlingshire	0	1		301	
05/10/2013	SC2	H	Peterhead	2	1		356	Lavery, O'Brien
12/10/2013	L	H	Elgin City	2	3		495	Lavery, Hoskins
19/10/2013	L	H	Clyde	0	1		472	
26/10/2013	L	A	Peterhead	1	1		503	Tulloch
02/11/2013	SC3	A	Culter	1	1		639	Notman
09/11/2013	SC3R	H	Culter	3	1		411	O'Brien, Dalziel, Lavery
16/11/2013	L	A	Annan Athletic	2	3		395	Lavery 2
20/11/2013	L	H	Montrose	1	1		227	L Currie
23/11/2013	L	H	Albion Rovers	2	1		388	Gielty, L Currie
30/11/2013	SC4	H	Dumbarton	1	3		406	L Currie
03/12/2013	L	A	Stirling Albion	1	3		378	L Currie
07/12/2013	L	A	Elgin City	0	2		543	
14/12/2013	L	H	East Stirlingshire	2	0		361	Lavery, L Currie
21/12/2014	L	A	Queen's Park	4	0		302	Dalziel 3, Lavery
28/12/2013	L	H	Peterhead	1	3		778	Notman
02/01/2014	L	A	Montrose	0	0		456	
11/01/2014	L	H	Annan Athletic	1	4		429	L Currie
18/01/2014	L	H	Stirling Albion	4	0		464	Lavery, Hoskins, P Currie, L Currie
25/01/2014	L	A	Albion Rovers	3	0		366	P Currie, L Currie 2
01/02/2014	L	A	Clyde	3	3		467	Dunlop, Morris, P Currie
08/02/2014	L	H	Queen's Park	1	0		443	Lavery
15/02/2014	L	H	Elgin City	2	3		412	L Currie, Fairburn
22/02/2014	L	A	East Stirlingshire	1	1		341	L Currie
01/03/2014	L	A	Annan Athletic	0	4		473	
08/03/2014	L	H	Montrose	5	0		410	Lavery, Notman, L Currie 2, Dalziel
15/03/2014	L	A	Peterhead	0	3		497	
22/03/2014	L	H	Clyde	3	0		519	Lavery, L Currie 2
29/03/2014	L	H	Albion Rovers	3	1		471	P Currie, Gray, Dalziel
05/04/2014	L	A	Stirling Albion	1	2		665	Lavery
12/04/2014	L	A	Elgin City	3	1		602	L Currie, Russell, Morris
19/04/2014	L	H	East Stirlingshire	1	0		582	Russell
26/04/2014	L	A	Queen's Park	3	1		420	L Currie, Dunlop, Russell
03/05/2014	L	H	Peterhead	1	2		586	L Currie

Friendly Matches			Versus	F	A	Att	Notes
7/7/13		Fr	A Ashington	1	1		
9/7/13		Fr	N Brechin City	3	2		at Peffermill
13/7/13		Fr	H Oxford United	1	2	247	
16/7/13		Fr	A Whitehill Welfare	2	4	119	
20/7/13		Fr	H Forfar Athletic	2	2	188	
23/7/13		Fr	A Musselburgh Athletic	2	1		
25/7/13		Fr	A Vale of Leithen	1	3		Res
27/7/13		Fr	A Penicuik Athletic	0	2		Res
30/7/13		Fr	A Tranent	2	3		Res
4/8/13		Fr	A Coldstream	3	2		Res
14/1/14		Fr	N Dumbarton	5	2		at Toryglen
27/1/14		Fr	A Penicuik Athletic	3	1		
15/4/14		CC	H Whitehill Welfare	1	2	102	City Cup Final

Date	Comp	H/A	Opponents	F	A	1	2	3	4	5	6	7	*	9	10	11	12	13	14	15	16	17	18
27/07/2013	RC1	H	Livingston (AET)	3	2	Grant	Turner	Gielty	Hoskins	Tulloch	Currie	Gray*	Notman	Dalziel"	Lavery+	Ronald	O'Brien*	Morris+	Miller*	Fairbairn	Bald		
03/08/2013	LC1	H	Cowdenbeath	0	5	Grant	Notman	Gielty	Hoskins	Tulloch	Currie	Gray"	Turner	Dalziel+	Lavery	Ronald+	O'Brien*	Morris+	Miller*	Brydon	Bald		
10/08/2013	L	A	Clyde	0	1	Grant	Notman	Brydon	Hoskins	Tulloch*	Currie	Gray"	Turner	Dalziel	Lavery	Ronald+	Gielty*	O'Brien*	Morris"	Miller	Bald		
17/08/2013	L	H	Queen's Park	4	0	Grant	Jacobs	Fairbairn	Hoskins	Notman"	Currie	O'Brien*	Gielty	Dalziel"	Lavery	Morris	Gray*	Miller+	Ronald"	Turner	Tufail		
24/08/2013	L	A	Montrose	1	1	Grant	Jacobs	Fairbairn	Hoskins	Notman	Currie	O'Brien	Gielty	Dalziel	Lavery+	Morris*	Gray*	Ronald+	Miller"	Turner	Tufail	Dunlop	
27/08/2013	RC2	A	Rangrs	0	2	Grant	Jacobs	Dunlop	Hoskins	Notman	Currie	O'Brien*	Janczyk"	Tulloch	Lavery	Gray*	Morris*	Gielty+	Dalziel"	Fairbairn	Bald		
31/08/2013	L	H	Annan Athletic	4	2	Grant	Jacobs	Dunlop	Hoskins	Notman	Currie	O'Brien*	Janczyk	Dalziel"	Lavery*	Tulloch	Morris*	Gielty+	Ronald"	Fairbairn	Bald	Miller	
14/09/2013	L	A	Albion Rovers	2	0	Grant	Jacobs	Dunlop	Hoskins	Notman	Currie	O'Brien+	Janczyk	Dalziel	Lavery*	Pullock	Gray*	Gielty+	Morris	Tufail	Carse		
21/09/2013	L	H	Stirling Albion	1	1	Grant	Jacobs	Dunlop	Hoskins	Notman	Currie	O'Brien"	Janczyk*	Dalziel+	Lavery	Pullock	Gielty*	Gray+	Carse"	Tufail	Morris		
28/09/2013	L	A	East Stirlingshire	0	1	Grant	Jacobs	Dunlop	Hoskins	Notman	Currie	Gray*	Janczyk*	Dalziel+	Lavery	Tulloch	Gray*	Carse+	Morris"	Gielty	Sloan		
05/10/2013	SC2	H	Peterhead	2	1	Bald	Jacobs	Dunlop	Hoskins	Notman"	Gielty	Gray*	Janczyk	Dalziel	Lavery+	Tulloch	O'Brien*	Morris+	O'Connor	Miller	Carse		Carse
12/10/2013	L	A	Elgin City	2	3	Grant	Jacobs	Dunlop+	Hoskins	Notman"	Gielty	O'Brien"	Janczyk	Dalziel	Lavery-	Currie	Gray*	Morris+	Ronald"	Carse	Bald		Fairbairn
19/10/2013	L	H	Clyde	0	1	Grant	Jacobs	Dunlop+	Hoskins	Notman"	Gielty	O'Brien"	Janczyk	Dalziel	Gray+	Currie	Gielty*	Morris+	Miller*	Lavery	Bald		
26/10/2013	L	H	Peterhead	1	1	Grant	Jacobs"	Dunlop	Hoskins	Notman	Tulloch	Gielty	Janczyk	Dalziel	Gray+	Currie	Morris*	Morris+	Miller*	Lavery	Bald		
02/11/2013	SC3	L	Culter	1	1	Bald	Jacobs	Dunlop	Hoskins	Notman	Tulloch	Gielty	Janczyk	Dalziel	Lavery*	Currie	Morris*	Miller	O'Connor	Miller	Gray	Brady	
09/11/2013	SC3R	H	Culter	3	1	O'Connor	Jacobs	Dunlop	Hoskins	Notman	Tulloch	O'Brien*	Janczyk+	Dalziel"	Lavery	Currie	Gray*	Gielty+	Carse"	Janczyk	O'Connor	Beveridge	
16/11/2013	L	A	Annan Athletic	2	3	Grant	Jacobs	Dunlop	Hoskins	Notman	Tulloch	O'Brien"	Janczyk	Gray*	Lavery+	Currie	Morris*	Gielty+	Janczyk	Ronald	O'Connor	Ronald	Carse
20/11/2013	L	H	Montrose	1	1	Andrews	Jacobs	Dunlop	Hoskins	Notman	Tulloch	O'Brien*	Dalziel"	Gray	Lavery	Currie	Morris*	Gielty+	Miller	Fairbairn	Miller		
23/11/2013	L	A	Albion Rovers	2	1	Grant	Jacobs	Dunlop	Hoskins	Notman	Tulloch	Gielty	Morris"	Dalziel+	O'Brien+	Currie	Lavery*	Dalziel"	Janczyk	Ronald	O'Connor	Carse	
30/11/2013	SC4	H	Dumbarton	1	3	Bald	Jacobs	Dunlop	Hoskins	Notman	Tulloch	Gielty+	Dalziel"	Gray	O'Brien"	Currie	Lavery*	Morris+	Janczyk	Miller	O'Connor	Carse	
03/12/2013	L	A	Stirling Albion	1	3	Grant	Jacobs	Dunlop	Hoskins+	Notman	Tulloch	Gielty	O'Brien"	Gray	Lavery	Currie	Dalziel*	Ronald+	Morris	Miller	Bald		
07/12/2013	L	H	Elgin City	0	2	Bald	Jacobs	Dunlop	Morris+	Notman	Gray	Gielty	O'Brien"	Dalziel	Ronald+	Currie	O'Brien*	Lavery+	Gray"	Janczyk	Grant		
14/12/2013	L	A	East Stirlingshire	2	0	Bald	Jacobs	Dunlop	Hoskins	Notman*	Gray	Gielty	Lavery+	Dalziel+	Ronald+	Currie	O'Brien*	Morris+	Fairbairn	Janczyk	Grant		
21/12/2013	L	H	Queen's Park	4	0	Bald	Jacobs	Dunlop	Hoskins	Notman+	Gray	Gielty	Lavery+	Dalziel	O'Brien*	Currie	Ronald*	Morris+	Miller*	Fairbain	Grant	Ronald	
28/12/2013	L	H	Peterhead	1	3	Bald	Jacobs	Dunlop	Hoskins	Notman	Gray*	Gielty	Lavery+	Dalziel	O'Brien*	Currie	Morris*	Carse+	Miller	Lavery	Bald	Carse	
02/01/2014	L	A	Montrose	0	0	Grant	Jacobs	Dunlop	Hoskins	Notman	Fairbairn	Gielty	Gray	Dalziel"	O'Brien"	Currie	Turner*	Carse	Miller	Lavery	Bald	Turner	
11/01/2014	L	H	Annan Athletic	1	4	Andrews	Jacobs*	Dunlop	Hoskins	Notman+	Fairbairn	P Currie	Gray	Dalziel"	Lavery*	Currie	Gielty*	Jancxyk+	Morris"	O'Brien	Bald	Carse	Turner
18/01/2014	L	A	Stirling Albion	4	0	Andrews	Jacobs	Dunlop	Hoskins	Notman	Cameron+	Gray	Dalziel+	Ronald	L Currie	Turner*	Morris+	O'Brien*	Fairburn	Fairburn	Bald		
25/01/2014	L	A	Albion Rovers	3	0	Andrews	Jacobs	Dunlop	Hoskins	Notman	Cameron*	P Currie	Gray+	Dalziel	L Currie	O'Brien*	Gielty*	Fairburn+	Giethy"	Fairburn	Miller	Bald	
01/02/2014	L	H	Clyde	3	3	Andrews	Jacobs	Dunlop+	Hoskins	Fairbairn	Cameron*	P Currie	Morris"	Dalziel"	L Currie	Miller*	O'Brien*	Downie+	O'Brien	Scott	Carse	Bald	
08/02/2014	L	H	Queen's Park	1	0	Andrews	Jacobs	Gielty	Hoskins	Fairbairn	Cameron+	P Currie	Gray+	Dalziel"	L Currie	Morris*	Miller*	O'Brien+	Dunlop	Giethy	Tulloch	Bald	
15/02/2014	L	A	Elgin City	2	3	Andrews	Jacobs	Notman	Hoskins	Gielty	Dunlop"	P Currie+	O'Brien	Dalziel"	Lavery+	L Currie	Miller*	Downie+	Morris"	Gielty	McMullen	Downie	Dunlop
22/02/2014	L	A	East Stirlingshire	1	1	Andrews	Jacobs	Drummond	Hoskins	Gielty	Dunlop"	P Currie+	Morris	Dalziel"	Lavery	L Currie	Russell*	Miller+	Fairbairn	Bald	Bald	Cameron	
01/03/2014	L	A	Annan Athletic	0	4	Andrews	Jacobs	Drummond	Hoskins	Notman+	Cameron"	Gray	Fairbairn	Dalziel"	Russell	L Currie	P Currie*	Morris+	Faibairn"	Bald	O'Brien	Morris	
08/03/2014	L	H	Montrose	5	0	Bald	Jacobs	Drummond	Tulloch	Notman+	Cameron"	Gray	Fairbairn	Dalziel"	Russell"	L Currie	P Currie*	Dalziel+	Giethy"	Andrews	Dunlop		
15/03/2014	L	A	Peterhead	0	3	Bald	Jacobs"	Drummond	Drummond	Drummond	Cameron"	Gray	Fairburn	Dalziel"	Russell+	L Currie	Hoskins*	Carse+	Giethy"	Hoskins	Andrews	Morris	
22/03/2014	L	H	Clyde	3	0	Bald	Jacobs"	Drummond	Tulloch	P Currie	Cameron"	Gray+	Fairburn	Lavery	Dalziel*	L Currie	Dalziel*	Carse+	Giethy"	Hoskins	Andrews	Miller	
29/03/2014	L	H	Albion Rovers	3	1	Bald	Jacobs	Drummond	Tulloch	P Currie	Cameron	Gray+	Fairburn	Lavery	Dalziel*	L Currie	Russell!!	Russell+	O'Brien	Hoskins	Andrews	Miller	
05/04/2014	L	A	Stirling Albion	1	2	Bald	Jacobs+	Drummond	Tulloch	P Currie	Cameron*	Gray+	Fairburn	Lavery	Dalziel	L Currie	Miller*	Downie+	O'Brien"	Scott	Carse	Miller	
12/04/2014	L	A	Elgin City	3	1	Bald	Dunlop+	Drummond	Tulloch	Miller"	Russell	Gray*	Fairburn	Lavery	Dalziel!	L Currie	Morris*	Downie+	Dunlop	Gielty	Tulloch	Downie	
19/04/2014	L	H	East Stirlingshire	1	0	Bald	Dunlop+	Drummond	Tulloch	Miller"	Russell	Gray+	Fairbairn	Lavery	Dalziel"	L Currie	Morris*	Hoskins+	Morris"	Bald	Downie		
26/04/2014	L	A	Queen's Park	3	1	Bald	Jacobs+	Drummond	Tulloch	P Currie	Russell	Gray+	Fairbairn	Lavery	P Currie*	L Currie	Dalziel*	Hoskins+	Jacobs"	Andrews	Downie	Cameron	
03/05/2014	L	H	Peterhead	1	2	Bald	Dunlop+	Drummond	Tulloch	Miller"	Russell	Gray*	Fairbairn	Lavery	Dalziel"	L Currie	Hoskins*	Jacobs+	Carse"	Andrews	Morris	Cameron	

Brechin City FC

Founded	1906
Ground	Glebe Park
Postcode	DD9 6BJ
Tel	01356 622856
Capacity	3960
Closest Railway Station	Montrose
Record Attendance	8122 v Aberdeen, SC 3/2/1973
Record Win	12-1 v Thornhill, SC, 28/1/1926
Record Defeat	0-10, v Airdrieonians, Albion Rovers & Cowdenbeath, 1937/8
Most League Goals in a Season	26 Ronald McIntosh, 1959/60
Most Goals in Career	131 Ian Campbell
Chairman	Ken Ferguson
Secretary	Angus Fairlie
Manager	Ray McKinnon
Assistant Manager	Grant Johnson & Darren Taylor
Colours 2013/14 Top	Red
Shorts	Red
Sponsor	Delson
Manufacturer	Pendle
Change Colours 2013/14 Top	Dark Blue with Yellow Flash
Shorts	Dark Blue
Nicknames	City
Web	www.brechincity.com

Brechin City were very much a mid-table side for 2013/14, never really threatening to make the play offs and keeping clear of the relegation zone.

In a bid to improve on this Manager Ray MacKinnon has made quite a few changes for 2014/15. Several experienced players have been allowed to move on and some decent newcomers have been signed. The nucleus of last season's team remains with striker Andy Jackson a key figure at Glebe Park.

Highlight of the season may have been running Rangers close in a 3-4 defeat - that result summed up Brechin's season - they scored plenty but conceded plenty as well.

The Glebe Park side continually work wonders on small crowds. Off the field they work tremendously hard to maintain a thriving football club in such a small town.

PREDICTION 2014/15
Could be a struggle for Brechin this season - mid table at best.

				L			SC			LC			RC						
Surname	First Name	DOB	Pos	A	S	G	A	S	G	A	S	G	A	S	G	UNS	Signed Previous Club	Notes	Contract
Anderson	Stuart	22/04/86	M	10	2		1			1			1			3	2013 Raith Rovers	Freed Jan 2014, joined Formartine United	
Antell	Calum	13/06/92	GK	4												1	2013 QOS (loan)	Returned to QOS	
Barr	Bobby	23/06/83	M	23	11	6	1						1	1	1		2013 East Fife		C (2015)
Boag	James															1	2013 Brechin City Youth		Youth
Brown	Jonathan	24/04/90	D	22	3	1	3			1			1			6	2012 Livingston	Joined Bonnyrigg Rose June 2014	F
Cameron	Greg	10/04/88	M	11	7											14	2013 Dundee United		C (2015)
Carcary	Derek	11/07/86	F	7	15	2	2	1		1			1			4	2011 Dumbarton	Joined Annan Athletic May 2014	F
Connolly	Aidan	15/08/95	F	1	3												2013 Dundee United (loan Sep-Oct)	Returned to Dundee United	
Donnelly	Ryan	23/10/91	M	8	6	2		2		1	2					5	2013 Airdrieonians	Freed Jan 2014, joined Albion Rovers	
Ferguson	Ryan	15/01/94	M	13	3												2014 Dundee United		C (2015)
Hay	Graham	11/06/87	D	31			3	3		1			1				2011 Lochee United	Joined Formartine United May 2014	
Jackson	Steven	27/08/92	D	17	8	3	2	1	1	1			1			10	2013 East Stirlingshire		C (2015)
Jackson	Andy	09/01/88	F	32	1	10	3		1	1			1				2012 Morton		C (2015)
Kenneth	Gary	21/06/87	D	5												3	2014 Bristol Rovers		F
McLaughlan	Gerry	08/03/89	D	24	1	1	1									10	2010 Montrose		C (2015)
McLean	Paul	02/02/90	D	26	3	3	2			1			1			3	2009 Norwich City		C (2015)
Molloy	Craig	26/04/86	M	24	7	3				1				1		3	2010 Stenhousemuir		C (2015)
Moyes	Ewan	30/03/90	D	17	1		2									13	2012 Gateshead	Joined East Fife June 2014	F
Nelson	Craig	25/08/71	GK													40	2004 St Johnstone		Coach
Petrie	Darren	26/07/95	M	23	1	1	3										2013 Dundee United (loan Sep-May)	Returned to Dundee United	
Robb	Steven	08/03/82	M	13	8	1	2									8	2013 Thai Port		F
Ryan	Andy	29/09/94	F	4		1											2013 Hamilton Accies (loan Oct-Nov)	Returned to Hamilton	
Smith	Graeme	08/06/83	GK	32			3			1		1					2013 East Stirlingshire		C (2016)
Thomson	Robert	28/05/93	F	12	2	7											2014 Dundee United		C (2015)
Tobin	Chris	18/10/93		1	1											8	2013 St Johnstone		
Tough	Ben	30/04/93	GK													2	2012 Luncarty	On loan to Kirrie Thistle	C (2015)
Trouten	Alan	08/11/85	M	25	2	12	3			3	1		1			3	2012 Ayr United		C (2015)
Walker	Allan	03/01/86	M	11	5			2	1	1			1			10	2013 Raith Rovers	Joined East Fife May 2014	
Own Goals						1				2	1	1			1				

NEW SIGNINGS 2014/15

Fusco	Gary																2014 Forfar Athletic		
Hamilton	Colin																2014 Arbroath		

Date	Comp	H/A	Opponents	F	A		Crowd	Scorers
27/07/2013	RC1	A	Peterhead	1	2		546	Strachan og
03/08/2013	LC1	A	Stranraer	3	4		291	Barr, Donnelly 2
10/08/2013	L	A	Rangers	1	4		44380	S Jackson
17/08/2013	L	H	East Fife	2	0		543	Donnelly, Trouten
24/08/2013	L	H	Forfar Athletic	2	1		724	Molloy, Trouten
31/08/2013	L	A	Arbroath	1	2		801	Barr
14/09/2013	L	H	Dunfermline Athletic	1	1		923	A Jackson
21/09/2013	L	A	Ayr United	2	2		987	Trouten, McLean
28/09/2013	L	H	Stranraer	1	1		455	Trouten
05/10/2013	L	A	Airdreonians	1	3		606	A Jackson
12/10/2013	L	A	Stenhousemuir	2	3		415	Mclean, S Jackson
19/10/2013	L	H	Rangers	3	4		3237	Hay, Brown, Trouten
26/10/2019	L	H	Arbroath	3	1		765	Hay, Ryan, Barr
02/11/2013	SC3	A	Arbroath	2	0		634	S Jackson, Trouten
09/11/2013	L	A	Forfar Athletic	0	2		663	
16/11/2013	L	H	Ayr United	1	1		518	A Jackson
23/11/2013	L	A	Dunfermline Athletic	1	3		2569	Mclean
30/11/2013	SC4	H	Forfar Athletic	1	1		724	Trouten
10/12/2013	SC4R	A	Forfar Athletic	3	3	AET, 3-4 pens	811	A Jackson, Trouten, Walker
14/12/2013	L	A	Stranraer	0	3		357	
17/12/2013	L	H	Airdreonians	4	3		445	Donnelly, Trouten 2, A Jackson
21/12/2013	L	A	East Fife	3	1		745	A Jackson, Barr, Carcary
28/12/2013	L	H	Stenhousemuir	0	1		507	
02/01/2014	L	H	Forfar Athletic	1	5		812	Barr
11/01/2014	L	A	Arbroath	1	0		777	Barr
18/01/2014	L	A	Ayr United	3	1		1018	McLaughlin, McAusland og, Hay
25/01/2014	L	H	Dunfermline Athletic	3	2		854	Carcary, A Jacson, Petrie
01/02/2014	L	A	Rangers	1	2		40377	Robb
08/02/2014	L	H	East Fife	3	0		523	Barr, A Jackson, Thomson
15/02/2014	L	A	Airdreonians	1	2		690	Thomson
22/02/2014	L	H	Stranraer	1	3		452	A Jackson
01/03/2014	L	H	Arbroath	2	4		668	A Jackson, Thomson
08/03/2014	L	A	Forfar Athletic	1	1		641	S Jackson
15/03/2014	L	A	Stenhousemuir	2	4		512	Trouten 2
23/03/2014	L	H	Rangers	1	2		3070	Thomson
29/03/2014	L	A	Dunfermline Athletic	1	2		2241	Thomson
05/04/2014	L	H	Ayr United	2	1		507	Thomson, Molloy
12/04/2014	L	H	Airdreonians	1	1		646	Molloy
19/04/2014	L	A	Stranraer	2	1		407	Trouten, Thomson
26/04/2014	L	A	East Fife	2	1		591	A Jackson, Trouten
03/05/2014	L	H	Stenhousemuir	1	3		543	Trouten

Friendly Matches

6/7/13	Fr	N	Cove Rangers	1	0	at Stirling University
9/7/13	Fr	N	Berwick Rangers	2	3	at Peffermill
14/7/13	Fr	N	Queen's Park	1	0	at NRC, Largs
16/7/13	Fr	N	Dumbarton	1	1	at Stirling University
20/7/13	Fr	A	Montrose	4	2	
30/7/13	Fr	A	Lochee United	0	2	

Date	Comp	H/A	Opponents	F	A	1	2	3	4	5	6	7	8	9	10	11	12	13	14	15	16	17	18
27/07/2013	RC1	A	Peterhead	1	2	Smith	S Jackson	McLean	Hay+	McLaughlin	Walker	Trouten	Anderson*	A Jackson	Barr	Carcary	Molloy*	Brown+	Nelson	Cameron	Moyes		
03/08/2013	LC1	A	Stranraer	3	4	Smith	S Jackson	McLean	Hay	Brown	Barr	Trouten	Anderson*	A Jackson	Molloy	Carcary	Barr*	Donnelly+	Donnelly"	Tobin	Nelson	Molloy	
10/08/2013	L	A	Rangers	1	4	Smith	S Jackson	Hay	McLaughlin	Robb	Walker+	Trouten	Anderson	Barr	Donnelly"	Carcary	A Jackson"	Cameron+	Brown"	Tobin	Nelson	Moyes	S Jackson
17/08/2013	L	H	East Fife	2	0	Smith	S Jackson	Hay	McLaughlin	Robb*	McLean	Trouten	Anderson	Barr	A Jackson"	Molloy	Donnelly*	Cameron*	Walker	Tobin	Nelson	Nelson	
24/08/2013	L	H	Forfar Athletic	2	1	Smith	Brown	Hay*	McLaughlin	Barr	McLean	Trouten	Anderson"	Barr	A Jackson"	Molloy	Donnelly*	Cameron*	Brown"	Tobin	Nelson	Nelson	
31/08/2013	L	A	Arbroath	1	2	Smith	Brown	Hay*	McLaughlin	McLaughlin	McLean	Donnelly	Anderson"	Barr	A Jackson	Molloy+	Barr*	Cameron"	Tobin"	Tobin	Nelson	Moyes	S Jackson
14/09/2013	L	A	Dunfermline Athletic	1	1	Smith	Brown	Hay	McLaughlin	McLaughlin	McLean	Trouten	Donnelly"	Barr	A Jackson	Molloy+	Barr	Robb+	S Jackson"	Tobin	Nelson	Carcary	Cameron
21/09/2013	L	A	Ayr United	2	2	Smith	Brown	Hay	McLaughlin	McLaughlin	McLean	Trouten	Robb+	Barr	A Jackson	Molloy+	Tobin"	Molloy+	S Jackson"	Cameron"	Nelson	Donnelly	Anderson
28/09/2013	L	H	Stranraer	1	1	Smith	Brown	Moyes	McLaughlin	Molloy*	McLean	Trouten	Anderson	Barr+	A Jackson	Molloy*	Walker*	Connolly*	Connolly"	Cameron	Nelson	S Jackson	Robb
05/10/2013	L	A	Airdreonians	1	3	Smith	Brown	Moyes	McLaughlin	McLaughlin	McLean	Trouten	Anderson"	Hay	A Jackson	Donnelly+	Walker*	Connolly*	Tobin	Cameron	Nelson	Molloy	Robb
12/10/2013	L	A	Stenhousemuir	2	3	Smith	Brown*	Moyes	McLaughlin+	McLaughlin	McLean	Trouten	Anderson"	Hay	A Jackson	Donnelly+	Barr*	Carcary+	S Jackson+	Cameron	Nelson	Molloy	Tobin
19/10/2013	L	H	Rangers	3	4	Smith	Brown	Moyes	McLaughlin	Walker*	McLean"	Molloy	Anderson"	Hay	A Jackson	Petrie	Barr*	Molloy*	S Jackson"	Cameron	Nelson	Donnelly	Robb
26/10/2019	L	H	Arbroath	3	1	Smith	Brown*	Moyes	Robb*	Ryan+	McLean	Molloy	Anderson"	Hay	A Jackson	Petrie	Barr*	Carcary+	McLaughlin"	Cameron	Nelson	Donnelly	McLaughlin
02/11/2013 SC3	L	A	Arbroath	2	0	Smith	Brown	Moyes*	Robb*	Trouten	McLean	Cameron+	Ryan"	Hay	A Jackson	Petrie	Molloy*	Carcary+	Barr"	Anderson	Nelson	S Jackson	McLaughlin
09/11/2013	L	A	Forfar Athletic	0	2	Smith	Brown	Moyes	Robb*	Trouten	S Jackson	Molloy"	Carcary+	Hay	A Jackson	Petrie	Molloy*	Carcary+	Barr*	Anderson	Nelson	Mclean	Walker
16/11/2013	L	A	Ayr United	1	1	Smith	McLean	McLean	Brown	Trouten	S Jackson	Molloy*	Carcary+	Hay	A Jackson	Petrie	Barr*	Donnelly+	Barr"	Anderson	Nelson	Mclean	McLaughlin
23/11/2013	L	A	Dunfermline Athletic	1	3	Smith	McLaughlin"	McLean	Brown	Trouten	S Jackson	Molloy"	Carcary	Hay	A Jackson	Petrie	Anderson+	Walker+	Donnelly"	Cameron	Nelson	Brown	McLaughlin
30/11/2013 SC4	L	H	Forfar Athletic	3	3	Anteil	McLaughlin*	Robb*	Donnelly+	Trouten	S Jackson	Molloy"	Carcary+	Anderson+	A Jackson"	Petrie	Walker*	Barr+	McLaughlin"	Anderson	Nelson	Robb	S Jackson
10/12/2013 SC4R	L	A	Forfar Athletic	0	3	Anteil	Donnelly"	Cameron*	Barr	Trouten	Cameron	Moyes	Carcary	Hay	A Jackson	Molloy	Barr"	Barr+	Donnelly"	Cameron	Nelson	Mclean	McLaughlin
14/12/2013	L	A	Stranraer	0	3	Anteil	Donnelly"	McLean	Donnelly+	Trouten	S Jackson	Moyes	Robb	Hay	A Jackson	Molloy	Anderson"	Robb	Robb	Walker	Nelson		
17/12/2013	L	A	Airdreonians	3	1	Anteil	McLaughlin"	McLean"	Barr	Trouten	McLaughlin	Moyes	Petrie"	Hay	A Jackson	Molloy	Barr*	Carcary+	Cameron"	Nelson	Walker	S Jackson	McLaughlin
21/12/2013	L	H	East Fife	1	1	Smith	Barr	McLean"	Donnelly"	Trouten	McLaughlin	Moyes	Petrie	Robb	A Jackson	Molloy	Barr"	Robb+	Brown"	Nelson	Walker	Donnelly	
28/12/2013	L	H	Stenhousemuir	0	1	Smith	Barr+	Carcary"	Robb	Cameron+	McLaughlin	Moyes	Petrie	Petrie	A Jackson	Molloy+	McLean*	Robb+	McLaughlin"	Antell	Cameron		
02/01/2014	L	A	Forfar Athletic	1	5	Smith	Barr	Mclean	Brown	Cameron+	S Jackson	Moyes"	Petrie	Petrie	A Jackson	Molloy"	Carcary*	Robb+	Trouten	Nelson	S Jackson	Moyes	Boag
11/01/2014	L	A	Ayr United	1	0	Smith	Barr	Mclean	Brown	Petrie	Petrie	Robb*	Ferguson"	Walker	A Jackson	Molloy*	Carcary*	Molloy+	Thomson"	Nelson	Cameron	Trouten	
18/01/2014	L	A	Dunfermline Athletic	3	1	Smith	Barr	Mclean	Brown	Petrie	McLaughlin	Robb*	Walker"	A Jackson	A Jackson	Ferguson"	Carcary*	S Jackson+	Petrie"	Nelson	S Jackson	Moyes	McLaughlin
25/01/2014	L	H	Dunfermline Athletic	3	2	Smith	Barr	Mclean	Brown	Kenneth"	McLaughlin	Robb*	Walker	Brown+	A Jackson	Ferguson*	Carcary"	Molloy+	Petrie"	Nelson	Cameron	Moyes	Moyes
01/02/2014	L	H	Rangers	1	2	Smith	Barr	Mclean	Brown+	Kenneth"	Thomson	Robb"	Walker"	Brown+	A Jackson	Ferguson"	Carcary"	Brown+	Carcary"	Nelson	S Jackson	Moyes	
08/02/2014	L	H	East Fife	3	0	Smith	Barr	Mclean	Petrie+	Kenneth"	Thomson	Robb"	S Jackson	Hay"	A Jackson	Molloy	Molloy*	Cameron+	Trouten"	Nelson	S Jackson	McLaughlin	
15/02/2014	L	A	Airdreonians	1	2	Smith	Barr	McLaughlin	Petrie	Ferguson	McLaughlin	Walker	S Jackson	Hay	A Jackson	Molloy	Trouten*	Barr+	Robb"	Nelson	Walker		
22/02/2014	L	H	Stranraer	1	3	Smith	Cameron*	McLaughlin	Petrie	Ferguson+	McLaughlin	Mclean	S Jackson	Hay	A Jackson	Molloy	Cameron*	Barr+	Mclean"	Nelson	Tough	Brown	
01/03/2014	L	A	Arbroath	2	4	Smith	Barr"	McLaughlin	Petrie	Brown+	Trouten	Mclean	S Jackson	Hay	Thomson	Molloy	Carcary*	Ferguson+	Moyes	Nelson	Tough		
08/03/2014	L	A	Forfar Athletic	1	1	Smith	Barr*	McLaughlin	Petrie	Cameron	Trouten	Ferguson	S Jackson	Hay	Thomson	Molloy	Carcary*	Walker	Carcary"	Nelson	Walker	Walker	
15/03/2014	L	A	Stenhousemuir	2	4	Smith	Barr	McLaughlin	Petrie	Cameron+	A Jackson"	Mclean	S Jackson	S Jackson	Thomson	Molloy	Carcary*	Moyes	Mclean	Nelson			
23/03/2014	L	H	Rangers	1	2	Smith	Barr+	McLaughlin"	Petrie	Brown+	Trouten	Ferguson	S Jackson	S Jackson	Thomson	Molloy	Cameron"	Walker	Carcary"	Nelson	Robb	Brown	Brown
29/03/2014	L	A	Dunfermline Athletic	1	2	Smith	Barr"	McLaughlin"	Petrie	Cameron	Trouten	Ferguson	S Jackson	S Jackson	Thomson	Molloy	Carcary*	Moyes	Mclean	Nelson	Moyes	Kenneth	Brown
05/04/2014	L	A	Ayr United	2	1	Smith	Barr	Mclaughlin	Petrie	Cameron	Trouten	Ferguson+	Mclean	Mclean	Thomson	Molloy	Carcary	Robb+	Carcary"	Nelson	Robb	Kenneth	Kenneth
12/04/2014	L	H	Airdreonians	1	1	Smith	Barr+	Moyes	McLaughlin	Brown+	Trouten	Ferguson	Mclean	Mclean	Thomson	Molloy	McLean*	Mclean	Carcary"	Nelson	Moyes	Moyes	McLaughlin
19/04/2014	L	A	Stranraer	2	1	Smith	Barr+	Ferguson"	McLaughlin"	Cameron	Trouten	A Jackson	Ferguson	S Jackson	Thomson	Molloy	S Jackson*	Ferguson+	Carcary"	Nelson	Robb	Moyes	Moyes
26/04/2014	A	East Fife	2	1		Smith	Kenneth+	Ferguson"	Petrie	Cameron*	Trouten	A Jackson"	Mclean	S Jackson	Thomson+	Barr	Robb*	S Jackson+	McLaughlian	Nelson	Brown	Moyes	McLaughlin
03/05/2014	L	H	Stenhousemuir	1	3	Smith	Kenneth	Ferguson	Petrie	Cameron*	Trouten	A Jackson	Mclean	Hay	Thomson+	Barr	Robb*	S Jackson+	McLaughlian	Nelson	Brown	Moyes	Carcary

Celtic FC

Founded	1888
Ground	Celtic Park
Postcode	G40 3RE
Tel	0871 226 1888
Capacity	60355
Closest Railway Station	Duke Street
Record Attendance	92000 v Rangers, Lge, 1/1/1938
Record Win	11-0 v Dundee, Lge, 26/10/1895
Record Defeat	0-8 v Motherwell, Lge, 30/4/1937
Most League Goals in a Season	50 Jimmy McGrory, 1935/6
Most Goals in Career	397 Jimmy McGrory
Chairman	Ian Bankier
Chief Executive	Peter Lawwell
Secretary	Michael Nicholson
Manager	Neil Lennon (until May) / Ronnie Deila
Assistant Manager	Johan Mjalby (Until May)
Colours 2013/14 Top	Green and White Hoops
Shorts	White
Sponsor	Magners
Manufacturer	Nike
Change Colours 2013/14 Top	Yellow with thin Green Bands
Shorts	Green
3rd Choice 2013/14 Top	Black
Shorts	Black
Nicknames	Tic, Bhoys
Web	www.celticfc.net

PREDICTION 2014/15
Champions again. May struggle to qualify for Champions League group stage

Neil Lennon's Summer departure came as a surprise to many but it may be that he thought he had taken Celtic as far as he could. Qualification for the Champions League, via a three-round qualifying process, was a major achievement and one that there is no guarantee of negotiating. The gap in resources when playing against Europe's real big hitters was fully demonstrated in 2013/14.

Domestically the League Championship race was effectively over by the turn of the year. The absence of Rangers from top flight football has been more of a problem for Celtic than any other club—season ticket sales remained good but match day attendances have dropped sharply. Celtic's Cup performances were disappointing.

The appointment of Ronnie Deila as Manager is bold and innovative. The same was said when Rangers appointed Paul Le Guen. Hopefully Deila gets more chance than Le Guen did. Deila will bring fresh and ideas and with John Collins assisting him we can expect to see attacking football from Celtic.

Surname	First Name	DOB	SQ	Pos	L A	L S	SC G A S	LC G A S	UC A S G	UNS	Signed	Previous Club	Notes	Contract
Ambrose	Efi	18/10/88	4	D	37	1	2 2	1	11 1		2012	Ashdod		C (2017)
Atajic	Bahrudin	16/11/93	37	F			3 1			12	2010	Malmo	On loan to Shrewsbury Town (Jan-May)	■
Balde	Amido	16/05/91	17	F	3	17	3 2		3	19	2013	Vitoria Guimaraes		C (2017)
Bangura	Mohamed	27/07/89		F							2011	AIK Stockholm	OL to Elfsborg, Free Jan 2014, joined Istanbul BB	
Biton	Nir	30/10/91	6	M	8	7	1	1	1 2	8	2013	Ashdod		C (2017)
Boerrigter	Derk	16/10/86	11	F	5	10	1 2	1	2 3	6	2013	Ajax Amsterdam		C (2016)
Brown	Scott	25/06/85	8	M	37	1	2 2	2 1	9		2007	Hibernian		C (2015)
Chalmers	Joe	03/01/94	43	D							2012	Celtic Youth	On loan to Falkirk Jan-May	OOC
Commons	Kris	30/08/83	15	M	32	2	27 2 3	1	10 1 2	1	2011	Derby County		OOC
Fasan	Leo	04/01/94	38	GK						1	2012	Celtic Youth		OOC
Fisher	Darnell	04/04/94	41	D	10	2	1			12	2011	Farnborough Town		F
Forrest	James	07/07/91	49	F	10	6	4 1		9 1 3		2010	Celtic Youth		C (2016)
Forster	Fraser	17/03/88	1	GK	37		2	12		1	2012	Newcastle United		C (2016)
Fraser	Marcus	23/06/94	44	D						1	2011	Celtic Youth		C (2015)
Fridjonsson	Holmbert	19/04/93	19	F						2	2013	Fram Reykjavik		C (2017)
Griffiths	Leigh	20/08/90	28	F	11	2	7			1	2014	Wolves		C (2017)
Henderson	Liam	25/04/96	53	M			4 4 1			10	2008	Hearts		C (2017)
Herron	John	01/02/94	31	M	1					4	2012	Celtic Youth		C (2015)
Hooper	Gary	26/01/88	88	F			1		1		2010	Scunthorpe United	Transferred to Norwich City July 2013, £5m	■
Irvine	Jackson	07/03/93	36	M			1				2010	Melbourne Victory	On Loan to Kilmarnock Aug 2013-May 2014	
Izaguirre	Emilio	10/05/86	3	D	34		2		10		2010	Motagua		C (2017)
Johansen	Stefan	08/01/91	25	M	13	3	2 1				2014	Stromsgodset		C (2017)
Johnstone	Denny	09/01/95	39	F						1	2012	Celtic Youth		OOC
Kayal	Beram	02/05/88	33	M	7	6			6 1 1	7	2010	Maccabi Haifa		C (2015)
Ledley	Joe	23/01/87	16	M	8	2	4 1	1	4 4		2010	Cardiff City	Transferred to Crystal Palace, Jan 2014	■
Lustig	Mikael	13/12/86	23	D	9	7	1	1 1	12 1		2011	Rosenborg Trondheim		C (2017)
Matthews	Adam	13/01/92	2	D	21	2	1 1	1	4 3		2011	Cardiff City		C (2016)
McGeouch	Dylan	15/01/93	46	M	1			1	1	8	2011	Celtic Youth		OOC
McGregor	Callum	14/06/93	42	M	1						2012	Celtic Youth	On loan to Notts County Aug 2013-May 2014	
Mouyokolo	Steven	24/01/87	22	D	1	1		1		8	2013	Wolves		OOC
Mulgrew	Charlie	06/03/86	21	D	27	1	6 1	1	8 2		2010	Aberdeen		C (2016)
O'Connell	Eoghan	13/08/95	34	D	1					11	2012	Avondale United		Youth
Pukki	Teemu	29/03/90	20	F	13	12	7 1 1		2 3	10	2013	Schalke 04		C (2017)
Rogic	Tom	16/12/92	18	M	1	2		1	3	15	2013	Central Coast Mariners	On Loan to Melbourne Victory Jan 2014-	C (2017)
Samaras	Giorgios	21/02/85	9	F	10	10	7 1		12 4	8	2008	Manchester City		F
Stokes	Anthony	25/07/88	10	F	30	3	20 2 1	1	8 3	1	2010	Hibernian		C (2017)
Twardzik	Filip	10/02/93	56	M	1					1	2009	Hertha Berlin		C (2015)
Twardzik	Patrick	10/02/93		F							2009	Hertha Berlin		F
Van Dijk	Virgil	08/07/91	5	M	35	1	5 2		7 1		2013	FC Groningen		C (2017)
Waters	Calum	10/03/96	59	D							2012	Celtic Youth		Youth
Watt	Tony	29/12/93	32	F	1	1			1	5	2011	Airdrie United	On Loan to SK Lierse Aug 2013-May 2014	C (2016)
Wilson	Kelvin	03/09/85	6	D					4		2011	Nottingham Forest	Sold to Nottingham Forest Aug 2013, £2.5m	■
Zaluska	Lukasz	16/06/82	24	GK	1			1		51	2009	Dundee United		C (2015)
Own Goals							2		1					

47

Date	Comp	H/A	Opponents	F	A		Crowd	Scorers
16/07/2013	ECL	A	Cliftonville	3	0		5442	Lustig, Samaras, Forrest
23/07/2013	ECL	H	Cliftonville	2	0		29758	Ambrose, Samaras
31/07/2013	ECL	H	Elfsborg Boras	1	0		40153	Commons
03/08/2013	Prem	H	Ross County	2	1		45705	Stokes 2
07/08/2013	ECL	A	Elfsborg Boras	0	0		9040	
17/08/2013	Prem	A	Aberdeen	2	0		20017	Commons, Forrest
20/08/2013	ECL	A	Shakther Karagandy	0	2		29950	
24/08/2013	Prem	H	Inverness CT	2	2		45160	Mulgrew, Matthews
28/08/2013	ECL	H	Shakther Karagandy	3	0		50063	Commons, Samaras, Forrest
31/08/2013	Prem	A	Dundee United	1	0		10586	Stokes
14/09/2013	Prem	A	Hearts	3	1		15928	Commons, Stokes, Pukki
18/09/2013	ECL	A	AC Milan	0	2		43000	
21/09/2013	Prem	H	St Johnstone	2	1		45220	Pukki, Mulgrew
24/09/2013	LC3	H	Morton	0	1	AET	15709	
28/09/2013	Prem	A	Kilmarnock	5	2		6149	Samaras 3, Commons, Balde
01/10/2013	ECL	H	CF Barcelona	0	1		58128	
05/10/2013	Prem	H	Motherwell	2	0		46608	Stokes, Commons
19/10/2013	Prem	A	Hibernian	1	1		14330	Forrest
22/10/2013	ECL	H	Ajax Amsterdam	2	1		58719	Kayal, Forrest
27/10/2013	Prem	A	Partick Thistle	2	1		7978	Samaras, Balde
02/11/2013	Prem	H	Dundee United	1	1		47386	Mulgrew
06/11/2013	ECL	A	Ajax Amsterdam	0	1		59908	
09/11/2013	Prem	A	Ross County	4	1		5982	Van Dijk 2, Ledley 2
23/11/2013	Prem	A	Aberdeen	3	1		49683	Commons 2, Boerrigter
26/11/2013	ECL	H	AC Milan	0	3		58619	
01/12/2013	SC4	A	Hearts	7	0		10636	Commokns 3, Brown 2, Ledley, Lustig
06/12/2013	Prem	A	Motherwell	5	0		9117	Commons 2, Ambrose, Stokes, Atajic
10/12/2013	ECL	A	Barcelona	1	6			Samaras
14/12/2013	Prem	H	Hibernian	1	0		46065	Pukki
21/12/2013	Prem	H	Hearts	2	0		46058	Commons, Forrest
26/12/2013	Prem	A	St Johnstone	1	0		7034	Van Dijk
29/12/2013	Prem	A	Inverness CT	1	0		6384	Commons
01/01/2014	Prem	H	Partick Thistle	1	0		52670	Ledley
05/01/2014	Prem	A	St Mirren	4	0		5778	Commons 2, Mulgrew, Stokes
18/01/2014	Prem	A	Motherwell	3	0		47489	Commons 2, McManus og
26/01/2014	Prem	H	Hibernian	4	0		12542	Commons 2, Van Dijkj, Pukki
29/01/2014	Prem	H	Kilmarnock	4	0		44271	Ledley, Ashcroft og, Mulgrew, Balde
02/02/2014	Prem	A	St Mirren	1	0		45014	Commons
08/02/2014	SC5	H	Aberdeen	1	2		30413	Stokes
16/02/2014	Prem	H	St Johnstone	3	0		45239	Stokes 3
22/02/2014	Prem	A	Hearts	2	0		15801	Griffiths, Pukki
25/02/2014	Prem	A	Aberdeen	1	2		16634	Forrest
01/03/2014	Prem	H	Inverness CT	5	0		46552	Griffiths 3, Mulgrew, Commons
14/03/2014	Prem	A	Kilmarnock	3	0		7495	Commons 3
22/03/2014	Prem	A	St Mirren	3	0		46536	Johansen, Griffiths, Stokes
26/03/2014	Prem	A	Partick Thistle	5	1		7549	Stokes 2, Hendreson, Johansen, Commons
29/03/2014	Prem	H	Ross County	1	1		49270	Commons
05/04/2014	Prem	A	Dundee United	2	0		11033	Samaras, Stokes
19/04/2014	Prem	A	Motherwell	3	3		7493	Stokes, Samaras, Griffiths
27/04/2014	Prem	H	Inverness CT	6	0		45712	Stokes 3, Griffiths, Ambrose, Pukki
03/05/2014	Prem	H	Aberdeen	5	2		47468	Brown 2, Stokes, Commons 2
07/05/2014	Prem	A	St Johnstone	3	3		4624	Commons, Pukki, Van Dijk
11/05/2014	Prem	H	Dundee United	3	1		52400	Stokes, Samaras, Commons

Friendly Matches

3/7/13	Fr	N	Sevastopol	0	1			at Furstenfeldbruck
6/7/13	Fr	N	CFR Cluj	1	2			at Kufstein
6/7/13	Fr	A	Clachnacuddin	2	1		U20	
9/7/13	Fr	A	Sp Vgg Greuther Furth	2	6		5260	
12/7/13	Fr	A	Union Berlin	0	3		22000	
20/7/13	Fr	A	Brentford	2	1		8253	
27/7/13	Fr	H	Borussia Moenchengladbach	1	2		17000	
30/7/13	Fr	A	East Fife	0	2		U20	
10/8/13	Fr	N	Liverpool	1	1			at Dublin
9/1/14	TnT	N	Trabzonspor	3	1			in Antalya
12/1/14	TnT	N	Galatasaray	0	0	4-5 pens		in Antalya

Date	Comp	H/A	Opponents	F	A		1	2	3	4	5	6	7	8	9	10	11	12	13	14	15	16	17	18
16/07/2013	ECL	A	Cliftonville	3	0		Forster	Lustig	Wilson	Ambrose	Izaguirre	Commons+	Brown	Kayal	Forrest"	Stokes	Samaras*	Watt*	Rogic+	McGeouch"	Amido	Irvine	Waters	Zaluska
23/07/2013	ECL	H	Cliftonville	2	0		Forster	Lustig	Wilson	Ambrose	Izaguirre	Commons	Brown	Kayal*	Forrest"	Stokes+	Samaras	Rogic*	Hooper+	Amido"	Watt	McGregor	Mouyokolo	Zaluska
31/07/2013	ECL	H	Elfsborg Boras	1	0		Forster	Lustig	Wilson	Ambrose	Izaguirre	Commons	Brown	Kayal*	Forrest	Stokes	Samaras+	Ledley*	Mulgrew+	Matthews	Watt	Balde	Mouyokolo	Zaluska
03/08/2013	Prem	H	Ross County	2	1		Forster	Lustig+	Mulgrew	Ambrose	Izaguirre	Commons	Brown	Ledley	Forrest"	Stokes	Boerrigter*	Watt*	Matthews+	Kayal"	Balde	McGeouch	Mouyokolo	Zaluska
07/08/2013	ECL	A	Elfsborg Boras	0	0		Forster	Lustig	Wilson	Ambrose	Izaguirre	Commons	Brown	Ledley	Forrest	Mulgrew"	Samaras*	Stokes*	Matthews+	Kayal	Balde	Watt	Mouyokolo	Zaluska
17/08/2013	Prem	A	Aberdeen	2	0		Forster	Mouyokolo	Mulgrew	Ambrose+	Izaguirre	Commons	Brown	Ledley	Matthews*	Kayal"	Samaras	Lustig*	Van Dijk+	Forrest"	McGeouch	Watt	Atajic	Zaluska
20/08/2013	ECL	A	Shakther Karagandy	0	2		Forster	Mouyokolo	Mulgrew	Van Dijk	Izaguirre+	Commons	Brown	Ledley	Forrest	Lustig*	Samaras	Matthews*	Balde+	Ambrose	Rogic	Kayal	Stokes	Zaluska
24/08/2013	Prem	H	Inverness CT	2	2		Forster	Ambrose	Mulgrew	Van Dijk+	Izaguirre	Matthews	Brown	Kayal*	Watt	Rogic"	Balde	Ledley*	Lustig+	Atajic"	McGeouch	Henderson	Mouyokolo	Zaluska
28/08/2013	ECL	H	Shakther Karagandy	3	0		Forster	Matthews	Mulgrew	Ambrose	Lustig	Commons*	Brown	Ledley	Forrest+	Stokes	Samaras	Boerrigter*	Van Dijk+	Izaguirre	McGeouch	Watt	Balde	Zaluska
31/08/2013	Prem	A	Dundee United	1	0		Forster	Matthews	Izaguirre	Ambrose	Lustig*	Commons	Brown	Ledley	Van Dijk	Stokes	Boerrigter+	Balde*	Rogic+	Atajic	McGeouch	Herron	Mouyokolo	Zaluska
14/09/2013	Prem	A	Hearts	3	1		Forster	Matthews*	Izaguirre	Ambrose	Lustig	Commons"	Brown	Ledley+	Van Dijk	Stokes	Boerrigter	Samaras*	Mulgrew+	Pukki"	Balde	Rogic	Atajic	Zaluska
18/09/2013	ECL	A	AC Milan	0	2		Forster	Matthews*	Izaguirre	Ambrose	Lustig	Commons+	Brown	Mulgrew"	Van Dijk	Stokes	Samaras	Boerrigter*	Pukki+	Biton"	Balde	Rogic	McGeouch	Zaluska
21/09/2013	Prem	H	St Johnstone	2	1		Forster	Matthews*	Izaguirre	Ambrose	Mulgrew	Commons+	Brown	Pukki"	Van Dijk	Stokes	Boerrigter	Biton*	Samaras+	Balde"	Atajic	Rogic	McGeouch	Zaluska
24/09/2013	LC3	H	Morton	0	1	AET	Zaluska	Van Dijk	Lustig	Ambrose	Mulgrew	Biton	Brown	Pukki	McGeouch*	Rogic+	Boerrigter"	Matthews*	Stokes+	Commons"	Balde	Fasan		
28/09/2013	Prem	A	Kilmarnock	5	2		Forster	Matthews*	Izaguirre	Ambrose	Mulgrew	Commons	Brown	Pukki+	Van Dijk	Stokes	Samaras"	Lustig*	Balde+	Atajic"	Biton	Rogic	Henderson	Zaluska
01/10/2013	ECL	H	CF Barcelona	0	1		Forster	Lustig+	Izaguirre	Ambrose	Mulgrew	Commons"	Brown	Matthews	Van Dijk	Stokes*	Samaras	Kayal*	Forrest+	Pukki"	Biton	Rogic	Balde	Zaluska
05/10/2013	Prem	H	Motherwell	2	0		Forster	Lustig	Izaguirre"	Ambrose	Mulgrew	Commons	Brown	Matthews*	Van Dijk	Stokes	Pukki+	Forrest*	Biton+	Balde"	Atajic	Kayal	Henderson	Zaluska
19/10/2013	Prem	A	Hibernian	1	1		Forster	Fisher	Kayal+	Ambrose	Mulgrew	Commons*	Brown	Pukki"	Van Dijk	Stokes	Samaras	Forrest*	Ledley+	Balde"	Biton	Rogic	Henderson	Zaluska
22/10/2013	ECL	H	Ajax Amsterdam	2	1		Forster	Lustig+	Izaguirre	Ambrose	Mulgrew	Kayal*	Forrest	Pukki"	Van Dijk	Stokes	Samaras	Ledley*	Biton+	Balde"	Atajic	Rogic	Fisher	Zaluska
27/10/2013	Prem	A	Partick Thistle	2	1		Forster	Lustig	Izaguirre"	Ambrose	Ledley	Kayal *	Brown	Pukki+	Van Dijk	Stokes	Samaras	Balde*	McGeouch+	Biton"	Atajic	Rogic	Fisher	Zaluska
02/11/2013	Prem	H	Dundee United	1	1		Forster	Fisher*	Izaguiire	Ambrose	Mulgrew	Ledley"	Brown	Forrest	Van Dijk	Stokes	Balde+	Lustig*	Pukki+	Boerrigter"	Biton	Rogic	Kayal	Zaluska
06/11/2013	ECL	A	Ajax Amsterdam	0	1		Forster	Lustig	Izaguirre	Ambrose	Mulgrew	Kayal+	Commons"	Forrest	Van Dijk	Stokes*	Samaras	Boerrigter*	Ledley+	Pukki"	Balde	Rogic	Fisher	Zaluska
09/11/2013	Prem	A	Ross County	4	1		Forster	Fisher	Izaguiire	Ambrose	Mulgrew	Ledley"	Brown	Forrest*	Van Dijk	Biton+	Pukki+	Stokes*	Rogic+	Boerrigter"	Commons	McGeouch	Balde	Zaluska
23/11/2013	Prem	H	Aberdeen	3	1		Forster	Fisher+	Izaguirre	Ambrose	Mulgrew	Ledley"	Brown	Commons	Van Dijk	Samaras	Pukki*	Boerrigter*	Lustig+	Balde"	Biton	Rogic	Kayal	Zaluska
26/11/2013	ECL	H	AC Milan	0	3		Forster	Lustig	Izaguirre	Ambrose	Mulgrew	Kayal*	Forrest"	Commons+	Van Dijk	Samaras	Boerrigter	Ledley*	Stokes+	Rogic"	Balde	Pukki	Fisher	Zaluska
01/12/2013	SC4	A	Hearts	7	0		Forster	Lustig+	Izaguirre	Ambrose	Mulgrew*	Ledley	Brown	Commons"	Van Dijk	Stokes	Biton	Pukki*	Fisher+	Boerrigter"	Balde	Samaras	Rogic	Zaluska
06/12/2013	Prem	A	Motherwell	5	0		Forster	Lustig	Izaguirre	Ambrose	Mulgrew	Ledley	Brown"	Commons*	Van Dijk	Stokes	Pukki+	Atajic*	Boerrigter+	Henderson"	Balde	Johnston	Fisher	Zaluska
10/12/2013	ECL	A	Barcelona	1	6		Forster	Lustig	Matthews"	Ambrose	Boerrigter	Ledley	Brown	Biton+	Van Dijk	Samaras	Pukki*	Mulgrew*	Commons+	Stokes"	Balde	Atajic	Fisher	Zaluska
14/12/2013	Prem	H	Hibernian	1	0		Forster	Lustig+	Izaguirre	Ambrose	Biton	Ledley	Brown	Commons	Van Dijk	Stokes	Pukki*	Samaras*	Matthews+	Henderson	Balde	Atajic	Fisher	Zaluska
21/12/2013	Prem	H	Hearts	2	0		Forster	Fisher	Izaguirre	Ambrose	Biton*	Ledley	Brown	Commons	Van Dijk	Stokes	Pukki+	Forrest*	Samaras+	Henderson	Balde	Atajic	O'Connell	Zaluska
26/12/2013	Prem	A	St Johnstone	1	0		Forster	Fisher	Izaguirre	Ambrose	Matthews*	Ledley	Brown	Commons"	Van Dijk	Stokes	Samaras+	Forrest*	Biton+	Balde"	Atajic	Pukki	Henderson	Zaluska
29/12/2013	Prem	A	Inverness CT	1	0		Forster	Forrest*	Izaguirre	Ambrose	Matthews	Ledley	Brown	Commons	Van Dijk	Stokes+	Samaras	Pukki*	Biton+	Balde	Atajic	Rogic	O'Connell	Zaluska
01/01/2014	Prem	H	Partick Thistle	1	0		Forster	Mulgrew*	Izaguirre	Ambrose	Matthews	Ledley	Brown	Commons"	Van Dijk	Pukki+	Forrest	Stokes*	Samaras+	Biton"	Balde	Fisher	Boerrigter	Zaluska
05/01/2014	Prem	A	St Mirren	4	0		Forster	Mulgrew*	Izaguirre	Ambrose	Matthews	Ledley	Brown+	Commons	Van Dijk	Stokes	Forrest"	Boerrigter*	Biton+	Balde"	Rogic	Pukki	Fisher	Zaluska
18/01/2014	Prem	H	Motherwell	3	0		Forster	Fisher	Izaguirre+	Ambrose	Mulgrew	Ledley	Brown	Commons*	Van Dijk	Stokes	Forrest	Pukki*	Balde+	Biton	Atajic	Henderson	O'Connell	Zaluska
26/01/2014	Prem	A	Hibernian	4	0		Forster	Fisher	Izaguirre	Ambrose	Mulgrew"	Ledley	Brown	Commons	Van Dijk	Samaras+	Biton*	Pukki*	Balde+	Johansen"	Boerrigter	Henderson	O'Connell	Zaluska
29/01/2014	Prem	H	Kilmarnock	4	0		Forster	Fisher	Izaguirre	Ambrose	Mulgrew"	Ledley	Brown	Commons	Van Dijk	Pukki*	Forrest+	Balde*	Boerrigter+	Johansen"	Biton	Samaras	O'Connell	Zaluska
02/02/2014	Prem	H	St Mirren	1	0		Forster	Fisher	Izaguirre	Ambrose	Mulgrew	Johansen	Brown	Commons+	Van Dijk	Stokes	Forrest*	Boerrigter*	Balde+	Biton	Samaras	Pukki	O'Connell	Zaluska
08/02/2014	SC5	H	Aberdeen	1	2		Forster	Matthews	Izaguiire	Ambrose	Commons"	Johansen	Brown	Samaras*	Van Dijk	Stokes+	Forrest	Griffiths*	Balde+	Boerrigter"	Biton	Pukki	Fisher	Zaluska
16/02/2014	Prem	H	St Johnstone	3	0		Forster	Matthews	Izaguirre*	Ambrose	Commons	Johansen	Brown+	Biton	Van Dijk	Stokes"	Griffiths	Fisher*	Boerrigter+	Pukki"	Samaras	Balde	O'Connell	Zaluska
22/02/2014	Prem	A	Hearts	2	0		Forster	Mattews	Mulgrew	Ambrose	Commons	Johansen+	Brown	Biton	Van Dijk	Stokes"	Griffiths*	Pukki*	Boerrigter+	Balde"	Samaras	Herron	Fisher	Zaluska
25/02/2014	Prem	A	Aberdeen	1	2		Forster	Matthews	Izaguirre"	Ambrose	Commons*	Mulgrew	Brown	Biton	Van Dijk	Stokes	Griffiths+	Forrest*	Samaras+	Balde"	Boerrigter	Pukki	Fisher	Zaluska
01/03/2014	Prem	H	Inverness CT	5	0		Forster	Matthews+	Izaguirre	Ambrose	Forrest	Mulgrew	Brown"	Biton	Van Dijk	Stokes*	Griffiths	Commons*	Fisher+	Johansen"	Samaras	Boerrigter	Kayal	Zaluska
14/03/2014	Prem	A	Kilmarnock	3	0		Forster	Matthews	Izaguirre	Ambrose	Commons	Mulgrew	Brown	Johansen"	Henderson+	Stokes	Griffiths*	Pukki*	Kayal+	Boerrigter"	Samaras	Balde	O'Connell	Zaluska
22/03/2014	Prem	H	St Mirren	3	0		Forster	Matthews	Izaguirre	Van Dijk	Commons+	Mulgrew	Brown	Johansen	Henderson*	Stokes	Griffiths"	Ambrose*	Pukki+	Samaras"	Twardzik	Fridjonson	Kayal	Zaluska
26/03/2014	Prem	A	Partick Thistle	5	1		Forster	Matthews*	Izaguirre	Ambrose	Commons	Mulgrew+	Brown	Johansen	Van Dijk	Stokes	Griffiths"	Henserson*	Kayal+	Samaras"	Balde	Pukki	O'Connell	Zaluska
29/03/2014	Prem	H	Ross County	1	1		Forster	Van Dijk	Izaguirre	Ambrose	Commons*	O'Connell+	Brown	Johansen	Henderson	Stokes	Griffiths"	Samaras*	Kayal+	Pukki"	Balde	Fraser	Herrpn	Zaluska
05/04/2014	Prem	A	Dundee United	2	0		Forster	Van Dijk	Izaguirre	Ambrose	Commons	Kayal	Brown	Johansen"	Henderson*	Stokes	Samaras+	Griffiths*	Balde+	Mouyokulo"	Pukki	Herron	O'Connell	Zaluska
19/04/2014	Prem	A	Motherwell	3	3		Forster	Van Dijk	Izaguirre	Ambrose	Herron+	Kayal*	Brown	Johansen	Commons	Stokes	Samaras	Griffiths*	Balde+	Pukki	O'Connell	Henderson	Fridjonsson	Zaluska
27/04/2014	Prem	H	Inverness CT	6	0		Forster	Van Dijk	Izaguirre	Ambrose	Matthews*	Mulgrew"	Brown	Johansen	Commons	Stokes+	Griffiths	Lustig*	Pukki+	Henderson"	Samaras	Balde	Kayal	Zaluska
03/05/2014	Prem	H	Aberdeen	5	2		Forster	Van Dijk	Izaguirre	Ambrose	Matthews	Mulgrew	Brown	Johansen*	Commons"	Stokes	Griffiths+	Kayal*	Lustig+	Henderson"	Boerrigter	Balde	Pukki	Zaluska
07/05/2014	Prem	A	St Johnstone	3	3		Zaluska	Van Dijk	Lustig	Ambrose	Matthews*	Mulgrew	Kayal	Johansen	Balde"	Boerrigter+	Pukki	Brown*	Commons+	Stokes"	Griffiths	Henderson	Mouyokolo	Forster
11/05/2014	Prem	H	Dundee United	3	1		Forster	Van Dijk	Lustig+	Ambrose	Twardzik"	Mulgrew	Brown	Johansen	Commons	Stokes	Griffiths*	Samaras*	Kayal+	Pukki"	Boerrigter	Henderson	Mouyokolo	Zaluska

Clyde FC

CLYDE	
Founded	1877
Ground	Broadwood Stadium
Postcode	G69 9NE
Capacity	7936
Tel	01236 451511
Closest Railway Station	Croy
Record Attendance	52000 v Rangers, 21/1/1908
Record Win	11-1 v Cowdenbeath, 6/10/1951
Record Defeat	0-11, v Dumbarton, SC 22/11/1879, v Rangers SC, 13/11/1880
Most League Goals in a Season	32 Billy Boyd, 1932/3
Most Goals in Career	124 Tommy Ring
Chairman	John Alexander
Secretary	Gordon Thomson
Manager	Jim Duffy (until May) / Barry Ferguson
Assistant Manager	Chic Charnley (until May) / Bob Malcolm
Colours 2013/14 Top	White
Shorts	Black
Sponsor	O'Neill Interiors
Manufacturer	Joma
Change Colours 2013/14 Top	Red
Shorts	White
3rd Colours 2013/14 Top	Black with White Band
Shorts	Black
Nicknames	Bully Wee
Web	www.clydefc.co.uk

Under Jim Duffy's management Clyde enjoyed a good season, qualifying for the promotion play offs. Duffy departed for the Manager's office at Morton. His replacement, Barry Ferguson, came as a bit of a surprise.

Clyde will be hoping that this works out in the way Paul Hartley did at Alloa. Ferguson is a young manager, keen to learn his trade, and obviously with ambitions way beyond the Broadwood side. He has a stage on which to demonstrate his potential.

Ferguson's intention is to be a player-manager. His class should shine through at League Two level.

Off the field there is still no real clarity about Clyde's long-term future in Cumbernauld. A potential move to East Kilbride seems to have stalled for the moment but it could be back on the agenda soon.

PREDICTION 2014/15
Potential league winners

Surname	First Name	DOB	Pos	L A	L S	L G	SC A	SC S	SC G	LC A	LC S	LC G	RC A	RC S	RC G	UNS	Signed	Previous Club	Notes	Contract
Barclay	Jamie	29/09/89	GK	27			2			1						2	2012	Berwick Rangers		C (2015)
Brown	Gavin	03/06/91	D	13	1		4			1						1	2010	Kilmarnock	Freed, Joined Cumnock	
Campbell	Gary	12/02/95	D													1	2013	Clyde Youth Academy		Youth
Capuano	Giuseppe	08/01/89	M	17	8		3	1								9	2013	Queen's Park		C (2015)
Coyne	Bradley	10/04/93	F		4											1	2014	Stirling Albion		F
Currie	Jack		F		1												2013	Clyde Youth Academy		Youth
Daly	Michael	24/11/85	F	24	8	9	1	2	1	1			1			2	2013	Annan Athletic		C (2015)
Dickie	Grant	05/12/94	F	5												15	2013	Clyde Youth Academy	On loan to Cumnock	F
Ferguson	Scott	28/01/95	F	30	5	10	2	1		1			1			3	2013	Clyde Youth Academy		C (2015)
Fitzharris	Sean	13/10/91	M	1						1						2	2012	Morton	Joined East Kilbride FC	
Frances	Ryan	19/03/92	D	12	5		2	2		1			1			23	2013	Vale of Clyde		C (2015)
George	Sam	06/03/95	GK													1	2013	Clyde Youth Academy		Youth
Gray	Iain	03/05/91	D	24	3		3	1								1	2010	St Mirren		C (2015)
Janczyk	Neil	07/04/83	M	12	2											1	2014	Berwick Rangers	Joined Penicuik Athletic June 2014	F
Marsh	David	06/04/90	D	31	1		2			1			1			3	2012	Cumbernauld United		C (2015)
McBeth	Ryan	29/04/91	M	3	3		1			1						16	2012	Partick Thistle		F
McCluskey	Stefan	22/08/90	F	28	4	11	3	1	1	1			1			1	2012	Shotts Bon Accord		F
McColm	Stuart	07/01/89	M	31	1	3	3	1		1						1	2012	Stranraer		C (2015)
McDonald	Kieran	21/07/93	M	36	4		4			1			1			1	2012	Motherwell	Joined Hamilton Accies June 2014	F
McGachie	Kieran	03/06/92	F	3						1						2	2013	Annan Athletic	On Loan to Bonnyrigg Rose Sep 2013	F
McGhee	Fraser	23/03/95	D	10	3											12	2013	Clyde Youth Academy		C (2015)
McGovern	Joe	02/03/94	GK	3													2014	Dundee United (Loan)	Returned to Dundee United	
McKinnon	Ross	09/10/92	D	6	3		1									6	2014	Elgin City (Loan)	Permanent from end of season	C (2015)
McQueen	Brian	01/01/91	D	33			2	2								4	2011	Hamilton Accies		C (2015)
Monaghan	Harry	24/03/93	M	3													2013	Annan Athletic	Joined Vikingur Reykjavik Apr 2014	
Orrick	Paul	25/09/95	M		2											1	2013	Clyde Youth Academy		Youth
Rajovic	Nic	21/02/93	GK	8			2									23	2012	Kilmarnock		C (2015)
Robertson	Michael		GK													1			Trialist, ex Celtic	
Scullion	Pat	02/03/86	F	20	10	1	3			1			1			9	2011	Stenhousemuir		C (2015)
Shaw	Chris		GK													13	2013	Clyde Youth Academy		Youth
Sweeney	John	16/04/87	M	38			4	4		1						1	2010	Pollok		C (2015)
Trialist																2				
Watt	Kevin	01/10/89	F	7	12	2	2	2	3	1			1			5	2012	Bo'ness United		C (2015)
Young	Gordon		M	2	3	1										15	2013	Clyde Youth Academy		C (2015)
Own Goal						1														

Date	Comp	H/A	Opponents	F	A		Crowd	Scorers
27/07/2013	RC1	H	Falkirk	1	2		935	McCluskey
03/08/2013	LC1	A	Falkirk	0	3	at Alloa	1154	
10/08/2013	L	H	Berwick Rangers	1	0		469	Daly
17/08/2013	L	A	Albion Rovers	0	3		528	
24/08/2013	L	H	Queen's Park	3	0		621	McDonald, Ferguson, Brough og
31/08/2013	L	A	Elgin City	0	1		544	
14/09/2013	L	H	East Stirlingshire	1	2		497	Sweeney
21/09/2013	L	A	Annan Athletic	2	1		483	Frances, Sweeney
28/09/2013	L	H	Montrose	0	3		464	
05/10/2013	SC2	A	Gala Fairydean Rovers	3	0		705	Watt, Daly, McColm
12/10/2013	L	A	Peterhead	1	1		562	McDonald
19/10/2013	L	A	Berwick Rangers	1	0		472	Frances
26/10/2013	L	H	Stirling Albion	2	1		676	Marsh, Ferguson
02/11/2013	SC3	H	Brora Rangers	2	1		686	McCluskey, Watt
09/11/2013	L	A	Queen's Park	1	1		704	McColm
16/11/2013	L	H	Elgin City	2	1		533	McCluskey, Scullion
23/11/2013	L	A	East Stirlingshire	1	0		452	McCluskey
30/11/2013	SC4	H	Stranraer	1	1		681	McDonald
03/12/2013	L	H	Annan Athletic	2	1		422	McColm 2
07/12/2013	L	H	Peterhead	1	3		498	Ferguson
10/12/2013	SC4R	A	Stranraer	1	4		454	Watt
14/12/2013	L	A	Montrose	2	0		410	Watt, Ferguson
21/12/2013	L	H	Albion Rovers	2	2		508	Daly, Ferguson
28/12/2013	L	A	Stirling Albion	1	1		859	Sweeney
04/01/2014	L	H	Queen's Park	1	2		751	McCluskey
11/01/2014	L	A	Elgin City	1	3		585	Ferguson
18/01/2014	L	A	Annan Athletic	1	0		456	McCluskey
25/01/2014	L	H	East Stirlingshire	1	0		473	McDonald
01/02/2014	L	H	Berwick Rangers	3	3		467	Daly, Ferguson, McQueen
15/02/2014	L	A	Peterhead	0	2		511	
22/02/2014	L	H	Montrose	1	1		418	McCluskey
25/02/2014	L	A	Albion Rovers	0	1		423	
01/03/2014	L	H	Elgin City	4	0		504	Daly 2, Ferguson, Young
08/03/2014	L	A	Queen's Park	3	1		608	McQueen, McCluskey, Daly
15/03/2014	L	H	Stirling Albion	1	0		673	McCluskey
22/03/2014	L	A	Berwick Rangers	0	3		519	
29/03/2014	L	A	East Stirlingshire	4	2		449	McDonald, McCluskey 2, Daly
05/04/2014	L	H	Annan Athletic	0	3		516	
12/04/2014	L	H	Peterhead	0	2		534	
19/04/2014	L	A	Montrose	2	0		422	Daly, McCluskey
26/04/2014	L	H	Albion Rovers	4	0		620	McCluskey, Daly, Sweeney, Watt
03/05/2014	L	A	Stirling Albion	1	4		1028	McKinnon
07/05/2014	PO	H	East Fife	1	0		1005	Ferguson
10/05/2014	PO	A	East Fife	1	2	AET, 6-7 p	1018	Ferguson

Friendly Matches

Date		H/A	Opponents	F	A	Scorers
2/7/13	Fr	A	Stenhousemuir	2	2	
10/7/13	Fr	H	Queen of the South	2	5	
13/7/13	Fr	H	Keith			
16/7/13	Fr	H	Dundee	0	5	
20/7/13	Fr	H	Celtic Nation	2	2	
23/7/13	Fr	A	East Kilbride	1	2	U19
27/7/13	Fr	A	Ashfield	1	2	U19
27/8/13	Fr	A	East Kilbride Thistle	3	1	U19

Date	Comp	H/A	Opponents	F	A	1	2	3	4	5	6	7	8	9	10	11	12	13	14	15	16	17	18
27/07/2013	RC1	H	Falkirk	1	2	Barclay	Scullion*	McDonald	Gray	Marsh	Frances	McBeth	Sweeney	Daly	McCluskey+	McColm	Ferguson*	Watt+	McGachie"	Rajovic	George		
03/08/2013	LC1	A	Falkirk	0	3	Rajovic	Brown	Marsh+	Gray	Watt"	Frances	McBeth	Sweeney	Daly	McDonald	McColm*	McCluskey*	Ferguson+	McGachie"	Scullion	George		at Alloa
10/08/2013	L	H	Berwick Rangers	1	0	Barclay	Brown*	Marsh"	Scullion"	McCluskey"	Frances	McBeth	Sweeney	Daly	MacDonald+	McColm	Watt*	Orrick+	McGachie"	Dickie	Ferguson	Watt	
17/08/2013	L	A	Albion Rovers	0	3	Barclay	Brown*	McQueen	Scullion"	Monaghan+	Frances	McBeth	Sweeney	Daly	MacDonald	McColm	Watt*	Ferguson+	Orrick"	Dickie	McGachie	Rajovic	
24/08/2013	L	H	Queen's Park	3	0	Barclay	Monaghan*	McQueen	Gray	Ferguson*	Frances	Watt+	Sweeney	Daly"	McDonald	McColm	Watt*	McBeth+	McGachie"	Scullion	Rajovic	Rajovic	
31/08/2013	L	A	Elgin City	0	1	Barclay	Brown	McQueen	Gray	Ferguson	Frances*	Watt+	Sweeney	Daly+	McDonald	McColm	McGachie*	Dickie+	Scullion"	Brown	McBeth	Rajovic	
14/09/2013	L	H	East Stirlingshire	1	2	Barclay	Brown"	McQueen	Gray	Ferguson	Frances*	McBeth+	Sweeney	Daly"	McDonald	McColm	McCluskey*	Scullion+	Watt"	Dickie	Rajovic	Orrick	Capuano
21/09/2013	L	A	Annan Athletic	2	1	Barclay	Brown"	McQueen	Capuano	Ferguson*	Frances	McCluskey+	Sweeney	Daly	McDonald	McColm	Gray*	Scullion+	Dickie"	Marsh	Rajovic	Watt	McBeth
28/09/2013	L	H	Montrose	0	3	Barclay	Watt*	Brown"	Capuano	Ferguson+	Frances	McCluskey+	Sweeney	Daly	McDonald	McColm	Daly*	Dickie+	McBeth"	Marsh	Rajovic	Scullion	McBeth
05/10/2013	SC2	H	Gala Fairydean Rovers	3	0	Barclay	Brown	McQueen	Scullion+	Ferguson"	Marsh	Watt*	Sweeney	Gray"	McDonald	McColm	McCluskey*	Daly+	Fitzharris"	Frances	Rajovic	Dickie	Fitzharris
12/10/2013	L	A	Peterhead	1	1	Barclay	Brown	Brown	Capuano+	Frances	Marsh	Watt+	Sweeney	Gray"	McDonald	McColm"	McCluskey*	Ferguson+	Scullion"	Dickie	Rajovic	Dickie	
19/10/2013	L	H	Berwick Rangers	1	0	Barclay	Brown	Scullion	Capuano	Frances*	Marsh	McCluskey	Sweeney	Gray	McDonald	McColm"	McQueen*	Daly+	McCluskey"	Dickie	Rajovic	Ferguson	McBeth
26/10/2013	L	A	Stirling Albion	2	1	Barclay	Brown	Scullion+	Capuano	Ferguson*	Marsh	McCluskey	Sweeney	McQueen	McDonald	McColm"	Watt*	Fitzharris+	Watt	Frances	Rajovic	Frances	McBeth
02/11/2013	SC3	H	Brora Rangers	2	1	Barclay	Brown	Scullion"	Gray	Ferguson	Marsh	McCluskey	Sweeney	McQueen	McDonald	McColm*	Daly*	Dickie+	Daley	Frances	McGhee	Frances	McBeth
09/11/2013	L	A	Queen's Park	1	1	Rajovic	Gray	Scullion"	Capuano	Ferguson	Marsh	McCluskey	Sweeney	McQueen	McDonald	McColm"	Daly*	Dickie+	McBeth	Frances	Rajovic	McGhee	McBeth
16/11/2013	L	H	Elgin City	2	1	Rajovic	Gray	Scullion	Capuano	Ferguson	Marsh	McCluskey+	Sweeney	McQueen	McDonald"	Brown*	Watt*	McGhee+	Frances"	Robertson	Trialist	Dickie	McGhee
23/11/2013	L	A	East Stirlingshire	1	0	Rajovic	Gray	Scullion+	Ferguson"	McColm	Marsh	McCluskey+	Sweeney	McQueen	McDonald	Brown*	Ferguson*	Watt+	McBeth"	McBeth	Trialist	Dickie	McGhee
30/11/2013	SC4	H	Stranraer	1	1	Rajovic	Gray"	Watt+	McColm	Marsh	McCluskey	Sweeney	McQueen	McDonald"	Brown*	Ferguson*	Watt+	Daley"	Frances	McBeth	McGhee	Shaw	
03/12/2013	L	H	Annan Athletic	2	1	Rajovic	Gray"	Scullion+	Capuano"	McColm*	Marsh	McCluskey	Sweeney	McQueen	McDonald"	Brown	Daly*	Ferguson+	Capuano"	McBeth	Frances	McGhee	Shaw
07/12/2013	L	A	Peterhead	1	3	Rajovic	Gray*	Scullion+	Capuano"	McColm"	Marsh	McCluskey	Sweeney	McQueen	McDonald"	Brown	Watt*	Daly+	Brown"	Marsh	Frances	Dickie	Shaw
10/12/2013	SC4R	A	Stranraer	1	4	Rajovic	Gray	Brown	Frances	McColm*	Daly	McCluskey*	Sweeney+	McQueen	McDonald	Watt	Ferguson*	Scullion+	McBeth"	Marsh	Dickie		
14/12/2013	L	A	Montrose	2	0	Rajovic	Gray	Scullion	Scullion	McColm+	Marsh*	Ferguson	Sweeney	Gray"	McDonald	Watt	Capuano"	Daly	Frances"	Shaw	Dickie		
21/12/2013	L	H	Albion Rovers	2	2	Rajovic	Gray	Brown	McColm+	Marsh*	Ferguson	Sweeney	McQueen	McDonald	Watt	McCluskey*	Daly+	Frances"	McGhee	Dickie	Capuano		
28/12/2013	L	A	Stirling Albion	1	1	Rajovic	Gray*	Daly"	McColm	McColm	Marsh*	Ferguson	Sweeney	McQueen	McDonald	McCluskey	Scullion*	Watt	Frances	Shaw	Dickie	McGhee	Young
04/01/2014	L	H	Queen's Park	1	2	McGovern	Gray*	Capuano	Scullion+	McColm	Marsh"	Ferguson	Sweeney	McQueen	McDonald	McCluskey	McGhee*	Frances	Shaw	Dickie	Young		
11/01/2014	L	A	Elgin City	1	3	McGovern	Gray*	Capuano	Daly	McColm	Marsh	Ferguson+	Sweeney	McQueen	McDonald	McCluskey	Coyne+	Campbell	Young				
18/01/2014	L	H	Annan Athletic	1	0	Barclay	Gray	Capuano	Daly"	McColm	Marsh*	Ferguson+	Sweeney	McQueen	McDonald	McCluskey	Coyne*	Janczyk+	Coyne"	Scullion	Barclay	McGhee	
25/01/2014	L	A	East Stirlingshire	1	0	Barclay	Gray*	Janczyk	Daly*	McColm	Marsh	Ferguson+	Sweeney	McQueen	McDonald	McCluskey	Frances*	Scullion+	Capuano	Young	McGhee	Shaw	
01/02/2014	L	H	Berwick Rangers	3	3	Barclay	Gray*	Janczyk+	Scullion+	McColm	Marsh	Ferguson	McKinnon*	Sweeney	McDonald	Capuano"	Currie*	Scullion"	Coyne	Young	Capuano	Shaw	
15/02/2014	L	A	Peterhead	0	2	Barclay	Gray*	Janczyk	Scullion+	McColm	Marsh	McCluskey	Sweeney	McQueen	McDonald	Daly	McCluskey*	McGhee+	Young	Frances	Shaw	Capuano	
22/02/2014	L	H	Montrose	1	1	Barclay	Gray	Janczyk*	Ferguson	McColm"	Marsh	McCluskey	Sweeney	McQueen	McDonald	Daly	Capuano*	Watt+	Frances	McKinnon	Young	McGhee	Young
25/02/2014	L	A	Albion Rovers	0	1	Barclay	Gray	Janczyk"	Ferguson+	McColm	Marsh+	McCluskey	Sweeney	McQueen	McDonald	Daly	Coyne*	Scullion+	Scullion	Young	Shaw	McGhee	McKinnon
01/03/2014	L	H	Elgin City	3	1	Barclay	McGhee	Janczyk	Ferguson*	McColm	Marsh	McCluskey	Sweeney	McQueen	McDonald	Daly+	Young"	Frances	Scullion	McKinnon	Young	Capuano	
08/03/2014	L	A	Queen's Park	4	0	Barclay	McGhee	Janczyk	Ferguson"	McColm+	Marsh	McCluskey	Sweeney	McQueen	McDonald	Daly+	McKinnon	Frances	Shaw	Young	Capuano	Shaw	
15/03/2014	L	H	Stirling Albion	1	0	Barclay	McGhee	Janczyk	Ferguson*	McColm	Marsh	McCluskey	Sweeney	McQueen	McDonald	Daly	Scullion*	Scullion+	Gray"	Shaw	Young	Capuano	Young
22/03/2014	L	A	Berwick Rangers	0	3	Barclay	Gray	Janczyk*	Ferguson+	McColm	Marsh	McCluskey"	Sweeney	McQueen	McDonald	Scullion	McKinnon+	McKinnon"	McBeth"	McGhee	Shaw	Capuano	Young
29/03/2014	L	H	East Stirlingshire	4	2	Barclay	Gray	Frances	Ferguson*	McColm+	Marsh	McCluskey	Sweeney	Frances	McDonald	Daly	Capuano*	Young*	Young	McGhee	Rajovic	Frances	Scullion
05/04/2014	L	A	Annan Athletic	0	3	Barclay	McCueen	McCueen	Ferguson	McColm	Marsh	McCluskey	Sweeney	Daly	McDonald	McQueen	Coyne*	Capuano"	McKinnon	McGhee	McBeth	McBeth	Young
12/04/2014	L	H	Peterhead	0	2	Barclay	McCueen	McGhee	Ferguson*	McColm	Marsh	McCluskey*	Sweeney	Scullion"	McDonald	McGhee	Young"	Capuano*	Capuano"	McKinnon	Rajovic	McBeth	Young
19/04/2014	L	A	Montrose	2	0	Barclay	McCueen	McKinnon	Ferguson"	McColm	Marsh	McCluskey	Sweeney	Scullion	Daly	McGhee	Capuano*	Janczyk"	McKinnon	Rajovic	McBeth	Watt	McBeth
26/04/2014	L	H	Albion Rovers	4	0	Rajovic	McCueen	McKinnon	Frances	McColm	Marsh	McCluskey"	Sweeney"	Scullion	Daly"	McGhee	Watt*	Janczyk*	McBeth"	Barclay	Rajovic	Capuano	McBeth
03/05/2014	L	A	Stirling Albion	1	4	Rajovic	McCueen	McKinnon	Frances	Marsh	McCluskey	Sweeney"	Scullion	Daly*	McGhee	Watt*	Ferguson+	McBeth"	McBeth	Watt	Rajovic	McBeth	
07/05/2014	PO	H	East Fife	1	0	Barclay	McCueen	McKinnon	Scullion+	Marsh	McDonald	Sweeney"	Scullion	Daly	McGhee	Frances	Scullion	McBeth	Young	Rajovic		
10/05/2014	PO	A	East Fife	1	2	Barclay	McCueen	McKinnon"	Ferguson	Marsh	Capuano	McDonald+	Sweeney	McCluskey	McDonald	McGhee	Capuano+	Capuano"	McBeth	Young	Rajovic	Frances	

Cowdenbeath FC

Founded	1882
Ground	Central Park
Postcode	KY4 9QQ
Tel	01383 610166
Capacity	4309
Closest Railway Station	Cowdenbeath
Record Attendance	25586 v Rangers, LC, 21/9/49
Record Win	12-0 v Johnstone, SC, 21/1/1928
Record Defeat	1-11, v Clyde, Lge, 6/10/51
Most League Goals in a Season	54, Rab Walls, 1938/9
Most Goals in Career	127 Willie Devlin
Chairman	Donald Findlay QC
Chief Executive	Alex Anderson
Secretary	Alex Anderson
Manager	Colin Cameron / Jimmy Nichol
Assistant Manager	Lee Makel
Colours 2013/14 Top	Blue
Shorts	White
Sponsor	Subsea
Manufacturer	Uhlsport
Change Colours 2013/14 Top	Red
Shorts	Blue
3rd Kit 2013/14 Top	Yellow
Shorts	Blue
Nicknames	Blue Brasil, Miners

Seldom have matches meant so much to a club as the end-of-season play offs did to Cowdenbeath. Victory over Ayr and Dunfermline ensured they retained their place in a Championship which will now include Hearts, Hibs and Rangers. Financially this was a huge boost for Cowdenbeath.

They did very well to come back from a crushing blow on the last day of the regular season. Six minutes into injury time against QOS they seemed to be safe from the play offs before they conceded a goal.

Manaher Jimmy Nichol has some re-building to do, particularly with the departure of both main strikers, Greg Stewart and Kane Hemmings. However, he will relish the challenge of once again keeping the Blue Brasil at a level that is really beyond all expectations.

PREDICTION 2014/15
Relegation struggle—bottom three placing.

				L			SC			LC			RC							
Surname	First Name	DOB	Pos	A	S	G	A	S	G	A	S	G	A	S	G	UNS	Signed	Previous Club	Notes	Contract
Adam	Grant	16/04/91	GK	11						2						8	2013	St Mirren	Freed Jan 2014, joined Airdrieonians	
Adamson	Kenny	21/08/88	D	24	2	1	1			2	1	1				9	2007	Livingston		C (2015)
Anthony	Ben	20/02/95	F	3												4	2012	Alloa		Youth
Armstrong	John	25/06/87	D	40	4	1				2		1				2	2005	Hearts		C (2015)
Brett	Dean	08/12/92	M	35	1					2		1				5	2008	Cowdenbeath Youths		C (2016)
Brownlie	Darren	10/04/94	D	15												1	2014	Partick Thistle (Loan)	Returned to Partick, then signed Jun 2014	C (2015)
Callaghan	Liam	10/10/94	M							1						8	2011	Cowdenbeath Youths		OOC
Cameron	Colin	23/10/72	M							1						1	2010	Dundee	Player Manager, left Nov 13, joined Berwick	
Cowan	David	05/03/82	D	7			1			1		1				9	2011	Livingston	Freed Jan 2014, joined East Fife	
Dunn	Liam	02/05/97	M							1						2	2013	Leith Athletic		Youth
Finnie	Dale	14/09/94	D													2	2011	Livingston		OOC
Flynn	Thomas	23/11/90	GK	24	1		1					1				17	2011	Hibernian		OOC
Fowler	James	26/10/80	D	10													2014	Kilmarnock (Loan)	Returned to Kilmarnock	
Gold	David	01/01/93	M	3	3											14	2013	Hibernian (Loan)	Returned to Hibernian	
Hemmings	Kane	08/04/92	F	34	1	19	1			1	1	4	1			1	2013	Rangers	Joined Barnsley, June 2014	OOC
Hunter	Shaun	12/03/96	GK													1	2013	Kelty Hearts Colts		Youth
Johnston	Craig	22/12/94	F	1												1	2011	East Fife		
Kane	Chris	31/05/93	M	7	25											6	2014	Dunfermline Athletic		C (2015)
Lynas	Aron	19/04/96	M													4	2012	Inverkeithing United		Youth
McKenzie	Marc	11/07/85	F	9	6		1			2	1					2	2010	East Stirlingshire	Joined Albion Rovers May 2014	F
McKeown	Rory	08/04/93	M	16	2												2014	Kilmarnock (Loan)	Returned to Kilmarnock	
Miller	Kyle	08/08/92	M	14	11	3	1			1	1	1	1			14	2010	Cowdenbeath Youths		OOC
Milne	Lewis	26/04/94	M	29	3	2	1			1		1				6	2010	Cowdenbeath Youths		C (2016)
Morton	Jordan	25/04/92	M	6	17	3	1			1	1	1				15	2013	Livingston		OOC
Nicholson	Jack	06/10/93	F													2	2012	Cowdenbeath Youths		OOC
O'Brien	Thomas	07/08/91	M	25	2	4	1			1		1				9	2007	Cowdenbeath Youths		C (2015)
Pyper	Jamie	22/08/93	M													8	2009	Hutchison Vale		F
Ramsay	Mark	24/01/86	M													1	2007	Dundonald Bluebell	Retired August 2013	
Robertson	Jon	25/04/89	M	29	5	1				1						1	2013	St Mirren		OOC
Russell	Andrew	30/03/93	F	4	8		1			2		1				7	2013	Livingston	Freed Mar 2014, joined Berwick Rangers	
Speedie	Callum	16/02/96	GK													2				Youth
Stevenson	Jamie	13/07/84	M	21	8	2	1	1		1						7	2012	Airdrie United	Joined Peterhead, June 2014	OOC
Stewart	Sammy	01/03/91	M	4	2	1				1						1	2014	Ambassadors		OOC
Stewart	Greg	17/03/90	F	31	6	16	1			1		1				1	2010	Syngenta Juveniles	Signed pre-contract with Dundee Jan 2014	
Usai	Sebastian	28/02/90	GK	5												13	2014	AFC United		F
Wedderburn	Nathaniel	30/06/91	D	37	1	1	1			1			1	1	1	1	2013	Corby Town		OOC
Wight	Craig	24/01/78	GK													2		Goalkeeping Coach		OOC

NEW SIGNINGS 2014/15

Brownlie	Darren	D		2014	Partick Thistle
Campbell	Ian	D		2014	Forfar Athletic

Date	Comp	H/A	Opponents	F	A		Crowd	Scorers
27/07/13	RC1	H	Dunfermline Athletic	1	3		1161	Wedderburn
03/08/13	LC1	A	Berwick Rangers	5	0		465	Hemmings 3, Miller, Adamson
10/08/13	L	A	Morton	0	2		1817	
17/08/13	L	H	Raith Rovers	3	4		837	Morton, Adamson, Stewart
24/08/11	L	A	Alloa	1	3		611	Hemmings
27/08/13	LC2	A	Partick Thistle	1	3	AET	1544	Hemmings
31/08/13	L	H	Dumbarton	3	2		384	Stevenson, Robertson, Hemmings
14/09/13	L	H	Falkirk	1	0		644	Stewart
21/09/13	L	A	Hamilton Accies	0	1		817	
28/09/13	L	A	Livingston	1	5		894	Hemmings
05/10/13	L	H	Dundee	0	2		1013	
12/10/13	L	A	Queen of the South	1	1		1514	Stewart
19/10/13	L	H	Morton	5	1		543	Hemmings 3, Morton, Stewart
26/10/13	L	A	Dumbarton	0	0		700	
02/11/13	SC3	A	Dumbarton	1	2		450	Stevenson
09/11/13	L	H	Alloa	0	2		346	
16/11/13	L	H	Hamilton Accies	2	4		401	Wedderburn, Milne
23/11/13	L	A	Falkirk	0	4		2550	
07/12/13	L	H	Livingston	2	3		363	Hemmings 2
14/12/13	L	A	Dundee	2	1		3533	Hemmings, Morton
21/12/13	L	A	Raith Rovers	3	3		1597	Stewart, Hemmings 2
28/12/13	L	H	Queen of the South	0	2		556	
02/01/14	L	A	Alloa	1	0		818	Hemmings
11/01/14	L	H	Dumbarton	2	4		434	Miller, Stevenson
18/01/14	L	H	Falkirk	0	2		566	
25/01/14	L	A	Hamilton Accies	4	3		944	Stewart 2, Hemmings 2
01/02/14	L	H	Raith Rovers	1	0		961	Hemmings
15/02/14	L	A	Morton	1	1		2087	Armstrong
22/02/14	L	H	Dundee	2	0		1419	McKeown, Stewart
01/03/14	L	A	Livingston	0	1		980	
08/03/14	L	H	Alloa	2	2		458	G Stewart 2
15/03/14	L	A	Dumbarton	1	5		687	Armstrong
22/03/14	L	A	Queen of the South	1	2		1619	S Stewart
25/03/14	L	H	Morton	3	0		318	Miller 2, G Stewart
29/03/14	L	H	Hamilton Accies	1	1		497	O'Brien
05/04/14	L	A	Falkirk	0	5		2830	
12/04/14	L	A	Dundee	0	4		4751	
19/04/14	L	H	Livingston	4	0		420	Armstrong 2, Hemmings 2
26/04/14	L	A	Raith Rovers	2	1		1760	McKeown, Milne
03/05/14	L	H	Queen of the South	1	1		1053	Hemmings
07/05/14	PO	A	Ayr United	2	1		1495	G Stewart 2
10/05/14	PO	H	Ayr United	3	1		933	G Stewart 2, O'Brien
14/05/14	PO	H	Dunfermline Athletic	1	1		3379	O'Brien
18/05/14	PO	A	Dunfermline Athletic	3	0		8288	G Stewart, Hemmings, O'Brien

Friendly Matches

Date		Comp	H/A	Opponents	F	A	Crowd	
6/7/13		Fr	H	Sheffield United	1	1	532	
10/7/13		Fr	H	St Johnstone	0	1	382	
13/7/13		Fr	A	East Fife	0	0	417	
20/7/13		Fr	H	Motherwell XI	0	5		
27/7/13		Fr	A	Hill of Beath Hawthorn	1	3	U19	
30/7/13		Fr	A	Kelty Hearts	4	1		at Loch Leven CC
4/8/13		Fr	A	Edinburgh City U19			U19	
28/11/13		FCP	A	East Fife	2	1	227	

Date	Comp	H/A	Opponents	F	A	1	2	3	4	5	6	7	8	9	10	11	12	13	14	15	16	17	18
27/07/13	RC1	H	Dunfermline Athletic	1	3	Flynn	Cowan+	Adamson	O'Brien	Armstrong	Wedderburn	McKenzie"	Milne	Stewart*	Russell	Morton	Hemmings*	Brett+	Miller"	Speedie	Ramsay		
03/08/13	LC1	A	Berwick Rangers	5	0	Adam	Cowan"	Adamson	Brett	Armstrong	Cameron	McKenzie"	Miller	Hemmings	Russell+	Morton*	Callaghan*	Stewart+	Dunn"	Nicholson	Flynn		
10/08/13	L	A	Morton	0	2	Adam	O'Brien	Adamson	Brett	Armstrong	Wedderburn"	McKenzie	Miller	Hemmings	Russell+	Morton	Stewart*	Stevenson+	Milne"	Dunn	Flynn	Callaghan	
17/08/13	L	H	Raith Rovers	3	4	Adam	Stevenson	Adamson	Brett	Armstrong	Wedderburn*	O'Brien	Miller*	Hemmings	Stewart+	Morton"	Milne*	Stewart+	Flynn"	Speedie	Callaghan		
24/08/11	L	A	Alloa	1	3	Flynn	Stevenson	Adamson	Brett	Armstrong	Wedderburn	O'Brien	McKenzie	Hemmings	Milne+	Morton"	Russell*	Stewart+	Miller"	Cowan	Flynn		
27/08/13	LC2	A	Partick Thistle	1	3	AET Adam	Stevenson	Adamson	Brett	Armstrong	Wedderburn	O'Brien	McKenzie+	Hemmings	Milne	Stewart"	Hemmings*	Morton+	Miller"	Cowan	Flynn	Miller	Miller
31/08/13	L	H	Dumbarton	3	2	Adam	Stevenson*	Adamson	Brett	Armstrong	Wedderburn+	O'Brien	McKenzie	Hemmings	Milne	Robertson	Morton*	Stewart+	Russell	Cowan	Flynn		
14/09/13	L	A	Falkirk	1	0	Adam	Russell*	Adamson	Brett	Armstrong	Wedderburn	O'Brien	McKenzie+	Hemmings	Milne*	Robertson	Morton*	Morton+	Russell	Cowan	Flynn	Miller	
21/09/13	L	A	Hamilton Accies	0	1	Adam	Stevenson	Adamson	Brett	Armstrong	Wedderburn	O'Brien	McKenzie+	Hemmings+	Milne+	Robertson	Stewart*	Morton+	Russell	Cowan	Flynn	Callaghan	Callaghan
28/09/13	L	H	Livingston	1	5	Flynn	Stevenson	Adamson	Cowan	Armstrong	Wedderburn	O'Brien	McKenzie+	Hemmings	Milne*	Robertson	Morton*	Morton+	Russell	Cowan	Flynn	Milne	
05/10/13	L	H	Dundee	0	2	Flynn	Stevenson"	Adamson	Cowan*	Armstrong	Wedderburn	O'Brien	Morton*	Hemmings	Morton*	Robertson	Stewart*	Miller+	McKenzie"	Brett	Adam	Milne	McKenzie
12/10/13	L	A	Queen of the South	1	1	Flynn	Stevenson"	Adamson	Cowan*	Armstrong	Wedderburn	O'Brien	Stewart+	Stewart	Stewart	Robertson	Miller*	McKenzie+	Russell"	Miller	Adam	Milne	Pyper
19/10/13	L	A	Morton	5	1	Flynn	Stevenson	Adamson	Cowan	Armstrong	Wedderburn"	O'Brien	Stewart	Hemmings	Morton	Robertson	Brett*	Russell+	McKenzie+	Brett	Adam	Milne	Lynas
26/10/13	L	H	Dumbarton	0	0	Flynn	Stevenson+	Adamson	Cowan	Armstrong	Wedderburn	O'Brien	Stewart	Hemmings+	Milne	Robertson	McKenzie*	McKenzie+	Russell	Brett	Adam	Pyper	Finnie
02/11/13	SC3	A	Dumbarton	1	2	Adam	Stevenson+	Adamson	Russell*	Armstrong	Wedderburn	Brett	Stewart	Stewart	Milne	Milne	Russell*	McKenzie+	Miller"	O'Brien	O'Brien	Milne	Lynas
09/11/13	L	A	Alloa	0	2	Flynn	Stevenson	Adamson	Cowan	Armstrong	Wedderburn	Brett	Hemmings	Stewart	Milne	Robertson	McKenzie	Miller+	Russell	Brett	Flynn	Morton	Miller
16/11/13	L	H	Hamilton Accies	2	4	Adam	Stevenson+	Adamson	Russell*	Armstrong	Wedderburn	Brett	Hemmings	Hemmings	Milne	Robertson	Russell*	McKenzie+	Cowan	Cowan	Flynn	McKenzie	Lynas
23/11/13	L	H	Falkirk	0	4	Adam	Stevenson	Adamson	Cowan	Armstrong	Wedderburn*	Brett	Hemmings	Hemmings	Milne	Robertson	McKenzie	Morton+	Cowan	Brett	Flynn	Russell	O'Brien
07/12/13	L	H	Livingston	2	3	Adam	Stewart"	Adamson	Cowan	Armstrong	O'Brien"	Brett	Hemmings	Miller	Milne+	Robertson+	Stewart*	Morton+	McKenzie"	Anthony	Flynn	Pyper	Morton
14/12/13	L	A	Dundee	2	1	Adam	Stewart*	Adamson	Cowan	Armstrong	O'Brien	Brett+	Miller	Miller	Milne+	Robertson*	O'Brien*	Morton+	Russell"	Anthony	Flynn	Pyper	Morton
21/12/13	L	A	Raith Rovers	3	3	Adam	Stewart"	Adamson	Cowan+	Armstrong	O'Brien	Brett	Miller	Miller	Stewart+	Robertson*	O'Brien+	Morton*	Russell"	Anthony	Adam	Pyper	Johnston
28/12/13	L	H	Queen of the South	0	2	Adam	Stevenson	Adamson	Cowan+	Armstrong	O'Brien	Brett	Hemmings+	Miller+	Milne+	Robertson	O'Brien*	Morton+	Nicholson	Pyper	Callaghan	Finnie	Kane
02/01/14	L	A	Alloa	2	4	Flynn	Stevenson	Adamson	Wedderburn	Armstrong	Fowler	Brett	Hemmings+	Miller+	Stewart*	Robertson	Russell*	Anthony+	Russell	Callaghan	Wedderburn	Finnie	Kane
11/01/14	L	H	Dumbarton	2	4	Flynn	Stevenson	Adamson	Wedderburn	Armstrong	Fowler	Brett	Hemmings	Hemmings	Gold*	Stewart	Morton*	McKenzie+	Robertson"	O'Brien	Callaghan	Hunter	Pyper
18/01/14	L	A	Falkirk	0	2	Flynn	Stevenson	Adamson	Brownlie	Armstrong	Fowler	Brett	Hemmings	Miller	Gold*	Stewart	Morton*	Anthony"	Anthony"	Morton	Miller	Wight	Robertson
25/01/14	L	H	Hamilton Accies	4	3	Flynn	Wedderburn	Adamson	Brownlie	Armstrong	Fowler	Brett	Hemmings*	Miller+	S Stewart	Stewart+	Morton*	Miller+	Robertson+	Callaghan	Miller	Kane	Callachan
01/02/14	L	A	Raith Rovers	1	0	Flynn	Wedderburn	Adamson	Brownlie	Armstrong	Fowler	Brett	Hemmings	Milne	Robertson	Stewart	Kane*	Morton	Gold	Miller	Kane	Kane	Callachan
15/02/14	L	A	Morton	1	1	Flynn	Wedderburn	McKeown	Brownlie	Armstrong	Fowler	Brett	Milne	Milne	Robertson	Stewart*	Anthony	O'Brien	Gold	Miller	Morton	Adamson	Callachan
22/02/14	L	H	Dundee	2	0	Flynn	Wedderburn	McKeown	Brownlie	Armstrong	Fowler	Brett	Milne	Milne	Robertson	Stewart	Stevenson*	Kane+	Gold	Usai	Morton	Miller	Miller
01/03/14	L	H	Livingston	0	1	Flynn	Wedderburn	McKeown	Brownlie	Armstrong	Fowler	Brett	Hemmings*	Hemmings"	Robertson	Stewart	Stevenson*	Kane+	Gold	Usai	Morton	Adamson	Morton
08/03/14	L	A	Alloa	2	2	Usai	Wedderburn	McKeown	Brownlie	Armstrong	Fowler	Brett	Kane*	Stevenson	S Stewart	G Stewart	Morton*	Stewart	Gold	Usai	Morton	Adamson	Morton
15/03/14	L	A	Dumbarton	1	5	Usai	Wedderburn	McKeown	Brownlie	Armstrong	G Stewart*	Brett'	Milne	Stevenson"	Robertson+	G Stewart	Morton*	Adamson	Gold	Usai	Morton	Gold	Miller
22/03/14	L	H	Queen of the South	1	2	Usai	Wedderburn	McKeown	Kane	Armstrong	G Stewart	Brett	Milne	Stevenson"	Robertson"	G Stewart	Miller*	Miller+	Miller"	Usai	O'Brien	Hemmings	Miller
25/03/14	L	H	Morton	3	0	Usai	Wedderburn	McKeown	Kane*	Armstrong	G Stewart"	Brett*	O'Brien	Miller	S Stewart	G Stewart	Stewart*	S Stewart+	Flynn	Usai	O'Brien	Gold	Miller
29/03/14	L	H	Hamilton Accies	1	1	Usai	Wedderburn	McKeown	Kane	Armstrong	G Stewart	Brett*	O'Brien	Miller	S Stewart	Hemmings	Gold*	Robertson+	Flynn	Flynn	Milne	Flynn	Kane
05/04/14	L	A	Falkirk	0	5	Flynn	Robertson*	McKeown	Milne	Armstrong	G Stewart	Brett*	O'Brien	Miller	Gold	Hemmings	Miller*	Robertson+	Flynn	Stevenson	Gold	Brownlie	
12/04/14	L	H	Dundee	0	4	Flynn	Wedderburn	McKeown	Milne	Armstrong	G Stewart	Brett*	O'Brien+	Miller+	Brownlie	Hemmings+	Milne*	Morton+	Stevenson+	Morton	Morton	Usai	
19/04/14	L	H	Livingston	4	0	Flynn	Wedderburn	McKeown	Milne	Armstrong	G Stewart	Brett	O'Brien	Kane	Brownlie	Hemmings	Wedderburn*	Adamson+	Johnston"	O'Brien	Gold	Usai	
26/04/14	L	A	Raith Rovers	2	1	Flynn	Wedderburn	Mcleown	Milne	Armstrong	G Stewart	Brett	O'Brien	Kane*	Brownlie	Hemmings	Robertson*	Miller+	Gold"	O'Brien	Morton	Usai	
03/05/14	L	H	Queen of the South	1	1	Flynn	Wedderburn	McKeown	Milne"	Armstrong	G Stewart"	Brett	O'Brien	Robertson	Brownlie	Hemmings	Kane*	Adamson	Gold"	Morton	Morton	Usai	
07/05/14	PO	A	Ayr United	2	1	Flynn	Wedderburn	McKeown	Milne	Armstrong	G Stewart	Brett	O'Brien	Robertson	Brownlie+	Hemmings	Kane*	Kane+	Stevenson	Adamson	Gold	Usai	
10/05/14	PO	H	Ayr United	3	1	Flynn	Wedderburn	McKeown	Milne	Armstrong	G Stewart	Brett*	O'Brien	Robertson	Gold	Hemmings	Stevenson	Kane	Gold"	Adamson	Morton	Usai	
14/05/14	PO	H	Dunfermline Athletic	1	1	Flynn	Wedderburn	McKeown"	Milne"	Armstrong	G Stewart	Brett*	O'Brien	Robertson	Brownlie	Hemmings	Stevenson	Stevenson+	Adamson"	Adamson	Morton	Usai	
18/05/14	PO	A	Dunfermline Athletic	3	0	Flynn	Wedderburn	McKeown"	Milne	Armstrong	G Stewart	Brett*	O'Brien	Robertson	Brownlie+	Hemmings	Miller"	Stevenson+	Adamson"	Morton	Gold	Usai	Kane

Dumbarton FC

Founded	1872
Ground	Bet Butler Stadium
Postcode	G82 1JJ
Tel	01389 762569
Capacity	2020
Closest Railway Station	Dumbarton East
Record Attendance	18000 v Raith Rovers, SC, 2/3/57
Record Win	13-1 v Kirkintilloch Central, SC, 1/1/1888
Record Defeat	1-11 v Albion Rovers, Lge, 30/1/1926; v Ayr United, LC, 13/8/52
Most League Goals in a Season	38 Kenny Wilson, 1971/2
Most Goals in Career	202 Hughie Gallacher
Chairman	Alan Jardine
Chief Executive	Gilbert Lawrie
Secretary	David Prophet
Manager	Iain Murray
Assistant Manager	Jack Ross
Colours 2013/14 Top	White with Black and Gold Chest Band
Shorts	White
Sponsor	Bet Butler
Manufacturer	1872
Change Colours 2013/14 Top	Gold with Black and White Chest Band
Shorts	Gold
Nicknames	Sons
Web	www.dumbartonfootballclub.com

Ian Murray has brought about a remarkable transformation in fortunes at Dumbarton. When he took over midway through 2012/13 the Sons looked doomed to relegation. He turned them around and the good form continued last season - at one point the club were genuine contenders for a promotion play off place.

Murray has elected to remain at the club despite being linked with other jobs. He has a solid team based on experience and a sound work ethic. They could be well placed to provide a challenge to some of the "so called" big guns in the Championship next season.

They have lost one or two players but Murray's dealings in the transfer market have produced some astute signings.

The club have been looking at the possibility of bringing in temporary stands / terracing to expand the capacity of their one-sided ground. They must seek to capitalise on the income potential from sell-out matches.

PREDICTION 2014/15
Should be capable of at least a mid-table finish and could pull off a few shock results along the way

				L			SC			LC			RC						
Surname	First Name	DOB	Pos	A	S	G	A	S	G	A	S	G	A	S	G	UNS	Signed Previous Club	Notes	Contract
Agnew	Scott	11/07/87	M	18	7	6	2	1		1			1			3	2011 Stranraer		C (2015)
Barry	Aaron	24/11/92	D	18			2			2							2013 Sheffield United (Loan)	Returned to Sheffield United	
Coleman	Joe	05/03/96	D													1	2013 Dumbarton Youth	On loan to Kilbirnie Ladeside	C (2015)
Ewings	Jamie	04/08/84	GK	27			2			1						5	2011 Alloa		C (2015)
Fleming	Garry	17/05/87	M	12	16	4	1	2		1	1		1	1			2012 Irvine Meadow		OOC
Gilhaney	Mark	04/11/84	M	31	3	2	4			1	1	1	1			1	2010 Alloa		C (2015)
Graham	Andy	22/09/83	D	36		2	4			2		1					2012 Morton		C (2015)
Grindlay	Stephen	13/03/82	GK	9			2									32	2010 Ayr United		OOC
Horne	Josh	25/05/93	D													4	2013 Dumbarton Youth	Freed Jan 2014 joined Pollok	
Kane	Chris	05/09/94	F	13	5	10	2										2014 St Johnstone (Loan)	Returned to St Johnstone	
Kirkpatrick	Jordan	06/03/92	M	24	8	6	4			2						2	2013 Airdrie United		C (2015)
Linton	Scott	06/09/89	D	29			4			1	1					1	2013 Cowdenbeath		C (2015)
Lumsden	Josh	12/08/96	GK													5	2013 Dumbarton Youth		C (2015)
McDougall	Stephen	17/06/86	F	4	14	2	1			2						14	2012 Dunfermline Athletic		C (2015)
McGinn	Paul	22/10/90	D	35			4			2			1				2013 St Mirren	Joined Dundee June2014	
McKerracher	Alistair	26/06/96	M	2			1						1			17	2012 Dumbarton Youth	On Loan To Kilbirnie Ladeside Jan 2014	C (2015)
McLaughlin	Mark	02/12/75	D	13			1	1								2	2013 Morton		C (2015)
McNiff	Martin	16/03/90	D										2			2	2008 Dumbarton Youth	Loan to Annan Athletic, then permanent from Jan	
Megginson	Mitch	27/07/92	F	32	3	10	4		1	1	1	1	1		1	1	2013 Aberdeen		OOC
Miller	Mikey	31/12/94	D	9			3	2		1							2014 Celtic (Loan)	Returned to Celtic	
Murray	Hugh	08/01/79	M	12	4		1			1						11	2013 Partick Thistle (Loan, then permanent from Jan 2014)		C (2015)
Nish	Colin	07/03/81	F	23	10	6	3	1	1	1							2013 Hartlepool United		OOC
Phinn	Nicky	14/10/88	M	1									1			13	2013 Stranraer		F
Prunty	Bryan	12/01/83	F	13	17	7	1	3	1	2						3	2011 Alloa		C (2015)
Ross	Jack	05/06/76	D													1	2013 Dunfermline Athletic	Coach	OOC
Smith	Scott	14/01/92	D	5			1			1						26	2013 Hibernian		F
Smith	Kevin	20/03/87	F	3	7	1	1	1	1	1						11	2013 Queen of the South	Joined East Fife Jan 2014	F
Thomson	Callum	30/01/95	D													9	2014 St Mirren (Loan)	Returned to St Mirren	
Turner	Chris	03/01/87	M	30			6	1		2							2012 Shamrock Rovers		C (2015)
Own Goal						1													

Date	Comp	H/A	Opponents	F A	Crowd	Scorers
27/07/2013	RC1	A	Stranraer	2 4	333	Fleming, K Smith
03/08/2013	LC1	H	Albion Rovers	1 0	506	Gilhaney
10/08/2013	L	H	Falkirk	1 1	1224	Prunty
17/08/2013	L	A	Hamilton Accies	1 4	995	Agnew
24/08/2013	L	H	Morton	3 1	1171	Megginson, Nish, McDougall
28/08/2013	LC2	H	Dundee United	2 3	1045	Megginson, K Smith
31/08/2013	L	A	Cowdenbeath	2 3	384	Turner 2
14/09/2013	L	A	Alloa	2 1	626	Graham, Agnew
21/09/2013	L	H	Livingston	1 2	759	Megginson
28/09/2013	L	A	Queen of the South	2 1	1693	Turner, Prunty
05/10/2013	L	H	Raith Rovers	2 4	843	Prunty 2
12/10/2013	L	H	Dundee	1 4	1175	Kirkpatrick
19/10/2013	L	A	Falkirk	2 1	2704	Fleming, Megginson
26/10/2013	L	H	Cowdenbeath	0 0	700	
02/11/2013	SC3	H	Cowdenbeath	2 1	450	Kirkpatrick 2
09/11/2013	L	A	Morton	0 2	1687	
16/11/2013	L	A	Livingston	3 1	1039	Megginson, Turner, Prunty
30/11/2013	SC4	A	Berwick Rangers	3 1	406	Prunty, Megginson, Linton
04/12/2013	L	H	Alloa	1 1	463	Prunty
07/12/2013	L	H	Queen of the South	0 1	824	
14/12/2013	L	A	Raith Rovers	1 2	1351	McDougall
21/12/2013	L	H	Hamilton Accies	2 1	642	Fleming, Graham
28/12/2013	L	A	Dundee	0 3	4489	
04/01/2014	L	H	Morton	2 0	1469	Prunty, Kane
11/01/2014	L	A	Cowdenbeath	4 2	434	Nish, Megginson 2, Kane
18/01/2014	L	A	Alloa	5 1	602	McLaughlin, Turner, Kane 2, Kirkpatrick
01/02/2014	L	A	Hamilton Accies	3 3	1061	Kirkpatrick, Hendrie og, Kane
05/02/2014	L	H	Livingston	2 2	562	Nish, Kane
08/02/2014	SC5	A	Alloa	1 0	749	Nish
15/02/2014	L	H	Falkirk	2 1	1003	Megginson, Kirkpatrick
22/02/2014	L	H	Raith Rovers	3 3	786	Nish, Kane, Agnew
01/03/2014	L	A	Queen of the South	1 3	1604	Miller
08/03/2014	SC6	A	Aberdeen	0 1	10600	
15/03/2014	L	H	Cowdenbeath	5 1	687	Megginson, Miller, Kirkpatrick, Fleming, Kane
22/03/2014	L	H	Dundee	0 1	1222	
25/03/2014	L	A	Falkirk	0 2	2489	
29/03/2014	L	H	Livingston	2 1	949	Turner, Kane
01/04/2014	L	A	Morton	0 3	826	
05/04/2014	L	H	Alloa	4 1	677	Gilhaney, Fleming, Agnew, Kane
12/04/2014	L	A	Raith Rovers	3 1	1602	Gilhaney, Megginson, Nish
19/04/2014	L	H	Queen of the South	0 3	1263	
26/04/2014	L	H	Hamilton Accies	4 1	1420	Agnew, Nish, Megginson, Kirkpatrick
03/05/2014	L	A	Dundee	1 2	10718	Agnew

Friendly Matches

29/6/13	Fr	H	Hibernian	1 1	1000	
13/7/13	Fr	H	Partick Thistle	3 4		
16/7/13	Fr	N	Brechin City	1 1		at Stirling University
18/7/13	Fr	A	Queen's Park	4 5		
23/7/13	StCF	H	Falkirk	3 2		2012/13 season
27/7/13	Fr	A	Campbeltown Pupils	2 0	U19	
30/7/13	Fr	H	Clydebank	5 1		
24/9/13	StCSF	A	Falkirk	1 3		

57

Date	Comp	H/A	Opponents	F	A	1	2	3	4	5	6	7	8	9	10	11	12	13	14	15	16	17	18
27/07/2013	RC1	A	Stranraer	2	4	Ewing	McGinn	Linton	Graham	S Smith	Phinn"	Gilhaney	Agnew	Fleming*	Prunty*	K Smith	McDougall+	Megginson*	Prunty+	McKerracher"	McNiff	Grindlay	
03/08/2013	LC1	H	Albion Rovers	1	0	Ewing	McGinn	Linton	Graham	Barry	Turner	Gilhaney	Agnew	Prunty*	Megginson	McDougall+	K Smith*	Fleming+	McKerracher"	S Smith	S Smith	Coleman	Grindlay
10/08/2013	L	H	Falkirk	1	1	Ewing	McGinn	Barry	Graham	S Smith"	Turner	Gilhaney	Agnew	Fleming+	Megginson	McDougall+	McDougall*	Kirkpatrick+	Fleming"	McKerracher	Grindlay	Phinn	Grindlay
17/08/2013	L	A	Hamilton Accies	1	4	Ewing	Graham	Barry	S Smith	Barry	Turner	Gilhaney	Agnew	Fleming+	K Smith+	McDougall+	Fleming*	McKerracher*	Prunty"	Home	Home	K Smith	Grindlay
24/08/2013	L	H	Morton	3	1	Ewing	Graham	McGinn	Linton	Barry	Turner	Gilhaney	McDougall"	Megginson*	Nish+	Murray	McDougall"	Fleming+	McDougall"	McKerracher	Home	Phinn	Grindlay
28/08/2013	LC2	H	Dundee United	2	3	Ewing	Graham	McGinn	Linton	Barry	Hunter	McDougall"	Murray	Prunty	Nish+	Murray	Agnew"	Prunty+	Fleming"	McKerracher	Grindlay	Kirkpatrick	Grindlay
31/08/2013	L	A	Cowdenbeath	2	3	Ewing	Graham	McGinn	Linton	Barry	Turner	Murray	Murray+	Megginson"	Nish+	Gilhaney	Fleming*	McDougall+	Megginson"	Home	Grindlay	K Smith	Linton
14/09/2013	L	A	Alloa	2	1	Ewing	Graham	McGinn	Linton	Barry	Turner+	Murray+	Fitzpatrick	Agnew*	Nish+	Gilhaney	Nish*	McDougall+	McKerracher"	Fleming	S Smith	Kirkpatrick	Grindlay
21/09/2013	L	H	Livingston	1	2	Ewing	Graham	McGinn	Linton	Barry	Turner	Murray"	Kirkpatrick	Agnew*	Nish+	Gilhaney	Nish*	Nish+	K Smith"	McKerracher	S Smith	K Smith	Grindlay
28/09/2013	L	A	Queen of the South	2	1	Ewing	Graham	McGinn	Linton	Barry	Turner	Murray	Kirkpatrick	Megginson*	Nish+	Gilhaney	Nish*	Fleming+	Kirkpatrick"	McKerracher	S Smith	Kirkpatrick	Grindlay
05/10/2013	L	H	Raith Rovers	2	4	Ewing	Graham	McGinn	Linton	Barry	Turner	Fleming*	Kirkpatrick	Prunty*	Nish	Gilhaney	Fleming*	McDougall+	K Smith"	McKerracher	S Smith	K Smith	Grindlay
12/10/2013	L	H	Dundee	2	4	Ewing	Graham	McGinn	Linton	Barry	Turner	Fleming"	Kirkpatrick	Prunty*	Prunty	Gilhaney	Prunty*	K Smith+	Kirkpatrick"	McKerracher	S Smith	K Smith	Grindlay
19/10/2013	L	A	Falkirk	2	1	Ewing	Graham	McGinn	Linton	Barry	Murray+	S Smith+	Kirkpatrick	Megginson*	Nish	Gilhaney	Agnew*	Kirkpatrick+	Kirkpatrick"	McKerracher	Grindlay	McDougall	
26/10/2013	L	H	Cowdenbeath	0	0	Ewing	Graham	McGinn	Linton	Barry	Murray+	Turner	Kirkpatrick*	Megginson+	Nish	Gilhaney	Prunty*	McKerracher+	K Smith"	Grindlay	Grindlay		
02/11/2013	SC3	L	Cowdenbeath	2	1	Ewing	Graham	McGinn	Linton	Barry	Turner	Murray+	Kirkpatrick	Fitzpatrick	Nish	Gilhaney	Agnew"	Phinn+	Nish"	McKerracher	Grindlay	McDougall	Phinn
09/11/2013	L	A	Morton	0	2	Ewing	Graham	McGinn	Linton	Barry	Turner	Murray	Kirkpatrick*	Kirkpatrick	Nish	Gilhaney	Prunty*	Agnew+	K Smith"	McKerracher	Grindlay	McDougall	Phinn
16/11/2013	L	A	Livingston	3	1	Ewing	Graham	McGinn	Linton	Barry	Turner	Murray	Kirkpatrick	Megginson+	Nish+	Gilhaney+	Agnew+	Prunty+	McKerracher+	McKerracher	Grindlay	McDougall	
30/11/2013	SC4	L	Berwick Rangers	3	1	Ewing	Graham	McGinn	Linton	Barry	Turner	Murray"	Kirkpatrick	Prunty*	Megginson"	Gilhaney	McDougall*	Nish+	Ross	Phinn	Grindlay	Smith	McKerracher
04/12/2013	L	H	Alloa	1	1	Ewing	Graham	McGinn	Linton	McLaughlin	Fleming"	Fleming"	Kirkpatrick	Megginson"	Prunty*	Gilhaney	Kane*	McDougall+	Smith	Phinn	Grindlay	Murray	S Smith
07/12/2013	L	A	Queen of the South	0	1	Ewing	Graham	McGinn	Linton	McLaughlin	Fleming"	Fleming"	Kirkpatrick	Prunty*	Megginson	Gilhaney	Agnew*	Fleming+	Smith"	Phinn	Grindlay	K Smith	S Smith
14/12/2013	L	A	Raith Rovers	1	2	Ewing	Graham	McGinn	Linton	McLaughlin	Turner	Murray"	Kirkpatrick	Megginson"	Megginson"	Gilhaney	Agnew"	Agnew+	Smith"	Phinn	Grindlay	McKerracher	S Smith
21/12/2013	L	A	Hamilton Accies	2	1	Ewing	Graham	McGinn	Linton	McGinn	Turner+	Turner	Kirkpatrick+	Prunty+	Megginson"	Gilhaney	Fleming*	Prunty+	McDougall"	Phinn	Grindlay	K Smith	S Smith
28/12/2013	L	H	Dundee	0	3	Grindlay	Graham	McGinn	Linton	McGinn	Nish	Turner	Kirkpatrick	Kane+	Megginson	Gilhaney	Kane*	Murray+	McKerracher+	Phinn	Grindlay	S Smith	Agnew
04/01/2014	L	H	Morton	2	0	Grindlay	Graham	McGinn	Linton	McGinn	Nish*	Turner	Kirkpatrick	Kane	Megginson	Megginson"	Nish*	Fleming+	McKerracher"	Phinn	Grindlay	S Smith	Agnew
11/01/2014	L	H	Cowdenbeath	4	2	Grindlay	Graham	McGinn	Linton	McGinn	Nish*	Turner	Kirkpatrick	Kane	Megginson	Megginson	Agnew*	Agnew+	McDougall"	McDougall"	Lumsden	Murray	McDougall
18/01/2014	L	A	Alloa	5	1	Grindlay	Graham	McGinn	Linton	McGinn	Nish*	Turner	Kirkpatrick	Kane	Megginson	Megginson	Agnew*	Prunty+	S Smith	K Smith	Lumsden	K Smith	McDougall
01/02/2014	L	A	Hamilton Accies	3	3	Grindlay	Graham	McGinn	Linton	McGinn	Gilhaney	Agnew	Kirkpatrick	Kane	Nish	Megginson+	Miller*	Fleming+	McDougall"	S Smith	Lumsden	McKerracher	McDougall
05/02/2014	L	H	Dundee	2	2	Grindlay	Graham	McGinn	Linton	McGinn	Gilhaney	Agnew	Kirkpatrick	Kane	Nish+	Megginson	Fleming*	Miller+	Prunty"	S Smith	Lumsden	Smith	Phinn
08/02/2014	SC5	L	Alloa	1	0	Grindlay	Graham	Miller	Linton	McGinn	Gilhaney	Agnew	Nish	Kane	Nish	Megginson	Miller*	Fleming+	Prunty"	S Smith	Lumsden	Thomson	McDougall
15/02/2014	L	H	Falkirk	2	1	Grindlay	Graham	Miller	Linton	McGinn	Gilhaney	Agnew*	McDougall"	Kane	Nish+	Megginson	Murray*	Fleming+	McDougall"	S Smith	Thomson	Thomson	Ewings
22/02/2014	L	A	Raith Rovers	3	3	Ewing	Graham	Miller	Linton	McGinn	Gilhaney	Agnew"	Kirkpatrick	Kane	Nish+	Megginson	Fleming+	S Smith+	Prunty"	S Smith	Thomson	Grindlay	McDougall
01/03/2014	L	A	Queen of the South	1	3	Ewing	Graham	Miller	Linton	McGinn	Linton*	McLaughlin	Kirkpatrick	Kane	Nish	Megginson"	Fleming+	Fleming+	McDougall"	K Smith	McDougall	McDougall	Murray
08/03/2014	SC6	L	Aberdeen	0	1	Grindlay	Graham	Gilhaney	Linton	McGinn	Kirkpatrick	McLaughlin	Nish	Kane	Nish+	Gilhaney	Prunty+	S Smith+	Prunty"	S Smith	Thomson	Grindlay	McDougall
15/03/2014	L	A	Cowdenbeath	5	1	Ewing	Graham	Gilhaney	Linton	McGinn	Kirkpatrick	McLaughlin	Fleming	Fleming	Nish+	Megginson	Kane+	Kane*	McDougall"	McDougall"	Thomson	Ewings	McDougall
22/03/2014	L	H	Dundee	0	1	Ewing	Graham	Miller	Turner"	McGinn	Kirkpatrick	McLaughlin	Fleming	Fleming"	Nish	Megginson"	Kane*	Agnew+	McDougall"	S Smith	McDougall	Ewings	Murray
25/03/2014	L	A	Falkirk	0	2	Ewing	Graham	Miller	Turner"	McGinn	Kirkpatrick	McLaughlin	McLaughlin	Fleming"	Agnew"	Megginson"	Agnew*	Prunty+	Megginson"	Agnew	Grindlay	Ewings	Prunty
29/03/2014	L	A	Livingston	2	1	Ewing	Graham	Miller	Turner"	McGinn	Kirkpatrick*	McLaughlin	McLaughlin	Fleming"	Agnew+	Megginson"	Agnew*	Kane+	Prunty"	S Smith	Grindlay	Ewings	Murray
01/04/2014	L	H	Morton	0	3	Ewing	Graham	Gilhaney	Turner"	McGinn	Kirkpatrick*	McLaughlin	McLaughlin	Fleming"	Prunty+	Megginson	Kane"	Agnew+	Fleming"	Agnew	Grindlay	Grindlay	Thomson
05/04/2014	L	A	Alloa	4	1	Ewing	Graham	Gilhaney	Turner"	McGinn	Agnew+	McLaughlin	McLaughlin	Fleming+	Turner	Megginson"	Nish*	Kane+	McDougall"	S Smith	Grindlay	Phinn	McDougall
12/04/2014	L	A	Raith Rovers	3	1	Ewing	Graham	Miller	Linton	McGinn	Agnew+	Gilhaney	Nish*	Kane	Turner	Megginson"	Nish*	Prunty+	Murray"	S Smith	Grindlay	Thomson	Murray
19/04/2014	L	A	Queen of the South	0	3	Ewing	Graham	Miller	Linton	McGinn	Agnew	Gilhaney	Nish*	Kane	Turner	Megginson"	Nish*	Kane+	McDougall"	S Smith	Grindlay	McDougall	Prunty
26/04/2014	L	H	Hamilton Accies	4	1	Ewing	Graham	Miller	Linton	McGinn	Agnew+	Gilhaney	Nish	Fleming+	Turner"	Megginson"	Nish*	Kirkpatrick+	Kane"	Murray	Grindlay	Phinn	Miller
03/05/2014	L	A	Dundee	1	2	Ewing	Graham	Miller	Linton	McGinn	Agnew	Gilhaney	Nish	Fleming+	Turner"	Megginson"	Kane*	Prunty+	Kirkpatrick"	Murray	Grindlay	McLaughlin	McDougall

Dundee FC

Founded	1893
Ground	Dens Park
Postcode	DD3 7JY
Tel	01382 889966
Capacity	11506
Closest Railway Station	Dundee
Record Attendance	43024, SC, v Rangers 7/2/1953
Record Win	10-0 v Alloa, Lge 9/3/47; v Dunfermline 22/3/47
Record Defeat	0-11 v Celtic, Lge, 26/10/1895
Chairman	Bill Colvin
Chief Executive	Scott Gardiner
Secretary	Laura Hayes
Manager	John Brown (until Feb 2014) / Paul Hartley
Assistant Manager	Gerry McCabe (from June)
Colours 2013/14 Top	Navy Blue
Shorts	White
Sponsor	Kilmac Energy
Manufacturer	Puma
Change Colours 2013/14 Top	Sky Blue
Shorts	Navy Blue
Nicknames	Dee, Dark Blues
Web	www.dundeefconline.co.uk

The potential of Dundee has never been in doubt and was reinforced by the sell-out crowd that witnessed their promotion against Dumbarton at the end of 2013/14. No club has suffered more from the reduced size of the top Division - since the mid 1970s Dundee have switched between the top two levels on far too many occasions.

Paul Hartley achieved an amazing treble in winning promotion for the third year running following two successive elevations with Alloa. His philosophy and methods have been a breath of fresh air and he has the potential to become a really top class Manager.

He's accepted that the squad that won promotion needed to be altered for the challenge ahead. He's brought in a combination of experienced players and promising young talent - finding the right blend on the park will be his immediate task at the start of the season.

The Tayside Derbies will be a highlight of the Premiership season. It promises to be an exciting season in the City of Discovery.

PREDICTION 2014/15
Should be good enough for a top ten finish, avoiding relegation and the play offs.

				L			SC			LC			RC						
Surname	First Name	DOB	Pos	A	S	G	A	S	G	A	S	G	A	S	G	UNS	Signed Previous Club	Notes	Contract
Beattie	Craig	16/01/84	F	8	10	5	1			1						1	2014 Barnet		F
Benedictus	Kyle	07/12/91	D	15	2	1							1	1		8	2008 Lincraig BC		OOC
Bonnett-Johnson	Sean															2	2014 Billericay Town		F
Boyle	Martin	25/04/93	F	18	11	4	1			1			1	1		7	2012 Montrose		C (2015)
Carberry	Thomas	26/11/96	F													4	2013 Clydebank U17		Youth
Conroy	Ryan	28/04/87	M	20	12	6	1			2			2	1		2	2011 Celtic		OOC
Cummins	Adam	03/03/93	D	2	1											12	2014 Motherwell (Loan)	Returned to Motherwell	
Davidson	Iain	14/01/84	M	25	1	3	1			1			2			1	2012 Raith Rovers	*	OOC
Doris	Steven	09/08/88	F	2	10					1			1	1		7	2013 Arbroath		C (2015)
Dyer	William	25/02/87	D	21						2			2	1		6	2013 Morton		C (2015)
Gallagher	Declan	13/02/91	D	36	4	1				2			3				2012 Clyde		OOC
Gibson	John	29/05/89	GK	1												7	2009 Dundee United	On loan to Elgin C Mar-May, joined Alloa May	F
Hughes	Stephen	14/11/82	M	1												1	2014 East Fife	Returned to East Fife	
Irvine	Gary	17/03/85	D	33			1			2			3			1	2011 St Johnstone		OOC
Kerr	Cameron	10/09/95	D	2	1											12	2012 Dundee Youths		C (2016)
Letheren	Kyle	26/12/87	GK	35			1			2			3				2013 Kilmarnock		C (2015)
Lockwood	Matt	17/10/76	D	17			1			1			1	1		12	2010 Colchester United	Joined Sutton United June 2014 as coach	
McAlister	Jim	02/11/85	M	36	4	1	1			2			1	3	1		2012 Hamilton Accies		C (2015)
McBride	Kevin	14/06/81	M	19	6	2				1			3			7	2012 Hamilton Accies		OOC
MacDonald	Peter	17/11/80	F	33	2	17	1			2			1	2	1	3	2013 Morton		OOC
McIntosh	Leighton	06/02/93	F	2												4	2010 Dundee Youths	On loan to Arbroath	
Monti	Carlo	10/07/90	F	7	1		1			1			2	1	1	10	2010 Pollok	Freed April 2014	
Nade	Christian	18/09/84	F	6	7	3										2	2014 PTT Rayong (Thailand)	Joined Raith Rovers June 2014	F
O'Donnell	Stephen	10/07/83	M	1												3	2010 St Mirren		F
Rae	Gavin	28/11/77	M	34	2	1	1			2			3				2013 Aberdeen		R
Reid	Jamie	11/01/94	M	4									1			6	2010 Dundee Youths	On loan to Montrose (Dec-)	F
Riley	Nick	10/05/86	M	18	9		1			1			2				2010 Hamilton Accies		OOC
Thomson	James	07/11/94	D													12	2012 Dundee United	Freed Jan 2014	
Twardzik	Dan	13/04/91	GK	1	1											31	2013 Aberdeen	Joined Motherwell May 2014	
Wighton	Craig	27/07/97	F	7	6	2	1									14	2013 Dundee Youths		Youth

Date	Comp	H/A	Opponents	F	A		Crowd	Scorers
27/07/2013	RC1	A	Alloa	1	0		880	Monti pen
10/08/2013	L	A	Queen of the South	3	4		2644	McDonald, Gallagher, Davidson
17/08/2013	L	H	Alloa	1	0		4167	McBride
20/08/2013	RC2	H	Forfar Athletic	3	1	AET	2052	McBride, McDonald 2
24/08/2013	L	A	Raith Rovers	0	0		2603	
27/08/2013	LC2	H	Forfar Athletic	2	1	AET	2027	McAllister, McDonald
30/08/2013	L	H	Livingston	3	0		3955	Monto, Gallagher, MacDonald
07/09/2013	RC3	H	Stenhousemuir	1	1	AET, 4-5 pens	1615	McDonald
14/09/2013	L	H	Hamilton Accies	0	0		4155	
21/09/2013	L	A	Falkirk	1	3		3349	Conroy
24/09/2013	LC3	H	Inverness CT	0	1		1682	
28/09/2013	L	H	Morton	3	1		3870	McDonald 2, Beattie
05/10/2013	L	A	Cowdenbeath	2	0		1013	Beattie, Conroy
12/10/2013	L	A	Dumbarton	4	1		1175	McDonald 2, Conroy, Rae
19/10/2013	L	H	Queen of the South	2	1		4357	McDonald, Beattie
26/10/2013	L	A	Livingston	1	2		1597	McDonald
09/11/2013	L	H	Raith Rovers	2	0		5064	Conroy, Wighton
16/11/2013	L	H	Falkirk	1	1		4661	Conroy
23/11/2013	L	A	Hamilton Accies	3	0		2077	Davidson, Gallagher, McDonald
30/11/2013	SC4	H	Raith Rovers	0	1		3184	
07/12/2013	L	A	Morton	2	1		1536	Beattie, Gallacher
14/12/2013	L	H	Cowdenbeath	1	2		3533	McAllister
21/12/2013	L	A	Alloa	1	0		1170	McDonald
28/12/2013	L	H	Dumbarton	3	0		4489	McDonald 2, McBride
02/01/2014	L	A	Raith Rovers	2	0		4039	McAllister 2
11/01/2014	L	H	Livingston	0	1		4367	
25/01/2014	L	A	Falkirk	0	2		4183	
01/02/2014	L	H	Alloa	1	1		4021	Conroy
08/02/2014	L	H	Hamilton Accies	1	0		5206	Boyle
15/02/2014	L	A	Queen of the South	1	0		2152	Conroy
22/02/2014	L	A	Cowdenbeath	0	2		1419	
01/03/2014	L	H	Morton	2	0		4488	Nade, McDonald
15/03/2014	L	A	Livingston	2	0		1759	McDonald, Benedictus
18/03/2014	L	H	Raith Rovers	0	0		4561	
22/03/2014	L	A	Dumbarton	1	0		1222	McDonald
25/03/2014	L	H	Queen of the South	1	0		3999	Davidson
29/03/2014	L	H	Falkirk	0	1		4919	
05/04/2014	L	A	Hamilton Accies	1	1		4529	Boyle
12/04/2014	L	H	Cowdenbeath	4	0		4751	Wighton, Boyle 2, McAllister
19/04/2014	L	A	Morton	0	1		2117	
26/04/2014	L	A	Alloa	3	0		2552	Nade, McDonald, Beattie
27/04/2014	L	H	Dumbarton	2	1		10718	Nade, McDonald

Friendly Matches

9/7/13	Fr	A	Montrose	5	1	600		
13/7/13	Fr	A	Forfar Athletic	1	0			
16/7/13	Fr	A	Clyde	5	0			
20/7/13	Fr	A	Rangers U20	3	2	U19	at Murray Park	
21/7/13	Fr	H	St Johnstone	1	1			
27/7/13	Tnt	N	Livingston U19	6	1	U19	at Broxburn	
28/7/13	Tnt	A	Broxburn Athletic	2	3	U19	at Broxburn	
30/7/13	Fr	A	Aberdeen U20			U19		
31/7/13	Fr	H	Rangers	1	1	5244		
3/8/13	Fr	A	Lochee United	4	1			

Date	Comp	H/A	Opponents	F	A	1	2	3	4	5	6	7	8	9	10	11	12	13	14	15	16	17	18
27/07/2013	RC1	A	Alloa	1	0	Letheren	Benedictus	Davidson	Gallagher	Irvine	Rae	McBride+	Conroy"	McAllister	McDonald	Monti*	Doris*	Riley+	Dyer"	Gibson	Boyle		
10/08/2013		A	Queen of the South	3	4	Letheren	Benedictus	Davidson	Gallagher	Irvine	Rae	McBride	Conroy"	McAllister	McDonald	Monti*	Doris*	Boyle+	Kerr	Dyer	Wighton	Reid	
17/08/2013		L	Alloa	1	0	Letheren	Benedictus	Davidson	Gallagher	Irvine	Rae+	McBride	Conroy*	McAllister	McDonald"	Monti+	Boyle*	Boyle"	Reid"	Dyer	Wighton	Lockwood	
20/08/2013	RC2	H	Forfar Athletic	3	1 AET	Letheren	Dyer	Davidson	Gallagher	Irvine	Rae+	McBride	Reid	McAllister	Doris"	Boyle"	MacDonald*	Conroy+	Monti"	Benedictus	Twardzik	Thomson	Carberry
24/08/2013		L	Raith Rovers	0	0	Letheren	Dyer	Lockwood	Gallagher	Irvine	Rae	McBride	Conroy"	McAllister	McDonald+	Monti*	Doris*	Boyle+	Reid"	Kerr	Twardzik	Thomson	
27/08/2013	LC2	A	Forfar Athletic	2	1 AET	Letheren	Dyer	Lockwood	Gallagher	Irvine	Rae	McBride	Conroy"	McAllister	McDonald	Monti*	Boyle*	Boyle+	Thomson	Carberry	Twardzik	Thomson	Boyle
30/08/2013		L	Livingston	3	0	Letheren	Dyer	Lockwood	Gallagher	Irvine	Rae	McBride+	Conroy+	McAllister	McDonald	Monti*	Riley*	Benedictus+	Reid"	Carberry	Twardzik	Thomson	Boyle
07/09/2013	LC3	H	Stenhousemuir	1	1 AET, 4-5 pens	Letheren	Dyer	Lockwood	Gallagher	Irvine	Rae	McBride+	Conroy+	McAllister	McDonald	Monti*	Riley*"	Benedictus+	Benedictus"	Carberry	Twardzik		
14/09/2013		H	Hamilton Accies	0	0	Letheren	Lockwood	Benedictus	Gallagher	Irvine	Rae	McBride"	Davidson	McAllister	Doris+	Beattie+	Riley"	Doris+	Conroy"	Monti	Twardzik	Lockwood	Wighton
21/09/2013		A	Falkirk	1	3	Letheren	Dyer	Riley"	Gallagher	Irvine	Rae	Conroy	Davidson	McAllister	Doris+	Monti+	Doris*	Beattie+	Boyle"	McBride"	Twardzik	Lockwood	Thomson
24/09/2013	LC3	H	Inverness CT	0	1	Letheren	Dyer	Riley+	Gallagher	Irvine	Rae	Conroy	Davidson	McAllister	McDonald"	Beattie"	MacDonald*	Monti	Thomson	Boyle"	Monti		
28/09/2013		H	Morton	3	1	Letheren	Dyer	Riley+	Gallagher	Irvine	Rae	Conroy	Davidson	McAllister	McDonald"	Beattie"	Monti*	Monti	Thomson	Boyle"	Twardzik	Monti	Doris
05/10/2013		L	Cowdenbeath	2	0	Letheren	Lockwood	Riley+	Gallagher	Irvine	Rae	Conroy	Davidson	McAllister	McDonald"	Beattie"	Wighton"	McBride+	Doris"	Boyle"	Twardzik	Reid	Benedictus
12/10/2013		L	Dumbarton	4	1	Letheren	Lockwood	Riley+	Gallagher	Irvine	Rae	Conroy	Davidson	McAllister	McDonald+	Beattie"	Wighton"	Doris+	Reid"	Monti	Twardzik	Monti	Thomson
19/10/2013		H	Queen of the South	2	1	Letheren	Lockwood	Riley+	Gallagher	Irvine	Rae	Conroy	Davidson	McAllister	McDonald"	Wighton"	Beattie*	Boyle+	Doris"	Kerr	Twardzik	Reid	Thomson
26/10/2013		L	Livingston	1	2	Letheren	Lockwood	Riley+	Gallagher	Irvine	Rae	Conroy	McBride	McAllister	McDonald"	Beattie"	Doris*	Boyle+	Kerr	Monti	Twardzik	Thomson	Wighton
09/11/2013		H	Raith Rovers	2	0	Letheren	Lockwood	Riley+	Gallagher	Irvine	Rae	Conroy	Davidson	McAllister	McDonald"	Wighton"	Boyle*	McBride+	Beattie"	Monti	Twardzik	Thomson	Doris
16/11/2013		L	Falkirk	1	1	Letheren	Lockwood	Riley+	Gallagher	Irvine	Rae	Conroy+	Davidson	McAllister	McDonald	Beattie+	McBride*	Monti+	Doris	Boyle	Twardzik	Thomson	O'Donnell
23/11/2013	SC4	A	Hamilton Accies	3	0	Letheren	Lockwood	Riley"	Gallagher	Irvine	Rae	Conroy"	Davidson	McAllister	McDonald+	Beattie"	Doris*	Beattie+	McBride"	Benedictus	Monti	Thomson	Doris
30/11/2013	SC4	H	Raith Rovers	0	1	Letheren	Lockwood*	Lockwood*	Gallagher	Irvine	Rae	Conroy	Davidson	McAllister	McDonald"	Boyle+	Boyle*	Beattie+	Monti*	McBride"	Twardzik	McIntosh	Wighton
07/12/2013		L	Morton	2	0	Letheren	Lockwood	Benedictus	Gallagher	Irvine	Rae	Conroy*	Benedictus	McAllister	McDonald	Boyle	Conroy*	Monti+	Monti	Benedictus	Twardzik	McBride	Wighton
14/12/2013		H	Cowdenbeath	1	2	Letheren	Lockwood"	Benedictus	Gallagher	Irvine	Rae	McBride*	Davidson	McAllister	McDonald+	Beattie"	Boyle*	Monti*	McBride"	Benedictus	Gibson	McIntosh	O'Donnell
21/12/2013		A	Alloa	2	0	Letheren	Lockwood"	Benedictus	Gallagher	Irvine	Rae	McBride+	Davidson	McAllister	McDonald+	Boyle+	Boyle+	Beattie+	Benedictus"	Dyer	Gibson	McIntosh	Kerr
28/12/2013		L	Dumbarton	3	0	Letheren	Conroy	Benedictus	Gallagher	Irvine	Rae	Conroy"	Davidson	McAllister	McDonald	Boyle+	Conroy*	Monti+	Monti*	Doris	Gibson	McIntosh	Kerr
02/01/2014		A	Raith Rovers	2	0	Letheren	Twardzik	Conroy	Gallagher	Irvine	Dyer	Conroy"	Davidson	McAllister	McDonald	Boyle*	McIntosh*	Rae+	McIntosh"	Dyer	McBride	Benedictus	Cummings
11/01/2014		L	Livingston	0	1	Letheren	Rae	Lockwood*	Gallagher	Irvine	Dyer	Hughes+	Davidson	McAllister	McDonald	Boyle"	Conroy*	Nade+	Boyle*	Gibson	Conroy	Hughes	Kerr
25/01/2014		A	Queen of the South	0	2	Letheren	Rae	Benedictus	Gallagher	Irvine	Dyer	McBride"	Davidson	McAllister	Wighton*	Monti"	Twardzik*	Nade+	McBride"	McBride	Cummins	Monti	Kerr
01/02/2014		H	Alloa	1	1	Letheren	Rae	Benedictus	Gallagher	Irvine	Dyer	McBride	Boyle"	McAllister	McDonald+	Monti*	Conroy"	Nade+	Boyle"	Gibson	Cummins	Hughes	Kerr
08/02/2014		H	Hamilton Accies	1	0	Letheren	Rae	Beattie+	Gallagher	Irvine	Dyer	McBride*	Boyle"	McAllister	McDonald	Boyle"	Wighton*	Nade+	Monti	Nade	Cummins	Twardzik	Kerr
15/02/2014		A	Queen of the South	1	0	Letheren	Rae	Rae	Gallagher	Irvine	Dyer	McBride"	Boyle	McAllister	McDonald+	Conroy*	Conroy	Nade+	Lockwood	Cummins	Bonnet-Johnston	Twardzik	Wighton
22/02/2014		L	Cowdenbeath	0	2	Letheren	Rae*	Riley"	Gallagher	Irvine	Dyer	McBride"	Boyle+	McAllister	McDonald+	Monti"	Monti*	Nade+	Lockwood"	Cummins	Bonnet-Johnston	Lockwood	Davidson
01/03/2014		H	Morton	2	0	Letheren	Rae	Riley+	Gallagher	Irvine	Dyer	Boyle"	Boyle+	McAllister	McDonald+	Riley*	Davidson*	Reilly+	Lockwood	Wighton	Twardzik	Lockwood	Twardzik
15/03/2014		L	Livingston	2	0	Letheren	Rae	Kerr+	Gallagher	Irvine	Dyer	McBride"	Boyle	McAllister	McDonald+	Nade+	Doris*	Riley+	Conroy"	Wighton"	Lockwood	Cummins	Gibson
18/03/2014		H	Raith Rovers	0	0	Letheren	Riley	Benedictus	Gallagher	Irvine	Dyer	Davidson	Boyle+	McAllister	Doris"	Doris"	Conroy*	Riley+	Lockwood	Wighton"	Wighton	Cummins	Reid
22/03/2014		A	Dumbarton	1	0	Letheren	Beattie+	Cummins	Gallagher	Irvine	Dyer	Davidson	McBride"	McAllister	McDonald+	Doris"	Conroy*	Riley+	Beattie"	Doris	Lockwood	Cummins	Gibson
25/03/2014		H	Queen of the South	1	0	Letheren	Riley"	Benedictus	Gallagher	Irvine	Dyer	Davidson	Rae	McAllister	McDonald+	Boyle	Conroy*	Conroy+	Lockwood	Doris	Twardzik	Reid	Twardzik
29/03/2014		L	Falkirk	0	1	Letheren	Beattie"	Cummins	Gallagher	Irvine	Dyer	Davidson"	Rae"	McAllister	McDonald"	Boyle	Conroy*	Nade+	Riley"	Doris	Benedictus	McBride	Kerr
05/04/2014		A	Hamilton Accies	1	1	Letheren	Riley+	Riley+	Gallagher	Wighton"	Dyer	Davidson+	Rae	McAllister	McDonald*	Boyle	Cummins*	Beattie+	Beattie*	Benedictus	Benedictus	Nade	Wighton
12/04/2014		L	Cowdenbeath	4	0	Letheren	Riley	Kerr+	Gallagher	Irvine	Dyer	Davidson"	Rae	McAllister	McDonald*	Boyle	Nade*	Beattie+	Beattie"	Benedictus"	Twardzik	Cummins	McBride
19/04/2014		A	Morton	0	1	Letheren	Riley	Nade*	Gallagher	Irvine	Dyer	Davidson	Rae	McAllister	McDonald	Boyle	Beattie*	Beattie"	Irvine	McBride"	Twardzik	Cummins	Conroy
26/04/2014		L	Alloa	3	0	Letheren	McBride"	Nade*	Gallagher	Irvine	Dyer	Davidson+	Rae	McAllister	McDonald	Boyle	Beattie*	Conroy+	Riley"	Cummins	Twardzik	Kerr	Wighton
27/04/2014		H	Dumbarton	2	1	Letheren	Benedictus	McBride	Gallagher	Irvine	Dyer	Nade+	Rae	McAllister	McDonald"	Boyle"	Conroy*	Riley+	Beattie"	Cummins	Twardzik	Kerr	Wighton

Dundee United FC

Founded	1909
Ground	Tannadice Park
Capacity	14229
Postcode	DD3 7JW
Tel	01382 833166
Closest Railway Station	Dundee
Record Attendance	28000 v Barcelona, Fairs Cup, 16/11/1966
Record Win	14-0 v Nithsdale Wanderers, SC, 17/1/1931
Record Defeat	1-12 v Motherwell, Lge, 23/1/1954
Most League Goals in a Season	40 John Coyle, 1955/6
Chairman	Stephen Thompson
Secretary	John Taylor
Manager	Jackie McNamara
Assistant Manager	Simon Donnelly
Colours 2013/14 Top	Tangerine
Shorts	Black
Sponsor	Calor
Manufacturer	Nike
Change Colours 2013/14 Top	White
Shorts	Tangerine
Nicknames	United, Terrors, Arabs
Web	www.dundeeunitedfc.co.uk

PREDICTION 2014/15
Another top four finish for United

For the neutral observer 2013/14 looked like a tremendously exciting season for Dundee United. At times they scored goals with abandon and produced some of the most convincing victories of any team. However, from the perspective of a Dundee United fan it may have been a bit different - disappointment at missing out on a European place and losing the Scottish Cup Final will have been hard to take.

However, they can take comfort in the emergence of a cohort of talented young players. In the meantime they can help seal top level performances and in the medium term they may provide financial stability for the Tannadice club.

Jackie McNamara would be the first to admit that he learned a lot during 2013/14 but he is the type of Manager who will only improve. He puts attack-minded teams on the park and recognises that entertainment is important. There was certainly no lack of that around Tannadice last season with the added bonus of the return of the Tayside derby.

SQUAD NUMBERS

				LA			SC			LC							
Surname	First Name	DOB	Pos	A	S	G	A	S	G	A	S	G	UNS	Signed Previous Club		Notes	Contract
Armstrong	Stuart	30/03/92	M	32	4	8	5			3	2		1	2009 Hamilton Accies			C (2016)
Butcher	Calum	26/02/91	D	6						2	1		12	2013 Hayes & Yeading			C (2015)
Cierzniak	Radoslaw	24/04/83	GK	37			5			3			1	2012 Cracovia			C (2015)
Ciftci	Nadir	12/02/92	F	27	5	11	5		4	2	1	2	3	2013 NAC Breda			C (2016)
Connolly	Aidan	15/08/95	F	2									5	2013 Queen's Park			C (2015)
Dillon	Sean	30/07/83	D	22	1	1	1			2			18	2007 Aston Villa			C (2015)
Dow	Ryan	07/06/91	F	16	10	3	2	2		1	1		13	2007 Dundee United Youth			C (2016)
El Alagui	Farid	10/02/85	F	4	9	3	2						6	2014 Brentford (Loan)		Returned to Brentford	
Erskine	Chris	08/02/87	M	4	3	1				1			8	2013 Partick Thistle		On loan to Partick Thistle, Jan 2014	C (2015)
Fraser	Scott	30/03/95		1									1	2011 Longforgan YC			Youth
Gardyne	Michael	23/01/86	M										2	2012 Ross County		on loan to Kilmarnock	C (2015)
Gauld	Ryan	16/12/95	M	21	10	6	3	1	1	2	1	1	4	2011 Brechin City BC			C (2017)
Gomis	Morgaro	14/07/85	M	5	11		4			1			13	2013 Birmingham City		Joined Hearts June 2014	F
Good	Curtis	23/03/93	D	4		1	1							2014 Newcastle United (Loan)		Returned to Newcastle United	
Goodwillie	David	28/03/89	F	9	10	3	1			2	3		3	2013 Blackburn Rovers (Loan)		Returned to Blackburn Rovers	
Graham	Brian	23/11/87	F	11	19	6	3	1	2	1			8	2013 Raith Rovers			C (2015)
Gunning	Gavin	29/01/91	D	26	1	3	4			1	2		1	2011 Blackburn Rovers		Joined Birmingham City June 2014	F
Mackay-Steven	Gary	31/08/90	F	27	8	7	5		3	1				2011 Airdrie United			C (2015)
McCallum	Mark	27/03/93	GK	1									45	2009 Aberdeen			C (2016)
Miller	Marc	23/02/88	M							1				2012 Falkirk		On loan to Falkirk	F
Oyenuga	Kudus	18/03/93	F	1									2	2013 Hayes & Yeading		On loan to Boreham Wood	C (2016)
Paton	Paul	18/04/87	M	36	1	2	5			3				2013 Partick Thistle			C (2015)
Petrie	Darren	26/07/95	M										3	2011 Carse Thistle		On loan to Brechin City	Youth
Rankin	John	27/06/83	M	35		2	5			2			2	2011 Hibernian			C (2016)
Robertson	Andrew	11/03/94	D	36		3	5		2	3			1	2013 Queen's Park			C (2016)
Smith	Brad	23/04/97	M	1									1	2014 Dundee United Youth			Youth
Souttar	John	25/09/96	D	21	1	1	2			1	1			2012 Brechin City BC			C (2016)
Watson	Keith	14/11/89	D	24	1	3	2	1		1	1		8	2006 Dundee United Youth			C (2015)
Wilson	Mark	05/06/84	D	14		3				2			19	2013 Bristol City			C (2015)
Own Goal					1												

NEW SIGNINGS 2014/15

Spittal	Blair	19/12/95	D		2014 Queen's Park
Telfer	Charlie	04/07/95	M		2014 Rangers

62

Date	Comp	H/A	Opponents	F	A		Crowd	Scorers
02/08/2013	Prem	A	Partick Thistle	0	0		7822	
10/08/2013	Prem	H	Inverness CT	0	1		6664	
17/08/2013	Prem	A	Hibernian	1	1		9171	Armstrong
25/08/2013	Prem	H	St Johnstone	4	0		6992	Watson, Goodwillie, Mackay-Steven, Armstrong
28/08/2013	LC2	A	Dumbarton	3	2		1045	Ciftci 2, Gauld
31/08/2013	Prem	H	Celtic	0	1		10586	
14/09/2013	Prem	A	Ross County	4	2		3005	Mackay-Steven, Armstrong, Gauld, Ciftci
22/09/2013	Prem	A	Motherwell	2	2		5808	Ciftci, Robertson
25/09/2013	LC3	H	Partick Thistle	4	1		3778	Goodwillie 3, Dow
28/09/2013	Prem	A	Hearts	0	0		13970	
05/10/2013	Prem	H	Kilmarnock	1	0		5850	Ciftici
19/10/2013	Prem	A	Aberdeen	0	1		12654	
26/10/2013	Prem	H	St Mirren	4	0		6331	Ciftci 2, Gauld, Erskine
29/10/2013	LC4	A	Inverness CT	1	2	AET	2133	Watson
02/11/2013	Prem	A	Celtic	1	1		47386	Armstrong
09/11/2013	Prem	A	Motherwell	4	0		5103	Gauld 2, Paton, Robertson
23/11/2013	Prem	H	Partick Thistle	4	1		6700	Mackay Steven 2, Robertson, Graham
29/11/2013	SC4	H	Kilmarnock	5	2		6979	Robertson 2, Armstron, Graham, Mackay-Steven
07/12/2013	Prem	H	Hearts	4	1		7808	Armstrong, Graham, McKay-Steven, Rankine
14/12/2013	Prem	A	Kilmarnock	4	1		3452	Watson, Gauld, Armstrong, Goodwillie
21/12/2013	Prem	H	Ross County	1	0		8029	McKay-Steven
26/12/2013	Prem	A	St Mirren	1	4		4780	Ciftci
29/12/2013	Prem	A	St Johnstone	0	3		7231	
01/01/2014	Prem	H	Aberdeen	1	2		12601	Souttar
05/01/2014	Prem	H	Hibernian	2	2		7862	Goodwillie, Graham
12/01/2014	Prem	A	Inverness CT	1	1		2980	Watson
18/01/2014	Prem	A	Ross County	0	3		3609	
01/02/2014	Prem	A	Partick Thistle	1	1		3748	El Alagui
08/02/2014	SC5	H	St Mirren	2	1		4952	Gauld, Ciftci
15/02/2014	Prem	H	Kilmarnock	3	2		6038	McKay-Steven, Good, Rankin
21/02/2014	Prem	H	Motherwell	3	1		7029	Dow, Gunning 2
28/02/2014	Prem	A	Hibernian	3	1		9608	Ciftci, Gunning, El Alagui
09/03/2014	SC6	A	Inverness CT	5	0		3164	Ciftci 2, Gunning, McKay-Steven, Armstrong
12/03/2014	Prem	H	St Johnstone	0	1		6720	
15/03/2014	Prem	H	St Mirren	3	2		6524	Graham, Armstrong, Ciftci
21/03/2014	Prem	A	Hearts	2	1		13448	Graham, Ciftci
26/03/2014	Prem	H	Inverness CT	2	1		6754	Gauld, Dow
29/03/2014	Prem	A	Aberdeen	1	1		14627	Paton
05/04/2014	Prem	H	Celtic	0	2		11033	
12/04/2014	SCSF	A	Rangers	3	1		41059	Ciftci, Armstrong, McKay-Steven
19/04/2014	Prem	A	St Johnstone	0	2		5223	
26/04/2014	Prem	H	Motherwell	5	1		6383	Ciftici 2, Armstrong, Dow, Graham
03/05/2014	Prem	A	Inverness CT	1	1		3428	El Alagui
06/05/2014	Prem	H	Aberdeen	1	3		8677	Dillon
11/05/2014	Prem	A	Celtic	1	3		52400	Twardzik og
17/05/2014	SCF	N	St Johnstone	0	2		47345	

Friendly Matches

Date		Comp	H/A	Opponents	F	A	Crowd		
7/7/13		Fr	A	Union Berlin	1	4	4118		
12/7/13		Fr	A	Energie Cottbus	0	2	5422		
16/7/13		Fr	N	Montrose	1	2		U20	at St Andrews
18/7/13		Fr	A	Cove Rangers	1	1		U20	
19/7/13		Fr	A	CD San Roque	1	3	150		
20/7/13		Fr	A	Buckie Thistle	5	0		U20	
23/7/13		Fr	A	Rangers U20	1	3		U20	at Murray Park
24/7/13		Fr	A	Dunfermline Athletic	3	1	1830		
24/7/13		Fr	A	Fraserburgh	4	1		U20	
26/7/13		Fr	A	Hutchison Vale	3	1		U20	
27/7/13		Fr	A	Wigan Athletic	1	0	3838		
29/7/13		Fr	A	Deveronvale	4	1		U20	
30/7/13		Fr	A	Tayport	0	2		U20	
27/8/13		FCF	H	St Johnstone	1	1	2-4 pens		

Date	Comp	H/A	Opponents	F	A	1	2	3	4	5	6	7	8	9	10	11	12	13	14	15	16	17	18
02/08/2013	Prem	A	Partick Thistle	0	0	Cierzniak	Dillon	Butcher	Watson	Robertson	Paton	Armstrong	Dow+	Gauld"	Goodwillie	Ciftci*	Mackay-Steven*	Graham+	Gardyne	Erskine"	Rankin	Souttar	McCallum
10/08/2013	Prem	H	Inverness CT	0	1	Cierzniak	Dillon	Butcher	Watson	Robertson	Paton	Armstrong+	Rankine*	Erskine+	Goodwillie"	Mackay-Steven	Graham*	Dow+	Ciftci"	Gunning	Gauld	Souttar	McCallum
17/08/2013	Prem	A	Hibernian	1	1	Cierzniak	Dillon	Butcher	Gunning	Robertson	Paton	Armstrong+	Rankine*	Dow"	Goodwillie"	Mackay-Steven"	Graham*	Gauld+	Erskine"	Watson	Ciftci	Souttar	McCallum
25/08/2013	Prem	H	St Johnstone	4	0	Cierzniak	Dillon	Butcher	Watson	Robertson	Paton	Armstrong+	Rankine	Dow*	Goodwillie+	Mackay-Steven	Ciftci*	Gauld+	Erskine"	Graham	Wilson	Souttar	McCallum
28/08/2013	LC2	A	Dumbarton	3	2	Cierzniak	Dillon	Butcher	Wilson*	Robertson	Paton	Souttar	Wilson*	Graham	Gauld"	Gauld"	Ciftci*	Erskine+	Miller"	Gardyne	Gardyne		McCallum
31/08/2013	Prem	H	Celtic	0	1	Cierzniak	Dillon	Gunning	Watson	Robertson	Paton	Armstrong	Rankine	Ciftci	Goodwillie+	Mackay-Steven	Gauld*	Butcher	Graham	Erskine	Wilson	Souttar	McCallum
14/09/2013	Prem	A	Ross County	4	2	Cierzniak	Dillon	Souttar	Watson	Robertson	Paton	Armstrong*	Rankine	Ciftci+	Gauld"	Mackay-Steven	Dow*	Goodwillie+	Graham*	Wilson	McCallum	Oyenuga	Petrie
22/09/2013	Prem	H	Motherwell	2	2	Cierzniak	Dillon	Souttar	Watson	Robertson	Paton	Armstrong	Rankine	Ciftci"	Gauld+	Dow*	Goodwillie*	Graham+	Oyenuga"	Wilson	McCallum	Butcher	Petrie
25/09/2013	LC3	H	Partick Thistle	4	1	Cierzniak	Dillon	Butcher	Gunning	Robertson	Paton	Armstrong	Rankine	Ciftci+	Graham"	Goodwillie	Dow*	Gauld+	Souttar"	Dillon	McCallum	Butcher	Petrie
28/09/2013	Prem	A	Hearts	0	0	Cierzniak	Dillon	Souttar	Watson"	Robertson	Paton	Armstrong+	Rankine	Ciftci"	Gauld*	Goodwillie	Dow*	Gauld+	Graham	Wilson	McCallum	Dow	Petrie
05/10/2013	Prem	H	Kilmarnock	1	0	Cierzniak	Dillon	Soutar	Watson"	Robertson	Paton	Armstrong+	Rankine	Ciftci	Gauld	Goodwillie	Mackay-Steven*	Butcher	Dow"	Wilson	McCallum	Butcher	Graham
19/10/2013	Prem	A	Aberdeen	0	1	Cierzniak	Dillon	Gunning	Watson"	Robertson	Paton	Armstrong+	Rankine	Ciftci	Ciftci"	Goodwillie"	Mackay-Steven"	Mackay-Steven+	Dow"	Wilson	McCallum	Butcher	Gomis
26/10/2013	Prem	H	St Mirren	4	0	Cierzniak	Wilson	Gunning	Souttar	Robertson	Paton+	Graham	Rankine	Ciftci"	Gauld*	McKay-Steven	Erskine*	Gomis+	Dow"	Butcher	McCallum	Armstrong	Goodwillie
29/10/2013	LC4	A	Inverness CT	1	2 AET	Cierzniak	Watson	Souttar	Dillon	Robertson"	Paton"	Armstrong*	Rankine	Ciftci	Gauld	McKay-Steven	Graham*	Gomis+	Butcher"	Goodwillie	McCallum		Gomis
02/11/2013	Prem	A	Celtic	1	1	Cierzniak	Wilson	Gunning	Souttar	Robertson	Gomis"	Armstrong	Rankine	Ciftci*	Graham+	McKay-Steven*	Paton*	Goodwillie+	Dow"	Dillon	McCallum	Butcher	Gauld
09/11/2013	Prem	H	Motherwell	4	0	Cierzniak	Watson	Wilson	Souttar	Robertson	Paton*	Armstrong+	Rankine	Ciftci"	Gauld*	McKay-Steven	Graham*	Goodwillie+	Gomis"	Dillon	McCallum	Dow	Watson
23/11/2013	SC4	H	Partick Thistle	4	1	Cierzniak	Wilson	Gunning	Souttar	Robertson"	Paton*	Armstrong+	Rankine	Ciftci*	Gauld	McKay-Steven	Gomis*	Goodwillie+	Gomis"	Dillon	McCallum	Dow	Watson
29/11/2013	SC4	A	Kilmarnock	5	2	Cierzniak	Wilson+	Gunning	Souttar	Robertson	Paton*	Armstrong+	Rankine"	Ciftci*	Gauld*	McKay-Steven	Graham*	Goodwillie+	Graham"	Dillon	McCallum	Dow	Watson
07/12/2013	Prem	H	Hearts	4	1	Cierzniak	Wilson+	Dillon	Souttar	Robertson"	Paton	Armstrong	Rankine	Graham*	Gauld	McKay-Steven	Goodwillie"	Watson+	Gomis"	Butcher	McCallum	Dow	Erskine
14/12/2013	Prem	A	Kilmarnock	4	1	Cierzniak	Watson	Gunning	Souttar	Robertson	Paton	Armstrong	Rankine	Graham*	Gauld"	McKay-Steven	Ciftci*	Gomis+	Goodwillie"	Dillon	McCallum	Dow	Erskine
21/12/2013	Prem	H	Ross County	1	0	Cierzniak	Wilson	Gunning	Souttar	Robertson	Paton	Armstrong+	Rankine	Graham*	Gauld*	McKay-Steven	Goodwillie"	Goodwillie+	Dillon	Erskine	McCallum	Dow	Erskine
26/12/2013	Prem	A	St Mirren	1	4	Cierzniak	Watson	Butcher	Dillon	Robertson	Paton	Armstrong+	Rankine	Ciftci	Gauld*	McKay-Steven	Ciftci*	Goodwillie+	Dillon	Erskine	McCallum	Dow	Gomis
29/12/2013	Prem	H	St Johnstone	0	3	Cierzniak	Wilson	Butcher	Gunning	Robertson	Paton+	Goodwillie"	Erskine+	Graham	Gomis	Dow"	Souttar"	Armstrong*	McKay-Steven+	Rankine	McCallum	Connelly	Ciftci
01/01/2014	Prem	A	Aberdeen	1	2	Cierzniak	Wilson	Gunning	Souttar	Robertson	Paton	Armstrong	Rankine	Ciftci"	Gauld+	McKay-Steven	Graham*	Gomis+	Dillon	Goodwillie"	McCallum	Dow	Erskine
05/01/2014	Prem	H	Hibernian	2	2	Cierzniak	Wilson+	Gunning	Dillon	Robertson	Paton	Armstrong+	Rankine	Ciftci*	Gauld"	McKay-Steven	Dillon+	Gauld+	Goodwillie"	Erskine	McCallum	Dow	Butcher
12/01/2014	Prem	A	Ross County	0	3	Cierzniak	Watson	Butcher	Gunning	Robertson	Paton	Armstrong+	Rankine"	Erskine"	Graham+	McKay-Steven	Ciftci*	Gauld+	Wilson	Butcher	McCallum	Dow	Gomis
18/01/2014	Prem	H	St Mirren	2	1	Cierzniak	Good	Souter	Wilson	Robertson	Paton	Armstrong*	Rankine	Ciftci"	Gauld*	McKay-Steven	Graham*	Armstrong+	Watson	Dow	Watson	Connelly	Oyenuga
01/02/2014	Prem	A	Partick Thistle	2	1	Cierzniak	Good	Soutar	Dillon	Robertson	Paton	Armstrong*	Erskine+	Ciftci"	Gomis	McKay-Steven	Graham*	Gauld+	Dillon	Dillon	Watson	Graham	McCallum
08/02/2014	SC5	H	St Mirren	2	1	Cierzniak	Good	Soutar	Watson	Robertson	Paton	Armstrong*	Rankine	Ciftci"	Ciftci"	McKay-Steven	Dow*	Gomis+	El Alagui"	Dillon	Watson	Graham	McCallum
15/02/2014	Prem	H	Kilmarnock	3	2	Cierzniak	Good	Soutar	Watson	Robertson	Paton	Armstrong*	Rankine	Ciftci	Gauld+	McKay-Steven	Dow*	Gomis+	Gomis"	Dillon	McCallum	Graham	Wilson
21/02/2014	Prem	A	Motherwell	3	1	Cierzniak	Good	Gunning	Watson	Robertson	Paton	Armstrong+	Rankine	Ciftci	Dow*	McKay-Steven	El Alagui+	Connolly+	Dillon	Wilson	McCallum	Graham	Gomis
28/02/2014	Prem	A	Hibernian	3	1	Cierzniak	Good	Gunning	Watson	Robertson	Paton	Armstrong	Rankine"	Ciftci+	Dow*	McKay-Steven	El Alagui+	Graham+	Gomis"	Wilson	McCallum	Dillon	Connolly
09/03/2014	SC6	A	Inverness CT	5	0	Cierzniak	Dillon"	Gunning	Watson	Robertson	Paton	Armstrong+	Ciftci+	Erskine	Dow*	McKay-Steven	El Alagui"	Gomis+	Graham"	Wilson	McCallum	Butcher	Souttar
12/03/2014	Prem	A	St Johnstone	0	1	Cierzniak	Dillon"	Gunning	Watson	Robertson	Paton	Armstrong	Rankine	Ciftci	Dow*	McKay-Steven	Gauld*	El Alagui+	Graham"	Wilson	McCallum	Souttar	Gomis
15/03/2014	Prem	H	St Mirren	2	1	Cierzniak	Dillon	Gunning	Wilson	Robertson	Paton"	Gauld+	Rankine	Ciftci	El Alagui"	McKay-Steven	Dow*	Armstrong+	Smith"	Butcher	McCallum	Dillon	Gomis
21/03/2014	Prem	A	Hearts	2	1	Cierzniak	Dillon	Gunning	Wilson	Robertson	Paton	Armstrong"	Rankine	Ciftci"	Dow	McKay-Steven	Graham*	Smith"	Gomis"	Watson	McCallum	Souttar	Gomis
26/03/2014	Prem	H	Inverness CT	2	1	Cierzniak	Dillon	Gunning	Wilson	Robertson	Paton	Armstrong*	Rankine	Ciftci+	Dow	McKay-Steven	Gauld+	Gomis+	Connolly"	El Alagui	McCallum	Smith	Connolly
29/03/2014	Prem	A	Aberdeen	1	1	Cierzniak	Dillon	Gunning	Wilson	Robertson	Paton+	Armstrong+	Rankine	Graham	Gauld+	McKay-Steven"	Graham*	Gauld+	Wilson	El Alagui	McCallum	Smith	El Alagui
05/04/2014	Prem	H	Celtic	1	3	Cierzniak	Dillon	Gunning	Dillon	Robertson	Paton	Armstrong	Rankine	Graham+	Dow+	Ciftci"	El Alagui	Gauld+	El Alagui"	Wilson	McCallum	Souttar	Dow
12/04/2014	SCSF	N	Rangers	3	1	Cierzniak	Watson	Gunning	Dillon	Robertson	Paton	Armstrong	Rankine	Gauld+	McKay-Steven	Ciftci	Watson"	Graham+	Gomis"	El Alagui	Connolly	Fraser	Dow
19/04/2014	Prem	H	St Johnstone	0	2	Cierzniak	Watson	Gunning	Souttar	Robertson	Paton	Armstrong	Rankine	Gauld+	McKay-Steven+	Ciftci	Dow*	Graham+	Gomis"	Wilson	McCallum	Gomis	El Alagui
26/04/2014	Prem	H	Motherwell	5	1	Cierzniak	Watson	Gunning	Dillon	Robertson	Paton	Armstrong*	Rankine	Ciftci"	McKay-Steven	McKay-Steven*	Graham*	Gauld+	Gomis"	Watson	McCallum	Souttar	El Alagui
29/04/2014	Prem	A	Inverness CT	1	1	Cierzniak	Watson	Gunning	Dillon	Robertson	Paton	Armstrong+	Rankine	Ciftci"	Dow	McKay-Steven*	El Alagui	Graham+	Connolly"	Wilson	McCallum	Smith	Connolly
03/05/2014	Prem	H	Celtic	1	3	Cierzniak	Wilson	Gunning	Dillon	Soutter	Paton	Gauld+	Rankine	Ciftci	El Alagui	Ciftci"	Graham"	El Alagui+	Wilson	El Alagui"	McCallum	Souttar	Gomis
06/05/2014	Prem	H	Celtic	1	3	McCallum	Wilson*	Gunning	Dillon	Robertson	Paton+	Armstrng	Gomis	Dow+	Gauld*	Ciftci	McKay-Steven"	Armstrong+	Fraser"	Gauld	Connolly	Robertson	Citernziak
11/05/2014	Prem	H	Celtic	1	3	Cierzniak	Wilson	Watson	Dillon	Robertson	Paton	Armstrong"	Gomis	Dow"	Dow*	El Alagui	McKay-Steven"	Graham+	Souttar	Graham	Ciftci	Gauld	McCallum
17/05/2014	SCF	N	St Johnstone	0	2	Cierzniak	Robertson	Robertson	Dillon	Watson	Paton+	Rankine"	Ciftci	Gomis	Armstrng	McKay-Steven"	Gauld"	Graham+	Souttar	Gomis	McCallum	Gauld	El Alagui

Dunfermline Athletic FC

Founded	1885
Ground	East End Park
Postcode	KY12 7RB
Tel	01383 724295
Capacity	11480
Closest Railway Station	Dunfermline Town
Record Attendance	27816, v Celtic, Lge, 30/4/68
Record Win	11-2 v Stenhousemuir, Lge 27/9/1930
Record Defeat	1-13 v St Bernards, SC, 15/9/1883
Most League Goals in a Season	53, Bobby Skinner, 1925/6
Chairman	Bob Garmary
General Managers	Ross McArthur, David McMorrine
Secretary	Shirley Johnston
Manager	Jim Jefferies
Assistant Manager	Neil McCann, John Potter
Colours 2013/14 Top	Black and White Stripes
Shorts	Black and White Stripes
Sponsor	Purvis Group
Manufacturer	Joma
Change Colours 2013/14 Top	Turqouise
Shorts	Black
Nicknames	Pars
Web	www.dafc.co.uk

It's not easy to classify 2013/14 for Dunfermline Athletic. The club and its strong support will have been bitterly disappointed to lose out in the promotion play offs to local rivals Cowdenbeath. Yet they should bear in mid that a year ago the very future of the club was in doubt and the fact that they mounted a promotion challenge at all was quite an achievement.

The troubles that the club have gone through seem to have galvanised the support. For several years the Pars seemed like a club going through the motions but now they appear to be on an upward curve.

Jim Jefferies has provided stability through a difficult period. He will know that he must get of to a flying start in 2014/15 because anything less than promotion will be deemed as failure. He's made some quality signings that should be stand-outs at this level.

PREDICTION 2014/15
Potential Champions

Surname	First Name	DOB	Pos	L A	L S	L G	SC A	SC S	SC G	LC A	LC S	LC G	RC A	RC S	RC G	UNS	Signed Previous Club	Notes	Contract
Byrne	Shaun	09/06/93	M	27	7	4	4			1	1		2			6	2013 Dunfermline Athletic Youth		C (2016)
Dargo	Craig	03/01/78	F	2	7	1	2			1	1		2			10	2012 Dumbarton	Player Coach	OOC
Drummond	Ross	20/03/1994	D	1	1											3	2011 Dunfermline Athletic Youth	On loan to Berwick Rangers	C (2015)
El Bakhtoui	Faissal	08/11/92	F	16	2	4	1						1			15	2012		C (2016)
Falkingham	Josh	25/08/1990	M	32	2	5	4			2			2			1	2012 Arbroath		C (2016)
Ferguson	Ryan	15/01/94	M	1	7		1			1			2	1		10	2013 Dundee United (loan Aug-Dec 2013)	Returned to Dundee Utd	
Forbes	Ross	03/03/89	M	11	6	3											2014 Partick Thistle		C (2015)
Geggan	Andy	08/05/1987	M	36	1	11	4			1	1	1	1				2012 Ayr United		C (2016)
Goodfellow	Ryan	26/05/1993	GK	2	2											41	2012 Dunfermline Athletic Youth		C (2015)
Graham	Finn	05/03/96		1												2	2012 Dunfermline Athletic Youth		Youth
Grainger	Danny	28/07/87	M	15	2												2014 St Mirren	Joined Carlisle United June 2014	
Hrivnak	Martin	05/03/1991	GK													3	2012 Brescia	Released Sep 2013	
Husband	Stephen	29/10/1990	M	24	11	5	1	1		1			1			3	2012 Blackpool		OOC
Johnston	Luke	03/09/1993	D	5	1					1						6	2013 Dundee United (loan Aug-Dec 2013)	Returned to Dundee Utd	
Kane	Chris	31/05/93	M	2	1					1			1			7	2012 Hearts	Joined Cowdenbeath Jan 2014	
Martin	Lewis	08/04/96	D	17	1	1	1									18	2012 Dunfermline Athletic Youth		
Mercer	Scott	18/06/95			1												2013 Dunfermline Athletic Youth	On loan to Albion Rovers Nov	C (2015)
Millen	Ross	28/09/94	D	23			1	4		2			1			14	2012 Dunfermline Athletic Youth		C (2015)
Moore	Jordan	19/02/1994	F	9	7	5	2	2		1	1	1	1			9	2013 Dundee United (loan Aug-Dec 2013)	Returned to Dundee Utd	
Morris	Callum	03/02/90	D	28	2	1	4			2			2	1		2	2012 Hayes & Yeading United	Joined Dundee United June 2014	
O'Kane	Declan	06/03/95	F	1												2	2012 Dunfermline Athletic Youth		Youth
Page	Jonathan	08/02/90	D	13	1											4	2014 Morton		OOC
Potter	John	15/12/1979	D													3	2011 St Mirren	Player Coach	OOC
Scully	Ryan	29/10/92	GK	38			4			2						1	2013 Partick Thistle (Loan)	Returned to Partick Thistle	
Shankland	Lawrence	10/08/95	F	11	2	7	1									1	2014 Aberdeen (Loan)	Returned to Aberdeen	
Smith	Allan	25/01/1994	F	7	17	4	2	1								8	2013 Brechin City		
Spence	Lewis	28/01/96	M	3	4											6	2012 Dunfermline Athletic Youth		Youth
Thomas	James															1	2014 Dunfermline Athletic Youth		C (2015)
Thomson	Ryan	14/03/91	M	17	7	4	2	1	1	2			2	1		1	2008 Dunfermline Athletic Youth		OOC
Thomson	Robert	28/05/93	F	7	2	1										2	2013 Dundee United	Freed Jan 2014, joined Brechin C	
Wallace	Ryan	30/07/90	M	23	4	10	3			2	2		1	2		1	2012 East Fife		C (2016)
Whittle	Alex	15/03/1993	M	30	3	1	3			1	2		2			4	2012 Nike Football Academy		C (2015)
Williamson	Ryan	14/03/1996	D	18	3		1									12	2012 Dunfermline Athletic Youth		C (2016)
Wilson	Jamie		GK													1	2014 Rangers		Youth
Young	Kerr	14/07/93	D	20	1		3			1	2					6	2011 Dunfermline Athletic Youth		C (2015)
Own Goals						2													

NEW SIGNINGS 2014/15

Buchanan	Gregor	2014 Airdrieonians
Stirling	Andrew	2014 Stranraer
Moffat	Michael	2014 Ayr United

Date	Comp	H/A	Opponents	F	A		Crowd	Scorers
27/07/13	RC1	A	Cowdenbeath	3	1		1161	Morris, Ferguson, Thomson
03/08/13	LC1	A	East Stirlingshire	2	0		1043	Wallace, Dargo
13/08/13	L	A	East Fife	1	0		1927	Wallace
17/08/13	L	H	Arbroath	2	3		3242	Morris, Byrne
20/08/13	RC2	H	Raith Rovers	0	2		3765	
24/08/13	L	A	Stenhousemuir	5	4		968	Moore 2, Geggan 2, Smith
27/08/13	LC2	A	Falkirk	1	2		3663	Moore
31/08/13	L	H	Stranraer	3	1		2585	Geggan, Johnston, Smith
14/09/13	L	A	Brechin City	1	1		923	Thomson
21/09/13	L	H	Airdrieonians	2	1		2607	Husband, Geggan
28/09/13	L	H	Ayr United	5	1		2743	Wallace 2, Whittle, Geggan, Falkingham
05/10/13	L	A	Forfar Athletic	0	4		968	
19/10/13	L	H	East Fife	1	2		3131	Moore
26/10/13	L	A	Stranraer	2	1		622	Husband, Falkingham
02/11/13	SC3	A	Elgin City	5	3		1108	Wallace 2, Moore 2, Whittle
06/11/13	L	A	Rangers	1	3		43082	Falkinghm
09/11/13	L	H	Stenhousemuir	3	2		2517	Byrne, Wallace, Smith
16/11/13	L	A	Airdrieonians	3	0		1219	Byrne, Smith, Dargo
23/11/13	L	H	Brechin City	3	1		2569	R Wallace 2, Moyes og
30/11/13	SC4	A	Ayr United	1	1		1391	Geggan
04/12/13	SC4R	H	Ayr United	1	0		1932	Thomson
07/12/13	L	H	Forfar Athletic	1	1		2469	Moore
14/12/13	L	A	Ayr United	4	2		643	Husband, Wallace 2, Moore
21/12/13	L	A	Arbroath	3	0		967	Geggan, Thomson, Falkingham
30/12/13	L	H	Rangers	0	4		10089	
02/01/14	L	A	Stenhousemuir	2	1		1556	El Bakhtoui, Geggan
11/01/14	L	H	Stranraer	3	2		2952	Thomson, Byrne, Shankland
18/01/14	L	H	Airdrieonians	0	1		2711	
25/01/14	L	A	Brechin City	2	3		854	Shankland, Wallace
01/02/14	L	A	East Fife	3	1		1872	Forbes, Wallace, Grainger
07/02/14	SC5	A	Rangers	0	4		19396	
15/02/14	L	A	Forfar Athletic	4	2		833	El Bakhtoui, Husband, Dofs og, Shankland
22/02/14	L	H	Ayr United	3	0		2773	Forbes, Shankland 2
25/02/14	L	H	Arbroath	3	0		1983	Husband, Forbes, Falkingham
01/03/14	L	A	Stranraer	1	3		704	Grainger
08/03/14	L	H	Stenhousemuir	0	0		2510	
15/03/14	L	A	Rangers	0	2		44110	
22/03/14	L	H	East Fife	1	2		2858	Shankland
29/03/14	L	H	Brechin City	2	1		2241	Shankland, Millen
05/04/14	L	A	Airdrieonians	0	2		1142	
12/04/14	L	H	Forfar Athletic	0	0		2634	
19/04/14	L	A	Ayr United	1	1		1272	Thomson
26/04/14	L	A	Arbroath	2	1		1079	Thomson, Geggan
03/05/14	L	H	Rangers	1	1		7605	Martin
07/05/14	PO	A	Stranraer	1	2		867	El Bakhtoui
10/05/14	PO	H	Stranraer	3	0	aet	4525	Geggan 2, El Bakhtoui
14/05/14	PO	A	Cowdenbeath	1	1		3379	Geggan
18/05/14	PO	H	Cowdenbeath	0	3		8288	

Friendly Matches

13/7/13	Fr	H	Hearts	1	2	4538	
20/7/13	Fr	H	Falkirk	2	2	1344	
24/7/13	Fr	H	Dundee United	1	3	1830	
25/7/13	Fr	A	Rosyth	2	5	U20	
30/7/13	Fr	A	Oakley United	4	2	Res	
2/9/13	Fr	A	Glenrothes	2	0	U20	
5/9/13	Fr	A	Ballingry Rovers	1	2	U20	

Date	Comp	H/A	Opponents	F	A	1	2	3	4	5	6	7	8	9	10	11	12	13	14	15	16	17	18
27/07/13	RC1	A	Cowdenbeath	3	1	Scully	Millen	Whittle	Young	Morris	Kane	Ferguson*	Byrne	Wallace+	Falkingham*	Ryan Thomson	Dargo*	El Bakhtoui+	Potter*	Williamson	Hrivnak		Goodfellow
03/08/13	LC1	A	East Stirlingshire	2	0	Scully	Millen	Whittle	Young	Morris	Kane	Ferguson+	Byrne*	Wallace*	Falkingham*	Ryan Thomson	Geggan*	Dargo+	Moore*	Johnston	Hrivnak	Williamson	Hrivnak
13/08/13	L	H	East Fife	1	0	Scully	Millen	Whittle	Young	Morris	Kane	Falkingham	Byrne*	Wallace	Geggan	Ryan Thomson	Falkingham*	Dargo++	Moore*	Moore	Johnston		
17/08/13	L	A	Arbroath	2	3	Scully	Millen*	Whittle	Young	Morris	Moore	Falkingham	Byrne*	Wallace+	Geggan	Ryan Thomson	Falkingham*	Dargo++	Potter*	Dargo	El Bakhtoui	Potter	
20/08/13	RC2	H	Raith Rovers	0	2	Scully	Ferguson*	Whittle	Young	Morris	Moore	Falkingham	Byrne	Dargo*	Geggan	Ryan Thomson	Smith*	Husband+	Smith*	Johnston	El Bakhtoui		
24/08/13	L	A	Stenhousemuir	5	4	Scully	Millen	Whittle	Young	Morris	Moore*	Falkingham	Husband+	Wallace	Geggan	Ryan Thomson*	Wallace	Byrne+	Dargo	Kane	El Bakhtoui	Ferguson	Goodfellow
27/08/13	LC2	A	Falkirk	3	1	Scully	Millen	Whittle	Johnston	Morris	Moore*	Falkingham	Husband	Wallace*	Geggan	Ryan Thomson*	Smith*	Ryan Thomson+	Byrne*	Kane	El Bakhtoui	Ferguson	Goodfellow
31/08/13	L	H	Stranraer	3	1	Scully	Millen	Whittle	Johnston	Morris	Moore*	Falkingham	Husband	Wallace*	Geggan	Rob Thomson	Smith*	Ryan Thomson+	Ferguson*	Young	El Bakhtoui	Byrne	Goodfellow
14/09/13	L	A	Brechin City	1	1	Scully	Millen	Whittle	Johnston	Morris	Moore*	Falkingham	Husband	Wallace+	Geggan	Rob Thomson	Smith*	Ryan Thomson+	Ferguson*	Kane	El Bakhtoui	Ferguson	Goodfellow
21/09/13	L	H	Airdrieonians	2	1	Scully	Millen	Whittle	Johnston	Morris	Wallace*	Falkingham	Husband	Byrne+	Geggan	Rob Thomson	Smith*	Wallace+	Ryan Thomson*	Young	El Bakhtoui	Ferguson	Goodfellow
28/09/13	L	A	Arbroath	5	1	Scully	Millen	Whittle	Johnston	Morris	Wallace+	Falkingham	Husband	Byrne*	Geggan*	Rob Thomson	Young*	Ryan Thomson+	Ryan Thomson*	Moore	Smith	Ferguson	Goodfellow
05/10/13	L	A	Forfar Athletic	0	4	Scully	Millen	Whittle*	Johnston	Morris	Wallace*	Falkingham	Husband	Byrne*	Geggan	Rob Thomson+	Byrne*	Smith++	Moore*	Young	El Bakhtoui	Martin	Goodfellow
19/10/13	L	H	East Fife	1	2	Scully	Millen	Whittle	Young	Morris	Wallace*	Falkingham	Husband	Byrne*	Geggan	Ryan Thomson*	Ferguson*	Ferguson+	Ferguson*	Dargo	El Bakhtoui	Martin	Goodfellow
26/10/13	L	A	Stranraer	2	1	Scully	Millen	Whittle	Young	Morris	Wallace+	Falkingham	Husband	Byrne+	Geggan	Ryan Thomson*	Smith+	Husband+	Dargo	Dargo	Ferguson	Martin	Goodfellow
02/11/13	SC3	H	Elgin City	5	3	Scully	Millen	Whittle	Young	Morris	Wallace*	Falkingham	Moore	Byrne	Geggan	Rob Thomson	Smith*	Smith+	Moore*	Johnston	Goodfellow	Martin	Williamson
06/11/13	L	H	Rangers	1	3	Scully	Millen	Whittle	Young	Morris	Wallace	Falkingham	Ryan Thomson	Byrne	Rob Thomson*	Smith	Ferguson*	Dargo+	Kane	Husband	Martin	Rob Thomson	Williamson
09/11/13	L	H	Stenhousemuir	3	2	Scully	Williamson	Williamson	Young	Morris	Wallace	Falkingham	Ryan Thomson*	Byrne	Geggan	Smith+	Dargo*	Ferguson++	Moore	Martin	Martin	Johnston	Goodfellow
16/11/13	L	A	Airdrieonians	3	1	Scully	Williamson	Williamson	Johnston	Morris	Wallace*	Falkingham	Ryan Thomson	Byrne	Geggan	Smith+	Dargo*	Ferguson+	Moore	Kane	Martin	Rob Thomson	Goodfellow
23/11/13	L	H	Brechin City	1	1	Scully	Millen	Whittle	Young	Morris	Wallace*	Falkingham	Ryan Thomson*	Byrne	Geggan	Smith*	Smith*	Husband+	Moore*	Husband	Martin	Johnston	Goodfellow
30/11/13	SC4	H	Ayr United	1	1	Scully	Millen	Whittle	Young	Morris	Wallace	Falkingham	Ryan Thomson*	Byrne	Geggan	Smith*	Dargo*	Ferguson++	Moore	Kane	Martin	Moore	Millen
04/12/13	SC4R	A	Ayr United	1	0	Scully	Millen	Whittle	Young	Morris	Wallace*	Falkingham	Ryan Thomson*	Byrne	Geggan	Smith*	Dargo*	Husband+	Moore+	Smith	Goodfellow	Drummond	Goodfellow
07/12/13	L	A	Forfar Athletic	1	1	Scully	Williamson	Williamson	Martin	Page	Wallace	Ryan Thomson+	Smith*	Byrne*	Millen*	Shankland	Husband*	Moore+	Kane*	Spence	Page	Drummond	Goodfellow
14/12/13	L	H	Ayr United	4	2	Scully	Williamson	Grainger	Martin	Morris	Wallace+	Falkingham	Forbes+	El Bakhtoui	Grainger	Shankland	Falkingham*	Husband+	Ryan Thomson*	Young	Whittle	El Bakhtoui	Goodfellow
21/12/13	L	A	Arbroath	3	0	Scully	Williamson	Whittle	Husband*	Morris	Shankland	Falkingham	Forbes+	El Bakhtoui*	Grainger	Geggan	Husband*	Shankland+	Moore*	Moore	Byrne	Millen	Goodfellow
30/12/13	L	H	Rangers	0	4	Scully	Williamson	Whittle*	Husband*	Martin	Shankland*	Falkingham*	Forbes+	El Bakhtoui*	Grainger	Geggan	Williamson*	Byrne+	Dargo*	Wallace	Martin	Whittle	Goodfellow
02/01/14	L	A	Stenhousemuir	0	2	Scully	Williamson	Whittle*	Husband+	Martin	Shankland*	Falkingham*	Forbes+	El Bakhtoui*	Grainger	Geggan	Whittle*	Thomson+	Smith	Martin	Millen	Byrne	Goodfellow
11/01/14	L	H	Rangers	3	2	Scully	Millen+	Whittle	Husband	Morris	Shankland*	Moore++	Forbes*	El Bakhtoui*	Grainger	Geggan	Smith*	Thomson+	Williamson*	Dargo	Martin	Spence	Williamson
18/01/14	L	A	Airdrieonians	3	1	Scully*	Millen*	Whittle*	Husband	Morris	Shankland*	Whittle+	Byrne	Byrne	Wallace*	Geggan	Goodfellow*	Spence+	Smith*	Thomson	Falkingham	Byrne	Williamson
25/01/14	L	A	Brechin City	2	3	Scully	Millen*	Williamson	Martin+	Morris	Shankland*	Whittle	Falkingham*	El Bakhtoui*	Wallace*	Geggan	Smith*	Forbes+	Ryan Thomson*	Byrne	Spence	Williamson	Goodfellow
01/02/14	L	H	East Fife	3	1	Scully	Millen*	Whittle	Husband	Morris	Shankland	Forbes	Falkingham*	El Bakhtoui+	Grainger	Geggan	Smith*	Smith+	Husband*	Byrne	Spence	Spence	Goodfellow
07/02/14	SC5	A	Rangers	0	4	Scully	Williamson	Whittle	Husband*	Morris*	Shankland	Smith+	Forbes+	Smith+	Wallace*	Shankland	Whittle*	Smith+	Byrne	Smith	El Bakhtoui	Graham	Millen
15/02/14	L	A	Forfar Athletic	4	2	Scully	Millen	Whittle	Martin	Page	Martin	Falkingham	Falkingham	Byrne*	Millen*	Geggan	Forbes*	Moore+	Forbes*	Young	Page	Drummond	Goodfellow
22/02/14	L	H	Ayr United	3	0	Scully	Williamson	Whittle	Husband+	Morris	Forbes*	Falkingham	Ryan Thomson*	Byrne*	Grainger	Shankland	Falkingham*	Husband+	Moore+	Young	Whittle	El Bakhtoui	Goodfellow
25/02/14	L	H	Arbroath	3	0	Williamson	Millen*	Whittle	Husband*	Morris	Potter+	Husband+	Ryan Thomson	Byrne	Grainger	Geggan	Husband*	El Bakhtoui*	Moore*	Wallace	Husband	Millen	Goodfellow
01/03/14	L	A	Stranraer	1	3	Scully	Martin	Whittle	Husband	Morris	El Bakhtoui	Graham*	Falkingham*	El Bakhtoui*	Wallace*	Geggan	Smith*	Shankland+	Smith	Martin	Martin	Martin	Williamson
08/03/14	L	H	Stenhousemuir	0	0	Scully	Millen*	Page	Husband*	Smith*	El Bakhtoui	Byrne	Falkingham*	El Bakhtoui*	Wallace*	Geggan	Goodfellow*	Byrne+	Smith*	Thomson	Falkingham	Spence	Williamson
15/03/14	L	A	Rangers	0	2	Scully*	Millen	Page	Husband	Byrne	Martin	Whittle	Byrne	Whittle	Ryan Thomson*	Geggan	Smith*	Spence+	Ryan Thomson*	Martin	Millen	Bakhtoui	Millen
22/03/14	L	H	East Fife	1	2	Scully	Millen	Page	Martin+	Morris	Shankland*	Whittle	Whittle	El Bakhtoui	Wallace*	Geggan	Smith*	Forbes+	Husband*	Byrne	Spence	Williamson	Goodfellow
29/03/14	L	A	Brechin City	2	1	Scully	Williamson	Page	Husband	Morris	Shankland	Forbes	El Bakhtoui	Forbes*	Grainger	Geggan	Whittle*	Smith+	Byrne	Martin	Spence	Graham	Williamson
05/04/14	L	H	Airdrieonians	0	2	Scully	Millen	Page	Husband*	Morris	Martin	Forbes	Falkingham*	Ryan Thomson*	Ryan Thomson*	Geggan	Whittle*	Smith+	Byrne	Martin	Spence	Shankland	Goodfellow
12/04/14	L	A	Forfar Athletic	1	1	Goodfellow	Williamson	Page	Husband+	Smith*	Martin	Whittle*	Falkingham*	El Bakhtoui*	Grainger	Geggan	Morris*	Geggan+	Page+	Millen	El Bakhtoui	Graham	Scully
19/04/14	L	H	Ayr United	1	1	Millen	Millen	Page	Spence+	Byrne	Martin	Whittle*	Husband+	Ryan Thomson	El Bakhtoui	Bakhtoui	Smith*	Byrne+	Forbes*	O'Kane	Smith	Williamson	Goodfellow
26/04/14	L	A	Arbroath	0	0	Scully	Williamson	Page	Geggan	Morris	Forbes*	Husband+	Whittle*	Ryan Thomson	Grainger	Dargo*	Spence*	Byrne+	Wallace*	Millen	O'Kane	Williamson	Goodfellow
03/05/14	L	H	Rangers	2	1	Goodfellow	Williamson	Whittle	Martin	Young	Martin	Graham*	Spence	Whittle	Smith	Dargo*	Husband*	Page+	Mercer*	Millen	Whittle	Thomas	Wilson
07/05/14	PO	H	Stranraer	1	1	Scully	Martin	Page	Geggan*	Morris	El Bakhtoui	Ryan Thomson*	Byrne	Spence	Grainger	Falkingham+	Forbes*	Smith+	Martin*	Smith	Whittle	Williamson	Goodfellow
10/05/14	PO	A	Stranraer	1	1	Scully	Martin	Young	Geggan	Williamson	Williamson*	Whittle	Whittle	Whittle	Grainger	Falkingham	Forbes*	Forbes+	Byrne*	Morris	Millen	Spence	Goodfellow
14/05/14	PO	H	Cowdenbeath	1	1	Scully	Martin	Young	Geggan	Williamson*	El Bakhtoui	Ryan Thomson*	Husband+	Whittle	Grainger	Falkingham	Smith*	Smith+	Morris*	Byrne	Page	Page	Goodfellow
18/05/14	PO	A	Cowdenbeath	0	3	Scully	Martin	Young	Husband*	Williamson	El Bakhtoui	Ryan Thomson*	Byrne*	Whittle	Grainger	Falkingham	Forbes*	Husband+	Dargo*	Page	Morris	Millen	Goodfellow

East Fife FC

Founded	1903
Ground	Bayview Stadium
Postcode	KY8 3RW
Tel	01333 426323
Capacity	1980
Closest Railway Station	Kirkcaldy
Record Attendance	22515 v Raith Rovers, 2/1/1950
Record Win	13-2 v Edinburgh City, Lge, 11/12/1937
Record Defeat	0-9, v Hearts, Lge, 5/10/1957
Most League Goals in a Season	41 Jock Wood 1926/7; Henry Morris 1947/8
Chairman	Lee Murray
Secretary	Jim Stevenson
Manager	Willie Aitchison (until Nov 2013) / Gary Naysmith
Assistant Manager	Kevin Drinkell (until Sep 2013), Robbie Neilson / Paul Hegarty
Colours 2013/14 Top	Black and Gold Stripes
Shorts	Black and Gold Stripes
Sponsor	Doe Sport
Manufacturer	1903 Club Branded
Change Colours 2013/14 Top	White with Black flashes
Shorts	
3rd Kit 2013/14 Top	Blue and White Saltire Design
Shorts	
Nicknames	Fifers
Web	www.eastfifefc.info

In 2012/13 East Fife escaped relegation through the Play offs but it wasn't to be in 2013/14. Once again they finished second bottom but after beating Clyde they lost out to Stirling Albion in the Final.

It was a season that turned out to be one of false hope. Pre-season all the talk was about big plans and big signings. Ultimately these came to very little and by mid season it was clear that the Fifers would be in a relegation battle. They chopped and changed their line-up in a search for consistency but were unable to halt a slide towards the foot of the table.

They also crashed out of all three Cups at the first hurdle which meant it was a tough season for their loyal group if supporters.

PREDICTION 2014/15
Should make the promotion play offs

Surname	First Name	DOB	Pos	L A	S	G	SC A	S	G	LC A	S	G	RC A	S	G	UNS	Signed Previous Club	Notes	Contract
Andrews	Michael	25/03/90	GK	4			1			1			1			13	2013 Brechin City	Freed Jan 2014, Joined Berwick Rangers	
Austin	Nathan	15/02/94	F	13	13	5	1			1			1			6	2013 Leven United		C (2015)
Barr	Lewis	26/04/94	M	11	6											8			C (2015)
Brown	Ross	10/06/93	M	15	6	2	1			1			1			2	2012 East Fife Youths		C (2015)
Buchanan	Liam	27/03/85	F	35	4	11	1			1	2	2	1	1		3	2013 Ayr United		F
Campbell	Steven	20/08/86	D	29	1	1	1									2	2009 Perth SC (Australia)		C (2016)
Clarke	Pat	18/05/85	F	11	12	1	1			1			1			5	2013 Raith Rovers		F
Cowan	David	05/03/82	D	11	2											1	2012 Cowdenbeath		F
Davidson	Jordan															1	2013 East Fife Youths		Youth
Durie	Scott	11/11/91	D	26	6	2	1			1			1			5	2010 Rangers		F
Dutot	Alexis	14/03/92	D	6	1					1						6	2012 Rouen B	Freed Jan 2014	
Falconer	Daryl															2	2013 East Fife Youths		Youth
Fisher	Gary	06/06/92	D	12	1	1										1	2013 Kilmarnock		F
Fotheringham	Greg	19/02/94	M	1												2	2013 Forfar Athletic	Joined Stenhousemuir June 2014	OOC
Grieve	Bradley							1								1			Youth
Hamilton	Jack		GK	2													2014 Hearts (Loan)	Returned to Hearts	
Henderson	Blair					3										2	2013 Dunfermline Athletic (Loan Dec-Jan)	Returned to Dunfermline	
Holmes	Derek	11/10/78	F	1														Trialist, Ex Arbroath etc	
Hughes	Stephen	14/11/82	M	19	2	2	1										2013 Aberdeen	Joined Dundee Jan, loaned to East Fife Feb	
Inkango	Bruce	18/05/84	F	4												5	2014 Denizlispor		F
Johnston	Craig	15/11/84	D	30	3	1	1			1	1		1			4	2010 Kennoway Amateurs		
Lennie	Ross					1										10	2013 East Fife Youths		Youth
Maskrey	David	19/01/96														1	2013 East Fife Youths		Youth
Mbu	Joe	14/02/82	D	27	1		1			1			1			7	2013 Cowdenbeath		
McBride	Scott	19/09/89	M	16	7	3	1			1			1			5	2012 Raith Rovers		
McKenzie	Marc	11/07/85	M	12	3	1										5	2014 Cowdenbeath (Loan)	Returned to Cowdenbeath	
Moosavi	Cyrus	31/01/91	M	4	4					1						5	2013 Edinburgh University		
Naysmith	Gary	16/11/78	D	10												1	2013 Aberdeen	Manager	R
Neilson	Robbie		D	5													2013 Falkirk	Joined Hearts May 2014	
O'Neill	Stephen	07/06/94	M	10	2	1										5	2014 Aberdeen (Loan)	Returned to Aberdeen	
Paterson	Greg	16/09/89	GK	32												8	2013 Forfar Athletic		F
Rooney	Dylan		GK	2	1											4	2013 East Fife Youths		C (2015)
Rutkiewicz	Kevin	10/05/80	D	13	1											1	2014 Carolina RailHawks		
Shaw	Connor		GK													15	2013 East Fife Youths	On Loan to Livingston United	Youth
Smith	Kevin	20/03/87	F	21	1	1	1									1	2013 Dumbarton (Loan)		C (2015)
Stewart	Johnny	12/02/90	M	21	7		1			1			1			10	2013 Brechin City		
Stewart	Ryan	06/10/93	M	8	10	1	1			1		1	1			9	2013 Brechin City		F
Thom	Gary	07/10/87	D	19	2	1				1						11	2013 Stirling Albion		F
Thomson	James	07/11/94	M	4												3	2013 Dundee (Loan)	Returned to Dundee	
Tuta	Cedric	31/01/88	D	5	4											1		Freed Jan 2014	
Willis	Paul	21/08/91	M	6	5		1			1						4	2013 Dunfermline Athletic		
Wilson	Kyle		M										1			2	2013 East Fife Youths		Youth
Woolley	Liam	08/06/96	M	2												2	2013 East Fife Youths		Youth
Own Goals				1															

NEW SIGNINGS 2014/15

Surname	First Name	Pos	Signed Previous Club
Cook	Alan	F	2014 Arbroath
McShane	Jon	F	2014 Celtic Nation
Walker	Allan	M	2014 Brechin City
McAleer	Caloan	F	2014 Partick Thistle
Moyes	Ewan	D	2014 Brechin City
Mullen	Fraser	D	2014 Raith Rovers

Date	Comp	H/A	Opponents	F	A		Crowd	Scorers
27/07/2013	RC1	A	Forfar Athletic	1	2		545	Buchanan pen
03/08/2013	LC1	H	Morton	2	6	AET	727	Buchanan 2
10/08/2013	L	H	Dunfermline Athletic	0	1		1927	
17/08/2013	L	A	Brechin City	0	2		543	
24/08/2013	L	H	Arbroath	2	1		809	Durie, Buchanan
31/08/2013	L	A	Rangers	0	5		42870	
14/09/2013	L	H	Forfar Athletic	1	3		796	Durie
21/09/2013	L	A	Stranraer	0	2		349	
28/09/2013	L	H	Airdrieonians	1	0		665	McBride
05/10/2013	L	A	Stenhousemuir	1	1		567	Johnstone
12/10/2013	L	H	Ayr United	1	4		753	Buchanan
19/10/2013	L	A	Dunfermline Athletic	2	1		3131	Brown, Buchanan
26/10/2013	L	H	Rangers	0	4		4700	
02/11/2013	SC3	A	Forfar Athletic	1	2		485	Johnstone
09/11/2013	L	A	Arbroath	2	2		603	Buchanan 2
16/11/2013	L	H	Stranraer	1	2		713	Buchanan
23/11/2013	L	A	Forfar Athletic	0	2		556	
07/12/2013	L	H	Stenhousemuir	1	0		561	Fisher
14/12/2011	L	A	Airdrieonians	3	1		624	Buchanan og, Brown, Hughes
21/12/2013	L	H	Brechin City	1	3		745	R Stewart
28/12/2013	L	A	Ayr United	0	2		1059	
02/01/2014	L	H	Arbroath	1	0		910	Austin
11/01/2014	L`	A	Rangers	0	2		42181	
18/01/2014	L	H	Forfar Athletic	2	1		685	McKenzie, O'Neill
01/02/2014	L	H	Dunfermline Athletic	1	3		1872	Willis
08/02/2014	L	A	Brechin City	0	3		523	
15/02/2014	L	A	Stenhousemuir	1	1		465	Buchanan
22/02/2014	L	H	Airdrieonians	0	0		815	
01/03/2014	L	H	Rangers	0	1		4020	
04/03/2014	L	A	Stranraer	0	2		407	
08/03/2014	L	A	Arbroath	1	2		679	Buchanan
15/03/2014	L	H	Ayr United	0	5		647	
22/03/2014	L	A	Dunfermline Athletic	2	1		2858	Buchanan, Austin
29/03/2014	L	A	Forfar Athletic	2	1		539	Buchanan, Austin
05/04/2014	L	H	Stranraer	1	1		636	Austin
12/04/2014	L	H	Stenhousemuir	1	2		639	Hughes
19/04/2014	L	A	Airdrieonians	1	2		1033	Campbell
26/04/2014	L	H	Brechin City	1	2		591	Clarke
03/05/2014	L	A	Ayr United	1	4		1952	Buchanan
07/05/2014	PO	A	Clyde	0	1		1005	
10/05/2014	PO	H	Clyde	2	1	aet 7-6p	1018	McBride, Smith
14/05/2014	PO	A	Stirling Albion	2	1		1501	McBride, Austin
18/05/2014	PO	H	Stirling Albion	0	2		1516	

Friendly Matches

6/7/13	Fr	A	Alloa	1	1			
10/7/13	Fr	H	Wolves	2	3			
13/7/13	Fr	H	Cowdenbeath	0	0		417	
17/7/13	Fr	H	Kilmarnock	0	1			
20/7/13	Fr	H	Hamilton Accies	0	4		301	
20/7/13	Tnt	N	Kennoway Star Hearts	0	4		U19	at Newburgh
21/7/13	Tnt	N	Raith Rovers U19			lost	U19	
30/7/13	Fr	H	Celtic XI	2	0			
7/9/13	Fr	E	Leven Amateurs	5	0			
28/11/13	FCP	H	Cowdenbeath	1	2		227	

Date	Comp	H/A	Opponents	F	A	1	2	3	4	5	6	7	8	9	10	11	12	13	14	15	16	17	18
27/07/2013	RC1	A	Forfar Athletic	1	2	Andrews	Durie	Johnston*	Thom	Mbu	J Stewart	Willis	McBride"	Clarke	Buchanan	Wilson+	Brown*	R Stewart+	Austin"	Paterson	G Fotheringham	Paterson	Lennie
03/08/2013	LC1	H	Morton	2	6 AET	Andrews	Durie	J Stewart*	Dutot	Mbu	Brown	Willis"	Johnstone	Clarke+	Buchanan	Moosavi	Grieve*	Austin+	P Stewart"	McBride	Falconer	Austin	Davidson
10/08/2013	L	H	Dunfermline Athletic	0	1	Andrews	Durie	J Stewart*	Thom	Mbu	McBride	Dutot+	Johnstone"	Moosavi	Buchanan	Tuta"	Clarke	Willis+	Brown"	Fotheringham	R Stewart	Barr	R Stewart
17/08/2013	L	A	Brechin City	0	2	Andrews	Durie	J Stewart"	Thom	Mbu	Brown	Willis	Johnstone"	Dutot*	Buchanan"	Tuta"	Clarke	R Stewart+	Brown"	Fotheringham	Paterson	Austin	McBride
24/08/2013	L	A	Arbroath	2	1	Andrews	Durie	J Stewart"	Thom	Mbu	Brown	Naysmith	Johnstone	Dutot+	Buchanan	Tuta"	Clarke*	Austin+	Clarke"	Moosavi	R Stewart	Barr	Durie
31/08/2013	L	H	Rangers	0	5	Paterson	Neilson	Durie	Thom+	Mbu	Austin	Willis	Johnstone	Clarke+	Buchanan	Tuta"	Brown*	Campbell+	Brown"	Moosavi	Andrews	Willis	Andrews
14/09/2013	L	A	Forfar Athletic	1	3	Paterson	Neilson	Thom	Thom	Campbell	McBride	Naysmith"	Johnstone	Clarke+	Buchanan	Willis	Brown*	Austin+	Tuta"	Moosavi	Andrews	Mbu	Durie
21/09/2013	L	A	Stranraer	0	2	Paterson	Neilson*	J Stewart*	Johnstone	Campbell	McBride	Naysmith	Johnstone	Clarke+	Buchanan	Tuta"	Durie*	Moosavi+	Tuta"	Dutot	Andrews	Andrews	Lennie
28/09/2013	L	H	Airdrieonians	1	0	Paterson	Neilson*	J Stewart*	Johnston	Campbell	McBride	Naysmith+	Johnstone	Clarke	Buchanan	Willis	Brown*	Austin+	Tuta"	Shaw	Andrews	Austin	Andrews
05/10/2013	L	A	Stenhousemuir	1	1	Paterson	Brown	Durie	Johnston	Mbu	McBride	Naysmith	Johnstone	Clarke	Buchanan	Brown"	Durie*	Moosavi+	Mbu"	Dutot	Shaw	Mbu	Lennie
12/10/2013	L	A	Ayr United	1	4	Paterson	J Stewart"	Durie	Thom	Mbu	McBride	Naysmith	Johnstone	Hughes*	Buchanan	Brown"	Durie*	Tuta+	Dutot"	Shaw	Austin	Mbu	Lennie
19/10/2013	L	H	Dunfermline Athletic	2	1	Paterson	Brown	Durie	Thom	Mbu	McBride"	Naysmith	Johnstone	Hughes*	Buchanan	R Stewart+	Durie"	Tuta+	Clarke"	J Stewart	Barr	Andrews	Andrews
26/10/2013	L	H	Rangers	0	4	Paterson	Brown	Dutot	Thom	Mbu	McBride	Naysmith	Johnstone"	Hughes"	Buchanan	R Stewart	Tuta*	Austin	Austin"	Andrews	Campbell	Durie	Moosavi
02/11/2013	SC3	A	Forfar Athletic	1	2	Andrews	Durie	Campbell+	Thom	Mbu	McBride	Brown*	Johnstone"	Hughes	Buchanan	R Stewart	Tuta"	Barr+	Durie"	Austin	Paterson	Dutot	Clark
09/11/2013	L	A	Arbroath	2	2	Paterson	McBride	Campbell	Johnstone*	Mbu	McBride	J Stewart"	Moosavi"	Fisher	Buchanan	Smith"	Clarke*	Moosavi+	Barr"	Andrews	Austin	Lennie	Wilson
16/11/2013	L	H	Forfar Athletic	1	2	Paterson	Thomson	Campbell	Johnston	Mbu	Brown	J Stewart"	Barr+	Fisher*	Buchanan	Smith"	Clarke*	Moosavi+	Holmes"	Andrews	R Stewart	Dutot	Tuta
23/11/2013	L	H	Forfar Athletic	0	2	Paterson	Thomson	Campbell	Johnston	Mbu	Brown	Thom	Barr	Fisher+	Buchanan+	Smith"	Clarke*	Henderson+	Holmes"	Durie	R Stewart	Thomson	Henderson
07/12/2013	L	A	Stenhousemuir	1	0	Paterson	Durie	Campbell	Johnston	Mbu	Brown*	Stewart	Barr	Fisher	Austin"	Smith	Durie*	Stewart+	Lennie"	Durie	Durie	Thom	Lennie
14/12/2011	L	A	Airdrieonians	3	1	Paterson	Durie	McBride"	Johnston"	Mbu	Brown*	J Stewart	Buchanan	Fisher	Austin+	Clarke	Hughes*	Stewart+	Lennie"	Barr	Durie	Barr	Thom
21/12/2013	L	A	Brechin City	1	3	Paterson	Durie	Campbell	Thom	Hughes	Brown+	J Stewart	Buchanan	Fisher	Austin"	Clarke+	R Stewart	Buchanan+	Henderson"	Andrews	Barr	Dutot	Henderson
28/12/2013	L	H	Ayr United	0	2	Paterson	Durie	Campbell	Johnston*	Mbu	Brown+	J Stewart	Buchanan	Fisher	R Stewart"	Clarke+	Willis*	Clarke+	Austin"	Andrews	J Stewart	Thom	Lennie
02/01/2014	L	A	Arbroath	1	0	Paterson	Durie	McBride"	Thom	Campbell	Willis*	Hughes	Buchanan	Fisher	R Stewart	Clarke"	Durie*+	Johnstone+	Clarke"	Andrews	Andrews	Thom	Shaw
11/01/2014	L'	A	Rangers	0	2	Paterson	Durie	Campbell+	Rutkiewicz	Mbu	Johnston	O'Neill	Buchanan	Johnstone	Smith	Smith	O'Neill*	Henderson"	Barr"	Thomson??	Willis	Willis	Shaw
18/01/2014	L	H	Forfar Athletic	1	3	Paterson	Durie	Campbell+	Rutkiewicz"	Mbu	McKenzie	O'Neill+	Buchanan	Fisher+	Smith"	Smith	Willis*	J Stewart+	Johnston	Thom	Barr	Brown	Shaw
01/02/2014	L	H	Dunfermline Athletic	1	3	Paterson	Durie	Campbell+	Rutkiewicz	Mbu	McKenzie	O'Neill	Buchanan	Fisher+	Smith"	Smith	Willis"	J Stewart+	Johnston	Barr	Brown	O'Neill	Shaw
08/02/2014	L	H	Brechin City	0	3	Hamilton	Durie	Cowan	J Stewart	Mbu	McKenzie	Campbell"	Buchanan	Fisher*	Smith+	O'Neill	R Stewart"	J Stewart+	Brown"	Naysmith	Naysmith	Austin	Shaw
15/02/2014	L	A	Stenhousemuir	1	1	Hamilton	Durie	Cowan	Rutkiewicz+	Mbu	Smith	Campbell"	Buchanan"	Fisher	Smith-	Johnstone	Rutkiewicz*	Johnstone+	McBride"	Willis	Willis	Falconer	Shaw
22/02/2014	L	A	Airdrieonians	0	0	Paterson	Durie	Cowan"	Rutkiewicz	Mbu	Smith	J Stewart+	Buchanan*	Fisher+	Smith-	Hughes	O'Neill*	Austin+	Barr"	Thom	J Stewart	Barr	Shaw
01/03/2014	L	H	Rangers	0	2	Paterson	Durie	Campbell	Johnston	Mbu	Smith+	Campbell*	Buchanan*	Fisher*	Smith+	Hughes	Johnstone*	Clarke+	Clarke"	Thom	J Stewart	Barr	Shaw
04/03/2014	L	A	Arbroath	0	2	Paterson	Durie*	Campbell	Rutkiewicz	Mbu	Smith+	Campbell*	Buchanan"	Fisher+	Smith-	Hughes	R Stewart*	Austin+	Clarke"	J Stewart	J Stewart	Campbell	Shaw
15/03/2014	L	H	Arbroath	1	2	Paterson	Durie	Campbell"	Johnston	Mbu	Smith+	Barr*	Buchanan"	Johnstone	Smith	Hughes	R Stewart*	Barr	Clarke"	Smith	O'Neill	Shaw	Shaw
22/03/2014	L	A	Dunfermline Athletic	2	1	Paterson	Durie*	Campbell	Johnston	Thom*	Smith"	Barr	McKenzie	O'Neill	Johnstone	Hughes+	Inkango*	J Stewart+	R Stewart"	Woolley	Woolley	McKenzie	McKenzie
29/03/2014	L	H	Forfar Athletic	2	1	Paterson*	Durie	Campbell"	Rutkiewicz	Mbu	Smith	Barr	Buchanan	O'Neill"	Johnstone+	Hughes+	McKenzie*	Thom+	J Stewart"	R Stewart	R Stewart	Clark	Inkango
05/04/2014	L	A	Stranraer	1	1	Paterson	Durie	Campbell	Rutkiewicz"	Austin*	Smith	J Stewart+	Buchanan	O'Neill	Johnstone"	Hughes	Inkango*	Cowan+	McBride"	Thom	Mbu	O'Neill	Paterson
12/04/2014	L	H	Stenhousemuir	1	2	Paterson	Durie	Campbell	Johnston	Austin	Smith	J Stewart"	Buchanan	Cowan+	McBride*	Hughes	Fisher*	Fisher+	O'Neill"	Inkango	McKenzie	McKenzie	Shaw
19/04/2014	L	A	Airdrieonians	1	2	Paterson	Durie	Campbell	Johnston	Austin	Smith	J Stewart"	Buchanan	Cowan"	McBride*	Hughes	McKenzie*	Inkango+	O'Neill"	Mbu	Johnstone	Clark	Rooney
26/04/2014	L	A	Brechin City	1	2	Paterson*	Durie*	Campbell	Johnston	Austin	Smith+	Mbu	Buchanan	Fisher*	McBride	J Stewart"	McKenzie+	Clarke+	Clarke"	R Stewart	R Stewart	O'Neill	Rooney
03/05/2014	L	H	Ayr United	1	2	Paterson	Durie	Campbell	Johnston	Cowan	Smith+	Mbu	Buchanan	O'Neill	McBride"	J Stewart+	Austin*	Barr+	Inkango*	Cowan	McKenzie	Maskrey	Rooney
07/05/2014	PO	A	Clyde	0	1	Paterson*	Durie	Campbell	Johnston	Cowan	Smith	Mbu	Buchanan+	Clark	Barr"	McKenzie+	Rooney*	Hughes+	Clarke"	Thom	J Stewart	O'Neill	Rooney
10/05/2014	PO	H	Clyde	2	1 aet 7-6p	Paterson" 7-6p	Durie	Campbell	Johnston	Cowan	Smith+	Mbu	Buchanan"	Austin	Barr"	McKenzie+	McBride*	Buchanan+	Brown"	Thom	J Stewart	Inkango	Clark
14/05/2014	PO	A	Stirling Albion	2	1	Rooney	Thomson	Campbell	Johnston	Cowan	Smith"	Mbu	Buchanan+	J Stewart	McKenzie+	McKenzie+	Rooney*	Austin+	Buchanan"	Clarke	O'Neill	R Stewart	Shaw
18/05/2014	PO	H	Stirling Albion	0	2	Rooney	Thom	Campbell	Johnston	Cowan	Smith+	Mbu	Clarke	J Stewart"	Barr	Austin+	Durie*	Brown+	Buchanan"	Mbu	McKenzie	Inkango	Paterson

East Stirlingshire FC

Founded	1880
Ground	Ochilview Park
Postcode	FK5 4QL (Ground)
Tel	01324 562992
Capacity	3746
Closest Railway Station	Larbert
Record Attendance	12000 v Partick Thistle, SC, 21/2/1921
Ground Record	2854 v Rangers, Lge, 17/1/2012
Record Win	1-2 v Vale of Bannock, SC, 22/9/1888
Record Defeat	1-12 v Dundee United, Lge, 13/4/1936
Most League Goals in a Season	36 Malcolm Morrison, 1938/9
Chairman	Tony Ford
Secretary	Tadek Kopszywa
Manager	John Coughlin (until May) / Craig Tully (from May)
Assistant Manager	Matt Kerr
Colours 2013/14 Top	Black and White Hoops
Shorts	Black
Sponsor	Larbert Mortgages
Manufacturer	Jako
Change Colours 2013/14 Top	Tangerine
Shorts	Tangerine
3rd Kit 2013/14 Top	Turquoise
Shorts	White
Nicknames	Shire
Web	www.eaststirlingshirefc.co.uk

Ten years ago the future of East Stirlingshire looked very bleak. Seemingly rooted to the bottom of the League, they were regarded as a bit of a laughing stock.

On the field things have been a roller-coaster since then. They've been in the promotion play offs and they've had seasons struggling in the nether regions. Off the field they've stabilised and the best news of 2013/14 was that plans for a new ground are finally taking shape.

Sharing with Stenhousemuir has worked out quite well for Shire but they now have plans to move to a brand new stadium at Little Kerse, not far from the Falkirk Stadium.

Shire have a new manager in charge for 2014/15 in the shape of Craig Tully. He was Assistant to Jim McInally at Peterhead and was keen to move into management in his own right.

His priority will be to avoid bottom spot and the potential for a play off to maintain their SPFL place.

PREDICTION 2014/15
Mid table is the likely prognosis for Shire - could sneak into the play off positions

Surname	First Name	DOB	Pos	L A	L S	L G	SC A	SC S	SC G	LC A	LC S	LC G	RC A	RC S	RC G	UNS	Signed Previous Club	Notes	Contract
Bolochowechyj	Michael		D	30	5	2	2			1			1				2013 Forfar Athletic		C (2015)
Devlin	Rhys		D	7	5		1									14	2012 Airdrie United		F
Gallagher	Callum		F	3	1	2											2014 Rangers (Loan Dec-Jan)		
Glasgow	Jamie		F	10	19	1	1			1			1			6	2012 Celtic Youth		C (2015)
Gordon	Craig		GK	3												37	2011 Queen's Park		F
Greenhill	David		M	31	3	4	2			2	1		1				2012 Berwick Rangers		C (2015)
Hay	Grant		GK	33			2			1			1			3	2011 Queen's Park		R
Hendrie	Christopher		M													3	2013 Hutchison Vale		
Herd	Michael		M	14	6		1									6	2012 Whitehill Welfare		F
Kelly	Conor		M		2								1			5	2013 Alloa		
Lamie	Ricky		M	4												1	2014 Airdrieonians (Loan Mar-Apr)		
Maxwell	Scott		M	28	2	2	1	1	1	1			1			3	2011 Dalkeith Thistle	Signed for Berwick Rangers May 2014	ONC
McAughie	David		F		4											14	2013 East Stirlingshire Youth	On loan to Luncarty Juniors Jan 2014	
McGowan	Michael		D	16			1	2		1			1				2013 Annan Athletic		R
McGregor	Graeme		M	26	6		2			1			1			3	2013 St Mirren		C (2015)
McKechnie	Jordan		M	17	5	3	1	1	1	1			1			6	2013 Annan Athletic		F
Miller	Ricky		D	14	3		1						1			6	2013 Vale of Leithen	On loan to Musselburgh Ath (Oct-Feb)	F
O'Donoghue	Ross		M	19	6		1	1		1			1			3	2013 Elgin City		F
Quinn	Paul		F	15	10	7							1			5	2011 Albion Rovers		F
Shepherd	Nathan		D	6	5	1										5	2012 Stranraer		C (2015)
Tapping	Jordan		D	10	3											19	2013 Larbert Athletic		C (2015)
Thomson	Iain		M	30	4	2				1			1			2	2013 Stenhousemuir		F
Townsley	Chris		D	35	3	2										2	2013 Berwick Rangers		C (2015)
Turner	Kevin		F	18	9	3	2			1	1		1			1	2013 St Mungo's Amateurs	Rejected new contract	ONC
Watt	Josh		F	2	3												2014 Stenhousemuir (Loan Jan-Feb)		
Wilson	Wallace		D													2	2013 Falkirk Juniors		
Wright	Max		F	25	5	6	1	1		1			1			3	2012 Stranraer		C (2015)
Own Goals						3													

NEW SIGNINGS 2014/15

Surname	First Name	Pos	Signed Previous Club
Niven	David	D	2014 Elgin City
McMullen	Paul	M	2014 Elgin City
Barnard	Richie	GK	2014 Camelon
McCabe	Neil	M	2014 Forfar Athletic
McKenna	David	F	2014 Stranraer

Date	Comp	H/A	Opponents	F	A	Crowd	Scorers
27/07/2013	RC1	A	Formartine United	0	2	186	
03/08/2013	LC1	H	Dunfermline Athletic	0	2	1043	
10/08/2013	L	A	Queen's Park	3	1	476	Thomson, Townsley 2
17/08/2013	L	H	Elgin City	3	0	254	Greenhill 2, McMullen og
24/08/2013	L	A	Stirling Albion	3	1	735	Bolochoweckyj, Quinn, Mckechnie
31/08/2013	L	H	Peterhead	1	4	286	Quinn
14/09/2013	L	A	Clyde	2	1	497	Wright 2
21/09/2013	L	H	Albion Rovers	1	4	336	Quinn
28/09/2013	L	H	Berwick Rangers	1	0	301	Bolochoweckyj
05/10/2013	SC2	H	Threave Rovers	6	0	288	Greenhill 2, Glasgow, Maxwell, McKechnie, Turner
19/10/2013	L	H	Queen's Park	1	1	339	McGowan
26/10/2013	L	A	Montrose	0	2	338	
29/10/2013	L	A	Annan Athletic	2	1	301	Thomson, McKechnie
03/11/2013	SC3	H	Raith Rovers	0	2	716	
09/11/2013	L	H	Stirling Albion	2	2	541	White og, Bolockoweckyj
16/11/2013	L	A	Peterhead	1	1	545	Mckechnie
23/11/2013	L	H	Clyde	0	1	452	
03/12/2013	L	A	Albion Rovers	2	3	323	Quinn 2
07/12/2013	L	H	Annan Athletic	1	1	218	Turner
14/12/2013	L	A	Berwick Rangers	0	2	361	
21/12/2013	L	A	Elgin City	1	0	502	Glasgow
28/12/2013	L	H	Montrose	2	2	244	Gallagher, Thomson
04/01/2014	L	A	Stirling Albion	1	2	639	Wright
11/01/2014	L	H	Peterhead	2	0	310	Townsley, Greenhill
18/01/2014	L	H	Albion Rovers	1	1	319	Gallagher
25/01/2014	L	A	Clyde	0	1	473	
01/02/2014	L	A	Queen's Park	0	0	337	
08/02/2014	L	H	Elgin City	3	0	309	Maxwell, Bolochoweckyj, Wright
15/02/2014	L	A	Annan Athletic	3	2	401	Wright, Greenhill, Shepherd
22/02/2014	L	H	Berwick Rangers	1	1	341	Quinn
01/03/2014	L	A	Peterhead	0	4	554	
08/03/2014	L	H	Stirling Albion	1	0	584	Thomson
15/03/2014	L	A	Montrose	0	2	333	
22/03/2014	L	H	Queen's Park	1	4	376	Quinn
29/03/2014	L	H	Clyde	2	4	449	McQueen og, Turner
05/04/2014	L	A	Albion Rovers	1	2	287	Maxwell
12/04/2014	L	H	Annan Athletic	2	1	253	Wright, Turner
19/04/2014	L	A	Berwick Rangers	0	1	582	
26/04/2014	L	A	Elgin City	0	5	588	
03/05/2014	L	H	Montrose	1	2	265	Bolochoweckyj

Friendly Matches

Date		Comp	H/A	Opponents	F	A		
6/7/13		Fr	N	Stranraer	0	1		at Ralston, Paisley
9/7/13		Fr	A	Stenhousemuir	1	3		
13/7/13		Fr	A	Craigroyston	2	1		
27/8/13		StC1	A	Alloa	2	2	4-2 pens	
8/10/13		StCSF	A	Stirling Albion	1	3		
30/11/13		Fr	A	Spartans	1	0		

Date	Comp	H/A	Opponents	F	A	1	2	3	4	5	6	7	8	9	10	11	12	13	14	15	16	17	18
27/07/2013	RC1	A	Formartine United	0	2	Hay	McGregor	McGowan	Miller	Bolochowecky	Thomson	O'Donohue	Greenhill*	Quinn	McKechnie+	Maxwell*	Glasgow*	Wright+	Kelly"	McCaughie	Gordon		
03/08/2013	LC1	H	Dunfermline Athletic	0	2	Hay	McGregor	McGowan	Miller	Bolochowecky	Thomson	O'Donohue	Greenhill	Turner"	Wright+	Maxwell	Glasgow*"+	McCaughie+	Kelly"	Townsley	Gordon	Miller	Kelly
10/08/2013	L	A	Queen's Park	3	1	Hay	McGregor	McGowan	Townsley	Bolochowecky	Thomson	O'Donohue"	Greenhill	Turner"	Wright *	Maxwell	Maxwell	McKechnie+	Quinn"	McCaughie	Gordon	Miller	Tapping
17/08/2013	L	H	Elgin City	3	0	Hay	McGregor	McGowan	Townsley	Bolochowecky	Thomson	Quinn	Greenhill"	Turner*	Wright	Glasgow+	Quinn*	McKechnie+	Kelly"	McCaughie	Gordon	Miller	Kelly
24/08/2013	L	A	Stirling Albion	3	1	Hay	McGregor	McGowan	Townsley	Bolochowecky	Thomson	Quinn	Greenhill"	Turner"	Wright*	Glasgow"	Kelly*	Wright*	McAughie"	Tapping	Gordon	Kelly	Wilson
31/08/2013	L	H	Peterhead	1	4	Hay	McGregor	McGowan	Townsley	Bolochowecky	Thomson	Quinn	Greenhill"	Turner"	Wright	Kelly"	Kelly"	McCaughie"	Glasgow"	McCaughie	Gordon	Miller	Tapping
14/09/2013	L	A	Clyde	2	1	Hay	McGregor	McGowan*	Townsley	Bolochowecky	Thomson	Quinn+	Greenhill	Maxwell*	Wright	McKechnie	O'Donohue*	Glasgow*	Miller*	McCaughie	Gordon	Miller	Tapping
21/09/2013	L	H	Albion Rovers	1	4	Hay	McGregor*	McGowan	Townsley	Bolochowecky	Thomson	O'Donohue	Greenhill	Maxwell+	Wright*	McKechnie	Turner*	Turner+	O'Donoghue"	McCaughie	Gordon	Kelly	Devlin
28/09/2013	L	H	Berwick Rangers	1	0	Hay	McGregor	McGowan	Townsley	Bolochowecky	Thomson	O'Donohue+	Greenhill"	Turner	Wright	McKechnie	Maxwell*	McCaughie+	Miller"	Hendrie	Gordon	McGauchie	
05/10/2013	SC2	H	Threave Rovers	6	0	Hay	McGregor	McGowan	Townsley"	Bolochowecky"	Thomson	O'Donohue"	Greenhill	Turner	Maxwell	McKechnie	Maxwell*	McCaughie"	Miller"	McCaughie	Gordon	Herd	Glasgow
19/10/2013	L	H	Queen's Park	1	1	Hay	McGregor	McGowan	Townsley	Bolochowecky	Thomson	O'Donohue	Greenhill	Turner	Maxwell	Glasgow*	Herd*	McKechnie	McCaughie-	Wilson	Gordon	Tapping	Devlin
26/10/2013	L	A	Montrose	0	2	Hay	McGregor	McGowan	Townsley	Bolochowecky	Thomson	O'Donohue	Greenhill"	Turner	Maxwell	Glasgow*	Herd*	McKechnie	McKechnie	McCaughie	Gordon		
29/10/2013	L	A	Annan Athletic	2	1	Hay	McGregor	McGowan	Townsley	Bolochowecky	Thomson	O'Donohue	Greenhill	Turner*	Maxwell*	McKechnie+	Herd*	Devlin	Hendry	Devlin"	Gordon		
03/11/2013	SC3	A	Raith Rovers	0	2	Hay	McGregor	McGowan	Townsley	Bolochowecky	Herd*	Herd*	Greenhill	Turner*	Maxwell*	McKechnie*	Wright*	Devlin+	McAughie"	Tapping	Gordon		
09/11/2013	L	H	Stirling Albion	2	2	Hay	McGregor+	McGowan	Townsley	Bolochowecky	Thomson	O'Donohue"	Greenhill	Turner	Maxwell+	McKechnie	Glasgow*	Herd+	McAughie"	Tapping	Gordon		
16/11/2013	L	A	Peterhead	1	1	Hay	McGregor+	McGowan	Townsley	Bolochowecky	Thomson	O'Donohue	Greenhill	Turner	Maxwell+	McKechnie	Glasgow*	Quinn+	McAughie"	Tapping	Gordon		
23/11/2013	L	H	Clyde	0	1	Hay	McGregor	McGowan	Townsley	Bolochowecky	Herd*	O'Donohue*	Greenhill	Quinn	Maxwell+	McKechnie	Glasgow*	Quinn+	Herd"	Tapping	Gordon	Devlin	
03/12/2013	L	A	Albion Rovers	2	3	Hay	McGregor	Devlin	Devlin	Bolochowecky	Herd*	O'Donohue*	Greenhill	Quinn	Thomson*	McKechnie	Tapping"	Wright+	Devlin	Townsley	Gordon	Devlin	McKechnie
07/12/2013	L	H	Annan Athletic	1	1	Hay	McGregor+	McGowan	Townsley	Bolochowecky	Glasgow"	O'Donohue"	Greenhill	Glasgow	Thomson	McKechnie+	Glasgow*	Quinn+	Tapping"	Tapping	Gordon	Shepherd	Shepherd
14/12/2013	L	A	Berwick Rangers	0	2	Hay	McGregor+	McGowan	Townsley	Bolochowecky	Quinn+	O'Donohue"	Glasgow*	Turner+	Thomson	McKechnie+	Turner*	Greenhill+	McGregor"	Maxwell	Gordon	Devlin	Devlin
21/12/2013	L	H	Elgin City	1	0	Hay	McGregor	McGowan	Townsley	Bolochowecky	Wright*	McGregor	Greenhill+	Gallagher	Thomson	McKechnie	Gallagher*	Glasgow+	Quinn	Tapping	Gordon	Shepherd	Turner
28/12/2013	L	H	Montrose	2	2	Hay	Maxwell	Herd	Townsley	Tapping	Wright*	Watt	Greenhill	Gallagher	Thomson	Miller+	McGregor*	Devlin+	McKechnie"	Tapping	Gordon	McKechnie	McKechnie
04/01/2014	L	A	Peterhead	2	0	Hay	Maxwell	Herd*	Townsley	Bolochowecky	Wright	Watt*	Greenhill"	Glasgow*	Thomson	Miller*	Watt	Devlin+	Quinn"	Tapping	Gordon	McKechnie	Shepherd
11/01/2014	L	H	Albion Rovers	1	1	Hay	Miller	Herd*	Townsley	Bolochowecky	Wright	Tapping	Greenhill	Thomson	Thomson*	Miller*	Watt*	Quinn"	McKechnie"	Tapping	Gordon	O'Donoghue	McGregor
18/01/2014	L	A	Clyde	0	1	Hay	Maxwell	Herd	Townsley	Tapping	Wright	Tapping	Greenhill	Quinn*	Thomson	Miller*	McGregor*	Glasgow+	Devlin"	Shepherd	Gordon	Devlin	Quinn
25/01/2014	L	A	Queen's Park	0	0	Hay	Maxwell	Herd	Townsley	McKechnie*	Wright*	Tapping	Greenhill	Quinn"	Thomson	Miller	Watt*	Glasgow+	Shepherd"	Tapping	Gordon	Glasgow	Devlin
01/02/2014	L	H	Elgin City	3	0	Hay	Maxwell	Herd	Townsley	McKechnie *	Wright	Tapping"	Greenhill	Quinn"	O'Donouhue*	Miller+	Shepherd*	Glasgow+	Devlin	Tapping	Gordon	O'Donoghue	Shepherd
08/02/2014	L	H	Annan Athletic	3	2	Hay	Maxwell"	McGregor	Townsley	Bolochowecky*	Wright	Tapping	Greenhill	Quinn	Thomson	Miller	Glasgow*	Devlin+	O'Donoghue"	O'Donoghue	Gordon	Shepherd	McKechnie
15/02/2014	L	A	Berwick Rangers	1	1	Hay	Maxwell	McGregor	Townsley	Bolochowecky	Wright	Wright	Greenhill	Quinn	Thomson	Miller"	Shepherd*	Glasgow+	McKechnie"	Devlin	Hay	Thomson	Shepherd
22/02/2014	L	H	Peterhead	0	4	Hay	Maxwell	Shepherd+	Townsley	Bolochowecky	Wright	Wright	Greenhill	McGregor	Thomson"	Miller	Devlin*	Quinn"	Mckechnie"	McGregor	Hay	Miller	Devlin
01/03/2014	L	H	Stirling Albion	1	0	Hay	Maxwell	Shepherd+	Townsley	Tapping	McGregor	Tapping	Greenhill	McGregor*	Turner*	Miller	O'Donoghue*	Tapping"	Glasgow	Devlin"	Hay	Maxwell	Miller
08/03/2014	L	A	Montrose	0	2	Gordon	Maxwell	Herd	Townsley	Bolochowecky	McGregor	Devlin	Greenhill	McGregor*	Wright	Miller	McKechnie*	Glasgow+	Quinn"	Mckechnie"	Gordon	Miller	Herd
15/03/2014	L	A	Queen's Park	1	4	Gordon	Maxwell	Herd	Townsley	Bolochowecky	Thomson	O'Donouhue"	Shepherd	Lamie	Wright	Glasgow*	Glasgow*	Tapping"	Glasgow"	Herd	Gordon	Devlin	McKechnie
22/03/2014	L	H	Clyde	2	4	Hay	Maxwell	Miller*	Townsley+	Bolochowecky	Thomson	Devlin"	Shepherd	Lamie	Quinn*	Turner"	Shepherd*	Greenhill+	Herd"	Herd	Gordon	Shepherd	
29/03/2014	L	A	Albion Rovers	1	2	Gordon	Maxwell*	Miller"	Townsley+	Bolochowecky	Thomson	Devlin	Shepherd	Turner"	Wright	Turner"	Glasgow*	Turner"	Quinn"	McKechnie	Gordon	Shepherd	
05/04/2014	L	H	Annan Athletic	2	1	Gordon	Maxwell	Miller*	Townsley+	Bolochowecky	McGregor	Devlin	Shepherd	Lamie	Turner*	Glasgow*	Glasgow*	Wright+	Herd"	Glasgow	Gordon	Shepherd	
12/04/2014	L	A	Berwick Rangers	0	1	Gordon	Maxwell	Greenhill	Townsley*	Bolochowecky+	Thomson	O'Donohue	Shepherd	Maxwell	Wright	Glasgow*	Turner"	Greenhill+	Herd"	Thomson	Hay	Thomson	Quinn
19/04/2014	L	A	Elgin City	0	5	Gordon	Tapping+	McGregor	Townsley+	Bolochowecky+	Thomson	Devlin"	Shepherd	Miller	Quinn*	Miller	Glasgow*	McGregor+	Quinn"	Devlin	Hay	Miller	Herd
26/04/2014	L	A	Elgin City	1	2	Gordon	Lamie	McGregor	Townsley	Bolochowecky	Thomson	Devlin"	Shepherd	Miller	Quinn*	Turner	Wright*	Glasgow+	Tapping"	Tapping	Hay	Maxwell	Herd
03/05/2014	L	H	Montrose	1	2	Hay	Maxwell	Herd	Townsley"	Bolochowecky]	Thomson	O'Donohue+	Greenhill*	Greenhill*	Wright	Turner	McGregor*	Glasgow+	McGregor"	Quinn	Gordon	Devlin	Lamie

Elgin City FC

Founded	1893
Ground	Boroughbriggs
Postcode	IV30 1AP
Tel	01343 551114
Capacity	4520
Closest Railway Station	Elgin
Record Attendance	12608 v Arbroath, SC, 17/2/1968
Record Win	18-1 v Brora Rangers, NOS Cup, 6/2/1960
Record Defeat	1-14 v Hearts, SC, 4/2/1939
Most League Goals in a Season	19 Martin Johnston 2005/6
Chairman	Graham Tatters
Secretary	Kate Taylor
Manager	Ross Jack / Barry Wilson
Assistant Manager	
Colours 2013/14 Top	Black and White Stripes
Shorts	Black
Sponsor	McDonald and Munro
Manufacturer	
Change Colours 2013/14 Top	Light Blue
Shorts	Light Blue
Nicknames	City
Web	www.elgincity.com

PREDICTION 2014/15
Mid table at best.

There was no shortage of entertainment for spectators at Elgin's matches last season. They fired in goals from all angles but also conceded them with alarming frequency. They pulled off some good wins but also suffered from very poor results - crashing out of the Ramsdens Cup by 5-1 to Formartine United being the most notable.

Manager Ross Jack left midway through the season when it became apparent that a play off place was beyond them. Barry Wilson came in and used the closing months as a way of trying out some younger players in a bid to get the right blend for 2014/15.

This season comes with a sting in the tail - the bottom side in League Two face a Play Off for survival against the winners of the Highland League or the Lowland League. Cynics have frequently observed that Elgin might be better back in the Highland League but nobody at the club thinks that way. Crowds last season held up well and the profile that goes with League football is important for the club and the town as a whole.

Surname	First Name	DOB	Pos	L A	L S	L G	SC A	SC S	SC G	LC A	LC S	LC G	RC A	RC S	RC G	UNS	Signed	Previous Club	Notes	Contract
Bayne	Graham	22/08/79	F	3	4	1										4	2014	Arbroath	Assistant Manager	
Beveridge	Graeme	07/10/90	D	23	6		2			1			2			6	2011	Raith Rovers		C (2015)
Birnstingl	Lucas	14/02/90	GK													1	2013	Trialist, ex Bo'ness United	Later signed for Q Park	
Black	Stewart	15/05/95	GK	4	1											30	2012	Elgin City Youths		C (2015)
Cameron	Brian	19/12/90	F	10	1	2	1			1		2					2008	Elgin City Youths		OOC
Crichton	Sean	26/03/90	D	33	1	1				1		1	2	1			2012	Montrose		OOC
Duff	Jamie	26/01/89	D	33	1	2	2			1	1		2				2010	Inverness CT		OOC
Dunbar	Robin	08/03/92														1	2013	Elgin City Youths		
Finlayson	Gordon	27/11/93	D	13													2014	Ross County (loan)	Returned to Ross County	
Gibson	John	29/05/89	GK	6													2014	Dundee (loan)	Returned to Dundee	
Gunn	Craig	17/07/87	F	36	15	2	2	1					2	1			2009	Ross County		C (2015)
Harkins	Paul	01/11/88	M	23	5	4	1	1		1			2			5	2012	Queen's Park		OOC
Jellema	Ray	27/09/85	GK	26		2				1			2			7	2013	Peterhead		OOC
Kaczan	Paul	03/02/83	D	1													2004	Partick Thistle		
Khutishvili	Dachi	29/10/93		2	4			1	1							10	2013	Inverness CT	Freed Jan 2014, joined Clachnacuddin	
MacAulay	Connor	31/07/95		1												10	2013	Elgin City Youths		Youth
Masson	Jamie	05/04/93		9	1												2014	Aberdeen (loan)	Returned to Aberdeen	
Mathieson	Scott		GK													2	2013	Inverurie Locos (loan)	Returned to Inverurie Locos	
McDonald	Calum	24/03/94	M	2	3											7	2014	Ross County (loan)	Returned to Ross County	
McHardy	Darryl		M	8	1		1					1				11	2013	Elgin City Youths	Jailed for 1 year, Dec 2013	C (2015)
McKenzie	Ally	05/08/90	M	24	7	1	2	2	1		2					2	2013	Strathspey Thistle		C (2015)
McKinnon	Ross	09/10/92		11	4	2	1			1						6	2013	SC Veendam	On loan to Clyde Jan-May	F
McLean	Ceiran	12/03/91	M	5	4	1		1		1		1					2010	Elgin City Youths	Jailed for 9 months, Dec 2013	C (2015)
McLeod	Adam	21/04/93		9	2							1				21	2012	Strathspey Thistle		
McMullen	Paul	13/03/84	D	19	2		1			1		1				2	2012	Clyde	Joined East Stirlingshire May 2014	F
Murray	Callum	27/10/96														5	2013	Elgin City Youths		Youth
Nicholson	Mark	25/06/88	M	19	1	1	1										2007	Ross County		C (2015)
Niven	David	27/12/87	D	19	1					1		2				2	2008	Ross County	Joined East Stirlingshire May 2014	
Sutherland	Shane	23/10/90	F	36	14	2				1		2	1				2013	Inverness CT		C (2015)
Urquhart	Sam	30/07/91	F	6	18	2		2			1					13	2013	Clachnacuddin		C (2015)
Vastano	Toto	04/11/94														3	2012	Strathspey Thistle	on loan to Strathspey Thistle, Jan 2014	
Wyness	Dennis	22/03/77	F	32	3	10	2		1		1	1				1	2012	Peterhead		C (2015)
Own Goals					1															

NEW SIGNINGS 2014/15

Moore	Daniel		2014 Nairn County
Cooper	Matthew		2014 Inverness CT
Finlayson	Gordon		2014 Ross County

Date	Comp	H/A	Opponents	F	A	Crowd	Scorers
27/07/2013	RC1	H	Montrose	2	0	505	Gunn, Sutherland
03/08/2013	LC1	H	Livingston	1	3	563	Crighton
10/08/2013	L	H	Albion Rovers	1	2	541	Gunn
17/08/2013	L	A	East Stirlingshire	0	3	254	
21/08/2013	RC2	A	Formartine United	1	5	480	Crichton
24/08/2013	L	A	Peterhead	2	2	543	Wyness, Gunn
31/08/2013	L	H	Clyde	1	0	544	Wyness
14/09/2013	L	H	Montrose	3	3	577	Niven, McKinnon, Crichton
21/09/2013	L	A	Queen's Park	3	3	342	Wyness, Gunn, Harkins
28/09/2013	L	H	Stirling Albion	4	0	623	Sutherland, Gunn 2, Cameron
05/10/2013	SC2	A	Keith	4	0	650	McKenzie 2, Gunn 2
12/10/2013	L	A	Berwick Rangers	3	2	495	Sutherland 2, Harkins
19/10/2013	L	A	Albion Rovers	0	0	337	
26/10/2013	L	H	Annan Athletic	2	3	648	Gunn, Cameron
02/11/2013	SC3	H	Dunfermline Athletic	3	5	1108	Duff, Wyness, Khutishvili
09/11/2013	L	H	Peterhead	2	4	622	Gunn, Urquhart
16/11/2013	L	A	Clyde	1	2	533	McHardy
23/11/2013	L	A	Montrose	3	3	398	Wyness 2, Gunn
30/11/2013	L	H	Queen's Park	3	2	608	Gunn 2, McKinnon
07/12/2013	L	H	Berwick Rangers	2	0	543	Sutherland 2
14/12/2013	L	H	East Stirlingshire	0	1	502	
28/12/2013	L	A	Annan Athletic	1	2	401	Sutherland
02/01/2014	L	A	Peterhead	1	2	737	Niven
11/01/2014	L	H	Clyde	3	1	585	Gunn, Sutherland 2
18/01/2014	L	A	Queen's Park	0	2	346	
25/01/2014	L	H	Montrose	2	3	550	Masson, Sutherland
01/02/2014	L	H	Albion Rovers	1	1	519	Duff
08/02/2014	L	A	East Stirlingshire	0	3	309	
15/02/2014	L	A	Berwick Rangers	3	2	412	Gunn, Wyness, Nicholson
22/02/2014	L	H	Stirling Albion	2	3	576	Crichton, Wyness
01/03/2014	L	A	Clyde	0	4	504	
08/03/2014	L	H	Peterhead	2	3	670	McKenzie, Sutherland
11/03/2014	L	A	Stirling Albion	1	1	681	Gunn
15/03/2014	L	H	Annan Athletic	2	3	485	Sutherland, Harkins
22/03/2014	L	A	Albion Rovers	2	5	286	Wyness, Sutherland
29/03/2014	L	A	Montrose	3	0	262	Sutherland, McLeod 2
05/04/2014	L	H	Queen's Park	1	1	555	Wyness
12/04/2014	L	H	Berwick Rangers	1	3	602	L Currie og
19/04/2014	L	A	Stirling Albion	2	2	640	Sutherland, Gunn
26/04/2014	L	H	East Stirlingshire	5	0	588	Bayne, Gunn, Urquhart, Duff, Harkins
03/05/2014	L	A	Annan Athletic	0	2	428	

Friendly Matches

Date	Comp	H/A	Opponents	F	A	Crowd	Scorers
5/7/13	Fr	A	Buckie Thistle	3	0		
7/7/13	Fr	N	Deveronvale	3	2		at Kinloss
10/7/13	Fr	H	Rangers	0	1	2382	
13/7/13	Fr	H	Inverness CT	0	2	559	
14/7/13	Fr	A	Strathspey Thistle	3	3		
17/7/13	Fr	A	Rothes	3	0		
19/7/13	Fr	A	Elgin City	4	0		
21/7/13	Fr	A	Huntly	5	2		
23/7/13	Fr	H	Aberdeen U20	2	1		
30/7/13	Fr	A	Dufftown	1	1		U19

Date	Comp	H/A	Opponents	F	A	1	2	3	4	5	6	7	8	9	10	11	12	13	14	15	16	17	18
27/07/2013	RC1	H	Montrose	2	0	Jellema	Niven	McMullen	Crighton	Duff	McLean*	Gunn	Harkins*	Cameron	Sutherland	Beveridge	Mackenzie*	McKinnon*	Urquhart	Wyness	Black	McHardy	
03/08/2013	LC1	H	Livingston	1	3	Jellema	Niven+	McMullen	Crighton	Duff	McLean"	Gunn"	Harkins"	Cameron	Sutherland	Beveridge	Mackenzie*	Urquhart+	Wyness"	McKinnon	Black		
10/08/2013	L	H	Albion Rovers	1	2	Jellema	McKinnon	McMullen+	Crighton	Duff	McLean*	Gunn	Harkins"	Cameron	Sutherland	Beveridge	Wyness*	McKenzie+	Urquhart"	MacLeod	Black		
17/08/2013	L	A	East Stirlingshire	0	3	Jellema	Niven	McMullen	McKinnon*	Duff	McLean"	Gunn"	Harkins"	Cameron	Sutherland	Beveridge	Mackenzie*	Urquhart*	McKenzie*	MacLean	Black	McHardy	McHardy
21/08/2013	RC2	A	Formartine United	1	5	Jellema	Niven	McMullen	McKinnon	Duff	Wyness	Gunn+	Harkins"	Cameron	Sutherland	Beveridge*	Mackenzie*	McKenzie+	McLeod"	MacLeod	Black	McMullen	Black
24/08/2013	L	A	Peterhead	2	2	Jellema	Niven	Crichton	McKinnon	Duff	Wyness	Gunn	Khutsishvili	Cameron	Sutherland	Beveridge	Harkins	McLean	Urquhart	Urquhart	MacAuley	McMullen	McMullen
31/08/2013	L	H	Clyde	1	0	Jellema	Niven	Crichton	McKinnon	Duff	Wyness	Gunn"	Khutsishvili	Cameron	Sutherland	Beveridge	McMullen*	McMullen+	Mackenzie+	MacLeod	Black	McLean	Harkins
14/09/2013	L	H	Montrose	3	3	Black	Niven	Crichton	McKinnon*	Duff	McLean*	Gunn"	Wyness	Cameron	Sutherland	McMullen	Mackenzie*	Mackenzie*	Beveridge	MacLeod	Birnsingl	Urquhart	Harkins
21/09/2013	L	A	Queen's Park	3	3	Jellema	MacKenzie	Crichton	McKinnon*	Duff	McLean*	Gunn"	Harkins	Cameron	Sutherland	Wyness	Wyness	Khutsishvili*	Beveridge+	Khutsishvili	Urquhart	Vastano	
28/09/2013	L	H	Stirling Albion	4	0	Jellema	MacKenzie	Crichton	McKinnon	Duff	Beveridge	Gunn	Harkins	Cameron	Sutherland	Wyness	Beveridge*	McMullen+	Khutsishvili"	MacLeod	McLean	Black	
05/10/2013	SC2	H	Keith	4	0	Jellema	MacKenzie	Crichton	McKinnon	Duff	Beveridge	Gunn*	Harkins	Cameron	Sutherland	Wyness	Urquhart*	McMullen"	Khutsishvili	Khutsishvili	McMullen	McLean	
12/10/2013	L	A	Berwick Rangers	3	2	Jellema	MacKenzie	Crichton	Crichton	Duff	McMullen	Gunn	Harkins*	Cameron	Sutherland	Wyness	Beveridge*	McLean	Khutsishvili	Khutsishvili	Black	Urquhart	MacLeod
19/10/2013	L	A	Albion Rovers	0	0	Jellema	MacKenzie	Crichton	Niven*	Duff	McMullen	Gunn*	Harkins*	Cameron"	Sutherland	Beveridge	McLean	Urquhart+	Khutsishvili	Khutsishvili	Black		McKinnon
26/10/2013	L	H	Annan Athletic	2	3	Jellema	MacKenzie	Crichton+	Niven	Duff	McMullen	Gunn	Harkins*	Cameron"	Sutherland	Wyness	McLean*	Khutsishvili+	Beveridge"	McHardy	Black	Urquhart	Beveridge
02/11/2013	SC3	H	Dunfermline Athletic	3	5	Jellema	MacKenzie+	Nicholson"	Niven*	Duff	McMullen	Gunn+	McLean+	Beveridge	Sutherland	Wyness	Harkins*	Khutsishvili*	Khutsishvili*	McHardy	Black	McLeod	
09/11/2013	L	H	Peterhead	2	4	Jellema	MacKenzie	Nicholson+	Niven	Duff	McMullen	Gunn	Harkins	Beveridge*	Sutherland	Wyness	Urquhart*	McHardy*	McKinnon"	McHardy	Black	Vastano	
16/11/2013	L	A	Clyde	1	2	Jellema	MacKenzie	Nicholson	Niven	Duff	McMullen	Gunn	McKinnon*	Crichton	Sutherland"	Wyness	McKinnon*	Urquhart	McHardy"	Khutsishvili	Black	McLeod	
23/11/2013	L	A	Montrose	3	2	Jellema	MacKenzie	Nicholson	Niven	Duff	McMullen	Gunn	McKinnon*	Crichton	Sutherland	Wyness	Beveridge*	McLeod*	McLeod	Khutsishvili	Black	McLean	Vastano
30/11/2013	L	H	Queen's Park	2	0	Jellema	MacKenzie	Nicholson	Niven	Duff	McMullen	Gunn	McKinnon*	Crichton	Sutherland	Wyness+	Urquhart*	McLeod*	McLeod	Khutsishvili	Beveridge	Beveridge	Harkins
07/12/2013	L	H	Berwick Rangers	0	1	Jellema	MacKenzie	Nicholson	Niven	Duff	McMullen+	Gunn	McKinnon+	Crichton	Sutherland	Wyness+	Cameron*	Cameron*	Harkins	Beveridge	Khutsishvili	McLeod	
14/12/2013	L	H	East Stirlingshire	1	2	Jellema	Urquhart	Nicholson	Niven	Duff	McMullen	Gunn	Harkins	Crichton	Sutherland	Wyness	Urquhart*	Urquhart+	Harkins	Beveridge	McKinnon		
28/12/2013	L	A	Peterhead	1	2	Jellema	Urquhart	Urquhart*	Niven*	Duff	McMullen	Gunn+	Masson	Crichton	Sutherland	Wyness	Khutsishvila*	Urquhart+	McKinnon	Beveridge	McAuley		
02/01/2014	L	A	Clyde	3	1	Black	McKenzie	Nicholson	McKenzie"	Duff	Niven	Gunn+	Masson	Crichton	Sutherland	Wyness*	Black*	McKenzie+	McKenzie+	McKinnon	McAuley	Black	Dunbar
11/01/2014	L	A	Queen's Park	0	2	Jellema	Beveridge	Nicholson	McKenzie*	McKenzie*	Harkins*	Gunn	Masson	Crichton	Sutherland	Wyness	McKenzie	Beveridge	McLeod	McKinnon	Niven	McLeod	
18/01/2014	L	A	Montrose	2	3	Jellema	Beveridge+	Nicholson*	McKenzie+	McKenzie*	Harkins+	Gunn"	Masson	Crichton	Sutherland	Wyness	Beveridge*	Urquhart+	McLeod	Black	McAuley	McLeod	
25/01/2014	L	H	Albion Rovers	1	1	Jellema	Beveridge	Nicholson	McKenzie	McKenzie*	Harkins	Gunn	McKenzie"	Crichton	Sutherland	Wyness	McKinnon*	Harkins+	Harkins"	Black			
01/02/2014	L	A	East Stirlingshire	0	3	Jellema	Beveridge	Urquhart*	McKenzie"	Duff	Harkins	Gunn	McKenzie"	Crichton	Sutherland	Wyness	Harkins*	Harkins+	Urquhart	Black	Bayne		
08/02/2014	L	H	Stirling Albion	2	3	Jellema	Beveridge	Kaczan*	Finlayson	Duff	Harkins	Gunn	McKenzie"	Crichton	Sutherland	Wyness*	McLean*	Bayne+	Black	MacAulay	McAuley	McAuley	
15/02/2014	L	A	Clyde	3	0	Jellema	Beveridge	Finlayson	Finlayson	Urquhart+	Harkins	Gunn+	McKenzie"	Crichton	Sutherland	Wyness*	Bayne*	McLeod+	McLeod"	Black	Black	Black	
22/02/2014	L	A	Peterhead	1	1	Black	Beveridge	Urquhart"	Finlayson	Duff	Harkins+	Gunn	McKenzie"	Crichton	Sutherland	Wyness	Bayne*	McLeod+	McLeod	Black	McDonald	McDonald	Murray
01/03/2014	L	H	Stirling Albion	1	3	Black	Beveridge+	MacAuley*	Finlayson	Bayne*	Harkins+	Gunn	McKenzie+	Crichton	Sutherland	Wyness	McLeod*	McKinnon+	McLeod	McAulay	Bayne	Black	Murray
08/03/2014	L	A	Annan Athletic	2	2	Black	Beveridge	McDonald*	Finlayson	Masson	Niven+	Gunn	Nicholson	Crichton	Sutherland	Wyness+	Bayne*	McAulay	McHardy"	McAulay	McDonald	McLeod	
11/03/2014	L	H	Albion Rovers	1	1	Black	Beveridge"	Duff	Finlayson	Finlayson	Niven+	Gunn*	Nicholson*	Crichton	Sutherland	Wyness	Bayne*	McLeod+	McLean+	Mathieson	McDonald	McLeod	
15/03/2014	L	H	Annan Athletic	2	3	Black	Beveridge"	Finlayson	Finlayson	Masson	Niven+	Gunn	Nicholson*	Crichton	Sutherland	Wyness	Urquhart*	Urquhart+	McLeod"	Murray	Bayne	McHardy	Jellema
22/03/2014	L	A	Albion Rovers	2	5	Black	Beveridge	Finlayson	Finlayson	Masson	Harkins+	Gunn+	McKenzie"	Crichton	Sutherland	Wyness	Urquhart*	McLeod+	McLeod"	McDonald	McHardy	McHardy	Jellema
29/03/2014	L	A	Queen's Park	3	0	Gibson	Beveridge*	Finlayson	Finlayson	Masson	Harkins+	Gunn	Harkins+	Crichton	Sutherland	Wyness	McLeod*	Nicolson+	McLeod"	Murray	McAulay	Urquhart	Jellema
05/04/2014	L	H	Queen's Park	1	1	Gibson	Beveridge	Finlayson	Finlayson	Beveridge	Harkins*	Gunn	Harkins+	Crichton	Sutherland	Wyness*	Duff*	McHardy+	McLeod"	McKenzie	Bayne	McAuley	Jellema
12/04/2014	L	A	Berwick Rangers	1	3	Gibson	Beveridge	Finlayson	Finlayson	Masson	Harkins+	Gunn	Harkins	Crichton	Sutherland	Wyness*	Niven*	McKenzie+	Harkins"	McHardy	McDonald	Black	Jellema
19/04/2014	L	A	Stirling Albion	2	2	Gibson	Beveridge	Duff	Finlayson	Masson	Niven+	Gunn	Harkins	Crichton	Sutherland	Harkins"	McHardy*	Wyness+	McLeod"	Urquhart	McDonald	Urquhart	Jellema
26/04/2014	L	H	East Stirlingshire	5	0	Gibson	Nicholson	Duff	Nicholson	Nicholson	Niven+	Gunn	Niven+	Crichton	Sutherland	Harkins"	McHardy*	Beveridge+	Harkins"	McLean	McLeod	McGardy	
03/05/2014	L	A	Annan Athletic	0	2	Gibson	Nicholson	Duff	Nicholson	Duff	McMullen	Urquhart	Harkins*	Urquhart	Sutherland	Wyness+	McHardy"	McLeod+	Murray"	Niven	McDonald	Mathieson	Black

Falkirk FC

Founded	1876
Ground	Falkirk Stadium
Postcode	FK2 9DX
Tel	01324 624121
Capacity	8750
Closest Railway Station	Falkirk Grahamston
Record Attendance	23100 v Celtic, SC, 21/2/1953
Record Win	11-1 v Tillicoultry, SC, 7/9/1889
Record Defeat	1-1 v Airdrieonians, Lge, 28/4/51
Most League Goals in a Season	43 Evelyn Morrison, 1928/9
Chairman	Martin Ritchie OBE
General Manager / Secretary	David White
Head Coach	Peter Houston
Coaches	
Technical Director	Alex Smith MBE
Colours 2013/14 Top	Navy Blue with White Flash
Shorts	White
Sponsor	Central Demolition
Manufacturer	Puma
Change Colours 2013/14 Top	White with Blue Flash
Shorts	Blue
3rd Kit 2013/14 Top	Yellow
Shorts	Navy Blue
Nicknames	Bairns
Web	www.falkirkfc.co.uk

Considering their small player pool and comparatively restricted budget Falkirk did very well in season 2013/14. They were still in contention for the title and automatic promotion going into the last few weeks of the season. The format of the play offs did nothing to help them with four games in quick succession proving too much of a hurdle.

The club can be delighted with the success of their youth system which has produced a succession of players for the first team. They have also proved effective at scouring the "Bosmans" for bargains who have gone on to be excellent signings.

Some Bairns fans had early reservations about Grant Holt as Manager but these had evaporated by the end of the season. It was, therefore, a disappointment to see him quit the club to return to Norwich during the Summer.

It remains to be seen whether the appointment of Peter Houston is a forward move or a step back.

PREDICTION 2014/15
Mid table, maybe scraping into the play offs

Surname	First Name	DOB	Pos	L A	L S	L G	Sc A	Sc S	Sc G	LC A	LC S	LC G	RC A	RC S	RC G	UNS	Signed	Previous Club	Notes	Contract
Alston	Blair	23/03/92	M	27	6	5	1			2	1		1	1	1	3	2010	Falkirk Youths		C (2015)
Beck	Martin	02/02/94	F	17	2	6											2014	Carlisle United (loan)	Returned to Carlisle United	
Bia Bi	Botti	08/03/96	F	1												4	2013	Falkirk Youths		Youth
Bingham	Rakish	25/10/93	F	2	9					1			1			3	2013	Wigan Athletic (loan)	Returned to Wigan	
Blair	Ryan	23/02/96	M													9	2013	Falkirk Youths		Youth
Bowman	Graham	02/01/93	GK	2									1			44	2012	Falkirk Youths		OOC
Chalmers	Joe	03/01/94	D	10	1											3	2014	Celtic (Loan)	Returned to Celtic	
Dick	Liam	18/09/95	D	2	5					1			1			12	2013	Falkirk Youths		OOC
Duffie	Kieran	04/03/92	D	26			1	1		3			3			1	2010	Falkirk Youths		OOC
Durojaiye	Ollie	20/10/92	M	7	11					2			2			17	2013	Norwich City		OOC
Faulds	Kris	03/07/94	M	2	1											2	2013	Falkirk Youths	On loan to Stenhousemuir	OOC
Flynn	Jonathan	18/11/89	D	18	8		1			1	1		1			8	2012	Ross County	Signed for Cliftonville May 2014	OOC
Fulton	Jay	04/04/94	M	19	2	2	1			2	1	1	2	1			2013	Falkirk Youths	Signed for Swansea City Jan 2014	
Grant	Thomas	31/05/95	M	4						1			1	1	2	3	2013	Falkirk Youths	Son of Brian Grant	C (2016)
Greene	Connor	08/01/96	D													2	2013	Falkirk Youths		Youth
Hogg	Connor	27/12/96	F	2												4	2013	Falkirk Youths	Son of Graeme Hogg	Youth
Kingsley	Stephen	23/07/94	D	39			1	1		3			2				2011	Falkirk Youths		OOC
Leahy	Luke	19/11/92	M	1	19		1			2			2			21	2012	Rugby Town		OOC
Loy	Rory	19/03/88	F	37		21	1			3			2	1			2013	Carlisle United		C (2015)
Martin	Michael	12/01/96	M							1							2013	Falkirk Youths		Youth
McCracken	David	16/10/81	D	26	1		2	1		2							2013	St Johnstone		OOC
McGovern	Michael	12/07/84	GK	38			1			3			2				2011	Ross County	Joined Hamilton Accies June 2014	OOC
McGrandles	Conor	24/09/95	F	40			5	1		2	1	1	3	1		1	2012	Falkirk Youths		C (2017)
McNab	Robbie	01/02/96	M													2	2013	Falkirk Youths		Youth
Miller	Mark	28/02/88	M	28	6	1											2013	Dundee United (loan)	Returned to Dundee United	
Roberts	Phil	07/04/94	F	25	1	5	1			2	1		2				2013	Arsenal	Signed Pre Contract for Dundee Jan 2014	
Rowan	Liam	05/02/95	D													4	2013	Falkirk Youths		Youth
Shepherd	Scott	29/05/96	F	2	16	1	1						2	1		13	2013	Falkirk Youths		Youth
Sibbald	Craig	18/10/95	M	33	5	5	1			3			2	1			2011	Falkirk Youths		OOC
Small	Lewis	26/01/95	F	5												12	2012	Falkirk Youths		C (2016)
Turnbull	Kyle	22/01/95	D	4	1					1			2			5	2013	Falkirk Youths		OOC
Vaulks	Will	13/09/93	D	37			1	1		3			3				2013	Workington		C (2016)
Own Goals						1							1							

Date	Comp	H/A	Opponents	F	A		Crowd	Scorers
27/07/2013	RC1	A	Clyde	2	1		935	Alston, McGrandles
03/08/2013	LC1	H	Clyde	3	0	at Alloa	1154	Alston, Roberts, Grant
10/08/2013	L	A	Dumbarton	1	1		1224	McGrandles
17/08/2013	L	H	Morton	3	1		3058	Loy 2, Roberts
20/08/2013	RC2	A	Ayr United	2	1	AET	921	Loy, Shepherd
24/08/2013	L	A	Livingston	3	0		1416	Roberts 3
27/08/2013	LC2	H	Dunfermline Athletic	2	1		3663	Morris og, Fulton
31/08/2013	L	H	Hamilton Accies	1	2		3266	Fulton
07/09/2013	RC3	A	Raith Rovers	0	1		1565	
14/09/2013	L	A	Cowdenbeath	0	1		644	
21/09/2013	L	H	Dundee	3	1		3349	Loy 2, Fulton
25/09/2013	LC3	H	Aberdeen	0	5		2838	
28/09/2013	L	A	Raith Rovers	1	1		1715	Faulds
05/10/2013	L	H	Queen of the South	2	1		3189	Loy 2
12/10/2013	L	A	Alloa	0	0		1625	
19/10/2013	L	H	Dumbarton	1	2		2704	Roberts
26/10/2013	L	A	Hamilton Accies	0	2		1340	
09/11/2013	L	H	Livingston	4	1		2878	Vaulks, Loy 2, Sibbald
16/11/2013	L	A	Dundee	1	1		4661	Leahy
23/11/2013	L	H	Cowdenbeath	4	0		2550	Miller 2, Loy, Shepherd
30/11/2013	SC4	H	Rangers	0	2		6228	
07/12/2013	L	H	Raith Rovers	3	1		2934	Sibbald, McGrandles, Kingsley
21/12/2013	L	A	Morton	2	0		1873	Duffie, Loy
28/12/2013	L	H	Alloa	0	0		3417	
04/01/2014	L	A	Livingston	1	0		1585	Loy
11/01/2014	L	H	Hamilton Accies	0	0		3099	
18/01/2014	L	A	Cowdenbeath	2	0		566	Miller, Loy
25/01/2014	L	H	Dundee	2	0		4183	McGrandles, Loy
01/02/2014	L	H	Morton	1	1		3120	Millar
08/02/2014	L	A	Queen of the South	0	2		1818	
15/02/2014	L	A	Dumbarton	1	2		1003	Loy
22/02/2014	L	H	Queen of the South	1	0		2862	Millar
01/03/2014	L	A	Raith Rovers	4	2		1729	Hill og, McCracken, Loy, Miller
08/03/2014	L	H	Livingston	1	1		2924	Alston
15/03/2014	L	A	Hamilton Accies	1	3		1706	Beck
22/03/2014	L	A	Alloa	0	3		1025	
25/03/2014	L	H	Dumbarton	2	0		2489	McCracken, Loy
29/03/2014	L	A	Dundee	1	0		4919	Beck
05/04/2014	L	H	Cowdenbeath	5	0		2830	Loy 3, Alston, Sibbald
12/04/2014	L	A	Queen of the South	2	1		1863	Alston, Beck
19/04/2014	L	H	Raith Rovers	2	1		3200	Loy, McGrandles
26/04/2014	L	A	Morton	1	1		1921	McGrandles
03/05/2014	L	H	Alloa	3	1		3998	Beck 2, Sibbald
06/05/2014	PO	A	Queen of the South	1	2		1996	Alston
10/05/2014	PO	H	Queen of the South	3	1	aet	4427	Loy, Sibbald, Alston
13/05/2014	PO	H	Hamilton Accies	1	1		4194	Beck
18/05/2014	PO	A	Hamilton Accies	0	1		4678	

Friendly Matches

Date	Comp	H/A	Opponents	F	A	Crowd	Scorers
29/6/13	Fr	A	Queen's Park	4	0		at Lesser Hampden
6/7/13	Fr	A	Stirling Albion	1	1	728	
8/7/13	Fr	A	Fraserburgh	1	0		
9/7/13	Fr	A	Selkirk	4	2	U20	
10/7/13	Fr	A	Huntly	6	2		
13/7/13	Fr	A	Turriff United	4	2		
16/7/13	Fr	A	Forfar Athletic	2	1		
20/7/13	Fr	A	Dunfermline Athletic	2	2	1344	
23/7/13	StCF	A	Dumbarton	2	3		2012/13 season
31/7/13	StC1	A	Stenhousemuir	1	0		
24/9/13	StCSF	H	Dumbarton	3	1		

Date	Comp	H/A	Opponents	F	A	1	2	3	4	5	6	7	8	9	10	11	12	13	14	15	16	17	18
27/07/2013	RC1	A	Clyde	2	1	McGovern	Duffie	Turnbull	Kingsley	Vaulks	Kingsley	McGrandles	Leahy	Roberts	J Fulton*	Alston+	Grant*	Sibbald+	Martin	Greene	Bowman		
03/08/2013	LC1	A	Clyde	3	0 at Alloa	McGovern	Duffie	Turnbull	Kingsley	Vaulks	Sibbald*	McGrandles*	Grant+	Durojaiye	Loy	Roberts	Alston+	Martin+	J Fulton*	Leahy	Bowman		
10/08/2013	L	H	Dumbarton	1	1	McGovern	Duffie	Turnbull	Kingsley*	Vaulks	Fulton*	McGrandles+	Alston+	Durojaiye	Loy	Roberts	Grant*	Sibbald+	Dick	Leahy	Bowman		
17/08/2013	L	H	Morton	3	1	McGovern	Duffie	Turnbull	Kingsley*	Vaulks	Fulton"	McGrandles+	Alston	Durojaiye	Loy	Grant"	Dick*	Grant"	Grant"	Leahy	Bowman		
20/08/2013	RC2	A	Ayr United	2	1 AET	McGovern	Duffie	Turnbull	Dick	Vaulks	Sibbald	McGrandles	Alston	Durojaiye	Loy	Grant"	Alston"	Fulton"	Shepherd"	Dick	Bowman		
24/08/2013	L	A	Livingston	3	0	McGovern	Duffie	Turnbull	Kingsley	Vaulks	Fulton	Sibbald*	McGrandles	Durojaiye	Loy"	Roberts	Sibbald*	Leahy+	Leahy"	Shepherd	Bowman		
27/08/2013	LC2	A	Dunfermline Athletic	2	1	McGovern	Duffie	Dick*	Kingsley	Vaulks	Fulton*	Sibbald	McGrandles	McGrandles	Loy	Roberts+	Alston"	Shepherd+	Leahy"	Shepherd	Bowman		
31/08/2013	L	H	Hamilton Accies	1	2	Bowman	Duffie	Tumbull*	Kingsley	Vaulks	Fulton*	McGrandles	Bingham+	McGrandles	Loy	Roberts	Flynn*	Grant"	Leahy"	Dick	Bowman		
07/09/2013	RC3	A	Raith Rovers	0	1	McGovern	Duffie	Flynn	Kingsley	Vaulks	Fulton*	McGrandles	Alston	Durojaiye	Loy	Roberts	Grant*	Shepherd+	Leahy"	McNabb	Bowman		
14/09/2013	L	A	Cowdenbeath	0	1	McGovern	Duffie	Flynn	Kingsley	Vaulks	Fulton	McGrandles	Durojaiye	Sibbald*	Loy	Roberts	Turnbull*	Bingham+	Turnbull	Turnbull	Bowman		
21/09/2013	L	H	Dundee	3	1	McGovern	Duffie	Flynn	Kingsley	Vaulks	Fulton*	McGrandles	Alston*	Sibbald	Loy+	Roberts	McCracken*	Bingham+	Leahy"	Turnbull	Bowman		
25/09/2013	LC3	H	Aberdeen	0	5	Bowman	Duffie	Flynn	Roberts	Roberts	Fulton+	McGrandles	Alston*	Sibbald	Loy"	McCracken	Bingham*	Leahy+	Leahy"	Turnbull	Bowman		
28/09/2013	L	A	Raith Rovers	1	1	McGovern	Duffie	Flynn	Kingsley	Vaulks	Fulton+	McGrandles	Alston	Sibbald*	Loy"	McCracken	Bingham*	Faulds+	Leahy"	Faulds	Bowman	Leahy	
05/10/2013	L	H	Queen of the South	2	1	McGovern	Duffie	Flynn	Kingsley	Vaulks	Fulton+	McGrandles	Bingham"	Sibbald"	Loy"	McCracken*	Bingham*	Grant+	Faulds"	Turnbull	Bowman		
12/10/2013	L	H	Alloa	0	0	Bowman	Duffie	Flynn	Kingsley	Vaulks	Fulton"	McGrandles	Alston	Sibbald+	Loy"	Roberts	Dick*	Bingham+	Small"	Sibbald	Grant		
19/10/2013	L	H	Dumbarton	1	2	McGovern	Duffie	Bingham+	Dick	Vaulks	Fulton"	McGrandles	Roberts*	Bingham*	Loy	McCracken	Leahy*	Shepherd+	Flynn"	Faulds	Bowman	Grant	Grant
26/10/2013	L	A	Hamilton Accies	0	2	McGovern	Duffie	Dick	Kingsley	Vaulks	Fulton"	McGrandles	Roberts*	Sibbald+	Loy"	McCracken	Bingham*	Alston+	Leahy"	Durojaiye"	Bowman	Green	Grant
09/11/2013	L	A	Livingston	4	1	McGovern	Duffie	Miller*	Kingsley	Vaulks	Fulton"	McGrandles	Roberts*	Roberts*	Loy"	McCracken	Flynn*	Flynn+	Shepherd"	Durojaiye"	Bowman	Bingham	Shepherd
16/11/2013	L	A	Dundee	1	1	McGovern	Duffie	Miller"	Kingsley	Vaulks	Fulton+	McGrandles	Roberts*	Sibbald	Loy+	Flynn	Bingham*	Leahy+	Leahy"	Durojaiye"	Bowman	Dick	Shepherd
23/11/2013	L	H	Cowdenbeath	4	0	McGovern	Duffie	Miller	Kingsley	Vaulks	Fulton	McGrandles	Roberts*	Sibbald	Loy"	McCracken	Bingham*	Leahy	Shepherd	Alston	Bowman	Bingham	Leahy
30/11/2013	SC4	L	Rangers	0	2	McGovern	Duffie	Miller	Kingsley	Vaulks	Fulton+	McGrandles	Roberts*	Sibbald	Loy"	McCracken	Alston+	Durojaiye+	Duzojaiye"	Durojaiye"	Bowman	Bingham	Leahy
07/12/2013	L	H	Raith Rovers	3	1	McGovern	Duffie	Miller	Kingsley	Vaulks	Fulton"	McGrandles	Shepherd"	Sibbald+	Loy"	McCracken	Flynn*	Leahy+	Flynn"	Duffie	Bowman	Shepherd	Flynn
21/12/2013	L	A	Morton	2	0	McGovern	Duffie	Miller	Kingsley	Vaulks	Fulton	McGrandles	Roberts"	Sibbald	Loy"	Roberts+	Flynn*	Durojaiye+	Durojaiye"	Durojaiye"	Bowman	Flynn	Small
28/12/2013	L	A	Alloa	0	0	McGovern	Duffie	Miller	Kingsley	Vaulks	Fulton	McGrandles	Roberts"	Sibbald	Loy"	McCracken*	Fulton*	Leahy	Bingham"	Duzojaiye"	Bowman	Flynn	Shepherd
04/01/2014	L	A	Livingston	1	0	McGovern	Duffie	Miller*	Kingsley	Vaulks	Alston+	McGrandles	Roberts"	Sibbald	Loy"	McCracken*	Small*	Beck+	Alston"	Blair	Bowman	Shepherd	Leahy
11/01/2014	L	H	Hamilton Accies	0	0	McGovern	Duffie	Miller	Kingsley	Vaulks	Alston	McGrandles	Roberts"	Sibbald	Loy"	Flynn	Shepherd*	Leahy+	Flynn"	Blair	Bowman	Small	Shepherd
18/01/2014	L	A	Cowdenbeath	2	0	McGovern	Duffie	Miller	Kingsley	Vaulks	Alston"	McGrandles	Roberts"	Sibbald+	Loy	Flynn	Roberts*	Sibbald+	Fulton"	Durojaiye"	Bowman	Small	Dick
25/01/2014	L	A	Dundee	2	0	McGovern	Duffie	Miller	Kingsley	Vaulks	Alston	McGrandles	Roberts"	Sibbald+	Loy"	Flynn	Beck*	Leahy+	Shepherd"	Duffie	Bowman	Small	Shepherd
01/02/2014	L	H	Morton	1	1	McGovern	Duffie	Miller	Kingsley	Vaulks	Alston	McGrandles	Roberts"	Shepherd"	Loy"	Flynn	Durojaiye*	Leahy+	Shepherd"	Leahy	Bowman	Blair	Chalmers
08/02/2014	L	A	Queen of the South	0	2	McGovern	Flynn	Alston+	Kingsley	Vaulks	Alston+	McGrandles	McGrandles	Sibbald	Loy	Chalmers	Shepherd*	Beck+	Flynn"	Durojaiye"	Bowman	Shepherd	McCracken
15/02/2014	L	A	Dumbarton	1	0	McGovern	Miller	Alston*	Kingsley*	Vaulks	McCracken	McGrandles	McGrandles	Sibbald*	Chalmers	Beck	Shepherd*	Leahy"	Flynn	Shepherd"	Bowman	Flynn	Chalmers
22/02/2014	L	H	Queen of the South	1	0	McGovern	Miller	Alston*	Kingsley	Vaulks	McCracken	McGrandles	Chalmers*	Roberts+	Loy	Beck	Roberts*	Leahy+	Durojaiye"	Durojaiye"	Bowman	Blair	Blair
01/03/2014	L	H	Raith Rovers	4	1	McGovern	Miller	Alston*	Kingsley*	Vaulks	McCracken	McGrandles	Chalmers*	Roberts	Chalmers	Beck"	Leahy*	Shepherd+	Shepherd"	Shepherd	Bowman	Flynn	Shepherd
08/03/2014	L	A	Livingston	1	1	McGovern	Flynn	Alston+	Kingsley	Vaulks	McCracken	McGrandles	Leahy+	Roberts	Chalmers	Beck"	Small*	Duzojaiye"	Alston"	Dick	Bowman	Durojaiye	Leahy
15/03/2014	L	H	Hamilton Accies	1	3	McGovern	Flynn	Alston*	Kingsley	Vaulks	McCracken	McGrandles	Roberts	Durojaiye"	Chalmers	Beck	Chalmers*	Shepherd+	Hogg"	Dick	Bowman	Blair	Chalmers
22/03/2014	L	A	Alloa	0	3	Bowman	Miller	Alston*	Kingsley	Vaulks	McCracken	McGrandles	Durojaiye"	Loy+	Flynn	Beck	Small*	Small+	Small	Dick	Bowman	Hogg	Shepherd
25/03/2014	L	H	Dumbarton	2	0	McGovern	Miller	Alston	Kinsley	Vaulks	McCracken	McGrandles	Sibbald	Loy"	Chalmers	Beck"	Dick*	Leahy+	Small	Durojaiye"	Bowman	Hogg	Hogg
29/03/2014	L	A	Queen of the South	1	0	McGovern	Miller	Alston	Kingsley	Vaulks	McCracken	McGrandles	Sibbald"	Loy	Chalmers	Beck"	Leahy*	Durojaiye+	Flynn"	Bowman	Bowman	Hogg	Small
05/04/2014	L	H	Cowdenbeath	5	0	McGovern	Miller	Alston	Kingsley	Vaulks	McCracken	McGrandles	Sibbald	Durojaiye	Loy	Beck*	Durojaiye*	Leahy+	Small"	Shepherd	Bowman	Flynn	Hogg
12/04/2014	L	A	Queen of the South	2	1	McGovern	Miller+	Alston+	Kingsley	Vaulks	McCracken	McCracken*	Sibbald	Loy	Chalmers	Beck	Shepherd*	Leahy	Small	Dick	Bowman	Shepherd	Hogg
19/04/2014	L	H	Raith Rovers	2	1	McGovern	Miller+	Alston	Kingsley	Vaulks	McCracken	McCracken	Sibbald	Loy	Loy	Beck	Durojaiye*	Shepherd+	Small	Dick	Bowman	Rowan	Blair
26/04/2014	L	A	Morton	1	1	McGovern	Miller+	Alston	Kingsley	Vaulks	McCracken	McCracken	Sibbald	Loy*	Loy"	Beck	Durojaiye*	Durojaiye	Flynn"	Dick	Bowman	Rowan	Bia Bi
03/05/2014	L	H	Alloa	3	1	McGovern	Miller+	Alston"	Kingsley	Vaulks	McCracken	McCracken	Sibbald	Flynn	Shepherd+	Beck	Shepherd*	Bia-Bi+	Small	Durojaiye	Small	Small	Leahy
06/05/2014	PO	H	Queen of the South	3	1 aet	McGovern	Flynn	Alston	Flynn	Vaulks	McCracken	McCracken	Sibbald*	Flynn	Loy	Beck"	Dick*	Durojaiye+	Shepherd"	Bowman	Bowman	Leahy	Bia Bi
10/05/2014	PO	A	Queen of the South	1	1	McGovern	Miller	Alston	Kingsley	Vaulks	Dick	McCracken	Sibbald+	Flynn	Loy	Beck*	Dick*	Durojaiye	Hogg"	Rowan	Small	Blair	Bia Bi
13/05/2014	PO	H	Hamilton Accies	1	1	McGovern	Miller	Alston	Kingsley	Vaulks	McCracken+	McCracken+	Sibbald*	Flynn	Loy	Beck	Shepherd*	Leahy	Flynn"	Leahy	Bowman	Leahy	Bia Bi
18/05/2014	PO	A	Hamilton Accies	0	1	McGovern	Miller	Alston"	Kingsley	Vaulks	McCracken	McCracken	Sibbald	Flynn	Loy	Beck	Shepherd"	Dick	Dick	Durojaiye	Bowman	Rowan	Bia Bi

Forfar Athletic FC

Founded	1885
Ground	Station Park
Postcode	DD8 3BT
Tel	01307 463576
Capacity	6777
Closest Railway Station	Dundee
Record Attendance	19780 v Rangers, SC, 2/2/1970
Record Win	14-1 v Lindertis, SC, 1/9/1888
Record Defeat	2-12 v King's Park, Lge, 2/1/1930
Most League Goals in a Season	46 David Kilgour, 1929/30
Chairman	Alasair Donald
Secretary	David McGregor
Manager	Dick Campbell
Assistant Manager	
Colours 2013/14 Top	Sky Blue with Navy Blue Flashes
Shorts	Navy Blue
Sponsor	Orchard Timber Products
Manufacturer	Pendle
Change Colours 2013/14 Top	White
Shorts	Blue
Nicknames	Loons
Web	www.forfarathletic.co.uk

Forfar Athletic are one of those clubs that it is hard not to have a soft spot for. Their ground at Station Park is a good old-fashioned stadium where you can change ends at half time and watch from the terracings. The club themselves have consistently punched above their weight and are always capable of producing shocks.

2013/14 was no different. The season started by knocking angers out of the League Cup and they reached the Fifth Round of the Scottish Cup.

Manager Dick Campbell likes to combine attacking flair with a steely resolve. What they lacked was the vital consistency which meant that they never aspired to better than a mid table finish. In Chris Templeman they have a genuinely talented player who seldom failed to entertain.

Off the field Forfar remain a model of how to run a small-town club. The installation of the artificial pitch at Station Park has been a great success and allowed the club to further develop its community aspect.

PREDICTION 2014/15
Likely to finish in mid table again

				L			SC			LC			RC							
Surname	First Name	DOB	Pos	A	S	G	A	S	G	A	S	G	A	S	G	UN	Signed	Previous Club	Notes	Contract
Andrews	Marvin	22/12/75	D	15	2		1			1							22 2013	Albion Rovers		F
Baxter	Mark	16/04/85	D	30	2		3			2			2				2013	Arbroath		C (2015)
Campbell	Iain	28/06/85	D	30	1	2	4			2	1	1					2009	Alloa	Joined Cowdenbeath June 2014	ONC
Campbell	Ross	11/07/83	M	8	19	3	3			2			2				8 2008	Spartans		F
Dale	James	13/10/93	M	18	11	2	1	1		2						1	6 2013	Stirling University		C (2015)
Deasley	Bryan	29/06/88	F	2									2				2 2013	Lochee United	On loan to Montrose, then permanent	▇
Dods	Darren	07/06/75	D	32	1	2	4			1			1				2013	Falkirk		ONC
Douglas	Rab	24/04/72	GK	17									1				19 2013	Dundee		C (2015)
Duggan	Chris	30/01/94	F	4	2	1											1 2013	Partick Thistle (Loan Mar-May)	Returned to Partick Thistle	▇
Dunlop	Michael	11/01/93	D	1													2012	Aberdeen	On loan to Berwick Rangers	C (2015)
Faero	Odmar	01/11/89	D	6			3										1 2012	B96 Thorshavn		C (2015)
Fotheringham	Martyn	23/03/83	M	13	7	4	2	1	1	1			1				4 2007	Cowdenbeath		C (2015)
Fusco	Gary	01/06/82	M	26	5		4			1			1				3 2013	Brechin City	Joined Brechin City May 2014	F
Gibson	Keith	01/05/81	D														6 2012	Arbroath		OTF
Gray	Connor	18/08/93	M														1 2012	Brechin City U19	Freed and joined Tayport	▇
Hay	Kerr	16/01/96	F														4 2013	Forfar Athletic Youths		Youth
Hill	Darren	03/12/81	GK	19						2			1				20 2013	Arbroath		C (2015)
Hilson	Dale	23/12/92	M	28	1	12	2	1	1	1			2				2013	Dundee United (Loan Sep-May)	Returned to Dundee United	▇
Kader	Omar	29/04/86	M	20	10	3	2			2			2	1			7 2012	Spartans		C (2015)
Keillor	Liam		M	2													3 2013	Forfar Athletic Youths		▇
Malcolm	Stuart	20/08/79	D	23			2	2	1	2			2	2			5 2013	Arbroath		C (2015)
Malin	Gavin	25/08/88	M	11	17	2		3	1	2			1				7 2012	Spartans		C (2015)
McCabe	Neil	10/07/90	M	14	3		1			1			1	1			13 2013	Kelty Hearts	Joined East Stirlingshire May 2014	▇
McCluskey	Jamie	06/11/87	M	8	6	2	2										7 2013	Unattached		▇
McCulloch	Mark	19/05/75	D							1			2				2009	Ross County		OTF
McLellan	Paul		M	2						1			1				7 2013	Forfar Athletic Youths		▇
McManus	Paul	26/12/82	F	5	8	4	1	1		1			2				1 2013	East Fife	Joined Arbroath Jan 2014	▇
Reid	Duncan		M														4 2012	Forfar Athletic Youths	On loan to Carnoustie Panmure	F
Salmon	Ross	04/09/93	GK														5 2013	Peterhead		Youth
Smith	Craig		M	1		1											7 2013	Forfar Athletic Youths		C (2015)
Storie	Craig	13/01/96	M	4													2013	Aberdeen (Loan)	Returned to Aberdeen	▇
Swankie	Gavin	24/11/83	F	27	2	10	4			1			2	2			2012	Arbroath		C (2015)
Templeman	Chris	11/09/80	F	35	1	5	4			3	2		1				2009	East Fife		C (2015)
Thomson	Gavin	10/04/85															2 2012	Forfar Athletic Youths		Youth

Date	Comp	H/A	Opponents	F	A		Crowd	Scorers
27/07/2013	RC1	H	East Fife	2	1		545	Kader, Malcolm
03/08/2013	LC1	H	Rangers	2	1	AET	4079	Swankie 2
10/08/2013	L	H	Airdrieonians	3	3		704	Malin, McManus 2
17/08/2013	L	A	Ayr United	0	2		1056	
20/08/2013	RC2	A	Dundee	1	3	AET	2052	Malcolm
24/08/2013	L	A	Brechin City	1	2		724	I Campbell
27/08/2013	LC2	A	Dundee	1	2	AET	2027	I Campbell
31/08/2013	L	H	Stenhousemuir	1	2		483	I Campbell
14/09/2013	L	A	East Fife	3	1		796	Dale, Hilson, Swankie
22/09/2013	L	H	Rangers	0	1		3776	
28/09/2013	L	A	Arbroath	0	3		855	
05/10/2013	L	H	Dunfermline Athletic	4	0		968	McManus, Malcolm, Maling, Hilson
12/10/2013	L	H	Stranraer	1	2		449	Templeman
19/10/2013	L	A	Airdrieonians	2	0		579	McCluskey, R Campbell
26/10/2013	L	A	Stenhousemuir	1	1		408	Hilson
02/11/2013	SC3	H	East Fife	2	1		485	Hilson, Templeman
09/11/2013	L	H	Brechin City	2	0		663	Hilson, R Campbell
23/11/2013	L	H	East Fife	2	0		556	Templeman, R Campbell
30/11/2013	SC4	A	Brechin City	1	1		724	Fotheringham
03/12/2013	L	A	Rangers	1	6		38745	Swankie
07/12/2013	L	A	Dunfermline Athletic	1	1		2469	Dods
10/12/2013	SC4R	H	Brechin City	3	3	AET, 4-3 p	811	Templeman 2, Malin
14/12/2013	L	H	Arbroath	1	1		609	McManus
21/12/2013	L	H	Ayr United	0	1		473	
02/01/2014	L	A	Brechin City	5	1		812	Templeman 2, Fotheringham, Dods, Hilson
11/01/2014	L	H	Stenhousemuir	3	0		485	Swankie, Fotheringham 2
20/01/2014	L	H	Rangers	0	2		2067	
25/01/2014	L	A	East Fife	1	2		685	
01/02/2014	L	H	Airdrieonians	1	1		542	Kader
08/02/2014	SC5	H	St Johnstone	0	4		1803	
15/02/2014	L	H	Dunfermline Athletic	2	4		833	Dale, Swankie
22/02/2014	L	A	Arbroath	3	2		823	Hilson, Swankie 2`
01/03/2014	L	A	Stenhousemuir	1	4		368	Malcolm
04/03/2014	L	A	Ayr United	3	2		656	Swankie 2, Templeman
08/03/2014	L	H	Brechin City	1	1		641	Hilson
11/03/2014	L	A	Stranraer	4	0		342	Hilson, Kader, Fotheringham, Swankie
15/03/2014	L	H	Stranraer	1	0		422	Hilson
22/03/2014	L	A	Airdrieonians	1	5		712	Hilson
29/03/2014	L	H	East Fife	1	2		539	Duggan
12/04/2014	L	A	Dunfermline Athletic	0	0		2364	
15/04/2014	L	A	Rangers	0	3		39704	
19/04/2014	L	H	Arbroath	0	2		833	
26/04/2014	L	H	Ayr United	4	2		532	McCluskey, Hilson 2, Kader
03/05/2014	L	A	Stranraer	1	3		501	Swankie

Friendly Matches

6/7/13	Fr	H	Turriff United	1	0
9/7/13	Fr	A	Spartans	2	0
13/7/13	Fr	H	Dundee	0	1
16/7/13	Fr	H	Falkirk	1	2
20/7/13	Fr	A	Berwick Rangers	2	2

Date	Comp	H/A	Opponents	F	A	1	2	3	4	5	6	7	8	9	10	11	12	13	14	15	16	17	18
27/07/2013	RC1	H	East Fife	2	1	Hill	McCabe	Baxter	M Fotheringham	Malcolm	McCulloch	Kader*	Malin	McManus*	Swankie	Deasley+	Dale*	R Campbell+	McLelland*	Thomson	Douglas		
03/08/2013	LC1	A	Rangers	2	1 AET	Hill	Andrews	Baxter	M Fotheringham	Malcolm	McCulloch	Kader	Malin	McCabe+	Swankie	Templeman	I Campbell*	Dale+	Deasley*	R Campbell	Douglas		
10/08/2013	L	H	Airdrieonians	3	3	Hill	Andrews	Baxter	Dods	Dale	Deasley*	Kader	Malin	McCabe	Swankie*	Templeman	McManus*	Fusco+	R Campbell*	Reid	Douglas	Malcolm	McClelland
17/08/2013	L	H	Ayr United	0	2	Hill	Andrews	Baxter	Dods	Dunlop+	Malcolm	Kader	Malin*	McCabe	Swankie	Templeman	Fusco*	Kader+	Swankie*	Deasley	Hill	Dale	
20/08/2013	RC2	A	Dundee	1	3 AET	Douglas	I Campbell	Baxter	Fotheringham+	McCulloch*	Malcolm	Kader*	Fusco	McManus*	Swankie	Deasley+	McCabe*	Templeman+	R Campbell*	Reid	Douglas	Dale	
24/08/2013	L	A	Brechin City	1	2	Hill	Andrews	Baxter	Dods	I Campbell	McCabe	Kader*	Malin+	Hilson*	Swankie	Templeman	Malin*	Dale+	Fusco*	Andrews	Douglas	Malcolm	
27/08/2013	LC2	A	Dundee	1	2 AET	Hill	Malcolm	Baxter	Dods	I Campbell	Malin	McCabe*	R Campbell+	Hilson*	Swankie	Templeman*	McManus*	Kader+	Fusco*	Andrews	Douglas	Malcolm	
31/08/2013	L	H	Stenhousemuir	1	2	Hill	Malcolm	Baxter	Dods	I Campbell	Fotheringham+	McCabe*	R Campbell	Hilson*	Swankie	Templeman	Malin*	Kader+	Dale*	Andrews	Douglas	Fusco	Reid
14/09/2013	L	A	East Fife	3	1	Hill	Andrews	Baxter	Dods	I Campbell	Dale*	McCabe*	R Campbell	Hilson+	Swankie	Templeman	Malin*	Kader+	Fusco*	R Campbell	Douglas	Malcolm	
21/09/2013	L	H	Rangers	0	1	Hill	Andrews	Baxter	Dods	I Campbell	Fotheringham+	McCabe	Kader+	Hilson	Swankie	Templeman+	McManus+	McManus+	McManus*	R Campbell	Douglas	Malcolm	Gray
28/09/2013	L	A	Arbroath	0	3	Hill	Malcolm	Baxter	Dods	I Campbell	Dale*	McCabe	Kader+	Hilson	Swankie	Templeman+	Malin+	Malin+	McManus*	Fusco	R Campbell	Douglas	Malcolm
05/10/2013	L	H	Dunfermline Athletic	4	0	Hill	Malcolm	Baxter	Dods	I Campbell	Dale*	Fusco	Malin+	McManus*	McManus*	Templeman	Kader*	R Campbell*	Keiller*	Andrews	Douglas	Smith	
12/10/2013	L	H	Stranraer	1	2	Hill	Andrews	Baxter	Dods	I Campbell	Dale*	Fusco	Swankie	Hilson+	McManus*	Templeman	Malin*	Kader+	McCuskey*	McCabe	Douglas	R Campbell	R Campbell
19/10/2013	L	A	Airdrieonians	2	0	Hill	Andrews*	Baxter*	Dods	I Campbell*	Malin	Fusco	Swankie	McCabe*	McManus*	Templeman	Fusco*	Kader+	R Campbell*	Dale	Douglas	McManus	Keillour
26/10/2013	L	A	Stenhousemuir	1	1	Hill	Andrews	Baxter	Dods*	I Campbell*	Malin+	McCuskey+	Swankie	Hilson+	McCuskey*	Templeman	Dale*	Kader+	Keiller	Kader	Salmon	McManus	Fotheringham
02/11/2013	SC3	H	East Fife	2	1	Douglas	Andrews*	Baxter*	Dods	I Campbell	Malin+	Fusco	Swankie	Hilson	McManus*	Templeman	Dale+	McManus*	Kader*	Kader	Salmon	R Campbell	Fotheringham
09/11/2013	L	A	Brechin City	2	0	Douglas	Malcolm	Baxter*	Dods	I Campbell	Malin+	Fusco	Swankie	Hilson+	McCuskey*	Templeman	Malcolm*	Fotheringham+	Malin*	Andrews	Salmon	Fotheringham	McCabe
23/11/2013	L	H	East Fife	2	0	Douglas	Malcolm	Baxter	Dods	I Campbell	Storie*	McCabe	Fusco*	Hilson+	McCuskey*	Templeman*	Kader*	R Campbell+	McCabe*	Hill	Hill	Kader	McCabe
30/11/2013	SC4	A	Brechin City	1	1	Douglas	Malcolm	Baxter	Dods	I Campbell	Storie*	McCabe*	Swankie	Hilson+	McCuskey*	Templeman*	Fotheringham*	Fotheringham*	Andrews	Andrews	Douglas	Kader	Fotheringham
03/12/2013	L	A	Rangers	1	6	Douglas	Andrews+	Baxter	Dods	I Campbell+	Faeron	Storie	Swankie	Hilson+	R Campbell	Templeman+	Fusco+	Fusco+	Malin	Malin	Douglas	R Campbell	Fotheringham
07/12/2013	L	H	Dunfermline Athletic	1	1	Hill	Fusco	McCabe+	Dods	I Campbell	Faeron	Storie	Swankie*	Dale	Kader+	Templeman	McManus*	McManus*	McManus*	Andrews	Hill	R Campbell	Andrews
10/12/2013	SC4R	H	Brechin City	3	3 AET, 4-3 p	Douglas	Malcolm	McCabe+	Dods	I Campbell	Faeron	Fotheringham+	Swankie*	Dale+	Kader+	Templeman	Smith*	Malin	McManus*	Andrews	Hill	R Campbell	Hay
24/12/2013	L	A	Arbroath	1	1	Douglas	Malcolm	Baxter*	Dods	I Campbell	Fotheringham+	Malin	McManus*	Dale+	Kader+	Templeman	Fotheringham*	R Campbell+	McCuskey*	Andrews	Smith	Smith	Hay
21/12/2013	L	H	Stenhousemuir	5	1	Douglas	Malcolm	Faeron	Dods	I Campbell	Fotheringham+	Malin+	McCuskey*	Dale	Hilson	Templeman	McManus*	McCuskey*	McManus*	Andrews	Hill	Kader	McLelland
02/01/2014	L	A	Brechin City	3	0	Douglas	Malcolm	Faeron	Dods	Dale+	Fotheringham*	Kader+	Fusco*	Dale	Hilson	Templeman	Kader+	McCluskey*	McLelland*	Andrews	Hill	Kader	Hay
11/01/2014	L	H	Stenhousemuir	0	2	Douglas	Malcolm	R Campbell	Dods	I Campbell	Malin+	Kader+	Fusco*	Swankie	Hilson*	Templeman	Dale*	McCluskey*	Malin*	Andrews	Hill	McCabe	Dale
20/01/2014	L	A	Rangers	0	2	Douglas	Malcolm*	Baxter*	Dods	I Campbell	Fotheringham*	Kader+	Fusco*	Swankie	Hilson+	Templeman*	Baxter*	Malin*	Dale*	Andrews	Hill	McCabe	Smith
25/01/2014	L	H	East Fife	1	1	Douglas	Andrews*	Faeron	Dods	I Campbell	Fotheringham*	Kader+	Fusco*	Swankie	Hilson+	Templeman*	R Campbell*	Malin+	I Campbell*	Andrews	Hill	McCabe	McCabe
01/02/2014	L	H	Airdrieonians	1	1	Douglas	Andrews+	Baxter	Dods	Dale+	Fotheringham*	Kader+	Fusco*	Swankie	McCabe*	Templeman*	Hilson*	R Campbell*	Malin+	Andrews	Hill	Malin	Smith
08/02/2014	SC5	A	St Johnstone	0	4	Douglas	Duggan	Baxter	Malcolm	I Campbell	Malin*	Faeroe	Fusco+	Fusco*	Faroe*	Templeman	Hilson*	R Campbell	Baxter*	Andrews	Hill	McCabe	McCabe
15/02/2014	L	H	Dunfermline Athletic	2	4	Douglas	Duggan+	Baxter	Malcolm	I Campbell	Dale*	Kader+	Fusco*	Swankie	McCabe*	Templeman*	Hilson*	I Campbell*	Hilson*	Andrews	Hill	McCluskey	Dale
22/02/2014	L	A	Arbroath	3	2	Hill	Dale*	Baxter	Malcolm	I Campbell	McCabe+	Faroe	Fusco	Swankie	Swankie	Templeman	Kader*	R Campbell*	McCabe	McCabe	Hill	McCuskey	McCabe
01/03/2014	L	H	Stenhousemuir	1	4	Hill	Andrews	Baxter	Malcolm	Kader+	McCabe	Faroe	Fusco	Swankie	Hilson	Templeman	Kader+	McCluskey+	Andrews+	Kader	Hill	McCabe	McCabe
04/03/2014	L	A	Ayr United	1	1	Hill	Andrews	Baxter*	Malcolm	I Campbell	Fotheringham+	Faroe	Fusco	Swankie	Hilson*	Templeman	Malin*	McCluskey+	R Campbell*	Andrews	Douglas	Malin	McCluskey
08/03/2014	L	A	Brechin City	1	1	Hill	Andrews	Baxter	Malcolm	I Campbell	Fotheringham*	R Campbell	Fusco	Swankie	Hilson	Templeman	Kader*	McCuskey*	Dale*	Malin	Hill	Faeroe	Malcolm
11/03/2014	L	A	Stranraer	4	0	Hill	Andrews	Baxter	Malcolm	I Campbell	Fotheringham+	Kader+	Fusco	Swankie+	Hilson*	Templeman	Dale*	Smith+	Dale*	R Campbell	Hill	McCabe	McCuskey
15/03/2014	L	H	Stranraer	1	0	Hill	Andrews+	Baxter	Malcolm	I Campbell	Fotheringham*	Kader+	Fusco*	Swankie	Hilson+	Templeman	Dale*	McCluskey+	R Campbell*	McCabe	Hill	McClelland	McCuskey
22/03/2014	L	A	Airdrieonians	1	5	Hill	Andrews*	Baxter	Malcolm	Dale	Fotheringham*	Kader+	Fusco	McCabe*	Hilson*	Templeman	Dods+	Smith+	Duggan*	Smith	Douglas	Malin	Dale
29/03/2014	L	H	East Fife	1	2	Hill	Duggan	Baxter	Malcolm	I Campbell	Fotheringham	Kader+	Fusco	Swankie+	McCabe*	Templeman*	Malin*	Swankie+	R Campbell*	Thomson	Smith	McClelland	Salmon
05/04/2014	SC	A	Dunfermline Athletic	0	3	Hill	Malin*	Baxter	Malcolm	I Campbell	McCuskey*	Kader+	Fusco*	Swankie	Hilson*	Templeman*	Kader*	R Campbell	Malin*	Andrews	McClelland	Gibson	Salmon
15/04/2014	L	H	Arbroath	0	2	Hill	Dale	Baxter	Malcolm	I Campbell	Kader	Dods	Fusco*	Swankie	Hilson+	Templeman+	Kader+	Fotheringham+	Malin*	Andrews	McClelland	Gibson	Salmon
26/04/2014	L	A	Ayr United	4	2	Hill	Andrews	Baxter	Kader	I Campbell	McCuskey*	Dods	Fusco*	Hilson*	Hilson*	Templeman+	Malin*	Duggan+	McLelland*	McCuskey	Keiller	Gibson	Douglas
03/05/2014	L	A	Rangers	1	3	Hill	Andrews	Malin*	Malcolm	I Campbell	McCuskey+	Dods	Kader	R Campbell	Hilson*	Templeman	Fotheringham*	Dale+	Keiller*	Gibson	McLelland	Smith	Duggan

Hamilton Accies FC

Founded	1874
Ground	New Douglas Park
Postcode	ML3 0FT
Tel	01698 368652
Capacity	6078
Closest Railway Station	Hamilton West
Record Attendance	28690 v Hearts, SC, 3/3/1937
Ground Record	5895 v Rangers, Lge, 28/2/2009
Record Win	9-0 v Gala Fairydean, SC, 28/1/1922
Record Defeat	1-1 v Hibernian, Lge, 6/11/1965
Most League Goals in a Season	35 David Wilson, 1936/7
Chairman	Les Gray
Secretary	Scott Struthers
Manager	Alex Neil
Assistant Manager	
Colours 2013/14 Top	Red and White Hoops
Shorts	White
Sponsor	M and H Logistics
Manufacturer	Nike
Change Colours 2013/14 Top	Blue and Black Stripes
Shorts	Black
Nicknames	Accies, Acas
Web	www.acciesfc.co.uk

2013/14 will certainly live long in the memory of Hamilton Accies fans. Fort most of the season the club were contesting top spot with Dundee - with the Dens Park side just pipping them for the automatic promotion spot.

Hamilton's final game of the regular season saw them record a remarkable 10-2 win over Morton.

In the Play Offs Hamilton accounted for Falkirk but looked to be outsiders after losing 2-0 at home to Hibs in the Final. However, an early goal at Easter Road paved the way to a memorable 2-0 win and the ensuing victory in a penalty shoot out.

That result was based on solid teamwork and a fantastic work ethic combined with flashes of inspiration from players like Jason Scotland. Manager Alex Neil deserves huge credit for producing the consistency required from the his squad to achieve such a remarkable promotion.

PREDICTION 2014/15
Finishing tenth would be a major success. Will be favourites to make an immediate return to the Championship.

Surname	First Name	DOB	Pos	L A	L S	L G	SC A	SC S	SC G	LC A	LC S	LC G	RC A	RC S	RC G	UNS	Signed	Previous Club	Notes	Contract
Andreu	Tony	22/05/88	M	32	6	16	1			2	2		1				2013	Livingston		C (2016)
Antoine-Curier	Mikael	05/03/83	F	18	15	12	1			2	1					1	2013	FC Atyrau (Kazakhstan)		OOC
Armstrong	Danny	11/10/97	M													1	2013	Hamilton Accies Youth		Youth
Brophy	Eamonn	10/03/96	M	1	6		1									1	2012	Hamilton Accies Youth	On loan to Queen's Park Jan 2014	OOC
Canning	Martin	03/12/81	D	38	1	1	3										2008	Hibernian		C (2015)
Crawford	Ali	30/07/91	M	36	4	6	1			3			1				2010	Hamilton Accies Youth		C (2015)
Currie	Blair	19/02/94	GK	2	1											42	2013	Rangers		OOC
Cuthbert	Kevin	08/09/82	GK	38			1			3			1				2012	Ayr United	Joined Raith Rovers June 2014	OOC
Devlin	Michael	03/10/93	D	25	2	1	1			3			1			10	2011	Hamilton Accies Youth		C (2015)
Docherty	Greg	10/09/96	M	3												14	2012	Hamilton Accies Youth		C (2015)
El Zubaidi	Ali	07/03/95	D													2	2013	Hamilton Accies Youth		Youth
Finnie	Ryan	19/02/95		1												7	2011	Hamilton Accies Youth	Freed Jan 2014, Joined Rangers U20	
Garcia-Tana	Jesus	07/06/90	D	19	3	1										13	2013	Livingston		OOC
George	Paul	27/01/94	F	1	5											9	2014	Celtic (loan)	Returned to Celtic	
Gillespie	Grant	02/07/91	M	35	2	1	1			2			1			2	2009	Hamilton Accies Youth		C (2015)
Gordon	Ziggy	23/04/83	D	38	2	1				3	1						2011	Hamilton Accies Youth		C (2016)
Hendrie	Stephen	08/01/95	D	19	3	1				2	1						2011	Hamilton Accies Youth		C (2015)
Keatings	James	20/01/92	F	30	2	13	2	2	1				3				2013	Celtic	Rejected new contract	OOC
Kilday	Lee	04/02/92	D	8	3					1						19	2012	Hamilton Accies Youth		F
Law	Scott	06/06/97	GK													2	2013	Hamilton Accies Youth		Youth
Longridge	Louis	05/07/91	F	21	10	7	1			1	1		1	1		4	2012	Bo'ness United		C (2016)
Lyon	Darren		M	1													2013	Hamilton Accies Youth		Youth
McGrath	Jaison	08/02/96	F				4									6	2013	Sunderland		Youth
McKinnon	Darian	09/12/85	M	34	1	4	1			3			1			1	2012	Clydebank		C (2015)
McMann	Scott		D													2	2013	Hamilton Accies Youth		Youth
McShane	Jon	14/09/91	F	8	5	1	1			1	2		1			3	2012	St Mirren	Released Jan 2014, Joined East Fife May 2014	
Neil	Alex	09/06/81	M	10	1					2	1					7	2005	Mansfield Town		C (2015)
Routledge	Jon	23/11/89	M	9	6					1	1		1			1	2012	Stockport County		C (2015)
Ryan	Andy	29/09/94	F	1	22	2	2									11	2011	Hamilton Accies Youth		C (2015)
Scotland	Jason	18/02/79	F	17	2	9											2014	Barnsley		OOC
Watson	Craig	13/02/95	M	5												8	2012	Hamilton Accies Youth		C (2015)
Own Goal									1						1					

NEW SIGNINGS 2014/15

McGovern	Michael	12/07/1984	GK	2014	Falkirk
Redmond	Danny	02/03/1991	M	2014	Wigan Athletic
Imrie	Dougie	03/08/1983	M	2014	Morton
McDonald	Kieran	21/07/1993	M	2014	Clyde

Date	Comp	H/A	Opponents	F	A		Crowd	Scorers
27/07/2013	RC1	A	Airdrieonians	1	2		807	Longridge
03/08/2013	LC1	A	Stirling Albion	3	0		556	Keatings 2, Smith og
10/08/2013	L	A	Raith Rovers	1	0		1652	Keatings
17/08/2013	L	H	Dumbarton	4	1		995	Keatings 2, Gillespie, Andreu
24/08/2013	L	H	Queen of the South	2	0		1367	MacKinnon, Ryan
27/08/2013	LC2	A	Kilmarnock	1	0		2033	Antoine-Curier
31/08/2013	L	A	Falkirk	2	1		3266	Antoine-Curier, Crawford
14/09/2013	L	A	Dundee	0	0		4155	
21/09/2013	L	H	Cowdenbeath	1	0		817	Gordon
24/09/2013	LC3	H	St Johnstone	0	3		1059	
28/09/2013	L	A	Alloa	0	1		653	
05/10/2013	L	H	Livingston	2	0		1059	Keatings 2
12/10/2013	L	A	Morton	1	1		2106	Andreu
19/10/2013	L	H	Raith Rovers	1	1		1113	Keatings
26/10/2013	L	H	Falkirk	2	0		1340	Andreu, Longridge
02/11/2013	SC3	A	Queen of the South	0	1		1324	
09/11/2013	L	A	Queen of the South	1	0		1557	Antonine-Curier
16/11/2013	L	A	Cowdenbeath	4	2		401	Tena, McKinnon, Gordon, Andreu
23/11/2013	L	H	Dundee	0	3		2077	
30/11/2013	L	H	Alloa	0	1		860	
14/12/2013	L	A	Livingston	0	0		794	
21/12/2013	L	A	Dumbarton	1	2		642	Keatings
28/12/2013	L	H	Morton	1	0		1472	Antoine-Curier
04/01/2014	L	H	Queen of the South	3	1		1366	Longridge, Antoine-Curier, Crawford
11/01/2014	L	A	Falkirk	0	0		3099	
25/01/2014	L	H	Cowdenbeath	3	4		944	Andreu 2, Keatings
01/02/2014	L	H	Dumbarton	3	3		1061	Keatings 2, Scotland
08/02/2014	L	A	Dundee	0	1		5206	
15/02/2014	L	A	Raith Rovers	4	2		1436	Andreu 2, Longridge, Keatings
21/02/2014	L	H	Livingston	2	0		1063	Scotland, Antoine-Curier
01/03/2014	L	A	Alloa	3	0		656	Longridge, Keatings, Andreu
08/03/2014	L	A	Queen of the South	1	1		1703	Canning
15/03/2014	L	H	Falkirk	3	1		1706	Scotland, McKinnon, Andreu
22/03/2014	L	A	Morton	4	3		1345	Scotland, Longridge 2, Antoine-Curier
25/03/2014	L	H	Raith Rovers	3	2		954	Andreu, Keatings, Scotland
29/03/2014	L	A	Cowdenbeath	1	1		497	Antoine-Curier
05/04/2014	L	H	Dundee	1	1		4529	Antoine-Curier
12/04/2014	L	A	Livingston	1	1		1133	Scotland
19/04/2014	L	H	Alloa	2	1		1087	Scotland, Ryan
26/04/2004	L	A	Dumbarton	1	4		1420	Scotland
03/05/2014	L	H	Morton	10	2		2034	Antonine-Curier 4, Andreu 3, Longridge, Devlin, Findlay og
13/05/2014	PO	A	Falkirk	1	1		4194	McKinnon
18/05/2014	PO	H	Falkirk	1	0		4678	Andreu
21/05/2014	PO	H	Hibernian	0	2		5322	
25/05/2014	PO	A	Hibernian	2	0 aet, 4-3pens	18031	Scotland, Andreu

Friendly Matches

Date	Comp	H/A	Opponents	F	A	Crowd	Scorers
16/7/13	Fr	A	Newcastle United XI	3	0		at Little Benton
18/7/13	Fr	A	Spennymoor	2	0		
20/7/13	Fr	A	East Fife	4	0	301	
22/7/13	Fr	A	Selkirk	6	0		
23/7/13	Fr	A	Bo'ness United	1	2		
27/7/13	Tnt	A	Broxburn Athletic	1	2	U19	
28/7/13	Tnt	N	Livingston U19	2	3	U19	at Broxburn
31/7/13	Fr	A	Petershill	2	3	U19	
7/5/14	Test	A	Blantyre Vics				at NDP

Date	Comp	H/A	Opponents	F	A	1	2	3	4	5	6	7	8	9	10	11	12	13	14	15	16	17	18
27/07/2013	RC1	A	Airdrieonians	1	2	Cuthbert	Gordon	Devlin	Kilday	Hendrie	Routledge	Gillespie+	Crawford	McKinnon	Keatings"	Longridge+	Andreu*	McShane"	Brophy"	Neil	Currie	Docherty	Finnie
03/08/2013	LC1	A	Stirling Albion	3	0	Cuthbert	Gordon	Devlin"	Manning	Crawford	Routledge	Gillespie	Neil+	McKinnon	Keatings	Longridge "	Andreu+	Andreu+	Kilday"	Hendry	Currie	McGrath	Kilday
10/08/2013	L	A	Raith Rovers	1	0	Cuthbert	Gordon	Devlin	Kilday	Crawford+	Hendry	Gillespie	Neil	McKinnon	Keatings"	McShane* *	Ryan*	Andreu+	Brophy"	Currie	Watson	Docherty	Finnie
17/08/2013	L	H	Dumbarton	4	1	Cuthbert	Gordon	Devlin	Canning	Crawford+	Hendry	Gillespie	Neil"	McKinnon	Keatings+	McShane"	Ryan*	Andreu+	McGrath"	Currie	Kilday	Docherty	Finnie
24/08/2013	L	A	Queen of the South	2	0	Cuthbert	Gordon	Devlin	Canning	Crawford"	Hendry	Gillespie"	Neil*	McKinnon	Keatings+	McShane	Andreu"	Ryan++	Watson"	Currie	Brophy *	Brophy *	McGrath
27/08/2013	LC2	A	Kilmarnock	1	0	Cuthbert	Gordon	Devlin	Canning	Crawford"	Hendry	Gillespie+	Andreu	McKinnon	Keatings+	Antoine-Curier*	Ryan*	McShane+	Neil*	Currie	Kilday	McGrath	Kilday
31/08/2013	L	A	Falkirk	2	1	Cuthbert	Gordon	Devlin	Canning	Crawford	Hendry	Gillespie+	Neil	McKinnon	Keatings+	Antoine-Curier"	Ryan*	Andreu+	McShane"	Currie	Longridge	Watson	Finnie
14/09/2013	L	A	Dundee	0	0	Cuthbert	Gordon*	Devlin	Canning	Crawford	Hendry	Gillespie+	Neil	McKinnon"	Keatings+	Antoine-Curier	Ryan*	Andreu+	McShane"	Currie	Longridge	Finnie	Garcia Tena
21/09/2013	L	H	Cowdenbeath	0	0	Cuthbert	Gordon	Devlin	Canning	Crawford	Hendry	Andreu+	Neil	McKinnon"	Keatings+	Antoine-Curier	Ryan*	Ryan+	Longridge"	Currie	McGrath	McGrath	Finnie
24/09/2013	LC3	H	St Johnstone	1	0	Cuthbert	Gordon	Devlin	Canning	Crawford*	Hendry+	Andreu+	Neil	McKinnon"	McShane	Antoine-Curier	Ryan*	Longridge+	Watson	Currie	Garcia Tena	Garcia Tena	Longridge
28/09/2013	L	A	Alloa	0	1	Cuthbert	Gordon	Devlin	Canning	Crawford	Neil	Gillespie"	Neil	McKinnon	Keatings"	Antoine-Curier	Andreu*	Finnie	Ryan"	Currie	Garcia Tena	Ryan	McShane
05/10/2013	L	H	Livingston	2	0	Cuthbert	Gordon	Devlin	Canning	Crawford+	Hendry	Gillespie	Andreu+	McKinnon	Keatings*	Antoine-Curier*	McShane*	Watson+	McGrath"	Currie	Garcia Tena	Finnie	Longridge
12/10/2013	L	H	Morton	1	1	Cuthbert	Gordon	Devlin	Canning	Crawford+	Hendry	Gillespie	Andreu+	McKinnon*	McShane*	Keatings"	McShane*	Watson++	McGrath"	Currie	Garcia Tena	Finnie	Neil
19/10/2013	L	H	Raith Rovers	1	1	Cuthbert	Gordon	Devlin	Canning	Crawford*	Hendry	Gillespie"	Andreu+	McKinnon*	Keatings	Antoine-Curier*	McGrath*	Longridge++	Brophy*	Currie	Garcia Tena	Kilday	Neil
26/10/2013	L	A	Falkirk	2	0	Cuthbert	Gordon	Devlin	Canning	Crawford*	Hendry	Gillespie	Andreu"	McKinnon*	McShane	Brophy+	McGrath*	Longridge++	Antoine-Curier*	Currie	Garcia Tena	Kilday	Neil
02/11/2013	SC3	A	Queen of the South	0	1	Cuthbert	Gordon*	Devlin	Canning	Crawford*	Hendry	Gillespie	Andreu	McKinnon	McShane	Brophy	Longridge"	Brophy+	Antoine-Curier*	Currie	Garcia Tena	Docherty	Docherty
09/11/2013	L	A	Queen of the South	1	0	Cuthbert	Gordon*	Devlin	Canning+	Crawford"	Hendry+	Gillespie+	Andreu	McKinnon"	McShane*	Brophy	Longridge"	Garcia-Tena+	McGrath	Currie	Kilday	Docherty	McGrath
16/11/2013	L	H	Cowdenbeath	4	2	Cuthbert	Gordon	Devlin	Canning+	Crawford*	Hendry	Andreu+	Neil	McKinnon	McShane"	Brophy	Longridge*	Longridge+	Watson"	Currie	Docherty	Docherty	McGrath
23/11/2013	L	A	Dundee	0	3	Cuthbert	Gordon	Devlin	Canning	Crawford*	Hendry+	Garcia-Tena	Andreu	McKinnon	McShane*	Keatings	Kilday*	Longridge+	Garcia-Tena"	Currie	Kilday	Watson	McGrath
30/11/2013		H	Alloa	0	1	Cuthbert	Gordon	Devlin	Canning	Crawford"	Hendry*	Gillespie	Andreu*	McKinnon+	Longridge*	Keatings	Ryan*	Docherty+	Brophy"	Currie	Brophy	McMann	Watson
14/12/2013		A	Livingston	0	0	Cuthbert	Gordon	Kilday	Canning	Crawford+	Garcia-Tena	McKinnon	Andreu	McKinnon+	Antoine-Curier	Keatings	Longridge*	Antoine-Curier"	Ryan*	Currie	Docherty	McMann	McShane
21/12/2013	L	A	Dumbarton	3	1	Cuthbert	Gillespie	Garcia-Tena	Canning	Kilday*	Devlin	McKinnon	Andreu+	McKinnon++	Antoine-Curier	Keatings+	Longridge*	Ryan+	Brophy	Currie	Docherty	McGrath	Kilday
28/12/2013	L	H	Morton	1	0	Currie	Gordon*	Kilday	Canning	Gordon	Devlin	McKinnon	Andreu*	McKinnon	Antoine-Curier	Keatings"	Longridge*	Ryan+	Brophy	Watson	McGrath	Garcia-Tena	Law
04/01/2014	L	A	Queen of the South	3	1	Currie	Gordon"	Hendry	Canning+	Crawford	Devlin	Gillespie	Andreu	Longridge	Antoine-Curier	Keatings	Docherty"	Ryan+	Kilday	Watson	Docherty	Garcia-Tena	Law
11/01/2014	L	A	Falkirk	0	0	Cuthbert	Gordon	Hendry	Canning	Crawford	Devlin	Gillespie*	Andreu	Longridge	Antoine-Curier+	Keatings	Ryan*	Brophy+	Routledge"	Watson	Docherty	Garcia-Tena	Currie
25/01/2014	L	A	Cowdenbeath	3	4	Cuthbert	Gordon	Gordon	Canning	Crawford	Devlin	George+	Andreu	Longridge++	Antoine-Curier+	Scotland	Antoine-Curier"	Crawgord+	Routledge"	Currie	Kilday	McKinnon	Ryan
01/02/2014	L	H	Dumbarton	3	3	Cuthbert	Gordon	Crawford	Canning	Routledge"	Devlin"	McKinnon	Andreu	Antoine-Curier*	Scotland	Keatings	McKinnon*	Gillespie+	Garcia-Tena"	Currie	Ryan	Gillespie	Longridge
08/02/2014	L	A	Dundee	0	1	Cuthbert	Gordon	Crawford	Canning	Canning	Longridge	McKinnon	Andreu	Garcia-Tena*	Scotland	Keatings+	Hendrie	Lyon+	Longridge*	Currie	George	George	Antoine-Curier
15/02/2014	L	A	Raith Rovers	4	2	Cuthbert	Gillespie	Crawford	Canning	Gordon	Longridge*	McKinnon	Andreu*	Garcia-Tena	Scotland+	Keatings+	Watson*	Antoine-Curier+	Antoine-Curier*	Currie	Ryan	Devlin	El-Zubaidi
21/02/2014	L	A	Alloa	3	0	Cuthbert	Gillespie	Crawford	Canning	Gordon	Longridge	McKinnon	Andreu+	Garcia-Tena	Scotland+	Keatings"	Hendrie*	Antoine-Curier+	Routledge*	Currie	Ryan	Devlin	Hendrie
01/03/2014	L	H	Alloa	3	0	Cuthbert	Gillespie*	Crawford	Canning	Gordon	Longridge	McKinnon	Andreu+	Garcia-Tena	Scotland+	Keatings"	Routledge*	Antoine-Curier+	Devlin"	Currie	Ryan	Hendrie	Routledge
08/03/2014	L	A	Queen of the South	4	3	Cuthbert	Gillespie*	Crawford	Canning	Gordon	Gordon	McKinnon	Andreu	Garcia-Tena*	Scotland+	Keatings"	George*	Hendrie*	Antoine-Curier+	Currie	Ryan	Devlin	George
15/03/2014	L	H	Falkirk	0	3	Cuthbert	Gillespie*	Crawford+	Canning	Gordon	Longridge+	McKinnon	Routledge	Garcia-Tena*	Scotland*	Keatings	Devlin*	Routledge+	Antoine-Curier*	Currie	Ryan	Hendrie	George
22/03/2014	L	H	Raith Rovers	4	3	Cuthbert	Gillespie	Crawford*	Canning	Gordon	Longridge+	McKinnon	Andreu	Devlin	Scotland"	Keatings++	Scotland*	Ryan+	Antoine-Curier*	Currie	Hendrie	Devlin	George
25/03/2014	L	A	Raith Rovers	3	2	Cuthbert	Gillespie	Crawford"	Canning	Gordon	Longridge+	McKinnon	Andreu	Garcia-Tena"	Antoine-Curier	Keatings++	Antoine-Curier*	George+	Routledge*	Currie	Garcia-Tena	Ryan	Kilday
29/03/2014	L	A	Cowdenbeath	1	1	Cuthbert	Kilday	Routledge	Canning	Gordon	Longridge+	McKinnon	Andreu	Devlin	Scotland+	Keatings"	Antoine-Curier*	Ryan+	Crawford"	Currie	Docherty	Neil	Gillespie
05/04/2014	L	H	Dundee	0	1	Cuthbert	Kilday*	Garcia-Tena	Canning	Gordon	Longridge	McKinnon	Andreu	Crawford	Scotland+	Keatings*	Antoine-Curier*	Ryan+	Gillespie*	Currie	George	Neil	Devlin
12/04/2014	H	Livingston	1	1	Cuthbert	Hendrie	Garcia-Tena	Canning	Gordon	Longridge	McKinnon+	Andreu	Crawford	Scotland	Antoine-Curier"	Ryan*	Neil	Kilday	Currie	George	Docherty	George
19/04/2014	H	Alloa	2	1	Cuthbert	Kilday	Garcia-Tena	Canning	Neil+	Longridge*	McKinnon*	Andreu"	Crawford"	Scotland	Gillespie	Ryan*	Docherty+	Antoine-Curier*	Currie	Devlin	Armstrong	George
26/04/2014	L	A	Dumbarton	2	4	Cuthbert	Devlin	Garcia-Tena	Canning	Gordon	Longridge*	Neil	Andreu*	Crawford"	Scotland	Gillespie	Keatings*	George+	Routledge*	Currie	Ryan	Kilday	George
03/05/2014	H	Morton			Cuthbert*	Devlin	Garcia-Tena	Routledge	Gordon	Longridge*	Kilday	Kilday	Ryan+	Antoine-Curier	Gillespie"	Currie*	George+	Crawford"	Keatings	Watson	Docherty	El-Zubaidi

Heart of Midlothian FC

Founded	1874
Ground	Tynecastle Park
Postcode	EH11 2NL
Tel	0131 200 7207
Capacity	17529
Closest Railway Station	Haymarket
Record Attendance	57857 v Barcelona, Friendly, 28/7/2007
Ground Record	53396 v Rangers, SC, 13/2/1932
Record Win	21-0 v Anchor, East of Scotland Cup, 30/10/1880
Record Defeat	1-8, v Vale of Leven, Scottish Cup, 1882
Most League Goals in a Season	44 Barney Battles, 1930/1
Most League Goals in Career	214 John Robertson
Chairman	Anne Budge
Chief Executive	
Secretary	David Southern
Manager	Gary Locke (until May) / Craig Levein
Assistant Manager	Billy Brown (until May) / Robbie Neilson
Colours 2013/14 Top	Maroon
Shorts	Maroon
Sponsor	Wonga.com
Manufacturer	Adidas
Change Colours 2013/14 Top	White
Shorts	White
Nicknames	Jam Tarts, Jambos
Web	www.heartsfc.co.uk

PREDICTION 2014/15

Hearts face a major challenge to get back in one season with Rangers and Hibs as opponents. But with the feelgood factor around Tynecastle these days they could easily seal the one automatic promotion place

Staring the season with a 15-point deduction, there was never much doubt that Hearts would be facing relegation. They were forced to play a team comprised mainly of inexperienced young players. At times, in the early to mid season, they looked out of their depth, but as the season progressed they improved greatly and produced some entertaining football and some fine results.

Relegation was inevitable but take away the points deduction and Hearts would have survived comfortably. Crowds held up well, but more importantly the off-field problems surrounding the club seem to have cleared.

It was an agonising wait for Hearts fans as legal deliberations in Lithuania were protracted and confusing. In the end things went in Hearts favour allowing long-term fan Anne Budge to take over as the major shareholder with the intention of selling the club back to the fans over the next few years.

Manager Gary Locke didn't survive the new regime who were quick to install Craig Levein as the man they see to lead Hearts back to the Premiership.

Season ticket sales are again booming and everything seems positive at Tynecastle these days.

Surname	First Name	DOB	Pos	L-A	L-S	L-G	SC-A	SC-S	SC-G	LC-A	LC-S	LC-G	UNS	Signed Previous Club	Notes	Contract
Beith	Angus	22/02/96	M										13	2013 Hearts Youths		Youth
Buchanan	Robbie		F										1	2013 Hearts Youths		Youth
Carrick	Dale	07/01/94	F	14	11	6		1		1	1		9	2013 Hearts Youths		C (2015)
Hamill	Jamie	29/07/86	D	34	1	5	1			4		4		2011 Kilmarnock	Joined Kilmarnock May 2014	F
Hamilton	Jack	22/03/94	GK										10	2009 Stenhousemuir		C (2015)
Holt	Jason	19/02/93	M	18	5	1				3			3	2011 Hearts Youths		C (2015)
King	Billy	12/05/94	F	7	25	3				1	1		5	2012 Hearts Youths		C (2015)
King	Adam	11/10/95	M	2				1					11	2013 Hearts Youth	Transferred to Swansea City Jan 2014	
McCallum	Paul	28/07/93	F	4	2					1			1	2014 West Ham United (Loan)	Returned to West Ham	
McDonald	Jamie	14/04/86	GK	37						4			1	2003 Musselburgh Athletic		F
McGhee	Jordan	24/07/96	D	13	3	1	1			1	1		23	2013 Hearts Youths		C (2015)
McGowan	Dylan	06/08/91	M	37						4			1	2010 Hearts Youths		C (2015)
McHattie	Kevin	15/07/93	D	36			1			4		1		2011 Hearts Youths		C (2015)
McKay	Brad	26/04/93	D	23	5					3			10	2010 Edinburgh City		C (2015)
Nicholson	Sam	20/01/95	M	14	10	2				1			10	2013 Hearts Youths		C (2017)
Oliver	Gary	14/07/95	F	1	7					1	1		23	2013 Hearts Youths		Youth
Paterson	Calum	13/10/94	F	36	1	11	1			4				2010 Tynecastle BC		C (2015)
Ridgers	Mark	09/08/90	GK	1						1			31	2007 Ross Youth	Joined St Mirren June 2014	F
Robinson	Scott	12/03/92	M	31	5	1	1			4				2008 Hearts Youths		C (2015)
Smith	David	01/03/93	F	18	14	1	1			1	1		2	2011 Hearts Youths		C (2015)
Smith	Liam												1	2013 Hearts Youths		Youth
Stevenson	Ryan	24/08/84	M	26	1	8	1			1	1	1	1	2012 Ipswich Town	Joined Partick Thistle June 2014	
Tapping	Callum	05/06/93	M	13	6					2			9	2012 Hearts Youths		F
Walker	Jamie	25/06/93	F	21	5	3	1			3			4	2011 Hearts Youths		C (2015)
Wilson	Danny	27/12/91	D	32		3	1			4		1		2013 Liverpool		C (2016)

NEW SIGNINGS 2014/15

Surname	First Name	Pos	Signed Previous Club
Gomis	Morgaro	M	2014 Dundee United
Keatings	James	F	2014 Hamilton Accies
El Hassnaoui	Soufain	F	2014 Sparta Rotterdam

Date	Comp	H/A	Opponents	F	A		Crowd	Scorers
03/08/2013	Prem	A	St Johnstone	0	1		6174	
11/08/2013	Prem	H	Hibernian	1	0		16621	Paterson
16/08/2013	Prem	A	Partick Thistle	1	1		6540	Walker
24/08/2013	Prem	H	Aberdeen	2	1		15218	Walker, McGhee
27/08/2013	LC2	A	Raith Rovers	1	1	AET, 5-4 pens	3688	Hamill
31/08/2013	Prem	A	Inverness CT	0	2		4034	
14/09/2013	Prem	H	Celtic	1	3		15928	Holt
21/09/2013	Prem	A	Ross County	1	2		4059	Paterson
25/09/2013	LC3	H	QOS	3	3	AET, 4-2 pens	8381	Hamill, Wilson, McHattie
28/09/2013	Prem	H	Dundee United	0	0		13970	
05/10/2013	Prem	H	St Mirren	0	2		14769	
19/10/2013	Prem	A	Motherwell	1	2		5350	Stevenson
26/10/2013	Prem	A	Kilmarnock	0	2		5090	
30/10/2013	LC4	A	Hibernian	1	0		16797	Stevenson
02/11/2013	Prem	H	St Johnstone	0	2		13175	
09/11/2013	Prem	A	Aberdeen	3	1		13940	Walker, Paterson, Stevenson
23/11/2013	Prem	H	Ross County	2	2		12508	Paterson, Stevenson
01/12/2013	SC4	H	Celtic	0	7		10636	
07/12/2013	Prem	A	Dundee United	1	4		7808	Hamill
14/12/2013	Prem	H	Inverness CT	0	2		11950	
21/12/2013	Prem	A	Celtic	0	2		46058	
26/12/2013	Prem	H	Kilmarnock	0	4		13684	
29/12/2013	Prem	A	St Mirren	1	1		4568	Hamill
02/01/2014	Prem	A	Hibernian	1	2		20106	D Smith
05/01/2014	Prem	H	Partick Thistle	0	2		13673	
11/01/2014	Prem	H	Motherwell	0	1		12888	
18/01/2014	Prem	A	St Johnstone	3	3		3395	Carrick, Nicholson, Wilson
25/01/2014	Prem	A	Ross County	2	1		4016	Paterson, Robinson
29/01/2014	Prem	H	St Mirren	2	1		12422	Paterson, Hamill
02/02/2014	LCSF	N	Inverness CT	2	2	AET, 2-4 pens	12762	Hamill 2
15/02/2014	Prem	A	Inverness CT	0	0		3392	
22/02/2014	Prem	H	Celtic	0	2		15801	
01/03/2014	Prem	A	Motherwell	1	4		4914	Paterson
08/03/2014	Prem	A	Kilmarnock	2	4		3510	Carrick, Nicholson
21/03/2014	Prem	H	Dundee United	1	2		13448	Wilson
30/03/2014	Prem	H	Hibernian	2	0		16873	Carrick, B King
02/04/2013	Prem	H	Aberdeen	1	1		13913	Hamill
05/04/2014	Prem	A	Partick Thistle	4	2		4262	Carrick, B King, Stevenson 2
19/04/2014	Prem	H	Ross County	2	0		13692	Hamill, Carrick
27/04/2014	Prem	A	Hibernian	2	1		14806	Paterson 2
04/05/2014	Prem	H	Kilmarnock	5	0		13656	Stevenson 3, B King, Paterson
07/05/2014	Prem	H	Partick Thistle	2	4		14059	Paterson, Wilson
10/05/2014	Prem	A	St Mirren	1	1		6311	Carrick

Friendly Matches

Date		Comp	H/A	Opponents	F	A			
6/7/13		Fr	A	Selkirk	6	2			
9/7/13		Fr	N	Dinamo Bucharest	1	5			at Leigh Sports Village
12/7/13		Fr	A	Hawick Royal Albert	6	1		U20	
13/7/13		Fr	A	Dunfermline Athletic	2	1	4538		
17/7/13		Fr	A	Raith Rovers	5	0			
20/7/13		Fr	A	Queen of the South	0	0			
25/7/13		TnT	N	Crusaders	2	0			at Glentoran
27/7/13		TnT	N	Liverpool U20	0	1			at Glentoran
30/7/13		Fr	A	Fauldhouse United	0	2		U20	

Date	Comp	H/A	Opponents	F	A	1	2	3	4	5	6	7	8	9	10	11	12	13	14	15	16	17	18
03/08/2013	Prem	A	St Johnstone	0	1	MacDonald	Hamill	Wilson	McGowan	McHattie	McKay	Robinson*	Stevenson	Tapping+	Walker"	Paterson	Holt*	B King+	Smith"	A King	Oliver	McGhee	Ridgers
11/08/2013	Prem	H	Hibernian	1	0	MacDonald	Hamill	Wilson	McGowan	McHattie	McKay	Robinson	Stevenson*	Holt	Smith*	Paterson	Walker*	B King"	Tapping	McGhee	Carrick	Nicholson	Ridgers
16/08/2013	Prem	A	Partick Thistle	1	1	MacDonald	Hamill	Wilson	McGowan	McHattie	McKay	Robinson+	Walker	Holt	Smith*	Paterson	B King*	Tapping+	Oliver	McGhee	Carrick	Carrick	Ridgers
24/08/2013	Prem	H	Aberdeen	2	1	MacDonald	Hamill	Wilson	McGowan	McHattie	McKay*	Robinson+	Walker"	Holt	B King+	Paterson	McGhee*	Tapping+	Smith"	A King	Oliver	Carrick	Ridgers
27/08/2013	LC2		Raith Rovers	1	1 AET, 5-4 pens	MacDonald*	Hamill	Wilson	McGowan	McHattie	McKay	Robinson+	Walker	Holt	B King+	Paterson	Ridgers*	Tapping*	Smith"	Tapping	McGhee	Nicholson	Ridgers
31/08/2013	Prem	H	Inverness CT	0	2	McGhee	Hamill	McGhee	McGowan	Smith*	McKay	Robinson	Walker"	Holt	Tapping+	Paterson	B King*	Oliver+	Nicholson"	A King	Beith	Buchanan	Ridgers
14/09/2013	Prem	A	Celtic	1	3	McDonald	Hamill	Wilson	McGowan	McHattie	McKay	Robinson	Walker"	Holt	B King+	Paterson	Smith*	Carrick+	Oliver"	Tapping	McGhee	Nicholson	Ridgers
21/09/2013	Prem	H	Ross County	1	2	McDonald	Hamill	Wilson	McGowan	McHattie	McKay	Robinson	Walker"	Holt	Smith*	Paterson	B King*	Nicholson+	Oliver	Tapping	McGhee	Carrick	Ridgers
25/09/2013	LC3	H	QOS	3	3 AET, 4-2 pens	McDonald	Hamill	Wilson	McGowan	McHattie	McGhee	Robinson"	Walker"	Holt	Oliver*	Paterson	B King*	McGhee+	Carrick"	Tapping	Ridgers	Carrick	Oliver
28/09/2013	Prem	H	Dundee United	0	0	McDonald	Hamill	Wilson	McGowan	McHattie	McGhee	Robinson*	Walker	Holt"	Smith+	Paterson	Tapping*	Holt+	Stevenson"	McKay	Ridgers	Carrick	Oliver
05/10/2013	Prem	A	St Mirren	0	2	McDonald	Hamill	Wilson	McGowan+	McHattie	McGhee	Robinson*	Stevenson"	Holt	Walker	Paterson	B King*	Tapping+	Carrick"	McKay	Ridgers	Smith	Oliver
19/10/2013	Prem	H	Motherwell	1	2	McDonald	Hamill	Wilson	McKay	Smith"	McGhee	McKay	Stevenson	Paterson*	Walker	Tapping+	Robinson*	Holt+	Nicholson"	B King	Ridgers	Carrick	Oliver
26/10/2013	Prem	A	Kilmarnock	0	2	McDonald	Hamill	Wilson	McGowan	McHattie	McGhee	Robinson*	Stevenson	Holt	Walker	Tapping+	Paterson*	McKay	Nicholson"	McGowan	Ridgers	Holt	Oliver
30/10/2013	LC4	A	Hibernian	1	0	McDonald	Hamill	Wilson	McGowan	McHattie	McGhee	Robinson+	Stevenson	Holt+	Walker*	Paterson	Tapping*	Carrick+	Nicholson	Carrick	Ridgers	McKay	Oliver
02/11/2013	Prem	A	St Johnstone	0	2	McDonald	Hamill	Wilson	McGowan	McHattie	McGhee	Robinson*	Stevenson	Holt	Walker*	Paterson+	Nicholson*	Carrick+	Smith"	Tapping	Ridgers	McKay	Oliver
09/11/2013	Prem	H	Aberdeen	3	1	McDonald	Hamill	Wilson	McGowan	McHattie	McKay	Robinson+	Stevenson	Holt+	Walker*	Paterson	Smith*	Carrick+	B King"	McKay	Ridgers	Nicholson	Oliver
23/11/2013	Prem	H	Ross County	2	2	McDonald	Hamill	Wilson	McGowan	McHattie	McHattie*	Robinson+	Stevenson	Tapping*	Walker+	Paterson	Nicholson*	B King+	Oliver	A King	Ridgers	Carrick	McKay
01/12/2013	SC4	H	Celtic	0	7	McDonald	Hamill	Wilson	McGowan	McHattie	McKay	Robinson	Stevenson+	Smith"	Walker+	Paterson	McKay*	Carrick+	A King"	B King	Hamilton	Tapping	Nicholson
07/12/2013	Prem	A	Dundee United	1	4	McDonald	Hamill	Wilson	McGowan	McHattie	McGhee	Robinson	Nicholson+	Tapping+	Walker	Paterson	B King*	Carrick+	A King	B King	Hamilton	Smith	Nicholson
14/12/2013	Prem	A	Inverness CT	0	2	McDonald	Hamill"	Wilson	McGowan	McHattie	McGhee	Robinson	Nicholson+	Tapping	Walker*	Paterson+	Smith*	Carrick"	B King+	McKay	Hamilton	A King	McGhee
21/12/2013	Prem	H	Celtic	0	2	McDonald	Hamill	Wilson	McGowan	McHattie	McKay	D Smith	A King"	Tapping+	Walker+	Paterson	Carrick*	Nicholson+	B King"	McGhee	Hamilton	Nicholson	
26/12/2013	Prem	A	Kilmarnock	0	4	McDonald	Hamill	McGhee	McGowan	McHattie	McKay	D Smith*	Stevenson	Tapping	Walker	Paterson	B King*	Robinson+	Oliver"	McGhee	Hamilton	Nicholson	
29/12/2013	Prem	H	St Mirren	1	1	McDonald	Hamill	McGhee	McGowan	McHattie	McGhee	Robinson	Stevenson	Tapping*	Walker	Paterson	Smith*	Carrick	B King"	A King	Hamilton	Nicholson	McGhee
05/01/2014	Prem	H	Partick Thistle	0	2	McDonald	D Smith*	McGhee	McGowan	McHattie	McGhee*	Robinson	Stevenson	Tapping	Walker"	Paterson+	B King*	Carrick+	Nicholson"	A King	Hamilton	Nicholson	
11/01/2014	Prem	A	Motherwell	0	1	McDonald	Hamill	McGhee	McGowan+	McHattie	McKay	Robinson	Stevenson	Holt+	Walker*	Paterson	Walker*	Oliver+	B King"	A King	Hamilton	Tapping	Oliver
18/01/2014	Prem	H	St Johnstone	3	3	McDonald	Hamill	Wilson	McGowan"	McHattie*	McKay	D Smith*	Stevenson	Holt+	Walker"	Paterson	Nicholson*	Oliver+	B King"	A King	Hamilton	Beith	Beith
25/01/2014	Prem	A	Ross County	2	1	McDonald	Hamill	Wilson	McGowan	McHattie	McKay	D Smith+	Nicholson+	Holt	Carrick	Paterson	Smith*	Tapping+	Oliver	McGhee	Hamilton	Beith	Beith
29/01/2014	Prem	H	St Mirren	2	1	McDonald	Hamill	Wilson	McGowan"	McHattie	McKay	D Smith*	Robinson	Holt"	Carrick*	Paterson	B King*	Tapping*	McGhee"	Tapping	Ridgers	Beith	Beith
02/02/2014	LCSF		Inverness CT	2	2 AET, 2-4 pens	McDonald	Hamill	Wilson	McGowan"	McHattie	McKay	McCallum"	Nicholson+	Nicholson+	Stevenson+	Paterson	Stevenson*	McCallum+	Tapping*	McGhee	Ridgers		
15/02/2014	Prem	A	Inverness CT	0	0	McDonald	Robinson	Wilson	McGowan	McGhee	McKay	McCallum"	Nicholson"	Robinson"	Stevenson+	Stevenson	B King"	Holt+	Oliver	Beith	Ridgers		
22/02/2014	Prem	H	Celtic	0	2	McDonald	Robinson	Wilson	McGowan	McHattie	McGhee	Carrick	Nicholson	Robinson"	Stevenson+	Paterson	Carrick*	Holt+	B King"	Beith	Ridgers	McGhee	Oliver
01/03/2014	Prem	A	Motherwell	1	4	McDonald	Hamill+	Wilson	McGowan	McHattie	McKay"	Carrick*	Nicholson	Stevenson+	Stevenson	Paterson*	Carrick*	McCallum+	B King"	Beith	Ridgers	McGhee	Oliver
08/03/2014	Prem	A	Kilmarnock	2	4	McDonald	Hamill	Wilson	McGowan	McHattie	McGhee"	Carrick	Carrick	Nicholson	Stevenson	Paterson*	B King*	McCallum+	McKay"	Beith	Ridgers	Holt	Oliver
21/03/2014	Prem	H	Dundee United	1	2	McDonald	Hamill	Wilson	McGowan	McHattie	D Smith+	McCallum*	McCallum"	Holt"	Stevenson	Paterson	Holt*	B King+	McKay"	Beith	Ridgers	McGhee	Walker
30/03/2014	Prem	H	Hibernian	2	0	McDonald	Hamill	Wilson	McGowan	McHattie	McKay	Carrick"	Nicholson	Holt	Stevenson	Paterson	McCallum+	B King*	Robinson"	McKay	Ridgers	McGhee	Oliver
05/04/2014	Prem	A	Aberdeen	1	1	McDonald	Hamill	Robinson*	McGowan	McHattie	Carrick+	McCallum*	B King+	Holt	Stevenson*	Paterson	Robinson*	B King+	Oliver+	Walker	Ridgers	McGhee	Walker
19/04/2014	Prem	H	Ross County	2	0	McDonald	Hamill	Nicholson"	McGowan	McHattie	Carrick+	McKay	B King+	Holt	Stevenson*	Paterson	Smith*	Robinson+	Smith"	Walker	Ridgers	McGhee	Oliver
27/04/2014	Prem	A	Partick Thistle	2	1	McDonald	Robinson	Wilson	McGowan	McHattie	Nicholson"	McKay	B King"	Holt	Stevenson	Paterson	Smith*	Walker+	McKay"	Oliver	Ridgers	McGhee	Beith
04/05/2014	Prem	H	Kilmarnock	5	0	McDonald	Robinson	Wilson	McGowan	McHattie	Nicholson	Carrick+	B King*	Holt	Stevenson*	Paterson	Smith*	Oliver+	Hamill"	Walker	Ridgers	McGhee	McCallum
05/05/2014	Prem	H	Partick Thistle	2	4	Ridgers	Robinson*	Wilson	McGowan	McHattie	Nicholson	Carrick	B King*	Holt	Stevenson"	Paterson	Walker*	Oliver+	McKay"	Oliver	McDonald	McGhee	Beith
10/05/2014	Prem	H	St Mirren	1	1	McDonald	Robinson	Wilson	McGowan	McHattioe	Nicholson	Carrick"	Walker+	Holt	Smith*	Paterson	McGhee*	King+	Oliver"	Beith	Ridgers	McKay	L Smith

Hibernian FC

Founded	1875
Ground	Easter Road Stadium
Postcode	EH7 5QG
Tel	0131 661 2159
Capacity	20421
Closest Railway Station	Edinburgh Waverley
Record Attendance	65860 v Hearts, Lge, 2/1/1950
Record Win	15-1 v Peebles Rovers, SC, 11/2/1961
Record Defeat	0-10 v Rangers, Lge, 24/12/1898
Most League Goals in a Season	42 Joe Baker, 1959/60
Chairman	Rod Petrie
Chief Executive	Leanne Dempster
Secretary	Garry O'Hagan
Manager	Pat Fenlon / Terry Butcher / ???
Assistant Manager	Jimmy Nicholl / Maurice Malpas / ???
Colours 2013/14 Top	Green with white sleeves
Shorts	White
Sponsor	Crabbies
Manufacturer	Nike
Change Colours 2013/14 Top	Black
Shorts	Black
Nicknames	Hibees
Web	www.hibernianfc.co.uk

PREDICTION 2014/15
At the time of writing (June 23) Hibernian were still managerless. Rumours that Alan Stubbs would be appointed had not been substantiated. Whoever takes the job has a big task on their hands - a play off spot may be the best they can aim for.

2013/14 proved to be the latest in a long line of disappointing seasons for Hibernian fans. In fact, "disappointing" just doesn't do it justice.

It began with a humiliation from Mlamo in the Europa League qualifiers. It continued with elimination from the League Cup at the hands of what was little more than a Hearts youth team. It ended with an inexorable slide down the table into the Play Offs, and another humiliation at the hands of Hamilton Accies.

The season cost two managers their jobs. Pat Fenlon's team looked disorganised and feckless. Terry Butcher took over and after a very brief improvement his teams looked even worse.

Rumours about "losing the dressing room" and similar didn't help. It was clear that there was no confidence at Easter Road and Butcher didn't seem to have any idea of what his best team was. In the end few supporters were greatly surprised by the final outcome, even after the 2-0 success away to Hamilton in the Play Off first leg.

				L			SC			LC			UC							
SQUAD NUMBERS			Pos	A	S	G	A	S	G	A	S	G	A	S	G	UNS	Signed Previous Club		Notes	Contract
Surname	**First Name**	**DOB**																		
Boateng	Daniel	02/09/92	D	1	2											7	2014 Arsenal (Loan)		Returned to Arsenal	
Cairney	Paul	29/08/87	M	14	5	1	1									8	2012 Partick Thistle			F
Caldwell	Ross	26/10/93	F	3				1		2				1		11	2010 Hibernian Youth		On loan to Alloa Jan 2014	OOC
Collins	James	01/12/90	F	27	9	6	2			2						4	2013 Swindon Town		Joined Shrewsbury Town June 2014	
Craig	Liam	27/12/86	M	33	3	6	2			2	3	2				2	2013 St Johnstone			C (2015)
Cummings	Jason	01/08/95	F	11	7	2										8	2013 Hutchison Vale			OOC
Forster	Jordan	23/09/93	D	26		4	2						2			10	2010 Celtic Youth			C (2016)
Grant	Paul	23/03/93	GK													4	2012 Hibernian Youth		On loan to Berwick Aug-Dec 2013	F
Handling	Danny	06/02/94	F	10	9	1	1			2						13	2010 Hibernian Youth			OOC
Hanlon	Paul	20/01/90	D	29		1	2			2						2	2007 Hibernian Youth			C (2016)
Harris	Alex	31/08/94	M	11	6		1						1	1			2012 Hibernian Youth			C (2017)
Haynes	Danny	19/01/88	F	8	2	1	1									4	2014 Notts County (Loan)		Returned to Notts County	
Heffernan	Paul	29/12/81	F	15	6	4	1									4	2013 Kilmarnock			C (2015)
Horribine	Dean	14/01/93	F		1											3	2011 Hibernian Youth			F
Maybury	Alex	08/08/78	D	16			1			1						18	2012 St Johnstone			F
McGivern	Ryan	08/01/90	D	33	2	1				1	1					2	2013 Manchester City			C (2015)
McPake	James	24/06/84	D	1	2					1					2	8	2012 Coventry City		Joined Dundee May 2014	
Mullen	Fraser	08/11/93	D	3										1		4	2013 Hearts		Freed Jan 2014, Joined Raith Rovers	
Murdoch	Sean	31/07/86	GK	1												42	2012 Accrington Stanley			F
Nelson	Michael	23/03/80	D	33	1	2	1	1	1							1	2013 Bradford City			C (2015)
Robertson	Scott	07/04/85	M	26		1	1			2						3	2013 Blackpool			C (2015)
Stanton	Sam	19/04/94	M	17	13	2	1	1		1			1			3	2011 Hibernian Youth			C (2018)
Stevenson	Lewis	05/01/88	M	35	2	1	2			2			2			3	2005 Hibernian Youth			C (2015)
Taiwo	Tom	27/02/90	M	17	5	1	1	1		2						2	2012 Carlisle United			F
Thomson	Kevin	14/10/84	M	15	4					1			2			4	2013 Middlesbrough		Joined Dundee May 2014	
Tudur Jones	Owain	15/10/84	M	8	8		1						1			14	2013 Inverness CT			C (2015)
Vine	Rowan	21/09/82	F	4	5					2			2			5	2013 St Johnstone		Freed Jan 2014, Joined Morton	
Watmore	Duncan	08/03/94	F	4	5	1	1									1	2013 Sunderland (Loan)		Returned to Sunderland	
Williams	Ben	27/08/82	GK	39			2						2			2	2012 Colchester United			F
Zoubir	Abdellah	05/12/91	M	3	10		1			1	1	1	1			6	2013 FC Istres (Loan)		Returned to FC Istres	
Own Goal												1								

Date	Comp	H/A	Opponents	F	A		Crowd	Scorers
18/07/2013	EUL	A	Malmo	0	2		8628	
25/07/2013	EUL	H	Malmo	0	7		16018	
03/08/2013	Prem	H	Motherwell	0	1		9237	
11/08/2013	Prem	A	Hearts	0	1		16621	
17/08/2013	Prem	H	Dundee United	1	1		9171	Robertson
24/08/2013	Prem	A	Kilmarnock	2	1		3807	Craig 2
31/08/2013	Prem	H	Ross County	0	0		9569	
14/09/2013	Prem	A	St Johnstone	2	1		4095	Heffernan, Collins
21/09/2013	Prem	H	St Mirren	2	0		9417	Collins, Heffernan
24/09/2013	LC3	H	Stranrær	5	3		6431	Craig 3, Zoubir, Rumsby og
28/09/2013	Prem	A	Inverness CT	0	3		4261	
07/10/2013	Prem	A	Partick Thistle	1	0		4521	Craig
19/10/2013	Prem	H	Celtic	1	1		14220	Heffernan
26/10/2013	Prem	H	Aberdeen	0	2		12810	
30/10/2013	LC4	H	Hearts	0	1		16797	
03/11/2013	Prem	A	Motherwell	0	1		3864	
09/11/2013	Prem	H	Inverness CT	0	2		8750	
23/11/2013	Prem	A	St Mirren	0	0		4451	
30/11/2013	SC4	A	Ross County	1	0		2213	Handling
07/12/2013	Prem	H	Partick Thistle	1	1		10431	Collins
14/12/2013	Prem	A	Celtic	0	1		46065	
21/12/2013	Prem	H	St Johnstone	0	0		8776	
26/12/2013	Prem	A	Ross County	2	0		3383	Nelson, Forster
29/12/2013	Prem	H	Kilmarnock	3	0		9683	Hanlon, Cairney, Stevenson
02/01/2014	Prem	H	Hearts	2	1		20106	Collins, Craig
05/01/2014	Prem	A	Dundee United	2	2		7862	Craig 2
10/01/2014	Prem	A	Aberdeen	0	1		12734	
18/01/2014	Prem	H	St Mirren	2	3		9610	Collins 2
26/01/2014	Prem	H	Celtic	0	4		12542	
08/02/2014	SC5	H	Raith Rovers	2	3		10503	Stanton, Nelson
15/02/2014	Prem	H	Ross County	2	1		8411	Stanton, Taiwo
22/02/2014	Prem	A	Kilmarnock	1	1		4036	Haynes
28/02/2014	Prem	H	Dundee United	1	3		9608	Forster
08/03/2014	Prem	H	Motherwell	3	3		8277	Forster, Nelson, Heffernan
12/03/2014	Prem	A	Inverness CT	0	0		2537	
15/03/2014	Prem	A	Partick Thistle	1	2		4448	Watmore
22/03/2014	Prem	A	St Johnstone	0	2		3553	
29/03/2014	Prem	A	Hearts	0	2		16873	
07/04/2014	Prem	H	Aberdeen	0	2		9321	
19/04/2014	Prem	A	St Mirren	0	2		5287	
27/04/2014	Prem	H	Hearts	1	2		14806	Forster
03/05/2014	Prem	H	Partick Thistle	1	1		10740	Stanton
06/05/2014	Prem	A	Ross County	0	1		3850	
10/05/2014	Prem	H	Kilmarnock	0	1		15057	
21/05/2014	PO	A	Hamilton Accies	2	0		5322	Cummings 2
25/05/2014	PO	H	Hamilton Accies	0	2	aet, 3-4p	18031	

Friendly Matches

29/6/13	Fr	A	Dumbarton	1	1		1000	
3/7/13	Fr	A	Gibraltar XI	3	1			
6/7/13	Fr	H	Vale of Leithen	2	0		U20	at Hibernian TC
6/7/13	Fr	N	Nottingham Forest	1	2			at Vila Real de Santa Antonio
10/7/13	Fr	A	Selkirk	7	0		U20	
12/7/13	Fr	A	Raith Rovers	2	0		2050	
13/7/13	Fr	H	Lothian Thistle HV	3	1			at Hibernian TC
16/7/13	Fr	A	Spartans	1	2		U20	
20/7/13	Fr	A	Civil Service Strollers	5	0		U20	
22/7/13	TnT	N	Institute	3	1		U20	Foyle Cup
30/7/13	Fr	H	Sunderland U20	2	2		U20	at Hibernian TC
30/7/13	Fr	A	Preston Athletic	1	0		U20	

Date	Comp	H/A	Opponents	F	A	1	2	3	4	5	6	7	8	9	10	11	12	13	14	15	16	17	18
18/07/2013	EUL	A	Malmo	0	2	Williams	Stevenson	Forster	McPake	Hanlon	Taiwo	Tudur-Jones+	Thomson*	Craig	Handling	Vine"	Caldwell"	Harris*	Cairney	Robertson+	Horribine	Mullen	Murdoch
25/07/2013	EUL	H	Malmo	0	7	Williams	Stevenson	Forster	McPake*	Hanlon	Taiwo+	Harris*	Thomson"	Craig	Handling	Vine	Mullen	Robertson+	Stanton*	Tudur-Jones	Horribine	Caldwell	Murdoch
03/08/2013	Prem	H	Motherwell	0	1	Williams	Stevenson	Mullen	Tudur-Jones"	Hanlon	Nelson	Harris*	Thomson"	Craig	Robertson+	Collins	Stanton"	Taiwo+	Stanton+	McGivern	Caldwell	Maybury	Murdoch
11/08/2013	Prem	A	Hearts	0	1	Williams	Stevenson	Mullen*	Tudur-Jones"	Hanlon	Nelson	Vine	Thomson	Craig	Robertson+	Collins	McGivern"	Taiwo +	Stanton*	Hanling	Caldwell	Forster	Murdoch
17/08/2013	Prem	H	Dundee United	1	1	Williams	Stevenson	Mullen*	Handling	Hanlon	Nelson	Vine+	Thomson	Craig	Robertson"	Collins*	McGivern"	Stanton+	Taiwo"	Maybury	Caldwell	Forster	Murdoch
24/08/2013	Prem	A	Kilmarnock	2	1	Williams	Stevenson	McGivern	Handling"	Hanlon	Nelson	Vine+	Taiwo"	Craig	Tudur-Jones	Collins*	Caldwell"	Stanton+	Horribine*	Maybury	Cummings	Forster	Murdoch
31/08/2013	Prem	A	Ross County	0	0	Williams	Stevenson	McGivern	Handling"	Hanlon	Nelson	Taiwo	Thomson	Craig"	Tudur-Jones	Collins+	Caldwell"	Heffernan+	Stanton"	Maybury	Robertson	Forster	Murdoch
14/09/2013	Prem	A	St Johnstone	2	1	Williams	Stevenson*	Maybury	Robertson	Hanlon	Nelson	Taiwo	Thomson	Craig"	Heffernan	Collins+	McPake*	Zoubir+	Stanton*	Vine	Caldwell	Forster	Murdoch
21/09/2013	Prem	H	St Mirren	2	0	Williams	Stevenson*	Maybury"	Robertson	Hanlon	Nelson	Taiwo*	Thomson	Craig	Heffernan	Collins+	Stanton*	Zoubir+	McGivern	Vine	McPake	Caldwell	Murdoch
24/09/2013	LC3	H	Stranraer	5	3	Williams	Stevenson	Maybury*	Robertson"	Hanlon	Nelson	Taiwo*	Vine"	Craig	Zoubir+	Collins	McGivern*	Stanton+	Caldwell"	McPake	Murdoch	Forster	Tudur-Jones
28/09/2013	Prem	A	Inverness CT	0	3	Williams	Stevenson	McGivern	Robertson"	Hanlon	Nelson	Taiwo*	Thomson"	Craig	Heffernan+	Collins"	McGivern"	Zoubir+	Caldwell"	McPake	Murdoch	Vine	Mullen
07/10/2013	Prem	A	Partick Thistle	1	0	Williams	Stevenson	McGivern"	Robertson"	Hanlon	Nelson	Taiwo+	Thomson	Craig+	Heffernan	Collins*	Tudur-Jones*	Zoubir+	Tudur-Jones*	McPake	Murdoch	Handling	Mullen
19/10/2013	Prem	H	Celtic	1	1	Williams	Stevenson	McGivern	Robertson	Hanlon	Nelson	Taiwo+	Thomson	Craig	Heffernan	Zoubir+	Zoubir+	Vine+	Caldwell"	Collins	Murdoch	Handling	Nelson
26/10/2013	Prem	H	Aberdeen	0	2	Williams	Maybury"	McGivern	Robertson	Hanlon	Nelson	Tudur-Jones*	Thomson"	Craig	Heffernan	Zoubir"	Collins"	Vine+	Caldwell"	Cairney	Murdoch	Forster	Thomson
30/10/2013	LC4	H	Hearts	0	1	Williams	Maybury	McGivern	Robertson*	Hanlon	McPake	Taiwo*	Handling"	Craig	Vine	Collins"	Caldwell"	Zoubir+	Caldwell"	Tudur-Jones	Murdoch	Mullen	Thomson
03/11/2013	Prem	A	Motherwell	0	1	Williams	Maybury	McGivern	Robertson	Hanlon	Forster	Taiwo*	Handling+	Craig	Heffernan	Zoubir+	Caldwell"	Vine*	Taiwo"	Tudur-Jones	Murdoch	McPake	Thomson
09/11/2013	Prem	H	Inverness CT	0	2	Williams	Maybury*	McGivern	Robertson*	Hanlon	Forster	Cairney*	Handling"	Collins"	Heffernan	Stevenson	Tudur-Jones*	Collins"	Nelson"	Taiwo	Murdoch	Zoubir	Zoubir
23/11/2013	Prem	A	St Mirren	1	1	Williams	Nelson	McGivern	Robertson	Hanlon	Forster	Cairney	Handling*	Craig	Heffernan	Stevenson	Cummings*	Zoubir"	Thomson"	Handling	Murdoch	Caldwell	Zoubir
30/11/2013	SC4	H	Ross County	1	0	Williams	Nelson	McGivern	Tudur-Jones	Hanlon	Forster	Cairney+	Cummings	Craig	Collins	Stevenson	Zoubir+	Vine+	Maybury	Handling	Murdoch	Caldwell	Zoubir
07/12/2013	Prem	H	Partick Thistle	1	1	Williams	Nelson	McGivern	Robertson	Hanlon	Forster	Cairney	Cummings*	Craig	Collins	Stevenson+	Cummings*	Zoubir+	Maybury	Stanton	Murdoch	Caldwell	Zoubir
14/12/2013	Prem	A	Celtic	0	1	Williams	Nelson	McGivern	Robertson*	Hanlon	Forster	Cairney	Cummings*	Craig	Collins+	Stevenson	Handling"	Tudur-Jones"	Maybury	Stanton	Murdoch	Caldwell	Stanton
21/12/2013	Prem	H	St Johnstone	0	0	Williams	Nelson	McGivern	Robertson	Hanlon+	Forster	Cairney*	Cummings*	Craig	Collins	Stevenson	Handling*	Tudur-Jones"	Maybury	Stanton	Murdoch	Caldwell	Zoubir
26/12/2013	Prem	A	Ross County	2	0	Williams	Nelson	McGivern*	Robertson*	Hanlon	Forster	Cairney*	Cummings*	Craig	Collins	Stevenson	Heffernan*	Tudur-Jones"	Handling"	Maybury	Murdoch	Handling	Zoubir
29/12/2013	Prem	H	Kilmarnock	3	0	Williams	Nelson	McGivern	Robertson	Hanlon+	Forster	Cairney*	Cummings*	Craig	Collins	Stevenson	Cummings"	Tudur-Jones"	Heffernan"	Handling	Murdoch	Cummings	Zoubir
02/01/2014	Prem	H	Hearts	2	1	Williams	Nelson	Stanton	Robertson*	Hanlon	Forster	Cairney*	Heffernan+	Craig	Collins	Stevenson*	Heffernan"	Stanton+	Stanton"	Maybury	Murdoch	Heffernan	Zoubir
05/01/2014	Prem	A	Dundee United	0	2	Williams	Nelson	Stanton	Taiwo"	Hanlon	Forster	Harris*	Watmore	Haynes*	Collins*	Collins*	Cairney*	Cummings+	Cummings"	Robertson	Boateng	Maybury	Tudur-Jones
10/01/2014	Prem	A	Aberdeen	0	1	Williams	Nelson	Stanton	Taiwo*	Hanlon	Foster	Harris+	McGivern	Haynes*	Collins*	Stevenson*	Cairney"	Zoubir+	Heffernan"	Maybury	Grant	Heffernan	Cummings
18/01/2014	Prem	A	St Mirren	2	3	Williams	Nelson	Stanton	Taiwo	Hanlon+	Foster	Harris	McGivern	Haynes*	Handling"	Handling+	Handling"	Cummings+	Collins"	Maybury	Boateng	Heffernan	Grant
26/01/2014	Prem	A	Celtic	0	4	Williams	Nelson	Stanton	Cairney"	Maybury	Foster	Harris	McGivern	Haynes+	Handling*	Craig	Stevenson*	Heffernan"	Handling"	Maybury	Boateng	Heffernan	Cummings
08/02/2014	SC5	H	Raith Rovers	2	3	Williams	Nelson	McGivern"	Cairney"	Maybury*	Foster	Collins	McGivern	Cummings*	Craig	Handling"	Cairney"	Craig+	Heffernan"	Handling	Cairney	Heffernan	Cummings
15/02/2014	Prem	A	Ross County	2	1	Williams	Nelson	McGivern	Cairney	Hanlon	Forster	Collins"	McGivern	Cairney+	Handling"	Stevenson	Heffernan"	Collins+	Boateng"	Robertson	Handling	Stevenson	Murdoch
22/02/2014	Prem	A	Kilmarnock	1	1	Williams	Nelson	McGivern	McGivern	Hanlon	Forster	Hayes	McGivern	Cairney*	Stanton"	Taiwo"	Handling"	Cairney+	Collins"	Maybury	Handling	Cummings	Murdoch
28/02/2014	Prem	A	Dundee United	1	3	Williams	Nelson	McGivern	McGivern	Hanlon+	Forster	Watmore*	McGivern*	Thomson	Stanton*	Taiwo	Harris*	Boateng+	Boateng	Stevenson	Boateng	Cummings	Murdoch
08/03/2014	Prem	A	Motherwell	3	3	Williams	Nelson	McGivern	Cairney+	Hanlon	Forster	Robertson"	Watmore	Thomson	Stanton*	Taiwo*	Harris+	Heffernan+	Handling"	McPake	Handling	Stevenson	Murdoch
12/03/2014	Prem	A	Inverness CT	0	0	Williams	Nelson	Maybury	Boateng	Craig	Forster	Robertson+	Watmore*	Thomson	Stanton*	Taiwo+	Cummings"	Craig+	Heffernan"	McPake	Collins	Cummings	Grant
15/03/2014	Prem	A	Partick Thistle	0	2	Williams	Forster	Maybury	Maybury	Stevenson	Forster	Robertson"	Thomson+	Handling*	Heffernan*	Taiwo*	Watmore*	Craig+	Haynes"	Collins	Grant	Heffernan	Murdoch
22/03/2014	Prem	A	St Johnstone	0	2	Murdoch	Forster	Maybury	Harris	Stevenson	Forster*	Robertson	Collins	Heffernan	Stanton	Haynes	Collins+	Cairney+	Stevenson"	Craig	Grant	Tudur-Jones	Murdoch
29/03/2014	Prem	H	Hearts	2	0	Williams	Nelson	Maybury	Harris	Stevenson	Harris+	Tudur-Jones+	Collins*	Handling"	Collins	Taiwo*	Watmore"	Cairney+	Haynes"	Boateng	Handling	Tudur-Jones	Murdoch
04/04/2014	Prem	A	Aberdeen	0	2	Williams	Nelson	Maybury	Harris	Craig	Harris*	Collins*	Craig	Cairney+	Cummings*	Cummings+	Watmore"	Thomson+	Stevenson"	Boateng	Handling	Tudur-Jones	Murdoch
19/04/2014	Prem	H	St Mirren	0	2	Williams	Nelson	Maybury	Stevenson	Stevenson	Harris*	Tudur-Jones+	Craig	Handling+	Cummings"	Cummings*	Tudur-Jones"	Watmore+	Cairney"	McPake	Collins	Tudur-Jones	Murdoch
27/04/2014	Prem	A	Hearts	1	2	Williams	Forster	Maybury	Stevenson	Stevenson	Harris	Robertson+	Craig	Stanton+	Collins	Heffernan	Stevenson"	Collins+	Cummings"	McPake	Boateng	Tudur-Jones	Grant
03/05/2014	Prem	H	Partick Thistle	1	1	Williams	Nelson	Maybury	Hanlon	McGiven	Harris+	Robertson+	Craig	Handling"	Cummings*	Heffernan"	Watmore*	Watmore+	Boateng	Foster	Cairney	Cairney	Murdoch
06/05/2014	Prem	A	Kilmarnock	0	1	Williams	Nelson	Maybury	Stevenson	McGiven	Watmore*	Craig	Craig	Stanton+	Cummings"	Heffernan"	Watmore*	Harris+	Handling"	Foster	Stevenson	Haynes	Murdoch
10/05/2014	Prem	H	Ross County	0	1	Williams	Forster	Maybury	Hanlon	McGiven	Watmore"	Craig	Craig	Stanton	Collins	Heffernan"	Tudur-Jones"	Tudur-Jones+	Cummings"	Cairney	Cairney	Thomson	Murdoch
21/05/2014	PO	H	Hamilton Accies	2	0	Williams	Nelson	Maybury	Stevenson	McGivern	Harris*	Craig	Craig	Stanton	Cummings	Heffernan"	Harris"+	Thomson+	Collins	Cairney	Cairney	Collins	Thomson
25/05/2014	PO	A	Hamilton Accies	0	2 aet, 3-4p	Williams	Nelson	Nelson	Stevenson	McGivern	Haynes*	Craig	Craig	Stanton	Cummings"	Heffernan"	Harris*	Thomson+	Tudur-Jones"	Foster	Cairney	Collins	Murdoch

Inverness Caledonian Thistle FC

Founded	1994
Ground	Caledonian Stadium
Postcode	IV1 1FF
Tel	01463 222880
Capacity	7800
Closest Railway Station	Inverness
Record Attendance	7753 v Rangers, Lge, 20/1/2008
Record Win	8-1 v Annan Athletic, SC 24/1/88
Record Defeat	0-6 v Airdrie Lge 21/9/2000; v Celtic LC 22/9/2010
Most League Goals in a Season	27 Iain Stewart 1996/7, Dennis Wyness 2002/3
Chairman	Kenny Cameron
Secretary	Jim Falconer
Manager	Terry Butcher/ John Hughes
Assistant Manager	Maurice Malpas / Russell Latapy
Colours 2013/14 Top	Blue with Red and Black Detail
Shorts	Blue
Sponsor	Orion Group
Manufacturer	Errea
Change Colours 2013/14 Top	Black with Red and Blue Detail
Shorts	Black
Nicknames	Caley
Web	www.ictfc.co.uk

PREDICTION 2014/15
It's difficult to see ICT maintaining their top six place but they should be good enough to steer clear of the relegation zone.

Season 2013/14 split into two distinct phases for fans of Inverness Caley Thistle. In the early part of the season, under Terry Butcher, they seemed to be maintaining the sort of consistency and level of performance of the previous year. They fully deserved their reputation as a difficult team to break down, hard working, quick on the break and potential challengers for a European place.

Butcher quit Inverness for the supposedly greener grass of Easter Road. His replacement was a former Hibs manager in the person of John Hughes.

He produced the highlight of the season - a League Cup Semi Final win over Hearts at Easter Road, achieved against all the odds with just nine men for the whole of extra time. The Final, against Aberdeen, was best forgotten.

In the League ICT lost their way a little. Results were inconsistent and the usually tight defence started to leak at times. However, Hughes did maintain their top six place and has a settled squad at his disposal for the new season.

Surname	First Name	DOB	Pos	L A	L S	L G	SC A	SC S	SC G	LC A	LC S	LC G	UNS	Signed Previous Club	Notes	Contract
Adgestein	Torbjorn	18/09/91	F	13			1			2			6	2013 Brighton	Released Jan 2014, joined IFK Haugesund	
Brill	Dean	02/12/85	GK	37			4			4			1	2013 Luton Town		C (2016)
Brown	Jason												2	2014 ICT Youths		Youth
Christie	Ryan	28/04/95	M	3	12	3	1			1			3	2012 ICT Youths		C (2016)
Cooper	Matthew	01/07/94	D										1	2012 Aberdeen	Signed for Elgin City May 2014	F
Devine	Danny	07/09/92	D	8	6					2	1		28	2013 Fleetwood Town		C (2015)
Doran	Aaron	13/05/91	M	35			5	3	1	3	3	1		2011 Blackburn Rovers		C (2016)
Draper	Ross	20/10/88	M	31	1	1	3			4	1			2012 Macclesfield Town		C (2016)
Esson	Ryan	19/03/80	GK	1									45	2008 Hereford United		C (2016)
Evans	Adam	03/05/94	F	2									6	2013 Burnley		OOC
Foran	Richie	16/06/80	M	23	1	4	2	1		3				2009 Southend United		C (2017)
Gorman	Joe	01/09/94	D										1	2013 Crewe Alexandra		OOC
Greenhalgh	Ben	16/04/92	M	1	5								17	2013 Concord Rangers	On loan to Stenhousemuir Mar-May	F
McKay	Billy	22/10/88	F	38		18	4		3	4		1		2011 Northampton Town		C (2015)
Meekings	Josh	02/09/92	D	34			4			4				2011 Ipswich Town		C (2015)
Pepper	Conor	04/05/94	F										14	2012 St Patricks Athletic	Joined Morton June 2014	F
Polworth	Liam	12/10/94	M	7	12	1	1	1		2			20	2010 ICT Youths		OOC
Raven	David	10/03/85	D	25	1	1	3			3			8	2012 Tranmere Rovers		OOC
Ross	Nick	11/11/91	M	25	8	1	2			2	2	2 1	6	2009 ICT Youths		OOC
Shinnie	Graeme	04/08/91	D	36		3	4			4			1	2009 ICT Youths		C (2015)
Sutherland	Alasdair												3	2013 ICT Youths		Youth
Tansey	Greg	21/11/88	M	15	1	2	3			2	1		1	2014 Stevenage		C (2016)
Tremarco	Carl	11/10/85	D	20	1		1			1	1		19	2013 Macclesfield Town		C (2017)
Vincent	James	27/09/89	M	19	2	1	3			3			3	2013 Kidderminster Harriers		C (2015)
Warren	Gary	16/08/84	D	34		2	4			2	1		1	2012 Newport County		C (2016)
Watkins	Marley	17/10/90	M	15	11	1	3	1		3				2013 Hereford United		C (2015)
Williams	Danny	25/01/88	M	11	9	1				3			15	2013 Kendal Town		C (2016)

Date	Comp	H/A	Opponents	F	A		Crowd	Scorers
03/08/2013	Prem	H	St Mirren	3	0		3215	Vincent, Doran, McKay
10/08/2013	Prem	A	Dundee United	1	0		6664	McKay
17/08/2013	Prem	H	Motherwell	2	0		3031	Foran, McKay
24/08/2013	Prem	A	Celtic	2	2		45160	Doran, Foran
31/08/2013	Prem	H	Hearts	2	0		4034	McKay 2
14/09/2013	Prem	A	Kilmarnock	2	1		3063	Foran, McKay
21/09/2013	Prem	A	Aberdeen	0	1		11251	
24/09/2013	LC3	A	Dundee	1	0		1682	McKay
28/09/2013	Prem	H	Hibernian	3	0		4261	McKay 2, Foran
05/10/2013	Prem	A	St Johnstone	0	4		3020	
20/10/2013	Prem	H	Partick Thistle	1	2		3154	Warren
29/10/2013	LC4	H	Dundee United	2	1	AET	2133	Warren, Draper
02/11/2013	Prem	H	Kilmarnock	2	1		2948	Doran, Shinnie
09/11/2013	Prem	A	Hibernian	2	0		8750	Ross, McKay
23/11/2013	Prem	H	St Johnstone	1	0		3255	McKay
30/11/2013	SC4	H	Morton	4	0			Ross, MacKay 2, Doran
07/12/2013	Prem	A	St Mirren	0	0		3305	
14/12/2013	Prem	A	Hearts	2	0		11950	McKay 2
21/12/2013	Prem	H	Aberdeen	3	4		4819	McKay 2, Shinnie
26/12/2013	Prem	A	Partick Thistle	0	0		2887	
29/12/2013	Prem	H	Celtic	0	1		6384	
01/01/2014	Prem	H	Ross County	1	2		4332	Doran
12/01/2014	Prem	H	Dundee United	1	1		2980	McKay
18/01/2014	Prem	A	Aberdeen	1	0		12021	Williams
25/01/2014	Prem	A	Kilmarnock	0	2		3035	
02/02/2014	LCSF	N	Hearts	2	2	AET, 4-2 pens	12762	Tansey, Ross
08/02/2014	SC5	A	Stranraer	2	2		722	Doran, McKay
15/02/2014	Prem	H	Hearts	0	0		3392	
18/02/2014	SC5R	H	Stranraer	2	0		1458	Ross, Doran
22/02/2014	Prem	A	St Johnstone	1	0		2415	Warren
25/02/2014	Prem	A	Ross County	3	0		4805	Raven, McKay, Watkins
01/03/2014	L	A	Celtic	0	5		46552	
09/03/2014	SC6	H	Dundee United	0	5		3164	
12/03/2014	Prem	H	Hibernian	0	0		2537	
16/03/2014	LCF	N	Aberdeen	0	0	AET, 2-4 pens	51143	
19/03/2014	Prem	A	Motherwell	0	2		3432	
22/03/2014	Prem	H	Partick Thistle	1	0		3093	McKay
26/03/2014	Prem	A	Dundee United	1	2		6754	Polworth
29/03/2014	Prem	H	St Mirren	2	2		3032	Draper, Tamsey
01/04/2014	Prem	H	Motherwell	1	2		2366	Christie
04/04/2014	Prem	A	Ross County	2	1		4433	Doran, McKay
19/04/2014	Prem	H	Aberdeen	0	0		4224	
27/04/2014	Prem	A	Celtic	0	6		45712	
03/05/2014	Prem	H	Dundee United	1	1		3428	Christie
07/05/2014	Prem	A	Motherwell	1	2		4482	Shinnie
11/05/2014	Prem	H	St Johnstone	2	0		3121	Christie, Tansey

Friendly Matches

Date	Comp	H/A	Opponents	F	A		Crowd	Scorers
6/7/13	Fr	A	Keith	9	0			
9/7/13	Fr	A	Forres Mechanics	3	0			
13/7/13	Fr	A	Elgin City	2	0		559	
16/7/13	Fr	A	Brora Rangers	2	1			
17/7/13	Fr	A	Clachnacuddin	4	0			
20/7/13	Fr	A	Raith Rovers	2	2			
23/7/13	Fr	A	Arbroath	7	1			
25/7/13	Fr	A	Wick Academy	5	1			
27/7/13	Fr	A	Charlton Athletic	1	0		2801	
27/8/13	Fr	A	Buckie Thistle					

Date	Comp	H/A	Opponents	F	A	1	2	3	4	5	6	7	8	9	10	11	12	13	14	15	16	17	18
03/08/2013	Prem	H	St Mirren	3	0	Brill	Warren	Raven"	Shinnie	Meekings	Vincent+	Doran"	Foran	Draper*	Ross	McKay	Polworth"	Adgestein+	Williams"	Devine	Greenhalgh	Tremarco	Esson
10/08/2013	Prem	A	Dundee United	1	0	Brill	Warren	Raven*	Shinnie	Meekings	Vincent	Doran+	Foran	Draper	Ross	McKay	Devine*	Polworth+	Greenhalgh	Tremarco	Williams	Agdestein	Esson
17/08/2013	Prem	H	Motherwell	2	0	Brill	Warren	Raven	Shinnie	Meekings	Vincent*	Doran*	Foran	Draper	Ross	McKay+	Polworth*	Adgestein+	Williams"	Devine	Greenhalgh	Pepper	Esson
24/08/2013	Prem	A	Celtic	2	2	Brill	Warren	Raven	Shinnie	Meekings	Vincent	Doran*	Foran	Draper	Ross	McKay+	Adgestein*	Greenhalgh+	Williams	Devine	Williams	Polworth	Esson
31/08/2013	Prem	H	Hearts	2	0	Brill	Warren	Raven	Shinnie	Meekings	Vincent+	Doran*	Foran	Draper	Ross	McKay*	Williams*	Greenhalgh+	Williams	Devine	Tremarco	Polworth	Esson
14/09/2013	Prem	A	Kilmarnock	2	1	Brill	Warren	Raven	Shinnie	Meekings	Vincent*	Doran	Foran	Draper	Ross	McKay*	Williams*	Polworth*	Greenhalgh	Devine	Tremarco	Polworth	Esson
21/09/2013	Prem	A	Aberdeen	0	1	Brill	Warren	Raven	Shinnie	Meekings	Vincent*	Doran	Foran	Draper	Ross	McKay+	Adgestein*	Polworth+	Williams"	Devine	Tremarco	Williams	Esson
24/09/2013	LC3	H	Dundee	1	0	Brill	Devine	Raven	Shinnie	Meekings	Vincent	Doran+	Foran+	Draper	Ross	McKay	Polworth*	Adgestein+	Greenhalgh	Tremarco	Esson	Williams	Devine
28/09/2013	Prem	H	Hibernian	3	0	Brill	Warren	Raven	Shinnie	Meekings	Vincent*	Doran"	Foran"	Draper"	Ross	McKay	Greenhalgh*	Polworth*	Greenhalgh	Tremarco	Esson	Greenhalgh	Devine
05/10/2013	Prem	A	St Johnstone	0	4	Brill	Warren	Raven	Shinnie	Meekings	Greenhalgh+	Doran"	Foran	Draper	Ross*	McKay*	Polworth*	Williams+	Williams"	Tremarco	Tremarco	Greenhalgh	Devine
20/10/2013	Prem	H	Partick Thistle	1	2	Brill	Warren	Raven	Shinnie	Meekings	Watkins*	Doran	Foran"	Draper	Ross+	McKay	Williams*	Watkins+	Adgestein"	Tremarco	Tremarco	Williams	Devine
29/10/2013	LC4	H	Dundee United	2	1 AET	Brill	Warren	Tremarco"	Shinnie	Meekings	Watkins*	Doran"	Foran	Draper	Ross"	McKay	Williams*	Polworth*	Polworth"	Devine	Esson	Greenhalgh	Adgestein
02/11/2013	Prem	A	Kilmarnock	2	1	Brill	Warren	Tremarco"	Shinnie	Meekings	Watkins*	Doran	Foran	Draper	Ross+	McKay	Polworth*	Raven	Devine	Raven	Esson	Pepper	Adgestein
09/11/2013	Prem	A	Hibernian	2	0	Brill	Warren	Tremarco	Shinnie	Meekings	Watkins	Doran	Foran	Draper	Ross	McKay	Devine*	Williams+	Devine	Raven	Esson	Polworth	Adgestein
23/11/2013	Prem	H	St Johnstone	1	0	Brill	Warren	Tremarco	Shinnie	Meekings	Watkins	Doran	Foran	Polworth	Ross	McKay	Williams*	Adgestein+	Greenhalgh	Polworth	Esson	Pepper	Devine
30/11/2013	SC4	H	Morton	4	0	Brill	Warren	Tremarco+	Shinnie	Meekings	Williams	Polworth	Foran	Foran	Ross+	McKay	Williams*	Devine	Greenhalgh	Polworth	Esson	Williams	Devine
07/12/2013	Prem	H	St Mirren	0	0	Brill	Warren	Vincent"	Shinnie	Meekings	Williams	Doran	Foran*	Foran	Ross	McKay	Raven	Williams+	Greenhalgh	Polworth	Esson	Raven	Adgestein
14/12/2013	Prem	A	Hearts	2	0	Brill	Warren	Vincent+	Shinnie	Meekings	Williams*	Doran"	Tansey	Foran*	Ross+	McKay	Adgestein*	Adgestein+	Greenhalgh	Polworth	Esson	Raven	Devine
21/12/2013	Prem	H	Aberdeen	3	4	Brill	Warren	Vincent*	Shinnie	Meekings	Williams*	Doran	Tansey	Foran"	Ross+	McKay	Williams*	Adgestein+	Greenhalgh	Polworth	Esson	Pepper	Devine
26/12/2013	Prem	A	Partick Thistle	0	0	Brill	Warren	Vincent	Shinnie	Meekings	Williams	Doran	Tansey	Foran*	Ross	McKay	Raven*	Christie+	Devine	Greenhalgh	Esson	Pepper	Raven
29/12/2013	Prem	H	Celtic	0	1	Brill	Warren	Vincent+	Shinnie	Meekings	Williams	Doran	Tansey	Foran*	Ross+	McKay	Raven"	Polworth*	Devine	Greenhalgh	Esson	Pepper	Raven
01/01/2014	Prem	H	Ross County	1	2	Brill	Raven"	Foran	Shinnie	Tremarco	Foran	Ross+	Tansey	Devine	Draper	McKay	Adgestein*	Vincent+	Evans"	Pepper	Esson	Raven	Christie
12/01/2014	Prem	A	Dundee United	1	1	Brill	Raven+	Vincent"	Shinnie	Tremarco	Watkins*	Doran+	Tansey	Warren	Draper	McKay	Greenhalgh*	Watkins+	Draper"	Greenhalgh	Esson	Christie	Pepper
18/01/2014	Prem	A	Aberdeen	1	0	Brill	Raven	Vincent	Shinnie	Tremarco	Foran	Doran+	Warren	Warren	Draper	McKay	Adgestein*	Ross+	Tremarco"	Tansey	Esson	Christie	Vincent
25/01/2014	Prem	H	Kilmarnock	0	2	Brill	Raven	Vincent*	Shinnie	Tremarco	Foran*	Doran	Warren	Warren	Draper	McKay	Christie*	Watkins+	Tremarco	Williams	Esson	Christie	Vincent
02/02/2014	LCSF	N	Hearts	2	2 AET, 4-2 pens	Brill	Raven	Foran	Shinnie	Tremarco	Foran"	Doran+	Warren	Warren	Draper+	McKay	Christie*	Christie+	Tremarco	Devine	Esson	Ross	Polworth
08/02/2014	SC5	H	Stranraer	2	2	Brill	Raven	Vincent*	Shinnie	Tremarco	Foran"	Doran"	Warren	Warren	Draper	McKay	Vincent+	Devine+	Warren+	Devine	Esson	Williams	Polworth
15/02/2014	SC5R	A	Stranraer	2	0	Brill	Raven	Vincent*	Shinnie	Tremarco	Foran	Draper"	Warren	Warren	Draper*	McKay	Tansey*	Ross+	Tremarco	Devine	Esson	Polworth	Pepper
18/02/2014	Prem	A	St Johnstone	1	0	Brill	Raven	Vincent+	Shinnie	Tremarco	Foran*	Draper	Warren"	Warren	Warren+	McKay*	Devine*	Vincent+	Christie"	Tremarco	Esson	Polworth	Pepper
22/02/2014	Prem	A	Ross County	3	0	Brill	Raven	Vincent	Shinnie	Tremarco	Devine	Doran	Warren	Warren	Ross+	McKay	Devine*	Tremarco+	Christie"	Devine	Esson	Polworth	Devine
25/02/2014	Prem	H	Celtic	0	5	Brill	Raven	Vincent	Shinnie	Tremarco	Meekings	Doran	Warren	Warren*	Watkins	McKay	Foran*	Ross	Shinnie	Devine	Esson	Ross	Devine
01/03/2014	L	H	Dundee United	0	5	Brill	Tremarco	Williams	Polworth	Tremarco	Foran	Doran	Warren	Warren	Draper	McKay*	Foran*	Watkins+	Warren	Tremarco	Esson	Ross	Pepper
09/03/2014	SC6	H	Dundee United	0	0 AET, 2-4 pens	Brill	Raven	Vincent	Shinnie	Tremarco	Foran	Doran	Warren	Warren	Draper	McKay*	Ross*	Polworth*	Watkins"	Tremarco	Esson	Greenhalgh	Pepper
12/03/2014	LCF	N	Aberdeen	0	0	Brill	Raven	Foran	Shinnie	Tremarco	Devine	Doran*	Devine	Devine	Vincent"	McKay	Ross*	Evans+	Ross"	Vincent	Brill	Ross	Polworth
16/03/2014	Prem	A	Motherwell	0	2	Brill	Raven	Vincent*	Shinnie	Tremarco	Ross	Ross	Tansey	Warren	Vincent"	McKay	Devine*	Ross+	Watkins"	Tremarco	Esson	Ross	Pepper
19/03/2014	Prem	H	Partick Thistle	1	0	Brill	Raven	Vincent+	Shinnie	Tremarco	Foran"	Doran	Tansey	Warren	Vincent*	McKay	Williams*	Watkins+	Polworth	Tremarco	Esson	Devine	Williams
22/03/2014	Prem	A	Dundee United	1	2	Brill	Raven	Williams	Polworth	Tremarco	Foran*	Doran	Tansey	Warren	Vincent	McKay*	Devine*	Christie+	Shinnie	Evans	Esson	Polworth	Polworth
26/03/2014	Prem	H	St Mirren	2	2	Esson	Raven+	Vincent*	Shinnie	Tremarco	Foran+	Doran	Tansey	Warren	Vincent*	McKay	Williams*	Watkins+	Christie"	Tremarco	Esson	Williams	Devine
29/03/2014	Prem	A	Motherwell	1	2	Brill	Raven	Polworth	Shinnie	Tremarco	Christie+	Draper"	Tansey*	Warren	Vincent	McKay	Polworth"	Christie*	Warren	Tremarco	Esson	Williams	Evans
01/04/2014	Prem	H	Ross County	2	1	Brill	Raven+	Meekings	Shinnie	Tremarco	Watkins	Doran	Tansey	Warren	McKay	McKay	Christie"	Williams	Watkins"	Evans	Brill	Ross	Polworth
04/04/2014	Prem	A	Aberdeen	0	0	Brill	Raven	Meekings	Shinnie	Tremarco	Watkins*	Doran	Tansey	Warren*	Vincent*	McKay	Christie*	Watkins+	Polworth	Evans	Esson	Ross	Devine
19/04/2014	Prem	H	Celtic	0	6	Brill	Shinnie	Devine	Draper+	Tremarco	Williams	Doran"	Tansey	Warren	McKay	Ross+	Christie*	Ross+	Esson	Esson	Ross	Williams	—
27/04/2014	Prem	A	Dundee United	1	1	Brill	Shinnie	Devine	Drper	Tremarco	Williams	Doran	Tansey	Warren	McKay	Watkins+	Williams"	Polworth"	Devine	Brown	Sutherland	Ross	Sutherland
03/05/2014	Prem	H	Motherwell	1	1	Brill	Shinnie	Devine	Draper	Tremarco	Raven	Doran*	Tansey	Vincent*	McKay	Christie"	Williams"	Christie+	Esson	Vincent	Ross	Polworth	—
07/05/2014	Prem	A	Motherwell	1	2	Brill	Shinnie	Devine	Draper	Tremarco	Raven	Doran*	Tansey	Vincent*	McKay	Watkins+	Williams"	Christie+	Esson	Brown	Sutherland	Polworth	Sutherland
11/05/2014	Prem	H	St Johnstone	2	0	Brill	Shinnie	Devine	Draper	Tremarco	Raven	Doran	Tansey	Vincent+	McKay+	McKay+	Watkins*	Williams+	Ross"	Brown	Esson	Polworth	Esson

Kilmarnock FC

Founded	1869
Ground	Rugby Park
Postcode	KA1 2DP
Tel	01563 545300
Capacity	18128
Closest Railway Station	Kilmarnock
Record Attendance	35995 v Rangers, SC, 10/3/1962
Record Win	11-1 v Paisley Academical, SC, 18/1/1930
Record Defeat	1-9 v Celtic, Lge 13/8/1938
Most League Goals in a Season	34 Harry Cunningham 1927/8, Andy Kerr 1960/1
Chairman	Michael Johnston
Secretary	Kirsten Callaghan
Manager	Allan Johnston
Assistant Manager	
Colours 2013/14 Top	Blue and White Stripes
Shorts	White
Sponsor	QTS
Manufacturer	1869
Change Colours 2013/14 Top	Red and White Stripes
Shorts	Red
Nicknames	Killie
Web	www.kilmarnockfc.co.uk

The story of 2013/14 for Kilmarnock was really all about one man - Kris Boyd. Without his goals the Rugby Park side would surely have been relegated, even with Hearts fifteen point deduction.

It was a difficult season for Killie. Pressure mounted on Chairman Michael Johnston from fans groups unhappy at the direction the club was taking. Manager Allan Johnston also took a lot of criticism as the results went against his team.

Crowds were generally poor, yet the potential of the club was shown with a huge travelling support at Easter Road for a crucial game at the business end of the season.

Killie do have some good young players coming through and they need to step up to the plate for 2014/15.

PREDICTION 2014/15

Much will depend on the striker role - if Kris Boyd resigns, or an adequate replacement can be sourced, then a mid table finish is likely. If not, then who knows?

Surname	First Name	DOB	Pos	L A	L S	L G	Sc A	Sc S	Sc G	LC A	LC S	LC G	UNS	Signed Previous Club	Notes	Contract
Ashcroft	Lee	29/08/93	D	23	2	1							6	2013 Kilmarnock Youth		OOC
Barbour	Ross	01/02/93	D	6	1								2	2008 Hamilton Accies		C (2016)
Barr	Darren	17/03/85	D	12			2		1	1		1		2013 Hearts		F
Bouzid	Ismael	21/07/83	D	4									3	2013 USM Alger		F
Boyd	Kris	18/08/83	F	35	1	22	1						1	2013 Portland		OOC
Brennan	Conor	30/03/94	GK										1	2013 Leicester City		Youth
Clingan	Sammy	13/01/84	M	13	5	1							7	2013 Doncaster Rovers		OOC
Clohessy	Sean	12/12/86	D	24			2		1	1			4	2013 Southend United		C (2015)
Davidson	Ross	28/10/93	M										2	2012 Kilmarnock Youth		C (2016)
Eremenko	Alexei	24/03/83	F	9	4	1							1	2014 Kairat Almaty		F
Fisher	Gary	06/06/92	M	1									4	2011 Kilmarnock Youth	On loan to East Fife	OOC
Fowler	James	26/10/80	M	6	3					1				1997 Kilmarnock Youth	On Loan to Cowdenbeath	F
Gardyne	Michael	23/01/86	M	17	6	1							5	2013 Dundee United (Loan)	Returned to Dundee Utd	
Gros	William	31/03/92	F	4	10		1		1				16	2010 Le Havre		C (2016)
Heffernan	Paul	29/12/81	F	4						1				2011 Sheffield Wednesday	Transferred to Hibernian Aug	
Ibrahim	Rabiu	15/01/91	M	6	4					1			6	2013 Celtic	Freed Jan 2014	
Irvine	Jackson	07/03/93	M	25	2	1	1			1			2	2013 Celtic (Loan)	Returned to Celtic	
Jacobs	Kyle	14/06/91	M	5						1			4	2013 Livingston	Freed Jan 2014, joined Livingston	
Johnston	Chris	03/09/94	M	15	6	3	1		1				9	2013 Kilmarnock Youth		C (2016)
Kiltie	Greg	18/01/97		3	2								2	2013 Kilmarnock Youth		Youth
Maksimenko	Vitalijs	08/12/90	M	8		1							8	2014 Brighton (loan)	Returned to Brighton	
McKenzie	Rory	07/10/93	F	28	5	4	1			1			1	2012 Kilmarnock Youth		C (2016)
McKeown	Rory	08/04/93	D	6	3					1			7	2011 Ipswich Town	On Loan to Cowdenbeath	C (2015)
Moberg-Karlsson	David	20/03/94	D	2	2								2	2014 Sunderland (loan)	Returned to Sunderland	
Muirhead	Robbie	08/03/96	F	10	11	2							5	2013 Kilmarnock Youth		Youth
Nicholson	Barry	24/08/78	M	14	9	2							11	2013 Fleetwood Town		F
O'Hara	Mark	12/12/95	D	11	3		1			1			10	2012 Kilmarnock Youth		F
Pascali	Manuel	09/09/81	D	29	2		1						2	2008 Parma		C (2015)
Pooler	Dylan	23/04/97	F										1	2013 Kilmarnock Youth		Youth
Reguero	Antonio	04/07/82	GK										39	2013 Inverness CT		C (2015)
Reuben	Gabriel	25/09/80	D	2			1							2013 Kano Pillars	Freed Jan 2014, joined Waasland-Beveren	
Samson	Craig	01/04/84	GK	38			1			1				2013 St Mirren		C (2015)
Silva	David	11/10/86	M	1	2								1	2013 Olhanense	Freed Jan 2014	
Slater	Craig	26/04/94	M	20	2	1	1						5	2013 Kilmarnock Youth		OOC
Stewart	Mark	22/06/88	F	1	3								1	2013 Dundee	Freed Jan, joined Derry City	
Tesselaar	Jereon	16/01/89	D	36			1			1				2012 St Mirren		OOC
Winchester	Jude	13/04/93	M	4									4	2011 Linfield	On loan to Cliftonville	
Own Goals						1										

NEW SIGNINGS 2014/15

Surname	First Name	DOB												Signed Previous Club
Hamill	Jamie	29/07/86	M											2014 Hearts

Date	Comp	H/A	Opponents	F	A	Crowd	Scorers
03/08/2013	Prem	A	Aberdeen	1	2	13149	Boyd
11/08/2013	Prem	H	St Johnstone	0	0	3550	
17/08/2013	Prem	A	St Mirren	1	1	4625	Boyd
24/08/2013	Prem	H	Hibernian	1	2	3807	Nicholson
27/08/2013	LC2	H	Hamilton Accies	0	1	2033	
31/08/2013	Prem	A	Motherwell	1	2	4353	Barr
14/09/2013	Prem	H	Inverness CT	1	2	3063	Nicholson
21/09/2013	Prem	A	Partick Thistle	1	1	4310	Boyd
28/09/2013	Prem	H	Celtic	2	5	6149	Clingan, Clohessy
05/10/2013	Prem	A	Dundee United	0	1	5850	
19/10/2013	Prem	H	Ross County	2	0	3582	Boyd, Irvine
26/10/2013	Prem	H	Hearts	2	0	5090	Boyd 2
02/11/2013	Prem	A	Inverness CT	1	2	2948	Barr
09/11/2013	Prem	A	St Johnstone	1	3	2855	Clohessy
23/11/2013	Prem	H	Motherwell	0	2	3704	
29/11/2013	SC4	A	Dundee United	2	5	6979	Barr, Johnston
07/12/2013	Prem	A	Ross County	2	1	2937	Johnston, Boyd
14/12/2013	Prem	H	Dundee United	1	4	3452	Boyd
21/12/2013	Prem	H	Partick Thistle	2	1	3865	Johnston, Boyd
26/12/2013	Prem	A	Hearts	4	0	13684	Boyd 2, Johnston, McKenzie
29/12/2013	Prem	A	Hibernian	0	3	9683	
02/01/2014	Prem	H	St Mirren	2	1	5410	McKenzie, Boyd
05/01/2014	Prem	H	Aberdeen	0	1	4073	
18/01/2014	Prem	A	Partick Thistle	1	1	4092	Muirhead
25/01/2014	Prem	H	Inverness CT	2	0	3035	Ashcroft, Boyd
29/01/2014	Prem	A	Celtic	0	4	44271	
01/02/2014	Prem	H	Ross County	2	2	3372	Boyd 2
15/02/2014	Prem	A	Dundee United	2	3	6038	Eremenko, Boyd
22/02/2014	Prem	H	Hibernian	1	1	4036	Mckenzie
01/03/2014	Prem	A	St Mirren	0	2	4650	
08/03/2014	Prem	H	Hearts	4	2	3510	Wilson og, Boyd 2, Gardyne
14/03/2014	Prem	H	Celtic	0	3	7495	
22/03/2014	Prem	A	Aberdeen	1	2	14029	Boyd
29/03/2014	Prem	A	Motherwell	2	1	4467	McKenzie, Slater
05/04/2014	Prem	H	St Johnstone	1	2	3665	Muirhead
19/04/2014	Prem	H	Partick Thistle	1	2	4980	Maksimenko
26/04/2014	Prem	A	Ross County	1	2	3401	Boyd
04/05/2014	Prem	A	Hearts	0	5	13656	
07/05/2014	Prem	H	St Mirren	1	0	4911	Boyd
10/05/2014	Prem	A	Hibernian	1	0	15057	Boyd

Friendly Games

17/7/13	Fr	A	East Fife	1	0		
20/7/13	Fr	A	Glentoran	2	0		
23/7/13	Fr	H	Gateshead	1	1		
26/7/13	Fr	H	Carlisle United	2	2	1324	
27/7/13	Fr	H	Newcastle Unitged XI	2	0	1000	
30/7/13	Fr	A	Kilwinning Rangers	2	0		U20
3/8/13	Fr	H	Dickinson College Pennsylvania				U20 at Klilwinning SC

Date	Comp	H/A	Opponents	F	A	1	2	3	4	5	6	7	8	9	10	11	12	13	14	15	16	17	18
03/08/2013	Prem	A	Aberdeen	1	2	Samson	Barr	Fowler	Tesselaar	McKeown	Jacobs	Fisher*	Johnston+	Heffernan	Gros*	McKenzie	Boyd*	Ibrahim+	Slater"	O'Hara	Davidson	Barbour	Reguero
11/08/2013	Prem	H	St Johnstone	0	0	Samson	Barr*	Fowler	Tesselaar	McKeown	Jacobs	O'Hara	Ibrahim*	Heffernan*	Boyd	McKenzie+	Johnston*	Gros+	Pascali"	Barbour	Davidson	Fisher	Reguero
17/08/2013	Prem	A	St Mirren	1	1	Samson	Barr	Clohessy	Tesselaar	McKeown	Jacobs	Nicholson"	Ibrahim+	Heffernan+*	Boyd	Irvine	Stewart*	Fowler+	Stewart*	Gros	Johnston	Fisher	Reguero
24/08/2013	Prem	H	Hibernian	1	2	Samson	Barr	Clohessy	Tesselaar	Fowler++	O'Hara	Nicholson	Ibrahim	Heffernan+*	Boyd	Irvine	Gros*	Johnston+	McKeown	Fisher	Slater	Pascali	Reguero
27/08/2013	LC2	H	Hamilton Accies	0	1	Samson	Barr	Clohessy	Tesselaar	McKeown*	O'Hara	Nicholson	Ibrahim+	Gros	Stewart"	Irvine	Fowler*	Heffernan+	McKenzie"	Nicholson	Ruguero	Pascali	Reguero
31/08/2013	Prem	A	Motherwell	1	2	Samson	Barr	Clohessy	Tesselaar	Fowler	Nicholson	Jacobs	McKenzie*	Gros*	Boyd	Irvine	Fowler*	Heffernan-	Pascali"	Fisher	Stewart	O'Hara	Reguero
14/09/2013	Prem	H	Inverness CT	1	2	Samson	McKeown	Clohessy	Tesselaar*	Fowler++	Nicholson	Jacobs"	Gardyne*	Gros*	Boyd	Irvine	Ibrahim*	Pascali+	Stewart*	Ashcroft	Pooler	O'Hara	Reguero
21/09/2013	Prem	A	Partick Thistle	1	1	Samson	Barr	Clohessy	Tesselaar*	Bouzid	Nicholson	Ibrahim+	Gardyne*	Pascali"	Boyd	Irvine	McKeown*	Stewart+	Gros*	O'Hara	Ashcroft	Jacobs	Reguero
28/09/2013	Prem	H	Celtic	2	5	Samson	Barr	Clohessy	McKeown	Bouzid	Nicholson"	Ibrahim+	Gardyne	Pascali"	Boyd	Clingan	O'Hara*	Silva+	McKenzie"	Fowler	Gros	Jacobs	Reguero
05/10/2013	Prem	A	Dundee United	0	1	Samson	Barr	Clohessy	O'Hara	Bouzid	Nicholson"	Silva++	McKenzie	Pascali"	Boyd	Clingan	Fowler"	Ibrahim+	Irvine"	Johnston	Gros	McKeown	Reguero
19/10/2013	Prem	H	Ross County	2	0	Samson	Barr	Clohessy	Tesselaar	Bouzid	Nicholson	Ibrahim*	Irvine	Pascali	Boyd*	Gardyne+	Silva*	McKenzie+	Fowler	Gros	O'Hara	Jacobs	Reguero
26/10/2013	Prem	A	Hearts	2	0	Samson	Barr*	Clohessy	Tesselaar	Johnston	McKenzie+	O'Hara	Irvine	Pascali	Boyd*	Gardyne"	Clingan*	McKenzie+	Muirhead"	Ashcroft	Fowler	Kittie	Reguero
02/11/2013	Prem	H	Inverness CT	1	2	Samson	Barr*	Clohessy	Tesselaar	Johnston	McKenzie"	O'Hara	Irvine	Pascali	Boyd*	Gardyne"	Clingan"	Gros-	Muirhead"	Gros	Fowler	Kittie	Reguero
09/11/2013	Prem	A	St Johnstone	1	3	Samson	Barr	Clohessy	Tesselaar	Clingan	Nicholson*	O'Hara	Irvine	Pascali	Boyd	Gardyne*	Fowler*	Ashcroft+	Gros	McKenzie	Ibrahim	Winchester	Reguero
23/11/2013	Prem	H	Motherwell	0	2	Samson	Johnston	Clohessy	Tesselaar	Clingan"	Nicholson*	O'Hara	Slater	Pascali	Boyd	Gardyne	McKenzie	Gros+	Winchester"	Ashcroft	Ibrahim	Jacobs	Reguero
29/11/2013	SC4	A	Ross County	2	1	Samson	Ashcroft	Clohessy*	Gabriel+	Gabriel	Irvine	Johnston"	Slater	Pascali	Boyd	McKenzie	O'Hara*	Gros+	Nicholson	Clingan	Ibrahim	Clingan	Reguero
07/12/2013	Prem	H	Dundee United	1	4	Samson	Barr	Clohessy*	Nicholson*	Nicholson"	Irvine	Johnston	Slater	McKeown	Boyd*	Gardyne+	Nicholson	Ashcroft-	Winchester"	Ashcroft	Ibrahim	Silva	Reguero
14/12/2013	Prem	A	Dundee United	1	4	Samson	Ashcroft	Clohessy	Gabriel	Gabriel	Irvine	Johnston+	Slater	Pascali	Boyd	McKenzie+	Nicholson*	McKeown+	Muirhead	Clingan	Ibrahim	Winchester	Reguero
21/12/2013	Prem	H	Partick Thistle	2	1	Samson	Ashcroft	Clohessy	Gardyne*	Gardyne*	Irvine	Johnston	Slater*	Pascali+	Boyd*	McKenzie	Gardyne*	Winchester+	Muirhead	Clingan	Ibrahim	McKeown	Reguero
26/12/2013	Prem	A	Hearts	4	0	Samson	Ashcroft	Clohessy	Gardyne*	Gardyne*	Irvine	Johnston	Slater	Pascali	Boyd*	McKenzie	Winchester*	McKeown+	Muirhead	Clingan	Gros	Nicholson	Reguero
29/12/2013	Prem	H	Hibernian	0	3	Samson	Ashcroft	Clohessy	Gardyne*	Gardyne*	Irvine	Johnstone	Slater	Pascali	Boyd*	McKenzie	Winchester*	Nicholson	Muirhead	Clingan	Gros	McKeown	Reguero
02/01/2014	Prem	A	St Mirren	2	1	Samson	Ashcroft	Clohessy	Gardyne*	Gardyne*	Irvine	Johnstone+	Slater	Pascali	Boyd*	McKenzie	Muirhead*	Nicholson+	O'Hara	Clingan	Winchester	McKeown	Reguero
05/01/2014	Prem	H	Aberdeen	0	1	Samson	Ashcroft	Clohessy	Muirhead	Clingan	Muirhead	Johnstone*	Slater*	Pascali	Boyd*	McKenzie+	Nicholson*	Gardyne+	O'Hara	Gros	Winchester	McKeown	Reguero
18/01/2014	Prem	A	Partick Thistle	1	1	Samson	Ashcroft	Muirhead	Clingan	Clingan	Irvine	Johnstone*	Slater	Pascali	Boyd*	McKenzie+	Nicholson*	Gros+	Nicholson	Clohessy	McKeown	Gardyne	Reguero
25/01/2014	Prem	H	Inverness CT	2	0	Samson	Ashcroft	Clohessy+	Muirhead	Clingan	Irvine	McKenzie	Slater	Pascali	Boyd	Kittie	Nicholson+	Johnston	Gros	Clohessy	Maksimenko	Johnston	Reguero
29/01/2014	Prem	A	Celtic	2	0	Samson	Ashcroft	Clohessy+	Muirhead*	Clingan	Irvine	McKenzie	Slater*	Pascali	Boyd	Kittie	Nicholson"	O'Hara+	Gardyne*	Clohessy	Maksimenko	McKeown	Reguero
01/02/2014	Prem	H	Ross County	2	2	Samson	Ashcroft	Muirhead*	Clingan	Clingan	Muirhead"	McKenzie	Slater	Pascali	Gros	Kittie*	Eremenko	Johnston+	Nicholson	Gardyne	Maksimenko	Johnston	Reguero
15/02/2014	Prem	A	Dundee United	2	3	Samson	Ashcroft	Muirhead*	Clingan	Clingan	McKenzie	McKenzie	Slater	Pascali	Boyd	Eremenko	Johnstone*	Nicholson	Nicholson	O'Hara	Brennan	Kittie	Moberg-Karlsson
22/02/2014	Prem	A	Aberdeen	1	1	Samson	Ashcroft	Clohessy	Tesselaar	Clingan*	O'Hara	McKenzie	Slater	Pascali	Boyd	Eremenko+	Kittie*	Gardyne+	Maksimenko	Irvine	Nicholson	Johnston	Reguero
25/02/2014	Prem	H	Hibernian	1	1	Samson	Ashcroft	Johnston"	Tesselaar	Clingan*	O'Hara	McKenzie+	Slater	Pascali	Boyd	Eremenko-	Irvine*	Muiread+	Moberg-Karlsson*	Gros	Gardyne	Maksimenko	Reguero
01/03/2014	Prem	A	St Mirren	0	2	Samson	Ashcroft	Johnston"	Moberg-Karlsson+	Moberg-Karlsson+	O'Hara	McKenzie*	Slater*	Pascali	Boyd	Gardyne*	Irvine*	Muiread+	Gros*	Johnston	Eremenko	Maksimenko	Reguero
03/03/2014	Prem	H	Hearts	4	2	Samson	Ashcroft	Clohessy	Tesselaar	Clingan*	O'Hara	McKenzie+	Slater*	Pascali	Boyd	Gardyne*	Eremenko-	Johnston+	Muirhead*	Nicholson	Eremenko	Maksimenko	Reguero
08/03/2014	Prem	H	Celtic	0	3	Samson	Ashcroft	Clohessy	Tesselaar	Maksimenko	Irvine	McKenzie+	Slater"	Pascali	Boyd	Gardyne*	Eremenko+	Johnston+	Irvine	O'Hara	Gros	Maksimenko	Reguero
14/03/2014	Prem	A	Celtic	1	2	Samson	Ashcroft	Clohessy"	Tesselaar	Maksimenko	Irvine	McKenzie+	Slater*	Muirhead	Boyd	Eremenko	Barbour*	Eremenko	Fowler	Gros	Gardyne	Bouzid	Reguero
22/03/2014	Prem	H	Aberdeen	1	2	Samson	Ashcroft	Barnour	Tesselaar	Maksimenko	Irvine	McKenzie*	Slater*	Muirhead"	Boyd	Eremenko*	Barbour*	Nicholson+	Johnston"	Gros	Slater	Muirhead	Reguero
29/03/2014	Prem	A	Motherwell	2	1	Samson	Ashcroft	Barbour	Tesselaar	Maksimenko	Irvine	McKenzie+	Slater*	Gardyne"	Boyd	Eremenko*	Gardyne*	Muirhead+	Johnston"	Clohessy	Bouzid	Fowler	Reguero
05/04/2014	Prem	H	St Johnstone	1	2	Samson	Ashcroft	Barbour	Tesselaar	Maksimenko	Irvine	McKenzie	Slater*	Muirhead+	Boyd	Eremenko-	Clingan*	Clingan+	Johnston"	Bouzid	Slater	Slater	Reguero
19/04/2014	Prem	H	Partick Thistle	1	2	Samson	Ashcroft	Barnour	Tesselaar	Maksimenko	Irvine	McKenzie	Pascali"	Gardyne*	Boyd	Eremenko-	Clingan*	Ashcroft+	Gros*	Fowler	Clohessy	Slater	Reguero
26/04/2014	Prem	A	Hearts	1	2	Samson	Ashcroft	Barbour	Tesselaar	Maksimenko	Slater	McKenzie	Pascali	Gardyne"	Boyd*	Muirhead*	Muirhead*	Clingan+	Johnston"	Fowler	Slater	Muirhead	Reguero
04/05/2014	Prem	H	Hearts	0	5	Samson	Clignan	Barbour	Tesselaar	Maksimenko	Slater	McKenzie+	Pascali	Johnston	Boyd*	Muirhead"	Gros*	Ashcroft+	Gros*	Gros	Nicholson	Moberg-Karlsson	Reguero
07/05/2014	Prem	A	St Mirren	1	0	Samson	Ashcroft	Barbour	Tesselaar	Maksimenko	Irvine	McKenzie+	Pascali	Fowler	Boyd*	Muirhead*	Eremenko	Nicholson+	Clingan	Gros	Slater	Johnston	Reguero
10/05/2014	Prem	H	Hibernian	1	0	Samson	Ashcroft	Barbour	Tesselaar	Maksimenko"	Irvine	McKenzie"	Pascali	Nicholson+	Boyd	Eremenko	Clingan*	Slater+	Muirhead"	Gros	Johnston	Bouzid	Reguero

Livingston FC

Founded	1943
Ground	Almondvale Stadium
Postcode	EH54 7DN
Tel	01506 417000
Capacity	9865
Closest Railway Station	Livingston North / Livingston South
Record Attendance	10024, Lge v Celtic, 18/8/2001
Record Win	7-0 v QOS, SC, 29/1/2000
Record Defeat	0-8 v Hamilton Accies, Lge, 14/12/74
Most League Goals in a Season	22 Leigh Griffiths 2008/9 / Iain Russell 2010/11
Chairman	Gordon McDougall
Chief Executive	Ged Nixon
Manager	Richie Burke (until Sep 2013) / John McGlynn
Assistant Manager	Mark Burchill
Colours 2013/14 Top	Yellow with Black Shoulder Panel
Shorts	Black
Sponsor	Energy Assets
Manufacturer	Adidas
Change Colours 2013/14 Top	Maroon and Blue Stripes
Shorts	Blue
Nicknames	Lions
Web	www.livingstonfc.co.uk

Livingston's fortunes have fluctuated since they changed their name and moved to the New Town in 1995. The most concerning feature must be the decline in attendances at Almondvale - a factor which must make the viability of full-time football very marginal indeed. At times home crowds dipped well below the 1000 mark.

2013/14 was an indifferent season. Manager Richie Burke was replaced by John McGlynn early in the season but the club never looked like progressing beyond mid-table.

Their ability to produce young talent continues with Mark McNulty and Stefan Scougall heading to Sheffield United and Coll Donaldson to QPR. Such sales are vital for the survival of the club but they also make the task of Managers and Coaches more difficult.

PREDICTION 2014/15
Looks like another season in mid table is the best that Livingston can hope for. They may be looking over their shoulders towards the foot of the league.

Surname	First Name	DOB	Pos	L A	L S	L G	SC A	SC S	SC G	LC A	LC S	LC G	RC A	RC S	RC G	UNS	Signed Previous Club	Notes	Contract
Barrowman	Andy	27/11/84	F	16	3	5	1			2	1						2013 Dunfermline Athletic		F
Beaumont	Jack	12/09/94	M	3						1	1		1			15	2010 Livingston Youths		C (2015)
Black	Taylor		F													1	2013 Livingston Youths		F
Burchill	Mark	18/08/80	F	6	14	2	1									3	2013 Esan United (Thailand)		C (2015)
Denholm	Danny	01/01/91	M	15	17	1	1			1	2	1				7	2013 Forfar Athletic	Joined Forfar Athletic May 2014	F
Docherty	Ross	23/01/93	M	5	3		2						1			5	2011 Livingston Youths		F
Donaldson	Coll	09/04/95	D	19			1	1		3			1				2011 Livingston Youths	Transferred to QPR Jan 2014, £154,000	
Downie	Jack	23/03/94								1						9	2011 Livingston Youths	Joined Berwick Rangers Feb 2014	
Fordyce	Callum	23/06/92	D	35			5	1		3			1	1			2009 Livingston Youths		C (2015)
Habai	Michal	30/07/85	D	4	3												2014 Morton		F
Hastings	Neil	02/04/92								1						3	2013 Unattached		Youth
Jacobs	Keaghan	09/09/89	M	28	4	4	1			1							2006 Livingston Youths		C (2015)
Jacobs	Kyle	14/06/91	M	13													2014 Kilmarnock		C (2015)
Jamieson	Darren	15/02/91	GK	31			2			1						6	2008 Livingston Youths		C (2015)
Lander	Kyle	21/01/96	F	5	1											15	2012 Livingston Youths		C (2015)
Mampuya	Moussa	17/01/83	D	14	1		1			1						6	2013 Enosis Neon (Cyprus)		F
McCaldon	Ian	14/09/74	GK													1	Goalkeeper Coach		
McDonald	Connor	15/04/94	D	3	2		2	1		1						2	2010 Livingston Youths		Youth
McNulty	Marc	14/09/92	F	32	3	17	1			2			1	1		1	2009 Livingston Youths	Signed for Sheffield United May 2015	
Mensing	Simon	27/06/82	D	27			2	1		3			1	1			2013 Raith Rovers		C (2015)
Mevlja	Nejc	12/06/90	D	12	1	1											2014 NK Maribor		F
Mullen	Danny	01/03/95	F	8	15	1	2			1						8	2012 Livingston Youths		C (2015)
Murphy	Sean		M													2	2013 Livingston Youths		F
O'Brien	Burton	10/06/81	M	30			1			1							2012 Falkirk		C (2015)
Prapotnik	Nejc	17/01/93	M	2	3											12	2013 Atalanta Bergamo		C (2015)
Rutherford	Shaun		D	1												9	2013 Livingston Youths		C (2015)
Scott	Martin "Jimmy"	15/02/86	M	26	7	4	1			3			1	1		2	2013 Hibernian	Joined Raith Rovers June 2014	F
Scougall	Stefan	07/12/92	M	16			2	1		1							2010 Dunfermline Athletic	Transferred to Sheffield United Jan 2014 £160,000	
Sives	Craig	09/04/86	D	11	1	2										3	2014 Hume City		C (2015)
Talbot	Jason	30/09/85	D	27	2	1	1			3			1			1	2008 Port Vale		C (2015)
Taylor	Billy		GK													1	2013 Livingston Youths		C (2015)
Twardzik	Patrick	10/02/93	F	1			1									4	2013 Celtic (Loan)	Returned to Celtic	
Walker	Kevin	12/09/91	GK	5			1			1						33	2013 Stirling University		C (2015)
Wilkie	Kyle	20/02/91	M	8	12					1	1	1	1			12	2013 Morton		F
Wilson	Scott		M													1	2013 Livingston Youths		F
Own Goals					2														

Comp	H/A	Opponents	F	A		Crowd	Scorers
RC1	A	Berwick Rangers	2	3	AET	460	McNulty, Mensing
LC1	A	Elgin City	3	1		563	Fordyce, Scott, McNulty
L	A	Alloa	0	1		714	
L	H	Queen of the South	3	3		1149	Fordyce 2, Denholm
L	H	Falkirk	0	3		1416	
LC2	A	Airdrieonians	2	0		483	Barrowman, Wilkie
L	A	Dundee	0	3		3955	
L	H	Morton	2	2		1077	Mensing, McNulty
L	A	Dumbarton	2	1		759	McNulty 2
LC3	H	Motherwell	1	2		1660	Denholm
L	H	Cowdenbeath	5	1		894	Fordyce 3, Barrowman, Burchill
L	A	Hamilton Accies	0	2		1059	
L	H	Alloa	3	2		869	Scougall, Donaldson, Barrowman
L	H	Dundee	2	1		1597	Kea Jacobs, Scott
L	A	Raith Rovers	0	1		1304	
L	A	Falkirk	1	4		2878	McCracken og
L	H	Dumbarton	1	3		1039	McNulty
L	A	Morton	5	1		1460	McNulty 3, Barrowman, Scott
SC4	A	St Johnstone	0	2		2294	
L	A	Cowdenbeath	3	2		363	McNulty 2, Barrowman
L	H	Hamilton Accies	0	0		794	
L	A	Queen of the South	2	2		1523	McNulty 2
L	H	Raith Rovers	3	0		1322	Thomson og, Scott, Scougall
L	H	Falkirk	0	1		1585	
L	A	Dundee	1	0		4367	Burchill
L	H	Morton	0	1		1245	
L	H	Queen of the South	1	2		1041	McNulty
L	A	Dumbarton	2	2		562	Kea Jacobs, Barrowman
L	A	Alloa	3	0		605	Mensing, Scott, Kea Jacobs
L	A	Hamilton Accies	0	2		1063	
L	H	Cowdenbeath	1	0		980	Talbot
L	A	Falkirk	1	1		2924	McNulty
L	H	Dundee	0	2		1759	
L	A	Raith Rovers	4	2		1329	Sives 2, McNulty 2
L	H	Alloa	2	0		709	McNulty, Kea Jacobs
L	H	Dumbarton	1	2		949	Mevlja
L	A	Morton	0	2		1009	
L	H	Hamilton Accies	1	1		1133	Kyle Jacobs
L	A	Cowdenbeath	0	4		420	
L	A	Queen of the South	0	2		1923	
L	H	Raith Rovers	2	0		1265	Mullen, McNulty

Friendly Games

Date	Comp	H/A	Opponents	F	A	Crowd	Team	Venue
30/6/13	Fr	N	Steaua Bucharest	1	4			at FAHQ, Burton
3/7/13	Fr	N	Dinamo Bucharefst	0	3			at Woodlesford, Leeds
4/7/13	Fr	N	Otelul Galati	0	0			at Carden Park Spa Resort
10/7/13	Fr	H	Rotherham United	0	2	389		
13/7/13	Fr	H	Wolves	1	2			
16/7/13	Fr	H	Partick Thistle	0	0			
17/7/13	Fr	H	Lothian Thistle HV	2	1		U20	at Almondvale Astro
18/7/13	Fr	A	Wick Academy	2	1			
19/7/13	Fr	A	Lybster	7	2			at Upper Bignold, Wick
20/7/13	Fr	A	Brora Rangers	1	0			
24/7/13	Fr	A	Craigroyston	4	0		U20	
27/7/13	TnT	N	Dundee U20	1	6		U20	at Broxburn
28/7/13	TnT	N	Hamilton Accies U20	3	2		U20	at Broxburn
30/7/13	Fr	A	Tynecastle				U20	
6/8/13	Fr	A	Musselburgh Athletic	1	0		U20	
27/8/13	Fr	H	Spartans EOSL	4	1		Res	
4/9/13	Fr	A	Gala Fairydean Rovers	4	0		Res	

Comp	H/A	Opponents	F	A	1	2	3	4	5	6	7	8	9	10	11	12	13	14	15	16	17	18
RC1	A	Berwick Rangers	2	3 AET	Jamieson	Mampuya	Talbot	Mensing	Donaldson	Fordyce+	Scott	Beaumont*	McNulty	Burchill	McDonald"	Wilkie+	Docherty*	Mullen"	Lander	Walker		
LC1	A	Elgin City	3	1	Jamieson	Docherty"	Talbot	Mensing	Donaldson	Fordyce	Scott+	Beaumont	McNulty	Wilkie*	McDonald	Denholm"	Mullen+	Downie"	Walker	Downie"	Lander	Murphy
L	A	Alloa	0	1	Jamieson	Docherty	Talbot	Mensing	Donaldson	Fordyce+	Scott	Beaumont*	McNulty	Wilkie	McDonald	Mullen"	Denholm+	Downie	Walker	Hastings	Lander	Rutherford
L	H	Queen of the South	3	3	Jamieson	Mampuya"	Talbot	Mensing	Donaldson	Fordyce	Scott	Beaumont+	McNulty*	Denholm+	McDonald"	Hastings"	Mullen+	Burchill"	Walker	Downie	Walker	Wilkie
L	H	Falkirk	0	3	Jamieson	Docherty	Talbot	Mensing	Donaldson	Fordyce	Scott	Barrowman	Mampuya	Denholm"	McDonald*	McDonald"	Lander+	Downie	Walker	Murphy	Wilson	
LC2	A	Airdrieonians	2	0	Walker	Docherty+	Talbot	Mensing	Donaldson	Fordyce	Scott	Barrowman	McNulty*	Denholm"	McDonald"	Wilkie+	Beaumont+	Mullen"	Jamieson	Lander		
L	A	Dundee	0	3	Walker	Mampuya	O'Brien	Mensing	Donaldson	Fordyce	Scott	Barrowman	Wilkie	Scougall+	McDonald"	Wilkie"	Lander+	Downie	Jamieson	Lander		Burchill
L	H	Morton	2	2	Walker	Mampuya	O'Brien	Mensing	Donaldson	Fordyce*	Scott"	Barrowman	Wilkie*	Wilkie*	McNulty	Wilkie*	Denholm+	Mullen"	Jamieson	Hastings	McDonald	Wilkie
L	A	Dumbarton	2	1	Jamieson	Mampuya	Talbot	Mensing	Donaldson	Fordyce*	Scott*	Barrowman	McNulty"	McNulty	McDonald	Jacobs*	Burchill+	Denholm"	Mullen	Lander	Walker	Rutherford
LC3	H	Motherwell	1	2	Jamieson	O'Brien	McDonald	Mensing	Donaldson	Fordyce	Scott	Barrowman"	McNulty	Scougall+	Kea Jacobs"	McDonald*	Denholm+	Burchill"	Walker	Wilkie	Mullen	Wilkie
L	A	Cowdenbeath	5	1	Jamieson	O'Brien	McDonald	Mensing	Donaldson	Fordyce	Scott	Barrowman"	McNulty+	Scougall*	Kea Jacobs	Burchill"	Denholm+	Wilkie"	Walker	Lander	Talbot	Beaumont
L	H	Hamilton Accies	0	2	Jamieson	O'Brien	Talbot	Mensing	Donaldson	Fordyce	Wilkie*	Barrowman"	McNulty+	Scougall"	Kea Jacobs	Denholm"	Mullen+	Mullen"	Walker	Lander	Downie	Praprotnik
L	H	Alloa	3	2	Jamieson	O'Brien	Talbot	Mensing	Donaldson	Fordyce	Wilkie*	Barrowman	McNulty+	Scougall*	Kea Jacobs	Denholm"	Mullen+	McDonald	Walker	Lander	Rutherford	Praprotnik
L	A	Dundee	2	1	Jamieson	O'Brien	Talbot	Mensing	Donaldson	Fordyce	Wilkie"	Barrowman	McNulty+	Scougall+	Kea Jacobs	Denholm"	Scott+	Mullen"	Walker	Lander	Mullen	Praprotnik
L	A	Raith Rovers	0	1	Walker	O'Brien	Talbot"	Mensing	Donaldson	Fordyce	Scott	Denholm	McNulty	Scougall"	Kea Jacobs	Wilkie"	Lander+	McDonald"	Walker	Wilkie	Lander	Praprotnik
L	H	Falkirk	1	4	Walker	O'Brien	Talbot"	McDonald	Donaldson	Fordyce	Scott*	Barrowman+	McNulty	Scougall+	Kea Jacobs	Scott*	McDonald+	McDonald"	Jamieson	Beaumont	Mullen	Mullen
L	H	Dumbarton	1	3	Jamieson	O'Brien	Talbot	Mensing	Donaldson	Fordyce"	Scott*	Barrowman"	McNulty	Scougall"	Kea Jacobs	Wilkie"	Wilkie+	Downie	Walker	Beaumont	Rutherford	Downie
SC4	A	Morton	5	1	Jamieson	O'Brien	Talbot	Mensing	Donaldson*	Fordyce	Scott*	Barrowman"	McNulty	Scougall	Kea Jacobs	Mullen"	Wilkie+	Wilkie"	Jamieson	Beaumont	Rutherford	Docherty
L	A	St Johnstone	0	2	Jamieson	O'Brien	Talbot*	Mensing	Donaldson	Fordyce	Scott*	Barrowman"	McNulty	Scougall+	Kea Jacobs	Denholm"	Twardzik+	Burchill"	Jamieson	Downie	Twardzik	Docherty
L	A	Cowdenbeath	3	2	Jamieson	Mampuya	Talbot	Mensing	Docherty	O'Brien	Scott*	Barrowman	Barrowman	Scougall+	Kea Jacobs	Twardzik"	Denholm+	Burchill"	Docherty	Beaumont	Twardzik	Taylor
L	H	Hamilton Accies	0	0	Jamieson	Mampuya	Mampuya	Mensing	Docherty*	Fordyce	Scott	Burchill*	Mullen+	O'Brien"	Kea Jacobs	Denholm"	Wilkie+	Burchill"	Walker	Beaumont	Mampuya	Mullen
L	A	Queen of the South	2	2	Walker	Mampuya"	Mampuya"	Mensing	Docherty*	Fordyce	Scott	Burchill+	Mullen	O'Brien	Kea Jacobs*	Wilkie"	Wilkie+	Downie	Walker	Beaumont	Twardzik	Docherty
L	H	Raith Rovers	3	0	Jamieson	Mampuya"	Talbot*	Mensing	Docherty*	Fordyce	Scott*	Burchill+	McNulty+	O'Brien	Kea Jacobs	Scott*	Burchill+	McDonald"	Walker	Beaumont	Rutherford	Downie
L	H	Falkirk	0	1	Jamieson	Mampuya	Talbot	Mensing	Donaldson	Fordyce	Scott	Burchill"	McNulty"	O'Brien	Kea Jacobs*	Mullen"	Denholm+	Burchill"	Denholm	Beaumont	Rutherford	Praprotnik
L	A	Dundee	1	0	Jamieson	Habai*	Talbot*	Mensing	Donaldson"	Fordyce	Scott	Mevlja	McNulty	Sives	Kea Jacobs	Burchill"	Wilkie+	Downie	Denholm	Rutherford	Mullen	Wilkie
L	H	Morton	0	1	Jamieson	Habai	Talbot*	Mensing	Habai*	Fordyce	Scott	Mevlja	McNulty	Sives	Kea Jacobs	Mullen"	Wilkie+	Mullen"	Walker	Walker	McCaldon	Praprotnik
L	H	Queen of the South	1	2	Jamieson	Habai+	Denholm"	Mensing	Kyl Jacobs	Fordyce	Mullen"	Mevlja	McNulty	Sives	Kea Jacobs	Wilkie"	Denholm+	Denholm"	Walker	Rutherford	Wilkie	Praprotnik
L	A	Dumbarton	2	2	Jamieson	Habai+	Denholm+	Mensing	Kyl Jacobs	Fordyce	Mullen+	Mevlja	McNulty	Sives	Kea Jacobs	Mullen"	Wilkie+	Mullen"	Walker	Wilkie	Wilkie	Praprotnik
L	A	Alloa	3	0	Jamieson	O'Brien	O'Brien	Mensing	Kyl Jacobs	Forduze	Mullen+	Mevlja	McNulty	Sives	Kea Jacobs	Wilkie"	Denholm+	Denholm"	Walker	Wilkie	Sives	Mampuya
L	H	Hamilton Accies	0	2	Jamieson	O'Brien	Denholm"	Mampuya+	Kyl Jacobs	Fordyce	Mullen"	Mevlja	McNulty	Sives	Kea Jacobs	Barrowman+	Barrowman+	Habai"	Walker	Wilkie	Mullen	Praprotnik
L	A	Cowdenbeath	1	0	Jamieson	O'Brien	Denholm*	Mampuya"	Kyl Jacobs	Fordyce	Mullen*	Mevlja	McNulty	Sives	Kea Jacobs	Docherty"	Docherty+	Burchill"	Walker	Lander	Mullen	Downie
L	A	Dundee	0	2	Jamieson	O'Brien	Denholm+	Mampuya*	Kyl Jacobs	Fordyce	Wilkie"	Mevlja	McNulty	Sives	Kea Jacobs	McNulty"	McNulty+	Sives*	Walker	Lander	Mampuya	Mullen
L	H	Raith Rovers	4	2	Jamieson	O'Brien	Mampuya"	Mampuya"	Kyl Jacobs	Fordyce	Wilkie"	Mevlja	McNulty	Burchill+	Burchill+	Barrowman"	Mullen+	Denholm"	Walker	Lander	Twardzik	Mampuya
L	H	Alloa	2	0	Jamieson	O'Brien	O'Brien	Scott"	Kyl Jacobs	Fordyce	Wilkie*	Mevlja	McNulty	Sives	Kea Jacobs	Barrowman*	Burchill+	Mampuya	Walker	Black	Rutherford	Downie
L	H	Dumbarton	1	2	Jamieson	O'Brien	Talbot	Beaumont+	Kyl Jacobs	Fordyce	Mevlja	Mevlja+	McNulty	Sives	Kea Jacobs	Prapotnik"	Burchill+	Denholm"	Walker	Beaumont	Denholm	Praprotnik
L	A	Morton	2	0	Jamieson	Mampuya"	Talbot	Scott	Kyl Jacobs	Fordyce	Prapotnik*	Mevlja*	McNulty	Sives	Kea Jacobs"	Scott*	Talbot+	Prapotnik"	Walker	Scott	Denholm	Wilkie
L	A	Hamilton Accies	1	1	Jamieson	O'Brien	Denholm+	Mensing	Kyl Jacobs	Fordyce	Mullen+	Mullen"	McNulty	Sives	Burchill+	Scott*	Burchill+	Burchill"	Walker	Beaumont	Denholm	Praprotnik
L	A	Cowdenbeath	0	4	Jamieson	O'Brien	O'Brien	Mensing	Kyl Jacobs	Fordyce	Mullen"	Mevlja	McNulty	Sives	Kea Jacobs	Wilkie*	Scott+	Mampuya	Walker	Denholm	Denholm	Praprotnik
L	A	Queen of the South	0	2	Jamieson	O'Brien	Talbot	Scott*	Kyl Jacobs	Fordyce	Wilkie"	Mevlja+	McNulty	Sives	Kea Jacobs	Lander*	Habai+	Wilkie"	Walker	Beaumont	Denholm	Rutherford
L	H	Raith Rovers	2	0	Jamieson	O'Brien	Talbot	Scott	Kyl Jacobs	Fordyce	Prapotnik"	Mullen+	McNulty"	Sives	Kea Jacobs	Mevlya"	Denholm+	Rutherford"	Walker	Beaumont	Burchill	Lander

Montrose FC

Founded	1879
Ground	Links Park
Postcode	DD10 8QD
Tel	01674 673200
Capacity	3292
Closest Railway Station	Montrose
Record Attendance	8983 v Dundee, SC, 17/3/1973
Record Win	12-0 v Vale of Leithen, SC, 4/1/1975
Record Defeat	0-13 v Aberdeen, 17/3/1951
Most League Goals in a Season	28 Brian Third, 1972/3
Chairman	Derek Sim
Secretary	Brian Petrie
Manager	Stuart Garden (Until April) / George Shields
Assistant Manager	George Shields (Until April) / Lee Wilkie
Colours 2013/14 Top	Blue with White Chevron
Shorts	Blue
Sponsor	John Lawrie Group
Manufacturer	Nike
Change Colours 2013/14 Top	Yellow
Shorts	Yellow
Nicknames	Gable Endies
Web	www.montrosefc.co.uk

PREDICTION 2014/15
Montrose will be looking for a Play Off spot but may have to settle for a mid table position, at best.

2013/14 saw Montrose struggling in the lower reaches of the League Two table. They also suffered a Scottish Cup exit at the hands of Highland League side Fraserburgh.

That result will raise the spectre of relegation at Links Park. In 2014/15 the bottom side in League Two will face a Play Off to retain their League status - if Montrose were to lose that they would find themselves in the Highland League.

The club have turned to George Shields as Manager to replace Stuart Garden who left in April. Traditionally the Gable Endies recruit from the Aberdeen and Dundee areas and they will have scoured the Juniors and Juveniles for potential signings. Their location make sit difficult to attract central-belt players.

At one time Montrose were one of the top part-time sides in Scotland. In 1976 they finished Third in Division One, reached the Semi Finals of the League Cup and Hearts needed 3 games to beat them in the Quarter Finals of the Scottish. Those were heady days and how the Montrose faithful must wish for a return to the status they enjoyed back then.

Name		DOB	Pos	L			SC			LC			RC			UNS	Signed	Signed From	Notes	Contract
				A	S	G	A	S	G	A	S	G	A	S	G					
Bell	Craig	24/01/1994	D	11	3								1			14	2013	Dundee United		C (2015)
Bonar	Lewis	19/01/1992	F	3	9		2			1	1					18	2013	Shepparton SC		F
Campbell	Alan	01/08/1984	D	27			2			1						1	2009	Carnoustie Panmure		OOC
Crawford	Jonathan	12/03/1990	D	24	3		2			1						5	2010	Aberdeen		C (2015)
Deasley	Bryan	29/06/1988	F	33	10	2										1	2013	Forfar Ath (loan until Jan, then perm)		C (2015)
Duguid	Craig	14/02/1994	D													11	2014	Aberdeen	Joined Cove Rangers June 2014	F
Easton	Dean	07/03/1995														10				Youth
Ferguson	Calum	12/02/1995	F	3	1												2014	Inverness CT (loan Feb 2014)	Returned to ICT	
Gray	David	27/06/1988	M	18	7	1	1			1			1			12	2012	Dumbarton		F
Johnston	Luke	03/09/1993	D	6													2013	Dundee United (loan)	Returned to DundeeUtd	
Johnston	Scott	22/08/1989	F	28	4	6	2			2		1					2011	East Stirlingshire		OOC
Johnston	Cameron															1	2013	Montrose Youths		Youth
Masson	Terry	03/07/1988	M	28	3	4	2			2		1				1	2010	Carnoustie Panmure		OOC
McCafferty	John	21/03/1985	GK													13	2014	Carnoustie Panmure		
McCord	Ross	18/02/1990	M	15	9		1			2	1	1	1	1		11	2013	Alloa		C (2015)
McIntosh	Ricky	26/02/1993	M	23	6		2			2		1				2	2013	St Johnstone		F
McKenzie	Stuart	06/01/1988	GK	36			2			2		1					2013	Cove Rangers		C (2015)
McLeod	Kyle															2	2013	Montrose Youths		C (2015)
McNally	Stephen	15/03/1984	D	18			2			1							2010	Forfar Athletic		OOC
Milne	Dedan															1	2013	Montrose Youths		C (2015)
Reid	Jamie	11/01/1994		7	2											3	2013	Dundee (loan)	Returned to Dundee	
Rodger	Gareth	22/02/1994	D	4			1	1									2013	St Johnstone (loan)	Returned to St Johnstone	
Sturrock	Kieran	23/08/1996	F	3	10		1			1			1			25	2013	Dundee		OOC
Trialist																2				
Watson	Paul	22/11/1985	D	34	8	2	1			1							2012	St Andrews United		OOC
Webster	Graham	10/12/1992	M	22	8	4	2	1	1	1			1			5	2013	Dundee		OOC
Wilson	Colin	10/05/1993	D	16	3		1			1	1		1			12	2013	Musselburgh Athletic		C (2015)
Winter	Jamie	04/08/1985	M				1			1	1		1				2010	Broughty Athletic	Joined Broughty Athletic Aug 2014	
Wood	Garry	27/01/1988	F	33	1	7	2			2		1				2	2012	Ross County		C (2015)
Wood	Sandy	02/05/1986	GK													13	2010	Tayport	Freed Jan 2014 and joined Arbroath	
Young	Lloyd	26/12/1985	M	4	3	2	1										2012	East Fife		OOC

Date	Comp	H/A	Opponents	F	A	Crowd	Scorers
27/07/2013	RC1	A	Elgin City	0	2	505	
03/08/2013	LC1	A	Arbroath	1	0	903	McCord
10/08/2013	L	H	Stirling Albion	1	2	486	Webster
17/08/2013	L	A	Annan Athletic	1	2	286	Wood
24/08/2013	L	H	Berwick Rangers	1	1	285	Watson
27/08/2013	LC2	A	Morton	0	4	918	
31/08/2013	L	A	Albion Rovers	2	0	311	Young, Deasley
14/09/2013	L	A	Elgin City	3	3	577	Deasley 2, Young
21/09/2013	L	H	Peterhead	2	1	434	Deasley 2
28/09/2013	L	A	Clyde	3	0	464	Wood, Rodger, S Johnston
05/10/2013	SC2	A	Dalbeattie Star	1	0	265	Wilson
19/10/2013	L	A	Stirling Albion	1	3	481	Deasley
26/10/2013	L	H	East Stirlingshire	2	0	338	McGowan og, Masson
29/10/2013	L	H	Queen's Park	1	2	358	Masson
02/11/2013	SC3	A	Fraserburgh	1	2	565	McCord
16/11/2013	L	H	Albion Rovers	2	1	343	Deasley 2
20/11/2013	L	A	Berwick Rangers	1	1	227	Webster
23/11/2013	L	H	Elgin City	3	3	398	Watson 2, S Johnston
30/11/2013	L	A	Peterhead	0	3	473	
07/12/2013	L	A	Queen's Park	1	0	357	S Johnston
14/12/2013	L	H	Clyde	0	2	410	
26/12/2013	L	H	Annan Athletic	0	2	350	
28/12/2013	L	A	East Stirlingshire	2	2	244	Wood, Webster
02/01/2014	L	H	Berwick Rangers	0	0	456	
11/01/2014	L	A	Albion Rovers	0	1	718	
18/01/2014	L	H	Peterhead	2	3	424	Wood, Masson
25/01/2014	L	A	Elgin City	3	2	550	Webster, S Johnston, Watson
01/02/2014	L	H	Stirling Albion	0	0	333	
08/02/2014	L	A	Annan Athletic	0	1	354	
15/02/2014	L	H	Queen's Park	1	0	301	Watson
22/02/2014	L	A	Clyde	1	1	418	S Johnston
01/03/2014	L	H	Albion Rovers	2	1	334	S Johnston, Masson
08/03/2014	L	A	Berwick Rangers	0	5	410	
15/03/2014	L	H	East Stirlingshire	2	0	333	Gray, Deasley
22/03/2014	L	A	Stirling Albion	2	2	529	Watson, Wood
29/03/2014	L	H	Elgin City	0	3	262	
05/04/2014	L	A	Peterhead	0	4	671	
12/04/2014	L	A	Queen's Park	1	1	251	Watson
19/04/2014	L	H	Clyde	0	2	422	
26/04/2014	L	H	Annan Athletic	2	1	264	Deasley, Wood
03/05/2014	L	A	East Stirlingshire	2	1	265	Wood, Watson

Friendly Games

6/7/13	Fr	H	Inverurie Loco Works	1	0		
9/7/13	Fr	H	Dundee	1	5	600	
13/7/13	Fr	H	Buckie Thistle	3	0		
16/7/13	Fr	N	Dundee United U20	2	1		at St Andrews
20/7/13	Fr	H	Brechin City	2	4		
23/7/13	Fr	A	Forfar Albion	1	2		U19
23/7/13	Fr	A	Kirrie Thistle	4	4		
27/7/13	Fr	A	East Craigie	3	3		U19
6/8/13	Fr	A	Downfield				U19

Date	Comp	H/A	Opponents	F	A	1	2	3	4	5	6	7	8	9	10	11	12	13	14	15	16	17	18
27/07/2013	RC1	A	Elgin City	0	2	McKenzie	Masson	McIntosh	Wilson	Campbell	Webster	Winter"	McCord	Wood	S.Johnston+	Watson+	Bell*	Sturrock+	Gray"	Crawford	Easton		
03/08/2013	LC1	A	Arbroath	1	0	McKenzie	Masson	Watson	Wilson	Campbell	Webster	McIntosh	McCord	Bonar*	S.Johnston	Wood	Winter*	Sturrock	Gray"	Crawford	Wood		
10/08/2013	L	H	Stirling Albion	1	2	McKenzie	Masson	McNally	Wilson	Campbell	Webster"	Watson	McCord	Bonar +	Sturrock	Sturrock*	Bell*	Sturrock+	Young"	Crawford	Easton		
17/08/2013	L	A	Annan Athletic	1	2	McKenzie	Masson"	McNally	Wilson	Campbell	Webster+	Watson	McCord+	Bonar	S.Johnston"	Wood	Bell*	Sturrock+	Young"	Crawford	Easton	Gray	
24/08/2013	L	H	Berwick Rangers	1	1	McKenzie	Masson*	McNally	Crawford	Campbell	Webster+	Watson	McCord+	McIntosh	S.Johnston"	Wood	Sturrock*	Gray+	Young"	Wilson	Easton		
27/08/2013	LC2	A	Morton	0	4	McKenzie	Masson	McNally	Crawford"	Campbell	Young+	Gray"	McCord*	McIntosh	S.Johnston	Wood	Webster*	Sturrock+	Bonar*	Bonar	Easton		
31/08/2013	L	A	Albion Rovers	2	0	McKenzie	Masson	McNally	Crawford"	Campbell	Young*	Gray"	McCord+	McIntosh	Deasley	Wood	S.Johnston*	Masson+	Webster"	Wilson	Easton	Sturrock	Masson
14/09/2013	L	A	Elgin City	3	3	McKenzie	Watson	McNally	Rodger	Campbell"	Young*	Gray	McCord	McIntosh	Deasley+	Wood	Crawford*	S.Johnston+	Bonar	Webster	Easton	Sturrock	McCord
21/09/2013	L	H	Peterhead	2	1	McKenzie	Watson	McNally	Rodger	Wilson*	Young	Gray+	McCord	McIntosh	Deasley	Wood	Bonar*	Webster+	S.Johnston"	Bell	Easton	Bonar	McCord
28/09/2013	L	H	Clyde	3	0	McKenzie	Watson	McNally	Rodger	Wilson	Young"	Gray+	Masson	McIntosh	Deasley"	Wood	S.Johnston*	Webster+	Sturrock"	Bell	Easton		
05/10/2013	SC2	A	Dalbeattie Star	1	0	McKenzie	Watson	McNally	Crawford	Wilson	S.Johnston+	Gray*	Masson	McIntosh	Deasley"	Wood	Webster*	Bonar+	Sturrock	Easton	McCord	Sturrock	
19/10/2013	L	A	Stirling Albion	1	3	McKenzie	Watson	McNally	Crawford	Wilson	S.Johnston"	Gray*	Masson*	McIntosh	Deasley	Wood	McCord*	Sturrock	Bonar*	Bell	S.Wood	McCord	Wilson
26/10/2013	L	H	East Stirlingshire	2	0	McKenzie	Watson	McNally	Crawford	Wilson	S.Johnston+	Gray*	Masson	McIntosh	Deasley	Wood	McCord*	Sturrock+	Bonar*	Bell	S.Wood	McCord	Gray
29/10/2013	L	A	Queen's Park	1	2	McKenzie	Watson	McNally	Crawford	Wilson"	S.Johnston+	Gray*	Masson	McIntosh	Deasley	Wood	McCord*	Sturrock+	Bonar*	Bell	S.Wood	Webster	
02/11/2013	SC3	A	Fraserburgh	1	2	McKenzie	Watson	McNally	Crawford	Rodger	S.Johnston"	McCord	Masson*	McIntosh+	Deasley	Wood	Webster*	Sturrock+	Bonar*	Bell	S.Wood	Gray	Wilson
16/11/2013	L	H	Albion Rovers	2	1	McKenzie	Wilson	McNally	Gray"	S.Johnston	Bell	McCord+	Masson	Webster*	Deasley	Wood	Johnston*	McIntosh*	Gray"	Sturrock	S.Wood	Wilson	
20/11/2013	L	A	Berwick Rangers	1	1	McKenzie	Wilson	McNally	Crawford	Watson	Bell	McCord+	Masson	Webster"	Deasley	Wood	Bonar*	Sturrock"	Sturrock	S.Wood	Bonar	McIntosh	
23/11/2013	L	H	Elgin City	3	3	McKenzie	Wilson	McNally	Crawford	Watson	Bell	McCord	Masson*	Webster"	Deasley	Wood+	Campbell	Campbell	Gray"	S.Wood	Sturrock	Gray	S.Wood
30/11/2013	L	H	Peterhead	1	0	McKenzie	McIntosh	McNally	Crawford	Watson	S.Johnston+	McCord+	Masson	Wood	Deasley	Wood*	S.Johnston"	Crawford+	Bonar	Bell	Gray	Webster	
07/12/2013	L	A	Queen's Park	1	0	McKenzie	McIntosh	McNally	Campbell	Watson	Wilson+	McCord+	Masson	S.Johnston	Deasley	Wood*	S.Johnston"	Crawford+	Bell"	C.Johnston	Sturrock		
14/12/2013	L	H	Clyde	0	2	McKenzie	Bell	Webster	Campbell	Watson*	L.Johnston	Wood	Masson	S.Johnston	Deasley	Reid+	Webster*	Gray	Bonar*	Gray	Bell		
28/12/2013	L	H	Annan Athletic	0	2	McKenzie	Bell+	Webster*	Campbell	Watson	S.Johnston	Wood	Masson	L.Johnston*	Deasley	Reid+	Crawford*	Gray+	McIntosh"	Sturrock	S.Wood	Bonar	Crawford
02/01/2014	L	H	Berwick Rangers	0	0	McKenzie	Bell+	McNally	Campbell	Watson	S.Johnston+	Webster"	Gray	S.Johnston"	Deasley	Wood	McCord*	McIntosh"	Reid+	Sturrock	S.Wood	Bonar	Crawford
11/01/2014	L	A	Albion Rovers	0	1	McKenzie	Bell+	Crawford	Campbell	McCord	L.Johnston	Webster"	Gray*	S.Johnston+	Deasley	Wood	Bonar*	Reid+	Wilson"	Reid	S.Wood	Sturrock	McCord
18/01/2014	L	H	Peterhead	3	2	McKenzie	McNally	McIntosh"	Campbell	Watson	Masson	Webster"	Reid	S.Johnston"	Deasley	Wood	Wilson"	Gray	Bonar"	McCord	Trialist	Sturrock	Gray
25/01/2014	L	H	Elgin City	3	2	McKenzie	Crawford	McIntosh"	Campbell	Watson	Masson	Webster*	Reid+	S.Johnston	Deasley	Wood	Ferguson*	Sturrock+	Wilson"	Gray	Trialist	Bonar	Gray
01/02/2014	L	H	Stirling Albion	0	0	McKenzie	Crawford	McIntosh	Campbell	Watson	Ferguson+	Webster	Reid+	S.Johnston"	Deasley	Wood	McCord*	Gray+	Wilson	McCord	Duguid	Sturrock	McCafferty
08/02/2014	L	A	Annan Athletic	0	1	McKenzie	Crawford	McIntosh	Campbell	Watson	Ferguson+	Webster	Reid+	S.Johnston	Deasley	Wood	McCord*	Gray+	Wilson	Gray	Duguid	Webster	McCafferty
15/02/2014	L	A	Queen's Park	1	0	McKenzie	Crawford	McIntosh	Campbell	Watson	Ferguson+	Masson	Webster+	S.Johnston	Deasley	Wood	McCord*	Gray*	Wilson	Duguid	Sturrock	Reid	McCafferty
22/02/2014	L	A	Clyde	1	1	McKenzie	Crawford	McIntosh	Campbell	Watson	Gray	Masson	Webster*	Wood	Deasley	Wood	Gray*	McCord+	Wilson	McCord	Sturrock	Bonar	McCafferty
01/03/2014	L	H	Albion Rovers	2	1	McKenzie	Crawford	Webster	Campbell	Watson	Gray	Masson	Webster*	S.Johnston*	Deasley	Wood	Reid*	Duguid	Wilson	McCord	Sturrock	Bonar	McCafferty
08/03/2014	L	A	Berwick Rangers	2	0	McKenzie	Crawford	McIntosh	Campbell	Watson	Gray*	Masson	Webster+	S.Johnston*	Deasley	Wilson	Sturrock*	McCord+	Sturrock	Bell	Sturrock	Bonar	Sturrock
15/03/2014	L	H	East Stirlingshire	2	0	McKenzie	Crawford	McIntosh	Campbell	Watson	Gray	Masson	Webster*	S.Johnston*	Deasley	Wilson	McCord*	Duguid	Sturrock	Bell	McCafferty	Bonar	
22/03/2014	L	A	Stirling Albion	2	2	McKenzie	Crawford	McIntosh	Campbell	Watson	Gray	Masson	Webster*	Wood	Deasley	Wilson	Bonar*	Sturrock	McCord	Bell	McCafferty	Duguid	
29/03/2014	L	H	Elgin City	0	3	McKenzie	Crawford	Wood	Campbell	Watson	Gray+	Bonar*	McCord	S.Johnston	Deasley	Wilson	Wood*	Bonar+	McCord	Bell	McCafferty	Duguid	Sturrock
05/04/2014	L	A	Peterhead	0	4	McKenzie	Crawford	Wood	Campbell	Watson	Gray*	Masson	Webster"	S.Johnston	Deasley	Wilson	McIntosh	Sturrock+	Wilson	Duguid	Mcafferty	Duguid	
12/04/2014	L	H	Queen's Park	1	1	McKenzie	Crawford	Wood	Campbell	Watson	Gray+	Bonar"	McCord	S.Johnston	Deasley	McIntosh	Masson*	Bonar+	Bonar	Duguid	Bonar	Duguid	Sturrock
19/04/2014	L	O	Clyde	0	2	McKenzie	Crawford	Wood	Campbell	Webster	Wilson*	Bell+	McCord	S.Johnston	Deasley	McIntosh	Masson*	R.McIntosh"	Bell	Gray	Bonar	McLeod	McCafferty
26/04/2014	L	A	Annan Athletic	2	1	McKenzie	Crawford	Wood	Campbell	Watson	Wilson*	Bell+	McCord	S.Johnston	Deasley	Masson	Gray"	Wilson"	Bonar	Duguid	McCafferty	Webster	Sturrock
03/05/2014	L	A	East Stirlingshire	2	1	McKenzie	Crawford	Wood	Campbell	Watson	Sturrock*	Bell+	McCord	S.Johnston	Deasley	Masson	Webster"	Wilson"	Bonar	Milne	McCafferty	Mcleod'	Gray

Morton FC

Founded	1874
Ground	Cappielow Park
Postcode	PA15 2TY
Tel	01475 723571
Capacity	11589
Closest Railway Station	Cartsdyke
Record Attendance	23500 v Celtic, 29/4/1922
Record Win	11-0 v Carfin Shamrock, SC, 13/11/1886
Record Defeat	1-10 v Port Glasgow, Lge, 5/5/1894 / v St Bernards Lge 14/10/1933
Most League Goals in a Season	58 Allan McGraw, 1963/4
Chairman	Douglas Rae
Chief Executive	Gillian Donaldson
Manager	Allan Moore (until Nov 2013) / Kenny Shiels (Until May) Jim Duffy (from May 2014)
Assistant Manager	Mark McNally (until Nov 2013) / David Hopkin
Colours 2013/14 Top	Blue and White Hoops
Shorts	White
Sponsor	Millions
Manufacturer	Puma
Change Colours 2013/14 Top	Black
Shorts	Black
3rd Kit 2013/14 Top	White
Shorts	Blue
Nicknames	Ton
Web	www.gmfc.net

Morton supporters will be glad to see the back of 2013/14. They started out with high hopes after enjoying so much success in 2012/13 but dreams quickly turned into nightmares.

League results were unremittingly poor. Big name signings proved to be unsuccessful. Long-serving Manager Allan Moore was replaced with Kenny Shiels but nothing much improved.

The only bright spot in an otherwise gloomy campaign was the League Cup win over Celtic at Parkhead.

The season ended in farce as Morton were beaten 10-2 by Hamilton Accies on the closing day of the season - the BBC reporter at the game saying that it looked as if half the team had downed tools and didn't care.

PREDICTION 2014/15
Might scrape into the play offs

Name		DOB	Pos	L			SC			LC			RC			UNS	Signed	Signed From	Notes	Contract
				A	S	G	A	S	G	A	S	G	A	S	G					
Bachirou	Fouad	15/04/90	M	35		1	4						1				2010	Paris St Germain		C (2015)
Cairnie	Jordan	26/03/96	F			1										4	2013	Morton Youths		Youth
Campbell	Archie	10/01/91	F	11	19	3	1			1	2	2				7	2011	Rangers		ONC
Caraux	Nicolas	04/03/91	GK	19		1	1			3			1			15	2013	RC Lens		C (2015)
Cham	Kabba-Modou	25/12/92	F	7	2	2				3	1	1	1			3	2013	KV St Truiden		F
Cole	Darren	03/01/92	D	18						2							2013	Rangers		ONC
Ferris	Aidan	07/07/96	M		1												2013	St Mirren		Youth
Findlay	Stuart	14/09/95	D	14													2014	Celtic (loan Jan-May)	Returned to Celtic	
Fitzpatrick	Marc	11/05/86	M	29	1	1	4	1	1							1	2013	Queen of the South	Joined Airdrieonians June 2014	
Fulton	Aiden	01/01/94	M	2	12						1					7	2013	St Mirren		ONC
Gaston	Derek	18/04/87	GK	17	1		1									22	2012	Albion Rovers		C (2015)
Habai	Michael	30/07/85	M	14	1	1	4	1	1							4	2013	SFN Senec	Transferred to Livingston Jan 2014	
Hands	Reece	06/10/93	M	9	1	3				3	1	1				2	2013	Blackburn Rovers		C (2015)
Imrie	Dougie	03/08/83	M	32	9	1				4	2	1				1	2013	St Mirren	Joined Hamilton Accies June 2014	
Irvine	Luke	03/06/96	D													1	2013	Barrhead YC		Youth
Jamieson	Nicky	03/08/96	D													1	2013	Gourock YAC		Youth
Knight	Craig	03/07/96	M	3	1											7	2013	Gourock YAC		Youth
McCormack	Jamie	01/02/92	D	10									1			7	2013	Wigan Athletic		ONC
McIntyre	Lewis	03/10/97	GK													3	2013	Tass Thistle		Youth
McKay	Barrie	30/12/94	F	14	4	3											2013	Rangers (loan)	Returned to Rangers	
McKee	Joseph	31/10/92	F	6	8		1			2	1					3	2013	Bolton Wanderers		C (2015)
McLaughlin	Mark	02/12/75	D	12		1				3	1	1				5	2012	Hamilton Accies	Transferred to Dumbarton Jan 2014	
McNeill	David	21/01/95	F	2	8					2	1					12	2013	Kilmarnock		Youth
Nicholson	Jake	19/07/92	D	3	1	1										1	2013	Tottenham Hotspur	Freed Nov 2013 and joined Wimbledon	
Novo	Nacho	26/03/79	F	8		1	1			1						1	2013	Huesca	Freed March 2014 and joined Carlisle United	
O'Brien	David	24/01/84	M	3	3		1			1	1					3	2010	Stirling Albion		ONC
O'Connor	Gary	07/05/83	F	9	2	1										3	2013	Tom Tomsk		F
O'Neill	Cameron	01/08/96	M													2	2013	Barrhead YC		Youth
O'Ware	Thomas	20/03/93	D	10	1	1	1									8	2011	Bonnyton Thistle		C (2015)
Page	Jonathan	08/02/90	D	10	2					2	1					2	2013	Hamilton Accies	Freed Mar 014 and joined Dunfermline Ath	
Peciar	Tomas	10/06/88	D	15	2	2				2		1				2	2013	AS Trencin	Freed Mar 2014	
Reid	Craig	26/02/86	D		9		1			1						1	2012	QOS	Freed Jan 2014 and joined Motherwell	
Robertson	David	23/09/86	M	14	2											1	2014	St Johnstone		ONC
Russell	Mark	22/03/96	D	4	8	1										9	2013	St Mirren BC		Youth
Sampayo	Ben	10/12/92	D		2											2	2014	Chelmsford City		ONC
Smith	Jack	27/12/94	F		2											3	2014	East Fife		Youth
Stirling	Stephen	05/01/90	M	8	3	1				1						1	2012	Stranraer	Freed Jan 2014 and joined Stranraer	
Taggart	Scott	27/12/91	M	29		1	3		1								2012	Hibernian		ONC
Verlaque	David	11/08/95	M													7	2013	Morton Youths		Youth
Vine	Rowan	21/09/82	F	12	4												2014	Hibernian		F
Wallace	Tony	22/02/91	M	8	6		2	2					1			6	2012	Dumbarton	on loan to Queen's Park Jan 2014	ONC

NEW SIGNINGS 2014/15

Name		DOB	Pos														Signed	Signed From		
Pepper	Conor	04/05/94	M														2014	Inverness CT		
Milojevic	Stefan	20/02/91	D														2014	Airdrieonians		

Date	Comp	H/A	Opponents	F	A		Crowd	Scorers
27/07/2013	RC1	A	Annan Athletic	0	1		732	
03/08/2013	LC1	A	East Fife	6	2	AET	727	Campbell 2, McNeil, Imrie, Habai, McLaughlin
10/08/2013	L	H	Cowdenbeath	2	0		1817	Hands, Campbell
17/08/2013	L	A	Falkirk	1	3		3058	Hands
24/08/2013	L	A	Dumbarton	1	3		1171	Imrie
27/08/2013	LC2	H	Montrose	4	0		918	Cham, Fitzpatrick, Hands, Fulton
31/08/2013	L	H	Raith Rovers	1	1		1545	Imrie
14/09/2013	L	A	Livingston	2	2		1077	Hands, Cham
21/09/2013	L	H	Queen of the South	0	2		1826	
24/09/2013	LC3	A	Celtic`	1	0		15709	Imrie
28/09/2013	L	A	Dundee	1	3		3870	Peciar
05/10/2013	L	H	Alloa	0	2		1478	
12/10/2013	L	H	Hamilton Accies	1	1		2106	Habai
19/10/2013	L	A	Cowdenbeath	1	5		543	Imrie
26/10/2013	L	A	Raith Rovers	1	2		1569	Novo
30/10/2013	LC4	H	St Johnstone	0	1		2619	
09/11/2013	L	H	Dumbarton	2	0		1687	McLauchlin, Peciar
16/11/2013	L	A	Queen of the South	0	2		1685	
23/11/2013	L	H	Livingston	1	5		1460	Cham
30/11/2013	SC4	A	Inverness CT	0	4			
07/12/2013	L	H	Dundee	1	2		1536	Imrie
14/12/2013	L	A	Alloa	0	2		546	
21/12/2013	L	H	Falkirk	0	2		1873	
28/12/2013	L	A	Hamilton Accies	0	1		1472	
04/01/2014	L	A	Dumbarton	0	2		1469	
11/01/2014	L	H	Raith Rovers	0	0		1745	
18/01/2014	L	A	Livingston	1	0		1245	McKay
29/01/2014	L	H	Queen of the South	1	1		2341	Campbell
01/02/2014	L	A	Falkirk	1	1		3120	Imrie
15/02/2014	L	H	Cowdenbeath	1	1		2087	Campbell
22/02/2014	L	H	Alloa	0	1		1628	
01/03/2014	L	A	Dundee	0	2		4488	
15/03/2014	L	A	Raith Rovers	1	2		1308	Vine
22/03/2014	L	H	Hamilton Accies	3	4		1245	Vine, Fitzpatrick, O'Connor
25/03/2014	L	A	Cowdenbeath	0	3		318	
29/03/2014	L	A	Queen of the South	0	3		1487	
01/04/2014	L	H	Dumbarton	3	0		826	Vine, O'Ware, McKay
05/04/2014	L	H	Livingston	2	0		1009	Imrie, McKay
12/04/2014	L	A	Alloa	0	2		615	
19/04/2014	L	H	Dundee	1	0		2117	Imrie
26/04/2014	L	H	Falkirk	1	1		1921	Vine
03/05/2014	L	A	Hamilton Accies	2	10		2034	Imrie 2

Friendly Games

3/7/13	Fr	H	Sheffield United		0	1	709	
9/7/13	Fr	H	Rotherham United		0	0	667	
11/7/13	Fr	N	Stranraer		2	7		Res
13/7/13	Test	H	St Johnstone		0	1	1014	Peter Weatherston Test
16/7/13	RCSF	H	Viewfield Rovers		9	0	233	
20/7/13	RCF	A	St Mirren		4	2	3703	
28/7/13	Fr	A	Largs Thistle		4	3		

Date	Comp	H/A	Opponents	F	A	1	2	3	4	5	6	7	8	9	10	11	12	13	14	15	16	17	18
27/07/2013	RC1	A	Annan Athletic	0	1	Caraux	Taggart	Fitzpatrick	Hands*	Peciar	Imrie	Bachirou+	McKee	O'Brien	Cham"	Habai	Campbell*	Fulton+	Wallace"	Irvine	Gaston		
03/08/2013	LC1	A	East Fife	6	2 AET	Gaston	Taggart	Fitzpatrick	McLaughlin	Habai	Imrie"	Bachirou"	McKee*	Hands	Campbell	Cham+	Wallace"	McNeil+	Fulton"	Page	Caraux		
10/08/2013	L	H	Cowdenbeath	2	0	Gaston	Taggart	Fitzpatrick	McLaughlin	Habai	Imrie"	Bachirou"	McKee+	Hands	Campbell	Cham*	McNeil*	Cham	Fulton"	Page	Caraux		
17/08/2013	L	A	Falkirk	1	3	Gaston	Taggart	Fitzpatrick	McLaughlin	Habai	Imrie	Bachirou	McKee*	Hands	Campbell"	Cham"	O'Brien*	Wallace+	Fulton"	Page	Caraux		
24/08/2013	L	A	Dumbarton	1	3	Gaston	Taggart	Peciar	McLaughlin+	Habai+	Imrie+	Bachirou"	Wallace"	Wallace"	Cham	O'Brien"	Campbell"	Wallace+	Fulton"	McNeill	Gaston	Fitzpatrick	
27/08/2013	LC2	H	Montrose	4	0	Caraux	Taggart	Fitzpatrick	McLaughlin	Habai"	Imrie+	Bachirou	Wallace	Wallace	Cham"	Page	Peciar*	Fulton+	Page+	Peciar	Gaston		
31/08/2013	L	H	Raith Rovers	1	1	Caraux	Taggart	Fitzpatrick	McLaughlin+	Habai+	Imrie	Bachirou	Wallace"	Wallace	Cham"	Page	Peciar*	Campbell+	McNeil"	Fulton	Gaston	Verlaque	McNeill
14/09/2013	L	A	Livingston	2	2	Caraux	Taggart	Fitzpatrick	McLaughlin+	Habai+	Imrie*	Bachirou	Wallace"	Wallace"	Cham	Page	Peciar*	Peciar*	McNeil"	Fulton	Gaston	Verlaque	McNeill
21/09/2013	L	H	Queen of the South	0	2	Caraux	Taggart	Fitzpatrick	McLaughlin+	Habai+	Imrie*	Bachirou	Page	Hands	Cham	Page	O'Brien*	Campbell+	O'Brien+	Peciar	Gaston	Verlaque	McNeill
24/09/2013	LC3	A	Celtic	0	1	Caraux	Taggart	Fitzpatrick	Peciar	Habai	Imrie	Bachirou	Page*	Hands	Cham+	Cham+	O'Brien*	Campbell+	Russell	Fulton	Gaston		
28/09/2013	L	H	Dundee	1	3	Caraux	Taggart	Fitzpatrick	Peciar	Habai*	Imrie	Bachirou	Page*	Page	Campbell+	Wallace	Stirling*	Campbell+	Campbell+"	Peciar	Gaston	Knight	
05/10/2013	L	A	Alloa	0	2	Caraux	Taggart	Fitzpatrick	Peciar	Habai	Imrie	Bachirou	Page	Page*	Campbell+	Fulton"	McKee*	McNeil+	McLaughlin"	Verlaque	Gaston		
12/10/2013	L	H	Hamilton Accies	1	1	Caraux	Taggart	Fitzpatrick	Peciar	Habai	Imrie	Bachirou	Page	Page	Novo	Stirling"	McKee*	Campbell	Fulton	Wallace	Gaston		
19/10/2013	L	A	Cowdenbeath	1	5	Caraux	Taggart*	Fitzpatrick	Peciar*	Habai	Imrie	Bachirou	Page	Reid	Novo+	Stirling	McKee*	Campbell+	McLaughlin+	Wallace	Gaston		
26/10/2013	L	A	Raith Rovers	1	2	Caraux	McLaughlin	Fitzpatrick*	Peciar*	Habai	Imrie	Bachirou	Mckee	Reid	Novo"	Wallace	Wallace+	Wallace+	Campbell*	Fulton	Gaston		Cham
30/10/2013	LC4	L	St Johnstone	0	1	Caraux	McLaughlin	Fitzpatrick	Peciar	Habai	Imrie"	Bachirou	McKee+	Reid	Novo	Wallace"	Page*	Campbell	Campbell	Cham	Gaston		
09/11/2013	L	H	Dumbarton	2	0	Gaston	McLaughlin	Page	Page	Campbell*	Imrie"	Bachirou	McKee+	Reid+	Novo	Wallace	Cham*	Stirling+	Russell*	Wallace	Gaston		Verlaque
16/11/2013	L	A	Cowdenbeath	0	4	Gaston	McLaughlin	McLaughlin"	McLaughlin"	McLaughlin	Imrie	Bachirou	Nicholson+	Reid	Novo"	Wallace"	Russell"	Stirling+	Cham"	Wallace	Gaston		Taggart
23/11/2013	L	H	Inverness CT	1	5	Caraux	McKay	Page	Fitzpatrick	Page	Imrie	Bachirou	Nicholson"	Reid+	Novo*	Cham	McKee*	Stirling-	McKee"	Campbell	Caraux	Mcneill	Stirling
30/11/2013	SC4	A	Queen of the South	0	4	Caraux	McLaughlin"	O'Ware"	Peciar	Stirling	Robertson*	Bachirou	Nicholson"	Reid	Novo"	Wallace	McNeil"	McKee+	Habai"	O'Ware	Gaston	Mcneill	O'Neill
07/12/2013	L	H	Dundee	1	2	Caraux	McKay	Fitzpatrick	Peciar	Stirling"	Imrie	Bachirou	Nicholson"	Reid	Cole	Russell+	Cham*	Stirling+	McKee*	Campbell	Gaston	Mcneill	Verlaque
14/12/2013	L	A	Alloa	0	2	Caraux	McKee*	Fitzpatrick*	Peciar	Stirling+	Imrie	Bachirou	Hands	McCormack	Cole	Fitzpatrick	Ferris*	McNeil+	Taggart	Russell	Gaston	Fulton	McKee
21/12/2013	L	H	Falkirk	0	1	Caraux	McKay	Fitzpatrick	Peciar	Stirling	Imrie*	Bachirou	Hands+	McCormack+	Cole	Habai	Nicholson"	McNeil"	Fulton"	Russell	Gaston	Hands	McLaughlin
22/12/2013	L	H	Hamilton Accies	0	1	Caraux	McKay"	Fitzpatrick	Peciar	Stirling	Imrie*	Bachirou	Robertson+	McCormack"	Cole	Cham	Campbell*	McNeil"	Russell"	Russell	Gaston	Novo	Habai
04/01/2014	L	A	Dumbarton	0	2	Caraux*	McKay"	Fitzpatrick	Peciar	Stirling*	Imrie	Bachirou	Robertson+	McCormack+	Cole	O'Connor	Wallace"	McNeil+	Campbell"	Wallace	Campbell	Tagart	McNeill
11/01/2014	L	H	Raith Rovers	0	0	Caraux	O'Ware+	Fitzpatrick	Peciar	Campbell+	Mackay	Bachirou	Robertson"	McCormack+	Cole	Campbell+	Fulton"	McNeil+	Russell"	Hands	McNeil	Habai	Cham
18/01/2014	L	A	Livingston	1	0	Caraux*	O'Ware+	Fitzpatrick	Mackay	Taggart	Imrie*	Bachirou"	McCormack"	Robertson+	Cole	O'Connor	Fulton*	Fulton+	Sampayo"	Wallace	McNeil	Jamieson	Sampayo
29/01/2014	L	H	Queen of the South	1	1	Caraux	Findlay	Fitzpatrick	Mackay	Taggart	Imrie*	Bachirou"	McCormack*	McCormack*	Cole	O'Connor	Fulton*	Campbell+	McKee	O'Ware	McNeil	O'Brien	McNeill
01/02/2014	L	A	Falkirk	1	1	Gaston	Findlay	Fitzpatrick	Mackay+	Taggart	Imrie	Bachirou"	Robertson"	McCormack*	Cole	O'Connor	O'Brien*	Campbell+	Robertson"	O'Ware	McIntyre	O'Brien	Cham
15/02/2014	L	H	Cowdenbeath	1	1	Gaston	Findlay	Fitzpatrick	Campbell	Taggart	O'Ware	Bachirou"	Vine	McCormack*	Cole	O'Connor	Campbell"	Campbell+	Smith"	O'Ware	O'Ware	Russell	Sampayo
22/02/2014	L	A	Alloa	0	1	Gaston	Findlay	Fitzpatrick*	O'Brien	Taggart"	O'Ware	Bachirou	Vine	McCormack+	Cole	O'Connor	Sampayo"	Campbell+	Smith"	McIntyre	O'Ware	McIntyre	Sampayo
01/03/2014	L	H	Dundee	0	2	Gaston	Findlay	Fitzpatrick	O'Brien	Taggart	O'Ware	Bachirou	Vine+	McCormack	Campbell"	Campbell	Robertson"*	McNeil+	O'Ware	O'Ware	Caraux	Russell	Russell
15/03/2014	L	A	Raith Rovers	1	2	Gaston	Findlay	Fitzpatrick	Knight"	Taggart	O'Ware	Robertson"	Vine*	McCormack	Cole+	Campbell	Campbell"	Russell+	Russell"	Knight	Caraux	Russell	Russell
22/03/2014	L	H	Hamilton Accies	3	4	Gaston	Findlay	Fitzpatrick*	Knight"	Taggart+	O'Ware	Bachirou	Vine+	Robertson	Cole+	O'Connor"	Fulton"	Campbell+	Cairnie"	Knight	Caraux	Fulton	O'Neill
25/03/2014	L	A	Cowdenbeath	0	3	Gaston	Findlay	Russell	McCormack	Taggart"	O'Ware	Bachirou	Vine	Wallace	Cole	O'Connor"	McKay"	Campbell+	Knight"	Imrie	Caraux	McCormack	McCormack
29/03/2014	L	H	Queen of the South	0	3	Gaston	Findlay	Russell	McCormack"	Taggart	Imrie	Bachirou	Imrie	Robertson+	Cole+	McKay+	McKay*	Campbell"	Knight"	Smith	Fulton	Wallace	Robertson
01/04/2014	L	H	Dumbarton	2	0	Gaston	Findlay	Russell	Robertson"	Taggart	Imrie	Bachirou	Imrie"	Vine	Cole	McKay+	McKay*	Russell+	Fulton"	O'Connor	Caraux	McCormack	Knight
05/04/2014	L	A	Livingston	2	0	Gaston*	Findlay	Russell	Robertson*	Taggart	Imrie	Bachirou	Imrie	Vine	Cole	McKay"	Smith*	Russell+	McKee"	Caraux	Cairnie	McCormack	Campbell
12/04/2014	L	H	Alloa	0	2	Gaston	Findlay	Russell	Robertson	Taggart	Imrie	Bachirou	Imrie"	Vine+	Cole	McKay"	McKee*	Campbell+	McNeil"	McNeill	Caraux	Smith	McCormack
19/04/2014	L	H	Dundee	1	0	Gaston	Findlay	Russell	Robertson	Taggart	Imrie	Bachirou	Imrie	Vine+	Cole	McKay"	McKee*+	McNeil+	McIntyre	Knight	Cairnie	McCormack	Cairnie
26/04/2014	L	H	Falkirk	1	1	Caraux	Findlay	Russell	Robertson	Taggart	Imrie	Bachirou	Imrie	Vine	Cole	McKay	Caraux*	McNeil"	McKee	Knight	Cairnie	McCormack	McNeill
03/05/2014	L	A	Hamilton Accies	2	10	Caraux	Findlay	Russell	Robertson*	Taggart	Imrie	Bachirou	Imrie	Vine	Cole	McKay	Campbell"	O'Connor	McKee	Knight	Cairnie	Gaston	McNeill

Motherwell FC

Founded	1886
Ground	Fir Park
Postcode	ML1 2QN
Tel	01698 333333
Capacity	13677
Closest Railway Station	Airbles
Record Attendance	35632, v Rangers SC, 12/3/1952
Record Win	12-1 v Dundee United, Lge, 23/1/1954
Record Defeat	0-8 v Aberdeen, Lge, 26/3/1979
Most League Goals in a Season	52 Willie McSpadyen, 1931/2
Hon President	John Chapman OBE
Chief Executive	Leeann Dempster (until May) / Alan Burrows
Manager	Stuart McCall
Assistant Manager	Kenny Black
Colours 2013/14 Top	Amber with Claret Band
Shorts	White
Sponsor	Cash Converters
Manufacturer	Puma
Change Colours 2013/14 Top	Black
Shorts	Black
Nicknames	Well, Steelmen
Web	www.motherwellfc.co.uk

Craig Reid's injury time winner for Motherwell at Aberdeen on the last day of the season sealed second place for Stuart McColl's side. Their performances over recent seasons have been astonishing considering the resources that hey have available to them.

Motherwell's success last season was based on a sound defence. Stephen McManus proved to be a great signing and Shaun Hutchison's performances earned him a move to Fulham. McCall will have to look around the bargain basements again to see who he can bring in to bolster his squad for 2014/15.

One face departing was that of James McFadden who had a disappointing season lightened by a few flashes of brilliance.

PREDICTION 2014/15
Top four finish once again for the Well

Surname	First Name	DOB	Pos	L A	L S	L G	SC A	SC S	SC G	LC A	LC S	LC G	UC A	UC S	UC G	UNS	Signed Previous Club	Notes	Contract
Ainsworth	Lionel	01/10/87	M	22	7	11	1		1							4	2013 Rotherham United (loan)	Returned to Rotherham	
Anier	Henri	17/12/90	F	19	14	8	1		1				1		1	2	2013 Viking Stavanger	Joined Erzgebirge Aue June 2014	
Cadden	Chris		M			3										6	2013 Motherwell Youths		Youth
Carswell	Stuart	09/09/92	M	24	3		1			2		1				3	2010 Motherwell Youths		C (2015)
Cummins	Adam	03/03/93	D	1	2					1		1				17	2011 Everton	On loan to Dundee	C (2015)
Erwin	Lee	19/03/94	F													8	2013 Motherwell Youths		Youth
Francis Angol	Zaine	30/06/93	D	21	12	3	1			2			2			2	2012 Tottenham Hotspur		C (2015)
Hamell	Stevie	18/02/82	D	34		1				2		2				2	2008 Southend United		C (2016)
Hollis	Lee	12/02/86	GK	14								1				6	2010 Airdrie United		OOC
Hutchison	Shaun	23/11/90	D	35		1	1			2		2					2007 Wallsend BC	Joined Fulham June 2014	
Kerr	Fraser	17/01/93	D	10	9		1					1	1			7	2013 Birmingham City		C (2015)
Lasley	Keith	21/09/79	M	37		2	1		1			2				2	2006 Plymouth Argyle		C (2016)
Lawson	Paul	15/05/84	M	5	12		1			2		2				7	2013 Ross County		C (2016)
Leitch	Jack	17/07/95	M	6	3		1									12	2013 Motherwell Youths		C (2016)
McCafferty	Paul		F													1	2013 Motherwell Youths		Youth
McFadden	James	14/04/83	F	21	6	4	1			1		1	1			5	2013 Sunderland		F
McHugh	Bob	16/07/91	F	3	5	1	1			1	1	1				11	2008 Motherwell Youths	On loan to QOS	C (2015)
McManus	Stephen	10/09/82	D	37		4	1			2		2					2013 Middlesbrough		C (2016)
Moore	Craig	16/08/94	F	3	15	1				1		1				13	2013 Motherwell Youths		C (2016)
Murray	Euan	20/01/94	D	1	2											20	2013 Motherwell Youths		Youth
Neill	Morgyn		D													1	2013 Motherwell Youths		Youth
Nielsen	Gunnar	07/10/86	GK	19			1			2		1				17	2013 Silkeborg		C (2015)
Ramsden	Simon	17/12/81	D	18						2		2					2012 Bradford City		C (2015)
Reid	Craig	26/02/86	D	13	1	1											2014 Morton		C (2016)
Shirkie	Dale		F				1									4	2013 Motherwell Youths		Youth
Stewart	Ross	16/04/95	GK													20	2013 Motherwell Youths		OOC
Sutton	John	26/12/83	F	37	1	22	1			1		1				1	2013 Hearts		C (2015)
Thomas	Dominic		M													12	2013 Motherwell Youths		Youth
Twardzik	Dan	13/04/91	GK	5													2013 Dundee (loan)	Returned to Dundee	
Vigurs	Iain	07/03/88	M	33	3	4				1		2					2013 Ross County		C (2015)
Own Goal						1													

NEW SIGNINGS 2014/15

Surname	First Name	DOB	Pos	Signed Previous Club
Twardzik	Dan	13/04/91	GK	2014 Dundee
Law	Josh	20/07/89	M	2014 Alfreton Town

Date	Comp	H/A	Opponents	F	A		Crowd	Scorers
01/08/2013	EUL	H	Kuban Krasnodar	0	2		6748	
03/08/2013	Prem	A	Hibernian	1	0		9237	Anier
08/08/2013	EUL	A	Kuban Krasnodar	0	1		31754	
11/08/2013	Prem	H	Aberdeen	1	3		6242	Anier
17/08/2013	Prem	A	Inverness CT	0	2		3031	
24/08/2013	Prem	H	Partick Thistle	1	0		5527	Sutton
31/08/2013	Prem	H	Kilmanock	2	1		4353	Anier, Sutton
14/09/2013	Prem	A	St Mirren	1	0		4012	Sutton
22/09/2013	Prem	A	Dundee United	2	2		5808	Anier, Ainsworth
25/09/2013	LC3	A	Livingston	2	1		1660	McHugh, McFadden
28/09/2013	Prem	A	Ross County	3	1		4263	Sutton 2, McHugh
05/10/2013	Prem	A	Celtic	0	2		46608	
19/10/2013	Prem	H	Hearts	2	1		5350	Moore, Hutchison
26/10/2013	Prem	A	St Johnstone	0	2		2449	
30/10/2013	LC4	H	Aberdeen	0	2		6995	
03/11/2013	Prem	H	Hibernian	1	0		3864	McManus
09/11/2013	Prem	H	Dundee United	0	4		5103	
23/11/2013	Prem	A	Kilmanock	2	0		3704	Sutton, Anier
30/11/2013	SC4	A	Albion Rovers	0	1	at Hamilton	2950	
06/12/2013	Prem	H	Celtic	0	5		9117	
14/12/2013	Prem	A	Ross County	2	1		2792	Sutton 2
21/12/2013	Prem	H	St Mirren	3	0		3867	Anier 2, Ainsworth
26/12/2013	Prem	A	Aberdeen	1	0		12494	Ainsworth
29/12/2013	Prem	A	Partick Thistle	5	1		4588	Lasley, Franis-Angol, McFadden, Ainsworth, Sutton
01/01/2014	Prem	H	St Johnstone	4	0		3763	Sutton, Vigurs, Ainsworth, McFadden
11/01/2014	Prem	A	Hearts	1	0		12888	Sutton
18/01/2014	Prem	A	Celtic	0	3		47489	
25/01/2014	Prem	H	Aberdeen	2	2		5756	McManus, Francis-Angol
15/02/2014	Prem	H	Partick Thistle	4	3		5048	Lasley, Ainsworth, McManus, Sutton
21/02/2014	Prem	A	Dundee United	1	3		7029	Sutton
25/02/2014	Prem	A	St Johnstone	0	3		1892	
01/03/2014	Prem	H	Hearts	4	1		4914	Vigurs, Ainsworth, Sutton, McFadden
08/03/2014	Prem	A	Hibernian	3	3		8277	Sutton 2, Ainsworth
12/03/2014	Prem	H	Inverness CT	2	0		3432	Ainsworth, Sutton
22/03/2014	Prem	H	Ross County	2	1		4080	McFadden, Sutton
29/03/2014	Prem	H	Kilmanock	1	2		4467	Vigurs
01/04/2014	Prem	A	Inverness CT	2	1		2366	Anier, Vigurs
05/04/2014	Prem	A	St Mirren	2	3		4377	Anier, Sutton
19/04/2014	Prem	H	Celtic	3	3		7493	Sutton 2, Francis-Angol
26/04/2014	Prem	A	Dundee United	1	5		6383	Ainsworth
03/05/2014	Prem	H	St Johnstone	2	1		7201	Ainsorth, McManus
07/05/2014	Prem	H	Inverness CT	2	1		4482	Sutton, Warren og
11/05/2014	Prem	A	Aberdeen	1	0		17016	Reid

Friendly Games

Date	Comp	H/A	Opponents	F	A	Crowd		
11/7/13	Fr	A	Craigroyston	2	0		U20	
13/7/13	Fr	A	Doncaster Rovers	0	0	1983		
16/7/13	Fr	H	Newcastle United	2	4	4475		
20/7/13	Fr	A	Cowdenbeath	5	0		Res	
20/7/13	Fr	A	Morecambe	2	1	1015		
26/7/13	Fr	H	Nottingham Forest	1	1	2230		
27/7/13	TnT	N	St Mirren U20	4	1		U20	at Irvine Meadow
28/7/13	TnT	N	Partick Thistle U20	2	3		U20	at Irvine Meadow
3/8/13	Fr	A	Wishaw				U20	
4/8/13	Fr	A	Bathgate Thistle	1	5		U20	

Date	Comp	H/A	Opponents	F	A	1	2	3	4	5	6	7	8	9	10	11	12	13	14	15	16	17	18
01/08/2013	EUL	H	Kuban Krasnodar	0	2	Hollis	Hamell	Hutchison	Ramsden	McManus	Francis-Angol	Lawson*	Vigurs	Lasley	McFadden+	Sutton	Anier*	Kerr+	Cummins	Carswell	McHugh	Moore	Nielsen
03/08/2013	EUL	A	Hibernian	1	0	Hollis	Hamell	Hutchison	Ramsden	McManus	McHugh*	Lawson*	Vigurs	Lasley	McFadden+	Sutton	Anier*	Francis-Angol+	Francis-Angol*	Cummins	Erwin	Kerr	Nielsen
08/08/2013	EUL	A	Kuban Krasnodar	0	1	Nielsen	Hamell	Hutchison	Ramsden	McManus	Francis-Angol	Sutton	Kerr	Lasley*	Carswell	Anier+	McHugh*	Cummins+	Moore*	Lawson	Carswell	McCafferty	Hollis
11/08/2013	Prem	A	Aberdeen	0	1	Hollis	Hamell	Hutchison	Ramsden	McManus	Francis-Angol	Sutton*	Vigurs	Lasley	McFadden+	Sutton	Kerr*	Anier+	Moore*	Moore	Carswell	Kerr	Nielsen
17/08/2013	Prem	H	Inverness CT	1	3	Hollis	Hamell	Hutchison	Ramsden	McManus	Francis-Angol*	Lawson*	Vigurs	Lasley	McFadden+	Sutton	McHugh*	McHugh+	Vigurs*	Erwin	Erwin	Erwin	Nielsen
24/08/2013	Prem	A	Partick Thistle	1	0	Hollis	Hamell	Hutchison	Ramsden	McManus	Anier*	Sutton	Anier+	Lasley	McFadden+	Sutton	Kerr*	Kerr+	Moore*	Moore	McHugh	Cummins	Nielsen
31/08/2013	Prem	H	Kilmarnock	1	0	Hollis	Hamell	Hutchison	Anier*	McManus	Francis-Angol	McHugh+	Vigurs+	Lasley	McFadden+	Sutton	Carswell*	Anier+	Kerr*	Moore	McHugh	Cummins	Nielsen
14/09/2013	Prem	A	St Mirren	1	0	Hollis	Hamell	Hutchison	Ramsden	McManus	Francis-Angol	Anier+	Vigurs*	Lasley	Anier+	Sutton	Lawson*	Kerr+	Lawson*	Moore	McHugh	Cummins	Nielsen
22/09/2013	Prem	H	Dundee United	2	2	Nielsen	Hamell	Hutchison	Ramsden	McManus	Francis-Angol	Carswell*	Vigurs*	Lasley	McFadden+*	Sutton	McHugh*	Francis-Angol+	Cummins*	Lawson	Ainsworth+	Leitch	Nielsen
25/09/2013	LC3	A	Livingston	2	1	Hollis	Hamell	Hutchison	Ramsden	McManus	Francis-Angol*	Carswell	Lawson*	Lasley	McFadden+	Sutton	Ainsworth*	McFadden+	Vigurs*	Sutton	Hollis	Kerr	Murray
28/09/2013	Prem	H	Ross County	3	1	Hollis	Hamell	Hutchison	Ramsden	McManus	Francis-Angol	Carswell	Vigurs	Lasley	Anier+	Sutton	Ainsworth*	McHugh+	Vigurs*	Lawson	Cummins	Kerr	Murray
05/10/2013	Prem	A	Celtic	0	2	Hollis	Hamell	Hutchison	Ramsden	McManus	Lawson	Carswell	Lawson*	Lasley	Ainsworth+	Sutton	Ainsworth*	Ainsworth+	Lawson*	Moore	Cummins	McHugh	Ainsworth
19/10/2013	Prem	H	Hearts	2	1	Nielsen	Hamell	Hutchison	Ramsden	McManus	Francis-Angol	Carswell*	Lawson*	Lasley	Moore+	Sutton	Moore*	Moore+	McHugh*	Kerr	Stewart	McHugh	Moore
26/10/2013	Prem	A	St Johnstone	0	2	Nielsen	Hamell	Hutchison	Ramsden	McManus	Francis-Angol	Carswell	Ainsworth	Lasley	Anier+	Sutton	Anier*	McHugh+	Lawson*	Kerr	Stewart	McHugh	Leitch
30/10/2013	LC4	H	Aberdeen	0	2	Nielsen	Hamell+	Hutchison	Ramsden+	McManus	McFadden*	Carswell	Lawson	Lasley	Moore+	Sutton+	Lawson*	McFadden+	McHugh*	Lawson	Kerr	McHugh	Carswell
03/11/2013	Prem	H	Hibernian	1	0	Nielsen	Hamell	Cummins*	Ramsden	McManus*	Ainsworth	Carswell+	Anier	Lasley	Anier+	McHugh+	Francis-Angol*	McFadden+	McFadden+	Stewart	Stewart	Stewart	Moore
09/11/2013	Prem	H	Dundee United	0	4	Nielsen	Hamell	Hutchison	Ramsden	McManus	Ainsworth+	Carswell+	Vigurs	Lasley	Anier+	Sutton	Moore+	Murray+	Vigurs*	Lawson	Vigurs	Anier	Leitch
23/11/2013	Prem	A	Kilmarnock	2	0	Nielsen	Kerr	Kerr	Vigurs	McManus	Ainsworth*	Carswell	Vigurs+	Lasley	Anier+	McFadden+	Anier*	Anier+	Moore*	Cummins	Moore	Murray	Francis-Angol
30/11/2013	SC4	A	Albion Rovers (at Hamilton)	0	1	Nielsen	Hamell	Hutchison	Kerr	McManus	Ainsworth*	Moore+	Kerr	Anier	McFadden+	Moore+	Kerr*	Leitch+	Kerr*	Lawson	Stewart	Murray	Ainsworth
06/12/2013	Prem	H	Hearts	0	5	Nielsen	Hamell	Hutchison	Ramsden	McManus	Ainsworth	Carswell	Vigurs*	Lasley	Moore+	Sutton	Cummins*	Anier+	Lawson*	Cummins	Stewart	McFadden	Leitch
14/12/2013	Prem	A	Ross County	2	1	Twardzik	Hamell	Hutchison	Ramsden	McManus	Ainsworth	Carswell	Vigurs*	Lasley	Anier+	Sutton	Moore*	McFadden+	Lawson*	Cummins	Moore	McHugh	Thomas
21/12/2013	Prem	H	St Mirren	3	0	Twardzik	Hamell	Hutchison	Ramsden	McManus	Ainsworth*	Carswell	Vigurs+	Lasley	Anier+	Sutton	Moore*	Anier+	McFadden*	Cummins	McHugh	Murray	Thomas
26/12/2013	Prem	A	Aberdeen	1	0	Twardzik	Hamell	Hutchison	Ramsden	McManus	Ainsworth+	Carswell	Vigurs	Lasley	Anier+	Sutton	Moore*	Anier+	Lawson*	Cummins	Moore	Murray	Thomas
29/12/2013	Prem	A	Partick Thistle	5	1	Twardzik	Hamell	Francis-Angol	Francis-Angol	McManus	Ainsworth	Carswell+	Kerr*	Lasley	Anier*	Sutton	Francis-Angol*	Francis-Angol+	McHugh*	Vigurs	Moore	Murray	Stewart
01/01/2014	Prem	H	St Johnstone	4	0	Twardzik	Hamell+	Hutchison	Ramsden	McManus	Ainsworth*	Carswell	Vigurs*	Lasley	McFadden+	McFadden+	Moore*	McFadden+	Lawson*	Cummins	McHugh	Francis-Angol	Leitch
11/01/2014	Prem	H	Hearts	1	0	Nielsen	Hamell	Hutchison	Ramsden	McManus	Ainsworth	Carswell	Vigurs	Lasley	McFadden*	Sutton+	Kerr*	Lawson+	Lawson*	Cummins	Moore	Murray	Thomas
18/01/2014	Prem	A	Celtic	0	3	Nielsen	Reid	Hutchison	Ramsden	McManus	Ainsworth*	Leitch	Vigurs	Lasley	McFadden+	Sutton	Anier*	Anier+	Leitch*	Stewart	Leitch	Shirkie	Thomas
25/01/2014	Prem	A	Aberdeen	2	3	Nielsen	Reid	Hutchison	Ramsden	McManus	Ainsworth*	Carswell	Kerr*	Lasley	McFadden+	McFadden+	Kerr*	Francis-Angol+	Francis-Angol+	Stewart	Hollis	Shirkie	Thomas
15/02/2014	Prem	A	Partick Thistle	2	1	Nielsen	Reid	Hutchison	Francis-Angol	McManus	Ainsworth	Carswell	Vigurs+	Lasley	McFadden	Sutton	Lawson*	Lawson+	Lawson*	Cummins	Leitch	Cadden	Stewart
22/02/2014	Prem	H	Dundee United	1	3	Nielsen	Reid	Hutchison	Francis-Angol	McManus	Ainsworth	Francis-Angol*	Vigurs*	Lasley	McFadden+	Sutton+	Anier*	Francis-Angol+	Lawson*	Stewart	Murray	Thomas	Thomas
25/02/2014	Prem	A	St Johnstone	0	1	Nielsen	Reid*	Hutchison	Francis-Angol	McManus	Ainsworth	Leitch*	Kerr	Lasley	McFadden+	Sutton	Reid*	Ainsworth+	Leitch*	Murray	Leitch	Thomas	Thomas
01/03/2014	Prem	H	Hearts	4	1	Hollis	Reid	Hutchison	Francis-Angol*	McManus	Ainsworth*	Leitch*	Vigurs+	Lasley	Moore*	McHugh+	McFadden*	Carswell+	Cadden*	Murray	Nielsen	Thomas	Leitch
08/03/2014	Prem	H	Hibernian	3	3	Nielsen	Reid	Hutchison	Murray	McManus	Ainsworth	Leitch*	Vigurs	Lasley	Moore*	Sutton	Murray*	Cadden+	Shirkie*	Murray	Stewart	Murray	Neill
12/03/2014	Prem	H	Inverness CT	2	0	Nielsen	Reid*	Hutchison	Hamell	McManus	Ainsworth	Leitch	Vigurs	Lasley+	Anier+	Sutton	Moore*	Cadden+	Shirkie*	Shirkie	Shirkie	Leitch	Thomas
22/03/2014	Prem	A	Ross County	2	1	Nielsen	Reid	Ainsworth+	Hamell	McManus	Ainsworth+	Francis-Angol	Vigurs	Lasley	Anier+	Sutton	Francis-Angol*	Francis-Angol+	Kerr*	Erwin	Ainsworth	Thomas	Thomas
29/03/2014	Prem	H	Kilmarnock	1	2	Nielsen	Reid	Hutchison	Hamell	McManus	Kerr	Francis-Angol+	Vigurs	Lasley	Anier+	Sutton	Moore*	Leitch+	Cadden*	Ainsworth+	Murray	Thomas	Stewart
01/04/2014	Prem	A	Inverness CT	2	1	Nielsen	Reid	Hutchison	Hamell	McManus	Kerr	Ainsworth	Vigurs*	Lasley+	Anier*	Sutton	Anier*	Moore+	Cadden*	Murray	Stewart	Thomas	Stewart
05/04/2014	Prem	H	St Mirren	2	3	Nielsen	Reid	Hutchison	Hamell	McManus	Kerr	Ainsworth+	Vigurs	Lasley	Anier*	Sutton	Moore*	Francis-Angol+	Francis-Angol*	Murray	Hollis	Thomas	Cadden
19/04/2014	Prem	A	Celtic	3	3	Hollis	Reid	Hutchison	Hamell	McManus	Kerr*	Ainsworth*	Vigurs*	Francis-Angol	Anier+	Sutton	Moore*	Moore+	Erwin	Hollis	Leitch	Thomas	Cadden
26/04/2014	Prem	H	Dundee United	1	5	Hollis	Reid	Hutchison	Hamell	McManus	Kerr	Ainsworth*	Vigurs	Lasley	Anier+	Sutton	Moore*	Ainsworth+	Moore*	Leitch	Leitch	McFadden	Cadden
03/05/2014	Prem	A	St Johnstone	2	1	Nielsen	Reid	Hutchison	Hamell	McManus	Francis-Angol	Ainsworth*	Vigurs*	Lasley	McFadden+	McFadden+	Moore*	Kerr+	Moore*	Leitch	Cadden	Thomas	Cadden
07/05/2014	Prem	H	Inverness CT	2	1	Hollis	Hollis	Hutchison	Hamell	McManus	Francis-Angol	Ainsworth+	Vigurs	Lasley	McFadden+	Sutton	Kerr*	Anier+	Moore*	Leitch	Leitch	Erwin	Nielsen
11/05/2014	Prem	A	Aberdeen	1	0	Nielsen	Reid	Hutchison	Hamell	McManus*	McManus*	Ainsworth*	Vigurs	Lasley	Kerr	Sutton	Anier*	Leitch+	McFadden*	Murray	Cadden	Erwin	Nielsen

Partick Thistle FC

Founded	1876
Ground	Firhill Stadium
Postcode	G20 7AL
Tel	0871 402 1971
Capacity	10102
Closest Railway Station	St Georges X / Kelvin Bridge (Subway)
Record Attendance	49838 v Rangers, Lge, 18/2/1922
Record Win	16-0 v Royal Albert, SC, 17/1/1931
Record Defeat	0-10 v Queen's Park, SC, 3/12/1881
Most League Goals in a Season	41 Alex Hair, 1926/7
Chairman	David Beattie
General Manager	Ian Maxwell
Manager	Alan Archibald
Assistant Manager	Scott Paterson
Colours 2013/14 Top	Red and Yellow Stripes
Shorts	Black
Sponsor	MacB Water
Manufacturer	Joma
Change Colours 2013/14 Top	Grey with Black Chest Band
Shorts	White
Nicknames	Jags, Harry Wraggs

The general view was that Partick Thistle would struggle on their return to the top flight. However, the doubters were proved wrong as the Jags were more than competitive and stayed up with a little to spare.

They took a long time to get their first home win but good counter-attacking performances away from hope helped boost their points haul.

Manager Alan Archibald did some shrewd deals in the January transfer window which injected more pace and striking quality into his team.

Attendances at some games demonstrated the potential that there is at Firhill - perhaps Friday night football should be something the club should look at on a more regular basis?

PREDICTION 2014/15
"Second season up" is always difficult but Thistle should have enough to push towards the top of the bottom half

Surname	First Name	DOB	Pos	LA	LS	LG	SCA	SCS	SCG	LCA	LCS	LCG	UNS	Signed	Previous Club	Notes	Contract
Baird	John	22/08/85	F	2	11					2	1		8	2013	Dundee	Released Jan 2014 and joined Raith Rovers	
Balatoni	Conrad	27/07/91	D	31		1	1			2		1		2012	Hearts		C (2015)
Bannigan	Stuart	17/09/92	M	33						1	1			2009	Partick Thistle U17		C (2016)
Basalaj	Scott	19/04/94	GK											2013	Wellington Phoenix		ONC
Buaben	Prince	23/04/88	M	9	2									2014	Carlisle United (loan)	Returned to Carlisle	
Colina Dominguez	Simon	07/02/95											1	2013	Barcelona		C (2015)
Craigen	James	28/03/91	M	26	6		1			1	1		6	2012	Edinburgh University		C (2015)
Doolan	Kris	11/12/86	F	22	14	11	1			1	1		1	2009	Auchinleck Talbot		C (2015)
Elliot	Christie	17/07/92	M	11	19	1	1	1		2	1	2	9	2011	Whitley Bay		C (2015)
Erskine	Chris	08/02/87	F	14	1	2								2014	Dundee United (loan)	Returned to Dundee Utd	
Forbes	Ross	03/03/89	M	1	14	1	1			3			8	2012	Motherwell	Joined Dunfermline Mar 2014	
Fox	Scott	28/06/87	GK	21			1			3			16	2010	Dundee		C (2015)
Fraser	Gary	02/07/94	M	18	1	2							9	2013	Bolton Wanderers (Loan)	Move made permanent during 2013/14	C (2017)
Gallacher	Paul	16/08/79	GK	17	1								24	2013	Ross County		C (2015)
Gallacher	Lee		M										1	2012	Partick Thistle U17		ONC
Higginbotham	Kallum	15/06/89	F	33	3	8	1			2				2013	Huddersfield Town		C (2015)
Keenan	Dale		D										3	2011	Celtic		ONC
Kerr	Mark	02/03/82	M				1			3			17	2013	Dundee	Freed Jan 2014 and joined QOS	
Lawless	Steven	12/04/91	F	17	11	4				1	2	1	9	2012	Motherwell		C(2015)
Lindsay	Liam	12/10/95	D	1										2012	Partick Thistle U17	Nephew of Ricky Gillies, ex St Mirren etc	ONC
Mair	Lee	09/12/80	D	17	2									2014	St Mirren		F
McDaid	Declan	22/11/95	W										1	2013	Morton		F
McMillan	Jordan	16/10/88	D	16		1							8	2013	Dunfermline Athletic		C (2015)
Meechan	Ross		D										2	2013	St Mirren		F
Moncur	George	18/08/93	M		2	1							11	2014	West Ham United (loan)	Returned to West Ham	
Muirhead	Aaron	30/08/90	D	18	2	3	1			1		1	6	2012	Annan Athletic		C (2015)
Mukendi	Henoc	20/11/93	F						1				3	2013	Liverpool (Loan)	Returned to Liverpool	
O'Donnell	Stephen	11/05/92	D	23	4					3		1	4	2011	Celtic		C (2015)
Osbourne	Isaac	22/06/86	M	11	1		1			1			5	2013	Aberdeen		F
Piccolo	Gabriel	15/10/89	D	15	2		1			3			12	2013	Rayo Vallecano B	Also known as Gabriel De La Vega	C (2015)
Sinclair	Aaron	08/04/91	D	36	2	1				3				2011	Montrose	Joined Wigan Athletic June 2014	
Taylor	Lyle	29/03/90	F	17	3	7								2014	Sheffield United (loan)	Returned to Sheffield Utd	
Waters	Marc	01/01/96	GK										1	2013	Partick Thistle U17		C (2015)
Welsh	Sean	15/03/90	D	10						1	1			2012	Hibernian		C (2015)
Wilson	David	15/03/90	D			1							11	2011	Raith Rovers BC		ONC

NEW SIGNINGS 2014/14

Surname	First Name	DOB	Signed	Previous Club
Stevenson	Ryan		2014	Hearts

Date	Comp	H/A	Opponents	F	A		Crowd	Scorers
02/08/2013	Prem	H	Dundee United	0	0		7822	
06/08/2013	LC1	H	Ayr United	2	1		2145	O'Donnell, Balatoni
10/08/2013	Prem	A	Ross County	3	1		3331	Doolan, Lawless 2
16/08/2013	Prem	H	Hearts	1	1		6540	Muirhead
24/08/2013	Prem	A	Motherwell	0	1		5527	
27/08/2013	LC2	H	Cowdenbeath	3	1	AET	1544	Elliot, Lawless, Muirhead
31/08/2013	Prem	A	St Mirren	2	1		5601	Higginbotham, Forbes
14/09/2013	Prem	H	Aberdeen	0	3		6193	
21/09/2013	Prem	H	Kilmarnock	1	1		4310	Muirhead
25/09/2013	LC3	A	Dundee United	1	4		3778	Elliot
28/09/2013	Prem	A	St Johnstone	1	1		3248	Doolan
07/10/2013	Prem	H	Hibernian	0	1		4521	
20/10/2013	Prem	A	Inverness CT	2	1		3154	Doolan 2
27/10/2013	Prem	H	Celtic	1	2		7978	Doolan
04/11/2013	Prem	A	Aberdeen	0	4		10057	
09/11/2013	Prem	H	St Mirren	0	3		4946	
23/11/2013	Prem	A	Dundee United	1	4		6700	Muirhead
01/12/2013	SC4	H	Aberdeen	0	1		3642	
07/12/2013	Prem	A	Hibernian	1	1		10431	Doolan
21/12/2013	Prem	A	Kilmarnock	1	2		3865	Dolan
26/12/2013	Prem	H	Inverness CT	0	0		2887	
29/12/2013	Prem	H	Motherwell	1	5		4588	Lawless
01/01/2014	Prem	A	Celtic	0	1		52670	
05/01/2014	Prem	A	Hearts	2	0		13763	Taylor, Sinclair
11/01/2014	Prem	H	Ross County	3	3		3539	Taylor 2, Lawless
18/01/2014	Prem	H	Kilmarnock	1	1		4092	Higginbotham
21/01/2014	Prem	H	St Johnstone	0	1		2719	
25/01/2014	Prem	A	St Mirren	0	0		4660	
01/02/2014	Prem	H	Dundee United	1	1		3748	Fraser
15/02/2014	Prem	A	Motherwell	3	4		5048	Erskine, Higginbotham 2
22/02/2014	Prem	H	Aberdeen	3	1		4554	Balatoni, Taylor 2
01/03/2014	Prem	A	Ross County	1	1		3441	Higginbotham
15/03/2014	Prem	H	Hibernian	3	1		4448	Erskine, Mair, Higginbotham
22/03/2014	Prem	A	Inverness CT	0	1		3093	
26/03/2014	Prem	H	Celtic	1	5		7549	Elliot
29/03/2014	Prem	A	St Johnstone	1	1		2999	Doolan
05/04/2014	Prem	H	Hearts	2	4		4262	Doolan, McMillan
19/04/2014	Prem	A	Kilmarnock	2	1		4980	Higinbotham, Sinclair
25/04/2014	Prem	H	St Mirren	1	1		5971	Doolan
03/05/2014	Prem	A	Hibernian	1	1		10740	Doolan
07/05/2014	Prem	A	Hearts	4	2		14059	Taylor, Fraser, Mair, Higginbotham
10/05/2014	Prem	H	Ross County	2	3		4390	Taylor, Moncur

Friendly Games

Date	Comp	H/A	Opponents	F	A		Crowd	Scorers
6/7/13	Fr	A	Gateshead	1	2		602	at Durham City
9/7/13	Fr	A	Annan Athletic	5	1			
13/7/13	Fr	A	Dumbarton	4	3			
16/7/13	Fr	A	Livingston	0	0			
20/7/13	Fr	A	Arbroath	0	1			
20/7/13	Fr	A	Petershill	2	1		U20	
24/7/13	Fr	A	Arthurlie	3	3		U20	
27/7/13	Fr	H	AEL Limassol	0	0			
27/7/13	TnT	A	Irvine Meadow	5	2		U20	
28/7/13	TnT	N	Motherwell U20	3	2		U20	at Irvine Meadow
18/1/14	Fr	A	Arthurlie	6	1		U20	

Date	Comp	H/A	Opponents	F	A		1	2	3	4	5	6	7	8	9	10	11	12	13	14	15	16	17	18
02/08/2013	Prem	H	Dundee United	0	0		Fox	O'Donnell	Sinclair	Muirhead	Balatoni	Welsh	Bannigan	Fraser*	Craigen+	Doolan*	Lawless	Baird*	Mukendi	Elliot+	Kerr	Osborne	Forbes"	Gallacher
06/08/2013	LC1	H	Ayr United	2	1		Fox	O'Donnell	Sinclair	De la Vega	Balatoni	Forbes"	Elliot*	Osborne+	Kerr	Baird	Lawless	Bannigan*	Welsh+	Mukendi"	Craigen	Osborne	Kerr	Gallacher
10/08/2013	Prem	A	Ross County	3	1		Fox	O'Donnell	Sinclair	Muirhead	Balatoni	Welsh	Bannigan+	Fraser	Craigen	Doolan+	Higginbotham	Baird*	Higginbotham*	Forbes	Elliot	Osborne	Kerr	Gallacher
16/08/2013	Prem	H	Hearts	1	1		Fox	O'Donnell	Sinclair	Muirhead	Balatoni	Welsh*	Bannigan	Fraser*	Craigen	Doolan+	Higginbotham	Higginbotham"	Baird+	Forbes	Elliot	Osborne	Kerr	Gallacher
24/08/2013	Prem	A	Motherwell	0	1		Fox	O'Donnell	Sinclair	Muirhead	Balatoni	Osbourne"	Bannigan	Fraser*	Craigen	Doolan*	Lawless	Higginbotham*	Baird*	Forbes"	Elliot"	De la Vega	Kerr	Gallacher
27/08/2013	LC2	A	Cowdenbeath	3	1	AET	Fox	O'Donnell	Sinclair	Muirhead	De La Vega	Forbes	Bannigan	Kerr"-	Craigen*	Baird*	Higginbotham"	Lawless*	Doolan+	Elliot"	Osbourne	Gallacher	Fraser	Gallacher
31/08/2013	Prem	A	St Mirren	2	1		Fox	O'Donnell	Sinclair	Muirhead	De la Vega	Osbourne+	Bannigan	Lawless"	Craigen+	Baird*	Higginbotham	Doolan+	Forbes+	Elliot*	Osbourne	De la Vega	Fraser	Gallacher
14/09/2013	Prem	H	Aberdeen	0	3		Fox	O'Donnell	Sinclair	Muirhead	De la Vega	Welsh*	Bannigan	Lawless"	Craigen+	Baird*	Higginbotham	Osbourne"	Forbes+	Doolan"	Elliot	Elliot	Fraser	Gallacher
21/09/2013	Prem	A	Kilmarnock	1	1		Fox	O'Donnell	Sinclair	Muirhead	Balatoni	Welsh	Bannigan	Lawless*	Osbourne	Baird"	Higginbotham	Elliot*	Forbes+	Doolan"	Kerr	Gallacher	Fraser	Baird
25/09/2013	LC3	A	Dundee United	1	4		Gallacher	De La Vega	Sinclair	De la Vega	Balatoni	Welsh	Forbes+	Lawless"	Kerr	Doolan*	Higginbotham"	Baird*	Lawless+	Craigen"	Osbourne	Gallacher"	Fraser	Fox
28/09/2013	Prem	H	St Johnstone	1	1		Fox	O'Donnell	Sinclair	Muirhead	Balatoni	Welsh	Forbes+	Elliot	Osbourne	Doolan	Higginbotham	Craigen*	Forbes	Lawless	Craigen	Kerr	Fraser	Fox
07/10/2013	Prem	H	Hibernian	0	1		Fox	O'Donnell	Sinclair	Muirhead	Balatoni	Welsh	Bannigan+	Lawless"	Osbourne	Doolan	Higginbotham	Elliot*	Baird+	Forbes*	Craigen	Gallacher	Fraser	De la Vega
20/10/2013	Prem	A	Inverness CT	2	1		Fox	O'Donnell	Sinclair	Muirhead	Balatoni	Welsh	Bannigan*	Craigen+	Osbourne	Doolan	Higginbotham+	Elliot*	Lawless+	Forbes	Wilson	Gallacher	Fraser	De la Vega
27/10/2013	Prem	H	Celtic	1	2		Fox	O'Donnell	Sinclair	McMillan*	Balatoni	Welsh	Bannigan*	Craigen+	Osbourne	Doolan	Higginbotham"	Elliot*	Forbes+	Baird*	Baird	Gallacher	Kerr	Mukendi
04/11/2013	Prem	A	Aberdeen	0	4		Fox	O'Donnell	Sinclair	McMillan*	De la Vega	Welsh	Bannigan"	Craigen+	Osbourne	Doolan*	Higginbotham"	Elliot*	Forbes+	Muirhead"	McMillan	Gallacher	Wilson	Baird
09/11/2013	Prem	A	St Mirren	0	3		Fox	O'Donnell	Sinclair	De la Vega*	Balatoni	Lawless+	Elliot*	Bannigan"	Craigen	Doolan	Higginbotham"	Elliot*	Elliot+	Baird	McMillan	Gallacher	Wilson	De la Vega
23/11/2013	Prem	H	Dundee United	1	4		Fox	McMillan	Sinclair	Muirhead	Balatoni	Forbes+	Elliot*	Bannigan"	Osbourne	Doolan	Higginbotham"	Lawless*	Elliot+	Baird	Kerr	Gallacher	Wilson	De la Vega
01/12/2013	SC4	H	Aberdeen	0	1		Fox	De La Vega	Sinclair	Kerr*	Balatoni	Forbes+	Elliot*	Bannigan	Craigen	Doolan*	Higginbotham	Welsh*	Lawless+	Baird*	Wilson	Gallacher	Mukendi	Meechan
07/12/2013	Prem	H	Hibernian	1	1		Fox	De La Vega	Sinclair	De la Vega	McMillan	Lawless*	Elliot+	Craigen+	Osbourne	Doolan*	Higginbotham+	Welsh*	Baird+	Lindsay"	Wilson	Gallacher	Kerr	Meechan
21/12/2013	Prem	A	Kilmarnock	1	2		Fox	De La Vega	Sinclair	De la Vega	Balatoni	Lawless*	Elliot+	Bannigan	Craigen	Doolan*	Higginbotham+	Elliot*	O'Donnell+	Forbes"	Wilson	Gallacher	Kerr	Muirhead
26/12/2013	Prem	H	Inverness CT	0	0		Fox	De La Vega	Sinclair	McMillan*	Balatoni	Lawless*	Bannigan	Elliot*	Osbourne	Doolan	Higginbotham	Elliot*	Forbes+	Baird"	Muirhead	Gallacher	Kerr	Muirhead
29/12/2013	Prem	H	Motherwell	1	5		Fox	De La Vega	Sinclair	O'Donnell	Balatoni	Lawless+	Bannigan	Elliot	Osbourne	Doolan	Higginbotham+	Forbes"	Lawless+	Wilson"	Wilson	P Gallacher	Kerr	L.Gallacher
01/01/2014	Prem	A	Celtic	0	4		Fox	De La Vega	Sinclair	O'Donnell	Balatoni	Muirhead"	Brannigan	Elliot	Osbourne	Taylor+	Higginbotham	Elliot*	Doolan+	Baird"	Forbes	P Gallacher	Kerr	Baird
05/01/2014	Prem	A	Hearts	2	0		Fox	McMillan	Sinclair	O'Donnell	Balatoni	Muirhead	Bannigan	Elliot	Lawless"	Taylor +	Higginbotham	Lawless*	Doolan+	McMillan	Forbes	P Gallacher	Wilson	McMillan
11/01/2014	Prem	A	Ross County	3	0		Fox	Mair	Sinclair	O'Donnell	Balatoni	Fraser*	Bannigan	Craigen+	Lawless +	Taylor	Higginbotham	Forbes*	Doolan+	Baird"	Forbes	P Gallacher	Fraser	Baird
18/01/2014	Prem	A	Kilmarnock	1	1		Gallacher	Mair	Sinclair	O'Donnell	Balatoni	Fraser*	Erskine	Craigen+	Erskine"	Taylor	Higginbotham	Elliot*	Elliot+	Doolan"	Wilson	Waters	McMillan	Forbes
21/01/2014	Prem	H	St Johnstone	0	1		Gallacher	Mair	McMillan	McMillan	Balatoni	Fraser*	Bannigan	Erskine	Lawless +	Taylor	Higginbotham+	Doolan"	O'Donnell+	Forbes"	Muirhead	Fox	De La Vega	Wilson
25/01/2014	Prem	A	St Mirren	0	0		Gallacher	Mair	Sinclair	McMillan	Balatoni	Muirhead	Bannigan	Erskine"	Erskine"	Taylor	Higginbotham+	Lawless*	Doolan+	Elliot*	O'Donnell	Fox	Fraser	Forbes
01/02/2014	Prem	H	Motherwell	3	4		Gallacher	Mair	Sinclair	McMillan*	Balatoni*	Fraser	Bannigan	Buaben"	Erskine+	Taylor	Higginbotham	O'Donnell*	Doolan+	Craigen"	Muirhead	Fox	Lawless	Moncur
15/02/2014	Prem	A	Aberdeen	3	4		Gallacher	Mair	Sinclair	McMillan	Balatoni	Fraser	Bannigan	Buaben	Erskine	Taylor*	Higginbotham	Doolan*	Elliot+	Craigen"	Muirhead	Fox	Lawless	O'Donnell
22/02/2014	Prem	H	Ross County	1	1		Gallacher	Mair	Sinclair	McMillan	Balatoni	Fraser*	Bannigan	Buaben	Erskine	Taylor*	Higginbotham	Doolan*	O'Donnell+	Lawless	Lawless	Fox	Elliot	Moncur
01/03/2014	Prem	H	Inverness CT	0	1		Gallacher	Mair	Sinclair	O'Donnell	De La Vega	Fraser*	Bannigan	Buaben	Erskine+	Taylor*	Higginbotham	Doolan*	Craigen	Lawless	De La Vega	Fox	Elliot	Moncur
15/03/2014	Prem	A	Celtic	1	5		Gallacher	Mair	Sinclair	McMillan	De La Vega	Fraser"	Doolan	Bannigan	Erskine+	Taylor*	Higginbotham+	Elliot*	Lawless+	Craigen"	De La Vega	Fox	McMillan	Moncur
22/03/2014	Prem	A	St Johnstone	1	1		Gallacher	Mair	Sinclair	McMillan	De La Vega	Fraser*	Buaben	Bannigan	Erskine+	Taylor*	Higginbotham+	Buaben"	Lawless+	Moncur"	Craigen	Fox	McMillan	Elliot
26/03/2014	Prem	H	Celtic	1	5		Gallacher	Mair	Sinclair	McMillan	Balatoni	Fraser"	Doolan	Bannigan	Erskine+	Taylor*	Higginbotham+	Elliot*	Lawless+	O'Donnell	O'Donnell	Fox	Moncur	Moncur
29/03/2014	Prem	A	St Johnstone	1	1		Gallacher	Mair	Sinclair	McMillan	Balatoni	Fraser"	Doolan	Buaben"	Erskine+	Taylor	Elliot	Doolan*	Lawless+	Craigen"	Craigen	Fox	Moncur	Keenan
05/04/2014	Prem	H	Hearts	2	4		Gallacher	Mair	Sinclair	McMillan	Balatoni	Fraser	Doolan	Bannigan	Erskine+	Taylor*	Higginbotham+	Buaben"	Lawless+	Doolan"	Craigen	Fox	Moncur	Moncur
19/04/2014	Prem	A	Kilmarnock	2	1		Gallacher	Mair	Sinclair	McMillan	Balatoni	Craigen	Doolan	Buaben"	Erskine"	Taylor	Higginbotham	Taylor*	Elliot*	Lawless"	O'Donnell	Fox	Fraser	Elliot
25/04/2014	Prem	H	St Mirren	1	1		Gallacher	Mair	Sinclair	McMillan	Balatoni	Fraser	Buaben"	Erskine"	Erskine"	Doolan+	Higginbotham	Taylor+	Elliot	Taylor"	Moncur	Fox	Lawless	De La Vega
03/05/2014	Prem	A	Hibernian	4	2		Gallacher	Mair+	Sinclair	McMillan	De La Vega	Fraser	Bannigan*	Craigen	Craigen	Taylor	Higginbotham	Fraser*	De La Vega+	Elliot"	Keenan	Fox	Lawless	Keenan
07/05/2014	Prem	A	Hearts	4	2		Gallacher	Mair	Sinclair	McMillan	Balatoni	Fraser	Elliot	Bannigan+	Craigen	Doolan+	Higginbotham	Erskine"	Doolan+	De La Vega"	Moncur	Fox	Lawless	Wilson
10/05/2014	Prem	H	Ross County	2	3		Fox+	De La Vega*	Sinclair	McMillan	Balatoni	Fraser	Elliot	Erskine"	Craigen	Taylor	Higginbotham	Lawless*	Gallagher+	Moncur"	Keenan	Wilson	McDaid	Dominguez

Peterhead FC

Founded	1891
Ground	Balmoor Stadium
Postcode	AB42 1EU
Tel	01779 478256
Capacity	3150
Closest Railway Station	Aberdeen
Record Attendance	8643 v Raith Rovers, SC, 25/2/1987
Ground Record	4855 v Rangers, Lge, 19/1/2013
Record Win	8-0 v Forfar Athletic, Lge, 30/9/2006
Record Defeat	0-13 v Aberdeen, SC, 10/2/1923
Most League Goals in a Season	21 Iain Stewart 2002/3, Scott Michie 2004/5, Rory McAllister 2012/13
Chairman	Rodger Morrison
Secretary	Nat Porter
Manager	Jim McInally
Assistant Manager	Craig Tully (until May)
Colours 2013/14 Top	Blue
Shorts	Blue
Sponsor	Kerloch Oil Tools
Manufacturer	Adidas
Change Colours 2013/14 Top	White
Shorts	Blue
Nicknames	Blue Toon
Web	www.peterheadfc.co.uk

Peterhead's sheer consistency during 2013/14 was very impressive. They pulled away from their promotion rivals over the winter period and never looked like being caught.

Jim McInally's side had two outstanding forward players in Rory McAllister and Andy Rodgers, both of whom were nominated for League Two Player of the Year.

However, their success was built on a settled line-up with a strong defence which gave little away over the course of the season.

The club have been at League One level before and will be hopeful of improving on their previous performances.

PREDICTION 2014/15
Should do enough to survive at League One level.

Surname	First Name	DOB	Pos	L			SC			LC			RC			UNS	Signed	Previous Club	Notes	Contract
				A	S	G	A	S	G	A	S	G	A	S	G					
Alexander	Greg	15/12/94														3	2012	Albion BC	On loan to Maud Aug-Jan	
Brown	Jordon	28/11/92	M	21	14	3	1			1			2	1		1	2013	Aberdeen		C (2015)
Buchan	Kevin	07/08/94	F	8						1			2			13	2013	Dundee		F
Cowie	Dean	13/03/14	M	26	2	2	1			1						2	2012	Fraserburgh		C (2015)
Cox	David	17/03/89	M	9	4	1	1			1			2	2		2	2012	Alloa		C (2015)
Donaldson	Reece	09/01/94	D	7												1	2013	Raith Rovers (loan)	Returned to Raith Rovers, then signed	
Fitzgerald	Jake	01/04/94	M													5	2012	East Stirlingshire		F
Gilfillan	Bryan	14/09/85	M	29	2	4							1			1	2013	Clyde		C (2015)
Jarvie	Paul	14/06/82	GK													36	2008	Inverurie Locos		C (2015)
Low	Tony	01/08/83	M	3												8				F
McAllister	Rory	13/05/87	F	32		31	1		1	1			1			1	2011	Brechin City		C (2015)
McCann	Ryan	21/09/81	M	11	15	1	1	1		1			1			6	2012	Einherji (Iceland)		ONC
McDonald	Callum	31/05/83														3	2006	Dundee		F
McGeever	Ryan	30/04/94	D	7	1	2	1									2	2013	Falkirk (loan)	Returned to Falkirk	
McGlinchey	Conner	22/05/93	M	5	10		1			1			2			15	2013	Hamilton Accies		
McLaren	Fraser	26/08/89	M	12	19	5	1									1	2013	Berwick Rangers		C (2015)
Noble	Steven	16/04/88	D	36			1			1			1			2	2012	Stranraer		C (2015)
O'Neill	Stephen	07/06/94	M	3	1											1	2013	Aberdeen	Transferred to East Fife Jan 2014	
Redman	Jamie	13/08/86	M	35	2		1			1						2	2011	Brechin City		C (2015)
Richardson	Dean	02/05/87	D	3	6		1									21	2013	Larkhall Thistle		C (2015)
Rodgers	Andy	18/10/83	F	23	8	10	1			1			1			1	2013	Stenhousemuir		C (2015)
Ross	Scott	19/04/91	D	30	2		1									2	2011	Aberdeen		C (2015)
Sharp	Graeme	03/05/84	D	34	2		1									2	2005	Montrose		C (2015)
Smith	Graeme	03/10/82	GK	36			1			1						2	2012	Partick Thistle		C (2015)
Smith	Ross	21/02/92	D	10												1	2014	Stenhousemuir		C (2015)
Strachan	Ryan	01/08/90	M	22	2	2	1						2			1	2009	Celtic		C (2015)
Tait	Jack	07/07/97	M													2	2013	Peterhead Youth		Youth
Trialist																1				
Tully	Craig	07/01/76		5												4	2011	Clyde	Joined East Stirlingshire as Manager	R
Own Goals									3											

NEW PLAYERS 2014/15

Surname	First Name	DOB		Signed	Previous Club
Donaldson	Reece	09/01/94		2014	Raith Rovers

Date	Comp	H/A	Opponents	F	A		Crowd	Scorers
27/07/13	RC1	H	Brechin City	2	1		546	Cox, Brown
03/08/13	LC1	H	Alloa	0	2		429	
10/08/13	L	H	Annan Athletic	2	2		504	Gilfillan, Cox
17/08/13	L	A	Stirling Albion	0	2		573	
20/08/13	RC2	H	Stenhousemuir	1	3	AET	427	Cox
24/08/13	L	H	Elgin City	2	2		543	McGeever, Gilfillan
31/08/13	L	A	East Stirlingshire	4	1		286	Brown, Redman, McGeever, O'Neill
14/09/13	L	H	Queen's Park	2	1		491	McAllister, McLaren
21/09/13	L	A	Montrose	1	2		434	McAllister
28/09/13	L	A	Albion Rovers	2	1		354	Ross, McAllister
05/10/13	SC2	A	Berwick Rangers	1	2		356	McAllister
12/10/13	L	H	Clyde	1	1		562	McLaren
26/10/13	L	H	Berwick Rangers	1	1		503	McAllister
05/11/13	L	A	Annan Athletic	0	2		277	
09/11/13	L	A	Elgin City	4	2		622	Rodgers, McAllister 2, Cowie
16/11/13	L	H	East Stirlingshire	1	1		545	Rodgers
23/11/13	L	A	Queen's Park	5	0		447	Rodgers 2, Sharp, Gilfillan, McAllister
30/11/13	L	H	Montrose	3	0		473	McAllister 2, McLaren
07/12/13	L	A	Clyde	3	1		498	Rodgers 2, Donaldson
14/12/13	L	H	Albion Rovers	1	1		423	McCann
21/12/13	L	H	Stirling Albion	3	1		521	McAllister 3
28/12/13	L	A	Berwick Rangers	3	1		778	McAllister 2, Cowie
02/01/14	L	H	Elgin City	2	1		737	Sharp, Redman
11/01/14	L	A	East Stirlingshire	0	2		310	
18/01/14	L	A	Montrose	3	2		424	McNally og, McAllister 2
25/01/14	L	H	Queen's Park	1	0		542	Ross
08/02/14	L	A	Stirling Albion	2	1		498	McAllister, McLaren
15/02/14	L	H	Clyde	2	0		511	Rodgers, McLaren
22/02/14	L	A	Albion Rovers	0	0		442	
01/03/14	L	H	East Stirlingshire	4	0		554	Brown, Tapping og, McAllister, Rogers
04/03/14	L	H	Annan Athletic	3	1		607	Strachan, McAllister, Noble
08/03/14	L	A	Elgin City	3	2		670	Rodgers, McAllister 2
15/03/14	L	H	Berwick Rangers	3	0		497	Gilfillan, McAllister, Brown
22/03/14	L	A	Annan Athletic	1	2		452	McAllister
29/03/14	L	A	Queen's Park	2	0		387	McAllister 2
05/04/14	L	H	Montrose	4	0		671	Strachan, McAllister 2, McIntosh og
12/04/14	L	A	Clyde	2	0		534	Rodgers, McAllister
19/04/14	L	H	Albion Rovers	2	0		775	McAllister 2
26/04/14	L	H	Stirling Albion	0	4		852	
03/05/14	L	A	Berwick Rangers	1	2		586	McAllister

Friendly Games

10/7/13	Fr	A	Cove Rangers	3	0		at Banks o' Dee
13/7/13	Fr	H	Ross County	2	0		
14/7/13	Fr	N	Alloa	1	2		at Banks o' Dee
20/7/13	Fr	A	Fraserburgh United			U19	
20/7/13	Fr	A	Inverurie Loco Works	2	0		
23/7/13	Fr	H	Aberdeen	3	2		

Date	Comp	H/A	Opponents	F	A	1	2	3	4	5	6	7	8	9	10	11	12	13	14	15	16	17	18
27/07/13	RC1	H	Brechin City	2	1	Smith	Sharp	Noble	Strachan	Ross*	Cowie"	Cox	Redman	McCallister	Brown	McCann+	McGlinchey*	Rodgers+	Buchan"	Richardson	Jarvie		
03/08/13	LC1	H	Alloa	0	2	Smith	Sharp	Noble	Strachan	McGlinchey	Cowie +	Cox"	Redman	McCallister	Brown	McCann *	Rodgers*	Gilfillan+	Buchan"	Richardson	Jarvie		
10/08/13	L	H	Annan Athletic	2	2	Smith	Sharp	Noble"	McGlinchey*	Ross +	Cowie"	Cox+	Redman	Gilfillan	Brown	McCann*	Rodgers*	McLaren+	Richardson+	Fitzgerald	Buchan	Jarvie	Buchan
17/08/13	L	A	Stirling Albion	0	2	Smith	Sharp	Noble	Strachan	Ross	Cowie"	Cox"	Redman	Gilfillan	Brown	McLaren	Rodgers*	McLaren+	McGlinchey"	Richardson	Janvie	Fitzgerald	Buchan
20/08/13	RC2	H	Stenhousemuir	1	3 AET	Smith	Sharp	Noble	Strachan	Ross	Cowie"	Cox"	Redman	Gilfillan+	Brown	McLaren	McGlinchey*	Buchan+	McCann"	Richardson	Jarvie		
24/08/13	L	H	Elgin City	2	2	Smith	Sharp	Noble	McGeever	Ross	Gilfillan	Cox*	Redman	McAllister	Brown*	McLaren	O'Neill	McGlinchey	Richardson	Buchan	Jarvie	Fitzgerald	Strachan
31/08/13	L	A	East Stirlingshire	4	1	Smith	McGlinchey	Noble	McGeever	Ross	O'Neill	Cox*	Redman	McAllister+	Brown*	McLaren+	Rodgers*	Buchan+	Richardson"	Fitzgerald	Jarvie		
14/09/13	L	H	Queen's Park	2	1	Smith	Sharp+	Noble	McGeever	Ross	O'Neill	Cox*	Redman	McAllister	Brown"	McLaren+	Cowie*	Rodgers+	McGlinchey"	Richardson	Jarvie	Jarvie	McCann
21/09/13	L	A	Montrose	1	2	Smith	Sharp	Noble	McGeever	Ross	O'Neill	Cox"	Redman	McAllister	Brown"	McLaren	Cowie"	Gilfillan+	Richardson	Rodgers	Jarvie	McGlinchey	McCann
28/09/13	L	A	Albion Rovers	2	1	Smith	Sharp	Noble	McGeever	Ross"	Brown"	Cox	Redman	McAllister*	Brown"	McLaren*	Cowie"	McCann+	McGlinchey"	Richardson"	Jarvie	Buchan	Brown
05/10/13	SC2	H	Berwick Rangers	1	2	Smith	McGlinchey	Noble	McGeever	Ross"	Brown"	Cox	Redman	McAllister*	Rodgers+	McLaren+	Cowie*	McCann+	Richardson"	McDonald	Buchan		
12/10/13	L	H	Clyde	1	1	Smith	McGlinchey	Noble	McGeever	McCann*	Sharp	Gilfillan	Redman	McAllister*	Cox*	McLaren	Cox*	Brown+	Richardson"	Buchan	McDonald	Tait	
26/10/13	L	H	Berwick Rangers	1	1	Smith	Brown+	Noble	Cowie	McCann	Sharp	Gilfillan	Redman	McAllister	Brown	McLaren	Buchan"	McGeever+	Jarvie	Trialist			
09/11/13	L	A	Annan Athletic	0	2	Smith	Richardson+	Noble	McGeever*	McCann	Sharp	Gilfillan"	Redman	McAllister	Brown	Cowie	Buchan"	McGlinchey+	Jarvie	Fitzgerald	Alexander		
05/11/13	L	H	Elgin City	1	1	Smith	Richardson*	Noble"	Cowie	Tully	Sharp	Gilfillan"	Redman	McAllister"	Brown	Rodgers+	McCann*	McGlinchey+	McLaren+	McGeever	Jarvie	McGlinchey	
16/11/13	L	A	East Stirlingshire	1	1	Smith	Richardson*	Noble	Donaldson	Tully	Sharp	Gilfillan"	Redman	McAllister*	Brown	Rodgers+	McLaren*	McCann+	Richardson"	Buchan	Jarvie	McGlinchey	McCann
23/11/13	L	H	Queen's Park	5	0	Smith	Ross	Noble	Donaldson"	Tully	Sharp	Gilfillan"	Redman	McAllister	Cowie	Rodgers+	McLaren*	McLaren+	Richardson"	Richardson	Jarvie	McCann	Buchan
30/11/13	L	H	Montrose	3	1	Smith	Ross	Noble	Donaldson"	Tully*	Sharp	Gilfillan"	Redman	McAllister*	Cowie	Rodgers+	Brown*	Brown+	Brown"	Richardson	Jarvie	McCann	McDonald
07/12/13	L	A	Clyde	3	1	Smith	Ross	Noble	Donaldson	Tully"	Sharp	Gilfillan+	Redman	McAllister"	Cowie	Rodgers	McLaren*	Brown+	Strachan"	Richardson	Jarvie	Buchan	McDonald
14/12/13	L	H	Albion Rovers	1	1	Smith	Ross	Noble	Donaldson	Strachan	Sharp*	Brown"	Redman	McAllister	Cowie	Rodgers	McCann*	McGlinchey	Tait	Jarvie	Jarvie	McGlinchey	
21/12/13	L	A	Stirling Albion	3	1	Smith	Ross	Noble	Donaldson	Strachan	Sharp*	Brown"	Redman	McCallister	Cowie	Rodgers"	McCann*	Gilfillan+	McLaren+	Buchan	Jarvie		
28/12/13	L	H	Berwick Rangers	3	1	Smith	Ross	Noble	Donaldson	Strachan	McCann	Gilfillan+	Redman	McAllister*	Cowie	Rodgers"	McCann*	Brown+	McGlinchey"	Jarvie	Jarvie		
02/01/14	L	H	Elgin City	2	1	Smith	Ross	Noble	McCann"	Strachan	Sharp	Gilfillan	Redman"	McAllister*	Cowie	Rodgers+	Brown*	Buchan+	McGlinchey"	Alexander	Jarvie		
11/01/14	L	A	East Stirlingshire	0	2	Smith	Ross	Noble	McCann+	Strachan	Sharp	Gilfillan"	Redman	McAllister+	Cowie	Rodgers*	Brown*	McGlinchey+	Buchan"	Buchan	Jarvie		
18/01/14	L	A	Montrose	0	2	Smith	Ross	Noble	McGlinchey	Strachan	Sharp	Gilfillan"	Redman	McAllister"	Cowie	Rodgers*	McLaren*	McCann+	Buchan"	Tully	Jarvie		
25/01/14	L	H	Queen's Park	1	0	Smith	Ross	Noble	McGlinchey+	Strachan	Sharp*	Gilfillan+	Redman"	McAllister	Cowie	Rodgers*	McLaren*	McCann+	Brown"	Buchan	Jarvie		
14/02/14	L	H	Stirling Albion	2	1	Smith	Ross	Noble	Brown	Strachan	Sharp*	Gilfillan"	Redman	McAllister	R Smith	Rodgers"	McCann*	McCann+	McGlinchey"	Buchan	Richardson	Richardson McDonald	
05/02/14	L	A	Albion Rovers	2	0	Smith	Ross	Noble	Brown+	Strachan	Sharp	McLaren	Redman	McAllister	R Smith	Rodgers"	McLaren*	McGlinchey+	Richardson	Alexander	Jarvie	Richardson	
15/02/14	L	A	Clyde	0	0	G Smith	Ross	Noble	Brown"	Strachan	Sharp"	Gilfillan	Redman	McCann	R Smith	Rodgers"	McLaren*	McCann+	McGlinchey"	Tully	Jarvie		
22/02/14	L	A	Albion Rovers	2	0	G Smith	Ross	Noble	Brown	Strachan	Sharp"	Gilfillan	Redman	McAllister*	R Smith	McLaren	McCann*	McGlinchey+	Richardson	Tully	Jarvie		
01/03/14	L	H	East Stirlingshire	4	0	G Smith	Ross	Noble	Brown	Strachan	Sharp	Gilfillan"	Redman	McAllister*	Rodgers*	McLaren	McGlinchey*	Richardson+	McGlinchey"	Tully	Jarvie		
03/03/14	L	A	Annan Athletic	3	1	G Smith	Ross	Noble+	Cowie	Strachan	Sharp	Gilfillan	Redman	McAllister"	R Smith	Rodgers*	McLaren*	Brown+	Low"	Richardson	Jarvie	Low	McGlinchey
08/03/14	L	A	Elgin City	3	0	G Smith	Ross	Noble	Cowie*	Strachan	Sharp	Gilfillan"	Redman	McAllister"	R Smith	Rodgers*	McLaren*	Brown+	McCann"	Richardson	Jarvie	Low	McGlinchey
15/03/14	L	H	Berwick Rangers	3	0	G Smith	Ross	Noble	Cowie	Strachan	Sharp	Gilfillan"	Redman	McAllister"	R Smith	Rodgers*	McCann*	McLaren+	McCann"	Richardson	Jarvie	Low	McGlinchey
22/03/14	L	A	Annan Athletic	2	0	G Smith	Ross	Noble	Cowie	Strachan	Sharp*	Gilfillan"	Redman	McAllister"	R Smith	Rodgers*	McCann*	McLaren+	Low	Richardson	Jarvie	Low	McGlinchey
29/03/14	L	A	Queen's Park	2	0	G Smith	Ross	Noble	Cowie	Strachan	Sharp"	Gilfillan"	Redman*	McAllister*	Brown	Rodgers+	McCann*	McLaren+	Cox"	Richardson	Jarvie	McGlinchey	Cox
05/04/14	L	H	Montrose	4	0	G Smith	Ross	Noble+	Cowie	Strachan	Sharp"	Gilfillan"	Redman	McAllister"	Brown	Rodgers+	McCann*	McLaren+	Low"	Richardson	Jarvie	Low	
12/04/14	L	H	Clyde	2	0	G Smith	Ross	Noble+	Brown*	Strachan	Sharp*	Gilfillan"	Redman	McAllister*	R Smith	Rodgers+	Cox*	Richardson+	R Smith"	Richardson	Jarvie	Low	Cox
19/04/14	L	A	Albion Rovers	0	4	G Smith	Ross	Noble	Cowie	Strachan+	Sharp	McCann	Redman"	McAllister"	R Smith	McLaren	Cox*	Cox+	Low"	McGlinchey	Jarvie	Richardson	Low
26/04/14	L	H	Stirling Albion	0	2	G Smith	Ross	Noble	Cowie	Strachan	Sharp	McCann	Gilfillan	Brown"	R Smith	McLaren	Cox*	Cox+	Gilfillan"	McAllister	Jarvie	Richardson	Low
03/05/14	L	A	Berwick Rangers	1	2	G Smith	Ross	Noble	Cowie	Strachan	Sharp	Cox*	Gilfillan	McAllister'	R Smith	McLaren+	Rodgers*	McCann+	Brown"	McGlinchey	Jarvie	Richardson	Low

Queen of the South FC

Founded	1919
Ground	Palmerston Park
Postcode	DG2 9BA
Tel	01387 254853
Capacity	7620
Closest Railway Station	Dumfries
Record Attendance	26552 v Hearts, SC, 23/2/1952
Record Win	11-1 v Stranraer, SC, 16/1/1932
Record Defeat	2-10 v Dundee, Lge 1/12/1962
Most League Goals in a Season	37 Jimmy Gray 1927/8
Chairman	Billy Hewitson
Secretary	Craig Paterson
Manager	Jim McIntyre
Assistant Manager	
Colours 2013/14 Top	Blue
Shorts	Blue
Sponsor	South West Mechanical Services
Manufacturer	Joma
Change Colours 2013/14 Top	Yellow
Shorts	Yellow
Nicknames	Doonhamers
Web	www.qosfc.com

PREDICTION 2014/15

It will be difficult for Queens with Rangers, Hearts and Hibs in the Championship. However, the likelihood is that they may take points from each other and Queens are one of the clubs best equipped to challenge them. Should finish in the top half again.

2013/14 must go down as a successful season for Queen of the South. The structure of the Play Off system always meant it would be a tall order for them to come through and so it proved.

However, establishing themselves as a solid Championship outfit over recent seasons has been quite an achievement. For many years in the 70s, 80s and 90s Queens languished at the lowest levels of Scottish football, failing to capitalise on their undoubted potential. Those days are long gone now and Queens are in a position to kick on from here.

There was no certainty how they would react to the loss of Manager Allan Johnston to Kilmarnock. Jim McIntyre grew into the job as the season progressed and made good use of the resources at is disposal.

Queens were largely a team without individual stars - one where teamwork and organisation were the key features. Perhaps if they could add one or two inspirational individuals they could make a concerted challenge to the perceived "big three" in the coming season.

Surname	First Name	DOB	Pos	L A	L S	L G	SC A	SC S	SC G	LC A	LC S	LC G	RC A	RC S	RC G	UNS	Signed Previous Club	Notes	Contract
Antell	Calum	13/06/92	GK	9	1					3			3			4	2013 Hibernian		F
Atkinson	Jim	06/01/95	GK	3	1											41	2011 QOS Youths		C (2015)
Burgess	Malcolm	13/05/95	F													1	2012 Gretna		Youth
Burns	Paul	18/05/84	M	23	3	1	2			2		1					2012 Dunfermline Athletic		C (2015)
Carmichael	Danny	21/06/90	F	10	18	1	2			1	1		1	1		8	2010 Gretna		C (2015)
Clark	Zander	26/06/92	GK	26			3						1				2013 St Johnstone (Loan)	Returned to St Johnstone	
Dowie	Andy	25/03/83	D	29	1	2				3			3			8	2013 Partick Thistle		C (2015)
Durnan	Mark	28/11/92	D	30		5	3			1			1			7	2012 St Johnstone		C (2015)
Dzierzawski	Kevin	01/07/92	M	10	5		1			1			1		1	19	2013 Dartmouth (USA)		C (2015)
Higgins	Chris	04/07/85	D	26	1	2	3			2			1	2		11	2011 Dunfermline Athletic		C (2015)
Holt	Kevin	25/01/93	D	30	2	1	3			3			3		1	6	2010 QOS Youths		C (2015)
Hooper	Scott	14/01/95	D	1												9	2011 QOS Youths		C (2015)
Kerr	Mark	02/03/82	M	12	1											1	2014 Partick Thistle		C (2015)
Kidd	Lewis	30/01/95	D	2	4											8	2014 Celtic (loan)	Returned to Celtic, then signed again	
Lyle	Derek	12/03/81	F	26	11	7	1	2	1	3		3	3	3			2012 Partick Thistle		C (2015)
McGuffie	Ryan	22/07/80	M	9	1	2				2	1	1	2			13	2010 Morton	Freed Feb 2014 and moved to Australia	
McHugh	Bob	16/07/91	F	11	3	4										2	2014 Motherwell (loan)	Returned to Motherwell	
McKenna	Stephen	25/11/85	M	17	6		2			2		1	3	2		1	2009 Airdrie United		C (2015)
McShane	Ian	20/12/92	M	26	4	3	3			1	1		2	1		8	2010 QOS Youths		C (2015)
Mitchell	Chris	21/07/88	D	32			3			2			2			6	2012 Bradford City		C (2015)
Orsi	Daniel	31/03/92	F	1												11	2010 QOS Youths	Freed Jan 2014, joined Annan Athletic	
Paton	Michael	25/03/89	F	24	6	3	1	1	1	3		2	3			2	2013 Aberdeen		C (2015)
Reilly	Gavin	10/05/93	F	19	15	12	2			3			3				2010 QOS Youths		C (2015)
Russell	Iain	14/11/82	F	30	6	13	3			1	2	1	2	1		18	2013 Livingston		C (2015)
Slatterty	Pat	03/06/93	M							1			1			18	2012 QOS Youths		C (2015)
Smith	Aidan	11/05/97	F													10	2013 QOS Youths		C (2015)
Young	Derek	27/05/80	M	12	6	1				2						5	2012 Morton		F

New Players 2014/15

Kidd	Lewis		2014 Celtic
Baird	John		2014 Raith Rovers

Date	Comp	H/A	Opponents	F	A		Crowd	Scorers
27/07/2013	RC1	H	Spartans	4	0		1224	McKenna 2, Lyle, Holt
03/08/2013	LC1	H	Annan Athletic	3	0		1588	Lyle 3
10/08/2013	L	H	Dundee	4	3		2644	Lyle, McGuffie, Russell, Paton
17/08/2013	L	A	Livingston	3	3		1149	Russell, McGuffie, Reilly
20/08/2013	RC2	A	Airdrieonians	2	0		637	Lyle 2
24/08/2013	L	A	Hamilton Accies	0	2		1367	
27/08/2013	LC2	H	St Mirren	2	1	AET	2073	Mckenna, Paton
31/08/2013	L	H	Alloa	0	0		1607	
14/09/2013	L	H	Raith Rovers	0	1		1620	
17/09/2013	RC3	H	Rangers	0	3		6155	
21/09/2013	L	A	Morton	2	0		1836	Lyle, Russell
25/09/2013	LC3	A	Hearts	3	3	AET, 2-4 pens	8381	McGuffie, Paton, Higgins
28/09/2013	L	H	Dumbarton	1	2		1693	Russell
05/10/2013	L	A	Falkirk	1	2		3189	Russell
12/10/2013	L	H	Cowdenbeath	1	1		1514	Dowie
19/10/2013	L	A	Dundee	1	2		4357	Lyle
26/10/2013	L	A	Alloa	3	0		727	Russell 2, Reilly
02/11/2013	SC3	H	Hamilton Accies	1	0		1324	Lyle
09/11/2013	L	H	Hamilton Accies	0	1		1557	
16/11/2013	L	H	Morton	2	0		1685	Reilly, McShane
23/11/2013	L	A	Raith Rovers	1	2		1497	Reilly
30/11/2013	SC4	H	St Mirren	2	2		2176	Russell, Paton
07/12/2013	L	A	Dumbarton	1	0		824	Russell
10/12/2013	SC4R	A	St Mirren	0	3		2775	
21/12/2013	L	H	Livingston	2	2		1523	Paton, Durnan
28/12/2013	L	A	Cowdenbeath	2	0		556	Burns, Russell
04/01/2014	L	A	Hamilton Accies	1	3		1366	Russell
11/01/2014	L	H	Alloa	3	1		1476	Paton, Reilly, Lyle
18/01/2014	L	H	Raith Rovers	1	0		1538	McShane
29/01/2014	L	A	Morton	1	1		2341	Russell
01/02/2014	L	A	Livingston	2	1		1041	Durnan, Lyle
08/02/2014	L	H	Falkirk	2	0		1818	Reilly 2
15/02/2014	L	H	Dundee	0	1		2152	
22/02/2014	L	A	Falkirk	0	1		2862	
01/03/2014	L	H	Dumbarton	3	1		1604	Durnan, Reilly, McHugh
08/03/2014	L	A	Hamilton Accies	1	1		1703	Reilly
15/03/2014	L	A	Alloa	1	0		644	Dowie
22/03/2014	L	H	Cowdenbeath	2	1		1619	Higgins, Reilly
25/03/2014	L	A	Dundee	0	1		3999	
29/03/2014	L	H	Morton	3	0		1487	Higgins, Lyle, Reilly
12/04/2014	L	H	Falkirk	1	2		1863	Reilly
15/04/2014	L	A	Raith Rovers	2	3		993	Durnan 2
19/04/2014	L	A	Dumbarton	3	0		1263	Russell, Lyle, Holt
26/04/2014	L	H	Livingston	2	0		1923	McShane, Russell
03/05/2014	L	A	Cowdenbeath	1	1		1053	Carmichael
06/05/2014	PO	H	Falkirk	2	1		1996	McHugh 2
10/05/2014	PO	A	Falkirk	1	3	AET	4427	McHugh

Friendly Games

Date	Comp	H/A	Opponents	F	A	Crowd	Scorers
10/7/13	Fr	A	Clyde	5	2		
13/7/13	Fr	A	Annan Athletic	2	0	710	
19/7/13	Fr	A	Nithsdale Wanderers				U19
20/7/13	Fr	H	Hearts	0	0		
24/7/13	Fr`	H	St Mirren	4	2		
27/7/13	Fr	A	Dalbeattie Star	3	2		U19
6/4/14	Test	H	Queen of the South 2008				Paul Burns Testimonial

Date	Comp	H/A	Opponents	F	A	1	2	3	4	5	6	7	8	9	10	11	12	13	14	15	16	17	18
27/07/2013	RC1	H	Spartans	4	0	Antell	Mitchell	Holt	Young"	Dowie	Higgins	McKenna	Burns	Lyle	Paton"	Carmichael+	Russell!*	Reilly+	McShane"	McGuffie	Atkinson		
03/08/2013	LC1	H	Annan Athletic	3	0	Antell	Mitchell	Holt	Higgins	Dowie	McGuffie	McKenna	Burns	Lyle+	Paton"	Russell!+	Reilly+	Orsi+	McShane"	Reilly	Atkinson		
10/08/2013	L	H	Dundee	4	3	Antell	Mitchell	Holt	Higgins	Dowie	McGuffie	McKenna	Burns	Lyle+	Paton"	Russell	Carmichael*	Reilly+	McShane"	Durman	Atkinson		
17/08/2013	L	A	Livingston	3	3	Antell	Mitchell	Holt	Higgins	Dowie	McGuffie	McKenna+	Burns	Lyle+	Paton*	Russell!*	Carmichael*	Reilly+	Orsi	Orsi	Atkinson	McShane	Durman
20/08/2013	RC2	A	Airdrieonians	2	0	Antell	Mitchell	Durman	McShane"	Dowie	McGuffie	McKenna	Holt	Lyle	Paton*	Russell!+	Carmichael*	Reilly+	Slattery"	Higgins	Atkinson		
24/08/2013	L	A	Hamilton Accies	0	2	Antell	Mitchell	Durman	Higgins	Dowie	McGuffie*	McKenna	Holt	Lyle	Carmichael	Carmichael"	Young*	Reilly+	Higgins"	Smith	Orsi	McShane	Atkinson
27/08/2013	LC2	H	St Mirren	2	1 (AET)	Antell	Mitchell	Durman	Burns*	Dowie	Young+	McKenna	Holt	Lyle	Paton	Paton	McGuffie*	Reilly+	Young"	Young+	Atkinson		
31/08/2013	L	H	Alloa	0	0	Antell	Mitchell"	Holt	Higgins	Dowie"	Young	McKenna*	McGuffie"	Lyle	Paton+	Carmichael"	McGuffie*	Reilly	McGuffie"	Higgins"	Atkinson	McShane	Slattery
14/09/2013	L	H	Raith Rovers	0	1	Antell	Mitchell"	Durman	Higgins	Dowie	Young+	McKenna	McGuffie	Lyle	Russell!*	Carmichael	Holt*	Dzierzawski*	Russell"	Orsi	Atkinson	McShane	Holt
17/09/2013	RC3	H	Rangers	0	3	Antell	McShane+	Holt	Higgins	Dowie	Young	McKenna*	McGuffie	Lyle	Russell	Carmichael	Reilly*	Reilly+	Holt"	Orsi	Atkinson		
21/09/2013	L	A	Morton	2	0	Antell	McShane	Holt	Higgins	Dowie	Young	Dzierzawski	McGuffie	Lyle+	Russell!"	Paton	Dzierzawski*	McKenna+	Paton"	Orsi	Atkinson	Mitchell	Slattery
25/09/2013	L	H	Hearts	3	3 (AET, 2-4 pens)	Antell	McShane	Holt	Higgins	Dowie	McGuffie+	Dzierzawski	Young"	Lyle"	Russell!+	Paton*	Reilly*	Reilly+	Smith	Orsi	Atkinson	Mitchell	Orsi
28/09/2013	L	H	Dumbarton	1	2	Antell	McShane	Holt	Higgins	Mitchell	McGuffie	Dzierzawski	Young	Lyle	Russell!"	Paton	Reilly"	Reilly+	Orsi"	Durman	Atkinson	Mitchell	Slattery
05/10/2013	L	A	Falkirk	1	2	Antell	McShane	Holt	Higgins	Mitchell	McGuffie	Dzierzawski	Young	Lyle	Russell!+	Paton*	Carmichael*	Orsi	Smith	Atkinson	Mitchell	Slattery
12/10/2013	L	H	Cowdenbeath	1	1	Clark	McShane	Holt	Higgins	Mitchell	Durman	Carmichael	Young"	Lyle	Russell	Paton*	Reilly*	Dzierzawski+	Smith	Mitchell	Atkinson	Smith	Holt
19/10/2013	L	A	Dundee	1	2	Clark	McShane*	Holt	Higgins	Mitchell	Durman	Dzierzawski	Young	Reilly"	Russell	Paton*	Reilly*	Lyle+	Orsi	Dowie	Atkinson	McGuffie	Dzierzawski
26/10/2013	L	A	Alloa	3	0	Clark	McShane"	Holt	Higgins	Mitchell	Durman	Dzierzawski	Young"	Reilly+	Russell	Paton*	Lyle+	Lyle+	Orsi	Dowie	Atkinson	McGuffie	Hooper
02/11/2013	SC3	H	Hamilton Accies	0	1	Clark	Carmichael+	Holt	Higgins	Mitchell	Durman	McShane	McShane	Reilly	Russell	Paton	Dzierzawski"	Paton+	McShane"	Slattery	Atkinson	McGuffie	Dzierzawski
09/11/2013	L	H	Hamilton Accies	0	1	Carmichael+	Carmichael	Holt	Higgins	Mitchell	Durman	McShane	McShane	Reilly	Russell	Lyle	Reilly*	Paton+	Orsi	Orsi	Atkinson	McGuffie	Dzierzawski
16/11/2013	L	A	Morton	2	0	Clark	Carmichael	Holt	Higgins	Mitchell	Durman	McShane	McShane	Reilly"	Russell	Paton	Carmichael+	Paton+	Paton"	Dowie	Atkinson	McGuffie	Dzierzawski
23/11/2013	L	A	Raith Rovers	2	2	Clark	Burns	Holt	Higgins	Mitchell	Durman	Dzierzawski"	McKenna	Reilly"	Russell"	Lyle	Burns*	McKenna+	Carmichael	Dowie	Atkinson	McGuffie	Dzierzawski
30/11/2013	SC4	H	St Mirren	2	2	Clark	Burns	Holt	Dowie	Mitchell	Durman	McShane	McKenna	Reilly	Russell	Lyle+	McKenna+	Burns*	Dowie	Slattery	Atkinson	McGuffie	Orsi
07/12/2013	L	H	Dumbarton	1	0	Clark	Burns	Holt	Dowie	Mitchell	Durman	McShane	McKenna	Lyle	Russell	Paton	Dzierzawski"	Smith	Carmichael	Slattery	Atkinson	McGuffie	Orsi
10/12/2013	SC4R	A	St Mirren	0	3	Clark	Burns	Holt	Higgins	Mitchell	Durman	Dzierzawski"	McKenna	Reilly"	Russell	Carmichael	Dzierzawski*	McKenna+	Dowie	Slattery	Atkinson	McGuffie	Orsi
21/12/2013	L	H	Livingston	2	0	Clark	Burns	Higgins	Higgins	Mitchell	Durman	Dzierzawski	McKenna	Lyle*	Russell	Paton+	Reilly*	Smith	McShane"	Higgins	Atkinson	McGuffie	Burgess
28/12/2013	L	A	Cowdenbeath	2	0	Clark	Burns	Higgins	Higgins	Mitchell	Durman	Lyle	McKenna	Lyle	Russell!+	Paton	Carmichael*	Carmichael+	McShane"	Slattery	Atkinson	McShane	Slattery
04/01/2014	L	A	Hamilton Accies	1	3	Atkinson	Burns	McShane*	Higgins	Mitchell	Durman	Burns	McKenna	Lyle+	Russell!+	Paton	McShane*	McShane+	Carmichael"	Slattery	Carmichael	Hooper	Holt
11/01/2014	L	H	Alloa	3	1	Atkinson	McShane*	Dowie	Higgins	Mitchell	Durman	Burns	McKenna	Lyle	Russell	Paton+	Reilly*	Carmichael+	McShane"	Slattery	Antell	Burgess	Dzierzawski
18/01/2014	L	A	Raith Rovers	1	1	Clark*	Burns	Dowie	McShane*	Mitchell	Durman	Burns	McKenna	Lyle+	Russell!+	Paton	Reilly*	Carmichael+	Smith	Slattery	Antell	McShane	Hooper
29/01/2014	L	H	Morton	2	0	Clark	Burns	Holt	Higgins	Mitchell	Durman	Burns	McKenna	Lyle	Russell	Paton+	Dzierzawski*	Dowie+	McHugh	McHugh	Antell	Hooper	Dzierzawski
01/02/2014	L	A	Livingston	2	1	Atkinson	Kerr	Dowie	Higgins	Mitchell	Durman	Burns	McKenna	McShane	McHugh	Paton	Atkinson*	Carmichael+	Slattery	Smith	Carmichael	Hooper	Smith
08/02/2014	L	H	Dundee	0	1	Clark	Kerr*	Dowie	Higgins	Mitchell	Durman	Burns	Lyle	McShane+	McHugh	Paton	Kerr*	Reilly	Kerr*	Hooper	Young	Young	Dzierzawski
15/02/2014	L	A	Falkirk	3	1	Clark	Kerr	Dowie	Higgins	Mitchell	Durman	Burns	Russell	McShane	McHugh+	Paton"	Antell*	Lyle+	Russell"	Higgins	Atkinson	Kidd	Dzierzawski
22/02/2014	L	H	Dundee	0	1	Clark	Kerr*	Holt	Higgins	Mitchell	Durman	Burns	Russell!*	McShane*	McHugh	Paton	Kerr*	Carmichael+	McHugh"	Higgins	Atkinson	Kidd	Dzierzawski
01/03/2014	L	A	Dumbarton	3	1	Clark	Kerr	Dowie	Higgins*	Mitchell	Durman	Burns	Russell*	McShane"	McHugh+	Reilly+	Antell*	Lyle+	Smith	Higgins	Atkinson	Kidd	Dzierzawski
08/03/2014	L	H	Hamilton Accies	1	0	Clark	Kerr	Holt	Higgins"	Mitchell	Durman	Burns	Russell"	McShane"	McHugh+	Reilly	Carmichael"	Lyle+	Paton	Hooper	Atkinson	Kidd	Dzierzawski
15/03/2014	L	A	Alloa	1	0	Clark	Holt	Dowie	Kerr*	Mitchell	Durman	Burns	Lyle	McHugh	Paton	Reilly"	Lyle*	Paton	Carmichael	Holt	Antell	Kidd	Dzierzawski
22/03/2014	L	H	Cowdenbeath	2	1	Clark	Kerr	Higgins	Kerr"	Mitchell	Kerr	Dzierzawski	McHugh*	McShane*	Paton+	Reilly	Russell"	Lyle+	Carmichael"	McKenna	Atkinson	Kidd	Holt
25/03/2014	L	A	Dundee	0	1	Clark	Kerr	Dowie	Hooper	Mitchell"	Durman	Burns	Russell	McHugh	Paton	Reilly"	Kidd*	Carmichael+	Russell"	Holt	Atkinson	Young	Dzierzawski
29/03/2014	L	A	Morton	3	0	Clark	McKenna*	Higgins	Kerr	Mitchell	Kidd	Kidd"	Russell"	Lyle"	Young	Reilly	Kidd*	Burns+	Kidd"	Young	Antell	Hooper	Young
12/04/2014	L	H	Falkirk	1	1	Clark	Holt	Dowie*	McKenna"	Mitchell	Durman	Dzierzawski	Russell!*	McShane+	Lyle	Reilly"	McHugh*	Young+	Holt"	Young	Atkinson	Higgins	Dzierzawski
19/04/2014	L	A	Raith Rovers	2	3	Clark	Holt	Dowie	Kerr	Higgins	Durman	Burns	Russell	McShane	Lyle+	Paton*	Russell"	Burns+	McKenna"	Carmichael	Atkinson	Mitchell	Dzierzawski
26/04/2014	L	H	Dumbarton	3	0	Clark	Holt	Dowie*	Kerr"	Higgins	Kidd	Burns	Russell	Lyle"	Lyle+	Reilly	Carmichael*	Young+	Kidd"	Slattery	Atkinson	Higgins	Dzierzawski
03/05/2014	PO	H	Cowdenbeath	1	1	Clark	Holt	Dowie	Kerr	Mitchell	Durman	Kidd"	Russell"	McShane	Lyle	Carmichael"	Young*	Young+	Kidd"	Hooper	Atkinson	Higgins	Kerr
10/05/2014	PO	A	Falkirk	1	3 (AET)	Clark	Holt	Dowie"	Kerr	Carmichael	Carmichael	Kidd"	Russell	McShane	Higgins	McHugh"	Young"	Lyle+	Dzierzawski"	Hooper	Atkinson	Smith	Slattery

Queen's Park FC

Founded	1867
Ground Share with Airdrie United FC	Until november 2014
Ground	Hampden Park
Postcode	G42 9BA
Tel	0141 620 4000
Capacity	52025
Closest Railway Station	Mount Florida
Record Attendance	95772 v Rangers, SC, 18/1/1930
Ground Record	149547, Scotland v England, 1937
Record Win	16-0 v St Peters, SC, 12/9/1885
Record Defeat	0-9 v Motherwell, Lge, 26/4/1930
Most League Goals in a Season	30 William Martin, 1937/8
President	Ron Jack
Secretary	Christine Wright
Manager	Gardner Spiers / Gus McPherson
Assistant Manager	R Dickson
Colours 2013/14 Top	Black and White Thin Hoops
Shorts	White
Sponsor	Irn Bru
Manufacturer	Underarmour
Change Colours 2013/14 Top	Red
Shorts	Red
Nicknames	Spiders
Web	www.queensparkfc.co.uk

There's no team in Scotland that needs to improve more than Queen's Park. At the end of 2014/15 the bottom club in League Two will face a Play off for League survival. Had that situation been in place for 2013/214 then it would have been Queen's Park facing Lowland League football.

Clearly 2013/14 was a season of transition. They had lost several key players to the professional ranks and the progress of the likes of Andrew Robertson at Dundee United demonstrates just how big a loss that was.

Coach Gardner Spiers also exited mid season and was replaced by Gus McPherson. He brought in a number of other talented youngsters and results showed signs of improvement. However, playing away from Hampden because of the Commonwealth Games did not help and they will have the same handicap for the first part of 2014/15.

PREDICTION 2014/15
Lower half of League Two.

SQUAD NUMBERS

Surname	First Name	DOB	Pos	L A	L S	L G	SC A	SC S	SC G	LC A	LC S	LC G	RC A	RC S	RC G	UNS	Signed	Previous Club	Notes	Contract
Anderson	David	07/06/83	M	21		2			1	1							2010	Kilbirnie Ladeside		
Baty	James	28/08/87	M	12	1											3	2013	Threave Rovers		ONC
Birstingl	Lucas	14/02/90	GK	19		1										4	2013	Bo'ness United		F
Brophy	Eamonn	10/03/96	F	8	1	7											2014	Hamilton Accies (loan)	Returned to Hamilton	
Brough	Jamie	21/12/88	D	24	2	2	1			1						2	2008	Queen's Park Youth		F
Brown	Michael	07/11/79	GK	4			1			1			1				2013	East Fife	Freed Sep 2013	
Burns	Sean	06/10/91	F	23	4	1	3			1			1			4	2011	St Mirren		ONC
Capuano	Giuseppe	08/01/89	M						1							2	2009	Queen's Park Youth	Freed Sep 2013, Joined Clyde	
Chalmers	Kyle		D	1													2013	Queen's Park Youth		Youth
Coll	Bernard	07/09/94	D	21	2					1						3	2013	Queen's Park Youth		ONC
Collins	Thomas	27/08/96	F	4	10	1										2	2013	Queen's Park Youth		Youth
Coyle	Brian		D													1	2013	Queen's Park Youth		Youth
Davison	Lee	12/09/95	F	1	17	1	1	2		1		1				3	2013	Queen's Park Youth		ONC
Fisher	Ross	20/08/93	D	21	1		3										2013	Kilmarnock		Youth
Gallagher	Paul	05/08/91	D	19	1	1	1	1		1						5	2009	Hibernian		
Gebbie	Kris	24/02/94	D				1									4	2013	Queen's Park Youth		F
Gibson	Scott	10/11/93	D	13	2											17	2013	Queen's Park Youth		
Gold	David	01/01/93	F	11		3											2013	Hibernian (loan)	Returned to Hibernian	
Gormley	Liam	19/03/93	F	7	19	3	1	1								4	2013	East Fife		F
Grier	Alex	24/08/95	D	1			1			1							2013	Queen's Park Youth		Youth
Keenan	Michael	27/01/85	M	29	3		3									3	2011	Arthurlie	Joined Irvine Meadow June	F
Lamie	Ricki	20/06/93	M	12	1		3	1								1	2013	Queen's Park (loan)	Returned to Airdrie	
Lochead	Blair	26/06/94	GK	14		2										24	2011	Partick Thistle		ONC
Marr	James		D	1													2013	Queen's Park Youth		Youth
McComish	Martin	25/10/90	D	5												2	2013	St Josephs Ams	Rejoined St Josephs Ams	
McKenna	Mark		M				1										2013	Queen's Park Youth		Youth
McLean	Ewan	11/09/94	M	1												2		Trialist, ex Morton		
McVey	Conor	15/04/94	M	14	10		2			1						11	2013	Queen's Park Youth		ONC
Mitchell	Gavin	31/12/95	D	16	2	1										9	2013	Queen's Park Youth		ONC
Mosson	Grant	02/03/92	M	5												3	2013	Brisbane Peninsula Power		F
Quinn	Tony	09/09/81	M	25	3	5	2			1		1	1		1		2001	Rob Roy U21		ONC
Rooney	Shaun	26/07/96	M	5	3			1		1		1				9	2013	Dundee United		ONC
Sinclair	Cameron	14/01/95	GK													4	2013	Queen's Park Youth		Youth
Spittal	Blair	19/12/95	M	35	1	8	3		4	1			1				2013	Queen's Park Youth		ONC
Sutherland	Craig	17/12/88	F	4													2014	Woking		F
Trialist																1				
Vitoria	Joao Pereira	21/04/89	F	7	11	3	1	1		1						5	2013	Giffnock North		F
Wallace	Tony	22/02/91	F	10		2											2014	Morton (loan)	Retured to Morton	
Winters	David	07/03/83	F	1														Trialist, Ex Ayr United	Joined Sauchie Juniors	
Own Goals									1											

New Signings

Fraser	Shaun		2014	Irvine Meadow
Miller	Darren		2014	Irvine Meadow
Berry	Vince		2014	Clydebank
McPherson	Ross		2014	Clydebank
Woods	Paul		2014	Petershill

Date	Comp	H/A	Opponents	F	A	Crowd	Scorers
27/07/2013	RC1	H	Ayr United	1	2	887	Quinn pen
03/08/2013	LC1	A	Raith Rovers	0	6	1219	
10/08/2013	L	H	East Stirlingshire	1	3	476	Spittal
17/08/2013	L	A	Berwick Rangers	0	4	439	
24/08/2013	L	A	Clyde	0	3	621	
31/08/2013	L	H	Stirling Albion	0	2	527	
14/09/2013	L	A	Peterhead	1	2	491	Quinn
21/09/2013	L	H	Elgin City	3	3	342	Quinn 2, Vitoria
28/09/2013	L	H	Annan Athletic	2	5	413	Vitoria, Gormley
05/10/2013	SC2	H	Preston Athletic	2	2	594	Spittal, Lamie
12/10/2013	SC2R	A	Preston Athletic	2	1	806	Spittal 2
19/10/2013	L	A	East Stirlingshire	1	1	339	Spittal
26/10/2013	L	H	Albion Rovers	1	1	541	Davison
29/10/2013	L	A	Montrose	2	1	358	Spittal, Gormley
02/11/2013	SC3	A	Ayr United	2	3	879	Brough, Spittal
09/11/2013	L	H	Clyde	1	1	704	Spittal
16/11/2013	L	A	Stirling Albion	0	3	681	
23/11/2013	L	H	Peterhead	0	5	447	
30/11/2013	L	A	Elgin City	2	3	608	Spittal, Quinn
07/12/2013	L	H	Montrose	0	1	357	
21/12/2013	L	H	Berwick Rangers	0	4	302	
28/12/2013	L	A	Albion Rovers	1	2	538	M Dunlop og
04/01/2014	L	A	Clyde	2	1	751	Spittal, Collins
11/01/2014	L	H	Stirling Albion	0	1	472	
18/01/2014	L	H	Elgin City	2	0	346	Gallagher, Vitoria
25/01/2014	L	A	Peterhead	0	1	542	
01/02/2014	L	H	East Stirlingshire	0	0	337	
08/02/2014	L	A	Berwick Rangers	0	1	443	
15/02/2014	L	A	Montrose	0	1	301	
22/02/2014	L	H	Annan Athletic	0	1	356	
25/02/2014	L	A	Annan Athletic	2	3	345	Wallace 2
01/03/2014	L	A	Stirling Albion	2	2	656	Spittal, Mitchell
08/03/2014	L	H	Clyde	1	3	608	Brophy
15/03/2014	L	H	Albion Rovers	4	0	361	Brough 2, Spittal, Gormley
22/03/2014	L	A	East Stirlingshire	4	1	376	Brophy 2, Quinn, Burns
29/03/2014	L	H	Peterhead	0	2	387	
05/04/2014	L	A	Elgin City	1	1	555	Brophy
12/04/2014	L	H	Montrose	1	1	251	Brophy
19/04/2014	L	A	Annan Athletic	1	1	560	Brophy
26/04/2014	L	H	Berwick Rangers	1	3	420	Brophy
03/05/2014	L	A	Albion Rovers	0	1	503	

Friendly Matches

29/6/13	Fr	H	Falkirk	0	4		at Lesser Hampden
9/7/13	Fr	H	Ayr United	0	3		at Lesser Hampden
14/7/13	Fr	N	Brechin City	0	1		at NRC, Largs
18/7/13	Fr	H	Dumbarton	5	4		
20/7/13	Fr	H	Alloa	0	0		
24/7/13	Fr	H	Blantyre Vics	1	2	U19	
29/7/13	Fr	H	Pollok	0	1		
31/7/13	Fr	H	Neilston	2	1		

Date	Comp	H/A	Opponents	F	A	1	2	3	4	5	6	7	8	9	10	11	12	13	14	15	16	17	18
27/07/2013	RC1	H	Ayr United	1	2	Gallacher	Coll	Quinn	Brough	Spittal	Anderson	Burns*	Vitoria	Rooney	Grier	Brown	Davison*	Trialist	Capuano	Keenan	Lochead		
03/08/2013	LC1	A	Raith Rovers	0	6	Brown	Gebbie	Grier	Brough	Burns	Capuano	Anderson*	McKenna	Rooney+	Spittal	Winters	Grier*	Davidson+	Capuano	Mitchell	Lochead		Rooney
10/08/2013	L	H	East Stirlingshire	1	3	Brown	Coll+	Lamie	Brough	Burns	Quinn	McVey*	Keenan	Rooney	Spittal	Vitoria	Burns*	Davidson+	Gebbie	Gebbie	Lochead		McComish
17/08/2013	L	A	Berwick Rangers	0	4	Brown	Coll	Mosson	Brough	Fisher	Quinn	Baty"	Keenan+	Anderson*	Spittal	Vitoria	Burns*	McVey+	Rooney"	Grier	Lochead		Gibson
24/08/2013	L	A	Clyde	0	3	Brown	McComish	Mosson	Brough	Burns*	Quinn+	Mitchell	Keenan	Rooney	Spittal	Vitoria	McVey*	Davidson+	Gebbie	Gibson	Lochead		Gallagher
31/08/2013	L	A	Stirling Albion	0	2	Brown	McComish	Mosson	Brough	Burns	Quinn	Mitchell	Keenan	Baty	Spittal	Vitoria*	Davison*	Rooney	McVey	Gibson	Lochead		Gallagher
07/09/2013	L	A	Peterhead	1	2	Lochead	McComish	Lamie	Brough	Burns+	Quinn	McVey	Keenan*	Gold	Spittal	Mitchell	Baty*	Mclean-	Brown	Gibson	Vitoria		Rooney
14/09/2013	L	H	Elgin City	3	3	Lochead	McComish	Lamie	Brough	Baty*	Quinn	McVey	Keenan+	Gold	Spittal	Mitchell	Burns*	Vitoria+	Rooney"	Sinclair	Sinclair	Mclean	Rooney
21/09/2013	L	H	Annan Athletic	2	5	Lochead	McComish	Lamie	Brough	Burns"	Quinn*	McVey	Keenan+	Gold	Spittal	Mitchell	Vitoria*	Gormley+	Rooney"	Sinclair	Mclean		Rooney
28/09/2013	L	A	Preston Athletic	2	2	Lochead	Fisher	Lamie	Anderson	Burns*	Quinn+	McVey*	Keenan*	Gold	Spittal	Vitoria+	Rooney"	Rooney"	Mitchell	Sinclair	Gibson	Mitchell	Mitchell
05/10/2013	SC2	H	Preston Athletic	2	1	Lochead	Fisher	Lamie	Anderson	Burns	Quinn	McVey*	Keenan	Gold	Spittal	Gallagher	Davison*	Gormley+	Vitoria	Sinclair	Sinclair	McComish	Rooney
12/10/2013	SC2R	A	Preston Athletic	1	1	Birmstingl	Fisher	Lamie	Anderson"	Burns	Quinn	McVey*	Keenan"	Gold	Spittal	Gallagher	McVey*	Gormley+	Vitoria	Sinclair	Sinclair	Mitchell	McComish
19/10/2013	L	H	East Stirlingshire	1	1	Birmstingl	Fisher	Lamie	Anderson	Anderson*	Brough	McVey*	Keenan"	Gold	Spittal	Gallagher	Quinn*	Gormley+	Gallacher"	Gibson	Lochead	Rooney	Gibson
26/10/2013	L	A	Albion Rovers	2	1	Birmstingl	Fisher	Lamie	Anderson	Burns	Brough	McVey"	Keenan	Gold	Spittal	Davison+	Quinn"	Coll"	Gallacher"	Brough	Brough	Baty	Gallagher
29/10/2013	L	A	Montrose	2	3	Lochead	Lochead	Lochead	Anderson	Burns	Brough	Quinn+	Keenan"	Gold	Spittal	Davison*	Gormley*	Coll"	Coll"	Gibson	Lochead	Baty	Gallagher
02/11/2013	SC3	A	Ayr United	1	1	Birmstingl	Fisher	Lamie	Anderson"	Burns	Coll	Quinn"	Keenan	Gold	Spittal	Davison	Vitoria"	Collins+	Coll"	Gallagher	Lochead	McVeigh	Rooney
09/11/2013	L	H	Clyde	0	3	Birmstingl	Fisher	Lamie	Anderson	Burns"	Gallacher	Vitoria"	Keenan	Gold	Spittal	Davison+	Gormley"	Collins+	Vitoria"	Gallagher	Lochead	McVeigh	McVeigh
16/11/2013	L	A	Stirling Albion	0	5	Birmstingl	Fisher	Gibson"	Anderson	Burns"	Brough	McVey"	Keenan	Gold	Spittal	Quinn	Collins"	Davidson+	Gormley"	Gallagher	Lochead	McVeigh	McVeigh
23/11/2013	L	H	Peterhead	2	3	Birmstingl	Fisher	Lamie"	Anderson	Burns	Brough	McVey"	Keenan	Gold	Spittal	Quinn+	Lamie*	Davidson+	Vitoria"	Coll	Lochead	Gormley	McVeigh
30/11/2013	L	A	Elgin City	0	4	Birmstingl	Fisher	Lamie	Anderson"	Burns	Brough	McVey	Keenan	Gold	Spittal	Quinn"	Vitoria*	Davidson+	Gormley"	Gibson	Lochead	Gormley	Rooney
17/12/2013	L	H	Berwick Rangers	0	1	Lochead	Lochead	Lochead	Anderson	Burns"	Brough	McVey	McVey	Davison+	Spittal	Quinn	Gallagher"	Davidson+	Gormley"	Mitchell	Birmstingl	Mitchell	Mitchell
21/12/2013	L	H	Berwick Rangers	1	2	Birmstingl	Fisher	Lamie	Anderson	Anderson	Brough	McVey	Rooney"	Gormley"	Spittal	Vitoria	McVey*	Gormley+	Coll"	Lamie	Birmstingl	Gibson	Gebbie
28/12/2013	L	A	Albion Rovers	0	1	Birmstingl	Fisher	Coll	Gibson	Anderson	Gibson	Gallagher"	Rooney"	Collins"	Spittal	Vitoria	Quinn*	Collins+	Davison"	Mitchell	Lochead	Baty	Gebbie
01/01/2014	L	H	Stirling Albion	0	1	Birmstingl	Fisher	Coll	Gibson	Anderson	McVey"	Gallagher	Mosson*	Collins*	Spittal"	Vitoria	Vitoria*	Burns*	Gormley"	Mitchell	Lochead	Lochead	Burns
11/01/2014	L	A	Stirling Albion	0	0	Birmstingl	Fisher	Coll	Gibson	Anderson	McVey	Gallagher	Anderson+	Collins+	Spittal"	Gormley	Davidson*	Gormley+	Keenan"	Mitchell	Lochead	Vitoria	Mosson
18/01/2014	L	H	Peterhead	0	1	Birmstingl	Fisher	Coll	Gibson	Anderson	McVey	Gallagher"	Anderson*	Quinn	Spittal	Gormley"	McVey*	McVey+	Collins"	McVey	Lochead	Mosson	Burns
25/01/2014	L	A	Elgin City	0	1	Birmstingl	Gibson+	Coll	Gibson	Batey	Davidson+	Gallagher	Anderson"	Quinn+	Spittal	Collins	Davidson+	Mitchell+	Collins"	Mitchell	Lochead	Burns	Collins
01/02/2014	L	A	East Stirlingshire	1	2	Lochead	Gibson+	Coll	Gibson	Batey	Wallace	Gallagher	Fisher*	Keenan"	Spittal"	Vitoria"	Vitoria*	Mitchell+	Keenan	Gormley	Baty	Baty	Mosson
08/02/2014	L	A	Berwick Rangers	0	1	Lochead	Gibson+	Coll	Gibson	Batey	Wallace	Gallagher"	Anderson"	Keenan	Spittal	Quinn	Quinn*	Gormley+	Davison"	Vitoria	Brough	Brough	Gibson
15/02/2014	L	H	Annan Athletic	2	3	Lochead	Brough	Coll	Brough	Batey*	Wallace"	Burns	Anderson+	Burns*	Spittal	Quinn	Collins*	Gormley+	Keenan"	Gibson	Davidson	Davidson	Burns
22/02/2014	L	A	Montrose	2	2	Lochead	Brough	Coll	Brough	Batey	Wallace"	Burns"	Anderson"	Burns"	Spittal	Gormley	Vitoria*	Keenan+	Davison"	Gibson	McVey	Lochead	Gebbie
25/02/2014	L	A	Annan Athletic	1	3	Lochead	Brough	Coll	Mitchell	Batey"	McVey	Burns"	Keenan"	Burns"	Spittal	Gormley	Collins*	Keenan+	Gibson"	Keenan	Lochead	Vitoria	Quinn
08/03/2014	L	H	Clyde	4	0	Lochead	Brough	Coll+	Mitchell	Batey	Wallace	Burns"	Keenan	Mosson	Spittal	Quinn	Brophy"	Gormley+	Davison"	Keenan	Lochead	Burns	McVey
15/03/2014	L	H	Albion Rovers	4	1	Lochead	Mitchell	Coll	Mitchell	Batey*	Wallace	Burns*	Keenan	Keenan	Spittal	Quinn	McVey*	Gormley+	Collins"	Davidson	Lochead	Davidson	Collins
22/03/2014	L	H	East Stirlingshire	0	2	Lochead	Mitchell	Coll	Mitchell	Batey	Wallace	Burns*	Keenan	Brophy	Spittal"	Quinn	McVey*	Keenan+	McVey"	McVey	Birmstingl	Davidson	Mosson
29/03/2014	L	H	Peterhead	1	1	Lochead	Mitchell	Coll	Mitchell	Batey	McVey	Burns"	Keenan	Brophy	Spittal	Quinn	McVey*	Gormley+	Davison"	Collins	Birmstingl	Gibson	Gibson
05/04/2014	L	H	Montrose	1	1	Lochead	Brough	Gallacher"	Gallagher"	Gibson"	Wallace	Wallace+	Keenan+	Brophy	Spittal	Sutherland"	Fisher*	Gormley+	Collins"	Collins	Birmstingl	Gallagher	Gormley
12/04/2014	L	H	Montrose	1	1	Lochead	Brough	Coll	Gallagher"	McVey	Wallace	Wallace"	Keenan*	Brophy	Spittal	Sutherland+	Davison"	Collins+	McVey"	Davidson	Birmstingl	Davidson	Vitoria
19/04/2014	L	H	Annan Athletic	1	3	Lochead	Fisher	Coll	Gallagher	Quinn	Mitchell	Wallace"	Keenan*	Brophy	Gormley	Sutherland+	Gormley"	Collins+	McVey"	Batey	Birmstingl	Davidson	Mosson
26/04/2014	L	H	Berwick Rangers	1	3	Lochead	Fisher	Gibson	Mitchell	Quinn	Mitchell	Wallace"	Keenan*	Brophy	Gormley	Burns	Gormley"	Davidson+	McVey	Birmstingl	Birmstingl	Davidson	Rooney
03/05/2014	L	A	Albion Rovers	0	1	Lochead	Marr	Gibson	Gibson	Quinn	Mitchell	Rooney	Keenan*	Brophy	Gormley	Sutherland+	Collins"	Spittal+	Chalmers"	Burns	Birmstingl	McVey	Wallace

Raith Rovers FC

Founded	1883
Ground	Stark's Park, Pratt Street
Postcode	KY1 1SA
Tel	01592 263514
Capacity	8473
Closest Railway Station	Kirkcaldy
Record Attendance	31306 v Hearts, SC, 7/2/1953
Record Win	10-1 v Coldstream, SC, 13/2/1954
Record Defeat	2-11 v Morton, Lge, 18/3/1936
Most League Goals in a Season	38 Norman Haywood, 1937/8
Chairman	Turnbull Hutton
Chief Executive / Secretary	Eric Drysdale
Manager	Grant Murray
Assistant Manager	Paul Smith
Colours 2013/14 Top	White with two blue hoops
Shorts	Shorts
Sponsor	O'Connells Bar and Diner
Manufacturer	Puma
Change Colours 2013/14 Top	Red
Shorts	Red
Nicknames	Rovers
Web	www.raithrovers.net

This was a strange season for Raith Rovers - at times it promised much, it delivered to some extent, but in League terms failed to live up to expectations.

Early on it looked as if Rovers would be involved in the battle for the promotion play offs. However, their form shaded and then dipped dramatically over the winter period.

Back in October Rovers had qualified for the Ramsdens Cup Final, when their form was good. By the time the Final came around in April their form had slumped - just three wins in their previous 17 games. However, Rovers nullified an insipid Rangers side and won the game with a late goal by John Baird.

By that time they were starting to worry about the prospect of a relegation play off. However, a timely win over Queen of the South relieved that pressure and they survived fairly comfortably.

Grant Murray's challenge for 2014/15 is to keep up with the promotion favourites. Raith beat both Rangers and Hibs last season, and took Hearts to penalties in the League Cup, so they have nothing to fear from the supposed big boys.

PREDICTION 2014/15
Top half of the table

Surname	First Name	DOB	Pos	L A	L S	L G	SC A	SC S	SC G	LC A	LC S	LC G	RC A	RC S	RC G	UNS	Signed	Previous Club	Notes	Contract
Anderson	Grant	20/08/86	M	29	4		4			2			5				2012	Hamilton Accies		ONC
Baird	John	22/08/85	F	14	1								1			1	2014	Partick Thistle	Joined QOS May 2014	
Bates	David	05/10/96	D													16	2013	Raith Rovers Youth		Youths
Booth	Callum	30/05/91	M	35			4			2			5				2013	Hibernian (Loan Aug-May)	Returned to Hibernian	
Callachan	Ross	04/09/93	M	16	12		3			2			1	1		8	2010	Raith Rovers Youth		C (2015)
Cardle	Joe	07/02/87	M	33			3			2			5				2013	Dunfermline Athletic	Joined Ross County May 2014	
Donaldson	Reece	09/01/94	D	8	2		1						1			22	2011	Raith Rovers Youth	On loan to Peterhead, signed for them May	F
Elliot	Callum	30/03/87	F	28	2		2			2			5				2013	Alloa		C (2015)
Ellis	Laurie	07/11/79	D	11	2		2	1		1			1			22	2008	Stirling Albion		C (2016)
Fox	Liam	02/02/84	M	29	1		3			2			5			2	2013	Livingston		C (2015)
Hill	Dougie	16/01/85	D	30			3			2			4			3	2009	Alloa		C (2015)
Laidlaw	Ross	12/07/92	GK	12	1		3									24	2012	Raith Rovers Youth		C (2015)
Matthews	Ross	23/01/96	M	1												23	2013	Raith Rovers Youth		Youths
McCann	Kevin	11/09/87	D	1	3		1									6	2013	Livingston	Freed Nov 2013, joined Warriors (Singapore)	
McCroary	Liam	23/07/96	M													2	2013	Raith Rovers Youth		Youths
McGurn	David	14/09/80	GK	10						2						4	2008	Morton		C (2015)
Moon	Kevin	08/06/87	M	8			1			4			2			4	2013	Alloa		C (2015)
Mullen	Fraser	08/11/93	D	7	3		1						1			7	2014	Hibernian		
Murray	Grant	29/08/75	D													2	2009	Kilmarnock		C (2016)
Roberts	Jordan	18/06/94	GK													11	2013	Raith Rovers Youth		Youths
Robertson	Callum	12/07/96	F													1	2013	Raith Rovers Youth		Youths
Robinson	Lee	02/07/86	GK	14			1									1	2014	Ostersunds		ONC
Smith	Gordon	14/02/91	F	16	17		3	1		2			1	2		3	2013	Hearts		
Spence	Greg	06/07/92	F	14	12		1	3		1			2	3		5	2012	Celtic		ONC
Stewart	Colin	10/01/80	GK													10	2013	Airdrieonians	Released March 2014	
Thomson	Jason	26/07/87	D	33			4			2			5				2012	Hearts		C (2015)
Vaughan	Lewis	19/12/95	M	5	16		1			2			1	1		19	2011	Raith Rovers Youth		C (2016)
Watson	Paul	20/12/90	D	22			2			2			5			1	2013	Livingston		C (2015)
Watson	Jamie		F													7	2012	Raith Rovers Youth		F

New Signings 2014/15

Surname	First Name	DOB	Pos	Signed	Previous Club
Scott	Martin "Jimmy"	15/02/86	M	2014	Livingston
Barr	Craig	29/03/87	D	2014	Airdrieonians
Cuthbert	Kevin	08/09/82	GK	2014	Hamilton Accies

Date	Comp	H/A	Opponents	F	A		Crowd	Scorers
27/07/2013	RC1	H	Stirling Albion	2	1		1111	Moon, Cardle
03/08/2013	LC1	H	Queen's Park	6	0		1219	Elliot 2, Smith, Cardle, Spence, Vaughan
10/08/2013	L	H	Hamilton Accies	0	1		1652	
17/08/2013	L	A	Cowdenbeath	4	3		837	Spence 3, Cardle
20/08/2013	RC2	A	Dunfermline Athletic	2	0		3765	Hill, Fox
24/08/2013	L	H	Dundee	0	0		2603	
27/08/2013	LC2	H	Hearts	1	1	AET, 4-5 pens	3668	Fox
31/08/2013	L	A	Morton	1	1		1545	Anderson
07/09/2013	RC3	H	Falkirk	1	0		1565	Spence
14/09/2013	L	A	Queen of the South	1	0		1620	Spence
21/09/2013	L	H	Alloa	4	2		1397	Cardle 2, Anderson, Elliot
28/09/2013	L	H	Falkirk	1	1		1715	Anderson
05/10/2013	L	A	Dumbarton	4	2		843	Elliot, Spence, Hill, Vaughan
13/10/2013	RCSF	H	Annan Athletic	3	0		2119	Spence, Elliot 2
19/10/2013	L	A	Hamilton Accies	1	1		1113	Elliot
26/10/2013	L	H	Morton	2	1		1569	Moon, Smith
29/10/2013	L	H	Livingston	1	0		1304	Smith
03/11/2013	SC3	A	East Stirlingshire	2	0		716	Smith, McGowan og
09/11/2013	L	A	Dundee	0	2		5064	
16/11/2013	L	A	Alloa	0	1		858	
23/11/2013	L	H	Queen of the South	2	1		1497	Elliot 2
30/11/2013	SC4	A	Dundee	1	0		3184	Irvine og
07/12/2013	L	A	Falkirk	1	3		2934	Spence
14/12/2013	L	H	Dumbarton	2	1		1351	Vaughan, Thomson
21/12/2013	L	H	Cowdenbeath	3	3		1597	Hill, Elliot, Booth
28/12/2013	L	A	Livingston	0	3		1322	
02/01/2014	L	H	Dundee	0	2		4039	
11/01/2014	L	A	Morton	0	0		1745	
18/01/2014	L	A	Queen of the South	0	1		1538	
01/02/2014	L	A	Cowdenbeath	0	1		961	
08/02/2014	SC5	A	Hibernian	3	2		10503	Moon, Hill, Anderson
15/02/2014	L	H	Hamilton Accies	2	4		1436	Cardle, Baird
22/02/2014	L	A	Dumbarton	3	3		786	Smith 2, Baird
25/02/2014	L	H	Alloa	1	1		978	Hill
01/03/2014	L	H	Falkirk	2	4		1729	Baird, Booth
08/03/2014	SC6	H	St Johnstone	1	3		3767	Cardle
15/03/2014	L	H	Morton	2	1		1308	Spence 2
18/03/2014	L	A	Dundee	0	0		4561	
22/03/2014	L	H	Livingston	2	4		1329	Baird, Thomson
25/03/2014	L	A	Hamilton Accies	2	3		954	Baird 2
29/03/2014	L	A	Alloa	1	0		726	Booth
06/04/2014	RCF	N	Rangers	1	0	AET	19983	Baird
12/04/2014	L	H	Dumbarton	1	3		1602	Smith
15/04/2014	L	H	Queen of the South	3	2		993	Cardle, Watson, Baird
19/04/2014	L	A	Falkirk	1	1		3200	Vaulks og
26/04/2014	L	H	Cowdenbeath	1	2		1760	Spence
03/05/2014	L	A	Livingston	0	2		1265	

Friendly Matches

Date		H/A	Opponents	F	A		Crowd	
10/7/13	Fr	H	Sheffield United	1	2		1054	
12/7/13	Fr	H	Hibernian	0	0		2050	
17/7/13	Fr	H	Hearts	0	5		1829	
20/7/13	Fr	H	Inverness CT	2	2			
20/7/13	TnT	A	Newburgh	2	5		U19	
21/7/13	TnT	N	East Fife U21			won	U19	at Newburgh
23/7/13	Fr	A	Spartans	3	2			
3/8/13	Fr	A	Tynecastle	1	5		U19	
6/8/13	Fr	A	Arniston Rangers				U19	

Date	Comp	H/A	Opponents	F	A		1	2	3	4	5	6	7	8	9	10	11	12	13	14	15	16	17	18
27/07/2013	RC1	H	Stirling Albion	2	1		McGurn	Thomson	Watson	Hill	Booth	Anderson	Fox	Moon	Cardle	Elliot	Smith*	Spence*	Vaughan	Callachan	Ellis	Laidlaw		
03/08/2013	LC1	H	Queen's Park	6	0		McGurn	Thomson	Watson	Hill	Booth	Anderson	Fox	Moon+	Cardle	Elliot*	Smith*	Spence*	Vaughan+	Callachan"	Ellis	Laidlaw		
10/08/2013	L	H	Hamilton Accies	0	1		McGurn	Thomson	Watson	Hill	Booth	Anderson	Fox	Moon	Cardle	Elliot	Smith*	Smith*	Callachan	Callachan	Ellis	Laidlaw	Matthews	Vaughan
17/08/2013	L	A	Cowdenbeath	4	3		McGurn	Thomson	Watson	Hill	Booth	Anderson*	Fox	Moon	Cardle	Elliot	Spence	Smith*	Ellis	Vaughan	Callachan	Laidlaw	Matthews	Donaldson
20/08/2013	RC2	A	Dunfermline Athletic	2	0		McGurn	Thomson	Watson	Hill	Booth	Anderson+	Fox	Moon	Cardle	Elliot	Spence	Smith*	Vaughan+	Smith*	Donaldson	Laidlaw		
24/08/2013	L	H	Dundee	0	0		McGurn	Thomson	Watson	Hill	Booth	Anderson	Vaughan	Moon	Cardle	Elliot	Smith	Murray	Watson	Callachan	Ellis	Donaldson	Matthews	
27/08/2013	LC2	H	Hearts	1	1	AET, 4-5 pens	McGurn	Thomson	Watson	Hill	Booth	Anderson	Fox	Moon+	Cardle"	Elliot	Smith*	Ellis*	Vaughan+	Callachan"	Roberts	Donaldson	Matthews	Roberts
31/08/2013	L	A	Morton	1	1		McGurn	Thomson	Watson	Hill	Booth	Anderson	Fox	Moon	Cardle	Elliot	Smith*	Vaughan*	Callachan+	Ellis	Roberts	Donaldson	Matthews	Watson
07/09/2013	RC3	H	Morton	1	0		McGurn	Thomson	Watson	Hill	Booth	Anderson*	Fox	Moon+	Cardle	Elliot	Vaughan"	Spence*	Smith	Roberts	Callachan	Donaldson		
14/09/2013	L	A	Queen of the South	1	0		McGurn	Thomson	Watson	Hill	Booth	Anderson"	Fox	Moon	Cardle	Elliot	Spence*	Smith*+	Vaughan+	Callachan"	Roberts	Donaldson	Matthews	Ellis
21/09/2013	L	H	Alloa	4	2		McGurn	Thomson	Watson	Hill	Booth	Anderson+	Fox	Moon*	Cardle+	Elliot	Spence*	Smith*	Vaughan+	Smith"	Roberts	Donaldson	Matthews	Bates
28/09/2013	L	H	Falkirk	1	1		McGurn	Thomson	Watson	Hill	Booth	Anderson	Fox	Moon	Cardle"	Elliot	Spence*	Donaldson*	Smith+	Roberts	Callachan	McCroary	Matthews	Bates
05/10/2013	L	A	Dumbarton	4	2		McGurn	Thomson	Watson	Hill*	Booth	Anderson"	Fox	Moon	Cardle"	Elliot"	Spence	Donaldson*	Callachan+	Vaughan"	Callachan	Laidlaw	Matthews	
13/10/2013	RCSF	H	Annan Athletic	3	0		McGurn	Thomson	Watson*	Hill	Booth	Anderson*	Fox	Moon*	Cardle*	Elliot"	Spence+	Donaldson*	Callachan+	Smith"	Vaughan	Laidlaw		
19/10/2013	L	H	Hamilton Accies	1	1		McGurn+	Thomson	Ellis	Hill	Booth	Anderson"	Fox	Moon	Cardle*	Elliot	Spence*	Callachan*	Smith+	Vaughan"	Bates	Laidlaw	Matthews	Vaughan
26/10/2013	L	H	Morton	2	1		McGurn+	Thomson	Ellis	Watson	Booth	Anderson	Fox	Moon*	Cardle	Elliot	Spence+	Callachan*	Laidlay+	Smith"	Donaldson	Donaldson	McCann	Roberts
29/10/2013	L	A	Livingston	1	0		Laidlaw	Thomson	Ellis	Watson	Booth	Anderson	Fox	Moon	McCann	Elliot	Smith*	Spence*	Hill	Hill	Donaldson	McCann	Vaughan	Vaughan
03/11/2013	SC3	A	East Stirlingshire	2	0		Laidlaw	Thomson	Ellis	Watson	McCann	Anderson"	Fox"	McCann	Cardle"	Elliot	Smith*	Spence*	Callachan+	Callachan	Donaldson	Roberts	Vaughan	Stewart
09/11/2013	L	H	Dundee	0	2		Laidlaw	Thomson	Ellis	Watson	Booth	Anderson	Fox	Moon	Cardle"	Elliot	Spence*	McCann*	Callachan	Callachan"	Donaldson	Roberts		
16/11/2013	L	A	Alloa	0	1		Laidlaw	Thomson	Hill	Watson	McCann	Anderson"	Callachan	Moon	Cardle	Elliot"	Smith*	Cardle"	Spence+	Callachan"	Callachan"	Robertson		
23/11/2013	L	H	Queen of the South	2	1		Laidlaw	Thomson	Hill+	Ellis	Booth	Anderson	Callachan	Moon	Cardle	Elliot	Spence*	Smith*	Vaughan+	McCann	Vaughan	Watson	Stewart	Matthews
30/11/2013	SC4	H	Dundee	1	0		Laidlaw	Thomson	Hill	Ellis	Booth	Anderson+	Callachan	Moon	Cardle+	Elliot	Smith*	Fox*	Ellis+	Bates	Bates	Matthews	Stewart	Watson
07/12/2013	L	A	Falkirk	1	3		Laidlaw	Thomson	Hill	Ellis	Booth	Anderson	Callachan	Moon	Cardle	Elliot	Smith+	McCann*	McCann+	McCann	Bates	Matthews	Stewart	Spence
14/12/2013	L	A	Dumbarton	2	1		Laidlaw	Thomson	Hill	Ellis+	Booth	Anderson	Callachan	Moon	Spence*	Elliot	Vaughan	McCann*	Vaughan+	McCann	Bates	Matthews	Stewart	
21/12/2013	L	H	Cowdenbeath	3	3		Laidlaw	Thomson	Hill	Ellis+	Booth	Fox	Callachan	Moon	Smith	Elliot+	Cardle	McCann*	McCann+	Watson	Bates	Matthews	Stewart	Stewart
28/12/2013	L	A	Livingston	0	3		Laidlaw	Thomson	Hill	Donaldson	Booth	Fox	Callachan+	Moon	Smith*	Elliot	Cardle	Smith*	Matthews+	Watson+	Matthews	Stewart		
02/01/2014	L	H	Dundee	0	2		Laidlaw	Thomson	Hill	Donaldson	Booth	Fox+	Callachan	Moon	Anderson+	Elliot+	Cardle	Spence*	Anderson+	Watson	Vaughan	Stewart		
11/01/2014	L	A	Morton	0	0		Laidlaw	Mullen	Hill	Donaldson	Booth	Fox*	Callachan	Moon*	Anderson*	Elliot*	Cardle	Vaughan*	Vaughan+	Spence	Ellis	Matthews		
18/01/2014	L	A	Queen of the South	0	1		Laidlaw	Thomson	Hill	Donaldson	Booth	Fox*	Callachan	Moon*	Anderson*	Elliot*	Cardle+	Anderson*	Spence+	Spence	Donaldson	Roberts		
01/02/2014	L	H	Cowdenbeath	0	1		Laidlaw	Thomson	Hill"	Donaldson*	Booth	Fox+	Callachan	Moon	Anderson*	Elliot*	Cardle	Moon*	Vaughan+	Vaughan	Donaldson	Ellis		
08/02/2014	SC5	A	Hamilton Accies	2	4		Robinson	Thomson	Ellis	Mullen	Booth	Smith	Callachan*	Moon	Baird+	Spence+	Cardle	Mullen*	Smith+	Smith"	Ellis	Ellis	Ellis	Bates
15/02/2014	L	H	Dumbarton	3	3		Robinson	Thomson	Watson	Donaldson*	Booth	Smith*	Baird	Moon	Anderson	Spence*	Cardle	Elliot*	Baird+	Ellis"	Vaughan	Roberts	Ellis	Mullen
22/02/2014	L	A	Dumbarton	1	1		Robinson	Thomson	Watson*	Hill	Donaldson*	Smith*	Baird	Moon	Anderson	Spence*	Cardle	Elliot*	Spence	Baird"	Donaldson	Roberts	Vaughan	Mullen
25/02/2014	L	H	Falkirk	2	4		Robinson	Thomson	Donaldson	Hill	Booth	Fox	Baird*	Moon*	Anderson	Baird	Cardle+	Elliot*	Spence+	Donaldson"	Donaldson	laidlaw	Matthews	Bates
01/03/2014	L	A	Alloa	1	1		Robinson	Thomson	Hill	Hill	Booth	Fox	Baird	Vaughan*	Anderson*	Baird	Cardle	Vaughan*	Vaughan+	Fox	Ellis	laidlaw	Matthews	Ellis
08/03/2014	SC6	H	St Johnstone	1	3		Robinson	Thomson	Watson	Hill	Booth	Fox	Baird"	Moon*	Anderson*	Smith+	Smith	Spence*	Smith+	Fox	Smith	laidlaw	Donaldson	Mullen
15/03/2014	L	A	Morton	2	1		Robinson	Thomson	Watson*	Hill	Booth	Fox	Baird	Moon+	Anderson*	Smith*	Cardle*	Donaldson*	Elliot+	Ellis	Donaldson	Mullen	Mullen	Matthews
18/03/2014	L	A	Dundee	0	0		Robinson	Thomson	Hill	Hill	Booth	Fox	Baird	Moon*	Anderson	Smith*	Cardle	Callachan*	Mullen+	Ellis	Ellis	laidlaw	Mullen	Matthews
22/03/2014	L	H	Livingston	2	4		Robinson	Thomson	Hill	Hill	Booth	Fox	Baird	Moon*	Anderson*	Spence*	Cardle	Callachan*	Elliot+	Smith"	Smith	laidlaw	Vaughan	Matthews
25/03/2014	L	H	Hamilton Accies	2	3		Robinson	Thomson	Watson	Hill	Booth	Fox	Baird	Mullen	Anderson*	Elliot+	Cardle	Moon*	Vaughan+	Vaughan"	Donaldson	laidlaw	Ellis	Mullen
29/03/2014	L	A	Alloa	1	0		Robinson	Thomson	Watson	Donaldson	Booth	Spence+	Baird	Mullen*	Anderson	Elliot+	Cardle	Mullen+	Smith+	Spence"	Ellis	laidlaw	Ellis	Matthews
06/04/2014	RCF	N	Rangers	1	0	AET	Robinson	Thomson	Watson	Hill	Booth	Fox	Baird+	Mullen	Smith+	Elliot	Smith	Callachan*	Vaughan+	Matthews	Callachan	laidlaw	Callachan	Smith
12/04/2014	L	H	Dumbarton	1	3		Robinson	Thomson	Watson	Hill	Booth	Fox	Baird	Moon*	Smith*	Elliot	Cardle*	Anderson*	Vaughan+	Spence"	Donaldson	laidlaw	Ellis	Bates
15/04/2014	L	A	Queen of the South	3	2		Robinson	Thomson	Watson	Hill	Booth	Spence	Baird"	Callachan	Anderson*	Elliot	Cardle	Anderson*	Spence+	Anderson"	Ellis	laidlaw	Ellis	Vaughan
19/04/2014	L	A	Falkirk	1	1		Robinson	Mullen	Watson	Donaldson	Booth	Fox	Baird	Callachan	Anderson*	Elliot	Cardle	Moon*	Spence+	Matthews	Ellis	laidlaw	Mullen	Bates
26/04/2014	L	H	Cowdenbeath	1	2		Robinson	Mullen	Watson	Donaldson	Booth	Fox	Baird	Callachan*	Anderson	Elliot	Cardle	Vaughan*	J Watson	Matthews	laidlaw	laidlaw	Vaughan	Bates
03/05/2014	L	A	Livingston	0	2		Robinson	Mullen	Watson	Hill	Booth	Fox	Baird	Callachan*	Anderson	Spence	Cardle	Vaughan*		Matthews	Ellis	laidlaw	McCroary	Bates

Rangers FC

Founded	1872
Ground	Ibrox Stadium
Postcode	G51 2XD
Tel	0141 580 8647
Capacity	50987
Closest Railway Station	Ibrox (Subway)
Record Attendance	118567 v Celtic, Lge, 2/1/1939
Record Win	14-2 v Blairgowrie, SC, 20/1/1934
Record Defeat	1-7 v Celtic, LC Final, 19/10/1957
Most League Goals in a Season	44 Sam English, 1931/2
Chairman	Sandy Easdale
Chief Executive	Craig Mathers (until Oct 2013) / Graham Wallace
Secretary	Andrew Dickson
Manager	Ally McCoist
Assistant Manager	Kenny McDowall
Colours 2013/14 Top	Blue
Shorts	White
Sponsor	Blackthorn
Manufacturer	Puma
Change Colours 2013/14 Top	White with Blue shoulder panel
Shorts	Blue
3rd Kit 2013/14 Top	Black
Shorts	Black
Nicknames	Gers
Web	www.rangers.co.uk

It's difficult to know how to sum up 2013/14 for Rangers. Winning League One with the resources at their disposal shouldn't be the cause for much celebration - but going the full season unbeaten is a great achievement at any level.

The biggest disappointment for Rangers fans must have been in the Cups. Elimination by Forfar in the League Cup, losing to Raith in the Ramsdens Final, and then being comfortably beaten by Dundee United at home in the Scottish Cup shows that the current Rangers side are still a long way from the top.

The Championship will be a tougher proposition. Their Manager has been criticised over tactical issues and it will be more important to get these right against better opponents. In particular, Rangers pressure game of long balls may not provide the same level of success as it did in Leagues One and Two,

PREDICTION 2014/15
Top three but by no means certain of the title

Surname	First Name	DOB	Pos	L			SC			LC			RC			UNS	Signed	Previous Club	Notes	Contract
				A	S	G	A	S	G	A	S	G	A	S	G					
Aird	Fraser	02/02/95	M	22	5	5	4	2	1		1	1	1	2		6	2012	Rangers Youth		C(2018)
Bell	Cammy	16/09/86	GK	31			5				3						2013	Kilmarnock		C(2017)
Black	Ian	14/03/85	M	32		2	5			1			4		1		2012	Hearts		C(2015)
Clark	Nicky	03/06/91	F	13	10	9	2	2			1	2				2	2013	Queen of the South		C(2016)
Crawford	Robbie	19/03/93	M	6	14	2		1	1		3					20	2009	Rangers Youth		C(2017)
Cribari	Emilson	06/03/80	D	4	3						2					22	2012	Cruzeiro		OOC
Daly	Jon	08/01/83	F	33		20	6		3		4		2			1	2013	Dundee United		C(2015)
Faure	Sebastien	03/01/91	D	22	4		2	2		1		2	2			11	2012	Olympique Lyonnais		C(2015)
Foster	Richard	31/07/85	D	19	4		4				3					5	2013	Bristol City		C(2015)
Gallacher	Scott	15/07/89	GK	3						1			2			4	2006	Rangers Youth		C(2015)
Gasparotto	Luca	09/03/95	D													7	2012	Rangers Youth	On loan to Stirling Albion Dec 2013	C(2015)
Halkett	Craig	29/05/95	D													1	2012	Rangers Youth		Youth
Hegarty	Chris	13/08/92	D	2		1				1						2	2011	Rangers Youth	Joined Linfield May 2014	F
Hutton	Kyle	05/02/91	M	2	8		2					1				4	2010	Rangers Youth		OOC
Kelly	Liam	23/01/95	GK													1	2012	Rangers Youth		Youth
Law	Nicky	29/03/88	M	32		9	6		1		4	2					2013	Motherwell		C(2016)
Little	Andy	12/05/89	F	13	8	5		3		1		3	1	1		2	2007	Rangers Youth		F
McAusland	Kyle	19/01/93	D	3	1					1			1			1	2010	Rangers Youth	On loan to Ayr United	C(2015)
McCulloch	Lee	14/05/78	D	34		17	6			1		5	1				2007	Wigan Athletic		C(2015)
McKay	Barrie	30/12/94	F	2						1		1	1			6	2011	Rangers Youth	On loan to Morton	C(2017)
McLeod	Lewis	16/06/94	M	16	2	5	2			1	3					1	2012	Rangers Youth		C(2017)
Mitchell	Andy	06/04/92	M							1							2010	Manchester City	Transferred to Annan Athletic Jan 2014	
Mohsni	Bilel	21/07/87	D	28		10	6		1		3	1					2013	Southend United		C(2015)
Murdoch	Andy	30/01/95	M	1												9	2011	Everton BC		Youth
Peralta	Arnold	29/03/89	M	17	3	1	3	1			2					10	2013	Vida		C(2017)
Shiels	Dean	01/02/85	F	13	5	8	3			1						12	2012	Kilmarnock		C(2016)
Simonsen	Steve	03/04/79	GK	2			1									39	2013	Dundee		F
Smith	Stevie	30/08/85	D	11	2	2	1		1		2					18	2012	Portland Timbers		C(2015)
Smith	Alan	25/05/93	GK													5	2010	Crumlin United		OOC
Telfer	Charlie	04/07/95	M	1												9	2011	Rangers Youth	Joined Dundee United June 2014	OOC
Templeton	David	07/01/89	F	9	11	3	2	2	3	1		1	3	1			2012	Hearts		C(2016)
Wallace	Lee	01/08/87	D	28		3	5			1	5					1	2011	Hearts		C(2017)
Gallagher	Calum	13/09/94	F	1	3	1	1						1			4	2010	Giffnock		C(2015)
Sinnamon	Ryan	22/07/96	M													2				Youth
Own Goals						3														

NEW SIGNINGS 2014/15

Miller	Kenny	23/12/79	F				2014 Vancouver Whitecaps

Date	Comp	H/A	Opponents	F	A		Crowd	Scorers
28/07/2013	RC1	A	Albion Rovers	4	0		5345	Law 2, Black, Templeton,
03/08/2013	LC1	A	Forfar Athletic	1	2	AET	4079	Aird
10/08/2013	L	H	Brechin City	4	1		44380	Hegarty, Law, Black, Shiels
17/08/2013	L	A	Stranraer	3	0		3473	Little, Mcleod, McCulloch
23/08/2013	L	A	Airdrieonians	6	0		9044	Daly 2, Law, Crawford, Little, Mcleod
27/08/2013	RC2	H	Berwick Rangers	2	0		16097	MacKay, Little
31/08/2013	L	H	East Fife	5	0		42870	Clark, McCulloch 3, McLeod
14/09/2013	L	A	Arbroath	5	1		43562	Mohsni, McCulloch 3, Little
17/09/2013	RC3	A	Queen of the South	3	0		6155	Mohsni, Daly, McCulloch
21/09/2013	L	A	Forfar Athletic	1	0		3776	Little
28/09/2013	L	H	Stenhousemuir	8	0		43877	Daly 4, Little, Wallace, Templeton, Mohsni
05/10/2013	L	A	Ayr United	2	0		8968	Mohsni, McLeod
19/10/2013	L	A	Brechin City	4	3		3237	Daly, Law, Mohsni, Clark
26/10/2013	L	A	East Fife	4	0		4700	Thom og, Daly 3
29/10/2013	RCSF	A	Stenhousemuir	1	0		2338	Daly
01/11/2013	SC3	H	Airdrieonians	3	0		22533	Daly 2, Templeton
06/11/2013	L	H	Dunfermline Athletic	3	1		43082	Daly, McCulloch, Mohsni
09/11/2013	L	A	Airdrieonians	2	0		43158	Daly, McCulloch
25/11/2013	L	A	Arbroath	3	0		3902	Daly, Donaldson og, Clark
30/11/2013	SC4	A	Falkirk	2	0		6228	Law, Templeton
03/12/2013	L	H	Forfar Athletic	6	1		38745	Clark 4, Wallace, McCulloch
07/12/2013	L	H	Ayr United	3	0		45227	Daly, Aird, Mohsni
26/12/2013	L	H	Stranraer	1	1		45462	McCulloch
30/12/2013	L	A	Dunfermline Athletic	4	0		10089	Aird, Clark, Law, Crawford
02/01/2014	L	A	Airdrieonians	1	0		6522	McLeod
05/01/2014	L	A	Stenhousemuir	2	0		2546	Law 2
11/01/2014	L	H	East Fife	2	0		42182	Shiels 2
20/01/2014	L	A	Forfar Athletic	2	0		2067	Mohsni, Templeton
25/01/2014	L	H	Arbroath	3	2		41207	Daly, Templeton, McCulloch
01/02/2014	L	H	Brechin City	2	1		40377	Shiels, Daly
07/02/2014	SC5	H	Dunfermline Athletic	4	0		19396	Shiels 3, Templeton
15/02/2014	L	A	Ayr United	2	0		8449	Law, Daly
22/02/2014	L	H	Stenhousemuir	3	3		41794	Law, McLaughlin og, Daly
25/02/2014	L	H	Stranraer	2	0		3024	Wallace, Daly
01/03/2014	L	A	East Fife	1	0		4020	McCulloch
09/03/2014	SC6	H	Albion Rovers	1	1		23976	Mohsni
12/03/2014	L	H	Airdrieonians	3	0		41343	McCulloch 3
15/03/2014	L	H	Dunfermline Athletic	2	0		44110	S Smith, Gallagher
17/03/2014	SC6R	A	Albion Rovers	2	0		5354	Aird, Daly
23/03/2014	L	A	Brechin City	2	1		3070	Aird, Clark
29/03/2014	L	A	Arbroath	2	1		3400	Daly, Aird
06/04/2014	RCF	N	Raith Rovers	0	1		19983	
12/04/2014	SCSF	H	Dundee United	1	3		41059	Smith
15/04/2014	L	H	Forfar Athletic	3	0		39704	Black, Mohsni, Shiels
19/04/2014	L	A	Stenhousemuir	4	0		2767	Smith, Shiels, McCulloch, Law
22/04/2014	L	H	Ayr United	2	1		40651	Mohsni 2
26/04/2014	L	H	Stranraer	3	0		46093	Aird, Peralta, Shiels
03/05/2014	L	A	Dunfermline Athletic	1	1		7605	Shiels

Friendlies

Date	Comp	H/A	Opponents	F	A	Crowd	Scorers	
7/7/13	Fr	A	Brora Rangers	2	0			
10/7/13	Fr	A	Elgin City	1	0	2382		
13/7/13	Fr	A	Bristol City	1	0	7874		
17/7/13	Fr	A	FC Gutersloh	1	0			
20/7/13	Fr	A	FC Emmen	1	0			
20/7/13	Fr	H	Dundee U19	2	3		U20	at Murray Park
23/7/13	Fr	H	Dundee United U20	3	1		U20	at Murray Park
24/7/13	Fr	A	Sheffield Wednesday	0	1			
31/7/13	Fr	A	Dundee	1	1	5244		
6/8/13	Fr	H	Newcastle United	1	1			
11/8/13	Fr	A	Cambuslang Rangers	3	1		U20	

Date	Comp	H/A	Opponents	F	A	1	2	3	4	5	6	7	8	9	10	11	12	13	14	15	16	17	18
28/07/2013	RC1	A	Albion Rovers	4	0	Gallacher	Faure	McCulloch	Cribari	Wallace	Black	Crawford+	Law	McLeod*	Little	Daly	Gasparotto	Templeton+	Aird+	McAusland	A Smith		
03/08/2013	LC1	A	Forfar Athletic	1	2 AET	Gallacher	Faure	McCulloch	Hegarty	Wallace	Black	Crawford"	Mitchell"	McLeod"	Little	Templeton+	McAusland*	Aird"	Aird"	Gasparotto	A Smith	Gasparotto	Murdoch
10/08/2013	L	H	Brechin City	4	1	Gallacher	Faure	Cribari*	Hegarty	Wallace	Black+	Crawford +	Law	McLeod	Little	Daly	McAusland"	Shiels+	Aird	McKay	A Smith	Gasparotto	Murdoch
17/08/2013	L	A	Stranraer	3	0	Gallacher	Faure	McCulloch	Hegarty	Wallace	Black+	Crawford	Law	McLeod*	Little+	Daly	Templeton*	Shiels+	Templeton"	Gasparotto	A Smith	Gasparotto	Murdoch
23/08/2013	L	A	Airdrieonians	6	0	Gallacher	Faure	McCulloch	McAusland	Wallace	Black+	Crawford	Law	McLeod	Little+	Daly	MacKay*	Shiels+	Aird	Gasparotto	A Smith	Telfer	Murdoch
27/08/2013	RC2	H	Berwick Rangers	2	0	Bell	Faure	Cribari	McCulloch	Wallace	Black+	Crawford	Shiels*	McLeod	Little+	Templeton+	MacKay*	Shiels+	Templeton+	Gasparotto	Kelly		Gallacher
31/08/2013	L	H	East Fife	5	1	Bell	Foster	Smith	McCulloch	Wallace	Peralta	Crawford*	McAusland	McAusland+	Little+	Templeton*	Templeton*	Murdoch+	Aird"	Gasparotto	Shiels	Forster	Simonsen
14/09/2013	L	A	Arbroath	3	0	Bell	Foster	Smith*	McCulloch	Mohsni	Peralta*	Crawford	Law	McLeod+	Little	Daly	Templeton*	Murdoch+	Murdoch+	McKay	Cribari		
17/09/2013	RC3	A	Queen of the South	1	0	Bell	Foster	Smith*	McCulloch	Mohsni	Peralta*	Crawford*	Law	McLeod	Little+	Wallace"	Faure*	Clark+	Smith"	McKay	Simonsen	Crawford	Simonsen
21/09/2013	L	A	Forfar Athletic	1	0	Bell	Foster	Black	McCulloch	Wallace	Hutton	Peralta*	Law	Clark"	Little	Daly	Little*	Templeton+	Hutton"	Templeton"	Clark	Smith	Simonsen
28/09/2013	L	H	Stenhousemuir	8	0	Bell	Foster	Smith	McCulloch	Wallace	Black*	Mohsni	Law	Daly+	Little	Daly+	Hutton*	MacKay+	Little"	Shiels	Aird	Smith	Simonsen
05/10/2013	L	A	Ayr United	2	0	Bell	Foster	Peralta*	McCulloch	Wallace	Black	Mohsni	Law	Daly	Clark	Daly+	Templeton*	Faure+	Hutton	Cribari	Faure	Faure	Simonsen
19/10/2013	L	A	Brechin City	4	3	Bell	Foster	Peralta"	McCulloch	Crawford*	Black+	Mohsni	Law	Daly	Clark+	Daly	Templeton*	Templeton+	Little+	Cribari	Aird	Faure	Simonsen
26/10/2013	L	H	East Fife	4	0	Bell	Foster	Peralta"	McCulloch	Wallace"	Black*	Mohsni	Law	Daly	Clark	Daly	Templeton*	Crawford+	Templeton"	Templeton"	Faure	CRawford	Simonsen
29/10/2013	RCSF	A	Stenhousemuir	1	0	Bell	Foster	Peralta*	McCulloch"	Wallace	Black+	Mohsni	Law	Daly	Clark	Templeton	Aird"	McLeod+	Crawford"	Faure	Templeton"	Crawford	Smith
01/11/2013	SC3	H	Airdrieonians	3	0	Bell	Foster	Aird*	McCulloch	Wallace	Black	Mohsni	Law	Daly	Clark+	Templeton+	McLeod*	Shiels+	Cribari	Cribari	Faure	Crawford	Hutton
06/11/2013	L	A	Dunfermline Athletic	3	1	Bell	Faure	Aird*	McCulloch	Wallace	Black	Mohsni	Law	Daly	Clark"	Templeton+	Foster*	Crawford+	Cribari	Cribari	Simonsen	Smith	Crawford
09/11/2013	L	H	Airdrieonians	2	0	Bell	Faure	Aird	McCulloch	Wallace	Black	Mohsni	Law	Daly	Clark*	McLeod	Crawford*	Crawford+	Cribari	Cribari	Faure	Smith	Crawford
25/11/2013	L	A	Airdrieonians	3	0	Bell	Faure	Peralta+	McCulloch	Wallace	Black	Mohsni	Law*	Daly	Clark+	McLeod	Foster*	Aird+	Cribari	Shiels	Simonsen	Smith	McKay
30/11/2013	SC4	A	Falkirk	2	0	Bell	Faure	Foster	McCulloch	Wallace	Foster	Mohsni	Law*	Daly	Little	McLeod	Templeton*	McKay	Cribari	Murdoch	Gallacher	Crawford	Crawford
07/12/2013	L	A	Forfar Athletic	6	1	Bell	Faure	Law"	McCulloch	Wallace	Black	Cribari	Aird*	Daly	Clark*	McLeod	Foster*	Cribari"	Peralta"	Peralta	Simonsen	Forster	McKay
26/12/2013	L	H	Ayr United	3	0	Bell	Faure*	Law	McCulloch	Wallace	Black	Cribari	Aird*	Daly	Clark	Smith*	Foster*	Cribari+	Crawford	Cribari	Simonsen	Cribari	Smith
30/12/2013	L	H	Stranraer	1	1	Bell	Faure	Peralta+	McCulloch	Wallace	Black	Mohsni	Aird+	Daly	Clark	McLeod+	Little*	Templeton+	Crawford	Cribari	Simonsen	Forster	Murdoch
02/01/2014	L	A	Airdrieonians	4	0	Bell	Foster	Law	McCulloch	Wallace	Black	Mohsni	Aird	Daly	McLeod	Smith*	Little*	Crawford+	Crawford	Cribari	Simonsen	Peralta	Shiels
05/01/2014	L	H	Airdrieonians	1	0	Bell	Foster	Law	McCulloch	Wallace	Black	Mohsni	Aird	Daly	Clark	McLeod+	Little*	Foster+	Smith	Cribari	Simonsen	Shiels	Shiels
11/01/2014	L	H	East Fife	2	0	Bell	Foster	Law	McCulloch	Wallace	Black	Mohsni	Aird	Daly+	Clark	Shiels*	Clark*	Shiels+	Cribari	Smith	Simonsen	Little	Murdoch
20/01/2014	L	A	Forfar Athletic	2	0	Simonsen	Foster	Law	McCulloch	Wallace	Foster	Mohsni	Aird	Daly	Templeton+	Shiels+	Little*	Little+	Cribari	Faure	Simonsen	Telfer	Crawford
25/01/2014	L	H	Arbroath	3	2	Bell	Foster	Law	McCulloch	Wallace	Black	Mohsni*	Aird*	Daly"	Templeton+	Shiels+	Little*	Little+	Cribari	Faure	Simonsen	Foster	Crawford
01/02/2014	L	H	Brechin City	2	1	Bell	Foster	Law	McCulloch	Wallace	Black+	Mohsni	Aird	Daly"	Templeton+	Shiels+	Clark*	Foster+	Cribari	Faure	Simonsen	Smith	Murdoch
07/02/2014	SC5	A	Dunfermline Athletic	4	0	Bell	Foster	Law"	McCulloch	Wallace	Black	Mohsni"	Aird+	Daly	Templeton	Templeton	Clark*	Peralta+	Templeton	Peralta	Simonsen	Foster	Foster
15/02/2014	L	A	Ayr United	3	3	Bell	Foster	Law	McCulloch	Peralta	Black	Mohsni	Aird	Daly	Smith	Templeton+	Crawford*	Aird+	Peralta	Crawford	Simonsen	Crawford	Halkett
22/02/2014	L	H	Stenhousemuir	3	0	Bell	Foster	Law	McCulloch	Wallace	Black	Mohsni	Aird	Daly"	Templeton	Templeton	Crawford*	Smith	Cribari	Crawford	Faure	Crawford	Peralta
25/02/2014	L	A	Stranraer	2	0	Bell	Foster	Law	McCulloch	Hutton	Black+	Mohsni	Aird	Daly"	Templeton	Templeton	Clark*	Cribari	Smith	Cribari	Simonsen	Daly	Peralta
01/03/2014	L	H	Ayr United	1	0	Bell	Foster	Faure	McCulloch	Wallace	Black"	Faure	Aird	Daly"	Templeton+	Templeton+	Faure*	Peralta+	Cribari"	Cribari	Simonsen	Smith	C Gallacher
09/03/2014	SC6	H	Albion Rovers	1	1	Bell	Foster	Law*	McCulloch	S Smith"	Black	Mohsni*	Aird	Crawford	Gallagher"	Clark	Cribari*	Hutton+	Gallagher"	Wallace	Simonsen	Cribari	Peralta
12/03/2014	L	H	Airdrieonians	3	0	Bell	Foster	Law	McCulloch	Wallace	Black+	Mohsni	Aird	Daly"	Gallagher	Hutton+	Clark*	Faure+	Peralta	Crawford	Simonsen	Cribari	Smith
15/03/2014	L	H	Dunfermline Athletic	2	0	Bell	Foster	Faure	McCulloch+	Wallace	Black	Mohsni	Aird	Daly	Crawford*	Clark	Clark*	Peralta+	Shiels	Crawford	Simonsen	Cribari	Shiels
17/03/2014	SC6R	A	Albion Rovers	2	0	Bell	Foster	Faure	McCulloch	Wallace	Black*	Mohsni	Aird	Daly+	Gallagher"	Little+	Clark*	Peralta+	Gallagher"	Faure	Simonsen	Crawford	Shiels
23/03/2014	L	A	Brechin City	2	1	Bell	Foster	Shiels+	McCulloch	Wallace	Black*	Mohsni	Aird	Daly+	Law	Shiels	Faure*	Hutton+	Peralta	Crawford	Simonsen	Daly	Telfer
29/03/2014	L	A	Arbroath	2	1	Bell	Foster	Shiels	McCulloch	Wallace	Peralta	Mohsni	Aird+	Daly	Law	Smith"	Clark*	Shiels+	Smith"	Cribari	Simonsen	Smith	Telfer
06/04/2014	RCF	N	Raith Rovers	0	1	Bell	Foster	Hutton*	McCulloch	Wallace*	Black	Mohsni	Aird	Daly	Law	Smith"	Clark*	Teifer+.	C Gallagher*	Shiels	Simonsen	Hegarty	Cribari
12/04/2014	SCSF	H	Dundee United	1	3	Simonsen	Foster	Shiels	McCulloch	Peralta	Black+	Mohsni	Aird	Daly	Law	Smith	Faure*	C Gallagher*	Faure	Crawford	S Gallagher	C Gallagher	Sinnamon
15/04/2014	L	H	Forfar Athletic	3	0	Simonsen	Foster	Shiels+	McCulloch	Peralta+	Black*	Mohsni	Aird	Daly	Law"	Smith	Clark*	Hutton+	Crawford"	Crawford	S Gallagher	Hegarty	C Gallagher
19/04/2014	L	A	Ayr United	4	0	Bell	Foster	Shiels*	McCulloch	Wallace+	Black"	Mohsni"	Aird	Daly+	Law	Smith	Clark*	Clark"	Clark"	Crawford	Simonsen	Faure	Telfer
22/04/2014	L	H	Ayr United	2	1	Bell	Foster	Shiels*	McCulloch	Peralta	Black*	Mohsni	Aird	Daly	Law	Smith	Clark*	C Gallagher*	Hutton"	Crawford	Simonsen	Faure	Peralta
26/04/2014	L	H	Stranraer	3	0	Bell	Foster	Shiels	McCulloch	Peralta	Black*	Mohsni	Aird	Daly+	Law	Smith	Little*	Clark+	Cribari"	Crawford	Simonsen	Faure	C Gallacher
03/05/2014	L	A	Dunfermline Athletic	1	1	Bell	Faure	Shiels+	McCulloch	Peralta*	Black+	Mohsni	Aird	Daly	Law	Smith	Little*	Clark+	Murdoch	Hutton	Simonsen	Crawford	Sinnamon

Ross County FC

Founded	1929
Ground	Victoria Park
Postcode	IN15 9QZ
Tel	01349 860860
Capacity	6541
Closest Railway Station	Dingwall
Record Attendance	6110 v Celtic, Lge, 18/8/2012
Record Win	11-0 v St Cuthbert Wanderers, SC, 1/12/1993
Record Defeat	0-7 v Kilmarnock, SC, 17/2/1962
Most League Goals in a Season	24 Andy Barrowman, 2007/8
Chairman	Roy McGregor
Secretary	Donnie McBean
Manager	Derek Adams
Assistant Manager	
Colours 2013/14 Top	Navy Blue
Shorts	Navy Blue
Sponsor	CRC Evans Offshore
Manufacturer	Diadora
Change Colours 2013/14 Top	White
Shorts	Red
Nicknames	Staggies
Web	www.rosscountyfootballclub.co.uk

County brought in quite a few new players for 2013/14 and early on it looked as if they might struggle. However, clever work in the January transfer window brought in some great signings and, in the end, they survived comfortably.

The success of the club is a huge tribute to the Board of Directors and Chairman who work so hard to provide a platform for full-time football in the far north. It's easy to forget that it is only 20 years since County were playing Highland League football in a very basic ground.

Cup performances were disappointing but were relatively unimportant compared with leaue survival.

PREDICTION 2014/15
Will probably be towards the top of the lower half

				L			SC			LC					
Surname	First Name	DOB	Pos	A	S	G	A	S	G	A	S	G	UNS	Signed Previous Club	Notes
Arquin	Yoann	15/04/88	F	14	2	4								2014 Notts County	OOC
Boyd	Scott	04/06/86	D	27	1	1	1						9	2008 Partick Thistle	C (2015)
Brittain	Richard	24/09/83	M	34	7	1	1		1					2008 St Mirren	OOC
Brown	Mark	28/02/91	GK	28			1			1			10	2012 Hibernian	C (2015)
Carey	Graham	20/05/89	F	31	5	3	1			1				2013 St Mirren	OOC
Cikos	Eric	31/07/88	D	14									1	2014 Slovan Bratislava (loan)	Returned to Slovan
Cooper	Alex	04/11/91	M	5	12	1							5	2011 Liverpool	F
De Leeuw	Melvin	25/04/88	F	19	14	9	1			1			3	2003 SC Cambuur	C (2015)
Dingwall	Tony	25/07/94	M										3	2013 Ross County Youth	C (2015)
Fraser	Michael	08/10/83	GK	10									21	2011 Birkirkara	F
Glen	Gary	22/03/90	F	4	10		1						12	2012 Hearts	F
Gordon	Ben	02/03/91	D	25	3	1							9	2013 Yeovil Town	OOC
Ikonomou	Evangelos	18/07/87	D	15									3	2014 Veria	F
Kettlewell	Stuart	04/06/84	M	22	3	2	1			1			2	2009 Clyde	OOC
Kiss	Filip	13/10/90	M	17	6									2014 Cardiff City (loan)	Returned to Cardiff
Klok	Marc	20/04/83	M	4	2								9	2013 FC Utrecht	C (2015)
Kovacevic	Mihael	06/03/88	D	13					1				3	2012 Zadar	Released Jan 2014
Luckassen	Kevin	27/07/93	F	9	5		1			1			4	2013 AZ Alkmaar	Released Jan 2014, joined Slovan Liberec
Maatesen	Daren	30/01/91	F	2	8	1	1						12	2013 Excelsior Maasluis	OOC
McCarthy	Sean	11/07/93	GK										9	2013 Ross County Youth	OOC
McLean	Brian	28/02/95	D	25	1		1			1			11	2013 Dundee United	OOC
McLeod	Kyle												1	2013 Ross County Youth	C (2015)
Micic	Branislav	17/04/90	D	8	1		1						13	2013 FC Sion	Freed Jan 2014
Munro	Grant	15/09/80	D	5	1					1			1	2011 Inverness CT	Freed Oct 2013 and joined Brora Rangers
Mustafi	Orhan	04/04/90	F	2	5					1	1		6	2013 Grasshoppers Zurich (loan)	Returned to Grasshoppers
Quinn	Rocco	07/09/86	M	20	9	2	1			1			9	2011 Queen of the South	OOC
Ross	Steven	29/08/93	M	5	5								8	2011 Ross County Youth	Joined Brora Rangers on loan Jn 2014 OOC
Saunders	Steven	30/03/91	D	4	8	1	1						6	2013 Motherwell	C (2015)
Slew	Jordan	07/09/92	F	17	3	1								2014 Blackburn Rovers (loan)	Returned to Blackburn
Songo'o	Yann	19/11/91	D	17	3									2014 Blackburn Rovers (loan)	Returned to Blackburn
Sproule	Ivan	18/02/81	M	7	3	2	1							2013 Hibernian	Released Nov 2013, Joined Linfield
Tidser	Michael	15/01/90	F	15	1									2014 Rotherham United (loan)	Returned to Rotherham

NEW SIGNINGS 2014/15

Jervis	Jake		2014 Portsmouth
Cardle	Joe		2014 Raith Rovers
Ferries	Scott		2014 Ross County Youths
McKillop	Ross		2014 Ross County Youths

Date	Comp	H/A	Opponents	F	A	Crowd	Scorers
03/08/2013	Prem	A	Celtic	1	2	45705	Maatsen
10/08/2013	Prem	H	Partick Thistle	1	3	3331	Carey
17/08/2013	Prem	A	St Johnstone	0	4	2833	
24/08/2013	Prem	H	St Mirren	3	0	3142	Kettlewell, Brittain 2
27/08/2013	LC2	A	Stranraer	2	3	215	Brittain, Mustafi
31/08/2013	Prem	A	Hibernian	0	0	9569	
14/09/2013	Prem	H	Dundee United	2	4	3005	Sproule, Quinn
21/09/2013	Prem	H	Hearts	2	1	4059	De Leeuw, Brittain
28/09/2013	Prem	A	Mothewell	1	3	4263	De Leeuw
05/10/2013	Prem	H	Aberdeen	1	0	5290	Quinn
19/10/2013	Prem	A	Kilmarnock	0	2	3582	
09/11/2013	Prem	H	Celtic	1	4	5982	Sproule
16/11/2013	Prem	A	St Mirren	1	2	4205	Saunders
23/11/2013	Prem	A	Hearts	2	2	12508	Carey, De Leeuw
30/11/2013	SC4	H	Hibernian	0	1	2213	
07/12/2013	Prem	H	Kilmarnock	1	2	2937	Kettlewell
14/12/2013	Prem	H	Mothewell	1	2	2792	De Leeuw
21/12/2013	Prem	A	Dundee United	0	1	8029	
26/12/2013	Prem	H	Hibernian	0	2	3383	
29/12/2013	Prem	A	Aberdeen	0	1	11602	
01/01/2014	Prem	A	Inverness CT	2	1	4332	Boyd, Cooper
04/01/2014	Prem	H	St Johnstone	1	0	3305	Carey
11/01/2014	Prem	A	Partick Thistle	3	3	2539	Kiss 2, Gordon
18/01/2014	Prem	H	Dundee United	3	0	3609	Kiss 2, Arquin
25/01/2014	Prem	H	Hearts	1	2	4016	Songo'o
01/02/2014	Prem	A	Kilmarnock	2	2	3372	Arquin, Songo'o
15/02/2014	Prem	A	Hibernian	1	2	8411	Brittain
22/02/2014	Prem	H	St Mirren	2	1	3394	Arquin, De Leeuw
25/02/2014	Prem	H	Inverness CT	0	3	4805	
01/03/2014	Prem	H	Partick Thistle	1	1	3441	Brittain
15/03/2014	Prem	A	St Johnstone	1	0	2213	De Leeuw
22/03/2014	Prem	A	Mothewell	1	2	4080	Songo'o
25/03/2014	Prem	H	Aberdeen	1	1	3775	De Leeuw
29/03/2014	Prem	A	Celtic	1	1	49270	De Leeuw
04/04/2014	Prem	H	Inverness CT	1	2	4433	Kiss
19/04/2014	Prem	A	Hearts	0	2	13692	
26/04/2014	Prem	H	Kilmarnock	2	1	3401	Kiss, Brittain
03/05/2014	Prem	A	St Mirren	0	1	4414	
06/05/2014	Prem	H	Hibernian	1	0	3850	Brittain
10/05/2014	Prem	A	Partick Thistle	3	2	4390	Slew, Arquin, De Leeuw

Friendly Games

3/7/13	Fr	A	Brora Rangers	0	2		
6/7/13	Fr	A	Forres Mechanics	2	0		
6/7/13	Fr	A	Strathspey Thistle	2	2		
9/7/13	Fr	A	Clachnacuddin	5	0		
13/7/13	Fr	A	Peterhead	0	2		
13/7/13	Fr	A	Rothes	3	2		U20
16/7/13	Fr	A	Nairn County	4	0		
20/7/13	Fr	H	Manchester United XI	2	2	4401	
20/7/13	Fr	A	Wick Academy	1	2		U20
23/7/13	Fr	A	Den Bosch	0	1	1000	
26/7/13	Fr	A	PEC Zwolle	1	5		
30/7/13	Fr	A	Burghead Thistle	8	0		U20

Date	Comp	H/A	Opponents	F	A	1	2	3	4	5	6	7	8	9	10	11	12	13	14	15	16	17	18
03/08/2013	Prem	A	Celtic	1	2	Brown	McLean	Munro	Kovacevic	Micic	Gordon	Quinn	Kettlewell	Carey+	Maatsen*	Luckassen"	Cooper*	Sanders+	Mustafi"	Ross	Klok	De Leeuw	Fraser
10/08/2013	Prem	H	Partick Thistle	1	3	Brown	McLean	Munro	Kovacevic	Micic+	Gordon	Quinn	Kettlewell	Carey+	Maatsen+	Mustafi"	De Leeuw*	Ross+	Glen"	Cooper	Klok	Sanders	Fraser
17/08/2013	Prem	A	St Johnstone	0	4	Brown	Boyd	Saunders	Brittain	Micic	Gordon	Quinn	Kettlewell	Carey	De Leeuw"	Sproule+	Ross*	De Leeuw+	Kettlewell+	Boyd	Fraser	McLean	Fraser
24/08/2013	Prem	H	St Mirren	3	0	Brown	McLean	Munro	Kovacevic	Brittain	Gordon	Quinn"	Kettlewell	Carey+	Luckassen"	Sproule+	Mustafi*	De Leeuw+	Maatsen"	Boyd	Micic	Mustafi	Fraser
27/08/2013	LC2	A	Stranraer	2	3	Brown	McLean	Munro	Kovacevic	Brittain	Gordon	Quinn	Kettlewell	Carey+	Luckassen	Sproule"	Mustafi*	Maatsen+	De Leeuw"	Boyd	Fraser	Ross	
31/08/2013	Prem	A	Hibernian	0	0	Brown	McLean	Munro	Kovacevic"	Brittain	Gordon	Quinn*	Kettlewell	Carey	Luckassen	Sproule	De Leeuw*	Maatsen+	Mustafi	Micic	Midic	Ross	Fraser
14/09/2013	Prem	H	Dundee United	2	4	Brown	McLean	Munro"	Kovacevic*	Brittain	Gordon+	Quinn	Kettlewell	Carey	Luckassen	Sproule	Mustafi*	De Leeuw*	Boyd"	Maatsen	Munro	Saunders	Brown
21/09/2013	Prem	H	Hearts	2	1	Brown	McLean	Boyd	Kovacevic	Brittain	Gordon"	Quinn*	Kettlewell	Carey	Ross	Sproule+	De Leeuw*	Glen+	De Leeuw+	Micic	Ross	Saunders	Brown
28/09/2013	Prem	A	Motherwell	1	3	Brown	McLean*	Boyd	Kovacevic	Brittain	Gordon	Quinn"	Kettlewell"	Carey	Ross"	De Leeuw+	De Leeuw*	Sproule+	Glen"	Micic	Ross	Glen	Brown
05/10/2013	Prem	A	Aberdeen	0	2	Brown	McLean	Boyd	Kovacevic	Brittain+	Gordon	Quinn"	Kettlewell"	Carey	Ross+	De Leeuw	Luckassen*	Luckassen+	Maatsen	Micic	Klok	Saunders	Brown
19/10/2013	Prem	H	Kilmarnock	0	2	Brown	McLean	Boyd	Kovacevic"	Brittain+	Gordon	Quinn	Kettlewell	De Leeuw	Ross"	Sproule"	Maatsen*	Luckassen"	Glen"	Micic	Ross	Luckassen	Brown
09/11/2013	Prem	A	Celtic	1	4	Brown	Kovacevic	Boyd	Saunders	Brittian	Micic	Quinn	Kettlewell	De Leeuw	Klok+	De Leeuw	Sproule*	Gordon+	Saunders"	Gordon	Klok	Kovacevic	Fraser
16/11/2013	Prem	A	St Mirren	1	2	Brown	Kovacevic	Boyd	Carey	Brittian	Micic	Quinn"	Kettlewell*	De Leeuw+	Luckassen+	Sproule	Carey*	Maatsen+	Ross"	Maatsen	Cooper	Mustafi	Brown
23/11/2013	Prem	H	Hearts	2	2	Brown	Micic	Boyd	Carey	Brittian	Micic	Quinn"	Kettlewell	De Leeuw+	Luckassen	Glen+	Klok*	Maatsen+	Ross	Kovacevic	Ross	Mustafi	Brown
30/11/2013	SC4	H	Hibernian	0	1	Brown	Saunders+	Mdean	Carey	Brittian	Micic	Quinn	Kettlewell	De Leeuw	Luckassen	Glen+	Saunders	Maatsen+	Kovacevic"	Klok	Klok	Dingwall	Brown
07/12/2013	Prem	A	Kilmarnock	1	2	Brown	Saunders*	Boyd	Brittain	Gordon	Micic*	Quinn	Kettlewell	De Leeuw	Luckassen+	Klok"	Glen*	Ross+	Mustafi"	Maatsen	Cooper	Ross	Brown
14/12/2013	Prem	H	Motherwell	1	2	Brown	Ikonomou	Boyd	Brittain	Gordon	Micic"	Quinn	Kettlewell	De Leeuw	Carey+	Klok"	Luckassen*	Glen+	Maatsen"	Micic	Cooper	Mustafi	Brown
21/12/2013	Prem	H	Dundee United	0	1	Brown	Ikonomou	Boyd	Brittain	Gordon	McLean	Quinn+	Kettlewell	De Leeuw*	Carey	Luckassen"	Glen*	Ross+	Maatsen"	Maatsen	Ross	Klok	Brown
26/12/2013	Prem	A	Hibernian	1	0	Brown	Ikonomou	Boyd	Brittain	Gordon"	McLean	Quinn	Kettlewell	De Leeuw+	Carey"	Luckassen*	Cooper*	Cooper+	Quinn"	Micic	Klok	De Leeuw	Brown
29/12/2013	Prem	A	Aberdeen	0	2	Brown	Ikonomou	Songo'o	Brittain	Gordon	McLean	Cooper"	Kettlewell"	Klok	Carey	Mustafi"	Glen*	Luckassen+	Quinn"	Micic	De Leeuw	Luckassen	Brown
01/01/2014	Prem	H	Inverness CT	2	1	Brown	Ikonomou	Songo'o	Brittain	Gordon	McLean	Cooper	Kiss"	Glen+	Carey	Siew	Glen*	De Leeuw+	Boyd	Micic	Klok	Luckassen	Brown
04/01/2014	Prem	A	Kilmarnock	2	2	Brown	Ikonomou"	Songo'o	Brittain	Gordon+	McLean	Cooper	Kiss*	Glen+	Carey	Siew	Micic*	De Leeuw+	Quinn"	Cikos	Boyd	Glen	Brown
11/01/2014	Prem	H	Partick Thistle	3	3	Brown	Ikonomou	Songo'o	Brittain	Gordon+	McLean	Tidser"	Kiss	Glen*	Carey	Siew	De Leeuw*	Kettlewell+	Gordon+	Kettlewell	Boyd	Glen	McCarthy
18/01/2014	Prem	A	Dundee United	1	2	Brown	Ikonomou	Songo'o	Brittain+	Gordon"	McLean	Tidser	Kiss	Arquin+	Carey"	Siew+	Quinn*	Tidser+	Quinn"	Glen	Quinn	Glen	McCarthy
25/01/2014	Prem	H	Hearts	1	2	Brown	Ikonomou	Songo'o	Brittain	Cikos	McLean	Tidser	Quinn*	Arquin"	Arquin"	Siew+	Cooper*	Cooper+	Quinn	Glen	Boyd	Glen	McCarthy
01/02/2014	Prem	A	Kilmarnock	2	2	Brown	Ikonomou+	Songo'o	Brittain+	Cikos	McLean	Tidser+	Kiss	Arquin	Carey"	Siew+	Cooper*	Cooper+	Saunders+	Glen	Boyd	McLean	McCarthy
15/02/2014	Prem	H	Hibernian	1	2	Brown	Ikonomou	Songo'o	Brittain	Cikos	McLean	Tidser+	Kiss	Arquin	Arquin	Siew"	Cooper*	Luckassen+	Gordon	Glen	Boyd	McLean	McCarthy
22/02/2014	Prem	A	St Mirren	2	1	Brown	Ikonomou"	Songo'o	Brittain+	Cikos	Kettlewell	Tidser	Kiss	Arquin	Arquin*	Siew	De Leeuw*	De Leeuw+	Saunders+	McLean	Gordon	Quinn	McCarthy
25/02/2014	Prem	H	Inverness CT	0	3	Brown	Ikonomou	Songo'o	Brittain	Cikos	De Leeuw"	Tidser+	Kiss*	Arquin	Cooper	Siew*	De Leeuw*	De Leeuw+	Gordon	Glen	Gordon	McLean	McCarthy
01/03/2014	Prem	H	Partick Thistle	1	1	Brown	Ikonomou+	Songo'o"	Brittain	Cikos"	De Leeuw*	Tidser*	Kiss	Arquin	Boyd	Siew	Carey*	Carey+	Gordon	Glen	Gordon	McLean	McCarthy
15/03/2014	Prem	A	St Johnstone	3	3	Brown	Ikonomou	Songo'o	Brittain	Cikos	De Leeuw"	Tidser*	Kiss	Arquin"	Boyd	Carey	Siew*	Glen+	McLean"	Gordon	Gordon	Saunders	McCarthy
22/03/2014	Prem	A	Aberdeen	1	2	Brown	Ikonomou	Songo'o	Brittain	Cikos	Quinn+	Tidser*	Kiss	Arquin"	Boyd	Carey	Siew*	Glen+	Arquin"	McLean	Quinn	McLeod	McCarthy
25/03/2014	Prem	H	Motherwell	1	1	Brown	Ikonomou	Songo'o	Brittain+	Cikos	De Leeuw+	Tidser	Kiss	Arquin	Boyd	Carey	Quinn*	Gordon+	Quinn"	Glen	Quinn	McLean	Fraser
29/03/2014	Prem	A	Celtic	1	1	Brown	Ikonomou	Songo'o	Brittain	Cikos	De Leeuw+	Kettlewell	Kiss	Arquin"	Boyd	Carey"	Cooper*	Siew+	Carey"	McLean	McLean	McLean	Saunders
04/04/2014	Prem	H	Inverness CT	1	2	Brown	Ikonomou	Songo'o	Brittain+	Cikos	De Leeuw+	Kettlewell"	Kiss	Slew	Boyd	Carey"	Kettlewell*	Saunders+	Arquin"	Gordon	Kettlewell	Saunders	Ikonomou
19/04/2014	Prem	H	Hearts	1	0	Brown	Ikonomou	Songo'o	Brittain	Cikos	De Leeuw+	Kettlewell+	Kiss	Slew	Boyd	Carey	Cooper*	Cooper+	Klok"	Quinn	Fraser	McLeod	Ikonomou
26/04/2014	Prem	A	Kilmarnock	2	1	Brown	Gordon	Songo'o	Brittain	Cikos	De Leeuw+	Carey	Kettlewell*	Slew	Slew	Carey"	Quinn*	Cooper+	Arquin"	Maatsen	Fraser	McLean	Saunders
03/05/2014	Prem	H	Hibernian	1	1	Brown	Gordon	Songo'o	Brittain	Cikos	De Leeuw+	Kettlewell	Kiss	Slew"	Slew	Carey"	Cooper*	Cooper+	Carey"	Fraser	Fraser	McLean	Ikonomou
06/05/2014	Prem	H	St Mirren	3	2	Brown	Gordon	Songo'o	Brittain	Cikos	De Leeuw+	Carey"	Kiss	Slew+	Slew"	Arquin	Quinn*	Cooper+	Carey"	Maatsen	Fraser	McLean	Ikonomou
10/05/2014	Prem	A	Partick Thistle	3	2	Brown	Gordon	Quinn	Quinn	Cikos	Cooper"	Cooper"	Kiss	Slew+	Boyd	Arquin"	De Leeuw*	Maatsen+	Klok+	McLean	Fraser	Dingwall	Ikonomou

St Johnstone FC

Founded	1884
Ground	McDiarmid Park
Postcode	PH1 2SJ
Tel	01738 459096
Capacity	10696
Closest Railway Station	Perth
Record Attendance	29972 v Dundee, SC, 10/2/1951
Ground Record	10545 v Dundee, Lge, 23/5/99
Record Win	9-0 v Albion Rovers, LC, 9/3/1946
Record Defeat	1-10 v Third Lanark, SC, 24/1/1903
Most League Goals in a Season	36 Jimmy Benson, 1931/2
Chairman	Steve Brown
Chief Executive	Chris Charalambous
Secretary	Paul Smith
Manager	Tommy Wright
Assistant Manager	Callum Davidson
Colours 2013/14 Top	Blue
Shorts	White
Sponsor	GS Brown Construction
Manufacturer	Joma
Change Colours 2013/14 Top	Red and Black Stripes
Shorts	Black
Nicknames	Saints, Sainties
Web	www.perthstjohnstonefc.co.uk

Winning the Scottish Cup and bringing a first-ever major trophy to Perth marked a momentous season for St Johnstone FC. Manager Tommy Wright believed that their early season European performances showed that they could match anyone over 90 minutes. He was right and the Cup Final performance was as impressive as it could have been.

The biggest frustration for the Perth club has been the low crowds at McDiarmid Park. 15,000 fans turned out for the Cup Final, and the best part of 9000 for European games - Saints need to harness a proportion of these on a more regular basis.

There was no shortage of entertainment on show. Striker Stevie May had a wonderful season and David Wotherspoon was a remarkable capture on a free from Hibernian.

PREDICTION 2014/15
Saints could improve on their league position and end up challenging for a top three or fur place

Surname	First Name	DOB	Pos	L A	L S	L G	SC A	SC S	SC G	LC A	LC S	LC G	UC A	UC S	UC G	UNS	Signed	Previous Club	Notes	Contract
Anderson	Steven	19/12/85	D	29			4			2			4			1	2004	Dundee		C (2016)
Banks	Steven	09/02/72	GK	4			1			1						43	2013	Dundee United		C (2015)
Brown	Scott	25/11/94	M	2	2		1									13	2013	Bradford City		C (2015)
Caddis	Liam	20/09/93	M	8			1						1			6	2011	St Johnstone Youth	On Loan to Alloa	C (2015)
Clancy	Tim	08/06/84	D	3	1											10	2014	Hibernian		F
Clark	Zander	26/06/92	GK													3	2008	St Johnstone Youth	On Loan to QOS	C (2016)
Cregg	Patrick	21/02/86	M	13	7		1	1		2			4			18	2012	Bury		F
Croft	Lee	21/06/85	M	10	8		2	1		1						3	2013	Oldham Athletic		C (2015)
Davidson	Murray	07/03/88	M	18	3		1				1		1				2009	Livingston		C Aug 2014
Dunne	James	18/09/89	M	13			3	1								2	2014	Stevenage (Loan)	Returned to Stevenage	
Easton	Brian	05/03/88	D	22	1		5			3				1		9	2013	Dundee		C (2015)
Easton	Dylan	06/04/94	M													2	2013	Berwick Rangers		C (2016)
Edwards	Gwion	01/05/93	M	4	9					1			3			7	2013	Swansea City (Loan)	Returned to Swansea	
Fallon	Rory	20/03/82	F	1	7		1			1			2			10	2013	Aberdeen	Freed Jan 14, joined Crawley Town	
Gilchrist	Ally	03/03/95	F													3	2013	St Johnstone Youth		Youth
Hasselbaink	Nigel	21/11/90	F	20	10		2			3			4			11	2012	St Mirren		F
Hurst	Mark		GK													3	2013	Livingston		Youth
Iwelumo	Chris	01/08/78	F	6			1			1						12	2014	Scunthorpe United		F
Jahic	Sanel	10/12/81	D	3	2		1									5	2013	Kardemir	Freed Jan 2014, Joined Grasshoppers	
Kane	Chris	05/09/94	F		2											2	2012	St Johnstone Youth	On Loan to Dumbarton	C (2015)
Mackay	David	02/05/80	D	37			5			3			4				2009	Livingston		C (2015)
Mannus	Alan	19/05/82	GK	34			4			2			4				2011	Shamrock Rovers		C (2015)
May	Stevie	02/11/92	F	34	4		5			3			2	1		10	2008	Youths		C (2015)
McDonald	Gary	10/04/82	M	26	3		3	1		3			4			3	2013	Morecambe		C (2015)
McLean	Steven	23/08/82	F	18	3		3	1		4							2012	Cheltenham Town		C (2016)
Millar	Chris	30/03/83	M	28	6		3	1		3			1	1		4	2008	Morton		C (2015)
Miller	Gary	15/04/87	D	16	6		1			1	2				2	19	2012	Ross County		C (2015)
O'Halloran	Michael	30/11/90	F	9	5		3	1		1						4	2013	Bolton Wanderers		C (2015)
Scobbie	Thomas	31/03/88	D	18	3		1						4			4	2012	Falkirk		C (2015)
Thomson	Craig	10/03/95	M		1											1	2011	St Johnstone Youth		Youth
Wotherspoon	David	16/01/90	M	32	6		4	1		2	1		4				2013	Hibernian		C (2015)
Wright	Frazer	23/12/79	D	24	1		3			3			4			1	2011	Kilmarnock		C (2015)

Date	Comp	H/A	Opponents	F	A		Crowd	Scorers
18/07/2013	EUL	A	Rosenborg Trondheim	1	0		5952	Wright
25/07/2013	EUL	H	Rosenborg Trondheim	1	1		7850	May
01/08/2013	EUL	A	FC Minsk	1	0	in Grodno	4000	McLean
03/08/2011	Prem	H	Hearts	1	0		6174	May
08/08/2011	EUL	H	FC Minsk	0	1	AET, 2-3 pens	8594	
11/08/2013	Prem	A	Kilmarnock	0	0		3550	
17/08/2013	Prem	H	Ross County	4	0		2833	Hasselbaink, May, Wotherspoon, MacKay
24/08/2013	Prem	A	Dundee United	0	4		6992	
31/08/2013	Prem	A	Aberdeen	0	0		9478	
14/09/2013	Prem	H	Hibernian	1	2		4095	May
21/09/2013	Prem	A	Celtic	1	2		45220	Caddis
24/09/2013	LC3	A	Hamilton Accies	3	0		1059	May 2, Edwards
28/09/2013	Prem	H	Partick Thistle	1	1		3248	McLean
05/10/2013	Prem	A	Inverness CT	4	0		3020	May, Mackay, McLean 2
19/10/2013	Prem	A	St Mirren	3	4		3739	McLean, Hasselbaink, Fallon
27/10/2013	Prem	H	Motherwell	2	0		2449	May, Hasselbaink
30/10/2013	LC4	A	Morton	1	0		2619	McDonald
02/11/2013	Prem	A	Hearts	2	0		13175	Hasselbaink, May
09/11/2013	Prem	H	Kilmarnock	3	1		2855	May 2, Hasselbaink
23/11/2013	Prem	A	Inverness CT	0	1		3255	
30/11/2013	SC4	H	Livingston	2	0		2294	May, Jahic
07/12/2013	Prem	H	Aberdeen	0	2		4711	
21/12/2013	Prem	A	Hibernian	0	0		8776	
26/12/2013	Prem	H	Celtic	0	1		7034	
29/12/2013	Prem	H	Dundee United	3	0		7231	May 3
01/01/2014	Prem	A	Motherwell	0	4		3763	
04/01/2014	Prem	A	Ross County	0	1		3305	
11/01/2014	Prem	H	St Mirren	2	0		2829	Davidson, May
18/01/2014	Prem	H	Hearts	3	3		3395	May 3
21/01/2014	Prem	A	Partick Thistle	1	0		2719	May
01/02/2014	LCSF	N	Aberdeen	0	4		16761	
08/02/2014	SC5	A	Forfar Athletic	4	0		1803	May, Wright, O'Halloran, Dunne
16/02/2014	Prem	A	Celtic	0	3		45239	
22/02/2014	Prem	H	Inverness CT	0	1		2415	
25/02/2014	Prem	H	Motherwell	3	0		1892	Mclean 2, G Miller
01/03/2014	Prem	A	Aberdeen	0	1		11487	
08/03/2014	SC6	A	Raith Rovers	3	1		3767	McDonald, Hasselbaink, Anderson
12/03/2014	Prem	A	Dundee United	1	0		6720	May
15/03/2014	Prem	H	Ross County	0	1		2213	
22/03/2014	Prem	H	Hibernian	2	0		3553	Mclean, McGivern og
25/03/2014	Prem	A	St Mirren	1	0		2817	McLean
29/03/2014	Prem	A	Partick Thistle	1	1		2999	May
05/04/2014	Prem	A	Kilmarnock	2	1		3665	Wright, Anderson
13/04/2014	SCSF	N	Aberdeen	2	1		19057	May 2
19/04/2013	Prem	H	Dundee United	2	0		5223	Anderson, May
26/04/2014	Prem	A	Aberdeen	1	1		10003	May
03/05/2014	Prem	A	Motherwell	1	2		7201	Mackay
07/05/2014	Prem	H	Celtic	3	3		4624	Clancy, Brown, O'Halloran
11/05/2014	Prem	A	Inverness CT	0	2		3121	
17/05/2014	SCF	N	Dundee United	2	0		47345	Anderson, McLean

Other Matches

10/7/13	Fr	A	Cowdenbeath	1	0		382	
12/7/13	Test	A	Fraserburgh	3	3			Russell McBride Test
13/7/13	Test	A	Morton	1	0		1013	Peter Weatherston Test
20/7/13	Fr	A	Morpeth Town	5	1		U20	
21/7/13	Fr	A	Dundee	1	1			
27/7/13	Fr	H	Morecambe	0	1			
30/7/13	Fr	A	Dundee North End				U20	
27/8/13	FCF	A	Dundee United	1	1	4-2 pens		

Date	Comp	H/A	Opponents	F	A	1	2	3	4	5	6	7	8	9	10	11	12	13	14	15	16	17	18
18/07/2013	EUL	A	Rosenborg Trondheim	1	0	Mannus	MacKay	Scobbie	Wright	Anderson	Cregg	C Millar	McDonald	Wotherspoon+	Maclean	Hasselbaink*	Edwards*	G Miller++	Caddis	B Easton	May	Fallon	Banks
25/07/2013	EUL	H	Rosenborg Trondheim	1	1	Mannus	MacKay	Scobbie	Wright	Anderson	Cregg	May*	McDonald	Wotherspoon+	Maclean	Hasselbaink*	Edwards*	G Miller+	Fallon*	Caddis	Easton D	Easton B	Clark
01/08/2013	EUL	A	FC Minsk (in Grodno)	1	0	Mannus	MacKay	Scobbie	Wright	Anderson	Cregg	Caddis	McDonald	Wotherspoon+	Maclean	Hasselbaink*	M Davidson*	May+	Fallon*	G Miller	Gwion Edwards	Caddis	Fallon
08/08/2013	EUL	H	FC Minsk	1	0	Mannus	MacKay	Scobbie	Wright	Anderson	Cregg	May*	McDonald	Wotherspoon+	Maclean	Hasselbaink*	M Davidson*	Edwards+	Fallon*	Cregg	Miller	Miller	Brown
08/08/2011	EUL	H	Hearts (AET, 2-3 pens)	0	1	Banks	MacKay	Scobbie	Wright	Anderson	Cregg	C Millar	Edwards	Davidson+	May	Hasselbaink*	M Davidson+	Edwards+	McLean*	Scobbie	Cregg	Edwards	Kane
11/08/2013	Prem	A	Kilmarnock	0	0	Banks	MacKay	Scobbie	Wright	Anderson	B Easton*	Wotherspoon*	Edwards	Davidson+	May	Hasselbaink*	Fallon*	M Davidson+	Wotherspoon*	Edwards	Scobbie	McDonald	Anderson
17/08/2013	Prem	H	Ross County	4	0	Banks	MacKay	Scobbie	Wright	Anderson	Cregg*	Caddis	McDonald	Davidson+	May	Hasselbaink*	Caddis+	Caddis+	McDonald+	Brown	Edwards	Cregg	Jahic
24/08/2013	Prem	A	Dundee United	0	4	Banks	MacKay	Scobbie	Wright	Wright	Cregg*	Wotherspoon*	Hasselbaink*	Davidson+	Maclean	Hasselbaink*	McDonald+	Fallon+	Fallon*	Hasselbaink	Miller	Brown	Jahic
31/08/2013	Prem	H	Aberdeen	0	0	Banks	MacKay	Scobbie	Wright	Wright	C Millar	Wotherspoon	McDonald	Davidson+	May	Hasselbaink*	Caddis+	Caddis+	Edwards*	Fallon	B Easton	Fallon	Kane
14/09/2013	Prem	A	Hibernian	1	2	Mannus	MacKay	Scobbie	Wright	Wright	Cregg*	Wotherspoon	McDonald	Davidson+	May	Hasselbaink*	Edwards+	Caddis+	Cregg*	Caddis	C Millar	McDonald	Edwards
21/09/2013	Prem	H	Celtic	1	2	Mannus	MacKay	Scobbie	Wright	Wright	Cregg*	Wotherspoon	McDonald	May	Maclean	C Millar	May*	Edwards+	Cregg*	Scobbie	Edwards	Edwards	Banks
24/09/2013	LC3	A	Hamilton Accies	3	0	Mannus	MacKay	B Easton	Scobbie	Anderson	Cregg	Hasselbaink*	McDonald	Davidson+	May	C Millar	G Miller*	Caddis+	Brown*	Scobbie	Caddis	Cregg	Fallon
28/09/2013	Prem	H	Partick Thistle	1	1	Mannus	MacKay	B Easton	Scobbie	Wright	Cregg	Wotherspoon*	McDonald	Davidson+	May	C Millar	Edwards*	Hasselbaink+	Cregg*	Edwards	Cregg	Cregg	Fallon
05/10/2013	Prem	A	Inverness CT	4	0	Mannus	MacKay	B Easton	Scobbie	Wright	Hasselbaink*	Hasselbaink*	McDonald	May	Maclean	C Millar	Edwards*	Davidson+	Edwards*	Scobbie	Banks	Caddis	Brown
19/10/2013	Prem	H	St Mirren	3	4	Mannus	MacKay	B Easton	Scobbie	Scobbie	G Miller	Hasselbaink*	McDonald	May	Maclean	C Millar	Scobbie*	Davidson+	Caddis*	Edwards	Edwards	Fallon	Kane
27/10/2013	Prem	A	Motherwell	2	0	Mannus	MacKay	B Easton	Scobbie	Scobbie	G Miller	Hasselbaink*	McDonald	May	Maclean	C Millar	Davidson+	Fallon+	Brown*	Scobbie	Scobbie	Scobbie	Anderson
30/10/2013	LC4	A	Morton	1	0	Mannus	Cregg	B Easton	Scobbie	Scobbie	Scobbie	Wotherspoon*	McDonald	May	Scobbie	C Millar	Edwards*	Caddis+	Fallon*	Brown	Edwards	Scobbie	Jahic
02/11/2013	Prem	H	Hearts	2	0	Mannus	MacKay	B Easton	Scobbie	Wright	G Miller*	Wotherspoon*	McDonald	May	May	C Millar*	Caddis*	Scobbie	Caddis*	G Miller	Banks	Croft	Jahic
09/11/2013	Prem	A	Kilmarnock	3	1	Mannus	MacKay	B Easton	Scobbie	Wright	G Miller+	Wotherspoon*	McDonald	May	May	C Millar*	Edwards+	Davidson+	Kane*	G Miller	Brown	Brown	Kane
23/11/2013	Prem	H	Inverness CT	0	1	Mannus	MacKay	B Easton	Scobbie	Wright	Davidson	Wotherspoon*	McDonald	May	May	G Miller	Fallon*	jahic+	B Easton*	Hasselbaink	Banks	Fallon	Edwards
30/11/2013	SC4	A	Livingston	2	0	Banks	McKay	B Easton	Wright	B Easton	Davidson	Croft*	McDonald+	May	Wotherspoon+	Hasselbaink*	Edwards*	Edwards+	Brown*	Cregg	Banks	Fallon	Edwards
07/12/2013	Prem	A	Aberdeen	0	2	Banks	McKay	B Easton	Wright	B Easton	Davidson*	Croft*	C Millar	May	May	Croft	Edwards*	Caddis+	C Millar*	Brown	Banks	C Millar	Brown
21/12/2013	Prem	H	Hibernian	0	0	Banks	McKay	B Easton	Wright	B Easton	Davidson*	Hasselbaink*	Cregg	McDonald	Hasselbaink	C Millar	Scobbie*	jahic+	Croft*	Hasselbaink	Banks	O'Halloran	Kane
26/12/2013	Prem	A	Partick Thistle	1	0	Mannus	McKay	B Easton	Wright	B Easton	Davidson*	Croft*	McDonald	McDonald	Wotherspoon+	McLean	Hasselbaink*	Edwards+	iwelumo*	Fallon	Hasselbaink	Fallon	Easton
29/12/2013	Prem	H	Celtic	0	1	Mannus	McKay	B Easton	B Easton	Anderson	Davidson	Croft*	McDonald	McDonald	Wotherspoon	McLean	O'Halloran*	Caddis+	Cregg*	Fallon	Banks	Brown	D Easton
01/01/2014	Prem	A	Dundee United	3	0	Banks	McKay	B Easton	B Easton	Anderson	Davidson	Wotherspoon*	McDonald	McDonald	May	Brown	iwelumo*	Fallon+	Kane*	G Miller	Hurst	Scobbie	Hasselbaink
04/01/2014	Prem	H	Motherwell	0	4	Banks	McKay	B Easton	B Easton	Anderson	Anderson	Croft*	McDonald	McDonald	Wotherspoon+	C Millar*	Clancy*	Edwards+	Brown*	G Miller	Hurst	Croft	Iwelumo
11/01/2014	Prem	A	Ross County	2	0	Banks	McKay	B Easton	B Easton	Anderson	Anderson	Hasselbaink	McDonald	McDonald	Wotherspoon*	McLean*	Wotherspoon*	Croft+	C Millar*	Cregg	Banks	Brown	O'Halloran
18/01/2014	Prem	H	St Mirren	3	3	Banks	McKay	B Easton	B Easton	Anderson	Anderson	Croft*	McDonald	May	Wotherspoon*	Croft	C Millar+	Hasselbaink+	C Millar*	G Miller	Banks	Wright	Gilchrist
21/01/2014	SC5	H	Partick Thistle	1	0	Mannus	McKay	Scobbie	Clancy	Clancy	Cregg*	May*	McDonald	McDonald	May	Croft	Croft+	Fallon+	Croft*	Fallon	Banks	Croft	Clancy
01/02/2014	LCSF	N	Aberdeen	0	4	Mannus	McKay	B Easton	Clancy	Clancy	Dunne*	Croft*	McDonald	McDonald	Wotherspoon*	McLean*	Cregg*	O'Halloran+	C Millar*	G Miller	Banks	Brown	Clancy
08/02/2014	SC5	A	Forfar Athletic	4	0	Mannus	McKay	B Easton	Clancy	Wright	Dunne	Croft*	McDonald	McDonald	May	Croft	Wright*	iwelumo+	C Millar*	Cregg	Banks	Dunne	Iwelumo
16/02/2014	Prem	A	Celtic	0	3	Mannus	McKay	B Easton	B Easton	Wright	Anderson	Hasselbaink	McDonald	McDonald	Wotherspoon+	McLean	Wotherspoon*	Wotherspoon+	Hasselbaink*	Hasselbaink	Banks	O'Halloran	Gilchrist
22/02/2014	Prem	H	Inverness CT	0	1	Mannus	McKay	B Easton	B Easton	Wright	Anderson	Croft*	McDonald	McDonald	Wotherspoon*	McLean*	C Millar+	G Miller+	Brown*	Cregg	Banks	Iwelumo	Clancy
25/02/2014	Prem	H	Motherwell	3	0	Mannus	McKay	B Easton	G Miller	Wright	Anderson*	Croft*	McDonald	May	May	McLean	Wotherspoon*	O'Halloran*	Cregg*	G Miller	Banks	Iwelumo	McDonald
01/03/2014	Prem	A	Aberdeen	0	1	Mannus	Wright	B Easton	G Miller	Easton	Anderson	Hasselbaink	McDonald	May	May	McLean	McLean*	Croft+	C Millar*	Hasselbaink	Banks	Iwelumo	Clancy
08/03/2014	SC6	A	Raith Rovers	3	1	Mannus	McKay	Clancy	Easton	Wright	Anderson	Croft*	McDonald	May	May	Croft	O'Halloran*	C Millar+	C Millar*	McDonald	Banks	O'Halloran	Clancy
12/03/2014	Prem	A	Dundee United	1	0	Mannus	McKay	B Easton	G Miller	Wright	Anderson	C Millar	McDonald	May	O'Halloran	McLean	Clancy*	Cregg*	iwelumo*	Hasselbaink	Banks	Iwelumo	Clancy
15/03/2014	Prem	A	Ross County	0	1	Mannus	McKay	B Easton	G Miller	Wright	Anderson	Wotherspoon*	McDonald	May	O'Halloran	McLean	Croft*	Cregg*	Cregg*	Fallon	Banks	Iwelumo	Clancy
22/03/2014	Prem	H	Hibernian	1	0	Mannus	McKay	B Easton	G Miller	G Miller	Anderson	Wotherspoon*	McDonald	May	O'Halloran	Hasselbaink*	Hasselbaink	Hasselbaink	Thompson*	Clancy	Banks	Iwelumo	Clancy
25/03/2014	Prem	A	St Mirren	1	0	Mannus	McKay	B Easton	G Miller	G Miller	Anderson	Wotherspoon*	McDonald	May	O'Halloran	McLean	Cregg*	McLean+	G Miller*	McDonald	Banks	Iwelumo	Clancy
29/03/2014	Prem	H	Partick Thistle	1	1	Mannus	McKay	B Easton	G Miller	G Miller	Anderson	Wotherspoon*	McDonald	May	O'Halloran	Hasselbaink*	Croft+	Wotherspoon+	McDonald+	Brown	Banks	Iwelumo	Thomson
05/04/2014	Prem	H	Aberdeen	2	1	Mannus	McKay	B Easton	B Easton	Easton	Dunne*	Croft*	McDonald	May	McLean	Croft	Hasselbaink+	iwelumo+	iwelumo*	Clancy	Banks	Iwelumo	Clancy
13/04/2014	SCSF	N	Aberdeen	2	1	Mannus	Wright	B Easton	B Easton	B Easton	C Millar	Wotherspoon*	McDonald	May	McLean	Croft	Croft*	McDonald+	May*	C Millar	Banks	Dunne	Clancy
19/04/2014	Prem	H	Dundee United	2	0	Mannus	McKay	Clancy	Wright	B Easton	C Millar	Wotherspoon*	McDonald	May	O'Halloran	Croft	Hasselbaink+	McLean+	G Miller*	Brown	Banks	Clancy	Gilchrist
26/04/2014	Prem	A	Motherwell	1	1	Mannus	McKay	Easton	G Miller	Wright	C Millar	Wotherspoon*	McDonald	May	O'Halloran	Croft	Croft*	Wotherspoon+	iwelumo*	Clancy	Banks	Iwelumo	Brown
03/05/2014	Prem	H	Inverness CT	3	3	Mannus	McKay	Clancy	G Miller	G Miller	C Millar	Wotherspoon*	McDonald	May	O'Halloran	Croft	Hasselbaink+	iwelumo+	May*	C Millar	Banks	Iwelumo	Hasselbaink
07/05/2014	Prem	A	Partick Thistle	2	1	Mannus	McKay	Clancy	Wright	G Miller	Anderson	Wotherspoon*	C Millar	May	Brown	Croft*	Croft*	McDonald+	McDonald*	McDonald	Banks	Clancy	Cregg
11/05/2014	Prem	H	Inverness CT	2	1	Mannus	McKay	Clancy	G Miller	Wright	C Millar	Wotherspoon*	McDonald	May*	McLean	Croft	iwelumo+	iwelumo+	May*	C Millar	Banks	Clancy	Brown
17/05/2014	SCF	N	Dundee United	2	0	Mannus	McKay	B Easton	Wright	Anderson	C Millar	Wotherspoon*	McDonald	May*	McLean	Dunne	Croft*	McDonald+	iwelumo*	G Miller	Banks	Hasselbaink	Cregg

St Mirren FC

Founded	1876
Ground	St Mirren Park, Greenhill Road
Postcode	PA3 1RU
Tel	0141 889 2558
Capacity	8023
Closest Railway Station	Paisley St James
Record Attendance	47438 v Celtic, LC, 20/8/49
Ground Record	7542 v Kilmarnock, 31/1/09
Record Win	15-0 v Glasgow University, SC, 30/1/1960
Record Defeat	0-9 v Rangersd, Lge, 4/12/1897
Most League Goals in a Season	45 Dunky Walker, 1921/2
Chairman	Stewart Gilmour
Chief Executive	Brian Caldwell
Manager	Danny Lennon / Tommy Craig
Assistant Manager	
Colours 2013/14 Top	Black and White Stripes
Shorts	White
Sponsor	Blacks Life Outdoors
Manufacturer	Diadora
Change Colours 2013/14 Top	Red with black side stripe
Shorts	Red
Third Kit 2013/14 Top	Yellow
Shorts	Black
Nicknames	Buddies
Web	www.saintmirren.net

St Mirren Manager Danny Lennon was under intense pressure in the early part of the season as results seemed to go against them. However, he weathered the storm and, at times, his team produced some excellent football.

A real positive was the emergence of a crop of home-grown youngsters who graduated to the first team and contributed well. Saints will hope to hold on to the likes of Kenny McLean and John McGinn for a while yet before possibly capitalising on their value.

Lennon's contract was not renewed and his job was given to Assistant Tommy Craig. Craig has vast experience of the Scottish game but is not used to the pressure associated with being the man in ultimate charge.

PREDICTION 2014/15
Could be a tough season for St Mirren, battling to avoid the relegation play off

			Pos	L A	S	SC G	A	S	LC G	A	S	G	UNS	Signed Previous Club	Notes	Contract
Surname	First Name	DOB														
Bahoken	Stephane	28/05/92	F	2	3								4	2013 OGC Nice (Loan)	Returned to OGC Nice	
Brady	Anton	07/02/92	M		1		1						12	2012 St Mirren Youth		Youth
Campbell	Adam	01/01/95	F	7	4	2	1						9	2014 Newcastle United (Loan)	Returned to Newcastle United	
Caprice	Jake	11/11/92	M		6				1				9	2013 Blackpool (Loan)	Returned to Blackpool	
Cornell	David	28/03/91	GK	5					1				8	2013 Swansea City(Loan)	Returned to Swansea City	
Cuddihy	Barry	19/12/96	M										3	2013 St Mirren Youth		Youth
Dillon	Kealan	21/02/94	M										2	2013 Hull City	Rele4ased Jan 2014, Joined Athlone Town	
Dilo	Christopher	05/01/94	GK	12	1								24	2013 Blackburn Rovers		ONC
Djemba Djemba	Eric	04/05/81	M	2		1							10	2014 Partizan Belgrade		F
Goodwin	Jim	20/11/81	M	31	1	3		1					1	2010 Hamilton Accies		C (2015)
Grainger	Danny	28/07/87	D	10	3	1		1					11	2013 Hearts	Released Jan 2014, Joined Dunfermline Ath	C (2015)
Harkins	Gary	02/01/85	M	7	8	1	1		1	1			5	2013 Dundee	On loan to Oldham Athletic Jan 2014	C (2015)
Hughes	Kieran	18/08/94	GK										3	2013 St Mirren Youth		Youth
Kello	Marian	05/09/82	GK	21		3							5	2013 Wolves		C (2015)
Kelly	Sean	18/01/93	D	32	1	1	2	1	1				3	2011 St Mirren Youth		C (2016)
Magennis	Josh	15/08/90	M	7	6									2014 Aberdeen (Loan)	Returned to Aberdeen	
Mair	Lee	09/12/80	D	5	1								13	2009 Aberdeen	Released Jan 2014, Joined Partick Thistle	
Mathers	Paul	17/01/70	GK										2		Goalkeeper Coach	
McAusland	Marc	13/09/88	D	30	2		3		1				2	2006 St Mirren Youth		C (2015)
McGinn	John	18/10/94	M	31	4	3	2		1				2	2012 St Mirren Youth		C (2015)
McGowan	Paul	07/10/87	F	33	3	4	2			1			1	2011 Celtic		F
McGregor	Darren	07/08/85	D	35			3						4	2010 Cowdenbeath		ONC
McLean	Kenny	08/01/92	M	28	2	7	3		1	1				2010 St Mirren Youth		ONC
Morgan	Lewis	30/09/96	M										4	2013 St Mirren Youth		Youth
Naismith	Jason	25/06/94	D	26	1	2	2						9	2012 St Mirren Youth		C (2017)
Newton	Conor	17/10/91	M	36	1	4	3		1	1				2013 Newcastle United (Loan)	Returned to Newcastle United	
Reilly	Thomas	15/09/94	F	1	7		2						24	2011 St Mirren Youth		C (2015)
Robertson	Jon	25/04/89	D	1	1								1	2012 Cowdenbeath	Joined Cowdenbeath Aug 2013	
Stewart	Jordan	05/03/96	M										1	2013 St Mirren Youth		Youth
Teale	Gary	21/07/78	M	6	9		1		1				4	2011 Sheffield Wednesday		C (2015)
Thompson	Steven	14/10/78	F	36		13	3		2	1		1		2011 Burnley		Option
Van Zanten	David	08/05/82	D	8	8		1			1			19	2010 Hamilton Accies		F
Williams	Mark	15/05/95	D										3	2013 St Mirren Youth		Youth
Wylde	Greg	23/03/91	M	6	11	2								2014 Aberdeen		C (2015)
Own Goals						1										

NEW SIGNINGS 2014/15

Ridgers	Mark		GK											2014 Hearts	

Date	Comp	H/A	Opponents	F	A		Crowd	Scorers
03/08/2013	Prem	A	Inverness CT	0	3		3215	
17/08/2013	Prem	H	Kilmarnock	1	1		4625	Harkins
24/08/2013	Prem	A	Ross County	0	3		3142	
27/08/2013	LC2	A	Queen of the South	1	2	AET	2073	Thompson
31/08/2013	Prem	H	Partick Thistle	1	2		5601	McLean
14/09/2013	Prem	H	Motherwell	0	1		4012	
21/09/2013	Prem	A	Hibernian	0	2		9417	
30/09/2013	Prem	H	Aberdeen	1	1		4051	Thompson
05/10/2013	Prem	A	Hearts	2	0		14769	McGinn, McGowan
19/10/2013	Prem	H	St Johnstone	4	3		3739	Mclean 2, McGowan, Thompson
26/10/2013	Prem	A	Dundee United	0	4		6331	
09/11/2013	Prem	A	Partick Thistle	3	0		4946	Thompson 2, Newton
17/11/2013	Prem	H	Ross County	2	1		4205	Mclean, Newton
23/11/2013	Prem	H	Hibernian	0	0		4451	
30/11/2013	SC4	A	Queen of the South	2	2		2176	Newton, Thompson
07/12/2013	Prem	H	Inverness CT	0	0		3305	
10/12/2013	SC4R	H	Queen of the South	3	0		2775	Harkins, Thomson, Kelly
14/12/2013	Prem	A	Aberdeen	0	2		9332	
21/12/2013	Prem	A	Motherwell	0	3		3867	
26/12/2013	Prem	H	Dundee United	4	1		4780	Thompson 2, McGinn, Naismith
29/12/2013	Prem	H	Hearts	1	1		4568	Thompson
02/01/2014	Prem	A	Kilmarnock	1	2		5410	Campbell
05/01/2014	Prem	H	Celtic	0	4		5778	
11/01/2014	Prem	A	St Johnstone	0	2		2829	
18/01/2014	Prem	A	Hibernian	3	2		9610	Williams og, Campbell, Thompson
25/01/2014	Prem	H	Partick Thistle	0	0		4660	
29/01/2014	Prem	A	Hearts	1	2		12422	Thompson
02/02/2014	Prem	A	Celtic	0	1		45014	
08/02/2014	SC5	A	Dundee United	1	2		4952	McLean
15/02/2014	Prem	H	Aberdeen	0	1		4073	Rooney
22/02/2014	Prem	A	Ross County	1	2		3394	McGinn
01/03/2014	Prem	H	Kilmarnock	2	0		4650	Nerwton, Wylde
15/03/2014	Prem	A	Dundee United	2	3		6524	McGowan, Thompson
22/03/2014	Prem	A	Celtic	0	3		46536	
25/03/2014	Prem	H	St Johnstone	0	1		2817	
29/03/2014	Prem	A	Inverness CT	2	2		3032	Naismith, Kelly
05/04/2014	Prem	H	Motherwell	3	2		4377	Thompson 2, McLean
19/04/2014	Prem	H	Hibernian	2	0		5287	Mclean, McGowan
25/04/2014	Prem	A	Partick Thistle	1	1		5971	McLean
03/05/2014	Prem	H	Ross County	1	0		4414	Wylde
07/05/2014	Prem	A	Kilmarnock	0	1		4911	
10/05/2014	Prem	H	Hearts	1	1		6311	Newton, Thompson

Friendly Matches

Date	Comp	H/A	Opponents	F	A	Crowd		
13/7/13	Fr	N	Charlton Athletic	0	4			at Marbella
13/7/13	TnT	N	Wrexham	1	6	205	U20	at Gretna
14/7/13	TnT	A	Gretna	0	2		U20	
17/7/13	RC1	H	Port Glasgow OBU	16	0			at Ralston
20/7/13	RCF	H	Morton	2	4	3703		
24/7/13	Fr	A	Queen of the South	2	4			
27/7/13	Fr	A	Stockport County	1	0	1171		
27/7/13	TnT	N	Motherwell U20	1	4		U20	at Irvine Meadow
28/7/13	TnT	A	Irvine Meadow	1	1		U20	
30/7/12	Fr	H	Newcastle United	0	2	4216		

Date	Comp	H/A	Opponents	F	A	1	2	3	4	5	6	7	8	9	10	11	12	13	14	15	16	17	18
03/08/2013	Prem	A	Inverness CT	0	3	Cornell	Van Zanten	Grainger	McAusland	Teale	Harkins	Goodwin	McGinn*	Thompson	McGowan+	Reilly	Robertson*	Kelly+	McGregor	Dillon	Naismith	Brady	Dilo
17/08/2013	Prem	H	Kilmarnock	1	1	Cornell	McGregor	Grainger+	McAusland	Teale	Harkins	Goodwin	Robertson	McLean*	McGowan	Newton	Reilly*	Kelly	McGinn+	Dillon	Naismith	Thompson	Dilo
24/08/2013	Prem	A	Ross County	0	3	Cornell	McGregor*	Grainger	McAusland	Teale+	Harkins+	Goodwin	Thompson	McLean*	McGowan	Newton	Van Zanten*	Reilly+	McGinn	Robertson	Naismith	Kelly	Dilo
27/08/2013	LC2	A	Queen of the South	1	2	Cornell	Van Zanten	Grainger	McAusland	Teale+	Harkins+	Goodwin	Thompson	McLean*	McGinn	Newton*	McGowan*	Caprice+	McGregor*	Reilly	Dilo	McGregor	Kelly
31/08/2013	Prem	H	Partick Thistle	1	2	Cornell	Van Zanten+	Grainger	McAusland	McGinn	Harkins*	Goodwin	Thompson	McLean*	Newton	Bahoken*	Teale*	McGowan+	Caprice*	Reilly	Dilo	McGregor	Mair
14/09/2013	Prem	A	Motherwell	0	1	Cornell	McGregor	Grainger+	McAusland	Teale	Harkins*	Goodwin	Thompson	McLean	Newton	Bahoken*	Caprice*	Harkins+	McGinn*	Van Zanten	Dilo	McGinn	Mair
21/09/2013	Prem	H	Hibernian	0	2	Dilo	Van Zanten+	Grainger	McAusland	Teale	Harkins*	Goodwin	Thompson+	McLean	Newton	McGowan*	Caprice*	Bahoken+	McGinn*	McGregor	Cornell	Mair	Reilly
30/09/2013	Prem	A	Aberdeen	1	1	Dilo	Van Zanten	Mair	McGregor	McGinn*	Kelly	Goodwin	Thompson+	McLean	Newton	McGowan*	Bahoken*	Teale	Naismith	Reilly	Cornell	Harkins	Caprice
05/10/2013	Prem	H	Hearts	2	0	Dilo	Van Zanten	Mair	McGregor	McGinn	Kelly	Goodwin+	Thompson	McLean	Newton	McGowan	Teale*	Bahoken	Harkins	Caprice	Cornell	Naismith	Grainger
19/10/2013	Prem	A	St Johnstone	4	3	Dilo	Van Zanten*	Mair	McGregor	McGinn*	Kelly	Goodwin++	Thompson	McLean	Newton	McGowan	Caprice*	Harkins+	Reilly	Bahoken	Cornell	Naismith	Grainger
26/10/2013	Prem	H	Dundee United	0	4	Kello	Van Zanten*	Mair	McGregor	McGinn*	Kelly	Goodwin++	Thompson	McLean	Newton	McGowan	Caprice*	Naismith+	Harkins*	Bahoken	Cornell	McAusland	Grainger
09/11/2013	Prem	A	Partick Thistle	3	0	Kello	McAusland	Naismith*	McGregor	McGregor	Kelly*	Goodwin	Thompson	McLean	Newton	McGowan*	Van Zanten*	Harkins+	Harkins*	Caprice	Cornell	Reilly	Bahoken
17/11/2013	Prem	H	Ross County	2	1	Kello	McAusland	Naismith	McGregor	McGinn	Kelly*	Goodwin	Thompson	McLean	Newton	McGowan*	Reilly*	Mair	Harkins	Caprice	Dilo	Mair	Grainger
23/11/2013	Prem	A	Hibernian	2	2	Kello	McAusland	Naismith	McGregor	McGinn*	Kelly	Van Zanten+	Thompson	McLean	Newton	McGowan*	Reilly*	Van Zanten	Harkins	Reilly	Dilo	Stewart	Grainger
30/11/2013	SC4	A	Queen of the South	2	2	Kello	McAusland	Naismith	McGregor	McGinn	Kelly	Goodwin	Thompson	McLean	Newton	McGowan*	Mair	Mair	Harkins	Reilly	Cornell	Caprice	Grainger
07/12/2013	Prem	H	Inverness CT	0	0	Kello	McAusland	Naismith	McGregor	McGinn	Kelly	Goodwin	Thompson+	McLean	Newton	McGowan*	Reilly*	Harkins*	Harkins*	Van Zanten	Dilo	Reilly	Grainger
10/12/2013	SC4R	H	Queen of the South	3	0	Kello	McAusland	Van Zanten	McGregor	McGinn*	Grainger*	Goodwin	Thompson	McLean	Newton	McGowan*	Caprice*	Reilly+	Brady*	Caprice	Dilo	Reilly	Grainger
14/12/2013	Prem	A	Aberdeen	0	2	Kello	McAusland	Naismith	McGregor	McGinn*	Kelly	Goodwin	Thompson+	McLean	Newton	Harkins*	Kelly*	Reilly+	Mair	Caprice	Dilo	Mair	Naismith
21/12/2013	Prem	H	Motherwell	0	3	Kello	Mair	Naismith	McGregor	McGinn*	Grainger	Goodwin	Thompson	McLean	Newton	McGowan	Harkins*	Harkins*	Brady*	Caprice	Dilo	Reilly	Grainger
26/12/2013	Prem	H	Dundee United	4	1	Kello	McAusland+	Naismith	McGregor	Harkins+	Kelly*	Goodwin*	Thompson	McLean	Newton*	McGowan	McGinn*	Reilly+	Van Zanten*	Caprice	Dilo	McAusland	Grainger
29/12/2013	Prem	A	Hearts	1	1	Kello	McAusland	Naismith	McGregor	McGinn	Kelly*	Goodwin	Thompson	McLean+	Newton	McGowan*	Reilly*	Grainger+	Harkins*	Reilly	Dilo	Mair	Brady
05/01/2014	Prem	A	Kilmarnock	1	2	Kello	McAusland	Naismith	McGregor	Harkins*	Kelly*	Goodwin*	Thompson	Grainger	Newton	McGowan+	Van Zanten*	Harkins+	Mair	Van Zanten	Dilo	Brady	Cuddihy
11/01/2014	SC5	H	Celtic	0	4	Dilo	McAusland	Naismith	McGregor	McGinn	Kelly*	Campbell	Campbell*	Grainger*	Newton	McGowan	Campbell*	Harkins*	Mair	Van Zanten	Dilo	Brady	Cuddihy
18/01/2014	Prem	A	St Johnstone	0	2	Dilo	Kello*	McGinn*	McGregor*	McGinn	Kelly	Goodwin	Thompson+	Grainger*	Newton	McGowan	Reilly*	Brady+	Reilly*	Van Zanten	Dilo	Williams	Cuddihy
25/01/2014	SC5R	H	Hibernian	3	2	Kello	Wylde	McGowan	McGregor	Campbell*	Kelly	Goodwin	Thompson*	Wylde	Newton	McGowan+	Bahoken*	Van Zanten	Brady	Hughes	Dilo	Mair	Morgan
25/01/2014	Prem	H	Partick Thistle	0	1	Kello	Wylde	Djemba-Djemba +	McGregor	McGinn	Kelly	Goodwin	Thompson	Campbell*	Newton+	McGowan+	Wylde*	Van Zanten+	Grainger*	Reilly	Dilo	Brady	Morgan
01/03/2014	Prem	A	Hearts	1	1	Kello	Wylde	Djemba-Djemba *	McGregor*	McGinn*	Kelly	Goodwin	Thompson	Campbell*	Wylde	McLean	Newton*	McAusland+	Campbell	Reilly	Dilo	Brady	Morgan
02/02/2014	Prem	H	Celtic	1	2	Kello	Naismith	McGowan*	McGregor	McGinn+	Kelly	McAusland	Thompson	Campbell*	Newton	McLean	Wylde*	Campbell+	Campbell	Reilly	Dilo	Hughes	Grainger
08/02/2014	Prem	A	Dundee United	0	2	Kello	Naismith"	McGowan"	McGregor"	McGinn	Kelly	McAusland	Thompson"	Campbell"	Newton	McLean	Wylde*	Teale+	Brady	Reilly	Dilo	Brady	Morgan
15/02/2014	Prem	H	Aberdeen	0	1	Kello*	Naismith	McGowan"	McGinn*	McGinn	Kelly	McAusland	Thompson	Magennis	Newton+	McLean	Wylde*	Goodwin+	Wylde*	Reilly	Dilo	Mair	Williams
22/02/2014	Prem	A	Ross County	1	2	Kello*	Naismith	Goodwin"	McGinn*	McGinn*	Kelly	Campbell+	Wylde*	Magennis	Newton+	McLean	Dilo*	Wylde*	Teale*	Van Zanten	Goodwin	Campbell	Djemba-Djemba
01/03/2014	Prem	H	Kilmarnock	2	0	Dilo	Naismith	Goodwin"	McGregor*	McGinn*	Kelly	Campbell+	Thompson	Wylde"	Newton+	McLean	Magennis*	Magennis*	Teale*	Van Zanten	Reilly	Mathers	Djemba-Djemba
15/03/2014	Prem	A	Dundee United	2	3	Dilo	Naismith+	Goodwin"	McGregor*	McGinn	Kelly	McAusland	Thompson*	McGowan*	Newton+	McLean	Wylde*	Wylde*	Teale"	Van Zanten	Campbell	Campbell	Djemba-Djemba
22/03/2014	Prem	H	Celtic	0	3	Dilo	Naismith	Goodwin	McGregor*	McGinn	Kelly	McAusland	Thompson	McGowan*	Newton	McLean	Magennis+	Wylde+	Teale"	Van Zanten	Teale	Kello	Djemba-Djemba
25/03/2014	Prem	A	St Johnstone	0	1	Dilo	Naismith	Goodwin	McGregor*	McGinn*	Kelly	McAusland	Thompson	McGowan*	Newton+	McLean	Wylde*	Magennis*	Van Zanten	Campbell	Teale	Kello	Djemba-Djemba
29/03/2014	Prem	A	Inverness CT	2	2	Dilo	Naismith	Goodwin"	McGregor*	McGinn*	Kelly	Campbell+	Thompson.	McGowan*	Newton+	McLean	Magennis*	Magennis-	Van Zanten	Campbell	Reilly	Campbell	Djemba-Djemba
05/04/2014	Prem	H	Motherwell	3	2	Dilo	Naismith	Goodwin"	McGregor	McGinn*	Kelly	McAusland	Wylde"	Wylde*	Newton	McLean	Wylde*	Wylde*	Teale"	Van Zanten	Campbell	Mathers	Djemba-Djemba
19/04/2014	Prem	H	Hibernian	2	0	Dilo	Naismith	Goodwin	McGregor*	McGinn+	Kelly	McAusland	Thompson	McGowan*	Newton+	McLean	Magennis*	Wylde*	Teale*	Van Zanten	Campbell	Kello	Djemba-Djemba
25/04/2014	Prem	A	Partick Thistle	1	1	Dilo	Naismith	Goodwin	McGregor*	McGinn*	Kelly	McAusland	Thompson	McGowan++	Newton+	McLean	Magennis*	Magennis*	Van Zanten	Campbell	Teale	Kello	Djemba-Djemba
03/05/2014	Prem	A	Ross County	1	0	Dilo	Goodwin"	Goodwin"	McGregor"	McGinn*	Kelly	McAusland	Thompson	McGowan*	Newton	McLean	Wylde*	Van Zanten	Teale*	Campbell	Teale	Kello	Djemba-Djemba
07/05/2014	Prem	A	Kilmarnock	0	1	Dilo	Naismith"	Goodwin"	McGregor	McGinn*	Kelly	McAusland	Thompson	Magennis	Newton+	McLean	Wylde*	Van Zanten	Teale"	Campbell	Van Zanten	Kello	Djemba-Djemba
10/05/2014	Prem	H	Hearts	1	1	Dilo	Naismith"	Goodwin"	McGregor	Teale*	Kelly	McAusland	Wylde	Magennis	Newton+	McLean	McGowan*	McGinn+	Van Zanten"	Reilly	Reilly	Kello	Djemba-Djemba

Stenhousemuir FC

Founded	1884
Ground	Ochilview Park
Postcode	FK5 4QL
Tel	01324 562 992
Capacity	3746
Closest Railway Station	Larbert
Record Attendance	12500 v East Fife, SC, 11/3/1950
Ground Record	01324 562992
Record Win	Ochilview
Record Defeat	2-11 v Dunfermline Athletic, 27/9/1930
Most League Goals in a Season	32 Robert Taylor, 1925/6
Chairman	Bill Darroch
General Manager	Margaret Kilpatrick
Manager	Martin Corrigan / Scott Booth
Assistant Manager	
Colours 2013/14 Top	Maroon
Shorts	White
Sponsor	Gulnar Indian Restaurant
Manufacturer	CIC (Own Brand)
Change Colours 2013/14 Top	Yellow with blue flash
Shorts	Blue
Nicknames	Warriors
Web	www.stenhousemuirfc.com

Stenhousemuir has an unremarkable season in League One during 2013/14, not really challenging at the top of the table and never in great danger of relegation. Towards the end of the season they appointed Scott Booth as Manager to take over from Martyn Corrigan.

Booth in an interesting appointment. He is a highly-regarded Coach and at Ochilview he will have a blank canvas to apply his own methods and techniques. He has cleared out quite a few players from last season as he looks to make his own mark.

Stenhousemuir have a well established youth and community policy and that has produced some good players for them in the past.

PREDICTION 2014/15
Likely to be in mid table again

Name		DOB	Pos	L A	S	G	SC A	S	G	LC A	S	G	RC A	S	G	UNS	Signed	Signed From	Notes	
Anderson	Craig	05/05/88	M	2	4					1			2	1		3	2012	Civil Service Strollers	Released during season	
Brash	Ross	22/05/93	M	1	4	1		1		1						11	2005	Stenhousemuir Youth		F
Devlin	Nicky	17/10/93	D	29	1	4		1		3						4	2013	Motherwell		F
Dickson	Sean	16/01/92	M	33	3	10	4	1	1	1	4						2008	Stenhousemuir Youth		C (2015)
Docherty	Charles	04/05/94	D													3	2009	Stenhousemuir Youth		F
Douglas	Errol	12/05/93	F	1	18	1	2	2	2	1			3	1		18	2013	Craigroyston	Joined Spartans May 2014	F
Duncan	Robbie	28/01/94	D	3									1		2		2010	Stenhousemuir Youth		C (2015)
Faulds	Kriss	03/07/94	M	5	4		2									8	2013	Falkirk (loan)		
Ferguson	Brown	04/06/81	M	9	3		1	2					2	1		11	2011	Partick Thistle		R
Gemmell	John	06/09/84	F	18	8	11	3			2	1		3	3			2012	Albion Rovers	Joined Albion Rovers May 2014	
Greacen	Stewart	31/03/82	D	18	1											1	2013	Derry City		C (2015)
Greenhalgh	Ben	16/04/92	M	6	3												2014	Inverness CT (Loan Mar-May)		
Higgins	Sean	29/10/84	F	29	1	9	1			1			4	2			2013	Falkirk	Joined Cowdenbeath June 2014	
Hodge	Bryan	23/09/87	M	27	1	2	1						1			1	2012	Brechin City		C (2015)
Kouider-Assa	Salim	22/03/96	F													3	2013	Motherwell		F
Lawson	Alan	18/07/94	D	2	4								1			3	2009	Stenhousemuir Youth		C (2015)
Lynch	Sean	31/01/87	M	26	4	3	4			1	1		2	1		4	2013	Airdrie United		F
Malone	Eddie	06/04/85	D	24	4	3	4			1			3				2013	Raith Rovers		F
McKinlay	Kevin	28/02/86	D	25	3	1	4			1			3			3	2011	Morton	Joined Ayr United June 2014	
McMillan	Ross	24/10/82	D	28				3		1	1	3				1	2011	Clyde		C (2015)
McNeill	Ross	01/11/91	F	7	17	3	1	2	3	1			3	1		12	2013	Rutherglen Glencairn U21	Joined Albion Rovers May 2014	F
Nimmo	Daniel			1			1						1			6		Stenhousemuir Youth		C (2015)
Rowson	David	14/09/76	M	22	4	1	2						3			2	2013	Partick Thistle		C (2015)
Shaw	Dean	09/09/94	GK	1												44	2009	Stenhousemuir Youth		C (2015)
Smith	Chris	05/03/86	GK	36			4			1		4					2013	St Mirren		C (2015)
Smith	Darren	27/03/88	F	19	7	7	2			1	1	4	1		2		2012	Stirling Albion		F
Smith	Ross	21/02/92	D	14		1	1						1			4	2013	Dundee United (loan)		
Summers	Ciaran			4												4		Stenhousemuir Youth		C (2015)
Thomson	Andrew	26/04/95	F													2	2009	Stenhousemuir Youth		F
Watt	Josh	31/08/93	F	8	3	1		2								10	2013	Akranes	on loan to East Stirlingshire, Jan 2014	C (2015)

NEW SIGNINGS 2014/15

Name		DOB	Pos	Signed	Signed From	Notes
McMenamin	Colin	12/02/81	F	2014	Celtic Nation	Coach
Grehan	Martin	09/10/84	F	2014	Stranraer	
Lithgow	Alan	12/03/88	D	2014	Ayr United	
Miller	Ryan		M	2014	Stirling University	
Sludden	Paul-John		F	2014	Stirling University	
Fotheringham	Greg	19/02/94	M	2013	East Fife	

Date	Comp	H/A	Opponents	F	A		Crowd	Scorers
27/07/2013	RC1	H	Arbroath	4	4	AET, 3-2 pens	280	Higgins, Gemmell 2, Douglas
03/08/2013	LC1	A	Airdrieonians	3	4		647	Smith, Dickson, McMillan
10/08/2013	L	H	Stranraer	1	0		483	Gemmell
17/08/2013	L	A	Airdrieonians	1	0		722	McNeil
20/08/2013	RC2	A	Peterhead	3	1	AET	427	Gemmell, D Smith, McNeil
24/08/2013	L	H	Dunfermline Athletic	4	5		968	Gemmell, R Smith, Lynch, Higgins
31/08/2013	L	A	Forfar Athletic	2	1		483	Higgins, D Smith
07/09/2013	RC3	A	Dundee	1	1	AET, 5-4 pens	1615	Higgins
14/09/2013	L	H	Ayr United	1	1		657	D Smith
21/09/2013	L	A	Arbroath	4	3		596	Hodge, Higgins, Gemmell, Dichson
28/09/2013	L	A	Rangers	0	8		43877	
05/10/2013	L	H	East Fife	1	1		567	Gemmell
12/10/2013	L	H	Brechin City	3	2		415	Gemmell 2, Dickson
19/10/2013	L	A	Stranraer	0	1		326	
26/10/2013	L	H	Forfar Athletic	1	1		408	Gemmell
29/10/2013	RCSF	H	Rangers	0	1		2338	
02/11/2013	SC3	H	Annan Athletic	2	2		309	Douglas, Gemmell
09/11/2013	L	A	Dunfermline Athletic	2	3		2517	McKinley, D Smith
12/11/2013	SC3R	A	Annan Athletic	4	2	AET	421	Gemmell, Dickson, Lynch, McNeil
16/11/2013	L	H	Arbroath	3	2		469	Lynch, Malone, Douglas
23/11/2013	L	A	Ayr United	3	4		986	Gemmell, Dickson, McNeil
30/11/2013	SC4	H	Fraserburgh	3	0		487	McNeil 2, Douglas
07/12/2013	L	A	East Fife	0	1		561	
21/12/2013	L	H	Airdrieonians	1	1		419	Dickson
28/12/2013	L	A	Brechin City	1	0		507	Hodge
02/01/2014	L	H	Dunfermline Athletic	1	2		1556	Lynch
05/01/2014	L	H	Rangers	0	2		2546	
11/01/2014	L	A	Forfar Athletic	0	3		485	
18/01/2014	L	A	Arbroath	1	2		498	D Smith
25/01/2014	L	H	Ayr United	1	1		467	Mcneil
01/02/2014	L	H	Stranraer	1	1		466	Malone
08/02/2014	SC5	A	Albion Rovers	0	2		748	
15/02/2014	L	H	East Fife	1	1		465	Malone
22/02/2014	L	A	Rangers	3	3		41794	Dickson, Higgins 2
25/02/2014	L	A	Airdrieonians	1	1		586	Greacen
01/03/2014	L	H	Forfar Athletic	4	1		368	D Smith 2, Dickson 2
08/03/2014	L	A	Dunfermline Athletic	0	0		2510	
15/03/2014	L	H	Brechin City	4	2		512	D Smith, Dickson, Watt, Gemmell
22/03/2014	L	A	Stranraer	1	1		403	Rowson
29/03/2014	L	A	Ayr United	3	2		992	Higgins 2, Greenhlagh
05/04/2014	L	H	Arbroath	2	2		518	Greenhalgh, Higgins
12/04/2014	L	A	East Fife	2	1		639	Dickson, Higgins
19/04/2014	L	H	Rangers	0	4		2767	
26/04/2014	L	H	Airdrieonians	1	2		812	Dickson
03/05/2014	L	A	Brechin City	3	1		543	Gemmell 2, Greenhalgh

Other Matches

29/6/13	Fr	H	Craigroyston	2	2
2/7/13	Fr	H	Clyde	2	2
6/7/13	Fr	H	Albion Rovers	0	1
9/7/13	Fr	H	East Stirlingshire	3	1
20/7/13	Fr	H	Stirling Albion	1	4
31/7/13	StC1	H	Falkirk	0	1

Date	Comp	H/A	Opponents	F	A		1	2	3	4	5	6	7	8	9	10	11	12	13	14	15	16	17	18
27/07/2013	RC1	H	Arbroath	4	4	AET, 3-2 pens	C Smith	Devlin	Rowson*	McMillan	McKinlay	Brash	Dickson+	Gemmell	D Smith	Malone	Higgins"	Anderson*	Douglas+	McNeill"	Shaw	Nimmo		
03/08/2013	UC1	A	Airdrieonians	3	4		C Smith	Higgins	Devlin	McMillan	McKinlay	Brash	Dickson*	Gemmell"	D Smith	Malone	Lynch	Anderson*	Douglas+	Shaw	McNeill	Nimmo		
10/08/2013	L	H	Stranraer	1	0		C Smith	R Smith	Devlin	McMillan	McKinlay	Ferguson	Dickson*	Gemmell"	D Smith	Anderson	Higgins+	McNeil*	Lynch+	Lawson"	Shaw	Douglas		
17/08/2013	L	A	Airdrieonians	1	0		C Smith	R Smith	Devlin	Lawson+	Lynch	Ferguson"	Dickson*	Gemmell	D Smith	Anderson	Higgins+	Malone*	Lynch+	McNeil"	Shaw	Douglas		
20/08/2013	RC2	A	Peterhead	4	5	AET	C Smith	R Smith	Malone	McMillan	McKinlay	Ferguson+	Dickson	Gemmell	D Smith	Anderson*	Higgins	McNeil*	Nimmo+	Duncan"	Shaw	Douglas	Lawson	Nimmo
24/08/2013	L	A	Dunfermline Athletic	4	5		C Smith	R Smith	Malone	McMillan	McKinlay	Ferguson+	Dickson	Gemmell	D Smith	Anderson*	Higgins*	McNeil*	Anderson+	McNeill"	Shaw	Douglas	Lawson	Devlin
31/08/2013	L	A	Forfar Athletic	2	1		C Smith	R Smith	Malone	McMillan	McKinlay	Ferguson	Dickson	Gemmell	D Smith+	Rowson*	Higgins*	Brash*	Lynch+	McNeill"	Anderson	Shaw		
07/09/2013	RC3	H	Dundee	1	1	AET, 5-4 pens	C Smith	Anderson*	Devlin	McMillan	McKinlay	Ferguson	Dickson	Gemmell	D Smith+	Rowson*	Higgins+	Douglas+	Malone+	McNeill"	Lawson	Shaw		
14/09/2013	L	H	Ayr United	1	1		C Smith	R Smith	Devlin	McMillan+	McKinlay	Ferguson	Dickson	Gemmell	D Smith	Lynch*	Higgins+	Anderson*	Malone+	McNeill"	Shaw	Douglas	Brash	Lynch
21/09/2013	L	A	Arbroath	4	3		C Smith	R Smith	Devlin	McMillan	McKinlay	Ferguson	Dickson	Gemmell	D Smith*	Hodge	Higgins+	Malone"	Malone+	Anderson"	Anderson	Shaw	Brash	Douglas
28/09/2013	L	A	Rangers	0	8		C Smith	R Smith	Devlin	McMillan	McKinlay+	Ferguson"	Dickson	Gemmell+	D Smith	Hodge	Higgins"	Lynch*	Malone+	McNeill*	Anderson	Shaw	McNeill	Watt
05/10/2013	L	H	East Fife	1	1		C Smith	R Smith	Devlin*	McKinley+	McKinley	Lynch+	Dickson+	Gemmell	D Smith	Hodge	Higgins"	Devlin*	Brash+	Douglas"	Shaw	Nimmo	Brash	Watt
12/10/2013	L	H	Brechin City	3	2		C Smith	R Smith	Malone*	Devlin*	McKinley	Lynch	Dickson	Gemmell	McNeil*	Hodge	Higgins	Ferguson"	Anderson+	Nimmo"	Shaw	Douglas	Brash	Watt
19/10/2013	L	A	Stranraer	0	1		C Smith	R Smith	Malone"	Devlin	McKinley	Lynch+	Dickson	Gemmell	McNeil"	Hodge	Higgins	Brash+	Douglas+	Ferguson"	Devlin*	Nimmo	Lynch	McNeill
26/10/2013	L	H	Forfar Athletic	1	1		C Smith	R Smith	Malone	Devlin	McKinley	Rowson+	Dickson+	Lynch	D Smith	Hodge	Higgins	Brash*	Douglas+	Ferguson	McMillan	Shaw		
29/10/2013	RC5F	H	Rangers	0	1		C Smith	McMillan	Malone	Devlin	McKinley	Rowson+	Dickson	Lynch	D Smith	Hodge*	Ferguson+	Douglas+	Douglas+	McNeill	R Smith	Shaw		
02/11/2013	SC3	H	Annan Athletic	2	2		C Smith	McMillan	Malone	Devlin	McKinley	Ferguson*	Dickson	Lynch	D Smith	Gemmell	Douglas"	Watt*	Shaw	Brash	McNeill	R Smith		
09/11/2013	L	A	Dunfermline Athletic	2	3		C Smith	McMillan	Malone	Devlin	McKinley	Ferguson*	Dickson	Lynch	D Smith+	Gemmell	Rowson*	Watt*	Smith+	Watt	Shaw	McNeill		
12/11/2013	SC3R	A	Annan Athletic	4	2	AET	C Smith	McMillan	Malone	McNeil+	McKinley	Brash*	Dickson*	Lynch	Douglas*	Gemmell	Rowson	McNeil*	Smith+	Ferguson"	Shaw	Docherty	Watt	Kouider-Aïssa
16/11/2013	L	A	Arbroath	3	2		C Smith	McMillan	Malone	McNeil"	McKinley	Brash*	Dickson+	Lynch	Douglas*	Gemmell	Rowson	Hodge*	Douglas"	Ferguson"	Anderson	Devlin	Watt	Kouider-Aïssa
23/11/2013	L	A	Ayr United	3	4		C Smith	McMillan	Malone	McNeil*	McKinley	Hodge	Dickson*	Lynch	R Smith	Gemmell+	Rowson*	Douglas"	Shaw	Watt*	Devlin	Docherty	Kouider-Aïssa	
30/11/2013	SC4	A	Fraserburgh	3	0		C Smith	McMillan	Malone	McNeil"	McKinley+	Hodge	Dickson"	McMillan	R Smith	Gemmell"	Faulds+	Douglas*	Kouider-Aïssa+	Watt*	R Smith	Kouider-Aïssa		
07/12/2013	L	A	East Fife	0	1		C Smith	Devlin	Rowson	McNeil	McKinley	Hodge	Dickson	McMillan	R Smith	Gemmell	Faulds+	Douglas*	Kouider-Aïssa+	Douglas	Watt	Watt	Duncan	
21/12/2013	L	H	Airdrieonians	1	1		C Smith	Devlin	Malone	McNeill	McKinley*	Hodge+	Rowson	McMillan	Ferguson"	Higgins+	Faulds"	Higgins*	Dickson+	McNeill	R Smith	Nimmo	Thomson	Faulds
28/12/2013	L	A	Dunfermline Athletic	1	0		C Smith	Devlin	Malone	Dickson*	McKinley	Hodge	Rowson	D Smith+	Douglas*	Higgins+	Lynch	Gemmell"	Faulds+	McNeill"	R Smith	Faulds	Thomson	D Smith
02/01/2014	L	H	Brechin City	1	2		C Smith	Devlin	Malone	Dickson*	McKinley	Hodge	Rowson	D Smith+	Faulds*	Higgins	Lynch	Gemmell*	McNeil+	Greacen	Shaw	Douglas	Shaw	Ferguson
05/01/2014	L	A	Rangers	0	2		C Smith	Devlin	Malone	Dickson+	McKinley	Hodge*	Rowson	McMillan	Greacen	Higgins"	Lynch	Gemmell"	D Smith+	McNeill	Devlin	Nimmo	Faulds	Ferguson
11/01/2014	L	A	Forfar Athletic	0	3		C Smith	Devlin	Malone	Dickson	McKinley+	Hodge	Rowson	McMillan	Greacen	Gemmell*	Faulds*	Douglas*	Douglas+	Hodge	Shaw	McNeill	Faulds	Ferguson
18/01/2014	L	A	Arbroath	1	2		C Smith	Devlin	Malone	Dickson	McKinley*	Hodge	Faulds	D Smith+	Greacen	Higgins	Lynch+	Rowson*	McNeil+	Douglas	Shaw	Ferguson	Thomson	Docherty
25/01/2014	L	H	Ayr United	1	1		C Smith	Devlin	Malone	Hodge+	McKinley	Hodge	Rowson	D Smith+	Greacen	Higgins	Lynch+	Douglas"	Dickson+	Summers	Shaw	Nimmo	Thomson	Faulds
25/01/2014	L	H	Stranraer	1	1		C Smith	Devlin	Malone	Hodge+	McMillan	Hodge	Rowson	D Smith+	Greacen	Higgins	Lynch+	Gemmell"	McNeil+	Summers	Shaw	Faulds		
08/02/2014	SC5	L	Albion Rovers	0	2		C Smith	Devlin	Malone	Hodge+	McMillan"	Faulds	Rowson	D Smith+	McMillan	Higgins	Lynch+	McNeil*	Douglas+	Nimmo"	Shaw	Ferguson		
15/02/2014	L	H	East Fife	1	1		C Smith	Devlin	Malone	Dickson*	Faulds"	Greacen	Rowson	Hodge	McMillan	Higgins"	Lynch	Watt*	McNeil	Nimmo"	McKinley	McKinley	Brash	Summers
22/02/2014	L	H	Rangers	3	3		C Smith	Devlin	Malone	Dickson*	D Smith"	Greacen	Rowson	Hodge+	McMillan	Higgins"	Watt*	Watt*	D Smith+	Douglas"	Shaw	Nimmo	McNeill	Brash
25/02/2014	L	A	Airdrieonians	1	1		C Smith	Devlin	Malone	Dickson+	McKinley"	Greacen	Rowson	Hodge+	McMillan	Higgins"	Lynch	Watt*	Watt+	McNeill"	Nimmo	Nimmo	Douglas	Brash
01/03/2014	L	H	Forfar Athletic	4	1		C Smith	Devlin	Malone	Dickson	D Smith*	Greacen	Rowson	Hodge	McMillan	Higgins+	Watt*	Lynch*	Douglas+	McKinley*	Shaw	Brash	McNeill	Ferguson
08/03/2014	L	A	Dunfermline Athletic	0	0		C Smith	Devlin	Malone	Dickson*	D Smith"	Greacen	Rowson	Hodge	McMillan	McKinley+	Lynch+	Douglas*	McKinley+	McNeill*	Shaw	Ferguson	Faulds	Watt
15/03/2014	L	H	Brechin City	4	2		C Smith	Devlin	Malone+	Dickson	D Smith	Greacen	Rowson	Hodge	McMillan	McNeill+	Lynch+	Gemmell*	Faulds+	Rowson"	Brash	Brash	McKinley	Douglas
22/03/2014	L	A	Brechin City	1	1		C Smith	Devlin"	Watt*	Dickson	Watt*	Greacen	Rowson	Hodge	McMillan	Higgins	Watt+	Gemmell"	Gemmell"	McNeill"	Shaw	Brash	Faulds	Douglas
29/03/2014	L	A	Ayr United	3	2		C Smith	Devlin"	Watt	Dickson+	McKinley	Greacen	D Smith	Greenhalgh	McMillan*	Higgins	Lynch*	Lawson"	Douglas"	Douglas"	Shaw	McNeill	Summers	Faulds
05/04/2014	L	H	Arbroath	2	2		C Smith	Duncan	Watt+	Hodge+	McKinley	Greacen	D Smith	Greenhalgh	Summers	Higgins	Rowson"	Dickson+	McNeill*	McNeill"	Shaw	Douglas	Duncan	Faulds
12/04/2014	L	A	East Fife	2	1		C Smith	Devlin	Watt	Hodge	McMillan	Greacen	Rowson+	Greenhalgh	Greacen	Higgins	Lynch+	Dickson*	Douglas+	Lawson	Shaw	D Smith	Devlin	Faulds
19/04/2014	L	H	Rangers	0	4		C Smith	Duncan	Watt	Hodge	McMillan	Greacen	Faulds"	Summers	Summers	Higgins	Lynch+	Dickson	Dickson+	Gemmell"	Shaw	Douglas	Lawson	Lynch
26/04/2014	L	A	Airdrieonians	1	2		C Smith	Devlin	Lynch	Hodge	McMillan*	Greacen	Faulds"	Greenhalgh*	Summers	Higgins	Dickson	Lawson*	D Smith+	Gemmell"	Shaw	Douglas	Rowson	Watt
03/05/2014	L	A	Brechin City	3	1		C Smith	Duncan	Lawson	Hodge	D Smith*	Greacen	Watt	Greenhalgh*	Summers	Gemmell	Dickson+	Shaw*	Faulds+	McNeill"	Douglas	Lynch	Rowson	McKinlay

Stirling Albion FC

Founded	1945
Ground	Forthbank Stadium
Postcode	FK7 7UJ
Tel	01786 450399
Capacity	3808
Closest Railway Station	Stirling
Record Attendance	26400 v Celtic, SC, 14/3/1959
Ground Record	3808 v Aberdeen, SC, 15/2/1996
Record Win	20-0 v Selkirk, SC, 8/12/1984
Record Defeat	0-9 v Dundee Utd, L, 30/12/1967; v Ross Co, SC, 6/2/2010
Most League Goals in a Season	27 Joe Hughes, 1969/70
Chairman	Stuart Brown
Secretary	Stuart Brown
Manager	Greig McDonald
Assistant Manager	Marc McCulloch
Colours 2013/14 Top	Red with white sleeves
Shorts	Red
Sponsor	Prudential
Manufacturer	Macron
Change Colours 2013/14 Top	Blue and Black Stripes
Shorts	Black
Nicknames	Binos
Web	www.stirlingalbionfc.co.uk

Stirling Albion hit form at exactly the right time to clinch a play off position. For much of the season they had been in mid table, capable of decent results, but also taking some bad defeats.

Key player was striker Jordan White who really found his shooting boots at the business end of the season. Stirling entered the Play Offs on a high and prevailed over Annan Athletic and East Fife to make the step up.

It's not something anyone would have predicted as late as March and the adjustment to League One football must be made quickly.

Stirling's ownership model means they will not over spend and they will have to look for bargain signings.

PREDICTION 2014/15
Will not find it easy and will be delighted to stay out of the bottom two

Surname	First Name	DOB	Pos	A	S	G	A	S	G	A	S	G	A	S	G	UNS	Signed	Previous Club	Notes	Contract
Allison	Brian	23/06/88	D														2008	Falkirk		
Ashe	Daniel	27/02/92	M	19	5		4									15	2010	SAFC Youths		F
Baillie	Stewart															1		Trialist, ex East Fife		
Bishop	Jamie	14/01/85	D	28	4	1	4			1		1				3	2012	Forfar Athletic		F
Boyle	Reece	13/01/95	D	1												5	2013	SAFC Youths		Youth
Clark	Jamie	08/05/93	D	1												19	2012	SAFC Youths	Freed Sep 2013, joined Bo'ness Utd	
Comrie	Craig	28/01/95	M	19	3	7										1	2014	Falkirk		C (2015)
Coyne	Bradley	10/04/93	F	4	9	2		2		1						5	2012	Forfar Athletic	Freed January 2014, Joined Clyde	
Crawford	David	30/06/85	GK	38			4			1		1				1	2013	Montrose		ONC
Cunningham	Sandy	05/04/95	F	10	20	7	2	2	1							6	2012	Falkirk		C (2015)
Day	Stephen	01/01/94	M	8	8		3			1		1				9	2012	SAFC Youths		F
Ferry	Mark	19/01/84	M	17	13	4	3		1	1		1				5	2012	Raith Rovers		F
Forsyth	Ross	20/01/82	D	29	1	5	3		1	1		1				2	2013	Dumbarton		ONC
Fulton	Dale	01/09/92	F	18	7	4	3									9	2013	Falkirk		C (2015)
Gasparotto	Luca	09/03/95		3													2013	Rangers (Loan)		
Hamilton	Lee	15/09/95	D	14	1											3	2012	SAFC Youths		C (2015)
Johnston	Phil	19/09/50	M	29	7	3	4			1		1					2013	Dumbarton		C (2015)
Lee	Michael		GK													1		Trialist, Ex Raith Rovers		
McAnespie	Kieran	11/09/79	M	14	3	2	3	1	1	1		1				5	2012	Arbroath	Retired March 2014	
McClune	David	08/02/83	M	26	4	2	4									3	2012	Brechin City		C (2015)
McCulloch	Marc	14/03/80	M													3	2011	East Fife		C (2015)
McCunnie	Jamie	15/04/83	D	1	1					1		1					2012	IR Reykjavik	Freed Sep joined Broughty Athletic	
McDonald	Greig	12/05/82	D													1	2010	East Fife		C (2015)
McGeachie	Ross	04/05/94	D	19	6					1		1				15	2012	SAFC Youths		C (2015)
Munn	Blair	17/04/95	M	1	1											16	2013	Alloa		Youth
O'Byrne	Michael	07/09/88	D	11												7	2014	Airdrieonians		F
Paton	Chris				1											3	2013	SAFC Youths		Youth
Reidford	Calum	26/05/87	GK	2	1											35	2013	Stenhousemuir		C (2015)
Robertson	Sean	24/08/96	GK													7	2013	Dunfermline Athletic		Youth
Smith	Chris	31/08/88	D	23		1	3			1		1					2013	Falkirk		C (2015)
Smith	Darren	04/06/80	M	11	2											2	2014	Arbroath		C (2015)
Weatherston	David	25/08/86	F	25	9	9	2									1	2013	Falkirk	Joined Alloa May 2014	
Weir	Graham	10/07/84	F	31	6	3	1	2	1	1		1				5	2012	Brechin City		C (2015)
White	Jordan	04/02/92	F	39	1	19	4		3	1		1	1		1		2012	Falkirk		ONC
Own Goals					2			1												

NEW SIGNINGS 2014/15

Surname	First Name		Pos		Signed	Previous Club
Paterson	Greg		GK		2014	East Fife
Wedderburn	Craig		D		2014	St Andrews United
Smith	Darren Lee		M		2014	Stenhousemuir

Date	Comp	H/A	Opponents	F	A	Crowd	Scorers
27/07/2013	RC1	A	Raith Rovers	1	2	1111	White pen
03/08/2013	LC1	H	Hamilton Accies	0	3	556	
10/08/2013	L	A	Montrose	2	1	486	Fulton, Ferry
17/08/2013	L	H	Peterhead	2	0	573	Fulton, Johnston
24/08/2013	L	H	East Stirlingshire	1	3	735	White
31/08/2013	L	A	Queen's Park	2	0	527	Cunningham, Ferry
14/09/2013	L	H	Annan Athletic	0	2	608	
21/09/2013	L	A	Berwick Rangers	1	1	491	Weatherston
28/09/2013	L	A	Elgin City	0	4	623	
05/10/2013	SC2	H	Whitehill Welfare	2	2	456	McAnespie, White
12/10/2013	SC2R	A	Whitehill Welfare	2	1	512	White, Cunningham
19/10/2013	L	H	Montrose	3	1	481	Smith, White, Cunningham
26/10/2013	L	A	Clyde	1	2	676	Coyne
29/10/2013	L	H	Albion Rovers	2	1	423	Johnston, Fulton
02/11/2013	SC3	A	Turriff United	3	0	490	Forsyth, Cumming og, Ferry
09/11/2013	L	A	East Stirlingshire	2	2	541	White 2
16/11/2013	L	H	Queen's Park	3	0	681	Fulton, Cunningham, Coyne
23/11/2013	L	A	Annan Athletic	4	4	384	McAnespie, Cunningham, White, Forsyth
30/11/2013	SC4	A	Alloa Athletic	2	3	1278	White, Weir
03/12/2013	L	H	Berwick Rangers	3	1	378	White, Notman og, Forsyth
07/12/2013	L	A	Albion Rovers	1	2	396	Bishop
21/12/2013	L	A	Peterhead	1	3	521	Forsyth
28/12/2013	L	H	Clyde	1	1	859	Weir
04/01/2014	L	H	East Stirlingshire	2	1	639	Comrie, Ferry
11/01/2014	L	A	Queen's Park	1	0	472	Ferry
18/01/2014	L	A	Berwick Rangers	0	4	464	
25/01/2014	L	H	Annan Athletic	1	1	509	White
01/02/2014	L	A	Montrose	0	0	333	
08/02/2014	L	H	Peterhead	1	2	498	White
15/02/2014	L	H	Albion Rovers	2	0	541	Weatherston, White
22/02/2014	L	A	Elgin City	3	2	576	White 2, McAnespie
01/03/2014	L	H	Queen's Park	2	2	656	Gibson og, Comrie
08/03/2014	L	A	East Stirlingshire	0	1	584	
11/03/2014	L	H	Elgin City	1	1	641	Cunningham
15/03/2014	L	A	Clyde	0	1	673	
22/03/2014	L	H	Montrose	2	2	529	Comrie, McClune
29/03/2014	L	A	Annan Athletic	2	1	479	Weatherston 2
05/04/2014	L	H	Berwick Rangers	2	1	665	Weatherston, Cunningham
12/04/2014	L	A	Albion Rovers	2	0	480	White, Weatherston
19/04/2014	L	H	Elgin City	2	2	640	White, Comrie
26/04/2014	L	A	Peterhead	4	0	852	Comrie 2, Weatherston, Weir
03/05/2014	L	H	Clyde	4	1	1028	White 2, Forsyth, Johnston
07/05/2014	PO	H	Annan Athletic	3	1	972	Weir, Weatherston 2
10/05/2014	PO	A	Annan Athletic	5	3	912	White 3, McClune, Comrie
14/05/2001	PO	H	East Fife	1	2	1501	Forsyth
18/05/2014	PO	A	East Fife	2	0	1516	White, Cunningham

Other Matches

6/7/13	Fr	H	Falkirk	1	1	728		
9/7/13	Fr	H	Bannockburn Amateurs	2	2		U19	at Forthbank Astro
13/7/13	TnT	A	Gretna	3	1			
14/7/13	TnT	N	Wrexham	0	3			at Gretna
18/7/13	Fr	A	Civil Service Strollers	6	1			
20/7/13	Fr	A	Stenhousemuir	4	1			
13/8/13	Fr	H	Spartans EOSL	2	0		U19	at Forthbank Astro
8/10/13	StCSF	H	East Stirlingshire	3	1			

Date	Comp	H/A	Opponents	F	A	1	2	3	4	5	6	7	8	9	10	11	12	13	14	15	16	17	18
27/07/2013	RC1	A	Raith Rovers	1	2	Crawford	McGeachie*	Bishop	Smith	Forsyth	Johnston	Ferry	McCunnie	McAnespie	White	Weir+	Cunningham*	Cunningham	Ashe	Clark	Lee		Clark
03/08/2013	LC1	A	Hamilton Accies	0	3	Crawford	McGeachie	Bishop	Smith	Forsyth	Johnston	Ferry+	McCunnie*	Day	White	Weir	Coyne*	McAnespie+	Ashe	Clark	Robertson	McGeachie	Day
10/08/2013	L	A	Montrose	2	1	Crawford	McAnespie	Bishop	Smith	Forsyth	Johnston	Ferry+	McCunnie	Fulton+	White	Weir+	McCunnie*	McClune+	Coyne+	Coyne	Robertson	Clark	Cunningham
17/08/2013	L	H	Peterhead	2	0	Crawford	McAnespie	Bishop	Smith	Forsyth	Johnston	Ferry+	McGeachie	Fulton*	White	Weir	Weatherston"	McClune"	McCunnie+	Ashe	Robertson	McCunnie	Bishop
24/08/2013	L	H	East Stirlingshire	1	3	Crawford	McAnespie	McGeachie*	Smith	Forsyth	Johnston	Ferry	Clark*	Fulton	White	Weir	Day+	Cunningham-	Coyne*	Ashe	Robertson	Clark	McCulloch
31/08/2013	L	A	Queen's Park	2	0	Crawford	McAnespie	McGeachie	Smith	Forsyth	Weatherston"	Weatherston"	Day*	Fulton+	White	Weatherston	Day-	Cunningham	Day-	Day"	Robertson	Clark	McGeachie
14/09/2013	L	H	Annan Athletic	0	2	Crawford	McAnespie*	McGeachie*	Smith	Forsyth	Johnston	Ferry	Day	Fulton+	White	Weatherston+	Johnston"	Cunningham+	Johnston*	Cunningham"	McAnespie	Cunningham	Coyne
21/09/2013	L	A	Berwick Rangers	1	1	Crawford	Bishop	McClune	Smith	Forsyth	Johnston	Ferry	Day*	Day	White+	Weatherston	Day"	Cunningham+	Cunningham+	Coyne"	Reidford	Clark	Paton
28/09/2013	L	H	Elgin City	0	4	Crawford	Bishop	McClune	Smith	Forsyth	Johnston	Ferry	Day*	Weir*	White-	Weatherston	Day*	Coyne	Coyne+	Coyne	Reidford	Clark	Munn
05/10/2013	SC2	A	Whitehill Welfare	1	3	Crawford	Bishop	McClune	Smith	Forsyth	Johnston+	Ferry	Day	White+	White	Weatherston+	Day-	Fulton+	Coyne	Clark	Reidford	Clark	Munn
12/10/2013	SC2R	H	Whitehill Welfare	2	1	Crawford	Bishop	McClune	McClune+	Forsyth	Johnston*	Ferry	Ashe	Weir"	White*	McAnespie	Cunningham*	Coyne+	McAnespie	McAnespie"	Reidford	Clark	Munn
19/10/2013	L	A	Montrose	3	1	Crawford	Bishop	McClune	McClune	Forsyth	Johnston*	Ferry	Ashe	Weir*	White*	McGeachie	Day*	Cunningham"	Day"	McAnespie*	Reidford	Clark	Munn
26/10/2013	L	H	Clyde	1	2	Crawford	Bishop	McClune-	Weir	Weir	Johnston"	Ferry	Ashe	Coyne-	White*	McGeachie	Weir"	Fulton+	McAnespie+	McGeachie"	McGeachie	Day	Weatherston
29/10/2013	L	A	Albion Rovers	2	1	Crawford	Bishop	McClune	McClune	Forsyth	Johnston*	Ferry	Ashe	Coyne*	White"	McAnespie	Coyne"	Day+	Coyne*	Clark	Reidford	Clark	Cleland
02/11/2013	SC3	A	Turriff United	3	0	Crawford*	Bishop*	McClune	McClune	Forsyth	Johnston"	Ferry*	Ashe	Coyne-	White*	Cunningham+	Coyne"	Day+	Coyne"	McGeachie"	Day	McGeachie	Munn
09/11/2013	L	A	East Stirlingshire	2	2	Crawford	Bishop	McClune	McAnespie	Forsyth*	Johnston+	Ferry*	Ashe	White	Fulton	Cunningham"	Coyne*	Day+	Coyne"	McGeachie"	Reidford	McGeachie	Paton
16/11/2013	L	H	Queen's Park	3	0	Reidford	Bishop	McClune	McAnespie	Forsyth*	Johnston+	Ferry*	Ashe	White	Fulton	Cunningham"	Weir"	Day+	Coyne"	McGeachie"	Reidford	Day	Munn
23/11/2013	L	A	Annan Athletic	4	4	Crawford	Reidford	McClune	McAnespie	Forsyth*	Johnston"	Ferry*	Ashe	White	Fulton+	Cunningham+	Weatherston"	Day+	Coyne"	McGeachie"	Reidford	Crawford	Patón
30/11/2013	SC4	A	Alloa Athletic	2	3	Crawford	Bishop	McClune	McAnespie	Forsyth"	Johnston'	Weatherston+	Ashe	White	Fulton"	Cunningham	Weir"	McAnespie+	Cunningham+	Clark	Crawford	McCunnie	Munn
03/12/2013	L	H	Berwick Rangers	3	1	Crawford	Bishop	McClune-	McAnespie	Forsyth	Coyne*	Weatherston+	Johnston	White	Fulton"	Weir	Coyne"	Reidford*	Munn"	Munn	Reidford	McGeachie	Munn
07/12/2013	L	A	Albion Rovers	1	2	Crawford	Bishop	McClune	McAnespie	Forsyth	Gasporotto	Weatherston	Weatherston	White	Ashe	Weir	McGeachie	Fulton+	Cunningham+	Munn	Reidford	McAnespie	Boyle
21/12/2013	L	A	Peterhead	1	3	Crawford	Bishop	Ashe"	McClune+	Forsyth	McGeachie	Weatherston	Weatherston*	White	Ferry*	Weir	Ferry*	McClune+	Cunningham"	Munn	Reidford	Hamilton	Boyle
28/12/2013	L	H	Clyde	1	1	Reidford	Bishop	Ashe	McClune	O'byrne	Gasporotto	Weatherston*	Fulton*	White	Cunningham	Cunningham+	Johnston"	McGeachie+	Comrie+	Munn	Reidford	Munn	McCulloch
04/01/2014	L	A	East Stirlingshire	2	1	Crawford	Bishop	Ashe	Ashe*	O'byrne	Gasporotto	Fulton	Weatherston+	White	Cunningham+	Weir	Weatherston"	Fulton+	Comrie"	Munn	Reidford	Munn	McCulloch
11/01/2014	L	H	Queen's Park	1	0	Crawford	Bishop*	Forsyth	Ashe+	O'byrne	Gasporotto	Fulton*	Weatherston+	White	Cunningham+	Weir"	Ashe"	Comrie	Ferry"	Munn	McGeachie	Munn	McClune
18/01/2014	L	A	Berwick Rangers	0	4	Crawford	Bishop	McGeachie	Ashe	O'byrne	Comrie	Ferry	Weatherston	White	D Smith	Day"	Johnston"*	McGeachie+	Cunningham+	Fulton	Reidford	McGeachie	Day
25/01/2014	L	A	Annan Athletic	1	1	Crawford	Hamilton	Hamilton	McClune	O'byrne*	Comrie	Ferry	Johnston	White	D Smith	Day*	Cunningham"	Cunningham"	Cunningham"	Fulton	Baillie	Coyne	Comrie
01/02/2014	L	H	Montrose	0	0	Crawford	Cunningham*	Hamilton*	McClune	O'byrne*	Comrie*	Ferry	Johnston	White"	D Smith	Hamilton*	Hamilton"	Cunningham	Weatherston"	Fulton	Reidford	McCunnie	Boyle
08/02/2014	L	A	Peterhead	1	2	Crawford	Bishop	Hamilton*	McClune	Mcgeachie	Comrie*	Ferry	Johnston	White"	D Smith	Day +	Weir"	McAnespie+	Comrie+	Munn	Reidford	McDonald	Hamilton
15/02/2014	L	H	Albion Rovers	2	0	Crawford	Bishop	Hamilton	McAnespie	D Smith*	Comrie	Ferry	Johnston	White	D Smith+	Hamilton"	Day"	McGeachie+	Comrie"	Weir	Weir	Boyle	Ashe
22/02/2014	L	A	Elgin City	3	2	Crawford	Bishop	Hamilton	Ashe*	D Smith*	Comrie	Weir	Cunningham	White	C Smith	Day	McClune"	Fulton+	Ferry"	Ferry	Reidford	Cunningham	Forsyth
01/03/2014	L	H	Queen's Park	2	2	Crawford	Bishop	Hamilton*	McClune	D Smith*	Comrie	Weir	Johnston	White	C Smith	Day"	Fulton"	D Smith+	Ashe"	Fulton	Reidford	Ashe	D Smith
08/03/2014	L	A	East Stirlingshire	0	1	Crawford	Forsyth	Hamilton	McClune	D Smith	Comrie*	Weir	Johnston*	White	C Smith	Cunningham*	Weatherston*	Ashe+	Cunningham+	Bishop	Reidford	Bishop	Ashe
11/03/2014	L	H	Elgin City	1	1	Crawford	Forsyth	Hamilton*	McClune	D Smith	Comrie	Weir	Johnston	White	C Smith	Weatherston	Bishop*	Ferry+	Boyle"	Fulton	Reidford	McAnespie	Fulton
15/03/2014	L	A	Clyde	0	1	Crawford	Forsyth	Hamilton	McClune	D Smith	Comrie+	Weir	Johnston	White	C Smith	Weatherston	Cunningham"	McGeachie"	Forsyth"	O'byrne	Reidford	Ferry	Fulton
22/03/2014	L	H	Montrose	2	2	Crawford	Forsyth	Hamilton	McClune	D Smith	Comrie	Weir*	Johnston	White	c smith	Weatherston*	Cunningham*	D Smith+	McAnespie"	O'byrne	Reidford	Ferry	Fulton
29/03/2014	L	A	Annan Athletic	2	1	Crawford	Forsyth	Hamilton	McClune	D Smith	Comrie*	Weir"	Johnston*	White"	C Smith	Weatherston+	Bishop"	Ferry+	Johnston+	O'byrne	Reidford	D Smith	Cunningham
05/04/2014	L	H	Berwick Rangers	2	1	Crawford	Forsyth	Hamilton	McClune	D Smith	Comrie+	Weir*	Johnston"	White	C Smith	Weatherston+	Ashe+	Ferry+	Hamilton"	O'byrne	Reidford	Cunningham	Ashe
12/04/2014	L	A	Albion Rovers	2	0	Crawford	Forsyth	Hamilton	McClune	D Smith	Comrie+	Weir*	Johnston"	White	C Smith	Weatherston+	Bishop"	Bishop+	Weatherston+	O'byrne	Reidford	Cunningham	Fulton
19/04/2014	L	H	Elgin City	2	2	Crawford	Forsyth	Hamilton*	McClune	D Smith	Comrie+	Weir+	Johnston	White	C Smith	Weatherston+	McGeachie"	Ashe+	Cunningham+	O'byrne	Reidford	Cunningham	McGeachie
26/04/2014	L	A	Peterhead	4	0	Crawford	Forsyth	Hamilton	McClune	D Smith	Comrie+	Weir	Johnston	White	C Smith	Weatherston*	McGeachie"	Fulton+	Ferry"	O'byrne	Reidford	Ashe	Cunningham
03/05/2014	L	H	Clyde	4	1	Crawford	Forsyth	Hamilton*	McClune	D Smith	Comrie+	Weir	Johnston	White*	C Smith	Weatherston	McGeachie"	Ferry+	Ashe"	O'byrne	Reidford	Ferry	Fulton
07/05/2014	PO	A	Annan Athletic	5	3	Crawford	Forsyth	Hamilton	McClune	D Smith	Comrie+	Weir*	Johnston"	White	C Smith	Weatherston"	Ashe+	Ferry+	Cunningham"	O'byrne	Reidford	Ashe	Fulton
10/05/2014	PO	L	Annan Athletic	3	2	Crawford	Forsyth	Hamilton"	McClune	D Smith	Comrie+	Weir	Johnston"	White	Bishop	Weatherston"	Cunningham"	Ferry+	Ferry"	O'byrne	Reidford	Ashe	Fulton
14/05/2014	PO	H	East Fife	1	2	Crawford	Forsyth	Hamilton	McClune	D Smith	Comrie+	Weir	Johnston*	Bishop	C Smith	Weatherston"	Cunningham"	Bishop"	McGeachie"	O'byrne	Reidford	Fulton	Cunningham
18/05/2014	PO	A	East Fife	2	0	Crawford	Forsyth	Hamilton	McClune	D Smith	Comrie+	Weir	Johnston"	White	C Smith	Weatherston"	Cunningham"	Bishop"	Ferry"	O'byrne	Reidford	Fulton	McGeachie

Stranraer FC

Founded	1870
Ground	Stair Park
Postcode	DG9 8BS
Tel	01776 703271
Capacity	2988
Closest Railway Station	Stranraer
Record Attendance	6500 v Rangers, 24/1/1948
Record Win	9-0 v St Cuthbert W, SC, 23/10/2010, v Wigtown & Bladnoch, SC, 22/10/2011
Record Defeat	1-11 v QOS, SC, 16/1/1932
Most League Goals in a Season	27 Derek Frye, 1977/8
Chairman	Robert Rice
Secretary	Hilde Law
Manager	Stephen Aitken
Assistant Manager	Stephen Farrell
Colours 2013/14 Top	Blues
Shorts	Blues
Sponsor	Stena Line
Manufacturer	Stanno
Change Colours 2013/14 Top	Red
Shorts	Red
Nicknames	Blues
Web	www.stranraerfc.org

Stranraer surprised many people with their performances, reaching the promotion play offs and doing well in Cup competitions. They had a very settled side which was strong in key areas. Their defence didn't give much away and up front they had several strikers capable of hitting the target.

Stranraer won many friends with their displays in the Cups. In the League Cup they beat Ross County and took Hibs to a 3-5 result at Easter Road. In the Scottish they held Inverness to a draw at Stair Park.

For 2014/15 they have lost several of the stars of last season. They will not have a big budget to bring in replacements so Stevie Aitken will wheel and deal to put together the best side he can.

PREDICTION 2014/15
May drop to the lower half of the League One table

Name		DOB	Pos	L A	S	G	SC A	S	G	LC A	S	G	RC A	S	G	UNS	Signed	Signed From	Notes	Contract
Aitken	Chris	31/03/81	M	15	6	4	3			3	2		3				2011	Stirling Albion		R
Baxter	Jonathan															2	2013	Stranraer Youths		Youth
Bell	Steven	24/02/85	M	16	7	3	3	1								4	2013	Dunfermline Athletic		C (2015)
Borris	Ryan	07/06/83	M	5	20		1	3		2	1	1	1			11	2012	Dumbarton	Joined Kilbirnie Ladeside June 2014	F
Corcoran	Mark	30/11/80	M	7	5	1		1		1	2		1	1		3	2013	Stenhousemuir		F
Docherty	Mark	15/05/88	D	32	2		6			1	1		2			4	2013	Alloa	Joined Alloa May 2014	
Fahey	Chris	28/06/78	GK													48	2013	Cumnock		C (2015)
Forde	Adam	11/10/95	F	15	1		3			1						16	2013	Stranraer Youths		Youth
Gallagher	Grant	11/01/91	M	36		2	6	1	3				2				2010	Celtic		C (2015)
Grehan	Martin	09/10/84	F	34	3	14	5	1	2	3		1	1	1	2		2013	Alloa	Joined Stenhousemuir June 2014	
Kinnaird	Lloyd	14/03/80	D	5	9		1			2				1		29	2012	Harmony Row U21		F
Longworth	Jamie	03/08/87	F	30	8	14	6		7	1	1	1	2				2013	Queen's Park		C (2015)
Maxwell	Kieron	28/10/95	M													2	2013	Stranraer Youths		Youth
McGregor	David	09/06/81	D	15	3		2			1	1		2			23	2011	Morton		F
McKenna	David	19/09/86	F	14	22	4	1	5		2	1	1	1	1	2		2013	Brechin City	Joined East Stirlingshire May 2014	F
McKeown	Frank	18/08/86	D	34		3	6	1	3				2				2011	Arthurlie		C (2015)
Mitchell	David	04/04/90	GK	38					6		3		2				2009	Ayr United		C (2015)
Rafferty	Kyle	03/09/95	M													2	2013	Stranraer Youths		F
Robertson	Scott	26/11/87	D	37		1	6			3		1	2				2013	Arbroath		C (2015)
Rumsby	Scott	01/01/94	D	29		1	3			2						1	2013	Aberdeen (Loan)	Signed permanenly May 2014	C (2015)
Stirling	Andrew	05/03/90	M	33	5	4	6		1	1			1			1	2013	Kitsap Pumas (USA)	Joined Dunfermline Ath, May 2014	
Stirling	Stephen	05/01/90	M	8	6	1										4	2014	Morton		C (2015)
Winter	Sean	31/08/87	M	30	4	4	4	1		2		1	1	1	1	2	2010	Arthurlie		C (2015)
Wood	Keiran	17/10/95	D													3	2012	St Mirren		Youth
Own Goal									1											

NEW SIGNINGS 2014/15

Pettigrew	Craig	25/11/86		2014 Auchinleck Talbot
Rumsby	Scott	01/01/94		2014 Aberdeen
Malcolm	Craig	30/12/85		2014 Ayr United
Russell	Barry	1/6/89		2014 Albion Rovers

Date	Comp	H/A	Opponents	F	A	Crowd	Scorers
27/07/2013	RC1	H	Dumbarton	4	2	333	Winter, Grehan, Aitken 2 (1 pen)
03/08/2013	LC1	H	Brechin City	4	3	291	Borris, Robertson, Aitken, McKenna
10/08/2013	L	A	Stenhousemuir	0	1	483	
17/08/2013	L	H	Rangers	0	3	3473	
20/08/2013	RC2	H	Annan Athletic	2	3	290	Aitken, Grehan
24/08/2013	L	H	Ayr United	1	1	845	Longworth
27/08/2013	LC2	H	Ross County	3	2	215	Winter, Aitken, Greham
31/08/2013	L	A	Dunfermline Athletic	1	3	2585	Grehan
14/09/2013	L	A	Airdrieonians	2	3	679	Aitken, Grehan
21/09/2013	L	H	East Fife	2	0	349	Grehan, Longworth
24/09/2013	LC3	A	Hibernian	3	5	6431	Longworth, Aitken, Nelson og
28/09/2013	L	A	Brechin City	1	1	455	Corcoran
05/10/2013	L	H	Arbroath	3	2	334	Grehan 2, Longworth
12/10/2013	L	A	Forfar Athletic	2	1	449	Longworth, Aitken
19/10/2013	L	H	Stenhousemuir	1	0	326	Aitken
26/10/2013	L	H	Dunfermline Athletic	1	2	622	Longworth
02/11/2013	SC3	H	Auchinleck Talbot	2	2	1170	Longworth 2
09/11/2013	SC3R	A	Auchinleck Talbot	3	2	1386	Longworth 2, Gallagher
12/11/2013	L	A	Ayr United	6	3	986	Longworth 3, Aitken 2, McKenna
16/11/2013	L	A	East Fife	2	1	713	Longworth, Bell
23/11/2013	L	H	Airdrieonians	3	1	461	Grehan, Winter, Stirling
30/11/2013	SC4	A	Clyde	1	1	681	Longworth
07/12/2013	L	A	Arbroath	2	1	521	Longworth, Aitken
10/12/2013	SC4R	H	Clyde	4	1	454	Stirling, McKeown, Longworth, Grehan
14/12/2013	L	H	Brechin City	3	0	357	Longworth, Grehan, Gallagher
26/12/2013	L	A	Rangers	1	1	45462	Longworth
04/01/2014	L	H	Ayr United	4	0	1097	Grehan 2, Stirling, Winter
11/01/2014	L	A	Dunfermline Athletic	2	3	2952	Bell, McKeown
25/01/2014	L	A	Airdrieonians	1	1	726	McKeown
01/02/2014	L	A	Stenhousemuir	1	1	466	A Stirling
08/02/2014	SC5	H	Inverness CT	2	2	722	Grehan, Longworth
15/02/2014	L	H	Arbroath	1	1	377	Gallagher
18/02/2014	SC5R	A	Inverness CT	0	2	1458	
22/02/2014	L	A	Brechin City	3	1	452	Grehan 3
25/02/2014	L	H	Rangers	0	2	3024	
01/03/2014	L	H	Dunfermline Athletic	3	1	704	Grehan, McKenna 2
04/03/2014	L	H	East Fife	2	0	407	Mckenna, S Stirling
08/03/2014	L	A	Ayr United	0	5	1141	
11/03/2014	L	H	Forfar Athletic	0	4	342	
15/03/2014	L	A	Forfar Athletic	0	1	422	
22/03/2014	L	H	Stenhousemuir	1	1	403	Longworth
29/03/2014	L	A	Airdrieonians	1	1	404	Longworth
05/04/2014	L	A	East Fife	1	1	636	Robertson
12/04/2014	L	A	Arbroath	2	4	528	Winter, Forde
19/04/2014	L	H	Brechin City	1	2	407	A Stirling
26/04/2014	L	A	Rangers	0	3	46093	
03/05/2014	L	H	Forfar Athletic	3	1	501	Winter, Rumsby, McKeown
07/05/2014	PO	H	Dunfermline Athletic	2	1	867	Grehan, Bell
10/05/2014	PO	A	Dunfermline Athletic	0	3	aet 4525	

Friendly Matches

6/7/13	Fr	N	East Stirlingshire	1	0		at Ralston, Paisley
11/7/13	Fr	H	Morton XI	7	2		
13/7/13	Fr	H	Wigtown & Bladnoch	5	1		
16/7/13	Fr	N	Albion Rovers	1	3		at St Ambrose HS, Coatbridge
20/7/13	Fr	H	Shildon	4	0		

Date	Comp	H/A	Opponents	F	A	1	2	3	4	5	6	7	8	9	10	11	12	13	14	15	16	17	18
27/07/2013	RC1	H	Dumbarton	4	2	Mitchell	McGregor	Docherty	Robertson"	McKeown"	Aitken	Winter	Gallagher	Longworth*	Borris+	Grehan	McKenna*	Corcoran+	Kinnaird"	Forde	Fahey	Wood	Fahey
03/08/2013	LC1	H	Brechin City	4	3	Mitchell	McGregor	Docherty	Robertson"	Robertson"	Aitken	Winter	Gallagher	McKenna*	Borris*	Grehan	Corcoran*	Forde+	Maxwell"	Kinnaird	Fahey	Kinnaird	Fahey
10/08/2013	L	A	Stenhousemuir	0	1	Mitchell	Kinnaird	Docherty	Robertson	Robertson	Aitken	Winter*	Gallagher"	Mckenna	Borris+	Grehan	Stirling*	Longworth+	Corcoran"	Forde	Fahey	Rafferty	Fahey
17/08/2013	L	H	Rangers	0	3	Mitchell	Robertson	Docherty+	McGregor	Robertson	Aitken	Winter*	Gallagher	Corcoran*	Longworth+	Grehan"	Borris"	Grehan"	Corcoran"	Kinnaird	Fahey	Wood	Fahey
20/08/2013	RC2	H	Annan Athletic	2	3	Mitchell	Robertson	Docherty+	McGregor	McGregor	Aitken	Stirling	Gallagher	Corcoran*	Corcoran*	Longworth	Grehan*	Winter+	McKenna"	Kinnaird	Fahey	Wood	
24/08/2013	L	H	Ayr United	1	1	Mitchell	Robertson	Rumsby	McGregor	McKeown	Winter	Winter"	Gallagher	Longworth*	Borris	Grehan+	McKenna*	Corcoran+	Wood"	Kinnaird	Fahey		Docherty
27/08/2013	LC2	H	Ross County	3	2	Mitchell	Robertson	Rumsby	Kinnaird	McKeown	Aitken	Winter*	Gallagher	McKenna*	Corcoran+	Grehan	Longworth*	Borris+	Forde"	Stirling	Fahey	Maxwell	
31/08/2013	L	A	Dunfermline Athletic	1	3	Mitchell	Robertson	Rumsby	McKeown	Rumsby	Aitken"	Winter*	Gallagher	Longworth+	Corcoran+	Corcoran+	Borris*	McKenna+	Corcoran+	Forde	Fahey		Docherty
14/09/2013	L	A	Airdrieonians	2	3	Mitchell	Robertson	McGregor	McKeown	Rumsby	Aitken	Winter*	Gallagher	Longworth+	Corcoran	Grehan	Stirling*	Stirling*	Longworth+	Kinnaird	Fahey		Docherty
21/09/2013	L	H	East Fife	2	0	Mitchell	Robertson	Stirling	McKeown	Rumsby	Aitken	Kinnaird	Gallagher	McKenna	Corcoran"	Grehan	Borris*	Borris+	Stirling"	Forde	Fahey		Docherty
24/09/2013	LC3	A	Hibernian	3	5	Mitchell	Robertson	Stirling"	McKeown	Rumsby	Aitken	Kinnaird	Gallagher"	McKenna*	Corcoran"	Grehan	Corcoran*	Longworth+	Docherty+	McGregor"	Fahey	McGregor	
28/09/2013	L	A	Brechin City	1	1	Mitchell	Robertson	Stirling"	McKeown	Docherty	Aitken	McGregor	Gallagher	Longworth	Corcoran"	Grehan	Docherty*	Borris+	Docherty"	Forde	Fahey	Winter	
05/10/2013	L	A	Arbroath	3	2	Mitchell	Robertson	Stirling"	McKeown	Docherty	Aitken	Stirling	Gallagher	Longworth+	Corcoran+	Grehan	Winter*	McKenna+	Borris"	Forde	Fahey	Borris	
12/10/2013	L	A	Forfar Athletic	2	1	Mitchell	Robertson	McGregor	McKeown	McKeown	Aitken	Stirling	Gallagher	McKenna*	Corcoran*	Grehan	McKenna*	McKenna+	Bell"	Kinnaird"	Fahey		
19/10/2013	L	H	Stenhousemuir	1	0	Mitchell	Robertson	McGregor	McKeown	McKeown	Aitken	Stirling	Gallagher	Longworth+	Corcoran*	Grehan	Corcoran*	Borris+	McKenna"	Kinnaird"	Fahey		
26/10/2013	L	H	Dunfermline Athletic	1	2	Mitchell	Robertson	McGregor	McKeown	Docherty	Aitken	Stirling"	Gallagher	Longworth	Bell"	Grehan	McKenna"	Corcoran+	McKenna"	Corcoran	Fahey		
02/11/2013	SC3	H	Auchinleck Talbot	2	2	Mitchell	Robertson	McGregor+	McKeown	Docherty	Aitken	Stirling"	Gallagher	Longworth"	Bell*	Grehan+	Borris*	McKenna+	Borris"	Corcoran	Fahey	Winter	Baxter
09/11/2013	SC3R	A	Auchinleck Talbot	3	2	Mitchell	Robertson+	Kinnaird	McKeown	Docherty	Aitken	Stirling	Gallagher	Longworth+	Bell"	Grehan+	McKenna*	McKenna+	Kinnaird	Bell	Fahey		
12/11/2013	L	A	Ayr United	6	3	Mitchell	Robertson	Kinnaird	McKeown	McKeown	Aitken	Stirling	Gallagher	Longworth*	Winter+	Grehan"	Borris*	Corcoran+	Corcoran"	Baxter	Fahey	Corcoran	
16/11/2013	L	H	East Fife	2	1	Mitchell	Robertson	McGregor	McKeown	McKeown	Aitken"	Stirling	Gallagher	Longworth	Winter+	Grehan*	McKenna*	Borris+	Borris"	Kinnaird"	Fahey	Corcoran	
23/11/2013	L	A	Airdrieonians	3	1	Mitchell	Robertson"	McGregor	McKeown	McKeown	Aitken*	Stirling	Gallagher	Longworth+	Winter+	Grehan*	McKenna*	Borris+	Bell"	Kinnaird"	Fahey		
30/11/2013	SC4	H	Clyde	1	1	Mitchell	Robertson	McGregor	McKeown	Docherty	S Stirling*	Stirling+	Gallagher	Longworth	Winter+	McKenna"	Grehan*	Kinnaird+	Borris"	McGregor	Fahey	Bell	
07/12/2013	L	A	Arbroath	2	1	Mitchell	Robertson	Rumsby	McKeown	Docherty	Bell"	Stirling	Gallagher	Longworth+	Winter+	Grehan	Forde*	Kinnaird+	Kinnaird"	McGregor	Fahey	Bell	
10/12/2013	SC4R	H	Clyde	4	1	Mitchell	Robertson"	Rumsby	McKeown	Docherty	S Stirling*	Stirling"	Gallagher	Longworth+	Winter	Grehan+	Grehan*	Kinnaird+	Forde"	McGregor	Fahey	Borris	Kinnaird
14/12/2013	L	H	Brechin City	3	0	Mitchell	Robertson	Rumsby	McKeown	McKeown	Aitken	Stirling	Gallagher	Longworth+	Winter+	Grehan*	Bell*	McKenna+	Kinnaird"	McGregor	Fahey	Borris	Kinnaird
26/12/2013	L	H	Rangers	1	1	Mitchell	Robertson	Rumsby	McKeown	McKeown	Bell"	Winter	Gallagher	Longworth+	Winter*	Grehan	McKenna*	Forde+	Kinnaird"	McGregor	Fahey		
04/01/2014	L	H	Ayr United	4	0	Mitchell	Robertson	Rumsby	McKeown	Docherty	Bell	McKenna"	Gallagher	McKenna*	Winter+	Grehan	Winter*	Forde+	Kinnaird"	McGregor	Fahey		Mckenna
11/01/2014	L	A	Dunfermline Athletic	2	3	Mitchell	Robertson	Rumsby	McKeown	McKeown	Bell	A Stirling	Gallagher	Longworth	McKenna*	Grehan-	Winter*	McKenna+	McKenna"	McGregor"	Fahey	Bell	Kinnaird
25/01/2014	L	A	Airdrieonians	1	1	Mitchell	Robertson+	Rumsby	McKeown	Docherty	S Stirling*	A Stirling	Gallagher	Longworth	Winter*	Grehan-	McKenna*	Longworth+	Kinnaird"	McGregor	Fahey	Borris	
01/02/2014	L	A	Stenhousemuir	1	1	Mitchell	Robertson	Rumsby	McKeown	Docherty	S Stirling*	A Stirling*	Gallagher	Longworth	S stirling"	Grehan+	Stirling*	Forde+	Bell"	McGregor	Fahey	Borris	
08/02/2014	SC5	H	Inverness CT	2	2	Mitchell	Robertson	Rumsby	McKeown	McKeown	Winter	A Stirling	Gallagher	McKenna*	Winter*	Grehan	McKenna*	Longworth+	Kinnaird"	McGregor"	Fahey	Rafferty	Kinnaird
15/02/2014	L	A	Arbroath	1	1	Mitchell	Robertson	Rumsby	McKeown	McKeown	Winter	A Stirling	Gallagher	S stirling"	Winter*	Grehan+	Winter*	Forde+	McKenna"	McGregor"	Fahey	Borris	
18/02/2014	SC5R	A	Inverness CT	0	2	Mitchell	Robertson	Rumsby"	McKeown	Docherty	Longworth"	A Stirling	Gallagher+	Longworth	Winter*	Grehan*	Borris*	McGregor+	Bell"	McGregor	Fahey		
22/02/2014	L	H	Brechin City	3	1	Mitchell	Robertson+	McGregor+	McKeown	Docherty	A Stirling	A Stirling	Gallagher	Longworth+	Winter*	Grehan-	McKenna*	Forde+	Forde"	McGregor+	Fahey	Borris	
25/02/2014	L	A	Rangers	0	2	Mitchell	Robertson"	Rumsby"	McKeown	McKeown	A Stirling	A Stirling	Gallagher"	Longworth	Winter*	Grehan+	McKenna*	Bell+	Forde"	Borris	Fahey		
01/03/2014	L	H	Dunfermline Athletic	3	1	Mitchell	Robertson+	McGregor+	McKeown	Docherty	A Stirling	A Stirling"	Gallagher	S Stirling*	McKenna+	Grehan	Winter*	McKenna+	Forde"	Bell	Fahey	Bell	Kinnaird
04/03/2014	L	A	East Fife	2	0	Mitchell	Robertson	Rumsby	McKeown	Docherty	A Stirling	A Stirling	Gallagher	S Stirling"	Winter*	McKenna+	Stirling*	Forde"	Kinnaird"	Bell	Fahey	Kinnaird	
08/03/2014	L	A	Arbroath	2	4	Mitchell	Robertson	Rumsby	McGregor	Docherty	A Stirling	A Stirling	Gallagher	S Stirling*	Winter*	Grehan	Winter*	Forde"	Forde"	Bell	Fahey	Borris	
11/03/2014	L	H	Brechin City	1	2	Mitchell	Robertson"	Rumsby	McGregor	Docherty	Winter+	A Stirling"	Gallagher	Mckenna	McKenna+	Grehan+	S Stirling*	Forde"	Forde"	Kinnaird	Fahey		
15/03/2014	L	H	Forfar Athletic	0	4	Mitchell	Mckeown	Rumsby	McGregor	Docherty	Winter"	A Stirling	Gallagher	Longworth+	Winter	Grehan"	Borris*	McKenna+	Forde"	Kinnaird	Fahey	McKenna	Borris
22/03/2014	L	H	Stenhousemuir	1	1	Mitchell	Robertson	Rumsby	McKeown	Docherty	Winter+	A Stirling"	Gallagher"	Longworth	Bell*	Grehan	Borris*	McKenna+	Forde"	Kinnaird	Fahey	Forde	
29/03/2014	L	H	Airdrieonians	1	1	Mitchell	Robertson	Rumsby	McKeown	Docherty	Winter+	McKenna	Gallagher	Longworth+	Bell*	Grehan-	Borris*	McKenna+	McGregor"	Kinnaird	Fahey	Forde	
05/04/2014	L	A	East Fife	1	1	Mitchell	Robertson	Rumsby	McGregor	Docherty	Winter+	A Stirling	Gallagher	McKenna	Bell	Grehan*	Borris*	McKenna+	McGregor	Kinnaird	Fahey	Forde	
12/04/2014	L	A	Arbroath	2	4	Mitchell	Robertson	Rumsby	McGregor	Docherty	Winter+	A Stirling	Gallagher	Longworth+	Bell*	McGregor	Borris*	McKenna+	Forde"	Forde	Fahey	S Stirling	
19/04/2014	L	A	Brechin City	1	2	Mitchell	Robertson	Rumsby	McKeown	Docherty	Winter+	A Stirling	Gallagher	Longworth	Borris	Grehan*	Borris*	S Stirling"	Forde"	Kinnaird	Fahey	Borris	
26/04/2014	L	H	Rangers	0	3	Mitchell	Robertson	Rumsby	McKeown	Docherty	Winter"	A Stirling	Gallagher	Longworth+	Bell*	Grehan*	S Stirling*	Bell+	Kinnaird"	Kinnaird	Fahey	Rumsby	
03/05/2014	L	H	Forfar Athletic	2	1	Mitchell	Robertson	McGregor	McGregor	Docherty	Winter+	A Stirling"	Gallagher	Longworth+	Bell*	Grehan*	McKenna*	McGregor+	Forde"	Kinnaird	Fahey	McGregor	McGregor
07/05/2014	PO	H	Dunfermline Athletic	2	1	Mitchell	Robertson	McGregor	McGregor	McGregor	Docherty	A Stirling	Gallagher	Longworth"	Bell"	Grehan"	McKenna*	S Stirling	S Stirling"	Kinnaird	Fahey	Forde	
10/05/2014	PO	A	Dunfermline Athletic	0	3 aet	Mitchell	Robertson+	Rumsby+	McGregor	Docherty	Winter	A Stirling	Gallagher	Longworth"	Bell"	Grehan*	McKenna*	S Stirling+	Forde"	Kinnaird	Fahey	Forde	

Scottish Professional Football League Tables 2013/14

SPFL PREMIERSHIP			W	D	L	F	A	W	D	L	F	A	GD	Pts
1	Celtic	38	16	3	0	50	10	15	3	1	52	15	77	99
2	Motherwell	38	13	2	4	39	29	9	2	8	25	31	4	70
3	Aberdeen	38	10	3	5	20	13	10	5	5	33	25	15	68
4	Dundee United	38	11	2	6	40	23	5	8	6	25	27	15	58
5	Inverness CT	38	8	6	5	26	16	8	3	8	18	28	0	57
6	St Johnstone	38	10	4	5	35	16	5	4	10	13	26	6	53
7	Ross County	38	8	2	9	25	29	3	5	11	19	33	-18	40
8	St Mirren	38	7	7	5	23	20	3	2	14	16	38	-19	39
9	Kilmarnock	38	7	3	9	25	30	4	3	12	20	36	-21	39
10	Partick Thistle	38	2	8	9	21	37	6	6	7	25	28	-19	38
11	Hibernian	38	4	7	9	20	29	4	4	10	11	22	-20	35
12	Hearts	38	6	3	10	21	29	4	5	10	24	36	-20	23*

SPFL CHAMPIONSHIP			H					A					GD	Pts
			W	D	L	F	A	W	D	L	F	A		
1	Dundee	36	11	4	3	27	9	10	2	6	27	17	28	69
2	Hamilton	36	12	3	3	43	21	7	7	4	25	20	27	67
3	Falkirk	36	12	4	2	38	13	7	5	6	21	20	26	66
4	Queen of South	36	9	4	5	28	17	7	3	8	25	22	14	55
5	Dumbarton	36	7	5	6	33	28	8	1	9	32	36	1	51
6	Livingston	36	7	4	7	27	24	6	3	9	24	32	-5	46
7	Raith Rovers	36	7	4	7	29	33	4	5	9	19	28	-13	42
8	Alloa Athletic	36	7	1	10	15	24	4	6	8	19	27	-17	40
9	Cowdenbeath	36	7	3	8	32	30	4	4	10	18	42	-22	40
10	Morton	36	5	6	7	20	23	1	2	15	12	48	-39	26

SPFL LEAGUE ONE			H					A					GD	Pts
			W	D	L	F	A	W	D	L	F	A		
1	Rangers	36	16	2	0	60	12	17	1	0	46	6	88	102
2	Dunfermline	36	9	4	5	33	23	10	2	6	35	31	14	63
3	Stranraer	36	9	4	5	30	22	5	5	8	27	35	0	51
4	Ayr United	36	8	3	7	39	33	6	4	8	26	33	-1	49
5	Stenhousemuir	36	5	8	5	30	31	7	4	7	27	35	-9	48
6	Airdrieonians	36	9	2	7	27	26	3	7	8	20	31	-10	45
7	Forfar Athletic	36	6	4	8	27	24	6	3	9	28	38	-7	43
8	Brechin City	36	7	4	7	32	34	5	2	11	25	37	-14	42
9	East Fife	36	5	2	11	15	33	4	3	11	16	36	-38	32
10	Arbroath	36	6	1	11	28	36	3	3	12	24	39	-23	31

SPFL LEAGUE TWO			H					A					GD	Pts
			W	D	L	F	A	W	D	L	F	A		
1	Peterhead	36	11	6	1	37	16	12	1	5	37	22	36	76
2	Annan Athletic	36	10	3	5	34	23	9	3	6	35	26	20	63
3	Stirling Albion	36	9	6	3	34	22	7	4	7	26	28	10	58
4	Clyde	36	9	3	6	29	24	8	3	7	21	24	2	57
5	Berwick Rangers	36	10	2	6	38	22	5	5	8	25	27	14	52
6	Montrose	36	7	4	7	21	24	5	6	7	23	32	-12	46
7	Albion Rovers	36	10	2	6	23	20	2	6	10	18	34	-13	44
8	East Stirlingshire	36	6	6	6	26	28	6	2	10	19	31	-14	44
9	Elgin City	36	6	3	9	37	33	3	6	9	25	40	-11	36
10	Queen's Park	36	2	5	11	17	36	3	4	11	19	32	-32	24

PREMIERSHIP PLAY OFF

Rd 1	06/05/2014	Queen of the South	Falkirk	2	1	
Rd 1	10/05/2014	Falkirk	Queen of the South	3	1	aet
SF	13/05/2014	Falkirk	Hamilton Accies	1	1	
SF	18/05/2014	Hamilton Accies	Falkirk	1	0	
F	21/05/2014	Hamilton Accies	Hibernian	0	2	
F	25/05/2014	Hibernian	Hamilton Accies	0	2	aet, 3-4 pens

CHAMPIONSHIP PLAY OFF

SF	07/05/2014	Ayr United	Cowdenbeath	1	2
SF	07/05/2014	Stranraer	Dunfermline Athletic	2	1
SF	10/05/2014	Cowdenbeath	Ayr United	3	1
SF	10/05/2014	Dunfermline Athletic	Stranraer	3	0
F	14/05/2014	Cowdenbeath	Dunfermline Athletic	1	1
F	18/05/2014	Dunfermline Athletic	Cowdenbeath	0	3

LEAGUE ONE PLAY OFF

SF	07/05/2014	Stirling Albion	Annan Athletic	3	1	
SF	07/05/2014	Clyde	East Fife	1	0	
SF	10/05/2014	Annan Athletic	Stirling Albion	3	5	
SF	10/05/2014	East Fife	Clyde	2	1	aet, 7-6 pens
F	14/05/2014	Stirling Albion	East Fife	1	2	
F	18/05/2014	East Fife	Stirling Albion	0	2	

SPFL MONTHLY AWARDS 2013/14

	Manager of the Month Premiership	Manager of the Month Championship	Manager of the Month League One	Manager of the Month League Two
August	Terry Butcher (ICT)	Alex Neil (Hamilton Accies)	Martyn Corrigan (Stenhousemuir)	John Coughlin (East Stirling)
September	Derek McInnes (Aberdeen)	Grant Murray (Raith Rovers)	Ally McCoist (Rangers)	Stuart Garden (Montrose)
October	Tommy Wright (St Johnstone)	Grant Murray (Raith Rovers)	Stephen Aitken (Stranraer)	Jim Duffy (Clyde)
November	Jackie McNamara (Dundee United)	Gary Holt (Falkirk)	Stephen Aitken (Stranraer)	Jim McInally (Peterhead)
December	Neil Lennon (Celtic)	John McGlynn (Livingston)	Stephen Aitken (Stranraer)	James Ward (Albion Rovers)
January	Neil Lennon (Celtic)	Ian Murray (Dumbarton)	Ally McCoist (Rangers)	Colin Cameron (Berwick Rangers)
February	Derek McInnes (Aberdeen)	Jimmy Nicholl (Cowdenbeath)	Jim Jefferies (Dunfermline)	Jim Chapman (Annan Athletic)
March	Neil Lennon (Celtic)	Alex Neil (Hamilton Accies)	Gary Bollan (Airdrieonians)	Jim McInally (Peterhead)
April	Gary Locke (Hearts)	Gary Holt (Falkirk)	Gary Bollan (Airdrieonians)	Greig McDonad (Stirling Albion)

	Player of the Month	Young Player of the Month
August	Richie Foran (ICT)	Stuart Bannigan (Partick Thistle)
September	Billy McKay (ICT)	Andrew Robertson (Dundee United)
October	Stevie May (St Johnstone)	Blair Spittal (Queen's Park)
November	Andrew Robertson (Dundee United)	Ryan Gauld (Dundee United)
December	Kris Commons (Celtic)	John McGinn (St Mirren)
January	Fraser Forster (Celtic)	Craig Slater (Kilmarnock)
February	Adam Rooney (Aberdeen)	Sam Stanton (Hibernian)
March	Rory McAllister (Peterhead)	Liam Henderson (Celtic)
April	Kenny McLean (St Mirren)	Callum Paterson (Hearts)

PFA SCOTLAND AWARDS 2013/14

Player of the Year	Kris Commons (Celtic)
Young Player of the Year	Andrew Robertson (Dundee United)
Manager of the Year	Derek McInnes (Aberdeen)
Championship Player of the Year	Kane Hemmings (Cowdenbeath)
League One Player of the Year	Lee Wallace (Rangers)
League Two Player of the Year	Rory McAllister (Peterhead)
Goal of the Season	Johnny Hayes (Aberdeen)
Special Merit Award	Frank McKeown (Stranraer)

SPFA Premiership Team of the Year	SPFA Championship Team of the Year	SPFA League One Team of the Year	SPFA League Two Team of the Year
Fraser Forster *Celtic*	Michael McGovern *Falkirk*	Cammy Bell *Rangers*	Graeme Smith *Peterhead*
Graeme Shinnie *Inverness CT*	Paul McGinn *Dumbarton*	Ryan Williamson *Dunfermline*	Devon Jacobs *Berwick Rangers*
Virgil Van Dijk *Celtic*	Will Vaulks *Falkirk*	Lee McCulloch *Rangers*	Steven Noble *Peterhead*
Mark Reynolds *Aberdeen*	Stephen Kingsley *Falkirk*	Callum Morris *Dunfermline*	Michael Dunlop *Albion Rovers*
Andrew Robertson *Dundee United*	Ziggy Gordon *Hamilton*	Lee Wallace *Rangers*	Kieran MacDonald *Clyde*
Stuart Armstrong *Dundee United*	Anthony Andreu *Hamilton*	Andy Stirling *Stranraer*	Blair Spittal *Queens Park*
Peter Pawlett *Aberdeen*	Mark Millar *Falkirk*	Andy Geggan *Dunfermline*	David Anderson *Queens Park*
Kris Commons *Celtic*	Ali Crawford *Hamilton*	Nicky Law *Rangers*	Lee Currie *Berwick Rangers*
Stevie May *St Johnstone*	Kane Hemmings *Cowdenbeath*	Michael Moffat *Ayr United*	Kenny MacKay *Annan Athletic*
Kris Boyd *Kilmarnock*	Rory Loy *Falkirk*	Jon Daly *Rangers*	Rory McAllister *Peterhead*
Nadir Ciftci *Dundee United*	Peter McDonald *Dundee*	Gavin Swankie *Forfar Athletic*	Andy Rodgers *Peterhead*

SCOTTISH FOOTBALL WRITERS AWARDS 2013/14

SCOTTISH FOOTBALL WRITERS PLAYER OF THE YEAR
Kris Commons (Celtic)

SCOTTISH FOOTBALL WRITERS YOUNG PLAYER OF THE YEAR
Stevie May (St Johnstone)

SCOTTISH FOOTBALL WRITERS MANAGER OF THE YEAR
Derek McInnes (Aberdeen)

LEAGUE POSITIONS SINCE 1994 (creation of the 4 Division structure)	94/5	95/6	96/7	97/8	98/9	99/0	00/1	01/2	02/3	03/4	04/5	05/6	06/7	07/8	08/9	09/10	10/1	11/2	12/3	13/4
Aberdeen	A9	A3	A6	A6	A8	A10	A7	A4	A8	A11	A4	A6	A3	A4	A4	A9	A9	A9	A8	A3
Airdrieonians	B4	B8	B2	B4	B4	B9	B8	B2												
Albion Rovers	D10	D10	D5	D5	D7	D10	D7	D3	D3	D8	D9	D8	D6	D7	D8	D5	D2+	C9	C10-	D7
Alloa	D5	D9	D4	D1+	C5	C2+	B10-	C2+	B9-	C7	C6	C9	C7	C4	C8	C2	C9-	D1+	C2+	B8
Annan Athleic															D7	D8	D4	D6	D8	D2
Arbroath	D7	D5	D10	D2+	C7	C4	C2+	B7	B10-	C8	C9-	D4	D2	D4+	C7	C9-	D1+	C2	C5	C10-
Ayr United	B9-	C6	C1+	B7	B3	B7	B2	B3	B6	B9-	C8	C6	C5	C7	C2+	B10-	C2+	B9-	C7	C4
Berwick Rangers	C5	C3	C10-	D6	D5	D2+	C3	C6	C5	C5	C10-	D2	D1+	C10-	D9	D6	D6	D7	D4	D5
Brechin City	C10-	D2+	C7	C10-	D3	D8	D3	D1+	C2+	B10-	C1+	B10-	C4	C6	C3	C4	C4	C8	C3	C8
Celtic	A4	A2	A2	A1	A2	A2	A1	A1	A2	A1	A2	A1	A1	A1	A2	A2	A2	A1	A1	A1
Clyde	C6	C5	C4	C8	C3	C1+	B5	B5	B2	B2	B3	B5	B5	B9	B10-	C10-	D10	D9	D9	D4
Clydebank / Airdrie*	B8	B7	B9-	C2+	B7	B10-	C5	C4	C3	C1+	B5	B6	B9-	C2+	B9	B9-	C6	C4+	B10-	C6
Cowdenbeath	D9	D8	D7	D8	D9	D5	D2+	C8	C10-	D5	D3	D1+	C6	C9-	D2+	C3+	B9-	C1+	B8	B9
Dumbarton	C2+	B10-	C9-	D10	D4	D6	D6	D2+	C6	C3	C7	C10-	D5	D8	D1+	C6	C7	C3+	B7	B5
Dundee	B3	B5	B3	B1+	A5	A7	A6	A9	A6	A7	A12-	B7	B3	B2	B4	B2	B6	B2+	A12-	B1+
Dundee United	A10-	B2+	A3	A7	A9	A8	A11	A8	A11	A5	A9	A9	A9	A5	A5	A3	A4	A4	A6	A4
Dunfermline Ath	B2	B1+	A5	A8	A10-	B2+	A9	A6	A5	A4	A11	A11	A12-	B5	B3	B3	B1+	A12-	B9-	C2
East Fife	C8	C2+	B10-	C6	C9-	D4	D4	D8	D2+	C9-	D8	D7	D4	D1+	C6	C7	C5	C6	C9	C9-
East Stirlingshire	D4	D7	D9	D4	D8	D7	D8	D7	D10	D10	D10	D10	D9	D3	D3	D9	D10	D10	D8	
Elgin City							D10	D6	D9	D9	D6	D5	D9	D6	D10	D9	D7	D4	D5	D9
Falkirk	A5	A10-	B5	B2	B2	B3	B3	B9	B1	B4	B1+	A10	A7	A7	A10	A12-	B3	B3	B3	B3
Forfar Athletic	D1+	C9-	D2+	C7	C10-	D3+	C8	C3	C4	C6	C5	C8	C10-	D10	D6	D2+	C3	C7	C4	C7
Gretna									D6	D3	D1+	C1+	B1+	A12-						
Hamilton Accies	B6	B9-	C2+	B8	B9-	C10-	D1+	C5	C8	C2+	B7	B3	B4	B1+	A9	A7	A12-	B4	B5	B2+
Hearts	A6	A4	A4	A3	A6	A3	A5	A3	A3	A3	A5	A2	A4	A8	A3	A6	A3	A5	A10	A12-
Hibernian	A3	A5	A9	A10-	B1+	A6	A3	A10	A7	A8	A3	A4	A6	A6	A4	A10	A11	A7		A11-
Inverness CT	D6	D3	D1+	C5	C2+	B6	B4	B6	B4	B1+	A8	A7	A8	A9	A12-	B1+	A7	A10	A4	A5
Kilmarnock	A7	A7	A7	A4	A4	A9	A4	A7	A4	A10	A7	A5	A5	A1	A8	A11	A5	A7	A9	A9
Livingston	C9-	D1+	C3	C3	C1+	B4	B1+	A3	A9	A9	A10	A12-	B6	B7	B7-	D1+	C1+	B5	B4	B6
Montrose	D2+	C10-	D6	D9	D10	D9	D9	D5	D7	D6	D5	D9	D8	D3	D5	D10	D8	D8	D6	D6
Morton	C1+	B3	B8	B5	B6	B8	B9-	C10-	D1+	C4	C3	C2	C1+	B8	B6	B8	B7	B8	B2	B10-
Motherwell	A2	A8	A8	A9	A7	A4	A8	A11	A12	A6	A6	A8	A10	A3	A7	A5	A6	A3	A2	A2
Partick Thistle	A8	A9-	B6	B9-	C8	C5	C1+	B1+	A10	A12-	C4+	B7	B6	B2	B6	B5	B6	B6	B1+	A10
Peterhead							D5	D4	D4	D4	D2+	C3	C8	C5	C4	C5	C10-	D5	D2	D1+
Queen of the S	C7	C7	C5	C4	C4	C9	C6	C1+	B5	B5	B4	B8	B8	B4	B5	B4	B4	B10-	C1+	B4
Queen's Park	D8	D6	D8	D7	D6	D1+	C9-	D10	D8	D7	D4	D6	D3+	C8	C9-	D4	D3	D2	D3	D10
Raith Rovers	B1+	A6	A10-	B3	B8	B5	B7	B10-	C1+	B8	B10-	C7	C3	C3	C1+	B7	B2	B7	B6	B7
Rangers	A1	A1	A1	A2	A1	A1	A2	A2	A1	A1	A2	A1	A3	A2	A1	A1	A1	A1	A1	C1+
Ross County	D3	D4	D3	D3	D1+	C3+	B6	B4	B8	B6	B6	B4	B10-	C1+	B8	B5	B8	B1+	A5	A7
St Johnstone	B5	B4	B1+	A5	A3	A5	A10	A12-	B3	B3	B8	B2	B2	B3	B1+	A8	A8	A6	A3	A6
St Mirren	B7	B6	B4	B6	B5	B1+	A12-	B8	B7	B7	B2	B1+	A11	A10	A11	A10	A11	A8	A11	A8
Stenhousemuir	C4	C4	C6	C9-	D2+	C8	C7	C9	C7	C10-	D7	D3	D7	D5	D4+	C8	C8	C5	C6	C5
Stirling Albion	C3	C1+	B7	B10-	C6	C7	C10-	D9	D5	D2+	C4	C5	C2+	B10-	C5	C1+	B10-	C10-	D7	D3+
Stranraer	B10-	C8	C8	C1+	B10-	C6	C4	C7	C9-	D1+	C2+	B9-	C9-	D2+	C10-	D7	D5	D3+	C8	C3

A Premier Division / Premiership
B Division One / Championship
C Division Two / League One
D Division Three / League Two

* Clydebank changed their name to Airdrie United in 2002, then to Airdrieonians in 2013

Scottish Cup   2013/14

Round	Date	Home	Away	F	A	Att	Notes
1	14/09/13	Brora Rangers	Vale of Leithen	1	0	300	
1	14/09/13	Coldstream	Wick Academy	0	6	100	
1	14/09/13	Deveronvale	Clachnacuddin	5	0	300	
1	14/09/13	Edinburgh University	Spartans	0	2	200	
1	14/09/13	Forres Mechanics	Keith	4	5	250	
1	14/09/13	Fort William	Newton Stewart	0	0	60	
1	14/09/13	Fraserburgh	Civil Service Strollers	4	0	246	
1	14/09/13	Gala Fairydean Rovers	Glasgow University	3	1	310	
1	14/09/13	Girvan	Auchinleck Talbot	1	5	592	
1	14/09/13	Golspie Sutherland	Edinburgh City	0	4	80	
1	14/09/13	Hawick Royal Albert	St Cuthbert Wanderers	0	1	120	
1	14/09/13	Huntly	Preston Athletic	3	4	200	
1	14/09/13	Inverurie Loco Works	Burntisland Shipyard	3	0	400	
1	14/09/13	Linlithgow Rose	Nairn County	2	0	850	
1	14/09/13	Lossiemouth	Culter	0	0	150	
1	14/09/13	Selkirk	Turriff United	1	3	135	
1	14/09/13	Threave Rovers	Rothes	3	0	100	
1	14/09/13	Wigtown & Bladnoch	Buckie Thistle	3	4	125	
1R	21/09/13	Culter	Lossiemouth	3	1	240	
1R	21/09/13	Newton Stewart	Forth William	3	1	60	
2	05/10/13	Albion Rovers	Spartans	1	0	437	
2	05/10/13	Auchinleck Talbot	St Cuthbert Wanderers	4	0	475	
2	05/10/13	Berwick Rangers	Peterhead	2	1	356	
2	05/10/13	Brora Rangers	Cove Rangers	1	1	350	
2	05/10/13	Buckie Thistle	Annan Athletic	0	0	320	
2	05/10/13	Dalbeattie Star	Montrose	0	1	265	
2	05/10/13	Deveronvale	Linlithgow Rose	2	2	800	
2	05/10/13	East Stirlingshire	Threave Rovers	6	0	288	
2	05/10/13	Edinburgh City	Fraserburgh	4	4	212	at Spart
2	05/10/13	Formartine United	Inverurie Loco Works	0	2	600	
2	05/10/13	Gala Fairydean Rovers	Clyde	0	3	705	
2	05/10/13	Keith	Elgin City	0	4	650	
2	05/10/13	Newton Stewart	Culter	0	6	115	
2	05/10/13	Queen's Park	Preston Athletic	2	2	594	
2	05/10/13	Stirling Albion	Whitehill Welfare	2	2	456	
2	05/10/13	Turriff United	Wick Academy	4	2	354	
2R	12/10/13	Cove Rangers	Brora Rangers	0	3	360	
2R	12/10/13	Fraserburgh	Edinburgh City	2	0	400	
2R	12/10/13	Linlithgow Rose	Deveronvale	1	3	1500	
2R	12/10/13	Preston Athletic	Queen's Park	1	2	806	
2R	12/10/13	Whitehill Welfare	Stirling Albion	1	2	512	
2R	19/10/13	Annan Athletic	Buckie Thistle	4	0	338	

Newton Stewart v Culter match was played at Wigtown due to building work

3	02/11/13	Albion Rovers	Deveronvale	1	0		484
3	02/11/13	Alloa	Inverurie Loco Works	3	0		403
3	02/11/13	Arbroath	Brechin City	0	2		634
3	02/11/13	Ayr United	Queen's Park	3	2		879
3	02/11/13	Clyde	Brora Rangers	2	1		686
3	02/11/13	Culter	Berwick Rangers	1	1		639
3	02/11/13	Dumbarton	Cowdenbeath	2	1		450
3	02/11/13	Elgin City	Dunfermline Athletic	3	5		1108
3	02/11/13	Forfar Athletic	East Fife	2	1		485
3	02/11/13	Fraserburgh	Montrose	2	1		565
3	02/11/13	Queen of the South	Hamilton Accies	1	0		1324
3	02/11/13	Rangers	Airdrieonians	3	0		22533
3	02/11/13	Stenhousemuir	Annan Athletic	2	2		309
3	02/11/13	Stranraer	Auchinleck Talbot	2	2		1170
3	02/11/13	Turriff United	Stirling Albion	0	3		490
3	03/11/13	East Stirlingshire	Raith Rovers	0	2		716
3R	09/11/13	Auchinleck Talbot	Stranraer	2	3		1386
3R	09/11/13	Berwick Rangers	Culter	3	1		411
3R	12/11/13	Annan Athletic	Stenhousemuir	2	4 aet		421
4	29/11/13	Dundee United	Kilmarnock	5	2		6979
4	30/11/13	Albion Rovers	Motherwell	1	0		2950 at Hamilton
4	30/11/13	Alloa	Stirling Albion	3	2		1278
4	30/11/13	Ayr United	Dunfermline Athletic	1	1		1391
4	30/11/13	Berwick Rangers	Dumbarton	1	3		406
4	30/11/13	Brechin City	Forfar Athletic	1	1		724
4	30/11/13	Clyde	Stranraer	1	1		681
4	30/11/13	Dundee	Raith Rovers	0	1		3184
4	30/11/13	Falkirk	Rangers	0	2		6228
4	30/11/13	Inverness CT	Morton	4	0		1500
4	30/11/13	Queen of the South	St Mirren	2	2		2176
4	30/11/13	Ross County	Hibernian	0	1		2213
4	30/11/13	St Johnstone	Livingston	2	0		2294
4	30/11/13	Stenhousemuir	Fraserburgh	3	0		487
4	01/12/13	Hearts`	Celtic	0	7		10636
4	01/12/13	Partick Thistle	Aberdeen	0	1		3642
4R	04/12/13	Dunfermline Athletic	Ayr United	1	0		1932
4R	10/12/13	Forfar Athletic	Brechin City	3	3 aet, 4-3 pens		811
4R	10/12/13	St Mirren	Queen of the South	3	0		2775
4R	10/12/13	Stranraer	Clyde	4	1		454
5	07/02/14	Rangers	Dunfermline Athletic	4	0		19396
5	08/02/14	Albion Rovers	Stenhousemuir	2	0		748
5	08/02/14	Alloa	Dumbarton	0	1		749
5	08/02/14	Celtic	Aberdeen	1	2		30413
5	08/02/14	Forfar Athletic	St Johnstone	0	4		1803
5	08/02/14	Hibernian	Raith Rovers	2	3		10503
5	08/02/14	Stranraer	Inverness CT	2	2		722
5	09/02/14	Dundee United	St Mirren	2	1		4952
5R	18/02/14	Inverness CT	Stranraer	2	0		1458
6	08/03/14	Aberdeen	Dumbarton	1	0		10600
6	08/03/14	Raith Rovers	St Johnstone	1	3		3767
6	09/03/14	Inverness CT	Dundee United	0	5		3164
6	09/03/14	Rangers	Albion Rovers	1	1		23976
6R	17/03/14	Albion Rovers	Rangers	0	2		5354 at Hamilton
SF	12/04/14	Rangers	Dundee United	1	3		41059 at Rangers
SF	13/04/14	St Johnstone	Aberdeen	2	1		19057 at Rangers
F	17/05/14	St Johnstone	Dundee United	2	0		47345 at Celtic

Scottish Cup Finals 1873-2014

Season	Winner	Score	Runner-up	Venue	Attendance
1873–74	Queen's Park (1)	2–0	Clydesdale	Hampden Park (original)	2,500
1874–75	Queen's Park (2)	3–0	Renton	Hampden Park (original)	7,000
1875–76	Queen's Park	1–1	3rd Lanark RV	Hamilton Crescent	6,000
(R)	Queen's Park (3)	2–0	3rd Lanark RV	Hampden Park (original)	10,000
1876–77	Vale of Leven	1–1	Rangers	Hamilton Crescent	8,000
(R)	Vale of Leven	1–1	Rangers	Hamilton Crescent	15,000
(SR)	Vale of Leven (1)	3–2	Rangers	Hampden Park (original)	12,000
1877–78	Vale of Leven (2)	1–0	3rd Lanark RV	Hampden Park (original)	5,000
1878–79	Vale of Leven	1–1	Rangers	Hampden Park (original)	9,000
(R)	Vale of Leven (3)	wo	Rangers	Hampden Park (original)	
1879–80	Queen's Park (4)	3–0	Thornliebank	Hampden Park (original)	4,000
1880–81	Queen's Park	2–1 *	Dumbarton	Kinning Park	15,000
(R)	Queen's Park (5)	3–1	Dumbarton	Kinning Park	10,000
1881–82	Queen's Park	2–2	Dumbarton	Cathkin Park (first)	12,500
(R)	Queen's Park (6)	4–1	Dumbarton	Cathkin Park (first)	14,000
1882–83	Dumbarton	2–2	Vale of Leven	Hampden Park (original)	15,000
(R)	Dumbarton (1)	2–1	Vale of Leven	Hampden Park (original)	12,000
1883–84	Queen's Park (7)	wo	Vale of Leven	Cathkin Park (first)	
1884–85	Renton	0–0	Vale of Leven	Hampden Park (second)	3,000
(R)	Renton (1)	3–1	Vale of Leven	Hampden Park (second)	5,500
1885–86	Queen's Park (8)	3–1	Renton	Cathkin Park (first)	7,000
1886–87	Hibernian (1)	2–1	Dumbarton	Hampden Park (second)	15,000
1887–88	Renton (2)	6–1	Cambuslang	Hampden Park (second)	10,000
1888–89	3rd Lanark RV	3–0 *	Celtic	Hampden Park (second)	17,000
(R)	3rd Lanark RV (1)	2–1	Celtic	Hampden Park (second)	13,000
1889–90	Queen's Park	1–1	Vale of Leven	Ibrox Park (first)	11,000
(R)	Queen's Park (9)	2–1	Vale of Leven	Ibrox Park (first)	13,000
1890–91	Heart of Midlothian (1)	1–0	Dumbarton	Hampden Park (second)	10,836
1891–92	Celtic	1–0 *	Queen's Park	Ibrox Park (first)	40,000
(R)	Celtic (1)	5–1	Queen's Park	Ibrox Park (first)	26,000
1892–93	Queen's Park	0–1 *	Celtic	Ibrox Park (first)	18,771
(R)	Queen's Park (10)	2–1	Celtic	Ibrox Park (first)	13,239
1893–94	Rangers (1)	3–1	Celtic	Hampden Park (second)	17,000
1894–95	St Bernard's (1)	2–1	Renton	Ibrox Park (first)	10,000
1895–96	Heart of Midlothian (2)	3–1	Hibernian	Logie Green	17,034
1896–97	Rangers (2)	5–1	Dumbarton	Hampden Park (second)	14,000
1897–98	Rangers (3)	2–0	Kilmarnock	Hampden Park (second)	13,000
1898–99	Celtic (2)	2–0	Rangers	Hampden Park (second)	25,000
1899–1900	Celtic (3)	4–3	Queen's Park	Ibrox Park	15,000
1900–01	Heart of Midlothian (3)	4–3	Celtic	Ibrox Park	15,000
1901–02	Hibernian (2)	1–0	Celtic	Celtic Park	16,000
1902–03	Rangers	1–1	Heart of Midlothian	Celtic Park	13,000
(R)	Rangers	0–0	Heart of Midlothian	Celtic Park	35,000
(SR)	Rangers (5)	2–0	Heart of Midlothian	Celtic Park	30,000
1903–04	Celtic (4)	3–2	Rangers	Hampden Park	64,472
1904–05	Third Lanark	0–0	Rangers	Hampden Park	54,000
(R)	Third Lanark (2)	3–1	Rangers	Hampden Park	55,000
1905–06	Heart of Midlothian (4)	1–0	Third Lanark	Ibrox Park	30,000
1906–07	Celtic (5)	3–0	Heart of Midlothian	Hampden Park	50,000
1907–08	Celtic (6)	5–1	St. Mirren	Hampden Park	58,000
1909–10	Dundee	2–2	Clyde	Ibrox Park	60,000
(R)	Dundee	0–0 AET	Clyde	Ibrox Park	25,000
(SR)	Dundee (1)	2–1	Clyde	Ibrox Park	25,000
1910–11	Celtic	0–0	Hamilton Academical	Ibrox Park	45,000

Season	Winner	Score	Runner-up	Venue	Attendance
(R)	Celtic (7)	2–0	Hamilton Academical	Ibrox Park	25,000
1911–12	Celtic (8)	2–0	Clyde	Ibrox Park	45,000
1912–13	Falkirk (1)	2–0	Raith Rovers	Celtic Park	45,000
1913–14	Celtic	0–0	Hibernian	Ibrox Park	56,000
(R)	Celtic (9)	4–1	Hibernian	Ibrox Park	40,000
1919–20	Kilmarnock (1)	3–2	Albion Rovers	Celtic Park	95,000
1920–21	Partick Thistle (1)	1–0	Rangers	Celtic Park	28,294
1921–22	Morton (1)	1–0	Rangers	Hampden Park	70,000
1922–23	Celtic (10)	1–0	Hibernian	Hampden Park	82,000
1923–24	Airdrieonians (1)	2–0	Hibernian	Ibrox Park	65,000
1924–25	Celtic (11)	2–1	Dundee	Hampden Park	75,317
1925–26	St. Mirren (1)	2–0	Celtic	Hampden Park	98,000
1926–27	Celtic (12)	3–1	East Fife	Hampden Park	80,070
1927–28	Rangers (6)	4–0	Celtic	Hampden Park	118,115
1928–29	Kilmarnock (2)	1–0	Rangers	Hampden Park	114,780
1929–30	Rangers	0–0	Partick Thistle	Hampden Park	107,475
(R)	Rangers (7)	2–1	Partick Thistle	Hampden Park	103,688
1930–31	Celtic	2–2	Motherwell	Hampden Park	104,863
(R)	Celtic (13)	4–2	Motherwell	Hampden Park	98,509
1931–32	Rangers	1–1	Kilmarnock	Hampden Park	112,000
(R)	Rangers (8)	3–0	Kilmarnock	Hampden Park	104,600
1932–33	Celtic (14)	1–0	Motherwell	Hampden Park	102,339
1933–34	Rangers (9)	5–0	St. Mirren	Hampden Park	113,430
1934–35	Rangers (10)	2–1	Hamilton Academical	Hampden Park	87,740
1935–36	Rangers (11)	1–0	Third Lanark	Hampden Park	88,859
1936–37	Celtic (15)	2–1	Aberdeen	Hampden Park	147,365
1937–38	East Fife	1–1	Kilmarnock	Hampden Park	80,091
(R)	East Fife (1)	4–2 AET	Kilmarnock	Hampden Park	92,716
1938–39	Clyde (1)	4–0	Motherwell	Hampden Park	94,000
1946–47	Aberdeen (1)	2–1	Hibernian	Hampden Park	82,140
1947–48	Rangers	1–1 AET	Morton	Hampden Park	129,176
(R)	Rangers (11)	1–0 AET	Morton	Hampden Park	133,750
1948–49	Rangers (12)	4–1	Clyde	Hampden Park	108,435
1949–50	Rangers (13)	3–0	East Fife	Hampden Park	118,262
1950–51	Celtic (16)	1–0	Motherwell	Hampden Park	131,943
1951–52	Motherwell (1)	4–0	Dundee	Hampden Park	136,274
1952–53	Rangers	1–1	Aberdeen	Hampden Park	129,761
(R)	Rangers (14)	1–0	Aberdeen	Hampden Park	113,700
1953–54	Celtic (17)	2–1	Aberdeen	Hampden Park	130,060
1954–55	Clyde	1–1	Celtic	Hampden Park	106,234
(R)	Clyde (2)	1–0	Celtic	Hampden Park	68,831
1955–56	Heart of Midlothian (5)	3–1	Celtic	Hampden Park	132,840
1956–57	Falkirk	1–1	Kilmarnock	Hampden Park	83,000
(R)	Falkirk (2)	2–1 AET	Kilmarnock	Hampden Park	79,785
1957–58	Clyde (3)	1–0	Hibernian	Hampden Park	95,123
1958–59	St. Mirren (2)	3–1	Aberdeen	Hampden Park	108,591
1959–60	Rangers (15)	2–0	Kilmarnock	Hampden Park	108,017
1960–61	Dunfermline Athletic	0–0	Celtic	Hampden Park	113,618
(R)	Dunfermline Athletic (1)	2–0	Celtic	Hampden Park	87,866
1961–62	Rangers (16)	2–0	St. Mirren	Hampden Park	127,940
1962–63	Rangers	1–1	Celtic	Hampden Park	129,643
(R)	Rangers (17)	3–0	Celtic	Hampden Park	120,273
1963–64	Rangers (18)	3–1	Dundee	Hampden Park	120,982
1964–65	Celtic (18)	3–2	Dunfermline Athletic	Hampden Park	108,800

Season	Winner	Score	Runner-up	Venue	Attendance
(R)	Rangers (19)	1–0	Celtic	Hampden Park	98,202
1966–67	Celtic (19)	2–0	Aberdeen	Hampden Park	126,102
1967–68	Dunfermline Athletic (3)	3–1	Heart of Midlothian	Hampden Park	56,365
1968–69	Celtic (20)	4–0	Rangers	Hampden Park	132,000
1969–70	Aberdeen (2)	3–1	Celtic	Hampden Park	108,434
1970–71	Celtic	1–1	Rangers	Hampden Park	120,092
(R)	Celtic (21)	2–1	Rangers	Hampden Park	103,332
1971–72	Celtic (22)	6–1	Hibernian	Hampden Park	106,102
1972–73	Rangers (20)	3–2	Celtic	Hampden Park	122,714
1973–74	Celtic (23)	3–0	Dundee United	Hampden Park	75,959
1974–75	Celtic (24)	3–1	Airdrieonians	Hampden Park	75,457
1975–76	Rangers (21)	3–1	Heart of Midlothian	Hampden Park	85,354
1976–77	Celtic (25)	1–0	Rangers	Hampden Park	54,252
1977–78	Rangers (22)	2–1	Aberdeen	Hampden Park	61,563
1978–79	Rangers	0–0	Hibernian	Hampden Park	50,610
(R)	Rangers	0–0 AET	Hibernian	Hampden Park	33,504
(SR)	Rangers (23)	3–2 AET	Hibernian	Hampden Park	30,602
1979–80	Celtic (26)	1–0	Rangers	Hampden Park	70,303
1980–81	Rangers	0–0AET	Dundee United	Hampden Park	53,000
(R)	Rangers (24)	4–1	Dundee United	Hampden Park	43,099
1981–82	Aberdeen (3)	4–1 AET	Rangers	Hampden Park	53,788
1982–83	Aberdeen (4)	1–0 AET	Rangers	Hampden Park	62,979
1983–84	Aberdeen (5)	2–1 AET	Celtic	Hampden Park	58,900
1984–85	Celtic (27)	2–1	Dundee United	Hampden Park	60,346
1985–86	Aberdeen (6)	3–0	Heart of Midlothian	Hampden Park	62,841
1986–87	St. Mirren (3)	1–0 AET	Dundee United	Hampden Park	51,782
1987–88	Celtic (28)	2–1	Dundee United	Hampden Park	74,000
1988–89	Celtic (29)	1–0	Rangers	Hampden Park	72,069
1989–90	Aberdeen (7)	0–0 †	Celtic	Hampden Park	60,493
1990–91	Motherwell (2)	4–3 AET	Dundee United	Hampden Park	57,319
1991–92	Rangers (25)	2–1	Airdrieonians	Hampden Park	44,045
1992–93	Rangers (26)	2–1	Aberdeen	Celtic Park	50,715
1993–94	Dundee United (1)	1–0	Rangers	Hampden Park	37,450
1994–95	Celtic (30)	1–0	Airdrieonians	Hampden Park	36,915
1995–96	Rangers (27)	5–1	Heart of Midlothian	Hampden Park	37,730
1996–97	Kilmarnock (3)	1–0	Falkirk	Ibrox Stadium	48,953
1997–98	Heart of Midlothian (6)	2–1	Rangers	Celtic Park	48,946
1998–99	Rangers (28)	1–0	Celtic	Hampden Park	52,670
1999–00	Rangers (29)	4–0	Aberdeen	Hampden Park	50,865
2000–01	Celtic (31)	3–0	Hibernian	Hampden Park	51,824
2001–02	Rangers (30)	3–2	Celtic	Hampden Park	51,138
2002–03	Rangers (31)	1–0	Dundee	Hampden Park	47,136
2003–04	Celtic (32)	3–1	Dunfermline Athletic	Hampden Park	50,846
2004–05	Celtic (33)	1–0	Dundee United	Hampden Park	50,635
2005–06	Heart of Midlothian (7)	1–1 AET + pk	Gretna	Hampden Park	51,232
2006–07	Celtic (34)	1–0	Dunfermline Athletic	Hampden Park	49,600
2007–08	Rangers (32)	3–2	Queen of the South	Hampden Park	48,821
2008–09	Rangers (33)	1–0	Falkirk	Hampden Park	50,956
2009–10	Dundee United (2)	3–0	Ross County	Hampden Park	47,122
2010–11	Celtic (35)	3–0	Motherwell	Hampden Park	49,618
2011–12	Heart of Midlothian (8)	5–1	Hibernian	Hampden Park	51,041
2012–13	Celtic (36)	3–0	Hibernian	Hampden Park	51,254
2013-14	St Johnstone (1)	2-0	Dundee United	Celtic Park	47,545

* Match Void

Scottish League Cup 2013/14

R1	3/8/13	Airdrieonians	Stenhousemuir	4 3	
R1	3/8/13	Arbroath	Montrose	0 1	
R1	3/8/13	Berwick Rangers	Cowdenbeath	0 5	
R1	3/8/13	Dumbarton	Albion Rovers	1 0	
R1	3/8/13	East Fife	Morton	2 6	AET
R1	3/8/13	East Stirlingshire	Dunfermline Athletic	0 2	
R1	3/8/13	Elgin City	Livingston	1 3	
R1<	3/8/13	Falkirk	Clyde	3 0	
R1	3/8/13	Forfar Athletic	Rangers	2 1	
R1	3/8/13	Peterhead	Alloa	0 2	
R1	3/8/13	Queen of the South	Annan Athletic	3 0	
R1	3/8/13	Raith Rovers	Queen's Park	6 0	
R1	3/8/13	Stirling Albion	Hamilton Accies	0 3	
R1	3/8/13	Stranraer	Brechin City	4 3	
R1	06/08/13	Partick Thistle	Ayr United	2 1	
R2	27/08/13	Aberdeen	Alloa	0 0	AET, 6-5 pens
R2	27/08/13	Airdrieonians	Livingston	9 2	
R2	27/08/13	Dundee	Forfar Athletic	2 1	
R2	27/08/13	Falkirk	Dunfermline Athletic	2 1	
R2	27/08/13	Kilmarnock	Hamilton Accies	0 1	
R2	27/08/13	Morton	Montrose	4 0	
R2	27/08/13	Partick Thistle	Cowdenbeath	3 1	
R2	27/08/13	Queen of the South	St Mirren	2 1	
R2	27/08/13	Raith Rovers	Hearts	1 1	AET, 4-5 pens
R2	27/08/13	Stranraer	Ross County	3 2	
R2	28/08/13	Dumbarton	Dundee United	2 3	
R3	24/09/13	Celtic	Morton	0 1	
R3	24/09/13	Dundee	Inverness CT	0 1	
R3	24/09/13	Hamilton Accies	St Johnstone	0 3	
R3	24/09/13	Hibernian	Stranraer	5 3	
R3	25/09/13	Dundee United	Partick Thistle	4 1	
R3	25/09/13	Falkirk	Aberdeen	0 5	
R3	25/09/13	Hearts	Queen of the South	3 3	AET, 4-2 pens
R3	25/09/13	Livingston	Motherwell	1 2	
QF	29/10/13	Inverness CT	Dundee United	2 1	
QF	30/10/13	Hibernian	Hearts	0 1	
QF	30/10/13	Morton	St Johnstone	0 1	
QF	30/10/13	Motherwell	Aberdeen	0 2	
SF*	01/02/14	Aberdeen	St Johnstone	4 0	
SF+	02/02/14	Hearts	Inverness CT	2 2	AET, 2-4 pens
F>	16/03/14	Aberdeen	Inverness CT	0 0	AET, 4-2 pens

< at Alloa
* at Tynecastle
+ at Easter Road
> at Celtic Park

Scottish League Cup Finals 1947-2014

Season	Winner	Score	Runner-up	Venue	Attendance
1946–47	Rangers	4 – 0	Aberdeen	Hampden Park	82,700
1947–48	East Fife	0 – 0 AET	Falkirk	Hampden Park	53,785
1947–48 (R)	East Fife	4 – 1	Falkirk	Hampden Park	31,000
1948–49	Rangers	2 – 0	Raith Rovers	Hampden Park	57,450
1949–50	East Fife	3 – 0	Dunfermline Athletic	Hampden Park	39,744
1950–51	Motherwell	3 – 0	Hibernian	Hampden Park	64,074
1951–52	Dundee	3 – 2	Rangers	Hampden Park	92,325
1952–53	Dundee	2 – 0	Kilmarnock	Hampden Park	51,830
1953–54	East Fife	3 – 2	Partick Thistle	Hampden Park	38,529
1954–55	Heart of Midlothian	4 – 2	Motherwell	Hampden Park	55,640
1955–56	Aberdeen	2 – 1	St. Mirren	Hampden Park	44,106
1956–57	Celtic	0 – 0 AET	Partick Thistle	Hampden Park	59,000
1956–57 (R)	Celtic	3 – 0	Partick Thistle	Hampden Park	
1957–58	Celtic	7 – 1	Rangers	Hampden Park	82,293
1958–59	Heart of Midlothian	5 – 1	Partick Thistle	Hampden Park	59,690
1959–60	Heart of Midlothian	2 – 1	Third Lanark	Hampden Park	57,994
1960–61	Rangers	2 – 0	Kilmarnock	Hampden Park	82,063
1961–62	Rangers	1 – 1 AET	Heart of Midlothian	Hampden Park	88,000
1961–62 (R)	Rangers	3 – 1	Heart of Midlothian	Hampden Park	47,500
1962–63	Heart of Midlothian	1 – 0	Kilmarnock	Hampden Park	51,000
1963–64	Rangers	5 – 0	Morton	Hampden Park	105,907
1964–65	Rangers	2 – 1	Celtic	Hampden Park	91,423
1965–66	Celtic	2 – 1	Rangers	Hampden Park	107,609
1966–67	Celtic	1 – 0	Rangers	Hampden Park	94,532
1967–68	Celtic	5 – 3	Dundee	Hampden Park	70,000
1968–69	Celtic	6 – 2	Hibernian	Hampden Park	74,240
1969–70	Celtic	1 – 0	St. Johnstone	Hampden Park	73,067
1970–71	Rangers	1 – 0	Celtic	Hampden Park	106,263
1971–72	Partick Thistle	4 – 1	Celtic	Hampden Park	62,740
1972–73	Hibernian	2 – 1	Celtic	Hampden Park	71,696
1973–74	Dundee	1 – 0	Celtic	Hampden Park	27,924
1974–75	Celtic	6 – 3	Hibernian	Hampden Park	53,848
1975–76	Rangers	1 – 0	Celtic	Hampden Park	58,806
1976–77	Aberdeen	2 – 1 AET	Celtic	Hampden Park	69,707
1977–78	Rangers	2 – 1 AET	Celtic	Hampden Park	60,168
1978–79	Rangers	2 – 1	Aberdeen	Hampden Park	54,000
1979–80	Dundee United	0 – 0 AET	Aberdeen	Hampden Park	27,173
1979–80 (R)	Dundee United	3 – 0	Aberdeen	Dens Park	28,933
1980–81	Dundee United	3 – 0	Dundee	Dens Park	24,466
1981–82	Rangers	2 – 1	Dundee United	Hampden Park	53,777
1982–83	Celtic	2 – 1	Rangers	Hampden Park	55,572
1983–84	Rangers	3 – 2 AET	Celtic	Hampden Park	66,369
1984–85	Rangers	1 – 0	Dundee United	Hampden Park	44,698
1985–86	Aberdeen	3 – 0	Hibernian	Hampden Park	40,061
1986–87	Rangers	2 – 1	Celtic	Hampden Park	74,219
1987–88	Rangers	3 – 3 AET + pk	Aberdeen	Hampden Park	71,961
1988–89	Rangers	3 – 2	Aberdeen	Hampden Park	72,122
1989–90	Aberdeen	2 – 1 AET	Rangers	Hampden Park	61,190
1990–91	Rangers	2 – 1 AET	Celtic	Hampden Park	62,817
1991–92	Hibernian	2 – 0	Dunfermline Athletic	Hampden Park	40,377
1992–93	Rangers	2 – 1 AET	Aberdeen	Hampden Park	54,298
1993–94	Rangers	2 – 1	Hibernian	Celtic Park	47,632
1994–95	Raith Rovers	2 – 2 AET + pk	Celtic	Ibrox Stadium	45,384
1995–96	Aberdeen	2 – 0	Dundee	Hampden Park	33,096
1996–97	Rangers	4 – 3	Heart of Midlothian	Celtic Park	48,559
1997–98	Celtic	3 – 0	Dundee United	Ibrox Stadium	49,305
1998–99	Rangers	2 – 1	St. Johnstone	Celtic Park	45,533
1999–00	Celtic	2 – 0	Aberdeen	Hampden Park	50,073
2000–01	Celtic	3 – 0	Kilmarnock	Hampden Park	48,830
2001–02	Rangers	4 – 0	Ayr United	Hampden Park	50,076
2002–03	Rangers	2 – 1	Celtic	Hampden Park	52,000
2003–04	Livingston	2 – 0	Hibernian	Hampden Park	45,500

Scottish League Challenge Cup 2013/14

PR	13/07/13	Spartans	Threave Rovers	4	2	
PR	20/07/13	Threave Rovers	Spartans	1	0	
R1	27/07/13	Airdrieonians	Hamilton Accies	2	1	
R1	27/07/13	Alloa	Dundee	0	1	
R1	27/07/13	Annan Athletic	Morton	1	0	
R1	27/07/13	Berwick Rangers	Livingston	3	2	
R1	27/07/13	Clyde	Falkirk	1	2	
R1	27/07/13	Cowdenbeath	Dunfermline Athletic	1	3	
R1	27/07/13	Elgin City	Montrose	2	0	
R1	27/07/13	Forfar Athletic	East Fife	2	1	
R1	27/07/13	Formartine United	East Stirlingshire	2	0	
R1	27/07/13	Peterhead	Brechin City	2	1	
R1	27/07/13	Queen of the South	Spartans	4	0	
R1	27/07/13	Queen's Park	Ayr United	1	2	
R1	27/07/13	Raith Rovers	Stirling Albion	2	1	
R1	27/07/13	Stenhousemuir	Arbroath	4	4	AET, 3-2 pens
R1	27/07/13	Stranraer	Dumbarton	4	2	
R1	28/07/13	Albion Rovers	Rangers	0	4	at Livingston
R2	20/08/13	Airdrieonians	Queen of the South	0	2	
R2	20/08/13	Ayr United	Falkirk	1	2	
R2	20/08/13	Dundee	Forfar Athletic	3	1	
R2	20/08/13	Dunfermline Athletic`	Raith Rovers	0	2	
R2	20/08/13	Peterhead	Stenhousemuir	1	3	
R2	20/08/13	Stranraer	Annan Athletic	2	3	
R2	21/08/13	Formartine United	Elgin City	5	1	
R2	27/08/13	Rangers	Berwick Rangers	2	0	
QF	07/09/13	Annan Athletic	Formartine United	4	0	
QF	07/09/13	Dundee	Stenhousemuir	1	1	AET, 4-5 pens
QF	07/09/13	Raith Rovers	Falkirk	1	0	
QF	17/09/13	Queen of the South	Rangers	0	3	
SF	13/10/13	Raith Rovers	Annan Athletic	3	0	
SF	29/10/13	Stenhousemuir	Rangers	0	1	
F	06/04/14	Raith Rovers	Rangers	1	0	AET at Hibernian

Scottish League Challenge Cup Finals 1991-2014

Season	Winner	Score	Runner-up	Venue	Att
1990–91	Dundee (1)	3–2 AET	Ayr United	Fir Park	11,506
1991–92	Hamilton Academical (1)	1–0	Ayr United	Fir Park	9,663
1992–93	Hamilton Academical (2)	3–2	Morton	Love Street	7,391
1993–94	Falkirk (1)	3–0	St. Mirren	Fir Park	13,763
1994–95	Airdrieonians (1)	3–2 AET	Dundee	McDiarmid Park	8,844
1995–96	Stenhousemuir (1)	0–0 aet + pens	Dundee United	McDiarmid Park	7,856
1996–97	Stranraer (1)	1–0	St. Johnstone	Broadwood	5,222
1997–98	Falkirk (2)	1–0	Queen of the South	Fir Park	9,735
1998–99	No competition				
1999–2000	Alloa Athletic (1)	4–4 aet + pens	Inverness Caledonian Thistle	Excelsior Stadium	4,043
2000–01	Airdrieonians (2)	2–2 aet + pens	Livingston	Broadwood	5,623
2001–02	Airdrieonians (3)	2–1	Alloa Athletic	Broadwood	4,548
2002–03	Queen of the South (1)	2–0	Brechin City	Broadwood	6,428
2003–04	Inverness Caledonian Thistle (1)	2–0	Airdrie United	McDiarmid Park	5,428
2004–05	Falkirk (3)	2–1	Ross County	McDiarmid Park	7,471
2005–06	St. Mirren (1)	2–1	Hamilton Academical	Excelsior Stadium	9,613
2006–07	Ross County (1)	1–1 aet + pens	Clyde	McDiarmid Park	4,062
2007–08	St. Johnstone (1)	3–2	Dunfermline Athletic	Dens Park	6,446
2008–09	Airdrie United (1)	2–2 aet + pens	Ross County	McDiarmid Park	4,091
2009–10	Dundee (2)	3–2	Inverness Caledonian Thistle	McDiarmid Park	8,031
2010–11	Ross County (2)	2–0	Queen of the South	McDiarmid Park	5,124
2011–12	Falkirk (4)	1–0	Hamilton Academical	Almondvale	5,210
2012–13	Queen of the South (2)	1–1 aet + pens	Partick Thistle	Almondvale	9,452
2013-14	Raith Rovers (1)	1-0 aet	Rangers	Easter Road	19,983

Scottish Reserve League 2013/14

	Air	All	Ann	Ayr	Ber	Cow	Dun	EF	ES	Liv	Mor	QOS	QP	RR	Ste	
Airdrieonians		Oct 7 1-0		Sep 30 1-0	Nov 18 5-3	Sep 23 2-2			Nov 4 2-0	Sep 9 0-1	Dec 17 0-4		Oct 21 0-2	Dec 9 3-0		
Alloa			Sep 30 2-0		Nov 11 1-7	Sep 16 1-4				Jan 13 1-3	Sep 2 3-0		Oct 14 1-6		Jan 20 2-4	
Annan Athletic	Dec 19 3-1			Dec 17 3-2				Jan 7 0-3	Sep 10 1-2		Sep 3 2-1	Oct 22 6-0	Dec 10 3-3		Oct 8 1-1	
Ayr United		Nov 18 1-1			Sep 17 6-1			Feb 4 5-0	Sep 3 1-0				Oct 14 2-1	Jan 27 1-5		
Berwick Rangers	Sep 24 8-2					Sep 10 2-1					Dec 10 2-2		Oct 8 0-1			
Cowdenbeath			Sep 17 0-1	Nov 5			Sep 3 1-2				Oct 15 3-3	Dec 3		Oct 1 1-4	Nov 18 0-0	
Dundee	Nov 12 4-1			Sep 10 2-2	Oct 28 6-2				Dec 9 3-1		Oct 8 3-3	Nov 26 2-0			Dec 17 3-0	
East Fife	Sep 16 7-0	Nov 4 4-0		Sep 2 3-1	Oct 21 1-3								Sep 30 0-0	Nov 18 1-0		
East Stirlingshire		Sep 11 2-2*	Feb 4 2-0*		Dec 17 1-5	Dec 11 1-1*	Oct 16 2-1*				Nov 27 1-4*	Oct 2 1-3*		Sep 25 0-4*	Nov 13 1-5*	* at Stirling University
Livingston				Oct 23 0-1*			Dec 2 2-1&	Oct 7 5-2*			Nov 18 1-2&			Sep 17 1-0*	Nov 4 4-1*	* at Blackburn United & at Broxburn
Morton				Dec 10 2-0	Oct 14 4-1				Nov 26 2-1*				Nov 11 3-2*		Sep 9 3-1	* at Parklea
Queen of the South	Sep 3 6-1	Feb 4 2-1			Dec 3 1-0	Oct 8 6-1			Nov 19 7-0	Jan 7 0-3				Nov 5 0-4		
Queen's Park	Dec 9 5-1*	Oct 14 2-0*					Nov 25 3-1*	Sep 30 2-2*			Nov 11 2-2*	Dec 23 2-0*		Jan 20 1-0*		* at Toryglen
Raith Rovers				Oct 8 5-1	Feb 4 5-1		Nov 19 2-3	Sep 24 1-0			Nov 5 2-2	Sep 10 0-3			Oct 22 3-1	
Stenhousemuir	Oct 15 4-2			Nov 26 4-2	Oct 1 3-3			Nov 12 0-4	Sep 17 2-3				Jan 28 2-2	Sep 3 3-0		

	P	W	D	L	F	A	PTS
Queen's Park	14	10	2	2	33	11	32
Dundee	14	9	3	2	39	19	30
Morton	14	9	2	3	30	23	29
Livingston	14	8	3	3	32	18	27
Raith Rovers	13	7	1	5	33	19	22
Queen of South	14	6	3	5	33	22	21
Ayr United	14	6	2	6	25	25	20
East Fife	13	6	1	6	26	21	19
Annan Athletic	12	5	2	5	22	21	17
Stenhousemuir	14	4	4	6	26	32	16
Airdrieonians	14	5	1	8	19	36	16
Berwick Rangers	13	3	2	8	29	40	11
East Stirlingshire	13	3	2	8	14	37	11
Cowdenbeath	14	2	4	8	23	31	10
Alloa Athletic	14	2	2	10	18	47	8

Scottish Reserve League Cup 2013/14

RESERVE LEAGUE CUP (West)

	Ai	AA	AU	L	M	QOS	QP			
Airdrieonians	■	Mar 18 2-1	Feb 10 1-2		Mar 6 2-3		Mar 25 0-2			
Annan Athletic		■		Mar 11 2-0	Mar 27 1-3		Apr 22 0-3			
Ayr United	Apr 9 0-2		■	Apr 2 2-2	Feb 17 1-7					
Livingston	Apr 15 2-2&			■		Mar 5 5-1	Apr 8 0-1*	* at Broxburn Athletic	& at Airdrie	
Morton				Feb 25 2-0	■	Mar 18 0-2*	Apr 15 0-3	* at Port Glasgow Juniors		
Queen of the South	Mar 11 2-1	Feb 11 2-3	Feb 25 2-2			■				
Queen's Park			Mar 10 0-4*			Feb 17 3-0*	■	* at Toryglen		

RESERVE LEAGUE CUP (East)

	All	Cow	D	EF	Es	RR	Sten			
Alloa	■	Mar 10 0-3	Mar 31 3-2	Mar 31 2-1	Feb 17 4-1	Feb 10 3-1				
Cowdenbeath		■	Mar 31 2-3		Feb 24 2-1	Mar 18 2-1				
Dundee			■							
East Fife		Apr 8 2-2	Apr 14 2-2	■	Mar 17 5-0					
East Stirlingshire		Apr 14 0-3>	Feb 25 2-1*		■	Apr 30 &		* at Alloa	& at Grangemouth Stadium	> at Stirling Uni
Raith Rovers			Apr 22 4-4	Feb 18 2-3		■	Apr 1 0-2			
Stenhousemuir	Apr 7 3-1		Feb 18 1-3	Mar 11 3-1	Feb 11 2-3		■			

	P	W	D	L	F	A	GD	Pts			P	W	D	L	F	A	Pts
Queen's Park	6	5	0	1	12	4	8	15		Cowdenbeath	6	4	1	1	14	7	13
Morton	6	4	0	2	15	9	6	12		Alloa Athletic	6	4	0	2	13	11	12
Annan Athletic	6	3	0	3	9	10	-1	9		Stenhousemuir	6	3	0	3	12	10	9
Ayr United	6	2	2	2	11	14	-3	8		East Fife	6	2	2	2	14	11	8
Queen of South	6	2	1	3	9	14	-5	7		Dundee	6	2	2	2	15	14	8
Livingston	6	1	2	3	9	10	-1	5		East Stirlingshire	5	2	0	3	6	15	6
Airdrieonians	6	1	1	4	8	12	-4	4		Raith Rovers	5	0	1	4	8	14	1

RESERVE LEAGUE CUP KO ROUNDS

SF	28/04/2014	Queen's Park	Alloa	1 0 at Airdrie
SF	28/04/2014	Cowdenbeath	Morton	2 1

F	08/05/2014	Cowdenbeath	Queen's Park	0 3 at Cowdenbeath

Scottish Under 20 League 2013/14

	A	C	DU	DA	F	HA	HM	HIB	ICT	K	M	PT	R	RC	SJ	SM
Aberdeen		Aug 20	Nov 27	Nov 19	Apr 1	Nov 5	Mar 11	Dec 17	Aug 6	Oct 14	Feb 26	Oct 1	Feb 11	Apr 22	Sep 10	May 7
		2-2%	2-1*	3-0*	0-2*	3-1*	4-0*	1-6*	0-1*	3-0*	3-2+	2-3*	1-2*	1-3*	1-4*	2-3>
Celtic	Jan 21		Aug 6	Oct 8	Apr 22	Feb 18	Feb 7	Apr 10	Dec 17	Sep 23	Apr 7	Feb 3	May 6	Mat 3	Sep 3	Mar 18
	1-2<		1-0*	2-1*	2-0%	3-0*	2-0&	0-2%	1-3>	2-1%	3-0&	4-0&	2-0&	5-0%	2-2*	3-2%
Dundee United	Apr 15	May 9		Sep 17	Apr 8	Feb 4	Nov 12	Oct 8	Dec 3	Sep 3	Mar 18	Jan 22	Oct 23	Feb 18	Aug 13	Mar 4
	1-0*	0-2*		0-1*	2-4<	5-0>	1-2%	2-3>	1-0%	3-2<	2-1<	2-2*	1-3&	0-1*	3-0<	
Dunfermline Athletic	Apr 8	Mar 24	Feb 11		Sep 9	Apr 1	Jan 28	Apr 22	Oct 1	Nov 4	Aug 26	Mar 11	Dec 17	Jan 7	Oct 14	Aug 6
	2-0*	1-0*	3-0*		2-2*	3-4*	5-0*	0-3*	2-3*	4-3*	1-1*	0-2*	3-0*	3-0*	3-2*	
Falkirk	Nov 12	Dec 3	Nov 19	Feb 4		Sep 3	Mar 18	Feb 18	Apr 15	Jan 21	Oct 22	Aug 13	May 2	Sep 17	Dec 10	Oct 8
	2-2*	2-3	3-1*	1-0*		3-1*	4-2*	2-2*	2-0*	4-2*	1-5*	0-4*	0-4*	2-1*	1-1*	0-0*
Hamilton Accies	Mar 18	Jan 7	Sep 10	Nov 12	Jan 28		Aug 20	Nov 27	Feb 11	Oct 22	Dec 17	Oct 15	Aug 6	Apr 8	Feb 24	Apr 22
	2-1%	1-3%	1-0%	2-0%	1-1%		5-1%	0-4%	3-2%	0-1%	0-0%	1-1%	0-0*	0-1%	3-0%	4-0%
Hearts	Oct 22	Apr 15	Apr 29	Mar 14	Nov 5	Jan 21		Sep 17	Nov 19	Dec 17	Mar 4	Dec 10	Apr 25	Feb 4	Dec 3	Feb 19
	0-5*	2-1*	0-2*	0-2*	1-1*	2-3%		2-2*	2-1*	0-2*	3-0*	5-1*	1-4*	4-0<	4-2*	1-3>
Hibernian	Aug 13	Mar 11	Feb 25	Dec 3	Oct 1	Apr 15	Feb 11		Oct 15	Apr 29	Sep 9	Apr 1	Mar 25	Dec 10	Nov 5	Aug 20
	2-1*	1-0*	1-1+	7-1*	4-2*	1-1*	3-2*		2-3*	1-1<	2-1*	2-0+	0-0<	5-0*	1-2*	0-2*
Inverness CT	Dec 10	Aug 13	Apr 22	Apr 24	Nov 26	Sep 17	Apr 8	Mar 27		Feb 4	Nov 12	Sep 3	Mar 18	Oct 8	Jan 20	Oct 22
	2-0*	1-0*	2-2*	3-1*	2-2*	0-1*	2-0*	1-3+		3-0*	2-3*	3-2*	1-2+	3-0*	3-0*	1-0*
Kilmarnock	Mar 4	Feb 11	Jan 28	Mar 18	Aug 19	Mar 11	May 8	Apr 8	Sep 10		Aug 6	Feb 25	Apr 22	Nov 12	Oct 1	Nov 26
	1-2%	0-1%	1-3%	0-0+	3-2*	3-3+	2-1*	3-3*	3-3*		0-1*	1-0%	1-2*	5-1*	3-0*	1-0*
Motherwell	Oct 8	Nov 19	Nov 5	Jan 21	Mar 11	Aug 13	Jan 14	Feb 4	Apr 2	Dec 10		Dec 3	Apr 29	Sep 3	Apr 15	Sep 17
	3-0*	0-5*	0-0>	2-1>	4-3>	2-4*	3-2>	0-3<	2-0>	2-3*		4-1>	1-2*	5-1*	3-0*	2-0%
Partick Thistle	Feb 18	Sep 9	Aug 20	Oct 22	Dec 17	Mar 3	Aug 7	Nov 12	Jan 28	Oct 8	Apr 22		Nov 26	Mar 17	Feb 11	Apr 8
	1-1%	1-0*	0-3*	2-1*	1-1%	1-3*	1-2*	2-0*	4-2%	2-0*	0-5%		0-3*	1-0%	2-2*	1-1%
Rangers	Sep 17	Mar 31	Mar 11	Aug 13	Dec 10	Dec 16	Dec 26	Nov 5	Dec 4	Oct 1	Apr 16			Jan 21	Nov 19	Feb 4
	0-2*	0-2>	1-0*	5-4*	5-0>	2-1*	1-1>	2-0>	2-2*	2-0>	4-0*			1-0*	2-2*	4-0>
Ross County	Mar 26	Oct 15	Oct 1	Apr 15	Feb 11	Apr 29	Sep 10	Aug 6	Apr 17	Apr 1	Jan 28	Nov 5	Aug 20		Mar 11	Dec 17
	1-1&	1-2*	2-3*	1-1&	3-0*	1-3&	1-1*	2-4*	2-0*	5-0*	0-3&	4-0*	2-3*		2-1*	3-3&
St Johnstone	Feb 4	Jan 28	Dec 17	Mar 4	Aug 6	Oct 8	Apr 22	Mar 18	Aug 20	Feb 18	May 5	Sep 17	Apr 8	Oct 22		Nov 12
	3-1&	0-1<	3-1>	0-3%	1-2*	1-3%	2-0%	1-3%	2-2%	2-2<	3-3%	4-1%	2-2%	6-1%		2-0%
St Mirren	Sep 3	Apr 30	Oct 15	Dec 11	May 5	Dec 3	Oct 1	Jan 22	Mar 11	Apr 15	Feb 11	Nov 19	Sep 10	Aug 13	Apr 1	
	0-0*	1-2*	1-0%	2-1%	4-2*	3-1*	1-1%	1-2*	1-0*	2-6*	1-2%	0-3%	1-2*	0-1*	3-0*	

KEY TO VENUES

	*	%	+	>	&
Aberdeen	Peterhead	Montrose	Arbroath	Brechin	
Celtic	Livingston	Lennoxtown	Morton	Dumbarton	
Dundee United	Tannadice	Arbroath	Airdrie	Raith	St Andrews Uni
Dunfermline Athletic	East End				
Falkirk	Falkirk Stadium				
Hamilton	Airdrie	New Douglas Pk			
Hearts	Newtongrange	Riccarton	Tynecastle	Airdrie	
Hibernian	Livingston	Hibernian TC	Airdrie		
Inverness CT	Caley Stadium	Highland Football Ac			
Kilmarnock	Rugby Park	Kilwinning SC	Clyde		
Motherwell	Fir Park	Bathgate	Broadwood	Airdrie	
Partick	Firhill	Airdrie			
Rangers	Dumbarton	Ibrox	Murray Park		
Ross County	Clach	Victoria Park			
St Johnstone	Stenhousemuir	McDiarmid Park	Airdrie	Forfar Ath	East Fife
St Mirren	St Mirren Park	Airdrie			

	P	W	D	L	F	A	GD	Pts
Celtic	30	21	2	7	60	27	33	65
Rangers	30	19	7	4	62	30	32	64
Hibernian	30	17	8	5	71	38	33	59
Hamilton	30	15	6	9	56	45	11	51
Motherwell	30	15	3	12	61	54	7	48
Inverness CT	30	13	4	13	56	51	5	43
Kilmarnock	30	11	6	13	48	53	-5	39
Falkirk	30	10	9	11	48	61	-13	39
Aberdeen	30	11	5	14	50	51	-1	38
Dunfermline	30	10	6	14	51	53	-2	36
St Johnstone	30	9	8	13	51	58	-7	35
Dundee Utd	30	10	4	16	40	43	-3	34
Ross County	30	10	4	16	43	63	-20	34
Partick Th	30	9	6	15	37	61	-24	33
St Mirren	30	9	5	16	37	53	-16	32
Hearts	30	7	5	18	40	70	-30	26

Scottish Under 19s League and League Cup 2013/14

SPFL UNDER 19S LEAGUE

	P	W	D	L	F	A	GD	Pts
Celtic	13	10	2	1	43	9	34	32
Clyde	13	8	3	2	30	17	13	27
Stirling Albion	13	8	2	3	31	21	10	26
Ayr United	13	6	5	2	38	18	20	23
Airdrieonians	13	7	2	4	32	25	7	23
Queen's Park	13	6	2	5	26	21	5	20
Arbroath	13	5	4	4	32	27	5	19
Forfar Athletic	13	5	3	5	38	28	10	18
Dundee	13	5	2	6	24	26	-2	17
Queen of South	13	3	6	4	25	29	-4	15
East Fife	13	3	3	7	25	44	-19	12
Cowdenbeath	13	3	2	8	21	37	-16	11
Dumbarton	13	2	1	10	23	40	-17	7
Montrose	13	1	1	11	7	53	-46	4

SPFL UNDER 19S LEAGUE CUP WEST TABLE

	P	W	D	L	F	A	GD	Pts
Ayr United	12	9	1	2	32	15	17	28
Celtic	12	9	0	3	36	10	26	27
Airdrieonians	12	8	2	2	30	16	14	26
Queen's Park	12	3	2	7	16	20	-4	11
Dumbarton	12	2	4	6	21	34	-13	10
Clyde	12	3	1	8	21	39	-18	10
Queen of the South	12	2	2	8	18	40	-22	8

SPFL UNDER 19S LEAGUE CUP EAST TABLE

	P	W	D	L	F	A	GD	Pts
Arbroath	10	7	3	0	28	11	17	24
Cowdenbeath	10	6	2	2	18	11	7	20
Dundee	10	4	2	4	22	24	-2	14
Stirling Albion	10	3	3	4	19	16	3	12
Forfar	10	3	2	5	29	31	-2	11
East Fife	10	1	0	9	10	33	-23	3

SPFL UNDER 19 LEAGUE CUP KO STAGES

SF	10/05/2014	Arbroath	Celtic	2 5
SF	11/05/2014	Ayr United	Cowdenbeath	2 1
F	18/05/2014	Ayr United	Celtic	1 2 aet

Scottish FA Youth Cup   2013/14

Rd 1	25/8/13	Airdrieonians	Edinburgh City	3	3	AET 2-4 pens
Rd 2	22/9/13	Hearts	Spartans	6	1	
Rd 2	22/9/13	Stirling Albion	Alloa	2	1	
Rd 2	22/9/13	Queen's Park	Forfar Athletic	1	0	
Rd 2	22/9/13	Stenhousemuir	Dundee	1	0	
Rd 2	22/9/13	Motherwell	East Fife	3	0	
Rd 2	29/9/13	Raith Rovers	Clyde	4	2	
Rd 2	22/9/13	Lossiemouth	Fraserburgh	0	1	
Rd 2	22/9/13	Ross County	Clachnacuddin	2	1	
Rd 2	22/9/13	Cove Rangers	Keith	6	1	
Rd 2	22/9/13	Hawick Royal Albert	Annan Athletic	2	7	
Rd 2	22/9/13	Edinburgh City	Arbroath	1	3	
Rd 3	20/10/13	St Johnstone	Stirling Albion	3	0	
Rd 3	20/10/13	Queen of the South	Annan Athletic	4	1	
Rd 3	20/10/13	Cove Rangers	Cowdenbeath	1	3	
Rd 3	20/10/13	Queen's Park	Inverness CT	2	2	AET, 4-1 pens
Rd 3	20/10/13	Dunfermline Athletic	Dundee United	1	0	
Rd 3	20/10/13	St Mirren	Partick Thistle	2	1	
Rd 3	20/10/13	Falkirk	Raith Rovers	1	3	
Rd 3	20/10/13	Livingston	Ayr United	0	1	
Rd 3	20/10/13	Morton	Fraserburgh	2	0	
Rd 3	20/10/13	Montrose	Motherwell	0	4	
Rd 3	27/10/13	Formartine United	Arbroath	3	2	
Rd 3	20/10/13	Kilmarnock	Aberdeen	3	0	
Rd 3	20/10/13	Rangers	Dumbarton	6	0	
Rd 3	30/10/13	Celtic	Stenhousemuir	4	0	at Dumbarton
Rd 3	20/10/13	Hamilton Accies	Hearts	2	4	
Rd 3	20/10/13	Hibernian	Ross County	5	1	
Rd 4	24/11/13	Rangers	Hibernian	5	1	
Rd 4	24/11/13	Queen's Park	Queen of the South	3	2	AET
Rd 4	1/12/13	Kilmarnock	Motherwell	3	1	
Rd 4	24/11/13	Raith Rovers	St Mirren	1	3	
Rd 4	24/11/13	Hearts	Formartine United	11	0	
Rd 4	1/12/13	Morton	Ayr United	3	2	
Rd 4	1/12/13	St Johnstone	Celtic	3	1	
Rd 4	24/11/13	Dunfermline Athletic	Cowdenbeath	3	1	
QF	23/2/14	Rangers	Dunfermline Athletic	2	0	
QF	23/2/14	Hearts	Queen's Park	3	0	
QF	2/3/14	St Johnstone	St Mirren	0	1	
QF	2/3/14	Kilmarnock	Morton	2	1	
SF	12/4/14	Hearts	Kilmarnock	3	0	
SF	13/4/14	St Mirren	Rangers	0	1	AET
F	13/5/14	Rangers	Hearts	2	2	AET, 8-7 pens at St Mirren

Junior Football

The structure and organisation of Junior football is quite complex and those not familiar with the Junior game can easily be confused by it. The Scottish Junior Football Association is the parent body for Junior football in Scotland. The name Junior does not imply any age-restriction - the use of the term Junior simply relates to the fact that in late Victorian times this grade of football was played on amore local basis than Senior football.

The Scottish Junior Cup is the only competition that is run by the SJFA. It was first contested in 1886/7 and is regarded as the "holy grail" of the Junior game. The SJFA acts as a parent body for the 3 Junior Regions, East, West and North.

This tri-partite system dates from the early 2000s. Prior to that, from 1968, there were six Junior regions - North, Tayside, Fife, Lothians, Central and Ayrshire. Prior to 1968 there were various County and District Junior Leagues and Cups, each of which was run independently.

The three Regions are responsible for League and Cup fixtures. The SJFA acts as a point of appeal if clubs dispute any decisions made by their Regional JFA. The number of Cups organised by the Regions has been greatly reduced in recent years. It is not so long since a club could participate in seven or eight different Cup competitions, in addition to their League games and the Scottish Junior Cup.

Junior football has been careful to guard its independence. In 2007 the Scottish Football Association decided to allow four Junior clubs to participate in the Scottish Cup each year - the three Regional Champions and the Scottish Junior Cup holders. They joined the Scottish Premier League, Scottish League and Senior Non League clubs in the draw. The results show that the top Junior clubs are amongst the most powerful "Non League" clubs in Scotland.

Attempts have been made to merge the Senior and Junior "Non League" games in Scotland. The Senior Highland League has existed for over one hundred years and recently the SFA created a Lowland League. Junior clubs were invited to apply but it appears that none have done so. The Lowland League has, in reality, become an expanded East of Scotland Senior League.

Why have Junior clubs not become involved? Most have no ambitions at all to be part of a pyramid system. They idea of the Lowland League is to create a pathway to promotion to the Scottish Professional Football League. So far not a single Junior club has seen this as a journey they wish to embark on.

Junior football thrives on local competition and rivalries. Crowds at the top level of Junior football reach a decent level, attracted by the cheap admission prices an the lack of regulation. The prospect of promotion to the lower reaches of the SPFL is not an attractive one for Junior clubs.

This does not mean that some clubs do not want to improve facilities and infrastructure. Linlithgow Rose are an excellent example. They have completed all the work necessary to become an SFA licensed club which means they should be admitted to the Scottish Cup on an annual basis. However, during the process of their application the goalposts were moved to include a commitment to the principle of a pyramid system. If Linlithgow are denied Scottish Cup participation on this basis then it will simply show that the football authorities in Scotland are even further out of touch with reality than people thought.

Junior football is the main grade of "Non League" football played in Scotland. It dominates the most populous areas and generates considerable local pride and interest.

The Annual General Meeting of the Scottish Junior FA takes place on the third Saturday in June. All fixtures require to be completed by then. The AGM is held in each of the three regions on a rotational

basis. All decisions are made on the basis of one club one vote and all motions are submitted by the clubs themselves. The AGM also votes on the admission of any new clubs to the SJFA. All new clubs making application for membership of the Scottish Junior Football Association must have a ground complying with the following requirements:
(a) Must be enclosed with a suitable fence to keep spectators from gaining entry to the ground without payment;
(b) Must have a pavilion situated inside the ground and closely adjacent to playing field with separate stripping accommodation for home and visiting teams and for match official, all with adequate toilet and washing facilities;
(c) The playing field must be properly fenced to keep spectators from encroaching on the field;
(d) Grounds and facilities must satisfy the inspection of the Scottish Junior Football Association. Ground inspection fee of £40 must accompany application for membership and clubs will be responsible for expenses incurred for any further inspections required.

SCOTTISH JUNIOR F.A. 2013/14
Hampden Park, Glasgow G42 9DD
Telephone: 0141-620 4560, Fax: 0141-620 4561
www.scottishjuniorfa.com
email: scottishjuniorfa@scottish-football.com

HON. PRESIDENTS
Peter Gardiner, ex President SFA
HON. VICE-PRESIDENTS
David Roy, Past President, Matt Spiers, Ayrshire Region, Ron Ross, Fife Region, J. Gordon Law, Past President, James Ferguson, Past President, Jack Whitehead, North Region, Ronnie Orr, Past President, John Reilly, Past President, Joseph P. Black (Assistant Secretary), John Brodie, Former Treasurer, Robert Smith, Past President, J.Scott Robertson, Secretary, West Region, George Rose, Past President, Tom Anderson, Past President
PRESIDENT
George Morton (Cumnock Juniors)
VICE PRESIDENT
Harry Lawrie (Fauldhouse United)
SECRETARY
Tom Johnston
ASST. SECRETARY
Joseph P. Black
TREASURER
Iain McQueen
AUDITORS
Peter Deans Chartered Accountants, 42 Stirling Street, Denny, FK6 6DJ

MANAGEMENT COMMITTEE 2013 - 2014
WEST REGION
Willie Wilson, (Kirkintilloch Rob Roy), Kennie Young, (Lugar Boswell Thistle), Matt Bamford, (Clydebank), Felix McKenna, (St.Anthony's)
EAST REGION
William L. Donaldson M.B.E., J.P., (Linlithgow Rose), Douglas Hynd (Oakley United), Ian Sherlock, (Whitburn), Larry Duncan, (Lochee United)
NORTH REGION
Norman Mackay, (Dyce Juniors), George Rose, (New Elgin)

REGIONAL SECRETARIES
WEST REGION
J. Scott Robertson (Secretary), John Fyfe (Assistant Secretary)
EAST REGION
John Reilly (Secretary), William Gunn (Assistant Secretary), Syd McAlpine (Discipline Secretary)
NORTH REGION
Richard Easton (Secretary). Ken Simpson (Assistant Secretary)

Scottish Junior Football Club Directory

Source: SJFA Website, last updated May 21 2014

Aberdeen East End Mr Dougie Yeats, 7 Gort Road, Aberdeen, AB24 2YS Tel. : (H) 01224 481910 (M) 07428683275 Alt.contact : Jim Kirkwood Tel. : (M) 07549513132 Ground : New Advocates Park, Aberdeen, AB24 1RG Tel. : 01224 276977

Annbank United Mr James Currie, 38 St Leonards Road, Ayr, KA7 2PT Tel. : (H) 01292 284455 (B) 01465 712284 (M) 07595609325 Alt.contact : Willie Fisher Tel. : (H) 01292 521156 (B) 01292 521156 (M) 07740951586 Ground : New Pebble Park, Weston Avenue, Annbank, KA6 5EE

Arbroath Victoria Mr Neil Hardie,73 Keptie Street, Arbroath, DD11 3AN Tel. : (H) 01241 876326 (B) 01307 473267 (M) 07774030028 Alt.contact : Russell Ruxton Tel. : (H) 01241 872855 (M) 07746024889 Ground : Ogilvy Park, Cairnie Loan, Arbroath, DD11 4DS

Ardeer Thistle Mr Peter Mcblain, 4 Darg Road, Stevenston, KA20 3AY Tel. : (M) 07767898818 Alt.contact : Peter Kean Tel. : (H) 01294 556481 (M) 0783418095 Ground : Ardeer Stadium, Stevenston, KA20 3JD

Ardrossan Winton Rovers Mr Bobby Macnamara, 3 Verona Place, Ardrossan, Ayrshire, KA22 8EJ Tel. : (H) 01294 604697 (M) 07969241895 Alt.contact : Douglas Rae Tel. : (H) 01294 466347 (M) 07946079443 Ground : Winton Park, Winton Street, Ardrossan, KA22 8JG

Armadale Thistle Mr James Smeaton11 Shaw Avenue, Armadale, West Lothian, EH48 3NE Tel. : (H) 01501 733401 Alt.contact : John Lee Tel. : (H) 01501 731366 (M) 07951936152 Ground : Volunteer Park, North Street, Armadale, EH48 3QD

Arniston Rangers Mr Alan Walker, 54 Peveril Terrace, Inch, Edinburgh, EH16 6DF Tel. : (H) 0131 664 8288 (M) 07951603626 Alt.contact : William Edmond Tel. : (H) 01875 820181 (M) 07921940324 Ground : Newbyres Park, 15 Hunterfield Road, Gorebridge, EH23 4TP

Arthurlie Mr Andrew Pollock, 3 / 3, 17 Paisley Road, Barrhead, East Renfrewshire, G78 1HG Tel. : (M) 07547676262 Alt.contact : David Blakey Tel. : (M) 07763192814 Ground : Dunterlie Park, 42 Carlibar Road, Barrhead, G78 1AA Tel. : 0141 580 1029

Ashfield Mr Thomas Robertson, 861 Crow Road, Flat 2 / 5, Anniesland, Glasgow, G13 1LE Tel. : (H) 0141 950 6991 (B) 0141 287 2279 (M) 07801394259 Alt.contact : Jim Ross Tel. : (H) 0141 762 1757 (M) 07979203543 Ground : Saracen Park, 404 Hawthorn Street, Glasgow, G22 6RU

Auchinleck Talbot Mr Henry Dumigan, 16 Main Street, Auchinleck, KA18 2AA Tel. : (H) 01290 421785 (M) 07929525494 Alt.contact : Morton Wright Tel. : (M) 07972719553 Ground : Beechwood Park, Beechwood Avenue, Auchinleck, KA18 2AR Tel. : 07786637584

Ballingry Rovers JFC Mr James Fox, 12 Capledrae Court, Ballingry, Lochgelly, KY5 8JG Tel. : (H) 01592 861011 (M) 07772996336 Alt.contact : Tammy Taylor Tel. : (H) 01592 219108 (M) 07881911326 Ground : Ore Park, Glencraig, Fife , KY58AB

Banchory St Ternan Mr Gordon Humble, 2 Forestside Road, Banchory, Kincardineshire, AB31 5ZH Tel. : (H) 01330 823969 (M) 07920110514 Alt.contact : John Watson Tel. : (H) 01330 811441 (M) 07831862070 Ground : Milton Park, Crathes by Banchory, AB31 5QH

Bankfoot Athletic Mr Graham Wilks, The Cottage, Prieston Road, Bankfoot, Perth, PH1 4BW Tel. : (H) 01738 787398 (M) 07766576262 Alt.contact : Donald MacDonald Tel. : (H) 01738 788092 (M) 07990622048 Ground : Coronation Park, Newhall Street, Bankfoot, PH1 4BQ

Banks o' Dee Mr John Irvine, 76 Union Grove, Aberdeen, AB10 6SA Tel. : (H) 01224 210678 (M) 07702103808 Alt.contact : Gordon Christie Tel. : (H) 01224 314482 (B) 01224 771122 (M) 07977682582 Ground : Spain Park, Abbotswell Road, Aberdeen, AB12 3AB

Bathgate Thistle Mr David Miller, 2 Birniehill Terrace, Bathgate, EH48 2RT Tel. : (H) 01506 676663 (M) 07714269406 Alt.contact : Robert Napier Tel. : (H) 01506 635594 (M) 07864071506 Ground : Creamery Park, Hardhill Road, Bathgate, EH48 2BW

Beith Mr Robert McCarter, 56 Crummock Gardens, Beith, KA15 2HF Tel. : (H) 01505 503800 (M) 07501897050 Alt.contact : John Boal Tel. : (M) 07831724969 Ground : Bellsdale Park, Meadowside Terrace, Beith, KA15 2AF

Bellshill Athletic Mr William Ward, 17 Secaurin Avenue, Stonehouse, Larkhall, ML9 3NZ Tel. : (H) 01698 793571 (M) 07543677932 Alt.contact : Scott Lennox Tel. : (H) 01698 299610 (M) 07722439337 Ground : Fullarton Park, Easterhill Street, Tollcross, Glasgow, G32

Benburb FC Mr Archie Wiseman, 115 Queensland Drive, Cardonald, Glasgow, G52 2NW Tel. : (M) 07969954415 Alt.contact : John Docherty Tel. : (M) 07841269213 Ground : Tinto Park, 1 Craigton Drive, G51 4XE

Bishopmill United Mr Colin Mitchell, 20 Spey Avenue, Fochabers, IV32 7QR Tel. : (H) 01343 821298 Alt.contact : tbc Ground : Pinefield, Elgin, IV30 6DF

Blackburn United Mr Paul Meechan, Dunroman Cottage, Strathloanhead, By Westfield, FK1 2JZ Tel. : (M) 07540434899 Alt.contact : Ian McGinty Tel. : (M) 07764681679 Ground : Blackburn United Community FC, Ash Grove, Blackburn, EH4 7LL

Blairgowrie Juniors Mr Mike Coyle, Lunelea, Sidlaw Road, Rattray, Blairgowrie, PH10 7DB Tel. : (H) 01250 872682 (M) 07905384521 Alt.contact : William Mackay Tel. : (H) 01250 874244 (M) 07518144537 Ground : Davie Park, Rattray, Blairgowrie, PH10 7BJ

Blantyre Victoria Mr Duncan Sinclair, 20 Caskie Drive, Blantyre, G72 9XG Tel. : (H) 01698 712906 (M) 07831327483 Alt.contact : Andrew McDade Tel. : (H) 01698 323790 (M) 07930128702 Ground : Castle Park, Forrest Street, Blantyre, G72 0JL

Bo'ness United Mr Douglas Argent, 7 Forthview Crescent, Bo'ness, EH51 0LR Tel. : (H) 01506 822896 (M) 07762947836 Alt.contact : John Aitchison Tel. : (H) 01506 511115 (M) 07899876296 Ground : Newtown Park, Jamieson Avenue, Boness, EH51 0DP Tel. : 01506 822313

Bonnyrigg Rose Mr Robert Dickson, 21 Quarryfoot Gardens, Bonnyrigg, Midlothian, EH19 2DH Tel. : (H) 0131 663 7498 Alt.contact : Charlie Kirkwood Tel. : (M) 07718933693 Ground : New Dundas Park, Town Centre, Bonnyrigg, EH19 3AE

Brechin Victoria Mr Bill Barclay, 88 Provost Buchan Road, Brechin, DD9 6DE Tel. : (H) 01356 625563 (M) 07949233245 Alt.contact : Brian Eaton Tel. : (H) 01356 623534 (M) 07740861898 Ground : Victoria Park, Behind Nursery Park Off River Street, Brechin, DD9 7EY

Bridge of Don Thistle Mr James Cruickshank, 22 Belmuir Gardens, Dyce, Aberdeen, AB21 7LS Tel. : (H) 01224 725122 (M) 07801129455 Alt.contact : Bobby Jarvie Tel. : (H) 01224 824807 (B) 01224 797078 (M) 07759144836 Ground : Hillhead Centre, Don Street, Old Aberdeen, Aberdeen, AB24 1XR

Broughty Athletic Mr Hugh Jamieson, 47 Forthill Road, Broughty Ferry, Dundee, DD5 3DQ Tel. : (H) 01382 732474 (B) 01382 775747 (M) 07963961322 Alt.contact : Gordon Deuchars Tel. : (H) 01382 736880 (B) 01382 770820 (M) 07788750760 Ground : Whitton Park, Arbroath Road, Broughty Ferry

Broxburn Athletic Mr Jim Provan, 24 Hillview Avenue, Broxburn, EH52 5SB Tel. : (H) 01506 854389 (M) 07753708841 Alt.contact : Alan Cunningham Tel. : (H) 01506 855458 (M) 07831391850 Ground : Albyn Park, Greendykes Road, Broxburn, EH52 5BY Tel. : 01506 858057

Buchanhaven Hearts Mr Graeme Mackie, 51 Richmondhill Road, Peterhead, AB42 3GJ Tel. : (H) 01779 481966 (B) 01779 480290 (M) 07950974466 Alt.contact : David Buchan Tel. : (H) 01779 470722 (B) 01779 480290 (M) 07518224499 Ground : Raemoss Park, Victoria Road, Peterhead, AB42 1UB

Buckie Rovers Mr David Roberts, 23 Ogilvie Park, Cullen, Buckie, AB56 4XZ Tel. : (H) 01542 840861 (B) 01542 840235 (M) 07929444254 Alt.contact : Alfie Morrison Tel. : (M) 07971210449 Ground : Merson Park, Barrhill Road, Buckie, AB56 1DS

Burghead Thistle Mr Robbie Russell, 3 Reid Street, Elgin, IV30 4HG Tel. : (H) 01343 545519 (M) 07583205280 Alt.contact : Ross Davidson Tel. : (H) 01343 835912 (B) 01343 814000 (M) 07973231907 Ground : Forrest Park, Burghead, IV30 5YJ

Cambuslang Rangers Mr Jim Logan, 37 Main Street, Cambuslang, G72 7HD Tel. : (M) 07912160450 Alt.contact : William Miller Tel. : (H) 0141 641 0255 (M) 07891199896 Ground : Somervell Park, Somervell Street, Cambuslang, G72 7EB

Camelon Juniors Mr Robert McTaggart, 284 Glasgow Road, Camelon, Falkirk, FK1 4JQ Tel. : (H) 01324 637796 (M) 07754151220 Alt.contact : Catherine Hughes Tel. : (H) 07999465231 Ground : Carmuirs Park, Fairlie Drive, Camelon Tel. : 01324 638060

Carluke Rovers Mr Tom Dickson, 148 Branchfield Drive, Wishaw, ML2 8QE Tel. : (H) 01698 382066 (M) 07954597688 Alt.contact : tbc Ground : John Cummings Stadium, Carluke, ML8 4EA

Carnoustie Panmure Mr Andrew Finlay, 156 Kinloch Street, Carnoustie, Angus, DD7 7JQ Tel. : (M) 07516000984 Alt.contact : Jim Armstrong Tel. : (M) 07776076144 Ground : Laing Park, Pitskelly Road, Carnoustie, DD7 7QX

Clydebank Mr Matt Bamford, 191 Broomhill Crescent, Bonhill, Alexandria, G83 9QZ Tel. : (H) 01389 710990 (M) 07961080310 Alt.contact : Gordon Robertson Tel. : (M) 07719431894 Ground : Holm Park, Clydebank, G81 1LX

Colony Park Juniors Mr Douglas Benzie, 39 Selbie Drive, Iverurie, Aberdeenshire, AB51 3YB Tel. : (H) 01467 629253 (M) 07712240583 Alt.contact : Sandy Robertson Tel. : (H) 01467 629235 (M) 07918721221 Ground : Colony Park, Harlaw Road, Inverurie, AB51 4SG

Coupar Angus Mr Les Stewart, 41 Princes Croft, Coupar Angus, PH13 9EH Tel. : (M) 07511595627 Alt.contact : Gillian McColl Tel. : (M) 07874364722 Ground : Foxhall Park, Forfar Road, Coupar Angus, PH13 9AN

Craigmark Burntonians Mr David Conway, 11 High Street, Dalmellington, Ayrshire, KA6 7QU Tel. : (H) 01292 551978 (M) 07748550589 Alt.contact : Derek Carruthers Tel. : (H) 01292 550530 (M) 07971629318 Ground : Station Park, Ayr Road, Dalmellington, KA6 7SJ

Crossgates Primrose Mr Kevan McArthur, 83 Droverhall Avenue, Crossgates, Cowdenbeath, KY4 8BP Tel. : (H) 01383 512963 (B) 01577 866207 (M) 07717835551 Alt.contact : Girvan Easton Tel. : (H) 01383 611906 (M) 07769730807 Ground : Humbug Park, Inverkeithing Road, Crossgates, Fife, KY4 8AT

Cruden Bay Mr Terry Dando, 16 Slains Crescent, Cruden Bay, Peterhead, AB42 0PZ Tel. : (H) 01779 812796 (B) 01224 711100 (M) 07931154524 Alt.contact : Kevin Smith Tel. : (H) 01779 812668 (M) 07890692425 Ground : Watson Park, Cruden Bay, AB42 0PJ

Culter JFC Mr Angus Johnstone, 153 Hardgate, Aberdeen, AB11 6XQ Tel. : (B) 01224 876733 (M) 07765256627 Alt.contact : Douglas Jamieson Tel. : (H) 01224 321663 (M) 07979346043 Ground : Crombie Park, Malcolm Road, Peterculter, AB14 0XB Tel. : 01224 735727

Cumbernauld United Mr Alan Robertson, 5 Southerness Drive, Westerwood, Cumbernauld, G67 0HU Tel. : (H) 01236 451850 (M) 07533194432 Alt.contact : George Watson Tel. : (H) 01236 720703 (M) 07977497605 Ground : Guys Meadow Stadium, Old Glasgow Road, Cumbernauld Village, G67 2SA 01236 722883

Cumnock Mr George Morton, 27 Gray Street, Cumnock, KA18 1EZ Tel. : (H) 01290 423992 (M) 07966 767405 Alt.contact : Owen Scott Tel. : (H) 01294 272328 (M) 07946730457 Ground : Townhead Park, Townhead Street, Cumnock, KA18 1LG Tel. : 01290 422027

Dalkeith Thistle Mr Duncan Purdie, 49 Echline Grove, South Queensferry, EH30 9RU Tel. : (H) 0131 331 5642 (M) 07762550391 Alt.contact : Tom Gilhooley Tel. : (H) 0131 663 5142 (M) 07905909346 Ground : Kings Park, Croft Street, Dalkeith, EH22 3BA

Dalry Thistle Mr Hugh Aitken, 45 Stockbridge Crescent, Kilbirnie, KA25 7HG Tel. : (H) 01505 683558 (M) 07968862364 Alt.contact : Steven Aitken Tel. : (H) 01505 683558 (M) 07790685946 Ground : Merksworth Park, Dalry, KA24 4BA

Darvel Mr James MacLachlan, 24 Lintmill Road, Darvel, KA17 0ES Tel. : (H) 01560 321487 (M) 07858430200 Alt.contact : Neil McPherson Tel. : (H) 0141 639 1567 (B) 01563 535363 (M) 07880744748 Ground : Recreation Park, Irvinebank Road, KA17 0HA

Deveronside Mr Ally Clark, 26 Erroll Place, Turriff, Aberdeenshire, AB53 4DB Tel. : (H) 01888 563101 (M) 07769214422 Alt.contact : Billy Allan Tel. : (H) 01261 815122 (M) 07770864119 Ground : Canal Park, Bridge Road, Banff Tel. : 01261 812769

Downfield Mr Philip Hart, 24 The Elms, Dundee, DD4 0XH Tel. : (H) 01382 505114 (M) 07743562168 Alt.contact : Alex Duncan Tel. : (M) 07505736928 Ground : Downfield Park, Balgowan Avenue, Dundee, DD3 0JB Tel. : 01382 810594

Dufftown Mr Harry Officer,16 Macduff Place, Dufftown, Keith, Banffshire, AB55 5AH Tel. : (M) 07875458405 Alt.contact : Gary Stephen Tel. : (H) 01340 820606 (B) 01340 822068 Ground : Westburn Park, Hill Street, AB55 4AW Tel. : 01340 821368

Dunbar United Kit Fraser, "Kilrush", Belhaven, Dunbar, EH42 1NS Tel. : (H) 01368 862888 (M) 07711912461 Alt.contact : Geoff Cornwall Tel. : (H) 01368 863951 (M) 07895144336 Ground : New Countess Park, Countess Road, Dunbar, EH42 1RF

Dundee East Craigie Mr Jack Stephenson, 92 Finella Terrace, Dundee, DD4 9NE Tel. : (H) 01382 502712 (M) 07773582908 Alt.contact : Adrian Shearer Tel. : (H) 01382 527649 (M) 07755750401 Ground : Craigie Park, Dundee, DD4 7HX

Dundee North End Mr Kenneth Grubb, 1 Beauly Avenue, Kirkton, Dundee, DD3 0DR Tel. : (M) 07402222343 Alt.contact : Robert Moran Tel. : (M) 07720972803 Ground : North End Park, Fairmuir Street, Dundee, DD3 8HU Tel. : 01382 810166

Dundee Violet JFC Mr Brian Coutts, 4 Bright Street, Lochee, Dundee, DD2 3DE Tel. : (B) 01382 505888 (M) 07720443374 Alt.contact : Dave Don Tel. : (H) 01382 457524 (M) 07780700349 Ground : Glenesk Park, Balfield Road, Dundee, DD3 6AG

Dundonald Bluebell Mr Andrew Davidson, 51 Denfield Avenue, Cardenden, Lochgelly, Fife, KY5 0BX Tel. : (H) 01592 721135 Alt.contact : Allan Halliday Tel. : (M) 07725199773 Ground : Moorside Park, Dundonald Park, Cardenden, KY5 0DG

Dunipace Mr Ian Duncan, 7 Spence Street, Bonnybridge, FK4 1NH Tel. : (H) 01324 813463 Alt.contact : Thomas Hunter Tel. : (H) 01324 825771 (M) 07812632019 Ground : Westfield Park, Townhouse Street, Denny, FK6 5DW

Dyce Mr Keith McIntosh, 5 Hopetoun Green, Bucksburn, Aberdeen, AB21 9QX Tel. : (H) 01224 713163 (B) 01224 332463 (M) 07787127574 Alt.contact : Norman Mackay Tel. : (H) 01224 311795 (M) 07768273630 Ground : Ian Mair Park, Dyce Drive, Dyce

East Kilbride Thistle Mr Martin Sutherland, 15 Galloway Road, Brancumhall, East Kilbride, G74 3NR Tel. : (M) 07941876698 Alt.contact : James Stewart Tel. : (M) 07717047543 Ground : Showpark, 17 Maxwell Drive, East Kilbride, G74 4HG Tel. : 01355 243066

Edinburgh United Mr Elliot Morgan, 10 Ormiston Road, Tranent, Edinburgh, EH33 2DR Tel. : (H) 01875 611844 (M) 07880320433 Alt.contact : Ronnie Jamieson Tel. : (H) 01383 432839 (M) 07976158155 Ground : Paties Road, Stadium, Katesmill Road, Edinburgh, EH14 1JF

Ellon United Mr Irvine Morris, 14 Hillhead Road, Ellon, Aberdeenshire, AB41 9LF Tel. : (H) 01358 721321 (M) 07791026406 Alt.contact : William Gordon Tel. : (H) 01358 721404 (M) 07922662250 Ground : The Meadows, Meadows Way, Ellon, AB41 9QJ Tel. : 01358 725162

Falkirk JFC Mr Alan Kerr, 14 Whiteside Loan, Brightons, Falkirk, FK2 0TB Tel. : (H) 01324 712661 (M) 07894806244 Alt.contact : Karl Lejman Tel. : (H) 01324 715605 (M) 07738086901 Ground : Grangemouth Stadium, Kersiebank Avenue, Grangemouth, FK3 0EE Tel. : 01324 504590

Fauldhouse United Mr Gordon Watson, 11-13 Blackfaulds Place, Fauldhouse, West Lothian, EH47 9AS Tel. : (H) 01501 773756 (B) 07967677441 (M) 07967677441 Alt.contact : Peter Lynch Tel. : (H) 01505 770592 (M) 07811071129 Ground : Parkview, Fauldhouse, EH47 9JS

Fochabers Mr Bryan Henderson, 9 High School View, New Elgin, IV30 6UF Tel. : (M) 07792747486 Alt.contact : Ron Smith Tel. : (M) 07967414418 Ground : Fochabers Playing Field, Fochabers, IV32 7EX

Forfar Albion Mr Douglas Reid, Ashbourne House, Glenogilvy, Glamis, Forfar, DD8 1UN Tel. : (H) 01307 840200 (B) 01307 475000 (M) 07768152762 Alt.contact : Michael Graham Tel. : (H) 01307 462141 (M) 07749893585 Ground : Guthrie Park, Lochside Road, Forfar, DD8 3JD

Forfar West End Mr Alan Morrison, 15 Gallowshade Road, Forfar, Angus, DD8 1LY Tel. : (H) 01307 460463 (M) 07979192149 Alt.contact : Gordon Roger Tel. : (H) 01307 465822 (M) 07931958959 Ground : Strathmore Park,Raig o' Loch Road, Forfar, DD8 1BT Tel. : 01307 462935

Forres Thistle Mr Alasdair Kennedy, 12 Califer Road, Forres, IV36 1HY Tel. : (H) 01309 676433 (M) 07506095034 Alt.contact : Stephen Johnston Tel. : (H) 01309 676722 (M) 07725217502 Ground : Logie Park, West Pilmuir, Forres, IV36 1PH

Forth Wanderers Mr James Kelly, 105 Main Street, Carnwath, Lanark, ML11 8HP Tel. : (H) 01555 840861 (M) 07715054638 Alt.contact : Stuart Smith Tel. : (H) 01555 811573 (M) 07807339725 Ground : Kingshill Park, Main Street, Forth

Fraserburgh United Mr Gordon Laird, 23 Ailsa Court, Fraserburgh,, Aberdeenshire, AB43 9SH Tel. : (H) 01346 516828 (M) 07890016153 Alt.contact : Colin Smith Tel. : (H) 01346 518035 (M) 07710662555 Ground : College Park, Henderson Road, Fraserburgh, AB43 9GA

Girvan JFC Mr Ronnie Hutcheson, 10 Glendoune Street, Girvan, KA26 0AB Tel. : (H) 01465 714780 (M) 07761867717 Alt.contact : Thomas McCreadie Tel. : (H) 01465 714681 (M) 07736397531 Ground : Hamilton Park, Vicerton Street, Girvan, KA26 9HF

Glasgow Perthshire Ms Carol Cunningham, 64 Mosspark Avenue, Glasgow, G52 1LQ Tel. : (H) 0141 419 9308 (B) 0141 248 5338 (M) 07854183775 Alt.contact : Billy Adams Tel. : (H) 0141 258 9233 (M) 07796511147 Ground : Keppoch Park, Ashfield Street, Possilpark, Glasgow, G22 5HE

Glenafton Athletic & Sporting Club Mr John Stewart, 1 Woodend Cottages, Drongan, Ayrshire, KA6 7BT Tel. : (H) 01292 591734 (B) 01292 590440 (M) 07831232638 Alt.contact : Ian Young Tel. : (H) 01290 338306 (M) 0776160004 Ground : Loch Park, 115 Main Street, New Cumnock, KA18 4AE Tel. : 01290 338022

Glenrothes Mr Willie Drew, 88 Falcon Drive, Glenrothes, Fife, KY7 5HR Tel. : (H) 01592 759189 (M) 07927385918 Alt.contact : Paul Aitken Tel. : (H) 01592 571453 Ground : Warout Stadium, Warout Road, Glenrothes, KY7 4JY

Glentanar Mr Bill Hay, 139 Lang Stracht, Aberdeen, AB15 6LB Tel. : (H) 01224 319148 (M) 07946464015 Alt.contact : Derek Thomson Tel. : (H) 01224 313522 (B) 01224 752677 (M) 07766248086 Ground : Woodside Sports Complex, Station Road, Woodside, Aberdeen, AB24 2UL Tel.01224 276141

Greenock Mr Liam Faulkner, 2A Old Inverkip Road, Greenock, PA16 9AQ Tel. : (H) 01475 797796 (B) 0141 814 5263 (M) 07833098858 Alt.contact : Neil Martin Tel. : (H) 01475 722570 (M) 07958450467 Ground : Ravenscraig Stadium, Greenock

Haddington Athletic Mr Thomas Thornton, 14 / 3 Redhall Place, Edinburgh, EH14 2DL Tel. : (H) 0131 443 7188 (B) 0131 549 3648 (M) 07878333586 Alt.contact : Drew Donaldson Tel. : (H) 01620 824704 (M) 07753513789 Ground : Millfield, Mill Wynd, Haddington, EH41 4DB Tel. : 01620 826547

Hall Russell United Mr John V. Carroll, 140 Osborne Place, Aberdeen, AB25 2DU Tel. : (H) 01224 641694 (B) 01224 643106 (M) 07749673786 Alt.contact : Iain Hay Tel. : (B) 01224 622868 (H) 01224 325400 (M) 07899901262 Ground : Denmore Park, Bridge of Don, Aberdeen, AB23 8JW

Harthill Royal Mr Patrick Beattie, 46 Bickerton Terrace, Whitburn, West Lothian, EH47 8HS Tel. : (M) 07472898696 Alt.contact : David Way Tel. : (H) 01501 743336 (M) 07810117401 Ground : Gibbshill Park, East Main Street, Harthill, ML7 5QQ

Hermes Mr Alex M. Fiddes, 345 Clifton Road, Aberdeen, AB24 4DT Tel. : (H) 01224 487466 (M) 07958080854 Alt.contact : Leslie Hutton Tel. : (H) 01224 317501 (M) 07816753128 Ground : Uniconn Park, Bridge of Don, Aberdeen, AB23 8JW

Hill of Beath Hawthorn Mr Stuart Black, 6 Wellbank, West Quarter, Falkirk, FK2 9SF Tel. : (H) 01324 719191 (B) 07702509246 (M) 07702509246 Alt.contact : Mark Stevens Tel. : (H) 01383 620038 (M) 07974425881 Ground : Keirs Park, Hawthorn Crescent, Hill of Beath, KY4 8EF

Hurlford United Mr George Jaconelli, 8 Mansewell Road, Prestwick, KA9 1BB Tel. : (H) 01292479722 (M) 07858667131 Alt.contact : Lorimer Headley Tel. : (H) 01563 539694 (M) 07748884377 Ground : Blair Park, Blair Road, Hurlford

Inverness City Ms Lara Pollard, 11 Willow Avenue, Inverness, IV2 6BT Tel. : (H) 01463 250944 (M) 07859407271 Alt.contact : alastair wardhaugh Tel. : (H) 01667 493278 (M) 07802461504 Ground : Bught Park, Inverness

Irvine Meadow XI Mrs Lyn McFarlane, 5 Norman Crescent, Irvine, Ayrshire, KA12 8SB Tel. : (H) 01294 272424 (M) 07854767062 Alt.contact : Robert Jeffrey Tel. : (H) 01294 272075 (M) 07971795730 Ground : Meadow Park, Wilson Avenue, Irvine, KA12 0TW Tel. : 01294 274459

Irvine Victoria Ms Sheena Thomson, 91 High Road, Saltcoats, Ayrshire, KA21 5SB Tel. : (H) 01294 468480 (M) 07980875410 Alt.contact : Robert Hanvey Tel. : (H) 01294 271346 (M) 07784317698 Ground : Victoria Park, Boyle Street, Irvine, KA12 8PG

Islavale Mr Brian Rae, Beechlea, 4 Muldearie View,Keith, AB55 5TF Tel. : (H) 01542 886336 (B) 01224 326321 (M) 07816346605 Alt.contact : Sandy McCombie Tel. : (M) 07740173436 Ground : Simpson Park, Westerton Road, Keith, AB55 5EP

Jeanfield Swifts Mr Eric Allan, 45 Cluny Terrace, Perth, PH1 2HP Tel. : (H) 01738 443504 (B) 07922721241 (M) 07922721241 Alt.contact : John Soutar Tel. : (H) 01738 636887 (B) 01583 684516 Ground : Riverside Stadium, Bute Drive, Perth, PH1 3BG

Johnstone Burgh Mr Ricky Cantwell, 11 Cruachan Avenue, Renfrew, PA4 0PH Tel. : (H) 0141 561 6010 (M) 07719323744 Alt.contact : George Walker Tel. : (H) 01505 337252 (B) 0141 887 8932 (M) 07836256849 Ground : Keanie Park, Auchenlodment Road, Johnstone, PA5 9PB Tel. : 01505 322200

Kello Rovers Ms Gillian Keggans, 32 Sandyknowe Crescent, Kelloholm, Dumfriesshire, DG4 6SX Tel. : (H) 01659 66632 (M) 07800864158 Alt.contact : John Campbell Tel. : (H) 01290 332540 (M) 07923170881 Ground : Nithside Park, Kirkconnel, DG4 6NB

Kelty Hearts Mr George Clark, Elgato, 13 Bath Street, Kelty, Fife, KY4 0AG Tel. : (H) 01383 831252 (M) 07900667736 Alt.contact : William McKenzie Tel. : (H) 01383 831517 (M) 07581316120 Ground : Central Park, Bath Street, Kelty, KY4 0AG

Kennoway Star Hearts Mr Kenny Bayne, 52 Sythrum Crescent, Glenrothes, Fife, KY7 5DH Tel. : (H) 01592 562165 (M) 07751115639 Alt.contact : Brian Davidson Tel. : (H) 01333 352392 (M) 07802772313 Ground : Treaton Park, Star, Fife, KY7 6LJ

Kilbirnie Ladeside Mr Gordon Ronney, Habost, Duchal Road, Kilmacolm, PA13 4AS Tel. : (H) 01505 874406 (B) 07881788854 (M) 07889403298 Alt.contact : Ian McDonald Tel. : (H) 01505 504201 (M) 07748416316 Ground : Valefield, Kirkland Road, Kilbirnie

Kilsyth Rangers Mr Russell McKay, 7 Jarvie Crescent, Kilsyth, G65 0LN Tel. : (H) 01236 824462 (M) 07946261384 Alt.contact : Stuart Dunbar Tel. : (H)

01236 821659 (M) 07843993012 Ground : Duncansfield, Haugh Road, Kilsyth, G65 9JX

Kilwinning Rangers Mr David Martin, 113 Sundrum Place, Pennyburn, Kilwinning, KA13 6SU Tel. : (H) 01294 559857 (M) 07427507078 Alt.contact : Danny Watt Tel. : (H) 01294 550889 (M) 07767258306 Ground : Abbey Park, Dovecot Lane, Kilwinning, KA13 6DU

Kinnoull Mr Charles Grieve, 46 South Inch Park, Perth, PH2 8BU Tel. : (H) 01738 446747 (B) 01738 815085 (M) 07557792832 Alt.contact : Chris Jones Tel. : (M) 07940814370 Ground : Tulloch Park, Tulloch Road, Perth, PH1 2RW

Kirkcaldy YMCA Mr James Douglas, 3 McIntosh Court, Kirkcaldy, KY2 6RQ Tel. : (H) 01592 649759 (B) 08451 555555 x 471789 (M) 07976838352 Alt.contact : Ramsay Budd Tel. : (H) 01592 202066 (M) 07504004067 Ground : Denfield Park, Den Road, Kirkcaldy, KY11 2ER

Kirkintilloch Rob Roy Mr Charles O'Brien, 33 Eastermains, Kirkintilloch, G66 2UT Tel. : (H) 0141 237 1927 (M) 07955095707 Alt.contact : James Black Tel. : (H) 0141 776 0316 (M) 07707048309 Ground : Adamslie Park, Glasgow Road, Kirkintilloch, G66 1BG Tel. : 0141 776 6393

Kirriemuir Thistle Mr Dave Petherick, 1 Middlefield Avenue, Kirriemuir, DD8 5AE Tel. : (H) 01575 570825 (M) 07940585786 Alt.contact : Bruce Mitchell Tel. : (H) 01575 575157 (M) 07790489975 Ground : Westview Park, Southmuir, Kirriemuir, DD8 5LG Tel. : 01575 572722

Lanark United Mr Tom Anderson, 45 Wellwood Avenue, Lanark, ML11 7HS Tel. : (H) 01555 663796 (M) 07721047708 Alt.contact : Mark McKenzie Tel. : (H) 01555 661361 (M) 07814449166 Ground : Moor Park, Hyndford Road, Lanark, ML11 9BG Tel. : 07721047708 (on match days)

Largs Thistle Ms Morag Soutter, 12 Cathcart Road, Largs, KA30 8JB Tel. : (H) 01475 687058 (M) 07533238655 Alt.contact : Margaret Brown Tel. : (H) 01475 673705 (M) 07903668428 Ground : Barrfields Stadium, Brisbane Road, Largs, KA30 8NN

Larkhall Thistle Mrs Fiona Tierney, 63 Earls Park Avenue, Glasgow, G43 2HE Tel. : (M) 07706681274 Alt.contact : Roy Gibson Tel. : (H) 01698 884686 (M) 07711308927 Ground : Gasworks Park, Raploch Street, Larkhall, ML9 1AJ

Lesmahagow Mr Andrew Irving, 60 Auldton Drive, Lesmahagow, ML11 0BY Tel. : (H) 01555 895828 (M) 07963770172 Alt.contact : George Brownlie Tel. : (H) 01555 892771 (M) 07989688219 Ground : Craighead, ML11 0AG

Lewis United Mr George Copland, 64 Summerhill Crescent, Aberdeen, AB15 6ED Tel. : (H) 01224 321683 (M) 07847059778 Alt.contact : Joanne Lancaster Tel. : (M) 07730532977 Ground : Aberdeen Sports Village, Linksfield Road, Aberdeen, AB24 5RU

Linlithgow Rose Mr James Harkins, 1 Pentland Way, Grangemouth, FK3 0EA Tel. : (H) 01324 482191 (B) 01506 842018 (M) 07763321040 Alt.contact : David Roy Tel. : (H) 01506 842197 (M) 07811220307 Ground : Prestonfield, Braehead Road, Linlithgow, EH49 6HF Tel. : 01506 843736

Livingston United Mr Scott Burgess, 162 Mayfield Drive, Armadale, West Lothian, EH48 2JH Tel. : (H) 01501 228485 (M) 07747195312 Alt.contact : Ann Dryburgh Tel. : (H) 01506 201790 (B) 0131 245 9712 (M) 07795143123 Ground : Station Park, Deans, Livingston, EH54

Lochee Harp Mr James Kelly, 20 Leven Street, Broughty Ferry, Dundee, DD5 3JE Tel. : (H) 01382 778006 (M) 0875262456 Alt.contact : Jack Kelly Tel. : (H) 01382 827457 Ground : Beechwood Park, Kings Cross Road, Dundee, DD3 2PU

Lochee United Mr Larry Duncan, 38 Lintrathen Gardens, Dundee, DD3 8EJ Tel. : (H) 01382 884188 (M) 07808587741 Alt.contact : Tom McMillan Tel. : (M) 01382 419462 (M) 07584102202 Ground : Thomson Park, Napier Drive, Lochee, Dundee, DD2 2SJ

Lochgelly Albert Mr James Brown, 18 Plantation Street, Lochgelly, Fife, KY5 9LP Tel. : (H) 01592 781889 (M) 07949382643 Alt.contact : John Kinnell Tel. : (H) 01592 781769 (M) 07568505304 Ground : Gardiners Park, South Street, Lochgelly, KY5 9LJ

Lochore Welfare Mr Gary Charles, 10 Zetland Place, Lochgelly, Fife, KY5 9BL Tel. : (H) 01592 781875 (M) 07718735150 Alt.contact : Stephen Nardone Tel. : (H) 01592 869151 Ground : Central Park, Crosshill, Fife, KY5 8AN

Longside Mr Gavin Davidson, 15 Bruce Brae, Longside, Peterhead, AB42 4SY Tel. : (B) 01779 471500 (M) 07748558461 Alt.contact : Alan Davidson Tel. : (H) 01779 821469 (B) 01779 821267 (M) 0831285904 Ground : Davidson Park, Off Station Road, Longside, AB42 4GR Tel. : (H) 01779 821789

Lossiemouth United Ms Alison Simpson, 21 King Street, Lossiemouth, IV31 6PZ Tel. : (H) 01343 814036 (M) 07999507500 Alt.contact : Ken Simpson Tel. : (H) 01343 814036 (M) 07967918725 Ground : Playing Fields, Coulardbank Road, Lossiemouth, IV31 6JW

Lugar Boswell Thistle Mr Kennie Young, 61 Brownhill Avenue, Douglas, Lanarkshire, ML11 0PE Tel. : (M) 07812046194 Alt.contact : tbc Ground : Rosebank Park, Lugar, KA18 3LT

Luncarty Mr Nigel Fielding, Beechgrove, 15 Croft Park, Craigie, Perth, PH2 0DX Tel. : (H) 01738 580234 (M) 07850349965 Alt.contact : James Meiklejohn Tel. : (H) 01738 828071 (M) 07535711182 Ground : Brownlands Park, Main Road, Luncarty, PH1 3EP Tel. : 01738 828836

Maryhill Mr Gordon Anderson, 14 Lomond Drive, Bishopbriggs, Glasgow, G64 3BZ Tel. : (H) 0141 563 0969 (B) 0141 287 2949 (M) 07693804869 Alt.contact : Gordon Boyd Tel. : (H) 0141 563 0483 (B) 0141 224 0521 0502 (M) 07984731365 Ground : Lochburn Park, 18 Lochburn Road, Glasgow, G20 9AQ Tel. : 0141 946 8850

Maud Mr Graham Lawson, 24 Burnside Road, Mintlaw, Peterhead, AB42 5GE Tel. : (H) 01771 623575 (B) 01224 216540 (M) 07825585524 Alt.contact : Alan Mathers Tel. : (H) 01771 613467 (M) 07766214993 Ground : Pleasure Park, In Village of Maud, AB42 4NP Tel. : 01771 613259

Maybole Mr Alex Meek, 2 Gardenrose Path, Maybole, KA19 8AG Tel. : (H) 01655 883419 Alt.contact : Archie Wotherspoon Tel. : (H) 01292 261390 (M) 07932955979 Ground : Ladywell Stadium, Dailly Road, Maybole, KA19 7AZ

Montrose Roselea Mr Alan Simpson, 20B Ramsay Street, Montrose, Angus, DD10 8BS Tel. : (H) 01674 677565 (M) 07593015043 Alt.contact : Roy Gill Tel. : (H) 01674 672920 (B) 01674 673651 (M) 07908763219 Ground : Broomfield Park, Broomfield Road, Montrose, DD10 8TZ

Muirkirk Mr Billy Tait, 17 Kings Way, Cumnock, KA18 1TN Tel. : (H) 01290 425377 (M) 07596089828 Alt.contact : Isabel Davidson Tel. : (H) 01290 661069 (M) 07814510259 Ground : Burnside Park, Furnace Road, Muirkirk, KA18 3RE

Musselburgh Athletic Ms May McGlynn, 47 Inchview Crescent, Wallyford, East Lothian, EH21 8LS Tel. : (H) 0131 665 5854 (M) 07951745018 Alt.contact : Charlie McGlynn Tel. : (H) 0131 665 5854 (M) 07951745018 Ground : Olivebank, Market Street, Musselburgh, EH21 6QA Tel. : 0131 653 3319

Nairn St Ninian Mr Derek Davidson, 8 Mill Road Terrace, Nairn, IV12 5EG Tel. : (H) 01667 459332 (M) 07743165525 Alt.contact : Ronald Sharp Tel. : (H) 01667 456183 (M) 07803604255 Ground : Showfield, Lodgehill Road, Nairn, IV12 4QL

Neilston Mr Hugh Blair, 33 Duncarnock Crescent, Neilston, G78 3HH Tel. : (H) 0141 881 8282 Alt.contact : Graham Walker Tel. : (H) 0141 571 5823 (M) 07947882947 Ground : Brig-o-Lea Stadium, Main Street, Neilston, G78 3LB Tel. : 0141 881 3008

New Elgin Mr George Rose, 10 Rowan Court, Elgin, Moray, IV30 4BB Tel. : (H) 01343 550734 (B) 07779999219 (M) 07580508190 Alt.contact : Joyce Rose Tel. : (H) 01343 550734 (M) 07967186467 Ground : Nicol-Togneri Park, Pinefield, Elgin, IV30 3AF

Newburgh Ms Denise Roberts, 7 Aipple Yaird, Newburgh, Fife, KY14 6EE Tel. : (H) 01337 842987 (M) 07715998303 Alt.contact : Jan Chebrika Tel. : (H) 01337 840225 (M) 07894797293 Ground : East Shore Park, Coach Road, Newburgh, Fife, KY14 6BY

Newmachar Ms Angela Cumming, 4 Station Road, Newmachar, Aberdeen, AB21 0PW Tel. : (H) 01651 862396 (M) 07731613405 Alt.contact : Paul Dunn Tel. : (H) 01651 863203 (M) 07843383850 Ground : Charlie Gordon Park, Newmachar, AB21 0QD

Newmains United Community Football Club Mr Thomas Hynes, 24 Lanark Avenue, , , Airdrie, ML6 9QX Tel. : (H) 01236 752105 (M) 07779191588 Alt.contact : Ian Rankin Tel. : (M) 07912076468 Ground : Victoria Park, Overtown Road, Newmains, ML2
Newtongrange Star Mr Gordon Stanners, 4 Corrie Court, Newtongrange, Midlothian, EH22 4QT Tel. : (H) 01875 823922 (M) 07736325087 Alt.contact : Stan Adams Tel. : (M) 07588326160 Ground : New Victoria Park, Dalhousie Road, Newtongrange, EH22 4NG Tel. : 0131 663 3362

Oakley United Mr Douglas Hynd, 4 Woodburn Crescent, Oakley, KY12 9RS Tel. : (H) 01383 851779 (B) 01383 424081 (M) 07775518846 Alt.contact : Alex Wright Tel. : (H) 01383 850593 (M) 07588410992 Ground : Blairwood Park, Blairwood Walk, KY12 9RA

Parkvale Mr Mike Kane, 54 Menzies Road, Torry, Aberdeen, AB11 9HJ Tel. : (H) (B) 01224 893330 (M) 07899758587 Alt.contact : Sandy Smith Tel. : (B) 01224 647620 (M) 07849714894 Ground : Findon Park, Portlethen Tel. : 01224 647620

Penicuik Athletic Mr Neil Gordon, 103 Rullion Road, Penicuik, EH26 9JA Tel. : (H) 01968 677395 (B) 0131 225 4433 (M) 07936156451 Alt.contact : John Fraser Tel. : (H) 01968 676515 (M) 07713247144 Ground : Penicuik Park, Carlops Road, Penicuik, EH26 9HU

Petershill Mr Derek Crozier, 6 Holly Drive, Glasgow, G21 4EQ Tel. : (H) 0141 557 2853 (M) 07711867748 Alt.contact : Peter Harding Tel. : (H) 0141 772 4445 (M) 07951462217 Ground : Petershill Park, 28/30 Adamswell Street, Springburn, Glasgow, G21 4DD Tel.: 0141 276 8446

Pollok Mr Francis McNeill, 68 Gleniora Drive, Glasgow, G53 6BH Tel. : (H) 0141 881 0026 (M) 07847542590 Alt.contact : Stuart McCulloch Tel. : (H) 01335 303204 (M) 07985741541 Ground : Newlandsfield Park, Glasgow, G43 2XR Tel. : 0141 632 4929

Port Glasgow Mr Peter Loughlin, 5J Killearn Road, Greenock, PA15 3DD Tel. : (H) 01475 719160 (M) 07946814951 Alt.contact : Iain Rorrison Tel. : (H) 01475 791457

(M) 07960699171 Ground : Port Glasgow Community Stadium, Parklea Playing Fields, Port Glasgow, PA14 6TR

Portgordon Victoria FC Mr Dennis Clark, 4 Findlater Street, Buckie, AB56 1SN Tel. : (H) 01542 488937 (B) 01542 835629 (M) 07530116485 Alt.contact : Peter Gordon Tel. : (H) 01542 835731 Ground : Gordon Park, Portgordon, AB56 5RB

Pumpherston Mr William Rogers, 5 Ormiston Drive, East Calder Tel. : (H) 01506 490981 (M) 07786021303 Alt.contact : Gordon Bastick Tel. : (M) 07412057830 Ground : Recreation Park, Pumpherston

RAF Lossiemouth Mr Jim Crabb, 63 Myreside Circle, Elgin, Moray, IV30 4PR Tel. : (M) 07799145318 Alt.contact : Howard Heap Tel. : (B) 01343 817249 Ground : RAF Lossiemouth, Moray, IV31 6SD

Renfrew Mr George Johnston, 4a Argosy Way, Renfrew, PA4 0NB Tel. : (M) 07724807774 Alt.contact : John Shaw Tel. : (M) 07951768012 Ground : Western Park, Inchinnan Road, Renfrew, PA4 8NG

Rossvale FC Mr Andy Sandilands, 49 Iona Ridge, Hamilton, ML3 8PZ Tel. : (H) 01698 477798 (B) 01355 245309 (M) 07908713302 Alt.contact : Dom McInally Tel. : (M) 07900928481 Ground : Petershill Park, 28/30 Adamswell Street, Springburn, Glasgow, G21 4DD Tel. : 0141 276 8446

Rosyth Mr Alfie Blair, 35 Hudson Road, Rosyth, Fife, KY11 2EW Tel. : (B) 01383 427470 (M) 07727188293 Alt.contact : Raymond Fairbairn Tel. : (H) 01383 416148 (M) 07817160420 Ground : Recreation Park, Admiralty Road, Rosyth, KY11 2BN

Royal Albert Athletic Mr Peter Higgins, 81 Margaretvale Drive, Larkhall, ML9 1EH Tel. : (H) 01698 888498 (B) 01355 585954 Alt.contact : Ross Stephen Tel. : (H) 01698 329606 (M) 07506070017 Ground : Tilework Park, Stonehouse

Rutherglen Glencairn Mr Alex J. Forbes, 83 Dryburgh Avenue, Rutherglen, G73 3ES Tel. : (H) 0141 643 1406 (M) 07787737654 Alt.contact : Alex McArthur Tel. : (M) 07967535513 Ground : Clyde Gateway Stadium, Toryglen Road, Rutherglen, G73 1JH

St. Andrews United Mr Mark Johnson, 3 Roundhill Road, St. Andrews, Fife, KY16 8HE Tel. : (H) 01334 476779 (M) 07825883608 Alt.contact : Johnny Strachan Tel. : (M) 07504053336 Ground : Recreation Park, Langlands Road, St Andrews, KY16 8BN Tel. : 01334 477365

St. Anthony's Mr Felix McKenna, 20 Overton Road, Glasgow, G72 7QP Tel. : (H) 0141 641 9659 (B) 0141 778 8300 (M) 07790169666 Alt.contact : James McKenna Tel. : (H) 01236 427696 (M) 07506957547 Ground : McKenna Park, Fulbar Road/Shieldhall Road, Glasgow, G51 4HU T

St. Rochs Mr Chris McMenamin, 114 Balgrayhill Road, Springburn,Glasgow, G21 3AE Tel. : (H) 0141 558 6601 (M) 07786528920 Alt.contact : Fergus Welsh Tel. : (M) 07591570693 Ground : James McGrory Park, 713 Royston Road, Glasgow , G21 2AA

Saltcoats Victoria Mr Gordon Hunter, 11 Wilson Street, Airdrie, ML6 0EE Tel. : (H) 01236 602828 (B) 01236 769218 (M) 07505488430 Alt.contact : Raymond Montgomerie Tel. : (H) 01294 601662 (B) 01294 463752 (M) 07766463658 Ground : Campbell Park, Blakery Road, Saltcoats, KA21 6AP

Sauchie Mr Noel Dalli, 16 Forthvale, Menstrie, Clackmannanshire, FK11 7AS Tel. : (H) 01259 763695 Alt.contact : Hamish Mitchell Tel. : (H) 01259 214600 Ground : Beechwood Park, Sauchie, FK10 3AX Tel. : 01259 722933

Scone Thistle Mr Scott Stewart, 48 Durleydene Crescent, Bridge of Earn, Perthshire, PH2 9RD Tel. : (H) 01738 629524 (M) 07990953576 Alt.contact : Jon Baker Tel. : (H) 01738 563144 (M) 07984408366 Ground : Farquharson Park, Stormont Road, Scone, PH2 6NT

Shettleston JFC Mr Les Turnbull, 401 Old Shettleston Road, Shettleston, Glasgow, G32 7JN Tel. : (M) 07415628354 Alt.contact : tba Ground : Greenfield Park, 401 Old Shettleston Road, Glasgow, G32 7JN Tel. : 0141 778 6415

Shotts Bon Accord Mr Alex Hendry, 42 Main Street, Fauldhouse, West Lothian, EH47 9HP Tel. : (H) 01501 771101 (B) 01501 824000 (M) 07760571381 Alt.contact : Tommy Brennan Tel. : (H) 01698 833585 (M) 07826459401 Ground : Hannah Park, Dykehead, Shotts, ML7 5EY Tel. : 01501 821542

Stonehaven Mr Ken Scott, 83 Slessor Drive, Aberdeen, AB12 5LT Tel. : (H) 01224 879786 (B) 01224 870502 (M) 07778359384 Alt.contact : Chuck Thorn Tel. : (H) 01224 745080 Ground : Glenbury Park, Stonehaven, AB39 2PY

Stoneyburn Mr Steven MacMillan, 1 Meadow Drive, Stoneyburn, EH47 8DZ Tel. : (H) 01501 762032 (M) 07824662273 Alt.contact : Derek Sutherland Tel. : (M) 07969346582 Ground : Beechwood Park, Strathyre Drive, EH47 8AZ

FC Stoneywood Mr David Burnett, 598 Holburn Street, Aberdeen, AB10 7LJ Tel. : (H) 01224 594950 (B) 01224 594808 (M) 07931623239 Alt.contact : Graeme Laird Tel. : (H) 01358 743246 (B) 07889971540 (M) 07884160674 Ground : Polo Park, Stoneywood, Aberdeen, AB21 9HX

Sunnybank Ms Yvonne Mearns, 3 Chapman Walk, Aberdeen, AB16 7DG Tel. : (H) 01224 696309 Alt.contact : Lesley Cochrane Tel. : (H) 01224 680242 (B) 01224 717500 (M) 07709192286 Ground : Heathryfold Park, Heathryfold, Aberdeen, AB16 7DS : 01224 696309

Tayport Mr Albert J. Oswald, 17 Reform Street, Tayport, DD6 9HX Tel. : (H) 01382 552644 (M) 07817532729 Alt.contact : Ken S. Smith Tel. : (M) 07881508396 Ground : The Canniepairt, Shanwell Road, Tayport, DD6 9DX

Thorniewood United Mr Ian McLaughlin, 75 Greenrig, Uddingston, G71 7TD Tel. : (H) 01698 810071 (B) 01698 201617 (M) 07758249811 Alt.contact : John Miller Tel. : (H) 01236 421465 (M) 07894709243 Ground : Robertson Park, Old Edinburgh Road, Uddingston, G71 6HQ Tel. : 01698 816471

Thornton Hibs Mr Craig Gilbert, Haslemere, Windygates Road, Leven, Fife, KY8 4DR Tel. : (H) 01333 423087 (M) 07769217025 Alt.contact : Audrey McDonald Tel. : (H) 01592 631135 (M) 07834095069 Ground : Memorial Park, Old Main Street, Thornton, Fife, KY1 4AL

Tranent Mr Robert McNeill, 11 Meadowmill Loan, Tranent, East Lothian, EH33 1FE Tel. : (H) 01875 611830 (M) 07724727813 Alt.contact : Henry Glynn Tel. : (H) 01875 613379 (B) 0131 300 1315 (M) 07522422832 Ground : Forresters Park, Lindores Drive, Tranent, EH33 1HY

Troon Ms Sharon Hamilton, Ground Right, 15 Gillies Street, Troon, KA10 6QH Tel. : (H) 01292 318076 (M) 07932214639 Alt.contact : Alasdair Kirkwood Tel. : (H) 01292 473619 (M) 07789225601 Ground : Portland Park, Portland Street, Troon, KA10 6QN

Vale of Clyde Mr Jim Wilson, 183 Easterhill Street, Tollcross, Glasgow, G32 8LD Tel. : (H) 0141 778 3340 (B) 0141 777 9050 (M) 07772973091 Alt.contact : Brian Kelly Tel. : (H) 0141 641 3086 (B) 0141 777 9050 (M) 07798881954 Ground : Fullarton Park, Easterhill Street, Tollcross , Glasgow, G32 8LD Tel. : 0141 778 3340 (Jim Wilson - Secretary)

Vale of Leven F&AC Mr Angus Wallace, 30 Whitehaugh Drive, Paisley, PA1 3PG Tel. : (H) 0141 840 1556 (B) 0141 810 2409 (M) 07950075210 Alt.contact : Hugh Hamill Tel. : (H) 01389 841050 (B) 0141 341 3922 (M) 07768670569 Ground : Millburn Park, Leven Street, Alexandria, G83 0SR Tel. : 01389 752164

West Calder United Ms Christine Wright, 64 Parkhead Crescent, West Calder, West Lothian, EH55 8AX Tel. : (H) 01506 794758 (M) 07523258772 Alt.contact : Lyndsay Lammie Tel. : (H) 01506 871903 (M) 07850567728 Ground : Hermand Park, Harburn Road, West Calder, EH55 8WW

Whitburn Ms Ann Haddow, 2 Loch Maree Way, Whitburn, EH47 0RW Tel. : (H) 01501 743316 (M) 07917753017 Alt.contact : Ian Sherlock Tel. : (H) 01501 743771 Ground : Central Park, East Main Street, Whitburn, EH47 0RE Tel. : 01501 740557

Whitehills Mr Martyn Tevendale, 8 Seafield Place, Whitehills, Banff, AB45 2NG Tel. : (H) 01261 861696 Alt.contact : Michael Watson Tel. : (H) 01261 861040 (M) 07946830509 Ground : School Park, Loch Street, Whitehills

Whitletts Victoria Mr Mark Porter, 2 Cowan Crescent, Ayr, KA8 9QU Tel. : (H) 01292 610489 (M) 07501614779 Alt.contact : John Dalton Tel. : (H) 01292 550033 (M) 07759637350 Ground : Dam Park Stadium, Content Avenue, Ayr, KA8 0ET Tel. : 01292 619595

Wishaw Mr Robert Andrew Watson, 16 Binniehill Road, Cumbernauld, G68 9JJ Tel. : (H) 01236 725042 (B) 01324 501558 (M) 07764223057 Alt.contact : William Kilgour Tel. : (M) 07824594754 Ground : The Beltane, Wishaw, ML2 0HL

Yoker Athletic Mr Campbell Bissland, 43 Mirren Drive, Duntocher, Clydebank, G81 6LE Tel. : (M) 07850150681 Alt.contact : Stephen Frew Tel. : (M) 07837637976 Ground : Holm Park, Yoker, G81 1LU

Three new teams are joining the North Region of the SJFA for 2014/15.

These are:

ABERDEEN UNIVERSITY
Hillhead Complex, Aberdeen
Colours - Blue and Yellow

GRANTOWN
Nethy Bridge Park, Nethybridge
Colours - Black and Gold

SPEY VALLEY
Cromdale Park, Cromdale
Colours - Red and Black Stripes

Two teams are entering abeyance for 2014/15:

COUPAR ANGUS JFC
FOCHABERS JFC

Three teams that were in abeyance are NOT returning:
STEELEND VICTORIA
BANKFOOT ATHLETIC
BISHOPMILL UNITED

One team that was in abeyance will return:
LOSSIEMOUTH UNITED

SCOTTISH JUNIOR CUP 2013/14

Round	Date	Home	Away	F	A
1	28/09/2013	Carnoustie Panmure	Edinburgh United	3	1
1	28/09/2013	Newmains United	Cambuslang Rangers	0	4
1	28/09/2013	Glenrothes	Livingston United	0	2
1	28/09/2013	Lochgelly Albert	Kelty Heats	3	1
1	28/09/2013	Arthurlie	Bridge of Don Thistle	3	0
1	28/09/2013	West Calder United	Sauchie	0	4
1	28/09/2013	Dundee North End	Ardeer Thistle	3	0
1	28/09/2013	Irvine Meadow	Scone Thistle	2	1
1	28/09/2013	Royal Albert	Stoneyburn	4	0
1	28/09/2013	Kirkcaldy YM	Falkirk	3	3
1	28/09/2013	Forth Wanderers	Coupar Angus	6	0
1	28/09/2013	Islavale	Tranent	1	1
1	28/09/2013	Dundee Violet	St Andrews United	0	1
1	28/09/2013	Cruden Bay	Glasgow Perthshire	2	2
1	28/09/2013	East Craigie	Wishaw	2	3
1	28/09/2013	Mussleburgh Athletic	Arniston Rangers	6	3
1	28/09/2013	Blairgowrie	Deveronside	0	2
1	28/09/2013	Crossgates Primrose	Vale of Clyde	1	2
1	28/09/2013	Dunbar United	Muirkirk	5	1
1	28/09/2013	Pollok	Luncarty	4	1
1	28/09/2013	Annbank United	Kello Rovers	3	1
1	28/09/2013	Kinnoull	Tayport	1	3
1	28/09/2013	Irvine Victoria	Greenock	1	2
1	28/09/2013	Glenafton Athletic	Inverness City	9	1
1	28/09/2013	Vale of Leven	Thornton Hibs	1	1
1	28/09/2013	Blackburn United	Largs Thistle	1	2
1	28/09/2013	Jeanfield Swifts	Yoker Athletic	1	3
1	28/09/2013	Bonnyrigg Rose	Bo'ness United	2	2
1	28/09/2013	Fochabers*	Kirrie Thistle	0	11
1	28/09/2013	Neilston	Port Glasgow	2	0
1	28/09/2013	Saltcoats Victoria	Blantyre Vics	1	2
1	05/10/2013	Bonnyrigg Rose	Bo'ness United	2	2
1R	05/10/2013	Thornton Hibs	Vale of Leven	0	2
1R	05/10/2013	Dyce	Maryhill	1	2
1R	05/10/2013	Glasgow Perthshire	Cruden Bay	1	2
1R	05/10/2013	Falkirk	Kirkcaldy YM	3	3 6-7 p
1R	05/10/2013	Tranent	Islavale	4	0
1R	12/10/2013	Bo'ness United	Bonnyrigg Rose	1	0
*		at Pinefield			

2	26/10/2013	Arbroath Vics	Beith	1	2
2	26/10/2013	Maryhill	Carnoustie Panmure	1	1
2	26/10/2013	Forfar Albion	Lanark United	0	6
2	26/10/2013	Kilsyth Rangers	Shettleston	5	1
2	26/10/2013	Blantyre Vics	Broughty Athletic	3	2
2	26/10/2013	FC Stoneywood	Shotts Bon Accord	1	4
2	26/10/2013	Neilston	Maud	2	1
2	26/10/2013	Cumnock	Troon	1	0
2	26/10/2013	Rossvale	Dunonald Bluebell	3	6
2	26/10/2013	Rosyth	Lochee United	0	6
2	26/10/2013	Culter	Ashfield	2	3
2	26/10/2013	Penicuik Athletic	Sunnybank	9	0
2	26/10/2013	Auchinleck Talbot	Broxburn Athletic	7	0
2	26/10/2013	Johnstone Burgh	Hill of Beath Hawthorn	0	2
2	26/10/2013	Sauchie	Tranent	4	0
2	26/10/2013	Carluke Rovers	Linlithgow Rose	1	1
2	26/10/2013	Mussleburgh Athletic	Armadale Thistle	3	0
2	26/10/2013	Livingston United	Vale of Clyde	4	0
2	26/10/2013	Dundee North End	Bo'ness United	1	2
2	26/10/2013	Tayport	Renfrew	4	2
2	26/10/2013	St Andrews United	Whitehills	17	1

2	26/10/2013	Hall Russell United	Cruden Bay	2	5
2	26/10/2013	Whitletts Vics	Bathgate Thistle	3	1
2	26/10/2013	Dunipace	Dunbar United	2	4
2	26/10/2013	Kilbirnie Ladeside	Newburgh	3	0
2	26/10/2013	Benburb	Lochgelly Albert	7	0
2	26/10/2013	Lewis United	Colony Park	0	2
2	26/10/2013	Haddington Athletic	Newtongrange Star	1	1
2	26/10/2013	St Rochs	Thorniewood United	3	5
2	26/10/2013	Forres Thistle	Kennoway Star Hearts	4	2
2	26/10/2013	Darvel	Wishaw	2	2
2	26/10/2013	St Anthonys	Petershill	3	3
2	26/10/2013	Maybole	Cumbernauld United	0	0
2	26/10/2013	Rutherglen Glencairn	Annbank United	7	1
2	26/10/2013	Greenock	Royal Albert	1	2
2	26/10/2013	Larkhall Thistle	Kirrie Thistle	7	3
2	26/10/2013	Brechin Vics	Aberdeen East End	1	2
2	26/10/2013	Hurlford United	New Elgin	8	0
2	26/10/2013	Kilwinning Rangers	Nairn St Ninian	12	0
2	26/10/2013	Irvine Meadow	Clydebank	3	2
2	26/10/2013	Dalkeith Thistle	Vale of Leven	6	1
2	26/10/2013	Yoker Athletic	Ardrossan Winton Rovers	4	2
2	26/10/2013	Stonehaven	Forfar West End	3	1
2	26/10/2013	Whitburn	Forth Wanderers	0	2
2	26/10/2013	Harthill	Craigmark Burntonians	7	0
2	26/10/2013	Dufftown	Pollok	1	5
2	26/10/2013	Lochee Harp	Kirkintilloch Rob Roy	1	7
2	26/10/2013	Downfield	Arthurlie	0	3
2	26/10/2013	Largs Thistle	Oakley United	2	1
2	26/10/2013	Hermes	Newmachar	9	0
2	26/10/2013	Banchory St Ternan	Pumpherston	6	1
2	26/10/2013	Cambuslang Rangers	Portgordon Victoria	7	1
2	26/10/2013	Bellshill Athletic	Deveronside	0	3
2	26/10/2013	Glentanar	Fauldhouse United	2	4
2	26/10/2013	Buchanhaven Hearts	Banks o' Dee	2	6
2	26/10/2013	Kirkcaldy YM	Longside	5	1
2	26/10/2013	Burghead Thistle	Parkvale	1	1
2	26/10/2013	Lochore Welfare	Ellon United	3	1
2	26/10/2013	Fraserburgh United	Ballingry Rovers	3	5
2	27/10/2013	Lugar Boswell Thistle	Glenafton Athletic	0	2
2	02/11/2013	East Kilbride Thistle	Montrose Roselea	1	1
2	02/11/2013	Dalry Thistle	Buckie Rovers	9	1
2	16/11/2013	Lesmahagow*	Camelon	2	4
2		Girvan	Bye		
2R	02/11/2013	Linlithgow Rose	Carluke Rovers	5	1
2R	02/11/2013	Newtongrange Star	Haddington Athletic	1	1 4-3 p
2R	02/11/2013	Wishaw	Darvel	2	3
2R	02/11/2013	Petershill	St Anthonys	3	0
2R	02/11/2013	Cumbernauld United	Maybole	2	1
2R	02/11/2013	Parkvale	Burghead Thistle	0	2
*		at Camelon			

From 2013/14 the Junior clubs who participate in the Scottish Cup proper were given guaranteed byes in Round One. Round One is used as an "equalisation" round to reduce the number of teams to 128. In 2013/14 this meant that Linlithgow Rose, Auchinleck Talbot, Hermes and Girvan were given byes - Girvan are unique in being full members of both the SJFA and the SFA, as a result of their move from the South Seniors to the Juniors a few years ago.

In 2013/14 Girvan struck it double lucky with another bye in Round Two - this came about as a result of the late withdrawal of Steelend Victoria who folded after the First Round draw had been made.

There was an unfortunate situation when the first round was drawn. SA miscalculation meant that four ties too few were drawn and an additional ballot had to be made a few hours after the draw itself.

3	23/11/2013	Montrose Roselea	Aberdeen East End	2	2
3	23/11/2013	Carnoustie Panmure	Colony Park	6	0
3	23/11/2013	St Andrews United	Thorniewood United	2	0
3	23/11/2013	Lochore Welfare	Pollok	1	5
3	23/11/2013	Newtongrange Star	Tayport	1	5
3	23/11/2013	Dunbar United	Arthurlie	3	2
3	23/11/2013	Bo'ness United	Auchinleck Talbot	1	0
3	23/11/2013	Camelon	Lochee United	4	1
3	23/11/2013	Irvine Meadow	Fauldhouse United	3	0
3	23/11/2013	Dalry Thistle	Burghead Thistle	4	2
3	23/11/2013	Banks o' Dee	Larkhall Thistle	1	2
3	23/11/2013	Banchory St Ternan	Whitletts Vics	1	6
3	23/11/2013	Glenafton Athletic	Royal Albert	2	2
3	23/11/2013	Petershill	Ballingry Rovers	1	0
3	23/11/2013	Deveronside	Musselburgh Athletic	3	3
3	23/11/2013	Largs Thistle	Kilbirnie Ladeside	2	1
3	30/11/2013	Dundonald Bluebell	Harthill Royal	4	0
3	30/11/2013	Cambuslang Rangers	Kennoway Star Hearts	2	1
3	30/11/2013	Neilston	Stonehaven	2	0
3	30/11/2013	Kilwinning Rangers	Hermes	4	2
3	30/11/2013	Cumbernauld United	Cruden Bay	4	0
3	30/11/2013	Kirkintilloch Rob Roy	Cumnock	2	3
3	30/11/2013	Yoker Athletic	Lanark United	2	0
3	30/11/2013	Benburb	Blantyre Vics	1	0
3	30/11/2013	Forth Wanderers	Hurlford United	1	1
3	30/11/2013	Darvel	Rutherglen Glencairn	1	2
3	30/11/2013	Beith	Sauchie	1	2
3	30/11/2013	Linlithgow Rose	Shotts Bon Accord	1	2
3	30/11/2013	Livingston United	Penicuik Athletic	1	3
3	07/12/2013	Dalkeith Thistle	Hill of Beath Hawthorn	1	4
3	30/11/2013	Ashfield	Girvan	4	4
3	30/11/2013	Kirkcaldy YM	Kilsyth Rangers	2	6
3R	30/11/2013	Musselburgh Athletic	Deveronside	3	1
3R	30/11/2013	Aberdeen East End	Montrose Roselea	0	2
3R	30/11/2013	Royal Albert	Glenafton Athletic	0	5
3R	07/12/2013	Girvan	Ashfield	4	3
3R	07/12/2013	Hurlford United	Forth Wanderers	4	0
4	18/01/2014	Irvine Meadow	Petershill	2	2
4	18/01/2014	Kilwinning Rangers	Sauchie	1	3
4	18/01/2014	Yoker Athletic	Montrose Roselea	3	2
4	18/01/2014	Cambuslang Rangers	Dundonald Bluebell	0	3
4	18/01/2014	Shotts Bon Accord	Dunbar United	2	2
4	18/01/2014	Camelon	Carnoustie Panmure	5	2
4	18/01/2014	Kilsyth Rangers	Largs Thistle	3	3
4	18/01/2014	Larkhall Thistle	Hurlford United	0	3
4	18/01/2014	Pollok	Penicuik Athletic	1	1
4	18/01/2014	Tayport	Hill of Beath Hawthorn	3	2
4	18/01/2014	St Andrews United	Bo'ness United	1	2
4	18/01/2014	Benburb	Whitletts Vics	2	3
4	18/01/2014	Cumnock	Neilston	4	1
4	18/01/2014	Musselburgh Athletic	Glenafton Athletic	1	4
4	22/02/2014	Girvan*	Rutherglen Glencairn	2	2
4	08/02/2014	Dalry Thistle	Cumbernauld United	5	2
4R	25/01/2014	Petershill	Irvine Meadow	0	2
4R	01/02/2014	Dunbar United	Shotts Bon Accord	4	4 3-4 p
4R	25/01/2014	Largs Thistle	Kilsyth Rangers	3	3 3-4 p
4R	01/02/2014	Penicuik Athletic	Pollok	2	1
4R	15/03/2014	Rutherglen Glencairn	Girvan	1	1 5-4 p
	*	at Largs			

5	22/02/2014	Penicuik Athletic	Irvine Meadow	0	0
5	22/02/2014	Whitletts Vics	Yoker Athletic	4	1
5	22/02/2014	Tayport	Hurlford United	1	2
5	22/02/2014	Glenafton Athletic	Shotts Bon Accord	3	2
5	15/02/2014	Dundonald Bluebell	Dalry Thistle	5	2
5	15/02/2014	Kilsyth Rangers	Cumnock	0	4
5	01/03/2014	Camelon	Sauchie	3	3
5	22/03/2014	Rutherglen Glencairn	Bo'ness United	1	2
5R	01/03/2014	Irvine Meadow	Penicuik Athletic	4	3
5R	15/03/2014	Sauchie	Camelon	1	3
6	15/03/2014	Cumnock	Glenafton Athletic	2	2
6	15/03/2014	Dundonald Bluebell	Hurlford United	0	3
6	29/03/2014	Camelon	Whitletts Vics	7	0
6	29/03/2014	Irvine Meadow	Bo'ness United	1	0
6R	22/03/2014	Glenafton Athletic	Cumnock	2	1
SF	19/04/2014	Hurlford United	Irvine Meadow	3	1
SF	13/04/2014	Camelon	Glenafton Athletic	1	1
SF	12/04/2014	Irvine Meadow	Hurlford United	2	1
SF	20/04/2014	Glenafton Athletic	Camelon	2	0
F	01/06/2014	Glenafton Athletic	Hurlford United	0	3

SCOTTISH JUNIOR CUP FINAL 2013/14
Sponsored by Barr Construction

Glenafton Athletic 0 Hurlford United 3
0-1 3mins   Stewart Kean (penalty)
0-2 30 mins Stewart kean (penalty)
0-3 80 mins Paul McKenzie
Att 5800

Glenafton Athletic	v	Hurlford United
Brian McGarrity	1	Ally Brown
Craig McEwan	2	Paul Cameron
Alan Cairns	3	Paul Byrbe
Ryan McChesney	4	Martin Brown
Craig Menzies	5	Glen Mitchell
Finlay Frye	6	Jamie Wilson
Jamie McGeoghan	7	Paul McKenzie
Jamie McKernon	8	Danny Mitchell
Aaron Connolly	9	Stewart Kean
Alan Kinney	10	Ross Robertson
Cameron Marlow	11	Calum Watt
Stevie Miller (for 11) (10)	12	John Dempster
Michael Reilly(for 3) (6)	14	Stevie Masterton
Darren McGill (for 9)	15	Jack Steele (11)
Craig Brown	16	Ewan Blair
Scott Adam	17	Stevie O'Neill
Tommy Bryce	M	Darren Henderson

Referee : Colin Steven
Assts : Simon MacLean and Craig King
4th Official : Gavin Ross

SCOTTISH JUNIOR FINALS

Season	Winners	Runners Up		
1886/87	Fairfield Govan	Edinburgh Woodburn	3 1	after protest
1887/88	Wishaw Thistle	Maryhill	3 1	after 2 protests
1888/89	Burnbank Swifts	West Benhar Violet	4 1	
1889/90	Burnbank Swifts	Benburb	3 1	after protest
1890/91	Vale of Clyde	Chrytson Athletic	2 0	after 1-1 draw
1891/92	Minerva	West Benhar Violet	5 2	
1892/93	Vale of Clyde	Dumbarton Fern	3 2	after 1-1 draw
1893/94	Ashfield	Renfrew Victoria	3 0	after 1-1 draw
1894/95	Ashfield	West Calder Wanderers	2 1	after 1-1 draw
1895/96	Cambuslang Hibs	Parkhead	2 1	
1896/97	Strathclyde	Dunfermline Juniors	2 0	
1897/98	Dalziel Rovers	Parkhead	2 1	
1898/99	Parkhead	Westmarch XI	4 1	
1899/00	Maryhill	Rugby XI	3 2	
1900/01	Burnbank Athletic	Maryhill	2 0	
1901/02	Glencairn	Maryhill	1 0	
1902/03	Parkhead	Larkhall Thistle	3 0	
1903/04	Vale of Clyde	Parkhead	3 0	
1904/05	Ashfield	Renfrew Victoria	2 1	
1905/06	Dunipace	Rob Roy	1 0	after 2-2 draw
1906/07	Strathclyde	Maryhill	1 0	after two 1-1 draws
1907/08	Larkhall Thistle	Queen's Park Hampden XI	1 0	
1908/09	Kilwinning Rangers	Strathclyde	1 0	ater 0-0 draw
1909/10	Ashfield	Kilwinning Rangers	3 0	after protest
1910/11	Burnbank Athletic	Petershill	1 0	after 2-2 draw
1911/12	Petershill	Denny Hibs	5 0	
1912/13	Inverkeithing United	Dunipace	1 0	
1913/14	Larkhall Thistle	Ashfield	1 0	after draws 0-0, 1-1
1914/15	Parkhead	Port Glasgow	2 0	
1915/16	Petershill	Parkhead	2 0	
1916/17	St Mirren Juniors	Renfrew	1 0	after 0-0 draw
1917/18	Petershill awarded cup			
1918/19	Glencairn	St Anthonys	1 0	after 1-1 draw
1919/20	Parkhead	Cambuslang Rangers	2 0	
1920/21	Rob Roy	Ashfield	1 0	
1921/22	St Rochs	Kilwinning Rangers	2 1	after protest
1922/23	Musselburgh Bruntonians	Arniston Rangers	2 0	
1923/24	Parkhead	Baillieston	3 1	after 1-1 draw
1924/25	Saltcoats Victoria	St Anthonys	2 1	after draws 1-1, 3-3
1925/26	Strathclyde	Bridgeton Waverley	2 0	after 1-1 draw
1926/27	Glencairn	Cambuslang Rangers	2 1	
1927/28	Maryhill Hibs	Burnbank Athletic	6 2	
1928/29	Dundee Violet	Denny Hibs	4 0	after protest and 2-2 draw
1929/30	Newtongrange Star	Hall Russell	3 0	
1930/31	Denny Hibs	Burnbank Athletic	1 0	
1931/32	Glasgow Perthshire	Rob Roy	2 1	
1932/33	Yoker Athletic	Tranent	4 2	after 0-0 draw
1933/34	Benburb	Bridgeton Waverley	2 1	
1934/35	Tranent	Petershill	6 1	
1935/36	Benburb	Yoker Athletic	1 0	after 1-1 draw
1936/37	Arthurlie	Rob Roy	5 1	
1937/38	Cambuslang Rangers'	Benburb	3 2	
1938/39	Glencairn	Shawfield	2 1	
1939/40	Maryhill	Morton Juniors	1 0	
1940/41	Glasgow Perthshire	Armadale Thistle	3 1	after draws 2-2, 0-0
1941/42	Clydebank	Vale of Clyde	4 2	
1942/43	Rob Roy	Benburb	3 1	after draws 1-1, 0-0
1943/44	Glasgow Perthshire	Blantyre Vics	1 0	
1944/45	Burnbank Athletic	Cambuslang Rangers	3 1	after protest
1945/46	Fauldhouse United	Arthurlie	2 0	
1946/47	Shawfield	Bo'ness United	2 1	after 1-1 draw
1947/48	Bo'ness United	Irvine Meadow	2 1	
1948/49	Auchinleck Talbot	Petershill	3 2	
1949/50	Blantyre Vics	Cumnock	3 0	
1950/51	Petershill	Irvine Meadow	1 0	
1951/52	Kilbimie Ladeside	Camelon	1 0	
1952/53	Vale of Leven	Annbank United	1 0	
1953/54	Sunnybank	Lochee Harp	2 1	
1954/55	Kilsyth Rangers	Duntocher Hibs	4 1	after 1-1 draw
1955/56	Petershill	Lugar Boswell Thistle	4 1	
1956/57	Banks o' Dee	Kilsyth Rangers	1 0	
1957/58	Shotts Bon Accord	Pumpherston	2 0	
1958/59	Irvine Meadow	Shettleston	2 1	
1959/60	St Andrews United	Greenock	3 1	
1960/61	Dunbar United	Cambuslang Rangers	2 0	after 2-2 draw
1961/62	Rob Roy	Renfrew	1 0	after 1-1 draw
1962/63	Irvine Meadow	Glenafton Athletic	2 1	
1963/64	Johnstone Burgh	Cambuslang Rangers	3 0	after 1-1 draw
1964/65	Linlithgow Rose	Baillieston	4 1	
1965/66	Bonnyrigg Rose	Whitburn	6 1	after 1-1 draw
1966/67	Kilsyth Rangers	Glencairn	3 1	after 1-1 draw
1967/68	Johnstone Burgh	Glenrothes	4 3	after 2-2 draw
1968/69	Cambuslang Rangers'	Rob Roy	1 0	
1969/70	Blantyre Vics	Penicuik Athletic	1 0	after 2-2 draw
1970/71	Cambuslang Rangers'	Newtongrange Star	2 1	
1971/72	Cambuslang Rangers'	Bonnyrigg Rose	3 2	after 1-1 draw
1972/73	Irvine Meadow	Cambuslang Rangers	1 0	after draws 3-3, 2-2
1973/74	Cambuslang Rangers'	Linlithgow Rose	3 1	
1974/75	Glenrothes	Glencairn	1 0	
1975/76	Bo'ness United	Darvel	3 0	
1976/77	Kilbimie Ladeside	Rob Roy	3 1	
1977/78	Bonnyrigg Rose	Stonehouse Violet	1 0	
1978/79	Cumnock	Bo'ness United	1 0	
1979/80	Baillieston	Benburb	2 0	AET and 2-2 draw
1980/81	Pollok	Arthurlie	1 0	
1981/82	Blantyre Vics	Baillieston	1 0	
1982/83	East Kilbride Thistle	Bo'ness United	2 0	
1983/84	Bo'ness United	Baillieston	2 0	
1984/85	Pollok	Petershill	3 1	after 1-1 draw
1985/86	Auchinleck Talbot	Pollok	3 2	
1986/87	Auchinleck Talbot	Kilbirnie Ladeside	1 0	after 1-1 draw
1987/88	Auchinleck Talbot	Petershill	1 0	
1988/89	Cumnock	Ormiston Primrose	1 0	
1989/90	Hill of Beath Hawthorn	Lesmahagow	1 0	
1990/91	Auchinleck Talbot	Newtongrange Star	1 0	
1991/92	Auchinleck Talbot	Glenafton Athletic	4 0	
1992/93	Glenafton Athletic	Tayport	1 0	
1993/94	Largs Thistle	Glenafton Athletic	1 0	
1994/95	Camelon	Whitburn	2 0	AET
1995/96	Tayport	Camelon	2 1	
1996/97	Pollok	Tayport	3 1	
1997/98	Arthurlie	Pollok	4 0	
1998/99	Kilwinning Rangers	Kelty Hearts	1 0	
1999/00	Whitburn	Johnstone Burgh	2 2	AET, 4-3 pens
2000/1	Renfrew	Carnoustie Panmure	0 0	AET, 6-5 pens
2001/2	Linlithgow Rose	Auchinleck Talbot	1 0	
2002/3	Tayport	Linlithgow Rose	1 0	
2003/4	Carnoustie Panmure	Tayport	0 0	AET, 6-5 pens
2004/5	Tayport	Lochee United	2 0	
2005/6	Auchinleck Talbot	Bathgate Thistle	2 1	
2006/7	Linlithgow Rose	Kelty Hearts	2 1	AET
2007/8	Bathgate Thistle	Cumnock	2 1	
2008/9	Auchinleck Talbot	Clydebank	2 1	
2009/10	Linlithgow Rose	Largs Thistle	1 0	
2010/11	Auchinleck Talbot	Musselburgh Athletic	2 1	AET

EAST JUNIORS

The East Region of Scottish Junior football extends from Montrose in the north to Dunbar in the south-east and Harthill in the south west. It includes the counties of Angus, Perthshire, Fife, East, Mid and West Lothian, Clackmannanshire, parts of Stirlingshire as well as the cities of Dundee and Edinburgh.

The East Region was formed in 2002 by the amalgamation of the Lowlands, Fife and Tayside Regions. Initially there as a Region wide Super League fed by three District Leagues. A premier Division (tier 2) was introduced in 2006. From 2013 the top two divisions were expanded to sixteen clubs and the three lower leagues amalgamated into two. This meant that the Fife clubs were split between the North and South Divisions.

Two teams are relegated and promoted between the Super and Premier Divisions with the 3rd bottom and 3rd top playing off. Two teams are promoted from each of the lower leagues with four relegated from the Premier Division. There is no official word on the composition of the lower leagues but presumably they will remain equal in size which raises the possibility of some teams switching divisions.

All clubs compete in the Scottish Junior Cup and the East of Scotland Junior Cup. Below that the Cup competitions are based on the old districts which existed until 2002—Tayside, Fife and Lothians.

The entrants to the long-established Fife and Lothians Cup are self explanatory. The Tayside clubs compete in a similar competition with the North (Aberdeen etc.) Juniors. There is also provision for a Fife-Tayside competition should there be room in the fixture list. These competions are known as Inter-District Cups.

Tayport represent a slight anomaly. Although located in Fife, the club chose to join the old Tayside Region when they joined the Juniors in 1990. They have regularly applied for membership of the Fife and Lothians FA but have always been rejected.

The season commences with the three Sectional League Cups, one in each of South, Central and North. These include the Super League, Premier League and District League teams. In recent years the 'domestic' knock-out cups have been pruned due to fixture congestion. Until a few years ago there were three knock out cups in each district; in 2009/10 just one was played in each District and from 2010/11 none at all.

SUPER LEAGUE (16)
Two teams relegated
One team in relegation Play Off

PREMIER LEAGUE (16)
Two teams promoted
One team in promotion Play Off
Four teams relegated

NORTH LEAGUE
Two teams promoted

SOUTH LEAGUE
Two teams promoted

Mcbookie.com East Super League 2013/14

	AT	BAL	BU	BON	BA	C	CP	HBH	KH	LR	LU	MA	NS	SAU	STAU	T
Armadale Thistle	—	Aug 10 0-1	Jan 11 0-7	Nov 16 0-1	Nov 9 0-1	Aug 24 0-2	Apr 19 4-0	Dec 28 0-3	Nov 30 2-1	Mar 15 0-2	Sep 21 3-2	Aug 31 2-3	Apr 5 0-5	May 7 1-3	Feb 1 3-2	Feb 8 3-2
Ballingry Rovers	Apr 12 2-1	—	Feb 1 1-4	Apr 26 0-1	Mar 22 0-3	Jun 2 2-3	Nov 30 2-1	Sep 7 1-3	Aug 13 1-1	May 17 0-3	Nov 16 0-3	Aug 17 1-2	Mar 15 2-1	Nov 2 0-8	May 3 4-3	Oct 12 2-2
Bo'ness United	Aug 13 2-1	Sep 21 4-2	—	Nov 30 0-3	Nov 2 6-1	May 12 4-0	Jan 4 3-0	Dec 21 2-1	Aug 17 5-0	Dec 28 4-1	May 28 5-1	Dec 14 2-1	Aug 31 4-2	May 17 4-1	Mar 15 3-0	Apr 12 3-0
Bonnyrigg Rose	Mar 8 2-0	Dec 28 0-0	Feb 22 0-1	—	Nov 23 3-0	Jan 11 0-1	Aug 10 4-0	Feb 1 1-1	Oct 26 2-2	May 10 2-0	Aug 31 3-0	Nov 2 0-0	Aug 24	Sep 21 1-4	Dec 7 4-3	Mar 22 3-2
Broxburn Athletic	Dec 21 1-3	Aug 31 2-0	Apr 23 2-2	Aug 13 1-1	—	Feb 1 2-3	Sep 21 0-2	Oct 19 3-2	Nov 16 1-0	Feb 8 1-0	Aug 17 2-1	Feb 22 1-1	Jan 18 2-1	Dec 28 1-1	Apr 5 4-2	Dec 7 2-1
Camelon	Apr 23 2-2	Dec 7 1-2	Sep 7 1-0	May 17 2-3	Sep 28 1-1	—	May 28 1-2	May 31 3-1	May 7 1-0	Aug 17 0-2	Jun 11 2-1	May 14 0-1	Nov 30 5-0	Aug 13 1-0	Jun 4 1-1	May 3 1-3
Carnoustie Panmure	Dec 14 5-2	Mar 1 1-1	Mar 8 1-2	Apr 12 1-3	Mar 29 0-1	Jun 14 0-5	—	2-2	May 10 2-1	Nov 16 2-3	Aug 13 0-2	Mar 15 1-2	Oct 5 0-2	Aug 17 3-2	Apr 30 4-2	Sep 7 3-1
Hill of Beath Hawthorn	Mar 22 4-1	Apr 22 0-0	0-1	Apr 12 2-0	May 14 3-2	Sep 21 1-1	Aug 31 5-1	—	Nov 2 2-0	Apr 19 1-3	Aug 13 5-0	Feb 8 4-0	May 17 1-2	Oct 12 2-2	May 28 4-3	Jan 11 3-1
Kelty Hearts	Sep 7 1-1	Nov 9 1-3	May 3 0-0	Feb 8 1-1	Jan 11 1-4	Dec 14 1-4	Oct 12 2-2	Aug 24 2-1	—	Jan 25 2-0	Nov 2 3-0	Mar 22 1-2	Dec 28 1-2	Mar 29 1-1	Feb 22 0-0	Dec 21 3-2
Linlithgow Rose	Dec 7 4-2	Aug 24 3-2	May 31 4-1	Jan 4 2-2	Aug 10 2-1	May 21 1-1	Mar 22 4-2	Feb 15 1-2	Aug 31 0-0	—	Feb 1 2-1	Sep 21 4-1	Apr 12 2-0	May 3 4-1	Oct 19 1-1	Jan 11 2-1
Lochee United	Mar 1 2-0	Jan 18 2-1	Apr 5 4-2	May 3 3-3	Dec 14 1-2	Aug 10 4-1	May 16 3-6	Sep 28 2-4	Mar 8 0-5	May 24 3-2	—	Oct 19 2-3	Apr 26 1-4	Jan 4 2-1	Sep 7 1-4	Aug 24 3-0
Musselburgh Athletic	Mar 29 0-1	Sep 14 5-0	Feb 8 3-3	Sep 7 1-1	Aug 24 1-2	Oct 12 1-1	May 3 4-1	Nov 16 0-1	Jan 4 2-3	Mar 8 0-1	Apr 12 4-2	—	Feb 1 2-3	Dec 7 3-2	Apr 19 1-1	Aug 10 3-1
Newtongrange Star	Sep 28 1-0	Oct 19 1-0	Apr 19 0-1	Mar 1 0-1	Sep 7 5-0	May 10 1-3	May 3 5-1	Aug 10 5-0	Dec 21 6-2	Mar 22 0-2	Aug 13 0-1		—	Nov 16 2-0	Feb 8 4-0	Jan 4 3-1
Sauchie	Oct 12 2-0	Apr 5 4-0	Aug 24 0-1	Dec 21 0-4	Apr 12 5-2	Apr 30 0-1	Jan 25 2-1+	Oct 19 2-0	Oct 12 2-1	Sep 7 0-3	May 9 1-5	May 10 1-3	Nov 16 1-3	—	Mar 22 4-2	Feb 1 1-1
St Andrews United	Nov 2 1-1	Feb 8 1-1	Aug 10 0-2	Mar 29 1-1	Oct 12 0-3	May 26 0-1	Aug 24 2-1	Apr 12 0-5	Sep 21 2-2	Apr 26 1-3	Nov 30 0-0	Dec 28 1-0	Mar 8 1-2	Aug 31 1-0	—	May 16 3-1
Tayport	Aug 17 0-2	Apr 19 2-0	Nov 16 2-1	Dec 14 0-4	Mar 15 3-4	Aug 31 1-2	May 7 3-1	May 19 1-0	Mar 1 0-0	Apr 5 1-1	Dec 28 1-3	Jan 25 1-1	Sep 21 0-2	Apr 26 0-2	Aug 13 1-1	—

+ at Alloa FC

			Home			Away						
	P	W	D	L	F	A	W	D	L	F	A	GD	PTS
1 Bo'ness United	30	14	0	1	51	14	8	3	4	28	18	47	69
2 Linlithgow Rose	30	10	4	1	39	19	10	2	3	31	14	37	66
3 Bonnyrigg Rose	30	8	4	3	28	15	9	6	0	32	13	32	61
4 Newtongrange Star	30	10	0	5	35	12	9	1	5	30	22	31	58
5 Camelon	30	6	3	6	22	19	10	3	2	29	16	16	54
6 Hill of Beath Hawthorn	30	8	4	3	37	19	6	8		24	25	17	49
7 Broxburn Athletic	30	7	4	4	25	23	7	2	6	28	33	-3	48
8 Musselburgh Athletic	30	5	4	6	30	23	7	3	5	23	28	2	43
9 Sauchie Juniors	30	7	1	7	25	27	5	3	7	30	26	2	40
10 Lochee United	30	6	1	8	32	40	6	0	9	25	32	-15	37
11 Armadale Thistle	30	5	0	10	18	35	3	3	9	17	29	-29	27
12 Carnoustie Panmure	30	5	2	8	25	31	3	1	11	18	43	-31	27
13 Ballingry Rovers	30	4	2	9	18	39	3	4	8	13	28	-36	27
14 Kelty Hearts	30	3	7	5	20	23	2	4	9	16	31	-18	26
15 Tayport	30	4	4	7	16	24	1	3	11	20	38	-26	22
16 St Andrews United	30	3	5	7	17	26	1	4	10	25	42	-26	21

Play Off Matches

4/6/14
Kelty Hearts v Dalkeith Thistle
4-0

11/6/14
Dalkeith Thistle v Kelty Hearts
0-1

Aggregate

Bo'ness United ultimately prevailed as Champions and earned due reward for their consistency over the season. The key result was probably a 4-1 win over rivals Linlithgow Rose at Newtown Park between Christmas and New Year. Linlithgow were having a hard time at that stage and fell too far behind to make up the ground. That was despite a great run in the latter stages of the season after the Prestonfield club had changed Managers, bringing in Danny Smith from Camelon to replace Mark Bradley.

Bo'ness Manager Allan McGonnigal based his team around experience. Robert Sloan, in the heart of midfield, was arguably the best player in the East Region this season. Up front Stevie Hislop was in terrific form, ably assisted by Nicky Walker and Darren Gribben. A decent run in the Scottish, and multiple postponements of Cup ties, threatened to derail the Bo'ness season but in the end they had enough about them to see things through.

Linlithgow endured a desperate spell early in 2014 including an unprecedented 6-0 Cup defeat at bottom of the table St Andrews. Rumours abounded of discontent behind the scenes and manager Mark Bradley fell on his sword. Linlithgow moved to entice their former player Danny Smith back from Junior Cup Semi Finalists Camelon and their results improved greatly under his regime.

Bonnyrigg and Newtongrange had good seasons but never really looked like title potential champions. However, both will regroup for 2014/15 and could mount a serious challenge. Camelon were left with a massive fixture backlog and considering the programme they faced in May, they did well to gain so many points. The Carmuirs club did well to reach the Semi Final of the Scottish Cup but they were

BO'NESS UNITED SQUAD

East Junior Super League - All Time Positions

	2002-3	2003-4	2004-5	2005-6	2006-7	2007-8	2008-9	2009-10	2010-11	2011-12	2012-13	2013-14
Armadale Thistle												11
Arniston Rangers	4	5	9	11								
Ballingry Rovers												13
Bathgate Thistle	3	7	7	2	7	8	8	3	8	11		
Bo'ness United		6	5	7	11		10	1	1	4	4	1
Bonnyrigg Rose	6	3	4	6	2	4	1	10	4	1	2	3
Broxburn Athletic											6	7
Camelon			11		10	3	2	6	10	6	3	5
Carnoustie Panmure	10		8	8	4	11				10	9	12
Dundee North End	9	12		12								
Dundee Violet	12											
Edinburgh United	11											
Forfar West End							11		6	Res		
Glenrothes	8	8	6	10		9	7	12				
Hill of Beath Haws	2	11		3	6	10	6	8	2	2	8	6
Kelty Hearts		10				7	5	9	9	5	5	14
Kinnoull				12								
Linlithgow Rose	5	1	3	5	1	5	3	2	3	3	1	2
Lochee United		4	1	9	5	1	9	5	5	7	10	10
Musselburgh Athletic								7	7	8	7	8
Newtongrange Star								4	12			4
Oakley United	7	9	10		9	12						
Sauchie											11	9
St Andrews United										9	12	16
Tayport	1	2	2	1	8	6	12		11			15
Thornton Hibs			12									
Whitburn				4	3	2	4	11				

	Apps
Goalkeepers	
Connor Wallace	6
Stewart Baillie	6
Mark Peat	37
Defenders	
Jamie Clark	2
Ross Campbell	15
Stewart Devine	33
Stuart Hunter	34
Tony Jaconelli	28
Will Snowdon	33
Midfield	
Andy Scott	33
Chris Donnelly	33
Ian Nimmo	32
Nicky Walker	41
Paul Murphy	37
Robert Sloan	40
Scott Gibb	13
Craig Scott	28
Forwards	
Darren Gribben	43
Jordan Burns	4
Keiran Anderson	26
Steven Hislop	35
Zander Miller	34

Source : Bo'ness United website

not helped by the departure of Danny Smith just a few says prior to the ties. Former player Davie Flynn stepped in as caretaker for the two Cup games before John Sludden was appointed as Manager on a permanent basis.

At the foot of the table it was a poor season for the two clubs from north-east Fife. St Andrews United and Tayport always looked likely to occupy the two relegation spots. The battle to avoid the play off spot was interesting. Kelty finished their league programme before their rivals and were eventually overhauled ay Armadale Thistle, Ballingry Rovers and Carnoustie Panmure. However, in the Play Off itself the gap between the Super League and the Premier League was apparent with Kelty running out handsome winners.

For 2014/15 the make-up of the Super League Division will be as follows:

Tayside (2)
Lochee United
Carnoustie Panmure

Fife (3)
Hill of Beath Hawthorn
Kelty Hearts
Ballingry Rovers

Lothians (11)
Linlithgow Rose
Sauchie
Bo'ness United
Broxburn Athletic
Armadale Thistle
Newtongrange Star
Fauldhouse United
Penicuik Athletic
Bonnyrigg Rose
Broxburn Athletic
Musselburgh Athletic

Bo'ness United will take part in the Scottish Cup. Linlithgow Rose, having achieved club licensing status, also believe that they will be eligible to take part in the Scottish Cup although this had still to be confirmed by the SFA at the time of going to press.

Rumours that Ballingry Rovers would fold or go into abeyance at the end of the season appear not to have been founded. Changes at committee level and the introduction of Lee Dair and Kevin Fortheringham as a new management team suggest that the Fife club have a decent future to look forward to.

Mcbookie.com East Premier League   2013/14

	AR	BT	BA	DT	DV	FU	G	JS	K	KYM	KT	LU	MR	OU	PA	P
Arniston Rangers		Jan 4	Aug 10	May 7	Oct 12	May 3	Oct 26	Nov 30	Mar 22	Aug 24	Apr 26	Apr 16	May 31	Dec 7	Apr 23	Nov 2
		3-1	0-0	2-3	2-3	3-2	1-1	2-1	1-0	2-1	5-1	6-1	3-3	1-2	4-2*	5-2
Bathgate Thistle	Mar 15		Feb 1	Aug 31	May 10	Aug 13	Dec 28	Sep 21	Aug 17	Nov 2	Mar 29	May 14	Oct 5	Apr 19	Dec 7	Apr 26
	0-1		2-0	6-1	2-4	3-3	7-4	1-3	6-1	2-1	2-0	2-3	3-2	6-1	3-5	9-0
Broughty Athletic	Dec 21	Oct 19		Sep 21	Aug 13	Aug 17	Feb 8	Mar 29	Nov 30	Mar 8	May 14	Aug 31	Mar 1	Mar 22	Nov 16	Apr 19
	4-3	2-2		2-3	3-4	2-1	2-3	1-2	1-2	3-1	8-0	3-0	2-0	0-2	3-2	10-0
Dalkeith Thistle	Aug 13	May 3	Apr 26		Aug 17	Sep 28	Mar 1	Jan 4	Mar 8	Sep 7	Apr 5	Oct 19	Nov 16	Oct 12	Apr 16	May 10
	4-0	2-1	3-3		1-3	3-4	4-2	3-2	4-2	4-2	3-0	3-2	3-1	2-2	0-2	4-2
Dundee Violet	Mar 1	Aug 10	Dec 14	Mar 15		Mar 22	May 31	Oct 26	Sep 21	Apr 26	Aug 24	Oct 5	May 14	Nov 9	Apr 12	Aug 31
	0-3	0-3	2-1	0-1		3-3	3-1	0-1	0-3	0-2	1-0	2-3	2-2	3-3	0-1	1-3
Fauldhouse United	Aug 31	Dec 21	Apr 5	Dec 28	Dec 7		Apr 26	Aug 10	Jan 18	Nov 16	Feb 8	Aug 24	Sep 21	Mar 1	Oct 19	Apr 12
	2-1	2-0	1-1	4-4	3-0		0-0	2-2	3-0	5-1	6-0	2-1	3-1	3-1	2-0	8-3
Glenrothes	Sep 21	Mar 22	Apr 12	Nov 2	Nov 16	Dec 14		Aug 24	Aug 31	Aug 10	Mar 15	Mar 29	May 10	May 3	May 21	Feb 15
	2-4	1-1	2-2	1-0	3-0	2-2		4-1	1-1	1-1	3-0	4-2	2-1	3-1	3-0	6-0
Jeanfield Swifts	Aug 17	Mar 1	Oct 12	Mar 22	Jan 18	Jan 25	Apr 19		Aug 13	Feb 15	Oct 19	Apr 26	Apr 5	Sep 7	Dec 28	Nov 16
	3-1	3-0	1-2	1-2	3-1	4-2	0-2		0-0	1-3	1-0	4-2	3-3	2-3	1-0	6-1
Kinnoull	Nov 16	Jan 25	May 3	Aug 10	Dec 28	Sep 7	Feb 22	Feb 1		Mar 29	May 10	Dec 21	Mar 15	Aug 24	Oct 12	Mar 1
	0-2	1-0	1-2	1-1	1-2	1-1	1-3	0-1		4-2	1-3	2-1	4-1	1-1	0-0	3-0
Kirkcaldy YM	Feb 1	Apr 5	Dec 28	Apr 12	Feb 22	Mar 15	Jan 11	Aug 31	Jan 4		Sep 21	Feb 8	Aug 17	Oct 19	Aug 13	Nov 9
	2-1	1-6	4-3	2-2	1-1	0-6	2-3	4-1	0-1		5-5	3-0	3-2	1-2	0-4	4-0
Kirrie Thistle	Jun 7	Oct 12	Sep 7	Oct 5	Apr 16	Apr 19	May 24	Apr 12	Dec 14	Mar 1		May 3	Aug 13	Mar 8	Mar 22	Aug 17
	0-0	0-3	2-3	1-4	0-2	0-1	0-2	0-1	3-1	1-3		2-1	2-1	1-2	0-3	1-0
Livingston United	May 17	Sep 7	Mar 15	May 12	Apr 19	Feb 1	Aug 17	Nov 2	Apr 12	Oct 12	Nov 16		Mar 22	Apr 5	May 7	Aug 13
	1-0	1-3	1-4	1-5	1-1	0-1	0-4	2-1	2-1	2-1	2-1		0-3	0-1	0-1	2-3
Montrose Roselea	Oct 19	Apr 12	Aug 24	May 24	Sep 7	Mar 8	Oct 12	Dec 14	Apr 19	Jan 25	Jan 11	Aug 10		Sep 28	May 3	Feb 1
	3-2	2-2	1-2	2-1	3-0	1-0	2-0	0-2	1-0	4-2	1-4	2-3		2-3	2-2	3-0
Oakley United	Apr 12	Nov 16	Nov 2	Feb 22	Mar 29	Nov 30	Aug 13	Dec 21	Feb 8	Jan 18	Aug 31	Sep 21	Apr 26		Aug 17	Jan 4
	3-1	4-1	2-2	1-0	1-1	0-5	2-1	0-4	0-1	6-2	4-3	2-3	1-0		2-3	5-1
Penicuik Athletic	Sep 7	Apr 30	May 24	Aug 24	Nov 2	May 17	Dec 21	May 14	Apr 5	Apr 19	Aug 10	Jan 4	Aug 31	Mar 15		Sep 21
	2-0	2-0	2-2	2-0	4-0	2-1	2-1	2-0	1-2	4-1	2-2	1-3	4-0	3-1		4-1
Pumpherston	Mar 29	Aug 24	Sep 28	Dec 21	May 3	Oct 12	Sep 7	Mar 15	Oct 19	Mar 22	Nov 30	Apr 23	May 17	Aug 10	Feb 8	
	1-4	0-10	1-4	0-4	0-3	1-8	2-2	0-3	2-3	2-5	0-1	1-1	1-3	0-4	0-3	

ABD

Sep 28 Penicuik v Bathgate
Nov 2   Kirrie Th v Fauldhouse Utd
Dec 14 Bathgate v Pumpherston
May 10 Penicuik Ath v Jeanfield S, Rain
* Arniston fielded suspended players, points awarded to Penicuik as a 1-0 win

		P	W	D	L	F	A	W	D	L	F	A	GD	Pts
1	Penicuik Athletic	30	11	2	2	41	13	9	2	4	27	16	39	64
2	Fauldhouse United	30	11	4	0	46	15	6	4	5	40	25	46	59
3	Dalkeith Thistle	30	10	2	3	43	27	7	3	5	31	26	21	56
4	Jeanfield Swifts	30	8	2	5	33	22	9	1	5	27	20	18	54
5	Glenrothes	30	9	5	1	38	16	6	3	6	28	28	22	53
6	Oakley United	30	8	2	5	33	28	8	3	4	28	31	2	53
7	Broughty Athletic	30	8	1	6	46	25	6	6	3	31	25	27	49
8	Bathgate Thistle	30	9	1	5	54	29	5	3	7	33	24	34	46
9	Arniston Rangers	30	8	3	4	36	22	5	1	9	23	27	10	43
10	Kinnoull	30	5	4	6	21	20	5	2	8	17	28	-10	36
11	Dundee Violet	30	3	3	9	17	30	7	3	5	24	28	-17	36
12	Montrose Roselea	30	8	2	5	29	23	2	3	10	24	35	-5	35
13	Kirkcaldy YM	30	6	3	6	32	37	4	2	9	29	39	-15	35
14	Livingston United	30	5	1	9	15	30	4	1	10	23	42	-34	29
15	Kirriemuir Thistle	30	4	1	10	13	27	4	1	10	21	43	-36	26
16	Pumpherston Juniors	30	0	2	13	11	58	2	0	13	16	71	-102	8

League Composition 2014/15

Tayside
Tayport
Jeanfield Swifts
Broughty Athletic
Kinnoull
Dundee Violet
Montrose Roselea
Dundee North End
Forfar West End

Fife
St Andrews United
Glenrothes
Oakley United
Dundonald Bluebell

Lothians
Dalkeith Thistle
Bathgate Thistle
Arniston Rangers
Edinburgh United

Penicuik Athletic Squad 2013/14

Goalkeepers
Chris Hill
Youssef Bejaoui

Defenders
Blair Dickson
Stehen Bunyan
Dougie Cunnison
Michael McDermott
Craig Meikle
Greg Ross
Darrell Young

Midfield
Ryan Gay
Gordon Harris
Jordan Lister
James McPartlin
Ross Montgomery

Forwards
Grant Killin
Ryan McCallum
Scott McCulloch
Craig Millar

East Premier Division - All Time Positions	2006-7	2007-8	2008-9	2009-10	2010-11	2011-12	2012-13	2013-14
Armadale Thistle	5	11		9	7	10	4	
Arniston Rangers	8	8	6	4	9	12		9
Ballingry Rovers			7	6	6	7	2	
Bathgate Thistle							6	8
Blairgowrie				8	11			
Bo'ness United			1					
Broughty Athletic					8	9	12	7
Broxburn Athletic					3	2		
Carnoustie Panmure			3	5	2			
Dalkeith Thistle							7	3
Downfield					11			
Dundee North End	6	5	12					
Dundee Violet							10	11
Dundonald Bluebell			9	11				
Fauldhouse United			9	10				2
Forfar West End		2		2				
Glenrothes	1				4	8	11	5
Jeanfield Swifts							8	4
Kelty Hearts	2							
Kinnoull		7	5	3	10			10
Kirkcaldy YM								13
Kirrie Thistle								15
Livingston United								14
Lochee Harp	11							
Montrose Roselea	7	10		12				12
Musselburgh Athletic	4	4	1					
Newtongrange Star		3	2			6	1	
Oakley United			10			5	9	6
Penicuik Athletic	9	6	4	7	5	4	5	1
Pumpherston								16
Rosyth	3	12						
Sauchie						1		
Scone Thistle	12							
St Andrews United	10				8	1		
Tayport					1		3	3
Thornton Hibs						12		
Whitburn						11		

With Penicuik being promoted, no club has now been "perma -members" of the Premier League.

Arniston Rangers will be at this level for the eighth time in nine seasons.

Edinburgh United have never played at this level. Although they were a Super League side at one time they were relegated at a time when there was no Premier Division and they went straight down to the Lothians League.

There was drama in the settling of all the issues in the East Premier Division. Fauldhouse United had their promotion spot sealed quite early but Penicuik Athletic came through a long backlog of postponed games to overtake them and win the title.

Glenrothes could have pipped Dalkeith for the pla off spot if they had defeated Violet in their final game - they lost, allowing Violet to escapefrom relegation.

The four teams who went down were all newcomers to this level. Pumpherston, having lost their entire management and playing staff that had won promotion, were doomed from the start. Livingston United and Kirrie Thistle had occasional spells of hope before they were relegated. Violet and Montrose Roselea effected last minute escapes to condemn Kirkcaldy YM to immediate relegation.

This was a high quality league with several ambitious clubs looing to progress. Jeanfield Swifts have a superb off-field set up and Arniston Rangers look to be on the cusp of a long-awaited revival.

Jeanfield, under the Management of Gavin Price and Alex Bone, have assembled a squad that should challenge for promotion in 2015. The duo moved from town rivals Kinnoull midway through the season but the Tulloch Park club weathered the storm and finished the season strongly.

Oakley United now have former Steelend and Lochgelly boss James Watt at the helm. The Blairwood Park club have enjoyed remarkable success over the past fifteen years on very small attendances.

There were signs of recovery at Glenrothes, The Warout club used to splash out big wages and signing fees but those days are long gone. Instead they have a decent squad of local players who could do well in 2014/15.

Relegated clubs St Andrews United and Tayport have big reputations but they will coiunt for nothing. Saints have appointed former Aberdeen ad Dunfermline player Phil McGuire as Manager and will have one of the bigger budgets.

Newcomers Edinburgh United, Dundonald Bluebell, Forfar West End and Dundee North End all have the potential to succeed. 2014/15 is likely to be a very competitive season with no real favourites for promotion or relegation.

McBookie.com East League North Division 2013/14

The main results grid lists each fixture as **date / score** (home team in the left column). A diagonal blank marks a team against itself.

	AV	B	BV	CA	D	DNE	EC	FA	FW	KSH	LH	LW	L	N	ST	TH
Arbroath Vics		May 3 / 3-2	Feb 8 / 2-0	Aug 10 / 4-1	Oct 12 / 3-3	Jan 18 / 2-5	Nov 30 / 3-2	Aug 24 / 5-1	Sep 7 / 2-4	Nov 16 / 2-4	Mar 8 / 1-1	Oct 19 / 2-2	Mar 22 / 3-2	Apr 5 / 4-2	Jan 4 / 4-5	Dec 21 / 3-3
Blairgowrie	Dec 28 / 5-1		Nov 30 / 2-1	Aug 13 / 4-0	Sep 7 / 3-3	Oct 19 / 1-3	Aug 10 / 3-2	Feb 15 / 2-1	Feb 8 / 1-0	Mar 29 / 1-2	Apr 19 / 3-2	Mar 15 / 3-1	Aug 24 / 1-2	Jan 25 / 1-4	Oct 12 / 5-1	Mar 8 / 2-1
Brechin Vics	Aug 13 / 0-1	Aug 17 / 2-1		Mar 8 / 4-0	Nov 16 / 2-3	Dec 14 / 0-8	Apr 19 / 0-0	Sep 7 / 3-1	Apr 12 / 2-3	Dec 21 / 1-2	Dec 28 / 3-0	Feb 22 / 0-1	Oct 12 / 0-3	Mar 22 / 2-3	Aug 10 / 1-0	/ 0-2
Coupar Angus	Mar 15 / 1-6	Dec 14 / 0-6	May 3 / 0-7		Aug 17 / 1-8	Nov 16 / 0-9	May 21 / 0-4	Nov 9 / 1-2	Mar 29 / 0-7	May 10 / 0-5	May 7 / 0-7	Nov 30 / 1-3	Sep 7 / 2-7	Oct 12 / 0-9	Apr 12 / 0-5	May 16 / 2-8
Downfield	Apr 12 / 4-1	Mar 22 / 2-0	May 7 / 3-1	Apr 6 / 4-1		Aug 31 / 0-0	Mar 1 / 1-0	Mar 8 / 5-0	Dec 14 / 2-1	Aug 26 / 0-0	Aug 24 / 5-1	Sep 21 / 2-0	Nov 9 / 1-0	Aug 10 / 2-2	May 24 / 1-3	Apr 30 / 0-4
Dundee North End	Nov 2 / 5-1	Mar 1 / 2-1	Feb 15 / 6-0	Jan 25 / 4-0	Mar 15 / 4-2		Aug 24 / 2-1	Nov 23 / 7-0	Feb 22 / 3-0	Aug 10 / 5-0	Jan 11 / 4-3	Dec 21 / 2-1	Apr 12 / 2-2	Dec 28 / 4-2	Sep 7 / 2-2	Oct 12 / 4-4
East Craigie	Mar 29 / 2-1	Apr 12 / 1-3	Aug 31 / 1-1	Sep 21 / 7-0	Aug 13 / 3-1	Jan 4 / 2-3		Nov 2 / 2-4	May 7 / 1-4	Mar 15 / 2-1	Feb 8 / 4-0	May 24 / 1-0	Dec 21 / 6-1	Feb 1 / 1-2	Oct 26 / 4-2	Aug 17 /
Forfar Albion	Feb 22 / 2-5	Nov 16 / 0-6	Jan 25 / 1-2	Aug 31 / 5-1	Jan 4 / 1-2	Feb 8 / 0-4	Apr 26 / 0-5		Aug 13 / 0-8	Sep 21 / 0-5	Dec 14 / 2-6	Mar 29 / 0-1	Oct 19 / 2-8	Mar 15 / 1-3	Aug 17 / 2-0	Nov 30 / 1-9
Forfar West End	Apr 26 / 2-1	Aug 31 / 3-2	Dec 28 / 4-0	Apr 19 / 3-0	Sep 21 / 3-0	Nov 16 / 2-1	Mar 1 / 4-0	/ 7-0		Mar 8 / 3-0	Mar 22 / 5-1	Apr 5 / 4-1	Aug 10 / 0-4	Sep 28 / 3-3	Nov 2 / 2-6	May 10 / 4-2
Kennoway Star Hearts	Mar 1 / 3-0	Jan 18 / 0-4	Apr 5 / 3-1	Oct 19 / 17-2	Sep 28 / 0-1	Apr 19 / 2-6	Oct 12 / 2-3	Mar 22 / 2-1	Aug 17 / 3-1		Feb 1 / 6-3	Aug 13 / 6-1	Dec 28 / 4-1	Sep 7 / 3-3	Dec 7 / 3-0	Aug 24 / 2-1
Lochee Harp	Sep 28 / 1-3	Feb 22 / 0-1	Mar 1 / 2-3	Dec 21 / 11-1	Aug 3 / 1-2	May 3 / 1-1	Aug 13 / 0-2	Sep 7 / 4-2	Oct 12 / 1-2	Nov 9 / 3-5		Oct 5 / 0-1	Aug 17 / 1-6	Apr 5 / 1-1	Apr 26 / 2-3	Mar 29 / 2-2
Lochore Welfare	Apr 19 / 4-3	Nov 2 / 3-2	Sep 28 / 3-1	May 13 / 9-0	May 21 / 2-2	Mar 22 / 0-1	Nov 9 / 0-3	Aug 10 / 6-1	Oct 12 / 3-3	Feb 8 / 0-4	Apr 12 / 4-3		May 19 / 5-1	Aug 24 / 1-3	May 3 / 2-0	Sep 7 / 4-1
Luncarty	Dec 14 / 5-0	Oct 26 / 2-6	Mar 15 / 1-0	Apr 30 / 10-1	May 10 / 0-1	Aug 17 / 2-3	May 3 / 2-3	Jan 18 / 5-2	Nov 30 / 1-0	Aug 31 / 4-1	Sep 21 / 4-1	Nov 16 / 2-2		May 24 / 2-2	Aug 13 / 7-0	Mar 1 / 1-3
Newburgh	Aug 17 / 3-1	May 10 / 3-2	Sep 21 / 2-2	Apr 19 / 6-0	Jan 18 / 2-0	Mar 29 / 1-2	Oct 19 / 4-1	Dec 21 / 10-0	May 3 / 0-1	Apr 12 / 3-2	Aug 31 / 1-3	Mar 1 / 2-2	Jan 4 / 2-3		Nov 16 / 4-1	Aug 13 / 4-2
Scone Thistle	Sep 21 / 1-1	Apr 26 / 2-2	Nov 9 / 3-0	Aug 24 / 5-0	Apr 5 / 1-2	Nov 30 / 0-7	Dec 14 / 4-3	Oct 26 / 3-1	Jan 18 / 3-2	Feb 22 / 0-3	Aug 10 / 2-2	Aug 31 / 1-2	Feb 1 / 3-0	May 16 / 1-2		Oct 19 / 6-2
Thornton Hibs	Aug 31 / 2-4	Sep 21 / 2-3	Nov 23 / 4-0	Oct 26 / 5-0	Nov 2 / 5-0	Feb 1 / 3-2	Mar 22 / 2-0	Apr 12 / 6-4	Mar 15 / 1-3	Nov 16 / 4-1	Apr 26 / 2-2	May 21 / 3-1	May 7 / 1-3	Apr 19 / 5-1	/	

ABANDONED

Oct 12	Kennoway Star Hearts v East Craigie, KSH had 5 players sent off
Nov 2	Brechin Vics v Kennoway Star Hearts, rain

			Home				Away						
		P	W	D	L	F	A	W	D	L	F	A	GD	Pts
1	Dundee North End	30	13	2	0	57	17	11	2	2	56	16	80	76
2	Forfar West End	30	12	1	2	49	21	8	1	6	39	23	44	62
3	Downfield	30	10	3	2	32	14	7	3	5	30	31	17	57
4	Newburgh	30	9	2	4	47	22	7	6	2	42	29	38	56
5	Kennoway Star Hearts	30	10	1	4	56	28	8	1	6	35	26	37	56
6	Blairgowrie	30	10	1	4	37	24	7	1	7	40	25	28	53
7	Thornton Hibs	30	10	0	5	50	26	6	3	6	47	36	35	51
8	Luncarty	30	8	2	5	48	25	8	0	7	42	33	32	50
9	Lochore Welfare	30	9	2	4	46	28	5	3	7	21	31	8	47
10	East Craigie	30	8	1	6	39	23	6	1	8	29	27	18	44
11	Arbroath Vics	30	7	4	4	43	37	5	1	9	29	40	-5	41
12	Scone Thistle	30	7	3	5	35	29	5	0	10	27	47	-14	39
13	Brechin Vics	30	5	1	9	26	28	3	2	10	19	37	-26	27
14	Lochee Harp	30	2	3	10	30	35	4	2	9	33	47	-19	23
15	Forfar Albion	30	2	0	13	17	65	2	0	13	20	68	-96	12
16	Coupar Angus	30	0	0	15	8	94	0	0	15	7	98	-177	0

Dundee North End were convincing winners, losing just twice in their 30-game league programme. Forfar West End eventually emerged to accompany them up to the Premier League but only after fighting off spirited challenges from Downfield, Newburgh and Kennoway Star Hearts.

KSH, in their debut season as a Junior club, performed beyond all expectations and demonstrated that they will be a force to be reckoned with.

Thornton Hibs finished the season very strongly and if they maintain the same squad they will be strongly fancied for 2014/15.

Coupar Angus struggled through the season without gaining a single point. Such was their situation that they played a late season game away to Lochore Welfare with just nine men. Hopefully 2014/15 will bring happier times for the friendly Angus side.

Also expect Brechin Vics to improve as Charlie King enters his second season as Player Manager.

The exact composition of the League remains to be confirmed at the East Region AGM. Kirrie Thistle, will drop down from the Premier League and it is possible, although unlikely, that either Lochore or Thornton could be moved to the South Division.

DUNDEE NORTH END SQUAD 2013/14

Dean Easton (GK)	Michael Stewart (D)
Mark Deuchars (D)	Darryl Gowans (D)
Jonathon Smart (D)	Adam Stevenson (D)
Reece Ritchie (M)	George Grier (M)
Connor MacLeod (F)	Barry McNaughton (M)
Scott McComiskie (F)	Gary Irons (F)
Jamie McCabe (M)	Jordan Colquhoun (F)
Sam Simpson (M)	Ben Sivewright
Robbie Shepherd	Calvin Colquhoun
Martyn McCabe (M)	Billy Hoon (GK)

East Juniors North Division - All Time Positions

	2006-7	2007-8	2008-9	2009-10	2010-11	2011-12	2012-13
Arbroath SC	2	9	6	10	6		
Arbroath Vics	10	5	5	3	5	4	6
Blairgowrie	4	1			8	9	8
Brechin Vics	12	11	11	9	9	7	10
Broughty Athletic	6	2	2	1			
Coupar Angus	11	10	9	12	13	11	12
Downfield	3	8	8	5	1		7
Dundee North End				8	2	2	5
East Craigie	7	7	7	7	11	5	3
Forfar Albion	9	12	12	11	12	10	11
Forfar West End	1						4
Kirrie Thistle	8	6	10	4	7	6	1
Lochee Harp		4	4	6	10	8	9
Montrose Roselea			1		4	3	2
Violet	5	3	3	2	3	1	

East Juniors Central Division - All Time Positions

	2006-7	2007-8	2008-9	2009-10	2010-11	2011-12	2012-13
Ballingry Rovers	3	1					
Bankfoot Athletic	12	10	7	7	6	5	12
Crossgates Primrose	10	6	8	10	9	9	10
Dundonald Bluebell	1			5	2	2	3
Jeanfield Swifts	7	5	4	4	4	1	
Kinnoull						3	1
Kirkcaldy YM	2	Ab	3	3	3	7	2
Lochgelly Albert	4	3	9	11	5	4	8
Lochore Welfare	5	7	6	6	7	11	5
Luncarty	6	11	13	14	13	13	13
Newburgh	11	9	12	12	11	6	4
Oakley United						2	1
Rosyth			2	8	12	10	6
Scone Thistle		8	11	13	10	Ab	11
St Andrews United			2	1			
Steelend Vics	8	12	10	9	8	12	9
Thornton Hibs	9	4	5	1		8	7

East Juniors South Division - All Time Positions

	2006-7	2007-8	2008-9	2009-10	2010-11	2011-12	2012-13
Armadale Thistle			1				
Arniston Rangers							4
Blackburn United	10	6	9	5	7	6	10
Broxburn Athletic	3	4	4	1			
Dalkeith Thistle	14	7	8	9	12	1	
Dunbar United	9	10	12	8	10	9	6
Edinburgh United	8	8	5	7	8	14	15
Falkirk JFC						3	13
Fauldhouse United	6	1			2	4	1
Haddington Athletic	5	2	11	10	4	2	5
Harthill Royal	7	3	7	12	14	15	14
Livingston United	15	12	14	13	3	7	3
Newtongrange Star	1						
Pumpherston	4	11	13	14	13	12	2
Sauchie	2	5	3	4	1		
Spartans				2	9	10	9
Stoneyburn	13	13	10	11	6	11	12
Tranent	11	12	2	3	5	5	7
West Calder United	12	9	6	6	11	13	11
Whitburn						8	8

From 2006 until 2013 the third tier of the East Region operated with three Divisions. The Perth area clubs were transferred from Tayside and grouped with the Fife clubs to form a Central Division. In 2013 a two-division set-up was established with the Central Division clubs split between the North and South Leagues. Spartans withdrew before the season started and Steelend Vics folded a few weeks into the season leaving an uneven split of 14 clubs in the South and 16 in the North.

McBookie.com East League South Division 2013/14

	BU	CP	DU	DB	EU	F	HA	HR	LA	R	SV	St	T	WC	Wh
Blackburn United		Mar 29	Sep 7	Aug 10	Nov 30	Oct 12	Apr 26	Jan 18	Jan 4	Nov 2	Aug 17	Mar 15	Mar 22	Aug 24	Apr 19
		4-3	4-2	2-2	0-3	3-0	3-5	3-0	3-1	7-1	5-2	4-3	3-0	2-1	1-0
Crossgates Primrose	Dec 14		Feb 22	May 3	Feb 15	Mar 15	Mar 22	Oct 12	Oct 5	Nov 16		Nov 30	Dec 28	Aug 10	Aug 24
	0-2		2-3	4-5	0-3	0-3	1-0	2-1	1-2	2-2		4-4	3-3	2-1	1-0
Dunbar United	Apr 12	Sep 21		Dec 21	Aug 10	Dec 7	Aug 13	Aug 17	Oct 19	Mar 15	Aug 31		Mar 1	Jan 11	Apr 26
	1-0	3-0		3-4	1-2	0-3	3-0	3-1	6-1	2-3	7-1		4-1	1-3	0-3
Dundonald Bluebell	Jan 11	Aug 13	Nov 2		Mar 22	Oct 19	Sep 21	Apr 5	Aug 31	Feb 22		Nov 16	Aug 17	Apr 19	Dec 28
	0-1	6-1	2-2		0-2	7-0	4-1	6-1	4-1	3-0		6-0	4-2	3-1	2-2
Edinburgh United	Mar 8	Nov 9	Jan 4	Sep 7			Jan 18	Mar 15	Dec 28	Feb 22	Dec 7	Feb 1	Dec 14	Nov 16	Nov 2
	2-2	3-0	6-3**	0-2			2-1	2-1	7-0	4-0	2-1	9-0	1-1	3-3	2-0
Falkirk	Feb 1	Aug 17	Aug 24	Apr 12	Mar 1			Nov 16	Sep 7	Dec 14	Feb 15	Dec 28	Aug 10	Dec 21	May 3
	1-5	4-3	4-0	2-3	3-2			1-3	7-1	5-0	1-0	2-1	2-3	1-2	1-3
Haddington Athletic	Dec 7	Nov 23	Dec 28	Mar 8	Jan 11	Apr 19		May 10	Aug 17	Aug 24	Sep 28	Nov 9	Apr 5	Sep 7	Feb 1
	1-6	6-0	0-1	3-1	1-2	3-3		5-0	3-2	3-0	4-2	8-2	6-1	3-1	5-4
Harthill Royal	Aug 13	Dec 21	Apr 19	Sep 28	Sep 21	Feb 22	Aug 31		Jan 11	Mar 29		Apr 12	Nov 2	Mar 15	Mar 22
	1-4	2-4	0-2	1-3	0-2	1-4	1-6		2-2	3-2		0-2	2-2	2-2	0-3
Lochgelly Albert	Nov 16	Nov 2	Apr 5	Feb 8	Dec 21	Mar 22	Jan 18	Aug 24		Aug 10		Oct 12	Dec 7	Feb 1	Sep 7
	0-4	1-2	4-2	0-4	1-4	1-3	1-2	6-0		3-1		2-3	4-2	5-1	4-3
Rosyth	Dec 28	Apr 19	Oct 12	Nov 9	Aug 31	Sep 21	May 7	Mar 1	Nov 23		Aug 13	Jan 11	Feb 8	Nov 30	Jan 18
	1-5	3-3	3-2	0-8	0-1	2-1	1-3	4-0	1-1		3-3	3-0	2-2	0-0	5-2
Steelend Vics				Aug 24				Aug 10					Sep 7		
				4-8%				3-3+					2-5%		
Stoneyburn	Oct 26	Jan 18	Mar 22	Apr 26	Aug 17	Mar 29	Jan 4	Dec 7	Mar 1	Sep 7			Aug 24	Apr 5	Aug 10
	1-0	2-2	3-1	0-1	2-7*	2-1	1-8	1-1	1-4	0-0			0-2	1-0	1-3
Tranent	Sep 21	Aug 31	Nov 16	Feb 1	Aug 13	Jan 4	Nov 30	Mar 8	Mar 15	Oct 19		Dec 21		Feb 22	Oct 12
	3-2	4-1	0-3	1-3	0-3	2-1	1-4	3-1	3-2	4-3		0-4		0-1	1-1
West Calder U	Mar 1	Dec 7	Mar 29	Oct 12	Feb 8	Oct 26	May 3	Oct 5	Sep 21	Apr 12	Aug 31	Aug 13	Nov 9		May 10
	3-2	2-0	0-3	1-3	1-3	2-2	2-1	2-2	3-3	2-3	3-1	2-0	0-1		0-2
Whitburn	Aug 31	Feb 8	Nov 30	Mar 1	Apr 5	Aug 13	May 17	Nov 16	Apr 12	Sep 28	Sep 21	Feb 22	Jan 11	Aug 17	
	2-1	8-2>	3-1	5-4	1-1	1-1	1-4	5-0	1-3	3-1	5-4	2-0>	3-3^	2-1	

* at West Calder
+ at Oakley
% at Rosyth
^ at Bo'ness
> at Whitburn Academy
** Edinburgh fielded ineligible player, points and goals deducted + £100 fine. Dunbar awarded 3 points.

ABD	Oct 12	Edinburgh United v Haddington, Referee Injured	
ABD	Oct 26	Crossgates v Edinburgh United, Player Injured	
ABD	Nov 2	Stoneyburn v West Calder United, Rain	

		Home					Away					
		P	W	D	L	F	A	W	D	L	F	A	PTS
1	Edinburgh United	26	8	3	1	37	11	11	1	1	35	10	61
2	Dundonald Bluebell	26	9	2	2	47	14	10	1	2	45	24	60
3	Blackburn United	26	10	1	2	39	21	7	1	5	34	16	53
4	Haddington Athletic	26	9	1	3	47	23	8	0	5	38	22	52
5	Whitburn Juniors	26	8	3	2	37	22	5	2	6	26	23	44
6	Dunbar United	26	7	0	6	34	22	5	1	6	22	26	40
7	Falkirk JFC	26	7	0	6	34	26	4	3	6	23	26	36
8	Tranent Juniors	26	6	1	6	22	29	2	6	5	22	34	31
9	Lochgelly Albert	26	6	0	7	32	31	3	3	7	22	37	30
10	West Calder United	26	4	4	5	20	24	3	3	7	17	25	28
11	Stoneyburn Juniors	26	4	3	6	15	30	4	1	8	21	47	28
12	Rosyth	26	5	4	4	25	28	1	2	10	14	34	24
13	Crossgates Primrose	26	4	3	6	22	29	2	2	9	21	48	23
14	Harthill Royal	26	1	3	9	15	38	0	2	11	8	54	8

Edinburgh Utd v Dunbar Utd, awarded as 0-1
Edinburgh fielded an ineligible player

EDINBURGH UNITED SQUAD 2013/14

Sinclair Inglis
Craig Hume
JamieStewart
David Heggie
Chris Gordon
Chris Inglis
Murray
Michael Fairnie
Matty Hunter
Kenny Fisher
Mark Smith
Grant Dick
Kayne Paterson
Kris Mitchell
Jordan Mack

Manager - Johnny Harvey

Dundonald Bluebell started the season as favourites having narrowly missed out on promotion the year before. As was the case in 2013/13 Bluebell scored freely but also conceded a fair few - in the end they had to settle for second place behind Edinburgh United.

The capital club were consistent throughout the season and thoroughly deserved to win the title. They managed to do despite having three points deducted for a registration irregularity in a victory over Dunbar United.

Haddington Athletic and Blackburn United were the "best of the rest". Both are ambitious clubs with decent off-field setups and deserve to go further. No doubt both will again be on contention for promotion next season. Blackburn spent their first full season at their new ground which is a splendid facility. Whitburn had to spend the second half of the season away from Central Park after the roof of their pavilion was blown away in a storm. They used the artificial pitch at Whitburn Academy but they were dogged by inconsistency all season.

Harthill finished bottom of the pile, possibly only because Steelend Vics folded after playing seven league games.

Next season will see Pumpherston and Livingston United return to the Division after a single season "upstairs" in the Premier League. It is likely that Kirkcaldy YM will also be allocated to the South Division.

EAST OF SCOTLAND JUNIOR CUP DRAW, 2014/15

Camelon v Carnoustie Panmure
Bo'ness United v Luncarty
Lochore Welfare v Newburgh
Jeanfield Swifts v Scone Thistle
Bonnyrigg Rose v Livingston United
Kennoway Star Hearts v Forfar West End
Kelty Hearts v Downfield
Blairgowrie v Blackburn United
Kinnoull v Forfar Albion
East Craigie v Arbroath Vics
Lochee United v Brechin Vics
Penicuik Athletic v Edinburgh United
Musselburgh Athletic v Falkirk Juniors
Whitburn v Sauchie
Hill of Beath Hawthorn v Dundee Violet
Newtongrange Star v Pumpherston
Thornton Hibs v Lochee Harp
Stoneyburn v Rosyth
Haddington Athletic v Armadale Thistle
Dundee North End v Fauldhouse United
Lochgelly Albert v West Calder United
St Andrews United v Dunbar United
Oakley United v Broughty Sthletic
Tranent v Broxburn Athletic
Tayport v Harthill Royal
Bathgate Thistle v Arniston Rangers
Crossgates Primrose v Kirriemuir Thistle
Montrose Roselea v Dalkeith Thistle
Linlithgow Rose v Kirkcaldy YM

Byes
Ballingry Rovers
Glenrothes
Dundonald Bluebell

East Region League Cup Competitions

These competitions were discontinued for 2013/14 due to the increased number of League fixtures.

Recent East (Central) Sectional League Cup Finals

Season	Winners	Runners Up	Score	Venue
2003/4	Rosyth Recreation	Thornton Hibs	2-1	Keir's Park, Hill of Beath
2004/5	Hill of Beath Hawthorn	Kircaldy YM	4-0	Ore Park, Glencraig
2005/6	Oakley United	Kelty Hearts	1-1, 4-3 pens	Recreation Park, Rosyth
2006/7	Kelty Hearts	Glenrothes	3-1	Recreation Park, Rosyth
2007/8	Hill of Beath Hawthorn	Glenrothes	2-1	Ore Park, Glencraig
2008/9	Hill of Beath Hawthorn	Glenrothes	1-1, 7-6 pens	Ore Park, Glencraig
2009/10	Glenrothes	Hill of Beath Hawthorn	1-1, 5-4 pens	Moorside Park, Dundonald
2010/1	Hill of Beath Hawthorn	Glenrothes	2-1	Central Park, Kelty
2011/2	Hill of Beath Hawthorn	Dundonald Bluebell	4-0	Keir's Park, Hill of Beath
2012/3	Jeanfield Swifts	Kelty Hearts	1-0	Blairwood Park, Oakley

Recent East (South) Sectional League Cup Finals

Season	Winners	Runners Up	Score	Venue
2004/5	Harthill Royal	Broxburn Athletic	2-0	Prestonfield, Linlithgow
2005/6	Musselburgh Athletic	Penicuik Athletic	1-0	New Victoria Park, Newtongrange
2006/7	Linlithgow Rose	Armadale Thistle	4-3	Carmuirs Park, Camelon
2007/8	Linlithgow Rose	Newtongrange Star	3-1	Prestonfield, Linlithgow
2008/9	Newtongrange Star	Camelon	1-1, 2-1 pens	Creamery Park, Bathgate
2009/10	Camelon	Linlithgow Rose	2-1	Prestonfield, Linlithgow
2010/1	Linlithgow Rose	Camelon	2-1	Creamery Park, Bathgate
2011/2	Linlithgow Rose	Newtongrange Star	3-0	Albyn Park, Broxburn
2012/3	Linlithgow Rose	Newtongrange Star	3-0	Albyn Park, Broxburn

Recent East (North) Sectional League Cup Finals

Season	Winners	Runners Up	Score	Venue
2000/1	Tayport	Dundee North End	2-0	Westfield Park, Carnoustie
2002/3	Montrose Roselea	Forfar West End	4-2	Westfield Park, Carnoustie
2003/4	Montrose Roselea	Carnoustie Panmure	3-0	Strathmore Park, Forfar
2004/5	Dundee North End	Scone Thistle	3-0	Westfield Park, Carnoustie
2005/6	Scone Thistle	Violet	4-1	Laing Park, Carnoustie
2006/7	Lochee United	Tayport	3-1	Laing Park, Carnoustie
2007/8	Lochee United	Tayport	2-2, 5-3 pens	Laing Park, Carnoustie
2008/9	Forfar West End	Lochee United	1-0	Laing Park, Carnoustie
2009/10	Montrose Roselea	Lochee United	0-0, 4-3 pens	Laing Park, Carnoustie
2010/1	Forfar West End	Tayport	2-2, 4-3 pens	Laing Park, Carnoustie
2011/2	Lochee United	Carnoustie Panmure	1-0	North End Park, Dundee
2012/3	Kirrie Thistle	Lochee United	2-1	Laing Park, Carnoustie

The new League structures, combined with a relatively mild winter, meant that some clubs were finished their fixtures very early in 2013/14. Some teams in the North an South Divisions were finished by April 5th.

Hopefully the East Region FA will consider introducing a voluntary Cup for competition in the latter part of the season to provide more fixtures for clubs affected in this way.

East of Scotland Junior Cup

Rd	Date	Home	Away	F	A	Notes
1	14/09/13	Camelon	Steelend Vics	6	1	'
1	14/09/13	Dunbar United	East Craigie	6	3	
1	14/09/13	Blackburn United	Kirkcaldy YM	3	0	
1	14/09/13	Bonnyrigg Rose	Haddington Athletic	4	0	
1	14/09/13	Thornton Hibs	Falkirk	5	2	
1	14/09/13	Lochgelly Albert	Coupar Angus	4	0	
1	14/09/13	Jeanfield Swifts	Arbroath Vics	3	4	
1	14/09/13	Blairgowrie	Crossgates Primrose	4	1	
1	14/09/13	Tranent	Newtongrange Star	1	4	
1	14/09/13	Tayport	Lochee Harp	4	1	
1	14/09/13	Oakley United	St Andrews United	2	2	4-5 pens
1	14/09/13	Forfar Albion	Dundee North End	0	3	
1	14/09/13	Dundee Violet	Kirrie Thistle	2	2	2-4 pens
1	14/09/13	Downfield	Broughty Athletic	1	5	
1	14/09/13	Stoneyburn	Livingston United	0	2	
1	14/09/13	Arniston Rangers	Lochore Welfare	5	0	
1	14/09/13	Kinnoull	Kelty Hearts	3	1	
1	14/09/13	Whitburn	Harthill Royal	1	1	3-1 pens
1	14/09/13	Newburgh	Edinburgh United	2	1	
1	14/09/13	Luncarty	Fauldhouse United	1	2	
1	14/09/13	West Calder United	Carnoustie Panmure	0	3	
1	14/09/13	Penicuik Athletic	Dundonald Bluebell	5	4	
1	14/09/13	Glenrothes	Brechin Vics	3	1	
1	14/09/13	Rosyth	Montrose Roselea	1	2	
1	14/09/13	Forfar West End	Sauchie	1	3	
1	14/09/13	Kennoway Star Hearts	Broxburn Athletic	1	1	7-6 pens
1	14/09/13	Armadale Thistle	Dalkeith Thistle	2	4	
1	14/09/13	Bo'ness United	Pumpherston	1	0	
1	14/09/13	Hill of Beath Hawthorn	Lochee United	3	2	
1	14/09/13	Bathgate Thistle	Scone Thistle	4	2	
1	28/09/13	Linlithgow Rose	Ballingry Rovers	4	1	
2	09/11/13	Arniston Rangers	Dunbar United	2	0	
2	09/11/13	Bathgate Thistle	Bonnyrigg Rose	0	0	2-4 pens
2	09/11/13	Blackburn United	Linlithgow Rose	0	5	
2	09/11/13	Blairgowrie	Newburgh	4	2	
2	09/11/13	Bo'ness United	Newtongrange Star	4	2	
2	09/11/13	Broughty Athletic	Sauchie	0	1	
2	09/11/13	Dalkeith Thistle	Lochgelly Albert	1	1	6-5 pens
2	09/11/13	Kennoway Star Hearts	Fauldhouse United	1	4	
2	09/11/13	Kirrie Thistle	Kinnoull	0	6	
2	09/11/13	Penicuik Athletic	Dundee North End	4	2	
2	09/11/13	Tayport	Arbroath Vics	2	1	
2	09/11/13	Thornton Hibs	Livingston United	2	3	
2	09/11/13	St Andrews United	Glenrothes	5	4	
2	21/12/13	Musselburgh Athletic	Camelon	0	3	
2	29/03/14	Tayport	Fauldhouse United	3	0	
2	29/03/14	Whitburn	Hill of Beath Hawthorn	1	5	at Whitburn Academy
3	05/04/14	Carnoustie Panmure	Blairgowrie	3	2	
3	19/04/14	Dalkeith Thistle	Sauchie	1	3	
3	07/05/14	Hill of Beath Hawthorn	Kinnoull	4	1	
3	28/04/14	Camelon	Livingston United	2	0	
3	19/04/14	Arniston Rangers	Bonnyrigg Rose	3	1	
3	26/04/14	Penicuik Athletic	Bo'ness United	2	2	3-4 pens
3	29/03/14	Tayport	Fauldhouse United	3	0	
3	01/03/14	St Andrews United	Linlithgow Rose	6	0	
QF	10/05/14	Tayport	St Andrews United	2	1	
QF	21/05/14	Sauchie	Hill of Beath Hawthorn	1	1	4-3 pens
QF	24/05/14	Camelon	Carnoustie Panmure	3	0	
QF	10/05/14	Arniston Rangers	Bo'ness United	4	2	

Recent East of Scotland Cup Finals

Season	Winners	Runners Up	Score	Venue	
1955/6	Loanhead Mayflower	Haddington Athletic	2-1	Tynecastle Park, Edinburgh	
1956/7	Haddington Athletic	Newtongrange Star	2-0	Easter Road, Edinburgh	
1957/8	Newtongrange Star	Arniston Rangers	2-0	Tynecastle Park, Edinburgh	
1958/9	Newtongrange Star	Musselburgh Athletic	5-3	Easter Road, Edinburgh	
1959/60	Tranent	Broxburn Athletic	1-0	Tynecastle Park, Edinburgh	
1960/1	Dunbar United	Bo'ness United	2-0	Easter Road, Edinburgh	
1961/2	Armadale Thistle	Arniston Rangers	2-1	Tynecastle Park, Edinburgh	
1962/3	Bonnyrigg Rose	Tranent	3-1		Replay
1963/4	Dunbar United	Bo'ness United	6-1	Olive Bank, Musselburgh	2nd Replay
1964/5	Linlithgow Rose	Armadale Thistle	3-1	Tynecastle Park, Edinburgh	
1965/6	Whitburn	Tranent	3-1	Easter Road, Edinburgh	
1966/7	Dalkeith Thistle	Newtongrange Star	2-0	Tynecastle Park, Edinburgh	
1967/8	Linlithgow Rose	Arniston Rangers	4-1	Tynecastle Park, Edinburgh	
1968/9	Whitburn	Bo'ness United	1-0	Tynecastle Park, Edinburgh	
1969/70	Whitburn	Newtongrange Star	3-0	Prestonfield, Linlithgow	Replay
1970/1	Arniston Rangers	Camelon	6-2	Meadowbank Stadium, Edinburgh	
1971/2	Dalkeith Thistle	Musselburgh Athletic	1-0	Newbyres Park, Gorebridge	Replay
1972/3	Haddington Athletic	Linlithgow Rose	1-0	Tynecastle Park, Edinburgh	
1973/4	Whitburn	Sauchie	2-1	Firs Park, Falkirk	
1974/5	Newtongrange Star	Broxburn Athletic	3-1	Olive Bank, Musselburgh	Replay
1975/6	Linlithgow Rose	Newtongrange Star	4-1	Tynecastle Park, Edinburgh	
1976/7	Newtongrange Star	Bonnyrigg Rose	1-0	Olive Bank, Musselburgh	
1977/8	Linlithgow Rose	Bonnyrigg Rose	3-2	Newbyres Park, Gorebridge	Replay
1978/9	Tranent	Camelon	3-1	Prestonfield, Linlithgow	
1979/80	Newtongrange Star	Penicuik Athletic	1-0	Newbyres Park, Gorebridge	
1980/1	Arniston Rangers	Newtongrange Star	3-2	New Dunas Park, Bonnyrigg	
1981/2	Newtongrange Star	Camelon	2-0	Prestonfield, Linlithgow	
1982/3	Sauchie	Camelon	2-1	Prestonfield, Linlithgow	
1983/4	Ormiston Primrose	Bo'ness United	4-1	Prestonfield, Linlithgow	Replay
1984/5	Bo'ness United	Linlithgow Rose	3-1	Newtown Park, Bo'ness	Replay
1985/6	Bonnyrigg Rose	Linlithgow Rose	3-1	Forresters Park, Tranent	
1986/7	Bonnyrigg Rose	Whitburn	2-1 AET	Prestonfield, Linlithgow	
1987/8	Broxburn Athletic	Linlithgow Rose	2-1 AET	Central Park Whitburn	Replay
1988/9	Linlithgow Rose	Broxburn Athletic	3-0	Central Park, Whitburn	
1989/90	Dunbar United	Whitburn	2-1	Forresters Park, Tranent	
1990/1	Linlithgow Rose	Bo'ness United	4-3	Central Park, Whitburn	
1991/2	Newtongrange Star	Whitburn	2-0	Newbyres Park, Gorebridge	
1992/3	Linlithgow Rose	Fauldhouse United	2-0	Volunteer Park, Armadale	
1993/4	Camelon	Livingston United	2-1	Prestonfield, Linlithgow	
1994/5	Ormiston Primrose	Dunbar United	2-1	Newbyres Park, Gorebridge	
1995/6	Linlithgow Rose	Camelon	3-0	Newtown Park, Bo'ness	
1996/7	Newtongrange Star	Bo'ness United	3-, 3-1 pens	Recreation Park, Pumpherston	
1997/8	Whitburn	Bonnybridge	2-0	Prestonfield, Linlithgow	
1998/9	Bo'ness United	Whitburn	2-0	Prestonfield, Linlithgow	
1999/00	Linlithgow Rose	Bo'ness United	2-1	Carmuirs Park, Camelon	
2000/1	Linlithgow Rose	Harthill Royal	5-0	Station Park, Livingston	
2001/2	Whitburn	Musselburgh Athletic	2-1	Newbyres Park, Gorebridge	
2002/3	Bonnyrigg Rose	Musselburgh Athletic	5-3	Newbyres Park, Gorebridge	
2003/4	Linlithgow Rose	Whitburn	1-0	Albyn Park, Broxburn	
2004/5	Linlithgow Rose	Newtongrange Star	1-0	Carmuirs Park, Camelon	
2005/6	Bonnyrigg Rose	Hill of Beath Hawthorn	2-1	Volunteer Park, Armadale	
2006/7	Bathgate Thistle	Rosyth	3-0	Recreation Park, Rosyth	
2007/8	Camelon	Bonnyrigg Rose	4-0	Prestonfield, Linlithgow	
2008/9	Lochee United	Glenrothes	3-0	Canniepairt, Tayport	
2009/10	Linlithgow Rose	Musselburgh Athletic	2-1	Creamery Park, Bathgate	
2010/1	Newtongrange Star	Dundee North End	2-0	Central Park, Kelty	
2011/2	St Andrews United	Kinnoull	2-1	Keir's Park, Hill of Beath	
2012/3	Bonnyrigg Rose	Linlithgow Rose	3-0	Creamery Park, Bathgate	
2013/4	Sauchie	Arniston Rangers	4-1	Prestonfield, Linlithgow	

The East of Scotland Junior Cup is now played for by all the member clubs of the East Region - from Montrose in the North to Dunbar in the South. In the 2013/14 season there were 64 clubs in the draw with Steelend Vics playing their First Round game before folding.

The Cup was expanded to its current format from 2004/5. Immediately before that it was a "Lothians" competition with Fife and Tayside having their own Junior Cups. If you go back long enough in history then Fife and Tayside clubs did play in the competition up to World War One - Denbeath Star won the Cup in 1916/17 and Brechin Harp reached the Final in 1903/4.

FINAL TIE 2013/14 - SPONSORED BY D J LAING
Sauchie v Arniston Rangers
June 14, at Prestonfield
4-1, Att c.700

At one point in the preceding week it seemed as if the Cup might be awarded to Arniston without a ball being kicked. Sauchie had a number of players going away on a pre-arranged stag do and the club asked for a change of date. They were unhappy as they felt that other ties could have been played earlier to accommodate an en earlier date for the Final. However, no change was permitted and Sauchie took the field minus several regulars, and with at least one who had driven from Manchester on the morning of the game.

Arniston: Ritchie, Brady, Forbes, Callaghan, Moriarty, Garden, McInally, Thomson, Court, Kataleza, Moffat. Subs Aitken, Lucas, Newll, McCaul, Marshall (Manager Stephen Osborne)
Sauchie: Halliwell, Munro, Syme, King, Kiczynski, McCulloch, Martin, Stevenson, Hendrie, Cummings, Samuel. Subs Tully, Bonnes, Docherty, Jackson (Manager Fraser Duncan)

1-0	21 mins	Darren Cummings
1-1	27 mins	Tadg Moriarty
2-1	37 mins	Darren Cummings
3-1	72 mins	Callum Hendrie
4-1	90+4 mins	Collin Samuel

Fife and Lothians Junior Cup 2013/14

1	05/10/13	Fauldhouse United	Ballingry Rovers	1	2	
1	05/10/13	Blackburn United	Dundonald Bluebell	2	3	
1	05/10/13	Rosyth	Sauchie	2	3	
1	05/10/13	Whitburn	St Andrews United	2	2	4-1 pens
1	05/10/13	Hill of Bath Hawthorn	Armadale Thistle	2	1	
1	05/10/13	Lochore Welfare	Stoneyburn	2	2	3-2 pens
1	05/10/13	Dunbar United	Glenrothes	1	1	1-3 pens
1	05/10/13	Arniston Rangers	Steelend Vics	wo	scr	
1	30/11/13	Newburgh	Falkirk	4	1	
1	18/01/14	Livingston United	Thornton Hibs	4	2	
2	05/10/13	Edinburgh United	Musselburgh Athletic	1	1	2-3 pens
2	09/11/13	Camelon	Harthill Royal	9	1	
2	23/11/13	Tranent	Whitburn	1	3	
2	30/11/13	Glenrothes	Bathgate Thistle	2	1	
2	30/11/13	Lochgelly Albert	Broxburn Athletic	3	5	
2	14/12/13	Arniston Rangers	Sauchie	3	2	
2	14/12/13	Ballingry Rovers	Newburgh	7	0	
2	14/12/13	Dalkeith Thistle	Newtongrange Star	1	1	4-3pens
2	14/12/13	Kirkcaldy YM	Dundonald Bluebell	2	4	
2	14/12/13	Lochore Welfare	Kennoway Star Hearts	5	6	
2	14/12/13	Oakley United	Penicuik Athleic	1	2	
2	18/01/14	West Calder United	Linlithgow Rose	1	4	
2	18/01/14	Pumpherston	Kelty Hearts	0	6	
2	15/03/14	Bonnyrigg Rose	Hill of Beath Hawthorn	1	1	2-3 pens
2	01/03/14	Bo'ness United	Crossgates Primrose	4	0	
2	01/03/14	Livingston United	Haddington Athletic	3	3	5-6 pens
3	15/03/14	Whitburn	Kelty Hearts	1	4	
3	29/03/14	Dalkeith Thistle	Linlithgow Rose	1	3	
3	29/03/14	Haddington Athletic	Dundonald Bluebell	4	0	
3	29/03/14	Penicuik Athletic	Ballingry Rovers	3	3	2-4 pens
3	15/04/14	Hill of Beath Hawthorn	Kennoway Star Hearts	2	2	7-6 pens
3	05/05/14	Camelon	Glenrothes	4	2	
3	01/03/14	Musselburgh	Broxburn Athletic	2	2	2-3 pens
3	05/05/14	Arniston Rangers	Bo'ness Utd	0	2	
QF	12/04/14	Haddington Athletic	Kelty Hearts	1	5	
QF	19/05/14	Camelon	Bo'ness	1	4	
QF	12/05/14	Ballingry Rovers	Hill of Beath Hawthorn	0	2	
QF	19/04/14	Broxburn Athletic	Linlithgow Rose	1	2	
SF	26/05/14	Bo'ness United	Kelty Hearts	2	0	
SF	26/05/14	Linlithgow Rose	Hill of Beath Hawthorn	1	0	
F	06/06/14	Bo'ness United	Linlithgow Rose	1	2	at Newtown Park

Recent Fife and Lothians Cup Finals

Season	Winners	Runners Up	Score	Venue
1986/7	Whitburn	Oakley United	3-0 AET	Prestonfield, Linlithgow
1987/8	Newtongrange Star	Kelty Hearts	1-0	Prestonfield, Linlithgow
1988/9	Edinburgh United	Camelon	1-1, 3-1 pens	Prestonfield, Linlithgow
1989/90	Newtongrange Star	Bo'ness United	2-0	Prestonfield, Linlithgow
1990/1	Newtongrange Star	Linlithgow Rose	2-1 aet	Newtown Park, Bo'ness
1991/2	Whitburn	Livingston United	2-1	Albyn Park, Broxburn
1992/3	Fauldhouse United	Bathgate Thistle	1-0	Volunteer Park, Armadale
1993/4	Bo'ness United	Hill of Beath Hawthorn	2-1	Carmuirs Park, Camelon
1994/5	St Andrews United	Hill of Beath Hawthorn	4-3	Warout Stadium, Glenrothes
1995/6	Hill of Beath Hawthorn	Whitburn	1-0	Prestonfield, Linlithgow
1996/7	Bo'ness United	Bonnybridge	3-1	Carmuirs Park, Camelon
1997/8	Arniston Rangers	Haddington Athletic	1-0	New Dundas Park, Bonnyrigg
1998/9	Whitburn	Bo'ness United	3-2 aet	Prestonfield, Linlithgow
1999/00	Linlithgow Rose	Stoneyburn	4-1	Carmuirs Park, Camelon
2000/1	Linlithgow Rose	Whitburn	5-1	Carmuirs Park, Camelon
2001/2	Linlithgow Rose	Hill of Beath Hawthorn	6-5	Carmuirs Park, Camelon
2002/3	Sauchie	Glenrothes	5-3	Carmuirs Park, Camelon
2003/4	Sauchie	Linlithgow Rose	4-0	Central Park, Whitburn
2004/5	Bonnyrigg Rose	St Andrews United	1-0	Central Park, Whitburn
2005/6	Camelon	Kelty Hearts	2-1 aet	Prestonfield, Linlithgow
2006/7	Bonnyrigg Rose	Musselburgh Athletic	2-0	Prestonfield, Linlithgow
2007/8	Camelon	Hill of Beath Hawthorn	5-0	Prestonfield, Linlithgow
2008/9	Linlithgow Rose	Thornton Hibs	1-0	Keir's Park, Hill of Beath
2009/10	Bathgate Thistle	Musselburgh Athletic	1-0	New Victoria Park, Newtongrange
2010/1	Linlithgow Rose	Bo'ness United	2-1	Prestonfield, Linlithgow
2011/2	Linlithgow Rose	Broxburn Athletic	3-1	Newtown Park, Bo'ness
2012/3	Linlithgow Rose	Camelon	5-3	Creamery Park, Bathgate
2013/4	Linlithgow Rose	Bo'ness United	2-1	Newtown Park, Bo'ness

The Fife and Lothians Cup was played for between 1934 and 1940 but then lapsed. It was revived in 1968 and has been played for continuously since then.

FINAL TIE 2013/14 - Sponsored by Dechmont Forklift Trucks
Bo'ness United v Linlithgow Rose, 1-2,
June 6, at Newtown Park
1-2, Att c.1900

The teams tossed a coin for choice of venue.

Bo'ness United: Peat, Devine (Miller), Hunter, Murphy, Donnelly, Jaconelli, Nimmo, Walker, Sloan, Hislop (Anderson), Gribben (Craig Scott) (Manager Allan McGonnigal)
Linlithgow Rose: Christie, Tyrell, McKillen, MacKenzie, Ovenstone, Nelson (Strickland) Shirra, Ruari MacLennan (Smith), Roddy MacLennan, Diack, Coyne (Meechan) (Manager Danny Smith)

1-0	26 mins	Nicky Walker
1-1	86 mins	Roddy McLennan
1-2	90 mins	Ian Diack

At the end of the season the Secretary of the Fife and Lothians FA, Ronnie Ross, retired after 54 years as a Junior official. He has been Secretary of Lochgelly Albert, the Fife Region and most recently the Fife and Lothians FA and is recognised by all as the grand old man of Fife Junior football.

NORTH JUNIORS

The structure of Junior football in the North was changed for 2013/14 as a result of the loss of a couple of clubs. This meant that the three division vertical structure had a very small third tier. It was decided to switch to a Super League with two parallel First Divisions (East and West). This served the double of purpose of providing decent sized leagues and reducing travel costs for some clubs.

In recent times several clubs have moved from the North Juniors into the Highland League. Inverurie Locos, Turriff United and Formartine United have enjoyed considerable success at Highland League level but Strathspey Thistle have found the transition more difficult. However, it is cleart that the top North Junior clubs are more than capable of handling themselves against Highland League opposition.

North Junior Super League   2013/14

	BST	BOD	C	DEV	DYC	EE	EU	FCS	HRU	H	L	M	NE	S
Banchory St Ternan		Sep 21 0-4	Mar 8 1-4	Apr 5 0-3	Nov 16 0-5	Dec 28 3-0	Aug 31 1-0	Sep 28 2-2	Aug 13 1-6	Aug 24 1-4	Mar 15 3-3	May 3 0-1	Feb 22 1-0	Apr 19 2-2
Banks o' Dee	Mar 1 6-2		Mar 12 1-3	Mar 26 2-0	Jan 4 3-1	Apr 26 4-1	Dec 7 1-0	Nov 16 4-1	Mar 21 6-1	Nov 2 3-3	Jan 11 8-2	Aug 6 2-2	Feb 8 3-1	Aug 20 6-0
Culter	Apr 26 8-2	Dec 28 2-1		May 10 3-1	May 20 3-1	Feb 8 4-0	Nov 16 2-1	Mar 22 7-3	Oct 12 3-1	Mar 1 1-2	Aug 24 6-0	Dec 21 2-2	Jan 18 5-1	Apr 22 2-1
Deveronside	Sep 14 5-1	Dec 14 2-5	Feb 1 1-4		May 17 2-1	Mar 22 4-1	Oct 5 1-1	Mar 1 2-2	Nov 2 0-1	Aug 3 4-3	Dec 28 2-1	Apr 29 2-0	Apr 26 2-4	May 3 1-0
Dyce	Mar 22 2-3	Apr 5 0-5	Nov 30 2-2	Oct 19 3-0		Aug 13 5-1	Nov 2 3-2	Apr 19 4-2	Jan 18 4-2	May 10 1-8	Mar 8 4-2	Aug 31 3-0	Dec 28 5-1	Nov 9 0-1
East End	Jan 25 1-3	Aug 24 3-3	Dec 14 0-3	Jan 4 1-1	Feb 1 1-3		Mar 1 1-0	Nov 16 1-3	Apr 22 1-2	Aug 22 1-1	Feb 22 0-1	Jan 11 0-2	Apr 5 1-0	2-0
Ellon United	Jan 18 1-3	Apr 19 1-0	Feb 22 2-4	Aug 13 2-2	Apr 26 3-1	Nov 9 1-2		Sep 14 4-2	Oct 19 3-1	Dec 28 4-1	Mar 29 0-1	Nov 23 1-3	Sep 7 0-1	Mar 22 2-0
FC Stoneywood	Feb 8 1-0	Mar 8 3-4+	Nov 23 0-1	Dec 21 2-2	Aug 20 0-1	Jan 18 5-1	Nov 30 4-5		Apr 5 0-1	Sep 21 1-4	Sep 7 4-1	Jan 4 3-3	Aug 24 1-1	Oct 12 2-1
Hall Russell United	Dec 14 1-4	Nov 9 0-3	Mar 29 1-4	Mar 8 1-3	Aug 24 2-3	Apr 19 2-2	Jan 4 2-0	Oct 5 1-2		May 1 3-3	Sep 21 2-0	May 17 0-3	Nov 23 1-2	Mar 1 0-1
Hermes	Jan 4 4-2	Apr 29 1-0	May 6 2-5	Mar 11 0-3	Dec 14 2-3	Aug 31 5-1	Apr 5 3-1	Jan 11 1-0	Aug 20 2-3		Mar 22 3-0	Aug 9 3-2	May 3 4-1	Oct 5 2-3
Longside	Nov 2 4-2	Oct 5 0-8	Jan 4 0-4	Jan 18 0-2	Nov 23 0-3	Feb 15 3-5	Aug 20 0-1	Dec 14 1-1	Nov 30 1-3	Oct 19 0-4		Apr 5 1-2	Mar 1 1-0	Sep 14 2-5
Maud	Nov 30 4-2	Jan 18 3-1	Apr 19 0-3	Aug 20 4-2	Mar 1 0-2	Oct 5 1-1	May 6 5-4	Nov 2 1-1	Dec 28 2-4	Mar 15 2-2	Nov 16 6-0		Sep 28 3-4	Dec 14 2-1
New Elgin	Oct 5 3-3	Nov 30 2-2	Aug 31 0-1	Aug 6 1-1	Mar 29 0-2	Nov 2 2-2	Dec 14 0-1	Feb 1 3-2	Feb 15 2-1	Nov 16 2-2	Nov 9 3-1	Mar 22 1-1		Jan 4 5-0
Stonehaven	Oct 19 4-3	Mar 29 1-1	Apr 29 2-1	Nov 16 3-2	May 6 2-1	Mar 8 3-3	Sep 28 0-0	Dec 28 2-2	Sep 7 0-2	Jan 18 1-5	Feb 22 3-2	Apr 26 1-1	Sep 21 4-0	

+ at Ellon

	P	W	D	L	F	A	GD	PTS
1. Culter	26	22	2	2	87	28	59	68
2. Banks o' Dee	26	16	5	5	86	35	51	53
3. Dyce Juniors	26	17	1	8	65	42	23	52
4. Hermes	26	15	5	6	74	45	29	50
5. Maud	26	11	8	7	53	45	8	41
6. Deveronside	26	11	6	9	50	46	4	39
7. Stonehaven	26	11	6	9	41	47	-6	39
8. New Elgin	26	9	7	10	44	51	-7	34
9. Hall Russell United	26	10	2	14	44	55	-11	32
10. Ellon United	26	8	3	15	37	48	-11	27
11. Banchory St Ternan	26	7	4	15	45	78	-33	25
12. FC Stoneywood	26	5	8	13	48	60	-12	23
13. East End	26	5	7	14	33	64	-31	22
14. Longside	26	2	2	22	25	88	-63	8

CULTER FC SQUAD 2013/14

Allan Youngson	Andrew Sim
Darryn Kelly	Davie Greig
Frank Smyth	George McBain
Grant Pennet	Hugh Robertson
Ian Leith	Jamie McAllister
Kieran Fowler	Lee Murray
Lewis McKimmie	Mark Robinson
Martin Crisp	Michael Taylor
Murray Rattray	Neil Duffy
Neil Reid	Philip McKibben
Richard Shand	Scott McArthur
Shaun Taylor	Steve Rintoul

Manager: Andy Gibson (resigned June 2014)

NORTH SUPER LEAGUE - ALL TIME GRID	2001-2	2002-3	2003-4	2004-5	2005-6	2006-7	2007-8	2008-9	2009-10	2010-11	2011-12	2012-13	2013-14
Banchory St Ternan								5	3	6	7	10	11
Banks o' Dee	5	8	6	6	3	3	1	1	5	4	5	4	2
Buchanhaven Hearts	14							13					
Cruden Bay	10	12	13										
Culter	2	2	1	1	1	1	3	3	2	1	4	1	1
Deveronside	13	14										5	6
Dyce						6	6	4	4	5	3	2	3
East End	6	4	11	12			9	9	14				13
Ellon United			13	7	12	5		10	10	11	8	9	10
FC Stoneywood	3	5	12	8	14				12	12	6	6	12
Formartine United	1	6	7	4	2	7	13						
Forres Thistle											13		
Fraserburgh United					13					14		14	
Glentanar	12	10	3	2	9	14							
Hall Russell United									11	2	10	12	9
Hermes	7	11	8	9	6	9	12	7	6	3	1	3	4
Islavale							13						
Lads Club		9	14										
Lewis United									11	8	8	11	13
Longside	9	3	10	5	11	8	11	6	9	13	9	11	14
Maud				14			4	8	7	9	12	8	5
New Elgin													8
Parkvale					12	10	14						
Stonehaven	8	7	4	11	10	4	8	14		10	2	7	7
Sunnybank	4	1	2	7	5	2	2	2	1	7	14		
Turriff United			5	3	8	5	7	12					
Wilsons XI / Hillhead	11	13	9	10	4	11	10	13					

Culter retained their North Super League crown and made it an impressive three titles in four years. Manager Andy Gibson, the former Aberdeen player, stepped down at the end of the season. Many people expected him to move into the Cove Rangers job but that did not come about.

The top four was made up of Banks o' Dee, Hermes and Dyce. These four clubs have had a firm grip on the Super League in recent years and have firmly established themselves as leading lights in the North. It's worthy of note that the Aberdeen area clubs should hold the first four places some distance ahead of the "provincial" clubs of Maud, Deveronside and Stonehaven.

New Elgin did well in their first venture at Super League level and looked comfortable in this Division. Longside were stranded from early on and ended an unbroken period of membership of the top flight. East End went down with them.

FC Stoneywood finally lost their quirky ground with its distinctive grandstand to housing development. They have moved to New Polo Park and will ne hoping to move forwards now that any uncertainty about their future has been removed.

North Junior First Division (West)   2013/14

Team	BR	BT	D	F	FT	IC	I	NSN	PV	W
Buckie Rovers		Jan 4	Nov 16	Aug 6	Oct 19	Nov 30	Sep 7	Oct 5	Dec 14	Aug 24
		1-3	4-1	2-1	1-4	1-3	0-2	3-0	0-5	2-5
		Feb 8		Mar 1		Mar 22		Feb 22	Feb 1	
		1-1		4-1		0-3		0-3	1-3	
Burghead Thistle	Sep 21		Aug 3	Nov 30	Feb 1	Oct 19	Jan 11	Mar 29	Nov 9	Dec 28
	1-3		0-0	0-2	1-1>	2-8	2-4	2-1	5-0	2-1
			Apr 26		Mar 1		May 3			Feb 22
			1-0		1-0		5-5			4-1
Dufftown	Sep 28	May 10		Aug 24	Sep 14	Dec 14	Aug 20	Nov 23	Nov 2	Oct 5
	1-0	3-1		5-0	1-2	2-2	3-3	3-0	4-1	8-1
	Jan 11			Mar 22			Mar 8	Apr 29	Apr 19	
	2-1			10-0			2-0	3-1		
Fochabers	Oct 26	Oct 5	Nov 9		Dec 14	Aug 31	Nov 2	Sep 21	Oct 19	Nov 23
	2-6	0-3	1-4		2-4	1-5	1-11	2-1	0-2	6-3
			Mar 8		Feb 8			Apr 5		Feb 1
	2-8				1-5			3-5		0-3
Forres Thistle	Aug 31	Aug 6	Nov 30	Oct 12		Nov 23	Dec 28	Nov 2	Sep 21	Sep 28
	1-3	0-4	0-2	4-0		2-2	0-2	3-2	3-1	3-1
	Jan 18		Feb 22			Jan 11	Apr 22			
	2-1		1-5			1-2	2-3			
Inverness City	Oct 12	Nov 16	Sep 21	Jan 4	Aug 13		Oct 26	Aug 6	Oct 5	Jan 18
	3-1	3-1	4-5	6-1	5-2		3-0	3-2	1-1	9-0
			Apr 19		Feb 22			Apr 12	Feb 8	Mar 15
			2-1		8-1			4-3	3-1	3-1
Islavale	Dec 21	Dec 14	Jan 4	Aug 13	Nov 9	Mar 1		Nov 16	Sep 14	Oct 19
	3-2	3-2	1-2	1-1	3-2	1-0		4-1	5-1	7-3
	Apr 19		Jan 18			Apr 26		Mar 8		
	0-2		4-0			2-5		1-0		
Nairn St Ninian	Dec 28	Aug 13	Oct 12	Feb 15	Aug 20	Nov 9	Feb 8		Nov 30	Aug 31
	1-2	2-2	1-2	5-2	0-1	0-2	3-2		2-3	3-1
	Mar 22				Mar 15				Jan 4	Mar 1
	0-4				0-2				1-0	5-0
Portgordon Victoria	Aug 20	Aug 24	Aug 31	Nov 16	Dec 7	Dec 28	Nov 23	Sep 28		Oct 12
	2-0	5-0	1-1	4-1	0-0	2-3*	1-2	5-1		4-2
	Feb 15	Jan 18	Dec 21	Mar 8			Mar 22			
	2-6+	1-0+	3-2	1-2+			0-0+			
Whitehills	Nov 9	Sep 14	Feb 8	Aug 20	Nov 16	Nov 2	Nov 30	Dec 14	Aug 17	
	1-3	1-3	2-2	1-4	3-1	2-6	1-4	0-5	3-4	
	Mar 8		Apr 12		Jan 4		Apr 5		Jan 11	
	1-0		0-2		0-3		1-2		0-4	

* at Nicol Togneri Park
+ at Pinefield
> at Lossie Playing Fields

		P	W	D	L	F	A	PTS
1	Inverness City	27	22	3	2	100	36	69
2	Dufftown	27	17	5	5	72	31	56
3	Islavale	27	17	4	6	75	45	55
4	Burghead Thistle	27	13	5	9	65	51	44
5	Portgordon Victoria	27	13	4	10	57	48	43
6	Forres Thistle	27	13	3	11	51	47	42
7	Buckie Rovers	27	10	1	16	44	55	31
8	Nairn St Ninian	27	8	1	18	48	59	22*
9	Whitehills	27	4	1	22	38	99	13
10	Fochabers	27	4	1	22	37	116	13

* 3 pts deducted for fielding ineligible player

Recent finishing positions in Divisions One and Two are included below.

North Juniors First Division 2003-2013

	2003-4	2004-5	2005-6	2006-7	2007-8	2008-9	2009-10	2010-11	2011-12	2012-13
Banchory St Ternan	6	4	6	3	1					
Bishopmill United							9	14		
Buchanhaven Hearts	8	9	12	5	4	1		5	11	13
Buckie Rovers	9					12	7	13	14	
Burghead Thistle	12	11	14					12	13	11
Cruden Bay		13	8	13	13	14				
Deveronside	3	6	10					5	9	3
Dufftown	13	12	11	10	10	13	13	11	12	
Dyce	10	7	1							
East End				5	1			10	5	2
Ellon United	2									
FC Stoneywood					11	12	4			
Formartine United						2				
Forres Thistle				7	9	8	11	2		10
Fraserburgh United	5	2		9	11	6	1		2	
Glentanar					7	11	4	3	4	4
Hall Russell United	4	10	13	12	8	5				
Hillhead / Bridge of Don Thistle							10	8	8	12
Inverness City							2	1	1	3
Islavale		3	2		6	9	12	6	9	5
Lads Club		8	7	6	3					
Lewis United	11	5	4	4	2					
Lossiemouth United						7	6	7	10	14
Maud	1		3	2						
Nairn St Ninian					14					9
New Elgin							8	4	6	1
Parkvale	7	1					10	14	7	6
Portgordon Vics										7
Stonehaven								3		
Strathspey Thistle					9	8	5	3		
Sunnybank										8
Whitehills	14									

North Juniors Second Division 2003-2013

	2003-4	2004-5	2005-6	2006-7	2007-8	2008-9	2009-10	2010-11	2011-12	2012-13
Bishopmill United	9	6	7	5	1	4		7		
Buckie Rovers		5	3	3						2
Burghead Thistle				8	5	5	1			
Colony Park							4	1		
Cruden Bay							5	7	5	4
Deveronside						6	3			
Fochabers	7	3	3	1	Ab	6	3	5	9	5
Forres Thistle	3	2	2							
Inverness City							1			
Islavale	1									
Kinloss	10	9	9							
Lossiemouth United	5	7	6	4	2					
Nairn St Ninian	6	5	4	2			7	2	4	2
New Elgin	4	1	1	6	4	2				
Newmachar United								2	3	3
Parkvale							1			
Portgordon Victoria								1		
RAF Lossiemouth	8	8	8	9	7	8	4	6	8	
Strathspey Thistle	2	4								
Whitehills		10	10	7	8	9	6	3	6	6

Prior to 2013/14 Inverness City's progress and ambitions were repeatedly thwarted by their lack of a home ground. That problem was finally solved when the club moved into a new facility adjacent to the Bught Park on the south side of the city. Their new home is known as Lister Park. This means they can take their promotion to the Super League, bringing this level of Junior football to Inverness for the first time.

They won their league by some distance, ahead of Dufftown and Islavale.

Portgordon Victoria found themselves thrown out of their ground midway through the season following a dispute over the lease. This relates to the previous Portgordon Juniors club and some uncertainty as to whether the two entities are one and the same thing, or not. Vics hope to play at the Linzee Gordon Park in Buckie for 2014/15.

Fochabers have opted to go into abeyance for 2014/15 but Lossiemouth United are returning to the fold after a year out. Sadly Bishopmill United, one of the oldest names in North Junior football, will not be returning.

Two new clubs were admitted to this division at the North Region AGM, subject to ratification at the Scottish Junior FA AGM on June 21st. Spey Valley Juniors will play at Cromdale and Grantown Juniors at Nethy Bridge.

INVERNESS CITY SQUAD 2013/14

Alan Kerr	Andy Devlin	Paul McDonald
Calum Neill	Chris McLeod	Steven McGregor
Colin Masson	Danny Murdoch	David Harrison
Duncan Lamont	Eddie Fuller	Finlay McLeod
Gary Anderson	Gary Miller	Graham Stewart
Iain Hughes	Iain Young	John MacLeod
Keith Mason	Kevin Fraser	Jordan MacDonald
Luke McKay	Mark Kennedy	Kelvin MacKenzie
Martin Clark	Michael Corbett	Mark McLennan
Michael Turner	Ross Thomson	Michael McKenzie
Ben Hosie	Stuart Pearce	Steven MacLennan
Chris Moir	Stuart Thomson	

North Junior First Division (East)   2013/14

	BDT	BH	CP	CB	FU	G	LU	NMU	P	S
Bridge of Don Thistle		Nov 9	Dec 14	Apr 12	Jan 4	Mar 29	Sep 7	Nov 16	Aug 17	Oct 12
		2-0	1-0	1-3	0-0*	1-1	0-0	4-0	2-2	4-1
			Feb 15	Mar 8		Apr 26			Apr 29	
			6-3	2-1		3-1			5-0	
Buchanhaven Hearts	Dec 28		Sep 21	Aug 20	Aug 13	Nov 16	Nov 30	Oct 12	Dec 14	Aug 31
	0-3		1-6	0-3	3-3	1-5	2-3	2-1	0-0	0-3
				Mar 22		Mar 1	Jan 18	May 6		Feb 8
				0-2		2-2	5-1	5-3		8-1
Colony Park	Aug 24	Nov 2		Nov 9	Oct 12	Oct 5	Aug 20	Jan 4	Sep 14	Oct 19
	2-4	12-2		1-1	8-1	4-1	5-0	3-1	1-1	1-3
		Mar 15		Mar 1	Mar 29					Jan 18
		1-1		1-2	1-0					1-0
Cruden Bay	Jan 18	Apr 5	Aug 31		Apr 19	Dec 28	Sep 14	Oct 19	Jan 4	Nov 16
	0-3	2-0	1-1		2-1	1-1	4-3	4-0	3-3	5-2
					Apr 29	Feb 22		Apr 26	Mar 29	Mar 15
					4-0	2-3		3-1	5-1	1-0
Fraserburgh United	Nov 2	Nov 23	Jan 11	Sep 7		Aug 24	Nov 9	Sep 14	May 10	Dec 28
	3-2	6-2	1-3	0-3		2-6	1-2	2-1	4-2	4-1
		Mar 8				Mar 22		Apr 5		Feb 22
		4-3				1-5		8-1		2-3
Glentanar	Sep 14	Oct 19	Nov 30	Aug 6	Dec 14		Jan 4	Sep 7	Nov 9	Aug 10
	1-4	11-3	3-2	1-1	2-5		5-2	7-1	3-2	3-0
	Apr 5		Feb 8				Mar 8	Apr 19	Jan 18	
	1-1		3-4				5-3	2-2	0-0	
Lewis United	Nov 23	Oct 5	Nov 16	Jan 11	Sep 21	Oct 12		Dec 28	Aug 31	Dec 14
	2-2	6-3	3-3	3-1	2-1	4-4		3-2	1-1	1-1
	Mar 15		Feb 22	Feb 8	Jan 25				May 1	
	1-6		2-3	2-3	4-1				0-1+	
Newmachar United	Aug 31	Feb 22	Sep 28	Dec 14	May 3	Nov 23	Nov 2		Oct 5	Nov 9
	1-2	5-6	3-4	2-3	2-1	2-2	1-0		1-3	4-3
	Mar 22		Apr 12				Mar 1		Mar 15	
	2-5		2-2				0-0		1-2	
Parkvale	Apr 22	Sep 28	Dec 28	May 3	Nov 16	Aug 20	Apr 26	Nov 30		Apr 5
	2-2	2-2	1-2	1-3	2-4	1-5	3-0	0-0		1-3
		Apr 12	Mar 22		May 17					May 6
		1-1	2-4		3-1					2-0
Sunnybank	Nov 30	Jan 4	Aug 17	Sep 21	Oct 5	Nov 2	Sep 28	Aug 20	Nov 23	
	1-1	1-3	1-2	1-2	6-5	1-0	1-8	3-2	0-3	
	Mar 1					Feb 15	Mar 22	Apr 22		
	2-2					2-3	0-4	2-0		

* at Ellon
+ at Hillhead

		P	W	D	L	F	A	PTS
1.	Cruden Bay	27	18	5	4	65	34	59
2.	Bridge of Don Thistle	27	16	9	2	70	31	57
3.	Colony Park	27	15	6	6	78	43	51
4.	Glentanar	27	13	9	5	85	54	48
5.	Lewis United	27	8	7	12	59	65	31
6.	Parkvale	27	7	10	10	42	53	31
7.	Fraserburgh United	27	9	2	16	62	76	29
8.	Sunnybank	27	8	3	16	42	72	27
9.	Buchanhaven Hearts	27	7	6	14	59	94	27
10.	Newmachar United	27	3	5	19	41	81	14

Cruden Bay emerged as Champions after a close race with Bridge of Don Thistle. It is more than ten years since the Bay were last in the Super League. They are a well-run club and will be hopeful of making the transition with some success.

Aberdeen East End and Longisde will be joining the Division following their relegation from the Super League.

Aberdeen University were admitted to the North Region at their AGM but they will need to be ratified at the Scottish Junior FA AGM on June 21st. This development poses a problem for Bridge of Don Thistle. The two clubs have shared the University's Hillhead Stadium for several years now. The North Juniors have no objection to inter-association ground shares so long as the Junior team have prioroty. However, they do not sanction ground shares between two Junior clubs. Should Aberdeen University's application be endorsed then it seems likely that Bridge of Don Thistle will either be kicked out or have to find a new ground at very short notice.

CRUDEN BAY SQUAD 2013/14

Cammy Buchan
Chris Cameron
Craig Findlay
Craig MacIntosh
Dale Nicoll
Daniel Glendinning
Daniel Watson
Jamie Ramsay
Jason McKessick
Jordan Abolghassem
Jordan Sangster
Kevin Anderson
Kevin Park
Lee Inglis
Lee Lawrence
Lee Wilby
Lewis Sime
Liam Reid
Owen Tocher
Scott Buchan
Scott Wisely
Stuart Ferris

Dominos Pizza North Regional Cup draw, 2014/15

Preliminary Round
Burghead Thistle v Portgordon Victoria
Colony Park v Culter
New Elgin v Whitehills
Newmachar United v Bridge of Don Thistle
FC Stoneywood v Aberdeen University (provisional)

First Round
Colony Park or Culter v Deveronside
Lewis United v Islavale
East End v Stonehaven
Banchory St Ternan v Newmachar United or Bridge of Don Thistle
Banks o' Dee v Forres Thistle
Cruden Bay v Lossiemouth United
Sunnybank v Fraserburgh United
Parkvale v Ellon United
Nairn St Ninian v New Elgin or Whitehills
Glentanar v Buckie Rovers
FC Stoneywood or Aberdeen University v Maud
Buchanhaven Hearts v Spey Valley FC (provisional)
Dyce Juniors v Longside
Hall Russell United v Burghead Thistle or Portgordon Victoria
Grantown FC (provisional) v Inverness City
Hermes v Dufftown

GA ENGINEERING CUP (North and Tayside) CUP DRAW 2014/15

Preliminary Round (North)
Buckie Rovers v Fraserburgh United
Whitehills v Islavale
Newmachar United v FC Stoneywood
Grantown FC (provisional) v Hermes

First Round (North)
Forres Thistle v Grantown FC or Hermes
East End v Banchory St Ternan
Inverness City v Buchanhaven Hearts
Lewis United v Longside
Maud v Banks o' Dee
Hall Russell United v Ellon United
Parkvale v Buckie Rovers or Fraserburgh United
Cruden Bay v Burghead Thistle
Dyce Juniors v Lossiemouth United
Nairn St Ninian v Culter
Sunnybank v New Elgin
Spey Valley FC (provisional) v Stonehaven
Deveronside v Glentanar
Colony Park v Whitehills or Islavale
Dufftown v Bridge of Don Thistle
Newmachar United or FC Stoneywood v Portgordon Victoria

GRILL LEAGUE CUP DRAW 2014/15

Section 1: Ellon United, Hall Russell United, Lossiemouth United, Sunnybank, Grantown FC (provisional)

Section 2: Portgordon Victoria, Parkvale, Buchanhaven Hearts, Nairn St Ninian, Spey Valley FC (provisional)

Section 3: Islavale, Deveronside, Stonehaven, Longside, Burghead Thistle

Section 4: Banchory St Ternan, Dyce Juniors, Dufftown, FC Stoneywood, Fraserburgh United

Section 5: Culter, Maud, Bridge of Don Thistle, Banks o' Dee

Section 6: Whitehills, Cruden Bay, New Elgin, Hermes

Section 7: Glentanar, Colony Park, Forres Thistle, Newmachar United

Section 8: Buckie Rovers, Inverness City, Lewis United, East End

Only the section winners qualify for the quarter finals.

Grill League Cup   2013/14

Section 1

	HRU	I	M	S	W
Hall Russell United		Aug 17 4-6	Aug 10 2-4		
Islavale				Aug 31 2-2	Aug 6 3-1
Maud		Aug 24 7-2			Aug 13 7-0
Stonehaven	Aug 6 0-1		Aug 17 0-3		
Whitehills	Aug 3 0-6			Aug 10 1-11	

Section 1	P	W	D	L	F	A	PTS
Maud	4	4	0	0	21	4	12
Islavale	4	2	1	1	13	14	7
Hall Russell United	4	2	0	2	13	10	6
Stonehaven	4	1	1	2	13	7	4
Whitehills	4	0	0	4	2	27	0

Section 2

	BST	CB	C	H	NMU
Banchory St Ternan		Aug 3 2-1			Aug 6 4-0
Cruden Bay			Aug 10 0-2	Aug 17 0-3	
Culter	Aug 20 8-3			Aug 6 2-2	
Hermes	Aug 10 10-5				Aug 13 6-0
Newmachar United		Aug 24 0-1	Aug 17 0-8		

Section 2	P	W	D	L	F	A	PTS
Culter	4	3	1	0	20	5	10
Hermes	4	3	1	0	21	7	10
Banchory St Ternan	4	2	0	2	14	19	6
Cruden Bay	4	1	0	3	2	7	3
Newmachar United	4	0	0	4	0	19	0

Section 3

	CP	DU	DY	PV
Colony Park		Aug 10 3-1		
Dufftown			Aug 17 4-4	Aug 6 5-0
Dyce	Aug 6 2-1			
Portgordon Victoria	Aug 3 1-6		Aug 10 1-3	

Section 3	P	W	D	L	F	A	PTS
Dyce	3	2	1	0	9	6	7
Colony Park	3	2	0	1	10	4	6
Dufftown	3	1	1	1	10	7	4
Portgordon Victoria	3	0	0	3	2	14	0

Section 4

	BOD	BR	EU	L
Banks o' Dee			Aug 10 4-1	
Buckie Rovers	Aug 3 0-5			
Ellon United		Aug 17 7-2		Aug 6 0-1
Longside	Aug 13 1-7	Aug 10 6-0		

Section 4	P	W	D	L	F	A	PTS
Banks o' Dee	3	3	0	0	16	2	9
Longside	3	2	0	1	8	7	6
Ellon United	3	1	0	2	8	7	3
Buckie Rovers	3	0	0	3	2	18	0

Section 5

	FCS	F	IC	LU
FC Stoneywood		Aug 17 7-1		Aug 6 4-0
Fochabers			Aug 3 0-2*	
Inverness City	Aug 10 2-1			
Lewis United		Aug 10 10-1	Aug 17 0-3+	

Section 5	P	W	D	L	F	A	PTS
Inverness City	3	3	0	0	7	1	9
FC Stoneywood	3	2	0	1	12	3	6
Lewis United	3	1	0	2	10	8	3
Fochabers	3	0	0	3	2	19	0

* at Lossiemouth Playing Fields
+ at Uniconn Park

	BH	D	EE	FT
Buchanhaven Hearts		Aug 17 1-2		
Deveronside				Aug 24 3-0
East End	Aug 6 5-0	Aug 10 2-2		
Forres Thistle	Aug 10 0-0		Aug 3 2-3	

Section 6	P	W	D	L	F	A	PTS
East End	3	2	1	0	10	4	7
Deveronside	3	2	1	0	7	3	7
Buchanhaven Hearts	3	0	1	2	1	7	1
Forres Thistle	3	0	1	2	2	6	1

	G	NSN	P	S
Glentanar		Aug 17 2-4		
Nairn St Ninian			Aug 10 3-1	Aug 24 2-4
Parkvale	Aug 13 4-3			Aug 6 4-5
Sunnybank	Aug 3 3-1			

Section 7	P	W	D	L	F	A	PTS
Sunnybank	3	3	0	0	12	7	9
Nairn St Ninian	3	2	0	1	9	7	6
Parkvale	3	2	0	1	9	11	6
Glentanar	3	0	0	3	6	11	0

	BDT	BT	FU	NE
Bridge of Don Thistle		Aug 6 3-0		
Burghead Thistle	Aug 10 4-0			Aug 20 1-5
Fraserburgh United		Aug 17 2-2		Aug 10 2-4
New Elgin	Aug 3 4-0			

Section 8	P	W	D	L	F	A	PTS
New Elgin	3	3	0	0	13	3	9
Burghead Thistle	3	1	1	1	7	7	4
Bridge of Don Thistle	3	1	0	2	3	8	3
Fraserburgh United	3	0	1	2	4	9	1

QF	14/09/13	Inverness City	Maud	3 3 3-4 pens
QF	14/09/13	New Elgin	Sunnybank	4 1
QF	13/09/13	Banks o' Dee	Dyce	2 0
QF	28/09/13	East End	Culter	2 4

SF	19/10/13	Banks o' Dee	New Elgin	4 3
SF	19/10/13	Culter	Maud	4 1

F	12/11/13	Banks o' Dee	Culter	0 0 4-2 pens at Hillhead

Banks o' Dee lifted the first silverware of the season by edging out Culter on penalties following a goal-less ninety minutes at the Hillhead Centre. Keith Horne struck the winning spot kick after George McBain had put his penalty wide and Hugh Robertson had seen his effort kept out by sponsors man of the match Michael Smith. Both sides had close calls during the regulation time. Smith brilliantly kept out Alan Youngson's free kick while Jamie McAllister and Ian Leith both missed good first half chances for Culter while Ross Forsyth was inches away from opening the scoring for Dee. After the break Jindrich Biskup had the best chance for Dee, but fired just over for Dee, while at the other end Michael Taylor's deflected effort struck the post in stoppage time. (Attendance 300)

Banks o' Dee: Michael Smith, Joe Priestley, Robert Turnbull, Jordan Reid, Darren Forbes, Kane Winton, Neale Allan, Ross Forsyth, Keith Horne, Jindrich Biscup, Max Alexander. Subs Stephen Jack
Culter: Neil Duffy, Andrew Sim, Hugh Robertson, Neil Reid, Darryn Kelly, Steve Rintoul, Davie Greig, Jamie McAllister, Allan Youngson, George McBain, Ian Leith.

Recent North Sectional League Cup Finals

Season	Winners	Runners Up	Score	Venue
1999/00	Sunnybank	Formartine United	4-3	Harlaw Park, Inverurie
2000/1	Sunnybank	Formartine United	2-0	Harlaw Park, Inverurie
2001/2	Sunnybank	Glentanar	1-0 aet	Keith Park, Aberdeen*
2002/3	Strathspey Thistle	Banks o' Dee	2-2, 4-3 pens	Keith Park, Aberdeen*
2003/4	Hermes	Glentanar	0-0, 4-3 pens	Heathryfold Park, Aberdeen
2004/5	Glentanar	Stonehaven	4-2	Heathryfold Park, Aberdeen
2005/6	Culter	Formartine United	2-0	Heathryfold Park, Aberdeen
2006/7	Turriff United	Hillhead	3-0	Heathryfold Park, Aberdeen
2007/8	Sunnybank	Culter	2-2, 5-4 pens	Hillhead Sports Centre, Aberdeen*
2008/9	Dyce	East End	0-0, 4-2 pens	Spain Park, Aberdeen
2009/10	Sunnybank	Longside	3-1	New Advocates Park, Aberdeen
2010/1	Culter	Inverness City	1-0	Merson Park, Buckie
2011/2	Maud	Inverness City	3-2	Simpson Park, Keith
2012/3	FC Stoneywood	Dyce	2-0	Hillhead Sports Centre, Aberdeen*
2013/4	Banks o' Dee	Culter	0-0, 4-2 pens	Hillhead Sports Centre, Aberdeen*

* Keith Park was later renamed Hillhead Sports Centre

North Regional Junior Cup　　2013/14

Prelim	24 August 2013 Lewis United	Inverness City	5	2		
Prelim	14 September 2013 East End	Fochabers	4	1		
Prelim	14 September 2013 Nairn St Ninian	Hall Russell United	0	1		
Rd 1	13 August 2013 Colony Park	Culter	2	3		
Rd 1	13 August 2013 Cruden Bay	FC Stoneywood	0	4		
Rd 1	13 August 2013 Portgordon Victoria	Dufftown	0	3		
Rd 1	13 August 2013 Stonehaven	Sunnybank	2	1		
Rd 1	17 August 2013 Banks o' Dee	Forres Thistle	4	0		
Rd 1	17 August 2013 New Elgin	Banchory St Ternan	6	1		
Rd 1	31 August 2013 Burghead Thistle	Longside	3	2		
Rd 1	14 September 2013 Buckie Rovers	Buchanhaven Hearts	3	0		
Rd 1	21 September 2013 Deveronside	Newmachar United	5	2		
Rd 1	21 September 2013 Glentanar	Bridge of Don Thistle	3	1		
Rd 1	21 September 2013 Islavale	Parkvale	3	0		
Rd 1	21 September 2013 Maud	Dyce	0	3		
Rd 1	21 September 2013 Whitehills	Ellon United	1	6		
Rd 1	28 September 2013 Hall Russell United	Hermes	2	1		
Rd 1	19 October 2013 East End	Lewis United	4	0		
Rd 1	Lossemouth United	Fraserburgh United	scr	wo		
Rd 2	15 March 2014 Buckie Rovers	Dufftown	0	2		
Rd 2	15 March 2014 East End	Burghead Thistle	2	1		
Rd 2	15 March 2014 Ellon United	Deveronside	2	3		
Rd 2	15 March 2014 FC Stoneywood	Dyce	0	0	5-4 pens	at Dyce
Rd 2	15 March 2014 Glentanar	Culter	1	2		
Rd 2	15 March 2014 Islavale	Hall Russell United	1	2		
Rd 2	15 March 2014 New Elgin	Fraserburgh United	2	1		
Rd 2	15 March 2014 Stonehaven	Banks o' Dee	2	3		
QF	05 April 2014 Culter	Burghead Thistle	5	1		
QF	05 April 2014 New Elgin	Dufftown	4	5		
QF	12 April 2014 Hall Russell United	Dyce	0	4		
QF	23 April 2014 Banks o' Dee	Deveronside	8	0		
SF	03 May 2014 Culter	Dyce	4	0		
SF	03 May 2014 Dufftown	Banks o' Dee	1	6		
F	31 May 2014 Culter	Banks o' Dee	0	0	4-2 pens	at Dyce

Culter completed a memorable season by adding the North Regional Trophy to the McLeman Cup and PMAC Superleague. The North Regional final kicked off in front of a healthy crowd and Culter had the better of the first half. McAllister rattled a post, McBain forced Smith into a fine one handed save then McBain again caused havoc nipping past the keeper only for Robertson to head his goal line shot away. McAllister headed over a Taylor cross and then shot wide. The half finishing with Youngson dancing his way into the box before firing a shot at Smith. Winton hit the inside of the post with a free kick from the edge of the box then Duffy was quick off the line to deny Biskup. Alexander lobbed well over when through on goal then headed past the post from a great position. With time running out Duffy produced a stunning one hand save to deny Anderson , at the Dee end Leith forced Smith into a diving save. The last chance fell to Murray in the dying seconds whose header just missed the target. The tie went into penalties and it was left McAllister, McBain(just) Leith and McKimmie to find the net from 12 yards and Neil Duffy to save two of the Dee spot kicks to start the celebrations.

Att 500

Season	Winners	Runners Up	Score	Venue
1988/9	Bon Accord	Culter	2-1 aet	Spain Park, Aberdeen
1989/90	Culter	Stonehaven	2-1	Spain Park, Aberdeen
1990/1	Stonehaven	FC Stoneywood	2-1	Spain Park, Aberdeen
1991/2	FC Stoneywood	Aberdeen East End	3-0	Heathryfold Park, Aberdeen
1992/3	Hall Russell United	Stonehaven	3-2	Heathryfold Park, Aberdeen
1993/4	Sunnybank	FC Stoneywood	0-0, 2-0 pens	Spain Park, Aberdeen
1994/5	FC Stoneywood	Sunnybank	2-1	Spain Park, Aberdeen
1995/6	Inverurie Locos	Bon Accord	3-1	Spain Park, Aberdeen
1996/7	Sunnybank	Bon Accord	3-1	New Advocates Park, Aberdeen
1997/8	Hermes	Cruden Bay	2-1	The Meadows, Ellon
1998/9	FC Stoneywood	Stonehaven	1-0	Heathryfold Park, Aberdeen
1999/00	Culter	Formartine United	2-1	Heathryfold Park, Aberdeen
2000/1	Inverurie Locos	Forres Thistle	3-1	The Haughs, Turriff
2001/2	Sunnybank	Culter	3-0	Pittodrie Stadium, Aberdeen
2002/3	Islavale	Banks o' Dee	3-2	Pittodrie Stadium, Aberdeen
2003/4	Hermes	Aberdeen East End	2-1	Pittodrie Stadium, Aberdeen
2004/5	Islavale	Banchory St Ternan	7-1	North Lodge Park, Pitmedden
2005/6	Islavale	Longside	3-1	The Haughs, Turriff
2006/7	Turriff United	Forres Thistle	2-1	Simpson Park, Keith
2007/8	Dyce	Turriff United	2-0	Pleasure Grounds, Maud
2008/9	Dyce	Formartine United	4-1	Heathryfold Park, Aberdeen
2009/10	FC Stoneywood	Hermes	5-3	Heathryfold Park, Aberdeen
2010/1	Banks o' Dee	Sunnybank	7-1	Crombie Park, Culter
2011/2	Culter	Inverness City	2-0	Kynoch Park, Keith
2012/3	Stonehaven	Maud	3-1	Ian Mair Park, Dyce
2013/4	Culter	Banks o' Dee	0-0, 4-2 pens	Ian Mair Park, Dyce

McLeman Cup   2013/14

The McLeman Cup is competed for by teams in the top division of the North Juniors.

McLeman Cup

Rd 1	25 January 2014	Dyce	Culter	2 4	
Rd 1	25 January 2014	FC Stoneywood	Maud	0 2	
Rd 1	25 January 2014	Longside	Deveronside	2 7	
Rd 1	25 January 2014	New Elgin	Banks o Dee	1 6	
Rd 1	25 January 2014	Stonehaven	Hall Russell	2 0	
Rd 1	08 March 2014	Hermes	Ellon United	2 0	
QF	12 April 2014	Culter	Deveronside	4 0	
QF	12 April 2014	Hermes	Banks o Dee	0 0	3-4 pens
QF	12 April 2014	Maud	Banchory St Ternan	6 2	
QF	12 April 2014	Stonehaven	East End	2 1	
SF	10 May 2014	Stonehaven	Maud	0 3	
SF	13 May 2014	Culter	Banks o Dee	2 0	
F	24 May 2014	Maud	Culter	1 2	at Colony Park

Recent McLeman Cup Finals

Season	Winners	Runners Up	Score	Venue
1988/9	Culter	Inverurie Loco Works	2-1	Heathryfold Park
1989/90	Bon Accord	East End	1-0	Spain Park
1990/1	Banks o' Dee	Crombie Sports	1-0	Heathryfold Park
1991/2	Lewis United	Sunnybank	2-1	Spain Park
1992/3	Culter	Longside	4-3	North Lodge Park
1993/4	FC Stoneywood	Culter	3-3, 3-2 pens	Spain Park
1994/5	Stonehaven	Hermes	3-1	Heathryfold Park
1995/6	Sunnybank	Banks o' Dee	3-1	New Advocates Park
1996/7	Sunnybank	Lads Club	4-0	New Advocates Park
1997/8	Sunnybank	Formartine United	3-2	New Advocates Park
1998/9	Formartine United	Stonehaven	1-0	Denmore Park
1999/00	Sunnybank	East End	2-1	Pittodrie
2000/1	Culter	Longside	4-1	Lochside Park
2001/2	Formartine United	Culter	1-0	Heathryfold Park
2002/3	Culter	Longside	1-0	Heathryfold Park
2003/4	Glentanar	Formartine United	2-1	Lochside Park
2004/5	Culter	Sunnybank	1-0	Lochside Park
2005/6	Formartine United	Parkvale	3-0	Heathryfold Park
2006/7	Sunnybank	Stonehaven	1-1, 4-3 pens	Keith Park
2007/8	Ellon United	Sunnybank	3-2	Lochside Park
2008/9	Hermes	Banks o' Dee	1-0	New Advocates Park
2009/10	Culter	Hermes	2-1	Keith Park
2010/1	Culter	Fraserburgh United	2-1	Longside
2011/2	Stonehaven	Hermes	1-1, 5-4 pens	Keith Park
2012/3	Culter	FC Stoneywood	3-1	Pittodrie
2013/14				
aka	Gordon Campbell Construction Trophy 1991-2001			
	Acorn Heating Trophy 2002-2006			
	ATR Group Cup 2006-7			

Morrison Cup   2013/14

For 2013/14 this cup was played for by Division 1 (East) clubs.

MTM Morrison Cup

Rd 1	25 January 2014	Glentanar	Parkvale	1 3
Rd 1	08 March 2014	Cruden Bay	Newmachar United	1 3
Rd 2	25 January 2014	Buchanhaven Hearts	Colony Park	3 0
Rd 2	25 January 2014	Sunnybank	Bridge of Don Thistle	1 0
Rd 2	01 March 2014	Parkvale	Fraserburgh United	2 1
Rd 2	29 March 2014	Newmachar United	Lewis United	2 3
SF	19 April 2014	Buchanhaven Hearts	Lewis United	3 1
SF	19 April 2014	Sunnybank	Parkvale	1 1 3-1 pens
F	18 May 2014	Sunnybank	Buchanhaven Hearts	1 1 4-3 pens at Ellon

Recent Morrison Cup Finals				
Season	**Winners**	**Runners Up**	**Score**	**Venue**
1988/9	Buchanhaven Hearts	Banks o' Dee	2-1	North Lodge Park
1989/90	Longside	Turriff United	2-1	North Lodge Park
1990/1	FC Stoneywood	Banks o' Dee	1-0	Heathryfold Park
1991/2	Lewis United	Dyce	3-1	New Advocates Park
1992/3	Lewis United	Hall Russell United	1-0	Keith Park
1993/4	Hermes	Banchory St Ternan	1-0	New Advocates Park
1994/5	Banchory St Ternan	Hermes	1-0	Crombie Park, Culter
1995/6	Banchory St Ternan	Buchanhaven Hearts	2-1	Denmore Park
1996/7	Hermes	Lewis United	2-1	Denmore Park
1997/8	Cruden Bay	East End	1-1, 4-3 pens	The Meadows, Ellon
1998/9	East End	Patkvale	2-1	Spain Park
1999/00	Cruden Bay	Buchanhaven Hearts	4-1	Davidson Park, Longside
2000/1	Lads Club	Glentanar	3-2	Ian Mair Park, Dyce
2001/2	Dyce	Lewis United	2-1	Woodside
2002/3	Lewis United	Parkvale	2-1	Ian Mair Park, Dyce
2003/4	Fraserburgh United	Banchory St Ternan	2-1	Ian Mair Park, Dyce
2004/5	Banchory St Ternan	Parkvale	2-1	Ian Mair Park, Dyce
2005/6	Banchory St Ternan	Lewis United	2-1	Ian Mair Park, Dyce
2006/7	East End	Maud	5-0	Ian Mair Park, Dyce
2007/8	Islavale	Hall Russell United	1-0	Pleasure Park, Maud
2008/9	Formartine United	Buckie Rovers	2-2, 5-4 pens	The Haughs, Turriff
2009/10	Stonehaven	Inverness City	2-2, 5-4 pens	Simpson Park, Keith
2010/1	Glentanar	Lossiemouth United	4-2	Pleasure Park, Maud
2011/2	New Elgin	Fraserburgh United	4-4, 4-3 pens	Colony Park, Inverurie
2012/3	East End	Inverness City	1-1, 5-4 pens	Simpson Park, Keith
2013/14	Sunnybank	Buchanhaven Hearts	1-1, 4-3 pens	The Meadows, Ellon
Until 91/2	played for by all North (East) clubs			
1991/2 onwards	played for by tier 2 clubs			

Elginshire Cup   2013/14

For 2013/14 this cup was played for by Division 1 (West) clubs.

Elginshire Refrigeration Cup

Rd 1	25 January 2014	Nairn St Ninians	Dufftown	0	6	
Rd 1	25 January 2014	Portgordon Victoria	Whitehills	5	1	at Pinefield
Rd 2	25 January 2014	Buckie Rovers	Fochabers	1	0	
Rd 2	25 January 2014	Inverness City	Burghead Thistle	6	0	
Rd 2	15 February 2014	Forres Thistle	Islavale	2	2	6-5 pens
Rd 2	01 March 2014	Dufftown	Portgordon Vics	5	2	
SF	29 March 2014	Buckie Rovers	Dufftown	2	0	
SF	29 March 2014	Forres Thistle	Inverness City	1	0	
F	04 March 2014	Forres Thistle	Buckie Rovers	3	1	at Elgin City FC

Recent Elginshire Cup Finals

Season	Winners	Runners Up	Score	Venue
1988/9	Bishopmill United	Deveronside	2-0	Forest Park, Burghead
1989/90	Islavale	Deveronside	2-1	Forest Park, Burghead
1990/1	Islavale	Forres Thistle	3-1	Merson Park, Buckie
1991/2	Nairn St Ninian	RAF Kinloss	2-1	Forest Park, Burghead
1992/3	Islavale	Nairn St Ninian	3-1	Logie Park, Forres
1993/4	Kinloss	Lossiemouth United	3-2	Logie Park, Forres
1994/5	New Elgin	Strathspey Thistle	2-1	Mosset Park, Forres
1995/6	Deveronside	Islavale	1-0	Gordon Park, Portgordon
1996/7	Deveronside	Islavale	2-2 aet, 4-3 pens	Mosset Park, Forres
1997/8	Deveronside	Lossiemouth United	5-2	Logie Park, Forres
1998/9	Islavale	Bishopmill United	2-1	Logie Park, Forres
1999/00	Nairn St Ninian	Islavale	1-0	Mosset Park, Forres
2000/1	Deveronside	Whitehills	3-2	Canal Park, Banff
2001/2	Strathspey Thistle	Islavale	3-2	Mosset Park, Forres
2002/3	Forres Thistle	Islavale	1-0	Merson Park, Buckie
2003/4	New Elgin	Lossiemouth United	2-0	Mosset Park, Forres
2004/5	Forres Thistle	New Elgin	4-3 aet	Mosset Park, Forres
2005/6	New Elgin	RAF Lossiemouth	1-1	Mosset Park, Forres
2006/7	Nairn St Ninian	Fochabers	1-1, 5-3 pens	Fochabers
2007/8	Burghead Thistle		wo	
2008/9	Inverness City	Bishopmill United	3-0	Logie Park, Forres
2009/10	Burghead Thistle	Cruden Bay	1-0	Merson Park, Buckie
2010/1	Newmachar United	Nairn St Ninian	1-0	Kynoch Park, Keith
2011/2	Nairn St Ninian	Portgordon Victoria	3-0	Logie Park, Forres
2012/3	Colony Park	Buckie Rovers	1-0	Boroughbriggs, Elgin
2013/14	Forres Thistle	Buckie Rovers	3-1	Boroughbriggs, Elgin

GA Inter-Regional Cup 2013/14

P (N)	10 August 2013	Newmachar United	Islavale	1 3	
P (N)	13 August 2013	Buckie Rovers	New Elgin	0 0	2-3 pens
P (N)	13 August 2013	Lewis United	Bridge of Don Thistle	3 4	
P (N)	31 August 2013	Fraserburgh Unitewd	FC Stoneywood	3 1	
P (N)	31 August 2013	Glentanar	Banks o' Dee	2 3	
P (N)	31 August 2013	Hall Russell United	Deveronside	1 2	
P (N)	07 September 2013	Buchanhaven	Dyce	1 2	
P (N)	07 September 2013	Colony Park	Banchory St Ternan	0 0	1-4 pens
P (N)	07 September 2013	Deveronside	Culter	3 3	4-2 pems
P (N)	07 September 2013	East End	Dufftown	1 0	
P (N)	07 September 2013	Fochabers	Nairn St Ninian	2 2	2-4 pens
P (N)	07 September 2013	Forres Thistle	Parkvale	2 3	
P (N)	07 September 2013	Hermes	Inverness City	7 4	
P (N)	07 September 2013	Portgordon Victoria	Maud	3 6	
P (N)	07 September 2013	Sunnybank	Banks o' Dee	0 6	
P (N)	07 September 2013	Whitehills	Burghead Thistle	2 5	
P (N)	28 September 2013	Fraserburgh United	Longside	1 9	
P (T)	05 October 2013	Brechin Vics	Blairgowrie	2 2	3-4 pens
P (T)	05 October 2013	Forfar Albion	Downfield	2 3	
P (T)	05 October 2013	Jeanfield Swifts	Forfar West End	1 3	
P (T)	05 October 2013	Lochee United	Arbroath Vics	3 2	
P (T)	05 October 2013	Tayport	Coupar Angus	4 0	
Rd 1 (N)	12 October 2013	Banchory St Ternan	Banks o' Dee	1 9	
Rd 1 (N)	12 October 2013	Cruden Bay	Parkvale	2 3	
Rd 1 (N)	12 October 2013	Deveronside	Longside	4 3	
Rd 1 (N)	12 October 2013	East End	Hermes	2 6	
Rd 1 (N)	12 October 2013	Ellon United	Maud	1 1	4-5 pens
Rd 1 (N)	12 October 2013	Islavale	Burghead Thistle	2 1	
Rd 1 (N)	12 October 2013	New Elgin	Dyce	0 2	
Rd 1 (N)	19 October 2013	Nairn St Ninian	Bridge of Don Thistle	0 2	
Rd 1 (T)	05 October 2013	Luncarty	Dundee North End	5 1	
Rd 1 (T)	05 October 2013	Broughty Athletic	Scone Thistle	5 0	
Rd 1 (T)	05 October 2013	Kinnoull	East Craigie	2 4	
Rd 1 (T)	30 November 2013	Violet	Downfield	1 1	1-4 pens
Rd 1 (T)	30 November 2013	Lochee Harp	Tayport	1 3	
Rd 1 (T)	21 December 2013	Lochee United	Carnoustie Panmure	4 4	3-2 pens
Rd 1 (T)	21 December 2013	Forfar West End	Kirrie Thistle	2 2	3-5 pens
Rd 1 (T)	21 December 2013	Montrose Roselea	Blairgowrie	4 0	
Rd 3	22 February 2014	Bridge of Don Thistle	Downfield	0 1	at Banks o 'Dee
Rd 3	22 February 2014	Broughty Athletic	Hermes	0 0	3-4 pns
Rd 3	22 February 2014	Deveronside	Kirrie Thistle	1 0	at Deveronvale
Rd 3	22 February 2014	Dyce	Montrose Roselea	0 2	
Rd 3	22 February 2014	Islavale	East Craigie	5 4	
Rd 3	22 February 2014	Lochee United	Parkvale	5 0	
Rd 3	22 February 2014	Luncarty	Banks o' Dee	4 2	
Rd 3	08 March 2014	Tayport	Maud	1 2	
QF	29 March 2014	Luncarty	Islavale	2 2	3-1 pens
QF	29 March 2014	Maud	Deveronside	1 2	
QF	29 March 2014	Montrose Roselea	Hermes	0 1	
QF	29 March 2014	Lochee United	Downfield	3 1	
SF	19 April 2014	Lochee United	Deveronside	6 1	
SF	19 April 2014	Hermes	Luncarty	0 0	6-7 pens
F	10 May 2014	Lochee United	Luncarty	1 1	4-3 pens at Dundee United FC

Recent North / Tayside Region Cup Finals

Season	Winners	Runners Up	Score	Venue
1988/9	Deveronside	Downfield	1-0	North End Park, Dundee
1989/90	Downfield	Banks o' Dee	2-1	Heathryfold Park, Aberdeen
1990/1	Downfield	Bon Accord	2-0	North End Park, Dundee
1991/2	Tayport	Forfar West End	2-0	North End Park, Dundee
1992/3	Forfar West End	Islavale	4-2	The Haughs, Turriff
1993/4	St Josephs	Downfield	3-1	North End Park, Dundee
1994/5	Tayport	Violet	4-2	North End Park, Dundee
1995/6	St Josephs	Downfield	2-1	North End Park, Dundee
1996/7	St Josephs	Tayport	2-1	North End Park, Dundee
1997/8	St Josephs	Dundee North End	0-0, 5-4 pens	Glenesk Park, Dundee
1998/9	Kirrie Thistle	Inverurie Locos	3-2	Heathryfold Park, Aberdeen
1999/00	Tayport	Lochee United	1-0	North End Park, Dundee
2000/1	Dundee North End	Broughty Athletic	2-2, 3-0 pens	Strathmore Park, Forfar
2001/2	Tayport	Sunnubank	5-1	Keith Park, Aberdeen
2002/3	Tayport	Dundee North End	3-0	Glenesk Park, Dundee
2003/4	Tayport	Lochee United	3-1 aet	North End Park, Dundee
2004/5	Tayport	Carnoustie Panmure	3-1	North End Park, Dundee
2005/6	Lochee United	Montrose Roselea	3-2	North End Park, Dundee
2006/7	Montrose Roselea	Forfar West End	1-1, 10-9 pens	Station Park, Forfar
2007/8	Forfar West End	Carnoustie Panmure	3-2	Westview Park, Kirriemuir
2008/9	Sunnybank	Blairgowrie	2-2, 4-3 pens	Hillhead, Aberdeen
2009/10	Sunnybank	Broughty Athletic	4-0	North End Park, Dundee
2010/1	Dundee North End	Broughty Athletic	3-2	Downfield Park, Dundee
2011/2	Jeanfield Swifts	Culter	3-0	Heathryfold Park, Aberdeen
2012/3	Jeanfield Swifts	Montrose Roselea	3-0	Whitton Park, Broughty Ferry
2013/14	Lochee United	Luncarty	1-1, 4-3 pens	Tannadice Park, Dundee

FINAL TIE 2013/14

May 10th at Tannadice Park
Lochee United v Luncarty
1-1, 4-3 pens
Lochee United: Mark Fotheringham, Mark Bannon, Greg Kirk, Dean Wallace, Scott Gates, Charlie Cargill (Danny Cavanagh 53), Ross Gallacher, Brian Clark, Phil Hagan, Jon Voigt, Paul Blackwood (Kevin Buchan 64). Subs not used: David Beedie, Chris Tawse, Marc Percy.

Luncarty: Mark Mitchell, Stuart Nicol, Jamie McKenzie, Ryan Ward, Joe Shields, Steve McAllister (Mark Shaw 19), Jon Kelly (Alex Williams 84), Kevyn Fowler, David Fyfe, Gavin Anderson, Dan Kelly (John Anderson 34). Subs not used: Nicky Robertson, Allan Hay.

0-1   3mins   Fyfe
1-1   44mins Hagan (pen)

WEST JUNIORS

The West Region has existed in its present format since 2002 when the Ayrshire and Central regions were merged.

The League structure has region-wide Super Premier and Super First Divisions, with 12 and 14 teams respectively. Below these are the District leagues - the Ayrshire District has a single Division while the Central District has two divisions.

For 2014/15 there is a considerable imbalance caused by the success of Ayrshire sides at the expense of Central teams. Subject to ratification at the Regional AGM, the make-up of the Leagues would be:

SUPER PREMIER (12)	SUPER FIRST (14)
8 Ayrshire, 4 Central	4 Ayrshire, 10 Central
Auchinleck Talbot	Kirkintilloch RR
Irvine Meadow	Pollok
Hurlford United	Largs Thistle
Clydebank	Maybole
Cumnock	Cumbernauld
Glenafton Athletic	Thorniewood
Kilbirnie Ladeside	Rutherglen
Petershill	Yoker
Troon	Greenock
Beith	Kilsyth R
Shotts Bon Accord	Irvine Vics
Arthurlie	Ardeer Th
	Neilston
	Shettleston

AYRSHIRE (12)	CENTRAL ONE (14)	CENTRAL TWO (11)
Kilwinning R	Ashfield	Camuslang
Whitletts	Renfrew	Johnstone B
Lugar BT	Lesmahagow	Glasgow Perthshire
Ardrossan WR	Benburb	Forth
Darvel	Bellshill	Royal Albert
Girvan	Carluke	Vale of Leven
Dalry	Dunipace	Rossvale
Saltcoats	Larkhall	Port Glasgow
Annbank	St Ants	St Rochs
Kello	Maryhill	EK Thistle
Muirkirk	Lanark	Newmains
Craigmark	Blantyre Vics	
	Vale of Clyde	
	Wishaw	

Some Central clubs have been unhappy that it is more difficult for them to achieve Super League status than it is for Ayrshire clubs. A simple solution would be to convert Central Divisions One and Two into parallel divisions based on geographical grounds.

West Junior Super League Premier Division 2013/14

	ART	AT	CLY	CUM	GA	HU	IM	KL	KRR	LT	PET	POL
Arthurlie		Nov 16	Aug 24	Apr 28	Oct 5	Nov 9	Oct 12	Nov 30	Mar 22	Mar 15	Sep 7	Apr 19
		1-1	2-5	2-0	1-3	1-2	0-4	1-1	4-1	1-2	2-2	1-1
Auchinleck Talbot	Aug 31		Nov 30	May 10	Oct 12	Sep 28	Apr 26	Feb 22	Jan 18	Apr 5	Aug 17	Mar 15
	6-0		2-0	2-1	2-1	1-1	1-2	3-0	4-0	3-0	3-1	2-0
Clydebank	Dec7	Mar 22		Apr 26	May 17	May 3	Sep 14	Apr 19	Aug 31	Nov 16	Oct 12	Aug 17
	3-1	3-0		1-2	0-1	0-1	1-1	2-1	2-0	3-2	0-2	1-2
Cumnock	Apr 12	Dec7	Sep 7		Nov 16	May 24	Apr 30	Oct 5	Nov 2	Aug 24	Mar 8	Mar 29
	0-3	0-1	1-1		1-2	4-4	0-0	1-4	3-0	5-1	1-3	1-1
Glenafton Athletic	May 10	Mar 1	Nov 9	May 3		Aug 31	Aug 17	Nov 2	Apr 5	Sep 14	Apr 26	Apr 28
	1-0	0-1	1-3	0-1		0-2	1-3	3-2	2-1	2-1	0-0	3-2
Hurlford United	Apr 26	Jun 9	Mar 29	Aug 17	Apr 30		Nov 16	May 14	Apr 28	Sep 7	Sep 21	Nov 2
	0-0	5-3	1-0	2-2	2-0		0-1	3-2	4-1	4-0	1-1	5-1
Irvine Meadow	Dec 28	Sep 21	Apr 28	Feb 1	Dec 21	May 12		Sep 7	Oct 5	Mar 22	Nov 30	Nov 9
	1-1	0-1	1-0	0-2	2-0	2-3		1-0	2-4	1-0	3-1	3-2
Kilbirnie Ladeside	Aug 17	Apr 12	Sep 28	Aug 31	Feb 1	Sep 14	Dec7		Mar 15	Jan 4	Nov 16	Jan 11
	3-0	0-1	0-0	1-1	2-1	3-0	1-2		1-1	1-2	3-0	2-0
Kirkintilloch Rob Roy	Sep 21	Sep 7	Apr 12	Dec 28	Dec7	Oct 12	Jan 11	Aug 24		Nov 9	Feb 1	Feb 15
	1-2	2-4	0-1	2-1	1-0	1-5	1-3	3-0		4-1	1-4	4-2
Largs Thistle	Nov 2	Jan 11	Feb 15	Apr 19	Mar 8	May 17	Aug 31	Oct 12	Aug 17		Dec 28	Nov 30
	1-2	1-2	1-3	1-2	3-0	1-0	1-1	3-0	2-3		2-1	2-1
Petershill	Feb 15	Jan 4	Jan 11	Nov 9	Aug 24	Mar 22	Mar 15	Dec 14	Sep 14	Oct 5		Aug 31
	1-2	1-1	2-1	0-1	1-2	0-0	2-3	1-5	1-1	2-0		3-3
Pollok	Sep 14	Aug 24	Mar 1	Oct 12	Sep 7	May 10	Jan 4	Mar 22	Nov 16	Feb 22	Dec7	
	2-0	1-4	3-4	0-2	2-2	2-5	1-2	5-4	3-1	3-2	2-5	

ABD May 19, Hurlford v Auchinleck, Rain

Pos	Team	Pld	W	D	L	F	A	GD	Pts
1	Auchinleck Talbot F.C.	22	16	3	3	48	20	28	51
2	Irvine Meadow F.C.	22	14	4	4	38	23	15	46
3	Hurlford United F.C.	22	13	6	3	50	26	24	45
4	Clydebank F.C.	22	10	3	9	34	29	5	33
5	Cumnock Juniors F.C.	22	8	6	8	32	31	1	30
6	Glenafton Athletic F.C.	22	9	2	11	27	33	-6	29
7	Kilbirnie Ladeside F.C.	22	8	4	10	40	32	8	28
8	Petershill F.C.	22	6	7	9	34	37	-3	25
9	Arthurlie F.C.	22	6	6	10	27	41	-14	24
10	Kirkintilloch Rob Roy F.C.	22	7	2	13	33	51	-18	23
11	Pollok F.C.	22	5	4	13	39	58	-19	19
12	Largs Thistle F.C.	22	6	1	15	27	48	-21	19

Promotion / Relegation Play Off

June 3rd
Kirkintilloch Rob Roy v Shotts Bon Accord   1-1

June 5th
Shotts Bon Accord v Kirkintilloch Rob Roy   4-1
Played at Greenfield Park, Shettleston

Aggregate
Shotts Bon Accord   5-1   Kirkintilloch Rob Roy

AUCHINLECK TALBOT SQUAD 2013/14

Andrew Leishman
Robert Kerr
Ally Park
James Latta
Joe O'Brien
Gavin Collins
Craig Pettigrew
Martin McGoldrick
William Lyle
Kenny Connolly
Mark Armour
Kyle Faulds
Steven White
Dwayne Hislop
Graham Wilson
Bryan Young
Keir Milliken
Colin Spence
Allan McKenzie
David Gormley
Michael Reilly
Mick McCann
Manager: Tommy Sloan

West Super League - All Time Positions

	2002-3	2003-4	2004-5	2005-6	2006-7	2007-8	2008-9	2009-10	2010-11	2011-12	2012-13	2013-14
Arthurlie	2	2	10	3	7	7	2	2	7	6		9
Ashfield										6	10	
Auchinleck Talbot	10	8	3	1	2	4	4	3	3	3	1	1
Beith						5	3	1	7	5	11	
Bellshill Athletic			6	9	9	9	9	11				
Benburb	12											
Clydebank										4	3	4
Cumnock	9	4	7	5	6	10	11		9	9	9	5
Glenafton Athletic	3	5	9	8	10	6	10				4	6
Hurlford United												3
Irvine Meadow	11					2	1	4	1	1	5	2
Johnstone Burgh	5	9	10	11								
Kilbirnie Ladeside	6	12						6	8	12		7
Kilsyth Rangers				7	8	12						
Kilwinning Rangers	4	1	11									
Kirkintilloch Rob Roy							6	8	6	8	7	10
Lanark United								10	11			
Largs Thistle								7	5	11		12
Larkhall Thistle	7	10	5	12								
Maryhill	8	6	4	6	11							
Neilston	2	11			4	8	12					
Petershill					7	3	5	9	10	2	2	8
Pollok	1	3	1	3	1	1	2	5	4	10	8	11
Renfrew			8	2	12							
Rutherglen Glencairn								12				
Shotts Bon Accord				4	5	11					12	
Troon		7	12									
Vale of Clyde								8	12			

Auchinleck Talbot comfortably retained their Super League title and qualified to take part in next season's Scottish Cup. It may be that their early exit from the Scottish Junior Cup at the hands of Bo'ness United eased their league progress—closest challengers Hurlford United and Irvine Meadow were involved in the later stages of the Cup competition. Talbot's domination of the West scene is such that they have not been out of the top three for five years now.

With Pollok being relegated Talbot are now the only "perma-members" of the West Super League. Pollok's decline in recent years has been a disappointment to their loyal support. A succession of managerial changes has failed to bring any improvement and it was no great surprise when they took the drop. Largs Thistle finished bottom but only on goal difference behind the Newlandsfield club. Kirkintilloch Rob Roy were comprehensively defeated in the Play Off by Super First Division side Shotts Bon Accord. Rob Roy also took their leave of Adamslie Park and will ground-share with Cumbernauld next season as they awit the completion of their own new ground.

Arthurlie and Petershill had disappointing seasons by their recent high standards. Big spending Hurlford achieved their main goal of winning the Scottish Cup—if they continue to challenge in the League next season then their success can be seen as more than a flash in the pan.

Joining Shotts in making the step up are two Ayrshire sides, Troon and Beith. Troon also enjoyed good Cup success and they look well placed to establish themselves in the top flight after a long gap. Beith stuttered to promotion and will be less confident of making an impact.

West Junior Super League First Division 2013/14

	ASH	BEI	CU	GRE	KILS	KILW	LES	MAY	REN	RUT	SBA	THO	TRO	YA
Ashfield	■	Apr 12	Apr 21	Sep 14	Apr 26	Jan 11	Dec 28	Nov 9	Jan 4	May 5	Feb 8	Oct 5	Aug 31	Aug 17
		0-3	0-2	1-1	2-3	1-3	3-0	1-5	1-4	0-5	1-4	4-1	4-2	1-2
Beith	Oct 12	■	Dec7	Apr 23	Dec 28	Jan 4	May 10	Jan 18	Aug 24	May 17	Mar 22	Sep 7	Sep 21	Apr 19
	2-0		3-2	2-0	3-1	3-2	7-1	0-0	4-2	5-1	3-2	4-3	4-1	0-0
Cumbernauld United	Sep 21	Apr 16	■	Apr 19	Jun 4	Apr 26	Aug 31	May 28	Oct 12	Apr 12	Aug 17	Dec 14	Nov 16	May 24
	2-0	1-2		4-1	1-4	1-1	3-0	0-2	4-1	4-0	2-4	0-6	1-2	1-1
Greenock	Apr 5	Mar 15	Sep 7	■	Dec7	Oct 12	Apr 16	Apr 28	Mar 29	Sep 21	Apr 12	Nov 30	Aug 17	May 12
	4-2	2-0	1-2		0-0	1-3	2-1	1-2	2-0	2-1	0-2	0-3	2-3	0-3
Kilsyth Rangers	Nov 2	Oct 5	Sep 14	Aug 31	■	Apr 30	Aug 17	Apr 12	Nov 16	May 3	Apr 16	Mar 22	Dec 14	Jan 4
	0-2	0-5	0-2	2-5		2-3	1-1	1-1	5-2	0-2	3-1	0-3	0-3	2-1
Kilwinning Rangers	Apr 28	Aug 31	Oct 5	Mar 22	Nov 9	■	Feb 8	Dec7	May 5	Dec 28	Sep 14	Aug 17	Mar 15	May 3
	1-2	2-4	1-2	2-3	2-3		4-1	0-1	6-0	2-0	0-4	3-1	0-2	1-1
Lesmahagow	Sep 7	Feb 15	May 19	Aug 24	Mar 29	Sep 28	■	May 3	Sep 21	May 24	Apr 21	Apr 28	Mar 1	Mar 22
	3-4	0-2*	2-1+	5-4	0-3*	0-2		5-3+	3-4	0-2+	0-3+	1-3+	0-1*	1-3*
Maybole	Apr 19	Sep 14	Mar 22	Nov 23	Sep 7	Aug 24	Jun 9	■	Nov 30	Jun 7	May 24	Mar 1	Sep 28	Apr 5
	1-2	0-3	3-1	2-2	0-0	1-0	2-3		1-1	3-2	0-4	2-0	2-2	2-2
Renfrew	Mar 22	Nov 9	Apr 30	Oct 5	Mar 15	Apr 16	Apr 19	Aug 17	■	Dec7	Apr 28	Dec 28	Sep 14	Aug 31
	1-6	2-2	1-3	1-1	0-1	2-3	2-1	1-3		0-2	0-4	1-0	0-3	2-2
Rutherglen Glencairn	Nov 16	Aug 17	May 31	May 14	Apr 21	May 10	Sep 14	Oct 5	Jan 11	■	Aug 31	Apr 16	May 19	Apr 26
	3-1	0-1	3-0	2-0	0-1	1-0	6-1	1-2	1-0		1-3	3-4	0-5	5-2
Shotts Bon Accord	Aug 24	May 3	Dec 28	Nov 9	Oct 12	May 17	Jan 4	May 10	Sep 7	Apr 19	■	Sep 21	Apr 26	Nov 16
	2-1	0-3	1-1	3-1	5-0	1-2	6-2	0-3	2-0	5-1		0-1	0-5	2-0
Thorniewood United	Apr 30	Mar 29	Aug 24	Apr 26	Apr 19	Nov 16	Apr 12	Aug 31	Apr 21	Oct 12	Dec7	■	Jan 11	Sep 14
	5-1	2-2	1-1	1-4	1-2	0-0	4-1	2-0	1-3	2-2	2-2		0-1	5-5
Troon	Jan 25	Apr 5	May 3	Jan 18	Aug 24	Nov 2	Feb 1	Dec 28	Nov 23	Sep 7	Oct 5	Nov 9	■	Dec7
	0-1	5-2	1-1	4-0	4-3	4-3	6-1	2-1	2-1	1-1	1-0	5-0		2-1
Yoker Athletic	Apr 16	Apr 30	Apr 28	Dec 28	Sep 21	Sep 7	Oct 5	Mar 15	Apr 12	Aug 24	Apr 23	May 7	May 10	■
	3-0	1-3	3-1	1-1	3-2	4-3	5-3	1-2	2-1	2-2	0-2	2-4	1-3	

* at Carluke
ABD
ABD Nov 2 Beith v Shotts (0-1), rain
+ at Stonehouse
ABD Apr 28 Beith v Rutherglen (1-0), injury

Pos	Team	Pld	W	D	L	F	A	GD	Pts	
1	Troon F.C.	26	20	3	3	70	29	41	63	
2	Beith Juniors F.C.	26	19	4	3	70	31	39	61	
3	Shotts Bon Accord F.C.	26	16	2	8	62	33	29	50	
4	Maybole Juniors F.C.	26	12	7	7	44	37	7	43	
5	Cumbernauld United F.C.	26	11	5	10	44	40	4	38	
6	Thorniewood United F.C.	26	10	6	10	55	49	6	36	
7	Rutherglen Glencairn F.C.	26	11	3	12	47	46	1	36	
8	Yoker Athletic F.C.	26	9	8	9	51	51	0	35	
9	Greenock Juniors F.C.	26	9	5	12	41	49	-8	32	
10	Kilsyth Rangers F.C.	26	9	4	13	36	55	-19	31	
11	Ashfield F.C.	26	9	1	16	41	62	-21	28	
12	Renfrew F.C.	26	5	4	17	32	65	-33	19	
13	Kilwinning Rangers F.C.	26	10	3	13	49	45	4	14	*-19
14	Lesmahagow Juniors F.C.	26	4	1	21	36	86	-50	13	

TROON JUNIORS SQUAD
2013/14

Goalkeepers
Darren Johnston
Marty Fraser

Defenders
Martin Ure
Cammy McKinnell
Gareth Armstrong
Neil McGowan
Dean Keenan
Gavin Collins

Midfield
Dougie Ramsay
Scott Chatham
Gareth Turner
Tony Murphy
Stevie Wilson
Neal Gilmour
Aaron Wylie

Forwards
Neil Sanderson
Dale Moore
David Gillies
Calum Hardie
Gareth "Bo" Armstrong

West Super League First Division All Time Positions

	2002-3	2003-4	2004-5	2005-6	2006-7	2007-8	2008-9	2009-10	2010-11	2011-12	2012-13	2013-14
Annbank United				10	8	9	9	9	14			
Ardrossan Winton Rovers									8	13		
Arthurlie	1											
Ashfield								8	1			11
Beith	4	5	4	4	2							2
Bellshill Athletic	3	1						12				
Benburb		11										
Cambuslang Rangers	11		10	14								
Clydebank						8	5	3	2			
Cumbernauld United	10	10	13						9	7	8	5
Cumnock								2				
Dalry Thistle									11	14		
Dunipace				13								
East Kilbride Thistle					9	7	8	6	6	11		
Girvan						14		4	5	4	13	
Glasgow Perthshire											11	
Glenafton Athletic								7	3	1		
Greenock												9
Hurlford United	9	8	6	8	11		14		10	10	1	
Irvine Meadow		7	11	1								
Johnstone Burgh				10	14							
Kello Rovers											12	
Kilbirnie Ladeside			12			4	2				2	
Kilsyth Rangers		4	1					10	13	4	9	10
Kilwinning Rangers						7	3	3	13		11	13
Kirkintilloch Rob Roy				8	11	1						
Lanark United								3			12	
Largs Thistle	12			3	6	5	1				3	
Larkhall Thistle					12							
Lesmahagow						7	13					14
Lugar Boswell T		9	7	9	13							
Maryhill					11							
Maybole				9	12		6	6	12		10	4
Neilston				5	1			14				
Petershill	6	6	3	2								
Port Glasgow								11				
Renfrew	8	2				10	7	4	8	3	7	12
Rutherglen Glencairn								1		6	6	7
Saltcoats Victoria			14									
Shettleston	5	12										
Shotts Bon Accord	7	3	2			12				7	2	3
Thorniewood United										5	4	6
Troon	2			5	5	12						1
Vale of Clyde					6	4	2			13		
Whitletts Victoria								10	5	9	14	
Yoker Athletic											5	8

As the table above shows, few teams linger for long in this League. With Renfrew suffering relegation to the Central Division, the "longest servants" Are now Cumbernauld United who embark on their fifth successive season at this level. At times during the season Cumbernauld looked potential promotion candidates but a big backlog of games caused them problems. However, reaching the Central KO Cup Final, in which they lost to Clydebank, was a significant achievement and suggests that better times may be just around the corner for the Guy's Meadow side.

Troon achieved back to back promotions to make it back to the Super League Premier Division after a nine year absence. They finished two points ahead of North Ayrshire rivals Beith. Troon also completed a memorable double by winning the Ayrshire Cup, defeating Scottish Cup winners Hurlford in the Final at Auchinleck.

Beith will be relieved to have bounced straight back following relegation in 2013. For a long time they looked to be outsiders but they came good at the right time and produced some decent results. The set-up at Bellsdale Park is worthy of Super Premier status and they will be happy to be back alongside so many of their traditional Ayrshire rivals.

Shotts Bon Accord triumphed over Kirkintilloch in the play-off. Following a 1 -1 draw at Adamslie Park, they outclassed the Rabs in the second leg, played at Shettleston's Greenfield Park. Manager Tommy McDonald and his Assistant John Gibson may need to build on their squad if they are to survive at the higher level. However, the ease with which they defeated Kirkintilloch suggests that they might do not too badly at the higher level.

Lesmahagow had a season to forget. As well as finishing bottom they saw the playing surface at Craighead Park washed away in the winter storms. They were forced to groundshare at Carluke and Stonehouse but will hopefully be back at home for the start of 2014/15.

Renfrew also had a miserable season. They finally seem to be on the verge of leaving dilapidated Western Park—they may return at the start of the new season or seek a groundshare until their new ground is built. Plans are in place for a new stadium just a few hundred yards from Western Park.

Ashfield suffered a second successive relegation following a poor season. The fourth relegated side was Kilwinning Rangers, crippled by a massive points deduction for fielding ineligible players.

That misdemeanour saved Kilsyth Rangers and Greenock from potential relegation.

With seven new teams for next season this will be a difficult league to predict. Pollok and Kirkintilloch must be fancied but it is never easy to bounce back first time round.

West Junior Ayrshire League   2013/14

	ANN	AT	AWR	CB	DAL	DAR	GIR	IV	KEL	LBT	MUI	SAL	WV
Annbank United		Nov 16	Apr 23	Apr 28	May 7	Jan 18	Apr 12	Apr 19	Oct 12	Mar 22	Aug 17	Nov 30	Sep 14
		3-4	1-1	6-1	8-4	3-4	3-2	1-2	3-2	2-2	3-0	2-1	1-1
Ardeer Thistle	Apr 26		Apr 12	Dec 21	Aug 24	Dec 28	Mar 29	Oct 26	Aug 31	Nov 23	Dec 7	Sep 14	Oct 12
	7-1		2-2	1-0	2-2	3-2	4-2	0-1	5-1	2-1	7-0	2-1	1-2
Ardrossan Winton Rovers	Nov 23	Nov 2		Aug 31	Sep 7	Aug 17	Oct 12	Mar 29	Mar 15	Apr 26	Jan 18	Dec 28	Dec 7
	3-0	1-4		8-0	3-2	4-1	2-2	0-5	4-0	3-2	8-1	4-3	3-3
Craigmark Burntonians	Oct 5	Nov 9	Nov 30		Mar 1	Nov 16	Apr 23	Jan 18	Mar 29	Mar 15	Sep 14	Aug 17	Apr 19
	2-6	0-5	1-6		1-3	1-6	1-4	1-4	2-10	1-7	2-3	1-8	1-4
Dalry Thistle	Mar 15	Apr 19	Apr 28	Sep 28		Apr 23	Aug 17	Nov 9	Apr 30	Apr 16	Oct 12	Mar 29	Aug 31
	2-0	0-3	3-2	3-0		1-1	3-2	1-3	4-4	3-4	5-1	2-2	1-4
Darvel	Sep 7	Mar 1	Apr 5	Feb 1	May 3		Aug 31	Apr 26	Dec 7	Nov 9	Mar 15	Oct 12	Sep 28
	4-0	1-5	1-6	6-0	4-4		1-0	0-4	4-1	4-4	4-2	1-3	4-1
Girvan	Nov 2	Oct 5	Apr 19	Aug 24	Nov 16	May 17		Sep 7	Apr 28	Dec 14	May 10	May 3	Dec 21
	3-2	3-2	1-1	6-1	0-2	1-1		1-0	6-1	3-0	2-2	1-2	1-2
Irvine Vics	Dec 7	Apr 5	Mar 1	Oct 12	Jan 11	Sep 14	Apr 30		Aug 17	Apr 28	Nov 16	Aug 31	Apr 16
	1-0	3-3	3-2	9-1	3-2	1-0	3-1		4-1	2-1	7-0	1-1	1-0
Kello Rovers	Mar 1	Mar 22	Sep 14	Jan 11	Apr 5	Oct 5	May 7	Nov 30			Aug 24	Apr 19	Nov 9	Apr 12
	1-5	4-3	3-2	3-3	2-4	3-3	1-2	0-0		0-5	3-3	2-1	2-4
Lugar Boswell Thistle	May 3	Aug 17	Nov 16	Feb 22	Sep 14	Mar 29	Sep 28	Apr 12	Apr 23		Aug 31	Jan 18	Nov 30
	2-3	2-2	2-2	6-0	4-3	0-2	3-1	2-1	3-1		3-0	4-0	1-2
Muirkirk	Mar 29	Sep 7	Nov 9	Mar 22	Dec 14	Aug 24	May 24	Oct 5	Oct 26	Mar 1		Apr 26	Apr 23
	2-1	0-2	0-4	1-0	3-4	0-6	2-3	0-7	0-4	0-8		0-3	1-3
Saltcoats Vics	Aug 24	Feb 22	Oct 5	Nov 23	Dec 7	Dec 21	Jan 11	Mar 15	Jan 4	Sep 7	Nov 2		Mar 1
	3-0	1-2	1-1	4-0	2-3	1-2	0-0	1-2	4-2	2-3	3-1		2-1
Whitletts Vics	Jan 11	Mar 15	Aug 24	Sep 7	Apr 25	Apr 30	Nov 9	Nov 2	Nov 16	Oct 5	Dec 28	Dec 14	
	7-2	1-3	2-2	1-0	3-2	1-3	1-0	2-0	7-1	1-3	5-2	2-2	

Pos	Team	Pld	W	D	L	F	A	GD	Pts
1	Irvine Victoria F.C.	24	18	3	3	67	21	46	57
2	Ardeer Thistle F.C.	24	16	5	3	74	33	41	53
3	Whitletts Victoria F.C.	24	14	4	6	60	39	21	46
4	Lugar Boswell Thistle F.C.	24	13	4	7	72	40	32	43
5	Ardrossan Winton Rovers F.C.	24	11	8	5	74	43	31	41
6	Darvel Juniors F.C.	24	12	5	7	65	49	16	41
7	Girvan F.C.	24	10	6	8	60	35	25	36
8	Dalry Thistle F.C.	24	9	5	10	63	63	0	32
9	Saltcoats Victoria F.C.	24	8	6	10	51	40	11	30
10	Annbank United F.C.	24	9	3	12	56	63	-7	30
11	Kello Rovers F.C.	24	5	5	14	52	81	-29	20
12	Muirkirk Juniors F.C.	24	3	1	20	22	100	-78	10
13	Craigmark Burntonians F.C.	24	0	1	23	19	128	-109	1

IRVINE VICTORIA SQUAD 2013/14

Kevin Adam
David Adams
Ricky Allan
David Anderson
Robert Burgess
Rory Campbell
Scott Chesney
Bobby Colligan
Stefan Johnstone
Chris Lamb
Ciaron McDermott
Alan McIlroy
Ross Munro
Antoni Paton
Ally Ross
Darren Russell
Gary Russell
Carlo Scaramuzza
Ryan Singleton
David Wilson

Co Manager: Iain McMillan and Stevie

Ayrshire District League - All Time Positions	2002-3	2003-4	2004-5	2005-6	2006-7	2007-8	2008-9	2009-10	2010-11	2011-12	2012-13	2013-14
Annbank United	10	4	2							5	8	10
Ardeer Thistle	11	12	11	5	5	9	12	12	8	9	4	2
Ardrossan Winton Rovers	9	9	3	9	6	5	4	4	1			5
Craigmark Burntonians	8	8	7	4	7	6	9	6	12	11	11	13
Dalry Thistle	5	13	10	8	3	4	1		2		10	8
Darvel	13	7	9	12	12	11	7	9	5	10	9	6
Girvan			4	2		2					7	7
Hurlford United					1		1					
Irvine Meadow				1								
Irvine Victoria	6	3	5	10	9	7	8	8	9	6	5	1
Kello Rovers	4	5	6	6	8	10	6	5	11	2		11
Kilbirnie Ladeside				3	1							
Kilwinning Rangers							2		4	1		
Largs Thistle			6	1								4
Lugar Boswell Thistle	1					8	3	3	7	12	3	
Maybole	2	1		2				4	1			
Muirkirk	3	11	8	13	11	13	10	11	10	8	12	12
Saltcoats Victoria	7	2		11	10	12	11	10	3	7	6	9
Troon							5	7	6	3	2	
Whitletts Victoria	12	10	12	7	4	3	2					3

Special mention must be made of Craigmark Burntonians who frequently had to field a very young side. Despite collecting just one point, they fulfilled all their fixtures and will hopefully return stronger for 2014/15.

Muirkirk appointed former Angolan international Jose Quitongo as their Manager mid season.

West Junior Central League First Division   2013/14

	BEL	BEN	CAM	CAR	DUN	GP	JB	LAN	LAR	MAR	NEI	SHE	STA
Bellshill Athletic		Oct 12	Sep 7	Nov30	Mar 22	Dec7	Sep 21	Jan 18	Mar 29	Apr 26	May 5	Mar 15	Apr 30
		4-0	2-1	0-2	1-2	3-2	3-0	2-1	1-1	5-1	2-1	1-1	3-0
Benburb	Apr 21		Sep 21	Dec 14	Feb 22	Aug 31	Mar 29	Mar 1	May 17	Aug 17	Mar 15	Apr 16	Dec7
	2-0+		1-1	3-3	1-0	2-1	2-1	3-1	0-3+	2-0	0-2	1-0+	3-1
Cambuslang Rangers	Mar 1	Mar 22		Aug 17	Apr 5	Sep 14	Apr 16	Apr 12	Oct 5	Aug 31	Nov 9	Dec7	Apr 19
	0-0	3-1		0-3	1-3	3-0	1-0	1-3	0-2	1-0	0-1	1-2	0-2
Carluke Rovers	Jan 11	Apr 26	Jan 4		Sep 21	Nov 23	Sep 7	Apr 19	Dec7	Feb 22	Feb 8	Aug 24	Oct 12
	1-1	3-1	3-2		0-2	6-0	3-2	0-2	1-2	1-3	0-1	2-1	1-2
Dunipace	Aug 31	Oct 5	Nov 2	Apr 12		Mar 1	May 3	Dec7	Apr 26	May 5	Sep 14	Apr 28	Aug 17
	2-3	1-0	1-0	1-3		5-0	3-0	0-2	1-0	4-1	0-0	1-2	2-2
Glasgow Perthshire	Apr 12	Jan 4	Apr 28	Feb 1	Sep 7		Nov 9	Sep 21	Nov 30	Apr 30	Aug 24	Apr 21	Mar 29
	1-1	0-1	0-8	0-5	2-4		3-2	1-6	2-5	2-4	1-3	2-4	1-5
Johnstone Burgh	Apr 19	Aug 24	Nov 16	Mar 22	Nov 30	Apr 23		May 17	Aug 31	Mar 15	May 10	Oct 5	Sep 14
	1-1	2-3	2-0	1-2	1-3	3-1		1-5	1-1	1-3	1-6	1-5	0-2
Lanark United	Nov 16	Apr 5	Oct 12	Aug 31	May 10	Mar 15	Aug 17		Jan 11	Sep 14	May 3	Mar 8	Dec 14
	0-2	1-1	1-2	5-1	3-3	2-0	2-2		1-2	0-2	2-3	1-1	2-3
Larkhall Thistle	Dec 14	May 3	Mar 15	Sep 14	Oct 12	Feb 22	May 12	Aug 24		Sep 21	Nov 16	Mar 22	Apr 12
	0-2	1-5	1-2	2-3	1-1	6-0	4-2	2-0		1-0	2-1	2-3	3-2
Maryhill	Apr 16	Apr 19	Apr 23	Nov 16	Aug 24	Mar 22	Dec7	Mar 29	May 24		Oct 12	Sep 7	May 12
	2-0	0-3	3-3	2-0	3-3	2-0	2-2	3-0	0-2		4-0	0-2	4-4
Neilston	Aug 17	Sep 7	Apr 26	Oct 5	Apr 30	May 7	Dec 28	Mar 22	Apr 19	Apr 12		May 14	Aug 31
	2-0	0-0	0-0	7-2	2-1	6-0	5-1	2-0	0-0	2-0		2-1	3-0
Shettleston	Sep 14	Nov 16	Jan 11	Mar 29	May 12	Oct 12	Apr 12	Apr 26	Aug 17	May 3	Sep 21		Mar 1
	1-1	0-2	2-1	3-4	3-0	5-1	5-1	2-1	3-1	4-0	2-0		4-3
St Anthonys	Oct 5	Feb 1	Aug 24	Dec 28	Mar 15	Nov 16	Jan 11	Sep 7	Nov 9	Apr 21	Apr 16	Nov 30	
	0-1	0-0	1-2	1-2	1-1	2-1	2-0	1-2	2-1	0-1	0-1	3-2	

ABD Nov 9 Carluke v Benburb
ABD Jan 11 Neilston v Glasgow Perthshire
ABD Mar 8, Carluke R v Benburb (High Winds)
+ at Neilston

Team	Pld	W	D	L	F	A	GD	Pts
Neilston Juniors F.C.	24	16	4	4	50	19	31	52
Shettleston F.C.	24	15	3	6	58	32	26	48
Benburb F.C.	24	13	5	6	37	28	9	44
Bellshill Athletic F.C.	24	12	7	5	39	25	14	43
Carluke Rovers F.C.	24	13	3	8	52	43	9	42
Dunipace F.C.	24	12	5	7	42	29	13	41
Larkhall Thistle F.C.	24	11	5	8	45	34	11	38
St. Anthony's F.C.	24	9	4	11	39	40	-1	31
Maryhill F.C.	24	9	4	11	40	44	-4	31
Lanark United F.C.	24	7	6	11	41	39	2	27
Cambuslang Rangers F.C.	24	8	3	13	32	35	-3	27
Johnstone Burgh F.C.	24	2	4	18	29	68	-39	10
Glasgow Perthshire F.C.	24	2	1	21	23	91	-68	7

In the course of the season Benburb vacated their old ground at Tinto Park and started to groundshare with Neilston. The Bens intend to build a new ground between Tinto Park and the M8. Tinto was one of the last of the grand old Junior grounds and will be greatly missed by the traditionalists.

Bellshill Athletic continued to groundshare with Vale of Clyde.

NEILSTON JFC SQUAD 2013/14

James Digney
Scott Perry
David Gordon
Keiran McDade
Martin McInnes
Robbie McNamara
Paul Young
Robert Campbell
James Lennox
Chris Cameron
Thomas Murdoch
Craig Murphy
James Canning
Stephen Docherty
Martin Hughes
Bryan Smith
Adam Nisanci
Darren Christie
Derek Kennedy
Matt McLean

Manager: Andy Whiteford

West Region Central Division One - All Time Positions	2002-3	2003-4	2004-5	2005-6	2006-7	2007-8	2008-9	2009-10	2010-11	2011-12	2012-13	2013-14
Ashfield						3	2					
Bellshill Athletic										10	9	4
Benburb			11			8	11			5	8	3
Blantyre Victoria	12				9	10		7	13			
Cambuslang Rangers		1			11		5	4	5	12		11
Carluke Rovers			12								7	5
Clydebank			2	8	2							
Cumbernauld United				5	3	5	6	1				
Dunipace		6	3		10	11		8	9	8	10	7
East Kilbride Thistle	6	5	6	2						14		
Glasgow Perthshire	8	12			13			10	6	1		13
Greenock	3	3	9	10				10	3	1		
Johnstone Burgh							12		12			12
Kilsyth Rangers	1								1			
Kirkintilloch Rob Roy	7	2			1							
Lanark United	5	11		6	7	2					6	10
Larkhall Thistle						7	8	12		6	3	6
Lesmahagow	11				1		9	11			2	
Maryhill							4	13				9
Neilston									4	4	11	1
Port Glasgow		10			4	1		9	8	7	12	
Rutherglen Glencairn	2	9	8	3	5	4	1					
Shettleston			7	12					11	9	4	2
Shotts Bon Accord								2				
St Anthonys		8	5	9	8	9	7	3	3	11	5	8
St Rochs	10					12					13	
Thorniewood United				11			3	6	2			
Vale of Clyde	9	7	1								14	
Vale of Leven	4	4	10	7	12		10	5	7	13		
Yoker Athletic			4	4	6	6				2		

West Junior Central League Second Division 2013/14

Team	BLA	FOR	EKT	NEW	POR	ROS	ROY	STR	VOC	VOL	WIS
Blantyre Vics		Mar 15 / 1-2	May 3 / 4-1	Oct 12 / 6-0	Aug 24 / 3-0	Jan 11 / 2-0	Apr 12 / 3-0	Apr 19 / 9-1	Dec7 / 3-2	Nov 9 / 3-3	Oct 5 / 3-0
Forth Wanderers	Sep 21 / 0-2		Apr 5 / 4-1	Apr 19 / 4-2	Sep 7 / 2-2	Nov 9 / 1-0	Oct 5 / 2-2	Mar 1 / 8-0	Jan 18 / 5-1	Mar 22 / 2-1	Aug 24 / 1-2
East Kilbride Thistle	Apr 16 / 0-1	Jan 11 / 4-4		Apr 12 / 2-2	Apr 19 / 3-0	Sep 21 / 1-5	Aug 24 / 0-1	Sep 7 / 0-6	Mar 15 / 1-2	Oct 12 / 1-3	Apr 28 / 1-2
Newmains United	Apr 26 / 0-3	Mar 29 / 1-3	Oct 5 / 3-2		Nov 9 / 0-5	Aug 24 / 0-4	Apr 16 / 2-4	May 3 / 2-2	Mar 22 / 2-8	Dec7 / 0-6	Sep 7 / 0-9
Port Glasgow	Mar 29 / 3-4	Apr 12 / 4-2	Aug 31 / 3-2	Jan 25 / 3-4		Nov 2 / 5-1	Oct 12 / 2-0	Aug 17 / 0-3	Nov 30 / 2-2	Sep 14 / 0-2	Nov 23 / 0-1
Rossvale	Sep 7 / 4-7	Oct 12 / 0-3	Mar 8 / 3-2	Nov 16 / 4-1	Feb 1 / 2-1		Dec 21 / 2-1	Dec7 / 2-1	Apr 5 / 0-3	Aug 17 / 2-3	Nov 30 / 1-0
Royal Albert	Aug 17 / 1-4	Aug 31 / 1-4	Nov 16 / 1-0	Sep 14 / 3-1	Mar 1 / 2-4	Mar 15 / 2-0		Apr 26 / 1-0	Mar 29 / 0-3	Apr 19 / 3-0	Sep 21 / 1-7
St Rochs	Aug 31 / 2-2	Sep 14 / 1-5	Mar 29 / 0-1	Apr 5 / 2-3	Mar 15 / 0-6	Oct 5 / 3-1	Mar 22 / 2-3		Sep 21 / 3-4	Dec 28 / 2-2	Apr 12 / 1-1
Vale of Clyde	Apr 21 / 1-2	Aug 17 / 3-1	Sep 14 / 8-0	Aug 31 / 5-2	Oct 5 / 5-1	Mar 1 / 4-0	May 2 / 4-3	Nov 16 / 5-4		Apr 12 / 3-2	Apr 19 / 3-2
Vale of Leven	Apr 5 / 3-4	Nov 2 / 1-3	Jan 4 / 3-0	Sep 21 / 6-0	Nov 16 / 3-3	Dec 14 / 4-2	Sep 7 / 1-2	Nov 30 / 4-1	Aug 24 / 1-2		Mar 15 / 0-1
Wishaw	Mar 22 / 0-4	Feb 22 / 3-1	Aug 17 / 2-1	Jan 18 / 4-3*	Apr 26 / 5-0	Sep 14 / 0-1	Dec7 / 3-1	Nov 9 / 1-2	Oct 12 / 2-0	Aug 31 / 6-2	

* ABD 89 mins due to fighting, result stands

#	Club	P	W	D	L	F	A	PTS
1	Blantyre Victoria F.C.	20	17	2	1	70	23	53
2	Vale of Clyde F.C.	20	15	1	4	68	36	46
3	Wishaw Juniors F.C.	20	13	1	6	51	26	40
4	Forth Wanderers F.C.	20	12	3	5	57	32	39
5	Royal Albert F.C.	20	9	1	10	32	44	28
6	Vale of Leven F.C.	20	8	3	9	50	40	27
7	Rossvale F.C.	20	9	0	11	34	44	27
8	Port Glasgow Juniors F.C.	20	7	3	10	44	46	24
9	St. Roch's F.C.	20	4	4	12	36	60	16
10	East Kilbride Thistle F.C.	20	2	2	16	23	57	8
11	Newmains United F.C.	20	3	2	15	28	85	8

Royal Albert's plans to move to a new ground at Ashgill appear to ha e stalled. In 2013/14 they used the old Stonehouse Violet ground at Tileworks Park and that arrangement will continue for 2014/15.

Towards the end of the season there was speculation that Port Glasgow Juniors might be "evicted" from the Port Glasgow Community Stadium. It remains to be seen if there was ay substance to these rumours.

Bishopbriggs-based Rossvale continue to groundshare with Petershill.

During the course of the season St Roch's ground at Provanmill Park was renamd the Jimmy McGrory Memorial Park in honour of the Candy's greatest ever player.

BLANTYRE VICS SQUAD 2013/14

Goalkeepers
Ryan Dakhil
Christopher Hanley
Paul Burns

Defenders
Mark O'Donnell
Michael Williams
Alexaner Amos
Bryan Mc:aughlin
Terry Hewitt
William Eadie
Paul Hanlo
Ross Mcntosh

Midfield
Ryan Barrett
Darren Burns
David Green
Gordon Duchess
Alan Christie
Ryan McGarry
Stuart Mills
David Gault
James Ronald

Forwards
David Kirkwood
Iain Reid
Stephen McDonald
Craig Smith

Manager: David Greig

West Region Central Division Two - All Time Positions

	2002-3	2003-4	2004-5	2005-6	2006-7	2007-8	2008-9	2009-10	2010-11	2011-12	2012-13	2013-14
Ashfield	4	7	5	4	1							
Baillieston	5											
Benburb				8	3			4	3			
Blantyre Vics		5	8	1			1			9	8	1
Cambuslang Rangers						3				1		
Carluke Rovers	12	2		7	5	4	4	6	7	1		
Clydebank		1										
Coltness United / Newmains United	11	13	13	W	9	Ab	10	11	12	10	11	11
Cumbernauld United												
Dunipace	3						2					
East Kilbride Thistle												10
Forth Wanderers	6	6	10	9	7	5	8	9	11	3	9	4
Glasgow Perthshire			12	3			3					
Greenock					4	6	7	3				
Johnstone Burgh								1		6	3	
Lanark United			1									
Larkhall Thistle									2			
Lesmahagow		4	3						9	4		
Maryhill									6	5	2	
Port Glasgow	2		4	2								8
Rossvale										8	5	7
Royal Albert	13	9	11	10	11	10	6	10	10	11	10	5
Shettleston					6	7	5	2				
St Anthonys	1											
St Rochs		8	7	5	2		9	7	4	2		9
Stonehouse Violet	10	12	6	6	10	8	Ab	Ab	5			
Thorniewood United	9	10	2		8	2						
Vale of Clyde											6	2
Vale of Leven						1					7	6
Wishaw	7	11	9	11	12	9	11	8	8	7	4	3
Yoker Athletic	8	3						5	1			
Ab = In Abeyance												
W = Withdrew												

Ardagh Ayrshire League Cup 2013/14

Section 1

	AWR	B	DT	KR	LT	SV
Ardrossan Winton Rovers		Aug 12 0-4	Aug 10 1-1			Aug 5 3-2
Beith				Aug 5 5-1		Aug 10 6-0
Dalry Thistle		Aug 7 1-3			Aug 5 2-1	
Kilwinning Rangers	Aug 14 9-1		Aug 12 1-1		Aug 10 3-0	
Largs Thistle	Aug 7 1-3	Aug 15 1-2				Aug 12 2-0
Saltcoats Victoria			Aug 15 0-5	Aug 7 0-5		

Section 1	P	W	D	L	F	A	PTS
Beith	5	5	0	0	20	3	15
Kilwinning Rangers	5	3	1	1	19	7	10
Dalry Thistle	5	2	2	1	10	6	8
Ardrossan Winton Rovers	5	2	1	2	8	17	7
Largs Thistle	5	1	0	4	5	10	3
Saltcoats Victoria	5	0	0	5	2	21	0

Largs Thistle's results suggested that they were in for a long hard season and that is how it transpired. Beith demonstrated that they would be up for the challenge of winning promotion from the Super League First Division.

Section 2

	AT	D	HU	IM	IV	KL
Ardeer Thistle		Aug 10 4-1		Aug 12 0-7		Aug 7 1-5
Darvel			Aug 14 1-6		Aug 7 1-2	
Hurlford United	Aug 5 9-0	Aug 12 6-1			Aug 10 4-0	
Irvine Meadow			Aug 7 2-2			Aug 10 0-4
Irvine Vics	Aug 14 2-0			Aug 5 0-5		Aug 12 1-3
Kilbirnie Ladeside	Aug 5 5-1	Aug 14 1-4				

Section 2	P	W	D	L	F	A	PTS
Hurlford United	5	4	1	0	25	4	13
Kilbirnie Ladeside	5	4	0	1	18	7	12
Irvine Meadow	5	3	1	1	20	7	10
Irvine Vics	5	2	0	3	5	13	6
Ardeer Thistle	5	1	0	4	5	24	3
Darvel	5	0	0	5	5	23	0

Hurlford spent big in pre-season and quickly established themselves as one of the teams to catch this season. With three top flight clubs this was always going to be an intriguing section - Hurlford's impressive 4-1 win at Kilbirnie was to prove decisive.

Section 3

	AU	CB	G	M	T	WV
Annbank United		Aug 10 7-1		Aug 14 3-7		Aug 12 2-3
Craigmark Burntonians				Aug 12 0-9	Aug 14 0-12	
Girvan	Aug 7 5-0	Aug 5 6-0		Aug 10 4-1		
Maybole					Aug 7 2-1	Aug 5 1-0
Troon	Aug 5 4-0		Aug 12 0-3			Aug 10 2-0
Whitletts Vics		Aug 7 5-1	Aug 14 1-1			

Section 3	P	W	D	L	F	A	PTS
Girvan	5	4	1	0	19	2	13
Maybole	5	4	0	1	20	8	12
Troon	5	3	0	2	19	5	9
Whitletts Vics	5	2	1	2	9	7	7
Annbank United	5	1	0	4	12	20	3
Craigmark Burntonians	5	0	0	5	2	39	0

By some distance the weakest section, it was Girvan who showed the consistency to make progress. Craigmark endured a desperate start to the season, including a 12-0 home defeat from Troon.

Section 4

	AT	C	GA	KR	LBT	M
Auchinleck Talbot			Aug 7 3-2	Aug 5 10-1		Aug 10 8-0
Cumnock	Aug 12 1-2		Aug 14 0-0	Aug 7 1-1		
Glenafton Athletic				Aug 10 7-1	Aug 5 1-7	
Kello Rovers					Aug 12 2-2	Aug 14 7-0
Lugar Boswell Thistle	Aug 14 0-9	Aug 10 1-4				Aug 7 5-0
Muirkirk		Aug 5 1-9	Aug 12 0-5			

Section 4	P	W	D	L	F	A	PTS
Auchinleck Talbot	5	5	0	0	32	4	15
Cumnock	5	2	2	1	15	5	8
Glenafton Athletic	5	2	1	2	15	11	7
Lugar Boswell Thistle	5	2	1	2	15	16	7
Kello Rovers	5	1	2	2	12	20	5
Muirkirk	5	0	0	5	1	34	0

Glenafton lost most of their squad to Hurlford in the Summer and had to build anew from scratch. Auchinleck looked imperious as they cruised through with the other teams beating each other. Poor Muirkirk were the exception with an average of almost seven goals conceded per game.

QF	21/08/13	Auchinleck Talbot	Maybole	3	1	
QF	21/08/13	Beith	Kilbirnie Ladeside	1	0	
QF	21/08/13	Hurlford United	Kilwinning Rangers	6	3	
QF	21/08/13	Girvan	Cumnock	1	1	3-4 pens

SF	28/08/13	Beith	Hurlford United	2	0
SF	28/08/13	Cumnock	Auchinleck Talbot	1	0

F	29/09/13	Cumnock	Beith	1	1	9-8 pens at Troon 1000

Cumnock: Semple, Lundie, McMenamin, Crawford, Wood, McKnight, Johnston, Williamson, Maguire, Love, Hanvey Subs ; Pierce, Robertson, Bradford, Reid, McInnes
Beith: Strain, Ryan, Wilson, Donnelly, McShane, McDonald, Gibson, Frize, McLean, Reid, Bradley Subs ; McKay, McGowan, Hobbs, Sheridan, Docherty

1-0	43mins	Crawford
1-1	75 mins	McLean (pen)

* The Kick Off had to be delayed for more than 15 minutes to allow the large ground in to Portland Park.

Recent Ayrshire Sectional League Cup Finals

Season	Winners	Runners Up	Score	Venue
1989/90	Auchinleck Talbot	Irvine Meadow	1-1, 5-3 pens	Rugby Park, Kilmarnock
1990/1	Auchinleck Talbot	Beith	2-1	Rugby Park, Kilmarnock
1991/2	Beith	Glenafton Athletic	2-1	Rugby Park, Kilmarnock
1992/3	Auchinleck Talbot	Irvine Meadow	1-1, 4-3 pens	Winton Park, Ardrossan
1993/4	Beith	Auchinleck Talbot	0-0, 4-3 pens	Somerset Park, Ayr
1994/5	Kilbirnie Ladeside	Auchinleck Talbot	0-0, 4-2 pens	Somerset Park, Ayr
1995/6	Cumnock	Ardeer Thistle	3-1	Somerset Park, Ayr
1996/7	Cumnock	Kilwinning Rangers	1-0	Somerset Park, Ayr
1997/8	Auchinleck Talbot	Beith	2-1	Somerset Park, Ayr
1998/9	Kilwinning Rangers	Auchinleck Talbot	2-1	Somerset Park, Ayr
1999/00	Glenafton Athletic	Kilwinning Rangers	4-1	Somerset Park, Ayr
2000/1	Cumnock	Kilwinning Rangers	2-2, 5-3 pens	Somerset Park, Ayr
2001/2	Cumnock	Irvine Meadow	3-2	Somerset Park, Ayr
2002/3	Auchinleck Talbot	Irvine Meadow	3-1	Somerset Park, Ayr
2003/4	Irvine Meadow	Auchinleck Talbot	2-0	Somerset Park, Ayr
2004/5	Beith	Auchinleck Talbot	1-1, 4-2 pens	Somerset Park, Ayr
2005/6	Glenafton Athletic	Cumnock	4-3	Somerset Park, Ayr
2006/7	Auchinleck Talbot	Cumnock	2-1	Somerset Park, Ayr
2007/8	Auchinleck Talbot	Irvine Meadow	2-1	Somerset Park, Ayr
2008/9	Irvine Meadow	Lugar Boswall Thistle	3-0	Meadow Park, Irvine
2009/10	Kilbirnie Ladeside	Cumnock	3-0	Meadow Park, Irvine
2010/1	Auchinleck Talbot	Irvine Meadow	1-1, 8-7 pens	Bellsdale Park, Beith
2011/2	Auchinleck Talbot	Irvine Meadow	3-0	Bellsdale Park, Beith
2012/3	Irvine Meadow	Auchinleck Talbot	4-4, 4-2 pens	Bellsdale Park, Beith
2013/4	Cumnock	Beith	1-1, 9-8 pens	Portland Park, Troon

Surridge Central Sectional League Cup 2013/14

Section 1

	LU	LT	L	RA
Lanark United		Aug 7 / 0-1		Aug 12 / 3-1
Larkhall Thistle			Aug 12 / 2-3	Aug 10 / 2-0
Lesmahagow	Aug 10 / 2-1			
Royal Albert			Aug 7 / 2-2	

	P	W	D	L	F	A	PTS
Lesmahagow	3	2	1	0	7	5	7
Larkhall Thistle	3	2	0	1	5	3	6
Lanark United	3	1	0	2	4	4	3
Royal Albert	3	0	1	2	3	7	1

Royal Albert took up residence at Tileworks Park in Stonehouse for the start of the season. Super League First Division side Lesmahagow, as expected, progressed against their three rivals from lower divisions.

Section 2

	CR	FW	NU	SBA	W
Carluke Rovers			Aug 8 / 11-0		Aug 15 / 3-0
Forth Wanderers	Aug 10 / 2-2		Aug 12 / 1-0		
Newmains United				Aug 14 / 0-9	Aug 5 / 0-4
Shotts Bon Accord	Aug 12 / 2-2	Aug 5 / 3-3			
Wishaw		Aug 7 / 2-0		Aug 10 / 0-4	

	P	W	D	L	F	A	PTS
Carluke Rovers	4	2	2	0	18	4	8
Shotts Bon Accord	4	2	2	0	18	5	8
Wishaw	4	2	0	2	6	7	6
Forth Wanderers	4	1	2	1	6	7	5
Newmains United	4	0	0	4	0	25	0

Quite an upset as Carluke Rovers progressed ahead of the highly-fancied Shotts Bon Accord side. Shotts dropped two points in their opening game at home to Forth Wanderers which ultimately cost them the section.

Section 3

	BA	P	SH	SR	TU
Bellshill Athletic		Aug 7 / 3-2	Aug 14 / 3-1		
Petershill			Aug 5 / 4-0		Aug 14 / 3-1
Shettleston				Aug 7 / 8-1	Aug 10 / 0-1
St Rochs	Aug 10 / 1-4	Aug 12 / 2-6			
Thorniewood United	Aug 12 / 1-0			Aug 5 / 1-0	

	P	W	D	L	F	A	PTS
Petershill	4	3	0	1	15	6	9
Bellshill Athletic	4	3	0	1	10	5	9
Thorniewood United	4	3	0	1	4	3	9
Shettleston	4	1	0	3	9	9	3
St Rochs	4	0	0	4	4	19	0

Bellshill and Thorniewood both ran Petershill close before the Super Premier side went through. St Rochs, unde rnew management and with an energetic new committee, failed to mak much impact on the field.

Section 4

	BV	CR	EKT	RG	VOC
Blantyre Vics		Aug 10 / 0-1	Aug 15 / 4-1		
Cambuslang Rangers			Aug 5 / 4-1	Aug 14 / 1-1	
East Kilbride Thistle				Aug 10 / 1-8	Aug 7 / 0-3
Rutherglen Glencairn	Aug 7 / 0-1	Aug 12 / 0-3			
Vale of Clyde	Aug 12 / 6-4			Aug 5 / 4-1	

	P	W	D	L	F	A	PTS
Vale of Clyde	4	3	1	0	14	6	10
Cambuslang Rangers	4	3	1	0	9	2	10
Blantyre Vics	4	2	0	2	9	8	6
Rutherglen Glencairn	4	1	0	3	9	9	3
East Kilbride Thistle	4	0	0	4	3	19	0

As expected this was a very tight section with Vale of Clyde emerging as unexpected winners. There was no sign of light at the end of the tunnel for East Kilbride Thistle who have endured hard times recently.

Section 5

	A	B	N	P	SA
Arthurlie		Aug 7 / 3-0	Aug 14 / 3-0		
Benburb			Aug 5 / 4-2		Aug 14 / 2-4
Neilston				Aug 7 / 1-2	Aug 10 / 4-3
Pollok	Aug 10 / 1-0	Aug 12 / 5-0			
St Anthonys	Aug 12 / 2-4			Aug 5 / 0-1	

	P	W	D	L	F	A	PTS
Pollok	4	4	0	0	9	1	12
Arthurlie	4	3	0	1	10	3	9
St Anthonys	4	1	0	3	9	11	3
Neilston	4	1	0	3	7	12	3
Benburb	4	1	0	3	6	14	3

Pollok won the "big one" against Arthurlie to go through to the Quarter Finals. None of the three other clubs showd much form to suggest a good season ahead.

Section 6

	A	C	GP	M	YA
Ashfield			Aug 12 / 4-1	Aug 14 / 1-3	
Clydebank	Aug 10 / 8-0			Aug 7 / 4-1	
Glasgow Perthshire		Aug 14 / 2-5			Aug 7 / 1-7
Maryhill			Aug 5 / 3-2		Aug 10 / 3-2
Yoker Athletic	Aug 5 / 2-2	Aug 12 / 0-1			

	P	W	D	L	F	A	PTS
Clydebank	4	4	0	0	18	3	12
Maryhill	4	3	0	1	10	9	9
Yoker Athletic	4	1	1	2	11	7	4
Ashfield	4	1	1	2	7	14	4
Glasgow Perthshire	4	0	0	4	6	19	0

Super Premier side Clydebank were never troubled as they won all four games against lower division opponents. Maryhill did well to finish second ahead of more fancied sides.

Section 7

	G	JB	PG	R	VOL
Greenock			Aug 5 / 1-2		Aug 14 / 2-2
Johnstone Burgh	Aug 7 / 1-1		Aug 14 / 0-1		
Port Glasgow				Aug 7 / 3-3	Aug 10 / 4-2
Renfrew	Aug 12 / 1-4	Aug 10 / 5-2			
Vale of Leven		Aug 12 / 5-0	Aug 5 / 2-1		

	P	W	D	L	F	A	PTS
Port Glasgow	4	3	1	0	10	6	10
Vale of Leven	4	2	1	1	11	7	7
Greenock	4	1	2	1	8	6	5
Renfrew	4	1	1	2	10	11	4
Johnstone Burgh	4	0	1	3	3	12	1

On paper this looked like a very close section. Port Glasgow got off to a good start with a derby win over Greenock. Renfrew were again a disappointment as they struggled to recapture former glories.

Section 8

	CU	D	KR	KRR	R
Cumbernauld United		Aug 10 / 5-4	Aug 14 / 2-4		Aug 7 / 0-0
Dunipace					Aug 5 / 3-0
Kilsyth Rangers		Aug 7 / 2-0		Aug 5 / 2-5	
Kirkintilloch Rob Roy	Aug 12 / 6-1	Aug 14 / 2-2			
Rossvale			Aug 12 / 3-1	Aug 10 / 2-3	

	P	W	D	L	F	A	PTS
Kirkintilloch Rob Roy	4	3	1	0	16	7	10
Kilsyth Rangers	4	2	0	2	9	10	6
Dunipace	4	1	1	2	9	9	4
Rossvale	4	1	1	2	5	7	4
Cumbernauld United	4	1	1	2	8	14	4

No problems for Kirkintilloch Rob Roy as they progressed at the expense of lower division opposition. Rossvale were delighted with a four-point tally against tricky opponents..

QF	21/08/13	Petershill	Vale of Clyde	4	1	
QF	21/08/13	Kirkintilloch Rob Roy	Pollok	2	3	
QF	21/08/13	Clydebank	Carluke Rovers	8	1	
QF	21/08/13	Lesmahagow	Port Glasgow	5	1	
SF	28/08/13	Pollok	Lesmahagow	3	1	
SF	28/08/13	Petershill	Clydebank	1	1	3-4 pens
F	22/09/13	Clydebank	Pollok	2	0	at Maryhill 881

Clydebank: L Campbell, Walker, McCann, Martin, Bell, R Campbell, J Campbell, Berry (Sub Gold), McPherson (Sub Andrew), Wilson, McElroy (Sub Paterson).
Pollok: Murdoch, McLennan, McGillion (Sub Waddell), Reilly, McGowan, Howie, Easton, Sinclair (Sub Hebburn), Barr, Diack, McAleenan.

1-0	71mins	McElroy
2-0	90mins `	Paterson

Recent Central Sectional League Cup Finals

Season	Winners	Runners Up	Score	Venue
1989/90	Dunipace	Arthurlie	2-2, 7-6 pens	Fir Park, Motherwell
1990/1	Pollok	Arthurlie	0-0, 4-3 pens	Fir Park, Motherwell
1991/2	Ruthergleb Glencairn	Arthurlie	4-1	Hannah Park, Shotts
1992/3	Pollok	Rutherglen Glencairn	3-1	Douglas Park, Hamilton
1993/4	Lesmahagow	Petershill	2-1	Kilbowie Park, Clydebank
1994/5	Petershill	Larkhall Thistle	2-1	Fir Park, Motherwell
1995/6	Blantyre Vics	Pollok	1-0	Fir Park, Motherwell
1996/7	Pollok	Shettleston	4-2	Fir Park, Motherwell
1997/8	Shotts Bon Accord	Arthurlie	0-0, 4-1 pens	Fir Park, Motherwell
1998/9	Neilston	Baillieston	5-0	Fir Park, Motherwell
1999/00	Pollok	Shotts Bon Accord	4-1	Firhill Stadium, Glasgow
2000/1	Cambuslang Rangers	Shotts Bon Accord	1-0	Firhill Stadium, Glasgow
2001/2	Bellshill Athletic	Larkhall Thistle	3-0	Firhill Stadium, Glasgow
2002/3	East Kilbride Thistle	Bellshill Athletic	2-0	Firhill Stadium, Glasgow
2003/4	Pollok	Kilsyth Rangers	1-1, 5-3 pens	Firhill Stadium, Glasgow
2004/5	Maryhill	Shotts Bon Accord	2-0	Firhill Stadium, Glasgow
2005/6	Neilston	East Kilbirde Thistle	0-0, 4-3 pens	Firhill Stadium, Glasgow
2006/7	Pollok	Clydebank	2-1	Lochburn Park, Glasgow
2007/8	Rutherglen Glencairn	Port Glasgow	2-1	Lochburn Park, Glasgow
2008/9	Arthurlie	Shotts Bon Accord	3-2	Lochburn Park, Glasgow
2009/10	Arthurlie	Shotts Bon Accord	1-0	Lochburn Park, Glasgow
2010/1	Shotts Bon Accord	Lanark United	1-0	New Southcroft, Rutherglen
2011/2	Petershill	Shotts Bon Accord	3-2	Lochburn Park, Glasgow
2012/3	Pollok	Renfrew	3-0	Lochburn Park, Glasgow
2013/4	Clydebank	Pollok	2-0	Lochburn Park, Glasgow

West of Scotland Junior Cup   2013/14

Round	Date	Home	Away			Notes
R1	12/10/13	Lesmahagow	St Rochs	6	1	
R1	19/10/13	Whitletts Vics	Arthurlie	0	3	
R1	19/10/13	Glenafton Athletic	Largs Thistle	2	3	
R1	19/10/13	Kilbirnie Ladeside	Ardrossan Winton Rovers	5	3	
R1	19/10/13	Greenock	Maryhill	4	4	
R1	19/10/13	Carluke Rovers	Glasgow Perthshire	5	4	
R1	19/10/13	Beith	Pollok	2	3	
R1	19/10/13	Vale of Leven	East Kilbride Thistle	7	0	
R1	19/10/13	Irvine Vics	Kello Rovers	3	1	
R1	19/10/13	Auchinleck Talbot	Bellshill Athletic	3	1	
R1	19/10/13	Shotts Bon Accord	Royal Albert	5	0	
R1	19/10/13	Cumnock	Lanark United	4	2	
R1	19/10/13	Kirkintilloch Rob Roy	Darvel	7	0	
R1	19/10/13	Irvine Meadow	Hurlford United	2	4	
R1	19/10/13	Petershill	Forth Wanderers	3	1	
R1	19/10/13	Cambuslang Rangers	Port Glasgow	3	0	
R1	19/10/13	St Anthonys	Kilwinning Rangers	2	3	
R1	19/10/13	Troon	Dalry Thistle	4	1	
R1	19/10/13	Maybole	Wishaw	2	0	
R1	19/10/13	Shettleston	Saltcoats Vics	9	1	
R1	19/10/13	Ashfield	Girvan	4	2	
R1	19/10/13	Muirkirk	Benburb	0	9	
R1	19/10/13	Ardeer Thistle	Larkhall Thistle	0	3	
R1	19/10/13	Kilsyth Rangers	Rossvale	5	0	
R1	09/11/13	Cumbernauld United	Vale of Clyde	1	1	4-3 pens
R1	02/11/13	Thorniewood United	Neilston	1	2	
R1	02/11/13	Newmains United	Johnstone Burgh	0	8	
R1	09/11/13	Dunipace	Rutherglen Glencairn	3	2	
R1	02/11/13	Clydebank	Lugar Boswell Thistle	3	2	
R1	02/11/13	Craigmark Burntonians	Blantyre Vics	1	11	
R1	09/11/13	Yoker Athletic	Annbank United	4	1	
R2	21/12/13	Kilbirnie Ladeside	Maybole	1	1	4-3 pens
R2	21/12/13	Lesmahagow	Shettleston	1	0	
R2	21/12/13	Carluke Rovers	Kirkintilloch Rob Roy	1	4	
R2	21/12/13	Irvine Vics	Troon	1	1	4-5 pens
R2	21/12/13	Cumnock	Largs Thistle	2	0	
R2	21/12/13	Pollok	Petershill	1	2	
R2	01/02/14	Dunipace	Greenock	1	0	
R2	01/02/14	Clydebank	Auchinleck Talbot	1	2	
R2	01/02/14	Arthurlie	Kilsyth Rangers	3	2	
R2	01/02/14	Renfrew	Johnstone Burgh	4	2	
R2	22/02/14	Cumbernauld United	Kilwinning Rangers	2	2	5-4 pens
R2	22/02/14	Muirkirk	Cambuslang Rangers	1	4	
R2	01/03/14	Larkhall Thistle	Shotts Bon Accord	2	3	
R2	01/03/14	Vale of Leven	Ashfield	3	4	
R2	01/03/14	Neilston	Yoker Athletic	6	1	
R2	01/03/14	Blantyre Vics	Hurlford United	0	4	at Hurlford
R3	29/03/14	Ashfield	Dunipace	1	2	
R3	29/03/14	Arthurlie	Kilbirnie Ladeside	1	2	
R3	29/03/14	Auchinleck Talbot	Kirkintilloch Rob Roy	3	0	
R3	29/03/14	Cambuslang Rangers	Troon	0	4	
R3	29/03/14	Neilston	Shotts Bon Accord	0	1	
R3	29/03/14	Cumbernauld United	Petershill	1	1	5-3 pens
R3	23/04/14	Hurlford United	Cumnock	2	0	
QF	19/04/14	Troon	Dunipace	1	0	
QF	03/05/14	Kilbirnie Ladeside	Auchinleck Talbot	0	2	
QF	05/05/14	Cumbernauld United	Hurlford United	2	1	
QF	05/05/14	Lesmahagow	Shotts Bon Accord	3	2	at Stonehouse
SF	17/05/14	Lesmahagow	Auchinleck Talbot	0	5	at Stonehouse
SF	17/05/14	Troon	Cumbernauld United	2	1	
F	24/05/14	Auchinleck Talbot	Troon	2	0	at Pollok

Recent West of Scotland Cup Finals

Season	Winners	Runners Up	Score	Venue
1988/9	Auchinleck Talbot	Shotts Bon Accord	1-0 aet	Rugby Park, Kilmarnock
1989/90	Irvine Meadow	Larkhall Thistle	4-1	Newlandsfield, Glasgow
1990/1	Largs Thistle	Renfrew	1-0	Somervell Park, Cambuslang
1991/2	Pollok	Beith	1-0	Somervell Park, Cambuslang
1992/3	Shettleston	Lesmahagow	2-0	Somervell Park, Cambuslang
1993/4	Kilwinning Rangers	Shettleston	2-0	Somervell Park, Cambuslang
1994/5	Shettleston	Pollok	1-1, 4-2 pens	Somervell Park, Cambuslang
1995/6	Petershill	Maryhill	2-0	Somervell Park, Cambuslang
1996/7	Arthurlie	Irvine Meadow	5-0	Somervell Park, Cambuslang
1997/8	Pollok	Petershill	3-1	Somervell Park, Cambuslang
1998/9	Kilwinning Rangers	Arthurlie	2-1	Newlandsfield, Glasgow
1999/00	Pollok	Glenafton Athletic	2-1	Somervell Park, Cambuslang
2000/1	Maryhill	Pollok	1-0	Somervell Park, Cambuslang
2001/2	Benburb	Johnstone Burgh	3-2	Newlandsfield, Glasgow
2002/3	Glenafton Athletic	Bellshill Athletic	4-2	Meadow Park, Irvine
2003/4	Maryhill	Bellshill Athletic	3-1	Newlandsfield, Glasgow
2004/5	Troon	Arthurlie	4-3	Newlandsfield, Glasgow
2005/6	Glenafton Athletic	Maryhill	1-1, 4-3 pens	Newlandsfield, Glasgow
2006/7	Petershill	Kilbirnie Ladeside	2-1	Newlandsfield, Glasgow
2007/8	Kilbirnie Ladeside	Pollok	5-1	Lochburn Park, Glasgow
2008/9	Beith	Auchinleck Talbot	2-1	Newlandsfield, Glasgow
2009/10	Irvine Meadow	Kirkintilloch Rob Roy	1-0	Newlandsfield, Glasgow
2010/1	Arthurlie	Pollok	1-0	Newlandsfield, Glasgow
2011/2	Irvine Meadow	Ashfield	2-0	Newlandsfield, Glasgow
2012/3	Glenafton Athletic	Glasgow Perthshire	2-2, 4-3 pens	Newlandsfield, Glasgow
2013/14	Auchinleck Talbot	Troon	2-0	Newlandsfield, Glasgow

WEST OF SCOTLAND CUP FINAL 2013/14
Auchinleck Talbot 2 Troon 0
Talbot – Leishman, Latta, Park, Pettigrew, McGoldrick, Spence, Young, White, Gormley, Wilson, Milliken
Subs – McCann, C Connolly, K Connolly, Armour, Kerr
Troon – Johnston, Murphy, Armstrong, McGowan, McKinnell, Chatham, Hardie, Wyllie, Gillies, Wilson, Moore. Subs – Armstrong, Keenan, Gilmour, Sanderson, Turner

1-0   1 min   Wilson,   2-0   49 mins   Wilson

AYRSHIRE CUP FINAL 2013/14
Troon 2 Hurlford United 0
Troon:1. Johnston, "Gaz" Armstrong, Keenan, McKinnell ©,Collins, Murphy (Sub Bo Armstrong), Hardie (Sub Ure), Chatham (Sub Turner), Gillies, Wilson, Moore

1-0   31minsGillies,   2-0   50 mins   Wilson

CENTRAL DISTRICT KO CUP FINAL 2013/14
Clydebank 3 Cumbernauld United 0 (Att 855)
Clydebank: Hamilton, Walker, Paterson, Martin, Bell, McCann, Gold, Berry (Sub Pearson), McPherson (Sub Shelvey), J Campbell, McElroy (Sub McCready)
Cumbernauld: Quinn, Steele, Fraser, Haxton (Sub Thomson), Boyle, Brown, McCafferty (Sub Gibson), Upton, Zok, Scott (Sub Foley), O'Halloran.

1-0   18mins McElroy,   2-0   33mins McElroy,   3-0   90 mins Pearson.

Ayrshire Junior Cup   2013/14

R1	08/02/14	Beith	Craigmark Burntonians	8	0		
R1	08/02/14	Ardeer Thistle	Cumnock	0	1		
R1	08/02/14	Annbank United	Kilbirnie Ladeside	0	4		at Kilbirnie
R1	08/02/14	Irvine Vics	Irvine Meadow	0	3		
R1	08/02/14	Hurlford United	Saltcoats Vics	4	1		
R1	22/02/14	Maybole	Kello Rovers	9	1		
R1	22/03/14	Dalry Thistle	Girvan	2	4		
R1	05/04/14	Lugar Boswell Thistle	Whitletts Vics	2	0		
R2	08/03/14	Darvel	Troon	2	3		at Troon
R2	01/03/14	Cumnock	Beith	2	2	2-4 pens	
R2	01/03/14	Kilbirnie Ladeside	Largs Thistle	1	2		
R2	08/03/14	Irvine Meadow	Auchinleck Talbot	3	2		
R2	08/03/14	Hurlford United	Ardrossan Winton Rovers	6	0		at Ardrossan
R2	29/03/14	Maybole	Glenafton Athletic	3	2		
R2	05/04/14	Muirkirk	Girvan	1	3		
R2	19/04/14	Kilwinning Rangers	Lugar Boswell Thistle	4	3		
QF	23/04/14	Irvine Meadow	Troon	1	2		
QF	26/04/14	Beith	Girvan	3	5		
QF	26/04/14	Largs Thistle	Maybole	2	4		
QF	07/05/14	Kilwinning Rangers	Hurlford United	0	6		
SF	05/05/14	Troon	Girvan	4	0		
SF	04/06/14	Maybole	Hurlford United	1	3		
F	12/06/14	Troon	Hurlford United	2	0		at Auchinleck

Recent Ayrshire Cup Finals

Season	Winners	Runners Up	Score	Venue
1988/9	Glenafton Athletic	Dalry Thistle	3-1	Meadow Park, Irvine
1989/90	Cumnock	Saltcoats Vics	3-0	Meadow Park, Irvine
1990/1	Beith	Largs Thistle	3-2 aet	Valefield, Kilbirnie
1991/2	Beith	Irvine Meadow	3-0	Valefield, Kilbirnie
1992/3	Glenafton Athletic	Cumnock	2-1	Townhead Park, Cumnock
1993/4	Auchinleck Talbot	Irvine Meadow	2-0	Abbey Park, Kilwinning
1994/5	Kilwinning Rangers	Largs Thistle	3-1	Meadow Park, Irvine
1995/6	Auchinleck Talbot	Cumnock	3-1	Beechwood Park, Auchinleck
1996/7	Auchinleck Talbot	Kilwinning Rangers	2-1	Meadow Park, Irvine
1997/8	Kilwinning Rangers	Troon	3-2 aet	Meadow Park, Irvine
1998/9	Kilwinning Rangers	Irvine Meadow	2-1	Meadow Park, Irvine
1999/00	Kilwinning Rangers	Auchinleck Talbot	3-2	Beechwood Park, Auchinleck
2000/1	Glenafton Athletic	Kilwinning Rangers	1-0	Meadow Park, Irvine
2001/2	Kilwinning Rangers	Lugar Boswall Thistle	2-0	Blair Park, Hurlford
2002/3	Beith	Kilwinning Rangers	3-1	Meadow Park, Irvine
2003/4	Beith	Lugar Boswall Thistle	2-0	Townhead Park, Cumnock
2004/5	Auchinleck Talbot	Kilbirnie Ladeside	5-0	Rosebank Park, Lugar
2005/6	Irvine Meadow	Kilwinning Rangers	2-1	Townhead Park, Cumnock
2006/7	Irvine Meadow	Dalry Thistle	7-0	Meadow Park, Irvine
2007/8	Cumnock	Kilwinning Rangers	5-0	Townhead Park, Cumnock
2008/9	Irvine Meadow	Auchinleck Talbot	2-1	Townhead Park, Cumnock
2009/10	Cumnock	Girvan	4-3	Beechwood Park, Auchinleck
2010/1	Auchinleck Talbot	Irvine Meadow	4-0	Beechwood Park, Auchinleck
2011/2	Auchinleck Talbot	Troon	5-1	Portland Park, Troon
2012/3	Largs Thistle	Cumnock	3-0	Bellsdale Park, Beith
2013/4	Troon	Hurlford United	2-0	Beechwood Park, Auchinleck

Central Regional Cup 2013/14

R1	08/02/14	Petershill	Bellshill Athletic	2	2	4-5 pens	
R1	08/02/14	Arthurlie	Larkhall Thistle	4	1		
R1	08/02/14	Clydebank	East Kilbride Thistle	4	1		
R1	08/03/14	Johnstone Burgh	Port Glasgow	4	2		at Port Glasgow
R1	22/02/13	Rossvale	Ashfield	2	3		
R1	15/03/14	Cumbernauld United	Newmains United	3	0		
R1	29/03/14	Rutherglen Glencairn	Yoker Athletic	1	1	4-2 pens	
R2	08/02/14	Blantyre Vics	Vale of Leven	3	5		at Vale of Leven
R2	08/02/14	Pollok	Renfrew	5	0		PROTEST
R2	08/02/14	Cambuslang Rangers	Vale of Clyde	0	1		at Vale of Clyde
R2	08/02/14	Dunipace	Forth Wanderers	2	0		
R2	08/02/14	Shettleston	Wishaw	4	1		
R2	08/02/14	Benburb	Thorniewood United	1	6		
R2	08/02/14	Maryhill	Royal Albert	1	1	4-2 pens	at Firhill Complex
R2	22/02/14	Greenock	Kirkintilloch Rob Roy	2	3		at Kirkintilloch
R2	22/02/14	St Rochs	Kilsyth Rangers	0	2		
R2	22/02/14	St Anthonys	Bellshill Athletic	4	0		
R2	22/02/14	Lanark United	Arthurlie	4	0		
R2	15/03/14	Ashfield	Lesmahagow	1	5		
R2	15/03/14	Shotts Bon Accord	Clydebank	0	2		
R2	05/04/14	Carluke Rovers	Cumbernauld United	2	2	2-4 pens	
R2	21/04/14	Johnstone Burgh	Neilston	1	1	6-7 pens	
R2ABD	05/04/14	Glasgow Perthshire	Rutherglen Glencairn	0	0		PROTEST
R3	23/04/14	Neilston	Clydebank	0	0	4-5 pens	
R3	23/04/14	Lesmahagow	Lanark United	3	0		at Lanark
R3	23/04/14	Thorniewood United	St Anthonys	2	0		
R3	23/04/14	Cumbernauld United	Dunipace	3	2		
R3	23/04/14	Vale of Leven	Rutherglen Glencairn	4	4	4-5 pens	
R3	23/04/14	Kirkintilloch Rob Roy	Renfrew	3	2		
R3	23/04/14	Shettleston	Vale of Clyde	3	2		
R3		Kilsyth Rangers	Maryhill	wo	scr		
QF	05/05/14	Kilsyth Rangers	Thorniewood United	2	0		PROTEST
QF	05/05/14	Clydebank	Shettleston	2	2	5-4 pens	
QF	07/05/14	Rutherglen Glencairn	Cumbernauld United	2	4		
QF	07/05/14	Lesmahagow	Kirkintilloch Rob Roy	2	3		at Stonehouse
SF	14/05/14	Clydebank	Thorniewood United	9	1		
SF	21/05/14	Cumbernauld United	Kirkintilloch Rob Roy	1	0		
F	11/06/14	Cumbernauld United	Clydebank	3	0		at Pollok

The 2013/14 competition was marred by several protests caused by registration problems:

Round 2 - Pollok were thrown out of the Cup for fielding ineligible players and enfrew were re-instated

Round 2 - The Glasgow Perthshire v Rutherglen Glencairn match, abandoned at half time due to rain, was never replayed. Perthshire were expelled for fielding an ineligible player

Round 3 - Maryhill scratched their tie against Kilsyth as they could not raise a team

QF - Kilsyth Rangers expelled for playing an ineligible player - Thoirniewood United reinstated

Recent Central District KO Cup Finals

Season	Winners	Runners Up	Score	Venue
1988/9	Pollok	Glasgow Perthshire	2-1	Greenfield Park, Glasgow
1989/90	Vale of Clyde	Shotts Bon Accord	5-1	Newlandsfield, Glasgow
1990/1	Arthurlie	Cambuslang Rangers	3-2	Newlandsfield, Glasgow
1991/2	Petershill	Shotts Bon Accord	1-0	Newlandsfield, Glasgow
1992/3	Lesmahagow	Bellshill Athletic	3-1	Newlandsfield, Glasgow
1993/4	Shotts Bon Accord	Shettleston	0-0, 4-2 pens	Newlandsfield, Glasgow
1994/5	not completed			
1995/6	Maryhill	Pollok	1-0	Somervell Park, Cambuslang
1996/7	Arthurlie	Pollok	2-1 aet	Somervell Park, Cambuslang
1997/8	Arthurlie	Shettleston	4-0	Newlandsfield, Glasgow
1998/9	Rutherglen Glencairn	Shettleston	4-1	Newlandsfield, Glasgow
1999/00	Benburb	Shettleston	2-1	Newlandsfield, Glasgow
2000/1	Bellshill Athletic	Pollok	0-0, 3-2 pens	Somervell Park, Cambuslang
2001/2	Shettleston	Johnstone Burgh	4-1	Petershill Park, Glasgow
2002/3	Arthurlie	Larkhall Thistle	2-1	Petershill Park, Glasgow
2003/4	Petershill	Maryhill	2-0	Adamslie Park, Kirkintilloch
2004/5	Pollok	Arthurlie	2-0	Petershill Park, Glasgow
2005/6	Maryhill	Greenock	2-1	Newlandsfield, Glasgow
2006/7	Lanark United	Kirkintilloch Rob Roy	2-1	Somervell Park, Cambuslang
2007/8	Arthurlie	Renfrew	3-0	Dunterlie Park, Barrhead
2008/9	Pollok	Kilsyth Rangers	1-1, 4-3 pens	Newlandsfield, Glasgow
2009/10	Clydebank	Ashfield	2-0	Newlandsfield, Glasgow
2010/1	Pollok	Shotts Bon Accord	7-3	Newlandsfield, Glasgow
2011/2	Clydebank	Shotts Bon Accord	3-0	Newlandsfield, Glasgow
2012/3	Pollok	Ashfield	3-0	Newlandsfield, Glasgow
2013/14	Clydebank	Cumbernauld United	3-0	Newlandsfield, Glasgow

Evening Times Champions Cup 2013/14

Prelim	01/05/14 Irvine Vics	Blantyre Vics	5 0	
SF	27/05/14 Neilston	Irvine Vics	1 0	
SF	28/05/14 Auchinleck Talbot	Troon	2 0	
F	07/06/14 Auchinleck Talbot	Neilston	7 1	at Pollok

Talbot – Leishman, Lyle, Park, Pettigrew, McGoldrick, Connolly, Latta, White, McCann, Wilson, Milliken Subs – Sloan, Anderson, Armour, Young, Kerr (gk)

Neilston – Digney, Murphy, Gordon, McDade, Young, Cameron, Canning, Hughes, Kennedy, Christie, Campbell. Subs – Smith, McLean, McNamara, Docherty, Perry (gk)

1-0	4mins	Wilson pen	
2-0	10mins	McCann pen	Neilston's cause was not helped by having
2-1	28mins	Canning	three players sent off during the match,
3-1	57mins	Milliken	including their goalkeeper after just 4
4-1	61mins	Wilson	minutes.
5-1	69mins	McCann	
6-1	82mins	Wilson	
7-1	90mins	McCann	

The Evening Times Trophy has been competed for since 1896/7 but in a variety of formats.

1896/7-1926/7   The trophy was the prize for the winners of the Glasgow Junior League.

1927/8-1930/1 This was the time of the "split" and the Evening Times Trophy was awarded to the overall Champions of the Scottish Intermediate League, following a play off between the winners of the East and West Divisions.

1931/2-1967/8   The trophy went to the winners of the Central League. Depending on the number of divisions there might be semi-finals or a preliminary round.

1968/9-1978/9   By now there were three Divisions A, B and C. The winners of B and C played off for the right to meet the A Division Champions. The lower league sides frequently won due to fixture congestion catching up on the A Division club.

1979/80-1981/2 The Evening Times Trophy was renamed the Evening Times Cup. It was contested for by the Central League's Division A Champions, the Sectional Cup winners, Central KO Cup winners and the McLeod Trophy winners

1982/3 to 2001/2 The 3 Central Division winners, plus the winners of the Sectional and KO League cups were entered.

2002/3 to 2011/2 Amalgamation of the Central and Ayrshire Juniors led to an expanded tournament. The five Divisional winners were joined by the West of Scotland , Ayrshire District, Central District KO, Ayrshire Sectional and Central Sectional Cups, giving a potential 10 entrants.

2012/13 - date Difficulties in fitting in dates for so many clubs meant the Cup was restricted to the 5 League Champions - it was renamed the Evening Times Champions Cup.

Evening Times Cup Winners Cup / Champions Cup - Recent Finals

Year	Winners	Runners Up	Score	Venue
1988/9	Arthurlie	Lesmahagow	2-1	Somervell Park, Cambuslang
1989/90	Vale of Clyde	Dunipace	1-0	Greenfield Park, Shettleston
1990/1	Cambuslang Rangers	Pollok	2-0 AET	Greenfield Park, Shettleston
1991/2	Petershill	Johnstone Burgh	3-1 AET	Somervell Park, Cambuslang
1992/3	Lesmahagow	Pollok	4-1	Somervell Park, Cambuslang
1993/4	Arthurlie	Shotts Bon Accord	3-1	Somervell Park, Cambuslang
1994/5	No competition			
1995/6	Maryhill	Blantyre Vics	3-0	Somervell Park, Cambuslang
1996/7	Maryhill	Pollok	2-1	Somervell Park, Cambuslang
1997/8	Maryhill	Greenock	5-1	Lochburn Park, Maryhill
1998/9	Dunipace	Rutherglen Glencairn	3-0	Somervell Park, Cambuslang
1999/00	Port Glasgow	Shettleston	3-1	Somervell Park, Cambuslang
2000/1	Arthurlie	Bellshill Athletic	2-0	Adamslie Park, Kirkintilloch
2001/2	Johnstone Burgh	Bellshill Athletic	3-1	Adamslie Park, Kirkintilloch
2002/3	Kilsyth Rangers	Larkhall Thistle	1-0	Petershill Park, Glasgow
2003/4	Pollok	Petershill	3-1	Lochburn Park, Maryhill
2004/5	Lanark United	Beith	2-0	Petershill Park, Glasgow
2005/6	Irvine Meadow	Maryhill	1-0	Newlandsfield, Pollok
2006/7	Pollok	Irvine Meadow	3-1	Somervell Park, Cambuslang
2007/8	Pollok	Cumnock	3-1	Lochburn Park, Maryhill
2008/9	Irvine Meadow	Pollok	1-0	Newlandsfield, Pollok
2009/10	Irvine Meadow	Kilbirnie Ladeside	4-0	Newlandsfield, Pollok
2010/11	Arthurlie	Shotts Bon Accord	1-0	Newlandsfield, Pollok
2011/2	Ashfield	Irvine Meadow	1-0	Newlandsfield, Pollok
2012/3	Auchinleck Talbot	Hurlford United	3-0	Newlandsfield, Pollok
2013/4	Auchinleck Talbot	Neilston	7-1	Newlandsfield, Pollok

SENIOR NON LEAGUE FITBA

2013/14 saw the inaugural season of the Lowland League which has been introduced by the SFA in a bid to create a pyramid system. The idea is that the Highland League and Lowland League Champions should play off at the end of 2014/15, with the winners then meeting the bottom club of SPFL Division Two for a place in the SPFL for 2015/16.

The hope was that the Lowland League would attract the best non-league sides from the southern half of the country. Sadly this has not happened—no Junior clubs have yet even applied for membership. The initial tranche of 12 clubs have now been augmented by two newcomers—Edinburgh University and Broomhill Sports Club from Glasgow. The latter have never fielded an adult team before. Crowds of more than 100 are very much the exception in the Lowland League and it cannot really be described as a suitable destination for any relegated SPFL side.

Moreover, Highland League Champions Brora Rangers have stated that they haver no interest in joining the Scottish Professional Football League should they win the title again next season. Chairman and financial backer Tony MacKay said: "Sorry to tell the Highland League - we're not going anywhere. We've got the pyramid system now - we have to deal with it. If it happens, it happens - we would never ever throw a game - but my preference is for Brora to go nowhere. I would like to do with Brora Rangers what happened with Huntly Football Club [in the 1990s] and dominate the Highland League. Nothing would give me more pleasure than that."

So, it remains to be seen if the m Play Offs for an SPFL place actually happen. Only some of the Lowland League clubs have the facilities and infrastructure required—in reality only Spartans are fully equipped to step up.

The East of Scotland League has been weakened by the loss of all its bigger clubs to the Lowland League. Two Lowland League sides field their reserves in the East of Scotland League, as did Hibernian and Berwick Rangers in 2013/14. These two have withdrawn leaving just 17 clubs in two divisions of 9 and 8. There is very little geographical overlap between the East of Scotland Senior and Junior sides—the Senior dominate in Edinburgh itself and in the Borders, with the Lothian counties remaining a Junior stronghold.

The South of Scotland League has expanded to 14 clubs thanks to the collapse of the Dumfries Amateur League. The South of Scotland may be "Level 2" of the SFA's Non League pyramid, but it also the lowest level of Saturday football played in the region. This simply emphasises the ill-thought out pyramid plan rushed through by the SFA.

In theory the East of Scotland and South of Scotland Leagues will act as feeders for the Lowland League.

Plans to split the Highland League into two divisions and create feeder divisions were booted into touch by the Highland League clubs who are quite happy with the set-up they currently have.

Finally, the SFA allegedly have plans to exclude "non licensed" clubs from the Scottish Cup from 2015. This has led to a rash of ground improvements at clubs such as Burntisland Shipyard, Edinburgh University, Civil Service Strollers and Coldstream as they seek to retain their Cup status and the SFA funding that goes with it.

Lowland League 2013/14

	DS	EK	EC	GFR	G	PA	SE	SP	SU	TR	VOL	WW
Dalbeattie Star		Nov 16	Aug 31	Nov 30	Apr 16	Nov 9	Sep 21	Oct 19	Sep 7	Aug 13	Apr 26	Dec 7
		2-0	0-1	4-1	1-1	3-3	9-1	2-2	3-3	0-0	4-0	1-5
East Kilbride	Oct 12		Nov 2	Mar 1	Jan 25	Sep 21	Aug 17	Aug 31	Nov 9	Dec 7	Aug 24	Aug 13
	0-3		1-3	2-3	1-1	2-0	4-1	1-0	1-2	1-1	0-1	1-0
Edinburgh City	Feb 8	Feb 15		Feb 1	Nov 30	Mar 1	Apr 12	Aug 10	Sep 28	Oct 19	May 10	Oct 26
	2-1	0-1		4-1	1-5	4-1	4-0	0-1	1-0	0-2	7-2	5-1
Gala Fairydean Rovers	Aug 17	Sep 28	Aug 13		Oct 19	Aug 24	Sep 7	Apr 5	Feb 8	Mar 29	Nov 9	Nov 9
	1-4	0-1	3-3		2-6	1-4	6-3	0-3	1-4	4-0	2-3	3-0
Gretna	Nov 2	Sep 7	Aug 17	Apr 12		May 10	Aug 13	Sep 21	Dec 7	Feb 8	Nov 9	Sep 28
	3-3	3-2	2-1	1-2		1-1	5-0	0-3	0-1	0-3	2-3	1-1
Preston Athletic	Aug 10	Nov 30	Aug 21	Nov 2	Apr 19		Feb 8	Sep 28	Aug 13	Sep 7	Aug 17	Oct 19
	3-4	1-2	2-1	5-2	0-2		3-1	2-1	1-3	3-0	1-2	2-9
Selkirk	Mar 29	Oct 5	May 3	May 10	Oct 12	Aug 31		Aug 21	Oct 19	Aug 10	Nov 16	Apr 26
	2-4	0-3	1-3	0-3	0-4	1-3		0-3	1-5	1-1	1-3	3-6
Spartans	May 3	Feb 8	Nov 9	Oct 12	Mar 29	Oct 26	Dec 7		Aug 17	Mar 1	Aug 13	Sep 7
	1-1	0-0	1-0	2-1	4-0	4-0	11-2		2-1	4-0	1-1	2-0
Stirling University	Apr 8	Aug 10	Apr 30	Aug 31	Aug 21	Feb 1	Apr 22	May 10		Nov 2	Sep 21	Mar 29
	0-1	2-1	3-1	2-2	0-0	3-0	3-2	3-2		2-0	4-1	0-2
Threave Rovers	May 26	Aug 20	Apr 19	Sep 21	Aug 31	May 3	Nov 9	Mar 26	Mar 22		Oct 12	Aug 17
	1-4	1-0	0-5	4-5	0-1	2-1	0-0	1-3	1-4		2-1	2-5
Vale of Leithen	Apr 22	Oct 19	Sep 7	Aug 21	Aug 10	Mar 29	Sep 28	Nov 2	May 3	Apr 12		Apr 19
	2-1	3-3	1-2	4-1	2-0	2-0	3-1	0-5	2-3	4-0		0-2
Whitehill Welfare	Sep 14	Feb 1	Sep 21	Aug 10	May 3	Apr 5	Nov 2	Apr 12	Mar 1	Nov 30	Aug 31	
	2-4	4-1	3-1	4-1	2-2	2-1	0-1	1-2	1-0	4-1	1-1	

	P	W	D	L	F	A	GD	Pts
Spartans	22	15	4	3	57	16	41	49
University of Stirling	22	14	3	5	48	26	22	45
Dalbeattie Star	22	11	7	4	59	34	25	40
Whitehill Welfare	22	12	3	7	56	36	20	39
Edinburgh City	22	12	1	9	49	32	17	37
Vale of Leithen	22	11	3	8	41	43	-2	36
Gretna 2008	22	8	7	7	40	33	7	31
East Kilbride	22	8	4	10	28	31	-3	28
Preston Athletic	22	7	3	12	40	53	-13	24
Gala Fairydean Rovers	22	7	2	13	46	63	-17	23
Threave Rovers	22	4	5	13	22	53	-31	17
Selkirk	22	1	2	19	20	86	-66	5

University of Stirling played their home League games at Forthbank Stadium. Some Cup ties were played at the Gannochy Sports Centre.

East Kilbride's artificial surface at the K-Park came in from criticism from some visiting sides who reckoned it was not as good as many of the other synthetic pitches around the country.

SPARTANS SQUAD 2013/14

Goalkeepers
Scott Bennett, Ross Gilpin,

Defenders
Danny O'Donnell, Gary Cennerrazzo, Neil MacCuish, Kevin Sivewright, Danny Main, Jack Blaikie, Ally MacKinnon

Midfield
John Grant, Alan Brown, Donal Henretty, Jack Beesley, Mark Whatley, Kevin Motion, Sean Muhsin, Jack Beacher

Forwards
Chris Anderson, Keith McLeod, Willie Bremner, Robbie Ross

Manager - Dougie Samuel

Lowland League Cup 2013/14

Section A

	GFR	PA	S	VOL
Gala Fairydean Rovers		Dec 14 / 3-1	Jan 4 / 3-1	Jan 18 / 0-2
Preston Athletic	Jan 11 / 7-0		Mar 22 / 2-2	Mar 4 / 3-1
Selkirk	Mar 8 / 5-1	Jan 18 / 3-4		Mar 1 / 1-3
Vale of Leithen	Mar 22 / 1-4	Mar 8 / 2-3	Jan 11 / 4-1	

ABD Dec 14 Selkirk v Vale of Leithen

	P	W	D	L	F	A	PTS
Preston Athletic	6	4	1	1	20	11	13
Vale of Leithen	6	3	0	3	13	12	9
Gala Fairydean R	6	3	0	3	11	17	9
Selkirk	6	1	1	4	13	17	4

Section B

	EC	S	SU	WW
Edinburgh City		Dec 14 / 1-3	Dec 28 / 0-3	Dec 21 / 1-0
Spartans	Jan 11 / 1-3		Dec 21 / 3-4	Dec 28 / 3-2
Stirling University	Jan 6 / 1-0	Jan 18 / 0-0		Jan 11 / 0-0
Whitehill Welfare	Jan 18 / 2-0	Mar 8 / 3-1	Dec 14 / 1-1	

	P	W	D	L	F	A	PTS
Stirling University	6	3	3	0	9	4	12
Whitehill Welfare	6	2	2	2	8	6	8
Spartans	6	2	1	3	11	13	7
Edinburgh City	6	2	0	4	5	10	6

Section C

	DS	G	EK	TR
Dalbeattie Star		Mar 22 / 4-3	Mar 8 / 1-1	Feb 15 / 6-1
Gretna	Mar 1 / 4-0		Dec 28 / 2-1	Jan 11 / 1-0
East Kilbride	Jan 11 / 3-2	Jan 4 / 2-0		Dec 21 / 6-0
Threave Rovers	Dec 28 / 1-4	Mar 8 / 3-3	Mar 19 / 0-1	

	P	W	D	L	F	A	PTS
East Kilbride	6	4	1	1	14	5	13
Dalbeattie Star	6	3	1	2	17	13	10
Gretna	6	3	1	2	13	10	10
Threave Rovers	6	0	1	5	5	21	1

SF   12/4/14   Dalbeattie Star   Preston Athletic   1 3
SF   12/4/14   East Kilbride   Stirling University 0 1

F   27/4/14   Preston Athletic   Stirling University 2 5 at Gala

Stirling University: Marshall, Nixon, Sutherland, Cuff, Faulds (Atkins 88), Williams-Mitchell (Leigh 46), Sludden, Jones (McWhirter 88), Geddes, McKee, Robertson. Unused Subs: Hughes, Sheridan, Donaghue-Kelly.
Preston Athletic: Gilbertson, Cherrie, O'Hara (Bingham 56), Morrison, Foster (Dodd 30), Ramsay, Stewart, Elliot, Osborne, Devlin, Moore. Subs: Davidson, Pennycuick.

1-0	4mins	Geddes	5-0	65mins	Geddes
2-0	24mins	Geddes	5-1	67mins	Bingham
3-0	48mins	Sludden	5-2	71mins	Elliot
4-0	59mins	Geddes			

Att approx 120

With only eighteen League fixtures in the Lowland League season the League Cup provided some essential "padding" for the fixture list. However, this necessitated a rather convoluted system with the three group winners and the "best loser" qualifying for the KO stages.

The choice of venue for the Final may have contributed to a very poor attendance with only around 100 spectators in the ground at Netherdale.

SFA South Region Challenge Cup 2013/14

When the Scottish Qualifying Cups (North and South) were scrapped in favour of an all-in Scottish Cup draw from 2007/8, the SFA sponsored tournaments to replace the Qualifying Cups in the fixture lists. The North Challenge Cup was dropped from the fixture list after a couple of years but the South competition carries on. It is open to all members of the Lowland, East and South of Scotland Leagues, as well as the 'odd' SFA member from the South—Glasgow University. Girvan are also eligible but have opted not to play in the competition in recent years.

Previous Finals

Year	Winners	Runners Up	Score	Venue
2007/8	Annan Athletic	Edinburgh City	3-2	Netherdale
2008/9	Spartans	Edinburgh Univ	6-0	Meadowbank
2009/10	Spartans	Gretna	3-1	Tynecastle
2010/11	Spartans	Edinburgh City	3-0	Tynecastle
2011/12	Stirling University	Duns	4-2	Netherdale
2012/13	Whitehill Welfare	Dalbeattie Star	3-1	Galabank
2013/14	East Kilbride	Dalbeattie Star	2-0	Palmerston

Rd 1 NE	26/10/13	Ormiston	Burntisland Shipyard	4 4 3-4 pens
Rd 1 NE	26/10/13	Gala Fairydean Rovers	Selkirk	5 2
Rd 1 NE	26/10/13	Civil Service Strollers	Stirling University	0 8
Rd 1 NE	26/10/13	Hawick Royal Albert	Leith Athletic	2 4
Rd 1 NE	26/10/13	Kelso United	Duns	4 2
Rd 1 NE	26/10/13	Edinburgh Uniersity	Easthouses Lily	0 3
Rd 1 NE	26/10/13	Coldstream	Eyemouth United	5 3
Rd 1 SW	26/10/13	Crichton	Dalbeattie Star	0 1
Rd 1 SW	26/10/13	Glasgow University	East Kilbride	0 1
Rd 1 SW	26/10/13	Gretna	Heston Rovers	5 1
Rd 1 SW	26/10/13	Mid Annandale	St Cuthbert Wanderers	0 5
Rd 1 SW	26/10/13	Newton Stewart	Fleet Star	4 4 AET, 3-4 pens
Rd 1 SW	26/10/13	Nithsdale Wanderers	Abbey Vale	3 1
Rd 1 SW	26/10/13	Threave Rovers	Creetown	9 1
Rd 1 SW	09/11/13	Lochar Thistle	Wigtown & Bladnoch	0 3
Rd 2 SW	23/11/13	East Kilbride	St Cuthbert Wanderers	4 2 AET
Rd 2 SW	23/11/13	Gretna	Dalbeattie Star	0 3
Rd 2 SW	23/11/13	Fleet Star	Threave Rovers	0 2
Rd 2 SW	30/11/13	Nithsdale Wanderers	Wigtown & Bladnoch	3 0
Rd 2 NE	23/11/13	Burntisand Shipyard	Leith Athletic	0 4
Rd 2 NE	30/11/13	Vale of Leithen	Kelso United	6 0
Rd 2 NE	30/11/13	Heriot Watt University	Craigroyston	3 1
Rd 2 NE	30/11/13	Stirling University	Tynecastle	4 1
Rd 2 NE	23/11/13	Easthouses Lily	Gala Fairydean	2 4
Rd 2 NE	23/11/13	Preston Athletic	Edinburgh City	3 0
Rd 2 NE	23/11/13	Spartans	Whitehill Welfare	3 2
Rd 2 NE	23/11/13	Lothian Thistle HV	Coldstream	4 2
Rd 3 NE	15/02/14	Gala Fairydean Rovers	Stirling University	1 5
Rd 3 NE	15/02/14	Spartans	Vale of Leithen	4 1
Rd 3 NE	15/02/14	Leith Athletic	Lothian Thistle HV	3 3 AET, 5-6 pens
Rd 3 NE	22/02/14	Preston Athletic	Heriot Watt University	5 1
QF	15/03/14	Lothian Thistle HV	Threave Rovers	2 1
QF	15/03/14	Preston Athletic	Dalbeattie Star	0 5
QF	15/03/14	Nithsdale Wanderers	Spartans	1 7
QF	15/03/14	East Kilbride	Stirling University	2 1 AET
SF	19/04/14	Lothian Thistle HV	East Kilbride	4 5 AET
SF	19/04/14	Spartans	Dalbeattie Star	2 3
F	24/05/14	East Kilbride	Dalbeattie Star	2 0 at QOS

2013/14 FINAL
Dalbeattie Star v East Kilbride, 0-2
Dalbeattie: Martin, Maxwell, Warren, Cameron, Wells, Cameron, Dunglinson (MacBeth 72), Fergusson, Park (Cook 82), Gordon, Sloan, Milligan
Subs not used: Anderson, Houston, Drysdale
East Kilbride: Stewart, Murdoch, Traynor, Templeton, Bronsky, Tierney, McLeish, Daw, Graham (Gallacher 83), McDougall (Atha 75), McLaughlin (McIntosh 58)
Subs not used: Fitzharris, Meldrum

0-1   McDougall (41)
0-2   Templeton (52pen)

Att approx 450

SFA South Challenge Cup Draw 2014/15

South & West Zone 1st Round
Creetown vs. Nithsdale Wanderers
BSC Glasgow vs. Lochar Thistle
Dalbeattie Star vs. Crichton
Fleet Star vs. Glasgow University

South & West Zone 2nd Round
Dalbeattie Star or Crichton vs. Threave Rovers
Newton Stewart vs. Mid Annandale
Gretna 2088 vs. Dumfries YMCA
BSC Glasgow or Lochar Thistle vs. Abbey Vale
Edusport Academy vs. Fleet Star or Glasgow University
East Kilbride vs. Heston Rovers
St Cuthbert Wanderers vs. Wigtown & Bladnoch
Upper Annandale vs. Creetown or Nithsdale Wanderers

North & East Zone 1st Round
Gala Fairydean Rovers vs Heriot-Watt University
Preston Athletic vs. University of Stirling
Craigroyston vs. Vale of Leithen
Peebles Rovers vs. Kelso United
Edinburgh University vs. Selkirk
Coldstream vs. Leith Athletic
Spartans vs. Burntisland Shipyard
Easthouses Lily MW vs. Edinburgh City

North & East Zone 2nd Round
Coldstream or Leith Athletic vs. Civil Service Strollers
Hawick Royal Albert vs. Gala Fairydean Rovers or Heriot-Watt University
Spartans or Burntisland Shipyard vs. Peebles Rovers or Kelso United
Edinburgh University or Selkirk vs. Preston Athletic or University of Stirling
Lothian Thistle HV vs. Easthouses Lily MW or Edinburgh City
Ormiston vs. Whitehill Welfare
Craigroyston or Vale of Leithen vs. Eyemouth United
Tynecastle vs. Duns

EAST SENIORS

CUP DRAWS 2014/15

Image Printers Cup
1ˢᵗ Round
Preston Athletic vs. Stirling University
Gretna 2008 vs. Kelso United
Craigroyston vs. Leith Athletic
Selkirk vs. Peebles Rovers
Duns vs. Civil Service Strollers
Eyemouth United vs. Easthouses Lily MW
Coldstream vs. Tynecastle
Whitehill Welfare vs. Ormiston
Edinburgh University vs. Hawick Royal Albert
East Kilbride vs. Lothian Thistle HV
2ⁿᵈ Round
Burntisland Shipyard vs. Spartans
Gretna 2008 or Kelso United vs. Edinburgh University or Hawick Royal Albert
Vale of Leithen vs. Gala Fairydean Rovers
Eyemouth United or Easthouses Lily MW vs. East Kilbride or Lothian Thistle HV
Whitehill Welfare or Ormiston vs Selkirk or Peebles Rovers
Duns or Civil Service Strollers vs Heriot-Watt University
Coldstream or Tynecastle vs. Edinburgh City
Craigroyston or Leith Athletic vs. Preston Athletic or Stirling University

East of Scotland Qualifying League
Section A: Civil Service Strollers, Eyemouth United, Burntisland Shipyard, Spartans
Section B: Lothian Thistle HV, Easthouses Lily MW, Heriot-Watt University, Hawick Royal Albert
Section C: Coldstream, Kelso United, Stirling University
Section D: Leith Athletic, Craigroyston, Ormiston
Section E: Duns, Tynecastle, Peebles Rovers

King Cup
1ˢᵗ Round
Hawick Royal Albert vs. Coldstream
2ⁿᵈ Round
Eyemouth United vs. Lothian Thistle HV
Spartans vs. Ormiston
Burntisland Shipyard vs. Leith Athletic
Kelso United vs. Hawick Royal Albert or Coldstream
Duns vs. Peebles Rovers
Tynecastle vs. Civil Service Strollers
Easthouses Lily MW vs. Heriot-Watt University
Stirling University vs. Craigroyston

Alex Jack Cup
1ˢᵗ Round
Kelso United vs. Tynecastle
Ormiston vs. Duns
2ⁿᵈ Round
Easthouses Lily MW vs. Peebles Rovers
Craigroyston vs. Heriot-Watt University
Kelso United or Tynecastle vs. Eyemouth United
Leith Athletic vs. Ormiston or Duns
3ʳᵈ Round
Leith Athletic or Ormiston or Duns vs. Craigroyston or Heriot-Watt University
Kelso United or Tynecastle or Eyemouth United vs. Easthouses Lily MW or Peebles Rovers

East of Scotland League Premier Division 2013/14

	CSS	CO	CR	EU	HWU	LA	LTHV	S	SU	T
Civil Service Strollers		Nov 30 0-3	Sep 21 1-2	Nov 23 1-6	Apr 19 3-1	Aug 17 3-2	Aug 24 1-3	Dec 7 0-4	Aug 31 1-1	Jan 18 2-4
Coldstream	Sep 7 0-2		Mar 29 0-2	Oct 19 1-1	Mar 1 0-1	Apr 19 1-2	Jan 11 0-4	Mar 22 2-0	Nov 16 1-2	Nov 9 1-4
Craigroyston	Nov 2 4-0	Oct 5 3-1		Aug 10 0-1	Jan 11 5-1	Mar 1 2-1	Oct 26 0-1	Sep 28 3-1	Nov 9 6-1	Dec 7 2-2
Edinburgh University	Sep 28 3-0	Dec 7 2-2	Apr 19 1-1		Sep 7 2-1	Nov 9 1-2	Apr 5 0-0	Nov 16 1-2	Oct 5 1-0	Jan 11 1-3
Heriot Watt University	Oct 5 3-2	Apr 12 1-2	Aug 31 1-3	Mar 29 0-0		Apr 8 2-2	Sep 28 3-2	Nov 9 0-0	Dec 7 0-1	Nov 2 3-4
Leith Athletic	Dec 14 7-3	Sep 28 1-3	Jan 18 0-0	Nov 30 1-1	Mar 22 1-0		Mar 11 0-4	Jan 11 3-3	Sep 21 1-4	Sep 7 2-1
Lothian Thistle HV	Nov 9 2-0	Aug 31 2-0	Apr 12 3-2	Sep 21 1-1	Mar 19 3-0	Dec 7 2-1		Apr 14 5-0	Apr 16 2-0	Mar 1 2-1
Spartans Reserves	Mar 1 0-2	Sep 20 4-0	Mar 8 0-0	Nov 2 2-1	Oct 25 2-0	Aug 31 2-2	Nov 30 2-3		Nov 22 6-2	Sep 14 1-2
Stirling University Reserves	Apr 12 0-1	Nov 2 2-3	Mar 22 2-1	Apr 9 2-2	Sep 14 2-1	Mar 29 1-4	Apr 23 2-1	Sep 7 3-1		Sep 28 5-0
Tynecastle	Mar 29 6-3	Aug 10 1-2	Oct 19 5-0	Aug 31 6-5	Sep 21 2-0	Apr 12 3-2	Apr 8 2-4	Apr 19 0-2	Oct 26 2-3	

	P	W	D	L	F	A	PTS
Lothian Thistle HV	18	15	1	2	46	16	46
Stirling University Reserves	18	10	2	6	35	34	32
Craigroyston	18	9	4	5	36	22	31
Tynecastle	18	9	1	8	45	40	28
Edinburgh University	18	5	8	5	30	25	23
Spartans Reserves	18	6	5	7	30	28	23
Leith Athletic	18	6	5	7	35	36	23
Coldstream	18	6	2	10	23	35	20
Civil Service Strollers	18	5	1	12	25	51	16
Heriot Watt University	18	3	3	12	19	37	12

The East of Scotland League was greatly weakened by the departures of its top clubs to join the Lowland League. Two of these teams, Spartans and Stirling University, retained reserve teams in the East of Scotland League. Controversially they were allowed to retain Premier Division status on the basis of "continuity".

Lothian Thistle / Hutchison Vale were runaway Champions, losing just two League games all season. They coped well with a backlog of fixtures to clinch the title. They also survived a change of Manager in November when Grant Carnie resigned following a disappointing defeat to Leith Athletic in the Alex Jack Cup Final. Carnie was sent from the dug out for comments made to match officials. Commenting on his departure, he said, "I put 100 per cent in, and I want the same back. I was disappointed with how I reacted at the cup final, but I felt my views were valid. I enjoyed my time at the club and I feel I brought the team on leaps and bounds. There are boys there who can win the league if they give enough effort, but I didn't feel I got that and that was one of the reasons for leaving." His replacement as Manager was Kevin Twaddle, the former Hearts and St Johnstone player, who had been coaching at the club the previous season. He then gave up the post to concentrate on his own painting and decorating business. Twaddle galvanised a very useful side that had the League's most potent attack and the tightest defence. Winning the title should entitle them to enter the Scottish Cup next season although the rules for entry remain to be clarified.

The most disappointing performances were from Edinburgh University and Coldstream who would both have been expecting to perform better.

Civil Service Strollers and Heriot Watt University finished in the relegation places. However, with an expansion of the Lowland League attracting applications from several East of Scotland League sides, the composition of the League for 2014/15 remained uncertain.

LOTHIAN THISTLE HUTCHISON VALE SQUAD 2013/14

Kevin Swain	Richie Wilkes	Craig Stevenson	Connor McDonald
Connan McDiarmid	Alan McDonagh	Omar Ali	
John McDonald	Callum Connelly	Jamie Butler	
Ross Elliot	Willis Hare	Chris Milligan	
Sean Wringe	John Williams	James Cuthbertson	
Callum Irvine	Paul Crawford	Steven Clee	
Scott Moffat	Grant Munro	Lloyd Dignan	

Manager: Grant Carnie, then Kevin Twaddle

East of Scotland League Premier Division - Recent Positions

	1987-8	1988-9	1989-90	1990-1	1991-2	1992-3	1993-4	1994-5	1995-6	1996-7	1997-8	1998-9	1999-00	2000-1	2001-2	2002-3	2003-4	2004-5	2005-6	2006-7	2007-8	2008-9	2009-10	2010-11	2011-12	2012-13	2013-14
Annan Athletic		8	1	7	9		5	3	3	5	4	3	1	1	3	2	4	2	6	1	7						
Berwick Rangers Reserves			7	5																							
Civil Service Strollers	4	2	2	9			7	4	10		6	4	7	11			7	9	10	12			5	8	7	8	9
Coldstream						6	7	10					8	9	9	11				10	9	11					8
Craigroyston	7	6	8	8	5	7	4	5	5	8	3	7	9	5	8	6	12		9	12							3
Dalbeattie Star																			8	11		6	2				
Easthouses Lily					1	6	8	9					10	12				9	7	9	11						
Edinburgh City	6	9		3	6	5	10		6	5	5	6	6	6	8	2	7	1	5	4	8	7	6	5	5		
Edinburgh University								8	8	^10					12		6	3	8	4	2	4	8	5	4	11	5
Eyemouth United			4	10																							
Gala Fairydean	3	1	3	1	4	3	3	2	2	3	9			10	10	4	5	11									
Gretna																										6	4
Hawick Royal Albert	9																										
Heriot Watt University																2	11			7	6	12				10	10
Kelso United	5	7	9												10	12											
Lothian Thistle (/ Hutchison Vale)											7	6	4	7	7	7	9	5	3	8	8	3	3	3	10	6	1
Manor Thistle / Edinburgh Athletic / Leith Athletic						8	9			4	10														11		7
Peebles Rovers				6	10								8	11			12					12					
Pencaitland	10						6	7	8	10																	
Pencaitland & Ormiston															11												
Preston Athletic							7	9								9	8	6	7	6	5	6	9	11		7	
Selkirk																							10	11	10	10	12
Spartans	8	5	5	4	8	2	6	7	4	1	2	2	3	4	1	3	1	1	4	2	3	1	1	1	2	3	
Spartans Reserves																											6
Stirling University																									2	1	2
Stirling University Reserves																											2
Threave Rovers														3	4	5	3										
Tollcross United / Tynecastle						9		10			9	12											4	9	9	12	4
Vale of Leithen	2	10		3	4	2	6	9					5	8	5	10	11								7	8	9
Whitehill Welfare	1	3	4	2	2	1	1	1	1	2	1	1	2	2	2	1	10	4	5	3	1	5	2	4	3	1	

HIBERNIAN EOS SQUAD 2013/14

Dougie Horne	Andrew Black	Ryan Baptie	Lewis Allan
Robert Wilson	Tom Gardiner	Euan Smith	Dean Horribine
Jamie Beaton	Jay Doyle	Cody Mulhall	Kevin Thomson
Jason Cummings	Aaron Dunsmore	Sean Brennan	
Taylor Hendry	Neil Martyniuk	Callum Crane	
Max Todd	Jordan Sinclair	Gareth McCaffrey	
Scott Martin	Kleton Perntrou		

David Paul tragically died midway through the season.

Manager- James McDonaugh

East of Scotland League First Division   2013/14

	BR	BS	D	EL	EU	HRA	H	KU	O	PR
Berwick Rangers Reserves		Apr 12	Apr 1	Mar 15	Apr 29	Feb 22	Sep 7	Sep 28	Nov 2	Mar 1
		1-0	3-0	2-0	7-2	4-2	0-1	0-2	1-2	2-0
Burntisland Shipyard	Aug 31		Sep 21	Nov 2	Mar 29	Jan 11	Dec 7	Oct 5	Feb 8	Apr 19
	0-3		2-1	2-7	3-1	3-1	1-1	3-3	1-0	1-2
Duns	Nov 9	Mar 22		Jan 11	Sep 7	Mar 29	Sep 28	Dec 7	Nov 16	Oct 5
	0-1	0-2		0-4	0-2	2-1	1-2	1-1	1-5	4-1
Easthouses Lily	Dec 14	Mar 8	Aug 31		Aug 21	Oct 5	Nov 9	Apr 12	Jan 18	Mar 29
	4-2	2-0	4-1		1-1	1-0	4-1	2-0	6-2	3-0
Eyemouth United	Nov 23	Nov 9	Jan 4	Sep 28		Dec 7	Mar 22	Mar 1	Aug 31	Sep 21
	3-1	3-3	3-4	2-5		3-2	1-4	0-1	2-4	3-2
Hawick Royal Albert	Sep 21	Mar 15	Mar 8	Nov 30	Apr 19		Apr 12	Sep 7	May 10	May 3
	1-0	4-0	3-3	1-3	1-0		0-3	3-2	2-0	2-5
Hibernian U20	Oct 5	Mar 1	Sep 14	Apr 19	Nov 30	Aug 31		Aug 15	Sep 21	Nov 2
	8-0	8-0	6-0	2-0	7-1	9-0		4-2	2-0	6-0
Kelso United	Sep 14	Apr 26	Jan 18	Sep 21	Nov 2	Apr 30	Mar 8		Mar 29	Aug 31
	1-4	1-2	1-5	2-2	4-2	2-1	3-2		0-1	0-0
Ormiston	Oct 12	Sep 7	Apr 19	Mar 1	Jan 11	Sep 28	Mar 15	Nov 9		Mar 8
	0-5	2-1	2-3	0-5	3-1	1-3	2-4	2-3		1-4
Peebles Rovers	Oct 19	Sep 28	Dec 14	Sep 7	Apr 12	Nov 9	Nov 16	Mar 15	Apr 26	
	1-6	3-0	3-3	1-1	1-1	3-2	1-2	4-0	4-0	

		P	W	D	L	F	A	PTS
1	Hibernian EOS	18	15	1	2	72	56	46
2	Easthouses Lily Miners Welfare	18	13	3	2	56	35	42
3	Berwick Rangers EOS	18	11	0	7	42	15	33
4	Peebles Rovers	18	7	4	7	37	-2	25
5	Kelso United	18	6	4	8	28	-10	22
6	Burntisland Shipyard	18	6	3	9	24	-19	21
7	Hawick Royal Albert	18	6	1	11	29	-15	19
8	Duns	18	5	3	10	29	-17	18
9	Ormiston	18	6	0	12	27	-21	18
10	Eyemouth United	18	4	3	11	31	-22	15

East of Scotland League First Division - Recent Positions

	1987-8	1988-9	1989-90	1990-1	1991-2	1992-3	1993-4	1994-5	1995-6	1996-7	1997-8	1998-9	1999-00	2000-1	2001-2	2002-3	2003-4	2004-5	2005-6	2006-7	2007-8	2008-9	2009-10	2010-11	2011-12	2012-13	2013-14
Annan Athletic	1			2																							
Berwick Rangers Reserves	5	2																			8			8	10	4	3
Burntisland Shipyard																										13	6
Civil Service Strollers					7	1				2				7	2					4	2						
Coldstream	4	6	1					7	5	11	7	3	3				9	10	6	2				9	7	2	
Craigroyston																6	1					5	3	6	5	1	
Dalbeattie Star																5	3	2		1							
Duns																									6	10	8
Easthouses MW / Lily	6	5	4	1					5	10	8	1			3	10	5	1					6	5	12	6	2
Edinburgh City			2					8	1																		
Edinburgh University	8	9	9	11	5	2							5	7	5	2		1									
Eyemouth United	2				3	9	10	10	11	8	11	12	13	6	7	6	12	12	12	8	9	10	10	3	4	5	10
Gala Fairydean															8	2			10	4	5	6	7	4	3	7	
Gretna																							4	4	1		
Hawick Royal Albert		4	7	4	5	3	9	3	9	4	9	6	8	4	12	9	10	9	11	11	10	12	12	12	13	14	7
Heriot Watt University	10	10	10	10	10	9	5	4	12	12	11	11	9	11	11	6	4	2			1					1	
Hibernian U20																											1
Kelso United					7	4	4	3	9	10	9	6	12	3	9	4	4	1			8	7	11	8	10	8	5
Lothian Thistle							3	1																			
Manor Thistle / Edinburgh Athletic / Leith Athletic				1			7	2					10	10	5	8	5	7	4	3	6	12	8	5	2	3	
Peebles Rovers	3	1			8	7	8	10	4	5	1					3	2	6	8	7	7	2	11	7	11	12	4
Pencaitland		3	8	5	6	6	6	1																			
Pencaitland & Ormiston / Ormiston													7	1		7	3	7	5	10	11	9	9	11	9	11	9
Preston Athletic						2			4	5	4	6	1														
Selkirk	9	8	5	6	3	8	4	6	6	3	10	9	11	10	10	8	8	3	2							9	
Stirling University																							3	1			
Threave Rovers							4	1																			
Tollcross United /Tynecastle	7	7	6	8	2	1		7	8	2						8	9	11	11	11	9	5	3	1			
Vale of Leithen		3	2			6	7	2						5	4	3	6	7	2								

East of Scotland Qualifying League 2013/14

Section A

	CSS	EU	KU	LTHV	T
Civil Service Strollers		Oct 12	Aug 10	Aug 13	Mar 22
		1-3	0-1	2-8	1-1
Eyemouth United	Feb 8		Dec 14	Aug 10	Aug 13
	1-1		1-3	1-6	4-6
Kelso United	Oct 19	Nov 16		Mar 22	Oct 12
	0-2	2-2		1-3	2-5
Lothian Thistle HV	Mar 8	Oct 19	Aug 21		Aug 17
	2-0	5-0	2-1		0-0
Tynecastle	Aug 20	Mar 15	Feb 8	Dec 14	
	6-0	2-0	4-1	0-1	

	P	W	D	L	F	A	PTS
Lothian Thistle HV	8	7	1	0	27	5	22
Tynecastle	8	5	2	1	24	9	17
Kelso United	8	2	1	5	11	19	7
Eyemouth United	8	1	2	5	12	26	5
Civil Service Strollers	8	1	2	5	7	22	5
Kelso United	8	2	1	5	11	19	7

Section B

	D	EU	HRA	O	SUR
Duns		Feb 1	Aug 13	Oct 19	Oct 12
		2-4	2-5	3-4	2-1
Edinburgh University	Aug 21		Feb 8	Dec 21	Aug 17
	3-1		2-0	4-0*	0-1
Hawick Royal Albert	Mar 1	Oct 12		Aug 17	Oct 19
	1-2+	2-4		2-1	1-1
Ormiston	Aug 10	Aug 13	Dec 14		Feb 1
	1-0	0-3	2-3		0-2
Stirling University Reserves	Mar 15	Mar 8	Aug 10	Aug 21	
	1-3	2-1>	3-0	5-0	

	P	W	D	L	F	A	PTS
Edinburgh University	8	6	0	2	21	8	18
Stirling University Reserves	8	5	1	2	16	7	16
Hawick Royal Albert	8	3	1	4	14	17	10
Duns	8	3	0	5	15	20	9
Ormiston	8	2	0	6	8	22	6

* at Ormiston
+ at Duns
> at Edinburgh Uni

Section C

	BSY	C	HWU	H	LA
Burntisland Shipyard		Aug 17	Oct 19	Aug 21	Dec 21
		4-5	1-3	1-3	2-4
Craigroyston	Dec 14		Dec 21	Feb 8	Aug 21
	1-2		3-0	1-2	3-1
Heriot Watt University	Aug 10	Aug 13		Dec 14	Feb 8
	3-0	1-3		1-1	2-2*
Hibernian U20	Feb 1	Oct 12	Aug 17		Oct 19
	4-0	1-1	8-0		3-3
Leith Athletic	Aug 13	Mar 15	Oct 12	Aug 10	
	5-1	1-2	4-4	1-1	

	P	W	D	L	F	A	PTS
Hibernian U20	8	4	4	0	23	8	16
Craigroyston	8	5	1	2	17	12	16
Leith Athletic	8	2	4	2	20	18	10
Heriot Watt Uni	8	2	3	3	14	22	9
Burntisland Shipyard	8	1	0	7	11	28	3

* at Meadowbank 3G

Section D

	BR	C	EL	PR	S
Berwick Rangers Reserves		Aug 13	Dec 7	Oct 26	Aug 24
		1-3	3-1	4-0	2-1
Coldstream	Mar 8		Feb 8	Aug 21	Aug 17
	0-3		4-2	1-1	3-2
Easthouses Lily	Aug 17	Oct 12		Dec 21	Oct 19
	2-2	3-4		5-1	3-3
Peebles Rovers	Aug 10	Feb 1	Aug 13		Oct 12
	1-3	0-4+	3-5		0-1
Spartans Reserves	Jan 18	Dec 14	Aug 10	Feb 8	
	7-3	2-0	4-0	5-0	

	P	W	D	L	F	A	PTS
Spartans Reserves	8	5	1	2	25	11	16
Berwick Rangers Reserves	8	5	1	2	21	15	16
Coldstream	8	5	1	2	19	14	16
Easthouses Lily	8	2	2	4	21	24	8
Peebles Rovers	8	0	1	7	6	28	1

+ at Peffermil

Top three teams in each section qualified for the East of Scotland League Cup (see next page). The four group winners received byes to the Quarter Final stage of the knock out Cup.

East of Scotland League Cup 2013/14

League Cup

Prelim	05/04/14	Tynecastle	Leith Athletic	1 2	
Prelim	05/04/14	Craigroyston	Coldstream	3 2	
Prelim	22/04/14	Berwick Rangers Reserves	Hawick Royal Albert	9 1	
Prelim	19/04/14	Stirling University	Kelso United	3 0	
1	03/05/14	Lothian Thistle HV	Leith Athletic	3 0	
1	26/04/14	Edinburgh University	Craigroyston	3 3	4-5 pens at Craigroyston
1	26/04/14	Hibernian	Berwick Rangers	3 1	
1	03/05/14	Stirling University	Spartans	1 5	
SF	05/05/14	Hibernian	Lothian Thistle HV	2 1	
SF	06/05/14	Craigroyston	Spartans	1 0	
F	10/05/14	Craigroyston	Hibernian	1 4	at Civil Service Strollers

Hibernian EOS: Perntreou, Dunsmore, Wilson, Martyniuk, Crane, Black, Sinclair, Horribine, Smith, Beaton, Allan. Subs: McCaffrey for Allan, Hendry for Sinclair, Todd for Beaton, Horne, Gardiner.
Craigroyston: Burnside, Ritchie, Hogarth, Jeffrey, Sommerville, Anderson, Dunn, Hendrie, Boggie, Dickson, G McCormack. Subs S McCormack for Boggie, Inglis for Sommerville, Barbiru, Greenhill, Rendall
1-0   8ins   Allan,   2-0 54 mins   Horribine,   2-1   63 mins Dunn,
3-1   67mins Sinclair 4-1 609 mins   Dunsmore
Att c.350

Recent East of Scotland League Cup Finals

Season	Winners	Runners Up	Score	Venue
1988/9	Whitehill Welfare	Spartans	1-0	Easter Road
1989/90	Berwick Rangers Reserves	Gala Fairydean	2-1 aet	Netherdale
1990/1	Whitehill Welfare	Spartans	1-0	Muirhouse
1991/2	Whitehill Welfare	Manor Thistle	4-1	Muirhouse
1992/3	Edinburgh City	Civil Service Strollers	1-0	Ferguson Park
1993/4	Gala Fairydean	Whitehill Welfare	0-0, 4-2pens	Whitestone Park
1994/5	Whitehill Welfare	Civil Service Strollers	2-0	Pennypit Park
1995/6	Whitehill Welfare	Annan Athletic	3-2 aet	Netherdale
1996/7	Whitehill Welfare	Vale of Leithen	2-0	Pennypit Park
1997/8	Whitehill Welfare	Craigroyston	3-0	Pennypit Park
1998/9	Whitehill Welfare	Threave Rovers	1-1, 5-4 pens	Netherdale
1999/00	Annan Athletic	Coldstream	2-1	Netherdale
2000/1	Civil Service Strollers	Edinburgh City	3-1	Ferguson Park
2001/2	Edinburgh City	Spartans	1-0	Ferguson Park
2002/3	Whitehill Welfare	Craigroyston	2-0	Saughton Enclosure
2003/4	Spartans	Edinburgh City	4-1	Saughton Enclosure
2004/5	Spartans	Edinburgh City	2-0	Ferguson Park
2005/6	Heriot Watt University	Easthouses Lily	2-0	Ferguson Park
2006/7	Whitehill Welfare	Annan Athletic	1-0	Islecroft Stadium
2007/8	Spartans	Whitehill Welfare	1-0	Pennypit Park
2008/9	Dalbeattie Star	Preston Athletic	2-0	Yarrow Park
2009/10	Spartans	Lothian Thistle	2-1	St Marks Park
2010/1	Spartans	Edinburgh University	4-2	Pennypit Park
2011/2	Whitehill Welfare	Edinburgh City	2-0	St Marks Park
2012/3	Edinburgh City	Spartans	2-0	Muirhouse
2013/4	Hibernian U20	Craigroyston	4-1	Muirhouse

Alex Jack Cup 2013/14

This competition, named after former League Secretary Alex 'Sandy' Jack, is for clubs which are not full members of the Scottish Football Association, and therefore do not play in the Scottish Cup. It was introduced to provide a parallel competition for the old Scottish Qualifying Cup (South).

Rd 1	17/08/13	Duns	Peebles Rovers	0 5	
Rd 1	17/08/13	Kelso United	Eyemouth United	2 3	
Rd 1	24/08/13	Heriot Watt University	Stirling University	0 4	
Rd 1	24/08/13	Easthouses Lily	Tynecastle	3 3 AET, 4-3 pens	
Rd 1	07/09/13	Craigroyston	Lothian Thistle	2 3 AET	
Rd 2	14/09/13	Lothian Thistle	Easthouses Lily	2 1 AET	
Rd 2	14/09/13	Eyemouth United	Ormiston Primrose	2 1	
Rd 2	14/09/13	Leith Athletic	Peebles Rovers	3 1	
Rd 2	14/09/13	Gretna	Stirling University	1 1 5-4 pens	* replay ordered
Rd 2	25/09/13	Gretna	Stirling University	0 3	
SF	05/10/13	Stirling University	Lothian Thistle	2 3 AET	
SF	05/10/13	Leith Athletic	Eyemouth United	6 1	
F	03/11/13	Leith Athletic	Lothian Thistle	2 1	at Muirhouse

Leith Athletic FC: Newman, Simpson, Hall, Black, Leslie, Burns, Cairns, Lauder, Campbell, Mason, Tracey. Subs: Gordon, Barrie, Martin, Lynch, Wright
Lothian Thistle HVFC: Swain, MacDonald, Stevenson, Horribine, Williams, Wilkes, Connolly, Elliot, Butler, Moffat, McDonaugh. Subs: Wringe, Milligan, Crawford, Deignon, Rooney
0-1 20 mins Butler 1-1 45 mins Manson 2-1 75mins Campbell
Att c.250

Complete Alex Jack Cup Finals

Season	Winners	Runners Up	Score	Venue
1988/9	Kelso United	Craigroyston	2-1	Netherdale, Galashiels
1989/90	Edinburgh City	Berwick Rangers 'A'	4-2	Ferguson Park, Rosewell
1990/1	Easthouses Lily	Pencaitland	2-1 aet	Ferguson Park, Rosewell
1991/2	Edinburgh City	Easthouses Lily	2-1	Ferguson Park, Rosewell
1992/3	Manor Thistle	Edinburgh City	1-0	Ferguson Park, Rosewell
1993/4	Craigroyston	Tollcross	1-0	Marine Drive, Edinburgh
1994/5	Preston Athletic	Craigroyston	2-0	Ferguson Park, Rosewell
1995/6	Manor Thistle	Lothian Thistle	2-0	Ferguson Park, Rosewell
1996/7	Edinburgh Athletic	Pencaitland	1-0	Ferguson Park, Rosewell
1997/8	Tollcross	Lothian Thistle	2-1 aet	Ferguson Park, Rosewell
1998/9	Easthouses Lily	Craigroyston	3-1	Ferguson Park, Rosewell
1999/00	Peebles Rovers	Easthouses Lily	1-1, 5-4 pens	Ferguson Park, Rosewell
2000/1	Lothian Thistle	Craigroyston	2-0	Ferguson Park, Rosewell
2001/2	Kelso United	Easthouses Lily	2-1	Victoria Park, Innerleithen
2002/3	Edinburgh Athletic	Lothian THistle	2-1	Ferguson Park, Rosewell
2003/4	Lothian THistle	Edinburgh Athletic	1-0	Ferguson Park, Rosewell
2004/5	Easthouses Lily	Lothian Thistle	1-1, 5-4 pens	Ferguson Park, Rosewell
2005/6	Lothian Thistle	Kelso United	2-1	Pennypit, Prestonpans
2006/7	Easthouses Lily	Tynecastle	2-0	Ferguson Park, Rosewell
2007/8	Lothian Thistle	Peebles Rovers	3-0	Victoria Park, Innerleithen
2008/9	Gretna	Tynecastle	4-2	Netherdale, Galashiels
2009/10	Leith Athletic	Eyemouth United	2-0	Pennypit, Prestonpans
2010/1	Stirling University	Lothian Thistle	8-0	Falkirk Stadium
2011/2	Stirling University	Gretna	3-0	Pennypit, Prestonpans
2012/3	Leith Athletic	Craigroyston	1-0	Ainslie Park, Edinburgh
2013/4	Leith Athletic	Lothian Thistle	2-1	Marine Drive, Edinburgh

Image Printers East of Scotland Qualifying Cup 2013/14

Rd 1	24/08/13	Peebles Rovers	Craigroyston	3 3	AET, 4-3 pens
Rd 1	24/08/13	Leith Athletic	Edinburgh Uniiversity	4 1	
Rd 1	24/08/13	Kelso United	Ormiston	2 4	Played for by East of
Rd 1	24/08/13	Eyemouth United	Hawick Royal Albert	2 5	Scotland FA members
Rd 1	24/08/13	Burntisland Shipyard	Duns	5 2	who are NOT members
Rd 1	24/08/13	Selkirk	Gretna	0 2	of the Scottish
Rd 1	24/08/13	Spartans	Edinburgh City	3 1	AET
Rd 1	24/08/13	Whitehill Welfare	Coldstream	3 1	
Rd 1	15/11/13	Easthouses Lily	Lothian Thistle HV	4 6	AET

Rd 2	05/10/13	Ormiston	Vale of Leithen	1 2	
Rd 2	15/11/13	Hawick Royal Albert	Gala Fairydean	0 5	
Rd 2	15/11/13	Heriot Watt University	Leith Athletic	1 2	AET
Rd 2	15/11/13	Whitehill Welfare	Civil Service Strollers	6 0	
Rd 2	15/11/13	Burntisland Shipyard	Preston Athletic	1 2	
Rd 2	15/11/13	Tynecastle	Stirling University	2 1	
Rd 2	15/11/13	Spartans	Gretna	2 0	
Rd 2	25/01/14	Lothian Thistle HV	Peebles Rovers	5 1	at Livingston FC Astro

Rd 3	25/01/14	Spartans	Vale of Leithen	4 0	
Rd 3	01/02/14	Tynecastle	Leith Athletic	1 3	
Rd 3	04/02/14	Preston Athletic	Whitehill Welfare	3 6	
Rd 3	05/02/14	Gala Fairydean Rovers	Lothian Thistle HV	1 4	

SF	22/02/14	Leith Athletic	Whitehill Welfare	3 4	
SF	22/02/14	Spartans	Lothian Thistle HV	2 1	

F	23/03/14	Spartans	Whitehill Welfare	2 2	AET, 4-5 pens at Craigroyston

Whitehill Welfare: Young, Hall (Sproule 69), Thom, Bruce, W Kidd, McGlashan, Dodds (McLaughlin 91), A Kidd, McIntosh, Somerville (Martin 106), Noon. Subs: Quinn, Cantley.
Spartans: Bennett, Grant, Cennerazzo, Sivewright, O'Donnell, Motion (Muhsin 91), Beesley (Henretty 111), Whatley, Bremner (Anderson 111), McLeod, Brown. Subs: Main, Gilpin

1-0	23mins	Noon	1-1	44 mins	Whatley
1-2	113 mins	Muhsin	2-2	120mins	Bruce

Att c.400.

Recent East of Scotland Qualifying Cup Finals

Season	Winners	Runners Up	Score	Venue
1988/9	Civil Service Strollers	Spartans	3-1	Ferguson Park, Rosewell
1989/90	Spartans	Edinburgh City	3-0	Tynecastle Park, Edinburgh
1990/1	Gala Fairydean	Whitehill Welfare	1-0	Victoria Park, Innerleithen
1991/2	Whitehill Welfare	Vale of Leithen	4-0	Netherdale, Galashiels
1992/3	Manor Thistle	Kelso United	2-2, 4-2 pens	Victoria Park, Innerleithen
1993/4	Whitehill Welfare	Selkirk	2-0	Netherdale, Galashiels
1994/5	Gala Fairydean	Kelso United	2-1	Netherdale, Galashiels
1995/6	Spartans	Edinburgh City	3-1	Pennypit Park, Prestonpans
1996/7	Lothian Thistle	Whitehill Welfare	2-1	Pennypit Park, Prestonpans
1997/8	Spartans	Gala Fairydean	2-0	Victoria Park, Innerleithen
1998/9	Whitehill Welfare	Lothian Thistle	2-0	Pennypit Park, Prestonpans
1999/00	Whitehill Welfare	Coldstream	4-2	Victoria Park, Innerleithen
2000/1	Whitehill Welfare	Lothian Thistle	2-0	Pennypit Park, Prestonpans
2001/2	Spartans	Whitehill Welfare	2-1 aet	Saughton Enclosure, Edinburgh
2002/3	Edinburgh City	Edinburgh University	2-1	Pennypit Park, Prestonpans
2003/4	Preston Athletic	Edinburgh City	2-1	Saughton Enclosure, Edinburgh
2004/5	Edinburgh University	Spartans	2-1 aet	Riccarton, Currie
2005/6	Spartans	Preston Athletic	6-4	Marine Drive, Edinburgh
2006/7	Spartans	Kelso United	3-0	Riccarton, Currie
2007/8	Selkirk	Lothian Thistle	3-1	Victoria Park, Innerleithen
2008/9	Whitehill Welfare	Edinburgh City	3-2	Pennypit Park, Prestonpans
2009/10	Gretna	Vale of Leithen	2-0	Albert Park, Hawick
2010/1	Spartans	Tynecastle	2-1 aet	St Marks Park, Edinburgh
2011/2	Edinburgh City	Whitehill Welfare	3-2	Ainslie Park, Edinburgh
2012/3	Gretna	Stirling University	2-1	Albert Park, Hawick
2013/4	Whitehill Welfare	Spartans	2-2 aet, 5-4 pens	St Marks Park, Edinburgh

King Cup   2013/14

1	30/11/13	Selkirk	Ormiston	3 1 AET	
1	30/11/13	Peebles Rovers	Duns	3 2	
1	25/01/14	Gala Fairydean Rovers	Hawick Royal Albert	5 1	
1	01/02/14	Heriot Watt University	Craigroyston	2 1	
1	22/01/14	Gretna	Tynecastle	2 2 AET 4-2 pens	
1	22/02/14	Burntisland Shipyard	Coldstream	1 2	
1	22/02/14	Easthouses Lily	Eyemouth United	6 0	
1	22/02/14	Edinburgh City	Civil Service Strollers	3 0	at Muirhouse
1	22/02/14	Kelso United	Edinburgh University	0 5	
1	18/03/14	Stirling University	Spartans	2 1	
1	25/03/14	Leith Athletic	Lothian Thistle HV	0 5	
2	15/03/14	Whitehill Welfare	Gala Fairydean Rovers	5 2	
2	15/03/14	Vale of Leithen	Edinburgh University	0 2	
2	15/03/14	Gretna	Coldstream	3 3 AET 5-4 pens	
2	22/03/14	Edinburgh City	Berwick Rangers Reserves	1 0	
2	15/04/14	Easthouses Lily	Peebles Rovers	4 3	
2	19/04/14	Selkirk	Stirling University	1 3	
2	30/04/14	Hibernian	Lothian Thistle HV	3 2 AET	
2	30/04/14	Heriot Watt University	Preston Athletic	2 3	
3	26/04/14	Gretna	Easthouses Lily	2 0	
3	06/05/14	Preston Athletic	Edinburgh City	2 4 AET	
3	07/05/14	Edinburgh University	Hibernian	1 0	
3	07/05/14	Whitehill Welfare	Stirling University	3 2	
SF	14/05/14	Whitehill Welfare	Gretna	3 1	
SF	14/05/14	Edinburgh University	Edinburgh City	1 0	at Meadowbank
F	18/05/14	Whitehill Welfare	Edinburgh University	0 1	at Preston Athletic

Whitehill Welfare: Young, Martin, Thom, Dodds, W Kidd, McGlashan, Manson, A Kidd, McIntosh, Somerville (Bruce 74), McLaughlin (Quinn 82). Subs: Sproule, Cantley.
Edinburgh University: Tait, MacFarlane, Murray, Flett, Black, Daniels, Ward, Gerrard, Guthrie (Coleman 87), Nikolaidis, Aitken (Habata 74). Subs: Hodgson, Maelger, Murray.
0-1   78 mins   Gerrard   Att c.200

Recent King Cup Finals
Season	Winners	Runners Up	Score	Venue
1989/90	Berwick Rangers Reserves	Civil Service Strollers	2-1	Rosewell
1990/1	Civil Service Strollers	Edinburgh University	3-0	Rosewell
1991/2	Vale of Leithen	Spartans	1-0	Rosewell
1992/3	Whitehill Welfare	Spartans	1-0	Muirhouse
1993/4	Whitehill Welfare	Craigroyston	3-1	Muirhouse
1994/5	Whitehill Welfare	Spartans	2-0 aet	Prestonpans
1995/6	Whitehill Welfare	Civil Service Strollers	3-0	Tynecastle Park, Hearts FC
1996/7	Craigroyston	Edinburgh Athletic	2-0	Prestonpans
1997/8	Whitehill Welfare	Civil Service Strollers	3-2	Rosewell
1998/9	Edinburgh City	Edinburgh University	3-1	Rosewell
1999/00	Edinburgh City	Whitehill Welfare	2-1	Rosewell
2000/1	Spartans	Vale of Leithen	2-0	Rosewell
2001/2	Spartans	Gala Fairydean	4-2	Prestonpans
2002/3	Spartans	Ormiston	2-0	Rosewell
2003/4	Lothian Thistle	Heriot Watt University	1-1 aet, 4-1 pens	Muirhouse
2004/5	Spartans	Edinburgh City	4-0	Muirhouse
2005/6	Spartans	Edinburgh City	6-1	Rosewell
2006/7	Edinburgh University	Lothian Thistle	2-0	Selkirk
2007/8	Spartans	Vale of Leithen	7-2	Rosewell
2008/9	Heriot Watt University	Vale of Leithen	1-0	Rosewell
2009/10	Spartans	Stirling University	2-0	Rosewell
2010/1	Spartans	Stirling University	2-1	Falkirk Stadium
2011/2	Stirling University	Spartans	2-1	Rosewell
2012/3	Spartans	Berwick Rangers Reser	3-1	St Marks Park, Edinburgh
2013/14	Edinburgh University	Whitehill Welfare	1-0	Prestonpans

East of Scotland City Cup 2013/14

The City Cup is now played between East of Scotland FA members who are outwith the top flight, plus the winners of he East of Scotland Qualifying Cup. In practice this has meant, in recent seasons, a single tie between Berwick Rangers and the Qualifying Cup winners. Previously both Meadowbank Thistle and Berwick took past, along with both finalists from the Qualifying Cup. It is unclear if Hearts will be required to play in it in 2014/15.

Tuesday April 15th, Shielfield Park, Berwick v Rangers v Whitehill Welfare, 1-2, Att. Approx 100
Berwick: Andrews, Downie, Hoskins, Elliot, Dinlop, Turner, Carse, O'Brien, Morris, Tulloch, Gill. (Sorer O'Brien)
Whitehill: Young, Hall, Thom, Bruce, McDiarmid, McGlashan, Martin, Kidd, McIntosh,McLaughlin, Sproule.
Subs Quinn, Sommerville, Dodds, Manson (scorers A Kidd, Sproule)

Recent City Cup Finals

1985/6	Meadowbank Thistle	Gala Fairydean	3-1		Netherdale
1986/7	Meadowbank Thistle	Berwick Rangers	0-1		Meadowbank
1987/8	Gala Fairydean	Berwick Rangers	1-1	4-2 pens	Shielfield
1988/9	Meadowbank Thistle	Berwick Rangers	2-1		Shielfield
1989/90	Meadowbank Thistle	Berwick Rangers	1-1	5-4 pens	Meadowbank
1990/1	Berwick Rangers	Meadowbank Thistle	2-1		Shielfield
1991/2	Vale of Leithen	Whitehill Welfare	4-1		Innerleithen
1992/3	Berwick Rangers	Meadowbank Thistle	2-1		Shielfield
1993/4	Whitehill Welfare	Berwick Rangers	2-2	6-5 pens	Shielfield
1994/5	Meadowbank Thistle	Kelso United	7-1		Netherdale
1995/6	Berwick Rangers	Livingston	5-2		Almondvale
1996/7	Livingston	Whitehill Welfare	2-1		Almondvale
1997/8	Spartans	Livingston	2-1		Almondvale
1998/9	Whitehill Welfare	Lothian Thistle	5-0		Rosewell
1999/00	Whitehill Welfare	Livingston	1-0		Rosewell
2000/1	Livingston	Lothian Thistle	3-0		Rosewell
2001/2	Berwick Rangers	Spartans	2-1		Rosewell
2002/3	Berwick Rangers	Edinburgh City	3-1		Shielfield
2003/4	Preston Athletic	Berwick Rangers	3-2		Prestonpans
2004/5	Spartans	Berwick Rangers	4-1		Shielfield
2005/6	Spartans	Berwick Rangers	2-1		Shielfield
2006/7	Spartans	Berwick Rangers	3-2		Shielfield
2007/8	Berwick Rangers	Lothian Thistle	2-0		Saughton
2008/9	Berwick Rangers	Whitehill Welfare	3-1		Shielfield
2009/10	Berwick Rangers	Gretna	2-0		Shielfield
2010/11	Berwick Rangers	Spartans	2-1		Shielfield
2011/12	Berwick Rangers	Edinburgh City	2-0		Shielfield
2012/13	Gretna	Berwick Rangers	4-2		Gretna
2013/14	Whitehill Welfare	Berwick Rangers	2-1		Shielfield

East of Scotland Shield 2013/14

Final, May 4th 2014
Hibernian Under 17 v Hearts Under 17, 2-0 (at Easter Road), Attendance approx 300
Hibernian: Sean Brennan, Matthew McInally, David Porcher, Ben Stirling, Jordan McGregor, Gregor Watson, Alistair Smith, Scott Martin, Conner Duthie, Dominic Docherty, Oliver Shaw (Kevin Waugh, 83). Unused substitutes: Ross Campbell, Stan Chitemere, David McKay, Adam Watson. Scorers - McGregor, Shaw
Hearts: Jamie Sneddon, Jack Simpson, Sam Daniels, Kai Wilson, Greig Page, Sean McKitdy, Lewis Moore, Aaron Scott, Murray Cockburn, Rhys Craigie, Ian Smith. Subs Kelby Mason, Jonny Grotlan, Scott Walker, Jonni Turner, Kiren Somerville, Taylor Queen.

NORTH SENIORS

Brora Rangers were worthy winners of the Highland League for the first time. The ambitious Sutherland club were magnificently backed by their main sponsor Sam Mac-Kay and he was rewarded with quality football. Brora's travelling supporters also added colour and passion to the grounds around the League.

Inverurie Locos and Nairn County ran them close but there was no denying that Brora were the top team over the course of the season. Formartine United and Fraserburgh can also be pleased with their season's work - Fraserburgh had a good Scottish Cup run before going out at Stenhousemui.

Deveronvale did the Highland League proud by beating a much-fancied Linlithgow Rose in the Scottish Cup. The Junior side seemed to be cruisingto victory in Banff before two late goals from Vale earned a draw. The Highland League team were convincing winners in the Replay.

Fort William again finished bottom with just one win this season. In fact, the bottom three of Fort, Rothes and Strathspey is becoming much too predictable and hopefully they can move up the table in 2014/15. Buckie Thistle and Clach will be particularly disappointed with their League performances when much more was expected of them.

	Pos	P	W	D	L	F	A	GD	PTS
Brora Rangers FC	1	34	31	2	1	123	16	107	95
Inverurie Loco Works FC	2	34	23	6	5	97	39	58	75
Nairn County FC	3	34	24	3	7	86	39	47	75
Formartine United FC	4	34	22	6	6	88	36	52	72
Fraserburgh FC	5	34	23	2	9	89	44	45	71
Deveronvale FC	6	34	20	5	9	64	43	21	65
Cove Rangers FC	7	34	16	7	11	91	62	29	55
Wick Academy FC	8	34	15	8	11	83	54	29	53
Forres Mechanics FC	9	34	15	7	12	68	50	18	52
Buckie Thistle FC	10	34	13	10	11	54	48	6	49
Clachnacuddin FC	11	34	13	7	14	67	64	3	46
Turriff United FC	12	34	13	5	16	60	57	3	44
Huntly FC	13	34	9	8	17	55	82	-27	35
Keith FC	14	34	9	2	23	50	98	-48	29
Lossiemouth FC	15	34	4	8	22	34	93	-59	20
Strathspey Thistle FC	16	34	3	3	28	28	116	-88	12
Rothes FC	17	34	3	3	28	36	136	-100	12
Fort William FC	18	34	1	6	27	35	131	-96	9

Highland League   2013/14

	BR	BT	Cl	CR	D	FU	FM	FW	Fr	H	IL	K	Lo	NC	Ro	ST	TU	WA
Brora Rangers	■	Aug 17 1-0	Aug 3 5-1	Jan 11 3-1	Oct 26 3-0	Mar 29 2-0	Jan 25 6-0	Sep 28 6-1	Dec 21 0-1	Nov 23 4-2	May 3 2-1	Feb 8 9-0	Sep 7 6-0	Dec 7 4-3	Nov 9 6-0	Feb 22 11-0	Mar 8 2-0	Dec 28 2-1
Buckie Thistle	Mar 5 0-5	■	Mar 29 2-2	Aug 24 2-2	Apr 26 0-1	Mar 8 0-0	Jan 11 1-1	Sep 7 0-0	Aug 10 2-1	Nov 9 1-0	Sep 28 2-1	Apr 16 5-0	Dec 28 4-0	Nov 23 1-3	Oct 26 2-2	Feb 8 3-0	Feb 22 1-0	Nov 30 2-1
Clachnacuddin	Nov 30 1-5	Nov 16 0-3	■	Aug 10 1-4	Sep 28 0-3	May 3 1-1	Aug 24 3-1	Mar 4 4-0	Apr 12 1-1	Oct 26 1-2	Sep 7 2-2	Jan 11 2-1	Dec 14 5-0	Mar 22 2-1	Oct 12 8-1	Mar 19 2-1	Feb 8 1-0	Nov 2 1-4
Cove Rangers	Aug 31 0-3	Dec 21 4-1	Apr 26 3-2	■	Mar 8 1-1	Nov 23 3-1	Sep 28 3-2	May 10 5-3	Jan 4 0-1	Aug 3 2-2	Feb 22 1-2	Mar 5 7-1	Mar 22 3-0	Aug 17 1-2	Mar 29 4-1	Mar 19 4-2	Nov 9 5-3	Jan 18 5-2
Deveronvale	Mar 15 0-4	May 3 1-0	Feb 1 1-1	Mar 12 3-2	■	Jan 18 2-1	Nov 16 0-4	Apr 12 2-0	Oct 19 3-2	Sep 21 2-2	Aug 10 1-2	Nov 30 5-2	Nov 30 3-0	Apr 26 0-1	Aug 31 3-0	Dec 14 5-1	Jan 4 0-0	Aug 24 0-4
Formartine United	Nov 16 4-3	Nov 2 1-0	Mar 15 1-2	Apr 12 2-1	Aug 3 1-4	■	Aug 10 0-4	Dec 14 2-0	Mar 22 2-3	Mar 19 1-2	Dec 28 1-2	Aug 24 4-2	Nov 30 4-2	Apr 26 1-2	Sep 28 3-0	Jan 11 8-0	Mar 5 3-0	Apr 19 3-1
Forres Mechanics	Sep 21 0-1	Aug 31 3-3	Dec 21 2-1	Feb 1 3-1	Mar 29 4-1	Apr 23 2-2	■	Feb 22 6-0	Apr 5 0-6	Apr 26 1-1	Apr 9 0-6	Apr 30 3-1	Oct 5 2-0	Aug 3 1-0	Dec 7 4-4	Mar 29 3-3	Aug 3 3-2	Feb 15 2-2
Fort William	Aug 23 2-5	Jan 18 3-1	May 16 3-0	Apr 19 2-6	Nov 23 0-3	Aug 17 2-2	Mar 26 2-0	■	Nov 16 1-3	Mar 29 4-3	Feb 8 0-2	Oct 26 1-3	Mar 12 5-1	Jan 4 1-2	Mar 8 4-1	Apr 26 6-2	Oct 26 1-0	May 3 3-2
Fraserburgh	Aug 24 1-4	Mar 12 5-2	Nov 23 3-0	Mar 19 1-3	Feb 22 2-5	Nov 9 0-1	Sep 7 2-0	Jan 25 9-0	■	Mar 29 4-3	Jan 11 1-5	Sep 28 4-0	Jan 11 3-1	Aug 3 1-0	Feb 8 6-0	Sep 7 1-1	Oct 26 2-4	Dec 14 3-2
Huntly	Apr 12 0-6	Mar 22 0-0	Jan 18 1-5	Nov 30 1-5	Jan 25 1-1	Oct 26 1-4	Dec 14 1-2	Aug 24 3-2	Mar 29 4-3	■	Mar 29 1-1	Apr 30 1-3	Apr 10 4-1	Nov 2 0-2	Dec 21 3-3	Nov 30 2-0	May 3 1-3	Oct 19 3-2
Inverurie Locos	Feb 15 1-2	Feb 1 1-1	Aug 31 1-2	Apr 23 2-2	Apr 16 3-1	Jan 4 2-3	Apr 26 2-2	Mar 22 3-0	Mar 5 1-3	Aug 31 3-1	■	Nov 16 3-1	Mar 1 4-1	Sep 21 2-5	Aug 17 5-0	Nov 23 4-2	Mar 29 1-3	Apr 12 2-2
Keith	Apr 5 0-3	Sep 21 0-2	Sep 21 2-1	Apr 9 4-1	Aug 3 1-4	Dec 21 0-2	Mar 1 0-6	Nov 2 2-3	Apr 19 3-1	Jan 4 1-3	Oct 26 0-3	■	Oct 19 5-2	Jan 18 1-8	Nov 23 7-0	Mar 8 2-2	May 3 4-3	Apr 12 7-0
Lossiemouth	Jan 18 0-3	Jan 4 3-1	Jan 4 1-1	Mar 26 0-0	Nov 9 0-1	Aug 3 0-3	Feb 8 1-1	Oct 12 5-1	Aug 31 2-3	Dec 7 2-3	Oct 26 1-4	Feb 22 1-3	■	Dec 21 0-5	Feb 22 3-1	Sep 28 2-2	May 3 1-3	Mar 22 0-1
Nairn County	Aug 10 0-2	Apr 12 1-0	Apr 12 1-0	Dec 14 3-3	Feb 8 1-1	Oct 26 4-1	Dec 28 3-1	Jan 11 3-0	Apr 9 2-3	Mar 8 1-0	Jan 25 1-2	Sep 7 1-2	Aug 24 1-1	■	Jan 25 5-1	Oct 19 2-0	Oct 12 1-0	Feb 1 0-0
Rothes	Mar 22 0-4	Mar 1 1-4	Feb 15 2-4	Nov 16 0-9	Apr 9 1-2	Feb 1 2-3	Nov 30 3-7	Aug 10 3-2	Mar 26 0-5	Oct 5 1-2	Aug 24 0-5	Dec 14 3-5	Apr 12 1-1	Apr 19 0-3	■	Oct 19 2-0	Sep 7 0-3	Sep 21 0-7
Strathspey Thistle	Mar 12 0-6	Oct 12 2-1	Oct 19 2-1	Mar 1 0-3	Aug 17 0-4	Aug 31 0-3	Mar 22 1-2	Nov 16 1-0	Feb 15 2-3	Feb 1 0-3	Aug 3 0-4	Apr 12 1-1	Nov 2 1-2	Feb 1 0-0	Jan 4 2-5	■	Apr 5 0-2	Aug 10 0-9
Turriff United	Apr 26 0-1	Apr 23 1-2	Mar 8 1-1	Mar 22 1-0	Dec 28 0-1	Sep 21 1-1	Apr 12 0-1	Nov 30 5-0	Aug 17 3-0	Feb 22 3-2	Dec 14 2-3	Aug 10 0-1	Nov 16 1-2	Aug 10 2-3	Jan 18 2-5	Aug 24 2-0	■	Aug 31 1-2
Wick Academy	Mar 26 0-1	Aug 3 2-0	Aug 3 1-1	Sep 7 1-1	Dec 21 2-3	Apr 5 1-1	Oct 12 0-1	Oct 26 8-1	Feb 22 3-2	Jan 11 4-1	Nov 23 2-2	Nov 9 1-0	Sep 28 5-2	Mar 29 1-2	Apr 26 3-2	May 10 6-1	Jan 11 4-1	■

ABD Dec 14 Buckie v Brora
ABD Mar 8 Forres v Inverurie, High Winds
ABD Apr 16, Fort William v Clach, Power Failure

Highland League - Recent Positions

	1980-1	1981-2	1982-3	1983-4	1984-5	1985-6	1986-7	1987-8	1988-9	1989-90	1990-1	1991-2	1992-3	1993-4	1994-5	1995-6	1996-7	1997-8	1998-9	1999-00	2000-1	2001-2	2002-3	2003-4	2004-5	2005-6	2006-7	2007-8	2008-9	2009-10	2010-11	2011-12	2012-13	2013-14
Brora Rangers	10	5	3	7	3	16	15	12	14	14	9	14	13	10	5	8	14	11	9	12	13	8	14	12	15	14	13	14	14	15	11	16	8	1
Buckie Thistle	5	14	13	5	5	7	5	2	9	10	11	7	9	8	10	12	13	10	12	3	3	3	4	2	6	3	3	4	6	1	1	5	12	10
Caledonian	9	1	1	1	2	4	2	1	10	2	2	2	4	2																				
Clachnacuddin	4	12	8	11	12	13	16	14	16	18	16	12	7	12	13	11	5	8	6	7	4	4	7	1	7	9	9	10	11	12	15	10	5	11
Cove Rangers							8	10	2	6	3	4	2	4	2	2	7	4	7	8	1	6	3	10	5	8	6	1	1	2	2	2	1	7
Deveronvale	13	11	14	14	14	17	17	11	13	16	15	13	11	14	9	9	8	9	10	11	6	2	1	4	4	1	4	3	2	3	4	7	7	6
Elgin City	3	4	2	4	7	2	3	7	5	1	7	8	1	6	8	7	9	5	4	9														
Formartine United																														6	9	11	2	4
Forres Mechanics	16	13	11	9	4	1	6	6	6	5	4	11	17	13	11	13	12	7	8	6	7	10	11	8	9	4	12	8	9	5	6	1	9	9
Fort William						12	11	17	18	13	12	16	16	16	12	14	16	15	16	16	14	13	15	15	13	15	15	15	15	17	18	18	18	18
Fraserburgh	2	7	6	8	13	14	13	13	11	7	13	15	10	9	7	5	6	2	5	2	8	1	6	3	3	7	8	5	7	4	13	6	6	5
Huntly	12	9	12	10	9	6	9	9	3	8	6	3	6	1	1	1	1	2	5	2	9	8	6	1	6	5	7	8	7	10	13	13	13	
Inverness Thistle	8	8	7	6	11	8	1	4	4	4	5	10	8	15																				
Inverurie Locos																						7	9	7	2	2	2	6	3	10	7	4	10	2
Keith	1	3	4	2	1	5	4	5	7	12	14	5	12	7	4	6	2	6	3	1	5	5	2	5	8	5	1	2	4	8	3	9	14	14
Lossiemouth	15	16	16	16	16	15	10	16	12	9	10	6	3	5	3	3	4	12	13	10	12	11	10	13	11	13	14	13	12	14	12	12	17	15
Nairn County	14	15	10	12	10	9	12	18	15	15	17	18	18	17	16	16	15	16	15	15	9	12	5	9	10	10	7	9	10	11	5	3	4	3
Peterhead	6	2	5	3	8	3	7	3	1	3	8	9	14	11	6	4	3	3	1	4														
Ross County	11	6	9	13	6	10	18	8	8	11	1	1	5	3																				
Rothes	7	10	15	15	15	11	14	15	17	17	18	17	15	18	15	15	11	13	11	13	11	15	12	14	14	11	10	12	13	16	16	15	16	17
Strathspey Thistle																														18	17	17	15	16
Turriff United																														13	8	14	11	12
Wick Academy															14	10	10	14	14	14	10	14	13	11	12	12	11	11	5	9	14	8	3	8

BRORA RANGERS SQUAD 2013/14

Ally MacDonald	Defence
Ally Ridgers	Goalkeeper
Andrew Grieg	Midfield/Forward
Dale Gillespie	Midfield
Danny MacKay	Defence
David Hind	Defence
Gavin Morrison	Midfield
Grant Innes	Midfield
Jack Theakston	Midfielder
James Ross	Defence
Joe Malin	Goalkeeper
John Allan	Goalkeeper
Jon Campbell	Midfielder
Liam Baxter	Striker
Martin MacLean	Midfield
Richie Hart	Midfield
Ross Tokley	Defence
Ryan Watson	Midfield
Scott Houston	Defence
Steven 'Sid' MacKay	Striker
Zander Sutherland	Forward

Aberdeenshire Cup 2013/14

1	06/08/2013	Turriff United	Keith	4 1	
1	07/08/2013	Buckie Thistle	Deveronvale	1 0	
2	27/08/2013	Inverurie Locos	Banks o' Dee	5 1	
2	28/08/2013	Formartine United	Turriff United	2 1	
2	21/08/2013	Buckie Thistle	Cove Rangers	2 3	
2	21/08/2013	Huntly	Fraserburgh	4 2	
SF	11/09/2013	Cove Rangers	Formartine United	0 2	
SF	04/09/2013	Inverurie Locos	Huntly	3 0	
F	19/10/2013	Formartine United	Inverurie Locos	3 2	at Fraserburgh

Final Details
Formartine United: Michael Ewen, Cammy Keith, Andy Shearer, Craig McKeown, Ross Campbell, Daniel Park (Sub Paul Napier), Joe Hamill, Gary Clark, Neil McVittie, Hamish Munro, Stuart Smith.
Inverurie Locos: Martin Bavidge, Neil McLean, Ross Anderson, Ryan Broadhurst, Mark Souter, Greg Mitchell, Andy Reid, David Ross, Dean Donaldson, Gordon Forsyth, Andy Hunter (Sub Andy Low)
Scorers 0-1 Bavidge 20, 0-2 Hunter 33, 1-2 McVittie 49, 2-2 McKeown 82, 3-2 Ewen 90.

Recent Aberdeenshire Cup Finals

Season	Winners	Runners Up	Score	Venue
1989/90	Aberdeen	Peterhead	3-0	Recreation Park, Peterhead
1990/1	Aberdeen	Huntly	1-0	Pittodrie, Aberdeen
1991/2	Huntly	Aberdeen	2-1	Christie Park, Huntly
1992/3	Aberdeen	Cove Rangers	1-0	Allan Park, Cove
1993/4	Huntly	Peterhead	1-0	Kynoch Park, Keith
1994/5	Huntly	Cove Rangers	3-0	Kynoch Park, Keith
1995/6	Huntly	Deveronvale	2-1	Kynoch Park, Keith
1996/7	Fraerburgh	Peterhead	3-2	Recreation Park, Peterhead
1997/8	Aberdeen	Deveronvale	5-1	Kynoch Park, Keith
1998/9	Peterhead	Aberdeen	3-1	Balmoor Stadium, Peterhead
1999/00	Huntly	Deveronvale	2-0	Christie Park, Huntly
2000/1	Deveronvale	Fraserburgh	2-1	Christie Park, Huntly
2001/2	Cove Rangers	Deveronvale	1-1. 5-4 pens	Christie Park, Huntly
2002/3	Aberdeen	Deveronvale	3-0	Harlaw Park, Inverurie
2003/4	Aberdeen	Inverurie Locos	4-0	Harlaw Park, Inverurie
2004/5	Aberdeen	Fraserburgh	4-1 aet	Bellslea Park, Fraserburgh
2005/6	Buckie Thistle	Deveronvale	2-2, 3-2 pens	Christie Park, Huntly
2006/7	Deveronvale	Inverurie Locos	1-0	Kynoch Park, Keith
2007/8	Buckie Thistle	Keith	1-0	Christie Park, Huntly
2008/9	Keith	Huntly	5-2	Harlaw Park, Inverurie
2009/10	Buckie Thistle	Cove Rangers	2-0	The Haughs, Turriff
2010/1	Cove Rangers	Buckie Thistle	3-0	Harlaw Park, Inverurie
2011/2	Deveronvale	Keith	5-4	Christie Park, Huntly
2012/3	Fraserburgh	Formartine United	2-2 aet, 3-1 pe	Victoria Park, Buckie
2013/14	Formartine United	Inverurie Locos	3-2	Bellslea Park, Fraserburgh

Aberdeenshire Shield 2013/14

1	22/10/2013	Aberdeen University	Fraserburgh	2 6	
1	22/10/2013	Cove Rangers	Banks o' Dee	4 2	
2	06/11/2013	Fraserburgh	Turriff United	3 3	3-4 pens
2	06/11/2013	Huntly	Formartine United	3 0	
2	05/11/2013	Cove Rangers	Keith	4 2	
2	12/11/2013	Inverurie Loco Works	Peterhead	3 2	
SF	18/02/2013	Cove Rangers	Turriff United	2 0	
SF	19/02/2014	Inverurie Loco Works	Huntly	2 1	aet
SF Rep	02/04/2014	Cove Rangers	Turriff United	0 1	at Inverurie
F	30/04/2014	Inverurie Loco Works	Turriff United	5 0	at Huntly

Recent Aberdeenshire Shield Finals

Season	Winners	Runners Up	Score	Venue
1990/1	Cove Rangers	Fraserburgh	1-0	Peterhead
1991/2	Fraserburgh	Deveronvale	2-2, 4-3 pens	Huntly
1992/3	Buckie Thistle	Huntly	3-2	Keith
1993/4	Fraserburgh	Keith	4-2	Huntly
1994/5	Deveronvale	Cove Rangers	1-0	Keith
1995/6	Fraserburgh	Peterhead	2-1	Huntly
1996/7	Fraserburgh	Peterhead	6-3 aet	Cove
1997/8	Keith	Peterhead	3-2	Banff
1998/9	Peterhead	Keith	3-1	Keith
1999/00	Fraserburgh	Keith	2-1	Keith
2000/1	Cove Rangers	Buckie Thistle	2-1	Peterhead
2001/2	Keith	Fraserburgh	3-2	Inverurie
2002/3	Deveronvale	Inverurie Locos	3-2	Keith
2003/4	Inverurie Locos	Deveronvale	5-1	Banff
2004/5	Keith	Inverurie Locos	3-1 aet	Inverurie
2005/6	Keith	Inverurie Locos	2-1	Banff
2006/7	Keith	Fraserburgh	3-0	Inverurie
2007/8	Buckie Thistle	Inverurie Locos	3-0	Huntly
2008/9	Cove Rangers	Banks o' Dee	2-0	Pittodrie
2009/10	Peterhead	Inverurie Locos	3-0	Peterhead
2010/11	Turriff United	Aberdeen	2-0	Peterhead
2011/12	Fraserburgh	Banks o' Dee	5-0	Peterhead
2012/13	Turriff United	Cove Rangers	6-1	Inverurie
2013/14	Inverurie Locos	Turriff United	5-0	Huntly

All Time Winners
6 - Fraserburgh, 5 - Keith, 3 - Cove Rangers, 2 - Buckie Thistle, Deveronvale, Peterhead, Inverurie Locos, Turriff United

The Semi Final tie between Cove Rangers and Turriff United was replayed after both teams fielded ineligible players. Cove included former Aberdeen defender Mark Perry and Turriff had an Amateur goalkeeper on the bench, both of whom had been signed after the deadline for availability.

Final Details
Inverurie Locos 5 (N, Gauld 4, C.Herd o.g. 46 M. Bavidge 51 & 62, A. Hunter 75) Turriff United 0

Inverurie: Andy Reid, Neil McLean, John Maitland, Scott Begg, Kieran Adams, Ryan Broadhurst, David Ross, Greg Mitchell (Ross Anderson 85), Neil Gauld, Martin Bavidge (Andy Hunter 67), Dean Donaldson (Mark Souter 74)
Turriff: Kierin McCaffrey, Lewis Davidson, Chris Herd, Stuart Cumming (James Brownie 53), Cammy Bowden, Paul Young, Aaron McKenna, Gary Davidson (Aaron Shand 56), Gary Harris, Gary McGowan (Ben Allan 67), Robert Allan.

The Aberdeenshire Shield competition started in 1990/1. The trophy used was formerly the Fleming Charity Shield competed for back in the early years of the 20th Century.

North of Scotland Cup 2013/14

Round	Date	Home	Away	F	A	Notes
1	27/07/2013	Fort William	Muir of Ord Rovers	1	0	
1	27/07/2013	Wick Academy	Brora Rangers	1	3	
1	30/07/2013	Brora Rangers	Inverness CT	1	1	3-0 pens
1	30/07/2013	Nairn County	Strathspey Thistle	3	1	
1	31/07/2013	Halkirk United	Clachnacuddin	4	5	
1	31/07/2013	Rothes	Lossiemouth	1	3	
2	07/08/2013	Lossiemouth	Forres Mechanics	0	3	
2	07/08/2013	Wick Academy	Clachnacuddin	4	3	
2	13/08/2013	Nairn County	Fort William	5	1	
2	13/08/2013	Thurso	Brora Rangers	0	5	at Halkirk
SF	04/09/2013	Brora Rangers	Wick Academy	6	2	
SF	03/09/2013	Nairn County	Forres Mechanics	2	0	
F	19/10/2013	Brora Rangers	Nairn County	3	0	at Clach

Brora: Joe Malin, Ross Tokeley, Scott Houston, Steven McKay, Zander Sutherland, Richard Hart, Martin McLean, Danny McKay, David Hind, Gavin Morrison, Andrew Greig. Subs Ally Ridgers, Ben Bruce, James Ross, Jon Campbell, Liam Baxter.
Nairn: Robert Duncanson, Archie McPhee, Adam Naismith, Callum Donaldson, Stuart Leslie, Conor Gethins, Martin McDonald, Daniel Moore, Sean Webb, Gregg Main, Wayne McIntosh. Subs Andrew Neill, Gary Kerr, Glenn Main, Ross Naismith, Sam McLean
Brora 3 Nairn 0, 1-0 Sutherland 1, 2-0 Hart 16, 3-0 Mclean 59.

Recent North of Scotland Cup Finals

Season	Winners	Runners Up	Score	Venue
1988/9	Elgin City	Brora Rangers	3-1	Kingsmills
1989/90	Elgin City	Inverness Thistle	0-0, 4-0 rep	Forres
1990/1	Brora Rangers	Forres Mechanics	2-1	Dingwall
1991/2	Ross County	Lossiemouth	0-0, 1-0 rep	Kingsmills
1992/3	Clachnacuddin	Inverness Thistle	4-2 aet	Caley
1993/4	Caledonian	Forres Mechanics	1-0	Kingsmills
1994/5	Lossiemouth	Fort William	4-0	Forres
1995/6	Lossiemouth	Clachnacuddin	1-0	Forres
1996/7	Lossiemouth	Forres Mechanics	4-1	Elgin
1997/8	Elgin City	Inverness CT	3-1	ICT
1998/9	Elgin City	Rothes	2-0	Forres
1999/00	Inverness CT	Lossiemouth	3-0	Forres
2000/1	Lossiemouth	Forres Mechanics	3-1	Forres
2001/2	Clachnacuddin	Inverness CT	2-0	ICT
2002/3	Lossiemouth	Rothes	3-1	Forres
2003/4	Elgin City	Inverness CT	1-0	Forres
2004/5	Forres Mechanics	Clachnacuddin	2-0	Dingwall
2005/6	Nairn County	Forres Mechanics	3-1	Clachnacuddin
2006/7	Ross County	Nairn County	3-0	Clachnacuddin
2007/8	Inverness CT	Elgin City	3-2	Forres
2008/9	Nairn County	Inverness CT	2-0	Clachnacuddin
2009/10	Inverness CT	Nairn County	3-2	Forres
2010/1	Forres Mechanics	Wick Academy	3-2	Brora
2011/2	Inverness CT	Forres Mechanics	4-3	Forres
2012/3	Nairn County	Wick Academy	2-1	Clachnacuddin

Highland League Cup 2013/14

Round	Date	Home	Away	Score	Notes
1	01/03/2014	Brora Rangers	Clachnacuddin	3 0	Protest, Brora thrown out
1	01/03/2014	Formartine United	Nairn County	1 4	
2	15/03/2014	Buckie Thistle	Cove Rangers	1 1	AET, 4-2 pens
2	15/03/2014	Fort William	Forres Mechanics	1 4	
2	15/03/2014	Huntly	Fraserburgh	3 2	
2	15/03/2014	Keith	Rothes	0 1	
2	15/03/2014	Nairn County	Turriff United	5 0	
2	15/03/2014	Strathspey Thistle	Inverurie Locos	0 4	
2	15/03/2014	Wick Academy	Lossiemouth	0 2	
2	26/03/2014	Clachnacuddin	Deveronvale	2 0	AET
QF	05/04/2014	Clachnacuddin	Rothes	7 0	
QF	05/04/2014	Forres Mechanics	Buckie Thistle	1 3	AET
QF	05/04/2014	Huntly	Lossiemouth	1 2	
QF	05/04/2014	Inverurie Locos	Nairn County	5 2	
SF	19/04/2014	Clachnacuddin	Lossiemouth	5 1	
SF	19/04/2013	Inverurie Locos	Buckie Thistle	1 3	
F	10/05/2014	Clachnacuddin	Buckie Thistle	3 3	4-3 pens, at Keith

Clach: Finnis, Lawrie, Skinner, McGurk, Graham, Morris, Laing, Campbell, Brindle, Callum, McKenzie. Subs Khutishvili, White, Dougal, McDonald, Grant
Buckie: Main, McKinnon, Baxter, Wood, Stewart, Munro, Low, Angus, Hegarty, Wood, Conway. Subs MacMillan, Strong, MacRae, Gauld K, Gauld S

1-0	47 mins	Brindle	2-0	60 mins	Morrison
2-1	63 mins	Baxter	3-1	71 mins	Brindle
3-2	83 mins	Low	3-3	85 mins	Conway

Recent Highland League Cup Finals

Season	Winners	Runners Up	Score	Venue
1988/9	Keith	Caledonian	1-1, Replay3-2	Boroughbriggs, Elgin
1989/90	Peterhead	Forres Mechanics	2-1	Boroughbriggs, Elgin
1990/1	Elgin City	Cove Rangers	2-1	Kynoch Park, Keith
1991/2	Ross County	Fraserburgh	3-1	Boroughbriggs, Elgin
1992/3	Huntly	Cove Rangers	1-1, 5-4 pens	Boroughbriggs, Elgin
1993/4	Huntly	Fraserburgh	4-1	Boroughbriggs, Elgin
1994/5	Cove Rangers	Lossiemouth	2-2, 5-3 pens	Christie Park, Huntly
1995/6	Huntly	Cove Rangers	2-1 aet	Kynoch Park, Keith
1996/7	Lossiemouth	Fraserburgh	2-1	Christie Park, Huntly
1997/8	Elgin City	Cove Rangers	1-0	Christie Park, Huntly
1998/9	Forres Mechanics	Keith	1-0	Boroughbriggs, Elgin
1999/00	Cove Rangers	Elgin City	4-3	Kynoch Park, Keith
2000/1	Forres Mechanics	Deveronvale	2-1	Christie Park, Huntly
2001/2	Forres Mechanics	Deveronvale	1-1, 4-3 pens	Kynoch Park, Keith
2002/3	Keith	Deveronvale	3-2	Harlaw Park, Inverurie
2003/4	Clachnacuddin	Forres Mechanics	3-0	Kynoch Park, Keith
2004/5	Cove Rangers	Deveronvale	2-0	Kynoch Park, Keith
2005/6	Fraserburgh	Cove Rangers	4-1	Kynoch Park, Keith
2006/7	Keith	Buckie Thistle	5-0	Princess Royal Park, Banff
2007/8	Inverurie LW	Cove Rangers	3-1	Christie Park, Huntly
2008/9	Inverurie LW	Fraserburgh	2-1 aet	Kynoch Park, Keith
2009/10	Forres Mechanics	Rothes	2-0	Victoria Park, Buckie
2010/1	Nairn County	Fraserburgh	4-0	Princess Royal Park, Banff
2011/2	Buckie Thistle	Cove Rangers	2-0	Princess Royal Park, Banff
2012/3	Keith	Inverurie LW	2-1	Princess Royal Park, Banff
2013/4	Clachnacuddin	Buckie Thistle	3-3, 4-3 pens	Kynoch Park, Keith

SOUTH SENIORS

South of Scotland League - Secretary's Report 2013/14
From the SOSL website

Season 2013-14 continued the theme of recent seasons with some major changes to the Scottish Football scene with the introduction of the Scottish Lowland Football League. At the 2013 AGM two new clubs were admitted to the League, East Kilbride and Lochar Thistle.

Following an Extraordinary General Meeting in June 2013 Dalbeattie Star, East Kilbride and Threave Rovers all left the South of Scotland Football League and became inaugural members of the new Scottish Lowland Football League.

The further on-going development of Scottish Football's "pyramid" will bring with it future opportunities as well as challenges. It was pleasing to see that South League teams beat Lowland League teams on 6 separate occasions throughout the season. The South of Scotland League season commenced on Saturday 29 July 2013 and was completed on Saturday 10 May 2014. In the League there was an exciting Championship which was decided in the penultimate fixture with Wigtown & Bladnoch securing their first title since 1991-92. What a tremendous season it was for Wigtown & Bladnoch with them eventually winning 5 trophies in all.

Wigtown & Bladnoch were pushed hard by St Cuthbert Wanderers & Newton Stewart but a final margin of 9 points between first and second place meant the title was well deserved. Once St Cuthbert Wanderers and Newton Stewart 3G pitches were complete it meant that there were 4 artificial pitches in use by teams in the League with Heston Rovers playing at Palmerston and Mid Annandale at Galabank. The benefit of the additional 3G surfaces coming into the Region was apparent and along with a wet but mild winter meant that there were very few postponements.

Creetown's long awaited new facilities were finally operational, and in my opinion, are excellent.
Lochar Thistle acquitted themselves very well during their first season in the League, finishing in a commendable mid table position. Mid Annandale had completed their League programme in February which presented problems of a different nature, in trying to keep them active prior to Cup competition fixtures.

The League website goes from strength to strength. To date we have had almost 400,000 "hits" including over 300,000 "hits" in the past season alone, which indicates just how popular the site has become. I am sure this has helped raise the profile of the League and acts as a point of reference for club officials, players, supporters as well as spectators looking to visit clubs in our League. I had hoped to develop the use of "social media" such as Facebook and Twitter to further enhance the awareness and grow the profile of the South of Scotland Football League but unfortunately this was one aspect that has had to take a back seat for now.

One unfortunate example of how not to use "social media" resulted in several long suspensions from the game, a learning point for us all. It is still a never ending, on-going challenge for us all, to continue to improve the level and quality of communication within all our organisations. Once again the League received task related payments from the Scottish FA. This has allowed the Executive Committee to provide each club with the opportunity to receive payments for improvements.
Applications from 4 clubs have been approved to date with 1 club receiving their grant. Now that we have established criteria for clubs wishing to join the League, it is felt that existing clubs should endeavour to ensure their facilities also match the same criteria.

The use of team sheets printed from the Scottish FA Admin Data System that list each club's registered players has been beneficial to me when compiling data. Each club remains responsible for the updating & maintaining the Data System including details of club Players, Officials, Committee, & Volunteers.
There was another meeting with the Manager and Coaches Union along with the Judicial Officer which was well attended. The South League continues to grow its reputation for supporting various initiatives. The League Cup final was played at St Mary's Park, Kirkcudbright on Saturday 8th February. Wigtown & Bladnoch triumphed over Lochar Thistle in front of an excellent crowd particularly taking into account the horrendous weather on the day. Once again results showed that any team could beat any other team on the day meaning that lots of the League clashes could have gone either way and the competitive nature of the season's League meant that teams went into fixtures with realistic expectations of winning.

Southern Counties FA - Secretary's Report 2013/14
From the SOSL website

With regards to our three SPFL member clubs, Queen of the South finished 4th in the Scottish Championship, Stranraer FC finished 3rd in Scottish League 1 and Annan Athletic finished 2nd in Scottish League 2. All 3 clubs qualified for their respective end of season play offs but unfortunately all failed to progress beyond their first matches.

In the Ramsdens Cup Threave Rovers lost out to Spartans in the Qualifying Round.
Following victories over Spartans and Airdrieonians Queen of the South went down 0-3 to Rangers in the quarter finals at Palmerston before a crowd of over 6,000 people.
Stranraer having beaten Championship side Dumbarton in Round 1 were then beaten in the second round, losing 2-3 in a local derby to Annan Athletic.
Annan Athletic had a great run to the Semi Final stage of this Cup. They beat Championship side Morton, local rivals Stranraer and Highland League side Formantine United, before going down 0-3 to another Championship side Raith Rovers.

In the League Cup Annan Athletic had a 0-3 defeat in a local derby with Queen of the South.
Having beaten Annan Athletic and Premier League St Mirren Queen of the South were eventually knocked out by another Premier League side Hearts, on penalties, having drawn the match 3-3 after extra time.
Stranraer progressed to Round three beating both Brechin City and Premier League team Ross County before going down 3-5 to another Premier League side Hibernian.

In the Scottish FA Cup Annan Athletic progressed to Round three beating Highland League Buckie Thistle after a replay before going down to Stenhousemuir again after a replay.
Having beaten Hamilton Academicals in round three Queen of the South were again matched with Premier League side St Mirren. The first match ended 2-2 but they lost the replay 0-3.
Stranraer having defeated both Auchinleck Talbot & Clyde drew their 4th Round tie with Premier League side Inverness Caledonian Thistle before losing the replay 0-2.
Dalbeattie Star entering the competition at round 2 lost 0-1 to Montrose.
Threave Rovers beat Rothes 3-0 in the first round before being beaten 0-6 by East Stirlingshire in round 2.
Newton Stewart beat Fort William 3-1 in a first round replay following a 0-0 draw in the first match, before losing 0-6 to Culter.
St Cuthbert Wanderers beat Hawick RA 1-0 in the first round before being knocked out 0-4 by Auchinleck Talbot.
Wigtown & Bladnoch went down 3-4 to Buckie Thistle in their first round match.

All 16 clubs in membership of the Southern Counties FA competed for the Challenge Cup.
The Challenge Cup competition began on 25 January 2014 and the Final was played on Friday 16 May 2014.
The Competition was won by Wigtown & Bladnoch FC who beat Dalbeattie Star FC in an excellent final.

The 11 South of Scotland Football League teams plus 2 Lowland League sides competed for the Potts Cup. The Potts Cup competition started in August 2013 and the Final was played on 07 May 2014. The Competition was won by Heston Rovers FC who beat Newton Stewart FC in the final to claim their first ever South silverware. Thanks go to St Cuthbert Wanderers FC for hosting the Final at very short notice after the pitch at Threave Rovers FC was deemed unplayable following heavy rain.

The 11 South of Scotland Football League teams competed for the J Haig Gordon Memorial Trophy The J Haig Gordon Cup started on 19 April 2014 and the Final was played on 21 May 2014. The Competition was won by Wigtown & Bladnoch FC who beat Newton Stewart FC in the final.

The decision to play Cup Finals on "neutral" grounds again appeared to be very popular.

252

SOUTH SENIORS

South of Scotland League 2013/14

	AV	Cree	Cri	FS	HR	LT	MA	NS	NW	StC	WB
Abbey Vale		Nov 9	Nov 30	Aug 2	Mar 22	Jul 27	Aug 17	Aug 31	Oct 5	Aug 13	Oct 12
		2-2	2-3	0-2	1-2	1-2	2-2	1-3	4-1	0-4	1-6
Creetown	Sep 7		Aug 31	Sep 28	Apr 12	Sep 21	Oct 12	Jan 11	Sep 14	Apr 26	Apr 28
	2-4		1-6	0-3	1-8	3-6	0-3	1-8	2-9	0-4	1-9
Crichton	Sep 14	Dec 7		Oct 5	Aug 3	Jul 31	Aug 24	Jul 27	Aug 7	Aug 17	Apr 12
	2-2	3-1		2-1	4-3	2-3	0-2	1-1	4-3	2-3	1-2
Fleet Star	Oct 19	Aug 13	Mar 29		Oct 12	Sep 14	Sep 21	Aug 17	Feb 22	Jul 27	Sep 7
	0-2	1-2	2-3		4-5	3-4	1-1	1-7	1-4	0-0	0-3
Heston Rovers	Aug 7	Aug 17	Nov 23	Mar 15		Jan 4	Oct 19	Feb 1	Apr 8	Jul 31	Oct 5
	6-0	6-0	3-4	3-3		3-5	2-2	1-3	4-2	4-1	2-2
Lochar Thistle	Apr 12	Mar 29	Oct 19	Nov 16	Aug 31		Oct 5	Aug 3	Oct 12	Aug 10	Aug 17
	5-1	4-1	0-5	4-0	0-1		3-1	1-2	2-4	1-4	0-1
Mid Annandale	Nov 2	Jul 31	Aug 12	Nov 9	Sep 14	Nov 30		Feb 22	Aug 10	Aug 7	Feb 1
	4-2	3-1	3-3	2-2	1-5	2-1		2-3	3-0	2-3	0-3
Newton Stewart	Feb 15	Nov 23	Nov 2	Jan 4	Nov 30	Mar 15	Dec 7		Oct 19	Jan 18	May 10
	12-0	3-0	5-1	7-0	6-0	1-1	4-3		2-3	2-0	0-5
Nithsdale Wanderers	Jul 31	Aug 3	Apr 16	Dec 7	Jul 27	Aug 13	Nov 16	Mar 1		Apr 12	Aug 24
	4-1	10-0	2-2	5-1	4-1	4-3	4-2	0-3		0-2	1-0
St Cuthbert Wanderers	Mar 8	Oct 19	Mar 15	Nov 30	Nov 2	Mar 1	Jan 4	Oct 12	Nov 9		May 3
	5-1	6-1	3-0	2-1	2-1	5-1	6-0	3-0	2-1		0-3
Wigtown & Bladnoch	Mar 1	Mar 15	Mar 22	Jul 31	Nov 16	Mar 8	Jul 27	Aug 13	Aug 31	Aug 3	
	5-0	6-1	3-1	5-1	2-1	7-1	3-0	5-1	2-1	3-0	

Pos	Team	P	W	D	L	F	A	GD	PTS
1	Wigtown & Bladnoch	20	18	1	1	75	13	62	55
2	St Cuthbert Wanderers	20	15	1	4	55	23	32	46
3	Newton Stewart	20	14	2	4	73	29	44	44
4	Nithsdale Wanderers	20	11	1	8	63	41	22	34
5	Crichton	20	9	4	7	49	45	4	31
6	Heston Rovers	20	9	3	8	61	47	14	30
7	Lochar Thistle	20	9	1	10	47	51	-4	28
8	Mid Annandale	20	6	5	9	38	48	-10	23
9	Abbey Vale	20	3	3	14	27	72	-45	12
10	Fleet Star	20	2	4	14	27	61	-34	10
11	Creetown	20	1	1	18	20	105	-85	4

SOUTH OF SCOTLAND CUP DRAWS 2014/15

Southern Counties Cup
Newton Stewart v Dalbeattie Star
Edusport Academy v Creetown
Crichton v Fleet Star
Byes Abbey Vale, Annan Athletic, Dumfries
YMCA, Heston Rovers, Lochar Thistle, Mid
Annandale, Nithsdale Wanderers, Queen of the
South, St Cuthbert Wanderers, Stranraer,
Threave Rovers, Upper Annandale and
Wigtown & Bladnoch.

South of Scotland League Cup
Edusport Academy v Creetown
Fleet Star v Crichton
Nithsdale Wanderers v Mid Annandale
Upper Annandale v Wigtown
St Cuthbert Wanderers v Abbey Vale
Lochar Thistle v Dumfries YMC

byes for - Newton Stewart and Heston Rovers.

Potts Cup
Nithsdale Wanderers v Edusport Academy
Upper Annandale v Wigtown
Abbey Vale v Mid Annandale
Fleet Star v Newton Stewart
St Cuthbert Wanderers v Lochar Thistle
Creetown v Dumfries YMCA

byes for - Crichton and Heston Rovers.

Haig Gordon Trophy
Upper Annandale v Heston Rovers
Crichton v Mid Annandale
Newton Stewart v Abbey Vale
Fleet Star v Creetown
St Cuthbert Wanderers v Wigtown
Edusport Academy v Nithsdale Wanderers

byes for - Dumfries YMCA and Lochar Thistle.

Tweedie Cup
Nithsdale Wanderers v Fleet Star
Edusport Academy v Crichton
Heston Rovers v Mid Annandale
Dumfries YMCA v Wigtown & Bladnoch
Lochar Thistle v Newton Stewart
Creetown v Upper Annandale

byes for - Abbey Vale and St Cuthbert
Wanderers

Cree Lodge Cup
Edusport Academy v Fleet Star
Heston Rovers v Lochar Thistle
Dumfries YMCA v Abbey Vale
Creetown v Mid Annandale
Nithsdale Wanderers v Newton Stewart
Crichton v Wigtown & Bladnoch

byes for - St Cuthbert Wanderers, Upper
Annandale

South of Scotland League - Recent Placings

Team	2013-14	2012-13	2011-12	2010-11	2009-10	2008-9	2007-8	2006-7	2005-6	2004-5	2003-4	2002-3	2001-2	2000-1	1999-00	1998-9	1997-8	1996-7	1995-6	1994-5	1993-4	1992-3	1991-2	1990-1	1989-90	1988-9	1987-8	1986-7	1985-6	1984-5	1983-4	1982-3	1981-2	1980-1
Abbey Vale	9					9	12	12	3	8	12	6	14											9			3	1	4	2	1	3	2	3
Annan Athletic	5	9	8	5	5	6	10	6	2	3	5	13	7	8	5	5	8	2	7	8	7	5	9		7	7			9	3	9	9	5	8
Annan Athletic Reserves					11	13		8	11	11	16		4	7	8	4	4	10	12		10	12	3	11	5	5	10	10	1	1	2	4	3	6
Blackwood Dynamoes / Crichton Royal / Crichton	11	1	13	2	2	7	6	8		2		11		3	2	4	6	13	10	6	5	2	3	4	3	1	5	2		8	2		3	
Creetown			1		10	10	4	4	10	13	14		8	5	13	7	6	5	3	4	8		4	7	1	8	9	8	8	7	6	5		5
Dalbeattie Star	6	5	3	8			15	9	13	6	14	14	6	9	11	2	3	9	4	7	3	9	4	5	8	4	9	6	7	4	7	6	8	
Dalbeattie Star Reserves		12	1		13	14	11	11	14	10		8	2		11	12	7	8	8	3	8	7	2	6	4	3	1	3	10	5	10		4	6
Dumfries HSFP / Dumfries / Heston Rovers										13	14	4	9		3		10	13				8												
Fleet Star	5	5	3	13	10	14		9	13		14	8				2	3	5	4	3	8	6		1	1	8	9	8	8	7	4	8	7	1
Girvan Amateurs / Girvan			1	11	12		11	11	14	10	2	14	8	6	11	12	7	9	7	7	2	8	7	7	1		1	3	7	8	7	2		8
Gretna Reserves	6	5	3	8	10	13	6	4	10		1	4	2	9	11	3	10			3	6	4	4			4			10	6	3	6	6	6
Lochar Thistle					12	14	15		13	10	4	3															1	7	10	9	5	1	8	7
Maxwelltown HSFP							11		14		7	11											8	5	8				2	6	4	1	4	1
Mid Annandale											4			10	3	3									1	1	9	8	5	9	5	3	8	
Newton Stewart		10	3	7	9	11	14		9	9	11	15	15	10	4	9	5	8	13	9	11	7	7	5	8	4	6	3	7		7	5	8	4
Nithsdale Wanderers	12	11	13	12	8	12	9	10	12	14	10	9	11		6	9	9	7	1	5	11	8	4	6	4	3	1	7	10	6	3	7	7	7
Queen of the South Reserves	7	5	3	8	3	5	5	5	6	5	2	5	3	1	4	9	9	1	1	3	2	8	2	1	8	8	1	8	2	5	10	1	1	5
St Cuthbert Wanderers	8	10	6	7	9	4	5	5	4	1	1	1	5	6	4	1	1	3	1	5	1	9	6	1	4	4	1	3	1	6	4	8	1	6
Stranraer Athletic	3	6	9	9	3	1	2	3	1	9		9	2	13	6	12	3	4	2	3	11	7	7	7	4	3	1	7	10	9	5	2	8	4
Stranraer Reserves	2											1	9	2	1	3	4	11	11		11	8	8	1	8	2	6	9	2	6	5	6	4	5
Tarff Rovers			4	4	4	3	2	1	1	4	4	5	1	6	1	1	1	6	2	9	11	7	5	6	6	6	7	7	7	9	5	6	6	
Threave Rovers			7	1	4	1	13	7	1	1	9	12	10	13	9	13	11	14	5	2	11	3	8	8	6	2	7	9	4	6	5		6	5
Threave Rovers Reserves		4	5	4	4	3	2	1	8	4		10	13	2	12	13	11	6	1	1	2	1	5	2	2	2	4	4	10	5	10	6	4	6
Wigtown & Bladnoch	1	3	10	10	4	3	13	7	8	12	9	10	13		9									3										

South of Scotland League Cup   2013/14

Rd 1	10/08/2013	Creetown	Wigtown & Bladnoch	0	8	
Rd 1	10/08/2013	Crichton	Newton Stewart	4	2	AET
Rd 1	10/08/2013	Fleet Star	Heston Rovers	1	3	
QF	21/09/2013	Abbey Vale	Wigtown & Bladnoch	1	10	
QF	21/09/2013	Heston Rovers	Nithsdale Wanderers	2	0	
QF	21/09/2013	St Cuthbert Wanderers	Crichton	5	2	at Crichton
QF	29/08/2013	Mid Annandale	Lochar Thistle	1	2	
SF	07/12/2013	Lochar Thistle	Heston Rovers	3	1	
SF	07/12/2013	St Cuthbert Wanderers	Wigtown & Bladnoch	1	3	
F	08/02/2014	Lochar Thistle	Wigtown & Bladnoch	1	5	at Kirkcudbright

Recent South of Scotland League Cup Finals

Season	Winners	Runners Up	Score	Venue
1988/9	Dalbeattie Star	Threave Rovers	3-2	2 legs
1989/90	Threave Rovers	Dalbeattie Star	3-2	2 legs
1990/1	Threave Rovers	Maxwelltown HSFP	3-2	2 legs
1991/2	Girvan Amateurs	Dalbeattie Star	6-1	2 legs
1992/3	Dalbeattie Star	Wigtown & Bladnoch	2-2, 4-3 pens	2 legs
1993/4	Threave Rovers	Wigtown & Bladnoch	4-1	2 legs
1994/5	Wigtown & Bladnoch	Annan Athletic	4-2	2 legs
1995/6	St Cuthbert Wanderers	Maxwelltown HSFP	4-3	2 legs
1996/7	QOS Reserves	Stranraer Athletic	5-3	2 legs
1997/8	Tarff Rovers	Threave Rovers	5-2	2 legs
1998/9	Tarff Rovers	QOS Reserves	5-4	2 legs
1999/00	Tarff Rovers	Threave Rovers	2-0	Kirkcowan
2000/1	Newton Stewart	St Cuthbert Wanderers	5-0	Newton Stewart
2001/2	Girvan	Stranraer Athletic	2-1	Girvan
2002/3	Crichton	Nithsdale Wanderers	4-1	Crichton
2003/4	Stranraer Athletic	Girvan	3-1	Girvan
2004/5	Annan Athletic Reserves	St Cuthbert Wanderers	5-0	Kirkcudbright
2005/6	Creetown	Stranraer Athletic	1-0	Creetown
2006/7	Threave Rovers	Crichton	2-1	Castle Douglas
2007/8	St Cuthbert Wanderers	Stranraer Reserves	4-2	Kirkcudbright
2008/9	St Cuthbert Wanderers	Crichton	1-0	Crichton
2009/10	Stranraer Reserves	St Cuthbert Wanderers	3-0	Stranraer
2010/1	Dalbeattie Star	Threave Rovers	1-0	Castle Douglas
2011/2	Dalbeattie Star	St Cuthbert Wanderers	4-1	Dalbeattie
2012/3	Dalbeattie Star	Threave Rovers	3-1	Palmerston Park
2013/4	Wigtown & Bladnoch	Lochar Thistle	5-1	Kirkcudbright

Potts Cup   (SCFA)   2013/14

Potts Cup

Rd 1	12/08/2013	Creetown	Heston Rovers	1	10
Rd 1	12/08/2013	Fleet Star	Dalbeattie Star	1	3
Rd 1	12/08/2013	Lochar Thistle	Threave Rovers	3	7
Rd 1	12/08/2013	Newton Stewart	Abbey Vale	10	1
Rd 1	31/08/2013	Mid Annandale	St Cuthbert Wanderers	0	1
Rd 2	28/09/2013	Dalbeattie Star	Newton Stewart	1	2
Rd 2	28/09/2013	St Cuthbert Wanderers	Crichton	2	4
Rd 2	28/09/2013	Wigtown & Bladnoch	Nithsdale Wanderers	6	1
Rd 2	27/09/2013	Heston Rovers	Threave Rovers	3	2
SF	29/03/2014	Newton Stewart	Wigtown & Bladnoch	3	2
SF	08/11/2013	Heston Rovers	Crichton	3	2
F	07/05/2014	Newton Stewart	Heston Rovers	1	3	at Kirkcudbright

Recent Potts Cup Finals

Season	Winners	Runners Up	Score	Venue
1988/9	St Cuthbert Wanderers	Threave Rovers	3-2	Castle Douglas
1989/90	Wigtown & Bladnoch	St Cuthbert Wanderers	3-2	Wigtown
1990/1	Threave Rovers	Dalbeattie Star	5-0	Dalbeattie
1991/2	Dalbeattie Star	Wigtown & Bladnoch	1-0 aet	Dalbeattie
1992/3	Dalbeattie Star	Newton Stewart	4-1	Dalbeattie
1993/4	Threave Rovers	Dalbeattie Star	5-2	Dalbeattie
1994/5	Threave Rovers	Dumfries HSFP	4-2	David Keswick Centre
1995/6	Stranraer Athletic	Dumfries HSFP	2-1	Stair Park
1996/7	St Cuthbert Wanderers	Maxwelltown HSFP	2-0	Maxwelltown HS
1997/8	Tarff Rovers	Newton Stewart	3-0	Newton Stewart
1998/9	Dalbeattie Star	Dumfries HSFP	1-0	Dalbeattie
1999/00	Dalbeattie Star	Creetown	5-1	Creetown
2000/1	Season abandoned			
2001/2	Tarff Rovers	St Cuthbert Wanderers	3-1	Kirkcudbright
2002/3	Annan Athletic Reserves	Tarff Rovers	3-0	Annan
2003/4	Stranraer Athletic	Creetown	4-0	Creetown
2004/5	Stranraer Athletic	Newton Stewart	3-0	Newton Stewart
2005/6	Nithsdale Wanderers	Threave Rovers	2-0	Sanquhar
2006/7	Wigtown & Bladnoch	Crichton	3-1	Crichton
2007/8	Stranraer Reserves	Creetown	1-1, 4-1 pens	Creetown
2008/9	Wigtown & Bladnoch	St Cuthbert Wanderers	3-1	Wigtown
2009/10	Stranraer Reserves	St Cuthbert Wanderers	2-0	Kirkcudbright
2010/1	Threave Rovers	Crichton	0-0, 3-0 pens	Crichton
2011/2	Dalbeattie Star	Threave Rovers	2-0	Dalbeattie
2012/3	Wigtown & Bladnoch	Newton Stewart	2-0	Stair Park
2013/4	Heston Rovers	Newton Stewart	3-1	Kirkcudbright

Cree Lodge Cup (Wigtownshire FA) 2013/14

Rd 1	07/08/2013	Fleet Star	Wigtown & Bladnoch	1	4			
Rd 1	07/09/2013	Heston Rovers	Nithsdale Wanderers	9	0			
Rd 1	07/08/2013	Newton Stewart	Mid Annandale	6	0			
Rd 1	07/09/2013	St Cuthbert Wanderers	Lochar Thistle	6	3	AET		at Lochar Thistle
Rd 2	16/11/2013	Abbey Vale	Crichton	0	0	AET, 4-1 pens		
Rd 2	16/11/2013	St Cuthbert Wanderers	Creetown	4	0			
Rd 2	16/11/2013	Threave Rovers	Newton Stewart	3	1			
Rd 2	18/03/2014	Heston Rovers	Wigtown & Bladnoch	2	1			
SF	02/04/2014	Threave Rovers	Abbey Vale	5	3	AET		
SF	15/04/2014	Heston Rovers	St Cuthbert Wanderers	3	2			
F	14/05/2014	Threave Rovers	Heston Rovers	2	3			at Dalbeattie

Recent Cree Lodge Cup Finals

Season	Winners	Runners Up	Score	Venue
1988/9	St Cuthbert Wanderers	Threave Rovers	3-1	Castle Douglas
1989/90	No competition			
1990/1	Annan Athletic	Stranraer Reserves	2-1	Stair Park
1991/2	No competition			
1992/3	Threave Rovers	Girvan	2-1	Girvan
1993/4	Annan Athletic	Threave Rovers	3-0	Annan
1994/5	Annan Athletic	Threave Rovers	7-1	Annan
1995/6	Annan Athletic	Stranraer Athletic	3-2	Stair Park
1996/7	Threave Rovers	Tarff Rovers	4-0	Castle Douglas
1997/8	Tarff Rovers	Threave Rovers	1-0	Castle Douglas
1998/9	Tarff Rovers	Dumfries HSFP	1-0	David Keswick Centre
1999/00	Tarff Rovers	Creetown	3-1	Kirkcowan
2000/1	Not completed			
2001/2	Girvan	St Cuthbert Wanderers	1-0 aet	Girvan
2002/3	Annan Athletic Reserves	Dumfries	3-2	Annan
2003/4	Creetown	Annan Athletic Reserves	2-0	Annan
2004/5	Creetown	Mid Annandale	4-0	Lockerbie
2005/6	Threave Rovers	Wigtown & Bladnoch	2-1	Wigtown
2006/7	Stranraer Athletic	Creetown	1-1, 8-7 pens	Stranraer High School
2007/8	Crichton	St Cuthbert Wanderers	3-0	Crichton
2008/9	Threave Rovers	Nithsdale Wanderers	6-2	Sanquhar
2009/10	Stranraer Reserves	St Cuthbert Wanderers	1-1, 8-7 pens	Stair Park
2010/1	Threave Rovers	St Cuthbert Wanderers	5-1	Kirkcudbright
2011/2	Threave Rovers	St Cuthbert Wanderers	4-2	Castle Douglas
2012/3	St Cuthbert Wanderers	Nithsdale Wanderers	5-2	Dalbeattie
2013/14	Heston Rovers	Threave Rovers	3-2	Dalbeattie

Haig Gordon Memorial Trophy (SCFA)   2013/14

Rd 1	19/04/2014 Heston Rovers	Creetown	2	1		
Rd 1	19/04/2014 Nithsdale Wanderers	Lochar Thistle	1	6		
Rd 1	19/04/2014 Wigtown & Bladnoch	St Cuthbert Wanderers	4	0		
Rd 2	26/04/2014 Mid Annandale	Abbey Vale	2	3		
Rd 2	26/04/2014 Newton Stewart	Heston Rovers	2	0		
Rd 2	30/04/2014 Crichton	Fleet Star	10	2		
Rd 2	30/04/2014 Lochar Thistle	Wigtown & Bladnoch	2	2	3-4 pens	
SF	05/05/2014 Newton Stewart	Crichton	3	1		
SF	06/05/2014 Wigtown & Bladnoch	Abbey Vale	1	1	3-0 pens	
F	21/05/2014 Newton Stewart	Wigtown & Bladnoch	2	1		at Creetown

Recent Haig Gordon Memorial Trophy Finals

Season	Winners	Runners Up	Score	Venue
1988/9	Dalbeattie Star	Annan Athletic	3-1	Dalbeattie
1989/90	Threave Rovers	Newton Stewart	4-3 aet	Castle Douglas
1990/1	Wigton & Bladnoch	Dalbeattie Star	2-1	Wigtown
1991/2	Maxwelltown HSFP	Annan Athletic	1-0	Maxwelltown HS
1992/3	Annan Athletic	St Cuthbert Wanderers	5-2	Annan
1993/4	Annan Athletic	Wigtown & Bladnoch	0-0, 7-6 pens	Wigtown
1994/5	No competition			
1995/6	Annan Athletic	Dumfries HSFP	5-0	Glencaple
1996/7	Stranraer Athletic	Dumfries HSFP	0-0, 5-3 pens	Glencaple
1997/8	St Cuthbert Wanderers	Newton Stewart	4-1	Newton Stewart
1998/9	Tarff Rovers	Newton Stewart	1-1, 6-5 pens	Newton Stewart
1999/00	Tarff Rovers	St Cuthbert Wanderers	3-1	Castle Douglas
2000/1	Not completed			
2001/2	Tarff Rovers	Crichton	4-1	Crichton
2002/3	Gretna	Tarff Rovers	5-3	Kirkcowan
2003/4	Creetown	Dumfries	6-3	Glencaple
2004/5	Stranraer Athletic	Threave Rovers	1-0	Stair Park, Stranraer
2005/6	Annan Athletic	Wigtown & Bladnoch	3-2	Wigtown
2006/7	Stranraer Athletic	Mid Annandale	3-0	Lockerbie
2007/8	Annan Athletic	St Cuthbert Wanderrs	3-3, 4-1 pens	Kirkcudbright
2008/9	Nithsdale Wanderers	Creetown	5-5, 5-4 pens	Sanquhar
2009/10	St Cuthbert Wanderers	Dalbeattie Star	2-1	Kirkcudbright
2010/1	Queen of the South	Threave Rovers	2-2, 4-2 pens	Palmerston Park, Dumfries
2011/2	Dalbeattie Star	Threave Rovers	3-0	Dalbeattie
2012/3	Wigtown & Bladcoch	St Cuthbert Wanderers	2-1 AET	Kirkcudbright
2013/14	Wigtown & Bladcoch	Newton Stewart	2-1	Creetown

Southern Counties FA Challenge Cup   2013/14

Rd 1	22/01/2014 Stranraer	Threave Rovers	1	6	
Rd 1	25/01/2014 Lochar Thistle	Queen of the South	4	2	
Rd 1	25/01/2014 Mid Annandale	Crichton	1	5	
Rd 1	25/01/2014 Newton Stewart	Heston Rovers	0	2	
Rd 1	28/01/2014 Fleet Star	Annan Athletic	1	6	at Kirkcudbright
Rd 1	22/02/2014 Dalbeattie Star	St Cuthbert Wanderers	7	1	
Rd 1	22/02/2014 Wigtown & Bladnoch	Creetown	12	1	
Rd 1	29/03/2014 Abbey Vale	Nithsdale Wanderers	2	4	
Rd 2	22/02/2014 Crichton	Annan Athletic	3	2	
Rd 2	22/02/2014 Heston Rovers	Lochar Thistle	5	3	aet
Rd 2	05/04/2014 Dalbeattie Star	Nithsdale Wanderers	9	0	
Rd 2	16/04/2014 Threave Rovers	Wigtown & Bladnoch	1	2	
SF	26/04/2014 Wigtown & Bladnoch	Crichton	6	1	
SF	30/04/2014 Heston Rovers	Dalbeattie Star	0	7	
F	16/05/2014 Wigtown & Bladnoch	Dalbeattie Star	2	1	at Kirkcudbright

Recent Southern Counties Challenge Cup Finals

Season	Winners	Runners Up	Score	Venue
1988/9	Stranraer	Queen of the South	2-1	Palmerston Park
1989/90	Annan Athletic	Threave Rovers	1-0	Galabank
1990/1	Queen of the South	Annan Athletic	2-2, 4-3 pens	Palmerston Park
1991/2	Stranraer	Dalbeattie Star	2-1	Islecroft Stadium
1992/3	Dalbeattie Star	Annan Athletic	4-2	Islecroft Stadium
1993/4	Stranraer	Wigtown & Bladnoch	3-1	Trammondford Park
1994/5	Stranraer	Annan Athletic	3-1	Galabank
1995/6	Annan Athletic	Stranraer	4-0	Galabank
1996/7	Queen of the South	Annan Athletic	2-0	Palmerston Park
1997/8	Threave Rovers	Newton Stewart	5-1	Blairmount Park
1998/9	Annan Athletic	Stranraer Athletic	4-0	Galabank
1999/00	Queen of the South	Tarff Rovers	5-2 aet	Palmerston Park
2000/1	Not completed			
2001/2	Tarff Rovers	Annan Athletic	3-0	Ballgreen Park
2002/3	Queen of the South	Stranraer Athletic	2-0	Stranraer High School
2003/4	Queen of the South	Threave Rovers	3-1	Palmerston Park
2004/5	Gretna	Stranraer	4-3	Raydale Park
2005/6	Annan Athletic	Creetown	3-1	Galabank
2006/7	Dalbeattie Star	Stranraer Athletic	4-1	Islecroft Stadium
2007/8	Threave Rovers	Mid Annandale	4-0	Meadow Park
2008/9	Dalbeattie Star	Annan Athletic	4-1	Galabank
2009/10	St Cuthbert Wanderers	Wigtown & Bladnoch	3-1	St Marys Park
2010/1	Annan Athletic	Newton Stewart	3-2	Blairmount Park
2011/2	Dalbeattie Star	Queen of the South	8-1	Galabank
2012/3	Dalbeattie Star	Nithsdale Wanderers	6-2	Annan
2013/14	Wigtown & Bladnoch	Dalbeattie Star	2-1	St Marys Park

Tweedie Cup (Wigtownshire FA)   2013/14

Rd 1	11/01/2014	Crichton	Abbey Vale	5	0	
Rd 1	11/01/2014	Lochar Thistle	Nithsdale Wanderers	2	2	6-7 pens
Rd 1	11/01/2014	St Cuthbert Wanderers	Heston Rovers	2	1	
Rd 1	11/01/2014	Wigtown & Bladnoch	Fleet Star	6	0	
Rd 2	08/03/2014	Mid Annandale	Crichton	4	6	
Rd 2	22/03/2014	Creetown	Nithsdale Wanderers	1	4	
Rd 2	09/04/2014	St Cuthbert Wanderers	Threave Rovers	0	1	
Rd 2	25/03/2004	Newton Stewart	Wigtown & Bladnoch	1	2	
SF	23/04/2014	Threave Rovers	Nithsdale Wanderers	2	0	
SF	23/04/2014	Wigtown & Bladnoch	Crichton	3	0	
F	23/05/2014	Wigtown & Bladnoch	Threave Rovers	4	2 AET	at Newton Stewart

Recent Tweedie Cup Finals

Season	Winners	Runners Up	Score	Venue
1988/9	No competition			
1989/90	St Cuthbert Wanderers	Threave Rovers	4-2	Kirkcudbright
1990/1	No competition			
1991/2	Newton Stewart	Wigtow & Bladnoch	1-0	Newton Stewart
1992/3	No competition			
1993/4	Maxwelltown HSFP	Dalbeattie Star	2-1	Maxwelltown HS
1994/5	No competition			
1995/6	Annan Athletic	Stranraer Athletic	3-1	Annan
1996/7	Threave Rovers	Annan Athletic	3-1	Castle Douglas
1997/8	Tarff Rovers	Annan Athletic	2-0	Annan
1998/9	Tarff Rovers	Creetown	2-2, 6-5 pens	Creetown
1999/00	Dalbattie Star	Threave Rovers	3-0	Kirkcowan
2000/1	Not completed			
2001/2	St Cuthbert Wanderers	Gretna	2-1	Kirkcudbright
2002/3	Creetown	Girvan	4-0	Creetown
2003/4	Creetown	Gretna	2-0	Creetown
2004/5	Annan Athletic	Stranraer Athletic	3-1	Annan
2005/6	Abbey Vale	Wigtow & Bladnoch	2-1	Abbey Vale
2006/7	Annan Athletic	Stranraer Athletic	6-2	Annan
2007/8	Creetown	St Cuthberts Wanderers	3-1	Creetown
2008/9	St Cuthbert Wanderers	Newton Stewart	2-0	Newton Stewart
2009/10	Crichton	Threave Rovers	3-3, 4-3 pens	Crichton
2010/1	Stranraer	Heston Rovers	6-3	Heston Rovers
2011/2	Threave Rovers	Newton Stewart	1-0	Castle Douglas
2012/3	Dalbeattie Star	Threave Rovers	2-1 AET	Annan
2013/14	Wigtown & Bladnoch	Threave Rovers	4-2 AET	Newton Stewart

Senior Non League Clubs - Highland League

Club	Brora Rangers
Formed	1878
Joined HL	1962
Ground	Dudgeon Park
Tel	01408 621231
Postcode	KW9 6QH
Capacity	2000
Secretary	Kevin Mackay
E Mail	brorarangersfc@highlandleague.com
Home Top 2013/14	Red
Shorts	Red
Nickname(s)	Cattachs

Club	Deveronvale
Formed	1938
Joined HL	1938
Ground	Princess Royal Park, Banff
Postcode	AB45 1AZ
Tel	01261 818303
Capacity	5000
Secretary	Stewart McPherson
E Mail	deveronvalefc@highlandleague.com
Home Top 2013/14	Red
Shorts	Red
Nickname(s)	Vale

Club	Buckie Thistle
Formed	1889
Joined HL	1909
Ground	Victoria Park
Tel	01542 831454
Postcode	AB56 1BJ
Capacity	5000
Secretary	Marc Macrae
E Mail	buckiethistlefc@highlandleague.com
Home Top 2013/14	Green and White Hoops
Shorts	White
Nickname(s)	Jags

Club	Formartine United
Formed	1946
Joined HL	2009
Ground	North Lodge Park, Pitmedden
Tel	01651 843266
Postcode	AB41 7PA
Capacity	2500
Secretary	Martin Johnston
E Mail	formartineunitedfc@highlandleague.com
Home Top 2013/14	Red and White Stripes
Shorts	White
Nickname(s)	

Club	Clachnacuddin
Formed	1886
Joined HL	1893 (Founder Members)
Ground	Grant Street Park
Tel	01463 718261
Postcode	IV3 8DR
Capacity	1500
Secretary	Douglas Noble
E Mail	clachnacuddinfc@highlandleague.com
Home Top 2013/14	White
Shorts	Black
Nickname(s)	Lilywhites

Club	Forres Mechanics
Formed	1884
Joined HL	1893 (Founder Members)
Ground	Mosset Park
Postcode	IV36 1AU
Tel	01309 675096
Capacity	1500
Secretary	David McDonald
E Mail	forresmechanicsfc@highlandleague.com
Home Top 2013/14	Yellow and Brown Hoops
Shorts	Yellow
Nickname(s)	Can Cans

Club	Cove Rangers
Formed	1922
Joined HL	1986
Ground	Allan Park
Postcode	AB12 3NR
Tel	01224 890433
Capacity	2300
Secretary	Duncan Little
E Mail	coverangersfc@highlandleague.com
Home Top 2013/14	Blue
Shorts	Blue
Nickname(s)	Cove

Club	Fort William
Formed	1984
Joined HL	1985
Ground	Claggan Park
Postcode	PH33 6TE
Tel	01397 698003
Capacity	4000
Secretary	Marie McMillan
E Mail	fortwilliamfc@highlandleague.com
Home Top 2013/14	Tangerine
Shorts	Black
Nickname(s)	Fort

Club	Fraserburgh		Club	Lossiemouth
Formed	1910		Formed	1945
Joined HL			Joined HL	1946
Ground	Bellslea Park		Ground	Grant Park
Postcode	AB43 9BB		Postcode	IV31 6JG
Tel	01346 518444		Tel	01343 813717
Capacity	3000		Capacity	2400
Secretary	Finlay Noble		Secretary	Alan McIntosh
E-Mail	fraserburghfc@highlandleague.com		E Mail	lossiemouthfc@highlandleague.com
Home Top 2013/14	Black and White Stripes		Home Top 2013/14	Red
Shorts	Black		Shorts	Red
Nickname(s)	Broch		Nickname(s)	Coasters

Club	Huntly		Club	Nairn County
Formed	1928		Formed	1914
Joined HL	1928		Joined HL	1919
Ground	Christie Park		Ground	Station Park
Postcode	AB54 8JE		Postcode	IV12 5LT
Tel	01466 793548		Tel	01667 454298
Capacity	1800		Capacity	3000
Secretary	Alix Turner		Secretary	Donald Mathieson
E Mail	huntlyfc@highlandleague.com		E Mail	nairncountyfc@highlandleague.com
Home Top 2013/14	Black and Gold Stripes		Home Top 2013/14	Yellow and Black Hoops
Shorts	Black		Shorts	Black
Nickname(s)			Nickname(s)	County

Club	Inverurie Locos		Club	Rothes
Formed	1903		Formed	1938
Joined HL	2001		Joined HL	1938
Ground	Harlaw Park		Ground	MacKessack Park
Postcode	AB51 4SG		Postcode	AB38 7AD
Tel	01467 622168		Tel	01340 831972
Capacity	2500		Capacity	1731
Secretary	Billy Thomson		Secretary	Andrew Simpson
E Mail	inverurielocoworksfc@highlandleague.com		E Mail	rothesfc@highlandleague.com
Home Top 2013/14	Red and Black Stripes		Home Top 2013/14	Orange
Shorts	Black		Shorts	Black
Nickname(s)	Locos		Nickname(s)	Speysiders

Club	Keith		Club	Strathspey Thistle
Formed	1910		Formed	1993
Joined HL	1924		Joined HL	2009
Ground	Kynoch Park		Ground	Seafield Park
Postcode	AB55 5EN		Postcode	PH26 3HY
Tel	01542 882629		Tel	
Capacity	4000		Capacity	2000
Secretary	Alex E Stables		Secretary	Malky Taylor
E Mail	keithfc@highlandleague.com		E Mail	strathspeythistlefc@highlandleague.com
Home Top 2013/14	Maroon		Home Top 2013/14	Blue
Shorts	Maroon		Shorts	Blue
Nickname(s)	Maroons		Nickname(s)	

Club	Turriff United
Formed	1954
Joined HL	2009
Ground	The Haughs
Postcode	AB53 4ER
Tel	01888 562169
Capacity	1200
Secretary	Gairn Ritchie
E Mail	turriffunitedfc@highlandleague.com
Home Top 2013/14	Blue
Shorts	Blue
Nickname(s)	Turra

Club	Wick Academy
Formed	1893
Joined HL	1994
Ground	Harmsworth Park
Postcode	KW1 5NH
Tel	01955 602446
Capacity	2000
Secretary	Alan Farquhar
E Mail	wickacademyfc@highlandleague.com
Home Top 2013/14	Black and White Stripes
Shorts	Black
Nickname(s)	Scorries

Senior Non League Clubs - Lowland League

Club	BSC (Glasgow)
Formed	
Joined LL	
Ground	Saracen Park
Postcode	
Tel	
E Mail	
Capacity	
Secretary	
Home Top 2013/14	
Shorts	
Nickname(s)	

Club	Dalbeattie Star
Formed	c1900
Joined LL	2013
Ground	Islecroft Stadium
Postcode	DG5 4HE
Tel	07712110574 (Match Sec Mobile)
E Mail	kennydbtstar@hotmail.com
Capacity	c1500
Match Secretary	Kenny Murray
Home Top 2013/14	Red and Black
Shorts	Black
Nickname(s)	Star

Club	East Kilbride
Formed	2010
Joined LL	2013
Ground	K Park
Postcode	G74 2AG
Tel	07757 859368 (Match Sec Mobile)
E Mail	eastkilbride@slfl.co.uk
Capacity	c800
Match Secretary	Peter Hickey
Home Top 2013/14	Blue and Gold Halves
Shorts	Blue
Nickname(s)	Kilby

Club	Edinburgh City
Formed	1928
Joined LL	2013
Ground	Meadowbank Stadium
Postcode	EH7 6AE
Tel	07773547732 (Sec Mobile)
	0131 661 5351 (Stadium)
E Mail	edinburghcity@slfl.co.uk
Capacity	7500
Secretary	Grant Coffin
Home Top 2013/14	White
Shorts	Black
Nickname(s)	City

Club	Edinburgh University
Formed	1877
Joined LL	2014
Ground	East Peffermill
Postcode	EH16 5LL
Tel	0131 650 2346
E Mail	info@euafc.com
Capacity	c1500
Secretary	Andrew Reid
Home Top 2013/14	Green / Blue
Shorts	Blue
Nickname(s)	Uni

Club	Gala Fairydean Rovers
Formed	2013
Joined LL	2013
Ground	Netherdale
Postcode	TD1 3HE
Tel	01896 754797
E Mail	graememciver@btinternet.com
Capacity	c2500
Secretary	Graeme McIver
Home Top 2013/14	Red and Black
Shorts	White
Nickname(s)	Gala

Club	Gretna
Formed	2008
Joined LL	2013
Ground	Raydale Park
Postcode	DG16 5AP
Tel	Sec Mobile: 07947 687293
E Mail	sandrabowdon@live.co.uk
Capacity	c1500
Secretary	Sandra Bowdon
Home Top 2013/14	White and Black
Shorts	Black
Nickname(s)	

Club	Threave Rovers
Formed	1953
Joined LL	2013
Ground	Meadow Park, Castle Douglas
Postcode	DG7 1DJ
Tel	01556 504536
E Mail	ianmunro443@hotmail.com
Capacity	c1500
Secretary	Ian Munro
Home Top 2013/14	Black and White Stripes
Shorts	Black
Nickname(s)	

Club	Preston Athletic
Formed	1945
Joined LL	2013
Ground	Pennypit Park
Postcode	EH32 9JQ
Tel	01875 815221
E Mail	preston@eastofscotlandfa.co.uk
Capacity	c3000
Secretary	Paula Redpath
Home Top 2013/14	Blue
Shorts	Blue
Nickname(s)	Panners

Club	Vale of Leithen
Formed	1891
Joined LL	2013
Ground	Victoria Park, Innerleithen
Postcode	EH44 6RB (approx)
Tel	Mobile: 07528 521332
E Mail	a.currie.7@btinternet.com
Capacity	c1500
Secretary	Alex Currie
Home Top 2013/14	Navy Blue
Shorts	Navy Blue
Nickname(s)	Vale

Club	Selkirk
Formed	1880
Joined LL	2013
Ground	Yarrow Park
Postcode	TD7 5AX
Tel	07984 984572 (Sec Mob)
E Mail	steve.davison@signum.freeserve.co.uk
Capacity	c2000
Secretary	Sheree Davidson
Home Top 2013/14	Blue
Shorts	Blue
Nickname(s)	Souters

Club	University of Stirling
Formed	
Joined LL	2013
Ground	Forthbank Stadium
Postcode	FK7 7UJ
Tel	Mobile: 07740 500140
E Mail	r.n.gowrie@stirling.ac.uk
Capacity	3800
Secretary	Raleigh Gowrie
Home Top 2013/14	Green and White
Shorts	Green and White
Nickname(s)	Uni

Club	Spartans
Formed	1951
Joined LL	2013
Ground	Ainslie Park, Edinburgh
Postcode	EH5 2HF
Tel	0131 552 7854
E Mail	macabiteam@hotmail.com
Capacity	c2500
Secretary	John McCabe
Home Top 2013/14	White
Shorts	Red
Nickname(s)	

Club	Whitehill Welfare
Formed	1953
Joined LL	2013
Ground	Ferguson Park, Rosewell
Postcode	EH24 9DS
Tel	0131 440 0115
E Mail	whitehillwelfare@gmail.com
Capacity	c1500
Secretary	Andrew Renwick
Home Top 2013/14	Maroon with Sky Blue Sleeves
Shorts	White
Nickname(s)	Welfare

Senior Non League Clubs - East of Scotland League

Club	Burntisland Shipyard
Formed	1925
Joined ESL	2012
Ground	Shipyard Recreation Ground
Postcode	KY3 0JG
Tel	07867 795898 (Sec Mobile)
E Mail	abeveridge.shipyard@sky.com
Capacity	c1500
Secretary	Andrew Beveridge
Home Top 2013/14	White
Shorts	Black
Nickname(s)	Shippy

Club	Duns
Formed	1882
Joined ESL	2011 (Rejoined)
Ground	New Hawthorn Park
Postcode	TD11 3QQ (approx)
Tel	Sec 07866 883 092
E Mail	colinpike598@gmail.com
Capacity	c1200
Secretary	Mark Dixon
Home Top 2013/14	Red and Black Stripes
Shorts	Black
Nickname(s)	Dingers

Club	Civil Service Strollers
Formed	1908
Joined ESL	
Ground	Marine Drive
Postcode	EH4 5EJ
Tel	0131 332 1175
E Mail	keith.l.stewart@bt.com
Capacity	c1000
Secretary	Keith Stewart
Home Top 2013/14	White
Shorts	Navy
Nickname(s)	Civvy

Club	Easthouses Lily
Formed	1969
Joined ESL	1981
Ground	Newbattle Complex
Postcode	EH22 4DP
Tel	Sec 0131 237 1351
E Mail	
Capacity	c1200
Secretary	Robert Paul
Home Top 2013/14	White
Shorts	Red
Nickname(s)	Lily

Club	Coldstream
Formed	1895
Joined ESL	
Ground	Home Park
Postcode	TD12 4DT
Tel	01890 883085
E Mail	allan@integrityifa.com
Capacity	c1500
Secretary	Allan Easton
Home Top 2013/14	Blue
Shorts	Blue
Nickname(s)	Streamers

Club	Eyemouth United
Formed	1945
Joined ESL	1945
Ground	Warner Park
Postcode	TD14 5DX
Tel	Sec 07526 244 570
E Mail	tcollin71@hotmail.com
Capacity	c1000
Secretary	Tommy Collin
Home Top 2013/14	Maroon
Shorts	Maroon
Nickname(s)	Fishermen

Club	Craigroyston
Formed	1976
Joined ESL	1976
Ground	St Mark Park
Postcode	EH7 4HN
Tel	Sec 07817 530 152
E Mail	jimsivewright@hotmail.co.uk
Capacity	c1500
Secretary	Jim Sivewright
Home Top 2013/14	Yellow
Shorts	Royal Blue
Nickname(s)	Craigie

Club	Hawick Royal Albert
Formed	1947
Joined ESL	1953
Ground	Albert Park
Postcode	TD9 8AG
Tel	01450 374231
E Mail	douglas.purves@nhslothian.scot.nhs.uk
Capacity	c2000
Secretary	Douglas Purves
Home Top 2013/14	Blue and Red
Shorts	White
Nickname(s)	Albert

Club Heriot Watt University
Formed 1971
Joined ESL 1971
Ground Riccarton Campus
Postcode EH14 4AS
Tel Sec 07747 616 402
E Mail info@hwufc.org.uk
Capacity c1000
Secretary Alasdair Matheson
Home Top 2013/14 Yellow
Shorts Blue
Nickname(s) Watt

Club Kelso United
Formed 1924
Joined ESL 1967
Ground Woodside Park
Postcode TD5 7BP
Tel Sec 07776 204 325
E Mail george.riley@royalcanin.com
Capacity c1000
Secretary George Riley
Home Top 2013/14 White and Black
Shorts Black
Nickname(s)

Club Leith Athletic
Formed 1996
Joined ESL 1991 (as Manor Th)
Ground Meadowbank 3G
Postcode EH7 6AE
Tel Sec 07850 772 706
E Mail tam.currie@leithathleticfc.com
Capacity c200
Secretary Tam Currie
Home Top 2013/14 White and Black Stripes
Shorts Black
Nickname(s)

Club Lothian Thistle Hutchison Vale
Formed 1969
Joined ESL 1995
Ground Saughton Enclosure
Postcode EH11 3BQ
Tel Sec 07730 256 783
E Mail tom@lothianthistlefc.co.uk
Capacity c3000
Secretary Tom Allison
Home Top 2013/14 Black and Yellow
Shorts White
Nickname(s) Hutchie

Club Ormiston
Formed 1999
Joined ESL 1999
Ground Recreation Ground
Postcode EH35 5LQ
Tel Sec 07740 680 904
E Mail secretary@ormistonfc.co.uk
Capacity c2000
Secretary John Greenhorn
Home Top 2013/14 Maroon
Shorts Maroon
Nickname(s) Ormy

Club Peebles Rovers
Formed 1893
Joined ESL 1979 (Rejoined)
Ground Whitestone Park
Postcode EH45 8BE
Tel Sec 07711 562 909
E Mail ac70@btinternet.com
Capacity c1500
Secretary Iain Clark
Home Top 2013/14 Red
Shorts Red
Nickname(s) Rovers

Club Spartans EOS
Formed 1951
Joined ESL 2013
Ground Ainslie Park
Postcode EH5 2HF
Tel
E Mail
Capacity c1500
Secretary
Home Top 2013/14 White
Shorts Red
Nickname(s)

Club Stirling University EOS
Formed
Joined ESL 2013
Ground Gannochy Sports Complex
Postcode FK9 4LA
Tel 07774 687 205
E Mail elliot.sutcliffe@yahoo.com
Capacity c1000
Secretary Elliot Sutcliffe
Home Top 2013/14 Green
Shorts Green
Nickname(s)

Club Tynecastle
Formed 1928
Joined ESL 1987
Ground Fernieside Recreation Ground
Postcode EH17 7HY
Tel Sec 07889 931 054
E Mail alistair@wilkielaw.co.uk
Capacity c1000
Secretary Alistair Wilkie
Home Top 2013/14 Maroon
Shorts White

Senior Non League Clubs - South of Scotland League

Club	Abbey Vale
Formed	1971
Joined SOSL	2001
Ground	Maryfield Park, New Abbey
Postcode	DG2 8BY
Tel	01387256004 (Sec)
E Mail	info@abbeyvalefc.co.uk
Capacity	c1000
Secretary	David Morton
Home Top 2013/14	Black / Amber
Shorts	Black
Nickname(s)	Vale

Club	Edusports Academy
Formed	
Joined SOSL	2014
Ground	Hamilton Palace Grounds, Hamilton
Postcode	ML3 6EF
Tel	07795807927
E Mail	
Capacity	c800
Secretary	Chris Ewing
Home Top 2013/14	
Shorts	
Nickname(s)	

Club	Creetown
Formed	1905
Joined SOSL	1946
Ground	Castle Cary Park
Postcode	
Tel	01671820628 (Sec)
E Mail	
Capacity	c1000
Secretary	Steve Dorrans
Home Top 2013/14	Yellow
Shorts	Black
Nickname(s)	Ferrytoun

Club	Fleet Star
Formed	1948
Joined SOSL	2004
Ground	Garries Park, Gatehouse of Fleet
Postcode	DG7 2HU
Tel	Sec 01557814829
E Mail	invinghannah6@gmail.com
Capacity	c1000
Secretary	Irvine Hannah
Home Top 2013/14	Royal Blue
Shorts	
Nickname(s)	

Club	Crichton
Formed	1972
Joined SOSL	1992
Ground	Crichton Hospital Park
Postcode	DG1 4ZE (Approx)
Tel	01387 263285 (sec)
E Mail	
Capacity	c1500
Secretary	Tommy Parker
Home Top 2013/14	Blue
Shorts	Blue
Nickname(s)	

Club	Heston Rovers
Formed	1978
Joined SOSL	2008
Ground	Palmerston Park, Dumfries
Postcode	DG2 9BA
Tel	Sec 07779289748
E Mail	
Capacity	7620
Secretary	Bobby Lumsden
Home Top 2013/14	Black and White stripes
Shorts	Black
Nickname(s)	

Club	Dumfries YMCA
Formed	
Joined SOSL	2014
Ground	Kingholm (MacLeod Pavilion)
Postcode	DG1 4SR
Tel	01576202438 (Sec)
E Mail	
Capacity	c1000
Secretary	Blair Crossan
Home Top 2013/14	Red
Shorts	
Nickname(s)	YM

Club	Lochar Thistle
Formed	
Joined SOSL	2013
Ground	Maxwelltown High School
Postcode	DG2 0EL
Tel	Sec 07828160408
E Mail	r.caskie@btinternet.com
Capacity	c1000
Secretary	Russell Caskie
Home Top 2013/14	Red and Black Stripes
Shorts	Black
Nickname(s)	

Club	Mid Annandale
Formed	1959
Joined SOSL	2003
Ground	Galabank, Annan
Postcode	DG12 5DQ
Tel	Sec 01576 202757
E Mail	
Capacity	2514
Secretary	George Trudt
Home Top 2013/14	Yellow
Shorts	Black
Nickname(s)	Mids

Club	Upper Annandale
Formed	1966
Joined SOSL	2014
Ground	Moffat Academy
Postcode	DG10 9QF
Tel	07776166835 (Sec Mob)
E Mail	
Capacity	c800
Secretary	Bob Smith
Home Top 2013/14	Black and White
Shorts	Black
Nickname(s)	

Club	Newton Stewart
Formed	1884
Joined SOSL	1946
Ground	Blairmount Park, Newton Stewart
Postcode	DG8 6NU
Tel	07702871739 (Sec Mob)
E Mail	j.mcnaught731@btinternet.com
Capacity	c1000
Secretary	John McNaught
Home Top 2013/14	Black and White Stripes
Shorts	Black
Nickname(s)	Creesiders

Club	Wigtown & Bladnoch
Formed	1888
Joined SOSL	1946
Ground	Trammondford Park, Wigtown
Postcode	DG8 9DY (approx)
Tel	07849 432008 (Sec Mob)
E Mail	sturen@btinternet.com
Capacity	c2000
Secretary	James McColm
Home Top 2013/14	Red
Shorts	Red
Nickname(s)	

Club	Nithsdale Wanderers
Formed	2001
Joined SOSL	2001
Ground	Lorimer Park, Sanquhar
Postcode	DG4 6DB
Tel	0165950822 (Sec)
E Mail	
Capacity	c1000
Secretary	Stephen Cook
Home Top 2013/14	Blue
Shorts	White
Nickname(s)	

Club	St Cuthbert Wanderers
Formed	1879
Joined SOSL	1946
Ground	St Mary's Park, Kirkcudbright
Postcode	DG6 4AW
Tel	07703 723846 (Sec Mob)
E Mail	saints1879@hotmail.co.uk
Capacity	c 1000
Secretary	James Richardson
Home Top 2013/14	Blue and White Hoops
Shorts	Blue
Nickname(s)	Saints

MISCELLANEOUS FITBA

North Caledonian League   2013/14

	P	W	D	L	F	A	GD	Pts
Halkirk United	12	9	3	0	43	13	30	30
Golspie Sutherland	12	8	1	3	45	24	21	25
Muir of Ord Rovers	12	6	2	4	26	25	1	20
Clachnacuddin	12	5	2	5	29	32	-3	17
Thurso	12	3	4	5	13	16	-3	13
Alness United	12	3	1	8	18	32	-14	10
Sutherland United	12	1	1	10	16	48	-32	4

League Champions 1970-date

1970/1	Dingwall Thistle
1971/2	Dingwall Thistle
1972/3	Alness
1973/4	Alness
1974/5	Golspie Sutherland
1975/6	Golspie Sutherland
1976/7	Invergordon
1977/8	Dingwall Thistle
1978/9	Wick Academy
1979/80	Wick Academy
1980/1	Wick Academy
1981/2	Wick Academy
1982/3	Bunillidh Thistle
1983/4	Muir of Ord
1984/5	Fort William
1985/6	Muir of Ord
1986/7	Wick Academy
1987/8	Invergordon
1988/9	Bunillidh Thistle
1989/90	Balintore
1990/1	Balintore
1991/2	Clachnacuddin
1992/3	Golspie Sutherland
1993/4	Halkirk United
1994/5	Caledonian Thistle
1995/6	Fearn Thistle
1996/7	Ross County
1997/8	Inverness Caledonian Thistle
1998/9	Golspie Sutherland
1999/00	Thurso
2000/1	Alness United
2001/2	Invergordon
2002/3	Thurso
2003/4	Golspie Sutherland
2004/5	THurso
2005/6	Balintore
2006/7	Golspie Sutherland
2007/8	Golspie Sutherland
2008/9	Golspie Sutherland
2009/10	Thurso
2010/1	Halkirk United
2011/2	Halkirk United
2012/3	Thurso
2013/4	Halkirk United

NORTH CALEDONIAN CUP

1	Sep 21	Orkney	Halkirk United	2	3	
1	Sep 21	Thurso	Shetland	1	1	AET, 3-5p
QF	Oct 5	Halkirk United	Muir of Ord Rovers	1	2	
QF	Oct 5	Sutherland United	Clachnacuddin	1	3	
QF	Oct 5	Shetland	Golspie Sutherland	2	3	
QF	Oct 12	Alness United	Lewis & Harris	1	0	
SF	Oct 19	Golspie Sutherland	Muir of Ord Rovers	2	6	
SF	Oct 19	Clachnacuddin	Alness United	2	4	
F	Nov 9	Muir of Ord Rovers	Alness United	1	3	@ Muir of Ord

FOOTBALL TIMES CUP

QF	Mar 1	Clachnacuddin	Halkirk United	2	0	
QF	Mar 1	Golspie Sutherland	Muir of Ord Rovers	2	0	
QF	Mar 1	Sutherland United	Thurso	0	0	AET, 3-4p
QF	Mar 22	Orkney	Alness United	2	0	
SF	Apr 12	Thurso	Halkirk United	1	0	
SF	Apr 12	Golspie Sutherland	Orkney	3	1	
F	Apr 26	Golspie Sutherland	Thurso	2	1	Morrison Park

SWL CUP

QF	Nov 16	Clachnacuddin	Orkney	2	0	
QF	Nov 16	Golspie Sutherland	Sutherland United	4	0	
QF	Nov 16	Muir of Ord Rovers	Alness United	3	2	
QF	Nov 16	Thurso	Halkirk United	3	1	
SF	Nov 30	Thurso	Clachnacuddin	5	0	
SF	Nov 30	Golspie Sutherland	Muir of Ord Rovers	4	3	
F	Apr 19	Golspie Sutherland	Thurso	5	0	@ Golspie

NESS CUP

R1	Mar 29	Alness United	Sutherland United	3	0	
R1	Mar 22	Halkirk United	Thurso	1	1	
R1	Mar 22	Muir of Ord Rovers	Golspie Sutherland	0	2	
R1	Mar 15	Clachnacuddin	Halkirk	1	4	
R1	Mar 15	Golspie Sutherland	Alness United	9	1	
R1	Mar 15	Sutherland United	Muir of Ord Rovers	3	1	
R1	Mar 8	Alness United	Halkirk	1	2	
R1	Mar 8	Thurso	Clachnacuddin	0	0	
R1	Feb 22	Alness United	Clachnacuddin	2	6	
R1	Feb 22	Halkirk United	Golspie Sutherland	2	0	
R1	Feb 22	Muir of Ord Rovers	Thurso	2	2	
R1	Feb 8	Clachnacuddin	Muir of Ord Rovers	4	0	
R1	Feb 8	Sutherland United	Golspie Sutherland	0	0	
R1	Feb 8	Thurso	Alness United	3	1	
R1	Jan 25	Golspie Sutherland	Clachnacuddin	1	2	
R1	Jan 25	Thurso	Sutherland United	2	1	
R1	Jan 18	Clachnacuddin	Sutherland United	4	0	
R1	Jan 18	Golspie Sutherland	Thurso	2	1	
R1	Jan 18	Halkirk United	Muir of Ord Rovers	0	0	
R1	Jan 11	Muir of Ord Rovers	Alness United	1	1	
R1	Jan 11	Sutherland United	Halkirk	0	3	
SF	Apr 2	Halkirk United	Thurso	2	2	4-5p
SF	Apr 5	Clachnacuddin	Golspie Sutherland	1	5	
F	May 10	Thurso	Golspie Sutherland	2	4	aet @ Thurso

JOCK MACKAY MEMORIAL CUP

1	Feb 15	Halkirk United	Golspie Sutherland	0	3	
QF	Feb 15	Clachnacuddin	Thurso	1	1	AET, 4-3p
QF	Feb 15	Golspie Sutherland	Alness United	6	0	
QF	Feb 22	Shetland	Sutherland United	2	0	
QF	Mar 8	Muir of Ord Rovers	Orkney	3	4	AET
SF	Mar 29	Orkney	Clachnacuddin	4	1	
SF	Mar 29	Shetland	Golspie Sutherland	1	1	AET, 1-3p
F	May 3	Orkney	Golspie Sutherland	0	4	@ Invergordon

Senior County Cup Competitions

Once regarded as important, these matches are now frequently unplayed. When they do take place it is often with below-strength team line-ups. They are included only for the sake of completeness.

EAST OF SCOTLAND SHIELD 2013/14
May 4th 2014
Hibernian Under 17 v Heaerts Under 17, 2-0 (at Easter Road), Attendance approx 300
Hibernian: Sean Brennan, Matthew McInally, David Porcher, Ben Stirling, Jordan McGregor, Gregor Watson, Alistair Smith, Scott Martin, Conner Duthie, Dominic Docherty, Oliver Shaw (Kevin Waugh, 83). Unused substitutes: Ross Campbell, Stan Chitemere, David McKay, Adam Watson. Scorers - McGregor, Shaw
Hearts: Jamie Sneddon, Jack Simpson, Sam Daniels, Kai Wilson, Greig Page, Sean McKitdy, Lewis Moore, Aaron Scott, Murray Cockburn, Rhys Craigie, Ian Smith. Subs Kelby Mason, Jonny Grotlan, Scott Walker, Jonni Turner, Kiren Somerville, Taylor Queen.

FIFE CUP 2013/14

Preliminary Round
28/11/13   East Fife v Cowdenbeath, 1-2

Semi Finals
Cowdenbeath v Dunfermline Athletic, Not played
Raith Rovers v Burntisland Shipyard, Not played

Cup was awarded to Cowdenbeath

FORFARSHIRE CUP 2013/14

The 2013/14 competition was not played.
The final of the 2011/12 competition was played this season:
27/8/13 Dundee United v St Johnstone, 1-1, 2-4pens

Draw 2014/15
Rd 1
Forfar Athletic v Brechin City
Dundee v St Johntone
Arbroath v Montrose
Bye Dundee United

SF
Arbroath or Montrose v Dundee United
Forfar Athletic or Brechin City v Dundee or St Johnstone

RENFREWSHIRE CUP
The two Semi Finals are contested by the two finalists of the Renfrewshire Victoria Cup (for Amateurs) who meet Morton and St Mirren. The Final is usually played pre-season in the following season. Sometimes it has been played before the Semi Finals in which case it has been billed as a Friendly.

The 2012/13 competition was held at the start of 2013/14:

Semi Finals
16/7/13 Morton v Viewfield Rovers, 9-0
17/7/13 St Mirren v Port Glasgow OBU, 16-0

Final
20/7/13 St Mirren v Morton, 2-4

STIRLINGSHIRE CUP

The Final of the 2012/13 competition was played at the start of 2013/14.
23/7/14 Dumbarton v   Falkirk, 3-2

The Final of the 2013/14 competition was held over until the start of 2014/15.

Other Results:

Round 1
31/7/13 Stenhousemuir v Falkirk, 0-1
27/8/13 Alloa v East Stirlingshire, 2-2, 2-4 pens

Semi Finals
24/9/13 Falkirk v Dumbarton, 3-1
8/10/13 Stirling Albion v East Stirlingshire, 3-1

Draw for 2014/15
Round 1
Stenhousemuir v Stirling Albion
Dumbarton v Falkirk

Semi Finals
East Stirlingshire v Dumbarton / Falkirk
Alloa v Stenhousemuir / Stirling Albion

University Football

Over many years the biggest prize in Scottish University football was the Queen's Park Shield, competed for on Wednesday afternoon's by the Scottish seats of learning. Nowadays the top Scottish sides compete in the various divisions of the UK-wide British Universities and Colleges Sport (BUCS) tournaments. The Queen's Park Shield is still played for but it is now a knock out competition rather than a League.

BRITISH UNIVERSITIES MENS PREMIER DIVISION NORTH

	P	W	D	L	GD	PTS	ADJ
1 Stirling 1st	10	5	3	2	8	18	
2 Nottingham 1st	10	5	2	3	2	17	
3 Durham 1st	10	5	1	4	8	16	
4 Loughborough 1st	10	4	1	5	1	13	
5 Sheffield Hallam 1st	10	3	2	5	-3	11	
6 Northumbria 1st	10	3	1	6	-16	10	

SCOTTISH DIVISION 1A

	P	W	D	L	GD	Pts
1 Stirling 2nd	8	6	0	2	7	18
2 Heriot-Watt 1st	8	5	1	2	3	16
3 Edinburgh 1st	7	5	1	1	13	16
4 Edinburgh Napier 1st	8	2	0	6	-9	6
5 Aberdeen 1st	7	0	0	7	-14	0

SCOTTISH DIVISION 2A

1 Abertay 1st	8	3	3	2	7	12
2 Robert Gordon 1st	8	3	3	2	2	12
3 St Andrews 1st	8	3	2	3	-2	11
4 Glasgow 1st	8	2	4	2	1	10
5 Edinburgh 2nd	8	1	4	3	-8	7

SCOTTISH DIVISION 3A

1 Strathclyde 1st	8	7	1	0	20	22
2 Glasgow Caledonian 1st	8	5	0	3	9	15
3 Dundee 1st	8	3	1	4	-10	10
4 Stirling 3rd	8	2	1	5	0	7
5 Glasgow 2nd	8	1	1	6	-19	4

SCOTTISH DIVISION 4A

1 Heriot-Watt 2nd	8	7	0	1	21	21
2 Edinburgh 3rd	8	6	0	2	18	18
3 Edinburgh 4th	8	2	1	5	-12	7
4 Robert Gordon 2nd	8	2	1	5	-20	7
5 Heriot-Watt 3rd	8	2	0	6	-7	6

SCOTTISH DIVISION 5A

1 Strathclyde 2nd	8	5	1	2	15	16
2 Aberdeen 2nd	8	4	1	3	0	13
3 Stirling 4th	8	3	3	2	9	12
4 Edinburgh Napier 2nd	8	2	2	4	-9	8
5 Strathclyde 3rd	8	2	1	5	-15	7

SCOTTISH DIVISION 6A

1 Glasgow 3rd	8	5	3	0	6	18
2 Dundee 2nd	8	5	2	1	14	17
3 Aberdeen 3rd	8	3	3	2	2	12
4 Abertay 2nd	8	3	0	5	1	6
5 Edinburgh Napier 3rd	8	0	0	8	-23	-6

Matches take place on Wednesday afternoons, usually from September until April.

Full details are shown on the BUCS website.

SCOTTISH DIVISION 7A

1 West of Scotland 2nd (Hamilton)	8	8	0	0	22	24
2 St Andrews 2nd	8	4	1	3	4	13
3 Stirling 5th	8	3	1	4	-1	10
4 Dundee 3rd	8	2	1	5	-9	7
5 Glasgow Caledonian 2nd	8	1	1	6	-16	4

SCOTTISH DIVISION 8A

1 West of Scotland 1st (Paisley)	8	7	0	1	18	21
2 St Andrews 3rd	8	7	0	1	21	21
3 Aberdeen 4th	8	3	1	4	-9	10
4 Queen Margaret 1st	7	1	1	5	-19	4
5 Scot' Rural 1st (Ayr)	7	0	0	7	-11	-15

SCOTTISH DIVISION 9A

1 Heriot-Watt 4th	8	5	3	0	11	18
2 Edinburgh Napier 4th	8	5	0	3	3	15
3 Stirling 6th	8	4	2	2	15	14
4 Dundee 4th	8	1	2	5	-18	5
5 Glasgow Caledonian 3rd	8	1	1	6	-11	4

BRITISH UNIVERSITIES KO CUP

R16	Stirling 1st		BYE	
R16	Bath 1st	Sheffield Hallam 1st	5 1	
R16	SW Pontypridd & Cardiff		BYE	
R16	Durham 1st	Gloucester 1st	4 1	
R16	UWE (Hartpury) 1st		BYE	
R16	Loughborough 1st	Cambridge 1st	6 2	
R16	Nottingham 1st		BYE	
R16	Chichester 1st	Northumbria 1st	4 1	
QF	Stirling 1st	Bath 1st	3 2	
QF	SW Pontypridd & Cardiff	Durham 1st	1 0	
QF	UWEn (Hartpury) 1st	Loughborough 1st	1 1	1-3 pens
QF	Nottingham 1st	Chichester 1st	1 2	
SF	Stirling 1st	SW Pontypridd & Cardiff	1 0	
SF	Loughborough 1st	Chichester 1st	4 0	
F	Stirling 1st	Loughborough 1st	2 1	
	at Surrey Sports Park, London			

QUEEN'S PARK SHIELD

				Venue
P1	Kilmarnock College	Cardonald College	12 1	St Josephs Acad
P1	Edinburgh College	Cumbernauld College	4 3	Muirhouse
P2	Glasgow Caledonian	Napier	3 1	Firhill Complex
P2	Kilmarnock College	Dundee	2 3	Kilwinning SC
P2	Aberdeen	Abertay	0 3	Hillhead
P2	Edinburgh College	Strathclyde	3 2	Muirhouse
P2	St Andredws	Edinburgh	0 5	St Andrews
P2	Glasgow	Robert Gordons	3 4	Garscube
QF	Stirling	Glasgow Caledonian	2 1	Gannochy
QF	Dundee	Abertay	2 2 1-3 pens	Riverside
QF	Heriot Watt	Edinburgh College	2 1	Riccarton
QF	Edinburgh	Robert Gordons	6 1	Peffermill
SF	Stirling	Abertay	3 2	Gannochy
SF	Heriot Watt	Edinburgh	1 1 5-4 pens	Riccarton
F	Stirling	Heriot Watt	0 0 5-4 pens	Spartans FC

AMATEUR FITBA

SCOTTISH AMATEUR FA 2013/14

Office Bearers

Hon. President
Hugh Knapp (

Hon. Senior Vice President
Stuart Urquhart

Hon. Junior Vice President
Alex McDowall

Hon. Treasurer
G Dingwall

National Secretary
Thomas McKeown

Technical Advisor
Stephen McLaughlin

Administrator
Mary Jardine

National Committees

Executive & Finance Committee

H. Knapp (Chairman), S. Urquhart, A. McDowall, G. Dingwall, C R Gallacher, J. Rodgers, G.Butler, I. Cowden, R.J. Hughes, J. Napier

Appeals Committee
G. Dingwall (Chairman), G. Farmer, L Wallace, I Cowden, G. Butler, J Locke.

General Purposes Committee
G. Butler (Chairman) , R. Baird, C. Lowrie, J. McKerley, J. Rodgers, G. Mair, Gary Watson, J McFarlane

National Disciplinary Committee (North)
A McDowall (Chairman) R. J. Hughes, T. Berry, J. Napier, A. Martin, M. Nicol, A. Denny, G Farmer.

National Disciplinary Committee (South)
S. Urquhart (Chairman) I. Cowden, G. Mair, T. Williamson, G. Watson, R. Baird, R Campbell, L. Wallace

National Disciplinary Committee (Highland)
H. Knapp (President - Chairman), A. Mackay (Caithness AFA), M. MacKay, D MacKenzie, H Morrison, E Campbell, K Smith, J Thomson.

National Review Committee
A McDowall (Chairman) G Farmer, A Irvine, J. Napier, J. McGunnigle, A J G Cox, J Nicoll.

District Committees

Western District Executive Committee

F. McCann, K. Lindsay, G. Mair, J. Rodgers, K. Liebow, L. Wallace, J. Robert, J. Soutar.
Secretary: John Rodgers
Match Secretary: Morris Tonner

East of Scotland Executive Committee

C R Gallacher (Chairman), DJ Ramage (Secretary/Match Secretary), J Ballantine, I Welsh, K. Keir, I. Sommerville, J Clark, and L Walls.
Secretary/ Match Sectretary: DJ Ramage

North Of Tay Executive Committee

T Berry (Chairman), G Farmer(Match Secretary), R.J. Hughes, T Latto, M Nicoll, A Martin (Secretary), S. McSwiggan
Secretary: A Martin
Match Secretary: G Farmer

Fife Executive Committee

A Melville (Chairman), A Denny (Secretary/Match Secretary), T. Boyle, W Moodie, J Hastie, C Justice, J McCombie and D Arthur
Secretary/ Match Secretary: A Denny

North of Scotland Executive Committee

J Napier(Chairman), J McGunnigle(Secretary), B Christie, D Strath, J Irvine, S Summers, B. Derrett and G McPherson.
Secretary/ Match Secretary: J McGunnigle

South of Scotland Executive Committee

D F Grant (Chairman), AJG Cox(Secretary), T Williamson, R. Campbell, S. Todd, D. Swan and C. LowrieSecretary/Match Secretary: AJG Cox

Highland & Islands Executive Committee

M MacKay(Chairman), A Mackay (Secretary/Match Secretary), I Whitehead, E Campbell, H Morrison, W MacIver, G MacLeod, K MacLeod and D MacKenzie
Secretary/Match Secretary: A. Mackay

Western District (Sunday) Executive Committee

J McKerley(Chairman), R Baird, W Mahomet, A. Coleman, J. Black, A. Black and G. Wood Secretary:

ABERDEEN SUNDAY AMATEUR FA 2013/14

Secretary: Mr. Brian Derrett, 6d Seaton Avenue, Aberdeen AB24 1XB
(M) 07923 066033. Email: bderrett@hotmail.co.uk (Senior Sunday)

League Website: http://www.asafl.co.uk/

Games in this Association are usually played with a 10.30am Kick Off.
Venues are variable.

League Tables

Premier Division	P	W	D	L	F	A	GD	PTS
KINCORTH	22	21	0	1	154	25	129	63
GREAT WESTERN	22	19	0	3	108	32	76	57
FOUNTAIN BAR	22	16	0	6	86	38	28	48
FOUNDRY BAR	22	13	1	8	93	59	34	40
WESTDYCE	22	12	1	9	88	64	24	37
MS SERVICES	22	12	1	9	79	56	23	37
HILLHEAD	22	9	5	8	71	61	10	32
SHIRLAWS	22	7	1	14	64	67	-3	22

First Division	P	W	D	L	F	A	GD	PTS
POLICE	22	10	4	8	68	77	-9	34
DRUMMONDS	22	11	1	10	60	71	-11	34
SHEDDOCKSLEY	22	7	7	8	52	61	-9	28
HYDRASUN	22	6	3	13	52	98	-46	21
BRIG O DEE DONS	22	6	1	15	55	127	-72	19
W.T.R	22	4	5	13	49	96	-47	17
GRANITE THISTLE	22	4	5	13	34	87	-53	17
MAILIBU	22	1	1	20	32	126	-94	4

Cup Finals

Gavin Robertson Memorial Cup
Great Western Star 3 Kincorth
Rovers 3 (3-1 pens)

Jim Lumsden Cup Final
(at Jamieson Park)
Kincorth Rovers 1 Fountain Bar 3

Rotosearch Cup
(at Jamieson Park)
Hydrasun 4 Brig o Dee Dons 1

ABERDEENSHIRE AMATEUR FA 2013/14

Secretary: Brian Christie, 69 Corthan Crescent, Aberdeen AB12 5BA   Telephone – 01224 895851 (h) or 07730 611960 (m)   Email – aafasecretary@hotmail.co.uk

League website: http://www.aberdeenshireafa.com

This is the main Saturday Amateur League in the North East of Scotland. It serves the City of Aberdeen and surrounding areas as far north as Huntly and Turriff and as far south as Laurencekirk. Over the years several clubs have stepped up to the Juniors from this league.

Final Tables

PREMIER	P	W	D	L	F	A	GD	Pts
Sportsmans Club	24	19	1	4	81	40	41	58
Woodside	24	16	3	5	82	29	53	51
Cove Thistle	24	15	4	5	93	43	50	49
Cowie Thistle	24	13	2	9	61	53	8	41
Hazlehead United	24	13	1	10	60	66	-6	40
MS United	24	11	2	11	68	59	9	35
Kincorth	24	10	4	10	73	76	-3	34
Westdyke	24	9	5	10	49	55	-6	32
University	24	8	5	11	58	68	-10	29
Luthermuir	24	8	4	12	39	58	-19	28
Beacon Rangers	24	7	3	14	60	65	-5	24
Feughside	24	5	1	18	36	102	-66	16
Insch	24	3	3	18	37	83	-46	12

Div One (N)	P	W	D	L	F	A	GD	Pts
Rothie Rovers	26	20	4	2	80	41	39	64
Great Northern Athletic	26	19	1	6	84	44	40	58
Johnshaven Athletic	26	15	7	4	69	35	34	52
Dee Amateurs	26	15	4	7	74	49	25	49
Tarves	26	13	2	11	73	52	21	41
Halliburton	26	12	2	12	52	45	7	38
Echt	26	11	5	10	63	44	19	38
Alford	26	11	5	10	58	52	6	38
Dyce ITC Hydraulics	26	10	5	11	58	57	1	35
Stoneywood Amateurs	26	10	4	12	53	53	0	34
Glendale	26	8	0	18	48	74	-26	24
Turriff Thistle *	26	7	6	13	49	60	-11	21
Bon Accord City	26	6	3	17	52	82	-30	21
Glendale XI *	26	1	0	25	19	144	-125	0

* Pts Deducted for registration issues

DIV ONE (E)	P	W	D	L	F	A	GD	Pts
RGU	26	20	3	3	87	31	56	63
Ellon Amateurs	26	17	5	4	72	40	32	56
AC Mill Inn	26	16	5	5	75	45	30	53
Newtonhill	26	15	6	5	73	44	29	51
Blackburn	26	14	3	9	72	54	18	45
Rattrays XI	26	12	6	8	43	39	4	42
Don Athletic	26	11	2	13	52	77	-25	35
Kaimhill United	26	10	4	12	59	56	3	34
Nicolls Amateurs	26	10	3	13	52	59	-7	33
Great Western United	26	8	6	12	57	70	-13	30
Northern United	26	9	2	15	48	62	-14	29
Bervie Caledonian	26	7	6	13	60	74	-14	27
Old Aberdonians	26	3	2	21	27	58	-31	11
Highland Hotel *	26	1	5	20	35	103	-68	2

* Pts Deducted for registration issues

DIV TWO (N)	P	W	D	L	F	A	GD	Pts
Granite City	26	20	3	3	89	36	53	63
Torry Select	26	19	3	4	92	35	57	60
Lads Club Amateurs	26	18	4	4	70	36	34	58
St Laurence	26	17	3	6	76	50	26	54
Ellon Thistle	26	14	3	9	72	53	19	45
Stonehaven Athletic	26	12	2	12	65	53	12	38
FC Polska	26	12	1	13	66	77	-11	37
Cammachmore	26	10	3	13	53	67	-14	33
Torphins	26	8	3	15	63	76	-13	27
Banchory Amateurs	26	7	3	16	56	88	-32	24
Scotstown Rovers	26	7	2	17	64	89	-25	23
Torry United	26	7	2	17	34	73	-39	23
Newburgh Thistle *	26	7	4	15	69	87	-18	16
Continental	26	3	6	17	34	83	-49	15

* Pts Deducted for registration issues

DIV TWO (E)	P	W	D	L	F	A	GD	Pts
Grammar FPs	26	20	0	6	89	50	39	60
West End	26	18	2	6	92	52	40	56
Bankhead	26	17	2	7	116	49	67	53
University Strollers	26	16	3	7	80	51	29	51
JS XI	26	16	3	7	92	48	44	51
Summerhill	26	13	2	11	75	61	14	41
Burghmuir	26	12	4	10	73	68	5	40
Glentanar Reflex	26	11	3	12	61	64	-3	36
University Colts	26	10	2	14	58	86	-28	32
Kemnay Youth	26	10	1	15	60	86	-26	31
Ferryhill	26	8	3	15	80	98	-18	27
Kintore	26	8	2	16	48	72	-24	26
Byron	26	3	4	19	50	100	-50	13
Trophies International	26	4	1	21	31	120	-89	13

DIV THREE	P	W	D	L	F	A	GD	Pts
BSFC	30	24	2	4	114	62	52	74
Glendale Youth	30	18	7	5	107	70	37	61
Theologians	30	19	3	8	104	57	47	60
Fintray Thistle	30	17	7	6	85	47	38	58
Westhill *	30	20	5	5	99	51	48	56
Bridge of Don	30	17	5	8	99	54	45	56
Formartine United	30	17	4	9	90	48	42	55
Monymusk	30	16	5	9	89	77	12	53
Postal ALC	30	16	3	11	83	64	19	51
ARI Thistle	30	10	4	16	73	72	1	34
McTeagle	30	8	4	18	37	76	-39	28
Auchnagatt Barons	30	7	4	19	51	89	-38	25
Huntly Amateurs *	30	8	3	19	58	81	-23	24
AFC Murdos	30	6	3	21	55	88	-53	21
RAM	30	3	3	24	39	139	-100	12
Aboyne	30	2	2	26	44	132	-88	8

* Pts Deducted for registration issues

Clubs in Membership 2013/14				
Club	Division	Ground	Home Colours	Change Colours
Aboyne	Three	Aboyne Green	Black/White	Red/White/Black
AC Mill Inn	One (East)	Mineralwell Park, Stonehaven	Red/Black	White
AFC Murdos	Three	Sheddocksley	Red/White	Black/White
Alford	One (North)	Alford Pleasure Park	Black/Blue	White/Blue
ARI Thistle	Three	Inverdee	Navy/White	Red/White
Auchnagatt Barons	Three	Auchnagatt	White/Navy	Blue/Black
Banchory Amateurs	Two (North)	George V Park, Banchory	Blue/White	Red/Black
Bankhead	Two (East)	Potterton	Gold/Black	Blue/White/Black
Beacon Rangers	Premier	Strathburn Park, Inverurie	Red/Navy	Black/White
Bervie Caledonian	One (East)	Booth Park, Gourdoun	Orange/Black	Maroon/Sky Blue
Blackburn	Premier	Blackburn Pleasure Park	Black/White	Wine
Bon Accord City	One (North)	Balgownie	Black/Pink	Orange/Black
Bridge of Don	Three	Westfield Park, Bridge of Don	Black/Blue	Red/White
BSFC	Three	Balgownie	Blue	Red
Burghmuir	Two (East)	Strathburn Park, Inverurie	Red/Yellow	Blue
Byron Amateurs	Two (East)	Jamieson Park, Lads Club	Red/Black	Black
Cammachmore	Two (North)	Newtonhill	Grey/Blue	Maroon
Continental	Two (North)	Webster Park, Kingswells	Blue	Red/Black
Cove Thistle	Premier	Catto Park, Cove	Blue	Red
Cowie Thistle	Premier	Mineralwell Park, Stonehaven	Blue/White	Red/White
Dee Amateurs	One (North)	Tullos	Blue	White/Blue
Don Athletic	One (East)	Westfield Park, Bridge of Don	Black/White	Blue/White
Dyce ITC Hydraulics	One (North)	Pitmedden Road, Dyce	Black/Gold	Red/White
Echt	One (East)	Echt Pleasure Park	Red	Blue
Ellon Amateurs	One (East)	The Meadows, Ellon	Red/Black	Red/White/Blue
Ellon Thistle	Two (North)	The Meadows, Ellon	Blue/White/Black	Yellow/Black
FC Polska	Two (North)	Inverdee	Green/Black	Orange/Black
Ferryhill	Two (East)	Beach Park, Balmedie	Black	White/Blue
Feughside	Premier	Farquharson Park, Finzean	Royal Blue	Black
Fintray Thistle	Three	Strathburn Park, Inverurie	Red/Black	Orange/Black
Formartine United	Three	Oldmeldrum Pleasure Park	Red/White	Blue
Glendale	One (North)	Corbie Park, Maryculter	Blue/Maroon	Blue/Black
Glendale XI	One (North)	Sheddocksley	Black/White	Claret/Blue
Glendale Youth	Three	Lads Club, Woodside	Blue	Yellow/Black
Glentanar Reflex	Two (East)	Hazlehead	Yellow/Blue	Blue/Navy/Black
Grammar FPs	Two (East)	Rubislaw	Navy/White	Black
Granite City	Two (North)	Potterton	Orange/White/Black	Navy/Red
Great Northern Athletic	One (North)	Jamieson Park, Lads Club	Orange	White
Great Western United	One (East)	Woodside Sports Complex	Blue/White/Black	Red
Halliburton	One (North)	Lawsondale, Westhill	Green/Black	Red/White/Black
Hazlehead United	Premier	Hazlehead Academy	Green	Black
Highland Hotel	One (East)	Inverdee	Red	Yellow
Huntly Amateurs	Three	The Meadows, Huntly	Amber/Black	Blue
Insch	Premier	Recreation Park, Insch	Blue/Yellow	Black
Johnshaven Athletic	One (North)	Wairds Park, Johnshaven	Purple/Black	Red/Black
JS XI	Two (East)	Hazlehead	Orange	Yellow/Black
Kaimhill United	One (East)	Kaimhill (Grass)	Red	Black
Kemnay Youth	Two (East)	Bogbeth Park, Kemnay	Black/White	Red/Navy
Kincorth	Premier	Kincorth Academy	Black	White/Black
Kintore	Two (East)	Kintore Pleasure Park	Blue/White	Red/White
Lads Club Amateurs	Two (North)	Lads Club, Woodside	Sky Blue/Claret	White/Black
Luthermuir	Premier	Luthermuir	Yellow/Black	Red/Black
McTeagle	Three	Sheddocksley	Black	Red
Monymusk	Three	Deer Park, Monymusk	White/Red	Black/Blue
MS United	Premier	New Advocates Park	Red/Black	Green
Newburgh Thistle	Two (North)	Gallowhill Park, Newburgh	Black	White/Blue
Newtonhill	One (East)	Newtonhill	Red/Black	Blue
Nicolls Amateurs	One (East)	Denmore Park	Maroon/Blue	Black/Amber
Northern United	One (East)	Inverdee	Blue/White	Red
Old Aberdonians	One (East)	Balgownie	Red/Black	Yellow/Navy
Postal ALC	Three	Lads Club, Woodside	Sky Blue/Maroon	Blue/White

CUP FINALS

Aberdeen FC Trophy

Cove Thistle v Luthermuir   1-0

(All clubs)

Association Trophy

Cowie Thistle v Sportsmans Club   3-0

(Prem + Div 1 Clubs)

Dickie Trophy

Bankhead v JS XI   2-1

(Div 2 + Div 3 clubs)

Edmond Trophy

Cowie Thistle v Johnshaven   2-1

(Teams kod in R1 of AFC Trophy)

Bowie Cup

AC Mill Inn v Feughside   2-2, 5-6 p

(Teams kod in R1 of Assoc Trophy)

Hans Fyfe Trophy

Continetal v Granite City   0-4

(Teams kod in R1 of Dickie Trophy)

Premier Trophy

Cove Thistle v Luthermuir   3-0

(Prem Div clubs)

Stephen Shield

Rothie Rovers v Tarves   1-3

(Div 1 North Clubs)

White Cup

Ellon Amateurs v RGU   1-1, 3-5 p

(Div 1 East Clubs)

Castle Rovers Cup

FC Polska v Granite City   1-3

(Div 2 North clubs)

Barclay Cook Cup

JS XI v West End   5-2

(Division 2 East clubs)

Chattan Rovers Cup

Fintray Thistle v Formartine United   2-0

(Div 3 clubs)

ABERDEENSHIRE AFA CHAMPIONS

1947-48 Cove Rangers
1948-49 Cove Rangers
1949-50 Ellon United
1950-51 Ellon United
1951-52 Millburn FC
1952-53 Millburn FC
1953-54 Cove Rangers
1954-55 Cove Rangers
1955-56 Cove Rangers
1956-57 Cove Rangers
1957-58 Cove Rangers
1958-59 Nicoll's XI
1959-60 Cove Rangers
1960-61 Cove Rangers
1961-62 Ellon United
1962-63 Ellon United
1963-64 Bon Accord FC
1964-65 Cove Rangers
1965-66 Aboyne
1966-67 Aberdeen City Police
1967-68 Aberdeen City Police
1968-69 Aberdeen City Police
1969-70 Aberdeen City Police
1970-71 Maud
1971-72 Kemnay
1972-73 Culter
1973-74 Culter
1974-75 Culter
1975-76 Culter
1976-77 Cove Rangers
1977-78 Kemnay
1978-79 Culter
1979-80 Culter
1980-81 Culter
1981-82 Grandholm Rosslyn
1982-83 Cove Rangers
1983-84 Aberdeen Shamrock
1984-85 Cove Rangers
1985-86 Crombie Sports
1986-87 Mugiemoss Amateurs
1987-88 Longside
1988-89 Hall Russell United
1989-90 Great Western United
1990-91 Kincorth
1991-92 Kincorth
1992-93 Kincorth
1993-94 Kincorth
1994-95 Dyce
1995-96 Hilton
1996-97 Echt
1997-98 Hilton
1998-99 Hilton
1999-00 Hilton
2000-01 Echt
2001-02 Echt
2002-03 Kincorth
2003-04 Kincorth
2004-05 Sunnybank Amateurs
2005-06 Sunnybank Amateurs
2006-07 Echt
2007-08 Echt
2008-09 Cove Thistle

AIRDRIE AND COATBRIDGE
SUNDAY AMATEUR LEAGUE 2013/14

Secretary: Mr A Coleman, 5 Portland Street, Coatbridge, Lanarkshire ML5 3LH. (H) 01236 608046. (Senior Sunday). Email: archiec@blueyonder.co.uk

Website: http://www.leaguewebsite.co.uk/airdrieandcoatbridgeafl

Matches in this league are usually 1.30pm Kick Offs.

This Sunday League appears to be thriving - seven new teams have joined for 2014/15.

LATEST AVAILABLELEAGUE TABLES

PREMIER DIVISION	P	W	D	L	F	A	GD	Pts
Thrashbush	13	11	1	1	44	19	25	34
Calderbank	13	9	0	4	41	24	17	27
Haghill	11	8	1	2	36	20	16	25
Jerviston	12	5	2	5	26	22	4	17
East End Utd	14	5	2	7	28	37	-9	17
Big Shop	14	5	1	8	32	51	-19	16
Blantyre Rangers	14	4	3	7	37	30	7	15
Lochgreen	14	4	1	9	35	53	-18	13
Cellarbar Colts	13	2	1	10	31	54	-23	7

FIRST DIVISION	P	W	D	L	F	A	GD	Pts
Rolling Barrell	20	19	0	1	133	25	108	57
Forgewood	18	17	0	1	80	25	55	51
Gartcairn Thistle	19	11	1	7	93	36	57	34
Real Albion	18	10	1	7	72	67	5	31
Millers Utd	19	9	1	9	73	56	17	28
Airdrie Workmans	17	9	0	8	66	74	-8	27
Greengairs Dynamo	20	8	3	9	55	68	-13	27
Kirkstyle Thistle	18	6	4	8	41	82	-41	22
Redbridge Rovers	19	4	3	12	35	67	-32	15
Monklands Utd	20	4	2	14	38	86	-48	14
Imperial Albion	18	3	1	14	37	86	-49	10
Unity	14	2	0	12	25	76	-51	6

Cup Final Results

Dee Sports Cup
Real Albion 3, Greengairs 2

Harkness Cup
Thrashbush 5Gartcairn 1

League Cup
Rollinbarrel 4 Haghill 1

All three finals were played at Airdrieonians FC.

AYRSHIRE AMATEUR F.A. 2013/14

Secretary: Mr. M Tonner, 17 Annandale Gardens, Crosshouse, Ayrshire KA2 0LE (H) 01563 531061 (M) 07980 971367 Email: mt@ayrshireafa.com
Senior Saturday. Partly Sunday.

Website: http://www.ayrshireafa.co.uk/

PREMIER DIVISION	P	W	D	L	F	A	GD	Pts
Hurlford Thistle	22	18	3	1	102	30	72	57
Clark Drive	22	13	4	5	49	28	21	43
Tarbolton	22	13	3	6	54	40	14	42
Galston United	22	11	3	8	56	37	19	33
Winlinton Wolves	22	10	3	9	54	54	0	33
Stewarton United	22	9	4	9	53	46	7	31
Carrick	22	7	6	9	26	29	-3	27
Ardrossan Castle Rovers	22	6	6	10	36	44	-8	24
West Kilbride	22	7	3	12	25	59	-34	24
Knockentiber	22	6	1	15	37	59	-22	19
Glenburn MW	22	6	1	15	29	75	-46	19
Mossblown	22	7	1	14	44	64	-20	18

FIRST DIVISION	P	W	D	L	F	A	GD	Pts
Dirrans Athletic	20	18	1	1	77	13	64	55
Lochan	20	12	3	5	45	30	15	39
Dailly	20	12	0	8	36	38	-2	36
Kilbirnie	20	10	2	8	45	33	12	32
Fenwick Thistle	20	7	4	9	29	46	-17	25
Glenmuir Thistle	20	9	2	9	46	44	2	23
Crosshill Thistle	20	6	2	12	44	66	-22	23
Cunninghame	20	6	3	11	46	53	-7	21
Troon Dundonald	20	6	3	11	43	56	-13	21
Kilmarnock AFC	20	5	6	9	42	59	-17	21
Beith	20	5	2	13	37	52	-15	14
Kilmarnock Town	0	0	0	0	0	0	0	0

SECOND DIVISION	P	W	D	L	F	A	GD	Pts
Netherthird	22	20	1	1	96	15	81	61
Westkirk Thistle	22	15	3	4	68	32	36	48
Mauchline United	22	15	3	4	62	31	31	48
Kilbride Thistle	22	13	2	7	69	38	31	41
Prestwick	22	9	4	9	54	63	-9	31
Dean	22	8	6	8	57	64	-7	30
Vale of Girvan	22	9	1	12	56	68	-12	28
Drumley United	22	8	1	13	58	73	-15	25
Crookedholm	22	4	7	11	36	79	-43	23
Stewarton Annick	22	4	1	17	51	90	-39	13
Loudoun	22	3	6	13	34	68	-34	8
Auchinleck Boswell	22	4	5	13	32	52	-20	1

THIRD DIVISION	P	W	D	L	F	A	GD	Pts
KSC Wolves	22	19	2	1	95	26	69	59
Irvine Town	22	18	2	2	82	31	51	56
Wallacetoun Sporting Club	22	17	2	3	84	40	44	53
Shortlees	22	10	5	7	56	47	9	35
Ayr Athletic	22	12	3	7	59	37	22	33
Craigie	22	10	3	9	59	55	4	33
Drongan United	22	9	3	10	31	44	-13	30
Coylton	22	6	1	13	40	63	-23	22
Darvel Victoria	22	7	3	12	44	59	-15	18
Largs	22	4	3	15	42	74	-32	18
Symington Caledonian	22	2	4	16	36	89	-53	10
Minishant	22	0	5	17	29	97	-68	5

FOURTH DIVISION	P	W	D	L	F	A	GD	Pts
Doon	24	21	3	0	130	37	93	66
Troon Athletic	24	19	1	4	124	42	82	58
Hurlford AFC	24	19	2	3	140	31	109	53
Ochiltree United	24	12	0	12	89	66	23	36
Ardrossan Winton Rovers	24	9	2	13	86	78	8	29
Crosshouse	24	10	1	13	57	84	-27	28
Dalmilling	24	9	0	15	68	77	-9	27
Troon United	24	4	1	19	37	151	-114	16
Dalmellington United	24	0	0	24	17	182	-165	-3

CUP FINALS

Ayrshire Cup
30/05/2014   Hurlford Thistle v Clark Drive   1-2 aet   at Auchinleck Talbot

James Scott Trophy
09/05/2014   Clark Drive v Winlinton Wolves   1-1aet, ⸌at Ardeer Thistle

Thistle Bar Trophy
25/04/2014   Hurlford Thistle v Galston United 3-2   at Hulford United

Donsport Trophy
16/05/2014   Wallacetoun SC v Galston United 3-4   at Cumnock Juniors

AYRSHIRE A.F.A. : PROPOSED LEAGUE FORMATIONS FOR SEASON 2014/15

PREMIER LEAGUE
Ardrossan Castle Rovers	
Carrick	
Clark Drive	
Dirrans Athletic	Promoted
Galston United	
Hurlford Thistle	
Knockentiber	
Lochan	Promoted
Stewarton United	
Tarbolton	
West Kilbride	
Winlinton Wolves	

FIRST DIVISION
Crosshill Thistle	
Cunninghame	
Dailly	
Fenwick Thistle	
Glenburn Miners Welfare	Relegated
Glenmuir Thistle	
Kilbirnie	
Mauchline United	Promoted (3rd)
Mossblown	Relegated
Netherthird	Promoted
Troon Dundonald	
Westkirk Thistle	Promoted

SECOND DIVISION
Beith	Relegated
Crookedholm	
Dean	
Drumley United	
Irvine Town	Promoted
Kilbride Thistle	
Kilmarnock AFC	Relegated
KSC Wolves	Promoted
Prestwick	
Stewarton Annick	
Vale of Girvan	
Wallacetoun Sporting Club	Promoted (3rd)

THIRD DIVISION
Auchinleck Boswell	Relegated
Ayr Athletic	
Coylton	
Craigie	
Darvel Victoria	
Doon	Promoted
Drongan United	
Hurlford AFC	Promoted (3rd)
Largs	
Loudoun	Relegated
Shortlees	
Troon Athletic	Promoted

FOURTH DIVISION
Ardrossan Winton Rovers	
Catrine	New Club
Crosshouse	
Dalmellington United	
Dalmilling	
Minishant	Relegated
New Farm Loch	New Club
Ochiltree United	
Symington Caledonian	Relegated

Proposed that Fourth Division Clubs play each other 3 times

Regional Cup Changes Since 2013/14
James Scott Memorial Trophy	Kilmarnock Town out, New Farm Loch in
Thistle Bar Trophy	Troon United out, Catrine in

ARDROSSAN CASTLE ROVERS　　St Matthews, Saltcoats
Colours Red top, black shorts, red sox Alt: Light blue/White stripes.
Blue shorts & sox
Secretary John McBreen, 6 Mayfield Place, Saltcoats, KA21 5RH
Phones McBreen 01294 471776; 07970 591319

ARDROSSAN WINTON ROVERS　　Ardeer Quarry, Stevenston
Colours Black/White hoops, Black shorts & sox Alt: Red/White hoops,
black shorts & sox
Secretary Liz Morgan, 8 Galloway Place, Saltcoats KA21 5BD
Phones Morgan 01294 605348; 07552 324605

AUCHINLECK BOSWELL　　Merlin Park, Auchinleck
Colours Black/Yellow Alt: Blue, Navy Blue & Black
Secretary Scott Smith, 82 Cameron Drive, Auchinleck KA18 2JG
Phones Smith: 01290 420318; 07429 021575

AYR ATHLETIC　　King George V Playing
Fields, Ayr
Colours Red/White Alt: Blue/White
Secretary Michael Fairlie, 11 Orkney Drive, Kilmarnock KA3 2HP
Phones Fairlie: 01563 521689; 07866 948874

BEITH AMATEURS　　Beith Astro Turf
Colours Black/White Stripes Alt: Red
Secretary Colin Hunter, 4 Crummock Street, Beith KA15 2BD
Phones Hunter: 01505 500407; 07856 744082

CARRICK　　Glebe Park, Maybole
Colours Navy/White Alt: White/Black
Secretary Reid Logan, 29 Cairnfield Avenue, Maybole KA19 7HY
Phones Logan: 01655 884261; 07870 845387

CLARK DRIVE　　Irvine Sports Club
Colours Royal Blue Alt: Red/Black vertical stripes
Secretary Jimmy Locke, 1 Gregory Street, Mauchline KA5 6BY
Phones Locke: 01290 550439; 07854 285901

COYLTON　　Coylon Public Park
Colours Orange & Black Alt: Maroon
Secretary James Ross, 5 Lochfergus Place, Coylton KA6 6GD
Phones Ross: 01292 571157; 07719 434810 Kay: 01292 571369;
07717 593119
Queen: 01292 570574; 07738 300455

CRAIGIE　　Newlands Drive,
Kilmarnock
Colours Blue/White Alt: Red/White
Secretary Campbell Scoular, 86 Tourhill Road, Kilmarnock KA3 2DG
Phones Scoular: 07916 148424

CROOKEDHOLM　　Crookedholm Public Park
Colours Black Tops, Yellow Shorts & Sox Alt: Red/Black Tops, Black
Shorts & Sox
Secretary Brian McLaren, 35 Annandale View, Crosshouse, Kilmarnock
KA2 0ER
Phones McLaren: 07920 827140

CROSSHILL THISTLE　　Crosshill Public Park
Colours Blue/white hoops Alt: Red
Secretary David McDowall, 18 Carrick Drive, Crosshill, Maybole KA19
7RH
Phones McDowall: 01655 740426; 07977 582123

CROSSHOUSE　　Lindsay Park, Crosshouse
Colours Red/Black Alt: White/Black
Secretary Jim McClements, 18 Annandale View, Crosshouse,
Kilmarnock KA2 0ER
Phones McClements: 01563 542739; 07527 223162

CUNNINGHAME　　Ardeer Quarry, Stevenston
Colours White/Red Alt: Black/Red
Secretary Derek Rennie. 8 Bute Court, Stevenston KA20 3JB
Phones Rennie 01294 607927; 07716 482619

DAILLY　　Riverside Park, Dailly
Colours Maroon/Blue Alt: Blue/White
Secretary Scott Kirkwood, 21 Ardmillan Road, Girvan KA26 9EF
Phones Kirkwood: 01465 712566; 07743 649463

DALMELLINGTON UNITED　　Running Track,
Dalmellington
Colours Green/Yellow
Secretary Stewart McPhail, 4 Park Crescent, Dalmellington KA6 7RP
Phones McPhail: 01292 551988; 07748 873845

DALMILLING　　King George V, Ayr
Colours Royal Blue/White Trim Alt:: White/Red Trim
Secretary Fiona Campbell, 52 Westwood Avenue, Ayr KA8 0QR
Phones Campbell: 07401 979729

DARVEL VICTORIA　　Gavin Hamilton Centre, Darvel
Colours Red/Black Alt: Blue
Secretary Martin McAvoy, 21 Dublin Road, Darvel KA17 0EQ
Phones McAvoy 01560 321421; 07528 744383

DEAN　　Dean Park, Kilmarnock
Colours Red/Black Alt: Blue
Secretary Ian Swan, 14 Sanda Place, Kilmarnock KA3 2JZ
Phones Swan: 01563 543057; 07879 012203

DIRRANS ATHLETIC　　Kilwinning S.C.,
Pennyburn
Colours Royal Blue Alt: White
Secretary David Faddes, 83 Blacklands Crescent, Kilwinning KA13
6HT
Phones Faddes: 01294 556907; 07449 372592

DOON　　Running Track,
Dalmellington
Colours Orange/Black Alt: Blue/White
Secretary Lee McPhail, 7 Gateside Street, Dalmellington KA6 7RT
Phones McPhail: 01292 551611; 07919 401667

DRONGAN UNITED　　Drongan Playing Field
Colours Sky Blue/White Alt: Royal Blue
Secretary Stewart Kean, 65 Hannahston Avenue, Drongan KA6 7AX
Phones Kean: 01292 590380; 07986 222287

DRUMLEY UNITED　　Toll Park, Mossblown
Colours Black/Royal Blue stripes Alt: White/Red trim/Red shorts and
sox
Secretary Kevin McKnight, 24 Mount Oliphant Crescent, Ayr KA7
3EQ
Phones McKnight: 01292 520193; 07704 751506

FENWICK THISTLE　　Fairlie Park, Fenwick
Colours Royal Blue Alt: Claret tops/Sky Blue shorts
Secretary Derek Brown, 3 Ken Road, Kilmarnock KA1 3QR
Phones Brown: 01563 534633; 07850 247856

GALSTON UNITED　　Barmill Stadium, Galston
Colours Red/Black Alt: Orange
Secretary Gordon Russell, 21 Carnalea Court, Galston KA5 8HY
Phones Russell: 01563 820644; 07957 847003

GLENBURN MINERS WELFARE　　Prestwick Academy,
Prestwick
Colours Yellow/Blue Alt: Red/White
Secretary Ricky Bicker, 24 Mossbank, Prestwick KA9 1DS
Phones Bicker: 01292 479973; 07588 421463

GLENMUIR THISTLE　　Logan P.F.
Colours Grey/Black Alt: Blue
Secretary Neil Murray, 49 Menzies Avenue, Cumnock KA18 3DP
Phones Murray: 07450 077997

HURLFORD AMATEURS　　Richardson Park, Hurlford
Colours Red/Black Alt: Blue/Yellow
Secretary Jillian Castle, 21 Roxburgh Road, Kilmarnock KA1 5BW
Phones Castle: 07884 005435

HURLFORD THISTLE　　Richardson Park, Hurlford
Colours Yellow/Blue Alt: All Yellow/Navy or Purple
Secretary Thomas McAvoy, 48 Hareshaw Gardens, Kilmarnock KA3
2ET
Phones McAvoy: 01563 570824; 07825 881823; 07789 377498

IRVINE TOWN Springside Public Park
Colours Royal Blue/Yellow piping Alt: Black/Yellow piping
Secretary Keith Graham, 74 Bank Street, Irvine KA12 0LP

Phones Graham: 01294 650707; 07446

280

KILBIRNIE Valefield, Kilbirnie
Colours Amber/Black Alt: Black
Secretary Steve Wilson, 41 Milton Road, Kilbirnie KA25 7EP
Phones Wilson: 01505 683474; 07791 525787

KILBRIDE THISTLE St Matthews Academy, Saltcoats
Colours Amber/Black Alt: Red/Blue
Secretary John Bell, 6 Blackshaw Drive, West Kilbride KA23 9BW
Phones Bell: 01294 823422; 07818 804356; 01294 826127 W

KILMARNOCK AFC Dean Park, Kilmarnock
Colours Blue/White Alt: Red
Secretary Bryan Thurston, 19B Gillesburn Gardens, Kilmarnock KA3 1DZ
Phones Thurston: 01563 549938; 07842 794222

KILMARNOCK TOWN Scott Ellis PF, Kilmarnock
Colours Navy/Yellow Alt: All Red or All Blue
Secretary Martin Swift, 102 Barnweil Drive, Hurlford, Kilmarnock KA1 5BA
Phones Swift: 01563 526571; 07779 617047

KNOCKENTIBER Knockentiber Public Park
Colours Royal Blue/White Alt: Red/Black
Secretary Cliff Jamieson, 34 Kilmaurs Road, Knockentiber, Kilmarnock KA2 0DY
Phones Jamieson: 01563 538255; 07841 867650

KSC WOLVES Kilwinning SC, Pennyburn
Colours Blue/White hoops Alt: Red/White
Secretary Jim Cochrane, 70 Glenapp Place, Kilwinning KA13 6TE
Phones Cochrane: 01294 554683; 07895 214447

LARGS Bowencraig, Largs
Colours Royal Blue Alt: Black
Secretary Jamie McDowell, Flat 1/1, 1 Harwood Crt, Campbell St .,Greenock PA16 7QA
Phones McDowell: 07944 581891

LOCHAN Riccarton Park, Kilmarnock
Colours Royal Blue/Black stripes Alt: Royal Blue/White hoops
Secretary Graham McCall, 14 Witchknowe Court, Kilmarnock KA1 4LF
Phones McCall: 01563 540951;

LOUDOUN Scott Ellis PF, Kilmarnock
Colours Blue Alt: Red
Secretary Stevie Lorimer, 21 Wardneuk Drive, Kilmarnock KA3 2EF
Phones Lorimer: 01563 520297; 07923 541876

MAUCHLINE UNITED Beechgrove Park, Mauchline
Colours Blue/Black stripes Alt: White
Secretary Andy Murdoch, 34 Loudon Street, Mauchline KA5 5BT
Phones Murdoch: 01290 553258; 07801 760471

MINISHANT Kewnston Park, Minishant
Colours Red/Yellow Alt: Black/White
Secretary John Sherwin, 25 Monkwood Crescent, Minishant KA19 8EZ
Phones Sherwin: 01292 445251; 07766 161096

MOSSBLOWN Goodwin Drive, Annbank
Colours Blue Alt: Orange/Black
Secretary Stephen Barrett, 79 Paterson Street, Ayr KA8 9HD
Phones Barrett: 01292 285962; 07985 612046; 01292 262050

NETHERTHIRD Netherthird PF, Cumnock
Colours Light Blue/Navy Alt: Yellow/Navy
Secretary Neil Gibson, 59 Dalgleish Avenue, Cumnock KA18 1QG
Phones Gibson: 01290 422197; 07983 997085

OCHILTREE UNITED Kay Park, Ochiltree
Colours White/Red Alt: Navy Blue
Secretary Brian Christie, 24 McDonald Street, Cumnock KA18 1DE
Phones Christie: 01290 423333; 07500 600447

PRESTWICK The Oval, Prestwick
Colours Blue/Black Alt: Tangerine
Secretary Ken Sinclair, 8 Englewood Avenue, Ayr KA8 9EF
Phones Sinclair: 01292 264298; 07594 659839

SHORTLEES Burnpark, Shortlees, Kilmarnock
Colours Red/Black Alt: White
Secretary John Sivewright, 6 Treesbank Road, Shortlees, Kilmarnock KA1 4RU
Phones Sivewright: 01563 574277; 07838 622436

STEWARTON ANNICK Stewarton Sports Centre
Colours White/Blue Alt: Red/Black
Secretary Alan Byrne, 29 Lloyd Walk, Stewarton KA3 3DF
Phones Byrne: 07969 442251

STEWARTON UNITED Cocklebie Park, Stewarton
Colours Red/Yellow Alt: Blue/White/Black or Orange/Black
Secretary James Taylor, 27a Bowes Rigg, Stewarton KA3 5EL
Phones Taylor: 01560 485232; 07545 264231

SYMINGTON CALEDONIAN Shaw Park, Symington
Colours Red/Black Alt: Orange
Secretary Mark Milligan, 5 Kiln Grove, Mossblown KA6 5BF
Phones Milligan: 01292 520678; 07446 352827; 01292 613072 (W)

TARBOLTON Tarbolton Public Park (Wilson Park)
Colours Royal Blue Alt: White/Royal
Secretary Danny Baird, 1 Margaret Sloan Place, Tarbolton KA5 5SD
Phones Baird: 01292 541806; 07713 592065; 01292 610932(W)

TROON ATHLETIC Marr College PF, Troon
Colours Black/Red stripes Alt: Yellow/Black
Secretary Craig Dewar, 13 Ayr Street Flat 2, Troon KA10 6ER
Phones Dewar: 01292 310302; 07793 238699

TROON DUNDONALD Marr College PF, Troon
Colours Maroon Alt: Sky Blue/Navy Blue stripes
Secretary Jim McDonald, 42 Lang Road, Barassie, Troon KA10 6TR
Phones McDonald: 01292 315140; 07799 802785

TROON UNITED Hosiery Park, Troon
Colours Red/Black stripes Alt: Yellow
Secretary Derek Murray, 1 Kenmore Place, Troon KA10 6PA
Phones Murray: 01292 319780; 07500 339367

VALE OF GIRVAN Victory Park, Girvan
Colours Maroon/White Alt: Red/Black
Secretary Robert Armstrong, 31 Willow Drive, Girvan KA26 0DE
Phones Armstrong: 01465 715509; 07443 000214

WALLACETOUN SPORTING CLUB King George V, Ayr
Colours All White Alt: Black
Secretary Jamie Tait, 55 Somerset Gardens, Ayr KA8 9TG
Phones Tait: 07706 822609; 01292 280636

WEST KILBRIDE Kirktonhall Glen, West Kilbride
Colours Amber/Black Alt: Black/White
Secretary Jean Musker, 14 Bellard Road, West Kilbride KA23 9JU
Phones Musker: 01294 823325; 07778 027696

WESTKIRK THISTLE Broomfield PF, Cumnock
Colours Black/White Alt: Blue
Secretary John Stewart, 45 McCall Avenue, Cumnock KA18 1LP
Contacts Stewart: 01290 426328; 07925 061074

WINLINTON WOLVES Greenwood Academy, Dreghorn
Colours Old Gold/Black Alt: Black with Yellow trim
Secretary Tommy Spooner, 92 Mill Road, Irvine KA12 0LA
Contacts Spooner: 01294 650336; 07974 285317

BORDER AMATEUR F.A. 2013/14

Secretary: Mr C. H. Campbell, 27 Oliver Park, Hawick, Roxburghshire TD9 9PL
(H) 01450 373840 Email: colinhcam@tiscali.co.uk   Senior Saturday
Website: http://bafl.leaguerepublic.com

Border Amateur FA Clubs 2013/14

Club	Ground	Colours
Ancrum	Bridgend	Yellow
Biggar	Hartree Mill	Blue / Black
	Kerfield Park	
	King George V Park, Carnwath	
	Monteith Park, Castairs	
CFC Bowholm	Canonbie Playing Field	Tangerine / Black
Chirnside United	Comrades Park	Green / Black
Chirnside United Colts	Chirside Primary School	Black
Coldtream Amateurs	Home Park	Blue
Earlston Rhymers	Runciman Park	Blue / White
Eyemouth Amateurs	Warner Park	Maroon
Gala Fairydean Rovers	Netherdale	Red / Black
Gala Hotspur	Netherdale	Blue / White
Gordon	Stewart Park	Black / Gold
Greenlaw	WS Happer Memorial ark	Green / Black
Hawick Legion	Wilton Lodge Park	Green / Black
Hawick Legion Rovers	Wilton Lodge Park	Light Blue / White
Hawick United	Albert Park	Gold / Black
Hawick Waverley	Wilton Lodge Park	Yellow / Black
Hears of Liddesdale	Liddle View Park	Maroon
Jed Legion	Elliot Park	Blue
Kelso Thistle	Woodside Park	Black / White
Langholm Legion	Castleholm	Yellow / Black
Lauder	Woodcot Pavilion	Yellow / Black
Leithen Rovers	Victoria Park	Blue
Linton Hotspur	New Moor Road	Blue / White
	Penicuik 3G	
	Wellington School	
Melrose	Tweedbank	Yellow / Black
Newtown	King George V Park	Black
Selkirk Victoria	Yarrow Park	Blue
St Boswells	Jenny Moore's Road	Maroon
Stow	Stow Park	Yellow / Black
Tweeddale Rovers	Kerfield Park, Peebles	Red / White
Tweedmouth Ams	Five Arches	Black / Gold
West Barns Star	West Barns Park	Maroon

Division A	P	W	D	L	F	A	GD	Pts
1 Chirnside Utd	20	12	5	3	62	40	22	41
2 Leithen Rovers	20	11	3	6	48	38	10	36
3 Stow	20	10	3	7	48	31	17	33
4 West Barns Star	20	10	2	8	68	60	8	32
5 Hawick Waverley	20	9	5	6	48	40	8	32
6 Greenlaw	20	9	3	8	45	50	-5	30
7 Newtown	20	8	5	7	43	37	6	29
8 Ancrum	20	8	5	7	55	58	-3	29
9 Gala Fairydean Rovers	20	7	2	11	54	59	-5	23
10 Tweeddale Rovers	20	6	3	11	37	44	-7	21
11 Hearts of Liddesdale	20	1	2	17	27	78	-51	-1 *

* Points Deducted By The B A F A Executive

Division B	P	W	D	L	F	A	+/-	Pts
1 Gordon	20	17	1	2	100	17	83	52
2 Jed Legion	20	17	0	3	71	19	52	51
3 Hawick Utd	20	12	2	6	64	62	2	38
4 Langholm Legion	20	10	3	7	64	44	20	33
5 Hawick Legion	20	9	4	7	69	48	21	31
6 Coldstream Ams	20	9	2	9	45	35	10	29
7 Eyemouth Ams	20	8	4	8	68	54	14	28
8 Gala Hotspur	20	7	3	10	54	53	1	24
9 Linton Hotspur	20	6	1	13	46	55	-9	19
10 Biggar	20	3	2	15	35	71	-36	5 *
11 Selkirk Victoria	20	1	0	19	10	168	-158	-3 *

* Points Deducted By The B A F A Executive

Division C	W	D	L	F	A	+/-	Pts
1 Chirnside Utd Colts	16	11	2	3	57	30	27	35
2 Earlston Rhymers	16	10	3	3	37	22	15	33
3 Kelso Thistle	16	10	2	4	40	25	15	32
4 St.Boswells	16	6	4	6	37	36	1	22
5 Melrose	16	6	2	8	44	40	4	20
6 Lauder	16	5	5	6	34	36	-2	20
7 Tweedmouth Ams	16	6	3	7	33	40	-7	18 *
8 CFC Bowholm	16	4	2	10	25	41	-16	14
9 Hawick Legion Rovers	16	2	1	13	28	65	-37	4 *

* Points Deducted By The B A F A Executive

CUP FINALS 2013/14

Waddell Cup
(All Teams, May 10 at Greenlaw)
Greenlaw v Gordon
4-1

Forsyth Cup (All Teams, at Earlston)
Biggar v St Boswalls
2-1 aet

Beveridge Cup
(Division A, May 16, at Greenlaw)
Newtown v Gala Fairydean Rovers
3-0

Border Cup
(Division A, October 12, at Greenlaw)
Leithen Rovers v West Barns Star
1-1 aet, 4-5 pens

Walls Cup
(Division B, May 3 at Tweeddale Rovers)
Biggar v Gordon
2-3

Wright Cup
(Division B, October 26, at Lauder)
Gordon v Jed Legion
4-0

Sanderson Cup
(Division C, April 12, at Selkirk)
Chirnside United Colts v Lauder, 4-3

Collie Cup
(October 5, at Earlston)
Kelso Thistle v Lauder, 2-4

RECENT BORDER LEAGUE CHAMPIONS

1974/5	Greenlaw	1984/5	Hawick United	1994/5	Chirnside	2004/5	Hawick Waverley
1975/6	Hawick British Legion	1985/6	Hawick United	1995/6	Gala Rovers	2005/6	Pencaitland
1976/7	Leithen Rovers	1986/7	Gala Rovers	1996/7	Chirnside	2006/7	Leithen Rovers
1977/8	Gala Rovers	1987/8	Eyemouth Legion	1997/8	Duns Legion	2007/8	Pencaitland
1978/9	Gala Hotspur	1988/9	Spittal Rovers	1998/9	Duns Legion	2008/9	Chirnside
1979/80	Gala Hotspur	1989/90	Duns Legion	1999/0C	Gala Rovers	2009/0	Leithen Rovers
1980/1	Gala Hotspur	1990/1	Duns Legion	2000/1	Gala Rovers	2010/1	Duns Ams
1981/2	Hawick United	1991/2	Hawick Legion	2001/2	Gala Rovers	2011/2	Pencaitland
1982/3	Hawick United	1992/3	Chirnside	2002/3	Earlston Rhymers	2012/3	Gala Rovers
1983/4	Eyemouth Legion	1993/4	Hawick Waverley	2003/4	Gala Rovers	2013/4	Chirnside

CAITHNESS AMATEUR F.A. 2013

Secretary: Mr Michael Gray, Bellmaya, Dunnett, By Thurso, Caithness, KW14 8YD. E mail michael-gray@rolls-royce.com. Tel 01847 851821

Division One	P	W	D	L	F	A	GD	Pts
Wick Groats	14	11	3	0	61	17	44	36
Pentland United	14	10	3	1	52	13	39	33
Thurso Acks	14	9	1	4	47	21	26	28
John O'Groats	14	8	1	5	40	29	11	25
Staxigoe United	14	5	2	7	38	31	7	17
Thurso Swifts	14	5	0	9	22	53	-31	15
Halkirk	14	3	0	11	21	55	-34	9
Thurso Pentland	14	0	0	14	17	79	-62	0

Division Two	P	W	D	L	F	A	GD	Pts
Castletown	14	13	1	0	82	11	71	40
Lybster	14	11	1	2	88	18	70	34
Wick Thistle	14	9	1	4	52	30	22	28
Francis Street Club	14	6	1	7	34	49	-15	19
Keiss	14	5	1	8	28	56	-28	16
Top Joes	14	5	0	9	31	49	-18	15
High Ormlie Hotspur	14	3	1	10	30	47	-17	10
Watten	14	1	0	13	15	100	-85	3

Watten FC's pitch was originally laid out within the notorious Camp 165 POW facility. This was a top-secret camp designated for top ranking Nazis.

This is a Summer League. Game are frequently played on Tuesday / Wednesday and Friday evenings.

Teams - Year of Formation: Castletown (1900) Francis St Club (1980) Halkirk (1926) Lybster (1887) John O Groats (1982) Thurso Pentlands(1918) Keiss (1927) Top Joes (1983) Pentland United (1948) Wick Thistle (1889) Thurso Acks (1898) Wick Rovers (1960) Thurso Swifts (1897) Wick Groats (1893)

Club Directory

	Colours	
Castletown	Green and White Hoops	Back Park, Castletown
John O' Groats	Orane and Black	John O' Groats
Lybster	Claret and Sky	Lybster
Pentland United	Claret and Sky	Ham Park, Dunnett
Staxigoe United	Yellow and black	Lower Bignold Park, Wick
Thurso Acks	Yellow and blue	The Dammies
Thurso Swifts	Black and White	The Dammies
Wick Groats	Red and Black Hoops	Upper Bignold Park
Francis Street Club	Red and Blue	Upper Bignold Park
Halkirk	Red and Black	Recreation Park, Halkirk
High Ormlie Hotspur	Green and White	Ormlie Park, Thurso
Keiss	Royal Blue and White	Keiss
Thurso Pentland	Green and Black	The Dammies
Top Joes	Maroon	Ormlie Park, Thurso
Watten		Watten
Wick Thistle	Blue and White	Upper Bignold Park

CALEDONIAN AMATEUR LEAGUE 2013/14

Secretary: Mr K. Lindsay, 35 Harris Close, Newton Mearns, Glasgow G77 6TU.
(H) 0141 639 3886 (B & M) 07899 750240 Email: kenny.lindsay@sky.com
Senior Saturday.

CUP FINALS 2013/14
William Turner Challenge Cup (at Broadwood)
Strathclyde University v Milton, 0-2

Douglas Smith League Cup (at Broadwood)
Cambusbarron Rovers v Glasgow Harp, 0-2

The Caledonian League was established in 1983. It aimed to provide a competition for ambitious Amateur clubs with a decent level of facilities. At the time it was the "top" Amateur League in the country - today the Central Scottish Amateur League would dispute that claim. The clubs are primarily from West Central Scotland and Stirlingshire. In the past the League has included tams from Edinburgh and the East but none of them remain.

Club Directory 2013/14

Member Club	Match Secretary	Contact Tel : No	Ground Postcode	Ground Tel : No
Balmore	Alan Crawford	07918 185501	M8 5EZ	07824340594
Bearsden	David Patey	07989 746592	G61 4BP	07989746592
Cambria	David Hill	07729 113 772	G33 6ND	0141 9464748
Cambusbarron Rvr	Gary Grahamslaw	07590 913525	FK7 9LP	07736 723845
Cumbernauld Colts	Richard McKenzie	07807 233671	G68 9NE	01236 856262
Dalziel HSFP	Peter Langford	07952 320930	ML1 5RZ	01698 862918
Doune Castle	William Docherty	07886 698529	FK16 6DJ	07886 698529
Drumchapel FP	David McLeary	07904 818345	G15 8SX	0141 2760774
Dumbarton Acad FP	John O'Neill	07970 806742	G82 2BL	07970 806742
EKFC	Brian McCormick	07957 966051	G75 0OZ	01355 279204
East Kilbride YM	Mike Smith	07767 317391	G74 3EU	01355 237 731
Gartcosh United	Stuart Hegarty	07837 529142	G69 8AO	01236 872674
Giffnock North	Andrew Davies	07801 052576	G46 6HU	0141 6382117
Glasgow Harp	Michael O'Neill	07947 691830	G64 2NE	0141 7721330
Glasgow University	Donald Fergusson	07789 545439	G20 0SP	0141 3305363
Hamilton FP	Ian Loose	07747 057371	ML3 6BY	01698 424101
Milngavie Wanderers	Robert Baxter	07906 186274	G62 7LN	07906 186274
Milton	Martin Conway	07803 897901	FK7 0EN	01786 811296
Rhu	Bobby Dunn	07912 312535	G84 8RX	07761103171
Rothesay Brandane	David Meldrum	07928 667979	PA20	01700 505384
St.Mungo's	John McClymont	07968 380775	G64 2PZ	0141 7726711
Strathclyde Uni	Michael McKenzie	07896 633773	G33 6ND	0141 7794341
Symington Tinto	Douglas McMillan	07798 755200	ML126LL	07917 634053
Viewfield Rovers	Justin Curry	07704 687967	PA124DE	07801591554
Weirs Recreation	Martin Guthrie	07754 549 056	G43 2HA	07971 802470
Westerlands	Liam McIntyre	07818 247 403	G20 0SP	0141 3305 363

	P	W	D	L	F	A	G/D	PTS
1 Glasgow Harp	22	13	5	4	57	31	26	44
2 Milton	22	11	6	5	55	40	15	39
3 Glasgow University	22	12	2	8	44	37	7	38
4 Doune Castle	22	10	7	4	60	43	17	37
5 EKFC	22	11	4	7	52	46	6	37
6 Dumbarton Academy	22	9	5	8	32	32	0	32
7 St Mungo's	22	8	6	8	39	47	-8	30
8 Giffnock North AAC	22	9	1	12	33	37	-4	28
9 Westerlands	22	8	3	11	32	47	-15	27
10 Gartcosh United	22	6	5	11	43	53	-10	20
11 Cambria	22	6	1	15	40	53	-13	19
12 Cambusbarron Rovers	22	6	1	15	36	57	-21	19

Gartcosh United deducted 3points (Player infringement)

	P	W	D	L	F	A	G/D	PTS
1 Dalziel HSFP	26	20	3	3	79	31	48	63
2 Strathclyde University	26	20	2	4	95	39	56	62
3 Bearsden	26	20	1	5	64	25	39	61
4 Milngavie Wanderers	26	16	2	8	83	47	36	50
5 Rothesay Brandane	26	15	2	9	66	52	14	47
6 Drumchapel FP	26	15	0	11	73	66	7	45
7 Balmore	26	12	1	13	50	57	-7	37
8 Hamilton FP	26	11	1	14	62	66	-4	34
9 Viewfield Rovers	26	11	2	13	68	57	11	35
10 East Kilbride YM	26	10	1	15	68	62	5	31
11 Cumbernauld Colts	26	9	0	17	49	76	-27	27
12 Rhu	26	6	4	16	58	97	-39	19
13 Weirs Recreation	26	3	3	20	40	87	-47	12
14 Symington Tinto	26	2	2	22	24	118	-94	5

Rhu 3 points deducted (Player infringement)
Symington Tinto deducted 3 points (Player infringement)
Unplayed Fixtures:-
Balmore* v Symington Tinto
Strathclyde Uni v Cumb. Colts*
* awarded 3 pts

CALEDONIAN LEAGUE CHAMPIONS

1983/4	Drumchapel Ams
	Queen's Park Hampden XI
1984/5	Bannockburn
1985/6	Muirend
1986/7	Stanley
1987/8	Stanley
1988/9	Queen's Park Hampden XI
1989/90	Liberton Cropley
1990/1	Stanley
1991/2	Dalziel HSFP
1992/3	Milngavie Wanderers
1993/4	Dalziel HSFP
1994/5	Dalziel HSFP
1995/6	Dalziel HSFP
1996/7	Bannockburn
1997/8	Dalziel HSFP
1998/9	Milton Ams
1999/00	Bannockburn
2000/1	Bannockburn
2001/2	Drumchapel Ams
2002/3	Netherton
2003/4	Coatbridge CC
2004/5	Bannockburn
2005/6	Dumbarton Academy FP
2006/7	Bannockburn
2007/8	Bannockburn
2008/9	Bannockburn
2009/10	Strathclyde University
2010/1	Bannockburn
2011/2	Glasgow Harp
2012/3	Giffnock North
2013/4	Glasgow Harp

The location of some teams is not immediately apparent from their name. Milton Amateurs are from Whins of Milton, near Stirling, but play at Bluebellwood Park in Bannockburn. St Mungo's, Westerlands and Cambria are Glasgow-based. Dalziel HSFP come from Motherwell. Viewfield Rovers are from Lochwinnoch and are occasional qualifiers for the senior Renfrewshire Cup. Weirs Recreation are another Glasgow-based club. Balmore and Symington Tinto are both Lanarkshire clubs.

CARLUKE AND DISTRICT AMATEUR LEAGUE 2013/14

Secretary: Mr Raymond Napier, 11 Angus Road, Carluke, ML8 4NX
(H) 01555 751710
E-Mail: thevics97@hotmail.co.uk
Website: www.http://cdafl.leaguerepublic.com
Sunday Afternoon League

FINAL TABLES 2013/14

Premier Division	P	W	D	L	F	A	GD	PTS
1 Bullfrog	16	13	3	0	84	20	64	42
2 Cleland Club	16	13	1	2	83	27	56	40
3 Dykehead AFC	16	9	4	3	76	47	29	31
4 Woodpecker AFC	16	8	2	6	50	38	12	26
5 Motherwell War Office	16	5	3	8	33	36	-3	18
6 Belhaven Amateurs	16	5	3	8	41	61	-20	18
7 Holytown Phoenix	16	4	2	10	24	86	-62	14
8 Carluke Victoria	16	2	2	12	26	71	-45	8
9 Allanton Amateurs	16	2	2	12	21	52	-31	8

First Division	P	W	D	L	F	A	GD	PTS
1 Coalburn Amateurs FC	18	15	0	3	65	25	40	45
2 AFC Airdrie Albion	18	14	1	3	78	24	54	43
3 Alpha FC	18	12	0	6	77	40	37	36
4 Wishaw athletic	18	10	0	8	55	55	0	30
5 Clarkston United	18	9	1	8	44	49	-5	28
6 Mac's bar	18	8	0	10	54	47	7	24
7 New Stevenston United	18	7	2	9	42	53	-11	23
8 AC Hamilton	18	7	2	9	45	48	-3	23
9 Carluke Thistle	18	4	2	12	47	63	-16	14
10 Lanarkshire Deaf Football Club	18	0	0	18	21	124	-103	0

CUP FINALS 2011/12

Premier Division Cup (May 11, at Vics Park, Shotts)
Dykehead v Cleland Club
2-2, 3-1 pens

First Division Cup
(May 11, at Hamilton Palace Grounds)
Coalburn Amateurs v Alpha
1-4

Mark Glackin Memorial Trophy
(May 25 at Vics Park, Shotts)
Dykehead v Cleland Club

League Cup
(May 18 at Vics Park, Shotts)
Dykhead v AFC Airdrie Albion
2-1

CENTRAL SCOTTISH AMATEUR LEAGUE 2013/14

Secretary: Mr G. Dingwall, 27 Owendale Avenue, Bellshill, Lanarkshire ML4 1NS

(M) 07747 821274

Email: colville.park@btinternet.com   Senior Saturday

Club Directory 2013/14		
Aikenhead Thistle	All Red	Firhill Complex, Glasgow, G20 7HH
Arthurlie United	Sky Blue	Thornley Park Campus, Paisley
Ashvale Victoria	All Blue	Cowan Park, Barrhead, G78 2SJ
Bannockburn	Maroon / White	Ladywell Park, Bannockburn, FK7 8LF
Blantyre Celtic	Green / White	Jock Stein Complex, Hamilton, ML3 9TU
Cambusnethan Talbot	Red	Dalziel Park, Motherwell, ML1 5RZ
Campsie Minerva	All Red	High Park, Lennoxtown, G66 7EJ
Chryston	Yellow / Blue	Carrick Park, Glenboig, ML5 2QS
Colville Park	All Blue	Colville Park, Motherwell, ML1 4UG
Condorrat Club	Blue / Yellow	Lomond Grove, Cumbernauld, G67 4JN
Drumchapel Amateurs	Red	Glenhead Park, Duntocher
East Kilbride	Red	Murray Public Parks, EK, G75 9AH
Eastfield	Gold / Navy	Earl's Hill, Cumbernauld, G69 9BZ
Garrowhill Thistle	Black / White	Lochend HS, Easterhouse, G34 0NZ
Gourock Athletic	Red / Black	Gourock Playing Fields, PA19 1YT
Greenock HSFP	Royal Blue	Battery Park, Greenock, PA16 7QG
Harestanes	Red	Merkland Park, Kirkintilloch, G66 3SN
Kilsyth	Green / Black	Kilsyth Sports Field, G65 9JX
Kirkintilloch MW	Black	Huntershill Park, G64 1RW
Linwood	Blue	Linwood Sports Centre, PA3 3RA
Mearns	Royal Blue	Crookfur Park, Glasgow, G77 6DT
Mill United	Red & Black Stripes	Fairhill Park, Hamilton, ML3 8HX
Pollok	Black / White	Nethercraigs Playing Fields, Glasgow G52 1RR
Postal United	Red	Glasgow Club, Haghill, G31 3LS
Redbrae	Blue	Merkland Playing Fields, Kirkintilloch
St Patricks FP	Green / White	Posties Park, Dumbarton, G82 4BG
Stedfast	Blue / Amber	Temple Playing Fields, Glasgow, G13 2TE
Steins Thistle	Red / Black	Allandale Park, FK4 2HD
Stirling City	Red	King's Park, Stirling, FK8 2JT
Uddingston Anvil	Red	Tannochside 3G, G71 5RH
Waterside	Blue	Waterside Park, Kirkintilloch, G66 3LL
Wellhouse	All Back	Greenfield Playing Fields, Shettleston, G32 6TP
WishawHSFP	Blue / Yellow	King George V Park, Wishaw, ML2 0DP

CUP FINALS 2013/14

Bunrigh Trophy League Cup
(May 26, at Cambuslang Rangers FC)
Wellhouse v Pollok   1-1aet, 3-2 pens

Fosters Cinema Cup
(June 2, at Kilsyth Rangers FC)
Colville Park v Wellhouse   1-0

McAvoy & McIntyre Trophy
(May 31, at Carluke Rovers FC)
Harestanes v Wellhouse   1-5

Robert Whyte Trophy
(May 31, at Colville Park)
Blantyre Celtic v Stirling City   8-0

PREMIER DIVISION	P	W	D	L	F	A	GD	Pts
BANNOCKBURN	20	14	4	2	66	33	33	46
HARESTANES	20	12	4	4	50	31	19	40
COLVILLE PARK	20	10	6	4	44	26	18	36
WELLHOUSE	20	9	5	6	43	31	12	32
CAMPSIE MINERVA	20	10	2	8	42	36	6	32
GREENOCK HSFP	20	9	4	7	49	45	4	31
DRUMCHAPEL	20	9	4	7	45	46	-1	31
EASTFIELD	20	7	2	11	37	47	-10	23
ST PATRICKS FP	20	6	2	12	29	39	-10	20
UDDINGSTON ANVIL	20	2	3	15	17	50	-33	9
ASHVALE VICTORIA	20	2	4	14	25	63	-38	7

Division 1A	P	W	D	L	F	A	GD	Pts
AIKENHEAD THISTLE	20	16	3	1	69	20	49	51
BLANTYRE CELTIC	20	16	2	2	74	24	50	50
GARROWHILL THISTLE	19	11	1	6	52	32	20	37
ARTHURLIE UTD	20	10	6	4	62	39	23	36
KILSYTH	20	8	3	9	39	42	-3	27
MILL UNITED	20	5	6	9	31	44	-13	21
LINWOOD	19	6	3	9	35	52	-17	21
CONDORRAT CLUB	20	6	1	13	54	60	-6	19
REDBRAE	20	5	4	11	30	54	-24	19
STEDFAST	20	4	4	12	43	83	-40	16
EAST KILBRIDE	20	3	3	14	35	74	-39	12

Division 1B	P	W	D	L	F	A	GD	Pts
POSTAL UTD	20	15	3	2	57	26	31	48
POLLOK	20	12	5	3	70	41	29	41
STEINS THISTLE	20	11	5	4	68	40	28	38
WATERSIDE	20	16	1	3	84	34	50	34
WISHAW HSFP	20	7	4	9	39	44	-5	25
KIRKINTILLOCH MW	20	5	6	9	44	52	-8	21
GOUROCK ATH.	20	6	3	11	41	60	-19	21
CAMBUSNETHAN TALBOT	20	5	5	10	37	43	-6	20
MEARNS	20	5	3	12	41	69	-28	18
CHRYSTON	20	4	3	13	30	68	-38	15
STIRLING CITY	20	4	2	14	38	72	-34	14

CHAMPIONS	PREMIER DIV
1988/9	Knightswood
1989/90	Bankhall Villa
1990/1	Bankhall Villa
1991/2	St Benedicts AFC
1992/3	Cardross Rock
1993/4	Cardross Rock
1994/5	Bellshill YMCA
1995/6	Bankhall Villa
1996/7	Killermont
1997/8	Harestanes
1998/9	Balmore
1999/00	Harestanes
2000/1	Harestanes
2001/2	Balmore
2002/3	Harestanes
2003/4	Kilsyth Ams
2004/5	Drumchapel Utd
2005/6	Redbrae
2006/7	Colville Park
2007/8	Drumchapel Utd
2008/9	Drumchapel Utd
2009/10	Drumchapel Utd
2010/1	Drumchapel Utd
2011/2	Colville Park
2012/3	Colville Park
2013/4	Bannockburn

DUMFRIES & DISTRICT AMATEUR LEAGUE 2013/14

Secretary: Mr. Graham Lockhart, Underwoodhouse, Kirkpatrick-Fleming,
Lockerbie, Dumfriesshire DG11 3AS (H) 01461 800223.
Email: underwoodhouse@tiscali.co.uk   Senior Saturday

Season 2013/14 proved to be the final one for the Dumfries and District Amateur League, which
was formed in 1954 out of the ashes of the old Dumfries Junior League.   Reduced to just 7
clubs, it was decided to call it a day.

Of the 7 clubs, both Upper Annandale and Dumfries YMCA have now joined the South of Scotland League.   Maxwelltown   Thistle   joined   the   Lanarkshire   Amateurs   whilst
orton Thistle moved into the Stewartry Summer League. Dynamo Star have folded and at the
time of going to press the future for Lochmaben and Terregles was unclear.

	P	W	D	L	F	A	PTS
Lochmaben	18	16	1	1	96	26	46*
Upper Annandale	18	11	2	5	49	27	35
Terregles Athletic	18	9	3	6	70	46	30
Maxwelltown Thistle	18	9	2	7	45	53	29
Morton Thistle	18	8	1	9	61	68	25
Dynamo Star	18	2	4	12	36	78	10
YMCA	18	1	1	16	34	95	4

* 3 pts deducted

Cup Finals 2013/14

Nivison Cup Final (May 2 2014, at Annan Athletic
FC)
Lochmaben v Upper Annandale   1-2

British Legion Cup Final (May 9 2014, at David
Keswick Centre)
Lochmaben v Terregles Athletuc   1-3

Burns Cup Final (May 24 2014 at David Keswick
Centre)
Lochmaben v Terregles Athletic   2-3

Queen of the South Cup Final (May 22 2014, at
QOTS FC)
Lochmaben v Morton Thistle   3-0

Tayleurian Cup Final (April 18 2014, at)
Upper Annandale v Lochmaben   1-0

League Cup Final (Nov 8 2013)
Upper Annandale v Maxwelltown Thistle   2-0

The Dumfries Amateur League website carries superb historical records of their competitions. We have reproduced some of these below, to give aflavour of the rich history of their competitions.

See: www.dumfriesamateurfootball.co.uk

Over the years so many clubs have moved on to the South of Scotland League tat it was perhaps inevitable that the Dumfries League would fold. However, the Sunday section remains buoyant.

	League Championship		Division 2		Queen of the South Cup	
Year	Winners	Runners Up	Champions	Runners Up	Winners	Runners Up
1954-55	Dumfries Amateurs	Hearts of Heath				
1955-56	Lincluden	Maxwelltown Thistle				
1956-57	Hearts of Heath	Millbrae				
1957-58	Not awarded				Drungans Swifts	Hearts of Heath
1958-59	Troqueer Amateurs	Hearts of Heath			Troqueer Amateurs	Hearts of Heath
1959-60	Western Thistle	Troqueer Amateurs			Hearts of Heath	Drungans Swifts
1960-61	Penmans Athletic	Troqueer Amateurs			Penmans United	Drungans Swifts
1961-62	Troqueer Amateurs	Loreburn Star			Troqueer Amateurs	Crichton RoyAL
1962-63	Lincluden Swifts	Crichton Royal			Lincluden swifts	Nalgo
1963-64	Lincluden Swifts	Crichton Royal			Lincluden swifts	Noblehill
1964-65	Lincluden Swifts	St Andrews			St Andrews	Noblehill
1965-66	Lincluden Swifts	Crichton Royal			Lincluden swifts	Royal Infirmary
1966-67	Green Colts	Lincluden Swifts			Crichton Royal	Royal Infirmary
1967-68	Lincluden Swifts	Troqueer Amateurs			Mid Annandale	Troqueer Amateurs
1968-69	Lincluden Swifts	Green Colts	Morton Thistle	Dumfries HSFP	Morton Thistle	Lincluden Swifts
1969-70	Colts*	Lincluden Swifts	Nithsdale Amateurs	Parkhead	Lincluden swifts	Royal Infirmary
1970-71	Upper Annandale	Colts	Lochmaben	Ashfield Rovers	Upper Annandale	Lincluden Swifts
1971-72	Lincluden Swifts	Colts	Parkhead	Mid Annandale	Lincluden swifts	Mid Annandale
1972-73	Lincluden Swifts	Colts	Dumfries HSFP	Lochar Thistle	Nithsdale Amateurs	Lincluden Swifts
1973-74	Nithsdale Amateurs	Lincluden Swifts	Glenmarlin	Young's Paint	Nithsdale Amateurs	Crichton RoyAL
1974-75	Nithsdale Amateurs	Lincluden Swifts	Upper Annandale	Kirkconnel Ams	Nithsdale Amateurs	Lochar Thistle
1975-76	Nithsdale Amateurs	Glenmarlin Thistle	Green Colts	Galloway Rovers	Nithsdale Amateurs	Young's Paints
1976-77	Nithsdale Amateurs	Heathhall Hearts	Lochar Amateurs	Locchmaben	Nithsdale Amateurs	Heathhall Hearts
1977-78	Mid Annandale	Heathhall Hearts	Lochar Amateurs	Bellevue Rovers	Morton Thistle	Nithsdale Amateurs
1978-79	Morton Thistle	Mid Annandale	Blackwood Dynamos	Terregles Athletic	Morton Thistle	Lochar Thistle
1979-80	Heathhall Hearts	Mid Annandale	Lochar Amateurs	Noblehill	Heathhall Hearts	Nithsdale Amateurs
1980-81	Nithsdale Amateurs	Lochar Thistle	YMCA	Annan Athletic Colts	Nithsdale Amateurs	Galloway Rovers
1981-82	Annan Athletic Colts	Lochar Thistle	Dumfries HSFP	Glenmarlin Thistle	Dumfries HSFP	Lochar Amateurs
1982-83	Lochar Thistle	Galloway Rovers	Lincluden Colts	Annan Athletic Colts	Morton Thistle	Kirkconnel Amateurs
1983-84	YMCA	Upper Annandale	Annan Thistle	Abbey Vale	Lochar Thistle	Upper Annandale
1984-85	YMCA	Kirkconnel Amateurs	Lochar Amateurs	Lincluden Colts	Kirkconnel Amateurs	Nithsdale Amateurs
1985-86	YMCA	Lochar Amateurs	Hoddam Rangers	Blackwood Dynamos	YMCA	Nithsdale Amateurs
1986-87	Kirkconnel Amateurs	YMCA	Dumfries HSFP	Gretna Community	YMCA	Lincluden Colts
1987-88	YMCA	Kirkconnel Amateurs	Lochmaben	Mid Annandale	Maxwelltown HSFP	Lochar Thistle
1988-89	Kirkconnel Amateurs	Nithsdale Amateurs	Abbey Vale	Lochar Thistle	Maxwelltown HSFP	Kirkconnel Amateurs
1989-90	Lincluden Colts	Maxwelltown HSFP	Dumfries AFP	Hoddam Rangers	Lincluden Colts	Heathhall Hearts
1990-91	Kirkconnel Amateurs	YMCA	Upper Annandale	Glaxochem	Kirkconnel Amateurs	Dumfries HSFP
1991-92	YMCA	Kirkconnel Amateurs	Lochmaben	Kirkton	Galloway Rovers	Glenmarlin
1992-93	YMCA	Lincluden Colts	Glenmarlin	Mid Annandale	Lincluden Colts	Upper Annandale
1993-94	Kirkconnel Amateurs	Lincluden Colts	Morton Thistle	Kelloholm	Kirkconnel Amateurs	Abbey Vale
1994-95	Lincluden Colts	Kirkconnel Amateurs	Lochar Thistle	Morton Thistle	Kirkconnel Amateurs	Lochmaben
1995-96	Lochmaben	Abbey Vale	Kirkpatrick Fleming	Loreburn	YMCA	Nithsdale Amateurs
1996-97	Kirkconnel Amateurs	Nithsdale Amateurs	Lochar Thistle	Kirkpatrick Fleming	Kirkconnel Amateurs	Kirkpatrick Fleming
1997-98	Kirkconnel Amateurs	Nithsdale Amateurs	Mid Annandale	Lochar Thistle	Mid Annandale	Kirkconnel Amateurs
1998-99	Kirkconnel Amateurs	YMCA	Dumfries Amateurs	Dalbeattie Star Colts	Kirkconnel Amateurs	Upper Annandale
1999-00	Dumfries Amateurs (2)	YMCA	Abbey Vale	Lochar Thistle	Mid Annandale	Abbey Vale
2000-01	Kirkconnel Amateurs	YMCA	Upper Annandale	Kelloholm	Kirkconnel Amateurs	Upper Annandale
2001-02	Kirkconnel Amateurs	Lochmaben	Kelloholm	Bellevue Rovers	Mid Annandale	Lochar Thistle
2002-03	Kirkconnel Amateurs	YMCA	Lochar Thistle		Kirkconnel Amateurs	Upper Annandale
2003-04	Kirkconnel Amateurs	Lochmaben	Upper Annandale		Kirkconnel Amateurs	Kelloholm
2004-05	Lochmaben	YMCA			Kirkconnel Amateurs	Lochmaben
2005-06	Lochmaben	Kelloholm			Lochar Thistle	Kirkconnel Amateurs
2006-07	Upper Annandale	Lochmaben			Kirkconnel Amateurs	Lochmaben
2007-08	Upper Annandale	Maxwelltown Thistle			Upper Annandale	Maxwelltown Thistle
2008-09	Upper Annandale	Lochar Thistle			Dynamo Star	Maxwelltown Thistle
2009-10	Upper Annandale	Lochmaben			Lochmaben	Lochar Thistle
2010-11	Lochar Thistle	Lochmaben			Lochar Thistle	Upper Annandale
2011-12	Lochar Thistle	Lochmaben			Lochmaben	Lochar Thistle
2012-13	Lochmaben	Lochar Thistle			Dynamo Star	Lochar Thistle

	Tayleurian Cup		British Legion Cup		Nivison Cup	
Year	Winners	Runners Up	Winners	Runners Up	Winners	Runners Up
1954-55	Lincluden	Maxwelltown Thistle				
1955-56	Millbrae	Hearts of Heath				
1956-57	Hearts of Heath	Millbrae				
1957-58	Unknown		Dumfries Amateurs	Unknown		
1958-59	Troqueer Amateurs	Hearts of Heath	Troqueer Amateurs	Drungans Swifts		
1959-60	Hearts of Heath	Penmans United	Western Thistle	Hearts of Heath		
1960-61	Troqueer Amateurs	Penmans United	Troqueer Amateurs	Penmans United		
1961-62	Troqueer Amateurs	Loreburn Star	Linduden Swifts	Crichton Royal		
1962-63	Lincluden Swifts	Loreburn Star	Linduden Swifts	Loreburn Star		
1963-64	Lincluden Swifts	Haleys	Linduden Swifts	Royal Infirmary		
1964-65	Lincluden Swifts	Unknown	Linduden Swifts	Noblehill		
1965-66	Lincluden Swifts	Crichton Royal	Drungans Swifts	Crichton Royal		
1966-67	Kirkconnel Amateurs	Terregles Athletic	Green Colts	Troqueer Amateurs		
1967-68	Green Colts	Lincluden Swifts	Green Colts	Lincluden Swifts		
1968-69	Lincluden Swifts	Dunfries HSFP	Linduden Swifts	Green Colts		
1969-70	Lincluden Swifts	Lochar Thistle	Morton Thistle	Royal Infirmary		
1970-71	Colts	Lochar Thistle	Linduden Swifts	Colts		
1971-72	Upper Annandale	Morton Thistle	Linduden Swifts	Upper Annandale		
1972-73	Nithsdale Amateurs	Lincluden Swifts	Morton Thistle	Lincluden Swifts		
1973-74	Nithsdale Amateurs	Lincluden Swifts	Mid Annandale	Nithsdale Amateurs		
1974-75	Nithsdale Amateurs	Ashfield Rovers	Nithsdale Amateurs	Lincluden Swifts		
1975-76	Glenmarlin	Nithsdale Amateurs	Heathhall Hearts	Nithsdale Amateurs		
1976-77	Lochar Amateurs	Mid Annandale	Nithsdale Amateurs	Heathhall Hearts		
1977-78	Glenmarlin	Heathhall Hearts	Nithsdale Amateurs	Glenmarlin Thistle		
1978-79	No competition		Morton Thistle	Lochar Thistle		
1979-80	Mid Annandale	Blackwood Dynamos	Unplayed			
1980-81	Nithsdale Amateurs	Lincluden Colts	Linduden Swifts	Lochar Thistle		
1981-82	Nithsdale Amateurs	Abbey Vale	Annan Athletic Colts	Noblehill		
1982-83	Galloway Rovers	Kirkconnel Amateurs	Dumfries HSFP	Morton Thistle		
1983-84	Upper Annandale	Annan Athletic Colts	Blackwood Dynamos	Upper Annandale		
1984-85	Galloway Rovers	Nithsdale Amateurs	Lochar Thistle	Galloway Rovers		
1985-86	Upper Annandale	Queens Colts	YMCA	Heathhall Hearts		
1986-87	Galloway Rovers	Upper Annandale	Maxwelltown Hearts	YMCA	YMCA	Kello Rovers
1987-88	Maxwelltown HSFP	Dunfries HSFP	YMCA	Lochar Thistle	Kello Rovers	Unknown
1988-89	Maxwelltown HSFP	Lochar Thistle	Kirkconnel Amateurs	YMCA	Maxwelltown HSFP	Lochar Thistle
1989-90	Lincluden Colts	Upper Annandale	Linduden Colts	Abbey Vale	Kirkconnel Amateurs	Dumfries AFP
1990-91	Dumfries HSFP	Nithsdale Amateurs	YMCA	Lincluden Colts	Abbey Vale	Mid Annandale
1991-92	Kirkconnel Amateurs	Dumfries AFP	Linduden Colts	Upper Annandale	YMCA	Abbey Vale
1992-93	Abbey Vale	Upper Annandale	Dumfries HSFP	Abbey Vale	Dumfries AFP	Upper Annandale
1993-94	Kirkconnel Amateurs	YMCA	YMCA	Lochmaben	Abbey Vale	Mid Annandale
1994-95	Nithsdale Amateurs	YMCA	Linduden Colts	Mid Annandale	YMCA	Lincluden Colts
1995-96	Nithsdale Amateurs	Lochmaben	Nithsdale Amateurs	Kirkconnel Amateurs	Lochmaben	Kirkton
1996-97	Lochmaben	YMCA	Kirkconnel Amateurs	YMCA	Lochmaben	Kirkton
1997-98	Kelloholm	Loreburn	Loreburn	Lochar Thistle	Upper Annandale	Morton Thistle
1998-99	YMCA	Mid Annandale	Kirkconnel Amateurs	Kirkpatrick Fleming	Loreburn	Nithsdale Amateurs
1999-00	Kirkconnel Amateurs	Abbey Vale	Mid Annandale	Kirkconnel Amateurs	Nithsdale Amateurs	Abbey Vale
2000-01	Kirkconnel Amateurs	Lochmaben	Unplayed		Unplayed	
2001-02	Kirkconnel Amateurs	Kelloholm	Kirkconnel Amateurs	Lochmaben	Kirkconnel Amateurs	Dumfries FC Colts
2002-03	Upper Annandale	Terregles Athletic	Kirkconnel Amateurs	Upper Annandale	Kirkconnel Amateurs	Dumfries FC Colts
2003-04	Hearts of Liddesdale	Kirkconnel Amateurs	Lochmaben	Kelloholm	Hearts of Liddesdale	Lochmaben
2004-05	Lochmaben	Hearts of Liddesdale	Kirkconnel Amateurs	Lochmaben	Kirkconnel Amateurs	Lochar Thistle
2005-06	Kirkconnel Amateurs	Upper Annandale	Lochar Thistle	Upper Annandale	Lochar Thistle	Kirkconnel Amateurs
2006-07	Upper Annandale	Terregles Athletic	Upper Annandale	Lochar Thistle	Kirkconnel Amateurs	Lochmaben
2007-08	Maxwelltown Thistle	Kirkconnel Amateurs	Maxwelltown Thistle	Upper Annandale	Lochmaben	Kirkconnel Amateurs
2008-09	Lochmaben	Maxwelltown Thistle	Maxwelltown Thistle	Lochar Thistle	Lochar Thistle	Upper Annandale
2009-10	Lochmaben	Dynamo Star	Lochmaben	Lochar Thistle	Upper Annandale	Lochmaben
2010-11	Lochar Thistle	Upper Annandale	Lochmaben	Lochar Thistle	Lochmaben	Lochar Thistle
2011-12	Lochar Thistle	Upper Annandale	YMCA	Upper Annandale	Morton Thistle	Upper Annandale
2012-13	Lochar Thistle	Lochmaben	Morton Thistle	Upper Annandale	Lochmaben	Terregles Athletic
2013-14	Upper Annandale	Lochmaben	Terregles Athletic	Lochmaben	Upper Annandale	Lochmaben

Year	Burns Cup Winners	Burns Cup Runners Up	League Cup Winners	League Cup Runners Up
1954-55				
1955-56				
1956-57				
1957-58				
1958-59				
1959-60				
1960-61				
1961-62				
1962-63				
1963-64				
1964-65				
1965-66				
1966-67				
1967-68				
1968-69			Lincluden Swifts	Greystone Rovers
1969-70			Lincluden Swifts	Colts
1970-71			Lincluden Swifts	Colts
1971-72			Lincluden Swifts	Nithsdale Amateurs
1972-73			Crichton Royal	Nithsdale Amateurs
1973-74			Nithsdale Amateurs	Dumfries HSFP
1974-75			Nithsdale Amateurs	Lincluden Swifts
1975-76			Nithsdale Amateurs	Heathhall Hearts
1976-77			Youngs Painters	Nithsdale Amateurs
1977-78			Nithsdale Amateurs	Mid Annandale
1978-79			Heathhall Hearts	Youngs Painters
1979-80			Youngs Painters	Heathhall Hearts
1980-81			Nithsdale Amateurs	YMCA
1981-82			Glenmarlin Thistle	Lochar Thistle
1982-83			YMCA	Dumfries HSFP
1983-84			Galloway Rovers	YMCA
1984-85			Kirkconnel Amateurs	Annan Thistle
1985-86			YMCA	Nithsdale Amateurs
1986-87			Kirkconnel Amateurs	YMCA
1987-88			Dumfries HSFP	Kirkconnel Amateurs
1988-89			Maxwelltown HSFP	Lochmaveb
1989-90			Nithsdale Amateurs	YMCA
1990-91			Nithsdale Amateurs	Upper Annandale
1991-92			YMCA	Kirkconnel Amateurs
1992-93			Dunfries AFP	Lochar Thistle
1993-94			Kirkconnel Amateurs	Dumfries HSFP
1994-95			Kirkconnel Amateurs	Lincluden Colts
1995-96			Lochmaben	Kelloholm
1996-97	Lochmaben	YMCA	Nithsdale Amateurs	YMCA
1997-98	YMCA	Abbey Vale	Mid Annandale	YMCA
1998-99	Loreburn	Kirkconnel Amateurs	Kirkconnel Amateurs	Nithsdale Amateurs
1999-00	Lochmaben	Dunfries Amateurs	Kirkconnel Amateurs	Dumfries Amateurs
2000-01	Kirkconnel Amateurs	Nithsdale Amateurs	Unplayed	
2001-02	Kirkconnel Amateurs	YMCA	Upper Annandale	Mid Annandale
2002-03	Lochmaben	Morton Thistle	Kirkconnel Amateurs	Lochmaben
2003-04	Kirkconnel Amateurs	Lochmaben	Kirkconnel Amateurs	Lochmaben
2004-05	Kirkconnel Amateurs	Lochar Thistle	Kirkconnel Amateurs	Hearts of Liddesdale
2005-06	Lochmaben	Bellevue Rovers	Upper Annandale	Lochmaben
2006-07	Lochar Thistle	Kirkconnel Amateurs	Upper Annandale	Dumfries FC Colts
2007-08	Upper Annandale	Lochar Thistle	Morton Thistle	Maxwelltown Thistle
2008-09	Lochmaben	Maxwelltown Thistle	Lochar Thistle	Upper Annandale
2009-10	Lochar Thistle	Upper Annandale	Upper Annandale	Lochar Thistle
2010-11	Lochmaben	Maxwelltown Thistle	Lochmaben	Lochar Thistle
2011-12	Lochmaben	Lochar Thistle	Lochar Thistle	Upper Annandale
2012-13			Lochmaben	Upper Annandale
2013-14	Terregles Athletic	Lochmaben	Upper Annandale	Maxwelltown Thistle

DUMFRIES SUNDAY AMATEUR FA 2013/14

Secretary: Mr Richard Irving, 12 MacDonald Loaning, Heathhall, Dumfries
DG1 3RX. (H) 01387 261592 (M) 07840 968700
Email: totti14@btinternet.com   Senior Sunday

PREMIER DIVISION	P	W	D	L	F	A	GD	Pts
Moffat Thistle 2010	21	15	4	2	63	26	37	49
Five Arches Bombers	21	13	3	5	66	50	16	42
Kings Arms	21	12	3	6	66	48	18	39
Loreburn Thistle	21	10	1	10	73	53	20	31
Palmerston Colts	21	8	3	10	53	66	-13	24
Scaur	21	6	5	10	53	60	-7	23
Normandy Star	21	5	2	14	47	78	-31	17
Black Bull Rovers	21	3	3	15	29	69	-40	12

FIRST DIVISION	P	W	D	L	F	A	GD	Pts
Annan Town	18	17	0	1	114	25	89	51
Nithside	18	15	1	2	116	38	78	46
Hole In the Wa	18	15	1	2	110	40	70	46
Jolly Harvester	18	10	2	6	73	65	8	32
Ruthwell Rovers	18	6	1	11	43	54	-11	19
Park Thistle	18	5	2	11	47	74	-27	17
Hendersons Colts	18	5	2	11	59	92	-33	17
Youth United	18	4	3	11	42	91	-49	15
Dumfries Athletic	18	3	1	14	26	97	-71	10
Summerhill	18	2	3	13	36	90	-54	9

The Dumfries Sunday Amateur FA will continue to operate despite the folding of the Saturday Amateurs. In fact, the Sunday League may gain one or two teams as a result of this.

The league was formed in time for the kick off for the 1977/78 season and has been running for nearly 40 seasons. For most of the time there have been two divisions.

Cup Finals 2013/14

**Houliston Cup
(April 27 2014))**
Ruthwell Rovers v Nithside   0-1

**League Cup
(May 15 2014)**
Normandy Star v King's Arms   2-3

**Turning Point Challenge Trophy
(May 11 2014, at Kelloholm)**
Moffat Thistle 2010 v Annan Town 3-0

**Heathhall Garden Centre Cup Final
(May 18 2014, at Palmerston Park)**
Moffat Thistle 2010 3 Scaur 1 (AET)

RECENT CHAMPIONS

2000/1	Globetrotters
2001/2	Balmoral
2002/3	Loreburn Thistle
2003/4	Hoddam Rangers
2004/5	Hoddam Rangers
2005/6	Balmoral
2006/7	Lochside Colts
2007/8	Lochside Colts
2008/9	Scaur
2009/10	Hole In The Wa
2010/1	The Famous Star
2011/2	Scaur
2012/3	Scaur
2013/4	Moffat Thistle 2010

DUNDEE SATURDAY MORNING AMATEUR LEAGUE 2013/14

Secretary: Mr. Steven McSwiggan, Coldstream, Tealing, Dundee DD4 0RG
(H) 01382 380735 (B) 01382 660111 bleep 4258) (M) 07821 589881.
Email: s.j.mcswiggan@dundee.ac.uk   Senior Saturday.

Website: http://www.dsmfl.co.uk/

Latest Available Tables

Premier Division	P	W	D	L	F	A	PTS
DC Athletic	22	16	4	2	69	34	52
Cannon Fodder	22	16	3	3	85	38	51
Sidlaw Thistle	22	15	1	6	82	38	46
Dundee Thistle	22	13	3	6	66	44	42
Hawkhill Athletic	22	11	6	5	65	51	39
DUMS	22	8	6	8	51	43	30
Camperdown	21	8	4	10	54	73	28
West End Athletic	21	7	3	12	37	62	24
Wellbeat United	22	7	1	14	54	82	22
Guardbridge Saints	21	6	1	14	39	62	19
Club 83	21	4	2	15	43	71	14
Riverside CSC	22	2	2	18	33	80	8

First Division							
AC Harleys	18	13	2	3	73	21	41
Riverside Plate	18	11	5	2	63	28	38
Dundee Rangers	18	11	4	3	79	45	37
Clarks Cowboys	18	11	2	5	58	39	35
Thomson Accies	18	11	2	5	65	30	35
Ferry Mechanics	18	6	3	9	44	51	21
Park Tool	18	5	3	10	48	61	18
Central Baptists	17	3	5	9	34	58	14
DK raiders	18	2	2	14	25	92	8
Springfield	17	2	0	15	23	87	6

Second Division							
Fintry Shamrock	22	21	0	1	138	32	63
Boyds Hibernia	22	20	1	1	102	32	61
Dundee Royal	22	16	1	5	100	44	49
Kellys Gunners	22	13	2	7	82	56	41
FC Boukir	22	11	2	9	71	50	35
Borussia Dexys	22	9	2	11	64	73	29
Fife Thistle	22	7	2	13	49	81	23
Maltman Athletic	22	7	2	13	61	112	23
Sidlaw Albion	22	6	3	13	49	69	21
Bridgend Athletic	22	6	2	14	48	77	20
Caird Park Athletic	22	3	3	16	56	109	12
Fintry Rovers	22	3	0	19	40	125	9

All games are played at either the University Grounds or the Riverside Playing Fields.

CUP FINALS 2013/4

Shaun Kelly Memorial Cup Final (May 31, North End Park)
DUMS v Sidlaw Thistle   2-2aet, 1-3 pens

George McArthur Memorial Cup (May 30, Invergowrie Park)
Dundee Thistle v Guardbridge Saints   5-0

Ross Kirk Prem Div Cup Final (May 28)
Sidlaw Thistle v Dundee Thistle   4-0

Trident Trophy Second Div Cup Final (May 7, University Show Pitch))
Fintry Shamrock v Dundee Royal   7-2

Balgay Bar Div 1 Cup (May 14, University Show Pitch)
Dundee Rangers v Riverside Plate 1-0

The Dundee Saturday Morning Amateur Football League affiliated to the SAFA in season 2009-2010 after existing for 17 years as a friendly league. The early years of the league's formation are sketchy though an initial loose collection of teams started out in the early 1990's playing at Riverside in Dundee. Founding members of the league that still play are Cowboys, Ferry Mechanics, Wellbeat and Springfield with a number of teams having joined in the past 10 years. In recent years the league has been the fastest growing in Scottish Amateur Football expanding from the original 14 clubs who affiliated to the SAFA, to 2013-14 with 34 clubs.

This expanded league now is split into three divisions, with the Premier League consisting of 12 teams, the 1st Division of 10 and 12 in the 2nd Division.

295

DUNDEE SUNDAY AMATEUR FA   2013/14

Secretary: Jim Martin, 07513 688612   Senior Sunday
Website: www.dsfafa.weebly.com/

The Association was formed in 2013 with the merger of the Sunday Amateiur
and Sunday Welfare Leagues.

Latest Table Available

	P	W	D	L	F	A	PTS
Dundee Argyle	27	24	2	1	127	33	74
Fairfield SLC	26	24	1	1	164	31	73
Tayport AFC	28	22	1	5	127	55	67
Fintry Athletic	28	18	2	8	85	51	56
Cutty Sark	28	16	4	8	128	78	52
Michelin Athletic	28	16	0	12	99	71	48
Downfield Harp	28	16	3	11	82	66	45
Bayview	28	14	5	12	94	109	38
Dundee Social Club	28	11	5	13	69	85	35
Burton Albion	28	10	4	15	81	90	31
Annfield	28	9	1	18	74	109	28
Ferraris	28	9	1	18	78	114	28
Planet Bar	27	9	2	19	61	102	20
Downfield AFC	28	6	1	25	30	126	7
Occidental	28	2	4	24	45	224	4
Lochee United AFC	w/d						
Boars Rock	w/d						
West End Albion	w/d						

CUP FINALS 2013/14

Alex Smith Cup Final (May 18)
Downfield Harp v Bayview
2-2, 1-3 pens

Direct Soccer Association Cup Final (May 11)
Fintry Athletic v Fairfield
0-2

League Cup (May 25)
Fairfield v Cutty Sark

Tayside Trophy (June 6)
Dundee Argyle v Fairfield SLC

EAST OF SCOTLAND CHURCHES A.F.A.

	P	W	D	L	F	A	GD	PTS
Fairmilehead	8	6	0	2	35	12	23	18
Loanhead PCFC	9	6	0	3	34	16	18	18
Lepra	7	5	1	1	19	12	7	16
Morningside	8	5	0	3	21	22	-1	15
Gorgie	8	3	1	4	17	19	-2	10
Wester Hailes	7	3	0	4	13	23	-10	9
Port Seton	9	2	0	7	15	24	-9	6
Ladywell	8	1	0	7	8	34	-26	3

Secretary: Mr Ian Midwinter, 20 Mosside
Terrace, Bathgate. Tel 07949742115
Email: ian.midwinter@salvationarmy,org.uk

Senior Saturday Mornings

This league used to have a good web
presence but that seems to have ended.
Virtually no information is available. The latest
available table from 2013/14 is shown here.

EDINBURGH AND DISTRICT SUNDAY A.F.A. 2013/14

Secretary: Mr Len Blackie, 7 Muirhouse Park, Edinburgh EH4 4RS.
(H) 0131 315 3058 (B) 07896 220145. Email: leadsafa@hotmail.com
Sunday
Website: http://www.leaguewebsite.co.uk/edinburghdistrictssundayafa

LATEST AVAILABLE TABLES 2013/14

PREMIER DIVISION	P	W	D	L	F	A	GD	Pts
REDHALL STAR	19	18	1	0	104	14	90	55
BOCA SENIORS	20	14	3	3	71	31	40	45
FOOTBALL CLUB of EDINBURGH	20	12	2	6	74	72	2	38
EDINBURGH THISTLE	19	11	1	7	60	33	27	34
DUDDINGSTON ATHLETIC	20	10	3	7	63	52	11	33
LONGSTONE UNITED	20	8	2	10	58	67	-9	26
ULTIMO GOCCIA 04	20	8	2	10	48	65	-17	26
DYNAMO HIBS	20	7	5	8	48	51	-3	23
HIBEERNIAN	20	6	0	14	44	72	-28	18
ABBEY ATHLETIC	20	5	0	15	43	83	-40	15
AC. MIDLOTHIAN	20	0	1	19	28	101	-73	1

FIRST DIVISION	P	W	D	L	F	A	GD	Pts
EDINBURGH ATHLETIC	18	17	0	1	99	23	76	51
ARNISTON ACFC	18	15	1	2	94	18	76	46
THE POLTON INN	18	10	2	6	68	50	18	32
LIMEKILN	18	9	3	6	81	55	26	30
LOCHEND STAR	18	7	6	5	45	41	4	27
CRAIGROYSTON	18	6	5	7	52	45	7	23
ARNISTON THISTLE	18	5	2	11	33	61	-28	17
LIBERTON UNITED	18	5	0	13	46	74	-28	15
PENTLAND THISTLE	18	3	1	14	25	124	-99	10
COWDEN PARK	18	3	0	15	26	78	-52	9

CUP COMPETITIONS— FINALS

All finals were played at Saughton Enclosure

Association Cup (May 25)
Boca Seniors v Redhall Star

J J McKenzie Trophy (May 18)
Edinburgh Thistle v Redhall Star
2-5

David Temple Memorial Cup (May 11)
Arniston AFC v Edinburgh Athletic
1-3

Premier Division Cup (May 4)
Redhall Star v Edinburgh Thistle
4-0

First Division Cup (April 27)
Arniston AFC v Edinburgh Thistle
4-2

FIFE AMATEUR FOOTBALL ASSOCIATION 2013/14

Secretary: Mr. A Denny, 9 Glen Artney Grove, Dunfermline, Fife KY11 8FD
(H) 01383 730932 (B) 0131 225 4460 (M) 07974 474172.
Email: archibald.denny@btinternet.com Senior Sat.

Premier Division	P	W	D	L	F	A	W	D	L	F	A	GD	Pts
Valleyfield	16	6	0	2	22	8	7	0	1	21	6	29	39
Burntisland United	16	6	2	0	22	9	5	0	3	19	13	19	35
Pittenweem Rovers	16	5	1	2	31	17	5	2	1	14	10	18	33
Dysart	16	4	1	3	15	17	3	1	4	21	20	-1	23
Kirkcaldy YMCA	16	5	1	2	20	20	1	2	5	8	20	-12	21
Rosyth	16	2	1	5	5	13	3	1	4	17	18	-9	17
St Andrews University	16	1	4	3	11	13	2	1	5	18	22	-6	14
St Andrews Amateurs	16	2	1	5	13	22	1	1	6	11	20	-18	11
Rosebank Rangers	16	2	1	5	13	21	0	4	4	11	23	-20	11

Division One	P	W	D	L	F	A	W	D	L	F	A	GD	Pts
Fossoway	18	7	2	0	30	8	7	2	0	28	11	39	46
Kingdom Athletic	18	8	1	0	19	6	4	1	4	19	13	19	38
Buckhaven Town	18	5	2	2	23	11	5	2	2	26	15	23	34
Leslie Hearts	18	4	3	2	32	14	3	5	1	19	15	22	29
Hearts of Beath	18	5	3	1	29	15	2	3	4	15	15	14	27
Auchtermuchty Bellvue	18	6	0	3	20	17	2	2	5	11	15	-1	26
Methilhill Strollers	18	4	2	3	26	22	3	1	5	18	20	2	24
Fife Thistle	18	3	2	4	22	24	2	0	7	10	40	-32	17
Glenrothes Strollers	18	2	2	5	10	19	1	1	7	13	30	-26	12
Lomond United	18	0	0	9	4	28	0	0	9	5	41	-60	0

Division Two	P	W	D	L	F	A	W	D	L	F	A	GD	Pts
AM Soccer	18	8	1	0	39	9	8	1	0	47	7	70	50
Denbeath	18	7	1	1	40	16	7	2	0	40	12	52	45
Inverkeithing Hillfield Swifts	18	5	1	3	26	13	5	2	2	34	16	31	33
St Monans Swallows	18	5	1	3	20	19	5	0	4	30	21	10	31
Kirkcaldy Rovers	18	3	2	4	24	23	4	1	4	24	24	1	24
United Colleges	18	2	2	5	23	28	5	1	3	24	19	0	24
Freuchie	18	4	1	4	11	20	3	2	4	18	27	-18	24
Kinglassie	18	2	2	5	14	31	2	0	7	14	27	-30	14
FC Bayside	18	2	0	7	17	42	2	2	5	11	19	-33	14
Glenrothes Athletic	18	0	0	9	6	54	0	0	9	13	48	-83	0

CUP COMPETITIONS—FINALS

League Cup Final (May 2)
(at Rosyth)
Pittenweem Rovers v Valleyfield
2-1

Bedlam Division 2 Cup Final (June 6)
(at Star Hearts)
Inverkeithing Hillfield Swifts v Denbeath
Abandoned due to crowd trouble

Tom McIntyre Cup Final (May 30)
At Kelty Hearts
Valleyfield v Kirkcaldy YM
3-1

Wallace Wright Division 1 Cup Final (May 23)
At Rosyth
Kingdom Athletic v Buckhaven Town
4-4 (Kingdom won 7-6 on pens)

Premier Division Cup Final (May 9)
Pittenweem Rovers v St Andrews University
(at Kelty Hearts)
4-1

FIFE SUNDAY AMATEUR FOOTBALL LEAGUE 2013/14

Secretary: Mr Craig Lindsay, 20 Monkstown, Ladybank, Fife KY15 7JX.
(H) 01337 831049 (M) 07789 761342.
Email: craig.lindsay1979@hotmail.co.uk Senior Sunday

Defence4Security PremierLeague   Home Park

Pos	Team	P	W	D	L	F	A	W	D	L	F	A	GD	Pts	
1	Rosyth AFC	16	6	0	2	37	23	7	1	0	28	11	31	40	Rosyth Institute
2	Brucefield AFC -3pts	16	6	0	2	37	10	7	0	1	47	14	60	39	Rex Park, Dunfermline
3	Crystal Barcelona -3pts	16	5	1	2	32	16	5	0	3	17	16	17	31	School View Park, Crossgates
4	Lochore Castle -3pts	16	5	1	2	20	13	4	2	2	24	15	16	30	Crosshill
5	Kinghorn Hearts -4pts	16	4	1	3	24	24	2	1	5	12	27	-15	20	Myres Park, Kinghorn
6	Limekilns AFC -3pts	16	4	0	4	17	24	2	1	5	18	31	-20	19	Limekilns
7	Bogarts AFC -3 pts	16	2	2	4	18	17	3	0	5	27	27	1	17	Ravescraig Park, Kirkcaldy
8	Kittys AFC -3pts	16	2	0	6	20	28	0	2	6	7	25	-26	8	Beveridge Park, Kirkcaldy
9	Crown Inn AFC	16	1	2	5	14	38	0	0	8	13	53	-64	5	KGV Park, Leven
10	Golden Acorn Folded	0	0	0	0	0	0	0	0	0	0	0	0	0	Warout Playing Fields, Glenrothes

Defence4Security 2ndDivision

Pos	Team	P	W	D	L	F	A	W	D	L	F	A	GD	Pts	
1	Minto Lounge	17	5	3	0	31	11	7	2	0	18	6	32	41	Moore Park, Lochgelly
2	CISWO AFC	18	6	2	1	28	11	3	4	2	16	14	19	33	Dovecot Park, Glenrothes
3	Kingdom United	18	3	1	5	21	18	6	1	2	24	14	13	29	Randolph Park, Kirkcaldy
4	Sky AFC	18	5	1	3	19	17	2	2	5	13	25	-10	24	Dalgety Bay Sports Centre
5	Society AFC	16	5	0	4	25	17	1	4	2	14	15	7	22	Randolph Park, Kirkcaldy
6	Coadys AFC	17	2	6	1	24	23	3	1	4	12	21	-8	22	St Leonards, Dunfermline
7	FC Brig	18	3	3	3	16	15	2	2	5	13	16	-2	20	KGV Park, Leven
8	Bar Toro AFC	18	2	1	6	10	19	4	1	4	17	30	-22	20	Randolph Park, Kirkcaldy
9	Dunfermline United	17	3	2	3	18	13	1	2	6	21	40	-14	16	Pitreavie Park, Dunfermlime
10	Torleys	17	2	2	4	18	21	1	2	6	17	29	-15	13	Moore Park, Lochgelly

Defence4Security 3rd Division

Pos	Team	P	W	D	L	F	A	W	D	L	F	A	GD	Pts	
1	Bayview AFC	20	10	0	0	56	7	10	0	0	44	7	86	60	Savoy Park, Leven
2	Lauders AFC -3 points	20	8	0	2	66	19	9	0	1	44	16	75	48	Townhill Park, Dunfermline
3	Styx AFC	20	8	0	2	40	11	5	2	3	23	21	31	41	Beveridge Park, Kirkcaldy
4	Jeffrey United AFC	20	6	0	4	34	24	6	0	4	20	18	12	36	Quarry Park, Leslie
5	Kennoway AFC	20	4	0	6	19	20	5	1	4	18	21	-4	28	KGV Park, Leven
6	Tams Bar	20	6	1	3	40	19	2	2	6	25	37	9	27	Muiredge, Buckhaven
7	Abbey AFC	20	3	1	6	34	37	3	1	6	23	57	-37	20	Beveridge Park, Kirkcaldy
8	Smeaton Boys Club	20	2	1	7	20	39	4	0	6	22	47	-44	19	Beveridge Park, Kirkcaldy
9	Athletico Dunfermline	20	4	1	5	19	29	2	0	8	13	56	-53	19	Duloch Park, Dunfermline
10	Novar Rovers	20	3	1	6	24	35	2	0	8	23	37	-25	16	Myres Park, Kinghorn
11	Legion Rovers	20	1	1	8	13	34	1	0	9	19	48	-50	7	Warout Playing Fields, Glenrothes

CUP COMPETITIONS—FINALS

J S Anderson Cup (may 19, Warout Stadium)
Railway Tavern v Dunfermline Thistle

League Cup (May 18, Warout Stadium)
Society v Lochore Castle   4-1

Fife Cup (May 25, Warout Stadium)
Rosyth v Kingdom United   3-2

FORFAR AND DISTRICT SUNDAY A.F.L. 2013/14

Secretary: Mr M. Nicoll, 6 Court Hillock, Kirriemuir DD8 4JZ
(H) 01575 575849 (B) 01307 466161 Email: mnickkirrie@btinternet.com
Senior Sunday. Morning

http://www.forfaranddistrictafa.co.uk

Latest Available Table

	P	W	D	L	F	A	GD	Pts
FC Porty	16	12	4	0	72	14	58	40
Finavon AFC	17	13	1	3	72	27	45	40
AFC Plough	17	11	3	3	57	34	23	36
Strathmore	17	11	2	4	84	30	54	35
Carnoustie All Stars	18	8	2	8	57	52	5	26
Westport Wanderers	16	7	0	9	51	66	-15	21
Millgate	17	6	2	9	35	48	-13	20
Kirrie Thistle Social Club	18	4	1	13	42	78	-36	13
Osnaburg	18	3	3	12	29	68	-39	12
Cliffburn Bandys	18	2	0	16	20	102	-82	6

FADAFA League Champions

2007/8	Forfar West End SC
2008/9	Strathmore
2009/10	Strathmore
2010/11	Finavon AFC
2011/2	Letham Hotel
2012/3	Finavon AFC
2013/4	FC Porty

GLASGOW & DISTRICT SATURDAY MORNING A.F.L. 2013/14

Secretary: Mr G. A. Fergusson, 12 Keystone Quadrant, Milngavie, Glasgow G62 6LA. (H) 0141 956 7371 (B) 0141 942 5855. Senior Saturday.

http://www.leaguewebsite.co.uk/gdsml

PREMIER DIVISION	P	W	D	L	F	A	GD	Pts
Invac	18	13	1	4	62	31	31	40
Red Star	18	11	3	4	49	37	12	36
Renfrew Town	18	9	3	6	47	32	15	30
Parklife	18	7	6	5	35	29	6	27
Ashfield AFC	18	8	2	8	45	40	5	26
Strathclyde University	18	7	4	7	32	31	1	25
Glasgow Islay	18	6	2	10	39	53	-14	20
Pursuers	18	4	6	8	51	69	-18	18
AC Milanda	18	6	0	12	42	65	-23	18
Blantyre AFC	18	5	1	12	35	50	-15	16

DIVISION ONE	P	W	D	L	F	A	GD	Pts
AFC Columba	18	12	3	3	53	21	32	39
Glasgow United AFC	18	11	5	2	42	20	22	38
Bellahouston	18	11	2	5	49	43	6	35
Kilpatrick Thistle	18	8	6	4	36	27	9	30
Hamilton Wanderers	18	8	1	9	48	52	-4	25
Crosslands	18	7	3	8	40	44	-4	24
Glasgow Caledonian	18	7	2	9	38	38	0	23
Milngavie BC	18	7	2	9	35	35	0	23
Garnethill Rovers	18	3	5	10	25	50	-25	14
Braehead AFC	18	0	3	15	17	53	-36	3

DIVISION TWO	P	W	D	L	F	A	GD	Pts
Bishopton	20	17	2	1	73	19	54	53
Finnieston Park AFC	20	15	2	3	82	29	53	47
Singer Community FC	20	12	2	6	68	48	20	38
Allander	20	11	1	8	54	53	1	34
Bellgrove Amateurs	20	10	2	8	67	44	23	32
Cambusglen AFC	20	9	4	7	55	50	5	31
Glenavon Thistle	20	8	2	10	52	67	-15	26
Abronhill Intrans	20	6	3	11	36	55	-19	21
FC Partick	20	5	3	12	43	57	-14	18
Cambuslang ROK	19	3	3	13	24	63	-39	12
Deanpark	19	0	2	17	20	89	-69	2

CUP FINALS 2013/14

All played at Kirkintilloch Rob Roy FC

Drummond Cup (April 12)
Renfrew Town v Invac 2-1

McGlinchey Cup (April 26)
Bellahouston v AFC Columba 3-0

John Rae Trophy (April 5)
Bishopton v Bellahouston 4-1

GDSML Cup (May 10 2014)
Invac v Kilpatrick Thistle 4-3

The Glasgow and District Saturday Morning League was officially founded at Glasgow University in 1968, although a number of the original member teams had previously played in the University Alchemist League, in some cases under different names.

There is some uncertainty about the actual teams, who commenced playing in the inaugural season, however the following clubs are believed to have formed the nucleus: Clydesdale, Sarsfield (Gilmorehill), Sky Blues, Gallardia, Mermaid, Steamboats, Duncanrig (Avondale), Park United, West of Scotland and Murray Classical.

In the early years most of the games were played almost entirely at Bellahouston Park or the Fifty Pitches,

GLASGOW COLLEGES A.F.A. 2013/14

Secretary: Mr R McGinley, 2 Chancellor Street, Partick, Glasgow G11 5RQ. (H) 0141 337 2210 (B) 0141 221 5072.
Email: management@eaglebuilding.biz   Senior Saturday (Mornings)

www.glasgowcollegesfa.co.uk

PREMIER DIVISION	P	W	D	L	F	A	GD	Pts
Jimmy Johnstone Academy	22	17	4	1	100	34	66	55
Saint Davids AFC	22	16	2	4	101	42	59	50
Gryffe Thistle	22	15	2	5	61	41	20	47
Clydeside Athletic	22	13	2	7	62	43	19	41
MSM	22	11	5	6	60	53	7	38
Central AFC	22	9	3	10	66	72	-6	30
Glasgow Islands	22	9	1	12	55	61	-6	28
Clyde Valley Rovers	22	8	2	12	51	70	-19	26
Hampden AFC	22	5	3	14	44	60	-16	18
SEMSA	22	5	2	15	41	81	-40	17
Rosehill United	22	4	2	16	43	87	-44	14
Sporto	22	3	4	15	28	68	-40	13

DIVISION ONE	P	W	D	L	F	A	GD	Pts
Maryhill Thistle	18	13	2	3	68	28	40	41
Saint Andrews AFC	18	13	1	4	62	26	36	40
Corinthians	18	11	2	5	50	41	9	35
Glasgow Ansar	18	11	1	6	60	48	12	34
FC Innter	18	9	4	5	73	58	15	31
UCS	18	8	2	8	60	51	9	26
Shawlands Accies	18	4	5	9	39	47	-8	17
Anderston Athletic	18	4	5	9	49	71	-22	17
Southside United	18	4	2	12	42	65	-23	14
Lokomotive Glasgow	18	0	2	16	24	92	-68	2

DIVISION TWO	P	W	D	L	F	A	GD	Pts
Silverburn	16	15	1	0	79	14	65	46
Burnbank AFC	16	11	3	2	54	17	37	36
Olympic Energetik	16	7	1	8	34	38	-4	22
Greater Glasgow AFC	16	7	1	8	30	43	-13	22
Glasgow Medics AFC	16	7	0	9	33	54	-21	21
Lomond Vale	16	5	4	7	34	48	-14	19
Newlands AFC	16	3	6	7	35	39	-4	15
Cambuslang United	16	4	2	10	40	60	-20	14
Ansar YFC	16	2	4	10	29	55	-26	10
JJA Colts	0	0	0	0	0	0	0	0

CUP FINALS 2013/14

CTB Cup (May 24)
At Firhill Complex
MSM v Glasgow Islands   2-2

GCFA Cup Final (May 10)
At Petershill Park
Jimmy Johnstone Academy v
Silverburn   2-3

League Cup Final (May 3)
At Petershill Park
Silverburn v Clydeside Ath   4-0

Jim Harvey Cup (April 26)
At Petershill Park
Jimmy Johnstone Academy v Saint
Andrews   2-1

Challenge Cup Final (April 19)
At Petershill Park
Silverburn v Maryhill Thistle   3-0

The Glasgow Colleges Football Association came into existence in the mid fifties with most of the teams as the name suggests connected with colleges from in and around the Glasgow area.

It included teams from Glasgow and Strathclyde Universities, Stow College, Central College of Commerce, Bell College to name but a few.

The university teams were mostly teams from the hall of residences.

GREATER GLASGOW PREMIER A.F.L.   2013/14

Secretary: Mr G. Butler, 40 Netherplace Road, Newton Mearns, Glasgow G77 6DG (H) & (B) 0141 639 5688 Fax 0141 616 0867 Email: james.butler93@ntlworld.com Senior Saturday.

http://www.greaterglasgow.co.uk

DIVISION ONE

		P	W	D	L	F	A	GD	Pts
1	Bannerman AFC	22	19	2	1	82	21	61	59
2	Myre Athletic FC	22	15	3	4	85	36	49	48
3	Dynamo East Kilbride AFC	22	12	4	6	77	49	28	40
4	Kelvin AFC	22	11	3	8	43	38	5	36
5	St. Patrick's FP AFC	22	8	4	10	42	42	0	28
6	Rannoch 'A' AFC	22	9	1	12	57	64	-7	28
7	Partick West AFC	22	8	2	12	51	68	-17	26
8	Orchard Parkmount 'A' AFC	22	8	2	12	37	64	-27	26
9	Eddlewood AFC	22	7	4	11	49	59	-10	25
10	Renfrew Thistle AFC	22	7	4	11	36	59	-23	25
11	Third Lanark Athletic Club	22	7	0	15	43	72	-29	21
12	Jordanhill Campus AFC	22	3	7	12	43	73	-30	16

DIVISION TWO

		P	W	D	L	F	A	GD	Pts
1	Erskine AFC	22	16	4	2	58	25	33	52
2	Baillieston Thistle AFC	22	16	1	5	70	40	30	49
3	Glasgow University 'A' AFC	22	14	4	4	71	42	29	46
4	Barrhead YM AFC	22	14	3	5	49	28	21	45
5	Calderglen AFC	22	14	2	6	64	31	33	44
6	Strathclyde University AFC	22	11	2	9	60	39	21	35
7	Craigneuk AFC	22	7	3	12	47	61	-14	24
8	Windlaw AFC	22	6	5	11	45	57	-12	23
9	East Kilbride Rolls Royce AFC	22	5	4	13	45	61	-16	19
10	Kilbowie Thistle AFC	22	6	1	15	37	72	-35	19
11	Dumbarton Academy FP AFC	22	4	2	16	22	77	-55	14
12	Weir Recreation AFC	22	2	3	17	39	74	-35	9

DIVISION THREE

		P	W	D	L	F	A	GD	Pts
1	Broomhouse FC	20	19	1	0	131	8	123	58
2	Kilbarchan Thistle AFC	20	14	2	4	60	26	34	44
3	Robslee AFC	20	11	2	7	50	50	0	35
4	Whiteinch FC	20	10	4	6	56	41	15	34
5	Westerlands AFC	20	9	3	8	54	53	1	30
6	Ashvale Victoria AFC	20	8	1	11	52	67	-15	25
7	Muirend AFC	20	7	3	10	59	63	-4	24
8	John Street AFC	20	7	1	12	51	74	-23	22
9	Harmony Row AFC	20	6	1	13	53	69	-16	19
10	Orchard Parkmount 'B' AFC	20	4	5	11	34	77	-43	17
11	Lennox Amateurs AFC	20	2	3	15	36	108	-72	9

DIVISION FOUR

		P	W	D	L	F	A	GD	Pts
1	Dumbarton Harp AFC	26	19	2	5	112	52	60	59
2	Cambria AFC	26	18	3	5	82	47	35	57
3	East Kilbride Y.M. AFC	26	18	2	6	89	47	42	56
4	Claremont AFC	26	17	2	7	64	45	19	53
5	Vale of Leven FP AFC	26	16	1	9	88	51	37	49
6	Glasgow University 'B' AFC *	26	13	8	5	75	59	16	44
7	St. Mungo's AFC	26	13	2	11	81	63	18	41
8	Hamilton Thistle AFC	26	13	2	11	62	58	4	41
9	Rannoch 'B' AFC	26	9	2	15	52	83	-31	32
10	Busby AFC	26	9	4	13	55	63	-8	31
11	Westerlands Glasgow Graduates AFC	26	8	3	15	37	70	-33	27
12	North Kelvin Utd AFC	26	5	2	19	48	103	-55	17
13	Bridgewell AFC	26	3	2	21	36	122	-86	11
14	Radnor Park AFC	26	2	3	21	33	51	-18	9

CUP FINALS 2013/14

Challenge Cup (June 6)
At Cambuslang Rangers
Broomhouse SC v East Kilbride

League Cup (May 24)
At Vale of Leven FC
Myre Athletic v Vale of Leven FP   5-3

Instituted in 1989, the Greater Glasgow Premier A.F.L., was intended to offer more competitive football to Glasgow Clubs 3rd participating in the Scottish Amateur Football League and playing in the Reserve or Lower Divisions.

The intention was to provide competitive football, with limited travel, and play on good grass pitches.

Initially, invitations were sent out to Clubs with at least three X1's and based in the South side of Glasgow. It was not long however, before other Clubs became aware of the possibility of a new League being formed, and expressed their interest.

In the summer of 1989, twenty Clubs were invited to meet in Rhuallan House, Giffnock, where George Butler had prepared a Draft Constitution, and it was agreed that the idea should be taken forward and proceed to found a new League.

Anniesland College, Cambria, Chryston, Dynamo East Kilbride, East Kilbride YMCA, Eastwood, Giffnock North, Glasgow University, Inchinnan United, Jordanhill College, Kilbarchan Thistle, Muirend, Rolls Royce East Kilbride, Rolls Royce Nerston, St. Mungo F.P., Stamperland, Strathclyde University, Third Lanark, Weir Recreation and Westerlands were the original members, and Clubs were drawn into two Sections of 10 Clubs, with the top 5 Clubs from each Section forming the 1st Division for Season 1990/91, and the remainder forming Division 2.

Club Directory

Club	Ground
Ashvale Victoria AFC	TBC
Baillieston Thistle AFC	Bannerman High School
Bannerman AFC	Lochend Community School.
Barrhead YM AFC	Cowan Park
Bridgewell AFC	St. Ambrose High School
Broomhouse FC	Greenfield 3G
Busby AFC	
Calderglen AFC	Lochwinnoch Public Park
Cambria AFC	Strathclyde University Playing Field.
Claremont AFC	
Craigneuk AFC	Muirhouse Park.
Dumbarton Academy FP AFC	Dumbarton Common.
Dumbarton Harp AFC	Wylie Park
Dynamo East Kilbride AFC	John Wright Sports Centre.
East Kilbride Rolls Royce AFC	Brancumhall.
East Kilbride Y.M. AFC	Kirktonholme Park
Eddlewood AFC	Eddlewood Public Park
Erskine AFC	Erskine
Glasgow University 'A' AFC	
Glasgow University 'B' AFC	
Hamilton Thistle AFC	
Harmony Row AFC	Drumoyne Sports Centre
John Street AFC	Glasgow Green
Jordanhill Campus AFC	Jordanhill Campus
Kelvin AFC	Kirklee Park
Kilbarchan Thistle AFC	Thomas Shanks Park
Kilbowie Thistle AFC	Blairdardie.
Lennox Amateurs AFC	Thorn Park.
Muirend AFC	Bogton Playing Fields
Myre Athletic FC	Howtshaws Park
North Kelvin Utd AFC	Netherton Park
Orchard Parkmount 'A' AFC	Bogton Playing Fields
Orchard Parkmount 'B' AFC	Bogton Playing Fields
Partick West AFC	Garscadden
Radnor Park AFC	Colquhoun Park, Bearsden
Rannoch 'A' AFC	King George V Bearsden
Rannoch 'B' AFC	King George V Bearsden
Renfrew Thistle AFC	King George V Playing Fields
Robslee AFC	Huntly Park
St. Mungo's AFC	Loretto Playing Fields
St. Patrick's FP AFC	Dumbarton Common
Strathclyde University AFC	Strathclyde University Playing Fields
Third Lanark Athletic Club	Peter Brownlee Pavilion
Vale of Leven FP AFC	
Weir Recreation AFC	Albert Park
Westerlands AFC	Greenfield Football Centre
Westerlands Glasgow Graduates AFC	Glasgow Green
Whiteinch FC	
Windlaw AFC	Barlia Sports Complex

INVERNESS A.F.A. 2013/14

93 Lawers Way, Inverness, IV3 8NX
Contact: Alan McDonald
E Mail ajmacdonald@tycoint.com
Tel 07598291522   Summer League
https://www.facebook.com/pages/Inverness-Football-Unofficial-Coverage

League Tables, Mid June 2014

PREMIER DIVISION	Pld	W	D	L	F	A	Diff	Pts
1 Ardersier	10	8	0	2	35	14	22	24
2 KDM	10	7	0	3	34	13	21	21
3 Merkinch	10	6	1	3	39	16	23	19
4 Muir of Ord United	10	5	2	3	29	22	7	17
5 Phoenix	10	4	2	4	27	37	-10	14
6 Gellions Loch Ness	10	6	1	3	39	28	11	10
7 Police	10	3	1	6	17	21	-4	10
8 Korrie	10	3	1	6	25	53	-28	10
9 The Exchange	10	2	1	7	18	43	-26	7
10 Tomatin	10	1	1	8	26	33	-7	4

DIVISION ONE	Pld	W	D	L	F	A	Diff	Pts
1 Hilton	11	10	1	0	45	14	31	31
2 Curry Hoose	11	8	0	3	45	25	20	24
3 Jewson	11	6	0	5	38	31	7	18
4 Hill Rovers	11	5	2	4	27	22	5	17
5 Inverness Central	11	5	2	4	26	29	-3	17
6 Culbokie	11	5	0	6	35	27	8	15
7 Heathmount (Keg)	10	4	2	4	30	28	2	14
8 Culloden Moor Inn	11	4	0	7	28	35	-7	12
9 Cairngorm	11	1	2	8	13	42	-29	5
10 Earthquakes	10	1	1	8	22	56	-34	4

305

KINGDOM CALEDONIAN A.F.A. 2013/14

Secretary: Mr J M Mitchell, 2 Newton Place, Rosyth, Dunfermline, Fife KY11 2LX.
(H) 01383 414339 (M) 07889 419328
Email: jjlpsmitch@aol.com   Senior Saturday

http://www.leaguewebsite.co.uk/kingdomcaledonianafa

LATEST AVAILABLE TABLE

	P	W	D	L	F	A	GD	Pts	
Leven United	24	16	4	4	75	30	45	54	King George V Park, Leven
Bowhill Rovers	22	16	4	2	78	23	55	52	Wallsgfreen Park, Bowhill
Rosyth Civil Service	23	17	1	5	75	30	45	52	Civil Service Sports Ground, Rosyth
Lumphinnans Utd	24	14	5	5	52	33	19	47	Ochilview Park, Gagarin Way, Lumphinnans
Greig Park Rangers	24	13	6	5	56	42	14	45	Greig Park, Windygates
Cupar Hearts	24	10	6	8	52	53	-1	36	Duffus Park, Cupar
Benarty	24	10	6	8	57	44	13	35	Dallas Doyle Park, Ballingry
Eastvale	23	10	2	11	48	45	3	32	Greig Park, Windygates
Kettle United	24	7	4	13	48	63	-15	25	Kettle Park, Kingskettle
Strathmiglo Utd	24	6	5	13	54	61	-7	23	King George V Park, Strathmiglo
Kinross	24	6	5	13	46	68	-22	23	The Myre, Kinross
Balgonie Scotia 1896	24	3	2	19	27	66	-39	11	King George V Park, Coaltown of Balgonie
Glenrothes	24	0	2	22	15	125	-110	2	
Blairhall	0	0	0	0	0	0	0	0	Village Park, Blairhall

CUP FINALS

Scottish Brewers Cup (July 5 at Star)
Leven United v Bowhill / Rosyth CS

Fence N Deck (Caledonian) Cup Final (June 28, at Star)
Bowhill Rovers v Lumphinnans United

Kingdom Cup Final (July 2, at Benarty)
Bowhill Rovers v Kinross

The Kingdom Caledonian FA was formed in 1984. At that time Amateur football in Fife was divided into two Associations—the Kirkcaldy and District AFA (West Fife) and the East Fife Amateur FA. The most ambitious sides from each, especially those with decent facilities, formed their own Association. Since then the Kirkcaldy and East Fife Associations have merged to form the Fife AFA. There have been rumours of a proposed merger between the KCAFA and FAFA over recent years but nothing has come of them.

LEWIS AND HARRIS A.F.A.

Secretary: Allan Macleod   3 Cross, Ness   (H) 810 660 (W) 704046
(M) 07884 242670

Senior Sat/Sun. Summer

http://www.lhfa.org.uk/

The Summer League played on Lewis and Harris is highly competitive. The latest available table for 2014 read:

	Pl	W	D	L	Gf	Ga	Gd	Pts
Westside	8	6	2	0	34	11	23	20
Lochs	8	5	2	1	15	8	7	17
Ness	7	5	0	2	23	10	13	15
Carloway	7	4	2	1	23	5	18	14
Athletic	8	4	0	4	26	17	9	12
Point	8	4	0	4	12	13	-1	12
Back	8	3	0	5	11	23	-12	9
United	8	1	0	7	8	29	-21	3
Harris	8	0	0	8	6	42	-36	0

LEWIS AND HARRIS LEAGUE HONOURS

Year	Champions	Runners-up	Third place
1980	Ness	Point	Stornoway Rovers
1981	Point	Ness	Stornoway Athletic
1982	Ness	Stornoway Athletic	Tolsta
1983	Harris	Point	Ness
1984	Ness	Back	Stornoway Athletic
1985	Ness	Point	Stornoway Athletic
1986	Ness	Point	Stornoway Athletic
1987	Ness	Stornoway Athletic	Lochs
1988	Stornoway Athletic	Ness	Lochs
1989	Ness	Lochs	Stornoway Athletic
1990	Ness	Stornoway Athletic	Stornoway Rovers
1991	Ness	Stornoway Athletic	Lochs
1992	Ness	Point	Stornoway Athletic
1993	Point	Ness	Harris
1994	Ness	Back	Point
1995	Lochs	Back	Ness
1996	Point	Ness	Harris
1997	Point	Stornoway Athletic	Harris
1998	Point	Stornoway Athletic	Harris
1999	Ness	Point	Harris
2000	Back	Harris	Point
2001	Harris	Ness	Lochs
2002	Point	Harris	Back
2003	Lochs	Back	Point
2004	Point	Back	Lochs
2005	Lochs	Stornoway Athletic	Back
2006	Stornoway Athletic	Lochs	Point
2007	Lochs	Back	Stornoway Athletic
2008	Lochs	Back	Carloway
2009	Lochs	Back	Carloway
2010	Lochs	Back	West Side
2011	Back	Carloway	West Side
2012	Stornoway Athletic	Back	Lochs
2013	Carloway	Stornoway Athletic	West Side

CUP COMPETITIONS 2014

Acres Boys Club Cup
Final
May 9, at Garrabost
Westside v Carloway, 5-0

Co-op Cup Final
August 23

Jock Stein Cup
Final
July 25

Eilean an Fhraoich Cup
Final
August 8

Moldova Lewis Cup
Final
September 6

Island clubs also participate in the prestigious Highland Amateur Cup.

There is also at least one Lewis and Harris Select match each year. In 2014 this will be against Orkney. Various Scottish League clubs have travelled to Stornoway's Goathill Park to provide opposition for the League Select in the past - notably Dundee, Dunfermline, Hibernian, Morton and Aberdeen.

LOTHIAN AND EDINBURGH A.F.A. 2013/14

Secretary: Mr D. J. Ramage, 13 Currievale Drive, Currie, Midlothian EH14 5RN.
(H) 0131 538 3222 (M) 07906 817706. Email: djramage@blueyonder.co.uk
Senior Sat/Sun.
www.leafa.co.uk

SATURDAY SECTION

Premier Division 1	P	W	D	L	Pts
Heriot Vale	20	15	3	2	48
ESV	20	14	3	3	45
Tollcross Th	20	11	5	4	38
Fernieside	20	8	6	6	30
Edinburgh Rose	20	7	7	6	28
East Linton	20	7	6	7	27
Musselburgh Ams	20	7	5	8	26
New'hall Leith Vics	20	6	7	7	25
Sandys	20	5	6	9	21
The Spartans	20	5	1	14	16
Loanhead MW	20	0	1	19	1

Premier Division 2	P	W	D	L	Pts
Lochend	22	12	7	3	43
Cramond FC	22	11	5	6	38
Mayfield & Easthouses	22	12	1	9	37
Linlithgow Th	22	10	4	8	34
Penicuik Utd	22	10	2	10	32
Edin University	22	9	3	10	30
Danderhall MW	22	9	3	10	30
Bathgate Th	22	8	4	10	28
Whitburn Bluebell	22	9	4	9	28 * 3 Pts Deducted
Uphall Station	22	7	6	9	27
Barca-Milton 97	22	8	1	13	25
East Calder Utd	22	5	4	13	19

Lothian West	P	W	D	L	Pts
South Gyle AFC	20	15	1	4	46
North Merchiston Vale	20	12	1	7	37
Dunalba FC	20	10	3	7	33
Lauriston Th	20	10	2	8	32
North Edinburgh Wdrs	20	9	3	8	30
Victoria Loco	20	9	3	8	30
Edinburgh Utd Alba	20	8	2	10	26
Blackridge Vale of Craig	20	7	4	9	25
Links Utd	20	6	4	10	22
Seaforth Highlanders	20	5	4	11	19
Heriot Watt	20	5	1	14	16

Lothian East	P	W	D	L	Pts
Newtongrange Star A	18	15	2	1	47
Inverleith FC	18	15	1	2	46
Tynecastle FC	18	14	2	2	44
Haddington Ath	18	9	2	7	29
Musselburgh Windsor	18	7	2	9	23
Pathhead	18	7	0	11	21
Edin Southern	18	5	1	12	16
Salters Ath	18	4	2	12	14
Scottish Widows	18	2	1	15	7
Lothian Star	18	5	1	12	4 * 12 Pts Deducted

Edinburgh West	P	W	D	L	Pts
Shotts Victoria	15	14	0	1	42
Forth Community Ams	16	11	2	3	35
Polbeth Utd	16	11	1	4	28 * 6 Pts Deducted
Armadale Th	16	8	1	7	25
Balerno Ath	16	5	4	7	19
Queensferry Ath	15	6	0	9	18
Sporting Livi	16	5	0	11	15
West Lothian	16	4	2	10	14
Ratho Ath	16	1	0	15	3

Edinburgh East	P	W	D	L	Pts
Pencaitland FC	20	18	1	1	55
Easthouses FC	20	15	3	2	48
North Berwick	20	14	1	5	43
Clermiston Star	20	12	1	7	37
Dunedin Ath	20	9	1	10	28
Edin Uni Reserves	20	8	1	11	25
Edinburgh Academicals	20	6	5	9	23
Musselburgh Utd	20	6	2	12	20
St Bernards	20	6	3	11	18 * 3 Pts Deducted
Dunbar Ath	20	2	2	16	8
Whitson Star	20	3	2	15	8 * 3 Pts Deducted

Edinburgh Central	P	W	D	L	Pts
Redhall Star	16	15	0	1	45
Hermiston Vale	16	14	1	1	43
LBG Strollers	16	8	2	6	26
C S Strollers	16	8	1	7	25
Redpath Albion	16	7	1	8	22
Mashucubia FC	16	7	0	9	21
Standard Life	16	4	1	11	13
Sporting Icapb	16	3	0	13	9
Melville Rovers	16	2	2	12	8

307

SUNDAY MORNING	P	W	D	L	Pts	
Broxburn AFC	18	14	1	3	43	
Partizan FC	18	12	1	5	37	
Stables FC	18	12	0	6	36	
Roseburn Th	18	11	2	5	35	
Craigshill Th	18	11	1	6	34	
Fountainbridge FC	18	8	3	7	27	
Gotham City	18	7	2	9	23	
Burgh Vale	18	6	3	9	21	
Hunterfield Th	18	1	1	16	4	
Meadowbank Wed	18	1	0	17	3	

SUNDAY AFTERNOON						
Premier Division 1	P	W	D	L	Pts	
Roslin da Vinci	16	12	2	2	38	
Pavilion FC	16	9	1	6	28	
Royal Penicuik	16	8	1	7	25	
Bilston Utd	16	8	0	8	24	
The Standard	16	6	3	7	21	
Bonnyrigg Sports Bar	16	6	3	7	21	
St Bernards	16	6	2	8	20	
Dunalba FC	16	5	2	9	17	
Alba Th	16	2	4	10	9	* 1 Pts Deducted

Premier Division 2	P	W	D	L	Pts
Salters Ath	18	16	2	0	50
Waverley Hotel	18	13	3	2	42
Edin Caledonian	18	9	5	4	32
Falcon Th	18	8	5	5	29
Gilmerton FC	18	9	2	7	29
Bathgate Th	18	7	3	8	24
Dalkeith Ath	18	5	2	11	17
Edinburgh City	18	5	1	12	16
The Green Tree	18	4	3	11	15
Dilligaf FC	18	0	2	16	2

Division 1	P	W	D	L	Pts	
Salvesen FC	14	14	0	0	42	
Rosewell Miners	14	8	3	3	27	
The Spartans	14	9	1	4	25	* 3 Pts Deducted
Tranent Ath	14	6	3	5	21	
Victoria Park Rangers	14	4	3	7	15	
Alnwickhill FC	14	4	2	8	14	
Armadale Rose	14	3	2	9	11	
Pumpherston Th	14	1	0	13	3	

CUP FINALS SUNDAY SECTION

Presidents Cup
Salvesen v Waverley Hotel   3-0

Edinburgh Cup
The Spartans v Bilston United   1-0

FA League Cup
Partizan v Broxburn   3-1

Premier Div League Cup
Pavilion v Bilston United   2-1

Colin Campbell Cup
Bathgate Thistle v Falcon Thistle
3-2

IME Cup
The Spartans v Salvesen   1-1
(Spartans won on penalties)

CUP FINALS 2013/14

SATURDAY SECTION

Logan Cup (All clubs)
Heriot Vale v Edinburgh Rose   3-1

Miller Cup (Consolation Cup)
Whitburn Bluebell v Inverleith   9-1

Challenge Cup (Premier 1 and 2)
Heriot Vale v Newcraighall LV   1-0

Ian McDonald Cup (Lothian E and W)
Links United v Tynecastle   3-1aet

Anderson Cup (Edinburgh W,C & E)
Shotts Victoria v Pencaitland   2-0

Centenary Cup (All Clubs)
Musselburgh Ams v Shotts Vics 0-2

Blaikie Cup (Prem 1)
Heriot Vale v Fernieside   3-2

Victory Cup (Lothian W)
South Gyle v Victoria Loco   2-1

Cairns Cup (Prem 2)
Lochend v East Calder   3-1

Holyrood Cup (Lothian E)
Tynecastle v Newtongrange Star A

Dunedin Cup (Edinburgh W)
Shotts Vics v Forth Community   4-0

Robertson Cup (Edinburgh E)
Pencaitland v Clermiston Star   4-0

Stead & Simpson Cup (Edinburgh C)
Redhall Star v CSS   2-0AET

Ronnie Travers Cup
Newtongrange Star v Redpath Albion
7-4

MIDLANDS A.F.A. 2013/14

Secretary: Mr A. Martin, 3 Godfrey Street, Barnhill, Dundee DD5 2QZ.
(H) 01382 477903. email: ally.martin@blueyonder.co.uk Senior Saturday.

www.mafa.pitchero.com

CUP FINALS 2013/14

Bremner Cup (June 4 at Forfar Athletic)
Riverside Athletic v Lowson United
2-0

Gray Trophy (May 31)
Lowson United v Dundee City   1-0

Ferrari's Shield (May 30)
St James v Arbroath HSFP   6-3

Wallace Trophy (May 29 at Midmill)
Monifieth Tayside v Portcullis   2-0

Buckman Mackie Trophy (May 28)
Riverside Athletic v Bank Street Athletic
6-4

Mel Ross Trophy (May 21)
Arbroath HSFP A v NCR   2-2aet, 4-3p

Carne Trophy (May 14)
Menzieshill v Douglas Athletic   5-1

Alliance Cup (May 6)
St James v Arbroath CSC   2-1

Lunan Trophy (Apr 23)
Ayside Fire Brigade v NCR   2-1

Marquee Trophy (Mar 29)
St James v Riverside Ath   3-1

Tay Valley Shield (1) (Nov 2)
Merpro v Barnhill
4-1

Tay Valley Shield (2) (Sep 26)
Menzieshill Rovers v Menzieshill   2-1

PREMIER DIVISION	P	W	D	L	F	A	GD	PTS	ADJ
1 Riverside Athletic	21	17	4	1	78	24	54	55	
2 St.James	22	17	3	2	85	33	52	54	
3 Arbroath CSC	22	15	2	5	46	31	15	47	
4 Bank Street Athletic	22	13	4	5	47	36	11	43	
5 Broughty Utd	22	10	3	9	41	45	-4	33	
6 Arbroath HSFP	22	7	5	10	48	50	-2	26	
7 NCR	22	7	4	11	38	42	-4	25	
8 Tayside Fire Brigade	22	7	3	12	35	62	-27	24	
9 Carnoustie YM	22	6	5	11	33	49	-16	23	
10 Invergowrie	22	4	8	10	30	49	-19	20	
11 D&A College	22	4	2	16	24	62	-38	14	
12 SS Peter And Paul	22	3	1	18	44	66	-22	10	

DIVISION ONE									
1 Lowson Utd	18	14	1	3	59	31	28	43	
2 Barnhill	18	11	4	3	57	28	29	37	
3 Merpro	18	12	0	6	38	19	19	36	
4 Newport	18	10	2	6	68	53	15	32	
5 Dundee City	18	7	4	7	42	41	1	25	
6 Monifieth Tayside	18	8	1	9	40	41	-1	25	
7 Logie Harp	18	7	4	7	40	46	-6	25	
8 FC Claypotts	18	4	3	11	27	49	-22	15	
9 Portcullis AFC	18	4	3	11	27	51	-24	15	
10 Morgan Academy FP	18	1	2	15	33	72	-39	5	
11 Dundee East	0	0	0	0	0	0	0	0	
12 FC Polonia Dundee	0	0	0	0	0	0	0	0	

DIVISION TWO									
1 Menzieshill AFC	20	16	1	3	121	23	98	49	
2 Douglas Athletic	20	16	1	3	102	34	68	49	
3 Menzieshill Rovers	20	16	1	3	88	24	64	49	
4 Dundee University	19	13	2	4	60	29	31	41	
5 Carnoustie Ath	20	11	2	7	55	42	13	35	
6 Kelso AFC	20	9	2	9	47	51	-4	29	
7 Kirriemuir Youth AFC	20	6	4	10	49	62	-13	22	
8 Harris Academy FP	19	4	2	13	32	48	-16	14	
9 Wellbank AFC	20	4	1	15	22	67	-45	13	
10 Edzell Ath	20	0	1	19	22	193	-171	1	
11 Michelin Ath	0	0	0	0	0	0	0	0	
12 Arbroath Harp	20	4	3	13	38	63	-25	0	-15

ALLIANCE DIVISION									
1 Logie Harp	23	14	6	3	58	35	23	48	
2 Invergowrie	23	14	5	4	75	43	32	47	
3 Carnoustie YM	23	15	0	8	86	65	21	45	
4 Broughty Utd	23	13	4	6	77	43	34	43	
5 Tayside Fire Brigade	24	13	3	8	76	45	31	42	
6 Arbroath HSFP A	22	13	3	6	67	36	31	42	
7 NCR	23	13	3	7	83	57	26	42	
8 Morgan Academy FP	24	12	2	10	70	65	5	38	
9 Barnhill	23	11	2	10	67	73	-6	35	
10 Portcullis AFC	24	10	3	11	69	57	12	33	
11 St.James	21	10	3	8	76	67	9	33	
12 Arbroath CSC	23	9	3	11	56	45	11	30	
13 D&A College	22	9	3	10	51	66	-15	30	
14 Arbroath HSFP B	24	5	6	13	46	85	-39	21	
15 Monifieth Tayside	24	5	1	18	36	96	-60	16	
16 Arbroath Harp	24	3	3	18	23	81	-58	12	
17 Kelso	24	2	2	20	37	94	-57	8	

HOME GROUNDS 2013/14

Arbroath CSC	Hercules Den, Arbroath	P
Arbroath Harp	McDonald Park, Arbroath	2
Arbroath HSFP	Friockheim Park, Friockheim	P
Bank Street Athletic	Fintry Park 1, Dundee	P
Barnhill	Monifieth HS, Monifieth	1
Broughty United	Dawson Park, West Ferry	P
Carnoustie Athletic	Carlogie Park, Carnoustie	2
Carnoustie YM	Carlogie Park, Carnoustie	P
D&A College	Gardyne Road, Broughty Ferry	P
Douglas Athletic	Monymusk, Huntly Road, Dundee	2
Dundee City	St Pauls School, Dundee	1
Dundee East	St Saviours HS, Dundee	1
Dundee University	University Grounds, Riverside Drive	2
Edzell Athletic	Brechin Park, Brechin	2
FC Claypotts	Claypotts Park, Dundee	1
FC Polonia Dundee	Drumgeith Park 4, Dundee	1
Harris Academy FP	Eton Street, Dundee	2
Invergowrie	Memorial Park, Invergowrie	P
Kelso AFC	University Grounds, Riverside Drive	2
Kirriemuir Youth	Martin Park, Kirriemuir	2
Logie Harp	Fairmuir Pitch 2, Dundee	1
Lowson United	Lochside Park, Forfar	1
Menzieshill AFC	Menzieshill HS, Dundee	2
Menzieshill Rovers	DISC 3G, Dundee	2
Merpro	Broomfield Park, Montrose	1
Michelin Athletic	Michelin Sports Ground, Dundee	2
Monifieth Tayside	Riverview Park, Monifieth	1
Morgan Academy FP	Monymusk, Huntly Road, Dundee	1
NCR	Caird Park Stadium, Dundee	P
Newport	Waterstone Crook, Newport on Tay	1
Portcullis	Victoria Park, Arbroath	1
Riverside Athletic	Finlathen Park 1, Dundee	P
SS Peter and Paul	Fairmuir Pitch 5, Dundee	P
St James	Fairfield Park, Dundee	P
Tayside Fire Brigade	Downfield Pitch 3, Dundee	P
Wellbank	Wellbank Park, Kellas Road, Wellbank	2

NORTH AYRSHIRE SUNDAY A.F.A. 2013/14

Secretary: Sean McMillan, 23 Links Road, Saltcoats, Ayrshire, KA21 6BQ.
E-mail sean_mcmillan@hotmail.co.uk   Tel 07837 983013

www.northayrshirefootball.weebly.com/

Latest available table:

Pos	Team	P	W	D	L	F	A	GD	PTS
1	Geet	12	11	0	1	113	14	99	33
2	Dalry Turf	11	10	0	1	78	15	63	30
3	Revels	12	8	2	2	87	22	65	26
4	Kilwinning Rangers	12	6	1	5	36	42	-6	19
5	Charlies bar	9	5	0	5	32	40	-8	15
6	Crown United	11	4	2	5	66	45	21	14
7	Bobbys Bar	9	3	2	4	49	40	9	11
8	Sullivans	6	1	2	3	21	28	-7	5
9	Jacks United	13	1	1	11	29	129	-100	4
10	Crown Inn	12	1	0	11	12	137	-125	3

NORTH WEST SUTHERLAND A.F.A.

Secretary: Mr H. Morrison, Orcadia, Lerin, Durness, By Lairg,
Sutherland IV27 4QB. (H) 01971 511336 (M) 07884 113779.
Senior Saturday Summer.
Email: info@smoocavehotel.co.uk

League Table at start of June 2014

NWSAFA 2014								
POSITION	TEAM	PLAYED	WIN	DRAW	LOSS	FOR	AGAINST	GD	POINTS
1	EMBO	4	3	1	0	18	4	14	10
2	BRORA	3	3	0	0	21	3	18	9
3	GOLSPIE	2	2	0	0	5	3	2	6
4	LAIRG	2	1	0	1	12	6	6	3
5	HELMSDALE	3	1	0	2	9	5	4	3
6	LOCHINVER	1	1	0	0	6	2	4	3
7	MELVICH	2	1	0	1	6	11	-5	3
8	TONGUE	4	0	1	3	7	15	-8	1
9	DURNESS	5	0	0	5	3	38	-35	0

NORTH & SOUTH LANARKSHIRE A.F.A. 2013/14

Mr Craig C Denholm, 31 Cairnwood Drive, Cairnhill, Airdrie, ML6 9HR
.
Email: ccd.lafa1938@yahoo.co.uk   Tel 07919161077
Saturday League

http://www.nslafa-est2008.com/

Latest available tables

PREMIER DIVISION	P	W	D	L	F	A	GD	PTS
Blantyre Soccer Academy	15	10	4	1	47	18	29	34
Overtown Thistle	14	10	3	1	60	17	43	33
Blantyre Rangers	16	10	1	4	47	37	10	31
Woodhall Thistle	16	8	4	4	32	30	2	28
Carluke Hearts	15	6	3	6	44	42	2	21
Donaldson	15	5	3	7	41	44	-3	18
Holytown Colts Youth	16	3	3	9	33	41	-8	12
Motherwell Bridgeworks	16	3	2	11	27	67	-40	11
Mount Vernon Juniors	15	0	3	12	26	61	-35	3
Carnwath	0	0	0	0	0	0	0	0

CUP FINALS 2013/14

League Cup Final (May 16)
At Excelsior Stadium

John Roan Cup Final (May 23)
At Excelsior Stadium

Lanarkshire Cup Final (May 30)
At Excelsior Stadium

DIVISION ONE	P	W	D	L	F	A	GD	PTS
Mill United	18	14	2	2	65	23	42	44
Springhill	15	10	3	2	56	25	31	33
Mossend	16	9	2	4	48	26	12	29
Motgherwell Miners	18	9	2	7	53	44	9	29
Electric Bar	17	8	4	4	44	29	15	28
Hillside	16	6	5	5	34	38	-4	23
FC Dal Riata	18	6	1	11	43	52	-9	19
Blantyre RGM	16	6	0	9	35	55	-20	15
Calderwood Bluestar	15	2	1	12	26	60	-34	7
Bothwell United	17	0	2	14	23	65	-42	2

ORKNEY A.F.A.

Secretary: Mrs Inga Foubister, Garth, Deerness, Orkney KW17 2QQ.
(H) 01856 741278 (B) 01856 872311. Summer Saturday
Email: Inga.foubister@orkney.gov.uk

2013 Final Tables

DIVISION A	P	W	D	L	F	A	GD	PTS
1 Rovers	18	15	3	0	87	18	69	48
2 Thorfinn	18	13	2	3	58	15	43	41
3 Dounby	18	12	2	4	33	19	14	38
4 Hotspurs	18	11	2	5	58	37	21	35
5 Stromness	18	11	1	6	42	22	20	34
6 Rendall	18	10	0	8	55	23	32	30
7 Holm	18	4	2	12	29	76	-47	14
8 Kirkwall United	18	4	1	13	39	54	-15	13
9 St Andrews	18	3	0	15	18	82	-64	9
10 Burray	18	0	1	17	15	88	-73	1

DIVISION B	P	W	D	L	F	A	GD	PTS
1 Deerness	12	11	1	0	65	14	51	34
2 South Ronaldsay	12	9	2	1	44	20	24	29
3 Firth	12	5	3	4	37	25	12	18
4 Wanderers	12	5	0	7	29	32	-3	15
5 Harray	12	3	3	6	25	37	-12	12
6 Orphir	12	3	1	8	30	37	-7	10
7 Accies	12	1	0	11	12	77	-65	3

CUP FINALS 2013

Brown Cup (July 22)
West v East
1-0

Archer Shield (July 6)
Annual Challenge
Orkney v Caithness
0-2

Corinthian Cup (July 6)
Annual Challenge
Orkney Juniors v Caithness Juniors
4-3

Green Challenge Cup (June 29)
Annual Challenge)
Orkney v Wick Academy
1-3

Highland Fuels Jolly Cup (August 24)
South Ronaldsay v Firth
5-2

IR Swanney Thomson Cup (July 20)
South Ronaldsay v Orphir
3-1

KC Findlay Craigmyle Cup (Sep 6)
Dounby v Hotspurs
2-1

Lows Thornley Binders Cup (Sep 8)
Sandwick Parish v Firth Parish
4-1

Meridian Salmon Isaac Newlands Shield (May 10)
Rovers v Thorfinn
3-1

Milne Cup (July 26)
Annual Challenge)
Orkney v Shetland
4-1

OAFA Shield (April 19)
Rovers v Thorfinn
3-2

Orcadian Parish Cup (Aug 10)
St Ola Parish v Birsay Parish
4-1

PAISLEY & DISTRICT A.F.A. 2013/14

Secretary: Jackie Loughlin; Tel 07719659444
E-Mail jackiefbs@yahoo.co.uk

Senior Saturday.

Latest tables available:

CUP FINALS 2013/14

Fleming Cup
Gallowhill v Glentyan   5-5AET, 4-1p

CIBA Cup
Elderslie v Paisley Athletic   1-0

DIVISION ONE	P	W	D	L	Pts
Paisley Athletic	17	12	4	1	40
Gallowhill AFC	17	11	1	5	34
Glentyan AFC	17	10	3	4	33
Linwood Thistle	17	9	4	4	28
Glynhill Moorcroft AFC	15	8	3	4	27
Apex AFC	18	7	5	6	26
Glenburn Athletic	18	5	4	9	19
Fordbank Star	16	4	2	10	17
Abercorn AFC	17	3	1	13	10
Tannahill AFC	16	1	1	14	4

McCreadie Cup
Thorn Athletic v Fulbar AFC   3-1

McLean / Lothian Cup
Winners: Paisley Athletic

The first meeting of the League was held on 28th June 1953. The Clubs present were: Anchor Athletic, Barrhead Bourock Y.M.CA., Barrhead Rovers, Camphill F.P., 'D' Squadron Ayshire Yeomanry, JohnstoneBB Ex Members, Johnstone Victoria, Neilston Rovers, Newton Swift North Dene, Paisley Corinthian, Rowanvale Victoria and White's Amateurs.

DIVISION TWO	P	W	D	L	Pts
Dumbarton Wanderers AFC	15	11	1	3	34
Hazelwood AFC	16	10	1	5	31
Elderslie AFC	12	10	0	2	30
Erskine YFC	15	9	1	5	28
Arkelston Athletic	12	8	1	3	25
Abbey Athletic	16	6	0	10	15
Glasgow Deaf Athletic	15	4	2	9	14
Tannahill 'A' AFC	14	2	1	11	7
Linwood Spartans	13	0	1	12	1
Glasgow West AFC	0	0	0	0	0

Ratification of the league and confirmation of the Constitution were proposed by Rowanvale Victoria and seconded by Neilston Rovers. Mr. Hendry of Newton Swifts was proposed by Neilston Rovers for president. This was seconded by Barrhead Bourock.The League Secretary Iain McTweed was not present as he was on his honeymoon.

An entry fee of £1 - 10 - 0 (£1.50) and a 10/- (50p) deposit good faith money. Mr. Thomas Fleming, on behalf of his father Mr. James Fleming, Ex-President of the S.F.A., offered to donate the 'Fleming Trophy' to the Paisley & District Amateur Football League witch is still played for today.

DIVISION THREE	P	W	D	L	Pts
Boswell AFC	21	15	3	3	48
Thorn Athletic AFC	19	13	1	5	40
AFC Fulbar	20	8	4	8	28
FC Argyle	20	8	4	8	28
West End Athletic AFC	21	9	0	12	27
Brucehill United AFC	20	8	1	11	22
Clydesdale United AFC	20	6	2	12	20
Glentyan Thistle 'B' AFC	19	5	1	13	16

All the clubs in the Paisley area played in leagues such as the West of Scotland Amateur Football League or the Scottish Amateur Football league. In the case of both these Leagues there was considerable amount of travel involved. It could be Motherwell, Rothesay, Oban or Greenock The local Y.M.C.A League had been in operation for some years but it was, in the main, restrictive in who could play. The rules of the league lay down that clubs had to play the matches within seven miles of Paisley Cross and within Renfrewshire.

Source: PADAFA Website

PERTHSHIRE AMATEUR F.A. 2013/14

Secretary: Mr. Steve Bonthrone, 7 Stormont Way, Scone, Perth PH2 6SP.
(H) 01738 553189. Email: theperthshireamateur@blueyonder.co.uk

Www.perthshireamateur.webs.com/

Senior Saturday.

Latest available tables:

Division One	P	W	D	L	F	A	GD	PTS
Letham	18	15	3	0	87	21	66	48
Ballinluig	18	12	2	4	33	25	8	38
Balmoral Utd	18	8	6	4	35	29	6	30
Fairfield	18	8	4	6	48	39	9	28
Craigie	18	9	1	8	47	47	0	28
Vale Of Earn	18	8	3	7	36	40	-4	27
St Johns	18	6	1	11	38	42	-4	19
Coupar Angus	18	5	3	10	34	50	-16	18
Rattray	18	4	1	13	34	68	-34	13
Burrelton Rovers	18	2	2	14	27	58	-31	8

Division Two	P	W	D	L	F	A	GD	PTS
Alyth	18	15	3	0	63	14	49	48
Auchterarder Primrose	18	14	4	0	92	20	72	46
Breadalbane	18	12	4	2	51	18	33	40
Jeanfield Swifts	18	10	2	6	51	37	14	32
Wolfhill	18	8	1	9	40	41	-1	25
Strathearn Grove	18	6	2	10	40	53	-13	20
Bridgeton utd	18	6	0	12	41	54	-13	18
Vale Of Atholl	18	5	2	11	36	71	-35	17
Tay Thistle	18	3	3	12	30	64	-34	12
Comrie Rovers	18	0	1	17	18	90	-72	1

Division Three	P	W	D	L	F	A	GD	PTS
Methven	23	21	1	1	102	28	74	64
Perth United	24	19	2	3	106	45	61	59
Bridge Of Earn	24	12	6	6	73	47	26	42
Kinrossie/Caledonian	24	12	4	8	77	60	17	40
Kettins	24	10	5	9	61	67	-6	35
Luncarty	23	6	6	11	62	61	1	24
Pole Team	24	4	6	14	49	80	-31	18
Meigle Vics	24	2	5	17	41	108	-67	11
Portmoak	24	2	3	19	40	115	-75	9

CUP FINALS 2013/14

Birks Cup
Methven v Ballinluig — 2-0

Consolation Cup
Methven v Jeanfield Swifts — 3-2

Ashleigh Cup
Letham United v Balmoral — 4-2

North Perthshire Cup
Breadalbane v Methvedn — 2-1

Perth and District Cup
Letham v Tay Thistle — 4-0

Atholl Cup
Methven v Ballinluig — 4-3

Marshall Cup
Alyth v Balmoral United — 2-1

Perthshire Cup
Alyth v Fairfield — 4-2

Smith League Cup
Letham v Alyth — 3-0

West District Cup
Auchterarder Primrose v Vale of Earn — 6-2

PERTHSHIRE SUNDAY A.F.L. 2013/14

Secretary:: Mr. Scott Murray E-mail: murraytoad@hotmail.com

Tel: 07813451658   Senior Sunday

	P	W	D	L	F	A	GD	PTS
1 The Auld Hoose	20	19	1	0	163	29	134	58
2 The Vic	20	15	0	5	75	52	23	45
3 Inter Perth	20	13	3	4	78	45	33	42
4 Dunbarney Rovers	20	8	6	6	59	55	4	30
5 Christies	20	8	2	10	60	63	-3	26
6 Letham 1995	20	7	2	11	60	92	-32	23
7 Green Room	20	7	1	12	64	85	-21	22
8 Taybank FC	20	5	5	10	53	85	-32	20
9 Saints Club	20	5	4	11	70	97	-27	19
10 Perth College UHI	20	5	2	13	63	71	-8	17
11 Buddies	20	3	4	13	51	122	-71	13
12 Star Bar	0	0	0	0	0	0	0	0

CUP FINALS 2013/14

Consolation Cup
Letham 95 v Dunbarney Rovers
4-2aet

League Cup
Auld Hoose v Inter Perth
7-1

Both finals played at Jeanfield Swifts

PERTHSHIRE OVER 35s A.F.L. 2013/14

Secretary: Lee Swan Phone: 07952 231024

League Table (Mid June)

	P	W	D	L	F	A	GD	PTS
1 Murray Royal	7	5	2	0	33	13	20	17
2 Breadalbane	5	2	3	0	23	14	9	9
3 St Johns	6	2	2	2	22	17	5	8
4 Vale of Earn	7	2	0	5	21	30	-9	6
5 Luncarty Old Boys	6	1	2	3	13	17	-4	5
6 Scone Thistle	5	1	1	3	11	32	-21	4

This is a Summer League with games played mainly on Sundays.

Murray Royal come from Scone, Breadalbane from Aberfeldy, St johns from Perth and Vale of Earn from Crieff.

SCOTTISH AMATEUR FOOTBALL LEAGUE

Secretary: Mr. Sandy Buchan, Flat 9 The Elms, Millholm Road, Glasgow G44 3YQ.
Email: sadlsecretary@btconnect.com Senior Saturday.

PREMIER DIVISION

Team	P	W	D	L	F	A	GD	PTS
1 Oban Saints AFC	18	13	5	0	53	19	34	44
2 Haldane United AFC	18	12	3	3	54	28	26	39
3 St. Josephs FP AFC	18	11	4	3	56	32	24	37
4 Finnart AFC	18	9	3	6	47	37	10	30
5 Busby AFC	18	7	3	8	37	46	-9	24
6 Thorn Athletic AFC	18	6	3	9	28	33	-5	21
7 Castlemilk AFC	18	4	7	7	40	50	-10	19
8 Alba Thistle AFC	18	6	0	12	31	51	-20	18
9 Inverclyde AFC	18	4	4	10	33	44	-11	16
10 Kilbowie Union AFC	18	1	2	15	30	69	-39	5

PREMIER DIVISION 1

Team	P	W	D	L	F	A	GD	PTS
1 Campbeltown Pupils AFC	18	11	3	4	47	27	20	36
2 Kings Park Rangers AFC	18	11	0	7	41	33	8	33
3 Eaglesham AFC	18	10	2	6	41	27	14	32
4 Hillington AFC	18	9	3	6	49	40	9	30
5 Rutherglen AFC	18	8	4	6	38	35	3	28
6 Dunoon AFC	18	7	2	9	29	38	-9	23
7 East Kilbride Rolls Royce AFC	18	6	4	8	32	36	-4	22
8 Shawlands FP AFC	18	6	4	8	42	48	-6	22
9 Centre AFC	18	5	4	9	39	49	-10	19
10 Paisley AFC	18	3	2	13	23	48	-25	11

PREMIER DIVISION 2

Team	P	W	D	L	F	A	GD	PTS
1 East Kilbride FC	18	15	1	2	68	21	47	46 *
2 Goldenhill AFC	18	12	3	3	69	40	29	39
3 Jamestown AFC	18	11	1	6	54	41	13	34
4 Lochgilphead Red Star	18	9	4	5	48	39	9	31 *
5 Easthall Star AFC	18	9	2	7	47	48	-1	29
6 Port Glasgow AFC	18	6	3	9	38	39	-1	21
7 Clydebank AFC	18	6	1	11	26	37	-11	19 *
8 Dunoon Athletic AFC	18	5	2	11	43	60	-17	17 *
9 Port Glasgow United AFC	18	3	4	11	31	66	-35	13 *
10 Glencastle Sparta AFC	18	2	3	13	27	60	-33	9 *

* East Kilbride FC receive 3 points as a result of Glencastle Sparta being debt suspended 8th March 2014
* LRS Unfulfilled fixture v Glencastle 12th April 3 points to LRS
* Clydebank AFC receive 3 points for an unfulfilled fixture v Dunoon Athletic.
* Dunoon Ath debt suspended 26 April points awarded to Easthall Star
* Port Glasgow United receive 3 points as a result of Glencastle Sparta being debt suspended 15th March 2014
* Glencastle Sparta unfulfilled fixture 16th April 3 points to Easthall Star.

CUP FINALS 2013/14

Jimmy Marshall Cup (May 28)
Oban Saints v Inverclyde
2-0
At St Anthonys JFC

Coronation Cup (May 25)
South Camlachie v Ferguslie Star
4-3
At Cambuslang Rangers JFC

Centenary Cup (May 9)
Castlemilk v St Josephs
3-2
At St Anthonys JFC

DIVISION 1A

Team	P	W	D	L	F	A	GD	PTS	
1 Drumchapel Amateurs Colts	20	18	0	2	103	27	76	54	
2 Ferguslie Star AFC	20	17	2	1	112	24	88	53	
3 Eaglesham AFC (B)	20	14	1	5	85	37	48	43	
4 Tarbert AFC	19	10	4	5	68	36	32	34	*
5 Rosehill Star	20	10	1	9	58	59	-1	31	
6 Millerston Thistle AFC	20	8	2	10	55	70	-15	26	
7 Millbeg Villa AFC	20	7	3	10	62	70	-8	24	
8 Inverkip Thistle AFC	20	4	4	12	38	89	-51	16	
9 Shawlands F.P (B)	20	3	5	12	56	97	-41	14	*
10 Bothwell and Uddingston Albion	20	2	7	11	44	67	-23	13	
11 Rossvale AFC	19	0	3	16	21	126	-105	3	

* Tarbert awarded 3pts. Unfulfilled fixture v Millerston 3rd May.
* Shawlands (B) awarded 3pts. Unfulfilled fixture v Bothwell 9th Nov.

DIVISION 1B

Team	P	W	D	L	F	A	GD	PTS	
1 Motherwell Thistle AFC	19	15	2	2	70	24	46	47	
2 South Camlachie YP AFc	20	13	5	2	75	29	46	44	
3 Neilston AFC	20	13	2	5	87	36	51	41	
4 Port Glasgow Old Boys Union AF	20	10	5	5	61	50	11	35	
5 Strathaven Dynamo	20	9	3	8	62	52	10	30	
6 FC Clydebank	20	7	6	7	40	37	3	27	
7 Centre AFC (B)	20	6	5	9	41	63	-22	23	
8 Whitehill FP AFC	20	4	7	9	39	57	-18	19	
9 Carlton YMCA AFC	20	4	2	13	38	60	-22	14	*
10 East Kilbride YMCA AFC	19	6	2	11	35	57	-22	10	[1]
11 Kings Park Rangers (B)	20	1	1	17	28	111	-83	4	

* Carlton v KPR (B) 27th April. Unfulfilled fixture 3pts awarded to Carlton.

[1] Committee Decision

Membership 2013/14

Team	Ground	Div
Alba Thistle	Seedhill Park, Paisley	P
Bothwell & Uddingston Albion	Porterswell Park, Uddingston	D1
Busby AFC	Overlea Playiong Fields, Clarkston	P
Campbeltown Pupils FP	Kintyre Park, Campbeltown	P1
Carlton YMCA	Kibble Complex, Paisley	D2
Castlemilk	Peter Brownlie Park, Cambuslang	P
Centre	Ballerup Playong Fields, East Kilbride	P1
Centre AFC B	Ballerup Playing Fields, East Kilbride	D2
Clydebank FC	Peterson Colquhoun Park, Bearsden	P2
Drumchapel Ams Colts	Glenhead Park, Duntocher	D1
Dunoon	Dunoon Stadium, Dunoon	P1
Dunoon Athletic	Dunoon Stadium, Dunoon	P2
Eaglesham	Burnside Park, Eaglesham	P1
Eaglesham AFC B	Burnside Park, Eaglesham	D1
East Kilbride FC	K-Park, East Kilbride	P2
East Kilbride YM	East Kilbride Stadium	D2
Easthall Star	Stepford Complex, Glasgow	P2
EK Rolls Royce	The Murray, East Kilbride	P1
FC Clydebank	Colquhoun Park, Bearsden	D2
Ferguslie Star	Ferguslie Sports Centre, Paisley	D1
Finnart	Glasgow Green	P
Glencastle Sparta	Crownpoint Stadium, Glasgow	P2
Goldenhill	Clydebank HS, Clydebank	P2
Haldane United	Inler Park, Balloch	P
Hillington	Glasgow Club, Drumoyne, Govan	P1
Inverclyde	Battery Park, Gourock	P
Inverkip Thistle	Battery Park, Gourock	D1
Jamestown	Argyll Park, Alexandria	P2
Kilbowie Union	Knowes Complex, Faifley	P
King's Park Rangers	Glasgow Green	P1
King's Park Rangers B	Stonelaw HS, Rutherglen	D2
Lochgilphead Red Star	Ropework Park, Lochgilphead	P2
Millbeg Villa	Lochend HS, Easterhouse	D1
Millerston Thistle	Hamilton Palace, Hamilton	D1
Motherwell Thistle	Muirhouse Playing Fields, Motherwell	D2
Neilston AFC	Kingston Playing Fields, Neilston	D2
Oban Saints	Mossfield Complex, Oban	P
Paisley AFC	Seedhill Park, Paisley	P1
Port Glasgow AFC	Parklea Playing Fields, Port Glasgow	P2
Port Glasgow OBU	Parklea Playing Fields, Port Glasgow	D2
Port Glasgow United	Parklea Playing Fields, Port Glasgow	P2
Rosehill Star	Nether Pollok, Glasgow	D1
Rossvale	Huntershill Playing Fields, Bishopbriggs	D1
Rutherglen AFC	Burnhill Sports Centre, Rutherglen	P1
Shawlands FP	Nether Pollok, Glasgow	P1
Shawlands FP B	Nether Pollok, Glasgow	D1
South Camlachie YP	Crownpoint Stadium, Glasgow	D2
St Josephs FP	William Street, Duntocher	P
Strathaven Dynamo	John Hastie Park, Strathaven	D2
Tarbert	Oil Andreis, Tarbert	D1
Thorn Athletic	Johnstone Sports Complex, Johnstone	P
Whitehill FP	Glasgow Green	D2

SCOTTISH FUTSAL LEAGUE

Secretary: Mr. Mark Potter, 52 Maple Road, Perth PH1 1EX.
(H) 01738 639743 (B) 07977 208663. Email: markpotter14@btinternet.com

Futsal in Scotland in conjunction with the Scottish Football Association (SFA) and Scottish Amateur Football Association (SAFA) started Scotland's first league in Perth in 1997 and is the oldest in the UK. Futsal has a long history, having been invented in South America as long ago as the 1930s. Now the game is set to develop in Scotland and the SFA was the first of the four British associations to give official recognition to this five-a-side version of football.

Futsal is now played in areas across Scotland with Bathgate, Dundee, Glasgow and Stirling now embracing the version of the game.

DUNDEE DIVISION ONE

	P	W	D	L	F	A	+-	PTS
1 Ferry Mechanics	5	4	1	0	47	23	24	13
2 S.T.A.R.S. Ltd	5	3	1	1	42	30	12	10
3 Aldos All Stars	5	3	0	2	32	39	-7	9
4 FC Polonia	5	2	0	3	41	33	8	6
5 Dundee Zulus	5	2	0	3	33	31	2	6
6 Borussia Teeth	5	0	0	5	14	53	-39	0

PERTH LEAGUE ONE (PHASE

	P	W	D	L	F	A	+-	PTS
1 Perth Saltires	15	14	0	1	131	29	102	42
2 Fair City Santos	15	13	0	2	106	31	75	39
3 Athletico	15	12	0	3	129	43	86	36
4 Cherrybank FC	15	10	1	4	90	49	41	31
5 International FC	15	10	0	5	83	55	28	30
6 Benfeca	15	9	0	6	94	78	16	27
7 PYF Saltires	15	8	1	6	86	66	20	25
8 The Glen Bar	15	7	3	5	86	60	26	24
9 Peter Vardy	15	7	0	8	66	81	-15	21
10 Outer Milan	15	5	1	9	72	83	-11	16
11 FC Pumas	15	5	1	9	61	73	-12	16
12 Midnight Blazers	15	5	1	9	50	99	-49	16
13 Zenit St Johnston	15	4	1	10	65	92	-27	13
14 Dundee Futsal Club	15	3	3	9	51	71	-20	12
15 Steaua Perth	15	1	1	13	29	174	-145	4
16 Letham	15	0	1	14	39	154	-115	1

PERTH ELITE LEAGUE PHASE

	P	W	D	L	F	A	+-	PTS
1 Perth Saltires	10	8	1	1	58	25	33	25
2 Athletico	10	7	0	3	43	25	18	21
3 Fair City Santos	10	6	0	4	44	31	13	18
4 Cherrybank FC	10	6	0	4	46	44	2	18
5 International FC	10	2	1	7	35	56	-21	7
6 Benfeca	10	0	0	10	21	66	-45	0

PERTH LEAGUE ONE PHASE :

	P	W	D	L	F	A	+-	PTS
1 FC Pumas	8	7	0	1	42	20	22	21
2 Peter Vardy	8	5	0	3	34	33	1	15
3 Outer Milan	8	4	1	3	37	39	-2	13
4 PYF Saltires	8	1	2	5	27	34	-7	5
5 The Glen Bar	8	1	1	6	28	42	-14	4

PERTH LEAGUE TWO PHASE

	P	W	D	L	F	A	+-	PTS
1 Dundee Futsal Club	9	6	2	1	69	16	53	20
2 Zenit St Johnstoun	9	6	2	1	80	29	51	20
3 Midnight Blazers	8	2	4	2	41	39	2	10
4 Letham	8	2	2	4	31	65	-34	8
5 Steaua Perth	8	0	0	8	20	92	-72	0

SCOTTISH POLICE A.F.A.   2013/14

Match Secretary: Roland Fabiani

	P	W	D	L	F	A	GD	Pts
Glasgow North	12	12	0	0	51	7	44	36
North Lanarkshire	13	7	4	2	37	29	8	25
Glasgow Central	9	6	1	2	37	18	19	19
Glasgow South	12	6	0	6	36	41	-5	18
Dumbartonshire	11	4	2	5	33	39	-6	14
Renfrewshire	11	4	1	6	22	28	-6	13
South Lanarkshire	10	3	0	7	23	35	-12	9
Edinburgh	14	0	0	14	0	42	-42	0

SCOTTISH POLICE CUP

R1	16/09/2013	Glasgow Central	Dumfries	3 0	Loch Inch
R1	19/09/2013	South Lanarkshire	Fife	3 1	Loch Inch
R1	26/09/2013	Glasgow South	Edinburgh	3 0	Loch Inch
QF	11/11/2013	Forth Valley	Glasgow South	0 3	Stenhousemuir FC
QF	05/12/2013	North Lanarkshire	Tayside	2 3	Loch Inch
QF	20/02/2014	Glasgow Central	South Lanarkshire	0 3	Loch Inch
QF	10/03/2014	Renfrew	Glasgow North	1 6	Loch Inch
SF	18/03/2014	South Lanarkshire	Glasgow North	1 3	Loch Inch
SF	20/03/2014	Tayside	Glasgow South	3 0	Downfield JFC
F	19/05/2014	Glasgow North	Tayside	2 1	Petershill Park

Scotland West (formerly Strathclyde) won the Police Sports UK National KO Cup. They defeated the Police Service of Northern Ireland 3-0 in the Final. The match was played at Troon Juniors FC on May 27 2014, and all the goals were scored in extra time.

SCOTTISH SUPPORTERS A.F.L. 2013/14

Secretary: Mr W Mahomet, 02/43 Acre Road, Maryhill, Glasgow G20 0TR.
(M) 07769 941110 Email: williemo6@tiscali.co.uk

This is a Sunday afternoon Amateur League.

Latest Table Available for 2013/14

Teams	P	GD	Pts
Sandbank Rangers AFC	13	43	34
Airdrie Utd SAFC	11	32	30
Kerrydale Celtic AFC	14	12	28
Braes 04	14	16	25
Broadwood Clyde SAFC	12	-2	16
StMirrenoff AFC	14	-26	11
Cadzow Hamilton SAFC	10	-13	9
Dumbarton	12	-23	5
Aberdeen SAFC	12	-39	5

The Scottish Supporters League began in 1984 after several years in which Supporters of various Scottish League clubs had played semi-regular friendly matches. Meadowbank Thistle were the pioneers behind the League and at one time fielded two teams. The League included teams from all over Central Scotland. At its height there were three Divisions of ten clubs each.

SHETLAND A.F.A.

shetlandfa@yahoo.co.uk

www.shetlandfootball.co.uk

SHETLAND LEAGUE 2013

	P	W	D	L	F	A	GD	Pts
Spurs	12	11	0	1	36	9	27	33
Whitedale	11	9	0	2	31	17	14	27
Scalloway	11	4	3	4	24	27	-3	15
Celtic	12	4	2	6	17	20	-3	14
Delting	12	2	5	5	21	26	-5	11
Whalsay	12	3	1	9	18	26	-8	10
Thistle	12	1	3	8	17	41	-24	6

2014 Season (as at June 18)

LEAGUE A	P	W	D	L	F	A	GD	PTS
Spurs	5	4	0	1	8	1	7	12
Delting	5	3	2	0	13	7	6	11
Whitedale	6	2	3	1	16	10	6	9
Whalsay	5	2	2	1	9	9	0	8
Thistle	6	2	1	3	10	6	4	7
Celtic	6	2	1	3	8	14	-6	7
Ness Utd	7	1	3	3	4	10	-6	6
Scalloway	6	1	1	4	12	16	-4	4
Petrofac	4	0	3	1	7	14	-7	3

LEAGUE B	P	W	D	L	F	A	GD	PTS
Ness Utd	5	5	0	0	18	7	11	15
Whitedale	5	5	0	0	15	6	9	15
Spurs	6	3	0	3	15	12	3	9
Delting	3	2	0	1	9	7	2	6
Whalsay	5	2	0	3	12	12	0	6
Scalloway	6	2	0	4	9	18	-9	6
Thistle	4	1	0	3	5	6	-1	3
Yell	5	1	0	4	7	14	-7	3
Celtic	5	1	0	4	11	19	-8	3

WORKS LEAGUE	P	W	D	L	F	A	GD	PTS
Baroc Revolution	7	5	2	0	28	11	17	17
Services	7	4	2	1	14	15	-1	14
Wurltizers	6	3	3	0	25	6	19	12
Banks	6	4	0	2	19	10	9	12
Dynamo Chernobyl	7	3	2	2	17	14	3	11
West Side Rebels	7	1	2	4	9	13	-4	5
Wast Linga Ramblers	6	0	1	5	8	36	-28	1
Ness C	6	0	0	6	8	23	-15	0

CUP FINALS 2013

County Shield (Sep 7)
At Gilbertson Park
Spurs v Whitedale

Bloomfield Cup (Aug 31)
At Gilbertson Park
Petrofrac v Whalsay B
3-2

H Williamson & Son Fraser Cup
(Aug 10)
At Fraser Park
Whitedale v Spurs
3-2 AET

Milne Cup (Jul 27)
At Gilbertson Park
Shetland v Orkney
4-1

Joint Cup (Jul 20)
At Gilbertson Park
Celtic B v Chernobyl

Until a few years ago the Works League
was organised by a separate Shetland
Works FA. This has now been brought
under the umbrella of the Shetland FA.

The Shetland FA also runs a "Parish Cup",
quite separate from the club competitions.
(see next page).

Shetland Parish Cup Winners *(all info from the Shetland Football website)*

Parish Team	Total	Winning years
Whalsay	19	1961, 1966, 1968, 1969, 1970, 1972, 1973, 1974, 1977, 1978, 1980, 1984, 1989, 1991, 1992, 1999, 2006, 2010, 2011
Delting	13	1993, 1994, 1996, 1997, 1998, 2001, 2002, 2003, 2004, 2005, 2007, 2008, 2009
Whitedale	9	1975, 1979, 1983, 1985, 1986, 1987, 1988, 1990, 1995
Quendale	5	1955, 1956, 1957, 1958, 1959
Unst	5	1964, 1965, 1967, 2000, 2012
Sandwick	4	1952, 1960, 1962, 1963
Cunningsburgh	2	1971, 1976
Queen of the South (Virkie)	2	1953, 1954
Burra	1	1981
Southend United	1	1982
Westside United	1	2013
Bressay	0	
Yell	0	
Bigton	0	
Northmavine	0	
Southern Aces	0	

The current rules on player eligibility are:

(a) A player who is born or registered in a parish or who has accumulated five or more year's residence in a parish shall be eligible to play for that parish for all time.

(b) Where (a) does not apply, in order to be eligible to play for a parish a player must:

(i) have been resident for a minimum of three consecutive months at 30th April for the season ahead; and

(ii) be named on the most recent register of eligible players for that parish; and

(iii) be in permanent residence in that parish on the date of the fixture.

The Parish Cup draw is made at the AGM which is usually held in March. Ties are played as single legs over three rounds of matches, followed by the final which takes place in Lerwick traditionally on the Saturday afternoon of the Inter-club sailing regatta week during August. The final is a big day out for the teams who manage to get there and likewise for their supporters. Large crowds are commonplace and the Parish Cup final is without question the most eagerly anticipated and most watched cup final of any in the Shetland football calendar with spectator numbers often rivalling those of the Shetland v Orkney senior inter-county fixture. In recent years, the Committee has introduced new initiatives including the finalists being led on to the pitch by the Lerwick Pipe Band, pitch side segregation, match programmes and a post-match reception for both teams and sets of supporters, all of which adds to the whole match day experience.

SKYE AND LOCHALSH A.F.A.

Secretary: Heckie Cormack (Secretary), 1 Manse Lane, Portree, Isle of Skye IV51 9QR
07765 25025 / 01478 612558 (w) / secretary@slafa.org.uk

Placings at June 18

	Pl	W	D	L	Pts	
Portree	9	7	2	0	23	Portree High School
Sleat & Strath	9	7	0	2	21	Kinloch
Plockton	9	6	0	3	18	Plockton High School
Portree Juniors	9	5	2	2	17	Portree High School
GA United	9	4	3	2	15	Glebe Park, Gairloch
Kyleakin	8	4	0	5	12	Kyleakin Community Hall
Struan	9	3	0	6	9	Feorlaig
Dunvegan	9	1	2	6	5	Dunvegan Primary School
Kyle	9	1	2	6	5	Douglas Park, Kyle
Glenelg	9	1	1	7	4	Glenelg Community Hall
Staffin	0	0	0	0	0	Uig

Ross Cup Draw 2014

Round 1:
GA United v Portree Juniors
Dunvegan v Glenelg

Round 2:
Portree v Struan
Sleat & Strath v Kyle
Plockton v GA United / Portree Juniors
Dunvegan / Glenelg v Kyleakin

Semi Finals:
Portree / Struan v Sleat & Strath / Kyle
Plockton / GA United / Portree Juniors
v Dunvegan / Glenelg / Kyleakin

STEWARTRY SUNDAY A.F.A.

Secretary: Mr B. Mellon, Abbey View, Dundrennan, Kirkcudbright DG6 4QH. (H) & (B) 01557 500233. Senior Summer Sunday.
Email: a.nellon3lp@btinternet.com

Teams in membership, Season 2014:

Cum Ye Inn	Dalbeattie
Dalry United	St John's Town of Dalry
Ferrytoon	Creetown
Kirkcudbright Bay Hotel	Kirkcludbright
Market Inn	Castle Douglas
Morton Thistle	Dumfries
Park Athletic	
Ship Inn	Dumfries
Swan Inn	Stranraer
Twynholm	Twynholm
Wigtown and Bladnoch Reserves	Wigtown

Information about this League is very hard to obtain. Local newspapers are the best source for fixtures / results.

STIRLING AND DISTRICT A.F.A.

Secretary: Mr G. F. R. Japp, 3 Arnothill Court, Falkirk FK1 5SY
(H) 01324 613135 (M) 07753 775375. Email: gordon.japp@sky.com Senior
Saturday.

PREMIER DIVISION	P	W	D	L	Pts		DIVISION TWO	P	W	D	L	Pts
Bonnybridge YFP	20	16	3	1	51		Redbrae Athletic	20	17	3	0	54
Loganlea United	20	15	2	3	44		Polmont AFC	20	15	1	4	46
Stenhousemuir AFC	20	13	3	4	42		Doune Castle Ams.	20	10	6	4	36
Slamannan AFC	20	11	3	6	36		Linlithgow Rose Community FC	20	8	4	8	28
Barrhill AFC	20	10	1	9	31		Stirling B.C.	20	8	3	9	27
Stirling University	20	9	3	8	30		Glenvale AFC	20	8	2	10	26
Braehead AFC	20	9	2	9	29		Auchengeich Miners FC	20	7	3	10	24
Carronshore Athletic	20	7	3	10	24		Campsie FC	20	7	3	10	24
Zetland AFC	20	6	1	13	19		Cumbernauld Athletic	20	6	4	10	22
California AFC	20	3	1	16	10		Hillfoots Community FC	20	6	2	12	20
Tullibody Community AFC	20	0	0	20	-3		Condorrat AFC	20	1	3	16	6

DIVISION ONE	P	W	D	L	Pts		DIVISION THREE	P	W	D	L	Pts
Independent FC	22	19	1	2	58		Bo'ness Cadora	20	17	1	2	52
Milton FC	22	18	2	2	56		Grangemouth Rovers	20	15	3	2	48
Fallin AFC	22	16	2	4	50		MLS Leeds	20	15	2	3	47
Callander Thistle	22	13	2	7	41		Carse Thistle	20	12	3	5	39
Dunblane Thistle	22	8	2	12	26		Forth Thistle	20	8	4	8	28
Greenhill AFC	22	8	1	13	25		Denny Ams.	20	8	5	7	26
Sunnyside Thistle	22	8	4	10	25		Kildrum United	20	7	0	13	21
Maddiston AFC	22	7	3	12	24		Airth Castle Rovers	20	5	2	13	17
Drumpellier Thistle	22	6	5	11	23		Beechwood Albion	20	5	1	14	16
Riverside AFC	22	5	2	15	17		1FC Abronhill	20	3	1	16	7
Tillicoultry AFC	22	4	5	13	14		Cumbernauld Rovers	20	2	4	14	4
Gormac Thistle	22	5	1	16	13							

CUP FINALS 2013/14

JF Colley Trophy (May 28)
Stenhousemuir v Bo'ness Cadora
4-1
At Dunipace Juniors

Mathieson Trophy (May 30)
Braehead v MLS Leeds
3-0
At Cumbernauld United

David McKinnon Trophy (June 2)
Loganlea United v Barrhill
5-3
At Dunipace Juniors

Drysdale Trophy (Prem)
Carronshore Athletic v Braehead
2-1
At Little Kerse

Robertson Trophy (Div 1)
Independent v Fallin
5-3
At Little Kerse

Taylor Trophy (Div 2)
Redbrae Athletic v Polmont
5-4 aet
At Little Kerse

Cameron Craig Trophy (Div 3
Bo'ness Cadora v MLS Leeds
3-2
At Airdrieonians FC

STRANRAER & DISTRICT A.F.L.

Latest Table Available

	P	W	D	L	F	A	PTS
Hamilton Arms	7	6	1	0	42	11	19
Bar 12	8	5	1	2	32	20	16
Park Athletic	6	3	2	1	25	13	11
Wigtown & Bladnoch	10	3	2	5	31	33	11
Chasers	5	2	1	2	19	12	7
Stranraer Boswell	7	2	1	4	19	34	7
Num FC	7	0	0	7	10	55	0

This League was in danger of folding at the end of the 2013/14 season. Six teams have expressed an interest in participating for 2014/15 and a meeting was due on June 17 to decide the future of the League.

STRATHCLYDE EVANGELICAL CHURCHES A.F.L.

http://www.churchesleague.com

Senior Saturday (Matches usually Kick Off 10am)

PREMIER DIVISION	P	W	D	L	F	A	GD	Pts
1 Carluke Baptists	18	9	3	2	50	22	28	30
2 Anniesland	18	8	1	5	45	41	4	25
3 Greenbank BB	18	6	3	5	25	30	-5	21
4 Kirkintilloch Riverside	18	6	2	6	50	41	9	20
5 St Andrew's	18	5	3	6	29	39	-10	18
6 Avendale	18	4	4	6	25	24	1	16
7 Kilsyth Utd	18	4	3	7	29	34	-5	15
8 Houston and Killellan	18	3	3	8	22	44	-22	12
9 Dumbarton Lennox EC	18	0	0	0	0	0	0	0
10 Motherwell Ebenezer	18	0	0	0	0	0	0	0

DIVISION ONE	P	W	D	L	F	A	GD	Pts
1 Westwood BB	18	13	1	4	67	33	34	40
2 Cartsbridge	18	13	1	4	56	31	25	40
3 Hope Hall FC	18	12	2	4	76	37	39	38
4 West Glasgow	18	12	1	5	85	28	57	37
5 King's Church	18	10	1	7	43	40	3	31
6 Chryston Unity	18	9	1	8	54	32	22	28
7 East Kilbride Free Church	18	8	1	9	35	49	-14	25
8 Inverclyde Nazarene	18	6	2	10	44	76	-32	20
9 St. Ninian's FC	18	2	0	16	23	97	-74	6
10 East Kilbride Baptist	18	0	0	18	15	75	-60	0

DIVISION TWO	P	W	D	L	F	A	GD	Pts
1 Gartcairn (Clarkston) F.A.	18	14	3	1	101	20	81	45
2 St Silas	18	12	2	4	57	34	23	38
3 Bishopbriggs International	18	11	1	6	54	37	17	34
4 Greenock Mount Kirk	18	8	3	7	81	50	31	27
5 West End Vineyard	18	8	3	7	50	42	8	27
6 Parkhead Tollcross United	18	8	2	8	61	55	6	26
7 Irvine Nazarene	18	7	5	6	49	43	6	26
8 Govanhill Free Church	18	8	0	10	56	53	3	24
9 Troon Seagate	18	3	1	14	26	77	-51	10
10 Kings Park Baptist Football Club	18	1	0	17	23	147	-124	3

DIVISION THREE	P	W	D	L	F	A	GD	Pts
1 Law Parish	18	16	0	2	93	29	64	48
2 Machan United	18	14	1	3	78	32	46	43
3 Airdrie Ebenezer	18	11	0	7	55	43	12	33
4 Chalmers Parish	18	7	4	7	51	53	-2	25
5 United Churches of Ayr	18	7	4	7	35	42	-7	25
6 Fullarton Irvine	18	7	2	9	37	39	-2	23
7 Glasgow Elim	18	6	4	8	43	57	-14	22
8 Mearns Churches	18	5	5	8	29	42	-13	20
9 Lenzie Union	17	5	2	10	31	49	-18	17
10 Greenbank Church of Scotland	17	0	0	17	16	82	-66	0

CUP FINALS 2013/14

Fraser Trophy (May 31)
Carluke Baptists v Westwood
6-2
At Airdrieonians FC

Atholl Cup (Div 3) (May 31)
Machan United v Chalmers
2-1

Atholl Cup (Div 2) (May 17)
Gartcairn v Bishopbriggs
2-0

Atholl Cup (Div 1) (May 17)
West Glasgow v Westwood
2-2, 8-7 pens

Atholl Cup (Prem) (May 10)
Carluke Baptists v Kirkintilloch
7-0

Objectives of the Churches League

The use of football as a means of true Christian Fellowship and the proper use of said fellowship as a means of glorifying God and representing a good Christian witness.

STRATHCLYDE SATURDAY MORNING A.F.L.

Match Secretary: Mr. John Walker, 20 Hunter Street, Airdrie, ML6 6NW. Tel 07940165412 E-Mail jakemuldake@hotmail.com .
Saturday Morning   http://www.ssmafl.co.uk/

Premier Division

Team	P	W	D	L	F	A	GD	Pts
C1 Whitefield Rovers	20	18	2	0	91	22	69	56
2 Tynecastle	20	17	2	1	87	29	58	53
3 Blochairn Star	20	12	2	7	65	53	12	38
4 Dennistoun Vale	20	9	2	9	38	49	-11	29
5 East Dunbartonshire	20	7	3	9	44	57	-13	24
6 I.C.C.	19	6	5	7	33	47	-14	23
7 Cresswell Lane	20	6	2	12	38	49	-11	20
8 Victoria Croftfoot	20	5	4	11	47	63	-16	19
9 A.S. Airdrie	19	4	4	11	37	65	-28	16
10 Shawbridge	20	4	3	13	38	64	-26	15
11 Yoker	20	3	4	8	58	80	-22	7*
12 Blairdardie	0	0	0	0	0	0	0	0

*Yoker deducted 9 points

Division 1

Team	P	W	D	L	F	A	GD	Pts
C1 Blochairn Star B	20	16	1	3	94	35	59	49
2 Windlaw	22	14	2	6	66	35	31	44
3 Motherwell	21	10	8	3	61	47	14	38
4 Maryhill Black Star	22	12	4	6	74	46	28	37
5 Firhill Utd	21	11	4	6	61	43	18	37
6 Ravenscraig	22	10	4	8	51	42	9	34
7 Kilbride Villa	22	10	3	9	59	49	10	33
8 Quayside Th	21	9	3	9	57	54	3	30
9 Sth Lanarkshire Utd	21	6	2	13	52	78	-26	20
10 D.T.I.	22	5	3	14	35	81	-46	18
11 Coatbridge Colts	22	5	1	16	43	99	-56	16
12 E.K. Accies	22	2	3	17	38	82	-44	8
13 Whinhall Utd	0	0	0	0	0	0	0	0
14 Seafar Villa	0	0	0	0	0	0	0	0

*Maryhill 3 points deducted

*E.K Accies 1point deducted

Division 2A

Team	P	W	D	L	F	A	GD	Pts
C1 Whifflet Ath	18	13	4	1	61	21	40	43
2 Tantallon Victoria	18	12	2	4	55	33	22	38
3 Petershall Villa	18	9	5	4	55	30	25	32
4 Westwood	18	8	5	5	36	33	3	29
5 Bengal Lancers	18	3	3	12	27	46	-19	12
6 Kelvinbridge	18	2	5	11	32	48	-16	11
7 Hardgate	18	2	4	12	21	76	-55	10
8 Milan	0	0	0	0	0	0	0	0

Division 2B

Team	P	W	D	L	F	A	GD	Pts
C1 Hutchesontown	21	15	3	3	75	42	33	48
2 Hamilton West	21	14	2	5	92	37	55	44
3 Cambusnethan Talbot	21	12	5	4	67	40	27	41
4 Kirkintilloch Th	20	13	0	7	56	52	4	39
5 Barshaw	21	8	1	12	51	63	-12	25
6 Duntocher	21	5	4	12	57	55	2	19
7 Westbridge Villa	20	5	3	12	58	76	-18	18
8 Skye Wanderers	21	1	2	18	29	96	-67	5

CUP FINALS 2013/14

Strathclyde Cup (May 30)
Whitefield v Bochairn Star B
At Cambuslang Rangers JFC

Tommy Marshall Trophy (May 23)
Blochairn Star v Tynecastle
0-3
At Shettlesto JFC

Challenge Cup (May 16)
Blochairn Star v Tynecastle
4-2 aet
At Cambuslang Rangers JFC

Presidents Cup (May 9)
Firhill United vBlochairn Star B
4-3
At St Rochs JFC

STRATHCLYDE SATURDAY MORNING LEAGUE CHAMPIONS

Season	Premier Division	Division 1	Division 2A	Division 2B
2013/14	Whitefield Rovers	Blochairn Star B	Whifflet Ath	Hutchesontown
2012/13	Blochairn Star	Dennistoun Vale	Kilbride Villa	Motherwell
2011/12	Blochairn Star	Victoria Croftfoot	Dennistoun Vale	
2010/11	Tynecastle	Whitefield Rovers	Seafar Villa	
2009/10	Greenhills Dynamo	I.C.C.	Whitefield Rovers	
2008/09	Tynecastle	S.C.Y.P	I.C.C.	
2007/08	Blochairn Star	NC United	S.C.Y.P	
2006/07	Blochairn Star	Clydebank United	Kelvinbank Star	
2005/06	Windlaw	Dunbreac	NC United	
2004/05	Vale United	Greenbank United	Bridgeton United	
2003/04	Blochairn Star	Vale United		
2002/03	Windlaw	Blochairn Star		
2001/02	Windlaw	Telecom		
2000/01	Levern	Reidvale		
1999/00	Levern	Portcullis		
1998/99	Levern	Cowder Vaults		
1997/98	Patrick Thistle	Windlaw		
1996/97	St Ambrose	Patrick Thistle		
1995/96	GDC	Tynecastle		
1994/95	Rutherglen PO	St Ambrose		
1993/94	Levern	Rutherglen PO		
1992/93	GDC	Northill		
1991/92	Lorne Star	Levernbank		
1990/91	Parkhead	Minstrels		
1989/90	Parkhead	Levern	Tynecastle	
1988/89	Ellsworth	Giffnock	Morton	

SUNDAY CENTRAL A.F.L.

Secretary: Sunday Central AFL, c/o The Venue ,96-102 Main Street,
Rutherglen, Glasgow, G73 2HZ,   07447401529
Email: sundaycentral@live.co.uk   Senior Sunday.

http://www.sundaycentralafl.co.uk

Premier Division

Pos	Team	P	W	D	L	GF	GA	GD	Pts	Adj
1	Rutherglen Vogue	18	13	4	1	70	24	46	43	-
2	Treble 2	18	13	0	5	47	32	15	39	-
3	Castlemilk Dynamo	18	11	3	4	56	23	33	36	-
4	Milton of Colquhoun	18	10	1	7	48	36	12	31	-
5	Cranhill United	18	10	1	7	45	36	9	31	-
6	Queens Park Spiders	18	10	0	8	38	45	-7	30	-
7	Westhill	18	7	3	8	44	41	3	24	-
8	Castlemilk United	18	6	3	9	42	68	-26	21	-
9	MK Dynamo	18	1	1	16	21	63	-42	4	-
10	Thornwood	18	0	2	16	16	59	-43	2	-
11	Beechwood Athletic	0	0	0	0	0	0	0	0	-
12	Westburn	0	0	0	0	0	0	0	0	-

Division One

Pos	Team	P	W	D	L	GF	GA	GD	Pts	+/-
1	Northend	22	19	1	2	110	30	80	58	-
2	Westercommon Star	22	14	2	6	74	44	30	44	-
3	Manhattan Blacks	22	12	2	8	67	53	14	38	-
4	Castlemilk East	22	13	3	6	80	42	38	36	-6
5	Gartferry	22	11	3	8	63	57	6	36	-
6	FC Baillieston	22	12	0	10	48	61	-13	36	-
7	Springhall Spartans	22	10	4	8	59	64	-5	34	-
8	Southside Whitecart	22	10	1	11	74	73	1	31	-
9	Drumchapel Thistle	22	8	2	12	70	72	-2	26	-
10	Haldane United	22	6	0	16	56	76	-20	18	-
11	Cumbernauld Colts	22	5	0	17	44	103	-59	15	-
12	Stanley Athletic	22	3	0	19	35	105	-70	9	-

Division Two A

Pos	Team	P	W	D	L	GF	GA	GD	Pts	+/-
1	Hillview	14	9	3	2	65	29	36	30	-
2	Thomsons FC	14	8	3	3	54	36	18	27	-
3	Bellgrove	14	8	2	4	43	44	-1	26	-
4	Windlaw	14	6	3	5	38	30	8	21	-
5	Cleddans	14	5	3	6	43	47	-4	18	-
6	Eastfield Star	14	3	4	7	35	48	-13	13	-
7	Drumchapel FP	13	4	0	9	34	50	-16	12	-
8	Lanarkshire Eagles	13	2	2	9	23	51	-28	8	-

Division Two B

Pos	Team	P	W	D	L	GF	GA	GD	Pts	+/-
1	Old Kilpatrick United	14	9	0	5	52	29	23	27	-
2	The Hub	14	8	3	3	49	27	22	27	-
3	Overlee Partizans	14	8	3	3	48	38	10	27	-
4	Croftfoot Amateurs	14	7	2	5	52	41	11	23	-
5	Eastend Rovers	14	6	1	7	44	48	-4	19	-
6	Calderside	14	4	1	9	28	50	-22	13	-
7	Crownpoint United	14	3	0	11	26	65	-39	9	-
8	Newton Vale	14	5	2	7	37	38	-1	7	-10

Division Two C

Pos	Team	P	W	D	L	GF	GA	GD	Pts	+/-
1	Glasgow Rovers	10	9	0	1	34	20	14	27	-
2	Glasgow South	10	6	1	3	39	24	15	19	-
3	Glasgow Thistle	10	6	1	3	35	24	11	19	-
4	Westend United	10	3	1	6	35	37	-2	10	-
5	Rossvale Amateurs	10	2	1	7	17	34	-17	7	-
6	Glasgow Rangers AFC	10	2	0	8	20	41	-21	6	-
7	Dunbeth	0	0	0	0	0	0	0	0	-
8	FC Polonia Glasgow	0	0	0	0	0	0	0	0	-

CUP FINALS 2013/14

Presidents Cup (May 16)
The Hub v Windlaw
4-1

League Cup (May 30)
Castlemilk Dynamo v Rutherglen
Vogue
3-1
At Rutherglen Glencairn JFC

Glass-Go Cup
Castlemilk Dynamo v Northend
3-3

UIST AND BARRA A.F.A.

The best sources of information for this league are their Twitter feed at: @UistBarraLeague and their Facebook page.

League Table 2013

	P	W	D	L	F	A	GD	PTS	Home Ground
Iochdar Saints	18	15	0	3	89	24	65	45	
Barra	17	9	1	7	45	47	-2	28	
Benbecula	18	7	3	8	43	48	-5	24	
Southend	18	7	2	9	36	44	-8	23	
Eriskay	18	7	1	10	44	60	-16	22	
North Uist	17	4	1	12	37	62	-25	13	

Latest League Table 2014

Iochdar Saints	8	8	0	0	43	8	35	24	Sgiol Lionacleit
Barra	8	4	2	2	27	19	8	14	Castlebay
North Uist	8	3	1	4	19	22	-3	10	Paible School
Benbecula	8	3	1	4	14	22	-8	10	Sgiol Lionacleit
Southend	8	2	0	6	12	25	-13	6	Sgiol Lionacleit
Eriskay	8	1	2	5	13	32	-19	5	Eriskay

Cup Results 2014:
Calmac Cup Final (at Sgiol Lionacliet)
Eriskay 3 Barra 2

WEST LOTHIAN SUNDAY A.F.L.

www.westlothian.leaguerepublic.com
Sunday League

PREMIER DIVISION	P	W	D	L	F	A	GD	PTS
1 Harvester AFC	12	12	0	0	46	21	25	36
2 Cross Tavern	12	10	0	2	65	19	46	30
3 Broxburn Athletic	12	7	0	5	49	24	25	21
4 Daltons	12	7	0	5	37	34	3	21
5 Shotts Thistle	12	4	0	8	24	37	-13	12
6 Redding AFC	12	1	0	11	22	46	-24	3
7 Carmondean	12	1	0	11	19	81	-62	3

DIVISION ONE	P	W	D	L	F	A	GD	PTS
1 Livi Hearts	16	12	1	3	53	39	14	37
2 Blackburn	16	9	2	5	55	30	25	29
3 Riverside	16	9	2	5	59	45	14	29
4 Newpark	16	8	2	6	54	44	10	26
5 Wheatsheaf	16	8	1	7	48	39	9	25
6 Lothian Thistle	16	7	1	8	42	44	-2	22
7 Livingston AFC	16	6	2	8	44	57	-13	20
8 Knightshades 3550	16	5	2	9	51	50	1	17
9 Krossbar	16	1	1	14	30	88	-58	4

DIVISION TWO	P	W	D	L	F	A	GD	PTS
1 Livi North	16	14	1	1	80	32	48	43
2 Newtown	16	12	1	3	90	30	60	37
3 Clachan	16	11	0	5	62	32	30	33
4 West Lothian Athletic	16	8	1	7	56	58	-2	25
5 Saltire	16	7	1	8	55	53	2	22
6 Whitburn JSC	16	6	2	8	33	41	-8	20
7 Armadale	16	4	2	10	41	53	-12	14
8 Corrie Bar	16	4	0	12	33	64	-31	12
9 Uphall Athletic	16	2	0	14	18	105	-87	6

CUP FINALS 2013/14

Energywise Cup (May 25)
Broxburn Athletic v Daltons
3-3, 5-4 pens

ACE Exhausts KO Cup (May 25)
Newtown v Cross Tavern
3-1

McNee Cup (May 18)
Livi North v Shotts Thistle
3-2

Almond Cup (May 25)
Wheatsheaf v Livi Hearts
4-1

Premier Division Cup (June 1)
Cross Tavern v Daltons
2-1

League One Cup (May 18)
Riverside v Wheatsheaf
1-1, 14-13 pens

League Two Cup (June 1)
Clachan v Newtown
4-0

WEST AYRSHIRE SUNDAY A.F.L. 2013/14

WASAFA : DIVISION 1

Team Name		P	W	D	L	F	A	GD	PTS
1	Medda SB (Div 1 Champions)	20	18	0	2	123	33	+90	54
2	Bothan Afc	20	17	1	2	112	33	+79	52
3	The Craft	20	13	2	5	93	51	+42	41
4	Tap Shop	20	13	1	6	86	58	+28	40
5	Eglinton Arms	20	12	2	6	65	41	+24	38
6	Valley Thistle	20	8	1	11	50	70	-20	25
7	AC Drongan	20	7	0	13	61	67	-6	21

WASAFA : DIVISION 2

Team Name		P	W	D	L	F	A	GD	PTS
1	Coach & Horses (Div 2 Champions)	21	12	1	8	65	58	+7	37
2	Kilbirnie Utd	21	9	4	8	64	58	+6	31
3	Killie Athletic	21	9	1	11	60	63	-3	28
4	Dreghorn Inn	21	7	3	11	54	81	-27	24
5	Annick Tavern	21	6	2	13	36	87	-51	20
6	Tartan Bar	21	5	2	14	44	86	-42	17
7	Stevenston Thistle	21	4	2	15	34	85	-51	14
8	Irvine No.1 CSC	21	3	0	18	42	118	-76	9

CUP FINALS 2013/14

Wayne Bannerman Trophy (May 2)
Killie Athletic v Stevenston Thistle
3-1 AET
At Saltcoats Vics

Go-Vending Cup (May 9)
The Craft v Medda S[ports Bar
0-3
At Ardrossan Wointon Rovers

Robbie Sharp Cup (May 16)
Eglinton Arms v Medda Sports Bar
2- AET
At Ardeer Thistle

WEST OF SCOTLAND A.F.L.

Secretary: Garry Watson (T) 07473506834
E mail Garrwatson82@googlemail.com

www.leaguewebsite.co.uk/westofscotlandamateurfootballleague
Senior Saturday

Latest available tables:

PREMIER DIVISION	P	W	D	L	F	A	GD	Pts
Niaroo	16	16	0	0	100	18	82	48
Dennistoun	15	11	1	3	87	28	59	34
Possil YM	15	10	2	3	56	29	27	32
Oban Athletic AFC	16	8	2	6	54	36	18	26
Antonine	15	8	1	6	45	38	7	25
Cardross Amateurs	16	6	1	9	43	56	-13	19
Crown Park	16	3	1	12	30	66	-36	10
Helensburgh	16	1	2	13	25	97	-72	5
Belleaire	15	1	2	12	13	85	-72	5

FIRST DIVISION	P	W	D	L	F	A	GD	Pts
Giffnock Amateur Football Club	19	16	1	2	94	21	73	49
Corkerhill	18	16	1	1	95	23	72	49
Anderston Victoria	20	13	1	6	88	34	54	40
Carradale Amateur FC	20	13	1	6	86	39	47	40
St Andrews	20	9	2	9	40	50	-10	29
Third Lanark Athletic Club	20	9	0	11	50	70	-20	27
Minorities Youth Foundation	19	8	2	9	51	63	-12	26
Point Media	20	7	2	11	59	75	-16	23
Erskine Thistle	20	5	2	13	38	80	-42	17
Lochfyneside AFC	18	3	4	11	22	81	-59	13
Firhill Football Club	20	0	0	20	19	106	-87	0

CUP FINALS 2013/14

Thomson Trophy (june 14)
Nia Roo v Oban Athletic
Ay Broadwood Stadium

Challenge Shield (May 31)
Dennistoun v Antonine
3-0
At Broadwood Stadium

League Cup (June 21)
Nia Roo v Dennistoun
At Broadwood Stadium

FROM THE WOSAL website:

The West of Scotland Amateur Football League was formed in the year 1898, and with the exception of the period during the first world war has functioned continually since that far off year. We make claims to being the oldest amateur football league in Scotland, and in fact could be the oldest in minor football, if not, We are sure are amongst the oldest.

At its start the league had eleven clubs in membership ranging from Motherwell, Wishaw, Helensburgh, Greenock, and in and around the city. The annual subscription was 5/- .In 1908 we became so popular that we were in a position to form a second division. This also saw the introduction of neutral referees. It was agreed that the officials be paid the sum of 2/- with third class rail travel.

In 1909 we receieved an invitation to join the proposed new Scottish Amateur association. In 1914 we now come to the only break in the leagues history. In September of that year a special general meeting was called for the purpose, we quote the presidents opening remarks "The Tremendous uncertainty before the country regarding the terrible war which was setting all Europe aflame. At such a critical time in the history of our beloved country was an opportune time to carry on the west of Scotland Amateur Football League" The chairman then put it to the meeting to consider the position. After a free discussion it was unanimously decided to record the decision of the meeting in these terms. "That this league definitely discontinue organised football at present."

In August 1919, a meeting was called to again get the league in a peace time footing. Nothing eventful happened unit 1925. At the start of this season an endeavour was made for the league to have its first trophy. To raise the necessary capital the referees were asked to give over the fee during August, to which the referees association agreed providing there would be no victimisation. Each club subscribed 15/-s, and in this way the shield was bought for £30. The shield eventually became obsolete and was superseded by the Albion Motors cup gifted by the directors of the firm.

SCOTTISH AMATEUR CUP WINNERS

1909/10	John Neilson FP	(Paisley)
1910/11	Edinburgh Civil Service	
1911/12	Queen's Park Hampden XI	
1912/13	Leith Amateurs	
1913/14	Cameronians	(Stirling)
1919/20	Queen's Park Hampden XI	
1920/21	Edinburgh Civil Service	
1921/22	Greenock HSFP	
1922/23	Falkirk Amateurs	
1923/24	Moorpark	(Renfrew)
1924/25	Coldstream	
1925/26	Murrayfield Amateurs	(Edinburgh)
1926/27	Glasgow University	
1927/28	Queen's Park Hampden XI	
1928/29	Murrayfield Amateurs	(Edinburgh)
1929/30	Murrayfield Amateurs	(Edinburgh)
1930/31	Murrayfield Amateurs	(Edinburgh)
1931/32	Glasgow Corporation Transport	
1932/33	Queen's Park Hampden XI	
1933/34	Queen's Park Hampden XI	
1934/35	Camphill Secondary FP	(Paisley)
1935/36	Queen's Park Hampden XI	
1936/37	Gogarburn	(Edinburgh)
1937/38	Coats	(Paisley)
1938/39	Murrayfield Amateurs	(Edinburgh)
1945/46	Craigton Athletic	(Glasgow)
1946/47	Queen's Park Hampden XI	
1947/48	Mearns	
1948/49	Greenock HSFP	
1949/50	Queen's Park Hampden XI	
1950/51	Queen's Park Hampden XI	
1951/52	Port Glasgow Hibernian	
1952/53	Mearns	
1953/54	Royal Technical College	(Glasgow)
1954/55	Eglinton Ams	(Glasgow)
1955/56	Milanda	(Glasgow)
1956/57	Giffnock North	
1957/58	Weir Recreation	(Glasgow)
1958/59	Crosshill Athletic	(Glasgow)
1959/60	Minishant	
1960/61	Glenavon	
1961/62	Bearsden Ams	
1962/63	Queen's Park Hampden XI	
1963/64	Queen's Park Hampden XI	
1964/65	NCR	(Dundee)
1965/66	Jordanhill TC	(Glasgow)
1966/67	Rhu	
1967/68	Cambusbarron Rovers	
1968/69	Cambusbarron Rovers	
1969/70	Douglas	
1970/71	Dumbarton Academy FP	
1971/72	Douglas	
1972/73	Knockentiber	
1973/74	Douglas	
1974/75	Star Hearts	
1975/76	Colville Park	(Mothewell)
1976/77	Morriston YMCa	(Cambuslang)
1977/78	Cambusbarron Rovers	
1978/79	Crosshouse Waverley	
1979/80	Newarthill Hearts	
1980/81	Knockentiber	
1981/82	Avon Villa	(Hamilton)
1982/83	Strathclyde Police	
1983/84	Pencaitland	
1984/85	Drongan United	
1985/86	Coatbridge CC	
1986/87	Bannockburn	
1987/88	Coatbridge CC	
1988/89	Norton House	(Leven)
1989/90	St Patricks FP	(Dumbarton)
1990/91	Bannockburn	
1991/92	Heathside	(Ayr)
1992/93	Bankhall Villa	(Chapelhall)
1993/94	Bannockburn	
1994/95	Heathside	(Ayr)
1995/96	Bellshill YMCA	
1996/97	Knockentiber	
1997/98	Dalziel HSFP	(Motherwell)
1998/99	St Patricks FP	(Dumbarton)
1999/00	Liberton Royal Mail	(Edinburgh)
2000/1	Dalziel HSFP	(Motherwell)
2001/2	Harestanes	(Kirkintilloch)
2002/3	Harestanes	(Kirkintilloch)
2003/4	Viewfield Rovers	(Lochwinnoch)
2004/5	Drumchapel	
2005/6	St Patricks FP	(Dumbarton)
2006/7	Drumchapel United	
2007/8	Eddlewood	(Hamilton)
2008/9	Queen's Park Hampden XI	
2009/10	Eddlewood	(Hamilton)
2010/11	Wishaw HSFP	
2011/12	Hurlford Thistle	
2012/13	Wellhouse	(Glasgow)
2013/14	Hurlford Thistle	

SCOTTISH AMATEUR CUP 2013/14

R1W	Ravencraig	(SAFL)	v	Glasgow Harp	(CALE)	0	7					
R1W	Auldhouse	(SAFL)	v	Rosehill United	(GCAFA)	scr	wo					
R1W	Blantyre Celtic	(CSAFL)	v	Westend Athletic	(P&D)	11	0					
R1W	Boswell	(P&D)	v	South Camlachie YP	(SAFL)	0	3					
R1W	Bothwell & Uddingston Albion	(SAFL)	v	Cumbernauld Colts	(CALE)	1	8					
R1W	Calderglen	(GGPAFL)	v	Craigneuk	(GGPAFL)	3	0					
R1W	Cambusnethan Talbot	(CSAFL)	v	Troon Athletic	(AYR)	3	0					
R1W	Campsie Minerva	(CSAFL)	v	FC Clydebank	(SAFL)	3	1					
R1W	Carlton YMCA	(SAFL)	v	Machan United	(SECAFL)	9	2					
R1W	Clark Drive	(AYR)	v	Winlinton Wolves	(AYR)	3	0					
R1W	Clydebank AFC	(SAFL)	v	Eaglesham	(SAFL)	3	1	P				Protest
R1W	Colville Park	(CSAFL)	v	Corkerhill	(WOSAFL)	8	0					
R1W	Crookedholm	(AYR)	v	Wishaw HSFP	(CSAFL)	0	5					
R1W	Cumbernauld Athletic	(S&DAFA)	v	Kirkintilloch Miners Welfare	(CSAFL)	0	5					
R1W	Cunninghame	(AYR)	v	East Kilbride YM	(CALE)	5	4					
R1W	Dalziel HSFP	(CALE)	v	Oban Athletic	(WOSAFL)	4	1					
R1W	Darvel Victoria	(AYR)	v	Aikenhead Thistle	(CSAFL)	0	4					
R1W	DTI	(SSMFL)	v	Kilmarnock Town	(AYR)	2	4					
R1W	East Kilbride YM	(GGPAFL)	v	Maryhill Black Star	(SSMFL)	5	4	P				Protest
R1W	Eastwood Park	(G&DSMAFL)	v	Kings Park Rangers	(SAFL)	1	1		2	4aet		AET
R1W	Erskine Thistle	(WOSAFL)	v	Crownpark	(WOSAFL)	0	3					
R1W	Fenwick Thistle	(AYR)	v	Kilsyth United	(SECAFL)	0	0		2	5		
R1W	Fullarton Irvine	(SECAFL)	v	Irvine Town	(AYR)	1	3					
R1W	Greenock Mount Kirk	(SECAFL)	v	Electric Bar	(NSLAFA)	scr	wo					
R1W	Jordanhill Campus	(GGPAFL)	v	Apex	(P&D)	4	0					
R1W	Kilbarchan Thistle	(GGPAFL)	v	Dumbarton Wanderers	(P&DAFL)	0	3					
R1W	Kings Park Rovers	(G&DSMAFL)	v	Gartcosh United	(CALE)	scr	wo					
R1W	Lochgilphead Red Star	(SAFL)	v	Paisley AFC	(SAFL)	1	1		1	2		
R1W	Mill United	(CSAFL)	v	Millerston Thistle	(SAFL)	4	4		1	0		
R1W	Mill United	(NSLAFA)	v	Erskine YFC	(P&D)	5	2					
R1W	Millbeg Villa	(SAFL)	v	Claremont	(GGPAFL)	3	2					
R1W	Milngavie BC	(G&DSMAFL)	v	Kilsyth AFC	(CSAFL)	2	4					
R1W	Minishant	(AYR)	v	Strathclyde University	(GGPAFL)	0	4					
R1W	Motherwell Bridgework	(NSLAFA)	v	Mount Vernon Juniors	(NSLAFA)	1	2	·				
R1W	Motherwell Thistle	(SAFL)	v	Bellgrove	(G&DSMAFL)	5	2					
R1W	North Kelvin United	(GGPAFL)	v	Redbrae Athletic	(S&DAFA)	1	8					
R1W	Orchard Park Mount 'B'	(GGPAFL)	v	Helensburgh	(WOSAFL)	2	0					
R1W	Possil YM	(WOSAFL)	v	Anniesland	(SECAFL)	9	0					
R1W	Redbrae	(CSAFL)	v	Centre AFC	(SAFL)	0	0		4	6		
R1W	Robslee	(GGPAFL)	v	Gallowhill	(P&D)	A	A					
R1W	Rothesay Brandane	(CALE)	v	Glasgow Univerity	(CALE)	0	1					
R1W	Shawlands FP	(SAFL)	v	Mossend	(NSLAFA)	3	3	A	A			
R1W	St Patricks FP	(CSAFL)	v	Whifflet Athletic	(SSMFL)	8	0					
R1W	Thorn Athletic	(P&D)	v	Independent	(S&DAFA)	1	3					
R1W	Troon Dundonald	(AYR)	v	Blantyre (RGM)	(RGM)	1	1		3	2		
R1W	Victoria Croftfoot	(SSMFL)	v	East Kilbride AFC	(SAFL)	1	4					
R1W	Viewfield Rovers	(CALE)	v	Orchard Park	(GGPAFL)	5	2					
R1W	Weirs Recreation	(CALE)	v	Kirkmichael	(WOSAFL)	wo	scr					
R1W	Westerlands	(CALE)	v	Mearns	(CSAFL)	5	1					
R1W	Whitefield Rovers	(SSMFL)	v	Kirkintilloch Thistle	(SSMFL)	5	0					
R1E	AFC Milton	(S&DAFA)	v	Pencaitland	(LEAFA)	0	4					
R1E	Ancrum	(BAFA)	v	Sunnyside Thistle	(S&DAFA)	2	2		3	3aet,5-3p		AET, 5-3 pens
R1E	Auchtermuchty Bellevue	(FIFE)	v	Shotts Victoria	(LEAFA)	0	5					
R1E	Blairhall Village	(KCAFA)	v	Rosebank	(FIFE)	2	3					
R1E	Bonnybridge YFP	(S&DAFA)	v	Inverkeithing Hillfield Swifts	(FIFE)	5	1					
R1E	Bowhill Rovers	(KCAFA)	v	Bo'ness Community	(S&DAFA)	wo	scr					
R1E	Braehead	(S&DAFA)	v	Steins Thistle	(CSAFL)	1	2					
R1E	Caledonia Star	(LEAFA)	v	FC Bayside	(FIFE)	scr	wo					
R1E	Callander Thistle	(S&DAFA)	v	Tullibody Community	(S&DAFA)	4	2					
R1E	Denbeath	(FIFE)	v	Penicuik United	(LEAFA)	4	5					
R1E	Fallin	(S&DAFA)	v	Seaforth Highlanders	(LEAFA)	4	1					
R1E	Glenrothes Strollers	(FIFE)	v	The Spartans AFC	(LEAFA)	2	1					
R1E	Kinross	(KCAFA)	v	California	(S&DAFA)	5	5		2	3		

R2W	Belleaire	(WOSAFL)	v	Ardrossan Castle Rovers	(AYR)	0	10			
R2W	Bishopton	(G&DSMAFL)	v	Coatbridge Colts	(SSMFL)	7	0			
R2W	Blochairn Star	(SAFL)	v	Blantyre Soccer Academy	(NSLAFA)	5	1			
R2W	South Camlachie YP	(SAFL)	v	AFC Fulbar	(P&D)	6	0			
R2W	Cumbernauld Colts	(CALE)	v	Hardgate	(SSML)	11	0			
R2W	Brucehill United	(P&D)	v	John Street	(GGPAFL)	6	1			
R2W	Busby	(SAFL)	v	Harmony Row	(GGPAFL)	9	1			
R2W	Calderglen	(GGPAFL)	v	Hamilton FP	(CALE)	0	1			
R2W	Cambria	(CALE)	v	Glenvale	(S&DAFA)	5	0			
R2W	Cambusglen	(G&DSMAFL)	v	Third Lanark	(WOSAFL)	6	2			
R2W	Cambusnethan Talbot	(CSAFL)	v	Columba	(G&DSMAFL)	2	1			
R2W	Cambusnethan Talbot	(SSMFL)	v	Orchard Park Mount 'B'	(GGPAFL)	2	0			
R2W	Cardross	(WOSAFL)	v	Kilsyth United	(SECAFL)	4	3			
R2W	Carluke Baptists	(SECAFL)	v	Balmore	(CALE)	3	2			
R2W	Clyde Valley Rovers	(GCAFA)	v	Bannockburn	(CSAFL)	2	8			
R2W	Eaglesham	(SAFL)	v	Carlton YMCA	(SAFL)	2	2	2	1	
R2W	Clydesdale United	(P&D)	v	FC Argyle	(P&D)	1	5			
R2W	Colville Park	(CSAFL)	v	KSC Wolves	(AYR)	3	0			
R2W	Condorrat	(S&DAFA)	v	Shawlands FP	(SAFL)	0	6			
R2W	Condorrat Club	(CSAFL)	v	Linwood Thistle	(P&D)	3	3	3	1	
R2W	Corinthians	(GCAFA)	v	Seafar Villa	(SSMFL)	3	4			
R2W	Coylton	(AYR)	v	Stewarton United	(AYR)	0	3			
R2W	Craigie	(AYR)	v	Kelvin	(GGPAFL)	1	4			
R2W	Crosshill Thistle	(AYR)	v	Carradale	(WOSAFL)	2	5			
R2W	Crosshouse	(AYR)	v	Cunninghame	(AYR)	1	7			
R2W	CS United	(G&DSMAFL)	v	Eddlewood	(GGPAFL)	scr	wo			
R2W	Kirkintilloch Miners Welfare	(CSAFL)	v	Waterside	(CSAFL)	4	3			
R2W	Cumbernauld Rovers	(S&DAFA)	v	Glasgow Harp	(CALE)	0	9			
R2W	Dalmellington United	(AYR)	v	Carluke Hearts	(NSLAFA)	0	13			
R2W	Dalmilling	(AYR)	v	Drumchapel AFC	(CSAFL)	3	11			
R2W	Dalziel HSFP	(CALE)	v	Possil YM	(WOSAFL)	0	1			
R2W	Aikenhead Thistle	(CSAFL)	v	Goldenhill	(SAFL)	4	1			
R2W	Dean	(AYR)	v	Ferguslie Star	(SAFL)	3	5			
R2W	Dennistoun	(WOSAFL)	v	Gallowhill	(P&DAFL)	5	1			
R2W	Donaldson	(NSLAFA)	v	Quayside Thistle	(SSMFL)	2	6			
R2W	Doon	(AYR)	v	Mill United	(CSAFL)	0	1			
R2W	Drumchapel FP	(CALE)	v	St Josephs	(SAFL)	1	7			
R2W	Drumpellier Thistle	(S&DAFA)	v	East Kilbride Rolls-Royce	(SAFL)	1	5			
R2W	Kilmarnock Town	(AYR)	v	Prestwick	(AYR)	0	1			
R2W	Dumbarton Academy FP	(CALE)	v	Glasgow Caledonian	(G&DSMAFL)	6	1			
R2W	Dumbarton Harp	(GGPAFL)	v	Bridgewell	(GGPAFL)	8	0			
R2W	Dynamo East Kilbride	(GGPAFL)	v	Eastfield	(CSAFL)	5	5	1	2	
R2W	East Kilbride AFC	(CSAFL)	v	Dirrans Athletic	(AYR)	0	4			
R2W	Maryhill Black Star	(SSMFL)	v	Abbey Athletic	(P&D)	7	1			
R2W	East Kilbride YM	(SAFL)	v	Baillieston Thistle	(GGPAFL)	1	2			
R2W	King's Park Rangers	(SAFL)	v	Carnwath	(NSLAFA)	wo	scr			
R2W	Elderslie	(P&D)	v	Chryston	(CSAFL)	5	3			
R2W	Erskine	(GGPAFL)	v	Pollok AFC	(CSAFL)	0	8			
	* at Pollok									
R2W	FC Dal Riata	(NSLAFA)	v	Crosslands United	(G&DSMAFL)	2	2	3	3	3-5p
R2W	Finnart	(SAFL)	v	Troon United	(AYR)	24	1			
R2W	Firhill United	(SSMFL)	v	Arthurlie United	(CSAFL)	1	2			
R2W	Gartcaim	(SECAFL)	v	AS Airdrie	(SAFL)	2	2	3	2	
R2W	Giffnock	(WOSAFL)	v	Centre	(SAFL)	1	1	3	1	
R2W	Glasgow Deaf Athletic	(P&DAFL)	v	Dennistoun Vale	(SSMFL)	0	5			
R2W	Glenbum MW	(AYR)	v	Red Star	(G&DSMAFL)	2	1			
R2W	Glentyan Thistle	(P&DAFL)	v	Millbeg Villa	(SAFL)	5	2			
R2W	Gormac Thistle	(S&DAFA)	v	Petershall Villa	(SSMFL)	4	4	1	5	
R2W	Greenock HSFP	(CSAFL)	v	Westerlands	(GGPAFL)	4	0			
R2W	Hamilton FP	(GGPAFL)	v	Auchengeigh Miners	(S&DAFA)	scr	wo			
R2W	Hamilton West	(SSMFL)	v	Stedfast	(CSAFL)	1	2			
R2W	Harestanes	(CSAFL)	w/o-scr	Houston	(P&D)	wo	scr			
R2W	Hillside	(NSLAFA)	v	Giffnock North AAC	(CALE)	1	3			

Rnd	Team 1	Lge 1		Team 2	Lge 2					
R2W	Radnor Park	(GGPAFL)	v	Silverburn United	(SSMFL)	2	7			
R2W	Rannoch	(GGPAFL)	v	Milngavie Wanderers	(CALE)	0	3			
R2W	Rosehill Star	(SAFL)	v	Campsie Minerva	(CSAFL)	0	9			
	* at Campsie									
R2W	Glasgow University	(CALE)	v	Shawbridge	(SSMFL)	0	0	2	2	4-3p
R2W	Rutherglen	(SAFL)	v	Blairdardie United	(SAFL)	wo	scr			
R2W	Scotia Athletic	(CSAFL)	v	Crownpark	(WOSAFL)	5	2			
R2W	Southside United	(GCAFA)	v	Carrick	(AYR)	0	2			
	* at Carrick									
R2W	Springhill	(NSLAFA)	v	Kilmarnock AFC	(AYR)	3	0			
R2W	St Andrews	(WOSAFL)	w/o-scr	Cumbernauld Clyde	(CSAFL)	wo	scr			
R2W	St Davids	(GCAFA)	v	Vale of Girvan	(AYR)	6	0			
R2W	St Mungos	(CALE)	v	Whinhall United	(SSMFL)	7	0			
R2W	Stewarton Annick	(AYR)	v	EKFC Whitehills	(CALE)	1	3			
R2W	Symington Caledonian	(AYR)	v	Hazelwood	(P&D)	5	5	4	5	
R2W	Tannahill	(P&D)	v	Mill United	(NSLAFA)	2	3			
R2W	Tarbet	(SAFL)	v	Yoker AFC	(SSMFL)	5	5*	3	5	
	* at Yoker									
R2W	Tarbolton	(AYR)	v	Galston United	(AYR)	0	1			
R2W	Third Lanark	(GGPAFL)	v	Firhill	(WOSAFL)	8	1			
R2W	Thorn Athletic	(SAFL)	v	Irvine Town	(AYR)	4	0			
R2W	Troon Dundonald	(AYR)	v	Netherthird	(AYR)	1	5			
R2W	Uddingston Anvil	(CSAFL)	v	Campbeltown Pupils	(SAFL)	0	0	3	4	
R2W	Vale of Leven Academy	(GGPAFL)	v	Wallacetown	(AYR)	4	4	2	1	
R2W	East Kilbride AFC	(SAFL)	v	Motherwell Community Trust	(SSMFL)	5	0			
R2W	Viewfield Rovers	(CALE)	v	Jordanhill Campus	(GGPAFL)	4	2			
R2W	Weirs Recreation	(CALE)	v	Campsie	(S&DAFA)	5	1			
R2W	West Kilbride	(AYR)	v	Fordbank Star	(P&D)	5	1			
R2W	Westbridge Villa	(SSMFL)	v	Renfrew Thistle	(GGPAFL)	3	3	3	4	
R2W	Westerlands	(CALE)	v	Tantallon Victoria	(SSMFL)	3	2			
R2W	Westwood	(SSMFL)	v	Drumley United	(AYR)	3	3	4	3	
R2W	Whitefield Rovers	(SSMFL)	v	Broomhouse	(GGPAFL)	3	3	3	1	
R2W	Whiteinch	(GGPAFL)	v	Wishaw HSFP	(CSAFL)	2	5			
R2W	Windlaw	(GGPAFL)	v	Hurlford Thistle	(AYR)	0	10			
R2W	Woodhall Thistle	(NSLAFA)	v	Gartcosh United	(CALE)	2	2	1	3	
R2E	Pencaitland	(LEAFA)	v	Haddington Athletic AFC	(LEAFA)					
R2E	Ancrum	(BAFA)	v	Strathmiglo United	(KCAFA)	2	2	0	3	
R2E	Shotts Victoria	(LEAFA)	v	Musselburgh AFC	(LEAFA)	3	2			
R2E	Barca Milton 97	(LEAFA)	v	Steins Thistle	(CSAFL)	3	3	2	3	
R2E	Rosebank	(FIFE)	v	Bathgate Thistle B AFC	(LEAFA)	wo	scr			
R2E	Bo'ness Cadora	(S&DAFA)	w/o-scr	QueensferryAlbert	(FIFE)	wo	scr			
R2E	Bonnybridge YFP	(S&DAFA)	v	Callander Thistle	(S&DAFA)	2	3			
R2E	Bowhill Rovers	(KCAFA)	v	California	(S&DAFA)	2	1			
R2E	Buckhaven Town	(FIFE)	v	Denny	(S&DAFA)	3	2			
R2E	Cabrera Athletic	(LEAFA)	v	Benarty	(KCAFA)	scr	wo			
R2E	FC Bayside	(FIFE)	v	Pittenweem Rovers	(FIFE)	2	2	1	6	
R2E	Cambusbarron Rovers	(CALE)	v	ForthCommunity	(LEAFA)	3	2			
R2E	Carronshore Athletic	(S&DAFA)	v	Rosyth	(FIFE)	1	2			
R2E	Clermiston Star	(LEAFA)	v	Symington Tinto	(CALE)	2	0			
R2E	Dalgety Bay	(FIFE)	v	Whitburn Bluebell	(LEAFA)	scr	wo			
R2E	Penicuik United	(LEAFA_)	v	Dunedin Athletic	(LEAFA)	3	0			
R2E	Doune Castle	(CALE)	v	Lothian Star	(LEAFA)	7	0			
R2E	Doune Castle	(S&DAFA)	v	Danderhall Miners	(LEAFA)	2	4			
R2E	Dunalba	(LEAFA)	v	Musselburgh United	(LEAFA)	3	0			
R2E	Dunblane Thistle	(S&DAFA)	v	North Berwick	(LEAFA)	2	6			
R2E	Dundonald	(FIFE)	v	Melrose	(BAFA)	scr	wo			
R2E	Earlston Rhymers	(BAFA)	v	MelvilleRovers	(LEAFA)	1	1	4	2	
R2E	East Calder United	(LEAFA)	v	Lomond United	(FIFE)	7	0			
R2E	Easthouses	(LEAFA)	v	Burntisland United	(FIFE)	1	3			
R2E	Eastvale	(KCAFA)	v	Armadale Thistle AFC	(LEAFA)	5	0			
R2E	Edinburgh Rose	(LEAFA)v	v	Greig Park Rangers	(KCAFA)	4	2			
R2E	Edinburgh United Alba	(LEAFA)	v	Victoria Loco	(LEAFA)	5	3			
R2E	Edinburgh University	(LEAFA)	v	Newtongrange Star A AFC	(LEAFA)	2	3			

Round	Home	Assoc	v	Away	Assoc						
R2E	Valleyfield	(FIFE)	v	Beechwood Albion	(S&DAFA)	1	0				
R2E	Cupar Hearts	(KCAFA)	v	Tillicoultry	(S&DAFA)	0	1				
R2NT	Arbroath CSC	(MAFA)	v	Maltman Athletic	(DSMAFL)	17	0				
R2NT	Arbroath Harp	(MAFA)	v	Coupar Angus AFC	(PAFA)	3	1				
R2NT	Auchterarder Primrose	(PAFA)	v	Vale of Earn	(PAFA)	3	1				
R2NT	Bank Street Athletic	(MAFA)	v	Star of Atholl	(PAFA)	wo	scr				
R2NT	Bridge of Earn	(PAFA)	v	Broughty United	(MAFA)	0	1				
R2NT	Burrelton Rovers	(PAFA)	v	Kettins	(PAFA)	1	1	3	4		
R2NT	Carnoustie YM	(MAFA)	v	Balmoral United	(PAFA)	2	2	2	0		
R2NT	Craigie	(PAFA)	v	Ballinluig Edradour	(PAFA)	3	2				
R2NT	Dundee City	(MAFA)	v	Tayside Fire Brigade	(MAFA)	4	2				
R2NT	Dundee College	(MAFA)	v	St Johns	(PAFA)	2	3				
R2NT	Fairfield	(PAFA)	v	Rattray	(PAFA)	1	2				
R2NT	FC Polonia Dundee	(MAFA)	v	Dundee University	(MAFA)	2	5				
R2NT	Invergowrie	(MAFA)	v	Vale of Atholl	(PAFA)	5	0				
R2NT	Jeanfield Swifts AFC	(PAFA)	v	Kirriemuir Youth	(MAFA)	4	4	5	3		
R2NT	Kinrossie Caledonian	(PAFA)	v	Kelso AFC	(MAFA)	3	1				
R2NT	Logie Harp	(MAFA)	v	Carnoustie Athletic	(MAFA)	2	2	2	0		
R2NT	Lowson United	(MAFA)	v	SS Peter & Paul	(MAFA)	5	4				
R2NT	Luncarty AFC	(PAFA)	v	Barnhill	(MAFA)	3	5				
R2NT	Meigle Vics	(PAFA)	v	Arbroath HSFP	(MAFA)	0	6				
R2NT	Menzieshill	(MAFA)	v	Harris FP	(MAFA)	wo	scr				
R2NT	Menzieshill Roves	(MAFA)	v	St James	(MAFA)	1	2				
R2NT	Monifieth Tayside	(MAFA)	v	Michelin Athletic	(MAFA)	wo	scr				
R2NT	Morgan Academy	(MAFA)	v	Wellbank	(MAFA)	4	3				
R2NT	NCR	(MAFA)	v	Letham	(PAFA)	3	3	2	6		
R2NT	Newport	(MAFA)	v	Parktool Athletic	(DSMAFL)	11	0				
R2NT	Perth United	(PAFA)	v	Methven	(PAFA)	0	3				
R2NT	Riverside Athletic	(MAFA)	v	Merpro	(MAFA)	6	1				
R2NT	Sidlaw Thistle	(DSMAFL)	v	Thomson Academicals AFC	(DSMAFL)	5	3				
R2NT	Strathearn Grove	(PAFA)	v	Portmoak	(PAFA)	7	1				
R2NT	Tay Thistle	(PAFA)	v	Alyth	(PAFA)	3	5				
R2NT	West End Athletic	(DSMAFL)	v	Cannon Fodder	(DSMAFL)	2	5				
R2N	AC Mill Inn	(AAFA)	v	Cowie Thistle	(AAFA)	0	3				
R2N	Banchory	(AAFA)	v	Ellon Thistle	(AAFA)	3	3	3	4		
R2N	Bankhead	(AAFA)	v	Stonehaven Athletic	(AAFA)	3	2				
R2N	Bridge of Don	(AAFA)	v	Woodside	(AAFA)	2	5				
R2N	Dee	(AAFA)	v	Torphins	(AAFA)	5	1				
R2N	Ellon	(AAFA)	v	Alford	(AAFA)	2	1				
R2N	Grammar FPs	(AAFA)	v	Newburgh Thistle	(AAFA)	1	4				
R2N	Granite City	(AAFA)	v	Newtonhill	(AAFA)	3	4				
R2N	Great Western United	(AAFA)	v	MS United	(AAFA)	3	9				
R2N	Highland Hotel	(AAFA)	v	Northern United	(AAFA)	6	3				
R2N	Huntly AFC	(AAFA)	v	Kintore	(AAFA)	0	0	2	7		
R2N	Fintray Thistle	(AAFA)	v	Glendale	(AAFA)	1	4				
R2N	Kaimhill United	(AAFA)	v	Glendale Youth	(AAFA)	0	3				
R2N	Luthermuir	(AAFA)	v	Echt	(AAFA)	scr	wo				
R2N	Monymusk	(AAFA)	v	Bervie Caledonian	(AAFA)	2	4				
R2N	Rothie Rovers	(AAFA)	v	Kemnay Youth	(AAFA)	4	0				
R2N	Scotstown Rovers	(AAFA)	v	Halliburton	(AAFA)	0	9				
R2N	Theologians NE	(AAFA)	v	Glentanar Reflex	(AAFA)	2	0				
R2N	Torry Select	(AAFA)	v	Tarves	(AAFA)	1	6				
R2N	BS AFC	(AAFA)	v	Burghmuir	(AAFA)	3	3	A	A	1	6
R3	Airth Castle Rovers	(S&DAFA)	v	Grangemouth Rovers	(S&DAFA)	2	3				
R3	Aikenhead Thistle	(CSAFL)	v	Electric Bar	(NSLAFA)	8	2				
R3	Alyth	(PAFA)	v	Rattray	(PAFA)	2	1				
R3	Arbroath CSC	(MAFA)	v	St Mungos	(CALE)	0	2				
R3	Arbroath Harp	(MAFA)	v	Dysart	(FIFE)	1	2				
R3	Ardrossan Castle Rovers	(AYR)	v	Cambusnethan Talbot	(SSMFL)	3	0				
R3	Blantyre Rangers	(NSLAFA)	v	Dirrans Athletic	(AYR)	2	3				
R3	Auchterarder Primrose	(PAFA)	v	St Monan Swallows	(FIFE)	5	1				
R3	Bank Street Athletic	(MAFA)	v	Mill United	(NSLAFA)	5	0				
R3	Steins Thistle	(CSAFL)	v	Muirend	(GGPAFL)	7	0				

R3	East Kilbride	(SAFL)	v	Fife Thistle	(FIFE)	7	1				
R3	East Kilbride Rolls Royce	(SAFL)	v	Glencastle Sparta	(SAFL)	7	0				
R3	Edinburgh Southern	(LEAFA)	v	Sidlaw Thistle	(DSMAFL)	1	2				
R3	Edinburgh United Alba	(LEAFA)	v	Glendale Youth	(AAFA)	3	4				
R3	Elderslie	(P&D)	v	St Andrews	(WOSAFL)	4	2				
R3	Ellon Thistle	(AAFA)	v	Condorrat Club	(CSAFL)	0	4				
R3	Pollok AFC	(CSAFL)	v	EKFC Whitehills	(CALE)	2	4				
R3	Crosslands United	(G&DSMAFL)	v	Castlemilk	(SAFL)	3	1				
R3	Fernieside	(LEAFA)	v	Hermiston Vale	(LEAFA)	1	2				
R3	Finnart	(SAFL)	v	Giffnock	(WOSAFL)	4	1				
R3	Glasgow University	(CALE)	v	Earlston Rhymers	(BAFA)	wo	scr				
R3	Glenmuir Thistle	(AYR)	v	Campbeltown Pupils	(SAFL)	2	7				
R3	Glentyan Thistle	(P&DAFL)	v	Drumchapel	(CSAFL)	0	2				
R3	Gordon	(BAFA)	v	Gleburn Miners Welfare	(AYR)	2	1				
R3	Petershall Villa	(SSMFL)	v	Beith AFC	(AYR)	2	6				
R3	Stedfast	(CSAFL)	v	Inverclyde	(SAFL)	1	3				
R3	Harestanes	(CSAFL)	v	South Camlachie YP	(SAFL)	1	1	4	3		
R3	Hearts of Beath	(FIFE)	v	West Kilbride	(AYR)	1	4				
R3	Highland Hotel	(AAFA)	v	Logie Harp	(MAFA)	1	1	2	2	3-2 pens	
R3	Giffnock North AAC	(CALE)	v	Queensferry Athletic	(LEAfa)	5	1				
R3	Hurlford Thistle	(AYR)	v	Arthurlie United	(CSAFL)	1	1	4	1		
R3	Inchinnan Community Club	(SSMFL)	v	Redbrae Athletic	(S&DAFA)	6	0				
R3	Invergowrie	(MAFA)	v	Shortlees	(AYR)	3	3	4	1		
R3	Jimmy Johnstone Academy	(GCAFA)	v	Ellon	(AAFA)	3	4				
R3	Kettle United	(KCAFA)	v	St Josephs	(SAFL)	0	6				
R3	Kingdom Athletic	(FIFE)	v	Easthall Star	(SAFL)	2	4				
R3	Jeanfield Swifts AFC	(PAFA)	v	Kirkcaldy YMCA	(FIFE)	1	0				
R3	LBC Lochend	(LEAFA)	v	Haldane United	(SAFL)	1	3				
R3	Leslie Hearts	(FIFE)	v	Luthermuir	(AAFA)	3	3	2	3		
R3	Leven United	(KCAFA)	v	Morgan Academy	(MAFA)	3	2				
R3	Loanhead Miners Welfare	(LEAFA)	v	Kelvin	(GGPAFL)	5	0				
R3	Loganlea United	(S&DAFA)	v	Mossblown	(AYR)	6	1				
R3	Blantyre Celtic	(CSAFL)	v	Springhill	(NSLAFA)	8	0				
R3	Maryhill Black Star	(SSMFL)	v	Garrowhill Thistle	(CSAFL)	0	3				
R3	Mashucubia	(LEAFA)	v	Bearsden	(CALE)	0	5				
R3	Hillington	(SAFL)	v	Motherwell Miners	(NSLAFA)	3	3	1	0		
R3	Melrose	(BAFA)	v	Pencaitland	(LEAFA)	1	6				
R3	Menzieshill	(MAFA)	v	East Linton	(LEAFA)	8	2				
R3	Methven	(PAFA)	v	Shotts Victoria	(LEAFA	0	3				
R3	Milton	(CALE)	v	Carnoustie YM	(MAFA)	3	0				
R3	Milton	(S&DAFA)	v	Lumphinnans United	(KCAFA)	2	2	2	3		
R3	Monifieth Tayside	(MAFA)	v	Dee	(AAFA)	1	3				
R3	Motherwell Thistle	(SAFL)	v	Lochan	(AYR)	5	1				
R3	Myre Athletic	(GGPAFL)	v	East Calder United	(LEAFA)	2	2	4	0		
R3	Newtongrange Star A	(LEAFA)	v	Neilston AFC	(SAFL)	1	3				
R3	Newtonhill	(AAFA)	v	Halliburton	(AAFA)	4	2				
R3	Nia Roo	(WOSAFL)	v	ESV	(LEAFA)	3	2				
R3	Oban Saints	(SAFL)	v	Rosyth	(FIFE)	6	1				
R3	Overtown Thistle	(NSLAFA)	v	Kintore	(AAFA)	3	1				
R3	Pathhead	(LEAFA)	v	Eastvale	(KCAFA)	2	2	0	9		
R3	Penicuik United	(LEAFA)	v	Prestwick	(AYR)	4	1				
R3	Port Glasgow	(SAFL)	v	Whitburn Bluebell	(LEAFA)	1	2				
R3	Port Glasgow OBU	(SAFL)	v	Tarves	(AAFA)	0	5				
R3	Strathclyde University	(CALE)	v	Newport	(MAFA)	5	2				
R3	Possil YM	(WOSAFL)	v	Eddlewood	(GGPAFL)	1	0				
R3	Postal United	(CSAFL)	v	St Patricks FP	(CSAFL)	1	3				
R3	Rhu	(CALE)	v	Bankhead	(AAFA)	3	3	4	1		
R3	Riverside Athletic	(MAFA)	v	North Berwick	(LEAFA)	1	1	4	0		
R3	Rosebank	(FIFE)	v	Newburgh Thisle	(AAFA)	5	0				
R3	Campsie Minerva	(CSAFL)	v	Westwood	(SSMFL)	2	2	5	1		
R3	Rosyth Civil Service	(KCAFA)	v	Tollcross Thistle	(LEAFA)	3	5				
R3	Rothie Rovers	(AAFA)	v	Newcraighall Leith Vics	(LEAFA)	0	3				
R3	Rutherglen	(SAFL)	v	St Johns	(PAFA)	3	1				

Round	Home	v	Away						
R4	Giffnock North AAC	v	Beith AFC		3	1			
R4	Glendale	v	Rosebank		1	5			
R4	Ardrossan Castle Rovers	v	Cumbernauld Colts		1	2			
R4	Carluke Hearts	v	Dumbarton Academy FP		2	3			
R4	Wellhouse	v	Hillington		5	2			
R4	East Kilbride AFC	v	Luthermuir		6	1			
R4	Shotts Victoria	v	Silverburn		2	1			
R4	Harestanes	v	Milton (CALE)		3	2			
R4	South Gyle	v	Scotia		3	3	1	3	
R4	Danderhall Miners Welfare	v	Inchinnan Community Club		5	2			
R4	Linwood	v	Overtown Thistle		0	1			
R4	Loanhead MW	v	St Patricks FP		0	2			
R4	Neilston	v	Dennistoun Vale		0	2			
R4	Westerlands	v	Nia Roo		1	1	2	4	
R4	Bank Street Athletic	v	Motherwell Thistle'		6	0			
R4	Tarves	v	Stenhousemuir AFC		2	6			
R4	Gartcairn	v	Galston United		1	5			
R4	Tollcross Thistle	v	Bantyre Celtic		2	5			
R4	Riverside Athletic	v	St Josephs		3	4			
R4	Craigie	v	Haldane United		2	4			
R4	Vale of Leven Academy	v	Greenock HSFP		1	4			
R4	Campbeltown Pupils	v	Carradale		3	1			
R4	Ferguslie Star	v	Clermiston Star		6	1			
R4	Glasgow University (CALE)	v	Lumphinnans United		2	0			
R4	Whitburn Bluebell	v	Alyth		1	1	1	0	
R4	Wishaw HSFP	v	Whitefield Rovers		1	3			
R4	Possil YM	v	Dysart		12	2			
R4	Penicuik United	v	Bearsden		1	3			
R4	Newcraighall Leith Vics	v	East Kilbride Rolls-Royce		3	2			
R4	Burghmuir	v	Colville Park		0	9			
R4	King's Park Rangers	v	Loganlea United		1	3			
R4	Steins Thistle	v	Baillieston	Thistle	4	3			
R4	Myre Athletic	v	Eaglesham		5	2			
R4	Knockentiber	v	Strathclyde University (CALE)		3	4			
R4	Sidlaw Thistle	v	Bannockburn (CSAL)		1	8			
R4	Hermiston Villa	v	Carrick		0	0	1	0	
R4	Drumchapel AFC	v	Jeanfield Swifts		4	2			
R4	Rutherglen	v	Netherthird		2	2	1	1	2-3p
R4	Mill United	v	Benarty		2	4			
R4	Glasgow Harp	v	Auchterarder Primrose	Primrose	3	1			
R4	Viewfield Rovers	v	Campsie Minerva		0	2			
R4	Valleyfield	v	Kirkcaldy Rovers		7	0			
R4	Finnart	v	Condorrat Club		3	0			
R4	Dirrans Athletic	v	Crosslands United		4	1			
R4	Bowhill Rovers	v	Easthall Star		5	1			
R4	Invergowrie	v	Gordon		2	3			
R5	Possil YM	v	Carluke Baptists		0	3			
R5	Danderhall Miners Welfare	v	Overtown Thistle		2	6			
R5	Eastfield	v	Whitburn Bluebell		3	2			
R5	Bank Street Athletic	v	Giffnock North		3	2			
R5	Bowhill Rovers	v	Dennistoun		4	1			
R5	Elderslie	v	Nia Roo		2	3			
R5	Galston United	v	Loganlea United	United	5	3			
R5	Bannockburn	v	St Josephs		2	2	4	1	
R5	Glasgow University	v	Blantyre Celtic		0	2			
R5	Thorn Athletic	v	Drumchapel AFC		2	2	3	2	
R5	Harestanes	v	Bearsden		4	0			
R5	Dennistoun Vale	v	Oban Saints		0	1			
R5	Steins Thistle	v	East Kilbride AFC		0	1			
R5	Cumbernauld Colts	v	Aikenhead Thistle		1	1	1	3	
R5	EK Whitehills	v	Campeltown Pupils		1	3			
R5	Rosebank	v	Dirrans Athletic		4	1			

R7	Greenock HSFP	v	Hurlford Thistle	2	3	
R7	Harestanes	v	Bannockburn	A	A	2 teams expelled
R7	Nia-Roo	v	Finnart	0	1	
R7	Pittenweem Rovers	v	Carluke Baptists	1	3	
R7	Wellhouse	v	Bowhill Rovers	4	0	
R8	Hurlford Thistle		Bye			
R8	Carluke Baptists	v	Eastfield	3	3 1 3	
R8	Finnart	v	Colville Park	1	3	
R8	Glasgow Harp	v	Wellhouse	2	2 2 1	
SF	Colville Park	v	Glasgow Harp	3	1	at New Douglas Pk
SF	Eastfield	v	Hurlford Thistle	0	5	at New Douglas Pk
F	Hurlford Thistle	v	Colville Park	3	3	aet, 4-3 pens

SCOTTISH AMATEUR FA DISTRICT CUPS 2013/14

NORTH OF TAY

SF	St James	Letham Amateurs	7	0		Dundee Violet
SF	Riverside Athletic	Ballinluig	6	3		Kinnoull JFC Park
F	Riverside Athletic	St James	1	2		Dundee Violet

FIFE

SF	Pittenweem Rovers	Leven United	4	2		Glenrothes JFC
SF	Bowhill Rovers	Rosyth Civil Service	1	0		Glenrothes JFC
F	Pittenweem Rovers	Bowhill Rovers	2	3		Kelty Hearts

EAST

SF	Tollcross Thistle	Steins Thistle	1	2		Spartans
SF	Braehead	Slamannan	3	1		Falkirk FC
F	Steins Thistle	Braehead	1	1	aet, 3-2p	Livingston FC

WEST

SF	Hurlford Thistle	Bannockburn	3	2		Airdrieonians FC
SF	Giffnock North AAC /Eastfield	Blochairn Star B	1	0		Airdrieonians FC
F	Hurlford Thistle	Giffnock North	2	0		Hamilton Accies

SOUTH

SF	Carluke Baptists	Stow	4	1		Innerleithen
SF	Hawick Waverley	Leithen Rovers	2	4		Innerleithen
F	Carluke Baptists	Leithen Rovers	3	4		Innerleithen

NORTH

SF	Cowie Thistle	Cove Thistle	wo	scr		Aberdeen East End
SF	Woodside	Kincorth	2	1	aet	Aberdeen East End
F	Cove Thistle	Woodside	1	0		Cove Rangers

HIGHLAND (2013)

SF	Wick Groats	Golspie Stafford	2	1	aet	Helmsdale
SF	Kirkwall Thorfinn	Pentland United	2	1		Kirkwall
F	Wick Groats	Kirkwall Thorfinn	1	0		Inverness CT

SCOTTISH SUNDAY AMATEUR TROPHY 2013/14

R1W	Annick Tavern	(WASAFA)	v	DW Woodrove	(WASAFA)	1	3
R1W	Bellgrove	(SCAFL)	v	Glasgow Rangers	(SCAFL)	4	1
R1W	Broadwood Clyde	(SSAFL)	v	Forgewood	(A&CAFL)	3	6
R1W	Charlies Bar	(NASAFA)	v	Kirkstyle United	(A&CAFL)	wo	scr
R1W	Drumbank Thistle	(SCAFL)	v	Coach and Horses	(WASAFA)	scr	wo
R1W	Gartcairn Athletic	(A&CAFL)	v	Treble 222	(SCAFL)	3	1
R1W	Gartcairn United	(C&DAFL)	v	Scaur	(DSAFL)	wo	scr
R1W	Glasgow South	(SCAFL)	v	Rutherglen Vogue	(SCAFL)	1	13
R1W	Holytown Phonix	(C&DAFL)	v	Glasgow Rovers	(SCAFL)	4	2
R1W	Lesmahagow AFC	(C&DAFL)	v	Allanton	(C&DAFL)	1	2
R1W	Loreburn Thistle	(DSAFL)	v	AC Hamilton	(C&DAFL)	3	2
R1W	Motherwell War Office	(C&DAFL)	v	Carluke Thistle	(C&DAFL)	6	0
R1W	Real Albion	(A&CAFL)	v	Jerviston Boys Club	(A&CAFL)	2	7
R1W	Southside White Cart	(SCAFL)	v	Crown Inn B	(NASAFA)	20	2
R1W	Wishaw Athletic	(C&DAFL)	v	New Stevenston United	(C&DAFL)	3	4
R1E	Abbey	(FSAFL)	v	Victoria Park Rangers	(LEAFA Sunday)	3	3 4-5 pens
R1E	Beltane Rangers	(WLSAFL)	v	The Polton Inn	(E&DSAFA)	4	1
R1E	Broxburn	(LEAFA Sunday)	v	Tams Bar	(FSAFL)	8	2
R1E	Edinburgh Athletic	(E&DSAFA)	v	Club 3550	(WLSAFL)	6	2
R1E	Golden Acorn	(FSAFL)	v	Saltire	(WLSAFL)	2	2
R1E	Livingston AFC	(WLSAFL)	v	Corrie	(WLSAFL)	4	2
R1E	Lothian Thistle AFC	(WLSAFL)	v	Glory XI	(LEAFA Sunday)	2	1
R1E	Pavilion	(LEAFA Sunday)	v	Edinburgh Caledonian	(LEAFA Sunday)	1	1 3-1 pens
R1E	Salvesen	(LEAFA) Sunday	v	The Clachan	(WLSAFL)	6	1
R1E	The Standard	(LEAFA Sunday	v	Shotts Thistle	(WLSAFL)	1	2
R1E	Tranent Athletic	(LEAFA Sunday	v	Boca Seniors	(E&DSAFA	0	4
R1NOT	Dundee Argyle	(DSAFA)	v	Westend Albion	(DSAFA)	6	0
R1NOT	Strathmore Bar	(F&DSAFL)	v	Kirrie Thistle Social	(F&DSAFL)	7	2
R1N	The Foundry	(ASAFL)	v	MS Services	(ASAFL)	5	6
R2W	AFC Airdrie Albion	(C&DAFL)	v	AFC Carluke	(C&DAFL)	5	0
R2W	Gartcairn Airdrie	(SSAFL)	v	Kilbirnie United	(WASAFA)	5	2
R2W	Airdrie Workmans	(A&CAFL)	v	Tap Shop	(WASAFA)	0	2
R2W	Albion	(A&CAFL)	v	Beechwood Athletic	(SCAFL)	A	A
R2W	Alpha	(C&DAFL)	v	Gartferry	(SCAFL)	3	3 3-4 pens
R2W	Belhaven	(C&DAFL)	v	AFC Drongan	(WASAFA)	6	0
R2W	Bishopbriggs	(SCAFL)	v	New Stevenston United	(C&DAFL)	1	0
R2W	Bobby's Bar	(NASAFA)	v	Valley Thistle	(WASAFA)	3	1
R2W	Forgewood	(A&CAFL)	v	DW Woodgrove	(WASAFA)	5	2
R2W	Cadzow Hamilton	(SSAFL)	v	Stonehouse	(WASAFA)	4	3
R2W	Calderbank	(A&CAFL)	v	Bullfrog	(C&DAFL)	1	2
R2W	Calderside	(SCAFL)	v	The Geet	(NASAFA)	0	4
R2W	Carluke Victoria	(C&DAFL)	v	Holytown Phoenix	(C&DAFL)	3	6
R2W	Castlemilk East	(SCAFL)	v	Westhill	(SCAFL)	2	2 5-3 pens
R2W	Castlemilk United	(SCAFL)	v	The Hamilton Arms	(S&DAFA)	3	3 4-1 pens
R2W	Cellar Bar Colts	(A&CAFL)	v	The Craft	(WASAFA)	4	4 3-4 pens
R2W	Charlies Bar	(NASAFA)	v	Jerviston Boys Club	(A&CAFL)	4	3
R2W	Chasers	(S&DAFA)	v	Cadzow Harp	(C&DAFL)	1	1 4-3 pens
R2W	Clarkston United	(C&DAFL)	v	Thornwood	(SCAFL)	3	5
R2W	Cleland Club	(C&DAFL)	v	Bar 12	(S&DAFA)	8	1
R2W	Cumbernauld Colts	(SCAFL)	v	Kings Arms	(DSAFL)	2	2
R2W	Dreghorn Inn	(WASAFA)	v	Rossvale AFC	(SCAFL)	5	3
R2W	Coach and Horses	(WASAFA)	v	MK Dynamo	(SCAFL)	3	4
R2W	Drumchapel FP	(SCAFL)	v	Park Athletic	(S&DAFA)	5	6
R2W	Drumchapel Thistle	(SCAFL)	v	Annan Town	(C&DAFL)	4	0
R2W	Dumfries Athletic	(DSAFL)	v	Scaur	(DSAFL)	0	13
R2W	Dykehead	(C&DAFL)	v	Big Shop	(A&CAFL)	3	2
R2W	Eastend Athletic	(SCAFL)	v	Stanley Athletic	(SCAFL)	6	3
R2W	Eastfield Athletic	(SCAFL)	v	Killie Athletic	(WASAFA)	scr	wo
R2W	Gartcairn Athletic	(A&CAFL)	v	Cranhill United	(SCAFL)	0	3
R2W	Rutherglen Vogie	(SCAFL)	v	Allanton	(C&DAFL)	7	1
R2W	Glasgow Thistle	(SCAFL)	v	Westend United	(SCAFL)	4	0
R2W	Haghill	(A&CAFL)	v	Bothan	(WASAFA)	4	2

R2W	Lochgreen		v	Brunswick	(SCAFL)	3	2	
R2W	Loreburn Thistle	(DSAFL)	v	The Hub	(SCAFL)	2	2	
R2W	Mac's Bar	(C&DAFL)	v	Overlee Partizans	(SCAFL)	1	2	
R2W	Medda Sports Bar	Sports	v	Crownpoint United	(SCAFL)	6	1	
R2W	Millers United	(A&CAFL)	v	Manhattan Blacks	(SCAFL)	0	10	
R2W	Moffat Thistle 2010	(DSAFL)	v	Hole In The Wa	(DSAFL)	5	1	
R2W	Monkland United	(A&CAFL)	v	Rolling Barrell	(A&CAFL)	1	5	
R2W	Motherwell War Office	(C&DAFL)	v	Southside White Cart	(SCAFL)	0	4	
R2W	Normandy Star	(DSAFL)	v	Milton of Colquhoun	(SCAFL)	2	2	4-2 pens
R2W	Polonia Glasgow	(SCAFL)	v	Jolly Harvester	(DSAFL)	4	1	
R2W	Queens Park Spiders	(SCAFL)	v	Northend	(SCAFL)	3	0	
R2W	Revels	(NASAFA)	v	Hillview	(SCAFL)	1	1	4-5 pens
R2W	Stevenston Thistle	(WASAFA)	v	Woodpecker	(C&DAFL)	0	6	
R2W	Stranraer Boswell	(S&DAFA)	v	Springhall Spartans	(SCAFL)	0	3	
R2W	Tartan Bar	(WASAFA)	v	Castlemilk Dynamo	(SCAFL)	2	5	
R2W	The Num	(S&DAFA)	v	Jacks United	(NASAFA)	3	1	
R2W	Thomsons	(SCAFL)	v	Cleddans (SCAFL)	(SCAFL)	1	0	
R2W	Thrashbush	(A&CAFL)	v	Eastfield Star	(SCAFL)	2	1	
R2W	Unity	(A&CAFL)	v	Newton Vale	(SCAFL)	0	9	
R2W	Westburn	(SCAFL)	v	Eastend United	(A&CAFL)	5	4	
R2W	Windlaw	(SCAFL)	v	Bellgrove	(SCAFL)	4	1	
R2E	Abbey Athletic	(E&DSAFA)	v	Whitburn JSC	(WLSAFL)	4	5	
R2E	Alnwickhill	(LEAFA Sunday)	v	Dunalba	(LEAFA Sunday)	0	2	
R2E	Armadale Rose	(LEAFA Sunday)	v	Beltane Rangers	(WLSAFL)	2	1	
R2E	Armadale United	(WLSAFL)	v	Torleys	(FSAFL)	0	1	
R2E	Arniston	(E&DSAFA)	v	Stables	(LEAFA Sunday)	2	0	
R2E	Blackburn United AFC	(WLSAFL)	v	Longstone United	(E&DSAFA)	4	0	
R2E	Bonnyrigg Sportsbar	(LEAFA Sunday)	v	Society	(FSAFL)	0	2	
R2E	Brucefield	(FSAFL)	v	Cowden Park	(E&DSAFA)	11	0	
R2E	Burgh Vale	(LEAFA Sunday)	v	Bathgate Thistle AFC Sunday	(LEAFA Sunday)	0	2	
R2E	Carmondean Rovers	(WLSAFL)	v	East Calder Daltons	(WLSAFL)	3	3	4-5 pens
R2E	CISWO	(FSAFL)	v	Kinghorn Hearts	(FSAFL)	2	2	4-3 pens
R2E	Club Livingston	(WLSAFL)	v	Styx	(FSAFL)	scr	wo	
R2E	Craigshill Thistle	(LEAFA Sunday)	v	Limekilns	(FSAFL)	2	4	
R2E	Crown Park	(WLSAFL)	v	Limekilns	(E&DSAFA)	3	4	
R2E	Crystal Barcelona	(FSAFL)	v	Royal Penicuik	(LEAFA Sunday)	3	0	
R2E	Dalkeith Athletic	(LEAFA Sunday)	v	Cross Tavern	(WLSAFL)	0	9	
R2E	Duddingston Athletic	(E&DSAFA)	v	Broxburn	(LEAFA Sunday)	1	4	
R2E	Dunfermline United	(FSAFL)	v	Livingston Poznan	(WLSAFL)	4	2	
R2E	Dynamo Hibs	(E&DSAFA)	v	Riverside Tower	(WLSAFL)	1	5	
R2E	Edinburgh Athletic	(E&DSAFA)	v	Livingston AFC	(WLSAFL)	4	0	
R2E	Falcon Thistle	(LEAFA Sunday)	v	Livingston Hearts	(WLSAFL)	2	1	
R2E	FC Brig	(FSAFL)	v	Krossbar	(WLSAFL)	6	0	
R2E	Fountainbridge	(LEAFA Sunday)	v	Victoria Park Rangers	(LEAFA Sunday)	0	2	
R2E	Harthill Village	(WLSAFL)	v	Hibeernian	(E&DSAFA)	3	3	1-3 pens
R2E	Kennoway	(FSAFL)	v	Harvester	(WLSAFL)	0	8	
R2E	Kingdom United	(FSAFL)	v	Novar Rovers	(FSAFL)	6	4	
R2E	Kittys	(FSAFL)	v	Golden Acorn	(FSAFL)	3	1	
R2E	Lauders	(FSAFL)	v	Westside	(E&DSAFA)	4	3	
R2E	LBC	(FSAFL)	v	Jeffrey United		scr	wo	
R2E	Legion Rovers	(FSAFL)	v	Edinburgh City AFC	(LEAFA Sunday)	0	5	
R2E	Liberton United	(E&DSAFA)	v	Bilston United	(LEAFA Sunday)	4	3	
R2E	Livingston North	(WLSAFL)	v	Newpark	(WLSAFL)	2	1	
R2E	Lochore Castle	(FSAFL)	v	Alba Thistle	(LEAFA Sunday)	1	2	
R2E	Minto Lounge	(FSAFL)	v	Salvesen	(LEAFA Sunday)	2	1	
R2E	Partizan	(LEAFA Sunday)	v	Bruntsfield Park	(LEAFA Sunday)	4	2	
R2E	Pavilion	(LEAFA Sunday)	v	Bayview Bar	(FSAFL)	1	1	
R2E	Pentland Thistle	(E&DSAFA)	v	Bogarts	(FSAFL)	1	6	
R2E	Pumpherston Thistle	(LEAFA Sunday)	v	Craigroyston AFC	(E&DSAFA)	2	7	
R2E	Redding	(WLSAFL)	v	Gilmerton	(LEAFA Sunday)	10	2	
R2E	Redhall Star	(E&DSAFA)	v	Lothian Thistle AFC	(WLSAFL)	7	2	
R2E	Roseburn Thistle	(LEAFA Sunday)	v	St Bernards	(LEAFA Sunday)	0	10	
R2E	Rosewell Miners	(LEAFA Sunday)	v	Oxgangs AFC	(E&DSAFA)	wo	scr	

R2E	Ultimo Golcia 4	(E&DSAFA)	v	Shotts Thistle	(WLSAFL)	0	1	
R2E	Uphall Athletic	(WLSAFL)	v	Newtown	(WLSAFL)	2	5	
R2E	Waverley Hotel	(LEAFA Sunday)	v	Rosyth AFC	(FSAFL)	4	1	
R2E	West Lothian Athletic	(WLSAFL)	v	AC Midlothian	(E&DSAFA)	5	2	
R2NOT	AFC Plough	(F&DSAFL)	v	Lochee United AFC	(DSAFA)	wo	scr	
R2NOT	Buddies	(PSAFA)	v	Carnoustie Allstars	(F&DSAFL)	1	4	
R2NOT	Dundee Argyle	(DSAFA)	v	Star Hotel	(PSAFA)	12	1	
R2NOT	Fairfield SLC AFA	(DSAFA)	v	v	Strathmore	2	0	
R2NOT	FC Porty	(F&DSAFL)	v	Burton Albion	(DSAFA)	6	0	
R2NOT	FC Westy	(F&DSAFL)	v	Vic	(PSAFA)	0	2	
R2NOT	Fintry Athletic	(DSAFA)	v	Finavon	(F&DSAFL)	4	2	
R2NOT	Letham 95	(PSAFA)	v	Downfield Harp	(DSAFA)	1	11	
R2NOT	Planet	(DSAFA)	v	Cutty Sark	(DSAFA)	0	5	
R2NOT	Tayport AFC	(DSAFA)	v	Taybank	(PSAFA)	12	0	
R2NOT	West Port Wanderers	(F&DSAFL)	v	Osnaburg Bar	(F&DSAFL)	3	2	
R2N	Great Western Star	(ASAFL)	v	v	The	3	2	
R2N	Shirlaws	(ASAFL)	v	Fountain Bar	(ASAFL)	1	4	
R2N	Westdyce	(ASAFL)	v	Sheddocksley United	(ASAFL)	5	3	
R3	Airdrie Albion	(C&DAFL)	v	Kittys	(FSAFL)	4	2	
R3	Alba Thistle	(LEAFA	v	West Port Wanderers	(F&DSAFL)	2	4	
R3	Armadale Rose	(LEAFA	v	Moffat Thistle 2010	(DSAFL)	0	1	
R3	Bathgate Thistle AFC	(LEAFA	v	Park Athletic	(S&DAFA)	2	2	5-4 pens
R3	Bishopbriggs	(SCAFL)	v	Blackburn United AFC	(WLSAFL)	1	5	
R3	Broxburn	(LEAFA	v	Hillview	(SCAFL)	1	6	
R3	Brucefield	(FSAFL)	v	Beechwood Athletic	(A&CAFL)	0	2	
R3	Bullfrog	(C&DAFL)	v	Riverside Tower	(WLSAFL)	3	2	
R3	Carnoustie Allstars	(F&DSAFL)	v	Sky	(FSAFL)	1	2	
R3	Castlemilk United	(SCAFL)	v	Whitburn JSC	(WLSAFL)	9	0	
R3	Charlies Bar	(NASAFA)	v	Dreghorn Inn	(WASAFA)	6	1	
R3	Chasers	(S&DAFA)	v	The Geet	(SCAFL)	1	3	
R3	CISWO	(FSAFL)	v	Arniston	(E&DSAFA)	2	2	4-3 pens
R3	Cleland Club	(C&DAFL)	v	The Hub	(SCAFL)	3	2	
R3	Craigroyston AFC	(E&DSAFA)	v	Bayview	(FSAFL)	1	7	
R3	Cranhill United	(SCAFL)	v	Edinburgh Athletic	(E&DSAFA)	5	3	
R3	Crystal Barcelona	(FSAFL)	v	Edinburgh City AFC	(LEAFA	3	0	
R3	Cutty Sark	(DSAFA)	v	Salters Athletic	(LEAFA	4	6	
R3	Dunalba	(LEAFA	v	Thrashbush	(A&CAFL)	1	4	
R3	Dundee Argyle	(DSAFA)	v	Athletico Dunfermline	(FSAFL)	11	2	
R3	East Calder Daltons	(WLSAFL)	v	Midlothian Star	(LEAFA	scr	wo	
R3	Eastend Athletic	(SCAFL)	v	Lauders	(FSAFL)	4	2	
R3	Fairfield SLC AFA	(DSAFA)	v	Redhall Star	(E&DSAFA)	5	0	
R3	Falcon Thistle	(LEAFA	v	Bogarts	(FSAFL)	5	3	
R3	FC Brig	(FSAFL)	v	Springhall Spartans	(SCAFL)	A	A	0-1
R3	FC Porty	(F&DSAFL)	v	Irvine No 1 CSC	(WASAFA)	7	0	
R3	Fintry Athletic	(DSAFA)	v	Castlemilk East	(SCAFL)	1	1	6-5 pens
R3	Fountain Bar	(ASAFL)	v	Shotts Thistle	(WLSAFL)	0	2	
R3	Gartferry	(SCAFL)	v	The Num	(S&DAFA)	17	0	
R3	Great Western Star	(ASAFL)	v	Belhaven	(C&DAFL)	9	0	
R3	Haghill	(A&CAFL)	v	Rolling Barrell	(A&CAFL)	1	2	
R3	Haldane United	(SCAFL)	v	Harvester	(SCAFL)	3	4	
R3	Holytown Phoenix	(C&DAFL)	v	Cadzow Hamilton	(SSAFL)	0	11	
R3	Imperial Albion	(A&CAFL)	v	Dunfermline United	(FSAFL)	2	2	
R3	Jeffrey United	(FSAFL)	v	Newtown	(WLSAFL)	2	6	
R3	Kingdom United	(FSAFL)	v	Gartcairn Airdrie	(SSAFL)	2	1	
R3	Kings Arms	(DSAFL)	v	Lochgreen		3	1	
R3	Liberton United	(E&DSAFA)	v	Waverley Hotel	(LEAFA	3	3	2-4 pens
R3	Limekilns	(E&DSAFA)	v	Partizan	(LEAFA	5	6	
R3	Limekilns	(FSAFL)	v	Queen's Park Spiders	(SCAFL)	1	3	
R3	Livingston North	(WLSAFL)	v	Scaur	(DSAFL)	5	2	
R3	Manhattan Blacks	(SCAFL)	v	Plough	(F&DSAFL)	6	2	
R3	Medda Sports Bar	(WASAFA)	v	Downfield Harp	(DSAFA)	3	1	
R3	Minto Lounge	(FSAFL)	v	Forgewood	(A&CAFL)	6	0	

R3	St. Bernards	(LEAFA	v Hibeernian	(E&DSAFA)	3	2	
R3	Castlemilk Dynamo	(SCAFL)	v Bobby's Bar	(NASAFA)	5	1	
R3	Thomsons	(SCAFL)	v Styx	(FSAFL)	5	2	
R3	Torleys	(FSAFL)	v Thornwood	(SCAFL)	1	1 5-6 pens	
R3	Turf	(NASAFA)	v Westercommon Star	(SCAFL)	3	2	
R3	Vic	(PSAFA)	v Tayport AFC	(DSAFA)	2	5	
R3	Victoria Park Rangers	(LEAFA	v Drumchapel Thistle	(SCAFL)	0	2	
R3	West Lothian Athletic	(WLSAFL)	v Harbour	(WASAFA)	2	2 5-4 pens	
R3	Westburn	(SCAFL)	v Tap Shop	(WASAFA)	2	2 4-3 pens	
R3	Westdyce	(ASAFL)	v Cross Tavern	(WLSAFL)	1	8	
R3	Windlaw	(SCAFL)	v Polonia Glasgow	(SCAFL)	4	2	
R3	Woodpecker	(C&DAFL)	v Broxburn Athletic AFC	(WLSAFL)	0	1	
R4	Bathgate Thistle AFC		Cranhill United		3	5	
R4	Rutherglen Vogue		Manhattan Blacks		5	0	
R4	Tayport AFC		Airdrie Albion		3	1	
R4	Moffat Thistle 2010		Castlemilk Dynamo		3	3 4-5 pens	
R4	Hillview		Belhaven		3	1 Abd, 6-2	
R4	Beechwood Albion		Cleland Club		1	2	
R4	Bullfrog		Dunfermline United		5	3	
R4	Castlemilk United		West Port Wanderers		9	0	
R4	Crystal Barcelona		St Bernards		3	3 4-5 pens	
R4	Thrashbush		Shotts Thistle		2	2 18-19 pens	
R4	Dykehead		Skye		6	1	
R4	East End Athletic		Falcon Thistle		2	1	
R4	Springhall Spartans		Medda Sports Bar		0	5	
R4	FC Porty		Fintry Athletic		0	2	
R4	Gartferry		CISWO		3	1	
R4	Rolling Barrell		Bayview Bar		3	0	
R4	Harvester		Dundee Argyle		2	2 5-4 pens	
R4	Cadzow Hamilton		Glasgow Thistle		2	10	
R4	Kingdom United		Salters Athletic		0	2	
R4	Lochgreen		The Geet		1	5	
R4	Queen's Park Spiders		Blackburn United AFC		5	2	
R4	Minto Lounge		Westburn		2	2 4-3 pens	
R4	MK Dynamo		Charlie's Bar		4	5	
R4	Boca Seniors		Waverley Hotel		3	3 4-3 pens	
R4	The Craft		Jeffrey United		6	1	
R4	Redding		Livingston North		4	2	
R4	Newton Vale		Cross Tavern		2	2 3-0 pens	
R4	Thornwood		Thomsons		5	5 7-6 pens	
R4	Drumchapel Thistle		Partizan		2	0	
R4	West Lothian Athletic		East Calder Daltons		2	7	
R4	Windlaw		Turf Inn		3	1	
R4	Broxburn Athletic AFC		Fairfield SLC AFA		0	2	
R5	Castlemilk United		Medda Sports Bar		4	4 4-5 pens	
R5	Cleland Club		Minto Lounge		6	0	
R5	Fintry Athletic		Windlaw		2	1	
R5	Hillview		Gartferry		4	1	
R5	Shotts Thistle		Rutherglen Vogue		5	2	
R5	Castlemilk Dynamo		Rolling Barrell				
R5	Redding		Tayport		3	3 2-4 pens	
R5	Thornwood		Queen's Park Spiders		4	2	
R5	The Craft		East End Athletic		1	1 5-6 pens	
R5	Glasgow Thistle		East Calder Daltons		3	2	
R5	Harvester		Newton Vale		4	1	
R5	St Bernards		Drumchapel Thistle		1	1	
R5	Dykehead		Cranhill		2	2 1-4 pns	
R5	Charlie's Bar		Bullfrog		1	4	
R5	Salters Athletic		The Geet		0	0 3-4 pens	
R5	Boca Seniors		Fairfield SLC AFA		0	6	

QF	Fintry Athletic	Castlemilk Dynamo	5	0	
QF	Fairfield SAL AFA	Bullfrog	3	1	
QF	Hillview	Harvester	3	4	
QF	Tayport AFC	Cranhill	1	3	
SF	Harvester	Fintry Athletic	2	0	at Creamery Park, Bathgate
SF	Cranhill United	Fairfield SLC AFA	3	1	at North End Park, Dundee
F	Harvester	Cranhill United	1	0	at Livingston FC

SCOTTISH AMATEUR FA - PREVIOUS CUP WINNERS

	West	East	North of Tay	Fife
1923/24	Moorpark Ams			
1924/25	Greenock HSFP			
1925/26	Moorpark Ams			
1926/27	Whitehall Athletic			
1927/28	Castings Ams			
1928/29	Greenock HSFP		YMCA Anchorage	
1929/30	Greenock HSFP		Hillcrest	
1930/31	Pointhouse		Aeros (Leuchars)	
1931/32	Glasgow University		Woodside Rangers	Burntisland Shipyard
1932/33	Queen's Park		Pittenweem Rangers	Bishopshire Swifts
1933/34	Mavor's XI		YMCA Anchorage	Glencraig Victoria
1934/35	Camphill Sec School FP		Pittenweem Rovers	St Andrews University
1935/36	Glasgow Corporation Transport		St Monance Swifts	Crail
1936/37	Greenock HSFP		Pittenweem Rovers	Pittenweem Rovers
1937/38	Coats Ams		RAF Leuchars	Freuchie Rovers
1938/39	Cartha Athletic		Harris Academy FP	Pittenweem Rovers
1945/46	Queen's Park		Lochee Ams	Burntisland Shipyard
1946/47	Queen's Park		YMCA Anchorage	Gallatown
1947/48	Rothesay Brandane	Edinburgh University	Ashdale	Milton Violet
1948/49	Laidlaw Ams	Civil Service Strollers	YMCA Anchorage	Victoria Swifts
1949/50	Queen's Park	Torphichen Ams	YMCA Anchorage	Boreland
1950/51	Govan Ams	Eastern Ams	YMCA Anchorage	Ladybank Violet
1951/52	Gartsherrie United	Dalkeith Ams	YMCA Anchorage	Ladybank Violet
1952/53	Babcock & Wilcox	Cobbinshaw Rovers	Kinrossie	Boreland
1953/54	Albion Motors	Cobbinshaw Rovers	Windsor	Thornton Loco
1954/55	Albion Motors	Cobbinshaw Rovers	Invergowrie	Thornton Loco
1955/56	Queen's Park	Lorwood AFC	YMCA Anchorage	Boreland
1956/57	Shell Amateurs	Pathead AFC	Windsor	Thornton Loco
1957/58	Muirend Ams	Orphan Hospital AFC	YMCA Anchorage	St Andrews University
1958/59	Kilmacolm AFC	Lorwood AFC	YMCA Anchorage	Cupar YM
1959/60	Crosshill Thistle	Pathead AFC	Ballinluig	Westwood Wanderers
1960/61	Queen's Park	Grangemouth Refinery	NCR	Nairn Star
1961/62	Glenavon	Winchburgh Albion	NCR	Westwood Wanderers
1962/63	Lincluden Swifts	West Lothian Steel Foundry	Ballinluig	Nairn Star
1963/64	Fenwick Thistle	Lorwood AFC	NCR	St Monance Swallows
1964/65	Lincluden Swifts	Edinburgh Albion	NCR	St Monance Swallows
1965/66	Minishant	Blackrodge Welfare	Withheld	Cambusbarron Rovers
1966/67	Vale of Girvan	Lorwood AFC	NCR	Cambusbarron Rovers
1967/68	Vale of Girvan	Lorwood AFC	Westgrove Albion	Star Hearts

	West	East	North of Tay	Fife
1968/69	Bishopton AFC	Lorwood AFC	NCR	Star Hearts
1969/70	Fenwick Thistle	Bilston AFC	Broughty United	Star Hearts
1970/71	Douglas Ams	Cambusbarron Rovers	Newtyle Hearts	Star Hearts
1971/72	Morriston YMCA	Pathead AFC	Errol	St Monance Swallows
1972/73	Clyde United	Links United	Hillside BC	Methil United
1973/74	Knockentiber	Whitson Star	Auchterhouse	Star Hearts
1974/75	Morriston YMCA	Whitson Star	Auchterhouse	Star Hearts
1975/76	Nithsdale	Bilston MW	Auchterhouse	Star Hearts
1976/77	Weir Recreation	Pencaitland	Auchterhouse	Hill of Beath Hawthorn
1977/78	Morriston YMCA	Pencaitland	Auchterhouse	Windygates
1978/79	Newarthill Hearts	Pencaitland	Riverside Athletic	Star Hearts
1979/80	Muirend Ams	Windsor AFC	Harris Academy FP	Windygates
1980/81	Cambusbarron Rovers	Telman Star	SMT	Norton House
1981/82	Westerlands	Bilston Colliery	Harris Academy FP	Strathmiglo United
1982/83	Bannockburn Ams	Milton Ams	Fintry	Star Hearts
1983/84	Initial Star	Cropley AFC	Harris Academy FP	Norton House
1984/85	Hyster	Bilston Cropley	Harris Academy FP	Ballingry Rovers
1985/86	Muirend Ams	Bilston Cropley	Riverside Athletic	Strathmiglo United
1986/87	Drumchapel AFC	Lothian Thistle	Lawside FP	Norton House
1987/88	Coatbridge CC	Liberton Cropley	Lawside FP	Hill of Beath Ramblers
1988/89	Knightswood AFC	Telman Star	Riverside Athletic	Norton House
1989/90	Clark Drive	Liberton Cropley	Riverside Athletic	Burntisland Shipyard
1990/91	Bellshill YMCA	Fallin MW	Riverside Athletic	Star Hearts
1991/92	Clark Drive	Bentswood Inn	Kingsway Athletic	Burntisland Shipyard
1992/93	Milngavie Wanderers	Craigmillar AFC	Lawside FP	Norton House
1993/94	Heathside	Cambusbarron Rovers	Alyth	Benarty
1994/95	Dalziel HSFP	Fallin MW	SS Peter and Paul	Benarty
1995/96	Dalziel HSFP	Cambusbarron Rovers	Riverside Athletic	Kettle United
1996/97	Knockentiber	AVU	Riverside Athletic	Burntisland Shipyard
1997/98	Newmilns Vesuvius	Fallin MW	Fair City Athletic	Lomond Victoria
1998/99	West Kilbride	Royburn AFC	Riverside Athletic	Leven United
1999/00	Dalziel HSFP	Manfort AFC	Fair City Athletic	Norton House
2000/1	Bannockburn Ams	Spartans	Riverside Athletic	Norton House
2001/2	Bannockburn Ams	Aberforth Rangers	Fair City Athletic	Norton House
2002/3	Drumchapel AFC	Aberforth Rangers	Fair City Athletic	Norton House
2003/4	Wellhouse AFC	Tullibody	Tayside Fire Brigade	Valleyfield
2004/5	Drumchapel United	Falkirk Amateurs	Riverside Athletic	Kettle United
2005/6	Drumchapel United	Stenhouse Athletic	Riverside Athletic	Kirkland
2006/7	St Patricks FPs	Doune Castle	NCR	Cupar Hearts
2007/8	Drumchapel United	Links United	Carnoustie YMCA	Cupar Hearts
2008/9	Bannockburn Ams	Cambusbarron Rovers	Vale of Earn	Strathmiglo United
2009/10	Harestanes	Bluebell	Breadalbane	Cupar Hearts
2010/11	Drumchapel United	Falkirk Amateurs	Riverside Athletic	Cupar Hearts
2011/12	Dumbarton Academy FP	Doune Castle	Burrelton Rovers	Kennoway
2012/13	Colville Park	Edinburgh Rose	Arbroath CSC	Leven United
2013/14	Hurlford Thistle	Steins Thistle	St James	Bowhill Rovers

	North	South	Highland	Sunday
1949/50	Dyce			
1950/51	Aberdeen University			
1951/52	Invercairn United	Eyemouth Swifts		
1952/53	Millburn	Peebles YMCA		
1953/54	Cove Rangers	Gala Rovers		
1954/55	Invercairn United	Greenlaw		
1955/56	Fraserburgh Toolworks	Greenlaw		
1956/57	Fraserburgh Toolworks	Gordon Westruther		
1957/58	Fraserburgh Toolworks	Broughton United		
1958/59	Aberdeen University	Selkirk Thistle		
1959/60	Formartine United	Gordon Westruther		
1960/61	Bon Accord	Tweeddale Rovers		
1961/62	Old Meldrum	Morebattle		
1962/63	Bon Accord	Gala Rovers		
1963/64	Aberdeen Dockers	Gala Rovers		
1964/65	Ellon United	Gala Ams		
1965/66	Bon Accord	Tweeddale Rovers		
1966/67	Cove Rangers	Tweeddale Rovers		
1967/68	Aberdeen University	Tweeddale Rovers		
1968/69	Kemnay	Symington		
1969/70	Maud	Lauder		
1970/71	Culter	Symington		
1971/72	Kemnay	Hawick United		
1972/73	Culter	Kelso United		
1973/74	Kemnay	Tweeddale Rovers		
1974/75	Culter	Tweeddale Rovers		
1975/76	Culter	Tweeddale Rovers		
1976/77	Banchory	Dunbar Blue Circle		
1977/78	Newtonhall	Dunbar Blue Circle	Blackmuir	
1978/79	Kemnay	Lanark Thistle	South Ronaldsay	Liberton Cropley
1979/80	Chatton Rovers	Lanark Thistle	Thurso Pentland	GJs
1980/81	Mugiemoss	Shotts MD	Thurso Pentland	Elphinston / Hillburn
1981/82	Shamrock	Monteith	Halkirk	Cambridge United
1982/83	Cove Rangers	Monteith	Thurso Pentland	Duncraig
1983/84	Longside	Tweeddale Rovers	Ness	Cambridge United
1984/85	Shamrock	Douglas Thistle	Halkirk	CISWO
1985/86	Chatton Rovers	Monteith	Maryburgh	Cambridge United
1986/87	Culter	Hawick Legion	Pentland United	Househill
1987/88	Kemnay Youth	Maxwelltown HSFP	Kirkwall Thorfinn	Dolphin
1988/89	Kincorth	Chirnside	Dingwall Thistle	Linden 30 Club
1989/90	Glentanar	Rigside	Marybugh	Cambridge United
1990/91	Great Western United	Monteith	Ness	St Lawrence
1991/92	Kincorth	Duns Legion	Ness	FJR
1992/93	Wilsons XI	Shotts YM	Pentland United	Jolly Farmer
1993/94	Hilton	Monteith	Point	Gauntlet
1994/95	Echt	Shotts YM	Ness	Tower

	North	South	Highland	Sunday
1995/96	Echt	Kirk United	Dingwall Thistle	Finnart
1996/97	Hilton	Duns Legion	Kirkwall Rovers	Finnart
1997/98	Hilton	Duns Legion	Pentland United	Cathkin
1998/99	Hilton	Upper Annandale	Contin	Railway Hotel
1999/00	Wilsons XI	Coldstream	Pentland United	Finnart
2000/1	Echt	Symington Tinto	Wick Thistle	Centaur
2001/2	Great Western United	Kirkconnel	Pentland United	The Braes
2002/3	Mintlaw	Symington Tinto	Lochs	Cavendish
2003/4	Aberdeen SC	Monteith	Back	Harvester
2004/5	Mintlaw	Chirnside	Lochs	Cavendish
2005/6	Dyce	Hawick W	Avoch	Rowantree
2006/7	Echt	Leithen Rovers	Avoch	Finnart
2007/8	Cove Thistle	Gala Rovers	Pentland United	Finnart
2008/9	Hazlehead United	Chirnside	Kirkwall THorfinn	Gantry
2009/10	Sportsmans Club	Newtongrange Star A	Pentland United	Finnart
2010/11	Kincorth	Leithen Rovers	Avoch	Tower
2011/12	Cove Thistle	Leithen Rovers	Avoch	Finnart
2012/13	Cove Thistle	Pencaitland	Wick Groats	Rutherglen Vogue
2013/14	Cove Thistle	Leithen Rovers	Wick Groats	Harvester

WELFARE FOOTBALL

WINTER SEASON

CENTRAL SCOTTISH WELFARE F.A.

During 2013/14 this League appeared to be operating with just 4 members.

LATEST AVAILABLE TABLE

	P	W	D	L	F	A	GD	Pts
Maryhill United	3	3	0	0	29	4	25	9
Clydebank Co-op	4	2	0	2	12	12	0	6
Cairnhill	3	1	0	2	6	18	-12	3
Petershill	4	1	0	3	5	18	-13	3

FORTH VALLEY WELFARE F.A.

FINAL TABLE 2013/14

Most of the teams in this league are from Clackmannanshire, with a few from Stirling.

	P	W	D	L	F	A	GD	Pts
Bank	16	13	0	3	75	28	47	39
Dollar Glen	16	11	0	5	49	25	24	33
Horseshoe Bar	16	11	0	5	56	37	19	33
St Ninians Borestone	16	10	2	4	69	53	16	32
Star Inn	16	7	2	7	61	53	8	23
Kincardine	16	7	0	9	56	56	0	21
Tullibody Inn	16	6	1	9	44	55	-11	19
Gartmorn	16	3	2	11	32	71	-39	11
Vinney's Bar	16	0	1	15	28	92	-64	1

GREENOCK WELFARE F.A.

	P	W	D	L	F	A	GD	Pts
Maukinhill	11	11	0	0	52	7	45	33
Blackthorn Rovers F.C.	11	9	0	2	38	20	18	27
Clydeside Utd	11	9	0	2	34	16	18	27
MISC	11	7	0	4	34	15	19	21
Boca Bay	11	6	1	4	36	21	15	19
Hillend	11	5	1	5	30	27	3	16
Emporium	11	5	0	6	31	42	-11	15
Lighthouse Bar	11	4	1	6	23	38	-15	13
Slaemuir	11	3	2	6	28	41	-13	11
Rankin Park	11	2	0	9	15	35	-20	6
Whinhill	11	1	1	9	14	44	-30	4
Bayhome Builders	11	0	2	9	15	44	-29	2

MONTROSE AND DISTRICT WELFARE F.A.

		P	W	D	L	F	A	GD	PTS
1	Golf Inn	24	21	2	1	131	35	96	65
2	Hudsons	24	19	4	1	143	30	113	61
3	Fordoun Galaxy	24	18	2	4	142	53	89	56
4	Hillside	24	15	2	7	141	66	75	47
5	Fettercairn	24	14	1	9	94	52	42	43
6	St Cyrus	24	13	2	9	91	76	15	41
7	MCT	24	10	3	11	70	89	-19	33
8	Northern Vaults	24	9	3	12	103	74	29	30
9	The Old Bolag	24	8	5	11	77	76	1	29
10	Bervie	24	4	3	17	53	113	-60	15
11	Lochside United	24	3	5	16	56	107	-51	14
12	@Bar FC	24	4	0	20	53	229	-176	12
13	Marykirk	24	1	2	21	43	197	-154	5

SUMMER SEASON

FORRES AND NAIRN WELFARE F.A.

Latest available table, June 2014

	P	W	D	L	F	A	GD	Pts
Jackos	9	7	2	0	38	10	28	23
Galacticos	9	6	1	2	47	12	35	19
Kinloss Sappers	8	6	1	1	37	14	23	19
Nairn Utd	9	5	3	1	33	20	13	18
Elgin Thistle	9	6	0	3	28	16	12	18
Carisbrooke	10	5	2	3	39	23	16	17
FC Elgin	8	5	1	2	26	17	9	16
Carlton	9	3	2	4	21	24	-3	11
Mosset Tavern	9	2	0	7	8	30	-22	6
Uncle Bobs	9	1	1	7	19	41	-22	4
Elgin Rangers	9	1	1	7	15	50	-35	4
Elgin Caledonian	10	0	0	10	16	70	-54	0

FORTH AND ENDRICK WELFARE F.A.

Compared to most of the others, the Forth and Endrick Welfare Association is settled and thriving. Matches are mainly played on Saturday evenings between teams representing the small towns and villages in the area between Stirling and Loch Lomond. Cup ties are often played on Sundays, with fixtures on midweek evenings as well.

Members for 2014 are:

Balfron Rovers	Gargunnock	Gartocharn
Fintry	Killearn	Drymen
Kippen	Blanfield Thistle	Thornhill
Buchlyvie United	Aberfoyle Rob Roy	Deanston

MORAY WELFARE F.A.

PREMIER DIVISION	P	W	D	L	F	A	GD	Pts
Rothes Amatuers	16	12	3	1	72	37	35	39
Portsoy	16	11	2	3	59	27	32	35
Bishopmill Villa	16	10	3	3	50	38	12	33
Burghead United	16	10	2	4	58	34	24	32
The Broons	16	6	2	8	32	42	-10	20
Ugie United	16	4	2	10	41	49	-8	14
Buckie United	16	4	2	10	38	53	-15	14
Aberlour Villa	16	4	1	11	32	54	-22	13
Tomintoul	16	2	1	13	14	62	-48	7
Brander	0	0	0	0	0	0	0	0

The Moray Welfare FA is another relatively successful area for Welfare football. Many of the clubs are long-established and the League generates considerable interest and local pride over the Summer months.

FIRST DIVISION	P	W	D	L	F	A	GD	Pts
Mosstodloch	18	16	2	0	105	30	75	50
RAF Lossiemouth	18	11	3	4	83	35	48	36
Lhanbryde	18	10	1	7	56	51	5	31
Banff Rovers	18	10	0	8	45	34	11	30
FC Fochabers	18	9	3	6	50	41	9	30
Thunderton	18	8	4	6	60	48	12	28
Hopeman	18	8	2	8	47	63	-16	26
Lossiemouth Youths	18	4	3	11	42	66	-24	15
Cullen	18	3	3	12	44	78	-34	12
Elgin Albion	18	0	1	17	24	110	-86	1
Bowl 2000	0	0	0	0	0	0	0	0
St. Marnans	0	0	0	0	0	0	0	0

NORTH EAST / BUCHAN WELFARE F.A.

For season 2014 the North East Scotland and Buchan Welfare Leagues opted to merge creating a two division format.

Latest available table june 2014

2013 Tables

DIVISION ONE

		P	W	D	L	F	A	GD	PTS	AJ
1	Clinton Thistle	10	7	1	2	34	15	19	24	2
2	New Pitsligo	10	7	2	1	21	9	12	23	0
3	Faithlie United	9	6	1	2	30	12	18	19	0
4	St Combs	11	6	0	5	28	38	-10	18	0
5	Bellslea	9	5	0	4	20	14	6	15	0
6	Panasonic	8	4	2	2	24	15	9	14	0
7	Balmoor	10	3	2	5	20	21	-1	10	-1
8	Mintlaw Fc	9	3	1	5	20	27	-7	10	0
9	Methlick	10	2	0	8	19	45	-26	6	0
10	Longside Thistle	12	1	1	10	21	41	-20	4	0

DIVISION TWO

		P	W	D	L	F	A	GD	PTS	AJ
1	Rosehearty Thistle	10	8	2	0	46	15	31	26	0
2	Ardallie	10	8	0	2	40	19	21	24	0
3	New Deer	8	6	1	1	28	9	19	19	0
4	Invercairn	9	5	1	3	31	22	9	16	0
5	Mormond Thistle	8	3	2	3	17	20	-3	11	0
6	Elizabethan Link Up	9	3	1	5	24	26	-2	10	0
7	Buchanhaven FC	11	2	1	8	17	49	-32	7	0
8	Cuminestown	9	1	3	5	18	28	-10	6	0
9	Peterhead United	10	0	1	9	12	45	-33	1	0

NORTH EAST SCOTLAND LEAGUE 2013

	P	W	D	L	F	A	GD	PTS
New Pitsligo	18	16	0	2	87	25	62	48
Bellslea	18	15	2	1	89	19	70	47
Clinton Thistle	18	15	2	1	80	26	54	47
Mintlaw Fc	18	9	2	7	44	37	7	29
Faithlie United	18	9	2	7	42	36	6	29
St Combs	18	7	1	10	43	37	6	22
Elizabethan Link Up	18	5	1	12	37	82	-45	16
Mormond Thistle	18	2	2	14	23	92	-69	8
Invercairn	18	1	2	15	23	81	-58	5

BUCHAN WELFARE LEAGUE 2013

TEAM	P	W	D	L	GF	GA	GD	PTS
PANASONIC	18	16	0	2	83	18	65	48
HATTON	18	14	1	3	86	26	60	43
BALMOOR	18	10	2	6	75	32	43	32
METHLICK	18	10	2	6	58	49	9	32
ARDALLIE	18	9	1	8	49	51	-2	28
LONGSIDE TH	18	9	1	8	46	49	-3	28
CUMINESTOWN	18	5	4	9	44	48	-4	19
DALES FC	18	6	0	12	44	77	-33	18
GLENUGIE UNITED	18	3	1	14	35	83	-48	10
PHD PENSIONERS	18	1	0	17	17	101	-84	3

ROSS-SHIRE WELFARE F.A.

ROSS-SHIRE WELFARE FA - JUNE 2014

Pos	Team	Pld	W	D	L	F	A	Pts
1	Alness Athletic	7	7	0	0	33	9	21
2	Fortrose Union	8	7	0	1	23	7	21
3	Tain Thistle	8	3	3	2	17	13	12
4	Dornoch City	8	3	1	4	17	20	10
5	Balintore	8	2	2	4	20	27	8
6	Ross-shire Club	7	2	1	4	12	17	7
7	Invergordon Social Club	8	1	2	5	11	26	5
8	Contin	8	1	1	6	12	26	4

ROSS-SHIRE WELFARE FA - FINAL TABLE 2013

Pos	Team	Pld	W	D	L	F	A	Pts
1	Tain Thistle	12	8	2	2	42	17	26
2	Alness Athletic	12	8	2	2	42	20	26
3	Cromarty	12	7	1	4	41	25	22
4	Fortrose Union	12	5	0	7	27	33	15
5	Invergordon Social Club	12	5	0	7	25	36	15
6	Balintore	12	3	3	6	34	45	12
7	Ross-shire Club	12	2	0	10	18	53	6

STRATHSPEY AND BADENOCH WELFARE F.A.

	P	W	D	L	F	A	GD	PTS
Grantown	6	6	0	0	53	9	44	18
Carrbridge	6	5	0	1	36	12	24	15
Aviemore RBL	6	4	0	2	29	25	4	12
Grantown United	6	3	0	3	23	19	4	9
Tomatin United	6	3	0	3	12	21	-9	9
Aviemore Thistle	6	2	0	4	10	25	-15	6
Cromdale	6	0	1	5	11	32	-21	1
Boat of Garten	6	0	1	5	8	39	-31	1

FINAL TABLE 2013	P	W	D	L	F	A	GD	PTS
Strathspey Thistle	10	7	3	0	35	8	27	24
RBL Aviemore	10	5	4	1	34	19	15	19
Grantown United	10	6	0	4	33	29	14	18
Cromdale	10	4	1	5	19	23	-4	13
Aviemore Thistle	10	2	1	7	18	37	-19	7
Tomatin United	10	1	1	8	19	42	-23	4

The table shown is from June 2014. The future of this League is in some doubt with Grantown and Cromdale having applied for membership of the Scottish Junior FA.

League Winners 2013: Strathspey Thistle
McCook Cup Winners: Strathspey Thistle
Stuart Cup Winners: Strathspey Thistle
MacLean Cup Winners: Strathspey Thistle

LOCHABER WELFARE F.A.

	P	PTS
Caol United	4	12
Caol Cosmos	4	9
Lundavra	4	9
Ballachulish	4	6
Mallaig	4	6
Lochaber	3	3
Inverlochy	3	0
Nevis Range	4	0

Centred on the Fort William area, this League was revived for the Summer of 2014.

A League table from mid-June is shown.

SCOTTISH WELFARE CUPS

JACK BRYSON (SUNDAY)

R1	St Ninians	Dollar Glen	7	2
R1	Vinny's Bar	Maukinhill United	1	11
R1	Bar FC	Kincardine	1	15
R1	Clydeside United	St Cyrus	4	1
R1	Lochside United	Lighthouse Bar	0	6
R1	Horeshoe	Rankin Park	3	0
R1	Northern Vaults	Boca Bay Juniors	1	5
R1	Ugie United	MISC	1	3
R1	Blackthorn Rovers	Tullibody Inn	6	3
R1	Fordoun Galaxy	Hollytree	wo	scr
R1	Hillend	Hillside (Montrose)	4	2
R1	Thunderton	Bay Homes	3	0
R1	Whinhill	Bank	0	3
R1	Gartmorn	Slaemuir	2	3
R2	Slaemuir	Fordoun Galaxy	2	5
R2	St Ninians	Emporium Outlet	8	3
R2	Thunderton	Maunkhill United	1	2
R2	MISC	Lighthouse Bar	1	0
R2	Clydeside United	Bank	4	2
R2	Boca Bay Juniors	The Star	1	2
R2	Kincardine	Blackthorn Rovers	3	5
R2	Hillend	Horseshoe	1	0
QF	MISC	Blackthorn Rovers	0	2
QF	Fordoun Galaxy	Clydeside United	2	5
QF	Star	St Ninians	2	3
QF	Hillend	Maukinhill United	1	2
SF	Maukinhill United	Clydeside United	6	0 at Largs Thist;e
SF	Blackthorn Rovers	St Ninians	4	0 at Sauchie Juniors
F	Maukinhill United	Blackthorn Rovers	4	0 at Largs Thistle

DONALD McNAIR (SATURDAY)

R1	Bank	Maryhill United	A	A
R1	Mormond Thistle	Clinton Thistle	0	6
R2	Balmoor	Invercairn	5	1
R2	Vinny's Bar	St Ninians	3	4
R2	New Deer	Star Bar	4	6
R2	Golf Inn	Yoker Boys		
R2	Bank	Thunderton	2	1
R2	Panasonic	Hillside		
R2	Clinton Thistle	Old Bolag	7	0
R2	Fordoun Galaxy	Fettercairn		
R2	New Pitsligo	Dollar Glen	0	2
R2	Elizabethan Link Up	Gartmom	4	1
R2	Dales	Bellslea	1	3
R2	Glenugie United	Tullibody Inn	0	12
R2	Faithlie	Hollytree	wo	scr
R2	Ugie United	Cairnhill		
R2	Petershill Youths'	Kincardine	1	8
R2	Horseshoe Bar	Clydebank Co-op	3	0
R3	Bank	Bellslea	3	2
R3	Tullibody Inn	Balmoor	2	3
R3	Golf Inn	Dollar Glen	1	3
R3	St Ninians	Elizabethan Link Up	9	2
R3	Ugie United	Clinton Thistle	1	2
R3	Kincardine	Star Bar	3	2
R3	Horeshoe	Panasonic	3	4
R3	Fordoun Galaxy	Faithlie United	1	8
QF	Panasonic	St Ninians Borestone	3	3 3-4 pens
QF	Kincardine	Bank	0	1
QF	Faithlie United	Clinton		
QF	Balmoor	Dollar Glen	1	1 4-2 pens
SF	St Ninians	Clinton		at Alloa FC
SF	Balmoor	Bank	2	3
F	Bank	St Ninians	2	1 at Alloa FC

HIGHLAND WELFARE CUP
Run by the local Associations

DATE	RD	TEAM			TEAM
28.04.13	1	DALES FC	7	V	6 MOSSTODLOCH
28.04.13	1	ABERLOUR	1	V	3 ELGIN ALBION
02.06.13	2	ELGIN ALBION	2	V	4 PHD PENSIONERS
02.06.13	2	PORTSOY	2	V	4 BISHOPMILL VILLA
02.06.13	2	DALES FC	1	V	2 GALACATCOS
02.06.13	2	THE BROONS	4	V	1 RAF LOSSIEMOUTH
02.06.13	2	LOSIEMOUTH YOUTHS	6	V	1 MORMOND THISTLE
02.06.13	2	BRGHEAD UNITED	11	V	0 CULLEN
02.06.13	2	BALMOOR	4	V	0 HATTON
02.06.13	2	ST MARNANS	2	V	7 NEWDEER
02.06.13	2	TOMINTOUL	2	V	1 ROTHES
02.06.13	2	BANFF ROVERS	0	V	3 NEW PITSLIGO
02.06.13	2	CUMINESTOWN	wo	V scr	ELGIN THISTLE
02.06.13	2	LHANBRYDE	3	V 2aet	LONGSIDE THISTLE
02.06.13	2	HOPEMAN	0	V	5 FAITHLIE UNITED
15.06.13	2	MINTLAW FC	2	V	4 UGIE UNITED
02.06.13	2	THIUNDERTON	3	V	2 ELIZABETHAN LINK UP
02.06.13	2	CLINTON THISTLE	3	V	1 BELLSLEA
30.06.13	3	TOMINTOL	1	V	3 THUNDERTON
30.06.13	3	UGIE UTD	9	V	1 BALMOOR
30.06.13	3	CLINTON THISTLE	7	V	1 GALACTOUS
30.06.13	3	BISHOPMILL VILLA	wo	V scr	PHD PENSIONERS
30.06.13	3	LHANBRYDE	0	V	4 NEW PITSLIGO
30.06.13	3	BURGHEAD	6	V	1 NEW DEER
30.06.13	3	CUMINESTOWN, 4-2 on pens	3	V	3 FAITHLIE THISTLE
30.06.13	3	LOSSIE YOUTH	1	V	3 THE BROONS
28.07.13	Q/F	CLINTON TH	wo	V scr	THE BROONS
28.07.13	Q/F	CUMINESTOWN	Scr	V wo	BISHOPMILL VILLA
28.07.13	Q/F	NEW PITSLIGO	7	V	1 THUNDERTON
28.07.13	Q/F	BURGHEAD	3	V	1 UGIE UNITED
01.09.13	S/FI	BISHOPMILL VILLA	2	V	0 CLINTON THISTLE
01.09.13	S/FI	BURGHEAD	3	V	5 NEW PITSLIGO
	FIN/	BURGHEAD	1	V	4 NEW PITSLIGO

	Templeton Cup / Donald McNair Cup	Daily Record Cup / Jack Bryson Cup
1919/20	Beardmore Mossend	
1920/21	Coats Juniors	
1921/22	Coats Juniors	
1922/23	Coats Juniors	
1923/24	Cleansing	
1924/25	Coats Juniors	
1925/26	Clark Anchor	
1926/27	Coats Juniors	
1927/28	Phoenix	
1928/29	Seafield	
1929/30	Westfield	Renton Thistle
1930/31	Hydepark Loco Works	St Martins Guild
1931/32	Anniesland	Camelot Welfare
1932/33	Napier House	Withheld
1933/34	Napier House	Shawfield Chemicals
1934/35	St Pauls	Shawfield Chemicals
1935/36	Templeton Albert	Smith & McLean
1936/37	Templeton Albert	Carwadric
1937/38	Kelvindale	Kerse
1938/39	Clyde Alloy	Scotia
1939/40		Vulcan
1940/41		Queen's Society
1941/42		Forth and Clyde
1942/43		Ardnance
1943/44		Scottish Cables
1944/45		Phoenix
1945/46	Harland & Wolff Ordnance	RNAS
1946/47	Milton Welfare	Carron Primrose
1947/48	ICI Welfare	Cadder Welfare
1948/49	Loco	Seafield Athletic
1949/50	Singers	Germiston Works
1950/51	Dalmarnock Power	Dalmarnock Power
1951/52	Singers Athletic	Templeton Albert
1952/53	Templeton Albert	Provan Gas / Ferranti Thistle
1953/54	Dalmarnock Power	Singer Athletic
1954/55	Rolls Royce (Hillington)	Rolls Royce (Hillington)
1955/56	Metro Vics	Howdens Athletic
1956/57	Singers	British Legion Polmont
1957/58	Rolls Royce (Hillington)	St Bernards
1958/59	Clyde Trust	St Bernards
1959/60	Dalmarnock Power	Clyde Trust
1960/61	J and T Boyds	Shanks Welfare
1961/62	Dalmarnock Power	Quay United
1962/63	Burroughs (Cumbernauld)	Grangemouth Dockers
1963/64	Grangemouth Dockers	Shanks Welfare
1964/65	Grangemouth Dockers	Quay United
1965/66	Clyde Port Authority	Grangemouth Dockers

	Templeton Cup / Donald McNair Cup	Daily Record Cup / Jack Bryson Cup
1966/67	British Hydro Chemicals	Shanks Welfare
1967/68	Rolls Royce (Hillington)	Brown Land Boilers
1968/69	British Aluminium	Shanks Welfare
1969/70	British Aluminium	Hoods
1970/71	Waverly Thistle	British Aluminium
1971/72	Winchburgh	Waverly Thistle
1972/73	Waverly Thistle	Dukes Head
1973/74	Plean Welfare	Waverly Thistle
1974/75	Tennents Caledonia	Tennents Caledonina
1975/76	200 FC	Tennents
1976/77	Singers	Clyde Blowers
1977/78	Singers	Singers
1978/79	Grangemouth Dockers	Singers
1979/80	Tennents	GSL
1980/81	East Stirlingshire Social Club	200 FC
1981/82	John Brown Engineering	Tennents
1982/83	200 FC	Malvern Star
1983/84	Malvern Star	Possil
1984/85	Withheld	Westquarter Violet
1985/86	Springfield	Commercial
1986/87	Glen Star	Westquarter Violet
1987/88	Westquarter Violet	Withheld
1988/89	Gordon Athletic	Tennents
1989/90	Robert Rae FC	Westquarter Violet
1990/91	Concord Metals	John Brown Engineering
1991/92	Withheld	Robert Rae
1992/93	Aldbury	Kelty Villa
1993/94	Aldbury	Aldbury
1994/95	John Brown Engineering	Jamestown
1995/96	Templeton Albert	Valley Bar
1996/97	Summerhill	Summerhill
1997/98	St Peters	Summerhill
1998/99	Rosyth Ex Service Club	St Ninians
1999/00	Peppes	Valley Bar
2000/1	St Peters	Tullibody WMC
2001/2	Calton Athletic	Kelty Villa
2002/3	Clydeshore	Peppes
2003/4	Invercairn United	Jokers
2004/5	Lauders FC	Oakwood
2005/6	Valley Bar	Braehead
2006/7	Blairhall	St Ninians Borestone
2007/8	Linlithgow Rose B	Star Inn
2008/9	Oakwood	Valley Bar
2009/10	Peppes	Oakwood
2010/11	Oakwood	Blairhall
2011/12	Castleview	Treetops
2012/13	Horseshoe	MISC
2013/14	Bank	Maukenhill United

358

TOM HUNTER NORTH CUP
Summer -- Run by Scottish WFA

R1	Elgin Albion	Peterhead Pensioners	2	4
R1	Portsoy	Bishopmill Villa	2	4
R1	Dales FC	Galacticos	1	2
R1	The Broons	RAF Lossiemouth	4	1
R1	Lossie Youths	Mormond Thistle	6	1
R1	Bughead United	Cullen	11	0
R1	Balmoor	Hatton	4	0
R1	St Marnans	New Deer	2	7
R1	Tomintoul	Rothes	2	1
R1	Banff Rovers	New Pitsligo	0	3
R1	Cuminestown	Elgin Thistle	wo	scr
R1	Lhanbryde	Longside Thistle	3	2
R1	Hopeman	Faithlie United	0	5
R1	Mintlaw	Ugie United	scr	wo
R1	Thunderton	Elizabethan Link Up	3	2
R1	Clinton Thistle	Bellslea	3	1
R2	Tomintoul	Thunderton	1	3
R2	Ugie United	Balmoor	9	1
R2	Clinton Thistle	Galacticos	7	1
R2	Bishopmill Villa	Peterhead Pensioners	wo	scr
R2	Lossie Youths	The Broons	1	3
R2	Lhanbryde	New Pitsligo	0	4
R2	Burghead	New Deer	6	1
R2	Cuminestown	Faithlie United	3	3 w-l pens
QF	New Pitsligo	Thunderton	7	1
QF	Burghead United	Ugie United		
QF	Clinton Thistle	The Broons	wo	scr
QF	Cuminestown	Bishopmill Villa		
SF	Burghead	New Pitsligo	3	5 at Portsoy
SF	Clinton Thistle	Bishopmill Villa	0	1 at Longside JFC
F	New Pitsligo	Bishopmill Villa	4	1 at Elgin City FC

UNOFFICIAL FITBA

ISLE OF ARRAN LEAGUE

A five-team Summer League operates on Arran.

League table as of mid-June 2014 was as follows:

	P	W	D	L	F	A	PTS
South	3	2	0	1	12	2	6
Lamlash	2	2	0	0	9	1	6
Brodick	3	2	0	1	6	5	6
Shiskin	2	0	0	2	2	11	0
Northend	2	0	0	2	2	12	0

ISLAY FOOTBALL LEAGUE

The following four teams were involved in the 2014 Summer League and Cup competitions:

Kilchoman FC
Bowmore FC
Port Ellen FC
Islay Wanderers FC

Glasgow Islay FC also travelled over to play in the pre-season Easter Cup. An Islay Select XI have played several friendlies against mainland teams.

Most games are played at Port Mor, just south of the village of Port Charlotte.

YOUTH FITBA

Listed here are the results for the closing rounds of the various Age Group Scottish Cup competitions run by the Scottish Youth FA.

2001s (U12)

R5	Largs Spartans	Rangers SABC	0 6	
R5	Harmony Row	Carbrain BC	6 0	
R5	Blue Brazil	East Kilbride	1 3	
R5	Edina Hibs	Partans	2 2 5-4 pens	
R5	Newcraighall Leith Vics	Hutchison Vale Colts	6 0	
R5	Giffnock Soccer Centre	Jerviston	0 3	
R5	St Mirren YFC	Penicuik Athletic	1 0	
R5	Edinburgh City	Hutchison Vale	1 8	
QF	East Kilbride	Hutchison Vale	0 1	
QF	Harmony Row	Newcraighall Leith Vics	0 0 4-2 pens	
QF	Rangers SABC	Jerviston	4 0	
QF	St Mirren YFC	Edina Hibs	1 8	
SF	Edina Hibs	Hutchison Vale	1 0	at Dalkeith Thistle
SF	Harmony Row	Rangers SABC	1 3 aet	at St Anthonys
F	Edina Hibs	Rangers SABC	3 0	at Airdrieonians

2000s (U13)

R5	Seafar Villa Blues	Calderbraes BC	1 2	
R5	Celtic BC	Grahamston BC	10 0	
R5	Lenzie YC	Celtic Juniors B	1 2	
R5	Hamilton Accies	Dalkeith CYP	3 0	
R5	Crosshouse BC	Hillwood BC	2 3	
R5	Ayr Boswell BC	Broxburn Athletic	2 1	
R5	Milton	PFD United	4 0	
R5	Syngenta Juvs	Leith Athletic	3 1	
QF	Ayr Boswell BC	Milton	3 1	
QF	Celtic Juniors B	Celtic BC	2 1	
QF	Hamilton Accies	Syngenta Juvs	1 2 aet	
QF	Hillwood BC	Calderbraes BC	6 1	
SF	Ayr Boswell BC	Hillwood BC	4 2	at Ayr United
SF	Celtic Juniors B	Syngenta Juvs	1 2	at Cumbernauld Utd
F	Ayr Boswell BC	Syngenta Juvs	1 2	at Airdrieonians

1999s (U14)

R5	Westwood Rovers	Barrhead YC Yellows	5 3	
R5	Carnoustie Panmure	Hamilton Accies BC	1 6	
R5	Dyce BC	Tynecastle	0 2	
R5	Kilsyth Athletic	Spartans Reds	3 1	
R5	Wishaw Wycombe Wander	Fraserburgh Link Up	0 6	
R5	Blantyre BC yellows	Edina Hibs	5 0	
R5	Falkirk FC Community	Celtic BC	0 9	
R5	Rossvale	Townhill	1 3	
QF	Blantyre BC yellows	Townhill	2 1	
QF	Celtic BC	Hamilton Accies BC	1 2	
QF	Tynecastle	Fraserburgh Link Up	1 5	
QF	Westwood Rovers	Kilsyth Athletic	1 0	
SF	Hamilton Accies BC	Blantyre BC Yellows	2 0	at Thorniewood Utd
SF	Fraserburgh Link Up	Westwood Rovers	1 4	at Longside FC
F	Hamilton Accies BC	Westwood Rovers	5 0	at Airdrieonians

1998s (U15)

R5	Fernieside	Girvan Youth	8 6 AET	
R5	Crosshouse BC	Mill United	1 3	
R5	Albion BC	Craigie United	3 0	
R5	Rossvale Thistle	Tynecastle	4 2	
R5	Cumbernauld Colts	Hutchison Vale	1 1 3-4 pens	
R5	West Park Utd	Musselburgh Windsor	2 4	
R5	Renfrew Victoria	Harmony Row	1 5	
R5	Currie Star	Syngenta Juvs	2 3	
QF	Albion BC	Fernieside	2 3	
QF	Hutchison Vale	Harmony Row	3 2 aet	
QF	Musselburgh Windsor	Mill United	2 1	

1997s (U16)

R5	Glentanar BC	Deveronvale	3 2	
R5	Syngenta juvs	Wolves	1 0	
R5	Antonine Blacks	Southside	4 0	
R5	Clydebank Utd	Tynecastle	1 3	
R5	Barrhead Youth	Strathaven Dynamo	5 2 AET	
R5	Salvesen CFC	Mill United	2 3	
R5	Jeanfield Swifts	Gourock YAC	1 3	
R5	Kildrum United	Edina hibs	2 6	
QF	Antonine Blacks	Gourock YAC	3 0	
QF	Barrhead Youth	Tynecastle	2 3	
QF	Glentanar BC	Edina hibs	0 1	
QF	Mill United	Syngenta Juvs	1 3	
SF	Syngenta juvs	Antonine Blacks	1 3	at Falkirk FC
SF	Tynecastle	Edina hibs	5 3	at Craigroyston FC
F	Antonine Blacks	Tynecastle	3 3 6-5 pens	at Airdrionians

1995s (U18)

R5	East Kilbride Gold	Rossvale	2 1	
R5	FC Bonnybridge	Ardeer Thistle		
R5	Kikrinitlloch Rob Roy	Colony Park	2 4	
R5	West Park	Hamilton Accies Invercly	2 0	
R5	Bantyre BC	Glenburn MW	2 4	
R5	Musselburgh Windsor	Baillieston Juniors BC	3 5	
R5	Monifieth Athletic	North Merchiston BC	2 2 3-4 pens	
R5	Barrhead YC	Troon	4 0	
QF	Baillieston Juniors BC	North Merchiston BC	5 2	
QF	Colony Park	Glenburn MW	1 1 4-3 pens	
QF	East Kilbride Gold	FC Bonnynridge	0 2	
QF	West Park	Barrhead YC	3 3 5-6 pens	
SF	Barrhead YC	Baillieston Juniors BC	5 3 aet	at East Kilbride FC
SF	Colony Park	FC Bonnybridge	2 1	at Inverurie Locos
F	Barrhead YC	Colony Park	5 2	at Airdrieonians

1992s (U21)

R3	Goldenhill BC	Bye		
R3	Campsie BW	Leith Athletic	6 0	
R3	Johnstone Burgh	EK Rolls Royce	1 1 3-4 Rep	
R3	Mill United	Busby Amateurs	3 1	
R3	Tower Hearts	Rutherglen Glencairn	4 2	
R3	Pollok Juveniles	Arsenal BC	1 3	
R3	East Kilbride	Erskine YFC	4 0	
R3	Murieston United	Steins Thistle	5 1	
QF	Campsie BW	Murieston United	4 0	
QF	Goldenhill BC	Arsenal BC	2 1	
QF	Mill United	East Kilbride	3 2	
QF	Tower Hearts	Johnstone Burgh	2 1	
SF	Goldenhill BC	Tower Hearts	1 1 3-1 pens	at Yoker Athletic
SF	Campsie BW	Mill United	2 1 aet	at Kirkintilloch RR
F	Goldenhill BC	Campsie BW	1 1 2-4 pens	at Airdrieonians

SCHOOLS FITBA

Listed here are the results for the closing rounds of the various Age Group Scottish Cup competitions run by the Scottish Schools FA.

Senior Boys Shield (U18)

R5	18/01/2014	Clydebank HS	Kirkcaldy HS	8	2	
R5	18/01/2014	Firrhill HS	Greenfaulds HS	2	5	
R5	18/01/2014	Monifieth HS	Penicuik HS	3	1	
R5	18/01/2014	Dunfermline HS	St Columbas HS (reenock)	0	2	
R5	18/01/2014	Springburn Acad	St Columbas HS (Dunfermline)	4	0	
R5	18/01/2014	St Pauls HS	Glenrothes HS	4	1	
R5	18/01/2014	St Ambrose HS	Strathaven Acad	6	2	
R5	18/01/2014	Greenwood Acad	Our Lady & St Patricks HS	1	1 3-2 pens	
QF	22/02/2014	St Pauls HS	Greenfaulds HS	3	1	
QF	22/02/2014	Clydebank HS	St Ambrose HS	1	1 3-4 pens	
QF	22/02/2014	Monifieth HS	Greenwood Acad	3	1	
QF	22/02/2014	Springurn Acad	St Columbas HS (Greenock)	2	1	
SF	27/03/2014	St Pauls HS	St Ambrose HS	1	3	New Douglas Park
SF	28/03/2014	Springburn Acad	Monifieth HS	5	0	Recreation Park, Alloa
F	09/05/2014	Springburn Acad	St Ambrose HS	0	0 3-5 pens	New Douglas Park

Under 16 Shield

R5	18/01/2014	Grange Acad	Beath HS	3	3 4-3 pens	
R5	18/01/2014	Linlithgow Acad	Cardinal Newman HS	0	4	
R5	18/01/2014	St Johns HS	St Margarets HS	0	2	
R5	18/01/2014	Aberdeen GS	Paisley GS	2	3	
R5	18/01/2014	Bannerman HS	Woodmill HS	2	2 4-2 pens	
R5	18/01/2014	Holyrood Sec	St Ambrose HS	1	1 4-3 pens	
R5	18/01/2014	Penicuik HS	St Ninians HS (Giffnock)	2	4	
R5	18/01/2014	Taylor HS	Stranraer Acad	6	4	
QF	22/02/2014	Holyrood Sec	Cardinal Newman HS	3	1	
QF	22/02/2014	Grange Acad	St Ninians HS (Giffnock)	1	2	
QF	22/02/2014	St Margarets HS	Taylor HS	3	0	
QF	22/02/2014	Bannerman HS	Paisley GS	1	1 4-3 pens	
SF	01/04/2014	Bannerman HS	St Margarets HS	4	4 1-3 pens	at Wishaw Juniors
SF	02/04/2014	Holyrood Sec	St Ninians HS (Giffnock)	1	0	at Neilston Juniors
F	02/05/2014	St Margarets HS	Holyrood Acad	2	2 2-3 pens	at Airdrieonians

Under 15 Shield

R5	18/01/2014	Holyrood Sec	Kirkcaldy HS	2	1	
R5	18/01/2014	Craigmount HS	Bishopbriggs HS	2	4	
R5	18/01/2014	St Johns HS	Airdrie Acad	3	4	
R5	18/01/2014	Madras College	Strathaven Acad	0	3	
R5	18/01/2014	St Andrews & St Brides HS	Mintlaw Acad	2	1	
R5	18/01/2014	Notre Dame HS	Montrose Acad	6	0	
R5	18/01/2014	Braidhurst HS	Largs Acad	5	1	
R5	18/01/2014	Gracemount HS	Trinity HS (Rutherglen)	2	6	
QF	22/02/2014	Notre Dame HS	Bishopbriggs HS	3	3 5-6 pens	
QF	22/02/2014	Holyrood Sec	Braidhurst HS	2	4	
QF	22/02/2014	Airdrie Acad	Trinity HS (Rutherglen)	1	0	
QF	22/02/2014	St Andrews & St Brides HS	Strathaven Acad	1	3	
SF	31/03/2014	Bishopbriggs HS	Braidhurst HS	2	6	at Vale of Clyde
SF	02/04/2014	Strathaven Acad	Airdrie Acad	4	1	at Cambuslang R
F	07/05/2014	Strathaven Acad	Braidhurst HS	1	2	at Airdrieonians

Under 14 Shield

R5	18/01/2014	Cathkin HS	Arbroath HS	8	0	
R5	18/01/2014	Linlithgow Acad	Broughton HS	2	4	
R5	18/01/2014	Kirkcaldy HS	St Ambrose HS	2	5	
R5	18/01/2014	Monifeith HS	Braidhurst HS	1	5	
R5	18/01/2014	St Ninians HS (Giffnock)	Cults Acad	6	4	
R5	18/01/2014	Duncanrig Sec	St Columbas HS (Dunfermline)	10	0	
R5	18/01/2014	Lasswade HS	Trinity HS (Rutherglen)	5	7	
R5	18/01/2014	Graeme HS	St Peter the Apostle HS	4	1	
QF	22/02/2014	Duncanrig Sec	Broughton HS	3	1	
QF	22/02/2014	Cathkin HS	Trinity HS (Rutherglen)	1	1 4-5 pens	
QF	22/02/2014	St Ambrose HS	Graeme HS	1	5	

Under 13 Shield

R5	15/02/2014	Grange Acad	Aberdeen GS	7	0	
R5	15/02/2014	Royal HS	Broughton HS	0	1	
R5	15/02/2014	Balwearie HS	Larbert HS	1	0	
R5	15/02/2014	Cults Acad	Trinity HS (Rutherglen)	3	7	
R5	15/02/2014	Bannerman HS	Grove Acad	2	7	
R5	15/02/2014	Holyrood Sec	Lasswade HS	1	0	
R5	15/02/2014	Braidhurst HS	St Ninians HS (Giffnock)	4	1	
R5	15/02/2014	Graeme HS	Duncanrig Sec	10	0	
QF	15/03/2014	Holyrood Sec	Broughton HS	2	8	
QF	15/03/2014	Grange Acad	Braidhurst HS	3	3 5-6 pens	
QF	15/03/2014	Balwearie HS	Graeme HS	0	6	
QF	15/03/2014	Grove Acad	Trinity HS (Rutherglen)	3	4	
SF	28/04/2014	Trinity HS (Rutherglen)	Graeme HS	1	4	at Vale of Clyde
SF	30/04/2014	Broughton HS	Braidhurst HS	4	1	at Fauldhouse Utd
F	22/05/2014	Broughton HS	Graeme HS	2	1	at Hearts FC

Senior Girls Shield (U18)

R3	14/12/2013	Williamwood HS	St Andrews Sec	8	1	
R3	14/12/2013	Duncanrig Sec	Eastbank Acad	7	0	
R3	14/12/2013	St Peter the Apostle HS	Kilmarnock acad	0	3	
R3	14/12/2013	Braidhurst Acad	Galashiels Acad	4	3	
R3	14/12/2013	Nicolson Institute	Bathgate Acad	3	2	
R3	14/12/2013	Boroughmuir HS	Websters Acad	3	0	
R3	14/12/2013	Firhill HS	Kincorth Acad	3	0	
R3	14/12/2013	Mintlaw Acad	Preston Lodge HS	6	1	
QF	15/02/2014	Boroughmuir HS	Duncanrig Sec	2	2 2-4 pens	
QF	15/02/2014	Kilmarnock Acad	Williamwood HS	0	5	
QF	15/02/2014	Firrhill Acad	Braidhurst Acad	9	1	
QF	15/02/2014	Nicolson Institute	Mintlaw Acad	1	0	
SF	24/03/2014	Firhill HS	Williamwood HS	3	1	at Hamilton Palace
SF	26/03/2014	Duncanrig Sec	Nicolson Institute	1	4	HF Acad, Dingwall
F	23/04/2014	Nicolson Institute	Firhill HS	2	2 4-2 pens	at Clachnacuddin

Under 15 Girls Shield

R3	14/12/2013	Our Lady & St Patricks HS	Rosshall Acad	3	0	
R3	14/12/2013	Stranraer Acad	Holyrood Sec	3	0	
R3	14/12/2013	Duncanrig Sec	St Peter the Apostle HS	2	1	
R3	14/12/2013	St Ninians HS (Giffnock)	Bannerman HS	2	3	
R3	14/12/2013	Forfar Acad	Wallace HS	4	0	
R3	14/12/2013	Lasswade HS	Mintlaw Acad	4	2	
R3	14/12/2013	Preston Lodge HS	Cults Acad	1	6	
R3	14/12/2013	Nicolson Institute	Linlithgow Acad	2	4	
QF	15/02/2014	Lasswade HS	Stranraer Acad	10	1	
QF	15/02/2014	Duncanrig Sec	Our Lady & St Patricks HS	4	0	
QF	15/02/2014	Cults Acad	Bannerman HS	1	1 1-3 pens	
QF	15/02/2014	Forfar Acad	Linlithgow Acad	2	3	
SF	24/04/2014	Bannerman HS	Duncanrig Sec	5	2	at East Kilbride FC
SF	30/04/2014	Lasswade HS	Linlithgow Acad	2	0	Meggetland, Edinburgh
F	22/05/2014	Lasswade HS	Bannerman HS	7	0	at Spartans FC

Under 13 Plate Competition

R3	14/03/2014	Irvine Royal Academy	Stewarton Academy	6	0	
R3	14/03/2014	Oban HS	St Andrews & St Brides HS	0	8	
R3	14/03/2014	Paisley Grammar School	Cathkin HS	2	1	
R3	14/03/2014	Stirling HS	Dalkeith HS	3	0	
R3	14/03/2014	Coltness HS	St Margarets Academy	3	2	
R3	14/03/2014	Portobello HS	Linlithgow Academy	3	0	
R3	14/03/2014	Inverurie Academy	Perth Academy	3	0	
R3	14/03/2014	Arbroath HS	Woodmill HS	4	2	
QF	04/04/2014	Inverurie Academy	Portobello HS	1	3	
QF	04/04/2014	Irvine Royal Academy	Coltness HS	0	3	
QF	04/04/2014	Arbroath HS	Paisley Grammar School	0	0 5-4p	
QF	04/04/2014	St Andrews & St Brides HS	Stirling HS	3	1	
SF	28/04/2014	Coltness HS	St Andrews & St Brides HS	1	3	Cambuslang Rangers
SF	14/05/2014	Arbroath HS	Portobello HS	4	4 4-3p	Glenrothes Juniors
F	09/06/2014	Arbroath HS	St Andrews & St Brides HS			Broxburn Athletic

Under 14 Plate Competition

R4	14/03/2014	Madras College	Eastwood HS	1	4	
R4	14/03/2014	Gryffe HS	St Modans HS	7	0	
R4	14/03/2014	Firhill HS	Airdrie Academy	2	2 4-5p	
R4	14/03/2014	Barrhead HS	Larkhall Academy	4	0	
R4	14/03/2014	Oban HS	Carrick Academy	1	3	
R4	14/03/2014	Montrose HS	Banchory Academy	5	1	
R4	14/03/2014	Glenrothes HS	Stonelaw HS	4	2	
R4	14/03/2014	Grangmouth HS	St Margarets HS	1	1 6-5p	
QF	04/04/2014	Eastwood HS	Gryffe HS	3	1	
QF	04/04/2014	Airdrie Academy	Carrick Academy	2	2 4-2p	
QF	04/04/2014	Barrhead HS	Glenrothes HS	1	11	
QF	04/04/2014	Montrose HS	Grangemouth HS	1	0	
SF	08/05/2014	Montrose HS	Eastwood HS	2	2 4-3p	Spartans
SF	15/05/2014	Glenrothes HS	Airdrie Academy	6	3	Spartans
F	05/06/2014	Glenrothes HS	Montrose HS	2	0	Forfar Athletic FC

TSB Senior U18 National Cup

QF	23/1/14	Aberdeen	Paisley	2	2 5-3p	Banks o' Dee
QF	31/1/14	North of Scotland	Forth Valley	1	4	
QF	31/1/14	Glasgow	Fife	4	1	
QF	25/2/14	Lothians	Dundee	1	1 4-3p	Spartans
SF	12/3/14	Forth Valley	Lothian	2	2 2-4p	Stirling Albion
SF	31/3/14	Aberdeen	Glasgow	0	0 5-6p	
F	30/5/14	Lothian	Glasgow	2	1	Whitehill Welfare

TSB Under 15 National Cup

QF	31/1/14	Ayrshire	Forth Valley	4	0	
QF	31/1/14	Lanarkshire	Dumfries & Galloway	3	0	
QF	4/2/14	Aberdeenshire	Fife	3	1	Inverurie Locos
QF	4/2/14	Aberdeen	Dundee	2	2 4-5p	Banks o' Dee
SF	24/3/14	Dundee	Aberdeenshire	2	0	Broughty Athletic
SF	27/3/14	Lanarkshire	Ayrshire	2	4	Hamilton Palace
F	27/5/14	Ayrshire	Dundee	2	4	Broxburn Athletic

SCOTTISH SCHOOLS FA

SCOTTISH SCHOOLS FA

President's Committee

GORDON PATE
President

BILL BARCLAY
Vice President

JOHN C. WATSON
General Secretary
OFFICE: Hampden Park, Glasgow, G42 9AZ
Tel: 0141 620 4570
Fax: 0141 620 4571
Email: jcwatson@scottish-football.com

ALEX B. McMENEMY
Treasurer
OFFICE: Hampden Park, Glasgow, G42 9AZ
Tel: 0141 620 4572
Fax: 0141 620 4571
Email: alex.mcmenemy@scottish-football.com

W. LES DONALDSON
International Teams Secretary

ALASTAIR T. BORTHWICK
Assistant General Secretary

PETER CLARK
Assistant General Secretary

GRENVILLE DAWSON
Assistant General Secretary

DAVID GILCHRIST
Assistant General Secretary

RONNIE HAMILTON
Assistant General Secretary

J. STEWART TAYLOR
Assistant General Secretary and Child
Protection Officer

JOHN GOLD
S.F.A. Council Member

ROD HOUSTON
Past President and Minute Secretary

ROBERT M. DOCHERTY
Honorary Vice President

Council
NORTH
DUNCAN MASSIE
H. STEWART NEILSON

EAST
ALAN BOAG
JUNE BOUAOUN
KENNY FINDLAY
CHRIS SEELEY

SOUTH EAST
JOHN FRAME
WILLIAM HENDERSON
ANDY McARTHUR
IAN R. SMITH

WEST
ROBERT ALLAN
IAN BURNS
GILLIAN DUFFY
STEWART McLACHLAN
TOM POOL
NEIL ROSS

CENTRAL
JIM BETTLEY
COLIN BURKE
SCOTT DOUGLAS
DAVID ECCLES
CRAIG JOHNSTONE
CLARE SMITH

SOUTH WEST
MICHAEL DOWNIE
IAIN FLEMING
STEPHEN GILMOUR
IAIN PROUDFOOT
DAVID THOMSON
JOHN WILSON

CO-OPTED MEMBERS
JOE HARKINS
ALASTAIR MacPHERSON
JACK STEELE

OBITUARIES

These details have been drawn from various sources, most notably the pages of *Scottish Football Historian* and *Backpass* magazines.

WILF ALLSOP
Born 23 January 1931, Arbroath; Died 27 December 2013, Glenrothes, Aged 82
A Juvenile internationalist, Alsop joined Hearts in 1948. The Arbroath-lad was farmed out to Lochee Harp but he did not make the first team during four years at Tynecastle. Allsop signed for Stirling Albion in May 1953 and made an impressive start but he fell out of things and was transferred to Forfar Athletic. A season with Arbroath brought his senior career to an end in 1956. He concentrated on his career as a teacher and he was a long-serving Principal Teacher of English at Kirkcaldy High School. One of his pupils was Val McDernid who went on to become an award-winning crime writer.

GEORGE McCAFFERTY ANTON
Born 29 November 1935, Died November 2013, aged 77
Goalkeeper George Anton turned Senior in 1959, joining Kilmarnock from Whitletts Vics. He made just one first team appearance before moving on to Stranraer where he was the regular first choice for five seasons between 1960 and 1965. Thereafter he played for Ayr United before going back briefly to Stranraer. His last club was Annbank United in the Ayrshire Juniors.

GERARD AUSTIN BAKER
Born 11 April 1938, in New Rochelle (USA); Died 24 August 2013, in Wishaw
Gerry Baker's career may have been over-shadowed by his more famous brother Joe, but he was a superb player in his own right. Born in the USA but brought up in Lanarkshire, Gerry was as Scottish as they come. He began with Larkhall Thistle as a teenager and was signed by Chelsea but failed to settle in London. He returned home and signed for Motherwell but he was unable to make much impact there either. It was when he joined St Mirren in 1958 that his career took off. Gerry scored prolifically and helped his new club to the Scottish Cup Final. He scored one of the goals in the 3-1 win over Aberdeen at Hampden, and kept a record of having scored in every round. In 1960 he was sold to Manchester City for £17,000 but just over a year later he returned to join Hibs. Further scoring feats saw him move to England again in 1963, this time with Ipswich. While with Coventry in 1968/9 he won 7 full caps for the USA. On giving up full-time football he worked for Jaguar cars and acted as player-manager for Margate, Nuneaton Borough, Bedworth United and Racing Club Warwick. His daughtrer, Lorraine, finished fifth in the 800 metres at the 1984 Olympics.

GEORGE BENNIE
Died April 27 2014, Aged 78
Well-known as a senior football referee and linesman in the 1970s. Then based in Tillicoultry, he later moved to Buchlyvie. Outside of football he was a PE teacher.

HARRY BONTHRONE
Born 1934 in Perth; Died: July 2014, Aged 79.
A keen footballer, Mr Bonthrone played in the old half-holiday league before taking up coaching roles with Jeanfield Swifts, Perth Celtic, Letham and St Johns.

ASHLEY BOOTH
Born 22 October 1937 in Aberdeen; Died March 23 2014
Booth was a typical centre half of his time – tall, rugged and uncompromising. He learned his football with Aberdeen Junior side Banks o' Dee and was signed by St Johnstone in 1961. Booth was a regular in the Saints team in 1962/3 but was plagued by injuries. These led to his rfelease and he joined East Fife where he fared little better – a knee injury sustained against Dumbarton ending his professional career prematurely.

ALEXANDER DEWAR "SANDY" BROWN
Born 24 March 1939, Grangemouth. Died: 8 April 2014
Sandy was best known as a dependable full back for Everton in the 1960s. His career had started at Broxburn Athletic before he signed for Partick Thistle in 1957. Everton paid a then substantial fee £38,000 to take him to Goodison in September 1963. After more than 250 games for the Toffees he ended his career with spells at Shrewsbury Town and Stockport County.

WILLIAM BRUNTON
Died 4 September 2013, Aged 94
Willie was a dedicated committee man at Haddington Athletic. The covered enclosure at their Millfield ground was named in his honour when it was constructed in 1992.

BILLY CARMICHAEL
Died 29 December 2013, Aged 80
Carmichael made his debut for Clyde in August 1953 and scored in a 3-1 win over Rangers at Ibrox. However, he didn't ever establish himself as a first team regular and moved on to Dunfermline Athletic before quitting senior football at the ag of 24. Carmichael concentrated on his career and became Chairman of the Scottish Stock Exchange. He returned to Clyde as a Director in 1992 and became Chairman and major shareholder. For several years he effectively bankrolled the club, financing big signings under the management of Alex Smith, Gardner Spiers, Ronnie McDonald and Alan Kernaghan. Carmichael left Clyde in 2004 and wrote off large financial losses, allowing the club to survive.

IAN CASHMORE
Died April 28th 2014, Aged 53
Ian was a promising forward with Ayr United in the early 1980s. During a loan spell with Berwick Rangers he had scored eight goals in ten games when he suffered a freak training accident at his parent club. This left him paralysed. A fund raising committee raised tens of thousands of pounds to help buy a bungalow and specially adapted car for Ian. His son, Ian Junior, played for several Scottish League clubs.

JOHN ALEXANDER CHRISTIE
Born 26 September 1929, in Fraserburgh. Died: 9 March 2014
Christie was a brave and athletic goalkeeper who first came to prominence with Inverness Thistle in the Highland League. Ayr United snapped him up and after a season of impressive displays he was spotted by Southampton while on National Service at Farnborough. He signed on at The Dell in January 1951 and played over 200 games for Saints before moving to Walsall in 1959. With the Saddlers he won two successive promotions and helped establish Walsall in the second tier of English football. He left them in 1962 and continued to play with Burton Albion and Rugby Town.

NICOLE CLARK
Died: 15 November 2013
Turriff United Ladies player Nicole was fatally injured in a road accident, aged just 20.

ROBERT YOUNG COLLINS
Born 16 February 1931, in Glasgow; Died 13 January 2014
"The Wee Barra", Bobby Collins, was a highly influential player at all his clubs. He signed for Celtic in 1948 while working as a miner in the Fife coalfield. He quickly starred in the Celtic midfield area and was instrumental in the 7-1 thrashing of Rangers in the 1957/8 League Cup Final. Collins won 31 Scotland caps, including playing in all three games dcuring the 1958 World Cup in Sweden. His fine performances brought English clubs calling and Everton paid £23,500 to sign him in 1958. Collins shone like a beacon in a disappointing Everton side. In March 1962 he moved to Leeds United for £30,000. Don Revie was starting a revolution at Elland Road and thought that Collins was just the man to lead it. He orchestrated promotion to the top flight and ushered in the start of the great era of Leeds United before passing the baton on to the likes of Billy Bremner and Johnny Giles. Collins suffered a shattered thigh in 1965 but he fought back to sign for Bury in 1967. He finished his playing days with time at Morton, Oldham, Shamrock Rovers and in Australia. While with Morton he recommended that Leeds should sign a raw laddie out of the Cappielow reserve team – called Joe Jordan. Collins had unsuccessful management spells at Huddersfield, Hull and Barnsley. Later, he worked with a friend in wholesale fashion, then for some years as a driver for Leeds University. In 2002, he was diagnosed with Alzheimer's.

TOMMY CRAIG
Died June 14 2014
A familiar face in any Rangers team group from the late 60s and 70s was physio Tommy Craig. He was part of the backroom staff at Ibrox when Rangers won the European Cup Winners Cup in 1972. He left the club in the early 1980s and practised physiotherapy from his home on the south side of Glasgow. It is thought that he suffered a heart attack.

ANDREW DAVIDSON
Born 13 July 1932 in Douglas Water; Died 5 April 2014

Davidson went to Yorkshire to sign for Hull City as a 15-year old and quickly established himself in the side. He played over 600 senior games for Hull between 1952 and 1968, mainly as a full back. His background in the mining villages of South Lanarkshire stood him well as he endured three leg breaks early in his career. Rangers were keen to bring him back to Scotland at one point but Davidson was happy to remain the archetypal "one club man". Injury forced him into retirement in 1968 and served Hull City as a Coach and Scout for several years. He quit football in 1979 to start a new career as a fishmonger.

JOE DAVIN
Born 13 February 1042; Died 30 September 2013
David was a schoolboy international with S Patrick's HS in Dumbarton and played Juvenile for Drumchapel Amateurs. He joined Hibs in 1959 and was on the fringe of the first team for several years. Joining Ipswich in 1963, David made 77 League appearances over three seasons. He returned to Scotland with Morton in 1966 and latterly Dumbarton. After retiring from football he worked for Polaroid in the Vale of Leven.

CHARLIE DICKSON
Born 7 July 1934, in Edinburgh; Died 18 October 2013 in Whitburn
Revered as a "legend" at Dunfermline Athletic, scoring 215 goals for them in just over 300 appearances. He joined the Pars in January 1955 from Penicuik Athletic and scored twice on his debut against Stenhousemuir. Charlie scored the second goal in the 1961 Scottish Cup Final Replay when the Pars brought the Cup home to Fife. In 1964 he moved to Queen of the South for whom he netted 21 goals in 35 League appearances. In 1965 he moved to Australia and has a spell with South Coast United. In later life he was a publican in Midlothian and hotelier in Dunbar before returning to his original trade as an electrician with Blue Circle He also doted on his racing pigeons. For in a second sporting career, Dickson became one of Scotland's top pigeon fanciers, and he and his son Charlie held Scottish titles and bred and raced some of the fastest birds in the sport, including champions of long-distance races from France. Charlie lived latterly in Dunbar but was still a regular attendee at East End Park for former players events.

NEIL DUFFY
Died June 2013
Neil turned senior in 1958 when he joined East Stirlingshire from Ashfield Juniors. He quickly made an impact in a decent Shire side. In 1960 he moved on to Partick Thistle for a fee of £8000, enjoying more success at Firhill between then and 1965. After a spell with St Johnstone he moved to South Africa in 1967, playing for Addingtonj. Despite spending just five years at Partick, he made such an impact that he was later inducted into the club Hall of Fame. His son, also Neil Duffy, played for Dundee United and others in the 1980s and 90s.

DREW FERGUSON
Died 16 May 2013, Aged 24
Drew was well-known as a shinty and football player for the Fort William clubs. He scored the winning goal in one Fort's rare victories, against Strathspey Thistle, in 2012/13. Drew died on board the diving support vessel Skandi Arctic while it was working in the Cromarty Firth.

JOHN FLANAGAN
Born: 26 April 1942, in Glasgow. Died 30 September 1913
Flanagan was best known for his time with Partick Thistle in the late 1960s. Despite his small stature, he was a decent striker who joined the Jags from St Johnstone in 1965. In 1970 he moved on to Clyde where he ended his senior career. Flanagan continued in the Juniors with St Rochs into the mid 1970s.

HUGHIE GALLACHER
Born: 26 November, 1930, in Vale of Leven. Died: 14 June, 2013 in Clydebank, aged 82
Hugh Gallacher was a key figure for Dumbarton in the 1950s. He arrived at Boghead for the 1954/5 season after spells with Duntocher Hibs and Arbroath. His first season with the club saw him score 32 goals as the Sons won the Division C title. In less than eight seasons with the club he netted 205 goals in 231 games for the Sons. Gallacher was sold to Clyde in 1960 but returned to Boghead in less than a year having also spent time at Queen of the South. He lived and worked in the Dumbarton area all his life. Hughie was married twice. His first wife, Eileen, died in 1973, and he later married Paddy, who predeceased him in 2012.

JAMES EDWARD GARRETT

Born 1939 in Nethermill, Died February 2014

Eddie was a fiery and hard-working striker who signed for Queens from Glenafton in 1958. His National Service (alongside Ron Atkinson), disrupted his time with Queens but he scored a creditable 29 goals in 88 games, helping the club back to the top flight in 1962 after a three year spell in Division Two. After a fall out with manager George Farm, he moved on to Carlisle United in 1963 and then settled in North Wales, playing for several Welsh League clubs including Rhyl Town. He later successfully managed a few too, notably his home town, Prestatyn Town who were Welsh League runners up while he was in charge. Settling in Wales, he named his house "Palmerston" and followed the fortunes of the Doonhamers with interest.

WALTER GERRARD

Born: 1 November 1943 in Glasgow; Died: 30 March 2014, Aged 70

Gerrard was on Barnsley's books as a teen but never made the first team. The Yorkshire side had followed his progress with Possil YM and Campsie Black Watch before taking him south. He returned to Scotland and played with East Stirlingshire, Berwick Rangers and Clydebank. In Hong Kong in 1958, Glaswegian emigre Ian Petrie had formed a football club which he named after his beloved Rangers – even the new club's crest was a copy of that flying over Ibrox. In 1970, Petrie advertised for British professional footballers to come and try their luck with the club, and Gerrard, Derek Currie and Jackie Trainer arrived in the then colony on 10 September, 1970 They were the first European professionals to play in Hong Kong and were treated like royalty on arrival, greeted by an excited media pack and hordes of fans. He became a prolific centre forward, nicknamed the Water Buffalo. He later served the Seiko club as player and coach. His favourite football story came from a match against Santos when he played for Hong Kong's Caroline Hill. He was subbed at the same time as Pele, and as the pair were leaving the field he put his arm round the Brazilian and said "these coaches don't know a good footballer when they see one". When Walter retired, he became involved in the wines and spirits industry where he became very successful, latterly with Fine Vintage Wines.

JACK GILLESPIE

Born: 11 March 1926, in Kirkintilloch, Died: July 15 2013, Aged 87

A lifelong Rangers supporter, Lenzie garage-owner Jack Gillespie bought Matt Taylor's shareholding in the club in the mid 1970s, taking a seat on the Ibrox Board in 1977. He was a force for change at Ibrox in the 1980s, helping with the redevelopment of Ibrox and the modernisation of the club's signing policy. He was Vice Chairman of the club during the Souness era. In the early 2000s he became involved with Airdrie United, once providing the club with a £50,000 interest-free loan when their future was in doubt.

JEFF GRAY

Died 28 September 2013

Penicuik Athletic's popular physio died after suffering heart attack during a match against Bathgate Thistle. It was fitting that Penicuik went on to win their League Championship, dedicating their success to Jeff. Jeff had been with the club for 12 years since they rejoined the Junior ranks.

JOHN HAMILTON

Born: 22 January 1935; Died: 13 August 2013

Johnny Hamilton was a typical winger of his era, fast and blessed with great ball skills. He won the Scottish Juvenile Cup with Kirkmuirhill Juveniles in 1951. After that he played for Birkenshaw Welfare and Lesmahagow Juniors before joining Hearts in April 1955. From then until 1966/7 he was pretty much a first team regular. Hamilton won Under 23 and League international caps but didn't make the full team. Hamilton spent 1967/8 with Watford and then joined Berwick Rangers from 1968 until 1971. After quitting football he worked as a newsagent in Edinburgh.

GRAHAM HARKNESS

Died 29 August 2013

Graham Harkness, President of the Scottish Amateur Association passed away suddenly on Thursday 29th August. Graham was the General and Match Secretary of the Dumfries Sunday League for many years. He was the guiding force in the DSAFL and the current strength of the league is a testament to all of Graham's hard work. In recent times Graham has held the top position in the SAFA, driving the association forward with streamlining and modernisation. This was not always easy but Graham's strength of character helped instigate many positive changes.

GEORGE HUNTER
Died: 25 May 2014
Honorary President of Dunipace Juniors FC.

WILLIAM "SANDY" PULLAR JARDINE
Born 31 December 1948, in Edinburgh; Died 24 April 2014, in Edinburgh; Aged 65
Jardine grew up in Edinburgh not far from Tynecastle Park but it was Rangers who secured his signature in 1964. He served a long apprenticeship in the Ibrox reserve side before becoming a first team regular in the late 1960s/ His first team debut came one week after his club had been knocked out of the Scottish Cup by Berwick Rangers. Sandy was initially used in midfield but he quickly dropped back into the full back position. He was an accomplished defender but also liked to forage forwards when possible. After 687 first team games for Rangers he was released in 1982 and joined his boyhood favourites Hearts. Jardine was capped on 38 occasions by Scotland, often partnering Danny McGrain at the back. He captained Scotland on 9 occasions. He played for Hearts until 1986 when he was made Joint Manager with Alex McDonald. During that time he passed the 1000 senior games mark. In 1988 new owner Wallace Mercer sacked Jardine. He later returned to Rangers in various PR and Marketing capacities which he held until his passing. IT was anno8unced in November 1912 that Jardine was being treated for cancer.

FRANK KOPEL
Born 25 March 1949, in Falkirk; Died 16 April 2014, in Kirriemuir, Aged 65
Kopel is best-remembered as a stalwart defender for Dundee United between 1972 and 1982. After winning Scotland Schools caps Kopel joined Manchester United as a 15-year old and made his debut for the first team in 1967. He played 12 times for United beside names such as Charlton, Law and Best. Kopel then had a couple of years at Blackburn Rovers before returning to Scotland. After his time at Dundee United he was player-coach at Arbroath and then Assistant Manager of Forfar Athletic. In 2008 he was diagnosed with Alzheimer's Disease. Frank's son Scott also played for Dundee United and Forfar Athletic, amongst other team.

DAVID MACKIE
Died 1 November 2013, Aged 85
Mackie hailed from the Brightons area of Falkirk and played Juvenile for Westquarter Violet. Turning Junior with Bathgate Thistle and then Kirkintilloch Rob Roy, Mackie won four Junior caps before signing for St Johnstone in September 1952. A strong right half, he was in the first team squad at Muirton for a couple of seasons before moving to Stenhousemuir.

COLIN McADAM
Born: 28 August 1951; Died 1 August 2013, Aged 61
Colin McAdam was a well-known figure through the 1970s and early 80s and popular at all his clubs. His playing style earned him the nicknames "Hoof" and "Beastie" but there was far more to his game than physicality. Starting at Dumbarton in 1969, he later played for Motherwell and Partick Thistle before joining Rangers in 1980. After that he played in Australia for a spell before returning to Scotland with Hearts and Partick Thistle. In the late 1980s McAdam played with Irvine Meadow and Maryhill before hanging up his boots in 1990. During his time with Dumbarton he qualified as a PE teacher and he returned to that role when he gave up football. Colin's brother Tom was also a prominent player with Dumbarton, Dundee United and Celtic.

JAMES McCOLL
Died 8 August 2013, Aged 88.
McColl played Junior football for Polkemmet during World War Two. Hibernian might have signed him but McColl's father was a Coach at Easter Road and did not want to be accused of favouritism. Instead McColl signed for Queen's Park. A talented right back, he was selected for the Great Britain team for the 1948 Olympics in London. At the start of 1948/9 McColl had a brief spell with Dundee befopre signing for Queen of the South. He then played for Falkirk and Cowdenbeath before an ankle injury brought his career to a premature end. Jimmy set up home in Edinburgh and worked in insurance until his retirement in 2003.

FRED MARTIN
Born: 13 May 1929, in Carnoustie; Died: 20 August 1913, aged 84.
Aberdeen was Fred's only Senior club and he served them from 1946 until 1960. Although he was signed as an inside forward, the Dons converted him to a goalkeeper and he went on to win 6 full caps for Scotland. He played in the 1954 World Cup in Switzerland. After retiring he went into the whisky trade with Dewars. Fred was one of the inaugural inductees to the Aberdeen FC Hall of Fame in 2007.

NORRIE MARTIN
Born 7 May 1939 in Ladybank; Died: 10 October 2013
Martin was a goalkeeper at Rangers from 1958 until 1970 but never won a major honour. He started with Dalry Thistle and then joined Hamilton Accies before signing for Rangers. Through much of his time at Ibrox he played second fiddle to George Niven and Billy Ritchie. On two occasions when he looked to be claiming a regular starting place Martin sustained a fractured skull, first in 1958 and again in 1965. 1966/7 was his most consistent season when he finally took over as first choice – he played in losing Rangers teams in the League Cup and European Cup Winners Cup Finals, with Rangers also finishing second in the League and going out of the Scottish Cup to Berwick Rangers. Tall and athletic, Martin was eventually freed in April 1970 and ended his career with brief spells at East Fife, Queen of the Soutnhand back at Hamilton Accies.

PETER McAVOY
Died April 2014, in the USA
Peter McAvoy was born and raised in Dundee and played for several local Junior clubs including Tayport and Arbroath SC. He then moved to the US to study at Herkimer County Community College. As captain of the college soccer team, the 22-year-old was named the NSCAA Junior College Player of the Year in 2013 and led the Herkimer Generals to two national championships. He collapsed and died in his college dorm room just hours after completing a match.

JAMES McCLUSKEY
Born 1 November 1950 in Salsburgh; Died November 14 2013in Ayr, Aged 63.
McCluskey was a prominent referee during the 1990s, from Stewarton. His last professional match was the 2000 Scottish Cup Final in which Rangers defeated Aberdeen 4-0. He officiated at the 1994 UEFA Cup Final between Inter Milan and Casino Salzburg. At one stage during the 1990s Celtic fans hired a private dotective to try and prove, in vain, that he had "Rangers sympathies". Away from football he was a partner in a civil engineering firm in Lugton. As a youngster he had harboured hopes of a playing career. He spent two seasons on the books of Airdrieonians and then played for Lanark United and Shotts Bon Accord.

DAVID McFARLANE
Born 16 January 1967 in Irvine; Died 30 October 2013 in Kilmarnock
McFarlane joined Rangers from Ayr United Boys Club but made just nine first team appearances in four years. After loan spells at Dundee and Kilmarnock the tenacious midfield player moved to Rugby Park on a more permanent basis in October 1988. In 1990 he moved to Partick for a short spell before trying his luck in Australian football. McFarlane soon returned and embarked on a career in Junior football. He played in 3 Junior Cup Finals for Glenafton before hanging up his boots and working for a Glasgow pawnbroker.

PETER MILLER
Born 21 April 1950; Died 17 June 2013, Aged 62
Miller was well known in the 1970s when he played for Arbroath, Dunfermline Athletic, Motherwell and Dundee. A midfield player or defender, he stood out with his blond hair and aggressive tackling. He stepped up to Arbroath from Forth Wanderers but it was at Motherwell that he had his best years – winning a Scottish League Cap against the Football League in 1974. He finished his senior career with Dundee. On retiring from full-time football Peter took up a career in the Civil Service. He remained involved in Junior football and had a successful spells as manager of Shotts Bon Accord and Cambuslang Rangers.

JOHN MULGREW
Died July 2013 in Aberdeen, Aged 94
John was trainer, manager and eventually President of Lewis United for more than 50 years. He was a real stalwart for the Aberdeen Junior side.

CHARLES DRYSDALE NOTMAN
Born June 26 1946 in Edinburgh; Died March 15, 2014, in Brugge.
Charlie Notman signed for Morton in the early 1960s from Musselburgh Windsor but never made the breakthrough in senior football. He went Junior with Linlithgow Rose and was capped for Junior Scotland in 1967. Later that year he moved to Belgium. He had a reasonable career as a player there turning out for KRC Mechelen, Cercle Brugge KSV, VG Oostende and D'Echte. Notman became a Coach and worked with various teams includingKFC Heist, FC Zeemeeuw Zeebrugge. He married a Belgian woman and set up a business which grew into a massive transport and logistics company, Middlegate Europe. By now a leading entrepreneur in Belgium he published his autobiography Schot in de Roos around 2010.

ANDREW PATON

Born 2 January 1923 in Dreghorn; Died 8 February 2014

Paton's father and uncles had all played professionally for clubs such as Newcastle, Derby, Spurs and Swansea, so it was no surprise when he was signed by Motherwell from Kello Rovers in 1942. He went on to be a superb club player for Motherwell – fully deserving of that title "legend" which is bandied about with such abandon these days. He played over 500 games for the Steelmen, plus many more in wartime games, and won great admiration for his defensive play. In a time when many centre halfs were just "stoppers", Paton was a real footballer who could include craft and style on his c.v. He captained Motherwell to their first national triumph when they won the League Cup in 1950/1 and again when they won the Scottish Cup the following season. In 1958 he joined Hamilton Accies and had a year as a player before becoming Manager – a position he held for nine seasons, leading the Accies to promotion in 1965. In 2006, Motherwell rewarded him after being voted the 'Greatest Ever Player' by supporters at a ceremony at Fir Park. Andy, a true gentleman, was on hand to accept the award with a humble grace that typified his personality.

DAVID PAUL

Born 7 February 1995, Edinburgh. Died December 22 1913, Edinburgh.

Paul was a member of the Hibernian Under 20 squad and was rated as an outstanding prospect. Educated at George Watson's College, David was a quiet, engagingly unassuming individual, but also a confident and committed footballer, who scored goals regularly at youth level. He died in his sleep just over 5 years after his older sister, then 16, died of an undiagnosed heart condition.

JAMES LORIMER SALMOND PITHIE

Born 20 January 1928, Edinburgh; Died 18 January 2014, Edinburgh

Pithie played Junior for Newtongrange Star and rugby for Boroughmuir before signing for Hearts in 1946. He played five times in the Hearts first team in 1946/7 before falling ill with tuberculosis. The career of the promising defender was over and he concentrated on his career. He spent three decades working for the Meat and Livestock commission. Pithie maintained his sporting involvement as a bowler at the Whitehouse and Grange BC.

COLIN JAMES RANDALL

Died 24 November 2013, Cove, Aged 41

A former goalkeeper with Highland League side Deveronvale, Colin died suddenly of a heart attack.

IAN REDFORD

Born: 5 April 1960 in Perth; Died 10 January 2014, in Irvine, Aged 53

The sudden death of Ian Redford shocked Scottish football. He was a creative midfield player who had a long career after coming through the ranks at Dundee in the mid 1970s. Ian was born into a Perthshire farming family and started playing with Errol Rovers, a Juvenile club started by his father where the team included his cousin Gavin and future Scotland cap Raymond Stewart. Redford helped Dundee win promotion from the First Division before Rangers signed him for a Scottish record fee of £210,000 in 1980. He played over 250 games for Rangers before moving to Dundee United in 1985, helping them to the UEFA Cup Final two years later. Ipswich Town gave him his chance in English football in 1988. Three years later he returned to play for St Johnstone and then had spells at Brechin City and Raith Rovers, for whom he played in the 1994 League Cup Final. After retiring from football he had several different business ventures in the Perthshire area. Shortly before his death his autobiography was published in which he revealed much about his deafness and the impact of the death of his brother when he was a child. Redford's suicide was a shocking reminder of the torment which many former footballers can feel when their career is over.

LAWRIE REILLY

Born: 28 October 1928, in Edinburgh; Died 22 July 2013 in Edinburgh, Aged

Born and raised close to Tynecastle, Reilly learned his football in the competitive world of Edinburgh Juvenile football with Edinburgh Thistle. He joined Hibs in 1946 and went on to score 238 goals in 355 games. His gutsy determination and clever anticipation set him aside from other players. Reilly won 38 full caps for Scotland, including scoring 5 goals in 5 appearances against England at Wembley. He was known as "Last Minute Reilly", not just for his 90th minute equaliser against England in 1963 but also for numerous late goals in Hibernian colours. A recurring knee injury brought a premature end to his playing career. He then invested all his energies into running the Bowlers Rest in Leith.

JOHN RYDEN

Born 18 February 1931, Alexandria. Died: 16 August 2013

Ryden entered senior football with Alloa in 1951/2. He racked up over 100 games for the Wasps before joining a large Scottish contingent at Accrington Stanley. He was a great success there and was picked for the Division Three North Select in 1955/6. He was transferred to Spurs for £8000. His skills as a centre half were quickly recognised and he was a first team, regular during his early days at White Hart Lane. When

Bill Nicholson took over as Manager Ryden dropped out of the team and in 1961 he was freed and joined Watford. Ryden had two footballiong brothers – George (Dundee, St Johnstone and Stirling Albion and Hugh (Chester, Stockport, Bristol Rovers, Halifax and Morton).

ALEX SIMPSON
Died September 2013, Edinburgh
Alex was a prolific goalscorer for Buckie Rovers in the early 1960s. His exploits earned a 14-day tria;l with Cardiff City but he was not signed by the Bluebirds. He was picked for Junior Scotland in 1965/6 and was snapped up by the other Bluebirds, Inverness Caley. After one season with Caley Simpson moved to home town team Buckie Thistle with whom he spent two good seasons.

JAMIE SKINNER
Died 23 December 2013, Edinburgh.
Jamie Skinner was playing for Edinburgh-based Tynecastle FC's under-14 team yesterday morning when he collapsed during the game against Spartans FC. Parents and officials who were watching the game at Saughton in Edinburgh tried to resuscitate the teenager after he dropped to the ground, before paramedics arrived. Jamie had previously played for Hearts FC at age-group level and had moved to Tynecastle FC recently.

GORON MELVILLE SMITH
Born: 3 July 1954 in Glasgow; Died: April 5 2014
Smith was one of several very good players produced by St Johnstone in the 1970s. He was spotted by Scout Alex McLintock playing for Rangers Boys Club and was persuaded to join Saints in 1969. A defender or midfield player, he won Scotland Under 23 caps and helped Saints qualify for the first ever Premier Division in 1975. He was sold to Aston Villa for £80,000 and immediately helped to League Cup glory. Subsequently Smith played for Tottenham Hotspur and Wolves, but a series of debilitating injuries plagued his later career. His playing career finished with short spells in both South Africa and the USA. Gordon later ran his own business and was contracted to sell and install Champions League perimeter advertising at football grounds. This took him all over Europe and kept him in touch with many of his former colleagues.

DOUGLAS SOUTAR
Died August 2013, Aged 85
Douglas had two spells as a Director of Forfar Athletic in the 1980s and 1990s. he also co-write the Centenary History of the Station Park side, published in 1985. Away from football he was a Headmaster and Senior Lecturer at Dundee College of Education.

NEIL MACKINNON STIRRAT
Born May 19 1941, Died 7 August 2013
Neil was a member of the 1951 Irvine Meadow Scottish Cup Final side. He stepped up to Airdrieonians but went back to the Ayrshire Juniors. Neil played for Irvine Vics from 1957 until 1961. He joined the Vics from Largs Thistle. In later life Neil was a keen local historian.

RONALD LEWIS SWAN
Born: 13 November, 1928, in Edinburgh. Died: 3 March, 2014, in Edinburgh, aged 85
Ronnie Swan played football at Edinburgh University in the early 1950s. He had earlier played for Saughtonhall Juveniles, despite attending rugby-playing George Watsons College. He did National Service in the Middle East before enrolling at Edinburgh University to study dentistry. He took part in a match between Scottish and English Universities at Westerlands which was the first match to be televised live. When Ronnie graduated he joined Spartans, the club with which he was to be associated with for over 60 years. Firstly as a player, then as Secretary (for over 50 years), Treasurer and finally President, he was the public face of Spartans as they rose through the non-league ranks. He masterminded the move from Canal Field to City Park that allowed them to play in the Scottish Cup, and paved the way for their later move to Ainslie Park and emergence as one of the strongest non-league clubs in Scotland.

DAVID TAYLOR
Born 1954 in Forfar; Died June 2014
Born in Forfar in 1954, Taylor was educated at Dundee High School before graduating from Edinburgh University with a degree in law. Taylor was Chief Executive of the SFA for eight years from 1999 before joining European football's governing body UEFA. He oversaw the appointments of Berti Vogts and Walter Smith as Scotland manager before leaving the SFA in 2007 to succeed Lars-Christer Olsson as general secretary at Uefa.

SAMUEL McGREGOR TAYLOR
Born 23 September 1933 in Glasgow; Died 6 November 2013 in Preston.
Sammy spent one season with Falkirk in 1954/5 after stepping up from Dunipace Juniors. Preston North End were so impressed with the forward that they paid £8500 for him and he became understudy to Tom Finney. Taylor continued to be a great success at Preston. In 1961 he moved on to Carlisle United, then to Southport in 1964. Taylor ended his playing career at Morecambe in the Lancashire Combination. By that time he had settled in Preston where he worked for British Aerospace.

JAMES THOMSON
Died 4 June 2013, Aged 80
Jimmy "Tiger" Thomson was a wing half for Hibs in the 1950s, after signing up from Edinburgh City. He became a first team regular in 1955/6, playing in the first ever European Cup campaign. Thomson then dropped out of the fiurst team and he was freed at the end of 1958/9. He had short spells with Ayr United and Cowdenbeath before finishing his playing career at Vale of Leithen.

GEORGE TOSH
Died July 2013, Aged 72
Tosh's passion for football saw him play for Angus and Perthshire teams in his younger day, including Forfar West End, before he became involved in the founding of Strathmore Albion in 1972. The club won many honours in the Perthshire Amateur Football Association. The team continued until ill-health forced Mr Tosh to retire in 2004, when it disbanded. Honoured as a life member of the Perthshire Amateur Football Association, he saw Albion sides scoop a host of titles and he only hung his own boots up in 2003, having been known to pull on a strip to ensure a team could take to the field.

RONNIE TRAVERS
Died 11 February 2014, Aged 57
Ronnie was stalwart defender for Edinburgh City during the 1990s. He continued to play Amateur football with LBC Lochend until 2013.

ROLANDO UGOLINI
Born Lucca June 4 1924, Died April 10 2014
Ugolini arrived in Scotland as a child in the later 1920s. He left school to work in his parents chip shop and signed on for Armadale Thistle. An acrobatic goalkeeper, much more athletic than the norm for the time, he was picked up by Celtic in 1944. He found first team chances limited and was transferred to Middlesbrough for a fee of £7000 in 1948. He was to play over 300 first team games for the Ayresome Park club before ending his career with spells at Wrexham, Dundee United and Berwick Rangers. Once retired from football Ugolini was a successful bookmaker.

JAMES WATSON
Born Hamilton 1931, Died June 2014.
James Watson was a lifelong Hamilton Accies fan who joined the Board of Directors in 1969 when the club was going through a crisis. He resigned shortly afterwards but quickly returned when Clyde were trying to buy the Douglas Park side and move to East Kilbride. He became a controversial figure at Hamilton in the 1990s as the club went through further turmoil. Watson became Chairman of Deeka and Hamilton Stadium but left the club Board in 1994. He co-wrote a detailed history of the club, published in 2009.

DAVID WHITE
Born: 23 August 1933, in Motherwell, Died: 17 July 2013, Aged 80
It is disappointing that White is best-remembered for a short and unsuccessful spell as Manager of Rangers in the 1960s. He had earlier managed Clyde before joining Rangers as Assistant to Scott Symon. After being sacked by Rangers in 1969 he later became Manager of Dundee, winning the League Cup with them in 1973/4. As a player he spent his entire senior career with Clyde from 1957 until 1966, after stepping up from Royal Albert in the Juniors. White turned his back on employment in football in the mid 1970s but he continued to support Rangers from the Ibrox stands until his death.

LES WILSON
Died 4 July 2013, in Edinburgh
A former coach at Junior side Dunbar United.

LOST CLUBS AND GROUNDS

Several well-known Junior clubs have folded in the course of the past year. The costs associated with running a Junior club, even without paying wages, are substantial. Those clubs that take minimal income through the gate and come from small towns or villages are the most likely to "go under".

Steelend Victoria started the 2013/14 season but dropped out after a couple of months. The owner of their ground in the small Fife village had increased the rent to a level beyond what the club could pay. An arrangement to move to the old Tulliallan Juniors ground in Kincardine fell through at the last moment. Vics had to play home games at Oakley and Rosyth but the club was unsustainable, The work of keeping the club going fell on just two people and they could not subsidise the team indefinitely.

Coupar Angus have been whipping boys in Tayside Junior football for several years now. Towards the end of 2013/14 they were struggling badly, and played a game against Lochore Welfare with just nine men. Like Steelend they were being run by a tiny committee and they have chosen to take a year out. Hopefully they can return for 2015/16.

Bankfoot Athletic dropped out for 2014/15 and will not return for 2014/15. The Perthshire club have a long and illustrious history but latterly had been struggling to recruit players and committee members.

Bishopmill United of the North region fall into a similar category. They sat out last season hoping to make a return but have been unable to do so. Founded in 1882, this marks a sad to more than 130 years of football history.

Several iconic football grounds have also disappeared during 2013/14.

Tinto Park (above) home of Benburb, was one of the last remaining "classic" Junior grounds. Built on a massive scale, Tinto had fallen into disrepair and was a real millstone around the neck of the club. In the meantime they will share with Neilston Juniors until a new ground is built, adjacent to the old Tinto Park, between it and the motorway.

Renfrew Juniors, after years of false dawns, also finally moved out of their traditional home at Western Park. With the club expecting to move away for some time little had been done to maintain or modernise the ground. Work will shortly begin on a new stadium a few hundred years away. Renfrew will move into a groundshare arrangement, possibly with St Anthonys.

Kirkintlloch Rob Roy lost their old ground at Adamslie Park (above). New house building had already encroached on the social club ad the grandstand was removed a few years ago. Now the ground has been lost completely. Rob Roy will share with Cumbernauld United until their new facility is completed.

In the North Juniors FC Stoneywood vacated their ground at Polo Park. It had a very unusual wooden grandstand in one corner of the ground. The club will start 2014/15 at New Polo Park.